OLD TESTAMENT THEOLOGY

VOLUME TWO

Israel's Faith

JOHN GOLDINGAY

IVP Academic

An imprint of InterVarsity Press
Downers Grove, Illinois

Paternoster:
thinking faith

InterVarsity Press
P.O. Box 1400, Downers Grove, IL 60515-1426
World Wide Web: www.ivpress.com
E-mail: email@ivpress.com

Paternoster
An imprint of Authentic Media
9 Holdom Avenue, Bletchley, Milton Keynes MK1 1QR, England
World Wide Web: www.authenticmedia.co.uk/paternoster

Design: Cindy Kiple
Images: Réunion des Musées Nationaux / Art Resource, NY

USA ISBN-10: 0-8308-2562-2
USA ISBN-13: 978-0-8308-2562-2
UK ISBN-10: 1-84227-497-X
UK ISBN-13: 978-1-84227-497-2

Printed in the United States of America ∞

Library of Congress Cataloging-in-Publication Data

Goldingay, John.
  Israel's Gospel/John Goldingay.
    p. cm.—(Old Testament theology)
Includes bibliographical references and index.
  ISBN 0-8308-2561-4 (cloth: alk. paper)
  1. Bible. O.T.—Criticism, Narrative. 2. Narration in the Bible.
  I.
Title.
  BS1182.3.G65 2003
  230'.0411—dc21

                                                                    2003013828

P	20	19	18	17	16	15	14	13	12	11	10	9	8	7	6	5	4	3	2	1
Y	22	21	20	19	18	17	16	15	14	13	12	11	10	09	08	07	06			

To John Austin Baker and Alec Motyer,

my first Old Testament teachers,

who more than forty years ago conveyed

their enthusiasm for the Old Testament

to such effect that I caught it,

still remember their doing so, and still share it.

CONTENTS

ABBREVIATIONS

AB   Anchor Bible

ANET   *Ancient Near Eastern Texts Relating to the Old Testament.* Edited by
            James B. Pritchard. 3rd ed. Princeton: Princeton University Press,
            1969.

BDB   Francis Brown, S. R. Driver, and Charles A. Briggs. *A Hebrew and
            English Lexicon of the Old Testament.* Oxford/New York: Oxford
            University Press, corrected ed., 1962.

Bib   *Biblica*

BZAW   Beihefte zur Zeitschrift für die alttestamentliche Wissenschaft

ConBOT   Coniectanea Biblica: Old Testament Series

DCH   *The Dictionary of Classical Hebrew.* Edited by D. J. A. Clines. 8 vols.
            Sheffield: Sheffield Academic Press, 1993- .

DDD   *Dictionary of Deities and Demons in the Bible.* Edited by Karel van
            der Toorn, B. Becking and P. W. van der Horst. 2nd ed. Leiden:
            Brill/Grand Rapids, Mich.: Eerdmans, 1999.

EVV   English versions (chiefly NRSV, NIVI, JPSV)

f.   feminine

GKC   *Gesenius' Hebrew Grammar.* Edited and enlarged by E. Kautzsch.
            Translated by A. E. Cowley. 2nd ed. Oxford/New York: Oxford
            University Press, 1910; reprinted with corrections 1966.

HALOT   Koehler, L., and W. Baumgartner. *The Hebrew and Aramaic Lexicon
            of the Old Testament.* Revised by W. Baumgartner and J. J. Stamm
            et al. Translated by M. E. J. Richardson et al. 2 vols. Reprint, Bos-
            ton/Leiden: Brill, 2001.

HBT   *Horizons in Biblical Theology*

IBHS   Waltke, B. K., and M. O'Connor. *An Introduction to Biblical Hebrew
            Syntax.* Winona Lake, Ind.: Eisenbrauns, 1990.

Int   *Interpretation*

JBL   *Journal of Biblical Literature*

JM   Joüon, P. *A Grammar of Biblical Hebrew.* Translated and revised by
            T. Muraoka. 2 vols. Rome: PBI, 1991.

JPSV   JPS Hebrew-English Tanakh

JR   *Journal of Religion*

JSOT	*Journal for the Study of the Old Testament*
JSOTSup	Journal for the Study of the Old Testament Supplement
K	Kethib, the written (consonantal) Hebrew text; contrast Q
KJV	King James [Authorized] Version
LHBOTS	Library of Hebrew Bible/Old Testament Studies
LXX	Septuagint
m.	masculine
mg.	margin; marginal
MS(S)	manuscript(s)
MT	Masoretic Text
NICOT	New International Commentary of the Old Testament
NIDOTTE	*New International Dictionary of Old Testament Theology and Exegesis.* Edited by Willem A. VanGemeren. 5 vols. Grand Rapids, Mich.: Zondervan, 1996/Carlisle: Paternoster, 1997.
NIVI	New International Version, Inclusive Language Edition
NRSV	New Revised Standard Version
OTS	*Oudtestamentische Studiën*
OTT 1	Goldingay, John. *Old Testament Theology.* Vol. 1, *Israel's Gospel.* Downers Grove, Ill.: InterVarsity Press, 2003.
pl.	plural
1Q etc	Qumran manuscripts from cave 1, cave 2, etc.
Q	Qere, the Hebrew text as read out (i.e., with the vowels); contrast K
s.	singular
SBLDS	Society of Biblical Literature Dissertation Series
Sym	Symmachus's Greek translation
Syr.	Syriac text
TBü	Theologische Bücherei
TDOT	*Theological Dictionary of the Old Testament.* Edited by G. Johannes Botterweck and H. Ringgren. Translated by J. T. Willis, G. W. Bromiley and D. E. Green. 14 vols. Grand Rapids, Mich.: Eerdmans, 1974- .
TLOT	*Theological Lexicon of the Old Testament.* Edited by Ernst Jenni, with assistance from Claus Westermann. Translated by M. E. Biddle. 3 vols. Peabody, Mass.: Hendrickson, 1997.
Tg(s).	Targum(s); Targumic

USQR	*Union Seminary Quarterly Review*
Vg.	Vulgate
VT	*Vetus Testamentum*
VTSup	Vetus Testamentum Supplement
WBC	Word Biblical Commentary
WMANT	Wissenschaftliche Monographien zum Alten und Neuen Testament
ZAW	*Zeitschrift für die alttestamentliche Wissenshaft*

PREFACE

In the first volume,[1] Theophilus, I wrote about all that Yhwh did from the beginning, though not about what Yhwh began to teach. In the third volume I hope to write about Yhwh's teaching on how Israel was supposed to live. I shall be sixty-six if and when I finish it, and my father and both my grandfathers did not live that long. Having announced this project, I shall feel really stupid if I fail to complete it. But then I shall have other things to think about if that happens—or not to think about.[2]

In closing a panel discussion of the first volume at a meeting of the Society of Biblical Literature in San Antonio in 2004, Wonil Kim shrewdly asked what was the relationship between that work and my dissertation, *Theological Diversity and the Authority of the Old Testament.*[3] I think I replied that the latter (upon which I began work in the 1970s) had been undertaken within the framework of modernity; the more recent volume reflected an awareness of our postmodern context. One aspect of that is our recognition of the importance of narrative as a way of doing theology; it was odd that we had not spotted that the Scriptures spend so much time doing theology this way. In the course of writing that dissertation, and over the subsequent decade or two, I accumulated a folder full of outlines for an Old Testament theology that would work out its programmatic statement, but in moving to the United States in 1997 I trashed these, either accidentally or purposely. I had realized by then that if I ever wrote an Old Testament theology, it would need to take much more seriously the narrative nature of the bulk of the Scriptures,[4] and in my first volume I sought to do that. On the other hand, the nonnarrative parts of the Scriptures would still be amenable to the approach(es) I considered in that dissertation.

In volume one I described the New Testament as a series of Christian and ecclesial footnotes to the Old Testament[5] (and got into trouble for it; though a neat aspect of that discussion at San Antonio was a Jewish scholar accusing me

---

[1]*Old Testament Theology,* vol. 1, *Israel's Gospel* (Downers Grove, Ill.: InterVarsity Press, 2003).

[2]See section 6.9.

[3]Grand Rapids, Mich.: Eerdmans, 1986/Carlisle, U.K.: Paternoster, 1995.

[4]As I had implied in *Models for Scripture* (Grand Rapids: Eerdmans/Carlisle, U.K.: Paternoster, 1994) and *Models for Interpretation of Scripture* (Grand Rapids, Mich.: Eerdmans/Carlisle, U.K.: Paternoster, 1995).

[5]See *OTT,* 1:24.

of being too Christian and a Christian scholar accusing me of not being Christian enough). I believe the two Testaments are fundamentally at one in their understanding of God and humanity and the relationship between them. The New Testament confirms the perspectives of the First Testament and shows how God brought to its climax the purpose that God had been pursuing with Israel. In the final chapter, I therefore sought to suggest how the New Testament took the First Testament's story forward. I respect the argument that says that the proper exercise I should be involved in is biblical theology, but I have had to set against that the fact that my passion, expertise and vocation lie in letting the voice of the First Testament be heard. But in this volume I again seek to consider briefly what happens when one takes the footnotes into account.

In general, I do not discuss questions about the authorship of the biblical material and, for instance, simply assume that more than one prophet contributed to the book of Isaiah, and thus refer without comment to "Second Isaiah." On the other hand, when I say, for example, "Isaiah says," I do not necessarily imply the conviction that this is a prophecy of Isaiah ben Amoz; I mean "you will find this prophecy in the book called Isaiah." On exegetical questions on Psalms, Isaiah and Daniel, I have often presupposed arguments formulated in my commentaries on those books, which are listed in the bibliography. Translations of the biblical text are my own, except where otherwise indicated. While I have used inclusive translation in my own writing, I have often retained gendered language in translations in order to make clear when the text uses the singular and when it uses the plural.

I am again grateful to Fuller Theological Seminary for providing a congenial and supportive setting for this work and to my students for making me think furiously, even when I pretend they have not asked a question I have not thought about before. And I am grateful to Dan Reid at InterVarsity Press and to his anonymous readers, who made suggestions, identified mistakes and saved me from the fallout from some of my more outlandish statements. I hope some remain.

1

INTRODUCTION

I have discussed some introductory questions about writing an Old Testament theology (such as why I refer to "the First Testament") in the first of these three projected volumes,[1] but some introduction is appropriate to this one.

1.1 Narrative and Theology

If we wanted to help other people understand a person and what he or she stands for, there are at least two ways we might do that. We might tell the story of his or her life or make a film of it, and we would then discover the person through seeing him or her acting and being acted on in different contexts. We would see how different issues arise in different contexts. We would see what plot emerges from the person's life—what he or she sought to achieve and did achieve. But another way of seeking to help other people understand that individual would be to try to describe the person as he or she essentially is, to analyze traits, to portray qualities, to discern what makes the person tick, to identify the priorities that have concerned him or her. We would be standing back from the story of an individual life and asking what themes run through it or what emerges from the whole.

Neither of these approaches is better than the other. Each achieves things that the other could not. The story would have implications for an understanding of the person, and the description would depend upon the story of the person's life. The understanding of the person would be impossible without the material contained in the story, and the description would aid understanding of the story, but they would not be capable of being collapsed into one.

The Scriptures fulfill something like these two roles for God and for Jesus. Each Testament opens with long narratives that help us understand God or Jesus by telling their story. These long narratives (Genesis to Esther and Matthew to Acts) help us see what they were seeking to achieve, and portray them acting in and reacting to different situations. Each Testament then follows the narratives with material addressing people more directly with an account of who God and Jesus are and what their significance is for us. In the First Testament the Wisdom Books and the Prophets do that; so do the Psalms, though for the most part they are formally addressed to God rather than to Israel. In the New Testament, the Epistles and Revelation follow this precedent.

---

[1]See *OTT* 1:15-41.

I write this Old Testament theology in the conviction that this is not merely an aspect of the formal nature of the Scriptures, but that the form gives expression to something of substance. "Christian theology is poised between the poles of narrative and metaphysics, and both are required for an adequate theological method."[2] It is not surprising, then, to find them in dialogue in Scripture. "The story-teller comes first," but the metaphysician follows.[3] Given that each Testament goes on from narrative about what God has done to discursive statement about how things are and how they will be, it is appropriate that an Old Testament theology should do the same, and in my first two volumes I am following this twofold pattern. Volume one worked through Israel's story as the First Testament tells it, considering how "God Began," "God Started Over," "God Promised," "God Delivered" and so on. I reckoned that there was a theology in those verbs—a gospel theology, a good news theology—and a theology in the plot line that they formed. I also found in reflecting on the story that many other theological questions surfaced on the way along in different contexts: For instance, what is the nature of the people of God? How does history work? How does Israel experience God's presence? In focusing on the First Testament narrative, I made occasional reference to other parts of the First Testament, but generally kept to the narrative in order to seek to do justice to what we see by sticking to that focus that the Scriptures themselves press upon us.

In volume two I reverse this approach, again in following the Scriptures' pattern, in focusing on material that directly speaks of who God is (as opposed to what God has done), who Israel is (as opposed to what Israel has done), and so on. I thus begin from the way the Wisdom Books reflect on the nature of faith, the way the Prophets make it a matter for exhortation and the way the Psalms make it a matter for praise and prayer. Such statements about who God is and who Israel is are implicit in its narrative, and they are sometimes explicit there—for instance, in the classic formulation of Israelite systematic theology first stated in Exodus 34:6-7. I thus make some reference to the story that puts flesh on the bones of this speech (and I make some cross-reference to volume one), but I concentrate on what the books that work this way actually say. Volume one concerned Israel's gospel, the good news story that the First Testament tells. Volume two concerns Israel's faith, the understanding of God and us that emerges from the First Testament: not what Israelites actually believed, but what the First Testament suggests they should have believed.

---

[2]Stanley Hauerwas and L. Gregory Jones, eds., *Why Narrative?* (Grand Rapids, Mich.: Eerdmans, 1989), p. 9, summarizing the work of Nicholas Lash: see "Ideology, Metaphor and Analogy," *Why Narrative?* pp. 113-37; see p. 117, reprinted from his *Theology on the Way to Emmaus* (London: SCM Press, 1986), pp. 95-119; see p. 99.

[3]Lash, *Theology on the Way to Emmaus*, p. 117 = *Why Narrative?* p. 136.

1.2 Diversity and Unity in Old Testament Theology

Our postmodern context does not make it more difficult to affirm the supreme authority and entire trustworthiness of the Scriptures; perhaps it makes it easier. It does mean that we work out the implications of that affirmation in different ways and in light of different questions. Like some theology of the premodern period, we recognize that we perceive only the outskirts of God and of God's ways. As well as the importance of narrative, a second aspect of our postmodern context that seems significant for Old Testament theology is thus our recognition that our insights into the truth are partial and fragmentary. In keeping with this, at the beginning of his *Theology of the Old Testament* Walter Brueggemann notes that the Old Testament is characterized by a "pluralism of faith affirmations" that makes it impossible now to go back to the idea of "a singular coherent faith articulation in the text." Consequently "it is impossible to fashion a coherent statement concerning theological substance or themes in the Old Testament unless the themes or substance be framed so broadly or inclusively as to be useless."[4] My own starting point is in effect to grant the truth of this first sentence but deny the inference expressed in the second.[5] We cannot identify a single faith articulation in the text, but we might be able to construct one out of its diversity, even if we find ourselves leaving some ambiguities and antinomies, and even if we still grant that the end result needs to recognize once more that we see only the outskirts of God's ways. At least, it is this that I attempt in the present volume.

Norman Gottwald once suggested that "a proper beginning point for a theology of the Hebrew Bible is to take account of everything that the Bible says about God, everything that God says, and everything that people say to God. This would be to follow radically and faithfully the course of the text. . . . Unless and until this is done, . . . theological criticism will continue to build very selectively on narrow bases of God-talk."[6] He later acknowl-

---

[4]Walter Brueggemann, *Theology of the Old Testament* (Minneapolis: Fortress, 1997), pp. xv-xvi.

[5]Cf. Mark S. Kinzer's remarks (*Post-Missionary Messianic Judaism* [Grand Rapids, Mich.: Brazos, 2005], p. 39) regarding Richard S. Hays's analogous comments about different New Testament texts that stand in fundamental tension with each other in their attitude to Judaism (*The Moral Vision of the New Testament* [San Francisco: HarperSanFrancisco, 1996], pp. 408-9).

[6]Norman Gottwald, "Literary Criticism of the Hebrew Bible," in *Mappings of the Biblical Terrain*, ed. Vincent L. Tollers and John Maier (Lewisburg, Penn.: Bucknell University Press/ London: Associated University Presses, 1990), pp. 27-44; see p. 39. Gottwald also notes the significant diversity of the literary forms in which the First Testament's God-talk appears, with which I have tried to work. His threefold account of the Bible's subject matter (what it says about God, what God says, what people say to God) overlaps with Rolf Rendtorff's "In the first part of the canon *God acts*, in the second *God speaks*, and in the third part of the canon *people speak* to God and of God" (*The Canonical Hebrew Bible* [Leiden: Deo, 2005], p. 6). And my own threefold structure overlaps with both.

edged that this was a task of some magnitude.[7] I have tried to work with the spirit of Gottwald's ideal, in the interests of his crucial "unless and until," and I have reread the entire First Testament more than once in this connection. The way I have structured the volume emerged from the reading of the First Testament that I did while writing it. I have sought to let the categories of thinking be ones that emerge from the First Testament itself. Like the authors of classic Old Testament Theologies such as Walther Eichrodt,[8] Edmond Jacob[9] and Theodorus C. Vriezen,[10] I present it as an approach to structuring the faith that emerges from the First Testament in such a way as to do justice to its own dynamic (again, our postmodern setting means we are past the day when anyone would claim that their way of articulating this faith is the only way).

I begin with what the First Testament tells us about who God is and who Israel is (chaps. 2-3). I go on to the way it speaks of Israel's future, in warning of disaster and promising restoration (chaps. 4-5—volume one of course focuses on Israel's past). I then consider the nature of humanity in Israel and elsewhere (chap. 6) before letting the horizon broaden in keeping with the way the Scriptures' horizon does, so as to speak of the created world and the world of nations (chaps. 7-8). This structuring of the work by topics also happens to make it possible to be in dialogue with some major theological works such as those of Karl Barth, Wolfhart Pannenberg and Jürgen Moltmann as well as with the world of Old Testament scholarship.

1.3 Biblical Theology of the Old Testament

I have also added occasional New Testament footnotes and closed each chapter with a reflection on what happens when First Testament faith is set in the context of New Testament faith to generate what one might call "A Biblical Theology of the Old Testament."[11]

It is customary to see Christ as God's supreme revelation, and the New Testament as the record of that revelation. I do not object to that formulation, but its significance needs stating carefully. First, Christ did not come primarily to reveal something new. The First Testament already provided Israel,

---

[7]Norman Gottwald, "Rhetorical, Historical, and Ontological Counterpoints in Doing Old Testament Theology," in *God in the Fray*, ed. Tod Linafelt and Timothy K. Beal (Minneapolis: Fortress, 1998), pp. 11-23; see p. 12.

[8]Walter Eichrodt, *Theology of the Old Testament*, 2 vols. (London: SCM Press, 1961, 1967).

[9]Edmond Jacob, *Theology of the Old Testament* (London: Hodder, 1958).

[10]Theodorus C. Vriezen, *An Outline of Old Testament Theology* (reprint, Oxford: Blackwell, 1962; 2nd ed., Oxford: Blackwell/Newton, Mass.: Branford, 1970).

[11]For that expression, see, e.g., Karl Barth, *Church Dogmatics* (Edinburgh: T & T Clark, 1936-1969), I/2:79.

and even the world, with plenty of revelation. Israel's chief need, and the world's chief need, was not some more revelation. Christ came to do something, not to reveal something. He came to implement God's rule in the world. That fact is reflected in my focus on the biblical story in volume one. The First Testament is primarily the story of what God did to create the world and then put it right.

In acting to that end (for instance, in bringing the Israelites out of Egypt, letting them generally live in a way they chose rather than the way they were told, letting their nation collapse and then bringing it back to life), Yhwh did indeed indicate what God was like, but that was not the main point; arguably they could have known most of that in the Garden of Eden. Likewise, when Christ joined in God's acting to that end (for instance, in healing people and expelling demons from them, and then in letting people kill him and having God raise him to a transformed life), he did indeed reveal God, but this did not mean revealing something that was previously unknown. Yhwh had always been the Lord of life and death, the sovereign over powers of chaos and disorder, the God who submitted to people's rejection but insisted on coming back for more. Christ provided a visible embodiment of the self-revelation that God had already given Israel. Hebrews 1:1 does not say that God spoke in many partial ways to our ancestors through the prophets but has now spoken to us more fully through a Son. It says that God spoke in many different ways to our ancestors through the prophets, but has now spoken to us through a Son. The distinction lies in the form of the revelation—a huge distinction indeed—not in the content of it.

So did Jesus say nothing new? If that had been so, there would have been nothing to be ashamed of, precisely because he came to do something, not to reveal something. There is one point at which he claims to be saying something new, the sequence of sayings introduced by "But I say to you" (Mt 5:21-48). But those sayings relate primarily to Israel's life, not to Israel's faith. They concern what people need to do in light of what God has done, not what God has done or who God is. In general, Jesus avoids giving the impression of saying something new. The New Testament is utterly vital to Christian faith because it tells us the story of Jesus. In this story First Testament faith finds its ultimate expression. But the New Testament makes less difference to that faith than people think.

To rework my opening metaphor from Acts 1:1, my image for the Scriptures is to think of them as a photograph album. What the New Testament does is provide us with a new set of pictures. Their subject is the same as that of the preceding set, but they are not identical; they are taken from some new angles in some different light with some different lenses. They therefore tell us more and fill out the picture. But they do not offer a revolutionary new revelation.

And thus we can study the theology of the First Testament separately from that of the New Testament without losing too much—and certainly without losing as much as we do if we follow the church's practice of studying the New Testament separately from the First Testament, which it allegedly regards as Scripture.

2

GOD

It is a characteristic and central awareness of First Testament faith that there is one real God, the God whose name is Yhwh. Scoundrels may whisper in their heart of hearts, "God is not here" (Ps 14:1), and they may put God out of mind or turn their backs on God or rebel against God. But for all these declarations, "all of them 'Noes' to God, none of them amounts to a 'not'; even apostasy argues for the existence of God. . . . The existence of God is unquestionable. The questions are how God is and who God is."[1] Thus a consideration of First Testament faith starts not with general discussion about God but with the particularity of the God of Israel; this defines what the word *God* means.[2] "Israel does not begin with some generic notion of God, to which Yahweh conforms"; it does not begin from regular human assumptions about what God could or must be—for instance, God is the all-powerful, all-knowing, all-present one. "It begins its utterance, rather, in witness to what it has seen and heard and received from Yahweh."[3] Here, God is not a concept, but a person who can be personally known. Nor is God a person to be found at the depth of our being or as the ground of our being, but a person who lives outside of us and independently of us; the First Testament begins from God's act of self-revelation outside of us.[4] The real God is the God who speaks and acts in Israel's story.

Part of being a person is that our personhood emerges in response to contexts, and that is true of Yhwh, the one with whom personhood has its origin. As time goes by and contexts pass, a human person may come to demonstrate characteristics of which one would not have dreamed ten years previously, or this person's characteristics may receive fuller expression that was only hinted earlier, so that any account of the person's character will involve schematizing. So it is with God. From the beginning, for the world as a whole Yhwh was founder, former and giver. For Israel's ancestors, Yhwh was father, leader and

---

[1]Ludwig Köhler, *Old Testament Theology* (London: Lutterworth, 1957/Philadelphia: Westminster Press, 1958), p. 20.

[2]Cf. Karl Barth's comments on beginning dogmatics with the Trinity rather than with more generic questions such as whether a god exists (*Church Dogmatics* [Edinburgh: T & T Clark, 1936-1969], I/1:346).

[3]Walter Brueggemann, *Theology of the Old Testament* (Minneapolis: Fortress, 1997), p. 144.

[4]Cf. Barth, *Church Dogmatics*, II/1:261.

covenanter. At the exodus, Yhwh was warrior, guide and commander. In the time of the monarchy, Yhwh was king, shepherd and deliverer. For the preexilic prophets, Yhwh was lover, judge and disciplinarian. In Babylon, God was creator, restorer and mother. In the Second Temple period, Yhwh was Lord of heaven and revealer of mysteries.[5] What divine personality profile emerges from this story as a whole?

2.1 The God Yhwh

To much traditional and modern thinking, it may seem obvious that God "is unknowable and unnameable."[6] Israel's experience and thinking suggested the opposite: God was known and God had a name. Perhaps "any intelligent talk about God . . . must begin and end with confession of the inconceivable majesty of God which transcends all our concepts,"[7] but "by his own act of bestowing a name on himself, God chooses to be described as the definable, the distinctive, the individual."[8]

Yhwh is the holy one, the majestic one, the God who speaks and then acts. The immediate object of that speech and action is Israel, but it has positive implications for the whole world.

Yhwh as Holy One

"Holy One" is the most fundamental description of Yhwh.[9] Yhwh can swear "by his holiness" (Amos 4:2; cf. Ps 89:35 [MT 36]), and this is an even more emphatic expression than swearing "by himself" (e.g., Is 45:23; Jer 22:5) or "by his life/his very self [*nepeš*]" (Amos 6:8) or "by his name" (Jer 12:16; 44:26). It indicates that Yhwh has thought carefully about the subject of this oath and that all the solemn transcendent deity of Yhwh lies behind it. There is thus absolutely no possibility of its not coming about. It is therefore a telling rhetorical device when Psalm 89 craftily attributes such an oath to Yhwh when Yhwh has never explicitly made one, as the psalm makes its way toward the outspoken protest that will come in its closing verses. That leaves Amos 4:2 as the only occasion when Yhwh actually does swear "by his holiness," which is very bad news for the elegant well-to-do wives of Samaria.

"The transcendence of God is expressed most clearly by the word holi-

---

[5]The theme of *OTT* 1 is the way theology emerges through this story.

[6]Erhard S. Gerstenberger, *Yahweh the Patriarch* (Minneapolis: Fortress, 1996), p. v.

[7]Wolfhart Pannenberg, *Systematic Theology,* 3 vols. (Grand Rapids, Mich.: Eerdmans/Edinburgh: T & T Clark, 1991-1998), 1:337.

[8]Walther Eichrodt, *Theology of the Old Testament,* 2 vols. (London: SCM Press, 1961, 1967), 1:206.

[9]Cf. John G. Gammie, *Holiness in Israel* (Minneapolis: Fortress, 1989), pp. 2-3.

ness."[10] Holiness points to Yhwh's metaphysical distinctiveness over against humanity. In Christian parlance "holy" is a moral category; it points to the absolute integrity, uprightness, goodness and righteousness of God, to be reflected by those who claim to belong to God. Rudolf Otto notes that this is not the connotation of holiness in the First Testament. Here, as the holy one Yhwh is metaphysically the "wholly other."[11] Otto means that "holy" and "wholly other" refer to the human awareness of being confronted by the numinous, the *mysterium tremendum*.[12] He is right in what he denies (though in this chapter we will see how Yhwh's distinctive person redefines the meaning of holiness in a moral direction) but questionable in what he affirms.[13] In the context of the First Testament, "the holy one" and "wholly other" have different connotations from the ones he notes. Other heavenly beings than Yhwh can be described as "holy ones," even though they do not share Yhwh's unique deity, and other Middle Eastern peoples can describe their deities as holy, even though these deities can be stupid, devious, disorderly, ineffectual, mortal and not very "wholly other." This does not compromise their holiness; they still belong to a different metaphysical realm. Oddly (but typically in the use of theological terms), the First Testament uses the same theological terms as we do, but uses them with different meanings. Israelites are quite capable of being aware that they stand in the awesome presence of God (see, e.g., Ex 19), but they do not regularly speak of God's holiness in that connection. It is God's majesty rather than God's holiness that provokes a reaction of dread and wonder (e.g., Judg 6:22-23; 13:22; Is 6:5; Ezek 1:28; 2:1).[14] Only quite late on in the Sinai story does Yhwh declare, "I am holy" (Lev 19:2), and Yhwh's point there is not that people need to respond with dread and wonder.

Admittedly, Isaiah, the prophet of Israel's holy one, does so respond when confronted by Yhwh in exaltedness and holiness (Is 6:1-5). The meeting takes place "in the year King Uzziah died." Isaiah follows up the reference to King Uzziah's demise with a reference to Yhwh as "Lord." Elsewhere, translations

---

[10]Theodorus C. Vriezen, *An Outline of Old Testament Theology* (reprint, Oxford: Blackwell, 1962), p. 149 (not in the 2nd ed.).

[11]Rudolf Otto, *The Idea of the Holy*, 3rd ed. (London/New York: Oxford University Press, 1925), pp. 5, 25.

[12]Ibid., p. 12.

[13]Cf. Barth, *Church Dogmatics*, II/1:360-61, emphasizing that Yhwh is the Holy One *of Israel*. It is a description that suggests good news, not something fearful. See also Thomas Dozeman, "The Holiness of God in Contemporary Jewish and Christian Biblical Theology," in *God's Word for Our World*, ed. J. Harold Ellens et al., JSOTSup 389 (London/New York: T & T Clark, 2004), 2:24-36.

[14]See John Calvin, *Institutes of the Christian Religion*, ed. John T. McNeill, trans. Ford Lewis Battles, 2 vols. (Philadelphia: Westminster Press, 1960/London: SCM Press, 1961), 1.1.3.

replace the name "Yhwh" by "the LORD," and this makes the noun *Lord* sound more common and less pointed than it is. This is a vision of "the Lord sitting on a throne, high and exalted, his skirts filling the palace." Yhwh is a sovereign, seated in majesty. Isaiah may be speaking hyperbolically of Yhwh's robe filling the heavenly palace, or may imply that in his vision he sees the skirts of this robe filling the earthly temple (the image would then compare with the description of the covenant chest as Yhwh's footstool). Either way, Yhwh is high and exalted and has the attendants appropriate to a king, especially a heavenly King: "there were seraphs standing before him,[15] each with six wings; with two he would cover his face, with two he would cover his feet, with two he would fly."[16] The King's splendor or honor *(kābôd)* "fills the earth" (or the land), as a king's splendor fills his land. It is reflected and celebrated throughout his realm. At the same time, Yhwh is no "constitutional monarch" like those of some European countries, with outward splendor but with power circumscribed by a parliament. Yhwh's honor is not merely ceremonial. This is "Yhwh Armies," someone with all power in heaven and on earth. We do not know how to construe that odd expression, but its implications are clear enough.[17] While Isaiah does not make explicit whether the date of his experience is significant, it is striking that the occasion when he saw "the King, Yhwh Armies" is the year of the human king's death.

And the seraphs are calling out to one another, "Holy, holy, holy, is Yhwh Armies." It is as Yhwh Armies that Yhwh is the holy one. Holiness is a term for the distinctive, transcendent, heavenly, awesome, exalted nature of deity, for what marks deity over against humanity. Further, Yhwh is not merely the once holy one, or even the twice holy one, but the thrice holy one. Yhwh possesses holiness to the power of three. There are many holy ones, but Yhwh is a deity of unrivaled holiness.

Yhwh's Majesty

Yhwh's majestic splendor is the outward expression of Yhwh's holiness.

---

[15]Lit. "above him," the Lord being seated as king.

[16]The seraphs appear only here in Scripture. *śārap* means "burn," and in other passages *śārāp* means "serpent," so they may be burning serpents, but one would not work this out from Is 6, where they are flying creatures attending on, worshiping and serving Yhwh.

[17]Norman K. Gottwald describes it as a double-entendre in its capacity to refer both to the heavenly and the Israelite armies (*The Tribes of Yahweh* [Maryknoll, N.Y.: Orbis, 1979/London: SCM Press, 1980; reprint, Sheffield: Sheffield Academic Press, 1999]), p. 682. The LXX's *pantokratôr* adds the possibility that the word is an abstract plural suggesting great power, specifically power to make war: cf. Horst Dietrich Preuss, *Old Testament Theology*, 2 vols. (Louisville, Ky: Westminster John Knox/Edinburgh: T & T Clark, 1995, 1996), 1:144-46. See further Hans-Joachim Kraus, *Theology of the Psalms* (Minneapolis: Augsburg/London: SPCK, 1986), pp. 18-20.

Ezekiel's inaugural vision (Ezek 1) reminds his hearers that one cannot say very much directly about what God looks like. What he announces as a vision of God turns out to be a vision of God's limousine and God's throne—perhaps not a "vision of God" at all but rather a "divine vision," a vision *from* God. It is a vision of dark cloud, bright light and flashing fire, suggesting that Yhwh is characterized by deep mystery, dazzling intensity and burning danger, while also indicating that people are protected from actually seeing Yhwh. The experience parallels the story of Israel at Sinai (Ex 19); again, Ezekiel does not refer to Yhwh's "holiness." At Sinai, Yhwh appeared in a cloud and in fire. This made clear that Yhwh really was appearing and speaking, and also simultaneously protected the people from being overwhelmed by Yhwh's splendor, as if they had looked at the sun and been blinded, or grasped a cable and been electrocuted, or stood too close to a surge of nuclear power.

When Ezekiel gives us a detailed description of the four creatures that carry Yhwh's throne, the abundance of this detail underlines the impossibility of saying much about Yhwh in person. Their extravagance also serves to highlight the splendor of the one they serve. Indeed, it is the splendor of Yhwh that Ezekiel sees (Ezek 1:28). He does tell us that the one who sits on the throne is humanlike in form (Ezek 1:26; cf. Ezek 8:2). Something similar has already been said about the four creatures (Ezek 1:5), though they are also animal-like and birdlike. "Humanlike" apparently means standing on two legs; Ezekiel goes straight on from that to refer to the loins of the figure on the throne, and to the parts of the body above and below the loins (Ezek 1:27; cf. 8:2). The figure also has a humanlike hand with which it can grasp Ezekiel by the hair (Ezek 8:3). Yhwh is not animal-like or birdlike, like the creatures and like other deities—at least, not here, though elsewhere Yhwh is described as, for instance, like a lion or a mother hen. The description of the figure as humanlike is complemented and safeguarded by the references to its brightness, fire and radiance.

Ezekiel's instinctive reaction to his vision of Yhwh's awe-inspiring splendor, and Yhwh's response to Ezekiel, also indirectly indicate something of Yhwh's nature. Ezekiel falls on his face (Ezek 1:28). Yet Yhwh's response is to tell him to stand on his feet so that Yhwh may speak to him. Yhwh's form of address, *ben-ʾādām*, confirms Ezekiel's position as a (mere) human creature (Ezek 2:1).[18] Yet Yhwh intends to speak with him and use him.

One objective of the exodus was recognition of Yhwh's majesty and honor. If its aim had been only to free the Israelites from their serfdom, it could have been a much simpler affair. Yhwh brought about the people's deliverance in a

---

[18]The NIVI has "son of man"; NRSV and JPSV more idiomatically "mortal."

more complicated way, and then inspired the Pharaoh to pursue Israel and to follow them into the Red Sea bed "so that I may gain honor" (*kābēd* niphal; Ex 14:4, 17-18). In the context of the people's imminent second exodus from Babylon, Yhwh speaks in similar terms, declaring the intention not to let go of honor (Is 42:8; 48:11). Here the rivals for Yhwh's honor are the Babylonian deities rather than the Egyptian king. Psalm 29 challenges the gods as a group to give honor to Yhwh, and Psalm 96 so challenges the nations as a whole.[19] Similarly, Ezekiel is subsequently concerned for Yhwh's holy name to be acknowledged and not profaned (e.g., Ezek 36:22-23; 39:7).

Why should Yhwh be concerned to be honored? As a professor I have no desire for my colleagues and students to honor me, and I skip occasions designed to express honor to professors. Admittedly that is a cultural matter; Americans like that kind of thing, as God does. But why should God? Perhaps it is not a sign of insecurity but the opposite. Perhaps, unlike me, Yhwh is relaxed and secure about honor and therefore comfortable about it being recognized. And Yhwh does not have to hide from reality. Yhwh *is* the only God who counts. It is appropriate for that to be recognized.

The Living God

Yhwh is "the living God" or "the God of life" (e.g., Ps 42:2 [MT 3]). "Life is what differentiates Yahweh from other gods."[20] Baal can be overcome by the god Death; Yhwh cannot.[21] Death is alien to Yhwh; thus it is inappropriate for someone who has been in contact with death to come straight into Yhwh's presence. Similarly, women losing blood in menstruation and people afflicted by skin disease (so-called leprosy), which makes living persons look somewhat corpselike, have taboo status: they carry in their bodies a witness to themselves and to other people that Yhwh is the God of life.[22] Yhwh is also lord of the realm of death, but death does not affect Yhwh's own being, as it can other heavenly beings (see Ps 82). It is not a power over against God or a weapon in the hand of a great supernatural power in a dualistic world.[23] In a First Testament context, to speak of Death shepherding people (Ps 49:14 [MT 15]) or of Death's firstborn consuming them (Job 18:13) is a powerful metaphor rather than a literal theological statement. "See, now, that I—I am the one, and

---

[19]Cf. Brueggemann, *Theology of the OT*, pp. 283-85.

[20]Edmond Jacob, *Theology of the Old Testament* (London: Hodder, 1958), p. 39.

[21]Cf. Werner H. Schmidt, *The Faith of the Old Testament* (Oxford: Blackwell/Philadelphia: Westminster Press, 1983), pp. 156-63; Tryggve N. D. Mettinger, *In Search of God* (Philadelphia: Fortress, 1988), pp. 82-91.

[22]See section 6.9 "Life and Death."

[23]Gerhard von Rad, *Wisdom in Israel* (London: SCM Press/Nashville: Abingdon, 1972), pp. 304-5.

there is no God beside me," says Yhwh; "I make people die and I make people live, I wound and I heal" (Deut 32:39; cf. 1 Sam 2:6-7).

The contexts of the declaration that Yhwh is the living God often imply that it means Yhwh is the lively and active God. Things happen when this God is present. It is for this reason that this is not a God to be belittled or trifled with (e.g., Deut 5:26; Josh 3:10; 1 Sam 17:26; 2 Kings 19:4, 16; Jer 10:10; 23:36; Dan 6:20, 26 [MT 21, 27]; cf. Ps 18:46 [MT 47]).[24] The same implication attaches to the further formulas used in oaths, "as I live" or "as Yhwh lives."[25] In substance, "living God" thus has similar significance to "I am/will be what I am/will be."[26] It is not surprising, then, if "the living God" is "the central thought of Judaism."[27] Karl Barth, in turn, takes it as his starting point for expounding who God is, noting that (unlike most other statements about God) it is a literal rather than a metaphorical description.[28] The First Testament's many anthropomorphisms and anthropopathisms express Yhwh's alive-ness. God walks, speaks, acts, smells, whistles, laughs, shouts, fights, and feels joy, compassion, anger, sorrow, regret and hatred; that shows that God is alive.[29] For all the gold and silver they are made from, images have only pretend mouths, eyes, ears, nose, hands, feet and throat. Conversely, being in the heavens and having no earthly image does not stop Yhwh reaching out to act on earth—far from it (Ps 115:2-8). Yhwh's is "a personhood which is fully alive, and a life which is fully personal," like that of a human person.[30] Yhwh really has a mouth to speak to Israel, eyes to guide it on its way, ears to listen to its prayers, a nose to savor its offerings, hands to embrace or investigate or act, feet to lead, a throat to shout in triumph.[31] Yhwh has a form (Ps 17:15). Yhwh is as real a person as the suppliant and as the enemies in the Psalms, and has analogous features to those of human beings (or rather, Yhwh has the originals and human beings have equivalents through being made in God's image).

The fact that the Scriptures speak thus of God resists our spiritualizing God. It is a basis for God's being the creator and savior of both body and soul, and

---

[24]The specific implications in Hos 1:10 [MT 2:1]; Ps 42:2 [MT 3]; 84:2 [MT 3] are less clear.

[25]Cf. TDOT, 4:338-40.

[26]So Gustavo Gutiérrez, The God of Life (Maryknoll, N.Y.: Orbis, 1991), pp. 9-13.

[27]So Abraham J. Heschel, God in Search of Man (reprint, New York: Farrar, 1986), p. 25.

[28]Church Dogmatics, II/1:263.

[29]Vriezen, Outline of OT Theology, pp. 171-73 (2nd ed., Oxford: Blackwell/Newton, Mass.: Branford, 1970, pp. 319-22).

[30]Eichrodt, Theology of the OT, 1:211. Cf. Paul M. van Buren, A Theology of the Jewish-Christian Reality, 3 vols. (San Francisco: Harper & Row, 1980-1988), 1:106-10; John F. Kutsko, Between Heaven and Earth (Winona Lake, Ind.: Eisenbrauns, 2000), p. 1.

[31]Rex Mason thus has a chapter on "God as Human" in his Old Testament Pictures of God (Oxford: Regent's Park College/Macon, Ga.: Smyth & Helwys, 1993), pp. 75-90.

for God's being able to act at all. While Yhwh is spirit (Is 31:3), Yhwh is not merely spirit, so that bodily human beings would have difficulties relating to such a God and God might have difficulty becoming a bodily human being.[32] The First Testament ascribes human attributes to God in a way that is "neither restrained nor incidental; indeed, anthropomorphism is to be found on every page of the Old Testament in a wealth of detail, unashamed and even drastic." There is no development toward a less anthropomorphic representation within the First Testament. Anthropomorphisms are too useful. They "make God accessible" to human beings. "They hold open the door for encounter and controversy" between God's will and human wills. "They represent God as a person."[33] The visions of prophets, too, imply that human form is the natural form for God to take. The form is veiled to protect the prophet, because indeed God cannot be seen, but this is because that is too dangerous, not because God is invisible. "There is no such thing for Israel as a nonincarnate God."[34]

The God Who Speaks and Acts

As the living God, then, Yhwh speaks and acts. Other gods have no witnesses to their liveliness, because their witnesses have no acts to witness to, though they will not acknowledge the fact (Is 44:9-11). None of them will whisper that the emperor has no clothes. Jeremiah has the nations acknowledging this of their so-called gods (Jer 16:19-21). They are lies (šeqer): they give the impression of reality, but it is a false impression. They are emptiness (hebel), mere breath. And thus they cannot actually do anything. As usual the prophet declines to distinguish the divine images from the gods they represent. He takes the images' immobility and inactivity as a true reflection of the actual deity's powerlessness. The real God is one who acts, and who thus cannot be imaged satisfactorily.

In contrast to such images and the deities they represent, "the God Yhwh" is creator of the heavens and the earth, and also the one who has announced the first events, which have come, and is now announcing new events before they come (Is 42:5-9). Here the word for "God" is 'ēl, the term that appears most often in Genesis in compound expressions such as "El Shaddai."[35] It suggests the ex-

---

[32]Cf. the comments in Barth, *Church Dogmatics*, II/1:266-67.

[33]Köhler, *OT Theology*, p. 22. Köhler has just noted that God is unmentioned in Esther, so his "every page" involves hyperbole, but not much. Contrast the argument that anthropomorphism is more characteristic of early Israelite faith (e.g., Marjo C. A. Korpel, *A Rift in the Clouds* [Münster: Ugarit, 1990], p. 128), which seems influenced by the assumption that later is better and that reducing anthropomorphism implies progress, and also seems to involve circular argument (e.g., p. 92).

[34]Terence E. Fretheim, *The Suffering of God* (Philadelphia: Fortress, 1984), p. 106, concluding his discussion of this theme.

[35]I discuss names such as El Shaddai in *OTT* 1:243-44.

alted position of Yhwh as the one who holds the highest position in heaven. That matches Yhwh's self-description as creator, with its implications for Yhwh's sovereignty, and matches Yhwh's declaration of intent about opening blind eyes. All that leads into the insistence on being acknowledged and not confused with other entities. Yhwh insists on being the real ʾēl in the sense of being the true top heavenly being, and the real ʾēl in the sense of being the real God whose being contrasts with those pathetic images. All this is implicit in being ʾēl.

It is also implicit in being Yhwh. "I am Yhwh; that is my name" (Is 42:8) might sound tautologous and/or pointless, but in reality it is an elliptical but dense declaration. To say "I am Yhwh" is to draw attention to all that is conveyed by the name Yhwh; the additional reference to this being Yhwh's name further underlines that. It invites people to bring back to mind all that this name "Yhwh" denotes, some of which the previous lines have noted. Among other things, it establishes the splendor of Yhwh, the inherent grandeur reflected in expressions of Yhwh's might such as the creation of the world and of humanity and Yhwh's commitment to bringing light to people in darkness. Talking in the same breath about Yhwh and an image or about Yhwh and a god who can be represented by an image involves a travesty of the facts. The truth in all this is reinforced by the final comment in Isaiah 42:8-9, for Yhwh's proven capacity to announce intentions and fulfill them is what particularly evidences that Yhwh is in another league from those so-called gods. Yhwh is not a God who merely claims credit for events after they happen, like Marduk, to whom the Marduk priests eventually attributed the fall of Babylon, but did so only (as far as we know) when it had become an actuality.[36] Yhwh long ago declared the intention to deliver the Judeans from Babylon and to use the Medes as the means of putting Babylon down. And this follows a pattern in Yhwh's activity. Long ago, Yhwh had declared the intention to deliver Israel from Egypt and had then implemented this intention. That pattern is now in the midst of being repeated in Babylon.

Other gods do make declarations about the future. Second Isaiah's more specific interest lies in the claim that only Yhwh prospectively and retrospectively made sense of the fall of Babylon and the accession of Persia, which make it possible for the Judean exiles to return to Jerusalem. Behind that, only Yhwh claimed responsibility for bringing national disaster to God's own people. Further, only for Yhwh can someone "pursue a continuity of divine action through the whole of history in the reciprocal relationship of prophecy and fulfillment."[37]

---

[36]See Cyrus's account of the fall of Babylon on the "Cyrus Cylinder," *ANET*, pp. 315-16.

[37]Rainer Albertz, *A History of Israelite Religion in the Old Testament Period*, 2 vols. (London: SCM Press/Louisville, Ky: Westminster John Knox, 1994), 2:419.

Yhwh's Exclusivism and Universality

As this unique deity, what is Yhwh's relationship with the rest of the world? The narrative structure of the First Testament or of John's Gospel puts God's relationship with the world first and suggests God has a broader concern for the world than one that merely concerns Israel. On the other hand, the hypothetical tradition history of the First Testament puts God's acts in relation to Israel first, and the theory that Joshua-Kings was written before Genesis-Numbers does the same. It is also the nature of Matthew, Mark and Luke to set God's acts in relation to Israel first and to focus on these. Matthew and Luke do then eventually move from Israel to the world, though Mark confines attention to Israel. There are thus several possible ways of seeing Yhwh's relationship with the world as a whole. We might see God's sovereignty over the whole world as setting God's involvement with one people in a broader framework. David's praise in 1 Chronicles 29 opens and closes with the fact that Yhwh is God of the people's ancestors, but he soon moves to speak of Yhwh's lordship over the whole cosmos and the entire world. We might see the significance of God's sovereignty over the whole world as lying in God's capacity to be sovereign in the way the world affects Yhwh's special people, like Jehoshaphat's later prayer in 2 Chronicles 20. We might emphasize God's concern with the whole world and see a commitment to one people as a means to that end.

The First Testament makes exclusive claims for Yhwh and for Israelite faith. Only Yhwh has real power; the Babylonians' beliefs about Marduk are fundamentally false. There is no hope for people who insist on continuing to adhere to this religion rather than accept Yhwh's claims. First Testament faith is thus exclusivist and nationalist because it claims a link between this one God and a particular people. Yet this does not stop it being also open and inclusivist. "According to the Old Testament the whole world knows God"—the human world, the natural world, the cosmic world.[38] By virtue of the freedom with which it utilizes insights from other Middle Eastern religions, it implies that the faiths of contemporary peoples contain true insights. In terms of truth, First Testament faith and Canaanite or Babylonian or Persian faith are not simply set over against each other as truth over against falsehood. Yet this is not to undermine the fundamental importance of the declaration that Yhwh alone is God and is doing something of worldwide importance with Israel.

The invitation to other peoples to recognize the truth about Yhwh and their gods comes to a climax in Isaiah 45:20-25. There is an openness and a solemnity about this pronouncement. It begins as a sardonic challenge to the "survi-

---

[38]Köhler, *OT Theology*, p. 19.

vors of the nations" to "gather and come, draw near all at once." Yhwh's declarations have come true. In the prophet's vision, the empire is falling. The nations have been decimated. Only survivors are left, and they might constitute only the tattered evidence that a mighty empire once ruled here (compare the leftovers in Amos 3:12). They appear here to admit that they were wrong after all, though they are apparently still too stubborn to do so, because they are still clinging to "the wood of their images" (the odd expression, with construct and absolute in the opposite order to the one we would expect, underlines the fact that these are mere lumps of wood). They are still "making their plea with a god [*ʾēl*] who cannot deliver." Once again Yhwh challenges them about who did say ahead of time that this was going to happen, the answer of course being that it was Yhwh, the only God [*ʾēl*] who *can* deliver. Yhwh is Israel's "faithful God and deliverer; there is no one but me" (Is 45:21).[39]

This might seem merely a triumphalist I-told-you-so intended purely to encourage an audience of exiles. We are not prepared for the next line that invites earth's extremities to "turn to me and find deliverance." The word *deliver* thus comes for a third time and turns out to have something to say to the rest of the empire and not only to the Judeans. Might the invitation be going only to Judeans scattered over the world? The context points rather to its going to the world as a whole that is destined to "bend the knee" to Yhwh. The survivors of the nations may find deliverance with Yhwh; this is the other side to bending the knee and coming to "swear allegiance" to Yhwh. People who "rage" at Yhwh "come to be shamed" in Yhwh's presence, and they there acknowledge that Yhwh alone is the quintessence of faithfulness and strength. Their acknowledgment of this is not a sad one that does them no good, but a liberative one that enables them to call on Yhwh as deliverer instead of calling for deliverance from their useless images. They are invited to "turn their faces" to Yhwh ("turn" is *pānâ*, not *šûb*, the verb often translated "repent") as people looking to Yhwh for deliverance and blessing.

The prophecy does close with a declaration about Israel's vindication and exultation: "in Yhwh all the offspring of Israel will be in the right and will exult." That reflects the fact that the invitation to the nations does remain a nationalist and exclusivist one in the sense that the survivors of the nations will find deliverance only if they turn to Yhwh, and the people who immediately hear this declaration are the exiles themselves who thus have their own morale built up. But what they hear is a genuine declaration about the nations finding deliverance. The situation is repeated when the New Testament declares that the Gentile world can find deliverance only by acknowl-

---

[39]On "faithful[ness]," see section 2.6 "True Faithfulness."

edging the Jewish people's God and the Jewish people's Messiah.

The First Testament does not assume that the true faith belongs to Israel in such a way as to give no other people access to it. On the contrary, the very chapters that most stridently declare that the God of Israel alone is God are the chapters that most explicitly portray other peoples coming to acknowledge Yhwh and that invite them to do so.

Eternal

Yhwh is "the eternal God," *'ĕlōhê 'ôlām* (Is 40:28), "the God of age," the lasting God, the permanent God, the God whose being and activity have stood through the ages that have preceded, and will stand through the ages that will come. Before the world existed, Yhwh was there, and after the world ceases to exist, Yhwh will be there. Retrospectively, it has been possible for the Lord to be a refuge for Israel "in every generation" because "before the mountains were brought forth or you gave birth to earth and world, yes, from age to age you have been God" (Ps 90:1-2). Conversely, it is worth praying for one's children and grandchildren to dwell and endure before Yhwh because "of old you founded the earth, and the heavens are the work of your hands. These—they will perish, but you—you will endure. So they will all wear out like a garment; you will pass them on like clothing, they will pass on. But you are the one, your years will not come to an end" (Ps 102:26-28 [MT 27-30]). Habakkuk thus reminds Yhwh (!), "Are you not from of old, Yhwh? My holy God, you will not die."[40] He, too, asserts the eternity of deity working backwards and working forward. There was no moment when Yhwh came into being, and there will be no moment when Yhwh ceases to be. Therefore Yhwh has always been and can always be Israel's God. Yhwh's power and Yhwh's commitment to Israel are not constrained by time. God's eternity might seem something overwhelming, as if God might be dismissive of creatures that do not share this endlessness. Instead, it is an encouragement. When we are not here, God will still be here.

Our transience as human beings is self-evident. We last longer than a wild-flower that can flourish and die all within a few days in the spring, but the cycle we experience is analogous. We too flourish and then perish, just as inexorably. We come alive and then we lose our life. Neither of these facts applies to Yhwh (Ps 103:15-18). No matter how far back you go, you find Yhwh there. Further, you find Yhwh always characterized by commitment (*ḥesed*).[41] And no matter

---

[40]The MT has "we will not die," but this is one of the eighteen scribal corrections in MT designed to safeguard against scandalous ideas. Cf. JPSV and see Carmel McCarthy, *The Tiqqune Sopherim and Other Theological Corrections in the Masoretic Text of the Old Testament* (Göttingen: Vandenhoeck & Ruprecht, 1981).

[41]See section 2.6 "Commitment."

how long the world lasts, Yhwh will be there, still characterized by commitment. This is of more than academic interest to people who (as far as they knew) after their death will not themselves personally experience that commitment. Actually, they will continue to experience it in the sense that Yhwh will stay committed to their children and their grandchildren, about whom they naturally care so much and in whom the community continues in being. The present generation's faithfulness to Yhwh motivates and/or obliges Yhwh to be faithful to their children and grandchildren. Jesus takes this argument further. God is the God of Abraham, Isaac and Jacob, so they must continue in life and not just die, because God is God of the living not the dead (Mk 12:27).

"I am first and I am last, and apart from me there is no God," says Yhwh (Is 44:6). While the First Testament indeed assumes that Yhwh always has been and always will be, that is not the point of this assertion in its context. Yhwh's concern is with the span of Israel's history from its creative beginning to the present moment of its transformative renewal. The "first events" (e.g., Is 41:22; 42:9; 43:9, 18) may in different contexts be the creation itself and/or the summons of Abraham and/or the exodus and/or the fall of Jerusalem and/or the beginnings of the triumphs of Cyrus. The "last events" are then the fall of Babylon and the restoration of the community and of the city of Jerusalem. Yhwh first claims to be the first and to be *with* the last, to be involved in these last events that will bring about that final renewal of Israel (Is 41:4). To *be* uniquely the first and the last (Is 44:6) is to have been the only God present (and therefore in existence) through that story, the only one working out a purpose in that story in its entirety from its beginnings until this coming consummation. It is to be the only God.

It would also be impressive to be the first and the last in some more abstract metaphysical sense, the God who was there before creation and will be there to eternity, and it may be implicit in those other claims, but Yhwh's failure to articulate that claim shows that it is less significant. The important self-assertion is to be the God whose being spans history from creation, Abraham and the exodus to Cyrus.

In Isaiah 48:12-16, the declaration about being first and last is preceded by another absolute claim, "I am the one," *'ănî hû'*. It is followed initially by an allusion to creation, suggesting that being first is indeed a claim to have been the God who was involved in creation. The one who brought the world into being was Yhwh, not the gods to whom the Babylonians attributed creation. It is then followed by an allusion to Cyrus, suggesting that being last is indeed a claim also to be the God who is now involved in these last events. And as usual, the evidence for the claim is that Yhwh had declared the intention to bring about these events and had then done so. And Yhwh had not acted thus in secret or in hiddenness (an allusion back to Is 45:15, 19). Yhwh had been speaking openly from the beginning. Is this from creation, when God spoke with the first human beings? Is it from the time of Abraham, the one originally summoned from the east? Is it from the exodus, when we get the first clear references to Yhwh's declaring an intention and fulfilling it? Or is it from the time Yhwh formulated an intention with regard to Cyrus and announced it and summoned him? Any of these will undergird Yhwh's claim to be the one who is the first and the last.

Belief that God is eternal in the sense of embracing and present to all time opened Christian faith to a more Platonic belief in God as eternal in the sense of timeless. Augustine encouraged that understanding, though he also pointed to suggestive images for understanding how God can experience both time and eternity. When we hear a melody or a sentence or read a text such as a psalm, we hear or read a sequence of notes or words, yet we hear or understand it as a whole.[42] The First Testament's take on the idea of God's eternity is not that God is outside time but that God is throughout time. God makes plans, has changes of mind about plans, keeps in mind or puts out of mind events from the past, is slow to get angry, stays angry for a shorter rather than a longer time. God's experience of time is different from that of human beings, but it is still an experience of time in the sense that God knows about before and after, about shorter and longer time, about looking forward and looking back.[43] God embraces and is present to all time.

Creator

So Yhwh is the creator. When Amos warns Israel to be ready to meet Yhwh, there follows a description of the one they will meet; it is elaborated when similar phrases occur later (Amos 4:13; 5:8-9; 9:5-6). The descriptions take the form of participles,[44] which may suggest that they are hymnic. Some of the activities the participles describe take place in the present. Yhwh is one "who flashes destruction on the strong so that destruction comes on the fortress"; that would be especially significant for Israel. Others belong to Yhwh's original bringing of the world into being; for instance, Yhwh is "former of the mountains, creator of the wind" and "maker of Pleiades and Orion," the constellations of the stars. But the implication of the participles is that however firmly located in the past such acts are, they tell us something of ongoing significance concerning their subject. Yhwh *is* the former and creator, "the builder of his upper stories in the heavens and founder of his vault on the earth" that supports them.

---

[42]Augustine, *Confessions*, 11.26, 33; 28, 38; cf. Pannenberg, *Systematic Theology*, 1:403-10.

[43]Fretheim, *Suffering of God*, pp. 39-44.

[44]The exceptions prove the rule; the finite verbs continue the participial construction (cf. GKC 116x).

Indeed, it is because those acts tell us something about the ongoing nature of Yhwh that they provide the background for ongoing acts as "the one who turns darkness into morning, who darkens day into night," who "treads on the high places of the earth," who "calls the waters of the sea and pours them out on the face of the earth" as rain, who "touches the earth and it melts," makes the land shake or quiver with thunder.

For the most part these are threatening acts. It is therefore the more striking that the first of the ongoing acts is that Yhwh tells humanity "what he is thinking" or "what he is complaining about." The noun śēaḥ may refer to Yhwh's intention or to Yhwh's displeasure, but either way it gives the listeners a hint that they had better respond to the thinking of this powerful God. The context of the last episode in this description makes most explicit its threatening implication. It is this God whom no one can escape (cf. Amos 9:2-4).

Isaiah 40—55 also describes Yhwh as creator by using the participial form of bārā' and other verbs. It generally does so with more encouraging implications. Yhwh speaks as "creator and spreader of the heavens, beater of the earth and its produce, giver of breath to the people upon it, spirit to those who walk on it" (Is 42:5). The participles with their lack of temporal reference once again suggest that Yhwh's being creator is not just a reality of the past. It was indeed in the past that Yhwh exercised creative sovereignty in spreading the heavens like a desert sheik spreading his tent and in flattening the earth that forms the tent's floor (but also making it productive). It was in the past that Yhwh formed the first human beings to live there and gave life to them. But the participles draw attention to the fact that Yhwh continues to be that creator and giver (cf. Is 44:24), and this is what underlies Yhwh's summons to Jacob-Israel so that it can become "a covenant for people" (Is 42:6), the people in the world to whom Yhwh gave and gives the breath of life. Zechariah 12:1 nuances this note: Yhwh is "spreader of the heavens, founder of the earth, and shaper of the spirit of human beings within them."

Yhwh "created" the planets and stars (Is 40:26), the world (Is 45:18), humanity (Is 45:12), individual Israelites (Is 43:7) and foreign oppressors (Is 54:16), and on the eve of Babylon's fall Yhwh is acting creatively in Jacob-Israel's life (Is 41:20; 45:8). Once more creation is thus not essentially an act that belongs to the world's origins, though neither does the prophet think in terms of continuous creation. Nor is creation necessarily creative; in Isaiah 40—55, Yhwh is also the one who creates the destroyer so that he may ravage (Is 54:16). Creation is a recurrent punctiliar event, and the essence of its significance is that it is an act of power, an expression of Yhwh's sovereignty.[45] Being

---

[45]Cf. Jon D. Levenson, *Creation and the Persistence of Evil* (reissued Princeton, N.J./Chichester, U.K.: Princeton University Press, 1994), p. 3.

creator of the planets and stars means having authority over them; they make nothing happen on their own initiative (Is 40:25-26). It goes along with giving orders to the entire heavenly army (Is 45:12). It establishes sovereignty over people's destiny and activity (Is 43:7; 54:16-17). It means that the heavens and the earth must do Yhwh's bidding (Is 45:8), and it explains the extraordinary transformative events that take place when they do (Is 41:20). "His sovereignty—and here we have one of the most important if not the first forms of an insight rather curiously achieved during the exile—is that of the Creator of heaven and earth."[46]

Concretely, Israel can therefore ask Yhwh for rain in the season of the spring rain, crucial for bringing the crops to fruition, because "Yhwh is the one who makes the storm clouds, gives the rain storm to people, the growth in the field to everyone" (Zech 10:1).

Unique

One impetus behind First Testament worship is the fact that "Yhwh is the great God, the great king above all gods" (Ps 95:3). In a modern context that can seem a rather unadventurous declaration that colludes with the idea that there are lots of gods. In its own context it is an audacious one. Israel was surrounded by and intermingled with people who claimed with some plausibility that Marduk or Baal was a great God and a great king above all gods. The psalm declares that it is Yhwh who is the creator and owner of sea and land, canyons and mountains (Ps 95:4-5). Yhwh is "to be revered above all gods," as the one who made the heavens, whereas the ʾĕlōhîm of the peoples are actually ʾĕlîlîm, feeble godlets or nothings or nobodies (Ps 96:4-5).[47] Thus the First Testament affirms that there is only one real God, though it does not deny the existence of other gods. Its use of words for "god" corresponds to that in other Middle Eastern languages. There it can connote "not only major deities but also a wide variety of other phenomena: monstrous cosmic enemies; demons; some living kings; dead kings or the dead more generally; deities' images and standards as well as standing stones; and other cultic items and places"—in fact, anything that is not regular humanity.[48] Hebrew, too, thus uses the words translated "god" differently from the way we use the word god in English. But like the word holy, the very word god ends up having a different meaning when applied to Yhwh from the meaning it has when applied to a god such as Marduk.

---

[46]Karl Barth, Church Dogmatics, IV/3,i:105.

[47]See, e.g., TDOT.

[48]Mark S. Smith, The Origins of Biblical Monotheism (New York: Oxford University Press, 2001), p. 6.

Thus Israel saw its deliverance at the Red Sea as establishing not that Yhwh alone is divine but that Yhwh has a majesty and wonder-working power different from that of other deities: "Who is like you among the gods [*ʾēlim*], Yhwh, who is like you, majestic in holiness, awesome in glorious deeds, doing wonders?" (Ex 15:11). Both Yhwh and other supernatural entities are gods and are holy, but the wonder-working ability demonstrated to the Israelites establishes that Yhwh is majestic in holiness and that no other god resembles Yhwh. Yhwh is the "Most High" (*ʿelyôn*), the divine title used by Melchizedek as priest-king of Jerusalem (cf. Gen 14:18-22) that also came to be applied to Yhwh. In ordinary usage the adjective simply denotes something high. Applied to God, it suggests God's exaltation over humanity, over the world and over other deities, and it thus points to Yhwh's majesty and power (e.g., Ps 7:17 [MT 18]; 18:13 [MT 14]).

The question "Who is like you?" recurs, as a question about the mighty God surrounded in truthfulness who is committed to the king (Ps 89:8 [MT 9]), the God who delivers an ordinary individual weak person from people too strong for them (Ps 35:10; 71:19). It also recurs as a question about the God who "carries wrongdoing and passes over rebellions" (Mic 7:18). A form of the question addressed to other people is "Who is like Yhwh our God?" as one who sits enthroned on high but observes what is happening far below and reaches down to lift up the poor and needy so that they sit among the important people (Ps 113:5-8). Yhwh in person asks, "Who is like me?" in might (Jer 49:19; 50:44) or in my capacity to declare what will happen, because I am the one who then makes it happen (Is 44:7; 46:9). "There is no one like me," declares Yhwh to Pharaoh (Ex 9:14). And Israel responds, "There is no one like you" (2 Sam 7:22), no one who speaks and acts as images cannot (Jer 10:6-7), no one who keeps covenantal commitment and is generous and forgiving (1 Kings 8:23; Ps 86:8). "There is no one like Yhwh," who can afflict and relieve Egypt as Yhwh chooses to do (Ex 8:10 [MT 6]) and can ride through the heavens to come to Israel's aid (Deut 33:26) and can act to elevate a lowly person and put down the majestic (1 Sam 2:2). It is "Israel's most extreme witness about God."[49]

Admittedly, in the study of the First Testament, claims about Yhwh's uniqueness are inclined to lead to embarrassment. The description of Yhwh as God of history is a particular example, since other Middle Eastern gods also claimed to act in history.[50] The Canaanite god El is like Yhwh in being both powerful and caring. The rhetorical questions about uniqueness voiced by Yhwh and Israel might then seem to come adrift, as rhetorical questions some-

---

[49]Brueggemann, *Theology of the OT*, p. 143; the subsequent sentences also parallel Brueggemann's elaboration of this point.

[50]See classically, Bertil Albrektson, *History and the Gods*, ConBOT 1 (Lund: Gleerup, 1967).

times do. Or perhaps the apparent difficulty helps us to see the significance of their rhetorical claim. They were not making a point about comparative religion. The discovery that other religions made comparable claims for their gods does not imperil Israel's underlying claim, which concerns not the uniqueness of a theology but the uniqueness of a reality. To say that there is no one like Yhwh is to say that there is no other God. "There is no God like me" collapses into "There is no God besides me" ('immādî, Deut 32:39). Has any other people ever heard a god speaking out of fire and survived? Has any other god ever gone to take hold of a people from the midst of another nation and done the wonders to make that possible? Has any other god driven more powerful nations out of their land so as to give it over to this people? All this ought to make Israel "acknowledge that Yhwh is God; there is no one apart from him. . . . So you are to acknowledge today and bring back to your mind that Yhwh is God in the heavens above and on the earth below; there is no other" (Deut 4:35, 39).

Only God

Thus "Yhwh our God Yhwh one" (Deut 6:4). "The fact that God is one is decisive for talk about God in the Old Testament from beginning to end."[51] But it is impossible to know where to put the "is" in turning that Hebrew noun clause into an English sentence (NRSV offers four possibilities). The particular declaration that Yhwh is "one" is also allusive. I take it to reinforce the fact that Yhwh is the one and only God whom Israel is to worship, the one proper object of all Yhwh's commitment.[52] "God is one means He alone is truly real"; it signifies "the same," an inner unity, both love and power, both creator and redeemer.[53] It also suggests something affective. Yhwh is the one God for Israel to love.[54]

Indeed, that difference in wonder-working ability between Yhwh and other deities or holy ones is such as to undermine the application of the same words to them. The word god, or rather God, turns out to describe a category of being of which there can be only one. Yhwh alone is a being who had no beginning

---

[51]Claus Westermann, *Elements of Old Testament Theology* (Atlanta, Ga.: John Knox Press, 1982), p. 32. Rolf Rendtorff (*The Canonical Hebrew Bible* [Leiden: Deo, 2005], pp. 634-35) notes that this is of course the theological confession of the biblical text itself; study of the history of Israelite religion will acknowledge that Israelites often worshiped other gods.

[52]See, e.g., *TDOT* and *NIDOTT* on 'ehâd. The context does not suggest the idea that Yhwh is a unity over against the multiplicity of deities in a polytheistic religion (true though that is).

[53]Abraham J. Heschel, *Man Is Not Alone* (New York: Farrar, 1951), pp. 117-19.

[54]Cf. R. W. L. Moberly, "Toward an Interpretation of the Shema," in *Theological Exegesis*, ed. Christopher Seitz and Kathryn Greene-McCreight (Grand Rapids/Cambridge: Eerdmans, 1999), pp. 124-44; see pp. 132-33.

and will have no end (Is 43:10-13). "Before me no god was shaped," Yhwh says. Paradoxically, "god" is here ʾēl, the term to denote the most exalted God in the Canaanite pantheon and also a term for Yhwh as *the* God (e.g., Is 40:18). It is also, paradoxically, a term for an image (e.g., Is 44:10), as well as for deities in general (Ex 15:11, just quoted). The prophet thus pictures the way a deity comes into existence as like that by which the image that represents the god comes into existence. There is indeed a profound difference here between Yhwh and the Babylonian gods. The Babylonians' own story told of how their gods came into being. Yhwh was in existence before any other deity. Indeed, Yhwh never came into existence. Nor will Yhwh tolerate the coming into being of any other deities: "and after me none will come into being."

The implication or the basis of this statement is the fact that "I alone, I am Yhwh" (cf. Is 45:5, 6, 18). We have noted that superficially this is an unimpressive or trivial or uncontroversial statement, simply an equivalent to Marduk saying "I alone am Marduk." But the association with other statements such as the ones that appear in the preceding and following lines give the statement more significance. It means "I alone am Yhwh [and that means I alone am God]." So "there is no plainer description of the divinity of God" than this phrase.[55] The declaration "I alone am God" soon follows, but typically, the point is first spelled out as a statement about Yhwh, and about Yhwh's activity, specifically Yhwh's activity as deliverer.

Mono-Yahwism, acknowledging Yhwh alone, implies monotheism, but the prophet is not interested in that academic category, as a Wisdom writer might be.[56] Mono-Yahwism "serves to stress the radical exclusivity of Yahweh in Israel's earliest belief without simply assimilating it to later monotheism and without regarding it merely as a crude forerunner of full monotheism."[57] Mono-Yahwism means Yhwh alone is the deliverer. (Does this imply that when [for instance] India was delivered from British rule or Vietnam from American involvement, it was Yhwh who delivered them?) Throughout, the First Testament believes that Yhwh is absolutely unique in authority and sovereignty. No one rivals Yhwh's power and no one else achieves what they want in any realm of earthly life independently of Yhwh's initiative or enabling or connivance. In a sense, then, the First Testament is monotheistic. But the framework presupposed by the word *monotheism* does not come from the First Testament. Indeed, David Tracy describes monotheism as "an Enlighten-

---

[55]Barth, *Church Dogmatics*, II/1:301.

[56]Vriezen, *Outline of OT Theology*, pp. 23-25; 2nd ed., pp. 32-35. Jon D. Levenson offers a provocative Jewish study of the sense in which First Testament faith is monotheistic in *Sinai and Zion* (Minneapolis: Winston, 1985), pp. 56-70.

[57]Gottwald, *Tribes of Yahweh*, pp. 679-80.

ment invention," an aspect of evolutionary thinking.[58] Certainly the First Testament is not preoccupied by the arithmetical question "how many beings are there entitled to claim the word *God*: are there one or two or six or many, or what?" Nor is it preoccupied by the philosophical version of this arithmetical question that actually generated the word *monotheism*. It is preoccupied by the question "who is God?"—is it Baal or Marduk or Yhwh? Better, it is preoccupied by the question "Whom are you treating as God?"—is it Baal or Marduk or Yhwh?[59] It thus combines a theoretical polytheism with a practical monotheism, contrasting with the modern or postmodern world's theoretical monotheism but practical polytheism ("We all worship the same God").[60]

Mono-Yahwism could be socially functional, but in more than one way. It could encourage the development of an egalitarian community.[61] It could do the opposite. When there is one God and God is king, and this one God is brought into association with a human king as vice-regent, that is a recipe for hierarchy and oppression. Likewise monotheism could be a recipe for particularism or for universalism. To insist that there is only one God could imply an openness to other peoples, whose worship must be worship of this one God, or it could imply intolerance of them as a people who worship no-gods instead of the one God.[62]

Inimitable

A vital theological difference between Israel and the nations around is the conviction that God cannot be imaged. Israel is not to learn to follow "the way of the nations" (Jer 10:2) in making images of Yhwh as they make images of their deities. The second of the Ten Words already warns against this (Ex 20:4-5). There is to be no making of images, the form or shape *(těmûnâ)* of anything in

---

[58]David Tracy, "God as Trinitarian," in *Christianity in Jewish Terms*, ed. Tikva Frymer-Kensky et al. (Boulder, Colo./Oxford: Westview, 2000), pp. 77-84; see p. 78.

[59]On this discussion, see, e.g., Claus Westermann, *Isaiah 40-66* (Philadelphia: Westminster Press/London: SCM Press, 1966), pp. 16-17; Gerhard von Rad, *God at Work in Israel* (Nashville: Abingdon, 1980), pp. 128-38; Brevard S. Childs, *Biblical Theology of the Old and New Testaments* (Minneapolis: Fortress/London: SCM Press, 1992), pp. 355-56; Robert K. Gnuse, *No Other Gods*, JSOTSup 241 (Sheffield: Sheffield Academic Press, 1997); Hershal Shanks, ed., *Aspects of Monotheism* (Washington, D.C.: Biblical Archaeology Society, 1997); Nathan MacDonald, "Whose Monotheism? Which Rationality?" *OTS* 55 (2005): 168-82; Richard Bauckham, "Biblical Theology and the Problems of Monotheism," in *Out of Egypt*, ed. Craig Bartholomew et al. (Grand Rapids, Mich.: Zondervan/Milton Keynes: Paternoster, 2004), pp. 184-232.

[60]So Christopher R. Seitz, *Word Without End* (Grand Rapids/Cambridge: Eerdmans, 1998), pp. 255-57.

[61]So Gottwald, *Tribes of Yahweh*, e.g., pp. 611-21.

[62]Cf. Regina M. Schwartz, *The Curse of Cain* (Chicago/London: Chicago University Press, 1997), p. 33.

the heavens or on the earth or in the waters under the earth, and there is to be no bowing down to them or serving them. The reason for this is that when Yhwh appeared at Sinai, people heard a voice but saw no form (Deut 4:12, 15-20; cf. Ex 20:22-23). Yhwh was there in the midst of the cloud and shielded by it, and they thus stood before Yhwh, and in some sense "Yhwh our God has shown us his splendor and his greatness" (Deut 5:24 [MT 21]); the people testify to their experience in words that recall the experience denied to Moses, who wanted to see Yhwh's splendor. Yhwh spoke to Israel there, but did not directly appear. Moses does not quite say that Yhwh has no form; indeed, he had seen Yhwh's form (Num 12:8). We have noted that Yhwh has eyes, lips, ears, right hand, hand and face, and has manifested a humanlike capacity to act. But the Israelites did not see a form, and Israelites are forbidden to image Yhwh as a being with face, hands, feet and other body parts.

The fact that Yhwh cannot be imaged coheres with Yhwh's nature as the real, living, active, speaking creator God, who is like no other. Jeremiah 10:1-16 draws attention to two aspects of the religion of many Middle Eastern nations: they stand in awe of signs in the heavens, and they make images of their gods. The nature of Yhwh as a God who makes things happen in the world confronts both of these. On one hand, Yhwh is the real king of the nations, the one who controls their destinies. The planets and stars are at best Yhwh's underlings in this respect. They do not deserve awe. On the other hand, Yhwh has a power in the world that the images also do not have. Thus the planets and stars may truly determine things, but only on Yhwh's behalf; the images have nothing to do with Yhwh at all, and they cannot determine things at all. It is Yhwh who is the original creator, the lord of nature now and the one who exercises sovereignty in international affairs. These three are interrelated aspects of Yhwh's activity. In substance they are three distinguishable but linked aspects of Yhwh's sovereignty. And the evidence for one undergirds the evidence for the others. The nature of the images is assumed to be an accurate representation of the nature of the deities.

So "to whom would you liken God—what likeness compare with him?" It makes no sense to think you can represent the sovereign of the universe by means of a humanly made image (Is 40:18-20). To discourage Israelites from making images, prophets deride the image-making process in cynically quasifactual accounts of it that are more or less allowed to speak for themselves (e.g., Jer 10:1-16; Is 40:19-20; 44:12-20). These images are made by human skill from natural resources such as wood, gold and silver, nicely colored cloth. Their craftsmen have to make sure of choosing wood that won't rot (you don't want your god decomposing) and of fixing the images securely (you don't want your god falling over). And they are no more capable of speaking or moving than a scarecrow is. They have to be carried by human beings. They cannot do anything, good or bad, and thus they do not deserve any reverence. They have no *rûah* in them. It is self-evidently stupid to go through the process of making a god and then bow down to it as if it could deliver you. *Images are just blocks of wood*, the prophet shouts. They are a con. Their makers' insight is empty. Image-makers "delight" in their images, but the creation stories show that delight is a dangerous thing (Gen 2:9; 3:6; cf. Is 1:29), and in this case the things they delight in are actually useless. Images are pathetic things, and so are the gods they represent.

Jealous

To put the point another way, images are mere breath (*rûah* again!) and emptiness; image-makers are therefore emptiness too (Is 41:29; 44:9). There is nothing wrong with emptiness as a starting point; God could go about some shaping and could fill emptiness with beings made in God's image (Gen 1). But that requires God as the subject of the verb *shape*, not human beings. Here the sequence emptiness-God-shaping-humanity is replaced by the sequence humanity-shaping-emptiness. Images are the object of "shaping," when it is of the essence of genuine deity to be the subject of that verb; the real God is one who shapes (Is 43:1,7, 21; 44:2; Jer 10:16; 51:19). According to *Enuma Elish*, the actual Babylonian deities, too, were shaped within time out of existent raw materials. It is particularly paradoxical to talk about shaping a *ʾēl*, for we have noted that *ʾēl* is most often a term for God that especially suggests majesty and power, absoluteness and might (e.g., Is 40:18), even among the Canaanites. Of course in theory no one thought that the image-makers were making a deity; they were making an image. But one can imagine that this distinction became rather theoretical, and the prophets ignore it. After all, the point about an image was that it *could* adequately represent the deity, so that when you were in the image's presence, you were in the deity's presence. The fact that *ʾăšērâ* is both the name of a god and a term for a column representing the god is a symbol of the fact that Israelites involved in worship of Asherah would have made little distinction between the two meanings; they would have identified the cult symbol and the deity.[63]

The risk in making an image is that Yhwh is a passionate or jealous God (*ʾēl qannāʾ*). Indeed, Yhwh's very name is "Jealous." That is how radically Yhwh is "a jealous God" (Ex 34:14). Jealous passion is very close to the center of Yhwh's nature. Oddly, this reference to Yhwh's passion or jealousy comes after the second of the Ten Words, not the First, about not having other deities,

---

[63]Cf. Susan Ackerman's comments, "At Home with the Goddess," in *Symbiosis, Symbolism, and the Power of the Past*, ed. William G. Dever and Seymour Gitin (Winona Lake, Ind.: Eisenbrauns, 2003), pp. 455-68; see p. 457.

where the idea of Yhwh's jealousy would seem more at home (Ex 20:4-5). It thus makes sense to see this sanction as attached to the first two Words together, with the implication that while worship by means of an image might in theory be worship of Yhwh, it actually counts as worshiping another god, because a god who can be imaged cannot be Yhwh. Deuteronomy 4:15-24 similarly slides from talk about the people making images to talk about their bowing down to the heavenly army (the planets) and thus worshiping other deities, and thereby betraying their position as Yhwh's people, and similarly links the making of an image with Yhwh's jealous passion.

Whereas Israel's worship dishonors Yhwh by offering as sacrifices animals that are blind, lame, sick or stolen, "from sunrise to sunset my name is great among the nations, and in every place incense and a pure offering are to be brought to my name" (Mal 1:11). Yhwh's words take the form of noun clauses (there is no *is* or *are*), with the usual consequent uncertainty about how to turn them into English verbal clauses. The NIVI provides them with future verbs, but there is no concrete indication that they refer to the future rather than the present, while as statements about the present, it would require more evidence to reckon that they refer to pure worship being offered by Israelites in the dispersion or by Gentiles. More likely they make a statement about the greatness of Yhwh and the recognition Yhwh must receive. As a matter of fact, Yhwh is the great God, great in power throughout the world, active in history in the way Israel has witnessed. It is by Yhwh's sovereignty that the sun rises and sets each day. And thus offerings are to be brought to Yhwh. "I am a great king and my name is to be revered among the nations," Yhwh adds (Mal 1:14).[64] The objective facts about Yhwh's greatness over the entire world show up the enormity of the Israelites' disdaining of Yhwh. "The language is doxological. . . . God's sovereignty and greatness do not depend on what happens in the Temple."[65] But worship should correspond to the truths about God.

2.2 Yhwh's Aides and Representatives and Rivals

So the First Testament does not deny the existence of other "gods," though it affirms Yhwh's uniqueness and preeminence as God. We might be inclined to reckon that the human origin of the images of the gods points to the human origin of the actual deities; the entire religion was a human construction. But the First Testament does not work the logic that way. It does not argue for the nonexistence of heavenly beings other than Yhwh. These so-called deities do

---

[64]I take the niphal participle to have its common gerundive force, "to be revered," and interpret the hophal participle similarly, "to be brought."

[65]Eileen M. Schuller, "The Book of Malachi," *The New Interpreter's Bible*, vol. 7 (Nashville: Abingdon, 1996), pp. 841-77; see p. 860.

indeed exist, but they do not count as God, and they are subject to God's judgment.

Indeed, there is rather a variety of ways of speaking about supernatural entities other than God. There is the aide who mediates Yhwh's own presence and activity. There is the advocate or restorer who can speak on our behalf with Yhwh and the adversary who may speak against us. And there are the supernatural centers of power that can deliberately oppose Yhwh's purpose and Yhwh's people.

Yhwh's Underlings

Yhwh's relationship with other gods is in fact analogous to that with human powers. Yhwh could simply overwhelm them, yet does not do so but does sit supreme over them. "All gods have bowed down to him. . . . You, Yhwh, are most high over all the earth; you have ascended far above all gods" (Ps 97:7-9). Therefore the divine beings (*běnê ēlîm*) must "bestow on Yhwh honor and strength, bestow on Yhwh the honor of his name" (Ps 29:1-2). They are not merely urged to "ascribe" to Yhwh the honor and strength that Yhwh in any case possesses. They are urged to "give" honor and strength to Yhwh (*yāhab*, cf. Ps 96:7-8), the honor and strength that they possess as heavenly beings. If they hold on to honor and strength, they compromise Yhwh's. They are to yield them. The verses that follow implicitly provide the basis for this exhortation. "Yhwh's voice was over the waters, the glorious God thundered, Yhwh over the mighty waters, Yhwh's voice was with power, Yhwh's voice with majesty" (Ps 29:3-4). At the Beginning, Yhwh asserted authority over all other powers in connection with creating the world. Yhwh did not need to fight in order to do so, like a Babylonian god, but simply spoke, in such a way as to quell the forcefulness of the mighty waters that embody tumultuous power asserted against God. Yhwh demonstrated power and majesty; it is appropriate that other deities therefore surrender to Yhwh their own honor and strength. And they do: "In his palace each one in it is saying, 'In honor Yhwh took his seat over the flood, and Yhwh took his seat as king forever. May Yhwh give strength to his people; may Yhwh bless his people with well-being'" (Ps 29:9-11). They recognize that the mighty waters will never be able to assert themselves again, and they acknowledge that Yhwh is the one who possesses strength, by asking that Yhwh in turn bestow it on Israel.

Although Yhwh would be quite capable of running the world without any help (Is 40:13-14), for unexplained reasons Yhwh brought into existence many other heavenly beings who work with Yhwh administratively and practically and thus form Yhwh's court or cabinet. As a court in the legal sense, this meeting's task is to deliberate about wrongdoing on earth. As president of the court, Yhwh makes the actual decisions, but does so on the basis of cases argued by its members; for instance, it is there that the Babylonian-born high priest Joshua is accused of being unfit to be high priest (Zech 3). But this heavenly cabinet discusses and makes decisions about earthly events more broadly (see, e.g., 1 Kings 22:19-22; Ps 82; Is 6; Dan 7:9-14), and its members are then involved in the implementing of these decisions.

In doing so, they act as representatives of different nations, rightly concerned for their welfare. Chemosh, for instance, will argue Moab's cause (cf. the portrait of the "leaders of the nations" in Dan 10). Extraordinarily, in Psalm 29 what these heavenly beings are now doing is arguing on behalf of Israel. In urging Yhwh to give strength to Israel, they are indeed bestowing strength on Yhwh as well as ascribing it, in that they are implicitly making their resources available to Yhwh in connection with taking Israel to its destiny, by blessing Israel with well-being. "In the heavens they confess your wonders, Yhwh, yes, your truthfulness in the assembly of holy beings, because who in the sky compares with Yhwh, who is like Yhwh among the divine beings, God held in great awe in the council of holy beings, revered above all who surround him? Yhwh God Armies, who is like you, mighty Yah, with your truthfulness surrounding you?" (Ps 89:5-8 [MT 6-9]).

To put it in a way easier for Westerners to cope with, the gods form a body of mighty aides who do what Yhwh says, armies of ministers who put Yhwh's desires into effect (Ps 103:20-21). They do not rule the world. God does that; they are "nothing but servants."[66]

While sovereign over all the nations and ruling them via these aides, Yhwh relates in a different way to Israel. The God who is the former of everything, Yhwh Armies, is the "allocation of Jacob" *(ḥēleq)*—an allocation made by Yhwh, of course—while those other subordinate deities are allocated to the other nations. Conversely, Israel is Yhwh's own personal possession *(naḥălâ)* among the nations (Jer 10:16).

Deuteronomy 32:8-9 makes this point very sharply: "When the Most High allocated the nations, when he divided up humanity, he set the boundaries of the peoples in relation to the number of the divine beings,[67] because Yhwh's possession is his people, Jacob is his allocation."[68] Israel's being Yhwh's personal possession means it has no right to worship other gods, but does provide

---

[66]Barth, *Church Dogmatics*, III/3:463.

[67]I quote the reading in the LXX and the Qumran manuscripts (cf. NRSV). The MT has "Israelites," but this makes less sense in the context. See, e.g., J. G. McConville, *Deuteronomy* (Leicester/Downers Grove: InterVarsity Press, 2002), p. 448.

[68]Out of the context one might take Yhwh here as a subordinate god who receives Israel as his allocation from the Most High, but in the context in Deuteronomy that cannot be the lines' meaning. See, e.g., Mark S. Smith, *The Memoirs of God* (Minneapolis: Fortress, 2004), pp. 109-10.

it with a basis for encouragement and appeal to Yhwh (e.g., Ps 74:2; Mic 7:14). It need not rule out Yhwh's relating to the other nations. Yhwh belongs to Levi (Num 18:20) and to several people in prayers (see Ps 16:5; 73:26; 119:57; 142:5 [MT 6]; Lam 3:24), yet also belongs to the whole people. But a converse of the fact that Israel is Yhwh's allotment is indeed Yhwh's allotting to other peoples to bow down to and serve the planets (Deut 4:19; cf. Deut 29:24-27 [MT 23-26]). It might seem a rather heartless conclusion that Yhwh should have allocated these deities and their useless images to the nations. In the context, it is designed to provide Israel with grounds for taking their relationship with Yhwh seriously. It provides a form of explanation for the otherwise inexplicable fact that the nations do worship these deities. What else could be said? Clearly Yhwh did not allot it to the other peoples to serve Yhwh. Was it the case that the peoples themselves chose these gods or that the gods chose these peoples? Moses declares that it does not issue from the act of the deities of themselves. Nor does it issue from mere chance or from human initiative, as we might assume. Indeed, in the allocation of responsibilities in Yhwh's council, this is how things work out. It is "a part of the creative and governing work of the Lord of Israel."[69]

Yhwh's Gender

There is another aspect to the demotion of the gods—and goddesses. Gerda Lerner argues that the demotion of the goddess and the eventual triumph in Israel of the one God, identified as Lord and King, encouraged the subordination of women and their marginalization from the community, though she recognizes that patriarchy is much older than that and that this development was "a tragic accident of history."[70] But (Tikva Frymer-Kensky adds), in the ancient world "there was not one Goddess, there were many goddesses; they were not enshrined in a religion of women, but in the official religion of male-dominated societies; they were not evidence of ancient mother-worship, but served as an integral part of a religious system that mirrored and provided the sacred underpinnings of patriarchy."[71] In Sumeria, male and female gods fulfilled roles that reflected the roles of men and women in that male-dominated society. Thus mother goddesses care for their children or act as queens or fulfill women's roles such as weaving. The fact that goddesses fulfill these roles gives some status to women fulfilling these roles, but also limits them to these. Like

---

[69]Patrick D. Miller, *Israelite Religion and Biblical Theology*, JSOTSup 267 (Sheffield: Sheffield Academic Press, 2000), p. 600.

[70]Gerda Learner, *The Creation of Patriarchy* (New York/Oxford: Oxford University Press, 1986), p. 198.

[71]Tikva Frymer-Kensky, *In the Wake of the Goddesses* (reprint, New York: Fawcett Columbine, 1993), p. vii; and see pp. 14-80 for what follows.

women, goddesses play a key role in connection with fertility but not in governing the world. In the second millennium, goddesses became much more marginalized.[72]

In First Testament faith, goddesses are marginalized out of existence, but so in effect are gods.[73] Indeed, perhaps if there is no female deity, there is no male deity. In practice this is indeed so in the First Testament. Yhwh is referred to as "he" and in terms of gender role is described by mostly male images such as "lord" and "king," as traditionally in English. But Yhwh fulfills the roles of goddesses as well as gods and is described in humanly female terms as well as humanly male terms (e.g., Num 11:12; Deut 32:18; Is 49:15; 66:13). Yhwh has eyes, hands and a back, but no genitals. "God is asexual, or transsexual, or metasexual, . . . 'he' is never sexed. God does not behave in sexual ways. . . . God is not imaged in erotic terms, and sexuality was simply not part of the divine order"[74] (though Gen 6:1-3 suggests it could be part of the heavenly order). The First Testament's images for God are mostly male ones, but "it is scarcely true to say that any prominence at all is accorded to his masculinity." Indeed, Ezekiel vehemently attacks people who worship Yhwh with the aid of male images (Ezek 16:17). The First Testament avoids bringing sexuality into its portrait of Yhwh.[75] "'He' is neither 'man' nor 'woman' (Deut 4:16)."[76] "The extreme integration of divine characteristics, roles, and powers in Yahweh carries with it an absorption of the feminine dimension in deity reflected in the goddess."[77]

It is perhaps for that reason that sexual activity carries a taboo; one cannot have sex and then rush into God's presence (Ex 19:15; Lev 15:18; 1 Sam 21:4),[78] and perhaps this is one significance of the fact that the Song of Songs never mentions God. Sex is not part of God's being. God is concerned for the way hu-

---

[72]Inanna/Ishtar, goddess of love and war, is a puzzling exception to the rule about goddesses fulfilling standard female roles, as is Deborah in the First Testament story.

[73]This is not the case, of course, in the actual faith of Israel, for most of its history, when Israelites regularly worshiped goddesses (see esp. Jer 44) and other gods. See, e.g., Othmar Keel and Christoph Uehlinger, *Gods, Goddesses, and Images of God in Ancient Israel* (Minneapolis: Fortress/Edinburgh: T & T Clark, 1998).

[74]Frymer-Kensky, *In the Wake of the Goddesses*, pp. 188-89. Cf. Mark S. Smith, "Like Deities, Like Temples (Like People)," in *Temple and Worship in Biblical Israel*, ed. John Day, LHBOTS 422 (London/New York: T & T Clark, 2005), pp. 3-27; see pp. 14-16.

[75]Ronald E. Clements, *Old Testament Theology* (London: Marshall, Morgan & Scott, 1978), p. 59.

[76]Gerstenberger, *Yahweh the Patriarch*, p. 83.

[77]Miller, *Israelite Religion and Biblical Theology*, p. 202. Cf. Miller, *The Religion of Ancient Israel* (Louisville, Ky: Westminster John Knox, 2000), pp. 23-40. But on this section, see also the comments on Ms. Wisdom in section 3.1 "A Place to Learn."

[78]Frymer-Kensky, *In the Wake of the Goddesses*, p. 189.

man beings express their sexuality, but some distance between sex and God is required, as is the case with death,[79] since death and sex are the two most significant human realities that have no divine analog. Whereas other Middle Eastern peoples, like the modern Western world, located sexuality within the godhead and also had a god called Death, the First Testament sees sexuality as of exclusively human significance and knew that God was distanced from death and sex, even though sovereign over these realms; there are no other deities involved in these realms.[80] While taking over the functions fulfilled by a variety of gods in other religions, Yhwh holds back from the realms of death and sex. (In contrast, the First Testament does not require distance between food and God, but rather indicates that God likes food, and it interweaves eating and worship.)

Yhwh's Embodiment

As well as speaking in the plural about the army of aides that serves Yhwh and thus ministers to humanity, the First Testament speaks of individual heavenly figures that do that. Further, it gives such individual figures a role as representatives or advocates in relation to Yhwh.

On Israel's journey from Egypt, Yhwh's aide went before the people, and for the journey from Sinai, Yhwh again promises to send an aide before the people to act as guard and guide (Ex 14:19; 23:20-23; 33:2). In Israel's subsequent experience, "Yhwh's aide camps round people who revere him and delivers them" (Ps 34:7 [MT 8]). The aide evidently fulfills a military role, leading a substantial army in protecting people. The EVV translate mal'āk "angel," but the First Testaments "angels" do not fit the image of angels in Christian spirituality. They are not figures flitting about in wispy dresses but strong, assertive figures. Nor does Yhwh's aide have a merely defensive role. With regard to the suppliant's attackers, the next psalm urges that "they must be like chaff before wind, with Yhwh's aide driving; their way must be darkness and slipperiness, with Yhwh's aide pursuing them" (Ps 35:5-6). The aide this psalm speaks of recalls the one who acted at the exodus.[81] The driving like chaff that he indulges in is a frightening image; so is that of being pursued in the dark along slippery tracks through mountains and canyons.

Yhwh's aide is to be taken very seriously because "my name is in him" (Ex 23:21). The identity of a divine aide can thus be a slippery question, as is the case in stories in Genesis. People can assume they are meeting with Yhwh's representative but find they are meeting with Yhwh in person. In Zechariah 3

---

[79]See section 2.1 "The Living God."

[80]Gottwald, Tribes of Yahweh, p. 681.

[81]Cf. Konrad Schaefer, Psalms (Collegeville, Minn.: Liturgical Press, 2001), p. 86.

this question is obscure from the opening "he showed me." We are not told who is the "he"; it could be either Yhwh or Yhwh's aide (cf. Zech 1:9, 20 [MT 2:3]). In the vision Joshua is standing "before" Yhwh's aide, who is therefore not Zechariah's interpreter nor Joshua's advocate but the court president. But why is Yhwh not presiding? Indeed, the person who immediately speaks in anticipation of the accuser's arguing his case *is* Yhwh. The JPSV changes this so that it is Yhwh's aide who does so, which draws attention to the jumpiness of the portrayal. What this person says is "Yhwh dismisses you, accuser. Yes, Yhwh who chooses Jerusalem dismisses you." The third-person verb is more natural on the aide's lips, but quite possible on Yhwh's.[82]

Given that being in the very presence of Yhwh is a dangerous business, Yhwh's aide effectively brings an aspect of that presence, but does so without being overwhelming. Elsewhere in Zechariah an aide brings definitive explanations of the significance of the prophet's vision and of the message the prophet is to proclaim (Zech 1:9, 14-17, 18-21 [MT 2:1-4]). But there, too, there is an ambiguity. The aide identifies the four horns; Yhwh shows Zechariah four blacksmiths; Zechariah asks about these, and in reply "he said." Is this the aide or Yhwh? Indeed, there is some ambiguity about the relationship of these aides to one another. Is the aide to whom Yhwh responds with good, comforting words the same as the aide who appealed to Yhwh on behalf of Jerusalem and Judah, or a different one (cf. Zech 2:1-5 [MT 5-9])? These various ambiguities indicate that we should not reify these aides, though that is not to say that they do not correspond to something real. They provide a way of picturing the reality of Yhwh's involvement in the world. The unevennesses in the visions also mean they leave something of its mystery. We receive just glimpses of its workings.

A number of psalms suggest an analogous way of thinking. Psalm 43:3 urges Yhwh to "send your light and your truthfulness: they can lead me. They can bring me to your holy mountain, yes, to your dwelling." In Psalm 23:6 "good and commitment chase me all the days of my life," again with the result that I can return to (MT) or dwell in (LXX) Yhwh's house for long years. Psalm 25:21 prays, "May integrity and uprightness watch over/preserve me"; this is elsewhere Yhwh's task (e.g., Ps 32:7). Psalm 57:3 [MT 5] asks for God to send "his commitment and his truthfulness," which is here Yhwh's means of sending from the heavens to deliver the suppliant from the person who is "hounding" him. Psalm 61:7 [MT 8] asks God to "appoint commitment and truthfulness" to guard the king. The background of this possibility lies in the awareness that "faithfulness and authority are the foundation of your throne,

---

[82]The verb is usually translated as a jussive, but whoever is the speaker, the verb is more likely an indicative declaration, the definitive rejection of the accuser's case.

commitment and truthfulness stand before you" (Ps 89:14 [MT 15]); therefore Yhwh can send these associates as emissaries. In Psalm 85:9-13 [MT 10-14], the possibility of Yhwh's deliverance becoming a reality for Israel issues from the fact that "commitment and truthfulness have met, faithfulness and well-being kissed; truthfulness has flourished from the earth, faithfulness has looked down from heaven." The images of kissing and looking down make particularly clear that faithfulness and well-being are personal entities. The psalm continues by declaring how "faithfulness will go before him, set its foot on the journey"; preceding and setting foot are likewise actions of a personal entity).[83] In this psalm the personal connotations may also carry over to deliverance, which draws near, and honor, which dwells.[84] But as experiences of Israel, deliverance, well-being, and honor are surely one step removed from being personified aspects of God. Indeed, it seems that faithfulness and commitment (and deliverance?) are the realities that come from heaven, while truthfulness and well-being (and honor?) issue from earth.

The imagery of aides emphasizes the personal nature and authority of God's involvement in the world, though they distance Yhwh from this involvement. The imagery in the Psalms avoids this distancing and emphasizes the moral quality of this involvement. God's people really experience God's own light, truthfulness, good and commitment.

Advocate

Horsemen who had been sent by Yhwh to go about the earth report to Yhwh's aide that everything is quiet in the world. This might seem good news, but the aide responds by crying out to Yhwh (Zech 1:7-17). "Yhwh Armies, how long will you not have compassion on Jerusalem and on the cities of Judah, with which you have been enraged now seventy years?" (Zech 1:12). The heavenly aide's job corresponds to that of a prophet (in another sense, of course, the former is the paradigm for the latter). It thus has two aspects. The aide mediates between heaven and earth in explaining to Zechariah what is going on, but also in speaking out to Yhwh about what is going on. This is not a heavenly being who fails to feel any responsibility for affairs on earth, but one who exercises this responsibility, not least by that speaking out to Yhwh with the kind of protesting question that the people themselves express in their prayers (e.g., Ps 74:10). The aide speaks on the people's behalf. But the question "How long" also appears on Yhwh's own lips, addressed to the "gods" (Ps 82:2). It is as if

---

[83]Though Yhwh could be understood as subject of the last colon.

[84]The parallelism would allow the first line to refer to "his honor," but the context suggests it rather refers to Israel's honor, which will link with its enjoying good things and well-being, though it is still "his honor" in the sense of his gift.

the aide is turning the question back on Yhwh. Perhaps it offers the reassurance that the aides and Yhwh share a concern that oppression should not go on forever, though it also raises the question whether either side is in a position to stop it doing so.

The aide thus adds heavenly protest to the earthly protest of prophet and people. The aide's question also recalls statements of prophets to people. From the beginning Yhwh has reckoned to be a God characterized by compassion (Ex 33:19). In the context of the threat and the reality of exile, prophets had re-emphasized Yhwh's compassion, which would mean the people's restoration after the fall of Jerusalem and the exile (e.g., Is 49:13; 54:7-8; Jer 31:20; 33:26; Hos 2:23 [MT 25]). The fall of Babylon has meant exiled Judeans are free to return home, and some have done so, but Jerusalem still stands in ruins. The community is merely a beleaguered subprovince of another overlord, and in a sense it hardly seems that the exile is over. To judge from how things are on the ground, Yhwh continues to be enraged with it and condemn it. The continuation of peace in the life of the empire is a sign that Yhwh is not taking action to restore Judah. It continues to stand under Yhwh's rebuke. Jeremiah had spoken of seventy years in exile, a veritable lifetime, and over seventy years have passed since the exile in 597 of Jehoiachin and thousands of other people (including, for instance, Ezekiel), and the associated pillaging of the temple. How long will this continue?

"Yhwh answered with good words, comforting words, to the aide who spoke with me" (Zech 1:13). The expressions are familiar. Zechariah's predecessors had already spoken of "comfort" and had brought news of "good" (e.g., Is 40:1; 52:7, 9; Jer 31:13; 32:39, 42). We might be tempted to reckon that what the situation needs is actions, not words, but the reply perhaps implies that these are words that mean action, words that set action going, performative words. The aide speaks again: "Call out as follows: Yhwh Armies has said this: I feel a huge passion for Jerusalem, for Zion, and I feel a huge anger against the nations that are at peace, because I was a bit angry, but they helped for trouble" (Zech 1:14-15). Yhwh underlines the strength of these feelings by using an idiom that pairs a verb with its cognate noun, "I passioned a great passion, angered a great anger" (cf. Zech 8:2).[85] Yhwh has been showing no compassion[86] for Jerusalem, but only rage or condemnation. But Yhwh now speaks words of comfort: "I am returning to Jerusalem in compassion. My house will be built in it (Yhwh Armies' message). The line will be extended over Jerusalem. Call out further, Yhwh Armies has said this: My cities will

---

[85]See section 2.6 "Passion."

[86]There is no semantic link between the Hebrew words for "compassion" and "passion" comparable to the link between the English words.

again overflow with good, and Yhwh will again comfort Zion and again choose Jerusalem" (Zech 1:16-17). "Calling out" is a declaration that makes things happen.

Job speaks of his advocate in heaven, in a different connection (Job 16:18-21). He is casting about for some way he can get God to acknowledge that the way he has been treated is unfair and unjustified. He despairs of being able actually to argue this out with God, because God is just too big. It would be like an ordinary citizen trying to confront the king and accuse him of being unfair. But he knows that one thing on his side is the fact that the blood of the innocent does cry out from the ground, and he urges the ground not to cover his blood, demanding that his cry find no resting place. This might imply he thinks the only vindication he can now expect is after death, but it might mean he imagines his future cry already making its appeal. That appeal goes not to God—who is the one who is shedding his blood—but to someone in the court of heaven who will act as his advocate with God even now, to argue the case for his innocence and thus for his restoration. Eliphaz has already asked rhetorically to which of the holy ones Job will turn (Job 5:1), and Job takes up his challenge.[87] "No, now, there—my witness is in the heavens, my advocate on high," who "must argue for a man with God as a person will for his friend" (Job 16:19). There is no reason for the "improbably paradoxical" idea that the advocate *is* God, as if Job were appealing to God against God.[88] It is this advocate who must argue with God on his behalf, and whom he also shortly urges to accept his oath that his protestations of innocence are true (Job 17:3).

Restorer

Perhaps Job will have to settle for vindication after his death, as his blood continues to shout out. In Job 19:23-27 he starts from the fact that there seems to be no way he can get a meeting with God in order to have the chance to argue for his innocence and vindication. One possibility he thus envisages is that his words might be securely and permanently recorded somewhere so that there might be some possibility of his vindication in the future. That might come after his death. There is a sense in which the existence of the book of Job forms the answer to Job's longing, though his concern presumably continues to be

---

[87]"Line 20a presents several possibilities: 'My interpreter[s]/scorner[s] [is/are] my friend[s]/ thought[s]/shepherd[s]'" (Marvin H. Pope, *Job*, AB, 3rd ed. (Garden City, N.Y.: Doubleday, 1973), p. 125. It makes for a smoother reading to take the words as singular and as referring to the witness/advocate, but the endings are ones that usually denote plural. I have thus taken "my mediators, my friends" to refer to the broader circle of this court, those "holy ones."

[88]David J. A. Clines, *Job 1—20*, WBC (Dallas: Word, 1989), p. 391, against, e.g., Robert Gordis, *The Book of Job* (New York: Jewish Theological Seminary, 1978), pp. 526-28.

vindication with God. The other possible factor in bringing that about is the existence of some mediator or advocate such as he earlier spoke of, here described as a restorer *(gōʾēl)*. "Oh that . . . I myself knew that my restorer will live and will take his stand last on the earth" (Job 19:25). The English versions usually have Job simply declaring that he does "know" that his restorer lives, but this is not the kind of "knowledge" Job usually testifies to; his knowledge is usually rather negative (e.g., Job 9:2, 28). I take this "knowing" as part of the wish that opens the passage; it follows on his wishing that his testimony was on permanent record. If only he could know this about his restorer![89] The written testimony and the restorer might then together procure his vindication. The point about describing the restorer as alive will be to make the contrast with Job himself, who by then will be dead. In a subsequent debate on Job's case, this restorer will have the last word.

A restorer was a member of a person's family who was in a position to act on their behalf when they were in need and thus to "restore" the situation to what it should be. That might involve an act such as spending resources to get them out of debt or servitude, or taking action against someone who had wronged them. Job has just been lamenting the fact that God has quite alienated his family from him. Everyone has put him out of mind, turned against him (Job 19:13-19). If only he had an alternative restorer! "Restorer" thus becomes a way of understanding the role of a heavenly being like the mediator or advocate. It would again be someone who could take your side when you were overwhelmed by some circumstance or need. Here that need is for the vindication of your good name and thus your place in the community. In particular, this restorer will thus put Job's "friends" in their place (Job 19:28-29). "Restorer" can be a term to describe God (e.g., Is 44:24), and in the end God will act as Job's restorer, but here the idea is that some other heavenly being should act restoratively in a situation where God is not doing so.

"Yes, after my skin has been struck away, but from my flesh I would see God; I myself would see him and my eyes will have seen, not another" (Job 19:26). Does he envisage an after-death experience? The fact that this is an unparalleled hope hardly argues against it. But more likely it indicates a more wistful expression of longing for what he really wants now. Vindication after death is better than nothing but it is not the ideal.

Elihu does know he has a mediator, or at least knows it is a possibility. It is part of his threefold understanding of God's discipline of humanity.[90] God

---

[89]On varying interpretations of this passage, see, e.g., Clines, *Job 1—20*, pp. 463-65.

[90]I assume that the convictions of Elihu and Job's other three friends can in principle count as part of the First Testament's theological insight. One has to ask whether they fit in with the whole, even if they are irrelevant to Job.

sends dreams and visions to draw someone away from a lifestyle that might end up in Sheol; God sends suffering that may itself take a person to the edge of Sheol. But he can escape that "if there is an aide for him, a mediator, one of a thousand, to declare his uprightness for the man. Then he shows grace to him and says, redeem him from descending to the Pit, I have found a ransom" (Job 33:23-24). But there is a telling ambiguity in Elihu's words about the mediator. Does he indeed plead the individual's integrity? And is this that person's ransom price? If so, that is exactly what Job wanted from an advocate. Yet how does this fit with the person's subsequent acknowledgment of sinfulness, of which Elihu speaks? Does Elihu rather mean that the aide declares the nature of the uprightness God looks for in this person? The aide's role would then seem to be that of pleading for forgiveness for the person, not making a claim for their uprightness. And this plea and the aide's willingness to stand surety for the person would be their ransom price.

The previous passage about a restorer or redeemer being alive has provided Christians with phrases to illumine the significance of Jesus, but this has little to do with its meaning for Job, who is concerned for the vindication of the innocent, not the forgiveness of the guilty. But ironically, it may be that Elihu describes a role that Jesus will fulfill.

The Adversary

Negatively, an "accuser," an official prosecutor, also plays a key role in the processes of Yhwh's cabinet in its courtly functioning. One of the divine beings (literally, "sons of God/sons of gods") and thus one of the members of the heavenly cabinet has the task of bringing charges against people against whom this court should then take action (see Zech 3; Job 1—2). Perhaps there was one such being, who was the equivalent to a state prosecutor, or perhaps any member of the court could take on the role of accuser. On the earthly plane in Israel, legal proceedings were initiated by the person who felt wronged or by some third party (see 1 Kings 21:13). We know of no arrangement in the Middle East whereby anyone functioned as public prosecutor, nor of a heavenly figure with this role in the stories or theologies of other Middle Eastern peoples. So perhaps "the adversary/accuser" in Zechariah and in Job are simply regular members of Yhwh's staff who on these occasions bring a charge.[91]

The word for adversary/accuser is śāṭān, and EVV often transliterate this word as Satan, but this gives a doubly false impression. The word is not a name but a common noun; it has the article the.[92] *The earliest otherwise-known occur-*

---

[91]See Peggy L. Day, *An Adversary in Heaven* (Atlanta, Ga.: Scholars Press, 1988), pp. 34-43.

[92]In later usage, as the NT shows, one can put the article on a name, but this is not the practice in biblical Hebrew.

rences of Satan as a proper name come in Jewish writings from the second century, Jubilees and the Assumption of Moses. It is not a proper name in Enoch or at Qumran. Further, in Zechariah 3 and Job this adversary is not the embodiment of evil and of resistance to God's purpose, but a being who fulfills a task on behalf of the court as a whole, even if he may get too enthusiastic about that role. He may also appear in 1 Chronicles 21, though there he may not be a supernatural figure at all. Perhaps a human being suggests the census and in thus leading David astray acts as an adversary to Israel (cf. the "adversary" in 1 Kings 11:14, 23).[93] After all, *śāṭān* usually refers to human adversaries (e.g., 1 Sam 29:4); it is an equivalent to "enemy" (*'ōyēb*), but is less frequent than that word. Sometimes it is specifically a legal adversary, an accuser (most clearly, Ps 109:6).

"The adversary" is not a supernatural being with power over against Yhwh. His authority is strictly circumscribed. He can accuse, but he cannot judge (Zech 3). He can tempt, but he cannot overwhelm; he requires human cooperation (1 Chron 21). He can test, but only within boundaries that God allows (Job 1—2).

Sometimes Yhwh's supernatural aides do exercise their responsibility in the right way, but sometimes they do not. Sometimes they fail to exercise their vocation in a way that recognizes Israel's special position or that otherwise recognizes proper principles, and Yhwh may then intervene. Thus Yhwh may assert authority over Moab and Chemosh and they may go into exile (Jer 48:7). "Why has Milcom dispossessed Gad?" Yhwh asks (Jer 49:1). Milcom was the chief god of the Ammonites, and Jeremiah sees his activity behind the Ammonites' appropriation of territory that had belonged to one of the Israelite clans. If this were an isolated comment, one might take it as a figure of speech: the Ammonites saw things that way, and for the sake of argument Jeremiah expresses the matter thus. But this is not the only example of such speech. Jephthah speaks of Chemosh as the god who gave the Ammonites their land (Judg 11:24),[94] and Chemosh is the subject of a strange incident in the time of Elisha. Under attack by Israel, the king of Moab sacrifices his son to Chemosh, "and great wrath came on Israel, so that they withdrew from him and returned to the land" (2 Kings 3:27). The story does not quite say that Chemosh simply made that happen in response to the Moabite king's act of sacrifice, but it half invites the reader to make that inference.

---

[93]So Sara Japhet, *The Ideology of the Book of Chronicles and Its Place in Biblical Thought*, 2nd ed. (Frankfurt/New York: Lang, 1997), pp. 147-48.

[94]Presumably Jephthah is slightly confused theologically, which would not be surprising, though he understands that the Ammonites have a deity identified with them and that they are functionally monolatrous, like the Moabites who actually did worship Chemosh; cf. *DDD*.

The Judgment of the Gods

So the task of other "deities" is to serve Yhwh's purpose in the world. When they fail to do that, they are in trouble, as Psalm 82 shows. "God took his place in the divine assembly [the assembly of ʾel]; in the midst of the gods he would take decisions." There are points when the First Testament uses the word ʾĕlōhîm (and ʾēl) in such a way as to indicate that it applies uniquely to Yhwh. But we have noted that in other contexts it is used more broadly.[95] Here it is applied both to God, the figure of unique authority who takes the decisions in this psalm, and also to the gods among whom and for whom this God makes decisions. The psalm makes clear that there is a world of difference between this God and the other ʾĕlōhîm. But it does not make a point of safeguarding this assertion by confining the use of the word ʾĕlōhîm to the uniquely author-itative speaker in the psalm. In a sense there is thus not so much difference be-tween the assertions of this psalm and the picture in *Enuma Elish*, where Marduk comes to have unique authority over the other gods, though there the gods voluntarily agree to accept that authority, while here it is imposed on them.[96] In the context of the First Testament, the opening "God" must refer to Yhwh. The gods, the offspring of the Most High, become Yhwh's heavenly un-derlings; the term "leaders" (śārîm) again recalls the supernatural "leaders" of the nations in Daniel 10.[97]

The question is, "How long do you take wrongful decisions by exalting the person of the wicked?" (Ps 82:2). Whether we think of them as gods or as lesser heavenly beings (or as human leaders, as has been suggested), the direct thrust of the psalm concerns not their metaphysical status but their moral behavior. They are responsible for justice in the world, not merely in Israel, but also else-where. Their multiplicity links with that, as in Daniel (and cf. Deut 32:8), but the psalm now makes it explicit. God had delegated authority in the world to these entities, but the psalm now calls them to account: "take decisions for the poor and orphan, do right by the weak and destitute, rescue the poor and needy, save them from the power of the wicked" (Ps 82:4). But instead of using their authority in a way that thus serves what is right, they have used it to sup-

---

[95]See section 2.1 "Unique."

[96]Cf. Levenson, *Creation and the Persistence of Evil*, pp. 6-7, 131-32.

[97]There is no doubt that the word ʾĕlōhîm suggests one "God" in Ps 82:1a and 8 (because its verbs are singular) but that it denotes a number of "gods" in Ps 82:1b (where it is governed by the prepositional expression "in the midst of") and v. 6 (where the words in apposition are all plural). I take it that Ps 58:2 [1] also refers to these gods and calls them to account for engendering violence on earth, though this depends on the assumption that the line origi-nally read ʾēlim not ʾēlem (cf. NRSV). Likewise I understand Ps 58:11 [12] then to declare con-fidence that in light of God's action "there are indeed gods making decisions [ʾĕlōhîm šōpĕṭim] on earth."

port wrong structures in society in their different spheres of authority. "They have not acknowledged, nor have they understood. People live their life in darkness; all earth's foundations shake" (Ps 82:5). We can see that the vision refers to the realities of the world in which we live, in which the wicked often succeed in realms such as politics or business and dominate the lives of the poor, rather than using their power and resources to elevate the poor. The job of these entities is to ensure that this does not happen, but they have not recognized that and applied themselves to the task. As a result ordinary people live in the darkness of oppression and the very foundations of the earth are thereby shown to be tottering.

Like Isaiah or Zechariah taking part in a meeting of God's cabinet, in the last three lines the psalmist then personally intervenes (Ps 82:6-8).[98] This intervention first declares to the "gods" that whatever their metaphysical status, they are going to die. It then issues a challenge to God, not directly to bring that about (though this might be an implication) but to take the necessary action about the matter of substance. CEOs can never shelter behind their staff, and God cannot evade responsibility for the earth on the basis of having committed its government to incompetent aides. God claims the whole earth and must therefore take the decisions that need to be taken for it.

The psalm does not tell us what occasion it refers to. My working assumption is that it relates a visionary experience that the psalmist had, and the nature of such a vision is that one cannot discover from the vision its external reference. One might compare it with the vision of the servant in Isaiah 52:13—53:12. In both cases, the nature of such a vision is to constitute both a promise and a challenge. In God's reality, this scene has taken place and the psalmist has prayed the prayer in the last line. We may therefore trust it to become reality in the world, and we had better align ourselves with it.

The psalm assumes that these "gods" came into existence at some point, like Babylonian deities, though it does not tell us how or in what sense they are "offspring of the Most High," though it does assert that despite this status they can "die like human beings." Evidently as well as being subordinate to Yhwh they are metaphysically different from Yhwh, the one God with no possible beginning and no possible end.

A Day of Action Against the Heavens

Isaiah 34:4-5 describes Yhwh promising action of the kind the psalm urges. The prophecy speaks elsewhere of a judgment that will shrivel the earth, but

---

[98]Indeed, while it is usually reckoned that God speaks in vv. 2-5, there is no indication of this, and I rather reckon that the whole psalm is the words of the person who speaks in v. 8. But the theological point is not affected.

here the shriveling also extends to the heavens. "All the army of heaven will rot, the heavens will roll up like a scroll, all their army will wither, like foliage withering from a vine, like withering from a fig tree, because my sword has drunk its fill in the heavens." Its slaughter embraces not only earthly armies but also heavenly ones. Isaiah does not suggest a causal link between the two, as if the former are the earthly equivalent to the latter, though it may assume this. The announcement rather conveys the impression that we are simply reading about a quite comprehensive act of punishment.

Why do nations act in the ways they do, ways that are inexplicably wicked and also in the end inexplicably stupid? Part of the answer lies in their leadership—not only the leaders on earth who affect their destiny, but the leaders in the heavens. Thus Isaiah 24:21-23 similarly declares that "on that day Yhwh will attend on high to the army on high and on the land to the kings of the land." The main part of Isaiah 24 concerns the world as a whole, but these lines move to a different plane. The reference to the heavenly army suggests an involvement of supernatural forces in the transgression on earth that the chapter has deplored. That parallels Genesis 1—11 with its account of the activity of the supernatural beings who took human women (Gen 6:1-4). Yet the prophecy then immediately moves to talk about human beings who hold power. In Genesis 1—11, they recall Nimrod, the world's first great warrior and the first man with whom kingship is associated (Gen 10:8-10). So this vision relates not merely to the supernatural over against the earthly, but to the dominant powers in heaven and on earth over against people in general. Alongside the wasting of the world will be the specific putting down of those who exercise this forceful power.

It is a two-stage piece of good news for ordinary people. First, the heavenly armies and the earth's kings "will be gathered like prisoners gathered in a pit, locked up in a prison" (Is 24:22). While it may be a long time before Yhwh finally attends to these powers, things will not simply be left as they are until then. Yhwh will put the powers under constraint. They cannot do as they like. In slightly different terms, it promises that the challenge in Psalm 82 will be met. The gods, the heavenly beings subordinate to Yhwh the sole God, will die, will fall. "After many days they will be attended to, and the moon will be abashed and the sun shamed," in their capacity as representing heavenly beings subordinate to Yhwh and often revered in their own right as powers that determine events on earth (e.g., Deut 4:19; Jer 8:2). That will happen "when Yhwh Armies has begun to reign as king on Mount Zion and in Jerusalem, and before the elders there is glory" (Is 24:22-23).[99]

---

[99]On this notion of Yhwh "beginning to reign," see sections 2.3 "Kingship over All the Earth" and "Kingship over Israel."

2.3 Yhwh's Lordship

Yhwh is "Lord" ('ādôn, e.g., Is 1:24). Applied to God, the word usually appears in the anomalous form 'ădōnāy[100] (e.g., Is 6:1), which looks as if it should mean "my Lord," though Ugaritic usage suggests the suffix might be not be pronominal but rather simply reinforce the word's meaning, implying "supreme Lord." In different contexts the personal suffix or the emphatic suffix fits better, and I have assumed that the word might be understood either way.[101]

Ludwig Köhler calls Yhwh's Lordship the most basic statement in the theology of the First Testament, the "backbone" of that theology.[102] It suggests "Yahweh's capacity to govern and order in ways that assert sovereign authority and that assure a coherent ordering of life in the world."[103] "There is no realm above or beside him to limit his absolute sovereignty. He is utterly distinct from, and other than, the world; he is subject to no laws, no compulsions, or powers that transcend him."[104] *Lord* is a word that applies to the master of the household or the king of the realm or the owner of some property. Being lord means that your word goes. No one can flout your will regarding family or politics or possessions. Yhwh can do anything, be anywhere and know anything. In this sense Yhwh is omnipotent, omnipresent and omniscient. Admittedly, Yhwh does not always impose sovereignty, can choose to move away from people and sometimes gets to know things, so we must be wary of the implications of those abstractions. But certainly, when Yhwh chooses, nothing can escape Yhwh's sovereignty, Yhwh's reach or Yhwh's awareness. Yhwh is sovereign over nations, over earthly and heavenly powers, over the world and over human life, in ways we may like and ways we may not like.

Kingship over All the Earth

Kingship is thus a subset of lordship.[105] It has been said that kingship is a root metaphor for understanding Yhwh,[106] though if this is so, the plant keeps its

---

[100]It looks like a plural noun (which would thus usually mean lords) and it thus analogous to 'ĕlōhìm /'ĕlōhay, but it has a long vowel in the suffix.

[101]See the discussion in *TDOT*.

[102]Köhler, *OT Theology*, pp. 30, 35; cf. Jacob, *Theology of the OT*, p. 37.

[103]Brueggemann, *Theology of the OT*, p. 233.

[104]Yehezkel Kaufmann, *The Religion of Israel* (Chicago: University of Chicago Press, 1960/London: Allen and Unwin, 1961), p. 60.

[105]Cf. Köhler, *OT Theology*, p. 31. James W. McClendon starts from "God's kingdom" but takes "God's rule" as a broader frame: see *Systematic Theology: Doctrine* (Nashville: Abingdon, 1994), p. 64.

[106]So Mettinger, *In Search of God*, p. 92. Ben C. Ollenburger links it especially with the Jerusalem cult (*Zion, the City of the Great King*, JSOTSup 41 [Sheffield: JSOT Press, 1987]); cf. Mettinger, *In Search of God*, pp.100-105.

roots beneath the surface and waits a long time before thrusting its head above ground.[107] The First Testament includes many references to human kingship before explicitly speaking of Yhwh's kingship. Through Genesis a number of human kings appear, but there are none among Israel's ancestors,[108] and in Genesis Yhwh is never called king or described as reigning. It could make one wonder whether kingship is not an idea Yhwh is fond of;[109] the textual data make one reflect on the ideological danger of talk of God as king. It might provide an argument for Israel not having kings, or an argument for Israel having kings.

But "king" is "one of the few nouns that are used in describing God."[110] And Yhwh's kingly sovereignty does go back to the Beginning, when Yhwh set limits to the raging of the sea, ensured that darkness would each day give way to light, established the violent elements of weather as resources for battling in the world, and set up the stars and planets to rule the seasons (Job 38:8-38).[111] Yhwh then established authority over resistant powers and powers that would threaten the divine purpose, and made sure that the dynamic powers within creation operated within that purpose. That was when Yhwh "began to reign," so as to be able henceforth, as king clothed in majesty and might, to ensure that the world will stand firm, will not totter. "Your throne stands from of old; you are from eternity." Therefore when the great flood lifted its voice and lifted its pounding, "greater than the thunder of mighty waters, more majestic than the sea's breakers, majestic on high is Yhwh." In consequence, "your declarations are quite trustworthy" (Ps 93). Yhwh has made declarations about how things are to work out in the world, and these declarations can be relied on.

At the beginning of Israel's own story, a human ruler attempted to insist on reigning as king over Israel. This drives Yhwh into insisting on showing who is sovereign, which in turn leads to the Israelites declaring that Yhwh will "reign" forever (Ex 15:18).[112] This is the first application of the verb *mālak* to Yhwh. At the other end of the journey from Egypt to Canaan, another king attempts to exercise some control over Israel's destiny, and that leads to a recognition that actually "the shout of a king is among them" (Num 23:21).[113] This

---

[107]See the discussion in Eichrodt, *Theology of the OT,* 1:194-200.

[108]Though passages such as Gen 17:6 envisage them, and Gen 37:8 interestingly tests the rule.

[109]Cf. Terence E. Fretheim, *God and the World in the Old Testament* (Nashville: Abingdon, 2005), pp. 46-48.

[110]Rendtorff, *Canonical Hebrew Bible,* p. 611.

[111]On the event of creation, see *OTT* 1:42-130.

[112]See *OTT* 1:327-32.

[113]I leave the literalistic translation; I take the genitive as subjective and referring to the shout of warrior Yhwh, but it might be objective and refer to a shout of praise to Yhwh.

is the first application of the noun *melek* to Yhwh.

Yhwh's entering into Canaan with the Israelites is another assertion of that kingship. Psalm 47 urges all people to "clap hands, shout to God with resounding voice." Among the regular contexts for clapping and shouting are the coronation of a king, and here peoples are challenged to recognize their real king, the real king, the real Great King—who is not the Assyrian emperor (see 2 Kings 18:19). On the contrary, "Yhwh Most High is to be revered, the great king over all the earth" (Ps 47:2). The evidence for that is the way Yhwh asserted sovereignty in giving Israel its land, notwithstanding the views of the peoples already there. "He subjected peoples under us, countries under our feet. He chose our possession for us, the rising of Jacob that he loves. God has gone up with a shout, Yhwh with the sound of a horn" (Ps 47:3-5). Yhwh ascended from the Jordan into the Ephraimite and Judean highlands and then specifically to the city of Jerusalem, to rule from there over this land and over the world. The psalm's point is thus not that Yhwh always reigns as king, but that on this occasion (as on some others) Yhwh asserted kingly authority and began to reign. Yhwh's occupying of Canaan and setting up a throne in Zion constituted a first stage in asserting sovereignty over the world as a whole. "God has begun to reign over the nations; as God he has sat on his holy throne" (Ps 47:8). Thus the world's leaders, the "shields of the earth" (their defenders or protectors), come and join with Israel or join as Israel (the Hebrew is ambiguous) in acknowledging Yhwh as the one who has ascended so high (Ps 47:9). As king, then, Yhwh will not let the nations occupy "his land" (Ps 10:16).

Kingship over Israel

The supreme locus of description of Yhwh as king or as reigning is here in the Psalms, where noun and verb take up significances implicit in their background in Israel's story. As was the case in Egypt, Israel is usually under the authority of foreign kings, Assyrian, Babylonian, Persian or Greek. Declaring that Yhwh is king affirms who is the real sovereign in Israel's destiny. In the context of the exile the affirmation that Yhwh is king needs to be made again, and the stories in Daniel do that. Indeed the fact that Yhwh is "King of the nations" and "everlasting King" surely means that all the nations should revere Yhwh (cf. Jer 10:7, 10; also Mal 1:14).

At Sinai, however, Yhwh "became king over Jeshurun," a poetic term for Israel (Deut 33:5).[114] Yhwh is not merely king of all the earth but "our king" and "your king" (Is 43:15). The statement is correlative to the people's being

---

[114]"There was a [human] king in Jeshurun" (NRSV) fits the context less well. See McConville, *Deuteronomy*, p. 469.

Yhwh's servant, Yhwh's subjects. That gives them a responsibility of loyalty to the king and of willingness to serve him. It means they cannot accept the authority of some other king, such as the king of Assyria; that amounts to treason.[115] In the First Testament narrative, after Numbers 23:21 the next application of the noun "king" to Yhwh occurs in the context of Israel's own insistence on having a human king (1 Sam 12:12). Samuel's point is not merely that Yhwh is king but that Yhwh is king over Israel. In the Latter Prophets, the first application comes in the vision of Yhwh enthroned as king, in the year a human king of Judah died (Is 6:1, 5).[116] It is a plausible view that a significant context of the use of the Psalms with their affirmation of Yhwh's kingship is the sanctuaries in Jerusalem and in Ephraim with their royal patronage. Declaring that Yhwh is king once more affirms who is the real sovereign in Israel.

The exile will further tweak the significance of that affirmation. Some prophetic promises encourage hope for the reestablishment of the monarchy, but Isaiah 40—55 has a different take on this question. Here the expression "the king of Israel" (Is 44:6) has a different referent from elsewhere in the First Testament (cf. also "king of Jacob" in Is 41:21). It denotes Yhwh, not a human being. It also means the heavenly king is committed to them, responsible to deliver them when they need delivering; that was what was expected of the human king (e.g., Ps 72; cf. Is 33:17, 22). It is as king that Yhwh shows grace and compassion to Israel and responds to those who call out for deliverance (Ps 145:1, 8, 11, 18). Indeed, Yhwh is not just "our king" but "my king" (Ps 5:2 [MT 3]). There is no indication within the psalm that this applies only to a person such as the worship leader or David, who are mentioned in its heading. I am Yhwh's servant, committed to Yhwh; Yhwh is my sovereign, committed to me. Yhwh is my refuge. The First Testament makes little use of animal images to describe Yhwh, though it occasionally uses the image of a bull or a lion, but it delights to describe Yhwh as a rock or crag or cliff. Yes, Yhwh is a strong refuge.

Describing Yhwh as Lord and King is an aspect of the patriarchal cast to the First Testament. Julia Myers O'Brien notes that all the characters in Nahum, for instance, "are constructed according to the template of the same patriarchal shape-box" as Yhwh and the king of Assyria, constructed as males, are involved in a battle over "their" respective women, Judah and Nineveh. "Each has a shaped hole into which it is designed to fall."[117] For a people that was usually marginalized and powerless, and for the marginalized and powerless individuals who are usually the people praying to Yhwh in the First Testa-

---

[115]Cf. Levenson, *Sinai and Zion*, p. 72.

[116]See section 2.1 "Yhwh as Holy One."

[117]Julia Myers O'Brien, *Nahum* (London/New York: Sheffield Academic Press, 2002), p. 94.

ment, such metaphors offered important promise. Their point is not that Yhwh is king, not friend or lover. It is that Yhwh, not Pharaoh, is king. Yhwh, not Baal, is king. Yhwh, not Sennacherib, is king. Yhwh, not David, is king.

Asserting Kingship

The two sides to kingship, sovereignty and commitment, find expression in the metaphor of shepherding. A king is his people's shepherd; as Israel's king, Yhwh is its shepherd (Gen 49:24; Ps 80:2 [80:1 [MT 2]]), and is even the individual's shepherd (Ps 23:1). Like kingship, shepherding suggests on one hand absolute authority and the power of life and death, and on the other an obligation to see that the subjects of this authority and power are looked after properly. Thus in the exile Yhwh goes looking for lost sheep rather than writing them off, rescues them when they have been scattered, and takes them back to land where they can feed and drink well. Of course Yhwh does this as the one who had been responsible for the scattering. So the sovereign calamity-bringer becomes the sovereign restorer. And while binding up the injured and strengthening the weak, Yhwh will destroy the fat and strong (who have got fat and strong at the expense of the weak). Thus Yhwh "will shepherd them with authority" (mišpāṭ, Ezek 34:11-16).

The trouble is that Yhwh must often indeed have seemed something like a constitutional monarch. Israelite kings often exercised decisive authority in Israel and/or foreign kings shaped its destiny, while apparently Yhwh stood by and did not act like someone in authority. Before the exile, Israel regularly refuses Yhwh's kingship. During the exile, Yhwh does not reign in Israel insofar as city and temple stand in ruins, no longer a place with any relationship to reigning; hence Yhwh's declaration at the end of this period about starting to reign (Is 52:7). After the exile, Yhwh still seems not to reign, insofar as conditions stay uncomfortably similar to the ones that obtained during the exile. But Yhwh will become king. In due course John the Baptist and Jesus will say that this moment has arrived, as Second Isaiah did, and there will again be some signs that God is so asserting kingly authority, though God did not finally and effectively do so at that point any more than at the end of the exile. It is evident that God still does not reign in the world or on Mount Zion and in Jerusalem where Jews and Arabs still fight and few on either side recognize Jesus. But the moment will come when Yhwh does so reign, and when before the elders in Jerusalem there is a manifestation of God's splendor like the one at Sinai (Is 24:23; cf. Ex 24:9-11, 15-17). This prophecy thus envisages Yhwh reigning from Jerusalem over the whole world (indeed, the heavens as well as the earth), but it does not forget the importance and the wonder of Yhwh's truly being known among the people of Israel. Indeed, perhaps reigning over the nations paves the way for appearing in splendor to Israel, as in Exodus in the sequence of Exodus

15 and Exodus 24; or perhaps there is a reciprocal relationship between these.

In this context, the Psalms' use of the verb *mālak* has a double significance. It indicates that Yhwh is indeed committed to reigning and in some sense does reign. In the world outside worship it often seemed as if Yhwh did not reign; in the context of worship, Israel affirmed that Yhwh did reign and that this was the real truth even when it did not look like it. The use of the verb in the qatal (e.g., Ps 47:8 [MT 9]) also points to occasions when Yhwh has asserted sovereignty,[118] which the First Testament takes as clues to the real truth about Yhwh and the world. Yhwh's reigning is not merely a present but invisible and rather paradoxical reality and a future but yet-unexperienced reality (cf. Zech 14:9, 16, 17); Yhwh's reigning is a reality evidenced from time to time by events in the life of Israel. While there is a sense in which Yhwh always reigns, in general Yhwh's authority in Israel and in the world is somewhat nominal. A look at Israel's history and at world events soon establishes that they can hardly be reckoned an outworking of Yhwh's will. But from time to time Yhwh asserts authority, begins to reign, implements the divine will.

Israel therefore prays, "As one shepherding Israel, give ear, as one driving Joseph like a flock. As one sitting on the cherubim, shine out, before Ephraim, Benjamin, and Manasseh. Awaken your might, come to deliver us. God, restore us, make your face shine so that we may find deliverance" (Ps 80:1-3 [MT 2-4]). The shepherd image hangs over all those pleas, while the subsequent descriptions of Yhwh interact with the shepherd image. As shepherd, Yhwh is the one who drives or leads or guides the flock to its pasture and to still waters, but instead Yhwh has been giving Israel tears as its food and drink (Ps 80:5 [MT 6]). As shepherd, Yhwh goes before the clans to find the pasture, but this shepherd travels on in an imposing and fast limo (on the cherubim) and can shine light ahead (all of which aids in that process). As shepherd, Yhwh has the might to deliver the sheep from the perils that come to them, and to restore them.

Power and Authority

Yhwh is thus "Israel's mighty one" (Is 1:24). The God of Israel is never in the position of wanting to do something and not being able to do it. Of course God would never, for instance, want to lie or sin or die, because that would not be the kind of thing God wanted to do, so the question whether God's omnipotence extends to a capacity to do such things does not arise. Further, omnipotence does not mean omnicausality.[119] Our understanding of omnipotence

---

[118]The EVV translate *mālak* "is king" or "reigns," but if the psalm wanted to make such an assertion of Yhwh's ongoing sovereignty, it would be natural to use a yiqtol or a noun clause, such as do appear elsewhere in the psalm. See further section 5.1 "Yhwh's Arm Bared."

[119]Cf. Barth, *Church Dogmatics*, II/1:528-29.

must be determined by who God is, rather than vice versa. We do not first determine the nature of omnipotence and then assume it applies to God; we determine who God is and work out what omnipotence is when this being exercises it.[120]

Israel's mighty one is "the great warrior God whose name is Yhwh Armies" (Jer 32:18), one who has great power and exercises it by means of a strong hand and an extended arm and by performing extraordinary marvels (1 Kings 8:42). The supreme occasion when Yhwh did that was the exodus (e.g., Ex 6:6; Deut 4:34; 5:15; 7:19; 9:29; 11:2; 26:8; 2 Kings 17:36; Ps 136:12; Jer 32:21). That was the event that gave Israel the idea that Yhwh was such a God, as Yhwh won a spectacular victory against the gods and political powers of Egypt. The manner of Yhwh's activity at the exodus then provides a model for understanding creation. "I am the one who by my great power and my extended arm made the earth and the peoples and animals that are on the face of the earth" (Jer 27:5). "Lord Yhwh! Yes, you are the one who made the heavens and the earth by your great power and your extended arm. Nothing is too marvelous for you" (Jer 32:17). Creation was Yhwh's first marvel.

Jeremiah also turns Yhwh's exodus power into bad news. "I am the one who will fight you with hand extended and with strong arm" (Jer 21:5). Isaiah had already spoken thus: Yhwh's hand stands extended against the people (e.g., Is 5:25) as well as against the nations (Is 14:26-27). Ezekiel brings these two together in a declaration that is simultaneously good news and bad news. "As I live (Yhwh's message), if I do not reign over you with a strong hand and an extended arm and fury outpoured . . . I will bring you out from the peoples and gather you from the countries where you are scattered, with a strong hand and an extended arm and fury outpoured" (Ezek 20:33-34).

Positive and a negative sides to the exercise of Yhwh's power emerge from another description of Yhwh at the Red Sea, as "the giver of a way through the sea, a path through mighty waters, the leader of chariot and horse, army and powerful one, all at once; they lie down, they do not get up, they are extinguished, snuffed like a wick" (Is 43:16-17). On one hand, Yhwh is one who provides a way through mighty waters that would otherwise overwhelm. But in principle there was no reason for Israel to pass through those mighty waters. They could have journeyed around them. The reason why that was impossible was that an army committed to their destruction threatened them. The way through the sea was their escape from that army. There was no immediate need for Yhwh to go on to destroy the army. Yhwh could have simply stopped it in its tracks, for instance by inflicting upon it a temporary blindness. But its

---

[120]Cf. Ibid., II/1:524-25.

leader was incorrigibly unwilling to let Israel go and to recognize Yhwh's power. To judge from previous episodes in the story, another temperate exertion of pressure on Pharaoh to take his hands off Israel would work no more permanently than earlier ones. Pharaoh is terminally resistant to releasing Israel and recognizing Yhwh, and this is the moment for taking account of that. Indeed, Yhwh has been spoiling for this moment. Another reason why Israel has no reason to pass through these waters is that they had no need to be going that way and thus walking into a trap. What looked like a trap for them is actually a trap for Pharaoh. Yhwh makes this the moment to show who has power in the world. Yhwh is willing to take an army to its death in order finally to deliver Israel and show who actually has that power.

As the one who has begun to reign, Yhwh intends thus to exercise authority over the peoples with equity (Ps 96:10; cf. Ps 96:13), to exercise it in a way that confronts worldly power and thus blesses the weak. Yhwh is a king who is "dedicated to *mišpāṭ* (Ps 99:4; Is 61:8). Hence it is possible to urge, "decide for me [*šopṭēnî*] Yhwh, in accordance with my faithfulness and with my integrity, which are over me. . . . God decides for the faithful person; God expresses indignation always"[121] (Ps 7:8, 11 [MT 9, 12]). The fact that Yhwh is a *šōpēṭ*, one who exercises *mišpāṭ*, is an encouragement to the needy. The EVV routinely translate these nouns as "judge" and "justice," but these translations are misleading. The expressions are words about having the power to make decisions in a more general sense. God does make a decision about right and wrong and then take action.

When understood to have moral implications, these expressions suggest a commitment to acting against people who exercise their power to exact from the weak or in other ways to protect and further their own interests. But their point is then positive: they do refer to the making of decisions *against* the powerful who are in the wrong, but their aim is to make decisions *for* the weak who are in the right. "You have given decisive judgment for me, you have sat on your throne as one who makes decisions faithfully" (Ps 9:4 [MT 5]). Even Barth, in speaking of "the judge judged in our place," comments that as Judge, God "is the One whose concern is for order and peace, who must uphold the right and prevent the wrong, so that His existence and coming and work is not in itself and as such a matter for fear, but something which indicates a favour, the existence of One who brings salvation," as is implied in the work of *the* "Judges" in the book of Judges.[122] It is logical therefore to plead with Yhwh. "The metaphor of judge does not have its locus in a theory of law. It lives,

---

[121]See A. A. Macintosh, "A Consideration of Psalm vii. 12f.," *Journal of Theological Studies* n.s. 33 (1982): 481-90; see pp. 481-82.

[122]Barth, *Church Dogmatics*, IV/1:217.

rather, in a world of desperate, practical appeal of those who have no other ground of appeal or hope and in a world of righteous rage among those who are appalled at exploitative brutality that must be called to accountability."[123] "Yhwh is seated forever as one who establishes his throne for making decisions. He himself makes decisions for the world in faithfulness, exercises authority for the countries with uprightness" (Ps 9:8-9 [MT 9-10]). It is logical therefore for the earth to rejoice that Yhwh has begun to reign, as well as for Zion to do so (Ps 97:1, 8; cf. Ps 98:7-9).

Supremacy

If God is on your side, the divine power is thus good news. But it could seem overwhelming. If this God is against you, what can you do?

It is in this connection that Job asks, "How can a human being be right before God?" (Job 9:2-10). Job's point is not that the person cannot be righteous enough, but that a human being is too small to win the case. "If he wishes to dispute with him, he would not answer him once in a thousand. Wise of mind and mighty in strength—who has been difficult with him and come out whole?" Disputing with God is pointless. God is like the teacher of a sixth-grade class, who knows far more about the subject than the students, is much bigger than they are, and is known to be tough in treating people. Not many students take on this teacher in an argument and win. So God is known for his toughness with the world. God is "one who moves mountains without their acknowledging it, overturns them in his anger, shakes the earth from its place and its pillars quake, says to the sun that it is not to shine and seals over the stars" (Job 9:5-7). Once more, the bulk of this description takes the form of participles, which do not specify the time reference of acts and thus have the capacity to point to God's activity as an aspect of the divine character. Here the order in which Job speaks of events is striking. When a hill collapses in a mudslide, or thunder makes the ground shake, or sandstorm or eclipse obscures the sun and the stars, that is because God has given the order.

But then Job moves to speak unequivocally of events associated with the original creation. God is also the one who "alone stretched out the heavens and trod on the heights of the sea, made the Bear and Orion, the Pleiades and the storerooms of the south, performed deeds that are great, beyond fathoming, wonders beyond numbering." (Job 9:8-10). As well as maintaining the participial construction (it is hard to represent that continuity in English), initially he continues to speak of the tough, assertive aspect to God's activity: creation involved God in treading on the heights of the sea or treading on the back of

---

[123]Brueggemann, *Theology of the OT*, p. 238.

Sea, like a warrior winning the victory over a recalcitrant opponent. Then he speaks harmlessly about creating the stars: but it is these that God has already been prepared to seal over. Thus when we come to God's performing deeds beyond fathoming and marvels beyond numbering, this does not encourage us with wonder but undergirds the sense of threat and overwhelming power. God stretched out the heavens, won a victory over resistant powers, made the stars, did marvels, and thus has the ability to overturn and shake and seal. The argument parallels that in passages such as Amos 4:13; 5:8-9; 9:5-6. When human beings stand under this God's displeasure, there is no way of disputing its appropriateness. Questions of innocence or guilt are neither here or there. God is just too big to take on. Even though I were innocent, says Job, I would find myself pleading guilty because I was so overwhelmed, or I would find God able to turn my protestations of innocence into evidence of my guilt (Job 9:11-24). Further, there is no point determining to change my attitude to my suffering, or to cleanse myself from such dirt as clings to me because I am a human being and thus a sinner, or to find some arbiter who can mediate between us. All those possibilities are excluded by God's determination to treat me as in the wrong (Job 9:25-33).

Further, Job later declares, there is no way of getting access to God in order to pursue a case and get God to listen to him. "If only I knew how I might find him, come to his dwelling. . . . If I go forward, he is not there, or backward, I cannot perceive him, as he acts to the left, I cannot behold him, he turns right and I cannot see him" (Job 23:3, 8-9). Forward, backward, to the left and to the right represent one way of describing the four points of the compass. Job cannot reach God, no matter how far he goes in any direction. But the literal expressions also give an impression of Job as an individual wondering in what direction to look from where he is, but knowing that it makes no difference. God is simply not available anywhere to hear Job's case for the recognition of his integrity.

Energy

Second Isaiah confronts a people in exile that has lost any conviction that its situation will ever improve (Is 40:27-29). It laments, "My way has hidden from Yhwh, a decision for me escapes from my God." There are, after all, many things on God's agenda, and it looks to Jacob-Israel as if the question of fulfilling its destiny has fallen off the bottom of it. As decades pass without anything happening to implement Yhwh's vision, this might seem a pardonable inference. Yet the prophet does not see it that way. "Do you not acknowledge, have you not listened? Yhwh is the eternal God, creator of earth's ends." Such a conclusion is impossible to reconcile with what the community allegedly acknowledges about Yhwh, with what it says and sings and hears in its gatherings each week about "Yhwh" as "my God." In responding to an earlier voice that commented on the withered state of the community (Is 40:6-7), implicitly the chapter has already put together the fact that Yhwh is Israel's God with the fact that Yhwh has the power to achieve things and not to be put off by anything. A further summary of the faith to which Jacob-Israel is theoretically committed now does so more explicitly, in putting together that name "Yhwh" and the description that follows: "He does not get faint or weary; there is no plumbing of his understanding—one who gives strength to the faint, who makes vigor abound for people without resources" (Is 40:28-29). Perhaps the earlier passage put more emphasis on the fact that the powerful God is Israel's God, whereas these later lines put the emphasis on the converse fact, that Israel's God is the powerful God. Yhwh's power is constrained neither by time (Yhwh is the eternal God) nor by space (Yhwh is "creator of earth's ends," and therefore of everything in between, and as creator is sovereign over them).

Further, Yhwh is not the kind of CEO who lets items fall from the agenda, the kind who runs out of energy as the decades pass since the creative moment of the company's founding and as the CEO's years increase, the kind the shareholders need to find a way of kicking upstairs. This creative originator has astounding capacity to stay fresh as time passes. The more complex the problems and the challenges become, the more vision and insight this CEO shows. The young turks run to keep up. Or rather, the more energized they become. For this CEO's instinct is to share strength and vigor, as it had been to share power at the Beginning (Gen 1:28). This implies not letting go of people who run out of energy but encouraging and reinvigorating.

How does that work? It is the qualities of the CEO that have this invigorating effect. The fact that Yhwh *is* the eternal God and the sovereign over all the earth, the one whose understanding can never be plumbed and thus tested beyond its limits, is the fact that can reinvigorate the people of God when they are inclined to give up. The moment of crisis, when the CEO seems to have lost it, is the moment when they need to stay cool and remind themselves of the basis for believing that this could not happen.

Knowledge

Power requires knowledge. Fortunately Yhwh has limitless access to knowledge. "If someone goes into a hiding place, can I not see them (Yhwh's message)? Do I not fill the heavens and the earth?" (Jer 23:24; cf. Ps 94:7-11). "Yhwh's eyes are in every place, watching the bad and the good" (Prov 15:3). "Sheol and Abaddon are in front of Yhwh—yes, and the minds of human beings" (Prov 15:11). "All the ways of a person may be pure in their own eyes, but Yhwh weighs spirits" (Prov 16:2). "Yhwh's lamp searches the human spirit, searches all the inner rooms" (Prov 20:27).[124] We can try very hard to evaluate our actions, but we may not be able to perceive what is really going on inside us, what are our hidden motives. But Yhwh can do so. "The crucible for silver, the furnace for gold, and Yhwh tests minds" (Prov 17:3).

Psalm 139:1-6 expounds this point. The psalmist has a sense of Yhwh knowing everything about him or her: "Yhwh, you have examined me and come to know me; you have come to know when I sit and when I get up, you have discerned my thinking from far away." All the verbs in Psalm 139:1-6 are qatal or wayyiqtol. While a verb such as *yāda'* can refer in the qatal to the state of "knowing" as well as to the act of "coming to know," and EVV thus render some of the verbs in the present, much of the emphasis in the passage lies on Yhwh's finding things out. "You have sifted my journey and my lying down, you have become familiar with all my ways" (Ps 139:3). This knowledge has come about not because it is simply intrinsic to being God but because Yhwh finds out things; the capacity to find out anything *is* intrinsic to Yhwh. That is how Yhwh can know all about the psalmist's movements, journeyings, acts and words. None could be hidden from Yhwh.

Other psalms also emphasize how Yhwh knows on the basis of looking carefully. Yhwh "probes minds and hearts" to check out claims to integrity and faithfulness (Ps 7:9 [MT 10]), "examines" or tests people *(bāḥan)*, looking at them carefully to discover the real truth about them (Ps 11:4; cf. Ps 17:3; 26:2; 95:9; 139:23). "From the heavens Yhwh has looked, seen all humanity, from his dwelling place he has watched all earth's inhabitants; the one who shapes their mind, each one, is the one who discerns all their deeds" (Ps 33:13-15). Here three verbs underline the intentionality of Yhwh's looking, seeing and watching everyone down here on earth from the royal palace in the heavens, and the three come to a climax with the very rare verb *šāgaḥ* (it otherwise comes only at Is 14:16; Song 2:9). They are then summed up in the eventual reference to Yhwh's discerning. The fact that Yhwh is the shaper of people's minds carries with it the capacity to look into them, like a programmer who can always find a way into what people have done with a program.[125]

That might seem sinister, and it is capable of having sinister implications, though the psalm seems rather to stress its beneficence. Psalm 33:18-19 goes on to comment on the relative uselessness of armies and their equipment. They do not ensure that one escapes from crises and finds deliverance. It then adds, "No, Yhwh's eye is on people who revere him, on people who wait for his

---

[124]I follow NIVI in seeing the verb in the second colon as also applying in the first. Other EVV take the first colon as a noun clause, "The human spirit is Yhwh's lamp," but this is an odd and unparalleled idea.

[125]On the fact that Yhwh does not always utilize that capacity, see section 2.6 "Letdown."

commitment, to rescue them from death, to keep them alive when food is gone." All that watching is designed to keep an eye on humanity in a positive way. People who look to Yhwh rather than to their military resources find that Yhwh looks for them and that Yhwh's seeing leads to acting for them, so that the kind of crisis that war brings (such as famine) is averted.

Sovereignty over Nations

If Yhwh is Lord, that implies being sovereign: over nations, over governments, over the heavenly powers that other people reckoned controlled the world, over the world itself and over human life.

Isaiah 40 offers a particularly sustained exposition of Yhwh's sovereignty. It has a specific historical context, in the 540s, when the Persian king Cyrus is in the midst of challenging Babylonian control of the Middle East. After half a century under Babylonian sovereignty, it would not be surprising if Judeans in Babylon and in Judah itself had lost conviction about Yhwh, who either would not or could not get involved in their life any more. One of the first tasks that Isaiah 40—55 therefore attempts is the reestablishment of Yhwh in the eyes of the people whom subsequent chapters address.[126] It begins to undertake that task by reminding people of the sovereignty of Yhwh as creator. It speaks first of Yhwh's sovereignty over the nations (Is 40:12-17). But its statements about that sovereignty make little reference to historical specifics and thus particularly lend themselves to general theological formulation.

"Who measured the waters in his palm, could survey the heavens with his span, measured earth's dirt by the gallon, weighed the mountains with the balance, the hills with scales?" Middle Eastern peoples had other answers to the prophet's rhetorical questions; the Babylonians pictured Marduk holding earth's raw materials in scales. There is thus more than one polemical point that the prophet might be making. The questions might implicitly be a simple challenge to people to make up their mind about whose hands do hold the world, a little like Joshua's challenge to people to make up their minds whom they are going to serve (Josh 24). But perhaps more likely they do not imply that Judeans were actually defecting to another religion but rather that they need to reaffirm their conviction that Yhwh is at least as big as the Babylonians claimed Marduk to be (!). The Judeans are in a position more like that of Ephraimites in Elijah's day, hovering between two views (1 Kings 18:21). Their inconsistency lies in their still being formally committed to Yhwh but in their

---

[126]Cf. Westermann, *Isaiah 40—66*, e.g., pp. 14-15. It has become less fashionable to think in terms of a distinguishable prophet called Second Isaiah (or rather, not called Second Isaiah). I hold to the old-fashioned view, but to avoid being too dependent on that I express the point here as an observation about how Is 40—55 works rhetorically.

having lost conviction about Yhwh's nature, and specifically about Yhwh's sovereignty, so they believe less about Yhwh than the Babylonians believe about Marduk. The prophet invites them to believe that Yhwh is as great as Marduk, and more.

Marduk, after all, needed help with creation. In contrast, "Who could direct Yhwh's spirit; as for his adviser, who could make things known to him? With whom did he take advice so that he enlightened him, taught him the way to make decisions, taught him knowledge, made known to him the way of en-lightenment?" (Is 40:13-14). In Babylonian theology, creation was a team effort. Marduk needed advisers the way a king needs advisers. The Judeans knew in theory that Yhwh was quite capable of planning creation without such help (see Gen 1), or only with the help of the divine insight (Prov 8:22-31). Yhwh might use divine and human aides (cf. the "let us" of Gen 1:26?), but did so out of an instinct to share power and creativity or as a sign of authority and splen-dor rather than out of an inherent need to consult anyone before acting. Yhwh's person and activity embrace the total range of personal qualities and the capacity to undertake all divine roles. The Judeans know this in theory but do not let it inform their attitudes and hopes.

All this has a particular significance in the context of the rise of Cyrus. It means that Yhwh knows how to exercise authority in the world, how to make decisions about historical events (how to exercise *mišpāṭ*). The world empires may look very impressive to the Judeans in Babylon or in Palestine during or after the exile, but they do not look so impressive to Yhwh. "Now: nations count like a drop from a pan, like a cloud on scales. Now: foreign shores are like a thin cloud rising; Lebanon: there is not enough for burning, its animals: there are not enough for a whole offering. All the nations are as naught over against him; they count as less than nothing, emptiness to him" (Is 40:15-17). This does not mean Yhwh lacks concern for them. It means they do not threaten Yhwh or pose a problem for Yhwh or imperil Yhwh's purpose. Their animals are not even enough to constitute a decent sacrifice and thus a decent festive meal. There is thus no need for the Judeans to worry about them.

Over Earthly and Heavenly Powers

Mystifyingly, the Judeans will not recognize such facts (Is 40:21-24): "Do you not acknowledge, do you not listen, has it not been proclaimed from the very first to you, have you not understood the foundations of the earth?" Yhwh's sovereignty in politics is, after all, the very beginning of Israel's faith in the sense that the event that set Israel going as a people was Yhwh's assertion of authority over against the political authorities of Egypt. That event has been celebrated through the centuries since. Each Passover people relive the story. Every Sukkot also reminds them of it. Week in and week out they sing psalms that speak of that event and of subsequent assertions of that sovereignty. How can they not make a connection with contemporary events in Babylon? There is nothing new about the Israelite people being controlled by a colonial power. Can they not make the connection between their present experience and their past experience?

Yhwh is not merely a God who enters into an intimate relationship with them in their hearts and spirits (but is not involved in their outward lives) or a God who marvelously set the world going at the beginning (but now leaves it entirely to humanity to run). Yhwh is "the one who sits above the horizon of the earth, with its inhabitants like grasshoppers, the one who stretches out the heavens like a net, who spreads them like a tent to sit in" (Is 40:22). Yhwh lives within the cosmos, not outside it. Its skies are the tent that Yhwh pitches, to enjoy its shade in the heat of the day. So Yhwh sits high over the earth, though not in remote and detached fashion. From there Yhwh is in a position to keep an eye on what is going on down here, like a human being observing the processions of ants. And Yhwh is thus in a position to stamp on the ants at will. Yhwh is "the one who turns sovereigns into nothing, who makes earth's decision-makers like emptiness" (Is 40:23). There are figures that down here seem so powerful and impressive, sovereigns and world powers, but from a heavenly perspective they are only insects, easy to turn into nothing. They look as if they are very firmly established, as if they have been there forever and will be there forever, but a moment's reflection reveals that this is not so. It is less than a century since Babylon became the dominant power in the Middle East, which is a long time from a human perspective (no one alive would remember a time when Babylon did not rule) but only a moment from a divine perspective. Human decision makers "are not really planted, not really sown, their stem is not really rooting in the earth, and there: he blows on them and they wither, and a whirlwind carries them off like straw" (Is 40:24). Babylon is like a plant that has hardly had time to put its roots down. Yhwh will have no problem uprooting it. The Judeans need to look at the superpowers from Yhwh's perspective. Again we note that although these declarations speak to the circumstances of the 540s, Isaiah 40 expresses them as generalizations that this particular context indeed illustrates. The chapter is a comment on the ongoing sovereignty of Yhwh in the world. This is not a sovereignty such as ensures that every event that happens reflects the divine will, but it is a sovereignty that can at any moment turn upside down the settled political scene.

The Judean exiles might be tempted to think that there were indeed heavenly powers with that capacity, but that they were the planets and stars that determined human destiny. The prophet confronts this assumption, too. "To whom, then, can you liken me, to whom could I be comparable, says the holy one?" (Is 40:25). Yhwh is the transcendent and majestic one, the being who contains all real majestic transcendence. Yes, Yhwh is the one who is sovereign in the world of international politics. This question thus deconstructs, because it asks with whom one could compare Yhwh but closes by referring to Yhwh by means of an expression that implies Yhwh's uniqueness. If the hearers missed the rhetorical nature of Yhwh's question, then the prophet's own term for Yhwh, "holy one," spells it out. And if the hearers are still unconvinced, then the lines that follow spell out that uniqueness to make the point clearer. "Lift on high your eyes and look: who created these? The one who leads out their army by number, who summons each of them by name, through abundance of resources and as one mighty in strength. Not one lags behind" (Is 40:26). In Babylon people reckoned that there were those other entities that decide events of political life and personal life, the planets and the stars. But who decides the movements of the planets and stars, which allegedly reveal what those political and personal events will be? Yhwh controls them. The creation story in Genesis 1 tells how Yhwh put them in place and delegates to them what power they have to rule the earth, and Isaiah 40 affirms that this is not merely an act of delegation at the Beginning. These entities, which at least determine when day and night come, do so each day at Yhwh's personal behest.[127] Not one of the planets or stars dares be idle on parade when Yhwh is the drill sergeant. So why do obeisance to the infantry when the commander-in-chief invites your attention?

"Do not be in awe of signs in the heavens, because the nations are in awe of them" (Jer 10:2). Many Middle Eastern peoples assumed that the movements of the stars and planets determine and reveal coming events on earth. They therefore deserve some awe.[128] But Israel knows that Yhwh is the one who lies behind events. He alone deserves awe (cf. Jer 10:7).

Over the World

Isaiah 40:28 goes on to describe Yhwh as "creator of earth's ends" and therefore of everything in between. Once again, describing Yhwh as creator makes a point not so much about Yhwh's activity back at the Beginning but about Yhwh's sovereignty now. Being the creator means being the lord. So Yhwh is not, for instance, merely creator of Israel and therefore sovereign in the land of Israel but not elsewhere. Yhwh's sovereignty as creator extends to the ends of the world that have the land of Israel as their (theological) center. Yhwh's hand can extend from there to the ends of the earth. Psalm 29 similarly refers to the

---

[127]Cf. the quotation from G. K. Chesterton in section 7.1 "Regularity."

[128]The EVV have "dismay," but like other words of overlapping meaning *ḥātat* can have a positive as well as a negative meaning (see Mal 2:5 for the niphal), and the former fits the subsequent references to reverence (Jer 10:5, 7).

way Yhwh's voice thundered over the waters at the Beginning, putting resistant powers under control, but goes on to assert that thundering in the present: "Yhwh's voice is breaking cedars, Yhwh is breaking up the cedars of Lebanon, making them jump like a calf—Lebanon and Sirion, like young buffalo. Yhwh's voice is dividing flames of fire; Yhwh's voice convulses the wilderness. Yhwh convulses the wilderness of Kadesh; Yhwh's voice makes deer convulse and strips forests" (Ps 29:5-9). When the heavens thunder, when the land then shudders, when lightning flashes, when animals jump in panic, when storm strips foliage off trees or makes even the most impressive trees fall, Yhwh is (or can be) giving evidence of being sovereign in the earth, from the far north to the far south of Israel's world.

Yhwh's crazy commission to pay out money for land on the eve of the collapse of the state provokes Jeremiah into a powerful affirmation of Yhwh's sovereignty:

> Lord Yhwh, it was you who made the heavens and the earth by your great power and by your extended arm. Nothing is too extraordinary for you—one who keeps commitment to thousands but requites the wrongdoing of parents into their children's pockets[129] after them, the great God, the warrior, whose name is Yhwh Armies, great in planning and mighty in action. Your eyes are open to all the ways of human beings so as to give to each person according to their ways and according to the fruit of their deeds. You did signs and portents in the country of Egypt to this day[130] both within Israel and within humanity, and made a name for yourself to this very day. (Jer 32:17-20)

In turn Jeremiah's act of recognition, with the expression of astonishment at the instruction to pay money out for some family land, provokes Yhwh: "Yes, I am Yhwh, God of all flesh. Is anything too extraordinary for me? Therefore, Yhwh has said this: Yes, I am giving this city into the hand of the Babylonians. . . . Yes, I am gathering them from all the countries where I have driven them" (Jer 32:27-28, 37). It is difficult to be sure of the precise links between these various statements, but they hint at a number of theological convictions. They indicate that Yhwh is in a position to do anything in the world. Yhwh is good at seeing what needs doing but also powerful enough to see that it gets done. If there are any limitations to Yhwh's sovereignty, they are self-imposed and they could be abandoned any time Yhwh chooses. As maker of the heavens and the earth and as the God of all flesh, Yhwh can impose events on anyone—Israel, Egypt, Babylon or other peoples among whom Yhwh scatters

---

[129]Lit. "lap." Yhwh is like someone paying goods in full measure into the fold in the front of someone's garment; cf. Joseph Blenkinsopp, *Isaiah 56—66*, AB (New York: Doubleday, 2003), pp. 268, 273.

[130]The JPSV paraphrases "with lasting effect."

Israel. Both creation and the exodus are the past evidence of this, present events in Jerusalem are reflecting it again, and the Judeans' coming return to their land is guaranteed by it and will once more evidence it. To different degrees these are all "extraordinary" events (the verb *pālāʾ*). They may be wondrous or awful; Yhwh's sovereign power as great God and warrior implies the ability to perform acts that are extraordinary in both senses. Yhwh's keeping commitment and requiting wrongdoing seems here to apply not only to Israel (as it does in Ex 34:6-7), but to the world in general, the "all flesh" of which Yhwh is God (as it does in Jonah 4:2). Yhwh's extraordinary acts take place before the eyes of the world and not just before Israel's eyes.

How is this so? It is at least because they happen to an Israel that lives its life not in isolation from the world but in the midst of the world, in relation to peoples such as Egypt, Babylon and those among whom they are scattered and thus from whose midst they will be gathered. If there are any limits to Yhwh's knowledge of what goes on in the world, they are self-imposed, and they, too, can be abandoned any time Yhwh chooses. When it is a matter of seeing that people get their deserve, nothing escapes Yhwh's eye. It can see all that happens. Yet what happens is then "the fruit of their deeds." God's activity is involved: God gives. Natural cause-effect is involved: what people receive is the fruit of their actions.

Over Human Life

In human life there is a time for birth and death, planting and uprooting, slaying and healing, demolishing and building, weeping and laughing, and so on, and God "makes it all beautiful/fitting at its time" (Eccles 3:1-11). God is sovereign in all those events in human life. "Everything that God does will be there forever; to it there is no adding, from it there is no subtracting" (Eccles 3:14). "God's deeds" can be equated with "the deeds that are done under the sun" (Eccles 8:17). What happens in the world is what God does. "The faithful and the wise and their acts of service are in God's hand" (Eccles 9:1).

In themselves these words are encouraging, but in the context Qohelet does not find them so. The faithful and wise as much as anyone else live their lives vulnerable to God's decisions about what will happen to them. Qohelet also urges, "Do not be very faithless and do not be stupid: why die when it is not your time?" (Eccles 7:17). This puts a question mark by an understanding of Ecclesiastes 3 such as suggests that the time for one's dying is fixed. Perhaps "the time for dying" is a set of circumstances, a time when it is appropriate.[131]

"Whatever happens was named long ago, and what a person is was known,

---

[131]Cf. Tomáš Frydrych, *Living Under the Sun*, VTSup 110 (Leiden/Boston: Brill, 2002), p. 121.

and he cannot contend with something stronger than him" (Eccles 6:10). How much should one read from this statement? Minimally, what happens and who we are was known long ago, presumably to God. Maximally, what happens and who we are was actually predetermined long ago, presumably by God. Either way, it is no good fighting with that or with God, in the sense of trying to get it changed. I am British; I am a man; I am white; I have a sharp mind but little ball sense; I can sing in tune but not play an instrument; I have certain personality characteristics and so on. There are ways in which I have changed over the years and ways in which I will yet change, but the basic facts about me were fixed before I was born. I cannot fight any of that or fight God over making it something different. I have to work with what I am. The fact that so much is fixed and unalterable likewise does not make Qohelet infer that we may as well give up any attempt to control our lives, but he does reckon we have to be realistic about what is fixed. "Look at God's activity, because who can straighten what he has made crooked?" Good days and bad days come from God (Eccles 7:13-14). To the person who asks how it is possible for God to make things crooked, Qohelet answers that it is quite clear that there are things that are crooked "under the sun," and they cannot all be blamed on human sin. By definition, God is responsible for all that is.

It is not only the case that God gives us our life. It is God who gives people wealth and possessions. Further, it is God who gives them the power (šālaṭ hiphil) to use these, to accept their lot and to enjoy their toil. It is God's gift. God thus keeps them busy enjoying themselves. On the other hand, there are other people to whom God gives wealth, possessions and honor, and who may lack nothing that they desire, but to whom God does not give the power to use these (Eccles 5:19 [MT 18]—6:2).

Psalm 18 gives praise for the way God has acted in delivering king and people, but it goes on to point to four ways of seeing divine and human involvement in this event. It begins with a spectacular portrayal of Yhwh's spectacular action, parting the skies to appear over the earth in thunder, lightning and hail (Ps 18:7-15 [MT 8-16]). How does that spell itself out? The psalm goes on to speak of Yhwh reaching down to rescue the king from his attackers, lifting him up so that the king experiences an escape against all the odds (Ps 18:16-19 [MT 17-20]). Yet the king is not merely passive. He escapes because he is strong, because his legs stand firm, because his hands are good at fighting, because he can bend a bow. But all those reflect a third form of divine activity. It was Yhwh who had girded him with strength, made his legs stand firm, trained his hands (Ps 18:32-34 [MT 33-35]). It was Yhwh who made him the man he was. Thus (fourth) he can describe the battle simply in terms of human forces fighting, without referring to God's involvement (Ps 18:37-38 [MT 38-39]). If one had been there, it would have looked just like a battle, even if the result was unexpected.

Over the Bad Things That Happen

Yhwh kills and brings to life, impoverishes and makes rich, humbles and exalts (Deut 32:39; 1 Sam 2:6-7). Perhaps this does not indicate that Yhwh is behind every such event, only that Yhwh can do all these. But the sovereignty of Yhwh does give Yhwh some level of responsibility for whatever happens. There is no such thing as chance. When a man accidentally kills another man, it is because God delivered him into his hand (Ex 21:3). Dice fall as they do because God determines it (Prov 16:33). Everything happens by God's determination.[132] When a prophet delivers a false message, encouraging hopes for peace when there are no grounds for such hopes, Yhwh may be involved in this. When priests tell people that Yhwh welcomes the sacrifice of children, Yhwh may be involved in that. When the results of divination determine that a Babylonian king attacks Jerusalem, not Amman, and people in Jerusalem scoff, Yhwh may be involved in that (Ezek 21:18-23 [MT 23-28]). Israel asks, "Why do you make us stray from your ways, Yhwh, why toughen our heart so that we do not revere you?" (Is 63:17). The questions are part of an anguished prayer, and Yhwh might not accept the charges. But it fits with comments such as those of Ezekiel, and Yhwh's response does not deny the charge, only imply that there was good reason.[133] "Shall we accept good things from God and not accept bad things? (Job 2:10). Both come "from with God" *(mē'ēt hā'ĕlōhîm)*. "Shaper of light and creator of darkness, maker of *shalom* and creator of bad things, I am Yhwh, maker of all these" (Is 45:7). "Who has spoken and it has come about if the Lord has not commanded it? Is it not from the mouth of the Most High that good things and bad things come?" (Lam 3:38-39).

The opening of Genesis is ambiguous over whether God created darkness (cf. NIVI) or whether the existence of darkness is simply the backcloth to God's creative acts (cf. NRSV, JPSV). In Isaiah 45:7 Yhwh's declaration makes it unequivocal that Yhwh is not only shaper of light but creator of darkness. Yet it makes this point in a different connection from the one that concerns Genesis. When speaking of God's creative activity, Isaiah 40—55 regularly thinks in terms of an ongoing activity, not one focused in events at the Beginning. Here it is noticeable that the prophet mentions the creation of darkness after the

---

[132]Calvin, *Institutes*, 1.16.6.

[133]Blenkinsopp (*Isaiah 56—66*, p. 253) renders the question "why do you let us stray?" and *IBHS* 27.5 does allow for such a permissive or tolerative hiphil, but JM 54d warns about exaggerating the significance of this idea, and the context makes it unwise to tone down the force of the accusation. Blenkinsopp himself goes on (p. 263) to note the First Testament's willingness to speak in strong terms about Yhwh's responsibility for people's attitude, referring to Is 6:9-10.

shaping of light, and that, too, points to the fact that Yhwh's assertion concerns present activity, activity in history. In turn that puts us on the track of the significance of light and darkness in this context. They do not refer to the unchanging realities of nature. Light is a figure for all that is good, for blessing, success, fullness, richness; darkness is a figure for all that is bad, for calamity, trouble, disaster, loss (e.g., Is 9:2 [MT 1]; Amos 5:18-20). The parallel colon restates the point: Yhwh is maker of *shalom* and creator of what is bad. *Shalom* stands potentially for all forms of well-being. It covers peace, but it is another positive term that embraces much more than the absence of conflict; it suggests a community enjoying fullness of life, prosperity, contentment, harmony and happiness. Its antonym here is *ra‘*, an all-purpose word for what is "bad." Marcion assumed that the prophet was making Yhwh "creator of evil" (cf. KJV), but Tertullian already recognized that he had missed the point.[134] Like the word "bad," *ra‘* covers both evil and adversity. Here the context makes clear that Yhwh is claiming to be one who brings about adversity as well as well-being.

Second Isaiah again speaks more somberly than Genesis 1, which only has God bringing into being things that are "good." The second colon as a whole repeats the point made in the first. Yhwh claims a sovereignty in events that embraces both the good and the bad things that happen (cf. Job 2:10). "Does *rā‘â* come on a city and Yhwh did not do it?" (Amos 3:6). Amos's comment might be a universal one indicating that every event issues from Yhwh's causation or it might be a contextual one about current events in Ephraim that are Amos's concern, and the statement in Isaiah 45 can be read either way. "All these things" may embrace every event that happens, or may denote every *kind* of thing that happens—both light and darkness, *shalom* and *ra‘*. In the context, it will indicate that Yhwh is both the author of events such as the fall of Jerusalem and of events such as the city's restoration, both the achievements of Cyrus and the disaster he brings to the cities he conquers. Whether or not it makes Yhwh the author of all world events, it attributes to Yhwh the *capacity* to bring about all sorts of events at will.[135] Perhaps God is the author of the rise and fall of the British Empire and of the American empire; certainly God can choose to bring about such events.

"Yhwh made everything for its purpose, even wicked people for the day of trouble" (Prov 16:4). Yhwh's work as *creator* thus lies behind the contingent events of *history*. Why does evil exist? God uses it to bring trouble to those who

---

[134]See, e.g., Tertullian *Against Marcion* 11.2.

[135]Cf. the discussion in Fredrick Lindström, *God and the Origin of Evil,* ConBOT 21 (Lund: Gleerup, 1983); James L. Crenshaw, ed., *Theodicy in the Old Testament* (Philadelphia: Fortress/London: SPCK, 1983.

deserve it, like the Babylonians bringing trouble to faithless Judah. Will the wicked be allowed to flourish forever? God has destined them for their day of trouble.[136]

Over Ends and Means

In Job 1—2, Yhwh draws the adversary's attention to Job as a man of unparalleled commitment to God and moral probity. Is Yhwh implying that the adversary needs to have a close look at Job? The adversary does not need to be asked twice. His job description requires him to be suspicious and he is prepared to jump to the obvious conclusion. Job reveres Yhwh because it pays to do so. If Yhwh were to take away all that he has, we would soon hear him stop worshiping and start cursing Yhwh. Yhwh therefore gives the adversary permission to take away all that Job has, and later to attack him personally; and a series of disasters overcomes his servants and flocks, then his sons and daughters, then the man himself.

Is this really the way God behaves? It is hard to reconcile with other aspects of God's ways as they are described elsewhere in the Scriptures. Perhaps this aspect of the story of Job is simply part of the scene-setting for the book as a whole. "There is indeed no 'cause' in Job to provoke the horrible train of events that will unfold: his suffering is, on the narrative level, gratuitous. . . . But on the conceptual level, his suffering is indispensable if the archaic doctrine of piety leading inevitably to prosperity (as in v 2) is to be upset."[137] It would then be like the aspects of Jesus' parables that we should not press. As it used to be put, they are parables, not allegories. That would fit with the fact that the scene in heaven is never taken up later in the book. The adversary does not reappear at the end. On the other hand, it is not different from the story of Abraham and Isaac. Isaac does not lose his life, but a psychologist would expect to see him devastatingly scarred by his experience, and its devastating implications for his mother are caught by the midrash recording her collapse when she is told about Abraham's going off to sacrifice Isaac.[138]

As scene-setting, the introduction makes important points. First, part of the story's background is the fact that calamities such as these do actually happen.

---

[136]See Lennart Boström, *The God of the Sages*, ConBOT 29 (Stockholm: Almquist, 1990), pp. 61-62.

[137]Clines, *Job 1—20*, p. 27. The "archaic" doctrine is of course still alive and well, and the questioning of it is likely as old as the doctrine (as James L. Crenshaw hints in "Popular Questioning of the Justice of God in Ancient Israel," in *Studies in Ancient Israelite Wisdom*, ed. J. L. Crenshaw [New York: Ktav, 1976], pp. 289-304).

[138]See briefly *Genesis Rabbah* 58.4 (*Midrash Rabbah: Genesis II* [London: Soncino, 1939], p. 511); also, e.g., Louis Ginzberg, *Legends of the Jews* (reprint, Baltimore: Johns Hopkins, 1998), 7:286-87.

Terrible calamities fall on people, and sometimes, for instance, on children just because of who their parents are. The modern instinct is to declare that these are simply accidents, for which God is only responsible (if at all) in some ultimate sense, by virtue of having made a world that works in this way. The Job story does not imply that God is always directly responsible for such events, but it does make God fairly directly responsible for this one, and thus takes a brave stance about God's sovereignty. And God is indeed sometimes directly sovereign in this way.

The scene-setting also matches a later emphasis of the book in presupposing that humanity and individual human beings are not the center of the world. We are part of a bigger picture.

> "Jacob I loved, but Esau I hated." So what shall we say? Is there injustice with God? Certainly not, because he says to Moses, "I will have mercy on whomever I will have mercy, and I will pity whomever I pity." So it issues not from desire or effort but from God having mercy. Because the scripture says to Pharaoh, "For this I raised you up, so that I might reveal my power in you, and so that my name might be proclaimed in all the world." So he has mercy on whom he wishes and hardens whom he wishes. (Rom 9:13-18)

It is rare for the First Testament to be as tough as Paul, who is here less concerned to magnify God's mercy than Exodus is, but Job manages it. The ultimate concern of the book of Job is not the personal welfare of Job's family and household, or that of Job himself, but an ultimate cosmic question about the basis of God's relationship with the world as a whole. It is our privilege as human beings to be part of a much bigger story than the story of our own lives.

Yhwh's Freedom

In Job 12:13-25, Job starts from the fact that God is one who possesses all wisdom and power. What happens emerges from God's purpose and sovereignty. That extends to all sorts of events in the spheres of politics and nature and in the experience of ordinary people and leaders. "If he tears down, it cannot be built up; if he imprisons a person, he cannot be released. If he restrains the waters, they dry up, and if he lets them loose, they devastate the land." Cities fall, people are taken captive, water dries up or floods. People formulate mistaken policies, advisers make stupid recommendations, and decision makers do crazy things. "With him are strength and resourcefulness; the person who goes astray and the one who leads astray are his. He makes counselors walk naked and makes leaders go mad."

Such truths can be asserted in praise of God (e.g., Ps 107), in encouragement of God's people (e.g., Is 44:24-28), and in testimony to God's revealing things (e.g., Dan 2:20-23). They mean God can bring about the deliverance of Israel.

Job implicitly pushes their implications in a different direction. Perhaps one can sometimes see a purposefulness in God's action, but that is not always so, and one cannot be selective in claiming these truths. If God has this wisdom and power, that has devastating implications. God's wisdom and power are often applied in directions that seem to contribute nothing to God's moral or saving purpose. The actions Job describe as issuing from that wisdom and power all have negative results. They are all destructive. The reference to exalting and enlarging nations is the exception that proves the rule; it is merely the prelude to destruction and displacement. Perhaps there is some principle behind it all, but Job can see none. God just seems a God who pulls things down. He does not imply that this is all there is to God. He does imply that this aspect of God has to be taken seriously. The speeches in Job 38—39 go on to insist on "the absolute freedom of God," which from a human perspective looks like unpredictability, randomness or capriciousness. God's acts do not correlate to those of human beings, as if to focus on giving people what they deserve.[139]

Job is not just talking theological theory. He has seen it happen and heard it reported by other people who have also seen it happen. These are the real facts that have to be faced. They are important to him, of course, because he has also experienced them in his own life. It is this that has led him to insist on his friends facing them. But behind that, paradoxically he himself needs to be able to affirm them, because they help to make his experience part of a pattern rather than a mere surd.[140]

Events work out as they do because human beings make decisions. But they work out as they do because Yhwh is at work determining what happens. When David fled from Jerusalem, the astute Ahitophel proposed to Absalom that he should follow quickly with a relatively small force in order to take on David and his supporters when they were tired and discouraged. A secret supporter of David then gave contrary advice and carried the debate, "when Yhwh had ordained that the good counsel of Ahitophel should be made ineffectual, so that Yhwh might bring disaster on Absalom" (2 Sam 17:14).

The book of Isaiah offers the most systematic reflection on this process. It is Yhwh who calls up the Assyrian army from far away (Is 5:26; cf. Is 7:18-20). Yhwh sends Assyria; Yhwh gives Assyria its orders (Is 10:6). Of course Assyria has its own agenda. It wants to defeat a number of nations, and it does so on the basis of its confidence in its generals (Is 10:7-11). But Yhwh is behind this.

---

[139]R. N. Whybray, "Wisdom, Suffering and the Freedom of God in the Book of Job," in *In Search of True Wisdom*, ed. Edward Ball, JSOTSup 300 (Sheffield: Sheffield Academic Press, 1999), pp. 231-45; see p. 244.
[140]Cf. Clines, *Job 1—20*, p. 298.

In Isaiah 41—45, it is Cyrus who decides to put down Assyria's conqueror; but behind him is the purpose of Yhwh making sovereign decisions about what Cyrus will do.

Yhwh's Flexibility

Yhwh's freedom extends to doing that with some flexibility. Jehoiakim, Jeremiah says, is to die in such a way as to be unlamented and humiliated, buried like a donkey (that is, unburied); his corpse dragged out of the city and abandoned (Jer 22:18-19). And none of his descendants is to sit on David's throne (Jer 36:30). In the event, he simply "slept with his ancestors," like someone such as David or Hezekiah (1 Kings 2:10; 2 Kings 20:21), and his son succeeded him (2 Kings 24:6). On these occasions, at least, the implication is not that we should reckon that in some way Jeremiah's prophecies actually were literally fulfilled, or that the power of the lines lies in the utterance rather than the fulfillment, or that the prophecy allows for God's openness to change in view of the human response.[141] The utterance has power only insofar as it finds fulfillment, but the fulfillment can be of another kind than one that corresponds to the literal imagery. Jehoiakim certainly dies ignominiously and unmourned, not least because of Jeremiah's own words that still heap ignominy on him, and in this sense their power does lie in their utterance. And his son reigns only three months before being deposed by the Babylonians.

Conversely, during the siege of Jerusalem Yhwh tells Zedekiah, "You will not die by the sword. You will die in peace. Like the burning of incense for your ancestors, the previous kings who came before you, so people will burn incense for you and say in lament for you, 'Oh, sovereign!'" (Jer 34:4-5). In the event, soon afterward Zedekiah was captured by Nebuchadnezzar, blinded, taken to Babylon, and put in prison there until his death (Jer 52:4-11).

In Ezekiel 26—28 Yhwh declares at some length that Tyre will fall. The first of these declarations is dated just after the fall of Jerusalem in 587. As part of their campaign in the west, the Babylonians indeed laid siege to Tyre, but the old city of Tyre is an offshore island and a hard nut to crack. In 574 the siege ended (the city was not conquered until Alexander the Great laid more effective siege to it in 332, building a causeway from the mainland). In some sense Tyre seems to have passed into Babylonian control,[142] but nowhere near as decisively as Ezekiel had implied, and apparently without covering expenses. So

---

[141]Contrast, e.g., John A. Thompson, *The Book of Jeremiah*, NICOT (Grand Rapids, Mich.: Eerdmans, 1980), p. 480; William L. Holladay, *Jeremiah*, 2 vols. (Philadelphia: Fortress, 1986; and Minneapolis: Fortress, 1989), 1:598; Terence E. Fretheim, *Jeremiah* (Macon, Ga.: Smyth & Helwys, 2002), p. 321.

[142]See Leslie C. Allen, *Ezekiel*, 2 vols., WBC (Dallas: Word, 1994, 1990), 2:109.

in 571 Yhwh makes a new decision, to give Egypt to Nebuchadnezzar to make up for all the vain effort he had expended on Yhwh's behalf on Tyre (Ezek 29:17-20).

Ezekiel, Yhwh and the people who kept hold of Ezekiel's oracles seem quite relaxed about the fact that Ezekiel's oracle about Tyre has not come true. They do not fear that events imply that Ezekiel is a false prophet or that Yhwh is not really God because both have failed the tests that prophets and Yhwh set for such recognition. Perhaps they accept the dialectic between divine intention and human resourcefulness, like a father grinning when one of his children "defeats" him. Perhaps they are relaxed because they know that Yhwh and Ezekiel feel quite secure on the basis of being manifestly right much of the time (not least over the crucial example of the fall of Jerusalem), like a professor grinning when a student asks something to which the professor does not know the answer. On that basis, perhaps they are relaxed because they know things will come right in due course; Tyre will eventually get its comeuppance. It will indeed do so, in Alexander's day, though that seems to fail Ezekiel's own test about his prophecies being significant for the present and the foreseeable future, not the future beyond the concerns of anyone currently alive (cf. Ezek 12:21-28). Further, neither does Yhwh ever give Egypt to Nebuchadnezzar or to Babylon, yet Yhwh, Ezekiel and the people who kept hold of Ezekiel's oracles also preserved this second oracle that did not come true.[143]

Ezekiel's relaxedness seems to come more from an acceptance of that dialectic between divine will and human will. It is particularly striking that Ezekiel should be relaxed about this, given his strong emphasis elsewhere on the divine will and on divine sovereignty. He also recognizes that human beings exercise real freedom in the world and do not have to cooperate with God's will. When Tyre declines to lie down and die because that is what Yhwh intends for them to do, like Moses declining to die when Yhwh tries to kill him (Ex 4:24), Yhwh's response is not to overwhelm it by a literal hurricane or a tidal wave of the kind that Ezekiel poetically describes and Yhwh could certainly send, if Nebuchadnezzar's army is not enough. It is rather to rework the plan. Yhwh is still Lord.

2.4 Yhwh's Wisdom and Word

When Proverbs wishes to commend wisdom, it notes that wisdom is what en-

---

[143]It seems that Nebuchadnezzar did take on Egypt in 568/67 but it is not clear what was the result. For different views, see Walther Eichrodt, *Ezekiel* (London: SCM Press/Philadelphia: Westminster Press, 1970), pp. 408-9; Moshe Greenberg, *Ezekiel 21—37*, AB (New York: Doubleday, 1997), pp. 617. Nevertheless, the achievement did not amount to conquest.

ables rulers to govern, and then that wisdom is what enabled God to create the world (Prov 8:1-31). There is an underlying link between these. Yhwh's wisdom is expressed in the way Yhwh governs the world. We may again note Job's observation that "with him are wisdom and power; counsel and understanding are his" (Job 12:13). God's original counsel or plan (*'ēṣâ*) related to creating the world (Job 38:2-7). This entire world issued from divine planning, each element in it being part of a design. That capacity for wise planning and sovereign implementation of plans continues in the way God runs the world. After all, a sovereign king has power and responsibility for formulating purposeful policies for a people. And "the mighty God is a wonderful planner" (*pele' yôʿēṣ*, Is 9:6 [MT 5]).[144] "Yhwh is great in planning/purposing/formulating policy" (*'ēṣâ*, Jer 32:19).

Yhwh's Purpose in Politics

God thus has a plan for Israel's life. Perhaps it would be better to call it an intention or a purpose. God had a purpose for the whole of Israel's life from the beginning, the intention stated in God's promise to its ancestors. God intends that Israel should enjoy blessing, increase and possession of its land, and intends to have the whole world seek the blessing it sees in Israel (Gen 12:1-3). God's design is that all the nations should flock to Jerusalem to listen to God (Is 2:2-4). That design goes back to the design of the creation itself, where humanity as a whole (not just Israel) was created in God's image. But the First Testament does not refer to such intentions as a plan. When it speaks of God's plan for Israel, this is not a design for the detail of history or an itemized strategy for the whole of Israel's life from the beginning, but an intention for the present context. It is in such a connection that people in Judah say, "he can speed, he can hasten his deed, so that we can see it; the plan of Israel's holy one can hurry to come about so that we can acknowledge it" (Is 5:19). The assumption that everything that happens in the world emerges from God's plan stands in contrast with the more concrete way in which the Scriptures speak of God's plan. God's plan refers to the way God works out specific details of an overall vision as decades unfold, in interaction with human actions. It concerns specific intentions for Judah's immediate future. It relates to the sequence of events whereby God implements the intention to bring about the world's deliverance.[145]

Isaiah 41:1-4 has Yhwh making the point about purposefulness to the nations themselves. Yhwh challenges the nations to a debate about who is sovereign in world affairs. Admittedly, expressing it that way implies an openness

---

[144]See section 5.7 "One Who Brings *Shalom*."
[145]Cf. Barth, *Church Dogmatics*, II/1:520-21.

or equality that Yhwh does not manifest or offer. What Yhwh issues is a summons to a debate where the other party is not actually going to speak, partly because they will not have anything to say. The prophet mixes metaphors: Yhwh speaks like one party in a debate before a court, but also like a judge making an authoritative decision before whom the parties must be silent. The summons calls one side to come to listen to another side's case, but the result of this debate is a foregone conclusion.

The topic is, whose will is being worked out in political events? More concretely, whose will is being worked out in the rise of a certain victor from the east? "Who aroused from the east one whom faithfulness calls to its heel?" The anonymity of the victor leaves the hearers to work out whom the prophet is talking about, and they might reasonably conclude that it is Abraham or that it is Cyrus. Yhwh summoned both from the east. Both were the servants of Yhwh's faithful purpose (ṣedeq). Both put down nations and kings (for Abraham, see Gen 14). In the political context, Cyrus is the more obvious of these two referents as he rampages around the Middle East turning the Babylonian Empire into the Persian Empire. But to the hearers, Abraham might be the more obvious, for to judge from subsequent prophecies, they found it difficult to believe that Cyrus the Persian was Yhwh's agent in restoring Judah. How could that be? It will become clear that the prophet reckons that Yhwh summoned both Abraham and Cyrus as part of the pursuing of the same faithful purpose, and the parallels between them would be part of the argument for that. They instance the same pattern of working. If you can believe that Yhwh summoned Abraham, you should be able to believe that Yhwh summoned Cyrus, and vice versa. What Yhwh is doing now through Cyrus is of a piece with that summoning of Abraham. It is part of the activity of the one who "called the generations from the beginning," whose involvement with Israel goes back to Abraham. The sovereign activity of Yhwh spans the entire story of Israel. It is neither something that belongs only in the past nor is it a new initiative in the present. "I Yhwh am the first, and I am with the last" (Is 41:4). Or, if we take the preposition in the second colon as applying also in the first, "I Yhwh was with the first [Abraham] and I am with the last [Cyrus]."

Yhwh's Word and Politics

In a further debate in Isaiah 41:21-29, the issue changes slightly, and the language of planning becomes explicit. "The first events: what were they? Tell us so that we may apply our mind and recognize their outcome. Or inform us about things to come; tell us what is to happen after this, so that we may recognize that you are gods." The first question was, who is active in events? The related issue is, who can talk convincingly about these events? Who can offer an interpretation of the events that have taken place? Again, the questions specifically concern a certain conqueror known to prophet and hearers. "Who told about it from the beginning so that we might recognize him, from beforehand so that we might say 'Right'?" Again, the prophet may invite the hearers to think in terms of either Abraham or Cyrus; the point holds either way. Who can make sense of the long haul of Israel's history over the centuries, the story that has unfolded since Abraham and Sarah's day? And who can make sense of the recent events that have seen the rise of Cyrus? Further, who can tell where either of those stories is going?

There is a sharper question than the one concerning what theologico-political pundit can interpret those events now. Who has been speaking of these events in the past, so that we have had a chance to test their alleged insight? Who spoke about these events before they happened? Prophecy is very difficult, says the Chinese proverb, especially about the future.

Yhwh claims to have met these criteria. Israel's story told how Yhwh had set its history going, summoning Jacob-Israel in Abraham in the way the prophet has just now noted (Is 41:8-9), declaring a plan to bless the nations through him, announcing the intention to bring the Israelites out of Egypt into the land promised to Abraham. For that matter, Yhwh had gone on to announce the intention to take the Judeans off into exile to Babylon. Their records of the words of their prophets also included Yhwh's declaration of intent to put the Babylonians down and take Judah back home, and this by means of the Medes (notably in Is 13; if these prophecies are not much older than Second Isaiah, that little affects their testimony in this connection). The significance of this "argument from prophecy" is not merely that Yhwh knew what was going to happen. It is that Yhwh's capacity to say what is going to happen reflects the fact that Yhwh decides what is going to happen.

The Babylonian gods (and their priests and prophets) are in no position to make sense of the story of Israel over the long haul. That may have seemed not very important, though in the longer haul, it has been proved to be so. But even in Second Isaiah's day, it is a pretty important question for the Judeans, who are the immediate audience of the prophet's words. The Babylonian gods (and their Babylonian priests and prophets) are also in no position to make sense of the rise of Cyrus, which in the immediate context is an urgent question. In due course the priests give unintentional witness to that when, seeing which way the wind is blowing, they change sides and declare that Marduk indeed inspired Cyrus as an act of judgment on Babylon. It is like and unlike the stance of prophets such as Jeremiah in relation to Jerusalem. It is like Jeremiah's stance in its willingness to see the city's deity acting against the city. It is unlike it because it is a stance adopted only ex post facto. Israelite prophets (at least, the ones whose words appear in the First Testament) stuck their necks out regarding Yhwh's purpose before it was obvious which way the wind was blowing. None of those Babylonian gods was actually "planning" events. Yhwh was doing so and was therefore in a position to announce them. Deity implies being at work in political events, evidenced in the capacity to interpret them and announce them.

Yhwh is a potter shaping clay and a father determining a child's destiny (Is 45:9-11). Talk in terms of pot and potter especially recalls Jeremiah's discussion of Yhwh's involvement in the world (Jer 18; also Is 29:13-16), ever flexible in its way of working with the lumps of clay that stand for Israel and other peoples, but always working toward producing pots that will fulfill their purpose. History is still clay in the potter's hands, the potter is still shaping it, and having squashed the clay back into a ball (the exile) is now reworking it again. The reference to parenthood suggests that Yhwh is Cyrus's father and Cyrus Yhwh's son. It is a less sentimental image than we may take it. It means Yhwh relates to Cyrus with the authority of a father who has the power to decide what the son will do (the son always obeys, otherwise he will be imperiling his inheritance).

Yhwh is "One who sends out his command to the earth; his word runs quickly," with the result that snow, frost and hail fall. Then "he sends out his word so that it melts them." Likewise "he declares his words to Jacob, his laws and decrees to Israel" (Ps 147:15-19).

Yhwh's Constancy and Flexibility

In pursuing the purpose that goes back to the beginning and in formulating plans from time to time in connection with this, Yhwh manifests constancy and flexibility. Yhwh's own being goes back to a time that cannot be imagined to have had a beginning, and it will continue to a time that cannot be imagined to have an end, and Yhwh's character remains consistent throughout Israel's story. We have noted the way Psalm 102:25-27 [MT 26-28] speaks of the enduring nature of Yhwh over against the transient nature of the cosmos, and its declaration "you are the one; your years do not end." The EVV render the penultimate clause "you are the same," which makes the line a useful proof text, but it is doubtful whether one can read that with precision into 'attâ hû'. This confession corresponds to the declaration "I am the one" (see Deut 32:39; Is 41:4; 43:10, 13; 46:4; 48:12), and the context suggests it affirms the unique and unrivaled position of Yhwh as the God whose being extends back and forward in time and on whom Israel can therefore unfailingly rely. And in this sense "I am the one/you are the one" does imply consistency of character and action over the eons. Yhwh is "the one who sits enthroned of old, in whom there are no changes" (Ps 55:19 [MT 20]). Yhwh does not pass on like any human ruler or like an image (Is 2:18) or a human being (Job 9:25-26). "I am Yhwh, I have not changed; you are the children of Jacob, you have not ceased to be" (Mal 3:6), despite the way you have behaved.

"All the perfections of God's freedom and therefore of His love, and therefore the one whole divine essence, can and must be expressed by recognizing and saying that God is constant."[146] But this does not mean God is immutable, which would be close to saying that God is dead.[147] "His constancy consists in the fact that He is always the same in every change": for instance, showing integrity to people of integrity but refractoriness to people who are crooked (Ps 18:25 [MT 26]).[148] Indeed, God's omnipotence requires that God not be immutable and therefore powerless, like the Persian king lampooned in Daniel 6.[149]

The common Christian understanding of God's immutability derives from the influence of Greek thinking on the church fathers, via the Hellenistic Jewish philosopher Philo.[150] It is a philosophical assumption about God that has to be tested by Scripture. In fact, while affirming God's consistency, the First Testament also describes Yhwh as changing, and that in several senses.

For instance, Yhwh is sometimes deliverer, sometimes punisher, and one might wonder whether this makes a coherent understanding of Yhwh impossible. But just after declaring that Yhwh is about to act *against* Judah in a fashion that will correspond to the way Yhwh once acted *for* David, Isaiah delivers a parable. He asks, "Does someone who plows for sowing plow all day, opening up and harrowing his land?" (Is 28:24). Not so. Further, farmers sow different types of seed with skill, being well instructed by their God. And they know how to thresh or crush the different crops in such a way as to get the best out of each. "This also comes forth from Yhwh Armies; he is wonderful in planning, great in insight" (Is 28:29). The activity of a farmer involves different activities in different months, sometimes giving the land a hard time and sometimes not doing so, giving some crops a hard time and treating others more gently. Farmers know how to do that because they learn from Yhwh. That points to the fact that Yhwh knows this is also the way to work in the world. Different peoples need to be treated in different ways, and the same people need to be treated in different ways at different times. There is a consistency about Yhwh's work, but there is also change and flexibility.

Yhwh's Relenting

Yhwh is also changeable in the sense of being willing to decide on a course of action but to be open to having a change of heart about it. Yhwh recalls, "I said

---

[146]Cf. Ibid., II/1:491.

[147]Cf. Ibid., II/1:494.

[148]Cf. Ibid., II/1:496.

[149]Cf. Ibid., II/1:522-23.

[150]See, e.g., John Sanders, "Historical Considerations," in *The Openness of God*, by Clark Pinnock et al. (Downers Grove, Ill.: InterVarsity Press/Carlisle: Paternoster, 1994), pp. 59-100.

I would pour out my fury on them in the midst of the land of Egypt and again in the wilderness, to make an end of them." But then Yhwh did not do so, "for the sake of my name" (Ezek 20:8-9, 13-14; cf. 21-22). The EVV have "I thought" for "I said," and it may be that Yhwh only "said" this as part of an internal conversation. Even if so, Yhwh goes on, "Moreover, I swore to them in the wilderness that I would not bring them into the land; but then my eye had pity on them and I did not destroy them" (Ezek 20:15, 17). On the other hand, Yhwh did then swear to scatter Israel among the nations (Ezek 20:23), in a way that has indeed since come about and is now to come about further.

Further, with some paradox, Yhwh can declare the intention to act in a certain way and in the same breath urge people to pray for the opposite. Yhwh says of the Jerusalem prophets, "if they are prophets and if Yhwh's word is with them, they should then intercede with Yhwh Armies so that the accoutrements that are left in the house of Yhwh and in the house of the king of Judah and in Jerusalem should not go to Babylon." Then Yhwh adds the reason they should so intercede: "because [!] Yhwh has said this" about these accoutrements, "they are to be brought to Babylon and be there until I attend to them (Yhwh's message) and bring them up and return them to this place" (Jer 27:18-22). Such statements indicate that Yhwh intends prayer not as a way of aligning us with Yhwh's will but as the means of changing Yhwh's will.[151] Indeed, that is why Yhwh's will is revealed. When people know that Yhwh intends to bring trouble, they can pray for that intention to be changed. "The underlying image of God in Jer. 30—31 is that of divine changeability. YHWH is changeable and changing in relation to human history."[152] The God who is inimical now is not locked into that stance. Yhwh can turn from hostility to compassion.

So if a nation turns from wicked ways, Yhwh will "relent" or "have a change of heart" concerning the ill that has been planned for it (Jer 18:8). The verb (*nāḥam,* usually niphal) is an inherently affective word. Insofar as it suggests a change of mind, this is a change of mind that issues from a change of heart. The EVV often translate the verb "repent," but in English *repent* is inclined to suggest abandoning something wrong, and this is rather misleading. But the word does suggest regretting as well as relenting. Yhwh's commitment to relenting applies even to Nineveh (Jonah 3:9-10; 4:2) as well as specifically to Judah (Jer 26:3, 13, 19). Indeed, it had applied at Sinai (Ex 32:12, 14). It can also apply when Yhwh initiates a calamity and forestalls its consummation (Joel 2:12-14), so we can pray for Yhwh to relent when we know we have been the objects of wrath for a while (Ps 90:13; cf. Ps 106:45; Judg 2:18).

The verb *šûb* is also often translated "repent," though again this is mislead-

---

[151]See Miller, *Israelite Religion and Biblical Theology,* pp. 452-56.

[152]Bob Becking, *Between Fear and Freedom,* OTS 41 (Leiden/Boston: Brill, 2004), p. 276.

ing. The verb refers to the action of turning from one direction of behavior to another, rather than to the feelings that accompany the action. "The depth of dialogical reciprocity between heaven and earth is brought into its strongest expression" by the way the prophets use the verb *turn* to describe both God's action toward human beings and human beings' action toward God. Joel 2:12-14 and Jonah 3:8-10 both illustrate that, and both incorporate the tentative hope about God, "Who knows whether God may turn and relent?"[153] The dialogical reciprocity highlights the paradoxical nature of the sovereignty of God. The question "Who knows" suggests how a relationship with God (as with a human being?) has room for neither presumption nor despair.

Yhwh's Reliability

This fits with another feature of the prophets. Isaiah 40—55 speaks as if history is divinely predetermined and not dependent on the dialogue between prophet and God. So does Daniel. Yet the events they speak of do not come about wholly in the way Yhwh says, and that also implies that God assumes room to maneuver.

Yhwh can decide to relent without being asked (2 Sam 24:16). But Yhwh can also get tired of relenting (Jer 15:6). Indeed, earlier on in Jeremiah, Yhwh declares regarding the coming disaster, "I have spoken, I have planned; I have not relented, and I will not turn from it" (Jer 4:28). Amos prevails on Yhwh to relent about an intention to bring disaster on Ephraim, an intention so real it could be envisioned, which implies it is already a reality and not merely an idea. Indeed, Amos so prevails more than once (Amos 7:1-6). But Amos can also become aware of more resolute intentions on Yhwh's part that seem to foreclose the question of relenting (Amos 7:7-9; 8:1-3). That was the context in which Samaria fell, and in which Jerusalem fell (Ezek 24:14).

Having a change of heart can mean turning from a positive attitude to a negative one (e.g., Gen 6:6-7) or from a negative one to a positive one. While Yhwh does not abandon promises but does rejoice to abandon the plan to punish people, if a nation turns from faithful ways, then Yhwh may relent concerning the good that had been planned for it (Jer 18:10). Such turning was the context of Yhwh's change of heart about appointing Saul king (1 Sam 15:11, 35). Samuel does tell Saul that Yhwh "does not deceive or have a change of heart, because he is not human in having changes of heart" (1 Sam 15:29). Since Yhwh has just told Samuel about having a change of heart concerning making Saul king, and the First Testament so often refers elsewhere to Yhwh having a change of heart, Samuel can hardly mean that Yhwh never has a change of

---

[153]Martin Buber, *On the Bible* (New York: Schocken, 1968), pp. 176-77.

heart. His statement reassures the reader that Yhwh is not fickle. Yhwh does not relent about things in the way that a human being does. There is consistent principle about Yhwh's actions.

So God can have a change of heart about bringing calamity or about bringing blessing, but these are not possibilities of equal status. The order in which they come in Jeremiah 18 reflects the fact that the former is Yhwh's "true and proper" change of heart. It is God's nature to have a change of heart about bringing trouble. It is not God's nature to have a change of heart about bringing blessing, though God can do so if necessary. It is the gifts and calling of God that are irrevocable (Rom 11:29).[154] Thus "Yhwh swore and will not relent" that the Davidic king was established in his position forever (Ps 110:4). In connection with Yhwh's declaration of blessing on Israel, Balaam affirms, "God is not a human being so that he lies or a mortal so that he relents. Would he say something and not act, speak and not establish it?" (Num 23:19). There are thus two passages that say that God never relents, and forty or so indicating that God does.[155] Both denials make a link with lying, and they assure us that the point about their distinctive statements is to assure us that God is consistent and can be relied on.

Thus when Yhwh intends to forgive and bring blessing, a prophet's job is to agree and to urge Yhwh to act in accordance with such a revelation. When Hananiah declares that Yhwh intends soon to restore the exiles of 597, Jeremiah indeed does pray for Yhwh to fulfill this intention: "Yes! So may Yhwh do! May Yhwh establish the words that you have prophesied" (Jer 28:6). Of course he does so with irony, because he knows that Hananiah's declaration is false. Jonah, in contrast, behaves as a false prophet when he hears that Yhwh intends to forgive, and protests in the way a prophet is supposed to protest when Yhwh intends to punish (Jonah 4).

Has the Planner Perished or Fallen Asleep?

Micah 4:9 asks Jerusalem, "Why do you shout out? Is there no king in you, has your planner perished, that anguish has seized you like a woman birthing?" The questions can be read in two ways, though the implications are similar. People could take the king and planner to be the human king who has responsibility for formulating wise policy for the nation, in which case the fact that the city is in a state of panic is a witness to the king's failure and to the city's implicit failure to take the divine King seriously enough. Or they could take

---

[154]Cf. Barth, *Church Dogmatics*, II/1:498.

[155]Richard Rice, "Biblical Support for a New Perspective," in *The Openness of God*, by Clark Pinnock et al. (Downers Grove, Ill.: InterVarsity Press/Carlisle: Paternoster, 1994), pp. 11-58; see p. 32. Cf. Terence E. Fretheim, "The Repentance of God," *HBT* 10, no. 1 (1988): 47-70.

the city's king and planner to be Yhwh, in which case the city's panic again witnesses to its failure to take its real King seriously (cf. Zeph 3:15; also Jer 8:19, with a different irony; and for Yhwh's planning over against that of earthly planners, e.g., Is 14:24-27; 19:11-17).

The redactional context suggests we should at least include the second perspective. Yhwh is the one who formulates purposeful policies for the city. The preceding lines (Mic 4:6-8) declare that Yhwh intends to "gather the stumbling, assemble the strayed, that which I hurt." The stumbling and straying entity is feminine singular and presumably is the city—that is, the city's population. The prophecy describes the disaster that has come upon them by means of a telling sequence of verbs. The people have "limped" their way off into exile (cf. Zeph 3:19). Did they fall or were they pushed? Is it significant that the verb's only other occurrence refers to Jacob limping off after the wrestler disables him (Gen 32:32)? They are people who have strayed or been cast out: how should we render the niphal verb *(nādah)*? After the qal and the niphal comes a hiphil in which Yhwh claims responsibility for the people's hurting *(rāʿaʿ)*. Yes, Yhwh has been sovereign in the negative aspect of their experience. But the promise looks beyond a situation of disaster to one of restoration. "I will make the stumbling into leftovers, that which is gone out there into a strong nation" (Mic 4:7). Yhwh will also be sovereign in reversing the calamity. The people who stumbled and went off into exile will be turned into leftovers that become a strong nation.[156] And that will necessarily involve Yhwh's reigning as king over them. Yhwh's kingship in Jerusalem will be restored.[157] Yhwh will formulate policies that work in a more positive way for it.

Micah's subsequent words speak in similar terms of the way nations are assembled to attack the city. "But they—they do not acknowledge Yhwh's intentions, they do not consider his plan, that he has assembled them like sheaves at the threshing floor" (Mic 4:12). Often the plans of the nations conflict with Yhwh's own intention (Ps 2; 33:10-11; 35; 37; 46; 48; Is 7:1-9; 8:10; 28:23-29; 29:15; 30:1; 46:11; Job 12:13-25; 38:2; Prov 8:14). Here, like Judah, the nations assume that it is they who formulate intentions and plan out the future, but they are under a misapprehension. Yhwh also has a plan at work in their assembling against Jerusalem, a plan that will make them the victims of the harvest, not the agents of it.

---

[156]In isolation the first colon in Mic 4:7a seems to use "leftovers" *(šěʾērît)* as if it had an unequivocally positive sense, which would be unique, but the second colon clarifies the sense of the whole. Prosaically put, "I will make the stumbling people, who have gone out there, into leftovers that become a strong nation."

[157]Micah 4:8 promises the return of "the former rule," which could refer to the Davidic monarchy (cf. Mic 5:2 [MT 1]), but then also calls it a "reign," which clarifies the reference, since Micah only applies *mālak* and *melek* to Yhwh.

But we should not deceive ourselves into thinking that we have God fathomed or figured out. There are two sorts of contexts in which the First Testament speaks of Yhwh's abandonment of Israel or Jerusalem, as there are two sorts of contexts in which it speaks of Yhwh's abandonment of individuals. There are occasions when Yhwh abandons as a response to the faithlessness of people and/or city. But there are also occasions when Yhwh abandons despite the faithfulness of people or city. Psalm 44 is the most unequivocal about this as it speaks at some length about the way Yhwh has rejected and shamed Israel, letting the people be defeated and scattered, and asserts with boldness, "All this has come upon us and we have not put you out of mind or been false to your covenant. Our heart has not turned back; our steps have not veered from your path. . . . It is because of you that we have been slain all day long, reckoned sheep for slaughter." Initially the psalm's talk about faithfulness might be referring to the people's response to their reversals, but that last line makes it more likely that the psalm is claiming that there had been no reason in the people's earlier life for Yhwh to abandon them. Therefore, "Get up, why do you sleep, Lord? Wake up, do not reject forever. Why do you hide your face, ignore our weakness and oppression?" (Ps 44:17-24 [MT 18-25]).

"Are you to ignore me forever? How long are you to hide your face from me?" (Ps 13:1 [MT 2]). There are times when Yhwh is behaving as if asleep, hiding the face instead of looking at what is happening and therefore doing something about it. Psalm 121:4 denies that God ever drops off to sleep, but then there are also other psalms that urge God to wake up (e.g., Ps 7:6 [MT 7]; Ps 35:23) and passages that describe God doing so (e.g., Ps 78:65). We should be wary of weasel words about God "seeming to be asleep," which take the edge off the words of this psalm.

Randomness or Mystery

It is often difficult to see any purposefulness in the way things turn out for people and for individuals. What happens to them bears no relationship to their different deserves. Job thus comments, "It is all one, that is why I say, 'he destroys the person of integrity and the faithless.' When a scourge kills suddenly, he mocks at the plight/despair of the innocent. The earth is given into the power of the faithless person; he covers the eyes of its leaders. If not, then who does?" (Job 9:23-24).

We might reckon that God certainly does not laugh at the innocent sufferer's plight or despair.[158] Job would respond that it sure looks like it. Like the

---

[158]I link massâ with māsas rather than nāsâ, but māsas can cover both outer and inner melting away.

"love" and "hatred" of Malachi 1:2-3,[159] the verb refers not merely to an attitude but to an action. God does nothing when the innocent suffer. Therefore in effect God laughs at it. The evidence of that lies in the next line. All over the world we see faithless people exercising power over the nations as kings and presidents, and other leaders of these nations turning a blind eye to what their kings and presidents do. With unusual reticence, Job declines explicitly to make God responsible for who rules the world, but it would take little to infer who is the unidentified agent of the passive verb, even if we did not have the point then made explicit in the words about covering their eyes. The final colon that turns this line into a tricolon brings Job 9:1-24 to a thundering conclusion with its Calvinist question, "If not, then who does?" Is it not the case that God is supposed to be sovereign? So God is responsible for the moral randomness of the world. And that includes what has happened to Job, who is just an example of that theological rule. "Yhwh's hand has done this. In his hand is every living person and the breath of every human being" (Job 12:9-10). Isaiah 41:20 also declares that "Yhwh's hand has done this," but it has a specific reference to an act that brings about the downfall of a superpower and the release of captives. Job's use of these words has no such limited and comforting implication.

Such questions as the ones in Psalm 44 do not receive answers, as Zophar points out and Yhwh eventually confirms. If God is sovereign in the world, we would like to know why wicked leaders rule nations and oppress their people, and why innocent people suffer. "Are you going to discover the mystery of God, discover the limit of Shaddai?" Zophar asks. "The heights of the heavens—what can you do? Deeper than Sheol—what can you know? Its measure is longer than the earth, broader than the sea" (Job 11:7-9). Job has reckoned that he knows the implications of God's treatment of him: God's involvement in the world does not have a moral basis (see Job 9—10). He can see this on the canvas of world affairs and he can see it in his own life, where God had first related to him with commitment and attentiveness but was covertly intending to bring calamity to him. Zophar's point is that we do not in fact have access to the total rationale for God's actions in either sphere. Ironically, of course, Zophar presupposes that in the matter that concerns Job such access is possible, and he reckons he himself has it. He "knows" the basis of God's relating to human beings, which is that God makes things go well if we act rightly and makes them go ill if we do not. Therefore Job must have done deep wrong in order to be on the receiving end of the treatment he has experienced, God is punishing him less than he deserves (!), and Zophar knows on what terms Job

---

[159]See sections 2.7 "Repudiation"; 3.3 "Loved."

may find the restoration of his life. In this sense truth is accessible and he, Zophar, is the person who has access to it. But both Job and Zophar agree that the world is characterized by causality, rationality and intelligibility; so either Job has behaved in an immoral way, or God has.[160] Zophar is right about the impossibility of plumbing God's mystery; he just needs to listen to his words as much as Job needs to do so.

Indeed, Job himself goes beyond Zophar in recognizing that the mystery of God of which he is aware is itself still "not the whole mystery of God, but only the outermost edge of it."[161] "Now: these are only the outskirts of his ways, and what a whisper is the word we hear of him; who could understand the thunder of his mighty deeds?" (Job 26:14).

2.5 Yhwh's Presence

Yhwh is the God of heaven, and this might imply that the transcendent God is rather far away—interested in the world, perhaps, but not personally present in it. Christians often reckon that God is present with us especially in an inner, "spiritual," experiential sense. The First Testament knows that Yhwh is present in the world in much broader and dynamic senses. God has access to us anywhere (whether we like it or not) and grants us generous access to God in different ways.[162]

Yhwh's Omnipresence

Yhwh fills the whole earth (Jer 23:24). Affirmations that the whole world is full of Yhwh's commitment and of Yhwh's splendor (Ps 33:5; Is 6:3) spell out some implications of that. The world in its splendor reflects God's splendor, and in the way it continues to work and to provide for humanity, it reflects God's commitment. Yhwh is thus omnipresent in the world. Perhaps, indeed, God's sovereignty implies God's omnipresence, and God's love implies God's omnipresence.[163] God is thus not merely present but "lovingly present."[164] Yet actual declarations of God's omnipresence in Scripture are hard to find; Jeremiah 23:24 is Pannenberg's only proof text for this idea.[165] Certainly God is not

---

[160]Cf. Carol A. Newsom, "The Book of Job," *The New Interpreter's Bible*, vol. 4 (Nashville: Abingdon, 1996), p. 422.

[161]Von Rad, *Wisdom in Israel*, p. 109.

[162]On this theme in Exodus, see *OTT* 1:385-408.

[163]Cf. Barth, *Church Dogmatics*, II/1:461-64.

[164]Fretheim, *God and the World in the OT*, p. 24.

[165]Wolfhart Pannenberg, *Systematic Theology*, 1:410. "Preaching must begin with a particular presence," Kornelis Miskotte comments, following on the observation that "the 'omnipresence' of God as such is a specimen of mongrel philosophy which is an embarrassment to epistemology and hardly convincing to faith" (*When the Gods Are Silent* [New York: Harper/London: Collins, 1967], p. 261).

within nature, as a life force. While God breathes life into the animal world and bestows on the plant world the capacity to grow and reproduce and can appear and speak out of a desert bush, God is distinct from these.[166] Likewise, over against belief in a mystical presence in us, a presence in our spirit, the First Testament sees God as someone distinct from us and outside of us. Israelites do not look within to find God. Perhaps they recognize that God is far too wondrous for this to be a notion with any meaning. Again, over against an emphasis on a mere human sense or feeling of God's presence, the First Testament emphasizes an actual objective presence of God that makes a difference to what happens to people. Our statements about the divine presence are inclined to collapse into statements about us and our feelings or awareness rather than about God. We then use expressions such as "we want to see God" in a transferred sense. We mean we want to have a sense that God is present. But when God promises always to come to the people at the sanctuary to bless them (Ex 20:24 [MT 21]), this need not mean they have a sense of God's presence. The First Testament is more interested in the objective fact of God's presence, with its different implications. God's presence means God acts to bless. When Jacob senses that Yhwh is in a certain place (Gen 28:16-17), "this is not simply an expression of pious emotion. On the contrary, it describes the objective condition that lies at the basis of the whole covenant between God and man," in its particularity and concreteness.[167]

Such a more dynamic understanding of Yhwh's presence is characteristic of the First Testament. Thus Psalm 24:7-10 challenges gates and doors to open (the context suggests these are the gates and doors of Zion) so that Yhwh can enter. The one who enters does so as "the glorious king, . . . strong one and warrior, . . . battle warrior, . . . Yhwh Armies," suggesting Yhwh comes as military victor. This may imply a procession that recalls Yhwh's first coming to Zion as victor over the Canaanites, or Yhwh's return to Zion after going out to fight on Israel's behalf in a subsequent battle, or Yhwh's return from exile as victor over Babylon. Whichever of these applies, the psalm presupposes that Yhwh is not always present, or not always present in the same way. Yhwh goes and comes. Indeed, humanity has at least theoretical opportunity to exclude Yhwh's presence. As God can know anything but in practice apparently chooses what to know and what not to know, so God can be anywhere but in practice chooses to be present or not to be present, to come to or to move away from people. Scoundrels (rulers, priests, prophets) may declare, "Is not Yhwh in our midst? No trouble can come upon us" (Mic 3:11). Yhwh's response

---

[166]Cf. Thorkild Jacobsen, *The Treasures of Darkness* (New Haven/London: Yale University Press, 1976), p. 6.

[167]Cf. Barth, *Church Dogmatics*, II/1:479.

might be, "Yes, I am in the midst, and therefore trouble is coming on you," or alternatively, "No, I am not in the midst, and therefore you have no protection from trouble."

Yhwh's "natural" home is in the heavens, as the Lord's Prayer presupposes (cf. Is 66:1), perhaps in two senses. Metaphysically speaking, God's home is in heaven. Within creation, God's home is in the heavens; they are God's throne, the earth being God's footstool. God is thus not merely far off in an ethereal realm, but within creation, yet in a particular location. There God lives like a king, living in a palace but taking an active interest in what goes on in the rest of the city. "Yhwh in his holy palace, Yhwh whose throne is in the heavens; his eyes behold, his gaze examines, human beings" (Ps 11:4). Yhwh looks out from the heavens at human beings to see if there is anyone showing insight, seeking help from God (Ps 14:2). And while from a distance God can see and hear what is happening there, God also visits the city frequently to check out what is going on. People from the city often plead with God to intervene in its life, and this forms another stimulus for God to visit the city and get involved in events.

Forms of Yhwh's Presence

There are many ways in which Yhwh's presence can make itself felt on earth.[168] The whole of the heavens and the earth are indeed Yhwh's home. Yet there is an accompanying presence that goes with God's people. God is present guiding and providing, journeying with them on their travels. That presence accompanies Israel's ancestors on their journeys. God's presence goes with Israel itself as it makes its way from Egypt to the promised land, seeing the way and seeing to their needs. This accompanying presence is known through the column of cloud and fire, though the covenant chest is also a symbol of it (Num 10:35-36). The correlative human experience of God's presence is that people know which way to go and have their needs met.

Then there is a settled, local divine presence. God is present and can be sought out at particular places, worshiped and pleaded with there, for blessing, advice and help. The meeting tent (Ex 33:7-11) and the wilderness dwelling (Ex 25:8-9) instance this, though both were structures that kept on the move as the community kept on the move. Mountains provide natural places for such seeking, because they point to the heavens and suggest a link between the earth and the heavens. Some locations become such places because Yhwh appears there and thus designates them as portals between earth and heaven (e.g., Gen 12:7; 28:10-18; Ex 20:24). Others come into being on human initiative, to which Yhwh responds (e.g., Gen 4:3-7; cf. Gen 12:8? Ps 132?). Either way,

---

[168]Cf. Rendtorff, *Canonical Hebrew Bible*, pp. 522-25.

Yhwh can then decide to withdraw this presence from them, as happened to Jerusalem in 587 (Ezek 11:22-23), though such withdrawal can be reversed (Ezek 43:1-7). In an extended sense, the whole land of Canaan is Yhwh's dwelling (so, e.g., Ex 15:13-18). Yhwh is present throughout it.

There is an attentive presence: God is listening when someone cries out because they are in need, and speaks in response to people's pleas. That was so for Israel in Egypt, and could be so at an altar or sanctuary (e.g., 1 Kings 8:37-40). God is present in the sanctuary attending to Israel's life and responding to its faithlessness (e.g., Ps 50; Jer 7).

Linked to that is an active presence: God is present and active when people need healing or delivering. This presence is known through its results, as at the exodus and the Red Sea, though perhaps also sometimes through accompanying phenomena such as a storm (e.g., Ps 18; 97)—unless this is metaphor. It is mediated by the covenant chest, or it could be thought to be so mediated (1 Sam 4:3-9). Israel's deliverance comes from Yhwh who dwells in the heavens, but it comes out of Zion (Ps 14:2, 7; cf. Ps 20:2, 6 [MT 3, 7]; 76:1-3, 8 [MT 2-4, 9]; 80:1, 14 [MT 2, 15])[169] and thus when necessary comes in Zion (e.g., Ps 48; and paradoxically, Is 31:4-5). Likewise disaster for Israel can come not only because of Yhwh's absence but because of the same presence.[170]

There is a narrative presence: God is present in the telling of the story of the great acts whereby God created the world, brought Israel into being and has delivered it over the centuries. In the sanctuary a suppliant might "see" Yhwh in the sense of "beholding your power and honor" (Ps 63:2 [MT 3]). The liturgy of a festival makes it possible for people imaginatively to reexperience those great events in which Yhwh's power and glory has been manifest, like the worshiper who asks "Were you there when they crucified my Lord?"

There is a personal presence: God appears person-to-person in human form (and thus may be immediately recognized) to announce something of significance for the divine purpose (e.g., Gen 18). A heavenly aide brings the presence of Yhwh mediated through a less overwhelming heavenly person whose word is nevertheless as good as Yhwh's word. Or Yhwh may appear personally but indirectly, in a vision or a dream.

There is an intense presence: God is present in all God's divine splendor, for instance at Sinai and in the wilderness dwelling (Ex 40:34-38). Phenomena such as those of a storm point to the reality of this intense and awesome presence, which can make itself known in Babylon as much as in Israel (see Ezek 1—3)—not surprisingly, as it starts outside Israel, at Sinai. Fear is a reasonable response to the immediate presence of God, especially when God's form is not

---

[169]Ronald E. Clements, *God and Temple* (Oxford: Blackwell, 1965), p. 68.
[170]Ibid., p. 101.

veiled, so that the person to whom God appears may be encouraged not to be afraid, though a cloud often protects Israel from the dangerous impact of this intense presence.

As there are many ways in which God can be present, so there are many ways in which God can be absent. In theory, at least, there could be a general absence of God: except that this would surely cause the world to cease to exist. There is an accompanying absence: Yhwh did not go with Ephraim into exile. There is an attentive absence: Yhwh stops listening to people's prayers. There is an active absence: Israel experiences defeat. There is a personal absence: for personal appearances are granted only in special circumstances.[171]

Yhwh's Spirit and Yhwh's Face

There is nowhere one can go to be inaccessible to God's help or to escape God (Ps 139:7-12). That could be comforting or worrying. "God possesses space."[172] "Where could I go from your spirit, where could I flee from your face? If I went up to the heavens, you would be there, and if I made my bed in Sheol, there you would be." It is possible to imagine that there are realms beyond Yhwh's reach, and while it is perhaps odd to think of Yhwh not being present in the heavens (the skies) or in heaven (God's abode), it is easy to think of Yhwh not being present in Sheol. There are passages of the Scriptures that declare that Yhwh does not act there (e.g., Ps 88:10-12 [MT 11-13]). But that does not mean Sheol is inaccessible to Yhwh. "Were I to take up the wings of the morning and lie down at the farthest point west, even there your hand would direct me, your right hand would grasp me" (Ps 139:19). Geographically, the fact that Canaan is Yhwh's own land might seem to imply that Yhwh is not present in other countries, and Jonah thinks he can get away from God by fleeing to the farthest west. People often have good reason to try get away from Yhwh, because they have done wrong or they intend to do wrong, or because Yhwh wants them to undertake some task. People can also have good reason to fear that experiences such as persecution or their own wrongdoing may take them out of the realm where Yhwh is clearly present. Is Yhwh there? The psalm worries or comforts us with the fact that there is no realm to which Yhwh does not have access.

Likewise, Yhwh is one who at the beginning dispelled darkness and one

---

[171]Jack Miles, in *God: A Biography* (London/New York: Simon & Schuster, 1995), p. 253, suggests a spectrum of awarenesses of presence in the First Testament: presence, absent presence, present absence, absence. See also Daniel Strange, "A Little Dwelling on the Divine Presence," in *Heaven on Earth*, ed. T. Desmond Alexander and Simon Gathercole (Carlisle/Waynesboro, Ga.: Paternoster, 2004), pp. 211-29.

[172]Cf. Barth, *Church Dogmatics*, II/1:469.

who gives light, so we might think that darkness is a realm from which Yhwh is absent. The psalm rules out all such inferences. There is no place where Yhwh's spirit cannot reach and thus where Yhwh cannot act with dynamic power, no place where Yhwh's face cannot look to shine out with blessing or trouble. "Even darkness is not too dark for you, and night is light like day; darkness and light are the same" (Ps 139:12). Darkness does not inhibit Yhwh because Yhwh brings light into darkness. It's all the same to Yhwh.

The psalm puts in parallelism "your spirit," "your face" and "you." Hebrew has no abstract word for presence; the word most commonly translated "presence" is the regular word for "face" (cf. Ps 16:11; 51:11 [MT 13]; 68:8 [MT 9]; 95:2; 100:2). The face of a person is his or her outward expression. We can tell from someone's face whether he or she is really present with us, and we expect to find that this apparent attentiveness issues in action on our behalf when we need it. It is a person's face that conveys personal presence.

Similarly, the spirit of a person is his or her personal dynamic. Whereas *face* might seem a word at home with human beings but less so with God, the reverse is true with *spirit* (cf. Is 31:3). This is a word especially associated with God, though in a rather different sense from the one commonly inferred from John 4:24.[173] *Spirit* suggests supernatural life and supernatural dynamism. The First Testament twice uses the expression "holy spirit" (Ps 51:11, Is 63:10-11), but the expression is arguably tautologous, because both *holy* and *spirit* point to something supernatural. Perhaps the tautology suggests a reminder that there are many spirits, but this is *the* Holy Spirit.[174] Perhaps it simply emphasizes the point. The spirit of God really is the spirit of God.

Yhwh's Reach

The context of Jeremiah 23:24, Pannenberg's prooftext,[175] indicates that it, too, is concerned not merely with the fact that Yhwh is everywhere but with the fact that Yhwh can reach everywhere. Yhwh's living in Jerusalem and Yhwh's accessibility there does not mean people can escape from Yhwh by going to some far away place.

There is no doubt that in Amos this fact is worrying, as it was for Jonah. Amos 9:2-4 uses similar imagery to Psalm 139, with unequivocally threatening implications. There is no place where the people of God can get away from Yhwh's punishment. It is no use digging into Sheol: there is nothing to stop Yhwh reaching into there. No other power stands at Sheol's gate able to prevent Yhwh's entering (cf. Prov 15:11). The far reaches of the heavens cannot be

---

[173]Cf. Preuss, *OT Theology*, 1:160.

[174]Barth, *Church Dogmatics*, IV/1:647.

[175]See section 2.5 "Yhwh's "Omnipresence.""

far enough to evade Yhwh. The dense woods or caves of Carmel could provide a hiding place from humanity, but not from Yhwh. Like Sheol, the sea might seem a realm with potential, since it often seems the embodiment of forces independent of and hostile to Yhwh. Perhaps people could conceal themselves from Yhwh's eyes at the murky bottom of the ocean? But Yhwh can even use the sea serpent (another figure for such hostility) as agent there. Exile might seem the last escape, because exile is itself a punishment that takes the form of distancing from Yhwh in lands defiled by the worship of other deities, but Yhwh is sovereign there, too, and even the realm of punishment could turn out to offer no immunity or safety from worse fates. Even there Yhwh could command the sword to slay them.

In speaking of Yhwh's capacity to reach people anywhere, psalm and prophet affirm the total extent of Yhwh's sovereign reach. There is no metaphysical or cosmic or national realm that lies outside Yhwh's authority. The Scriptures' emphasis is thus that God *can be* anywhere rather than that God *is* everywhere. We might fear that we could end up somewhere where God would not be able to reach us—for instance, some place where our own wickedness or other people's wickedness makes that impossible. It cannot happen. We might think we can escape from God by going to the extreme height or depths of the cosmos, or merely to the extreme height or depths of the world, and we might be right if God chooses not to follow. But we will never be secure, because God *can* choose to follow. Like Joe LaFarge, the relentless pursuer of Butch Cassidy and the Sundance Kid, God may choose to keep pursuing, and then we will never escape. We might think that God does not operate beyond the promised land, but even exile may not save us if God chooses to follow (as Butch and Sundance also found).

"Yhwh is on high, but he sees ordinary people and knows important people, from a distance" (Ps 138:6). The NRSV attributes moral connotations to the words for "ordinary" and "important" *(šāpāl, gābōah)* and takes them to mean "lowly" and "haughty," but the words do not usually carry these implications. They refer to things that are physically low or high, and then to people who are low or high in status. When they have moral connotations, this is usually indicated by the addition of phrases such as "in spirit" or "in one's [own] eyes." Here there is no reason to introduce such connotations, for the context refers to the psalmist as someone who has been "down" in relation to attackers who are "on top," and to people such as kings who are by definition high in status and power. The NRSV also then naturally assumes that there is a contrast in the line Yhwh "regards the lowly; but the haughty he perceives from far away." More likely the psalm's point is that Yhwh's dwelling in heaven means that Yhwh is on high and far away in relation to all humanity, both important people and ordinary people. But being on high and far away does not stop

Yhwh seeing and knowing what is happening on earth. The psalmist's experience of Yhwh's answering prayer uttered in the midst of trouble and danger has proved once again that Yhwh sees and knows what important people are doing and what is happening to ordinary people, and is therefore in a position to do something about it.

Yhwh's Home

As well as the question of whether God can get to us, there is the question whether we can get to God. Neither for God nor for humanity was it enough for God to have a home in heaven and a home in the heavens. First, God also commissioned Israel to build a rather palatial mobile home (see Ex 25—31), and subsequently David asked for permission to replace this with a rather palatial fixed home in Jerusalem, to which Yhwh eventually but reluctantly agreed.[176] In order to meet human desire that there should be a place where one can always find God at home, God agrees always to be accessible there (subject to some relational and moral constraints). Yhwh is "seated on Zion"; there Yhwh hears people's cries, and receives people's praises for doing so (Ps 9:11-12 [MT 12-13]). "You are in our midst, Yhwh" (Jer 14:9).

Ezekiel relates two visions of God that between them hold together several of these realities—God's home being in the heavens, God's home being in the temple, and God's being able to appear elsewhere, even in unlikely places (Ezek 1; 8—11). The second of these draws attention to the scandalous and dangerous implications of the temple's being Yhwh's home. The people have been behaving like teenagers holding orgies in their parents' home. It is not surprising if there is a price to pay when the parents return. It is wonderful that Yhwh deigns to live in the temple in Jerusalem, but it is also perilous. One implication for the exiles is that Yhwh's capacity for appearing among them is also both encouraging and solemn.

Confronted by these abominations in the temple, "the splendor of Israel's God took itself up from over the cherub that it was on,[177] to the threshold of the house" (Ezek 9:3; 10:4). It is on the way to withdrawing. But before it finally does so, Yhwh has further tasks to perform: to mark the people who disassociate themselves from the abominations and to commission the killing of everyone else and the burning of the city itself. Then the cherubim transport gets itself ready, "and Yhwh's splendor went out from the threshold of the house

---

[176]I refer to the order of events as the First Testament relates them; on the usual critical view, the actual original mobile structure was simply the rather less palatial meeting tent of Ex 33:7-11 and the prescription in Ex 25—31 is really something like a vision for a subsequent future. On these, see *OTT* 1:392-401.

[177]The reference here is to the cherub[im] in the inner sanctuary.

and stopped over the cherubim." They rose, and then "it stopped at the entrance of the east gate of Yhwh's house. The splendor of Israel's God was above them" (Ezek 10:18-19). Once more there is a delay as Yhwh has Ezekiel prophesy against Jerusalemites who are involved in the deaths of other people but are convinced that their future is secure, and has him promise a future for people in exile. Then the cherubim transport again gets going, "and Yhwh's splendor went up from over the midst of the city and stopped over the mountain east of the city," the Mount of Olives (Ezek 11:23). Even now the splendor has not actually left. It is not over until it is over. Yhwh does not wish to leave that home in Jerusalem.

People who knew that Yhwh lived in the Jerusalem temple might again wonder whether being taken off into exile meant being taken away from Yhwh's presence. Ezekiel's first vision affirms that this is not so. Yhwh is not present in the temple in such a way as to make it impossible to appear somewhere else. Yhwh has not cast off the exiles so completely as to have no inclination to appear in exile. In his first vision, the skies part so that Ezekiel in Babylonia sees a vision of God or a divine vision, sees God coming from the heavens (Ezek 1). Subsequently the same figure appears to him again (Ezek 8:2) preparatory to his being transported to Jerusalem to the temple court, to "my sanctuary," to "Yhwh's house," to "Yhwh's palace" (Ezek 8:6, 14, 16).[178] Further, "the splendor of Israel's God was there, like the vision I had seen in the vale" (Ezek 8:4). "When the prophet arrives in the temple area, 'the Majesty of the God of Israel' is there waiting for him; it is free to appear anywhere at any time."[179] It is free to leave; and it is free to return. Subsequently Second Isaiah will encourage the exiles with the declaration from Yhwh, "I am with you" (Is 41:10), a declaration that again has dynamic implications. Yhwh's presence suggests action on their behalf.

"The dwelling place of God is particular and spatial. It is not universal and everywhere. . . . God's dwelling is still with Israel and is still cultural and spatial at the end," as it remains when Revelation 21 takes up the image of a new Jerusalem.[180]

Yhwh's Accessibility

The temptation for Israel, as for other peoples, is to reckon that they need to devise elaborate means whereby they can access God's presence. Yhwh denies

---

[178]The EVV often translate *bayit* and *hêkāl* as "temple," but they are the ordinary words for "house" and "palace" reused to apply to God, so I use these words also in connection with divine abodes.

[179]Moshe Greenberg, *Ezekiel 1—20*, AB (Garden City, N.Y.: Doubleday, 1983), p. 197.

[180]Miller, *Israelite Religion and Biblical Theology*, pp. 678-79.

this and promises "in every place where I cause my name to be proclaimed I will come to you and bless you" (Ex 20:21).

From the beginning, the temple was thus an ambiguous affair. People wanted a place where they could be sure to find God (and everyone else had a temple, so it was odd not to have one). So God went along with that. But it was always something God had mixed feelings about, and something that even Solomon recognized embodied a contradiction (see 2 Sam 7; 1 Kings 8).[181] The God who lives there is the God of heaven and earth, so how can such a God live there? The theology of temple deconstructs.

In connection with its rebuilding after the exile, the issues surface again (Is 66:1-2). "The heavens are my throne, the earth is my footstool. Where, then, could you build a house for me, where, then, is the place for me to settle down? My hand made all these things, so that all these things came into being." Yhwh has already described the second temple as "the place of my sanctuary, the place where my feet rest" (Is 60:13), but here Yhwh offers a very different comment relating to it. If the heavens and the earth are Yhwh's home, then the idea of human beings manufacturing a home for Yhwh becomes somewhat ridiculous.

The temple's ambiguity would have different implications in different contexts. During the exile itself and immediately after the return of some Judeans to the city, it might offer some comfort. If people were longing to rebuild the temple and could not do so because they lacked the resources, it reminds them that the temple is not really necessary. They are a people who are weak and broken-spirited (cf. Is 57:15) and trembling at the word of Yhwh that brought calamity to them and upbraided them for their faithlessness. But, Yhwh says, those are just the people Yhwh has regard for. Their inability to rebuild the temple does not mean Yhwh is absent, as if Yhwh would never be here if the temple were not here. They must not get the temple out of proportion. "To this person I will pay attention: to the weak and broken-spirited, the one who trembles at my word" (Is 66:2). The EVV have the people as "humble and contrite" rather than "weak and broken-spirited," but this again introduces an alien moral note into Yhwh's comment.[182] The point is not that people must screw themselves up into contrition but that it is their weakness and discouragement that draws Yhwh to them. The promise is talking about Yhwh's grace and mercy.

A few decades later the comment would have different implications. Peo-

---

[181]See *OTT* 1:562-72.

[182]"Humble" as a rendering of *ʿanî* is fine if by it we designate an objective position rather than a subjective attitude. "Broken" is *nākēh*, which in its other occurrences refers to broken limbs; the verb *nākâ* means "hit."

ple are now in a position to build the temple, and are thus in danger of forgetting that it is not as indispensable or central to Yhwh's presence as they are
inclined to think. That will be a special temptation to the religious leadership
of the community, such as its priests and prophets. Over against them, the
weak and broken-spirited would now stand not for the community as a whole
but for its marginalized. The passage declares that Yhwh pays attention to
them and not to the building that means so much to priests and prophets. Is
the word at which they tremble now the tough word that threatens expulsion
from the community to people involved in foreign marriages (Ezra 10:3, 8; cf.
Is 66:5)?[183] Centuries later, Jesus will similarly declare that God is closer to despised tax-collectors than to prestigious Scripture scholars. This is a hard word
for Scripture scholars, but one they have to come to terms with.

Yhwh's Name

Whereas there are religions in which the god's name is a secret, perhaps because it gives away the mystery of the person, in Israel everyone knows
Yhwh's name.[184] The temple is a place that bears Yhwh's name. Literally, it is
a place over which Yhwh's name has been called, a place where Yhwh's name
dwells (Jer 7:10-12). It is therefore a place that suggests God's presence.[185]
Christians may find that whispering the name "Jesus" suggests the reality of
Christ's presence; similarly uttering the name "Yhwh" suggests the reality of
the presence of the one whose person that name expresses.

There are three senses in which the name may point to the person. Occasionally names have meaning. People may name their child "Grace" or
"Mercy" and intend this to signify a recognition of the child's significance.
Similarly the name El Olam signified that Yhwh was the lasting God. Second,
occasionally names are given new meaning on the basis of paronomasia. Thus
the names Yhwh or Abraham gain a meaning that derives from their similarity
to words for "be" or "father of a multitude."[186] But third, even when names
have no inherent meaning that people are aware of and do not have associations on the basis of similarity to significant words, they are significant because of the person they refer to. The name "John Goldingay" strikes fear into
the heart of some people, but this is not because they are frightened of the idea

---

[183]So Blenkinsopp, *Isaiah 56—66*, p. 297.

[184]Cf. Gerhard von Rad, *Old Testament Theology*, 2 vols. (Edinburgh: Oliver & Boyd/New
York: Harper, 1962, 1965), 1:184-85.

[185]Thus speaking in terms of God's name does not imply the conviction that God is not really
present. Deuteronomy speaks both in terms of the presence of Yhwh's name and in terms
of things happening "before Yhwh," implying "in Yhwh's presence": see Ian Wilson, *Out
of the Midst of the Fire*, SBLDS 151 (Atlanta, Ga.: Scholars Press, 1995).

[186]I have discussed the name Yhwh as expounded in Ex 3 in *OTT* 1:334-40.

that Yhwh is gracious (probably the meaning of antecedents of the name John) nor because they know anything about the village called Goldenhay, from which some of my ancestors may have come. It is because they know the person to whom the name refers. In a parallel way, to judge from the lack of references to the meaning of the name Yhwh in the First Testament, most Israelites were not especially aware of the meaning of the name Yhwh, yet nevertheless this name was very significant for them because they knew the one to whom it referred. The name stands for the person, not because the name means something and is thus inherently revelatory but because the name refers to someone. When Californians spell my name Goldengay, I have to work hard to tell myself that this does not matter. It feels as if they have slighted me by misspelling my name. When I myself cannot remember someone's name, I feel guilty because I feel as if I have slighted them. The name points to the person. It is God's name that sets the king on high (Ps 20:1 [MT 2]), that is the means by which I am delivered or rescued; God's name is thus "good," and is the object of my praise (Ps 54:1, 6 [MT 3, 8]).

Yhwh therefore acts "for the sake of my name, that it should not be profaned before the eyes of the nations" among whom Yhwh had declared the intention to bring the Israelites out of Egypt (Ezek 20:9). For its sake Yhwh does not act in wrath on Israel because of its worship of Egyptian gods. Yhwh had declared the intention to bring the Israelites out of Egypt into a new and special land, and had required the Israelites to give up worshiping Egyptian gods. If Yhwh did act in wrath because the Israelites failed to do as they had been bidden, what Yhwh had declared as the intention would not happen. That would discredit Yhwh because one of the key characteristics of the one to whom the name "Yhwh" belongs and a characteristic that distinguishes this deity from others is the habit of declaring the intention to do something and then doing it. Whether or not that is the meaning of the name Yhwh, it is the character of the one to whom that name belongs. "Profaning Yhwh's name" thus does not refer to profanity in the sense of using Yhwh's name in frivolous oaths or as an expletive. Profane is the opposite of holy, and profaning (ḥālal hiphil) is the opposite of making holy or sanctifying.[187] To sanctify Yhwh's name is to recognize that Yhwh is the holy one and acknowledge Yhwh. To profane Yhwh's name is to deny that Yhwh is the holy one, to deny that Yhwh is God. One can see then how failing to finish a task would cast doubts on Yhwh's word or power and thus on Yhwh's deity.

It was likewise "for the sake of my name" that Yhwh would not abandon Israel in the wilderness (Ezek 20:22). When Ezekiel talks about Yhwh's eye

---

[187]See, e.g., NIDOTTE.

having pity on Israel (*ḥûs*), this stands alongside the declaration that Yhwh acts "for the sake of my name" (Ezek 20:14, 17). And when Yhwh restores Israel, "the nations will acknowledge that it was because of its wrongdoing that the household of Israel went into exile, because they disdained me and I hid my face from them and gave them into the power of their adversaries" (Ezek 39:23). It was not because Yhwh was incapable of looking after them or behaved in a fickle way.

2.6 Yhwh's Love

What of Yhwh's character traits? Everyone knows that the Old Testament God is a God of wrath; the New Testament God a God of love. Oh no they don't.

Fatherly Dedication

The many Israelite names compounded with the word *father* (e.g., Abijah, "Yah is my father"; Joab, "Yo is father") indicate that Israel takes for granted the idea that God is our father and that this applies to individuals, as did other Middle Eastern peoples.[188] Perhaps it is precisely the familiarity of this image that makes the First Testament itself otherwise reticent in using it. People too easily view God as father. Indeed, the fact that Yhwh is father could be a basis for critique of Israel. "A son honors a father and a servant his master. If I am a father, where is my honor? If I am a master, where is my revering?" (Mal 1:6; cf. Deut 32:6, 18; Is 1:2-3; Jer 3:19-20).[189] It can of course be a basis for encouragement: "The everlasting Father is a ruler with *shalom*" (Is 9:6 [MT 5]).[190] The father cannot finally cast out his firstborn son (Jer 31:9).

"God in his holy dwelling is father of orphans, champion of widows; God enables people who are alone to live at home, brings out captives, in fetters, but rebels live in dry land" (Ps 68:5-6 [MT 6-7]). Dwelling in the heavens does not mean God is oblivious to what happens on earth and is therefore uninvolved. Specifically, for these different needy groups God acts in the way they need. If people lack parents and therefore have no one to provide for them and protect them, Yhwh acts as their father. If a woman is a widow and therefore subject to being swindled out of her land or home, Yhwh acts as her champion or advocate. If people are in other ways alone, members of no family and homeless (for instance, because of debt or because they have moved from elsewhere because of famine), Yhwh acts to see that they come to have a home. If

---

[188]See, e.g., Jacobsen, *Treasures of Darkness*, pp. 145-64.

[189]Mal 2:10-16 may begin with another reference to God as father, which is then the basis for lamenting the people's faithlessness to one another (so JPSV, NIVI), but it may be referring to Abraham as father (so NRSV); we are uncertain of the meaning of the whole passage.

[190]See section 5.7 "One Who Brings *Shalom*."

people are captives to a foreign power or to people who enslave them, Yhwh acts to see they get their freedom. And to those ends, God sees to the casting out of rebels (the kind of people who oppress orphans, widows and migrants, and who impose captivity on people).

Is it really so? Often it does not look like it. The psalm goes on to provide the implicit basis for its conviction, in the story of God's dealings with Israel. Yhwh acted thus in bringing Israel to its land, for instance, in pouring rain on this land, not merely in the form of the powerful thunderstorm that suggests God's power, but also in the form of the "generous," plentiful, fructifying rains that provide for the land when it languishes. That in itself was and is a way "you provide for the weak with your goodness" (Ps 68:10 [MT 11]). Alongside that, and corresponding to the comment about rebels, is Yhwh's more directly political action in scattering kings and their armies (Ps 68:11-14 [MT 12-15]). Whereas other Middle Eastern peoples were inclined to use the images of father and begetting to describe God's relationship with humanity as creator, the First Testament is more inclined to see the exodus as the moment when God became Israel's father[191] and when God thus claims this son from Pharaoh (Ex 4:22-23). It is in this connection, too, that "God our Father means God our Creator" (cf. Deut 32:6; Is 64:7)—that is, the Lord of our existence, the one who keeps us in being now.[192] Karl Barth notes that "Yhwh" is set alongside "Father" (Deut 32:6; Mal 1:6) and comments that it is not the case that human beings as such are the children of God; it is *Israel* that is adopted as the children of *Yhwh* (cf. Hos 11:1).[193] This is not merely a covenant commitment that by its nature comes about as a result of a special decision to enter into a relationship and can be suspended or terminated. By its nature, parenthood lasts forever; parents cannot divorce their children.

After the exile, there were Israelites who could not imagine Abraham and Israel acknowledging them, perhaps because they were such a small remnant compared with their ancestors in their heyday. The people make the point as background to expressing a confidence that it need not matter too much, because *Yhwh* looks on them like a father even if Abraham and Israel do not (Is 63:16; cf. Is 64:8 [MT 7]). "Yahweh is made subject to Israel because of his fatherhood"; whereas *king* is a natural term for God when Israel has kings, when there are no kings, this family term is natural.[194]

The father cannot but have motherly compassion for his children, even

---

[191]Cf. Mason, *OT Pictures of God*, pp. 45-74.

[192]Barth, *Church Dogmatics*, I/1:447.

[193]Ibid., I/1:444.

[194]Gerstenberger, *Yahweh the Patriarch*, pp. 4, 5, though he notes (p. 7) that Yhwh is king as well as father in Malachi.

when they go off the rails (Ps 103:9-14). Father is not an inherently patriarchal image for God, at least if we follow the First Testament in seeing God as a motherly father.[195] Indeed, it might subvert patriarchal authority, for if God is father, this relativizes the authority of earthly fathers. Yet the fact that people in the First Testament rarely address and/or speak of God as father (hardly more often than they speak of God in motherly terms?) suggests that this need not be a dominant image for God. Further, it is suggestive that the First Testament's reticence may reflect overuse or misleading resonances attaching to the image in the surrounding religious culture. We, too, will be inclined to understand the fatherhood of God in light of what fatherhood means in our culture or in our own experience. The First Testament's relative reticence about calling God "Lord" similarly raises questions about the dominance of this image in Christian faith. The Second Temple community saw reason to give up addressing God as Yhwh and to address God as Lord and as Father instead. The Third Millennium community might need to think through the implications of the way the idea of God as Lord and Father was transformed in Christendom, when Christian faith lost hold of the aspects of provision and compassion that belonged to lordship and fatherhood in both Testaments and in earlier Christian thinking.[196]

Parental Carrier

God is identified with Israel. Yhwh speaks about "my bad neighbors" (Jer 12:14): Judah's neighbors are Yhwh's neighbors. Yhwh is Israel's "deliverer in time of trouble" (Jer 14:8), and Yhwh addresses Israel as "your restorer [$g\bar{o}\,{}^{\circ}\bar{e}l$]" (Is 44:24). Indeed, as father Yhwh will also be their restorer (Is 63:16). It is a striking statement, because by definition a restorer was a relative who had to accept responsibility when a person had no member of their nuclear family to help them.[197] As restorer, Yhwh behaves like a member of Israel's family who has resources that this weaker member of the family does not possess. Such a person has a moral obligation to apply those resources to the needs of members of the family, to get them back on their feet or buy them back their freedom or provide them with the security they lack. As the story of Ruth shows, this is only a moral obligation; it can be evaded. But Yhwh is not that kind of person. Being part of Yhwh's extended family guarantees Israel its restoration.

But before being Israel's restorer, Yhwh was its shaper. Jeremiah speaks of being shaped by Yhwh *in* the womb (Jer 1:5), while Second Isaiah speaks of a

---

[195]Cf. Jürgen Moltmann, *History and the Triune God* (London: SCM Press, 1991), p. xiv.

[196]Moltmann (ibid., p. 6) draws particular attention to the *Treatise on the Anger of God* by Lactantius (260-330) (*ANF* 7:259-80).

[197]See section 2.2 "Restorer."

shaping that takes place *from* the womb (cf. Is 44:2, 24; 49:5). The change in prepositions goes along with the prophet's characteristic use of participles to describe Yhwh, which are also inclined to suggest that they refer to more than a one-time event. Yhwh has been shaping Israel through its life from the womb, like a potter who keeps working at a lump of clay. It is then the fact that Yhwh is the shaper (whether on a one-time or an ongoing basis) that is the background to Yhwh's being the restorer. The fact that the potter's shaping is not very successful (cf. Jer 18) does not make the potter give up rather than continuing to seek to remold the pot into one the potter will be proud of. Isaiah 44:24 undergirds Yhwh role as Israel's shaper with the fact that Yhwh is also the world's maker. It means Yhwh has the power to achieve that purpose with Israel, even if it long seems to fail. Indeed, Yhwh is "Israel's creator" (Is 43:15; 44:2).

Yhwh is also Israel's carrier. Yhwh's supremacy to the so-called deities of Babylon is expressed in another way in an imaginative account of the fall of Babylon (Is 46:1-4). In imagination the prophet sees the Babylonian gods, Bel and Nebo, collapsing to be loaded onto pack animals, being taken off into captivity (perhaps because victors often took the images of gods back to their capital as trophies).

The key motif in this vision is that of carrying. The prophet uses three different verbs to make the point. One point about a God is being one who carries you as a people. Yhwh had been that in bringing the people from Egypt to Canaan, carrying Israel like an eagle or like a parent carrying a child, and continuing to carry them over the years (e.g., Ex 19:4; Deut 1:31; Ps 68:19 [MT 20]; Is 63:9). The prophet sidesteps the idea that the fall of Jerusalem was the moment Yhwh dropped the people (but would no doubt say "Yes, Yhwh did, and we deserved it")[198] and focuses on the fact that Yhwh will carry the exiles back to Canaan like a shepherd carrying lambs (Is 40:11). In contrast, the trouble with the magnificent images of Bel and Nebo is that their worshipers have to carry them, or get animals to do so. The carrying relationship between deity and people is reversed. The gods become a burden to their worshipers. Instead of rescuing their worshipers from exile, they are carried off into exile. It is a nice fact that the root of the word for "image" (*ʿāṣāb*) is identical with another root for pain and vexation. Instead of removing weariness from the people, the deity is a source of weariness (contrast Is 40:27-31).

The gods who bow down in this vision are gods of key significance: they gave their names, for instance, to Nebuchadnezzar, Nabonidus and Belshazzar. Their fall symbolizes the fall of the empire itself; the fall of the empire sym-

---

[198]Perhaps there is an allusion to that in the way Yhwh addresses the people as "leftovers" in Is 46:4, which may take up the way they described themselves in their prayers.

bolizes their fall. Yhwh is in a position to claim a different relationship with Israel. Yhwh has carried them from when they were children (cf. Hos 11:1-9) and will carry them till their old age.

Motherly Compassion

Yhwh is "the rock that bore you, . . . the God who birthed you" (Deut 32:18).[199] But Israel put its mother out of mind, and then it seemed that Yhwh had returned the compliment (Is 49:14-15). "Zion said, Yhwh has abandoned me, my Lord has put me out of mind." Zion's inference is a reasonable one; indeed, Yhwh admits having abandoned Zion (Is 54:7), though never admits putting her out of mind, and here emphatically denies that this would ever be possible. "Can a woman put her baby out of mind so as not to show compassion for the child from inside her? Yes, these may put them out of mind, but I—I will not put you out of mind." The verb šākaḥ is conventionally translated "forget," but this gives a misleading impression, like that which attaches to translating zākar "remember." Both commonly refer to intentional acts, setting one's mind on something or keeping it in mind, or deliberately putting it out of mind. Zion does not complain that she has accidentally slipped from Yhwh's mind because Yhwh has other things to think about. Rather Yhwh has deliberately disregarded her. Yhwh is like a husband who has abandoned his wife.

In response, Yhwh implies a different comparison, implying the claim to be more like a mother than a husband. Yhwh first asks a rhetorical question to which we would assume the answer is "No"; a woman does not stop thinking about her baby. The word for "baby" (ʿûl) literally denotes a suckling, and this may suggest why a mother cannot put her baby out of mind. Physiologically, her body continues to remind her that she is equipped for suckling her baby. And the act of suckling establishes a deep bond between mother and baby. How could a woman put her baby out of mind or forget it when she has been used to feeding it? The companion colon underlines the point. Keeping in mind implies caring for or having compassion for. We might say that in this sense a mother is hardwired for such caring; there are aspects of her chemical makeup that push her in this direction. Israel makes a similar point by means of its language, for the word "compassion" (raḥămîm) is the plural of the word for the womb (reḥem).[200] Isaiah 47 has already implicitly worked with this link in critiquing Ms. Babylon for failing to show the womanly attitude of compassion. While Israelites might have not have thought about motherhood every

---

[199]It may be that the first colon refers to Yhwh's *begetting* Israel (so JPSV), though it would be the only such reference, and *yālad* more often means "bear." But the second colon certainly refers to a mother's birthing.

[200]See Phyllis Trible, *God and the Rhetoric of Sexuality* (Philadelphia: Fortress, 1978), pp. 31-71.

time they used the word *raḥămîm*, as we can use the word *compassion* without thinking about the fact that etymologically it suggests "suffering with" someone, the context here brings the etymology of *raḥămîm* nearer the surface. A woman shows compassion for the child that came from inside her.[201] The feeling of compassion is the natural one for a mother to show. Compassion is not confined to mothers, but it is an especially motherly feeling.

Admittedly mothers do sometimes behave in unmotherly ways toward their children, and the prophet seems to recognize that. The rhetoric works by implying that the answer to the question in the second line is actually "Yes." Mothers can put their babies out of mind; Yhwh will not do that to Zion. Think of the best example of human compassion, the passage says, then double it to get a truer impression of Yhwh's compassion. Through Hosea Yhwh had warned, "I will no longer have compassion on the household of Israel" (Hos 1:6). Hosea presupposes that Yhwh has long been having compassion on Israel; according to Israel's story, that started at Sinai (Ex 34:6). But Hosea says there comes a moment when it stops. Isaiah 49 implies either that Yhwh did not fulfill that threat, or that the action that looked like an abandonment of compassion coexisted with an attitude of compassion.

"I will have compassion on whomever I will have compassion" (Ex 33:19). The implication is not "*only* on those" but "on *all* those."[202] This compassion issues from the free being of Yhwh in person and reaches out to all those to whom Yhwh wills to reach out, unconditioned by who they are.[203] It "lies in His readiness to share in sympathy the distress of another, a readiness which springs from His inmost nature and stamps all His being and doing."[204]

Attentiveness

Psalm 79:5-9 also links compassion and keeping things in mind, but in a different profile. In asking whether Yhwh is going to be angry with the people forever, Yhwh's passion burning with unquenchable fire, it begs, "Do not keep in mind against us former wrongdoings." The NRSV and NIVI take the "former wrongdoings" to be those of earlier generations, but the verses do go on to refer to "our shortcomings," and more likely JPSV is right that this phrase refers to the present generation's own. In any case that later line makes clear that the speakers accept that they have done wrong. Yet they are astonishingly dispas-

---

[201]The EVV have "from her womb," but the word is the more general term *beṭen*, which refers to the insides of a woman or a man.

[202]See *OTT* 1:406-7.

[203]Barth, *Church Dogmatics*, II/1:353.

[204]Ibid., II/1:369. Barth is describing God's "mercy" (*Barmherzigkeit*), but the First Testament passages he refers to in the context are ones that speak of God's *raḥămîm*.

sionate about this. The psalm contains no actual confession of sin, even though those words presuppose there is sin to confess. They leap over confession of sin to appeal for forgiveness, in the also-astonishing form of an appeal to Yhwh to "expiate our shortcomings."[205] They appeal further for Yhwh's compassion to "draw near to us quickly," but the basis for their appeals is "the honor of your name"; the motif runs through the psalm. The problem about what has happened is that foreigners have defiled Yhwh's holy palace and violated Yhwh's servants, foreigners who do not acknowledge Yhwh or call on Yhwh's name but throw scorn at Yhwh. If Yhwh does not act, they will continue saying "Where is their God?" For all the reality of Jerusalem's failure in relation to Yhwh, that of its attackers is surely greater. The basis for appeal is not so much what the attackers have done to the community that prays this prayer; it is what they have done to Yhwh (cf., e.g., Ps 83).

Thus Yhwh can abandon, but not put out of mind. It is easier either to abandon and put out of mind, or not to abandon and not to put out of mind. Yhwh lives with a tension between abandoning in the sense of standing back and declining to intervene on Zion's behalf, yet still watching and grieving over its suffering. It is the stance God will take at the cross, when God abandons Jesus, declining to intervene to stop his execution, yet does not stop watching what goes on, grieving over his suffering and thus suffering with him. Norbert Hoffmann has suggested that in "the Christ who died for us" we discover the eternal "God is for us." "Only with the doctrine of the Trinity is the historical truth of the cross given theological illumination."[206] For Gentiles that is so, but Israel already knew the eternal "God for us," and it is its understanding of God that provides the theological illumination for the cross, which the later doctrine of the Trinity spells out. Likewise, for Gentiles "the God whom Jesus proclaims as 'my Father' is first of all only his God; not our God nor the God of our Father. Only through the proclamation of Jesus and the way in which he turns towards other men and women does his God become their God and his Father become our Father."[207] But for Israel, God is already father, mother, husband, next-of-kin—"father of orphans" (Ps 68:6), indeed.[208] In subsequent Christian faith the community lost the confidence of its own belonging to God's family and its entitlement to call on God as "Abba" and to trust God as its shepherd, and the priest or senior "pastor" came to be its "father" and shepherd. The priest or pastor had access to God; it was not clear that the congre-

---

[205]On this verb, see section 2.6 "Cleansing."

[206]Norbert Hoffmann, *Kreuz und Trinität* (Einsiedeln: Johannes, 1982), p. 52, as translated in Moltmann, *History and the Triune God*, p. xvii.

[207]Moltmann, *History and the Triune God*, p. 14.

[208]As Moltmann goes on to note (ibid. p. 14).

gation had its access except via the priest or pastor.

Israel, too, might have thought it needed to devise means to keep itself in Yhwh's mind and before Yhwh's eyes. Actually Yhwh had taken that action. "There, on my palms I have inscribed you; your walls are before me continually" (Is 49:16). Every look at the hands is a reminder. Perhaps the companion colon implies that Yhwh has engraved a picture of the walls there. There is no way Yhwh can get Jerusalem out of mind. "Yhwh's eyes are towards the faithful and his ears to their cry for help. . . . People cry out and Yhwh listens; from all their troubles he rescues them. Yhwh is near people who are broken inside; he will deliver the crushed in spirit" (Ps 34:15-18 [MT 16-19]). Yhwh is "one who listens to prayer" (Ps 65:2 [MT 3]).

Mercy

In Isaiah 57:14-21, Yhwh has just been indicting the people for their adherence to traditional religious observances with their sexual rites, sacrifice of children and sacrifices to the King of Sheol. Yhwh goes on to declare, "I dwell on high as the holy one, and with the crushed and low in spirit" (Is 57:15).[209] There might seem to be a tension between these two, but the prophet implies none. Yhwh does not have to do something odd in order to associate with the crushed. This assumption coheres with the one that is more explicit in Hosea 11, where Yhwh's holiness manifests itself in showing tender concern. Here in Isaiah 57 Yhwh is "on high, exalted," one whose "name is holy," that is, Yhwh *is* "the holy one of Israel," the title that often appears in Isaiah (and see Is 6:1). Yhwh dwells in heaven, in another realm without the constraints of the material realm, and/or lives in the heavens and sits enthroned there, using earth as a footstool. Either description establishes the exalted position of Yhwh and the distinctiveness of Yhwh's being and life over against the world. Yhwh's position parallels that of a king such as Solomon in his palace at the height of the city, separated in splendor from the ordinary citizenry. Further, Yhwh dwells there "forever," with none of the transience that characterizes the human community. Again that is mirrored in the permanence of the king in his palace with the promise that his dynasty will continue, which contrasts with the vulnerability of ordinary people who may lose their homes or their freedom to poverty or fraud.

But being the king means being occupied with the task of seeing to the welfare of the city, and that includes seeing that the crushed and low are lifted up.

---

[209]The NRSV translates *dakkāʾ ûšĕpal-rûaḥ* "contrite and humble in spirit," but the regular meaning of *dakkāʾ* is "crush," and of *ûšĕpal*, "low." To introduce a moral note here obscures the point, as in Is 66:1-2 (see section 2.5 "Yhwh's Accessibility"). *Crushed* is the word used of Yhwh's servant in Is 53:5, 10.

Much of the time the king will do that by commissioning aides to act on his behalf, but from time to time he will get down into the city to see for himself and to act directly.[210] Always working from the palace risks remoteness. Even in trying to do a good job of ruling the country, he will not have fulfilled his vocation. All this imitates the instinct of the God who models the true nature of kingship (if there can be such a thing). Yhwh's desire as the one on high is not to stay as the sole high one but to lift up the low, "to revive the spirit of the low, to revive the heart of the crushed" (Is 57:15) (for instance, the people of Jerusalem in the sixth century). And Yhwh does that through "dwelling" with them, being present with them. That does not mean merely being present with them like a friend who sits with someone who is sick but is unable to do anything to make them better. It is more like a doctor who can be with them and take action to bring about healing.

"By linking 'Holy One' to the term 'of Israel,' Israel's testimony asserts that this completely separated One is the characteristically related One." The idea of holiness is thus recharacterized by bringing it into association with Yhwh's own distinctive nature. The holy one who dwells on high is the one who dwells with people who are humiliated and crushed.[211]

Healing

Paradoxically, Yhwh maintains that attitude even though being the one who crushed the community and made it low. Yhwh gets angry, but does not stay angry. The people's "wrongdoing inspired by greed" (Is 57:17; lit., "their wrongdoing of greed" or greedy wrongdoing) could not finally be ignored. "I hit them as I hid and was angry." But having put the people down, Yhwh is free to lift them up again. Having attacked, Yhwh is free to defend. Having hit, Yhwh is free to heal. "I saw their way but I will heal them." Yhwh's declarations perhaps take up the challenges of their prayers, as Isaiah 40—66 often does. People say, "Yhwh has crushed us and cast us down. He will always be against us, angry with us forever." "No!" Yhwh says. The very fact that Yhwh made us a living, breathing humanity, but one whose spirit thus grows faint when its creator withdraws, means that Yhwh cannot turn away forever.

It is to this end that Isaiah 57:14-21 begins with Yhwh's commissioning the carving of a highway: "build up, build up, clear a road, lift high the obstructions from the way to my people!" Its talk of removing the obstacles from (literally) "the way of my people" might suggest this is a highway for the people to travel (cf. Is 35). It might then be a highway that leads back to God, a highway that the people have to build by their turning from the wrong way to the

---

[210]Cf. section 2.5 "Yhwh's Omnipresence."

[211]Brueggemann, *Theology of the OT*, pp. 289, 292.

right way (cf. Mt 3:1-3). But the context rather suggests a highway for Yhwh to travel (cf. Is 40:3-5). Yhwh wants to get back to this people, reversing the hiding that endorsed their own going away from Yhwh. It is by returning to them in this way that Yhwh will come to build up the crushed and raise up the low in spirit. Yhwh's aides are involved in Yhwh's action, but they are only making sure the road is clear for Yhwh to come to act in person.

Yhwh will undertake this despite the fact that there has been no movement on the part of the people themselves. They are crushed and low in spirit, but with the characteristic perversity of the people of God they are still carrying on in their own way. Yhwh sees that this is true but still says "I will heal them"; or rather, Yhwh sees that this is true and *therefore* says "I will heal them." It is no use waiting for them to turn and reckoning then to heal them. Their very persisting in following their own inclinations reflects their being crushed and low. It will be a long time before they turn on their own. Yhwh needs to heal them. Their inclination is to walk in their own way, so Yhwh will take responsibility for leading them and guiding them. Yhwh will "repay them with comfort," a paradoxical expression. Comfort is certainly what the crushed and low-spirited need, both comfort in the sense of encouragement and comfort in the sense of restoration. But it is paradoxical to call this "payment." The only payment they deserve is more crushing. In paying them comfort for persisting in going their own way, Yhwh is turning regular ways of thinking upside down.[212] Something similar will be true about "creating fruit for their lips."[213] This people's lips are unfruitful, or rather they give forth only bad produce, and their lips are stained by what they have said (cf. Is 6:5; 59:3). Sometimes people honor Yhwh with their lips but not with their inner beings (Is 29:13), but now in their mourning they are saying nothing at all. And Yhwh knows it is no good simply bidding them to put their speech right. Yhwh is creating fruit for their lips, words that represent true recognition of Yhwh. Yes, "things are going to be well, things are going to be well" (*shalom, shalom;* Is 57:19).

It is still the case that "the faithless are like the sea tossing because it cannot keep still" (Is 57:20). Yhwh's action does not simply remove human responsibility, as if healing happens without the patient's cooperation. People who stay faithless do not find things are all well (Is 57:21).

---

[212]But there may be some play on words in this line. The LXX *parekalesa auton* points to the fact that 'anḥēhû recalls the verb nûaḥ as well as nāḥâ and thus hints at "I will give them relief" as well as "I will lead them" The LXX then implies that wa'ăsallēm means something like "restore" (cf. NIVI), which suggests a link with šālôm—plausibly, since that word comes twice in the next line.

[213]"Fruit of the lips" comes only here, but expressions such as "fruit of the mouth" come a number of times in Proverbs (e.g., Prov 18:20-21) to suggest the good things that can issue from a person's words.

Commitment

The fact that Yhwh is prepared to threaten but then relent is a sign of Yhwh's ongoing "commitment" to people, Yhwh's *hesed* (EVV translate by words such as "steadfast love"). There are two contexts in which *hesed* especially operates. Sometimes someone's action involves making an extraordinary commitment to a person with whom they have no prior relationship (e.g., Rahab, Josh 2:12). That is *hesed*. It is closely related to grace *(hēn)*. Sometimes *hesed* presupposes that there is a relationship, and that one party maintains that commitment against all odds—for instance, even when the other party does not, or when it does not look like it (as in Naomi's comment in Ruth 2:20). The New Testament Greek word *agapē* is a later equivalent to *hesed*. To say "God so loved the world" (Jn 3:16) is to say that God's sending Jesus is an expression of Yhwh's *hesed*.

The close of Psalm 62 points to "one thing . . . two things" about God, two key truths of divine revelation to offer encouragement under the pressure of other people's attacks. They are that might and commitment belong to God. The order in a numerical saying of this kind may be significant. Unlike the attackers, God is not only powerful but also committed. That means God does reward people who are faithful, the psalm infers. (It is of course not on this basis that Israel comes to be the people of God, but once they are the people of God, they must be committed to faithfulness if their lives before God are to work out.) Although Psalm 62:11-12 [MT 12-13] thus relates to its context, it also encapsulates a double truth about God's nature that is not bound to its context, a neat summary of fundamentals of First Testament theology.[214]

So, Psalm 103 declares, Yhwh is one who "pardons all your wrongdoing, heals all your illnesses, restores your life from the Pit, festoons you with commitment and compassion," and thereby shows that "Yhwh is compassionate and gracious, long-tempered and big in commitment." Indeed, "as high as heaven above the earth has his commitment prevailed above people who revere him; as distant as east is from west has he distanced our rebellions from us." The psalm goes on again to underline Yhwh's compassion over people, then notes the feeble origins and transience of humanity. This provides further reason for Yhwh's commitment, though the psalm also goes on to make it the basis for another point. In contrast to human transience, "Yhwh's commitment stands from age to age above people who revere him and his faithfulness for grandchildren" (Ps 103:3-18).

So the height of heaven is not a threat, as if it distanced God from us. It is

---

[214]So Georg Fohrer, *Theologische Grundstrukturen des Alten Testaments* (Berlin/New York: Walter de Gruyter, 1972), p. 99. Cf. Helmer Ringgren, *The Faith of the Psalmists* (Philadelphia: Fortress/London: SCM Press, 1963), p. 47.

good news, as a figure of how completely God's commitment prevails above us. The prepositional expression is an odd one, repeated three times. Very rarely does anyone have commitment or compassion "over" someone. Initially, at least, the preposition continues the vertical spatial image. God's commitment towers high over us. Likewise the horizontal spatial relationship of east and west or sunrise and sunset become a positive image. Literal geographical distance can be a problem in religious life (e.g., Ps 42). So can metaphorical geographical distance (e.g., Ps 22:1, 11, 19 [MT 2, 12, 20]), not least when it is an image for the effect of wrongdoing on a relationship (e.g., Prov 15:29). But it can also be a figure for the distance God sets, not between us and God, but between us and our acts of rebellion, and so it is here. The relationship of distance and wrongdoing becomes a happy one rather than an unhappy one. Again, the psalm presupposes, a parent stands high over a child, and that spatial relationship can be a threat. But here, once more, the threat is turned into good news; it is a father's compassion over a son that provides an image for Yhwh's. Humanity is one with God, so that images from human life can represent realities about God. Humanity is one with heaven. But humanity is also one with earth, specifically in its frailty. As the hot Middle Eastern wind withers the grass and wildflowers soon after they spring up, so human beings eventually wither. Yet God's commitment means that God does not dismiss humanity in its oneness with earth, because of God's own oneness with humanity as a fatherlike person.

True Faithfulness

Yhwh is the "true God" (*'ēl 'ĕmet*, Ps 31:5 [MT 6]). Yhwh is "one who keeps truthfulness forever, exercises authority for the oppressed" (Ps 146:6-7). Psalm 146 therefore urges people not to put their reliance for deliverance on human beings who look impressive. They are only human. They will die, and their plans to help will die with them. That affirmation of Yhwh's truthfulness stands between descriptions of Yhwh as creator and as one who acts on behalf of the needy. Yhwh's being the creator is a past expression of that truthfulness and is the basis for declaring that this truthfulness stands forever. It expresses itself further in action to meet the needs of the oppressed, hungry, captive, blind, disabled, aliens, orphans and widows, and more generally in commitment to the faithful and against the faithless, to frustrate their efforts and/or put them down.

Job can describe God as someone who does not care about truth. He imagines himself challenging God in a court but unable to win the case, not because he is in the wrong but because God is simply bigger than he is (Job 9). Paradoxically, he then speaks confidently to his "friends" about God's just commitment to the truth. God will surely be aroused by their untruth (Job 13:7-10).

What Job says about God when speaking to others is very different from what he says about God when speaking to himself. He shows a confidence in God's commitment to truth that is extraordinary in light of his earlier statements, though perhaps it shows that one of the points of those earlier statements was to arouse the God who overheard them to disprove them. He knows that God loathes theological statements that are designed to honor God but fail to do so (for instance, because we are really concerned to protect statements that make us feel more comfortable even if they do not face facts). Either we do not take the dreadful majesty of God seriously, or we will soon find ourselves its victims, or both. Our theology is mere ash. Bulwarks designed to defend a city but made of the ash-remains of preceding buildings, or made of clay rather than rock, will soon collapse. The same is true of the arguments the friends use to defend God. Given that he sees himself as involved in a trial between himself and God, they are bearing false witness, for reasons that lie inside themselves. "Job is demanding that theological language be held to the same strict standards of truth required of participants in a trial."[215] He believes God will not tolerate false witness, even though superficially glorified by it. He will prove to be right (see Job 42:7).

Yhwh is also a faithful God (ṣaddîq) and a deliverer (môšîaʿ, Is 45:21). The fact that European languages have no equivalent to ṣĕdāqā and are reduced to translating it by dikaiosunē and then by iustitia and then by "justice" or "righteousness" "has cast a shadow over the whole of the old covenant."[216] The EVV conventionally translate ʾēl ṣaddîq "a righteous God" or "a just God" and Christian faith has often seen a tension between God's being righteous or just and being saving or forgiving. First Testament faith does not feel such a tension, partly because it does not understand Yhwh's relationship with us primarily in legal terms. Yhwh's ṣĕdāqâ is not a justice that is subservient to an impartial objectivity which is itself a higher ideal. Yhwh's ṣĕdāqâ is a commitment to doing the right thing by the people with whom one stands in relationship. It "is not a juristic concept but one having reference to relationships." Ruling over people in the context of fellowship in such a way as to help and protect them is what makes Yhwh ṣaddîq.[217] It is thus as the one who is ṣaddîq that Yhwh rains fire and sulfur on the faithless when they attack people (Ps 11:6-7). And there is no tension between being ṣaddîq and being môšîaʿ. Yhwh does not have to feel guilty about having an instinct to forgive people and deliver or restore them. It is an expression of faithfulness. Indeed, Yhwh's honor lies in being faithful; kābôd and ṣĕdāqâ appear together (e.g., Ps 85:9-13 [MT 10-

---

[215]Newsom, "The Book of Job," p. 433.

[216]Hans Urs von Balthasar, *The Glory of the Lord*, vol. 6 (Edinburgh: T & T Clark, 1991), p. 163.

[217]Köhler, *OT Theology*, p. 35.

14]; 97:6; 145:5-7; Is 58:8).[218] Yhwh is "dedicated to faithfulness," *'ōhēb ṣĕdāqā* (Ps 33:5). Yhwh loves faithfulness, is enthusiastic about it, is given to it. Yhwh is thus "my faithful God," *'ĕlōhê ṣidqî* (Ps 4:1 [MT 2]).

Psalm 71 contains the densest concentration of references to God's faithfulness in the First Testament. Here God's faithfulness is expressed in listening to people's pleas and responding by saving, rescuing and delivering (Ps 71:2). More systematically, God's faithfulness will therefore be the subject of the suppliant's proclamation, commemoration, confession and talk when it has issued in deliverance. (Ps 71:15-16, 19, 22, 24). The dominating topic of Israel's praise is here the fact that God is faithful, which is not merely something continuous and persistent but something dynamic and vigorous. God's faithfulness expresses itself not merely in being a consistent presence but in acting on Israel's behalf when action is what is needed.

Passion

If compassion is Yhwh's characteristic as a mother or father, passion, eroslike love, is Yhwh's characteristic as a husband or wife. Ezekiel's portrayal of God as the lover of an unfaithful wife makes the point powerfully, though distastefully in a modern Western context. Jerusalem was like an illegitimate, unwanted and abandoned child, like a baby whose mother has left her in the trash, wrapped in newspaper. God was thus first the compassionate foster-father who gave her the gift of life, made it possible for her to grow into a child and an adolescent girl. Then God gave her the gift of love. For *love* Ezekiel does not use the word *'ahăbâ* but *dôd*, a word used most often for the love of a man and a woman, especially in the Song of Songs. "I spread my robe over you and covered your nakedness, and pledged myself to you and entered into covenant with you (the Lord Yhwh's message) and you became mine" (Ezek 16:8). Yhwh goes on to recall bathing her, perfuming her, clothing her richly and adorning her with jewelry, and watching her become more and more beautiful, queenlike. No one else had seen her beauty. Indeed, there was not beauty there to be seen; as often happens, beauty emerged from being the object of love.

The story goes on to focus at great length on the enormity of the girl's subsequent gross unfaithfulness and the jealous anger this arouses. She has broken the covenant. "But I myself will be mindful of my covenant with you in your young days, and I will establish for you a lasting covenant. And you will be mindful of your ways and be humiliated . . . and you will acknowledge that I am Yhwh, so that you will be mindful and be humiliated, and there will be no more opening of the mouth for you, in the face of your shame, when I make

---

[218]José P. Miranda, *Marx and the Bible* (Maryknoll, N.Y.: Orbis, 1974/London: SCM Press, 1977), pp. 235-36.

expiation for you for all you have done" (Ezek 16:60-63).

There is no sentimentality in Ezekiel, and Yhwh resembles a jealous husband who cannot imagine instantly forgetting what his wife has done and
wants to see the look of shame on her face. But that adds power to the commitment here expressed. The fact that his wife has gone back on the marriage covenant does not mean he just forgets it. He reminds himself of it and confirms
it. One might have imagined his now making it a more explicitly conditional
covenant, but he moves in the opposite direction, making it explicitly a covenant that will last *(bĕrît ʿôlām)* notwithstanding the way his wife has behaved.
It resembles the covenants with Noah or Abraham or David, which required
obedience in response, but were not conditional upon it (e.g., Gen 9:16; 17:13,
19; 2 Sam 23:5). Yhwh's love is electing—that is, free (Deut 7:6-7; 14:2). It is purifying. And it is creative, because it inspires love (Deut 6:5; 30:6).[219] It "is not
merely not conditioned by any reciprocity of love. It is also not conditioned by
any worthiness to be loved on the part of the loved" (cf. Deut 7:8); God's love
issues from who God is.[220]

Yhwh's passion is a key factor in Israel's destiny. Zechariah reports, "Yhwh
has said this: I have a huge passion for Zion, I have a fierce passion for her"
(Zech 8:2). More literally, "I passion for Zion a big passion, a fierce passion I
passion for her." While the language of passion is not confined to a man-
woman relationship, it is especially at home there (e.g., Prov 6:34; Song 8:6).
Yhwh speaks like a man viscerally moved in his feelings about the woman he
loves. If his woman had been unfaithful to him, that passion could imply jealousy and a strength of feeling that issues in hostility toward her, but when the
verb is used with *l* it suggests feelings that work in her favor (cf. Zech 1:14).
Thus when Yhwh goes on to describe these feelings as characterized by *hēmâ*,
as fierce (JPSV) or burning (NIVI) or wrathful (NRSV), that does not add to the
threat to Zion but adds to their positive message (cf. Is 42:13). Yhwh is not like
a man who has discovered that another man has been courting his woman but
like a man who has discovered that another man has been beating his woman.
One expects that this passion will therefore issue in a determination to take it
out on her attacker (so Zech 1:14-15, where the knee-jerk expression of passion
acts toward the nations and the compassion for Jerusalem comes second). In
Zechariah 8, Yhwh bypasses the nations. Instead of leaving Zion in her state of
distress while venting on her attacker, Yhwh's passion issues immediately in
concern for her: "Yhwh has said this: I am turning to Zion and I shall dwell in
the midst of Jerusalem'" (Zech 8:3).

[219]Barth, *Church Dogmatics*, IV/2:751-83.
[220]Ibid., II/1:278-79.

Cleansing

Yhwh therefore intends to make expiation for Jerusalem (*kipper*, Ezek 16:63). We do not know the precise meaning of this key verb. It may literally imply white out or wash off,[221] but either way the metaphor clearly indicates an action that results in offenses no longer counting, no longer having any effect.[222] The verb is traditionally translated "atone for," and there is no doubt that it generally refers to a human act whereby people atone for sin and put things right with God. Understandably, there are not many occasions when Yhwh is its subject (Deut 21:8; 32:43; 2 Chron 30:18; Ps 65:4 [MT 3]; 78:38; 79:9; Jer 18:23), and only three actually affirm that God does make expiation. The verb then suggests that God is taking responsibility for an intrinsically human obligation. If someone is to reestablish the relationship that their spouse has imperiled by unfaithfulness, that requires an extraordinary willingness on the part of the wronged party to deal with the offense they have received rather than yielding to the reasonable conclusion that the marriage is over. It is an extraordinary expression of grace that God atones for the wrongs that people have done to God. And perhaps Ezekiel implies that it will be this act of love on Yhwh's part that will issue in some mindfulness on Jerusalem's part that responds to Yhwh's, a mindfulness that owns failure and issues in an awareness of humiliation and shame and in an abandonment of self-assured assertiveness. That is a painful experience to impose on her, but a necessary one. Facts have to be faced. Without that, there can be no progress. In due course, her husband will also need to forget as well as forgive.

The image of washing off is explicit elsewhere. "Wash me thoroughly from my waywardness, purify me of my failure" a suppliant pleads (Ps 51:2 [MT 4]; cf. 7 [MT 9]). Sin is like the stain that comes on someone through something such as contact with a corpse, or on someone who has worshiped other deities or has killed someone. It would therefore be appropriate for the only, living, faithful God to have no contact with us, because our beings are redolent of other deities, of death and of wrongdoing. The psalm asks God to overcome this logic and act to purify us so that contact continues to be possible (it is the action that Jesus repeats when he reaches out to touch someone with a skin disease or touches a dead man's coffin or lets a "sinner" touch him (Lk 5:13; 7:14, 39).

"Decontaminate me with hyssop," the psalm adds (Ps 51:7 [MT 9]). *Decontaminate* (*ḥāṭā'* piel) comes from the verb "fail, fall short, sin," which is related to the noun for failure or shortcoming (Ps 51:2 [MT 4]). The failure the psalm

---

[221]See the discussion in, e.g., *NIDOTTE*.
[222]Cf. Roy Gane, *Cult and Character* (Winona Lake, Ind.: Eisenbrauns, 2005), pp. 193-94.

has spoken of has left a stain that needs removing. That word *failure* can also denote an offering for failure or sin, a purification offering. Such an offering dealt with stain in general and with the staining effect of wrongdoing (not directly with the sin itself, which would require repentance and some way of making up for the wrongdoing). In the psalm this becomes a metaphor for something that Yhwh does, rather like the appeal to Yhwh to make expiation for us. Alongside sacrifice, sprinkling with water by means of a branch of hyssop could be part of the process whereby something was cleansed (the same form of this verb is used in connection with the cleansing of a tent where someone has died, in Numbers 19:14-19). The suppliant asks God to act like the friend who sprinkles the people who live in that tent, the tent itself and its furnishings, to decontaminate people and tent so that the people can resume their ordinary lives.

There are acts and words that can ensure that stains are covered or removed and declare that they have been so dealt with. But these need to stand for the fact that God is the one who washes, purifies, decontaminates, expiates and speaks the words that bring joy. A person who has done wrong needs to hear God say, "It's OK." Until that happens, the entire person, body and spirit, is overcome by a crushed and crushing sadness. But hearing those words from God brings joyful relief (Ps 51:8 [MT 10]).

"I myself am the one who wipes out your rebellions, for my own sake, and your shortcoming I do not call to mind" (Is 43:25). The key expression at the center of the line applies to both clauses: I act "for my own sake." As Israel's moral strength and religious faithfulness did not bring about Yhwh's commitment to it in the first place, so its moral feebleness and religious faithlessness cannot terminate Yhwh's commitment. Whoever said that God will pardon because it is his business[223] was encapsulating a key truth, even if people are inclined to dismiss the observation because it is also a dangerous one. In a strange sense Yhwh has no alternative but to stay committed to Israel even when meeting with no reciprocal commitment. The people of God load their shortcomings on God and thus make God their servant, reversing the natural relationship between them (Is 43:24), and God says "All right, then," and shoulders the burden.

There is admittedly some contradiction in Yhwh's statement. The paragraph in which it is set comprises a reminder of Israel's shortcomings. How can Yhwh then claim not to bring these to mind? Perhaps the answer is the practical one, that Yhwh refers to the practical effects of this action. Bearing sin in mind easily

---

[223]The statement has been attributed both to Catherine the Great and to Heinrich Heine: See *The Oxford Dictionary of Quotations*, 4th ed. (Oxford/New York: Oxford University Press, 1996), pp. 185, 331.

means holding grudges. Yhwh does not do that. Some talking about past sin and punishment may be necessary, in order to be realistic and to encourage Israel toward change. But Yhwh is determined that past sin should not spoil the present and future relationship with Israel, not on Yhwh's side.

Carrying

Alongside the image of cleansing are the images of covering and carrying. "You have carried your people's wrongdoing, you have covered all their shortcomings, you have withdrawn all your fury, you have turned from your angry burning" (Ps 85:2-3 [MT 3-4]). It is impossible for wrongdoers to cover their sin. It is impossible to cover over shed blood. But God can do what is forbidden or impossible.

It is by carrying the wrongdoing that God covers it. Either the carrying and covering issue from the abandonment of anger or they make possible the abandonment of anger, or both. One who gives up anger is determined to carry and cover; one who carries and covers removes the cause for anger. The verb *carry* (*nāśā'*) is the word most often translated "forgive." When people do wrong, someone has to "carry" it, to accept responsibility for it, pay the cost of it, bear the burden of it, shoulder the consequences of it. The First Testament often speaks of people "carrying" their wrongdoing. They bear the responsibility and shoulder the consequences. But when one person has been wronged by another, the wronged person may choose to carry or share the consequences, to choose not to let the wrong spoil the relationship or not to seek redress. The First Testament suggests an analogous understanding of Yhwh's relationship with our wrongdoing. Yhwh chooses to pay the price for it rather than making us do so. Yhwh thus declines to let the relationship with Israel be broken by Israel's wrongdoing. God bears the cost of human sin. "What marks out God above all false gods is that they are not capable and ready for this. In their otherworldliness and supernaturalness and otherness, etc., the gods are a reflection of the human pride which will not unbend, which will not stoop to that which is beneath it. God is not proud. In His high majesty He is humble. It is in this high humility that He speaks and acts as the God who reconciles the world to Himself."[224]

This only properly works if it meets with a response from Israel. If it meets with no response, then the relationship is spoiled, and Israel has to live with

---

[224]Barth, *Church Dogmatics*, IV/1:159. On the expression "carry sin," see Baruch J. Schwartz, "The Bearing of Sin in the Priestly Literature," in *Pomegranates and Golden Bells*, ed. David P. Wright et al. (Winona Lake, Ind.: Eisenbrauns: 1995), pp. 3-21, though I do not follow his distinction between "carrying sin" in the sense of bearing one's own guilt and "carrying sin" in the sense of taking it off somewhere. See also Gane, *Cult and Character*, pp. 101-3.

its consequences. Either people carry their sin, or God carries it. It is thus God's self-giving for enemies that makes possible their "reception into the eternal communion of God."[225] That can work via the sacrificial system, though it is not dependent on that; God continued to carry Israel's wrongdoing through the exile, when no sacrifices could be offered. And after A.D. 70 "instead of plunging into despair because there were now no means of cleansing the people's sins, [Israel] turned to its father in heaven and remembered that it is he who forgives sins and he can do so with or without the Temple."[226]

There are occasions when prophets warn that Yhwh will totally cast off Israel and totally destroy the people, but Yhwh never quite manages to do that, as Micah 7 notes. There are always some leftovers. "Who is a God like you, carrying wrongdoing, getting over rebellion for the leftovers of his possession?" The leftovers do not then simply get left, as if they survive only to be witnesses to Yhwh's act of destruction. That would not count as commitment, the kind of commitment and truthfulness that Yhwh has to show in order to be faithful to the promises sworn to Abraham. For these leftovers, Yhwh turns out indeed to be one who carries wrongdoing. "He will not keep hold of his anger forever, because he is one who likes commitment. He will again have compassion on us, he will trample on our wrongdoings. You will throw all their failures into the depths of the sea. You will show truthfulness to Jacob, commitment to Abraham, you who swore to our ancestors from days of old" (Mic 7:18-20). In this context, the distinctiveness of the familiar image of carrying sin lies in the way it follows an earlier reference to carrying. "I shall carry Yhwh's indignation, because I have failed him, until Yhwh contends for me" (Mic 7:9). For a while Jerusalem indeed carried Yhwh's indignation, but a time came when the direction of this carrying was reversed and Yhwh resumed the carrying of Israel's sin that is more usually the way carrying works.

Getting Over

In the Micah passage, alongside the image of carrying is another; Yhwh "gets over" their rebellion. The verb is the common ʿābar used in an unusual way. Yhwh is like the human being who proves the possession of insight by being slow-tempered rather than quick-tempered and who proves to be a fine person by "getting over" rebellion (Prov 19:11). Barth notes the long-tempered stance God takes to Cain, to humanity after the flood and to Nineveh,[227] and the way the whole story of Israel and of the church is a story of divine long-temperedness. Admittedly Yhwh reached a point of deciding not to pass by Is-

[225]Miroslav Volf, *Exclusion and Embrace* (Nashville: Abingdon, 1996), p. 23.
[226]Michael Wyschogrod, *The Body of Faith* (San Francisco: Harper & Row, 1989), p. 17.
[227]*Church Dogmatics*, II/1:412-14.

rael any longer (Amos 7:8; 8:2), but Micah here looks beyond the implementing of that resolve and expresses the conviction that it is not Yhwh's last word.
"Getting over" rebellion suggests more than merely "overlooking" it (BDB),
something more deliberate and less distanced. When we speak of "getting
over" something and "getting beyond" it or "getting through" it, we reflect the
fact that we have been affected by whatever has happened. Getting over/
through/beyond requires time, but also a certain willingness not to get stuck.
Yhwh decided for a while not to carry on putting up with rebellion, but then
determined not to get stuck in a stand-off with Israel but to get over its rebellion for the sake of "the leftovers of his possession," for what was left of the
people who belonged to Yhwh.

To put it another way, Yhwh gets angry, but does not hold on to anger so
that it becomes a permanent running resentment that makes it impossible to
restore the relationship. To put it yet another way, Yhwh treats the people's
wrongdoings like an enemy one defeats in battle. In hand-to-hand fighting the
warriors that get shot or stabbed fall and get trampled underfoot. At the exodus the warriors got thrown into the depths of the sea; Micah pictures Yhwh
doing that to Israel's failures. Micah's "Who is a God like you?" is a familiar
rhetorical question (e.g., Ex 15:11), but it usually points to the fact that there is
no god as powerful as Yhwh. Here the question points to a quite different characteristic that marks Yhwh off from other gods. Yhwh casts Israel's sins, not
Israel's enemies, into the depths of the sea. Yhwh loves the sinner but hates the
sin in the sense of being committed to the sinner but repudiating, opposing
and attacking the sin so it can no more stand as an obstacle that makes it hard
for Yhwh to relate to the people.[228] Trampling and throwing are different images for the same reality as carrying and getting over. The reverse way to express that is to ask, "Do not expel me from before your face" (Ps 51:11 [MT 13]).
The stain of wrongdoing would make it impossible for us to come before God
in worship; we would inevitably be thrown out, like someone in dirty clothes
at a royal banquet. There is a dress code here. But the fact that God cleanses
and renews makes it possible for God to keep us there.

So anger can become spent and punishment is something that has limits.
Half a century after Jerusalem was destroyed, Yhwh declares that its people
can be comforted, "because she has completed her service, because her wrongdoing is paid for, because she has received from Yhwh's hand double for all
her failings" (Is 40:2). While there are contexts in which Yhwh carries the people's wrongdoing, on this occasion the city has carried its own wrongdoing.
That is what the exile was about. But city and people are assured that it has

---

[228]See section 2.7 "Repudiation."

come to the end of the time of hard, fruitless toil, an experience like the service required of someone in the draft. This is not the unearned toughness in human experience of which Job speaks (Job 7:1; 14:14) but the earned toughness of the city's destruction and desolation. But Jerusalem has finished paying for its wrongdoing. What exactly Yhwh means by its paying double is not clear, but it is quite clear that it has paid quite adequately for all those failings of the period up to 587, for its people's faithlessness to Yhwh and their faithlessness to one another.

Pardon

Admittedly there is some contradiction involved in Psalm 51. Its being prayed presupposes that sin does not separate us from God, that a sinner can pray and be sure of being heard. Yhwh is not separated from Adam and Eve or Cain by their sin, but carries on relating to them. But sin has the potential to separate us from God, if we do not seek to put things right. "Right to you all flesh come with deeds of waywardness."[229] "Whereas our rebellions are too mighty for me [MT]/us [LXX], you are the one who expiates them" (Ps 65:2-3 [MT 3-4]). When we come to God, we come "with" praise (Ps 100:2) and "with" sacrifices (Ps 66:13), but we also come "with" sins. One might have thought this impossible, but it is not so. Indeed, we come "right to" God (ʿad) with them. Our rebellions might be too much for us to do anything about; we cannot compensate for them, as we think about coming into the presence of the king against whom we have rebelled. But they are not too much for God, who is again said to expiate them or atone for them, to cover them or wash them off. Atoning for sin is naturally the sinners' business, but it may be an impossible task, and the situation might then seem hopeless. Actually, this is not the case. Paradoxically, when there are acts whose offensiveness would seem to make it impossible for people to come to God, God makes that possible. God declines to be offended, and the offenses therefore cease to exist.

Yhwh once commissioned a search of the streets and squares of Jerusalem to try to find one individual who made right decisions and sought steadfastness, "so that I may pardon Jerusalem" (sālaḥ). But there are none, so "for what reason should I pardon you?" (Jer 5:1, 7). Yet when Yhwh commissions Jeremiah to write down all his prophecies, the aim is that the Judeans may turn from their evil ways "so that I may pardon their wrongdoing and their failure" (Jer 36:3). Yhwh is thus not like a judge in a Western law court, because such a judge has no power or right to pardon someone on the basis of their changing their way of life. They still have to pay their penalty. But pardon as the right of

---

[229]I associate the first clause of v. 3 with what precedes, which provides more balanced lines than MT's, though MT's versification also implies the point.

a king or president works within a power framework rather than a legal framework. It presupposes that wrongdoing is an offense against the king or the president, or against the nation whom this leader represents. It presupposes that the person who gives the pardon is prepared to bear the wrongdoing. If the wrongdoing is seen as an offense against the king, an act of rebellion against his authority, the king bears it. If it is seen as an offense against the nation, the president assumes the power to determine that the nation will bear it. So the king will cancel the record: "Blot out my rebellions," a suppliant asks (Ps 51:1 [MT 3]). And God agrees.

To put it yet another way, God avoids looking at our sins. "Hide your face from my failures" (Ps 51:9 [MT 11]), we ask. As acts, our sins lie in the past, but Hebrew thinking (more logically than English thinking) sees the past as lying in front of us, whereas the future lies behind us; we cannot see it. So for the psalmist, "my shortcomings are in front of me all the time" (Ps 51:3 [MT 5]). They must surely also stand before God, continually accusing us before God's eyes. But God has more control of the mechanisms of looking, thinking and forgetting than we have. God can decide to turn away from my shortcomings and not look at them anymore. As far as God is concerned, they cease to exist. "The God who remembers also knows how to forget."[230]

Risk

The fact that we can turn our backs on Yhwh means that relating to us involves Yhwh in risk. In bidding Abraham to sacrifice Isaac, Yhwh is testing him, acting to discover whether he will give up his son, and when he has shown that he will, Yhwh comments, "Now I know that you revere God" (Gen 22:1, 12). Yhwh did not know until then. The opening of Job has similar implications, though the word *test* does not come. It is Yhwh who says to the adversary, fresh from going about the earth to check out what is going on, "Have you considered my servant Job?" When the adversary raises the question about Job's motivation for a life of integrity and submission to Yhwh, Yhwh's response is not to declare assurance based on knowing Job from the inside, but to agree that the adversary should test him (Job 1:8-12). The results are mixed; the end of the story has Yhwh both rebuking Job and commending him.

While the earlier speeches of Job's friends focus on being irrelevant rather than wrong, eventually Job goads Eliphaz into talking vicious nonsense. His falsehood focuses on maligning Job's character, but he begins with a series of rhetorical questions: "To God, can a man be of service? Can a person of understanding be of service to him? Does it bring pleasure to the Almighty if you are

---

[230]Gutiérrez, *The God of Life*, p. 37.

faithful, or gain if you show integrity in your ways?" (Job 22:2-3). Eliphaz's questions abound in ironies. On the broadest canvas he might seem to be quite right. God is self-sufficient and does not "need" us. God's freedom (cf. Ex 3:14)[231] means God is unconditioned, uncontrolled and self-sufficient. God loves and acts out of self-sufficiency, not out of need or incompleteness. Extending the rhetorical questions so that they also cover wrongdoing, Elihu infers that "your faithlessness affects [only] a person like you, and your faithlessness affects [only] a human being [like you]" (Job 35:6-8). Yet the Scriptures never make that point, and in reporting that God created humanity to look after the world on God's behalf, as God's servants, they imply that human beings can be of service to God. They can certainly bring pleasure (ḥēpeṣ) to God (e.g., 1 Sam 15:22; Ps 51:19 [MT 21]).

More specifically, Eliphaz seems to be questioning a premise that emerges from the book's opening scenes, which neither he nor Job knows about. There Yhwh gained a vested interest in Job's integrity. Yhwh's reputation and insight came to be hitched to Job's faithfulness. If God is wrong about Job, God will look really stupid the next time the cabinet meets. God has a lot to lose now. Indeed, the prologue raised a darker question. Overtly it asked whether Job was in a relationship with God only for the sake of what he got out of it. But covertly it raised the question whether God was in this relationship for the same reason. Is it simply because God likes all that obedience and worship, which indeed brings pleasure to God? Eliphaz's actual words also unwittingly add a barb to his question along these lines. The repeated verb sākan usually means "be of service, benefit." Elihu interestingly takes up the verb in reworking Eliphaz's point, when he has Job say that avoiding sin brings no benefit to us (Job 35:2-8). Eliphaz himself uses the hiphil again later, apparently to mean something like "submit" (Job 22:21). But it (or a homonym) can also mean "harm" (Eccles 10:9). Can a man harm God or endanger God or bring risk to God? Actually, yes.

Sadness

In relating to Israel and to people such as Abraham and Job, God thus sometimes receives reassurances, but also surprises and disappointments. Relating to us involves Yhwh in sorrow and sadness. "What can I do for you, Ephraim, what can I do for you Judah, when your commitment is like morning cloud or like dew, going so early?" (Hos 6:4). The Prophets suggest a number of images to convey Yhwh's disappointment at how things have worked out with Israel. Yhwh's relationship with Israel is like a marriage, for instance, but when

---

Yhwh looks back over this relationship at the beginning of the main body of Jeremiah's prophecies (Jer 2:1-8), it is with despondency and disappointment. Yhwh calls to mind the bliss with which the marriage started (time has given a rosy tint to the memory), but also the way Jerusalem subsequently turned its back on its husband.

The response to human sinfulness in Isaiah begins not with God's anger or God's judgment for disobedience to a code of laws, but with God's sorrow and disappointment as a parent.[232] Almost the first words in the book, in a chapter that previews many of its themes, are "I reared children, brought them up, but they—they rebelled against me. An ox acknowledges its owner, an ass its master's trough, but Israel does not acknowledge, my people does not pay attention" (Is 1:2-3). Parents cannot force their children to become the sort of people they wish them to be. Like any other parent, God is helpless before the freedom of these children. And thus God knows the inconsolable sadness of watching children make the wrong decisions and pay for it. "If only you had paid attention to my commands. Then your well-being would have been like a river, your faithfulness like the waves of the sea" (Is 48:18). Only here in Scripture does Yhwh say "if only" with regard to the past, to a situation that cannot now be altered in the sense that the loss cannot be prevented, though it can be altered for the future. God grieves over not having been able to grant the well-being and show the faithfulness that are God's instinct. As father or mother Yhwh did everything a doting parent could do, but Israel was bent on turning away from Yhwh (Hos 11:7).

Isaiah goes on to picture Yhwh as a vine-grower who had done all the necessary work to make sure of a good crop of grapes and thus "expected" that it would happen, but found his expectations disappointed (Is 5:2, 4). Yhwh was expecting to find authority being exercised in a faithful way in the community but instead found blood flowing and the oppressed crying out (Is 5:7). It was not what Yhwh thought would happen. "I myself had said how I would put you among my children and give you a delightful country, the loveliest possession of the nations. And I said you would call me 'my father' and not turn from me. But in fact, as a woman breaks faith with her lover, so you broke faith with me, household of Israel" (Jer 3:19-20). The word ʾākēn ("but in fact") is often used after "I said [to myself]" as a way of indicating a marked contrast, "expressing the reality, in opp. to what had been wrongly imagined"[233] (Is 49:4; 53:4; Ps 31:22 [MT 23]; Job 32:8). Here it indicates that Yhwh also goes through that human experience of imagining how things will work out and finding

---

[232] Abraham J. Heschel, *The Prophets* (reprint, New York: HarperCollins, 2001), p. 101; cf. Fretheim, *Suffering of God*, p. 114.
[233] BDB.

they do the opposite (cf. Zeph 3:7). "He said, 'They are indeed my people, children who will not act falsely'" (Is 63:8). But things turned out differently from the hopes those words express.[234]

Letdown

God's disappointment thus conveys an impression of surprise, of not having foreseen what would happen. The First Testament often assumes that Yhwh can, for instance, know about future events, largely through being the one who decides them. Prophecy announces what Yhwh intends to do. But it also indicates that Yhwh does not always know what will happen; perhaps the implication is the converse, that this is partly because Yhwh is not always the one who decides what happens. Human beings often make their own decisions independently of Yhwh. Even then, I assume Yhwh could choose to know what will happen, but if so, the First Testament indicates that Yhwh does not always do so. Likewise it often assumes that God can look inside people and know their thoughts (e.g., Ps 44:21 [MT 22]), perhaps in the way that a human being can sometimes know what another person is thinking. But on occasions such as the ones we are considering, it indicates that God does not do so, and it seems arbitrary to declare that this form of statement is anthropomorphic in a way that other statements are not, and not really true. The Greek doctrine of divine omniscience assumes that God has an intrinsic knowledge of absolutely everything. The First Testament picture overlaps with that doctrine, but it is not identical with it, and it is striking that Wolfhart Pannenberg's only proof text for divine omniscience is in the deuterocanonical writings, in Sirach 42:18-19.[235] Karl Barth's only First Testament proof text is 1 Samuel 2:3, which refers to omniscience only in English translations; more literally it simply describes Yhwh as "God of knowledge."[236] The way the First Testament speaks suggests that, while indeed having the capacity for such knowledge, Yhwh does not "automatically" know everything.

We have noted that often God knows things as a result of discovering them; what distinguishes God in this connection is a limitless and irresistible *capacity* to know what is going on in the world and in people's hearts, what is happening in the present and what will happen in the future.[237] It is apparently up to God whether to turn that capacity into actuality, and it seems that God does

---

[234]See further section 4.1 "The Mystery of Sin."

[235]*Systematic Theology*, 1:381.

[236]Barth, *Church Dogmatics*, II/1:554. The word for "knowledge" is plural, suggesting abundant knowledge (GKC 124c). Barth's NT proof text is 1 Jn 3:2; he quotes other texts that affirm that God *can* know anything.

[237]See section 2.3 "Knowledge."

not always do so. Commissioning Jeremiah to speak to the people in the temple court, Yhwh comments, "Perhaps they will listen and turn, each of them, from their ill-doing, and I can relent about the ill that I am planning to do to them" (Jer 26:3; cf. Jer 36:3). Commissioning Ezekiel to act out a prophecy, Yhwh comments, "Perhaps they will look, because they are a rebellious household" (Ezek 12:3). In both cases, evidently Yhwh does not actually know. No doubt God can envisage the many possibilities that may arise in the world and knows the vast boundaries of human capacity. In this sense life holds no nasty surprises for God. God does not get caught off guard. Yet among the various possibilities open to humanity (or to members of the celestial world) God does not always know precisely how things will work out.[238] Since God's being coexists with all time (as well as perhaps extending beyond time), events that are future from our perspective are present from God's, and that might be a basis for God being able to know about acts of mine that I have not yet decided to undertake. So it might be quite possible for God to know about decisions I have not yet made. And the First Testament makes clear that Yhwh sometimes knows what people are going to do. Yet it also makes clear that Yhwh does not always choose to do so. And thus God experiences letdown when people do not do as hoped.

So while God sometimes shows a knowledge of the future and a knowledge of what goes on inside people, experiencing surprise and disappointment indicates that God does not always exercise the capacity for such knowledge. Perhaps God holds back from it in order to stay in a more real relationship with people, like a father or mother wanting to develop a free, mutual relationship with a child.[239]

Grief

When disappointed, Yhwh feels the pain of a foster father whose daughter went wrong, of a guardian whose charge ran amok, of a lover whose gifts have become the means of attracting other men, of a husband whose wife went off with someone else, of a father who has found he is married to a child-killer (Ezek 16). Indeed, the first emotion that the First Testament attributes to Yhwh is grief, when Yhwh's heart was saddened at how the world turned out (ʿāṣab hitpael; Gen 6:5-6). Grief has been part of God's experience even from near the beginning of things.[240] It was then part of God's experience with Israel from its beginning (Ps 78:40-41; Is 63:10). These passages illustrate how grief, like anger, is a reaction to loss and to being let down and

---

[238]Cf. Fretheim, *Suffering of God*, pp. 45-47.

[239]See, e.g., Gordon D. Kaufman, *Systematic Theology* (New York: Scribner's, 1968), pp. 155-56.

[240]Fretheim, *Suffering of God*, p. 112.

abandoned. When calamity comes to Judah, many people will lose their lives, but some will survive to be taken into exile. There "they will think about me among the nations where they have been taken captive, how I was broken with their immoral heart that turned away from me and with their immoral eyes that turned away to their pillars" (Ezek 6:9). In the words of the tough-minded Ezekiel, the description of Yhwh as broken by the people's unfaithfulness is especially remarkable. It is Yhwh's own experience that is mirrored in the fate of the people's incense altars and pillars (Ezek 6:4, 6), and in the fate of Jerusalem, its prophet and its people (e.g. Jer 14:17; 23:9—the same verb, *šābar* niphal), or vice versa. Yhwh's brokenness (Ezek 6) has to be set alongside Yhwh's anger (Ezek 5). Both are aspects of Yhwh's passion or pathos.[241] Behind the anger is Yhwh's brokenness, behind the brokenness is Yhwh's anger.

To a people who know they have been overwhelmed by calamity that resulted from their wrongdoing, Yhwh declares, "As if I want the death of the faithless rather than that the faithless turn from their way and live on"(Ezek 33:11). "Condemnation is neither God's first nor God's final word."[242] Indeed, human arrogance and sinfulness is folly, bondage and torment, and as such it is the object of God's compassion. "The God who is provoked to anger is not only angry, but for the sake of that which provokes Him sets bounds to His anger and is compassionate," because that is God's intrinsic nature. God "Himself suffers pain because of our sin and guilt," indeed, a greater sorrow than we can feel for ourselves.[243] Kazoh Kitamori takes the phrase "my heart is troubled" in Jeremiah 31:20 as his way in to considering "theology of the pain of God," which stands between God's love and God's wrath. It refers to "God's pain in loving sinful men,"[244] something different from Isaiah 63:9, which just means sharing in human pain. Scripture thus corrects the idea of the impassibility of God, the idea that pain does not belong properly to God, which comes from outside Scripture.[245]

---

[241]For this word, see Heschel, *Prophets*, pp. 285-382; further, Jürgen Moltmann, *The Trinity and the Kingdom of God* (London: SCM Press/New York: Harper, 1981), pp. 21-60, and his references.

[242]L. Gregory Jones, *Embodying Forgiveness* (Grand Rapids, Mich.: Eerdmans, 1995), p. 107.

[243]Barth, *Church Dogmatics*, II/1:371, 373.

[244]Kazoh Kitamori, *Theology of the Pain of God* (Atlanta, Ga.: John Knox Press, 1965/London: SCM Press, 1966), p. 59.

[245]Ibid., p. 60. A number of earlier passages in Jeremiah speak of grief, distress, desolation and sickness of heart at the suffering of the people (e.g., Jer 8:18-22 [9:1]), and these have been taken as expressing Yhwh's distress, but they more likely express Jeremiah's (cf. Joseph M. Henderson, "Who Weeps in Jeremiah viii 23 [ix 1]?" *VT* 52 [2002]: 191-206).

2.7 Yhwh's Hostility

No, Israel's God is not simply a God of wrath. But Yhwh *is* a God of wrath. God gets fed up with the way we turn away, withdraws in response, lets anger find expression, and does so in ruthless fashion.

Weary Skepticism

The letdown may reach a point when Yhwh says, "Right, that's it." When Yhwh brings disaster because the people have broken the covenant, "they will cry out to me but I will not listen to them." And therefore neither can Jeremiah pray for them. They are in no position to come into Yhwh's house to pray and offer sacrifice when they are also involved with other deities (Jer 11:11-17). Of course, if they do turn away from these deities and have recourse to Yhwh alone, it is unlikely that Yhwh would be able to resist their prayer. But in the context of the exile, such a declaration explains why disaster had to come. Whatever prayers were prayed, Yhwh did not listen. "Before they call, I will answer" (Is 65:24). But this can involve Yhwh's anticipating the prophet's prayer and giving notice that it will not be granted. "You—do not plead for this people or raise a cry or a plea on their behalf or intervene with me, because I am not listening when they call to me on account of their calamity" (Jer 11:14).

There was a terrible drought in Judah. The cisterns were empty. The crops were not growing. There was no grass for the animals to eat. "Jerusalem's wail goes up." Surely Yhwh will answer such a prayer? Implicitly or explicitly a prayer like this either needs to affirm that there is no reason for Yhwh's neglect of the people and therefore to appeal for a demonstration of Yhwh's faithfulness, or it has to acknowledge that the people's wrongdoing has made them deserve chastisement and therefore to appeal to Yhwh to show mercy. On this occasion the people do the latter (Jer 14:1-10). They acknowledge their turnings and their failings and throw themselves on Yhwh's mercy. Surely this is an acceptance of responsibility to which Yhwh will respond? On the contrary, Yhwh says, "They so love to wander; they do not hold their feet back." The people of God cannot assume that Yhwh will respond positively to them, even when they acknowledge their wrongdoing. A wife whose husband is unfaithful to her may have him back once and then twice, but the third time may say "No," at least until there is evidence that this time there will be real change. "Yhwh has said this to this people: Yhwh does not accept them; he will now keep in mind their wrongdoing, attend to their failures." The people have been directly addressing Yhwh, and Yhwh at first seems to be addressing them back. But in the words that follow there is neither an "I" nor a "you" responding to the people's "we" and "you," and we have to reconsider the introductory words and ask whether they more likely mean "Yhwh has said this with regard to this people." Yhwh does not speak to them as an "I" to a "you," but gives Jeremiah words to speak about Yhwh and about "them." Yhwh accepts the accusation of relating to them like a passing stranger ("This land is not my home, I'm just a-passing through") rather than a citizen who cares about the country, or like a warrior who has forgotten how to fight for them, and implicitly points out that such indifference or inaction is quite deserved.

Yhwh therefore has nothing to say to them, and does not wish to hear any more from them, or from Jeremiah about them. "Do not plead on behalf of this people, for their welfare. When they fast, I will not be listening to their cry. When they offer burnt offering and grain offering, I will not be accepting them, because I will be consuming them by the sword, by famine, and by epidemic" (Jer 14:11-12). Neither intercession, nor fasting, nor supplication, nor offerings can turn away Yhwh's intention to devastate the people. Prayer does not avail when unaccompanied by change, whether it is the prayer of people for themselves or the prayer of others for them. To underline the point, Jeremiah 14:17—15:9 makes it again. "I am tired of relenting," Yhwh says (Jer 15:6). There are feelings here and there is awareness of Judah's terrible suffering, but there is not pity. Here it is the other side to Yhwh's feelings that predominate. Yhwh has been rejected and feels rejected, and is tired of behaving like the wife who always has her philandering husband back. Yhwh is going to let the natural and reasonable wrath of such a woman receive expression.

Hiddenness/Withdrawal/Absence

Discussion of God's hiddenness or absence is confusing. First, there is a sense in which God is actually present when God's face (that is, presence) is hidden.[246] In Esther, the pointed nature of the series of passages where God and faith lie between the lines means that "God, as a character of the story, becomes more conspicuous the more he is absent."[247] There is also a sense in which God is hidden even when present. "Everything the OT says of God's self-unveiling stands *eo ipso* under apparently the very opposite sign as well: 'Am I a God at hand, saith the Lord, and not (also) a God afar off?'" (Jer 23:23).[248] Indeed, in that respect the New Testament matches it: "the mark of the New Testament saving event is a deep *hiddenness on God's part*," for here God sets aside what we would normally reckon as divine glory and acts in veiled form, in weak-

---

[246]Samuel Terrien's emphasis in *The Elusive Presence* (New York: Harper, 1978), e.g., p. 251. Cf. G. Tom Milazzo, *The Protest and the Silence* (Minneapolis: Fortress, 1992), pp. 31-32, and his references.

[247]David J. A. Clines, *Ezra, Nehemiah, Esther* (London: Marshall, Morgan & Scott/Grand Rapids, Mich.: Eerdmans, 1984), p. 269; cf. *OTT* 1:784.

[248]Barth, *Church Dogmatics*, I/1:370. Cf. Samuel E. Balentine, *The Hidden God* (Oxford/New York: Oxford University Press, 1982), p. 175.

ness and shame.[249] In the First Testament, the face or presence of God is so bright and fiery that it would blind someone who looked at it, and on occasions the First Testament therefore describes people as protected from it (classically, Ex 33:12-23), but this does not mean God is absent. But the First Testament does not take such gracious hiddenness as the main key to understanding the ambiguity of presence and absence, as if absence is always a veiled form of presence.

On other occasions, God's hiddenness means God's absence, and sometimes this absence is hard to account for. The agonized cries in Job or the Psalms (e.g., Ps 69:17 [MT 18]; 88:14 [MT 15]; 143:7) imply that God really is absent. If it is like being in a room when someone is present but hiding beneath the sofa, the trouble is that this means that person is present but hiding when their friend is being beaten up, and that is not much of a presence. The psalms' "Why?" perhaps implies such a presence. God is present enough to be addressed, but not present enough to act. That experience may lead to formulating a theology of hope, but it is a hope that this absent presence will be replaced by active presence.

On yet other occasions, there are perceptible reasons for Yhwh's absence: this withdrawal is a response to human wrongdoing. In effect people withdraw from Yhwh, and Yhwh withdraws from them, like a mother who gets angry with her children and walks out on them for a while. "You are indeed a God who hides, God of Israel, deliverer," foreign nations declare (Is 45:15). In the coming fall of Babylon, peoples such as Egypt, Sudan and Ethiopia see the God who has been hiding from Israel now becoming once more the God who delivers.

A whole theology has been built on this phrase in Isaiah, understood to describe Yhwh as the "hidden God." Rather, a whole theology takes this as its tag phrase; it has little to do with the phrase's meaning in the context, nor with any broader First Testament theme. "The prophets do not speak of the *hidden God* but of the *hiding God*. His hiding is . . . an act not a permanent state."[250] It is not the case that "for Israel's faith, God is essentially hidden,"[251] though it is no doubt the case that God would be hidden were it not for the fact that God wills to be known,[252] as is the case with any person. Before Isaiah 40—55, "the notion that God is inscrutable, loftily mysterious, and beyond the comprehension of

---

[249]Von Rad, *OT Theology*, 2:374.

[250]Heschel, *Man Is Not Alone*, p. 153. Cf. Kutsko, *Between Heaven and Earth*, e.g., pp. 1-2, 150, for the move between presence and absence in Ezekiel.

[251]So Wolfhart Pannenberg, *Basic Questions in Theology*, 3 vols. (London: SCM Press, 1970-1973), 2:154.

[252]Cf. Barth, *Church Dogmatics*, II/1:179-204.

mere men, though standard in the received, popular notion of God, is all but absent from the biblical presentations of him"; it is now introduced to make it possible to say something new (cf. Is 43:19).[253] The acknowledgment of Yhwh as one who hides recognizes that God sometimes hides from Israel but then returns. Thus Israel may ask, "How long, Yhwh? Will you hide forever?" (Ps 89:46 [MT 47]). Twentieth-century history provides an example of Yhwh's hiding and then delivering in this way. For a decade from the mid-1930s to the mid-1940s, the God of Israel hid from the Jewish people and they paid a terrible price for being a people who stood for God. But in the late 1940s God turned from being one who hides to being one who delivers, and the State of Israel was born.[254]

In Isaiah 45:19, however, it looks as if Yhwh even denies hiding, or at least qualifies the appropriateness of this framework. "It was not in hiddenness that I spoke, in a place in a dark land. I did not say to the offspring of Jacob, 'Seek help from me in a wasteland.'" In the exile, after all, Yhwh's withdrawal issued from Israel's sinfulness, so it was not the inexplicable kind of hiding that, for instance, Psalm 89 referred to.[255] Over the centuries and in the exile Yhwh has been accessible to the people, not playing games with them by expecting them to seek out someone who could not really be easily reached. The question is whether they have been turning to Yhwh (cf. Is 43:22; 48:16).

Anger

Like English, Hebrew has a range of terms for the strong feelings with which we react to being wronged or seeing that someone else has been wronged. *Anger* (*'ap*) is the regular word for human anger, though it is also used of God. *Wrath* (*qeṣep*) usually refers to divine anger with its distinctive force. *Rage* (*zaʿam*) suggests a personal sense of outrage at the way one has been treated, at someone's affront or failure to meet their obligations, an indignation that issues in speech and thus in action; it is close to meaning "curse."[256] *Fury* (*ḥēmâ*) suggests something hotly felt rather than merely cool, rational and objective. The First Testament uses words for anger three times as often in connection with God than it does in connection with human beings.[257] Yhwh's anger is my resource when people attack me for no reason as if they are themselves con-

---

[253]Miles, *God*, p. 227.

[254]Cf. Eliezer Berkovits, *Faith After the Holocaust* (New York: Ktav, 1973), see esp. pp. 63-66, 101, 117.

[255]If Ps 89 reflects the exile, perhaps it reflects a time when the exile has gone on a long time and Yhwh seems to have permanently hidden.

[256]In Num 23:7-8 it appears in parallelism with *'ārar* and *qābab*.

[257]Elsie Johnson, *TDOT*, 1:356.

sumed with anger. I can urge, "Rise Yhwh in your anger, lift yourself up at the outbursts of my assailants" (Ps 7:6 [MT 7]). Psalm 18:7-15 [MT 8-16] describes Yhwh's coming in terms of the violence of a thunderstorm that makes the ground shudder and flashes the fire of lightning across the terrain.[258] The violence of these phenomena is an expression of Yhwh's rage; Yhwh is breathing fire. Both the rage and the violence are good news for Israel and its leader when they are pressed hard by attackers. Yhwh is enraged (as well as amused) when the nations work against the divine purpose (Ps 2:4-5, 11; cf. Ps 59:8 [MT 9]). Yhwh can then be ruthless in wrath toward them in order to frustrate that purpose, seeing to their future (their offspring) as well as to their present (Ps 21:8-12 [MT 9-13]). The psalm provides Paul with frightening language to use not merely with regard to people's earthly destiny but with regard to their eternal destiny as it talks about flaming fire and eternal destruction "from the presence of the Lord" (2 Thess1:8-9).[259] When Psalm 7:11 [MT 12] promises that Yhwh "expresses indignation always," LXX adds a negative to reassure the reader, but MT's version of the promise is itself reassuring. Of course, the psalm goes on to note, it is only if a wicked person fails to turn that Yhwh goes on to act out that indignation.

As with love and hatred, in the First Testament anger refers as much to the action associated with strong feelings as to the feelings themselves. The way one knows Yhwh is angry is through experiencing its violent results. In Psalm 38, for instance the suppliant has felt God's hand come down and felt God's arrows pierce, and therefore knows that God is angry. When forces from the north overwhelm Judah and make its country a wasteland, people will wail, "Yhwh's angry fury has not turned from us" (Jer 4:8; cf. 23). In Psalm 18, the suppliant has seen calamity fall on attackers and knows that God's anger has been aroused (cf., e.g., Ex 15:7; 32:12-13; Ps 69:24 [MT 25]; 78:49; 88:16 [MT 17]). In some psalms, the suppliants thus know that God has a basis for anger, though when they are its victims, more often they express bewilderment about this; they are not aware of wrongdoing that would explain God's anger.

In due course the exile happened because "I was angry with my people" (Is 47:6). Yhwh drove Judah into exile "in anger and fury and great rage" (Jer 32:37). As the decades then pass and Jerusalem remains in ruins, the question arises whether Yhwh is going to be angry forever; this is the question with which Lamentations closes (Lam 5:22). Everything depends on perspective. From the perspective of a human generation, Yhwh's anger may seem to go on

---

[258] I doubt whether the imagery made people think of earthquakes or volcanoes; see section 7.2 "The Realm Below and the Realm Above."

[259] The EVV read "separation from the presence of the Lord," but this addition seems unjustified (contrast KJV).

forever. In a broader time frame, this may not seem so. "In a burst of anger I hid my face from you for a moment" is all Yhwh will admit, and hastily goes on to the fact that the brevity of this time of anger contrasts with the lasting commitment Yhwh will henceforth show; "I hereby swear that I will not be angry with you" (Is 54:8-9; cf. Is 57:16-18; 60:10).

Zechariah is rather ambivalent about how angry Yhwh really was and how far the agents of Yhwh's anger went further than Yhwh intended (Zech 1:2, 15; 7:12; 8:14-15). Yhwh professes to be really angry with the nations that are at peace (once again, "the nations" refers to the empire): "I am angry [with] big anger." It is this anger that will generate action. Yes, Yhwh had been angry with Judah, but nothing like as angry as would be implied by the severity of the nations' action toward it (Is 47:6; 54:8; contrast Zech 1:2; 7:12; also Lam 5:22). The nations helped Yhwh, Zechariah seems to imply with a strange formulation, but helped in such a way as to bring about trouble such as Yhwh did not want. So now Yhwh is really angry with the nations that have gone so much further than Yhwh intended.

Thus "'anger' was indeed for Israel more than a meted-out punishment; it was above all a reality which could no longer be accommodated to human ideas of order," and in Job, talk about God's anger features more on Job's own lips (e.g., Job 9:5; 10:17; 14:13; 16:9; 19:11) than on those of the friends (e.g., Job 4:9; 20:23, 28; 35:15).[260] If one reckons that trouble is the appropriate punishment for sin, one has less need to refer to anger than if trouble seems an unwarranted and inexplicable outburst. "Don't be angry with me" may imply "don't burst out at me for no apparent reason." And thus, while the book of Job is about human suffering, it is even more about God.[261]

Rage

Jeremiah speaks of wrath going forth and a storm whirling (Jer 23:19-20), and this distances Yhwh from it, as if the wrath and the storm were forces semi-independent of Yhwh. One might even think of them as destructive forces let loose by human wrongdoing. Yet they are also *Yhwh's* storm and *Yhwh's* anger, which makes clear that Yhwh identifies with them. Similarly Yhwh sends a *rûaḥ rāʿâ*, a bad spirit ("evil spirit" is a misleading translation) between Abimelech and the people of Shechem (Judg 9:23) and another to torment Saul (1 Sam 16:14-23; 18:10), replacing the spirit from Yhwh that formerly came on him. Yhwh sent a deceptive spirit to mislead some prophets, to punish Ahab (1 Kings 22:19-23), spread over Israel a spirit of deep sleep to stop them heed-

[260]Von Rad, *Wisdom in Israel*, p. 221. See also Alastair V. Campbell, *The Gospel of Anger* (London: SPCK, 1986), esp. pp. 92-94.
[261]Von Rad, *Wisdom in Israel*, p. 221.

ing the message that came to them (Is 29:10), and put a spirit in Sennacherib that led him to go home to be assassinated (Is 37:7). These expressions, too, suggest a dynamic semipersonal force, semi-independent of Yhwh, the negative equivalent to Yhwh's commitment and steadfastness as forces that are semi-independent of Yhwh, forces Yhwh sends off to do things (Ps 23:6; 43:3). Anger is not a divine attribute in the same sense as love is; the instinct to love emerges from God without any outside stimulus, but God gets angry only as a reaction to outside stimulus. Yet God does get angry.[262]

So anger involves action, but it does also involve strong feelings. Another limitation of "judgment" talk[263] is that in the tradition of Western justice, a judge is disengaged from the parties involved in a case and suspends personal feelings in order to act objectively. In contrast, Yhwh as judge acts with very strong feelings indeed. By acting to punish, "My anger will be complete, and I will give rest to my fury on them and relieve myself [*nāḥam* niphal], and they will acknowledge that I, Yhwh, spoke in my passion, when I complete my fury on them" (Ezek 5:13). While rulers are capable of acting in anger, such strength of feeling is more characteristic of parents and spouses. It is an indication of personal affront and hurt, of the kind Yhwh indeed expresses. Israel has repudiated the decisions of the head of the household, committed loathsome acts in Yhwh's house such as defile Yhwh's sanctuary.

Significantly, this language recurs in Ezekiel in a specifically marriage context.[264] Yhwh has behaved like a caring foster father and then an amorous lover, but his wife has not just been unfaithful by giving in to one temptation but scattered her sexual favors far and wide. Therefore Yhwh acts with violence against her in "passionate fury." Thus "I will release my fury on you; and my passion will turn from you and I will be quiet and not be angry any more" (Ezek 16:42). "Anger is an emotion that drives the body to want to get rid of whatever is experienced as intolerable."[265]

The strong feelings involved in punishment provide part of the energy needed for its implementing. They guard against the danger that the authority who is supposed to implement the punishment cannot be bothered to do so. Judah's self-indulgence, made possible by depriving people of fair legal treatment and (thus?) of their land and its skepticism about Yhwh's warnings of

---

[262]Cf. Fretheim, *Jeremiah*, p. 337.

[263]See section 2.3 "Power and Authority"; section 2.6 "Risk."

[264]See section 2.6 "Passion."

[265]Pietro Bovati, *Re-Establishing Justice*, JSOTSup 105 (Sheffield: Sheffield Academic Press, 1994), p. 53. Bovati goes on to suggest that wrath is an outworking either of pride or of justice, but there are other alternatives. Like love and mercy, both divine and human wrath can issue from strength of appropriate personal feelings that issue from a relationship, but not a judicial one.

the calamity that will follow, make God really angry. "That is why Yhwh's anger burned against his people and he extended his hand against them and hit them, so that mountains shook, and their corpses became like trash in the middle of the streets" (Is 5:25). Horror, paradox and inevitability are written into the words. We are talking about a relationship between Yhwh and "his people," a special relationship like that between parents and children (Isaiah's first image for the relationship, in Is 1:2). That relationship implies a certain stance toward Yhwh and a certain stance toward other members of the community. All this is lacking. They have turned their backs on Yhwh, not to serve other gods but just to run their lives their own way and ignore Yhwh. The fact that they also offer Yhwh enthusiastic worship only makes matters worse. Yhwh is therefore infuriated and reacts accordingly, behaving like a mother whose temper finally breaks because of the way her children behave toward her and toward each other, and who therefore lashes out at them in anger and frustration. Once she has done that, she feels better, because she has expressed her feelings, though also worse, because she is sorry she has hurt the children (even if she also still reckons she did the necessary thing).

Yhwh has equivalent feelings. "I regret the disaster I caused to you," Yhwh says after the fall of Jerusalem (Jer 42:10). The verb (again *nāḥam* niphal) hardly indicates that Yhwh is going back on the decision to cause the city to fall. There are too many continuing affirmations of that act, including subsequent reference to the fact that Yhwh had not regretted/relented (Zech 8:14). Further, if Yhwh regretted it in this sense, one would expect speedy action to reverse it. More likely Yhwh regrets the fact that this necessary act caused so much death and destruction, yet does not go back on the necessity of bringing it about. This regret will thus be the converse of Yhwh's regret at creating humanity (Gen 6:6-7), which does not (quite) make Yhwh destroy humanity but does suggest that it had worked out in a different way from the one Yhwh envisaged and that Yhwh regrets that fact, but does not (quite) go back on the decision to create humanity.

If Isaiah 5:25 refers to the earthquake in Judah in Uzziah's time (Amos 1:1), one might then have thought that this would be the end of the matter; Yhwh's anger has received expression. But the frightening aspect to this oracle then comes in the last line, which indicates that this is not so: "for all this, his anger has not turned away; his hand is still extended." This line will be repeated (Is 9:12, 17, 21; 10:4). The horror of the earthquake has not exhausted Yhwh's anger. There is more to come.

Redress

Thus, Yhwh says, "I will get relief from my foes, exact punishment from my enemies" (Is 1:24). The nightmare that threatens Judah has profoundly negative implications for the people who are on the receiving end of Yhwh's action, partly because it brings such strong relief to Yhwh. Yhwh's own personal energy therefore goes into the action; it is designed to make Yhwh feel better. Yhwh is acting to punish personal enemies.

While the implications of these statements are thus profoundly negative, they are not wholly negative. The need to get relief reflects the strong feeling aroused in Yhwh by the scandalous events in Jerusalem that previous verses have described, the way the city that was designed to be secure and trustworthy has become a place where orphan and widow are despised and money is all that matters (Is 1:21-23). Yhwh is deeply involved with Jerusalem and has an inner compulsion to act against the people who have turned Secure/Trustworthy Town upside down. In a strange way, then, there is a positive aspect to Yhwh's acting against the city in order to stop having to bottle up those feelings.

The same point emerges from the fact that Yhwh's enemies are thus getting their due punishment. Yhwh is not just letting oppression continue. The notion of taking redress (*nāqam*) presupposes the existence of a cosmic moral order; Yhwh will not countenance its imperiling. The conventional translation of the verb as "avenge" and of *nāqām* as "vengeance" suggests retaliation that is excessively personal. The words rather denote the implementation of justice by a legitimate authority in such a way as to put right things that were wrong.[266] And the object of such action is "redress, righting a lost balance and restoring the damaged integrity of a kinship group," so that it links closely with the idea of "restoration," which can appear in parallelism with it (see Is 63:4; also Is 47:3-4), a task undertaken by a close relative within the kin group.[267]

Yet Yhwh's talk of "my enemies" indicates that there is indeed a personal aspect to this punishment. Yhwh is not merely an impartial judge imposing penalties for the breaking of laws that the judge had no hand in framing and may even disagree with. Yhwh is identified with the cosmic moral order; it reflects Yhwh's own being. To flout that order is thus to flout Yhwh and to make oneself liable to Yhwh's acting for the sake of that order with which Yhwh is identified. Even the fact that Yhwh's hand turns against us thus has a positive side. Yhwh might simply not care about moral and social order and abandon the world to its sin.

Psalm 94 thus begins its prayer for deliverance by addressing Yhwh as *ʾēl nĕqāmôt*. The suppliant wants "the God of redress," as the one who exercises authority over the earth (*šōpēṭ hāʾāreṣ*), to arise to "give back to the lofty their

---

[266]See G. L. Peels, *The Vengeance of God*, OTS 31 (Leiden/New York: Brill, 1995); in the end, he rather oddly retains the translation "vengeance."

[267]Blenkinsopp, *Isaiah 56—66*, p. 250.

recompense" (*gĕmûl*, Ps 94:1-2). Indeed, Yhwh is also "God of recompense" (Jer 51:56). At present the lofty, important people are in a position to exult and go about talking big even as they act faithlessly and destroy the community, crushing Yhwh's own people by killing the widow, the foreigner and the orphan, convinced that Yhwh takes no notice. The suppliant knows that Yhwh does listen, see, chastise and rebuke (Ps 94:3-10). When powerful and important people take advantage of the weak and vulnerable, Yhwh is not one who simply leaves them to it. Yhwh is "God of redress." On any translation, it is still a chilling epithet, the more so because it can work against Israel as a whole when Yhwh exacts "covenant redress" (Lev 26:25). But for the suppliant it is one full of hope. "Who will rise up for me against evil people, who will take a stand for me against people who do harm?" Humanly speaking the answer is "no one"; the people who have the power to do so are themselves the wrongdoers. Thus "were Yhwh not a help for me, I would soon have dwelt in silence"—that is, in Sheol. But "Yhwh's commitment—it supports me." It is impossible to imagine a "seat of destruction" (that is, a court that makes decisions destructive of the community by conspiring to condemn the innocent to death, a court that "shapes suffering by statute") being "associated" with Yhwh (Ps 94:16-21). "But Yhwh has become for me my haven, my God has become the crag where I take refuge, and he is bringing back their wickedness upon them;[268] he will put an end to them through their evildoing—Yhwh our God will put an end to them" (Ps 94:22-23). Yhwh is providing the suppliant with a refuge, but that is an interim arrangement pending the act of redress that will put things right and restore order.

Self-Assertion

The redress Yhwh brings is thus designed to restore things to their proper state. Similarly the lofty majesty of Jerusalem needs to be put down in order to reinstate that reality in which Yhwh is manifestly the awesome, majestic one who towers over the world. Then "human loftiness will bow, the exaltedness of people will drop down; Yhwh alone will tower on that day" (Is 2:10-17). Yhwh's day will again restore things to their proper state. Yhwh will tower above people and they will drop down and throw away the religious resources they have devised for themselves, the images made of gold and silver and the impressive churches with their state-of-the-art sound systems. Then they will be driven to take refuge from Yhwh's awesomeness and majesty "when he arises to overawe the earth" (Is 2:19, 21). As the problem with the people of God is not exactly pride but achievement and impressiveness, so the problem

---

[268]I take the wayyiqtol as equivalent to an instantaneous qatal. The subsequent yiqtols put the point more literally.

with Yhwh is not inspiring terror before a judgment but inspiring a sense of awed realism about who Yhwh is and who they are in their real unimpressiveness when they see the truth about Yhwh. Isaiah later repeats that "human beings bow, people drop down, lofty human eyes drop down," and adds, "And Yhwh Armies is lofty in decision making, the holy God shows himself holy in faithfulness" (Is 5:15-16). The exaltation of Yhwh in holiness necessitates the putting down of humanity in its misleading exaltedness.

Yhwh is Israel's vinedresser. The vinedresser did all the right things for his vineyard, digging the ground and clearing it of stones, building a tower from which he could watch over the vineyard and protect it from predators, carving out a wine vat. He was also prepared to be tough, as a farmer has to be. When it did not produce good fruit, he declared the intention to remove the hedge and wall that protect it and leave it to be wasteland that produces only briars and thistles. The vinedresser will also bid the clouds not rain on it. One can imagine an angry farmer doing that, but at this point in the allegory we see the face of the divine vinedresser behind the allegory. Yhwh is a vinedresser who loves his vineyard, but precisely because of that he is prepared to devastate it when it disappoints him (Is 5:1-7).

Christians would conventionally speak of such an act as God's acting in judgment. While this is appropriate insofar as the prophets utilize a quasi-legal framework for the way they express Israel's wrongdoing and the consequences that will follow, we have noted that the Hebrew terms for "judgment" are broader in meaning than this conventional translation implies, covering authoritative decision making in general.[269] "Judgment" is a much less common image than we might think. But punishment indeed involves the exercise of authority in decision making. Humanly speaking, such exercise of authority is the responsibility of the king, and it is as king that Yhwh exercises authority in exacting punishment.[270] It again follows that the activity of the human or the divine king as judge and punisher is the hope of the oppressed. Punishing their oppressors is an act of love toward them.[271]

Pardon and forgiveness are ambiguous acts. If someone who has been wronged confronts the people who did the wrong and they acknowledge what they have done and put things right, then this reestablishes justice and right relationships. The confrontation has fulfilled its purpose. If such a matter reaches the courts, this is probably a sign that the person is not acknowledging his or her wrongdoing. If a court then pardons the offender, this risks belittling the importance of the law and of moral behavior, encouraging the offender

---

[269] Again, see section 2.3 "Power and Authority."

[270] See Peels, *Vengeance of God*, pp. 276-81.

[271] Ibid., pp. 292-95.

and other people not to take the offender's wrongdoing seriously. Indeed, when individuals forgive someone who has wronged them, this carries equivalent risks. "If grace is shown to the faithless, they do not learn faithfulness. In the land of straightforwardness they act perversely and do not consider the majesty of Yhwh" (Is 26:10). Conversely, "the rod and reproof give insight" (Prov 29:15),[272] or at least may do so. It is not enough for God simply to turn a blind eye and put up with things.

Repudiation

"You hate all evildoers" (Ps 5:5 [MT 6]); so NRSV. The rendering suggests that the psalmist would disagree with the mantra "God hates the sin but loves the sinner," and this is probably so, notwithstanding Micah 7:18-20.[273] The psalm speaks in similar terms of Yhwh's attitude to the sin and to the sinner, perhaps on the assumption that the former only has reality as embodied in the latter. How can one take an attitude to sin in the abstract?

But the standard translation of $\acute{s}\bar{a}n\bar{e}^{\circ}$ as "hate" is misleading, like the translation of $^{\circ}\bar{a}h\bar{e}b$ as "love." Hatred is an emotion, and Hebrew has a number of words for this emotion, such as $g\bar{a}^{\circ}al$, $m\bar{a}^{\circ}as$, and $q\hat{u}\d{s}$. But $\acute{s}\bar{a}n\bar{e}^{\circ}$ designates a stance, an activity, an expression of commitment. It may involve feelings, but it need not do so. "My enemy" is literally "one who hates me," but this hatred is hostility in action more than negativity in attitude (as "anger" often suggests action more than feelings). It involves having nothing to do with someone or something, being totally against the person or the thing. "You are not a God who delights in faithlessness; evil/an evil person cannot stay with you. Wild people cannot take their stand before your eyes; you are against all who do harm. You destroy those who speak falsehood; the person who seeks bloodshed by fraudulence Yhwh repudiates" (Ps 5:4-6 [MT 5-7]). Yet those lines begin with that understatement referring to God's attitude; the parallel colon about evil or evil people not being able to "stay" with Yhwh suggests that Yhwh's not "delighting" in faithlessness refers to Yhwh's not accepting their worship (cf., e.g., Ps 51:16, 19 [MT 18, 21]; Is 1:11; Hos 6:6) and not accepting the worshipers. The door to Yhwh's house is barred to them. They cannot come and stand before Yhwh to seek Yhwh's help or guidance. And the lines close with the verb $t\bar{a}^{\circ}\bar{e}b$, which suggests regarding something or someone as loathsome and thus wishing to have nothing to do with it (the noun $t\hat{o}^{\circ}\bar{e}b\hat{a}$ is translated "abomination"). In the context, then, the emotional connotation of "hate" may well apply to $\acute{s}\bar{a}n\bar{e}^{\circ}$. Yhwh loathes and wishes to have nothing to do with sin and sinner. Indeed, "his $nepe\check{s}$ is against [$\acute{s}\bar{a}n\bar{e}^{\circ}$] the person dedicated to

---

[272]Bovati, *Re-Establishing Justice,* pp. 169-70.
[273]See section 2.6 "Carrying."

[*ʾāhēb*] violence" (Ps 11:5). Judah's worship is *tôʿēbâ* and Yhwh is against it (*śānēʾ*, Is 1:13-14).

"Why, God, have you rejected us forever, why does your anger fume against the flock you shepherd?" (Ps 74:1). The question doubly denies Yhwh elbow room to query the presuppositions of the question, though this would not stop Yhwh doing so. At the beginning of the colon the question "Why" presupposes that rejection is a fact; the only uncertainty concerns its explanation. At the end of the colon the adverbial expression "forever" presupposes it again. Now the only uncertainty concerns its finality.

As with declarations concerning Yhwh's anger, the comment relates to how Israel experiences things. Israel knows Yhwh has rejected it because of the phenomena it goes on to recall. Enemies have invaded the sanctuary and burned it, and burned other meeting places throughout the land; the community has received no signs or words that point to an end to these attacks; the enemies have reviled Yhwh's name. And God does nothing. That constitutes rejection. If in theory Israel is still Yhwh's people, that has no cash value. For practical purposes, Yhwh has rejected Israel. The parallel colon well expresses the implied paradox: Why is shepherding combined with anger?

"Look to the covenant," the psalm urges Yhwh (Ps 74:20). Here the presupposition is presumably that Yhwh has not finally rejected the people, otherwise this exhortation would hardly make sense.

Ruthlessness

"I will not pity. I will not spare. I will not have compassion so as not to destroy them" (Jer 13:14). Yhwh looks in the eye the implications of bringing calamity on Israel and affirms these. "I will do to you what I have not done and the likes of which I will not do again, because of all your abominations. Thus parents will eat children in your midst and children will eat their parents. . . . I will shear and my eye will not pity, yes, I will show no mercy." A third will die of epidemic or famine, another third will die in battle, then Yhwh will scatter the remaining third and even chase them with a sword. The people will be turned into a ruin and a horrific warning to the world of what Yhwh is capable of doing (Ezek 5:7-17). Subsequently Ezekiel makes explicit that the lack of pity extends to the vulnerable in the community—women and children, the old and the young (Ezek 9:5-6). The slaughter is to begin at "my sanctuary," as one of the great loci of faithlessness, and Yhwh also looks in the eye the fact that such slaughter will defile this house (Ezek 9:7). It involves a horrific parody of the Passover, as a mark is once again put on people who are to be exempted from the slaughter, but the people to be slain are Israelites, not foreigners. If they behave like Egyptians or Canaanites, they will be treated thus.

While the significance of Yhwh's action can be understated, it can also be stated in frightening terms. Yhwh is like a maggot eating Ephraim up, or like a cancer rotting its bones, or like a lion tearing at it and walking off with it in the certainty that no one will be able to rescue it from its grasp (Hos 5:12-13), or like a man abusing his wife and children (Hos 2:2-13 [MT 4-15]). What people did in seeking the help of other deities in order to have their everyday needs fulfilled looked sensible, but it was actually mindless stupidity. Their gifts (grain, wine, wool, linen) came from their original "husband," and he intends to take them back. Indeed, the husband will confine his wife to the house and stop her seeking out her lovers and put a trace on her cell phone calls. Yhwh's willingness to be described in terms of a husband punishing his wife for her unfaithfulness involves taking a risk. Yhwh could seem to be validating the male violence against women (and children?) that is a feature of patriarchal society. Yhwh is prepared to take that risk for the sake of getting a point home to Israel. If that is the kind of attitude that the men in the society take to their wives and children, and if they fear that their wives are having affairs, how much more powerful is the declaration that they are themselves just that kind of woman.

Israel "is not a people with understanding; therefore its maker will not have compassion on it, its shaper will not show grace to it" (Is 27:11). While recognizing that being without understanding is a matter for critique because it implies a rejection of understanding and commitment to Yhwh, Hans Wildberger nevertheless comments, "radical grace, which is great enough to include the godless as well or which actually reaches its high point in bestowing grace on sinners, is simply not to be found in the OT."[274] It is an odd remark, for the First Testament certainly reckons that Yhwh bestows grace on godless sinners, within Israel and without.[275] This passage on its own would indeed give a gloomy view of Yhwh's relationship with the world, but (as Wildberger hints) affirmations of grace without warnings of possible trouble raise their own questions. If the First Testament affirmed that God showed compassion and grace to all even if they rejected God's wisdom, it would seem that Jesus, with his warnings about weeping and gnashing of teeth, was taking a harsher line than the First Testament does. (That of course is the case insofar as he warns about hell, not a topic the First Testament speaks of. I heard a theologian asked if hell would be the way Jonathan Edwards pictured it. One might have ex-

---

[274]Hans Wildberger, *Isaiah 13—27* (Minneapolis: Fortress, 1997), p. 597.

[275]In his own hostile comments on the passage, Joseph Blenkinsopp does note the contrast with the stance taken in Jonah (*Isaiah 1—39,* AB [New York: Doubleday, 2000], p. 379). One problem in both commentators' treatment is their starting point in a hypothesis about the passage's original historical context and reference, when the passage itself offers no information on these matters.

pected him to say that it would not be as gory as that, but then to add that of
course eternal separation from God was a terrible thing. Instead the theologian
simply answered, "It will be worse.")

Slayer

So Yhwh's preparedness to take punitive action is good news for people who
need someone to fight for them, but bad news for its victims. The familiar
name Shaddai can be used to make the point. When the First Testament speaks
of "destruction coming from Shaddai" (Is 13:6; Joel 1:15) it implies a link between the name and the verb *šādad*, "destruction is coming from the Destroyer"—perhaps more a paronomasia than something implying a conviction
about the name's origin.[276]

From the Beginning, Yhwh has been prepared to take violent action against
forces that oppose the divine purpose and thus imperil people. "You rule over
the swelling of the sea; when its waves rise, you still them. You crushed Rahab
like a corpse; with your powerful arm you scattered your enemies" (Ps 89:9-10
[MT 10-11]). Yhwh's arm stands for Yhwh taking forceful action. Yhwh has a
reputation for acting violently against the powers of disorder and the forces
that threaten death, but in the present Yhwh leaves those powers to rule the
world. Isaiah 51:9-11 therefore urges, "Wake up, wake up, put on strength, arm
of Yhwh! Wake up as in days of old, generations long past!" There have been
two supreme moments when Yhwh thus acted forcefully, at creation and at the
exodus. Isaiah 51 initially seems to be referring to an event such as the exodus,
because talk of Yhwh's acts "in days of old" suggests events in Israel's story.
But it goes on, "Aren't you the very hacker of Rahab, the slayer of the sea
dragon?" That suggests reference to events associated with creation, since the
slaying of the monster appears in other Middle Eastern stories about events
outside of history. Back in association with creating the world, Yhwh asserted
authority over any forces that might oppose the bringing of order and blessing
in the world, and did so in such a decisive way that we can be sure that the life
of the cosmos is secure.

Then the next line turns to another concept that makes things more ambiguous: "Aren't you the very drier of Sea, of the waters of the Great Deep?" (Is
51:10). That is another good Middle Eastern way of picturing a victory over
turbulent powers before creation, a victory such as ensures that the tumultu-

---

[276]Does Naomi also make this link? See Ruth 1:20-21. We do not know the name's actual etymology. There is no indication in the First Testament that Israelites made a connection with
the word *šad*, "breast" or with Akkadian *šadû*, "mountain," nor do we know the basis for
LXX's common translation "All-powerful." The name is most common in Job and then in
Genesis, and it thus functions as a name used by people in contexts where one would not
expect the name Yhwh to be known (cf. Ex 6:3). Balaam also uses it (Num 24:4, 16).

ous energy symbolized by the crashing and engulfing power of the sea can never overwhelm the cosmos. But it also recalls Yhwh's assertion of authority over Egypt, itself an embodiment of turbulent powers asserted against the divine purpose. Further, Isaiah 51 goes on to describe Yhwh as "turner of the depths of Sea into a way for the restored to cross," indicating decisively that the passage refers to that victory. Yhwh's violent assertion of authority over the tumultuous power of the sea embodied in the Red Sea turned that sea into an escape route for the Israelites.

Isaiah 51 thus certainly refers to the latter of these two victories and probably also refers to the former. Either way, the passage affirms how important it is that Yhwh is prepared to act violently to put down resistant powers, and it affirms that in the past Yhwh has done so. Indeed, by using participles to describe these events (hacker, slayer, drier, turner) it once again points to the fact that these are not just one-time acts but acts representative of who Yhwh consistently is. The trouble is that Yhwh is not acting so now. This is not because Yhwh has decided now to opt for nonviolent conflict resolution. This is not within the purview, any more than it is in the New Testament, which also speaks of the violent putting down of powers that resist God (e.g., Rev 18—19). The problem is not that Yhwh acts violently but that Yhwh fails to do so. So Yhwh (or the prophet or the people, or all three) urges Yhwh's arm once again to assert itself against the powers that hold Israel in exile and keep Jerusalem in ruins. Then Yhwh's people will be able to come back to Zion, with joy, and the promise of Isaiah 35:10 (repeated here) can be fulfilled.

Warrior

In response to the urging in Isaiah 51:9-11 comes the declaration, "Yhwh is baring his holy arm before the eyes of all the nations" (Is 52:10). But the basis of the exhortation has already been laid in Isaiah 42:13-16: "Yhwh will go out like a warrior, arise like a man of battle. With force he will shout, with anger he will roar, he will act the warrior against his enemies."

The divine warrior is "one of the central Old Testament images for the nature and activity of God,"[277] indeed "one of the most pervasive of all biblical themes."[278] The declaration that "Yhwh is a man of war," a *gibbôr* (Ex 15:3), was proven by the exodus and even more by Yhwh's defeat of the Pharaoh at the Red Sea,[279] and then again by Yhwh's defeat of the powers of Canaan. Yhwh's acting as a war-maker appears at these crucial points at the beginning

---

[277]Miller, *Israelite Religion and Biblical Theology*, p. 356.

[278]Tremper Longman and Daniel G. Reid, *God Is a Warrior* (Grand Rapids, Mich.: Zondervan, 1995), p. 13.

[279]I have discussed Ex 15:1-18, the basic text for the idea of Yhwh as warrior, in *OTT* 1:325-26.

of Israel's story, and continues through the story. Yhwh's war making is very prominent in Chronicles, at quite a late stage in Israel's story. There is no development toward more emphasis on peace in the First Testament,[280] as there is not in the New Testament, which ends with a book that much emphasizes God's activity as warrior.

Yet although the First Testament speaks a number of times about Yhwh engaged in violent action, these can seem a small number of occasions when one considers that the story spans so many centuries. Many people therefore never see Yhwh act thus in their whole lifetime, when they need Yhwh to do so because they live under tyranny. Yhwh recognizes that. "I have kept quiet for a long time" (Is 42:14)—*mēʿôlām*, from eternity; so it feels to people under such domination. The JPSV translates "far too long," which is certainly how it seems to people living in the darkness that Yhwh goes on to refer to. "I have been keeping still, restraining myself." The yiqtol verbs also suggest an inactivity that has gone on and on.[281] As ever, Yhwh has been caught between acting in judgment on people because of their wrongdoing, which Yhwh would not wish to do if it can be avoided, and acting in judgment on these people for the sake of their victims, which Yhwh would wish to do. But there are times when judgment cannot be postponed any longer and when compassion for one party has to yield to compassion for the other.

So there are occasions when the time comes and Yhwh puts the instinct to restraint on hold. Yhwh arises or wakes up (it is the same verb as appears in Is 51:9). Then extraordinary restraint gives way to extraordinary dynamism. There are no half-measures with Yhwh. It is either breathtaking mercy that makes people complain, or breathtaking forcefulness that makes people complain. Yes, Yhwh then acts like a warrior charging into battle, adrenaline racing, or like a woman involved in her extraordinarily energetic struggle to give birth: "like a birthing woman I will scream" (Is 42:14). Like the members of a rampaging army Yhwh will lay waste to the land of the nation that needs to be forced to release the people it has been keeping in captivity. But the images are insufficient for the scale of what Yhwh will do; Yhwh will do more than an ancient army could do, though not more than a modern one can do. Yhwh has already spoken of turning desert into well-watered, fertile countryside for a people that cries out in thirst (Is 41:17-20). Yhwh will do the reverse to those who make them their victims, putting them down so as to be able to release into the light the people in darkness and lead them home.

---

[280]Cf. Preuss, *OT Theology*, 1:137-38.

[281]I take the yiqtols as having past imperfect significance, though the point is little affected if they are equivalent to aorists.

Yhwh as warrior is the one who acts like a true judge and king, insisting that divine decisions about history are implemented and divine rule becomes a reality in the world. "Yahweh as warrior is one who actively and vigorously intervenes with decisive power. The warrior is not simply a king who issues decrees or a judge who renders verdicts. This is an agent forcibly engaged."[282] When Yhwh acts as warrior, that means no one else who claims power succeeds in exercising it. Yhwh's being a warrior is good news for a little people such as Israel that itself has no capacity for winning wars and lives most of its life under the domination of one superpower or another. The fact that Yhwh has won military victories in Israel's experience provides evidence that powers of disorder will not triumph in the world. Yhwh has already demonstrated power over them, not in an unseen world but in the empirical world. Israel's God is "Yhwh Armies." Thus little Israel need not finally fear the various superpowers that often sought to dominate it. The pattern of Yhwh's violent activity in the past gives hope for the future, when Israel once again needs delivering from imprisonment.

Yhwh's being a warrior can be bad news when Yhwh decides it is time to make war on Israel.[283] When acting against the nations, Yhwh will roar like a lion (Jer 25:30; 49:19-20; 50:44) or soar like a vulture (Jer 49:22), and if the lion is on your side, then its roar is good news rather than bad news (cf. Hos 11:10-11; Joel 3:16 [MT 4:16]). On the other hand, when Israel puts Yhwh out of mind, Yhwh becomes to them like a lion or a leopard or a bear robbed of her young (Hos 13:7-8). It is possible to think that the lion is roaring against your foes and find it is roaring at you (Amos 1:2). Yhwh starts off as the warrior who fights on Israel's behalf, but becomes the warrior who fights against Israel, though that is not the end of the story; God will once again fight for Israel's deliverance.[284]

Enemy

The necessity for such action on Israel's behalf continued into the Persian period, and no one arose to put the matter right. "Yhwh saw and was displeased that there was no decisive action; he saw that there was no one and he was appalled that there was no one intervening" (Is 59:15-16). In some sense it is a matter of justice. The Judeans have no reason to be under the

---

[282]Brueggemann, *Theology of the OT*, pp. 241, 243. Mettinger (*In Search of God*, p. 92) likewise makes "The Battling Deity" his subtitle for his chapter "The Lord as 'King.'" On the other hand, Rendtorff (*Canonical Hebrew Bible*, p. 614) distinguishes between being judge (which implies active intervention) and being king (which implies a continuous, powerful presence).

[283]See W. L. Moran, "The End of the Unholy War and the Anti-Exodus," *Bib* 44 (1963): 333-42.

[284]Cf. Longman and Reid, *God Is a Warrior*, p. 17.

domination of the Babylonians in the middle of the sixth century or under pressure from their neighbors in the Persian period. The Babylonians have had their time as agents of Yhwh's punishment and the neighbors are just taking advantage of Judean weakness. But no one is doing anything about sorting out the rights and wrongs here. (We need not ask who might do so or whether this seems to discount Cyrus through whom Yhwh actually acted or whether it refers to his successors who as leaders of the Persian superpower should have kept order in its Levantine empire; this would be to press a metaphor too far.)

So Yhwh will take action (Is 59:16-20). "So his arm delivered for him, his faithfulness—it sustained him. He put on faithfulness as a breastplate, deliverance as a helmet on his head. As clothing he put on redress garments, he wrapped on passion as a coat." Military action is what is required to lay the foundation for restoring Judah, so military action is what Yhwh will take. While Genesis shows that being a warrior is not first nature to Yhwh, the exodus story shows that Yhwh can turn into a fighter when necessary (Ex 15:1-3).[285] Yhwh puts on the appropriate armor and clothing, though its nature is remarkable. It comprises faithfulness, deliverance, redress and passion. *Faithfulness (şĕdāqâ)* is Yhwh's commitment to doing the right thing by Israel. *Deliverance (yĕšûʿâ)* is the content of that right thing at a time when Israel is under the domination of a superpower or under pressure from a stronger neighbor. *Redress (nāqām)* is what such powers deserve because of their action. *Passion (qinʾâ)* is the energy that drives Yhwh to take the required action for Judah and against their and Yhwh's enemies, and guarantees the fulfilling of Yhwh's purpose and promise concerning Israel (Is 9:7 [MT 6]).

"According to deserts, so he will repay wrath to his foes, recompense to his enemies. Recompense to foreign shores he will repay, so that from the west people will revere Yhwh's name, from the rising of the sun his splendor. For he will come as an enemy, like the torrent that Yhwh's wind drives on" (Is 59:18-19). The eventual result of Yhwh's action will be to cause the world as a whole to acknowledge Yhwh. (Beyond Babylon and Edom, the reference to foreign shores and peoples from west and east makes us think of the Greek domination of Palestine that will follow that of the Persians.) What they will be struck by is this decisive might of Yhwh. The Assyrian is not the only one who comes down like a wolf on the fold[286] or like an overflowing torrent.

---

[285]The suggestion that Gen 1 with its lack of conflict has priority over, e.g., Ex 15 because it comes first in the story (cf. J. Richard Middleton, *The Liberating Image* [Grand Rapids, Mich.: Brazos, 2005], 268-69) fits with Jesus' comments about what was so from the beginning (Mk 10:1-9), but the prevalence of conflict imagery in the Scriptures suggests that it says something normative and significant.

Yhwh will so come. But the aim of the redress and the recompense that this coming brings is the restoration of Israel: it will enable Yhwh to "come as restorer to Zion and to people in Jacob who turn from rebellion" (Is 59:20). Without putting down those foes, there can be no raising up of their victims.

The prophecy does have a sting in its tail as it promises this restoration not simply for Zion in its entirety but for people in Jacob who turn from their rebellion.[287] If the community does not take action to sort out questions of *mišpāṭ* and *ṣĕdāqâ* in its own life, it cannot necessarily expect Yhwh to sort out those questions as they affect the way other peoples treat Judah. Indeed, Israel knows, Yhwh can become its enemy (Lam 2:5).

Vintner

The Judeans have even less reason to be under pressure from the Edomites specifically, when in the Persian period they take advantage of continuing Judean weakness to extend their territory. Someone ought to sort things out. In the absence of anyone else doing anything about the situation, a prophet imagines Yhwh doing so (Is 63:1-6). "Who is this coming from Edom, from Bozrah red in garments—this one splendid in his attire, leaning forward in his mighty greatness?" Just now the prophet was referring to lookouts who were to watch keenly for Yhwh's coming to restore Jerusalem. It is such a lookout who speaks. He can see a powerful warrior advancing on the city, and we are perhaps to infer that this constitutes an answer to the intercession that the prophet urged on these lookouts. The lookout asks, "Why is your attire red, your garments like someone treading the winepress?"

The warrior is stained red, which makes one think of grapes, but also of blood. Admittedly we should not be literalistic about the vision; the word *blood*

---

[286]I allude to the opening of Lord Byron's poem "The Destruction of Sennacherib." My translation of the penultimate line of the Isaiah passage (Is 59:19b) is idiosyncratic. It is usual to assume that the enemy is an earthly figure from whom Yhwh brings deliverance (but this requires a sharp change of subject) or to translate it "he will come like a constrained torrent" (but the noun has the article and the adjective does not, which is odd, and the meaning of the adjective *ṣar* has to be stretched).

[287]This also hints at a link with the context, which is otherwise puzzling. Is 59:15b-20 follows on a confession of the community's own lack of faithfulness and action on behalf of what is right (Is 59:9-15a), and in substance this vision of Yhwh's taking action does not follow that confession, until this last phrase. The material in Isaiah 56—66 is arranged chiastically. At the center is the vision of Jerusalem's restoration in Is 60—62. Outside these chapters are two visions of the action to put down oppressors, its precondition (Is 59:15b-21; 63:1-6). Outside these visions are prayers (Is 59:9-15a; 63:7—64:12), and outside these indictments and challenges (Is 56:9—59:8; 65:1—66:16). The varied material stands in theological conversation rather than taking the form of a linear argument; Yhwh's taking action against Israel's oppressors is not a response to Israel's failure to take action in its own life. But at the end this passage does hint at a link.

never comes,[288] and the vision speaks only of the warrior as stained with grape juice like someone who has been treading grapes. The vision is thus milder than the New Testament's portrayal of the warrior King of kings dipping his robe in blood (Rev 19:11-16).[289] One reason for the imagery in Isaiah 63 is that "Bozrah" (boṣrâ) resembles a word for "vintage" (bāṣîr) and "Edom" itself means "red," but it is also the case that dām is blood. So geography, language, social life and prophetic traditions (for instance, the talk of a cup of poison) come together to provide the raw material for the vision to portray Yhwh's act of punishment as like the treading of grapes—not a pleasant experience for the grapes. But there is no literal portrayal of the act of punishment or of any massacre. The red of the warrior's garments is—grape juice.

The warrior thus advances on the city as mighty but messy. The lookout anxiously asks who he is. The answer is slightly enigmatic but is evidently designed to reassure. He has been involved in a task that served ṣĕdāqâ and brought about deliverance. He was prepared to behave in rage to that end. The unfamiliar imagery serves a familiar agenda, the deliverance of Israel in fulfillment of Yhwh's commitment to do right by the people. Edom, grapes and blood come together as Yhwh was prepared to get messy in order to tread down Israel's assailant because no one else was doing so. "I have trodden the wine vat on my own, from the peoples there was no one with me. I trod them in my anger, trampled them in my rage. Their juice spattered my garments; I stained all my attire" (Is 63:3).

Yhwh speaks not merely of punishing Edom but of punishing "peoples." Although there was never any love lost between the descendants of Jacob and of Esau, and the Edomites did advance into Judean territory over the centuries (they were still there in New Testament times), the Edomites were not in the same league as Assyria or Babylon. They were more like Samaria or Moab. It is likely, then, that Edom is also either a suggestive figure for nations because its name suggests the image of treading grapes and/or is simply the direction from which the warrior comes (cf. Judg 5:4-5).

The situation Isaiah 63 presupposes is somewhat like that in the 540s, when the time had arrived for punishing Babylon and making it possible for the Judeans to return to their land. On that occasion Cyrus was available to be the means of bringing about these two events. On this occasion there seems to be no one like that to deal with Judah's southern neighbor. This raises questions

---

[288]Contrast Blenkinsopp's comment (Isaiah 56—66, p. 250) that "'blood' (dām) is the dominant motif in this poem."

[289]I assume that the blood is that of the peoples under judgment, though the other references to the fate of these peoples perhaps means it makes little difference if it is the blood of the martyrs; the fate of the people under judgment is still sealed.

about the relationship of divine initiative to history. After all, Yhwh had raised up or commissioned the Medes and Cyrus to put Babylon down and restore Judah (e.g., Is 13:17-18; 41:2-4; 45:1-7). So why can Yhwh not raise up someone to act in this way again? Is the implication that there is a more dynamic relationship between Yhwh's initiatives and human initiatives? Yhwh no doubt could be interventionist and make something happen that would never have happened, but the rise of Cyrus is an event that Yhwh becomes aligned with rather than one that Yhwh generates in an interventionist way. And the same is true about the rise and fall of other empires. In this vision, there is no one on the horizon for Yhwh to harness, nor does Yhwh raise up someone. Yhwh acts in person.[290] He is the people's champion, the person who fights on their behalf. "The day of redress [nāqām] was in my mind; my year of restoration came. I looked, but there was no helper; I stared, but there was no support. So my arm delivered for me, my rage supported me. I trampled peoples in my anger, made them drunk with my fury, poured their juice on the earth." In the vision, the time has arrived for the punishment of a troublemaker and thus for the restoration of Yhwh's people. Joseph Blenkinsopp finds the picture involves "such violent and lurid images as to repel the reader of even mildly liberal instincts" and notes that it was this passage that led Friedrich Delitzsch to give up on the First Testament. But he does go on to observe that part of the problem lies in the common use of the English word "vengeance" as an equivalent for nāqām.[291]

2.8 Two Sides to Yhwh's Person and Activity

So Yhwh is characterized by power and love, mercy and anger, forgiveness and rejection, violence and sorrow. Yhwh's person and activity embrace the total range of personal qualities, the capacity to undertake all divine roles and the total potential for sovereignty. Yhwh is a war god, a fertility god, a healing god, a rain god and more. Instead of these different roles being shared among a number of gods, one God fulfills them all. Yhwh is master over all reality. This means that conflict among the gods cannot be the explanation for defeat, infertility, epidemic and drought. Either humanity is to blame and such experiences are the one God's responses to its faithlessness, or the one God has a dark side.[292] "There is no God besides me. I myself kill and enliven; I wounded

---

[290]It is customary to locate the difference between "prophetic" and "apocalyptic" thinking here. Prophetic thinking sees Yhwh at work through ordinary historical processes; apocalyptic thinking does not see Yhwh acting through these processes. See Paul D. Hanson, *The Dawn of Apocalyptic* (Philadelphia: Fortress, 1975).

[291]Blenkinsopp, *Isaiah 56—66*, p. 250; he refers to Friedrich Delitzsch's *Zweiter Vortrag über Babel und Bibel* (Stuttgart: Deutsche, 1903). On nāqām, see section 2.7 "Redress."

and I will heal," Yhwh personally says (Deut 32:39). There is no "Mr. Nice" and "Mr. Nasty." It is not the case that one parent is the disciplinarian, the other the comforter. When Marcion denied that God had any feelings and made this part of his reason for rejecting the First Testament because there God had strong feelings of anger, Tertullian's response was to agree that the Father had no anger and to attribute anger to the Son.[293] Modern Christians are more inclined to believe in a harsh God but a nice Jesus. Yhwh accepts both roles, moving between *tôʿēbâ* and *rāṣôn* (between finding things disgusting and finding them lovely; e.g., Prov 11:1, 20).

How do these relate to each other? Is Yhwh's personality coherent?

Power and Faithfulness

Yhwh is a powerful and sovereign God. But that would not be not enough. "We are more anxious to know whether there is a God of justice than to learn whether there is a God of order. Is there a God who collects the tears, who honors hope and rewards the ordeals of the guiltless?"[294] In his study of Mesopotamian religion, Thorkild Jacobsen notes an irony that also appears in the First Testament. While acknowledging God as the mighty, transcendent Lord, awesome in holiness, Mesopotamian and Israelite religion also assume that God can be totally focused on me and my needs.[295]

Thus Psalm 50 begins with a particularly fulsome and solemn naming of God. First it designates God as "El," the great creator, sovereign among the heavenly beings (cf. Jerome's translation *fortis*), a title that links Israelite faith with the faith of other peoples around. Then God is *ʾĕlōhîm*, deity over against humanity. The psalm goes on to designate God as "Yhwh," the name revealed to Israel as the one especially active in Israel's story, and also as "our God"; other psalms address this mighty being as "my God" (e.g., Ps 5:2 [MT 3]). "The oddness and the enduring power of Yahweh to compel our attention is that the sovereign One who is marked by glory, holiness, and jealousy is the One who has engaged Israel in a relationship of enduring fidelity."[296] Yhwh is faithful as well as Most High (Ps 7:17 [MT 18]).

Both aspects of Yhwh's character are necessary for Yhwh to be a God who

---

[292]Cf. Frymer-Kensky, *In the Wake of the Goddesses*, pp. 100-107. But Antti Laato and Johannes C. de Moor in their introduction to *Theodicy in the World of the Bible* (Leiden/Boston: Brill, 2003), p. xxii, warn against the idea that polytheism simply solves the problem of theodicy; different polytheisms look at the question in different ways.

[293]See Tertullian *Against Marcion* 2.27; cf. Heschel, *Prophets*, pp. 383-85.

[294]Heschel, *Man Is Not Alone*, p. 55.

[295]See Jacobsen, *Treasures of Darkness*, pp. 147-64.

[296]Brueggemann, *Theology of the OT*, p. 296; though perhaps Jacobsen's observation means this is not so odd.

delivers. "For Israel, power and solidarity are held together, and . . . both are crucial for Israel's normative utterance about Yahweh." Thus Yhwh is both mighty warrior, returning, conquering, military hero, *and* shepherd or nurse-maid acting with inordinate gentleness and tenderness.[297] Each of these metaphors acts as a balance, corrective and safeguard in relation to the other. What Israel found in its God was "power in behalf of just rule."[298]

The fact that *ṣĕdāqâ* signifies faithfulness as much as justice helps to explain how "God's righteousness does not really stand alongside His mercy, but . . . as revealed in its necessary connexion, according to Scripture, with the plight of the poor and wretched, it is itself God's mercy. Just because He is righteous God has mercy."[299] In behaving with compassion, the God who embodies *ṣĕdāqâ* is not responding to the deserve of people but expressing the essential nature of the God who has made a commitment to them for reasons that are nothing to do with their deserve or lack of it, and who must act in accordance with that intrinsic divine nature.[300] Conversely, that action implies justice as much as faithfulness because its expression requires that God pay the price for this faithfulness, in the way that comes to ultimate expression on the cross. "One of the most disastrous errors in the history of Christianity is to have tried—under the influence of Greek definitions—to distinguish between love and justice."[301] Love expresses itself in a concern for justice, and justice involves faithfulness. It is in response to the Red Sea deliverance that Israel acknowledges Yhwh as the holy one and in response to Yhwh's answering her prayer that Hannah does so (Ex 15:11; 1 Sam 2:2), and it is Israel's holy one who is Israel's restorer (e.g., Is 41:14).[302] "Just because He is gracious God shows His holiness, and as the Holy God He manifests His grace." Thus in Scripture "we do not find the Law alongside the Gospel but in the Gospel."[303]

Power needs to be complemented by faithfulness, and faithfulness needs to be complemented by power. Zechariah 1:12-17 speaks of Yhwh's great passion for Jerusalem.[304] Yhwh here speaks words of comfort and declares that compassion has begun, and at the same time speaks of great anger toward the nations who so ill-treated Jerusalem and Judah. Compassion and rage are

---

[297]Ibid., pp. 143, 232.
[298]Miller, *Israelite Religion and Biblical Theology,* p. 419; emphasis in original.
[299]Barth, *Church Dogmatics,* II/1:387.
[300]Cf. Ibid., II/1:389-90.
[301]Miranda, *Marx and the Bible,* p. 61.
[302]Barth, *Church Dogmatics,* II/1:361.
[303]Ibid., II/1:364, 363.
[304]See section 2.2 "Advocate."

necessarily the two sides to Yhwh's passion.

Creator and Liberator

Much mid-twentieth-century study of Old Testament theology focused on the question of its "center." What was the key idea around which it should be structured? This question reached an impasse. In subsequent decades, a number of scholars suggested that the central dynamic of the First Testament was binary in nature. It involved a tension between "Creation and Liberation."[305] As the creator, Yhwh is the God who made the world an orderly place and undergirds its order, blesses the beings in the world so that they can multiply and makes things grow. The divine order of creation is itself undergirded by the ordering structures of a society such as the monarchy, expressed in the Davidic covenant, which make for stability and security. The localization of God in a fixed temple contributes to this stable order. Although the Scriptures often dissociate Israel from its neighbors, this understanding of God is open to comparison with what Morton Smith called "the common theology of the ancient Near East"[306] with its belief in one supreme god, active in history and in nature, just and merciful, promising blessing in return for obedience.

Israel's origins lie, however, in the Mosaic covenant with its background in a context in Egypt where the orderly structures of the state have become a means of oppression rather than blessing. As the one who liberates, Yhwh is the God who is prepared to overturn those structures of order. The locus of Yhwh's activity is then not the realm of nature with its continuities and consistencies but the realm of political history with its rifts and upheavals. Here the divine instinct for liberation needs to subvert the ordering structures of regular political life and foment revolution. Further, Yhwh is not a God who settles down but one who stays on the move, out of the control of the people and their leadership. When Israel's kings become only too like those of the nations, this "paganization" of Israel[307] affects Israel's own life as it affected the life of the nation from which it was rescued at the beginning.

---

[305]The title of an inaugural lecture by George Landes, published in *USQR* 33 (1977-78): 79-89; and in *Creation in the Old Testament,* ed. Bernhard W. Anderson, pp. 135-51 (London: SPCK/Philadelphia: Fortress, 1984). I have discussed this polarity in my *Theological Diversity and the Authority of the Old Testament* (Grand Rapids, Mich.: Eerdmans, 1986/Carlisle, U.K.: Paternoster, 1995), pp. 200-239. Walter Brueggemann has traced these two trajectories and the scholarly literature in a number of places: e.g., *Old Testament Theology: Essays on Structure, Theme, and Text* (Minneapolis: Fortress, 1992), pp. 1-44, 95-110; *A Social Reading of the Old Testament* (Minneapolis: Fortress, 1994).

[306]Morton Smith, "The Common Theology of the Ancient Near East," *JBL* 71 (1952): 135-47. Cf. Levenson, *Sinai and Zion,* p. 113, with particular reference to Ugarit.

[307]G. E. Mendenhall, "The Monarchy," *Int* 29 (1975): 155-70; see p. 155.

Of course if "Yhwh our God Yhwh one," we would expect to find that when being creator Yhwh acts as liberator, and when being liberator Yhwh acts as creator. These two activities interweave. Creation is an act of liberation even as it is an act of ordering, and it is an egalitarian act even though it is then undergirded by a hierarchical social structure. In the context of exile when Yhwh the God of history is not acting as the liberating lord of history, talk of creation serves liberation concerns. Liberation is an act designed to restore proper order and blessing to the community's life. But Yhwh does have to move between being one who supports order and one who subverts and overturns it, one who encourages revolution and one who reckons that for the time being the cost of liberation will be greater than the gain from it. Isaiah is a Jerusalem prophet who presupposes the validity of the Davidic monarchy even while critiquing it; Josiah uses his position as Davidic king to authorize a Torah-inspired religious revolution. Neither Ezekiel nor Isaiah 40—55 can be identified with one of the paradigms (creation/order or liberation/revolution) rather than the other.

Compassionate and Forgiving

Yhwh's personality profile is outlined near the beginning of the First Testament story. The one who appears to Moses is

> Yhwh, Yhwh, God compassionate and gracious, long-tempered and big in commitment and trustworthiness, extending commitment to thousands [of generations], carrying wrongdoing, rebellion, and failure, but certainly not acquitting, attending to the wrongdoing of parents on children and grandchildren, on those of the third and fourth [generation]. (Ex 34:5-8)

The popular impression that the First Testament God is a God of wrath reflects the impression that wrath has priority over mercy, but at this key point when the First Testament directly speaks to that question, it affirms the opposite. "God's compassion has the last word."[308] The location of the statement and the recurrence of its phrases elsewhere in the First Testament suggest that this self-description stands at the heart of First Testament theology. Yhwh has already anticipated it, more briefly, in the Ten Words (Ex 20:5-6); Jeremiah's formulation is that Yhwh "keeps commitment to thousands but requites the wrongdoing of parents into their children's pockets[309] after them" (Jer 32:18). The parents make the "investment" but the children pay the price.

The two sides to Yhwh's statements and the relative balance between them reflect the events with which they interweave. Already, Yhwh has been both

---

[308] Rendtorff, *Canonical Hebrew Bible*, p. 628.

[309] On this expression, see section 2.3 "Over the World."

keeping commitment and attending to wrongdoing. Even for Israel at Sinai, "you were a God who carries . . . but one who brings redress for their wrongdoings" (Ps 99:8).[310] The dynamic recurs in Numbers 14, where Moses appeals to the first part of the formulation, but Yhwh implies a necessity also to reflect the second part.[311] It is a basis for praise (Ps 145:8) and for appeal for oneself (Ps 86:15). Nahum 1:3 puts the stress on the second part, to Israel's benefit, while Jonah 4:1-2 regrets the application of the first part to Israel's oppressors. "Yet the tension between the divine mercy and justice is far from fully explicated. . . . It does not explain . . . the basis for the distinction between the iniquity which Yahweh 'forgives' and the iniquity of the fathers which Yahweh 'visits upon the children' as far as three or four generations. Are some sins forgivable and others unforgivable? Or, are the same wrongdoings involved in both cases, with the distinction that those persisted in are to be punished?" One might even ask whether Yhwh makes such a distinction; perhaps Yhwh can be carrying wrongdoing even while attending to it, in the sense of not letting it be a basis for casting off the people. "The most that is asserted is that Yahweh is acting true to 'his' nature when forgiving sin and when punishing sin."[312] Subsequent accounts of Yhwh's forgiving and punishing resolve this ambiguity in different ways.

Holy in the Faithful Exercise of Authority

Isaiah expresses this ambiguity in the way he speaks of Yhwh's holiness. "Human beings bow, people drop down, lofty human eyes drop down, But Yhwh Armies is lofty in authority and the holy God shows himself holy in faithfulness" (Is 5:15-16). In Isaiah's day Judah is doing rather well, and gives an impression of lofty stature. Unfortunately that imperils recognition of Yhwh's own lofty stature. Further, socially and religiously it is not doing so well; it is characterized by self-indulgence and failure to pay attention to what Yhwh is doing. All this makes necessary an assertion of Yhwh's holiness.

Among other things, this will mean a revelation of the distinctive nature of that holiness. "Here is a virtual definition of God's holiness in moral, relational categories."[313] It expresses itself in *mišpāṭ* and *ṣĕdāqâ*, which together imply the faithful exercise of authority. The EVV translate these terms "justice and righteousness," but this gives a misleading impression. Acting in *mišpāṭ* denotes acting with authority, decisiveness and power; it can imply a legal context (so

---

[310]On this motif in the Sinai story, see *OTT* 1:408-25.

[311]Brueggemann, *Theology of the OT*, p. 220.

[312]Gottwald, *Tribes of Yahweh*, p. 686.

[313]Jo Bailey Wells, *God's Holy People*, JSOTSup 305 (Sheffield: Sheffield Academic Press, 2000), pp. 145-46.

it implies justice in judgment) but it is a broader idea than that.[314] Acting in *ṣĕdāqâ* denotes doing the right thing by people with whom one is in a relationship, something nearer "faithfulness" than "righteousness" or "justice." There is therefore some paradox in Isaiah's statement. Yhwh's acting in relation to Israel in *mišpāṭ* and *ṣĕdāqâ* should mean doing right by the people, for instance by protecting them from attackers.

Perhaps Isaiah thus here hints that the terrible calamity on Judah that he has just announced, which involves Sheol swallowing up the people (Is 5:14), will not be Yhwh's last word. This statement will then anticipate the subsequent recurring declaration that Israel's holy one is its restorer (e.g., Is 41:14). When exile and death seem to be the lords exercising sovereignty over Judah, that will not be the end of the story. A new self-assertion of the holy, exalted Yhwh will mean decisively doing the right thing by the people. It is thus good news that Yhwh is "your holy one" (Is 43:15).

Or perhaps Yhwh's faithful exercise of authority has to be understood more paradoxically. Yhwh is committed to a decisive faithfulness to Israel as a whole, but also to decisive faithfulness in other directions. One such direction is toward groups within Israel such as the people whose blood cries out to Yhwh from the ground (Is 5:7). Decisive faithfulness to them means acting against the people who have robbed them of their lives. It means acting on behalf of those who are the present and the potential victims of people who want to accumulate stuff and will let other people die in order to do so. It is of the essence of deity to act in decisive faithfulness; to fail to do so is thus to fail the test for deity. If Yhwh were to fail this test, it would make Yhwh liable to the condemnation and judgment of Psalm 82.

Yhwh also has to be decisively faithful to who Yhwh is. That, too, can mean that the faithful exercise of authority works against Israel as it works against other peoples. The tension finds expression again when Yhwh expresses deep grief over the destruction that has come on the people (for which Yhwh is implicitly responsible), then refuses to listen when the people plead for mercy.

Yhwh is one who does not insist on majesty and is prepared to be self-humbling, but as the majestic one insists on people's self-humbling. Yhwh is one who is resolutely active to bring the world into being and then to take the world and Israel to its destiny, one who speaks as well as acting, one who addresses Israel and calls Israel, who speaks the truth to Israel. Human pride is an insistence on one's importance, a pretense to a majesty one does not possess. But Yhwh's self-humbling activity and truthfulness will win in the end. Yhwh will

---

[314]Though also a narrower one, insofar as it is possible to exercise *mišpāṭ* in an unjust way.

give Israel real majesty, win it to obedience and make it a witness to truth.[315]

The Dilemma of Parenthood

As Yhwh experiences it, the parent-child relationship is just as one-sided as the parents of a teenager are inclined to feel (see Is 1:2-3). Hosea 11:1-9 suggests the closer analogy of a couple who have adopted a child. "When Israel was a boy, I loved him; from Egypt I called him my son." So Yhwh was like a father or mother who adopted a child when he was a boy. In Israel's case this means when he was in Egypt. Yhwh reached out in love to this child there and gave him the position of son. But in Canaan they heard all sorts of other calls and followed the voices of people who had no right to be making demands on them—or to follow LXX's expression, Yhwh kept addressing them as son and summoning them to work for Yhwh the way a son works for a father, but they persisted in declining. Instead they served the "Masters" (the Baals). This was so despite the fact that Yhwh was the one who taught them to walk, picked them up when they needed carrying and dressed their wounds when they fell over, let them walk but kept a harness on them to try to ensure they did not get into trouble, and bent down to feed them.[316] But they did not "acknowledge" Yhwh as the one who did that; Hosea uses the same verb as Isaiah 1:3. They refused to return to Yhwh. "My people—they are bent on turning from me."

So the parents will throw them out. One can see the suitcases and clothes in the driveway waiting for the recalcitrant teenager to come to collect them, unless the trash truck arrives first. Father lashes out in all directions with mutually contradictory threats. They will return to Egypt. Or they will come under the authority of Assyria. Or a supernatural sword will whirl over the country consuming the people—specifically the agents through whom they sought guidance instead of looking to Yhwh—and take vengeance for the political schemings that were also their way of running their life without taking Yhwh into account. Or they will be treated like a recalcitrant animal put under much more severe restraint than the one just referred to.

Except that parents cannot do such a thing to their child, the child they chose and adopted and brought up and cared for. "How can I give you up, Ephraim, how surrender you, Israel? How can I make you like Admah, treat you as Zeboiim?" Yhwh cannot treat Ephraim as if it were some obscure people no one has ever heard of. Before the child comes back home, the internal pressure toward throwing the teenager out is overcome by a different internal pressure, and the belongings are already back in his or her room. A change

---

[315] Adapted from Barth, *Church Dogmatics,* IV/1:79-154.

[316] But it may be that Hosea here changes the image and speaks of Ephraim as an ox that Yhwh keeps restrained but releases so that it can eat.

comes over the parent, a remorse at the idea of throwing the child out. "My heart is changed within me, all at once my remorse[317] kindles." The parent wants to throw arms round the stupid child rather than punishing it further. The reason is striking, for more than one reason. It is that "I am God and not a man, the Holy One in your midst" (Hos 11:9). The "problem" lies in the deity, the holiness of Yhwh. It is precisely that divine holiness that makes the expression of rage impossible. Yhwh's point is thus the reverse of the one often made when people suggest that Yhwh's holiness makes it is hard for Yhwh to forgive sin. For Yhwh, it is this holiness that makes it hard to punish sin. The holiness of Yhwh is the deity of Yhwh, the nature of Yhwh as God. Hosea's argument is not even that Yhwh is the Holy One *of Israel* and therefore must show compassion to "my people." Hosea appeals simply to the fact that Yhwh is the Holy One—period.

The implication is that the instinct to love, comfort and tolerate is nearer the heart of Yhwh than the instinct to act in rage. That is so because Yhwh is God, not a man. Now it may be that Yhwh is here suggesting that human beings find it easier to punish and to act in rage than God does. But Yhwh talks about being God rather than *ʾiš*, not God rather than *ʾādām*. While that might have the same meaning, the language raises the question whether Yhwh is specifically speaking of the qualities of a man as opposed to a woman. Stereotypically, at least, it is the man of the house who would be more likely to act tough than the woman of the house, and Yhwh is at this point suggesting a nature more like a mother than a father.

Of course there are other contexts where Yhwh does let rage overrule mercy, and this is not Yhwh's last word in Hosea. Indeed, the very next lines presuppose that Yhwh has thrown the children out of the house because these verses constitute a promise to fetch them back.[318] But Yhwh thus does promise to fetch them back. "There is an instant in his anger, a life in his acceptance. In evening weeping takes up lodging, but at morning there is resounding" (Ps 30:5 [MT 6]). The suppliant knows from experience that we normally live in the light of God's love and acceptance. That makes it possible to cope with occasional but temporary inexplicable experiences of God's having turned away from us. While the experience lasts, it may not seem to last only an instant, nor at evening may we have conviction that it will be gone by morning. But the other side of the experience (as with the mother looking back on her labor) it can seem so.

---

[317]The EVV have "compassion," as if the word were *raḥămîm* rather than *niḥûmîm*. Words from the root *nḥm* usually suggest comfort or change of heart; the latter entirely fits here.

[318]See, e.g., Hos 13:14-16, where Yhwh declines to let remorse have its way (see section 4.2 "Death").

Wrathful, But Not from the Heart

It is a commonplace of human experience that people have dominant aspects to their personality and also secondary aspects. They may, for instance, be more inclined to action or reflection, to idealism or realism, to planning or to serendipity, to firmness or flexibility, to orientation on the present or on the future. Both elements in each pair are good. We might be inclined to think that it would be ideal to have each of these in balance within the individual, though people are rarely like that. Perhaps God prefers to achieve that balance by having within the human body and within the body of Christ people who are more inclined to one or to the other, because this encourages us to live together rather than being self-sufficient. Whatever our dominant characteristics as individuals, however, we usually have some capacity to summon up their correlative characteristics when required. Our dominant side is complemented by a secondary side.

In this regard we are like God. It may be that God has some personality aspects in balance. God holds together idealism and realism, which often startles Bible readers who expect God to be wholly visionary and are surprised at the condescension to practicalities expressed in Moses' Teaching. God holds together firmness and flexibility, so that Moses' Teaching lays down the law in detail, yet does so in ways that reflect changes in the way God guided people over the centuries, and sometimes explicitly testifies to the way God can be flexible (e.g., Num 27; cf. 2 Chron 30:17-20). God holds together "structure legitimation" and "pain-embrace" and is "always in the process of deciding" which way to act.[319]

At other points there are dominant aspects to God's character and secondary aspects. For instance, while Genesis 1—2 indicate that God combines a capacity for planning and for serendipity, the biblical story as a whole suggests that God is more inclined to serendipity. Again, this surprises Bible readers who have inferred from references to God's planning and to God's sovereignty that God had a detailed plan for world history from the beginning, and for their own lives, but find that the Bible does not suggest that.[320]

Christians have sometimes spoken of God as combining love and justice in such a way that these have equal place in God's nature. God thus "has" to punish our sin, but punishes it by punishing his Son instead of punishing us. The First Testament does not thus see love and justice as equally balanced in God (nor, I think, does the New Testament). After line upon line of lament at Yhwh's (deserved) wrath and affliction, Lamentations 3 extraordinarily declares,

---

[319]Brueggemann, *OT Theology: Essays*, p. 43.
[320]See section 2.4.

This I call to mind;
    therefore I have hope
In Yhwh's commitments, because they have not ended,
    because his compassion has not finished.
They are new each morning;
    great is your truthfulness. . . .
Yhwh is good to people who wait for him,
    to the person who has recourse to him. . . .
Because the Lord
    does not reject forever
But causes suffering and has compassion,
    according to the abundance of his commitments.
Because it is not from the heart that he afflicts
    or makes human beings suffer. (Lam 3:21-33)

The EVV render that last line "he does not willingly afflict," which is itself a very striking statement. When God afflicts people, this is an unwilling action on God's part. So whose will is being put into effect? Who is causing God to act unwillingly? This compulsion can only be coming from within God's own person. The Hebrew expression coheres with that, though it nuances the point in indicating that affliction comes from God, but not come from God's heart, not from God's inner being. The model this suggests is that, as is the case with a human being, there are dominant or central or governing aspects to God's character, and also secondary, more marginal aspects. With regard to human beings, this can be referred to as their shadow side, though when applied to God, that can seem to suggest negative aspects. But a human being's shadow side is simply their less prominent side. Some professors, for instance, have a dominant side that is happiest when they are sitting alone at their desks researching, but their shadow side is capable of being relational and of projecting themselves to people, and they call on this shadow side when they are in the classroom.

Yhwh's Asymmetry

So toughness and softness or justice and mercy do not have an equal place in Yhwh's moral character. Yhwh can summon up the capacity to act tough from time to time, but this does not issue from Yhwh's heart. Yhwh's dominant side is to be loving and merciful; Lamentations' point is that afflicting people involves the realizing of God's secondary side. It is not the case that "wrath is not an attribute of God,"[321] that within the Godhead are only love and faithfulness, and not wrath. But it is the case that wrath has a secondary status within

---

[321]Pannenberg, *Systematic Theology,* 1:439.

God, compared with love and faithfulness.

Thus the exercise of anger issues from God's circumstantial will, which always stands in the service of God's absolute will for life and blessing.[322] Indeed, "if God does not meet us in His jealous zeal and wrath . . . then He does not meet us at all. . . . That man is not abandoned in this way, that God is really gracious to him, is shown in the fact that God confronts him in holiness. . . . The fact that God does not permit Israel . . . to perish means that He cannot allow them to go their own way, unaccused, uncondemned and unpunished, when they are and behave as if they were people who do not participate in this salvation and protection."[323] "If God did not make known His consuming opposition to sin and therefore to sinful man, how could He really hold fellowship with man, seeing He can do so only on the basis of grace and election?"[324] Thus "God's affection for Israel rings even in the denunciations. It is 'My people' who do not understand. . . . There is sorrow in God's anger. . . . Anger is not His disposition, but a state He waits to overcome." God's anger is "*suspended* love," "mercy withheld," but it is about to be shown again.[325] It is in line with this that God has made certain permanent commitments, expressions of love and faithfulness such as bind God henceforth. As Moses points out and God implicitly grants (Ex 34:10), God cannot get out of such commitments. The first (Gen 8:21-22) binds God to the whole world. The second (Gen 17:1-8) binds God to Abraham and his descendants via Isaac (Ishmael has his own covenant); it is to this commitment that Moses holds God. The third and fourth bind God to David and to Levi, as surely as God was bound to the earth (Jer 33:17-26).[326]

God indeed destines some to be vessels of mercy and others to be vessels of wrath (Rom 9:20-23), but these are not two coequal destinies because both serve God's purpose of mercy, and both may profit from it.[327] "While the wrath of God plays a fundamental role in the divine pleroma, God finally weaves the strands of divine action, of mercy and wrath and of sinful human action into a creative integration which is ultimately salvific."[328] Thus the Egyptian

---

[322]So Terence E. Fretheim, who thus rightly questions Brueggemann's statement that "there is a profound disjunction at the core" of Yhwh's life (*Theology of the OT*, p. 268) ("Some Reflections on Brueggemann's God," in *God in the Fray*, ed. Tod Linafelt and Timothy K. Beal [Minneapolis: Fortress, 1998], pp. 24-37; see p. 31). Fretheim also sees wrath as less an attribute of God than love (p. 30).

[323]Barth, *Church Dogmatics*, II/1:366.

[324]Ibid., II/1:367.

[325]Heschel, *Prophets*, pp. 103-5, 378.

[326]I here adapt remarks of Fretheim ("Some Reflections," p. 32), though I do not think he is justified to identify Yhwh's commitments as those to Noah, Abraham and Israel.

[327]Barth, *Church Dogmatics*, II/2:217-33.

[328]Jim Garrison, *The Darkness of God* (London: SCM Press, 1982), p. 114.

plagues issue in Israel's occupation of the promised land, the various outbursts of wrath in connection with the covenant chest and the divine wrath
that inspires David to count the people are part of the story that leads to the
building of the temple. The blinding of people in Jesus' time likewise leads to
the cross and the proclaiming of Jesus to the Gentile world. In this process our
personal destinies are subordinate to the process whereby God works toward
the restoring of all things. The wrath of God is "deadly yet positive, inexplicable and arbitrary yet sovereign and ultimately creative," leading inextricably
to the creation of a new world order.[329]

First Testament study has difficulty in accepting that there is both a compassionate and a rough side to Yhwh. For the most part First Testament study emphasizes the "positive" side, leaving it to a minority from time to time to draw
attention to the acts of Yhwh the "rough beast."[330] In Jewish understanding,
David Blumenthal notes, being a person implies that God is fair, God speaks
and listens, God is powerful (though not unlimited), God is loving (warm, affirming, forgiving, committed, demanding, frustrating, exclusive, inclusive,
intolerant), God gets angry, God is partisan. But he adds that in addition the
Scriptures and subsequent experience indicate that from time to time God acts
in a way that is so unjust in, for instance, allowing the Holocaust that it can
only be called "abusive." He refers to Psalm 44, where God does not respond
to Israel's protest about God's treatment of it, and to Job, to whom God responds but declines to offer a rationale for what has happened (of course, we
know the rationale, but may not like it).[331] J. Pedersen rather reverses the characterization, with considerable exaggeration, declaring that "the divine awfulness pervades the whole of the Old Testament," though going on to note that
the fear this allegedly induces coexists with love, and that pervaded by both
feelings "the Israelite is irradiated with happiness."[332]

Seeing Both Sides

Psalm 78 pictures the relationship between Yhwh and Israel as one in which

---

[329]Ibid., p. 116.

[330]See David Penchansky, *What Rough Beast?* (Louisville, Ky: Westminster John Knox, 1999),
    considering the irrational God (2 Sam 6), the vindictive God (2 Sam 24), the dangerous God
    (Lev 10), the malevolent God (Ex 4) and the abusive God (2 Kings 2).

[331]David Blumenthal, *Facing the Abusing God* (Louisville, Ky: Westminster John Knox, 1993),
    pp. 14-20, 247. See also Lindström's comments on Gen 32:23-32; Ex 4:24-26; 12:21-23 in *God
    and the Origin of Evil*, pp. 21-73; and Kalina Rose Stevenson's description of God as one who
    batters the earth ("If Earth Could Speak," in *The Earth Story in the Psalms and in the Prophets*,
    ed. Norman C. Habel (Sheffield: Sheffield Academic Press/Cleveland, Ohio: Pilgrim,
    2001), pp. 158-71 (see p. 158).

[332]J. Pedersen, *Israel* III-IV ([1926-1940] reprint, London: Oxford University Press, 1953), pp.
    625, 627.

Israel oscillates between trust and disobedience, and Yhwh oscillates between anger and compassion. Sometimes Yhwh's anger would issue in slaughter, and that would draw them back to obedience. But their trust would turn again into abandonment as they again had recourse to other gods. There is a maleficent illogic about their action and a beneficent illogic about Yhwh's. There is no true logic about their giving up their trust in Yhwh; the psalm keeps drawing attention to the wonder of what Yhwh had done for them. (It might even seem that there was no great logic about Yhwh's *punishment* making them come to trust Yhwh as their restorer.) There is also no logic about Yhwh's moving from anger to compassion and Yhwh's willingness personally to atone for their wrongdoing,[333] except a logic that emerges from Yhwh's character. Yhwh combines a capacity for compassion and a capacity for anger, and has to keep deciding which of these to express. The latter can never be dominant, but it cannot always be denied opportunity for expression, not because of pressures from inside Yhwh but because of the demands of right and wrong. The psalm thus several times speaks of Yhwh's anger arising, but sets these declarations in the context of comments on how "he would again and again turn his anger." He was capable of causing their days to end in emptiness, but also of taking into account the fact that they were mere flesh, like "a wind that passes and does not return." Therefore (in the next psalm) the people can plead, "Do not be mindful with regard to us of the wrongdoing of our predecessors; may your compassion come to meet us quickly. . . . Rescue us and atone for our failures, for the sake of your name"(Ps 79:8, 9).

It is hard for us to bring the two sides of Yhwh together. In this we resemble ourselves as small children in our attitude to our parents—and in our attitude to ourselves. Our instinct is to see our parents either as all good or as all bad in the sense that either they do what we want and they are all good, or they fail to do what we want, acting in ways that seem inexplicable, and they are all bad. Good and bad are thus not moral categories but relational ones that point to what seems good or bad from the perspective of our desires and perceptions. Growing toward maturity involves coming to see that our parents are neither all good nor all bad, in that sense (and in other senses). They are people in their own right with their own agendas and concerns, which include matters that are priorities to us but extend beyond those in ways we may not be able to understand. They are not all good or all bad in the way they approach our agenda, but a mixture.

Growing toward maturity involves coming to a related realization about ourselves, though here good and bad have more moral connotations. To see

---

[333]See section 2.6 "Cleansing."

oneself as wholly good or wholly bad is a sign of immaturity or delusion. We, too, are not all bad or all good, but a mixture. Maturity involves coming to own that ambivalence in ourselves.

Christians often expect God to be all good. In a moral sense that is presumably true, but our perspective on God's goodness is often that of children in relation to their parents' goodness. A major theme in Yhwh's confrontation of Job is that Yhwh's agenda and concern for the world is much broader than involving merely what is good for Job or even for humanity as a whole. As far as we are concerned, God does good and bad things, and often we cannot see how the things that feel bad and look bad (the acts of the rough beast) can be the acts of one who is good. Living by trust in God involves coming to believe that they may be so. As with our parents (if we are lucky), the evidence is the fact that many of God's acts do look good. We then trust God for the others. The First Testament shows us that this need by no means exclude protesting about them, or owning them by telling stories about them that do not at all pretend to "explain" them. If we have been able to come to recognize our parents as people who combine good and bad in the first sense, and ourselves as people who combine good and bad in the second sense, we may have an easier time accepting that God combines good and bad in the first sense. And we may have an easier time accepting that the appearance of bad in the second sense may indeed be only an appearance, even though we cannot see how that is so. Conversely, coming to accept who God is may help us accept our parents and ourselves.

There are acts of grace and roughness that are inexplicable, as there are acts of blessing and toughness that are explicable. Whether acting explicably or inexplicably, Yhwh's dominant side is to be loving and merciful. There is no invariable resolution of the tension between compassion and toughness. But there is a promise that compassion is at the heart of Yhwh's character. Yhwh is prepared to be Mr. Nasty, but finds it more natural to be Mr. Nice.

◆ ◆ ◆

The God and Father of Our Lord Jesus Christ

"Wherein does the plus of the *New* Testament lie? . . . What is new in the new *covenant* lies in the fact that the Word became flesh."[334] The real presence of God in places is succeeded by God's real presence in a person.[335] "In Jesus Christ we have to do with very God." Christ "is very God acting for us men,

---

[334]Miskotte, *When the Gods Are Silent*, pp. 163-64.

[335]Cf. Barth, *Church Dogmatics*, II/1:482.

God Himself become man."[336] And the God with whom we have to do in Christ is the God of Israel. Thus one should expect that the God whom the First Testament portrays is the God whom we see embodied in Christ, and that the person Christ is should give us clues to the identity of the God portrayed in the First Testament. For as God did not become any "flesh," but Jewish flesh, so the one who became flesh was not simply God, but the one who made a commitment to be the God of Abraham and Sarah and their progeny.[337] Thus the incarnation and the cross were "not a historical *novum,* not the arbitrary action of a *Deus ex machina,* but . . . the fulfilment—the superabundant fulfilment—of the will revealed in the Old Testament of . . . the gracious God who as such is able and willing and ready to condescend to the lowly and to undertake their case at His own cost."[338] In becoming flesh, God thus did not give up being God. If anything, God was here most manifestly God. That is especially so on the cross, where God goes to the uttermost in the bearing of human faithlessness that God has been doing through Israel's story, and where the pain of God becomes flesh. In Christ the First Testament's anthropomorphism reaches its apotheosis.

That awareness, and the pouring out of the Holy Spirit, eventually issues in the doctrine of the Trinity. Christians have often reckoned that this in some sense "solves" questions about God we have considered. God is the embodiment of divine toughness and Jesus the embodiment of divine mercy. The First Testament guards against this by making clear that both compassion and toughness inhere in God. That is so within Father, within Son and within Spirit.

Jürgen Moltmann sets the understanding of God as Trinity over against monotheism, to counter the latter's patriarchal implications;[339] but monotheism, like the doctrine of the Trinity, is a postbiblical development, and one may doubt whether the First Testament's own understanding of God has any more patriarchal implications than those of the New Testament. The fact that God is Trinity does mean that the people of God is welcomed into the fellowship of the Holy Spirit, which is a fellowship with the Father and the Son. If we may infer that within God, the Father, the Son and the Spirit live in interrelationship, the people of God is constituted through being drawn into this community.[340] This will mean that we conceptualize and articulate the nature of our relationship with God differently. Jesus addresses God as "Abba, Father," and

---

[336]Ibid., IV/1:128.

[337]Ibid., IV/1:166-69.

[338]Ibid., IV/1:170.

[339]Moltmann, *The Trinity and the Kingdom of God,* pp. 191-202.

[340]See, e.g., Moltmann, *History and the Triune God,* pp. xi-xiii.

the church does the same; it is the cry the Spirit inspires from within us (e.g., Rom 8:15). But the Psalms, for instance, show that Israel had just as real, confident and childlike a relationship with God. What Christ does is make clearer how that was possible (because its basis lay in God's willingness to die to self for us), and what the Spirit does is extend it to the Gentile world.

3

ISRAEL

Yhwh is the God of Israel, and Israel is the people of Yhwh. Israel is more fundamentally the people of Yhwh than it is a political, ethnic or geographical entity. Yhwh is the God of a people more fundamentally than the God of a city or of a holy place or of natural processes, or even of a land, or even of individual persons.[1] The First Testament suggests a number of ways of thinking of Israel. It is a family, a nation, a congregation; it is a son, a servant, a disciple, a rebel; its vocation is to be and to stay in being, to acknowledge and to worship, to pass on the story and to witness; it is chosen, covenanted, critiqued, rejected, restored.[2] The First Testament focuses on its story. Yhwh is not the God of Israel more fundamentally than being the God of the whole earth; the First Testament begins with Yhwh's purpose for the whole world, and Yhwh's involvement with Israel serves that purpose. But as the New Testament talks more about the church than about the world, so the First Testament talks more about Israel than about the world.

3.1 Yhwh's Family

To designate the people of God as "Israel" is to designate it as a family, the descendants of one man with that name. That points to some key aspects of the being of this people of God. It comes into existence by God's grace, not human choice. It is a people with a securely based unity. It is a place of learning and a place of challenge.

Household, Family, Clan

The Israelites started off as a family. Abraham is their father and Sarah is the one who bore them (Is 51:2). They are "the household of Jacob" (*bayit*, Ex 19:3). They are "the children of Israel." They are an extended "family" (*mišpāḥâ*, Amos 3:1). They are a "clan" (*šēbeṭ*, Ps 74:2). They are a "people" (*ʿam*, Gen 25:8). Even that is a kinship term; in drawing attention to its kinship basis, designating Israel as a people, an *ʿam*, itself "presents an understanding of a hu-

---

[1] See Norman K. Gottwald, *The Tribes of Yahweh* (Maryknoll, N.Y.: Orbis, 1979/London: SCM Press, 1980; reprint, Sheffield: Sheffield Academic Press, 1999), pp. 685, 688.

[2] See *OTT* 1:437-50. Paul D. Hanson studies the changing nature of the people of God through the biblical period in *The People Called* (San Francisco: Harper & Row, 1986).

man group in terms that are more internal than external."[3] As it grows, this
family comes to comprise a number of clans, groups that are large enough to be
political entities in their own right yet know themselves to be related to each
other.[4] The clans subdivide into extended families or villages and into nuclear
families or households[5] (see, e.g., Josh 7:14-18). Admittedly this language is not
used consistently; the term *household* might be applied to the extended family
or the clan as well as to the people as a whole. A city might comprise a number
of extended families, while a household might be large enough to require more
than one actual house.[6] The household is the basic economic unit, the context
for education and for some worship—notably, Passover—and thus for the continuity of Israel's relationship with God.[7] The village provides households with
mutual support and protection, potential wives and husbands, structures for
dispute resolution, and a context for some worship. The clan and cooperation
between the clans provide protection in relation to other peoples, the resolution
of broader disputes, and the celebration of the annual festivals.

While the First Testament can thus portray Israel as the family of Abraham
or Jacob, it can also see it as the family of Yhwh, the household of Yhwh, the
people of Yhwh. That broadens the kinship designation. Yhwh is part of the
family, or rather Israel is part of Yhwh's family. Its being Yhwh's people is then
the basis for Yhwh's protection, deliverance and restoration of Israel. The relationship is one to which the First Testament appeals especially in connection
with Yhwh and Israel's mutual address. Talk of "Yhwh's people" "belongs
mainly in the context of dialogue between Yhwh and Israel, and less so to the
situation of speaking about Israel."[8] We are "your people"; you are "my people" (e.g., Ps 28:9; Is 52:4-6).

Within this family, Yhwh is the father or mother, and Israel is Yhwh's children. This image is commonly used to suggest that Israel has not behaved like
children. It has fulfilled a parent's nightmare, that a son should turn out an incorrigible rebel (Is 1:2). Deuteronomy 21:18-21 prescribes the stoning of such a

---

[3]Horst Dietrich Preuss, *Old Testament Theology*, 2 vols. (Louisville, Ky: Westminster John
Knox/Edinburgh: T & T Clark, 1995, 1996), 1:50-51.

[4]It is thus better to speak of the "clans" of Israel than the tribes of Israel, since a tribe is usually
an entity set over against other tribes and not claiming a common ancestry with them.

[5]Though these might comprise four or more generations and thus might also be reckoned
small-scale extended families.

[6]See, e.g., Gottwald, *Tribes of Yahweh*, pp. 237-341.

[7]Cf. Christopher J. H. Wright, *God's People in God's Land* (Exeter: Paternoster/Grand Rapids,
Mich.: Eerdmans, 1990), pp. 72-89.

[8]Norbert Lohfink, "Beobachtungen zur Geschichte des Ausdrucks עַם יְהוָה," in *Probleme biblischer Theologie*, ed. Hans Walter Wolff (Munich: Kaiser 1971), pp. 275-305; see p. 280; cf.
Preuss, *OT Theology*, 1:285.

son. Like many other prescriptions, Israel seems not to have understood it literally, but it nevertheless might have the effect of making the Israelites listen with fear, not least in light of the possibility that Yhwh might treat them thus as rebellious children. In practice what Yhwh implicitly threatened to do was disown them, though also promising in due course to take them back as "children of the living God" (Hos 1:10 [MT 2:1]). They remain "my sons," "my daughters," people called by Yhwh's name as the members of a family are called by their father's name (Is 43:6-7).

The point may also be put individually. Israel as a people is Yhwh's child, begotten and birthed by Yhwh (Deut 32:18). It is Yhwh's son, one Yhwh loved, taught to walk and carried (Hos 11:1). It is therefore a child of which Yhwh has expectations, and one whom Yhwh will not allow to be kidnapped and treated as a servant by someone else when this son should be serving his father (Ex 4:22). It is a son to whom Yhwh continues to be committed when that experience is later repeated, and Yhwh recollects taking Israel as son (Jer 31:9). Or Israel is Yhwh's daughter, adopted when she was a foundling, abandoned at birth (Ezek 16:6). Israel is (literally) "the daughter my people" or "my daughter-people" or "my corporate daughter."[9] The expression is a term of endearment, suggesting the tender relationship of father to daughter as "my dear people." Or Israel is the wife Yhwh married at the time of the exodus and Sinai. For this image to work, this marriage is not the egalitarian relationship of the Song of Songs but the regular hierarchical relationship in which the husband is master.[10] Yhwh had then espoused the people *(bāʿalti)*, become its husband and lord (Jer 3:14; 31:32). She was then expected to stick to him *(dābaq,* e.g., Deut 11:22; 30:20; Josh 22:5) in the way that a man sticks to a woman (Gen 2:24).[11] As it did so, it would be for Yhwh "people, name, praise, and finery" (Jer 13:11; cf. Jer 33:9; Deut 26:19). Is the point that Israel's commitment to Yhwh would enhance Yhwh's reputation, praise and standing, or its own? It is hard to choose between these, and perhaps we do not need to do so.

Looking back (selectively) to the early days of this marriage, in the wilderness, Yhwh recalls how his bride followed him in committed fashion (Jer 2:2). The trouble is that his wife soon started going after other lovers (Jer 3:1). So he will throw her out. But that will not be the end. He will then renew the marriage and take her back (Is 54:5-6; Hos 2:14, 16 [MT 16, 18]).

---

[9]Not "the daughter of my people"; the construct is a genitive of definition (GKC 128f, k).

[10]Tikva Frymer-Kensky, *In the Wake of the Goddesses* (reprint, New York: Fawcett Columbine, 1993), p. 147.

[11]In a bizarre analogy, Israel was intended to stick as close to Yhwh as a man's underclothes stick to him (Jer 13:11). The verb is also used of Ruth's sticking with Naomi (Ruth 1:14), and the adjective *(dābāq)* is used of someone who sticks really close as a friend (Prov 18:24).

A Mark of Grace

Insofar as Israel is a family, the starting point of First Testament faith is ethnic. It is not exclusively so. A family can be open-walled or closed in on itself, can exist solely for the sake of its members or also for the sake of outsiders. Its kinship links can give it the strength to extend its arms to people outside it, in the manner of the First Testament's expectations of the hospitality and welcome to be given to the homeless. A family has clear boundaries, but it can be open to receiving people from outside. Indeed, arguably it does so every time one of its members gets married. Thus whereas in Western culture the family often seems an inherently self-focused, bounded entity, in the First Testament this is not so. Family points to a form of openness. The Israelite families take many other people with them when they leave Egypt, and members of a household who are not born Israelites may become so and take part in Passover (Ex 12:38, 43-49). As they reach Sinai, they welcome the Midianite Jethro to acknowledge what Yhwh has done for Israel and join in a family meal before Yhwh (Ex 18:1-12). On the edge of the promised land, they accept the Canaanite Rahab on the basis of her acknowledgment of Yhwh and her alignment with them. At the end of the judges period with the moral chaos that engulfs the Israelite family, it accepts the Moabite Ruth into family relationships in the household of Israel. In David's day, one of his warriors is a Hittite whose name, Uriah, suggests he is a worshiper of Yhwh. Conversely, a whole generation forfeits its family place in the promised land for declining to live its life on the basis of what Jethro and Rahab acknowledged, the story of what Yhwh had done in bringing Israel out of Egypt. It is possible to join a family or to be cut loose from its destiny.[12]

But the starting point of First Testament faith is ethnic. Why did God make it so, in choosing a family? Is Christian faith superior for not being ethnically based? (Or does claiming God's promise in Acts 2:39 "to you and your children" mean that there is also an ethnic streak, or at least a family-based streak, to Christian faith?) God could have chosen on the basis of some quality such as faith or piety or righteousness, or could have chosen people who were left-handed or people with curly hair (or white skin).

One result of God's choosing a family is that the chosen people is a corporate entity, a corporal entity and a group of people no better or worse than others. It is not the case that God's working via an ethnic group obscures the fact that God acts on the basis of grace.[13] On the contrary, it makes this fact clearer, and it makes clear that God is working sovereignly to achieve a purpose. If God's election depended on a human response of faith, people could escape or

---

[12]See further section 3.3 "An Open Community."

[13]As N. T. Wright seems to imply: see *The Climax of the Covenant* (Minneapolis: Fortress, 1992), p. 168; cf. Miroslav Volf, *Exclusion and Embrace* (Nashville: Abingdon, 1996), p. 45.

resign from that election. But through the choosing of a certain people, God's name is bound to the world in a way that cannot easily be dissolved.[14]

The point is made paradoxically in a passage that speaks of the people as "the household of Jacob," who "call themselves by the name of Israel," who "came forth from the waters of Judah" (Is 48:1). All these are honorable descriptions. They declare the community's relationship with its forebear Jacob-Israel to whose household they belong. It is as if they are a gargantuan extended family. Within that extended family, they belong in particular to the household of Judah—who became the senior son after Reuben, Simeon and Levi brought disfavor on themselves in different ways—and thus to the household to which David belonged. But there are implicit slights in the description. After all, who is Jacob but the person who swindled his brother, a person of down-to-earth, morally weak humanness? They call themselves by the name of Israel, but how appropriately do they do so? They came forth from the waters of Judah, but we know about Judah's sexual activity (Gen 38). Yhwh's association with this people shows that God acts on the basis of grace.

On the other hand, while it is birth that offers most people the possibility of belonging to Yhwh's people, their membership is made actual by their own confession.[15] If a man declines circumcision, he will be (or shall be) cut off from his people (Gen 17:14). The people's declaring that they will walk in Yhwh's ways is as essential to their relationship with Yhwh as Yhwh's choice of them (Deut 26:16-19). They have to make their confession that Yhwh is God, as Christians will later confess that Jesus is Lord (Josh 24). Their confession is both individual and communal. The people as a whole makes its decision, but the Torah shows how it has to be worked out in the lives of individuals. Individuals make their declaration, but they do not do so in an individualistic way, but rather as members of a people, as baptism makes us members of a people.

One People

In modern usage, the word *covenant* can suggest a mutual commitment in society, which for Israel would indicate "the bonding of decentralized social groups in a larger society of equals."[16] There is then "a dynamic of reciprocity" in covenant; it involves people freely taking on obligations that they commit themselves to keep, no matter how circumstances may change and indepen-

---

[14]Cf. Michael Wyschogrod, *The Body of Faith* (San Francisco: Harper, 1989), e.g., pp. xv, 65-68, 256; cf. R. Kendall Soulen, *The God of Israel and Christian Theology* (Minneapolis: Fortress, 1996, pp. 5-6.

[15]Contrast Wolfhart Pannenberg's formulation, *Systematic Theology*, 3 vols. (Grand Rapids, Mich.: Eerdmans/Edinburgh: T & T Clark, 1991-1998), 3:113. See further section 3.5 "Witness."

[16]Gottwald, *Tribes of Yahweh*, p. 692.

dent of what benefits or sacrifices they may turn out to entail.[17] Biblical covenants are not necessarily reciprocal, and this modern usage of covenant talk
does not correspond to the way the First Testament uses the word běrît. But the
First Testament does expect the people of Yhwh to be characterized by such
mutual commitment; it utilizes family images rather than covenant language
to make the point.

"In the West, theological ecclesiologies traditionally have their focal point
in the grounding of the authority of ministry in the church." The church exists
because the ministry exists.[18] As a family, the people of God is not defined by
its leadership. It has a hierarchical structure, and God may relate to the family
via its head; Yhwh is the God of Abraham, the God of Isaac and the God of Jacob. But the individual members of the family themselves relate to God, and
in origin there are no kings and no priests. The being of Israel is not defined by
its leadership. Power and authority are diffused rather than centralized.

The oneness of the people thus says something about status within this
community, something about agreement and disagreement, and something
about relationships between the generations. First, Israel itself began as a
twelve-clan unit in which all twelve clans equally belong. If some are more
equal than others (Ephraim, Judah), they cannot take their position for granted
(see, e.g., Ps 78; and cf. the argument of Rom 11:20-21).

Second, the oneness of the canon with the diversity of views it embodies suggests that the one people of God can hold in itself diversity of convictions without splitting into several different Israels. The authors of Chronicles, Qohelet
and Daniel belong to the same Israel, both the same spiritual Israel and the same
outward Israel. This is not to say that the people lacks bounds. Through much
of Israel's history, very many Israelites believed in a number of gods and worshiped Yhwh by means of images. The diversity of the canon does not embrace
such views. But within that framework, it has room for disagreement and argument that does not involve forming separate denominations.

Third, to the generation on the edge of the land, Moses declares, "Yhwh our
God sealed a covenant with us at Horeb, not with our ancestors . . . but with
us" (Deut 5:2-3; cf. Deut 4:9-14). He speaks to the people as if they were actually there at Sinai, notwithstanding his simultaneous recollection of the fact
that a key aspect of the current generation's identity is that they were *not*
among the Sinai generation whom God has required to die out. To make the

---

[17]Paul D. Hanson, "Covenant and Politics," in *Constituting the Community*, ed. John T. Strong
and Steven S. Tuell (Winona Lake, Ind.: Eisenbrauns, 2005), pp. 205-33; see p. 206. He is taking up the emphasis on covenant in Richard Niebuhr, "The Idea of Covenant and American
Democracy," *Church History* 23 (1954): 126-35.

[18]Jürgen Moltmann, *History and the Triune God* (London: SCM Press, 1991), p. 63.

point even more vividly and paradoxically, Moses urges his audience to recognize that it is they, not their children, who experienced the exodus and the journey to the edge of the land (Deut 11:2-7). In literal terms, he is addressing the children, but he urges them to see themselves as their parents. Conversely, he declares, "not with you alone am I sealing this sworn covenant, but both with you who are standing here with us today before Yhwh our God and those who are not here with us today" (Deut 29:14-15). The generations of the exodus and Sinai, of the plains of Moab and the entry into the land, and of ongoing life in Canaan are all one people.

A Place to Learn

As a family, Israel is a locus of teaching and learning. Deuteronomy emphasizes the individual family as the place where the story of what God has done is passed down from one generation to another. Much of Proverbs, which also constitutes the point of departure for the teaching in Qohelet and Job, represents insight that has accumulated and proved itself in the context of family life over the generations, and it commends itself as the insight passed on by a father and mother to their children (e.g., Prov 6:20; 15:20). People are wise to trust in this human teaching because it is "the proverbs of Solomon" or "the proverbs of Solomon which the men of Hezekiah, king of Judah, transcribed" or "the words of Lemuel . . . with which his mother admonished him" (Prov 1:1; 25:1; 31:1). These headings reflect that process of the passing on of wisdom from one generation to another. The father who speaks in Proverbs 4:1-9 claims to have received his wisdom from his father, and he now passes it on to his son. We learn from our own experience, but we can economize by learning from our parents and our culture with its tradition. We are thereby rescued from being confined not only to our individual perspectives and experience but to those of our own generation with its limitations, as Bildad argues (Job 8:8-10).

The fact that this insight is not presented as coming from God is not to imply that it represents "mere" human wisdom, any more than the words of the prophets dropped from heaven without being mediated through a human personality. It represents the best human wisdom, tested by experience and by time, accepted by the community and invested with the authority of Scripture. While God communicates through prophets in a way that (in theory or in principle) leaves no doubt that it is God who is doing the communicating, God also communicates in the form of teaching that is overtly more human. "It is Yhwh who gives wisdom" (Prov 2:6), but the authors of sayings do not feel that these were put onto their lips in the way that prophets may reckon happens with their oracles. Yhwh gives wisdom in the sense that Yhwh makes someone a person who can see, who reveres Yhwh, who has the kind of character that will see truth and live by it. And the composer thus generates sayings that are as

true and powerful as the words that come from a prophet's lips, so that it is as
if they came from Yhwh's lips as a prophet's words do. Proverbs 2:6 goes on,
"from his mouth come acknowledgment and discernment."[19] Divine dictation
does provide an analogy for the truth expressed in human insight. One accepts
instruction from Yhwh's mouth, puts Yhwh's words in one's mind (Job 22:22).
The point can also be expressed in terms of the activity of the human spirit and
that of the divine spirit. "Yes, it is the spirit in a person, it is the breath of Shaddai that gives them insight" (Job 32:8).[20] Wisdom is "advice," *ʿēṣâ* (e.g., Prov
1:25, 30), but this does not mean it is merely expression of opinion given on a
take-it-or-leave-it basis.[21] This is the kind of *ʿēṣâ* that stands and compels (cf.
Is 46:10). It is a clearly and decisively formulated declaration of how things
will be, to be ignored at one's peril.

Thus to describe wisdom as human is not to imply that it is merely subjective. Wisdom addresses us and urges us to pay attention to it (Prov 8:1-11). It
stands over against us. (True) understanding stands over against our own (so-
called) understanding (*bînâ*, Prov 8:1; 3:5). In urging, "my son, keep my words,
. . . keep my commands and live, my teaching as the apple of your eye, tie them
on your fingers, write them on the tablet of your mind" (Prov 7:1-3), a father
or mother speaks like Yhwh addressing the people through Moses. Or perhaps
it is the other way round and Moses speaks like a parent. Either way, there is
a similarity between the form and the content of the parents' wisdom and
those of Moses' words at Sinai and in Moab. The "ten commandments" were
actually ten "words" (e.g., Ex 20:1; 34:28), though of course they are also "commands" (e.g., Deut 5:10, 29, 31 [MT 26, 28]). They are Moses' "teaching" (e.g.,
Josh 8:31-32). They are to be "kept" (e.g., Deut 5:1, 32 [MT 29]). The promise of
life attaches to the keeping of Moses' teaching (e.g., Deut 4:1; 30:16). The commands are to be tied to people's hands and put on their minds, taught to people's children and talked about at home and attached to the doorposts of the
family's home (cf. Deut 6:8; 11:18). They are to be written on tablets, though in
the Torah these were stone tablets. Wisdom and Torah stand alongside each
other. One is not intrinsically subordinate to the other, so that the collapse of
one would imperil the other.

A Place of Challenge

The father and mother in Proverbs 1—9 know that for good and ill their son

---

[19]It may be that *mippeh* can mean "by the command" (so JPSV), but it commonly refers to actual words coming "from the mouth" of someone (e.g., Ezra 1:1; Jer 36:4; Zech 8:9).

[20]Cf. Michael V. Fox, *Proverbs 1—9*, AB (New York: Doubleday, 2000), p.113, though he draws
different inferences.

[21]Cf. William McKane, *Proverbs* (London: SCM Press, 1970), p. 304.

faces the blandishments of the opposite sex, and they reflect this in the content and the form of their teaching. They know that Ms. Stupidity sits in the door of her house on the heights of the town inviting in the naive, the people without sense, and promising them something sweet and tasty (Prov 9:13-18). But accepting her invitation means not life but death. Her house is the entrance to Sheol. The implicit portrayal of her as a whore suggests the nature of the non-wisdom that seeks to beguile young men. So father and mother imagine the alternative invitation of Ms. Wisdom, the positive seductress, which compares and contrasts with that. Ms. Wisdom's invitation actually comes first (Prov 9:1-6; cf. Prov 4:5-9), suggesting she has the priority, even epistemologically; Ms. Stupidity's invitation is a deceitful imitation of Ms. Wisdom's.

Ms. Wisdom also speaks like a goddess, of the kind that Israelites were familiar with in surrounding cultures; indeed, both the First Testament and archeological discoveries make clear how through much of Israel's history its people believed there were goddesses and other gods alongside Yhwh. Proverbs thus pictures Yhwh as indeed having a consort (or a daughter, Prov 8:22-31 may rather hint) who shares Yhwh's work in the world. Perhaps both men and women might like the idea of imagining this feminine figure speaking to them.[22] She is an aggressive woman, like prophets such as Miriam or Deborah or Huldah, not a demure and submissive wife (if there were any in Israel). She issues her invitation in the manner of goddesses such as Ishtar and Anat, though their invitations also turn out to lead to death rather than life.[23]

Ms. Wisdom speaks like a prophet standing at the street corner and urging people to listen to her message (e.g., Prov 8). She thus speaks like God. Speaking as God's representatives, prophets say "I" and they mean "God." Ms. Wisdom does that to even greater effect, warning people of the disastrous consequences that will follow from refusing to heed her (Prov 1:24-30). Like Yhwh, she speaks of calling and receiving no response (cf. Is 50:2; 65:1-2, 12; 66:4) and of laughing mockingly at people (Ps 2:4). When she explains that this reflects the fact that people have rejected reverence for Yhwh in refusing her advice, she sets herself in even closer relationship with Yhwh. Insight is indeed revealed from heaven as well as acquired by observation on earth and attentiveness to teaching.[24]

Deuteronomy also takes up the image of family as a basis for attitudes to other members of the community. Whatever hard-headed stance Israelites take to foreigners, they are not to use an Israelite's need as an occasion to im-

---

[22]See section 2.2 "Yhwh's Gender."

[23]See Roland E. Murphy, *Proverbs*, WBC (Nashville: Thomas Nelson, 1998), p. 59.

[24]Cf. Tomáš Frydrych, *Living Under the Sun*, VTSup 110 (Leiden/Boston: Brill, 2002), pp. 57-66.

prove their own financial position, because this is "your brother." They are not
to harden their hearts against such a brother but to lend to him generously. Being family means treating one another with a measure of understanding and
generosity when people get into economic difficulty (Deut 15:1-11). The same
consideration puts constraints on the appointment and behavior of kings
(Deut 17:14-20). They are to be appointed from within the family and are to be
wary of starting to elevate themselves above their brothers.

3.2 Yhwh's Covenant People

If 'am implies a kin relationship in a group, referring to Israel as Yhwh's people
could imply a natural familial relationship between Yhwh and Israel. In fact the
First Testament rather affirms that the bond between Yhwh and Israel is not one
inherent in nature but one Yhwh deliberately brought into being. This is an aspect
of the significance of calling the relationship a covenant. As Israel is holy because
the Holy One enters into an association with it, so another basis for its being one
people—rather than the fact that its members manage to stay together—is the fact
that there is one God who gathers this people.[25] But the covenant also makes demands on Israel; it begins with Yhwh's initiative but requires Israel's response.
The Torah is what gives content to the nature of that response.

A Commitment on Yhwh's Part

A covenant is a solemnly sealed pledge made by one party to another in a particular context.[26] It thus involves a commitment in a relationship, as opposed
to a mere acquaintance without obligation. As solemnly sealed, the commitment is something the person making the pledge thinks about and affirms
with some formal procedure; there will be no getting out of it.[27] And it comes
into being historically, as opposed to being a natural commitment or relationship.[28] "'Covenant' is the central expression of the distinctive faith of Israel as

---

[25]Cf. Jürgen Moltmann's comments on the creedal declaration of belief in one church, in *The
Church in the Power of the Spirit* (London: SCM Press, 1977), p. 338.

[26]On the sealing of a covenant at Sinai, see *OTT* 1:369-78.

[27]According to Gordon P. Hugenberger, a "widespread scholarly consensus" agrees that an
actual oath is indispensable to a covenant. He defines an oath as a "solemn declaration or
enactment which invokes the deity to act against the one who would be false to an attendant
commitment or affirmation." But then he grants that an oath may be simply a "solemn positive declaration" of one's commitment, uttered before God, in which any self-malediction
is purely implicit (*Marriage as a Covenant*, VTSup 52 [Leiden/New York: Brill, 1994], pp. 182,
193, 215).

[28]See Theodorus C. Vriezen, *An Outline of Old Testament Theology* (reprint, Oxford: Blackwell,
1962), pp. 140-41 (2nd ed., Oxford: Blackwell/Newton, Mass.: Branford, 1970, pp. 167-68);
cf. Frank M. Cross, *From Epic to Canon* (Baltimore/London: Johns Hopkins University Press,
1998), pp. 3-21.

'the people of Yahweh,' children of God by adoption and free decision rather than by nature or necessity."[29] There is no covenant between parents and children or between other members of a family or kinship group; such a commitment is inherent in the existence of these relationships. Parents do not have to covenant to look after their small children, nor do grown-up children have to covenant to look after their parents, notwithstanding whether they get anything out of it. That is built in to being parents and children. Covenant comes to be involved when people extend a commitment beyond such natural groupings, as happens when two people get married, or when a kinship group extends its membership to people who were not born within it, or when two nations enter into a covenant or treaty relationship. Covenant relationships can thus be quite varied. They may involve two people coming to an egalitarian mutual commitment, as in Western marriage and as in some relationships in the First Testament (e.g., between Abraham and Abimelech, and between Jacob and Laban; Gen 21:27; 31:44). But there is nothing inherently egalitarian or mutual about covenants. They can be hierarchical, and they can be one-sided.

So the covenant relationship between Yhwh and Israel is not a "natural" relationship, one built into creation. Walther Eichrodt declares that covenant is where "the relationship with God has the character of a relationship of grace, that is to say, it is founded on a primal act in history, maintained on definite conditions and protected by a powerful divine Guardian," though he then adds that the First Testament can be talking about such a relationship whether or not it uses the word *bĕrît*, the word most often translated "covenant."[30] Thus the declaration "I will be your God and you will be my people" (or the reverse) can be described as "a statement of the basic covenant relationship"[31] even if the word *bĕrît* does not appear in the context (e.g., Jer 7:23; 24:7; 30:22).[32] It would be in this sense that one could say that "the idea of the Covenant dominates the whole OT"[33] even though in the narrower sense one could also say

---

[29]Ernest W. Nicholson, *God and His People* (Oxford/New York: Oxford University Press, 1986), p. viii.

[30]Walther Eichrodt, *Theology of the Old Testament*, 2 vols. (London: SCM Press, 1961, 1967), 1:36-37. Rolf Rendtorff also notes that we should not confine our understanding of covenant to passages where *bĕrît* occurs; see *The Covenant Formula* (Edinburgh: T & T Clark, 1998).

[31]Peter R. Ackroyd, *Exile and Restoration* (London: SCM Press, 1968), p. 59.

[32]The history of the concept of covenant in Israel is controverted, and I assume it would be unwise to base theological statements on a position about that question; on which see Nicholson, *God and His People*; more recently, Scott Hahn, "Covenant in the Old and New Testaments," *Currents in Biblical Research* 3 (2005): 263-92; also Norbert Lohfink, "The Concept of 'Covenant' in Biblical Theology," in *The God of Israel and the Nations*, by Norbert Lohfink and Erich Zenger (Collegeville, Minn.: Liturgical Press, 2000), pp. 11-32.

[33]George A. F. Knight, *A Christian Theology of the Old Testament* (London: SCM Press, 1959), p. 218.

that "covenant consciousness did not dominate the preoccupations of the religious leaders of Israel."[34]

Conversely, the First Testament often uses the word *bĕrît* in a way that does not correspond to Eichrodt's definition of covenant; *bĕrît* can also refer to treaties and contracts, and thus covers bonds with a relational focus, a legal one or a political one. All this opens up a problem: it is hard to control discussion of covenant, which has been an unfocused notion in the history of theology (and politics). It is impossible to argue that there can be only one way of defining covenant, though Eichrodt's approach helps us see why explicit covenant talk is absent from Genesis 1—2. There was a "natural" mutual commitment implicit in God's creation of humanity, one that did not require to be sealed by a covenant. But when that collapsed through humanity's turning from God and God's punishment of the world, it became appropriate for God to initiate a covenant relationship with humanity, as God does with Noah and his descendants.

In this context, covenant is a one-sided affair. It suggests making a promise or undertaking an obligation. So it is with God's original covenant with Abraham in Genesis 15. Further, it is an ineluctably hierarchical relationship. Yhwh's covenant with Noah and his family, with Abraham and his descendants, and with Moses and his people is "my covenant" (e.g., Gen 6:18; 17:2; Ex 19:5). This relationship is not one that issues from negotiation between two equal parties.

A Commitment on Israel's Part

But God's covenant with Noah and his family requires them to enter the ark, and God's covenant with Noah and the rest of humanity after the flood follows on the requirements detailed in Genesis 9. While God's initial covenant with Abraham in Genesis 15 states no preconditions and carries no obligations, the covenant in Genesis 17 follows on the requirement that Abraham walk before God and live wholly for God, and it leads into the requirement of circumcision for males, whose neglect will mean being cut off from his kin. Then as a result of the meeting at Sinai, Israel becomes a "people committed to me [*hăsîday*], who sealed a covenant with me over sacrifice" (Ps 50:5). That is the definition of Israel. Once again, the covenant is Yhwh's; it comes into being on Yhwh's initiative. But it requires their responsive commitment, which they made through the solemn rite of sacrifice. Literally they "cut" this covenant. The implications may be spelled out a little by Genesis 15:7-21, so that

---

[34]Samuel Terrien, *The Elusive Presence* (San Francisco: Harper, 1978), p. 24. See also the critique in Claus Westermann, *Elements of Old Testament Theology* (Atlanta, Ga.: John Knox Press, 1982), pp. 42-45.

the cutting up of an animal for sacrifice implies a self-curse: May this happen to me if I go back on my commitment.

Exodus 19:3-6 makes the point in a further way. It begins by recalling what Yhwh did to Egypt and how Israel got where it is. Yhwh has a right to expect Israel's obedience and to impose covenant obligations because of that exercise of authority and power. Perhaps Yhwh also implies that rescuing Israel from Egypt was an act of compassion, but the emphasis lies on the exercise of power to take hold of Israel as a people. (Further, seeing "what I did to Egypt" conveys warning as well as encouragement: look what happened to a people that resisted Yhwh.)

The first of the Ten Words makes the same point. "I am Yhwh your God, who brought you out from the land of Egypt, from the household of slaves. You are to have no other gods besides me" (Ex 20:2-3). Yhwh has earned the right to Israel's exclusive allegiance, though the reference to "the household of slaves" again hints at the compassion that Yhwh's act of sovereignty also implied. Exodus 20:2 has thus been called a "formula of grace,"[35] but it is even more explicitly a formula of authority. Tellingly, at this point Walther Zimmerli closes his chapter on "The Gifts Bestowed by Yahweh" and opens a new chapter on "Yahweh's Commandment."[36] In Egypt, one conforms to world order; in Israel, to Yhwh.[37]

This covenant of Yhwh's Israel is now challenged to keep or guard (šāmar) by committing itself to doing what Yhwh says. To say that Israel is "required" to keep it might be too strong, but "invited" would be too weak. The covenant is like the noncovenantal relationship between parents and their grown-up children within the same extended family, the same household and the same family business. In other words, covenant brings into being just as solid and firm a commitment as the one that naturally obtains in families (in theory!); it is a way of extending family-type commitments to the realm outside the family.

Or the covenant is like the treaty relationship between a king and his subjects, which Hebrew also calls a běrît. When the Assyrian king "offers" a smaller nation a covenant relationship, the smaller nation can in theory say "Thanks, but no thanks," but the choice is not an equal one. The opportunity to say yes or no is really an opportunity to say yes. So it is when Yhwh offers Israel the opportunity to agree to listen to Yhwh's voice and keep Yhwh's covenant. Yhwh is like an emperor and Israel is like a junior power within Yhwh's empire. It is Yhwh who determines the terms of this covenant. Israel does not

---

[35]So A. Jepsen, "Beiträge zur Auslegung und Geschichte des Dekalogs," *ZAW* 79 (1967): 277-304.
[36]Walther Zimmerli, *Old Testament Theology in Outline* (Atlanta, Ga.: John Knox Press/Edinburgh: T & T Clark, 1978), p. 109.
[37]Preuss, *OT Theology*, 1:88.

get the opportunity to listen to its terms and think about whether to make some counterproposals.

Awareness of political treaties may have influenced the working out of the covenant in some periods of Israel's history. Although we should be wary of exaggerating the importance of this factor in the development of covenant thinking,[38] the political treaty with its stress on the sovereign might of the senior partner and the obligation it imposes on the junior partner offers an illuminating model for understanding Yhwh's relationship with Israel. Deuteronomy as a whole has been called a kind of countertreaty: Israel is under obligation to obey Yhwh, not the Assyrian king.[39] The fundamental covenant commitment requires love of God with one's entire being and energy, a loyalty to Yhwh that excludes reliance on other peoples, and thus may exclude other covenants (2 Chron 16:1-12), of course including covenants with other deities.

Divine Commitment and Human Obligation

A king is his people's shepherd and they are his flock. As Yhwh's people, Israel is Yhwh's flock, shepherded and provided for by Yhwh (Mic 7:14). Its shepherd pastures it, rests it, leads it, waters it, refreshes it, protects it and reassures it (Ps 23; 95:7). But it has to follow its shepherd. The obligations that the covenant places on Israel are worked out systematically in connection with the exodus. Their significance is reaffirmed by the prophets in a context where Israel is perhaps inclined to assume (like its neighbors) that its relationship with Yhwh is intrinsic and ineluctably secure. In that context, the idea of covenant emphasizes that this relationship, which emerges from divine choice, not necessity, requires that Israel make a responsive choice of self-commitment to Yhwh. Indeed, in some contexts covenant could be primarily an undertaking on Israel's part. It was quite possible for Israel to take the initiative in committing itself to Yhwh in covenant, specifically when it wished to restore its commitment to Yhwh's covenant after a period of apostasy (2 Chron 23:16; 34:29-33). The Israelites then become once again the committed ones (Ps 50:5).

So the covenant involves both a "divine commitment" and a "human obligation."[40] "Covenant is utterly giving and utterly demanding."[41] The "covenant formula," "I will be God for you and you will be a people for me," could put the emphasis on either aspect or equally on both.[42] While the cov-

---

[38]See Nicholson, *God and His People*, pp. 56-82.

[39]Preuss, *OT Theology*, 1:88, 92.

[40]See David Noel Freedman, "Divine Commitment and Human Obligation," *Int* 18 (1964): 419-31.

[41]Walter Brueggemann, *Theology of the Old Testament* (Minneapolis: Fortress, 1997), p. 419.

[42]See Rendtorff, *Covenant Formula*.

enant relationship in the First Testament was hierarchical and was in origin primarily an undertaking on God's part, it became a more mutual commitment, a covenant between Yhwh and Israel, Israel and Yhwh. T. C. Vriezen can therefore suggest that covenant means "something like 'bond of communion,'" even though unilateral in origin, as Yhwh is the one who makes the covenant. The covenant brought God and the people "into a communion, originating with God, in which Israel was bound to Him completely and made dependent on Him," as well as obliging Israel to do God's will.[43] The essence of Jewish religion is "the *awareness of God's interest in man*, the awareness of a *covenant*, of a responsibility that lies on Him as well as on us, . . . of the *reciprocity* of God and man, of man's *togetherness* with Him who abides in eternal otherness."[44]

The giving of the Torah is thus integral to the making of the covenant.[45] The Torah is a gift from God to identify Israel as Yhwh's, the means of bringing Yhwh's election to full realization. "It is the proclamation of the Decalogue over her which puts Israel's election into effect." The covenant being a two-sided relationship, "the proclamation of the divine will for justice is like a net thrown over Israel: it is the completion of her conveyance to Jahweh." The giving of these commands is thus "a saving event of the first rank." Through this gift Israel is "offered the saving gift of life."[46] The "law," then, is not a burden but a privilege, something one can imagine other peoples being jealous of (Deut 4:6-8). The extraordinary nature of its requirements lies in how *ṣaddîq* the requirements are; that is, they constitute expressions of Yhwh's faithfulness in doing the right thing by Israel. They are thus a cause of great joy rather than of fear to Israel (cf. Ps 119).[47] They are the secret to life. Of course you had to decide to obey them in order to have that life. If you made the opposite choice, you were choosing the curse, choosing death. Thus blessing is also made conditional on obedience (e.g., Deut 6:18; 7:12; 8:1; 11:8-9; 16:20; 24:18). Israel on the edge of the promised land, a generation after Sinai, or in whatever century Deuteronomy was written, still stands in a "today" located between election and salvation, still on the road to receiving Yhwh's blessing, and still needing to commit itself to obedience if it is to receive it.[48]

---

[43]Vriezen, *Outline of OT Theology*, pp. 141, 142 (2nd ed., pp. 168, 169). The second quotation is italicized in the original.

[44]Abraham J. Heschel, *Man Is Not Alone* (New York: Farrar, 1951), pp. 241-42.

[45]On this feature of the Sinai narrative, see *OTT* 1:378-85.

[46]Gerhard von Rad, *Old Testament Theology*, 2 vols. (Edinburgh: Oliver & Boyd/New York: Harper, 1962, 1965), 1:192-94.

[47]Cf. ibid., 1:196.

[48]Ibid., 1:230-31.

The Fragility of the Covenant

The covenant means that Israel's security depends originally on Yhwh's sovereignty and commitment and not on Israel's fickleness, but that Israel's commitment is an absolutely necessary corollary of Yhwh's commitment to Israel. It is not exactly that Yhwh's commitment to Israel is conditional on Israel's commitment. Rather, it demands it. As the one who brought the people out of Egypt, Yhwh requires that they "really listen to my voice and keep my covenant" (Ex 19:5). "Really listen" represents the Hebrew idiom whereby a verb is emphasized by adding its infinitive to its finite verb: "in listening you listen." And *šāmaʿ* can as easily be translated "obey"; hence "if you really obey my voice" (cf. NRSV). Listening and obeying are the way Israel will respond to what Yhwh has done and keep Yhwh's covenant. The implication is not that the covenant will come into effect only when the people is obedient. A covenant is not a contract. "The situation is rather the reverse. The covenant is made, and with it Israel receives the revelation of the commandments."[49] Thus the logic is, "You have become Yhwh's people, so attend to the voice of Yhwh your God and keep his commands" (Deut 27:9-10). The argument is like that in Romans 6: we do not give ourselves to God as servants of righteousness because otherwise we would lose the gift of eternal life, but because that was the object of Christ's dying and rising for us.

But if Israel does not meet the expectations of the covenant, it does imperil its position. It can make God expostulate, "You are not my people and I will not be yours" (Hos 1:9). The declaration attached to the name of Gomer's third child comes as the climax to a series of such negative assertions. Yhwh will bring an end to the dynasty in Ephraim. Yhwh will no more have compassion on the people. Worst of all, Yhwh will simply terminate the relationship—indeed, hereby does so. In due course Yhwh will hint at the more balanced formulation, "You are my people and I am your God" (cf. Hos 2:23 [MT 25]), that came to be an expression of the covenantal relationship between the two parties that was traced back to Sinai (Jer 11:3-4). Here Yhwh simply declares the intention not to be yours, not to be "for you" *(lākem)*. The prophet's not completing the formulation suggests a disparity between the stances of the two parties. It is not that they simultaneously make an agreement to split. It is that the Israelites have already split; they are already not Yhwh's people. They have let themselves be the people of the "Master," Baal, as well as Yhwh, and therefore instead of Yhwh. In response to that, Yhwh declares the intention not to be theirs in the future (the first clause is a noun clause—there is no "are"; the second is a verbal clause). Yhwh will not be there for Israel, will not be on Is-

---

[49]Ibid., 1:194; cf. Rolf Rendtorff, *The Canonical Hebrew Bible* (Leiden: Deo, 2005), p. 481.

rael's side (cf. Gen 31:42; Ps 124:1-2). The words thus undergird the declaration that calamity will come for Israel in Jezreel and that Yhwh will no longer have compassion. Yhwh is against the people rather than for them. The Yhwh who at Horeb told Moses "I will be with you" and "I will be what I will be," and bade him tell the people that "I will be" had sent him (Ex 3:11-14), now says, "I will not be, for you."

In the context of exile where Israel's failure has imperiled the covenant relationship, the emphasis of the Abraham covenant would remind Israel that its relationship with God originally rested on divine choice and that this failure of theirs need not mean its termination. The hierarchical nature of the covenant means that Israel's relationship with Yhwh rests on the immense security of its having come into being because of Yhwh's sovereignty. It does not rest on Yhwh's sentiment nor on the fickleness of Israel's choice of Yhwh. It is thus not so surprising that after a while Yhwh commissions messengers with the words "Comfort, comfort my people, says your God" (Is 40:1). Hosea's threat is reversed.

Taught by God

Like the family relationship, the covenant works because Israel is addressed by God and about God. It is such address that makes Israel's covenant response possible. Thus the account of the covenant in Exodus to Deuteronomy details Yhwh's expectations; this teaching confronts the community as something detailed by God in connection with setting up a relationship with Israel. "There is . . . no voice more central to Judaism than the voice heard on Mount Sinai. . . . Ultimately, the issue is whether God is or is not king. . . . Mount Sinai is the intersection of love and law, of gift and demand, the link between a past together and a future together."[50]

The Torah is then a possession (môrāšâ) of the congregation of Israel (Deut 33:4), like the land that the people as a whole possessed or the allocation of land held by a clan or family; it is something the individual acquires as a possession (the denominative nāḥal), again like the land (Ps 119:111). It belongs to the entire community, and the entire community is responsible for letting its life be shaped by it, in ways to be encouraged by various provisions in Deuteronomy (e.g., Deut 6:1-3, 20-23; 31:10-13).[51] Psalm 119 expresses to the Torah attitudes that are elsewhere expressed to God, suggesting that the Torah mediates God. One delights in it, clings to it, turns to it, reaches out to it (Ps 119:24, 31, 45, 48). This does not mean the Torah replaces God or comes be-

---

[50]Jon D. Levenson, *Sinai and Zion* (Minneapolis: Winston, 1985), p. 86.

[51]Moshe Greenberg, *Studies in the Bible and Jewish Thought* (Philadelphia: Jewish Publication Society, 1995), pp. 11-20.

tween people and God. Rather it links people and God. "The closeness to God through preoccupation with Torah is regarded by the psalmist as the most precious experience he can have."[52]

Psalm 19:7-11 [MT 8-12] likewise enthuses over Yhwh's word as key to the development of character. Do we wish to be people of integrity, reliability, uprightness, cleanness, purity and truthfulness? We learn the way from the teaching, declarations about expectations, charges, commands, reverence and decisions that come from Yhwh. They offer life, insight, joy and light in the eyes, and they stand firm and faithful. Paradoxically, they do that not least by giving us warnings to heed, boundaries to observe. Yhwh's words or sayings take the form of teaching (*tôrâ*), declarations ('*ēdâ*, '*ēdût*), charges (*piqqûd*), statutes (*ḥuqqâ*), commands (*ṣiwwâ*), rulings (*mišpāṭ*) and a way (*derek*). Particular status attaches in this connection to the "Ten Words" that open Yhwh's words at Sinai. It is noteworthy that this opening summary of religious and moral principles on which the people's life is founded[53] are described simply as "words," as are the promises on which Israel's life is also founded (see the references to trusting God's word in Ps 119). In these demands and in those promises Yhwh indeed *addresses* Israel, and these are two chief forms in which God's word comes.

Yhwh's instructions at Sinai are classically described as *tôrâ*. The word is conventionally translated "law," but this is usually inappropriate. The First Testament has several words for law, such as *ḥôq*, and such words do appear in connection with the covenant (e.g., Deut 4). There is a sense in which the covenant is a quasi-legal document, but *tôrâ* itself is not essentially a legal word. We have seen that "teaching" is transmitted by parents to children and by tutors to pupils (e.g., Prov 3:1), and *the* Torah is an expression of wisdom, the best wisdom there is. Much of the Torah is essentially similar to the content of the family insight expressed in Proverbs and/or other people's custom and law. It issues from human reflection, argument and experience. But paradoxically, the First Testament presents much of it as divine revelation, as dictated by Yhwh. It bears not only God's stamp of approval but God's stamp of authority. And even though *tôrâ* is not merely imperatival, as the whole Pentateuch is *tôrâ* (the story as well as the instruction), the word *tôrâ* has imperatival implications. Whether Israel heeds this teaching is not optional. Even though it is not transmitted by people with a place in a legal framework, teaching involves instruction, telling people what they should do.

---

[52]Ibid., p. 22.
[53]Cf. Preuss, *Old Testament Theology*, 1:89.

It Stands Written

The teaching in the Torah is in part written by God (in Exodus, though it is not clear whether any of that survived events at Sinai),[54] in part dictated by God on Sinai (in Exodus), in part dictated at the meeting tent (esp. in Leviticus), in part declaimed by Moses (esp. in Deuteronomy), in part written down by Moses (Deut 31:9, 19, 22).[55] (It is never transmitted or formulated by the king, in the manner of Hammurabi.) Dictation emphasizes the divine origin of the teaching, while exposition by Moses complements that in recognizing the way it is expounded in human words so as to speak to human beings afresh in each new generation. For such later generations, writing would suggest the highest degree of assured divine origin. This would fit with the actual status of the Ten Words (originally written by Yhwh) in the Jewish and Christian communities. And of course, in the form in which Israel eventually held on to it and lived by it, the Torah as a whole stands written.

Thus Yhwh's teaching, for the most part, started as the gift of Yhwh's voice or of Moses' voice, but in due course became the gift of someone's writing that is thus available for reading to the people as a means of shaping their lives in obedience to Yhwh (Deut 31:9-13). People do not have to climb into the heavens or sail across the sea to discover what Moses commanded; it is available for reading. Nor does God's revelation involve impenetrable mysteries; God's truth can be understood by ordinary people. "No, the word is very near you, in your mouth, in your mind, to do it" (Deut 30:11-14). It is on their lips as they read it out, and thus in their minds and open to being put into practice. But given Moses' expectation that the people will not maintain their commitment to Yhwh, the written form of the teaching is placed by the covenant chest as a witness against the people, and the song that follows is likewise available "to testify before them as a witness" by virtue of its ongoing use by the people (Deut 31:21, 26).

Jewish and Christian thinking came to see the whole of the Torah, the Prophets and the Writings as the deposit of God's communication or revela-

---

[54]Moses smashed the two stones that Yhwh originally inscribed, and there is no account of Yhwh actually inscribing some more, or what was on them if Yhwh did.

[55]What is "this teaching" (Deut 31:9)? The expression first comes in the introduction to Moses' address, and it recurs later, while the instructions about kingship presuppose the existence of a written version of "this teaching" (Deut 1:5; 4:8; 17:18-19), and Deut 28:58, 61; 29:21 [MT 20]; 30:10; 31:24 refer to this teaching being written down, explicitly or implicitly on a scroll. These passages would suggest that "this teaching" is something like Deut 1—30. On the other hand, Deut 27:3, 8 speak of "this teaching" being inscribed on stones, like the Ten Words (cf. Josh 8:32), and it seems unlikely that this refers to such a long document and more likely that it refers to something such as Deut 27—28 (as Josh 8:34 might imply), or to the Ten Words. Moses' own writing might refer to the shorter or the longer document.

tion or inspiration. The First Testament itself does not see its narratives (or psalmody or wisdom writing) as divinely inspired; it does not speak in terms of their being "the word of Yhwh," like the message of a prophet. In the framework of Christian doctrinal thinking, to say that would seem to undermine the authority of the narratives, but in the framework of First Testament thinking, this is not so. The narratives have supremely important and normative status as the true story of God's dealings with Israel. They have supreme authority. Their designation as "holy Scripture" implies the conviction that they have that status by God's will. These narratives came into being by human initiative, but they came to be holy. Human action sanctified them, but so did divine action, as human action but also divine action sanctified the temple. Human action took the initiative; divine action responded to it. The narratives have holy status, though without their being brought into being by God in the direct manner of the words of the Prophets, as the temple (brought into being by divine initiative and human response) contrasts with the wilderness dwelling (brought into being by divine initiative and human response). The narratives are not the results of divine communication but of true human witness and reflection and divine sanctification,[56] and they then have supreme authority for the community because they tell the true and divinely sanctified story of God's dealings with Israel. It is this story that shares with the words of God and the words of Moses the authority definitively to shape the faith and life of Israel.

3.3 Yhwh's Chosen

As a family and as a covenant people, Israel is Yhwh's chosen and Yhwh's beloved. It is Yhwh's possession and Yhwh's treasure, separate and distinct from the rest of the world. It is chosen for its own sake, but also for Yhwh's sake, and for the world's sake because Yhwh's intention is to reach out to the whole world through Israel.

Chosen

"Yhwh your God chose you" (Deut 7:6; cf., e.g., Deut 14:2; 1 Kings 3:8; Ps 33:12; 135:4; Is 41:8-9; 44:1; Ezek 20:5). In Christian thinking the notion of God's choice will come to apply to individuals, but in the First Testament Yhwh's choice centers on a people. The New Testament uses the term God's *chosen* specifically as a description of Christ (e.g., Lk 9:35), *the* individual on whose election all other election will then turn out theologically to depend, as well as of the church as coming to share in Israel's election.

---

[56]I owe the notion of the sanctification of Scripture to John Webster, *Holy Scripture* (Cambridge/New York: Cambridge University Press, 2003), pp. 17-30 (and the reference to this volume to Dan Reid), though I think I have reworked it.

Explicit talk in terms of choosing *(bāḥar)* is not an early feature of First Testament faith, whether one thinks historically or narratively, but is a fruit of Israel's reflection on Yhwh's dealings with it. In Genesis 18:19 Yhwh does speak of "acknowledging" Abraham *(yādaʿ*; EVV use the verb "choose"), and Amos 3:2 applies that word to Israel as a people, but the actual verb "choose" with Israel as object first appears in Deuteronomy, while in the Prophets it is first prominent in Isaiah 40—55.[57] Historically, talk about God's choice of special individuals such as the Davidic king may have preceded talk of God's choice of the people; the latter expression then "democratizes" the idea.[58] The First Testament also talks of Yhwh's choice of Jerusalem and of the land of Israel, though Yhwh is never "the God of Israel" in the sense of the God of this land; the Assyrians' use of such a term (2 Kings 17:26-27) proves the rule. While the land is called after Yhwh (it is Yhwh's possession), Yhwh is not called after the land.[59]

No, Yhwh is "the God of Israel" in the sense of the God of that people, "my/your/his/their God." And despite their wrongdoing, only if the sun could fall from the sky could Israel's offspring cease from being a nation or could Yhwh finally reject Israel's offspring (Jer 31:35-37). The other little nations of Israel's day did disappear from the face of the earth. There are no peoples who identify with the Canaanites, the Amorites, the Jebusites, the Ammonites, the Moabites, the Edomites and so on. The forces of history in Israel's day would surely suggest that Israel could go the same way. Could it survive its scattering through the world and the takeover of its land by other peoples who would themselves in due course disappear? Of course this is not merely a question about historical process. Christians have often reckoned that God did cast off Israel and replace it by the church. Might God reject Israel?

If God has done so, then Jeremiah must be a false prophet. His declarations of Yhwh's commitment to Israel are quite unequivocal. They establish Israel's position as a family or people, "Israel's offspring," and also as a "nation," an identifiable political entity, that will not disappear. Yhwh offers the most extravagant and extreme way of guaranteeing this, for even in a traditional society, the consistency, permanence, size and complexity of the cosmic order provide an image for that. It is not a conditional promise. We have noted that Yhwh's commitment to Israel indeed imposes obligations on Israel, but these are no more conditions for Yhwh's continuing commitment to Israel than they were conditions for Yhwh's original commitment. There is

---

[57]See the comments in Zimmerli, *OT Theology in Outline*, pp. 43-48; Westermann, *Elements of OT Theology*, pp. 41-42.

[58]For this notion see von Rad, *OT Theology*, 2:240.

[59]Ludwig Köhler, *Old Testament Theology* (London: Lutterworth, 1957/Philadelphia: Westminster Press, 1958), p. 38.

nothing other peoples can do, nothing Israel might do and nothing Yhwh will do to terminate Israel as Yhwh's people. "The Rejector can never cease being the Elector."[60] It is the case that the rejection of Israel stands over against the election of Israel, the two forming "an essential polarity." But like the love of God and the wrath of God, these are not two coequal notions. "As unthinkable it was that the creative power of God to establish the world would end, likewise was the thought that Israel would ever cease being a nation before God."[61] There is no First Testament doctrine of rejection to set alongside the doctrine of election.[62]

Possessed

To be chosen is to be summoned, separated out, seized, desired, acknowledged, restored, purchased, acquired, grasped and found.[63] It is to be taken as God's bride, to be drafted as Yhwh's army, to be adopted as Yhwh's son, to be purchased as Yhwh's servant, to be planted as Yhwh's vineyard, to be acquired as Yhwh's sheep, to be formed as Yhwh's vessel, to be separated as Yhwh's special possession.[64] "Israel was holy to Yhwh, the firstfruits of his harvest." That was part of its security. "Anyone who eats it is liable. Trouble comes on them" (Jer 2:3).

Israel is thus the "possession" Yhwh chose (*naḥălâ,* e.g., Deut 9:26, 29; Joel 2:17; 3:2 [MT 4:2]; Ps 28:9; 78:62, 71). The word is often translated "inheritance," in keeping with its etymology, and that translation correctly suggests the intrinsic and secure link between the possessor and the object possessed. But the application of the word to God makes clear something that also applies to more general usage, that the word's emphasis lies on the certainty of possession rather than the means whereby it was obtained. From whom would Yhwh have inherited this people, and to whom pass it on? Yhwh did not possess this people simply because of inheriting them; Yhwh *chose* this possession (Ps 33:12). "Your name has been proclaimed over us" (Jer 14:9), Israel affirms; it is a declaration of ownership. It was by an act of self-assertion that Yhwh took Israel itself as *naḥălâ* (e.g., Deut 4:20), and the land of Canaan becomes Israel's *naḥălâ* by Yhwh's gift.

Indeed, it is to land that the word *naḥălâ* directly applies. It refers to the tract

---

[60]Martin Buber, *On the Bible* (reprint, New York: Schocken, 1982), p. 92.

[61]Brevard S. Childs, *Biblical Theology of the Old and New Testaments* (Minneapolis: Fortress/ London: SCM Press, 1992), p. 427.

[62]Theodorus C. Vriezen, *Die Erwählung Israels nach dem Alten Testament* (Zürich: Zwingli, 1953), pp. 98-108; cf. *OTT* 1:216-17.

[63]See Preuss, *OT Theology,* 1:31.

[64]See Seock-Tae Sohn, *The Divine Election of Israel* (Grand Rapids, Mich.: Eerdmans, 1991).

of land belonging to a family (which normally it would have received as an inheritance from that family's earlier generations, and would be able to pass on to the next generation). To refer to this land as "property" could be misleading, because people do not usually regard land as a commodity that can be bought and sold like something humanly made. But a family does have a secure right of possession in relation to its land, and this is of monumental importance to it. One fundamental reason is the practical one, that possessing your land is key to survival. Only if you have land can you grow food. If you have no land, your position as a family is intrinsically insecure. You can live only on the basis of the charity of people who do possess land. There is thus a sense in which your land means everything to you. For a family, the fact that the land on which and from which you live has belonged to your family for generations would give it further value to you. And theologically, the fact that this is your portion of the land that Yhwh gave Israel as a people would enhance that preciousness. So a man such as Naboth would hardly be willing to exchange "my ancestors' *nahălâ*" for another perfectly good piece of land (indeed, on Ahaz's account, for a better one; 1 Kings 21:1-3).

All this would give significance to the idea of Israel being Yhwh's *nahălâ*. It means that Yhwh has an ownership of this people that is secure for Yhwh and secure for the people. They cannot escape from Yhwh's ownership, nor can they be removed from it by some other would-be owner. It means they mean something important to Yhwh. Surely Yhwh would never abandon this *nahălâ* (Ps 94:14), as a family would not do so.

This makes it natural and plausible to ask, "bless your possession" (Ps 28:9). And it is extraordinary that Yhwh should seem to behave in a way that suggested anger with this possession (Ps 78:62) and a loathing of it (Ps 106:40), that faithless people are allowed to afflict Yhwh's possession (Ps 94:5), and perhaps even more extraordinary that Yhwh grants, "I was angry with my people, I defiled my possession" (Is 47:6).

Treasured

To put it another way, Israel is Yhwh's treasure *(sĕgullâ)*. "You are a holy people for Yhwh your God. Yhwh your God chose you to be for him a specially treasured people" (Deut 7:6; cf., e.g., Deut 14:2; Ps 135:4). Being committed in covenant to Yhwh makes it possible for Israel to be the possession Yhwh especially values among all peoples, even though all the earth belongs to Yhwh (Ex 19:5).

Isaiah 43:1-7 expands on the value Yhwh places on Israel. It had meant so much to Yhwh that long ago Yhwh was willing not only to surrender Egypt and leave it to Pharaoh but also to throw in its neighbors as makeweights, in order to realize proper possession of Israel, which the Pharaoh wanted to treat as his own. Yhwh thus "restored" Israel (*gāʾal*).[65] It was as if Yhwh had acted like a slave master who had bought someone at an auction. Yhwh had looked at various possible good purchases and had settled on Israel, and had been prepared to stop bidding for those other peoples and let someone else have them. Israel was a valuable asset to acquire. Thus, says Yhwh, "I gave Egypt as your ransom, Sudan and Ethiopia for you, because you were valuable in my eyes, you were honorable and I dedicated myself to you" (Is 43:3-4). And Yhwh is prepared to act in the same way again. "I would give people for you, nations for your life." Such sacrifices would Yhwh make to bring the entire people back home from their exile. That gives Yhwh certain rights in relation to Israel. It puts Yhwh in a position to summon Jacob-Israel to do Yhwh's bidding. Jacob-Israel belongs to Yhwh.

In our world, belonging can be just a commercial business. It suggests no personal relationship. In a traditional society, that would often be different. The relationship of master and servant ideally involves a mutual commitment and a mutual appreciation, as the relationship of Abraham and his servant illustrates (Gen 24). In this relationship, there is no doubt that Yhwh is the boss, yet Yhwh knows that being a master entails moral obligations. The master stands by the servant. The servant is expected to honor the master, but the master also honors the servant. The servant is expected to love or be dedicated to the master, but the master also loves or is dedicated to the servant (*ʾāhēb*, Is 43:4). So if there should be a recurrence of the kind of disaster that the master originally rescued the servant from, then the master does not simply abandon the servant and write off the asset. If water or fire again threatens to overwhelm the servant, the master will be there. "I will be with you." Being with Israel does not mean being caring and solicitous. It means taking action to put the situation right. It means delivering people from the disaster that overwhelms, not consoling them in its midst. Floods will not overwhelm, fire not consume, because "Israel's holy one is—your deliverer."

Gathering Israel's offspring from every point of the compass (Is 43:5-6) is another way of making the point. It would be easy to reckon that the flood and fire of exile and dispersion would swallow this people, as history swallowed the Canaanites, the Philistines, the Edomites and the Moabites. Yhwh promises that the willingness to sacrifice Egypt, Sudan and Ethiopia for Israel carries with it the guarantee that this will not happen. The point is underlined by itemizing the four points of the compass, somewhat rhetorically: how many exiles were there across the Mediterranean at this point? The implication is that Yhwh will search under every rock to make sure that no one is missed.

---

[65]See section 2.2 "Restorer."

The point is underlined again by specifying women as well as men; it is the only point in Scripture where Yhwh specifically refers to "my daughters." Everyone counts, the last line affirms. Indeed it is in the context of their being members of the community that Yhwh relates to individuals; there is no personal relationship with God independent of the community. But let it not be said that Yhwh cares about the people but not about the individuals.

The last line (Is 43:7) also returns to the other side of the master-servant relationship. The security of the servant derives from—being a servant. The members of Israel are people "summoned" to Yhwh's service. They are summoned by their name and summoned in Yhwh's name. They are people Yhwh honors, and they are people created, shaped and made for Yhwh's honor.

Loved

So Israel "knows that it is loved, and it is this awareness that has enabled it to survive thousands of years of persecution without internalizing the anti-Semite's view of the Jew," even though it knows itself to have been severely punished by God.[66]

Back at the beginning, Yhwh was as thrilled with Israel as a farmer tasting the first tender, luscious figs of the season, or a person journeying through the wilderness, longing for something moist and succulent (there are no roadside diners), who suddenly sees a vine with grapes (Hos 9:10). The comment that this is "imagery which almost borders on the fantastic"[67] is almost an understatement. The Song of Songs makes much use of the imagery of fruit, including vines, grapes and figs.[68] It does not use the precise words that come here, but its usage suggests that in Hosea the imagery may not arise merely from the literal experience of enjoying fruit in that way. It is the regular language of love. The fact that Hosea speaks much of the relationship of a man and a woman supports the idea that here Yhwh speaks with the enthusiasm of a lover for the object of his love.

How devastating, then, is the fact that soon after Yhwh found them, the Israelites got involved with other "lovers" and "consecrated themselves to shame."[69] Hosea abandons the imagery of agriculture or love for a powerful theological metaphor. "Consecrated themselves" (*nāzar* niphal) is the verb that generates the word *Nazirite*, someone distinctively dedicated to Yhwh. But Is-

---

[66]Wyschograd, *Body of Faith*, p. 12.

[67]R. Bach, "Die Erwählung Israels in der Wüste" (diss., Bonn, 1952), p. 18, as quoted in Hans Walter Wolff, *Hosea* (Philadelphia: Fortress, 1974), p. 161.

[68]Cf. G. I. Davies, *Hosea* (London: Marshall Pickering/Grand Rapids, Mich.: Eerdmans, 1992), p. 226.

[69]For the story, see Num 25:1-5.

rael has moved in the opposite direction, and that sharply, and become dedicated to shame—that is, the shameful thing, the "Master." And the result is that it has moved from one extreme of enthusiastic appreciation to the other extreme of abhorrence and dissociation. Israel is as abhorrent as the one to whom they have now given themselves.

"I have loved Jacob but I have hated Esau," English versions have Yhwh saying in Malachi 1:2-3; we have noted that Paul finds the comment illuminating as he wrestles to understand the Jewish people's failure to recognize Jesus (Rom 9:13).[70] What is this love? The question is complicated for English-speakers because of the way our vocabulary works, which falls short of Hebrew and Greek vocabulary in different ways. C. S. Lewis wrote of "four loves,"[71] *storgē*, *philia, erōs* and *agapē*. Having these four words makes it easier for Greek to distinguish between family love, friendship love, romantic or sexual love, and love that expresses itself in extraordinary acts of self-giving. Not having read Lewis, the LXX uses *agapē* as a general-purposes word for love. But it hesitates to use it for Solomon's love for foreign women and Ahasuerus's love for Esther (1 Kings 11:1-2; Esther 2:17), for love of wrongdoing (Prov 17:19) and for Israel's or Jerusalem's lovers (Hos 2:5-13 [MT 7-15]; Lam 1:2, 19). Hebrew similarly has *ḥesed* (love that expresses itself in extraordinary acts of self-giving), *dôd* (loving affection) and words from the root *rāʿâ* (which can denote close friendship or romantic love), but the First Testament generally uses *ʾahăbâ* as an all-purpose word that covers all four of the Greek words. Yet the fact that *ʾahăbâ* thus commonly denotes a love that takes the form of commitment or self-giving gives it a different profile from the English word *love*, which is inclined essentially to suggest an emotion. Thus for different reasons, Hebrew *wāʾōhab ʾet yaʿăqōb* and Greek *ton Iakōb ēgapēsa* have different resonances from English "I have loved Jacob." Malachi's point concerns not Yhwh's feelings for Jacob but the way Yhwh has behaved toward Jacob; the JPSV has "I have accepted Jacob." In the previous section I translated this verb "dedicate oneself."

Similar considerations apply more strongly to the companion correlative verb translated "hate," *śānēʾ*, which can refer to an emotion but more characteristically refers to a commitment.[72] So JPSV renders the second clause, "and have rejected Esau." Yhwh's subsequent words also explicate the point: "I have made his mountains a desolation, the land he possesses into a wilderness for jackals." It may be that this qatal verb refers to an event that has recently happened, but we are uncertain about the chronology of Edomite history, and if this event has happened, the people's complaint becomes more puzzling. More likely it is an

---

[70]See section 2.3 "Over Ends and Means."

[71]C. S. Lewis, *The Four Loves* (New York: Harcourt, Brace, 1960).

[72]See section 2.7 "Repudiation."

event Yhwh is committed to that will evidence the truth in the statement, *wāʾōhab ʾet yaʿăqōb wĕʾet ʿēśāw śānēʾtî,* "I dedicated myself to Jacob and acted against Esau." Judah's problem is that for more than a century Edom has been occupying a significant part of Judah's territory; even Hebron is under Edomite occupation. That is surely evidence that Yhwh is committed to Edom, not Judah. There was no reason why this should be so. But Yhwh points out that although Esau and Jacob were brothers, Yhwh showed preferential treatment to Jacob. That gives a basis for trusting and hoping in Yhwh now.

The Object of Choosing

Why did God choose a particular people rather than relating to the whole world? It was for Israel's sake, for God's sake and for the world's sake.

It is for Israel's sake, in that election brings Israel into a special relationship with God of a kind that no other people enjoys. Yet at the same time, Deuteronomy indicates, the object of God's choice of Israel was simply for God to have a special people. In this sense it was for God's sake. Michael Wyschogrod suggests that there is something about love that requires it to be particular. Loving the world is all very well, but it is not the same as loving specifically.[73] Election thus explains what is involved in grace. God decides not to be self-sufficient (for God could be that; God does not get involved with humanity because of divine need) but in freedom to draw another into covenant relationship. Thus "the concept of election means that grace is truly grace. It means that God owes His grace to no one, and that no one can deserve it." But the electing into covenant relationship means it is an election of a people who will make this God their Lord.[74]

The same principle applied when God chose Levi for its role in worship rather than the other clans; it was for the sake of what Levi was going to do for Yhwh (1 Chron 15:2; 2 Chron 29:11). God's relationships with individuals also illustrate the point. The First Testament speaks of God "choosing" individuals such as Abraham, but it also illustrates it in describing the way God favors individuals such as Abel, Noah, Isaac and Jacob. They are God's elect not merely for their sake but for God's. Their vocation is that "they are silent when others speak; they confess when others deny; they stand when others falter; they adore when others blaspheme; they are joyful when others are sad, and sad when others are joyful; at peace when others are restless, and restless when others are at peace."[75] "The tradition could not be clearer as to the continually operative principle of the distinguishing choice; the freedom with

---

[73]Wyschogrod, *Body of Faith,* pp. 60-65; cf. Soulen, *God of Israel,* pp. 7-8.
[74]Karl Barth, *Church Dogmatics* (Edinburgh: T & T Clark, 1936-1969), II/2:10-12.
[75]Ibid., II/2:343, 345.

which this choice cuts across and contradicts all distinctions that are humanly regulated or planned on the basis of human predilections, and the relativity of the distinctions that are actually made; the fact that those who are cut off, who are not distinguished by actual choice, are not on that account utterly rejected, but do in their own way remain in a positive relation to the covenant of God.[76] The story of Saul and David illustrates the point further.[77]

It is also the case that God chose one people in order to further the divine purpose to bless the whole world. The broader context of Deuteronomy suggests that Yhwh's particular love of Israel is designed to be inclusive not exclusive. Choosing Levi did not imply rejecting the other clans. If the notion of God's choice began with David, then it is significant that this choice was not made for David's sake but for the sake of what David was going to do for the people (Ps 78:70-71). For other individuals who are summoned and chosen such as Abraham or Moses, Joshua or Gideon, Isaiah or Jeremiah, Andrew or Philip, Peter or Paul, election does convey a privileged personal relationship with God, but that pales into insignificance alongside the way God's choice of them sees them as "set in a function to be exercised between God and other men, between God and the world."[78] It is that call that matters. And as the object of choosing an individual is to use them in relation to the people as a whole, so the object of choosing the people is to use them in relation to the world as a whole. It belongs in the context of Yhwh's will to be sovereign of the whole world and to bless the whole world, and it serves that end. The aim of Yhwh's summons and acknowledgment of Abraham (and then of God's choice of Israel) related to that purpose (Gen 12:2-3).

A Gospel Idea

Thus paradoxically, "election faith and thought tend towards a certain universalism,"[79] because the chosen people is chosen to be the means of Yhwh's reaching out to the world, not of avoiding it. The people are chosen so that they may "summon the whole world to faith in Him."[80] Election is both for Israel's sake and for the world's. It reflects both God's concern for the world and God's "passion" for Israel.[81] The First Testament often speaks of the nations be-

---

[76]Ibid., II/2:356.

[77]Ibid., II/2:366-88.

[78]Ibid., IV/3.ii:592.

[79]Preuss, *OT Theology*, 2:285.

[80]Barth, *Church Dogmatics*, II/2:196.

[81]Jon D. Levenson, "The Universal Horizon of Jewish Particularism," in *Ethnicity and the Bible*, ed. Mark G. Brett, Biblical Interpretation Series 19 (Leiden/New York: Brill, 1996), pp. 143-69 (p. 156).

cause of their significance for Israel, yet it is also interested in the nations because they all belong to Yhwh, and it is interested in Israel because of its significance for them.[82]

So election is not the means of leaving out other people but the means of drawing them in. In answering the question "What is the church," the Heidelberg Catechism begins by declaring "that out of the whole human race the Son of God gathers, protects and upholds a community of the elect destined for eternal life." Here there is no suggestion that the church and its election relates to God's concern for the world.[83] Rather "the relation to the fellowship of a renewed humanity that is to be achieved in the future of God's dominion is constitutive for the concept of the church."[84] God indeed enters into a special relationship with Israel, which God then extends to the church, so that the catechism is not wrong in what it affirms, but its affirmation needs to be set in the context of that purpose. R. Kendall Soulen suggests that the three key expressions of Yhwh's blessing of Israel are peoplehood, Torah and land.[85] Yet whereas Yhwh's original words to Abraham make no reference to Torah, they do refer to the blessing of the nations.[86]

Election is thus a gospel idea. Not only is God's rejection subordinate to God's election with regard to Israel itself; with regard to the world as a whole, God's election of one people does not imply God's rejection of others. The First Testament "does not proclaim in the same breath both good and evil, both help and destruction, both life and death. It does, of course, throw a shadow. . . . In itself, however, it is light and not darkness. . . . The Yes cannot be heard unless the No is also heard. But the No is said for the sake of the Yes and not for its own sake. In substance, therefore, the first and last word is Yes and not No."[87] The grounds of election, after all, lie in the nature of God, and thus in God as love, and in God's love for the world.[88] Even when, for instance, Yhwh's choice of Israel leads to giving them a land that currently belonged to other peoples, that, too, is subordinate to Yhwh's purpose for the world. Indeed, there is a sense in which other individual peoples are elect, in the sense that God is also

---

[82]Cf. Barth, *Church Dogmatics*, IV/3.ii: 688-93.

[83]Cf. Moltmann, *The Church in the Power of the Spirit*, pp. 68, 69.

[84]Pannenberg, *Systematic Theology*, 3:26-27. Pannenberg goes on (p. 32) to contrast the church and Israel by suggesting that Israel's existence was not from the very first based on the breaking in of God's rule over all humanity. In fact, as the First Testament tells the story, this was surely so.

[85]Soulen, *God of Israel*, pp. 123-25.

[86]Soulen (ibid., p. 125) does go on to note that this blessing "is ordered to the inclusion of the other households of creation as well."

[87]Cf. Barth, *Church Dogmatics*, II/2:13.

[88]Cf. ibid., II/2:25.

involved in their histories in distinctive ways to bless and to judge (see Amos 1—2:4; 9:7). On the other hand, such nations may not apply the motif of Israel's unique election to themselves (as Britain and the U.S.A. have done).[89]

The fact that God gave the Torah to Israel alone does not mean it cannot be the basis for a single human family.[90] To begin with, the Sinai requirements of the covenant were not built into the original covenant, as Paul notes in Romans 4 and Michael Wyschogrod also affirms.[91] Yet even when the Sinai requirements become intrinsic to the covenant, Isaiah and Micah, at least, do not see this as implying that the Torah cannot be the basis for the world becoming one. Of course this project did not work, but that is no basis for Christians to claim that Christ has solved the problem, because neither has his death yet made the world into one family.

The Basis for Choice

Why did God not reach out to all humanity as a whole rather than via some members of the human race? The First Testament gives no answer to that question. All one can observe is that it is of a piece with much of God's work in the world, which reflects the way God created the world. It reflects humanity's interdependence. God designed humanity to learn from one another, and acting with one group as a means of reaching others fits that pattern.

And why did God work via a nation? As well as seeing God's choice of an ethnic group as a mark of grace,[92] Michael Wyschogrod adds the suggestion that it was because "the nation is most remote from God."[93] In theory it might be possible to save people as individuals irrespective of their national identity. One could simply ignore that, abandon national identity as irredeemable. There is a wide Christian strand of thought that made this assumption, and one can see its fallaciousness. In practice the national identity of Spain or Britain or Germany or Serbia or the United States wins the victory over the individual Christian commitment of their citizens nearly every time. It is their identity as Spaniards, Britishers, Germans, Serbians or Americans that decisively shapes them. Their Christian commitment does not overcome that. It is almost as hard to separate a person from their nationality as to separate soul from body. National identity is too strong a force. Yhwh's choice of a nation confirms the national order and signifies God's intention to redeem humanity in the true nature of its predicament.

---

[89]Cf. Pannenberg, *Systematic Theology*, 3:518-21.
[90]Against N. T. Wright, *Climax of the Covenant*, p. 173; cf. Volf, *Exclusion and Embrace*, pp. 44-45.
[91]Wyschogrod, *The Body of Faith*, p. 57.
[92]See section 3.1 "A Mark of Grace."
[93]Wyschogrod, *Body of Faith*, p. 68.

And why this nation in particular? It is the least answerable of the questions about election. Christians often look for the reasons that would justify God's choice of them. God must have chosen because of seeing some quality or some potential. People have speculated about a rationale behind God's choice of Israel. Is it some feature of the Jewish character? Is it the location of the land of Israel? Deuteronomy forestalls such questions, making clear some bad answers and then sidestepping any concrete good answer. "It was not because you were more numerous than all the other peoples that Yhwh fancied you and chose you, because you were the smallest of peoples, because it was on account of Yhwh's love for you and on account of keeping the promise he made to your ancestors" (Deut 7:7-8).[94] Israel is not to think that it is because of faithfulness or integrity that it possesses. It is rather because of the faithlessness of the other nations, as well as to fulfill the promise to Israel's ancestors. Israel, after all, is a stiff-necked people, one inclined to provoke Yhwh to anger and to be continually defiant, so it is certainly not the case that Israel deserves election (Deut 9:4-7). God does not elect a people on the basis of its obedience or of its potential for obedience, nor does God wait till Israel is obedient before using it. God uses it either way—obedient or disobedient.[95] Either way, it reflects the grace, commitment, faithfulness and compassion of God. God does not choose an obedient but an obdurate people, under whose obduracy God chooses to suffer curse and shame and death.[96]

Distinctive and Separate

So "election, as Israel presents it, means recruitment."[97] Israel is chosen to serve God's purpose in the world. Admittedly God's vision for the way it is to do this bemuses Christians. God does not commission Israel to go out on a mission or crusade. From the beginning, it fulfils its vocation more by being than by acting. To put it another way, the First Testament assumes that Yhwh's self-revelation to the world comes about through Yhwh's own action by means of Israel rather than by Israel's action or Israel's action that Israel interprets as Yhwh's action. The principle is established by Yhwh's first words to Abraham. Yhwh intends so to bless Abraham that he will become a blessing— that is, a means of other people's blessing. That will come about as all peoples

---

[94]See *OTT* 1:214-16.

[95]Cf. Barth, *Church Dogmatics*, II/2:206-7. Barth's comments come in the context of a sustained exposition of Rom 9—11 with their significance for an understanding of Israel's place within God's purpose.

[96]Barth, *Church Dogmatics*, II/2:206.

[97]Paul M. van Buren, *A Theology of the Jewish-Christian Reality*, 3 vols. (San Francisco: Harper & Row, 1980-1988), 2:117.

pray to be blessed as Abraham is blessed (Gen 12:1-3). It will not come about because he does something, except go where Yhwh tells him (and pray: see Gen 18). In Second Isaiah, "the Chosen People's business is to exist. . . . The mission of Israel consists in reflecting the glory of God by accepting His gifts and His judgment alike."[98]

Israel thus becomes a blessing in the midst of the world (Is 19:24).[99] In Roman Catholic thinking, the church is a sacrament, a means by which God not only embodies and communicates what it is to be God's people but conveys that reality to others and brings it about in them.[100] Being a blessing to the world is not merely something for which Israel or the church is responsible, something it has to go out and do or put into effect in its own life, but something that God does.

The concern with holiness in Leviticus and Deuteronomy fits within this framework assumption. Israel's food laws were designed to underline and preserve its distinctiveness (see Lev 11; Deut 14). There are animals that may be eaten and that may not; among the ones that may be eaten, there are animals that may be sacrificed and that may not. There may be some arbitrariness about which animal belongs to which category, to make the system easier to work; and/or practical factors may enter in (for instance, whether cultivation of pigs is easy in much of Canaan). Having such a system is not peculiar to Israel (and eating pork is forbidden by the Qur'an). Further, there may be a number of symbolisms about the distinctions. But the Torah's introduction of some systematizing of what to avoid make a theological point. The distinctions mirror and reinforce the distinction between Israelites and other peoples, and within Israel between priests and laypeople. This is reflected in the rationale for their abandonment by Jews who were called to get involved in telling the Gentile world about Jesus.[101] For the moment, Yhwh declares Israel to be a holy nation (Ex 19:6), a people with a distinctive position over against other peoples. It does not have to take steps to be holy or to maintain its holiness, though Yhwh will make that point in due course (see Lev 19:2). Holiness is its position as a result of an association with the holy one.

In the First Testament, God's missional concern works primarily in centripetal fashion. In the New Testament, it works more in centrifugal fashion. Indeed, in the First Testament it is not a missional concern but an attractional

---

[98]Martin-Achard, *A Light to the Nations*, p. 31.

[99]See further section 8.6 "Sharing Israel's Status."

[100]See Avery Dulles, *Models of the Church*, 2nd ed. (Dublin: Gill and Macmillan, 1988), pp. 63-75.

[101]See the discussion in Walter Houston, *Purity and Monotheism*, JSOTSup 140 (Sheffield: Sheffield Academic Press, 1993).

concern; it involves drawing people, not sending messengers to them. Admittedly that difference should not be exaggerated. Modern Christians "think they must adjust to the world instead of consciously and concertedly differentiating themselves from its rules and forms of life. But in the early days of Christianity the difference between the way Christians lived and the morally corrupt world around them was very effective in attracting people to their fellowship and faith."[102] The church grew by attraction. That is the First Testament norm.

An Open Community

The existence of Israel is an expression of God's mission in the world. Israel's was not a missionary faith, but it was a faith that made universal claims.[103] Israel embodies the fact that the people of God does not have a mission that it has to undertake. It is more the vehicle of God's mission, a movement from God in which Israel has its origin and arrives at its own movement, but which goes beyond Israel, finding its goal in the consummation of all creation in God.[104] The reason for Israel's existence lies in God's purpose for the world that goes back to creation. And the point of its existence is to be the means of God's reign spreading in the world—that is, of fulfilling God's original purpose that humanity should subdue the earth, make the earth a place under its control and thus (!) under God's control, fulfilling God's purpose. While God would eventually take steps toward that goal by having Christ commission his disciples to go out into the world to make the nations into his disciples, this does not mean that this is the only way God pursues that purpose. "The point is not to spread the church but to press the kingdom."[105] And again, this understanding needs not become a basis for reframing things we do as things that God is doing, disguising our conviction that it is our business to bring in God's kingdom.[106]

All we have to do is be holy. To fulfill its vocation, Israel needed to be a distinct entity over against other peoples and a whole entity in itself. Yet in order to fulfill its vocation, Israel also needed to be inclusive in relation to outsiders and exclusive in relation to insiders.

The distinction between Israel and other peoples is both ethnic and reli-

---

[102]Pannenberg, *Systematic Theology*, 3:492.

[103]Robert Martin-Achard, *A Light to the Nations* (Edinburgh: Oliver & Boyd, 1962), pp. 54-60; Levenson, *Sinai and Zion*, pp. 207-8.

[104]I follow Moltmann's words in *The Church in the Power of the Spirit*, p. 11, replacing "the church" with "Israel."

[105]Ibid., p. 11.

[106]See further section 5.1 "Yhwh's Arm Bared."

gious. But from the beginning the Israelite family had been open to outsiders who attached themselves to Yhwh.[107] Tacitly, it was always assumed that a member of another ethnic group could join Israel. Religious identification could thus trump ethnic difference. Perhaps such foreigners might often be adopted into an Israelite family and come to be thought of as full Israelites, so that their descendants might have no clue that they came from extra-Israelite stock. But awareness of their adoptive status was often preserved; Ruth was always "the Moabite," Uriah "the Hittite," even though Ruth came to commit herself to Yhwh and Uriah bears a Yhwh-name. They might then always find their position vulnerable, especially in contexts when Israel needed to define itself carefully rather than be overwhelmed by other peoples. The nations were forbidden to come into the sanctuary or the congregation, but Lamentations 1:10 mentions that in connection with the fact that the enemy has laid hands on the things that were precious there. People who have come to join themselves to Yhwh would be a different matter.

Indeed, in his new land, when the land is reallocated among the clans, Ezekiel envisages that such aliens will be allocated their own land within the regular clan allocations, like the Levites (Ezek 47:22-23). "They are to be to you as native Israelites." They fully belong to the people, and are no longer dependent on "charity." This is thus a more radical expression of love for the alien that Deuteronomy requires (Deut 10:19; cf., e.g., Deut 26:11). Since Ezekiel elsewhere bans from entering the sanctuary people who are "spiritually and physically uncircumcised" (Ezek 44:7-9), presumably he here assumes that these aliens have fully attached themselves to Yhwh. I assume that conversely the marriages broken up in Ezra's day were ones in which the non-Israelite partners kept their own faith. But one can imagine that there might be voices that argued for ethnic purity in Israel as there were voices that argued for ethnic openness, and one can imagine that this made longstanding converts nervous.[108]

An Open Ministry

Isaiah 56 complements Ezekiel's vision with the promise that foreigners who join themselves to Yhwh can "minister" to Yhwh (*šārat*), the role Ezekiel confines to the Levites. Foreigners who want to join themselves to Yhwh need not fear that "Yhwh may quite separate me from his people" (Is 56:3): the verb is *hibdîl*, the word the canons use for distinguishing between what is clean and

---

[107]Cf. section 3.1 "A Mark of Grace."

[108]Steven S. Tuell sees these foreigners as the offspring of mixed marriages: see "The Priesthood of the 'Foreigner,'" in *Constituting the Community*, ed. John T. Strong and Steven S. Tuell (Winona Lake, Ind.: Eisenbrauns, 2005), pp. 183-204.

what is taboo. Yhwh says, "I will bring them to my holy mountain and let them rejoice in my house of prayer; their whole offerings and sacrifices will be accepted on my altar, because my house will be called a house of prayer for all peoples." The God "who gathers the banished of Israel" thus declares, "I will yet gather more to their people who are gathered" (Is 56:7-8). Yhwh reaffirms the principle of openness.

Isaiah 56 advocates ethnic openness but religious strictness, and then follows up the logic of its position. If foreigners can be members of Yhwh's community and can share in the holding of Yhwh's land, can they not have the fullest position in the worship of Yhwh?

How radical is the prophecy? Rejoicing in Yhwh's house of prayer and having their offerings accepted on Yhwh's altar might imply simply that they are full lay members of the worshiping community. But earlier Isaiah 56 speaks of their ministering to Yhwh and serving Yhwh, and these terms rather suggest ministerial roles. Ezekiel 44 emphasizes how important it is that foreigners who are spiritually and physically uncircumcised do not join in the ministry of the temple. Isaiah 56 declares that foreigners who commit themselves to Yhwh may indeed join in this ministry. It may not be referring to priestly roles in the narrow sense (though Is 66:21 does so), but it is referring to more than the position of ordinary laypeople. Perhaps, then, the allusions to their rejoicing in Yhwh's house of prayer and having their offerings accepted refer to their taking part in officiating in the temple liturgy. Such participation would give vivid expression to the temple's destiny to be a house of prayer for all the peoples who are destined to find their way to Yhwh's holy mountain (cf. Is 2:2-4). They embody the way Yhwh's vision for the gathering of people scattered over the world extends beyond a gathering of scattered Israelites to a gathering of all peoples.

If the idea of such inclusion of foreigners in the temple service raised eyebrows, so might the passage's other insistence, that eunuchs also have an equal place in the worshiping community (Is 56:3-5). Other Middle Eastern peoples sometimes castrated men in connection with their service at court, and it may be that Isaiah's threat about Hezekiah's descendants being eunuchs in the palace of the Babylonian king (Is 39:7) had been literally fulfilled. While Moses' teaching does not specifically refer to eunuchs, it does exclude from Yhwh's assembly men who are sexually mutilated (Deut 23:1 [MT 2]), and one can imagine people reckoning that this applied to eunuchs. Thus some Israelites who came back from exile would find themselves excluded from the community. The passage stands against this and makes extravagant promises to them. No, they cannot have children, and thus they cannot contribute to the future of the community. But to make up for that, far from excluding them Yhwh will give them a special place within the very walls of the temple. They too must stick by the demands of the covenant, but given that, they are to be welcomed right inside Yhwh's house, and there to be given personal commemorative monuments. Their not having children would mean that there was no one to carry on their name; but these monuments will mean they are never forgotten. Perhaps the prophet speaks metaphorically. The image of a commemorative monument in Yhwh's house declares that Yhwh will never be able to forget them. There is a sense in which that is better than having sons and daughters.

Required to Respond

There are conditions. Third Isaiah does not disagree with Ezekiel, and perhaps not with Ezra. The foreigners to whom this assurance applies are people who have actually "joined themselves" to Yhwh. They thus fulfill the declaration in Isaiah 14:1 (cf. also Zech 2:11 [MT 15]). The verb, *lāwâ*, resembles the name of the clan Levi, and the prophecy may be hinting that the people who are to function as Levites or joiners must have done their joining (cf. the utilizing of this resemblance in Numbers 18:2, 4, and in connection with the joining involved in marriage, in Gen 29:34). Concretely, that joining is expressed in keeping the sabbath. In the exile, the sabbath became the marker of commitment to Yhwh that it has remained ever since. Back in Judah, too, when the community is surrounded by and interwoven with other peoples, willingness to keep the sabbath is a symbol of adherence to Yhwh. It is the way in which one demonstrates that one is holding on to Yhwh's covenant. So the key question for foreigners who want to minister to Yhwh, to be Yhwh's servants, is whether they keep the sabbath rather than profaning it, and thus stick firm by an expectation that is evidently seen as key to covenant commitment in the context. We might say that keeping the sabbath would be the sign of being spiritually circumcised.

Chosenness always calls for response. As Israel's original position as Yhwh's people depended entirely on Yhwh, yet required Israel's response, so Israel's restoration after the exile likewise depends entirely on Yhwh, yet requires Israel's response. "Get out of Babylon, flee from Chaldea," Isaiah 48:20 urges. The Judean community does nothing to bring about Cyrus's conquest of the Babylonian empire and his decree to let them go home. Yet they do actually have to make the journey from Babylon to Jerusalem. The reality and the language parallel the exodus, when Israel "got out" of Egypt and "fled" from there (e.g., Ex 12:31; 14:5). Once more, Yhwh does not intend to pick Israel up and compel them to go to Canaan on eagle's wings, despite Exodus 19:4 (and in the event, much of the community did not choose to go).

There is another response the community has to make, again following the pattern of the exodus. "Announce with a ringing voice, make this heard, take it out to the end of the earth." Israel's task will be to proclaim what Yhwh does, as it proclaimed it at the Red Sea and did so again in telling the story of the way Yhwh took it through the wilderness and made water flow when the people needed it. They are to shout out, "Yhwh is restoring his servant Jacob. They are not thirsty as he leads them through the wastes, he is making water flow from the rock for them, he is splitting the rock and water is gushing" (Is 48:20-21). Thus this second exodus will actually be better the first, for there they did thirst; this time they will not. And this time the news of this event is not confined to coming generations of Israel and to people such as Jethro and Rahab, or even Moabites and Canaanites in general. It is to be taken to the end of the earth.

3.4 Yhwh's Kingdom

On arrival at Sinai, Yhwh tells Jacob's household, "you will be for me a kingdom of priests, a holy nation" (Ex 19:6). The family becomes a huge people, and the people becomes a nation. As a kingdom, it lives under the authority of Yhwh as king, though rather surprisingly Yhwh agrees to its also having human kings, at least for a while. As a priesthood, it has special access to Yhwh.[109] As a nation, it is a people with its own land, though its land also becomes its temptation, and it can lose its land.

Nation

Becoming a great nation had been a promise to the people's ancestors since Genesis 12:2; Deuteronomy 26:5 sees it as having been fulfilled in Egypt. Designating Israel as a nation underlines the magnitude of its growth and gives another form to its external bounds.

It also gives another form to its significance in the world as it marks it off from the other nations among whom it lives. The world as God watched it develop through Genesis 1—11 became a world of nations. Genesis does not quite say that God willed this, but it does imply that this is the form that God's blessing of the world took. God wants to be involved in the world, and the world is a world of nations. It is therefore logical for God to form a nation through which to reach nations. As a nation, a *gôy*, Israel is a body involved in political relations with other nations *(gôyim)*. Its existence is lived like that of other nations in its world, and it is often in conflict with its neighbor nations (some ethnically or religiously related) and with more distant imperial powers that might be a military or political threat. It prays as a political entity

---

[109]There is no suggestion that it exercises this priesthood on other people's behalf; the idea that Israel has a role to play in relation to other peoples is expressed in other ways (see, e.g., section 3.3 "Distinctive and Separate").

under pressure from enemies without as well as from enemies within (e.g., Ps 46; 59; 79). And as a nation it engages in war, because that is what nations do. Yhwh goes into war with Ephraim as helmet and Judah as staff, battling with their aid (Ps 60:7 [9]). Israel is thus a people with God's praise on its lips and a sword in its hands to act for Yhwh against the nations (Ps 149:6), action that can lead to the nations coming to acknowledge Yhwh (Ps 47). Of course Israel might claim that it was acting in Yhwh's name when it was actually acting for self-aggrandizement. Yhwh's attitude to a people such as Assyria when it does that would suggest that Israel would then be in deep trouble. If it behaves like the nations, it will be treated like the nations. But designating it as a holy nation (Ex 19:6) safeguards its distinctiveness over against other nations. It is "a people that dwells apart and does not reckon itself among the nations" (Num 23:9).

Speaking of Israel as a nation also designates it as an institution, with a structure for decision making and thus some structure of authority. This does not mean it has to be hierarchical.[110] Indeed, designating it as kingdom for Yhwh points away from that. Israel is a people ruled by Yhwh as king. Israel was a people under the authority of Yhwh before it was a worldly kingdom. "It is of the utmost significance that the Torah, the law of the theo-polity, was, for all its diversity, always ascribed to Moses and not to David." Israel had its law before it had its king. Israel was "'a kingdom of priests and a holy nation' both before and after she was a kingdom of a more mundane kind."[111] But the spiritual and moral pressures of being a kingdom of a more mundane kind are usually overwhelming. People of God and state usually live in an uneasy relationship. If the people of God is a small and insignificant entity, it will likely have no problem with the state, but it can hardly then be fulfilling its role in the world. If it seeks to fulfill that role, it will likely find itself subject to pressure from the state, and it needs to keep living in light of the fact that Yhwh is its Lord. If it finds itself in political power, it will likely find itself corrupted by that power, and inclined to use it to maintain the status quo and/or to extend the power of the central state over its people or to extend the power of this particular state over other peoples. Thus living in light of the fact that Yhwh is Lord may be even harder.

Yhwh planned to make Israel a paradigm for the blessing of the nations. Unfortunately the nations became a paradigm for Israel's experience. Jeremiah is bidden to send word to the envoys of Edom, Moab and other countries who have come to Zedekiah, apparently in connection with the possibility of rebelling against Babylon, to tell them to submit to Nebuchad-

---

[110]Contrast Dulles, *Models of the Church*, pp. 34-46.

[111]Levenson, *Sinai and Zion*, p. 75.

nezzar as Yhwh's servant or find themselves in exile. He then speaks to Zedekiah "in just the same way" (Jer 27:12). He urges Judah to submit to Nebuchadnezzar's yoke and serve him rather than risking death by sword, famine and epidemic, and not to listen to prophets who advise otherwise. They are prophesying falsehood and listening to them will mean Judah will end up being driven out and perishing. All this corresponds to what "Yhwh has spoken concerning the nation that will not serve the king of Babylon" (Jer 27:13). Judah is just one more people. Judah and other nations are to submit to the power of Babylon (e.g., Jer 28). We might say it is commanded to take a nonviolent stance, and it is certainly noteworthy that the prophets consistently oppose rebellion against the powers of the day. They never commission violence. On the other hand, they do not commend this stance on the basis of a conviction that violence is wrong, and they certainly picture Yhwh using other nations' violence. They do not suggest that nonviolence is a strategy for achieving peaceful change. They do commend it as a strategy for avoiding the situation getting worse; they assume that it is better to be red than dead. And they commend it because of theological convictions about the place of the superpower in Yhwh's purpose.

Landed

"Is ownership of real property necessary for either individual or group fulfilment? Is the life of the *fellah* intrinsically better than that of the *bedouin* (many have thought quite the contrary)?"[112] But being a nation implies having a land; a nation without a land is virtually a contradiction in terms. Theologically, that reflects something about the way God created humanity. It is the corporate equivalent to the fact that God created individual human beings as people with bodies.[113] Thus as a nation, Israel is a territorial entity. God's original promise of nationhood stood alongside a commission to go to a new land, and God soon specifically attached a promise to give this land to Abraham's offspring (Gen 12:1-7). There was some inevitability about this. If Yhwh was to turn Abraham's family into a nation, this nation needed a land. The exodus was thus to mean freedom from servitude in one land to life in another land (Ex 3:8). Elmer A. Martens can thus see land as one of the four recurrent motifs that are key to Old Testament theology,[114] which contrasts with the fact that

---

[112]Robert C. Dentan, reviewing Walter Brueggemann, *The Land* (Philadelphia: Fortress, 1977/ London: SPCK, 1978) in *JBL* 97 (1978): 577-78; see p. 578.

[113]Cf. the comments of Thomas F. Torrance, "The Divine Vocation and Destiny of Israel in World History," in *The Witness of the Jews to God*, ed. David W. Torrance (Edinburgh: Handsel, 1982), pp. 85-104; see p. 103.

[114]Elmer A. Martens, *Plot and Purpose in the Old Testament* (Leicester: Inter-Varsity Press, 1981). Cf., e.g., C. J. H. Wright, *God's People in God's Land*, pp. 3-70.

"no texts of the religious environment of ancient Israel know of a promise of the land."[115]

The link between nationhood and land is indicated by the fact that other peoples also have their land as their possession (*yĕrussâ*), by Yhwh's gift, so that Israel is not allowed to dispossess them (e.g., Deut 2:5, 9, 19). Yhwh is of course in a position to take it from one set of occupants and give it to another. While Yhwh might not do so arbitrarily, the Canaanites have forfeited their land because of their behavior (Deut 9:4-5). So Yhwh can make it possible for Israel to dispossess them and take possession of their land (*yāraš*, e.g., Deut 1:8; 3:18, 20). Israel is thus able to "take" the land (*lāqah*, e.g., Deut 3:8), yet only because the land is God's gift (e.g., Deut 1:8; 3:18, 20). That also implies that the recipient becomes the long-term possessor of the gift, in keeping with the fact that the land was promised as a gift to Israel's ancestors "and to their offspring after them" (Deut 1:8). Giving presupposes that the giver is the possessor of the gift and is in a position to give it to someone else. Thus Yhwh can determine to give Israel the land east of the Jordan belonging to Sihon, and can manipulate Sihon into forfeiting it (Deut 2:30-31).

So the lands of other peoples can thus become the possession or allocation (*nahălâ*) of Israel (e.g., Deut 4:21; Ps 135:12), something the people possess securely in the context of others having their own *nahălâ*.[116] The term perhaps has its background in the fact that each family had its *nahălâ*; this provides an image for the significance of the land as a whole for Israel.[117] Joshua thus "allocates" the land to the people (Deut 3:28). Calling something one's *nahălâ* also suggests that one does not possess it by right or by one's own initiative, but one does possess it securely.[118]

Yhwh is glad to have reason to allocate this land to Israel because it is "a good and wide land, a land running with milk and honey" (Ex 3:8). There is plenty of room there, plenty of pasture for sheep and good soil for trees such as figs whose fruit produces sweet syrup. The evidence is the spectacular bunch of grapes the spies were able to bring back from the land. This land has cities, houses and cisterns, vineyards and olive groves, and the people will eat their fill there (Deut 6:10-11). It has a plentiful water supply, grows crops well and contains mineral resources (Deut 8:7-9). It is a land Yhwh looks after (Deut

---

[115]Preuss, *OT Theology*, 1:119.

[116]We noted in discussing Israel as Yhwh's "possession" that although this word is also often translated "inheritance," it does not intrinsically point to the possession being passed down within the family. See Norman C. Habel, *The Land Is Mine* (Minneapolis: Fortress, 1995), pp. 33-35.

[117]Cf. von Rad, *OT Theology*, 1:224.

[118]On the land as Israel's *nahălâ*, see Rendtorff, *Canonical Hebrew Bible*, pp. 458-60.

11:10-12). It contrasts with Egypt, even as the Egyptians experience Egypt, and with the wilderness, where resources could so easily run out. Yhwh "chose our possession for us, the rising of Jacob that he loves" (Ps 47:4 [MT 5]). English versions have the "pride" of Jacob, but that gives a misleading impression. The *gā'ôn* of Jacob is the impressive mountain country of Ephraim and Judah, which rises up from the Jordan and the coastal plain. Yhwh loves these highlands and thus swears by them (Amos 8:7), and having chosen Israel, therefore gives them to this people (EVV reckons it is Jacob that Yhwh loves, and therefore gives it the highlands; the result will be the same).[119]

Nevertheless, there is a sense in which the land continues to be Yhwh's. Israel does not own it but lives there as resident aliens *(gērîm)*, not now in relation to its human owners (e.g., Gen 15:13) but in relation to Yhwh (Lev 25:23). The land is referred to more often as "Yhwh's land" than as "Israel's land." Yhwh's continuing ownership is embodied in the requirement that Israel let the land rest one year in seven, leaving it to Yhwh (Lev 25:1-7, 20-22). Israelites cannot sell in perpetuity their own allocation of land to one another (Lev 25:23-24). You cannot sell something that does not really belong to you. You can sublet your land to someone else when you are in financial straits, but eventually things must get back to the way they were. The jubilee year is the year for "the restoration of the land."

Dispersed

But the land could become a distraction from keeping Yhwh in mind (Deut 6:10-15; 8:10-20). Israel could come to reckon that it had gained its prosperity by its own effort, forgetting the story of how Yhwh had brought it to the land. Or it could start following other gods, the deities of the peoples around them, deities whose activity focused on ensuring that people could "eat their fill." Instead, the land is to be a locus of obedience to Yhwh, a place where Israel gives itself to living by Yhwh's teaching (e.g., Deut 4:1-5, 14). It is free, for instance, to decide that it wants to be governed by a king, but the king must take steps to ensure that he lives by Yhwh's teaching (Deut 17:14-20). The land must not, for example, be defiled by the shedding of innocent blood (Deut 19:10) or by the sexual customs of the Canaanites (Lev 18; 20). If Israel fails here, it will find Yhwh devastating the land and/or expelling Israel from it (Lev 26:27-33; Deut 29:21-28 [MT 20-27]).

This expectation is a converse of the moral logic that opened up the land to Israel. Another misapprehension Israel might fall into was the idea that Yhwh gave it the land because of its moral superiority. It was not morally superior.

---

[119]On the gift of the land, see *OTT* 1:512-28.

Rather Yhwh was expelling the land's previous inhabitants because of their faithlessness (*riš'â*, Deut 9:4-5). This faithlessness expressed itself in abhorrent practices such as the sacrifice of children, forms of divination (which were allowed to the nations but are forbidden to Israel) and inquiring of the dead (of which perhaps the same was true) (Deut 18:9-14).

But Israel itself is characterized by faithlessness (*reša'*, Deut 9:27). It has a stiff neck (Deut 9:6), unwilling to turn in the direction Yhwh wishes. Such characteristics imperil its possession of the land as surely as they imperiled the Canaanites' possession of it. The claim that Yhwh owns the land but gives it to Israel might function ideologically, justifying Israel's taking it from other peoples. These warnings safeguard against that.

So Israel as a people is given up to subjection, death, exile, plundering and shame, a mere remnant of what it once was (Ezra 9:7, 13-15). In exile Israel weeps and remembers, is taunted and voiceless, reminds and looks for judgment (Ps 137). All that remains in Jerusalem or in dispersion is a group of survivors; Israel is a people grieved for and prayed for, confessed for and argued for (Ezra 1:4; Neh 1:4-11). It is a sign of God's grace that Israel survives at all with a toehold in its country and is able to feel encouraged through experiencing a little reviving even as it has to live under the authority of foreign kings (Ezra 9:8-9). For the history of rebellion never ends in Israel's annihilation, because saving it reveals Yhwh's power, because leaders such as Moses and Phinehas intervene on its behalf, standing between them and Yhwh's wrath, because Yhwh could not but hear its cry and remember the covenant relationship with them, because saving it could lead to testimony and glory (Ps 106). As the preserved remnant it is then challenged to be the responsive remnant (Ezra 10; Neh 9).

Isaiah 5:1-7 thus pictures the vinedresser abandoning the vine because it failed to produce good grapes, despite all the careful attention given it. On the other hand, Psalm 80 accuses Yhwh of abandoning the vineyard without such reason. It emphasizes the several sides to Yhwh's sovereignty. It was Yhwh who marvelously transplanted a vine from Egypt to Canaan, making space for it by clearing out the nations already there, and thus freed it to grow and flourish remarkably to the tops of the mountains and from the sea to the river (from the Mediterranean to the Euphrates?). But then in a dark equivalent to this movement between Yhwh's act and the vine's experience, Yhwh has broken down its wall, stopped protecting Israel, with the consequence that other peoples are free to ravage it. The vine is burned and cut down. The psalm then looks for a third exercise of Yhwh's sovereignty: for Yhwh to turn, to look, to see, to attend.

Vulnerable and Reduced to Leftovers

So apart from the question whether the people of God finds itself dispersed because it has failed God, it is the consistent experience of the people of God to be under attack from the rest of the world.[120] Its life confronts the world and inevitably provokes its attack. In Psalm 123 the people thus lift their eyes to Yhwh like servants looking to the hands of their masters and mistresses because they need Yhwh to show grace as they are overwhelmed by the scorn and contempt of their confident attackers. People have attacked it since its youth, though they have not overcome it (Ps 129). It prays as people who are weak and needy, seeking water and not finding any and thus being parched with thirst (Is 41:17). But it prays as a nation that from its beginning has known the difference it makes to have Yhwh on its side, and therefore not to be overwhelmed by peoples that sought to overwhelm it (Ps 124). It is rejected, abased, defeated, spoiled, slaughtered, scattered, discarded, taunted, shamed, broken, forgotten, cast off, oppressed, resourceless and powerless, like a bird at the mercy of predators (Ps 44; 74:19). The people of holy ones is subject to oppression and attack by mighty kings (Dan 7:21; 8:24-25). Loyalty to Yhwh seems to stimulate suffering rather than evade it (Dan 11). The experience of being turned into a mere remnant can come despite the fact that Israel lives in loyalty to the covenant and shapes its life by Yhwh's ways (Ps 44:17-26). Israel has escaped its enemies like a bird escaping a trap; if Yhwh had not been on Israel's side its enemies would have quite devoured it (Ps 124).

Yhwh's ownership of the land is an encouragement when Israel's possession of the land seems imperiled. Sometimes Israel experiences invasion and loss of part of the land, and sees this as evidencing Yhwh's rejection. But it can then remind itself of Yhwh's self-determination with regard to ownership and control of the land. Psalm 60 thus looks back to such a determination that Yhwh formulated near the beginning of Israel's story to exercise sovereignty over those who possessed Shechem and the Vale of Succot, and Gilead and Manasseh; both pairs of terms stand for the land as a whole, either side of the Jordan. Yhwh owns this land and is therefore in a position to allocate different parts of it to different clans, to measure it out among them. Yhwh will take possession of it in order to do so, by being the victorious warrior who acts via the Israelite clans. Thus Ephraim and Judah, the two clans that gave their names to the two parts of the land as a whole, are the warrior's helmet and scepter. The warrior is likewise in a position to treat other lands with sovereign freedom. Moab is the basin in which he washes off the grime and blood from his feet, Edom the place where he throws his dirty shoes as he does so. In light of that, the psalm snidely adds, Philistia (in the early monarchic period Israel's great rival for control of Canaan) can raise a battle shout if it wishes; it will not

---

[120]Cf. Barth's comments in *Church Dogmatics*, IV/3.ii:614-47, though he expresses this in terms of the individual.

be a threat to Yhwh! No, the warrior looks forward with confidence to battling against Edom, another foe that challenged Israel for possession of the land from another quarter (both in David's day and in the exile and after), and asks, where are the scouts who are going to show the way to its stronghold?

In a situation like that of Edomite occupation of much of the land in the exile and afterward, one can imagine the community asking whether God has abandoned them and challenging God to come to their aid again (Ps 60:10-11 [MT 12-12]). The fact that God declared sovereignty over this land in Joshua's day is their encouragement. "The staff of a faithless person will not rest over the allocation of the faithful" (Ps 125:3). The psalm apparently implies that at the moment that staff does exercise authority over the land Yhwh allocated to Israel, as happened during periods of time from the exile onward. But Yhwh surely cannot allow it to rest there, to stay there permanently.

Israel is taken away from a secure position in relation to land (Abraham), is settled in a land but without rights there (Abraham), is exiled from land (in Egypt), is given land as a possession and is able to control it (Joshua, David), is tempted by land, turfed off land to become settled forever elsewhere (Ephraim), turfed off land to become temporary settlers elsewhere (Judah), restored to land without political control (Sheshbazzar). Stories such as those of Ezra, Nehemiah, Esther and Daniel show it is possible to live a full Jewish life outside the land, but they also show in various ways how the land remains important for people who live elsewhere. It is to the land that Daniel prays, and Ezra and Nehemiah find themselves "returning" to this land that their forebears left long ago. It hardly makes sense to think of Israel as a people without a relationship to a land. If God had chosen to work through a nonethnic people, then that would have been quite possible, but God did not make that choice, and we have suggested that this reflects God's commitment to working with the realities of the actual world.

In turn that suggests that the Zionist quest for a return to the land fits with the purpose announced in the First Testament. But the principle on which Yhwh originally granted the land to Israel indicates that the Arab occupants of the land could not simply be expelled from it in the absence of any moral basis. So Yhwh's promise of the land does not imply support for Israel over against the Palestinians, and the First Testament illustrates the possibility of returning from exile to life in the land without statehood.

Yhwh's Kingdom in the Hands of a Human King

Rather surprisingly, the God who had resented the idea that anyone else should reign over Israel eventually issues a promise regarding a human king: "I will install him in my kingship/kingdom" (1 Chron 17:14). "Sit at my right hand, until I make your enemies a stool for your feet," Yhwh says, undertaking to make him dominate over his enemies (Ps 110:1-2). Perhaps even more surprisingly, alongside that promise is another declaration: "You are a priest forever, according to the order of Melchizedek" (Ps 110:4), a priest-king over the priestly kingdom. Yhwh apparently refers to the position in Jerusalem of a king such as Melchizedek, who exercised a priestly as well as a political role (cf. Gen 14:18-20). The First Testament seems not to infer that the king regularly took a leading role in the worship of the temple, though it does describe him as offering sacrifices and blessing the people on special occasions (e.g., 1 Chron 16:2). The main point of the promise is rather to undergird further his position as king in Jerusalem. He inherits a position that goes back centuries and that will hold "forever." Psalm 144:3 reflects on what an extraordinary commitment this is, adapting words that apply to all humanity: What is a man that Yhwh should so acknowledge him? "The good fortune of the people that has it so; the good fortune of the people that has Yhwh as its God!" (Ps 144:15). King and people live in symbiotic relationship. The people want to have a king to fight their battles (1 Sam 8:20). The king then needs their support and not least their prayer in order that he may do so successfully (Ps 20).

It is the king in particular whose experience provokes the declaration, "Yhwh is my cliff, my fastness, the one who enables me to escape. My God is my crag on which I take refuge, my shield, my peak that delivers, my haven" (Ps 18:2 [MT 3]). As Psalm 18 goes on to show, the king thus has special opportunity to testify to the experience of distress when threatened by enemies, calling on Yhwh and having Yhwh listen, come to take forceful action on his behalf and deliver him when he was otherwise lost (cf. also Ps 118). By such gifts of deliverance and by giving him long life rather than allowing him to lose his life in battle, Yhwh makes the king a blessing (Ps 21:6 [MT 7])—that is, so blesses him that other people make him the standard of blessing to which they aspire and for which they pray, like Abraham (Gen 12:2).

It is thus to Yhwh that the king must look for help, not to other resources: "Some people extol chariotry and others horses, but we—we extol the name of Yhwh our God" (Ps 20:2, 7 [MT 3, 8]). *Extolling* is a worship word. It implies looking at such resources the way one looks at Yhwh. Isaiah 30—31 similarly critiques "trust" in such resources. Yhwh is the one to trust. So the king is not to go down to Egypt for help (Is 30:1; 31:5). Isaiah 30 critiques people's applying words such as *refuge, shelter* and *protection* to Egypt as they put their trust in horses and chariotry. The king will not make that mistake but will extol only Yhwh.

The promise is given more detail in Psalm 89. The covenant with Abraham and the covenant with Israel are supplemented by a covenant with David and his successors, who will be able to relate to Yhwh like a son to a father (cf. Ps 2). The king's authorization comes from having been anointed by Yhwh, via the hands of a person such as a prophet or priest and/or by the people, via their representative. Further, this anointing signifies the commitment of the anointers to the anointed. By this rite the king receives Yhwh's support and the people's support. Anointing implies a covenantal commitment to the king by both these parties.[121] Psalm 89 speaks of no conditions attaching to Yhwh's covenant, but any Israelite would recognize that an unconditioned divine or human commitment implies expectations about the way the recipient of this commitment will serve Yhwh and people, as the unconditioned declaration "You are my son" implies expectations concerning the way the son honors the father.

Of course the irony is that Yhwh has done exactly the opposite: rejected, become angry, renounced the covenant, failed to keep commitment (Ps 89:38-51 [MT 39-52]). Like Elie Wiesel's stories, a psalm such as this refuses closure. It is "part of a process that destroys the enchantment of reality and reveals the jagged edges of events which have not been domesticated by memory and reduced to consonance."[122] The dissonance of story and psalm is what enables them to be a source of strength, because they face what is disturbing rather than avoiding it. It is noteworthy that Psalm 89 closes Book III of the Psalter. It thus stands in tension with Psalm 2 (virtually the beginning of Book I) and Psalm 72 (the end of Book II).[123] Psalm 2 made promises, Psalm 72 laid out expectations, Psalm 89 declares that the promises have failed and implies that the kings' failure to live up to the kingly ideal does not provide a satisfactory explanation because Yhwh had declared that the promise would stand even if the king did not live up to the ideal.

A Return to a Priestly Kingdom

"A king's mind is a water channel in Yhwh's hand; he inclines it wherever he wishes" (Prov 21:1). A farmer channels water as he wishes to irrigate his crops, and Yhwh does the same with the king's mind. Not only can Yhwh know what is going on in a person's mind, Yhwh can also project images of possible actions there, so that the king makes decisions in line with Yhwh's purpose. Yhwh thus pushes the king toward decisions that will have the beneficent effect of irrigation on the growth of the crops. Yet evidently Yhwh does not always act thus, and often presidents and prime ministers act in a way that

---

[121]On the significance of this practice in its Middle Eastern context, see Tryggve N. D. Mettinger, *King and Messiah*, ConBOT (Lund: Gleerup, 1976), pp. 185-232.

[122]Graham B. Walker, *Elie Wiesel* (Jefferson, N.C.: McFarland, 1988), p. 32, as quoted by Marvin E. Tate, *Psalms 51—100*, WBC (Dallas: Word), p. 430.

[123]Cf. Gerald H. Wilson, "The Use of Royal Psalms at the 'Seams' of the Hebrew Psalter," *JSOT* 35 (1986): 85-94.

benefits only themselves and their cronies rather than their people. "'All kings,' observed Huckleberry Finn, 'is mostly rapscallions,' and Solomon was no exception."[124] Nor were later Judean and Ephraimite kings, along with emperors, presidents and other such leaders.

Yet you have to serve somebody. In the last decades before the exile, and of course in the exile itself, Judah serves Babylon; Jeremiah wears a yoke that symbolizes that. But Yhwh intends to break that yoke and free the people to serve Yhwh and to serve David (Jer 30:8). They will serve a king from their own people rather than serving a stranger. Hosea perhaps recognizes that the nation will need leadership in some form. "The people of Judah and the people of Israel will assemble together and appoint for themselves one head" (Hos 1:11 [MT 2:2]). While "head" can apply to the king (1 Sam 15:17), avoiding the word *king* suggests the assumption that monarchy, never having been Yhwh's first choice, must be abandoned, even if the people do need some sort of single common leader. Yhwh intends to terminate the kingship of the household of Israel (Hos 1:4), and it is not to be reestablished, nor simply to be replaced by a Davidic kingship.

Once Judah is under the domination of a foreign empire and has lost its kings, it comes under the authority of an official appointed by the foreign power, though commonly a Judean. The first of these is Gedaliah (see Jer 39—41). The story hints that he was an honorable man who set about trying to fulfill the demanding task of standing between the Judeans and the Babylonians, but he was naive in his assessment of the difficulties of this position. He dismissed rumors of a plot against his life and paid for that with his life. Sadly, that meant people assassinated what otherwise looks like the best leader Israel had since Josiah, who also paid with his life for an unwise decision. Subsequently the portrayal of governors such as Zerubbabel and Nehemiah hints that rule by a governor is a wiser form of leadership than monarchy.

That fits with the way Second Isaiah "democratizes" Yhwh's promise to David, so that Isaiah 55:3-5 forms a response to the lament in Psalm 89.[125] It also fits the way Ezekiel has a place for someone called a prince in the renewed Jerusalem, but little place for a human king (Ezek 37:22-24 does speak of "my servant David" as king over them"). When the palace has been laid out, the real sovereign who abandoned the city can return (see Ezek 43:1-12). Looking out from the great eastern gateway, designed with this return in mind, Ezekiel

---

[124]Johnny E. Wiles, *Wise King—Royal Fool*, JSOTSup 399 (London/New York: T & T Clark, 2004), p. 39, quoting from Mark Twain, *Huckleberry Finn* (reprint, Berkeley: University of California, 2001), p. 199.

[125]See section 8.2 "Recognition for Yhwh's Sake." Wilson ("The Use of Royal Psalms at the 'Seams'") suggests that Psalms 90—106 also form a response to Ps 89.

sees the most electrifying and moving sight. "There—the splendor of the God of Israel was coming from the east, its sound like the sound of mighty waters. The earth shone with his splendor." Its appearance is the same as that in Ezekiel's vision in Babylonia and the same as his vision of Yhwh's splendor abandoning the city; it returns from the direction by which it had left (see Ezek 10—11). There is monumental reassurance in both these facts. "As Yhwh's splendor was going into the house by way of the gate that faced eastward, a spirit lifted me and took me into the inner court. And there, Yhwh's splendor was filling the palace" (Ezek 43:4-5). Yhwh in person addresses Ezekiel: "Mortal, this is the place for my throne and the place for the soles of my feet, where I will dwell in the midst of the Israelites forever" (Ezek 43:7). The fact that Yhwh in person speaks means there is no doubt that this will happen. Further, there is no doubt that this is a real presence. Yhwh is a real person who sits on a seat and has feet to put on a footstool. The down-to-earth anthropomorphic expressions "exclude all doubt about the reality of his presence."[126]

There is no doubt that this person is a king, for the seat is a throne, the only throne in the new Jerusalem. At first sight this commitment seems an unconditional one, though as usual Yhwh's apparently unqualified commitment makes demands on people, and these complicate the issue. Yhwh demands that the household of Israel and their kings do not again defile Yhwh by their (religious) promiscuity and by the commemoration of their kings in proximity to Yhwh's dwelling,[127] but also adds that then "I will dwell among them forever." The Scriptures' usual tension between unqualified and conditional commitment appears here.

Yhwh's people has never arrived; it is always on the way. It starts off as a people Yhwh commissions to go to a new place and to which Yhwh makes outlandish promises. It continues to be a people that finds itself on the move. It "finds itself": that is, this does not happen because it chooses to move; indeed, it usually resents it and wishes to go back to where it came from. It experiences partial fulfillment of those promises: always real fulfillment, but always partial fulfillment.

In its relationship with Yhwh, too, Israel is ever on the way to its destination. As the church is disunited and faithless as well as one and holy, so Israel

---

[126]Walther Eichrodt, *Ezekiel* (London: SCM Press/Philadelphia: Westminster Press, 1970), p. 555.

[127]It is not clear whether this refers to burial of them, memorials to them or offerings for them (see, e.g., Leslie C. Allen, *Ezekiel 20—48*, WBC [Dallas: Word, 1994], p. 257). Nor is it clear whether the offense lies in the kings' encroaching on the space of the great King or in the kings' involvement in the religious promiscuity or in the pollution involved in their corpses being located there or in the practices involved in the offerings made in connection with their commemoration.

is also Jacob, the deceiver. It is the "field of conflict between spirit and flesh, righteousness and sin, and presses, in intention, beyond its historical forms towards redemption, by virtue of its hope."[128] It is surprising neither that Israel (or the church) sometimes experiences God's blessing and the signs of God's deliverance, and sometimes walks God's way, nor that it sometimes does not. The former is a sign that God is taking it to its destination, to the age to come; the latter is an indication that it is not there yet, that we still live in this age.

3.5 Yhwh's Servant

It is in the context of Israel's exile and dispersion that the First Testament also develops the image of Israel as Yhwh's servant. "The modern notion of the servant Church . . . seems to lack any direct foundation in the Bible,"[129] in the sense that it does not speak of the people of God as designed to be a servant of the world, but the people of God is designed to be the servant of God.

It is naturally more common for the First Testament to use the expression "Yhwh's servant" to describe an individual such as Moses, David, Isaiah or Nebuchadnezzar. Describing Israel as Yhwh's servant stretches the implications of the word. It is a first instance of the way Isaiah 40—55 democratizes ideas, applying to the people as a whole images that by their nature apply more readily to an individual, and specifically to a king such as David (e.g., Is 37:35; Jer 33:21, 22, 26; Ezek 34:23, 24; 37:24, 25). The image suggests both the way, as Yhwh's servant, that Israel knows Yhwh's support and the way its task is to be the means of Yhwh's teaching coming to the world and to be a witness to the world, not least by its embodying how Yhwh's covenant with a people works out.

Supported

When the Persian king Cyrus is generating instability and panic through the Middle East, other peoples faced with the uncertainties of political events are anxiously shoring up their gods. Yhwh then reminds Jacob-Israel that being Yhwh's chosen people also means being Yhwh's servant (Is 41:8-16; cf. Ps 136:22; Jer 30:10-11).

Being someone's servant implies both subordination and status. Servants are subordinate to their bosses and have no choice about whether they do what their bosses require, but they are associated with their bosses and share something of their honor. In the context in Isaiah 41:8-16, the honored and

---

[128]Moltmann, *The Church in the Power of the Spirit*, p. 23, speaking of Israel. I am not sure in what sense the church or Israel presses or has such an intention or hope, but I know that God does, and this is what counts.

[129]Avery Dulles, *Models of the Church*, p. 100.

privileged status of servanthood has the emphasis. Other peoples are reacting quite rationally to this crisis, doing the best they can do in a situation that is genuinely threatening to their political future and the adequacy of their religious resources. Israel has no need to get caught up in their distress. Ultimately, the one who is causing the instability is Yhwh, and Jacob-Israel is Yhwh's servant, with the significance and security that attaches to a relationship with Yhwh. The whole people has the significance and security that attached to David.

As a servant, Israel is the one Yhwh chose. Yhwh acted like the "capable wife" of Proverbs 31:10-31, looking at possible workers at the job market and deciding which one to employ. So being chosen to be a servant conveys significant status. Yet it does leave a person only a servant, not, for instance, a son; so Yhwh adds a description that conveys much more status. Jacob-Israel is the offspring of Abraham, and as such is Yhwh's friend (Is 51:8).[130] In the context this suggests not merely a buddy-buddy relationship, which is not what Jacob-Israel needs as the Persian cavalry thunders over the hill toward Babylon. It suggests that Yhwh and Jacob-Israel are allies, like Hiram and David (1 Kings 5:1 [MT 15]). In this alliance Yhwh is the senior partner, like the U.S.A. in relation to the U.K., and in that sense friendship is not so different from servanthood. But the word *friend* points to a more-than-servile relationship between the two parties, while also further underlining the honor and security of Jacob-Israel's position in relation to Yhwh.

The description of Yhwh as "restorer" (gōʾēl) underlines that yet further, since a gōʾēl is a member of one's family with resources that one does not have, who takes action to restore a situation to what it should be.[131] The word thus has similar implications to the designation of Jacob-Israel as Yhwh's friend. It does not suggest an egalitarian relationship between the two parties. It is "Israel's holy one" who makes this commitment, the God who is transcendent and sovereign in relation to Israel, yet who is committed to Israel (Is 41:14). Indeed, its good news lies in the opposite direction from suggesting an egalitarian relationship. This restorer is a relative who is in a much better position, but has a commitment to a needy member of the extended family.

"You are my servant" is performative language. By this declaration, Jacob-Israel was turned into Yhwh's servant, as the king is turned into God's adoptive child by the declaration "You are my son" (Ps 2:7). That happened when

---

[130]Grammatically, "my friend" could be a description of Abraham (cf. 2 Chron 20:7), but the parallelism in the line suggests it is a description of the people, and this understanding makes the tricolon in Is 41:8 come to a climax, as one might expect, rather than ending more limply with a description that applies only to the people's ancestor.

[131]See the comments on this word in section 2.2 "Restorer."

Yhwh took hold of it from the ends of the earth, by taking hold of Abraham and Sarah and summoning them to move to Canaan. English versions have Yhwh thus "calling" them, but translating *qārā'* thus can give a wrong impression. This "call" is not like a vocation in our sense, and certainly not something you can choose whether to respond to. It is like a boss's summons. The employee has no choice but to come running. But that does also mean that the employee has the boss's support when, for instance, some other would-be boss threatens the servant. Of course bosses do let employees go, and Jacob-Israel's poor job performance over the centuries would entirely justify Yhwh's letting it go. The exile could look as if that is exactly what Yhwh has done. Indeed, Jacob-Israel thus sees itself as a mere worm (cf. Ps 22:6 [MT 7]); it is a mere relic of what it once was.

So Yhwh reassures Israel that it is still Yhwh's servant; it has not been let go. "I have not abandoned you/rejected you" (Is 41:9). The relationship holds. It is actually not in the boss's interest to let the servant be imperiled; the boss would not then be able to get the job done.

All this implies that being Yhwh's servant means Jacob-Israel has no need to be afraid, like Marduk's servants, who have good reason to be afraid. "I am with you," says the boss. You have my absolute support. Again, in our experience such an assurance on a boss's part can have ironic implications; it might be true today, but it has no implications for tomorrow if the boss's interests point in another direction. In Yhwh's case, "I am with you" is not a statement made from the security of the CEO's office on the top floor. It means Yhwh is present and active, strengthening, helping, upholding. The boss does not just leave the servant to get on with it and go off to the beach, especially when opposition hits the fan. When the servant is under attack, the boss stands alongside and acts in a faithful fashion *(ṣedeq)*. Yhwh is committed to restoring this servant.

Fulfilling Yhwh's Commission

Being Yhwh's servant is thus an encouragement, though the term *servant* implies that the position also brings responsibility. There will be a task for the servant to fulfill. There can be no ideological appropriation of belief in election.

There is huge variety in the roles that servants fulfill for masters and that servants such as Moses or David or Isaiah or Nebuchadnezzar fulfill for Yhwh. So what is Israel's particular task as servant? The description of the servant in Isaiah 42:1-4 begins resumptively. "You know that servant whom I chose and whom I uphold?" The opening makes clear that the prophecy takes up the description of Israel in the previous chapter. What we are to hear is a further description of that servant, in terms of his role, though the description omits to name the servant as Israel, which will turn out to be significant.

This servant is one "on whom I put my spirit" with the result that he is in a position to bring Yhwh's *mišpāṭ* to the nations (Is 42:1). Yhwh's spirit came on people such as the leaders in Judges, who are described as *šōpĕṭîm*, "leaders" or "people who act authoritatively." One could thus say that the result of their activity was to reestablish Yhwh's *mišpāṭ*, Yhwh's authority.[132] Israel had gone wrong in its attitude to Yhwh, and Yhwh had made things go wrong in its life. Yhwh has thus been acting with authority in a negative way—acting as judge, in fact, in our sense of the word. But the positive acts of these *šōpĕṭîm* established *mišpāṭ* in a more positive sense.

That is now this servant's role in relation to the nations. The implication is that the nations' experience rather resembles that of Israel in Judges (perhaps because their life resembles Israel's life in Judges, too). There, being under God's judgment (in our sense) made Israel cry out to Yhwh (*ṣāʿaq*, Judg 4:3). It was the same cry as they had cried in Egypt (*ṣaʿăqâ*, Ex 3:7, 9), though the Israelites were not the first to utter that cry. It was the cry that Abel's blood uttered and the cry that came up from Sodom (Gen 4:10; 18:21; 19:13). The prophet has already spoken of the fear and trembling of the nations as Cyrus advances (Is 41:5). What was true of Abel and the oppressed of Sodom is true of the nations as a whole. They are crying out, in their fear of what is going to happen to them, crying out like Israel in Egypt. They are thus waiting for the servant's teaching (Is 42:4). They may not be aware that this is what they are waiting for, but they need *something* that will speak to their fear and their cry.

Yhwh's servant will not cry out as Abel and Sodom and Israel once did. Confronted by nations that are like bent reeds or flickering candles, he does not trample them underfoot or blow out their flame, as one might expect a conqueror like Cyrus to do. He has a mission to bring them Yhwh's own truthfulness or steadfastness (*ʾĕmet*), and his bringing Yhwh's *mišpāṭ* is destined to have that effect in the world. And he will not waver until he has completed his task. How he does it—for instance, by taking certain sorts of action as well as by proclamation—is not made specific.

To put it another way, Jacob-Israel is the aide Yhwh sends (Is 42:19). Aides (*malʾāk*; EVV have "messenger" or "angel") act on behalf of the divine or human king in at least two ways. They are messengers, announcing the king's requirements or desires or intentions (e.g., Is 14:32; 18:2; 30:4; 37:9, 14; 44:26). They are also executors, empowered to act on the king's behalf (e.g., Is 37:36; 63:9; Prov 17:11). Describing Jacob-Israel as Yhwh's aide exalts both

---

[132]"Justice" (e.g., NRSV, NIVI) or "the true way" (JPSV) are involved, but these expressions do not catch the specific nuance of the word, as "judges" does not catch the meaning of *šōpĕṭîm*: see section 2.3 "Power and Authority."

the privilege of its position and its responsibility.[133]

The trouble is that this description comes in the context of declaring that this servant-aide is actually himself deaf and blind, both in the sense of sitting in the darkness of imprisonment and in the sense of lacking any insight into Yhwh's ways with him (Is 42:18-25). This servant cannot fulfill the role ascribed to the servant or that described in those words that follow.

Covenant

After the initial description of the servant's vocation, the prophet's reexpresses it in different words (Is 42:5-9). Yhwh speaks of summoning and taking by the hand, again picking up the language of that earlier encouragement to Israel that looked back to the summons and taking of Abraham and Sarah (Is 41:8-9). It again pushes its logic. Yhwh had then declared that Abraham would "become a blessing" to the nations (Gen 12:2). Abraham's experience of blessing would be such that other nations would want the same for themselves. Yhwh here uses an analogous expression in saying, "I made you a covenant of people, a light of nations."[134] The covenant relationship into which Yhwh entered with Abraham becomes a model for people in general of the kind of commitment Yhwh is prepared to make to them. Israel thus becomes a light for nations as they see the good things God gives Israel. In a way not here explained, this is a means of releasing people from the prison they are in; that is a related image to the picture of them as people crying out under oppression.

Against the background of Israel's actually being "despised in spirit, loathed by nations, servant of kings," Yhwh later restates much of this (Is 49:7-13). Israel indeed looks like a people that has been abandoned, but at last the moment has come when Yhwh is looking on this weak people with acceptance and favor instead of anger. At last Yhwh is answering them, responding to their sad cries of abandonment and acting to deliver them and "help" them (Is 49:8). (But ʿāzar denotes something more dynamic, decisive and indispensable than "help," as the collocation with "deliverance" suggests; "help" presupposes that people are helpless, not merely that one is adding a little to the efforts of people who are also "helping themselves," and that Yhwh is taking decisive action to rescue people who cannot help themselves.) Now Yhwh is

---

[133]On "aide," see section 2.2 "Yhwh's Embodiment." The passage also describes Jacob-Israel as *mĕšullām*, a puzzling expression that BDB takes to mean "one in a covenant of peace"; this would be another indicator of Yhwh's commitment to this servant.

[134]"Covenant of people" is an elliptical expression but the previous verse and the parallel phrase "light of nations" confirm that the "people" are people in the world in general, and the parallel phrase indicates that "covenant of people" is a kind of objective genitive, not a defining one. For "covenant people" (JPSV) one would expect the words in the reverse order.

keeping guard over them in this situation where other nations are imperiled.

Thus Yhwh is making them into a covenant for people; the phrase recurs from Isaiah 42:6. There Yhwh went on to state the aim of this, to free people from their imprisonment, and hinted at the way Yhwh would achieve this, by the method announced in the promise to Abraham. Here Yhwh takes that further. Yhwh's making them a covenant for people comes about in acts such as reallocating the land, freeing prisoners, providing for those who are on a journey and assembling those who are scattered to the four points of the compass. Some of these phrases could refer to the peoples of the world themselves, but some must refer to Yhwh's restoring Israel, which suggests that this is the significance of the phrases as a whole.

Yhwh speaks of restoring the land itself, which is not unoccupied but is still devastated by invasion and assumed to continue to be in a neglected state, with the owners of many parts of it in exile. Thus one aspect of restoring it is the bringing home of the exiles out of their bondage, providing for them on their journey back home and drawing their fellow Israelites from different points of the compass. It is by this that Yhwh will restore the land—and make Israel a covenant for people. They will provide a working model of what it means to be in covenant with Yhwh and a promise of what Yhwh intends for all peoples. It is therefore appropriate that the heavens and the earth should be drawn into rejoicing at the prospect of Yhwh's restoring Israel (Is 49:13). It means something for the destiny of the world as a whole.

Witness

The role of teacher, of one who brings news of Yhwh's purpose being implemented in the world, might also be pictured as the role of a witness (Is 43:8-13).

Outside the work of Karl Barth, in modern theology the idea of witness became a dead metaphor, even when (especially when) theologians routinely spoke of the "witness" of the Old Testament, until it became central to Walter Brueggemann's *Theology of the Old Testament*. It is a crucial category in Isaiah 40—55,[135] where it is new, alive and concrete. Oddly, its context is one of religious pluralism, so if we could bring the metaphor back to life, it might be a helpful one for us.

Here, then, the relationship between faiths is pictured as one of debate or disputation, like the debate that takes place in a civil court when a dispute between two parties regarding an issue such as the ownership of something or responsibility for some accident needs to be resolved. In such a disputation a key role is played by witnesses who can give testimony regarding the matter.

---

[135]Cf. Brueggemann, *Theology of the OT*, p. 120.

The disputed question is, "Who is at work in history, and specifically in current events in the Middle East? And thus who is the real God, the one the nations need to acknowledge?" The Babylonians, for instance, claim that Marduk is in control of events. Yhwh has summoned Israel to court for it to give contrasting testimony on the basis of its own experience. It can testify to the fact that Yhwh declared the intention to act in such a way as to deliver Israel by using the Medes to put down the Babylonians. That development is taking place before the world's eyes. Israel is in a singular position to testify to Yhwh's uniquely being the one responsible for it. Israel has eyes and ears; it has been listening to its prophets over the years and watching events that have happened. When the worshipers of the Babylonian gods attempt to provide evidence for their convictions, they and their gods are going to look stupid, because the Babylonians cannot provide any evidence that these gods have declared their intention and are now implementing it, as Yhwh has.

The trouble is that despite all this, Israel is blind and deaf. It has been unwilling to open its eyes and listen to what its prophets have said. So surely Yhwh will have to give up any hope of winning this argument or will have to look elsewhere for witnesses. And what is Yhwh doing in commissioning the court to bring out these deaf and blind witnesses and summoning the nations to come to listen to the debate? Is Yhwh not also set up for humiliation? Apparently Yhwh reckons this need not be so. Yhwh is prepared to parade Israel as witnesses in the conviction that they will come good.

It is an extraordinary evidence of Yhwh's commitment to Israel. It emerges from the fact that Yhwh *had* made that commitment and cannot get out of it. One might imagine Yhwh knowing that this commitment meant leaving Israel with the status of servant, but resolving to kick him upstairs and find someone else to do the strategic work as servant (roughly what some Christians think later happened). But this would not be a true honoring of that commitment. Yhwh had chosen Israel to do the work of servant, of witness, and still intends that Israel should fulfill its vocation.

Indeed, the object is not merely that the world should hear its testimony but that Israel should hear itself giving its testimony and thus come to acknowledge and believe in Yhwh, believe that Yhwh is the only real God, who antedated all other so-called gods and who will also postdate them. The witnesses are to convert themselves.

At present they themselves do not believe that Yhwh is involved in events in the way the prophet says. They do not see Yhwh's hand at work. Having to give their testimony will mean they have to listen to it, and perhaps they will thus come to believe it. One reason for this is that the characteristic attribute of Yhwh that their testimony will reflect is the fact that Yhwh is "deliverer," the one who "delivered." This is not merely a dispute about power in events but

about a gracious purposefulness. They will see themselves again as the beneficiaries of Yhwh's deliverance. At the moment they believe themselves cast
off by Yhwh. Being driven nevertheless to speak for Yhwh as witnesses will
provide the evidence that this is not so. They are not cast off. Yhwh is still committed to them. It is hard to imagine more impressive evidence than Yhwh's
insistence on still using them as witnesses when they are deaf and blind. In
both senses it will be the means of opening their eyes and ears.

It is thus through being called to be a witness that Israel hears the good
news to which it testifies. There is then a reciprocal relationship between its
giving its witness and its enjoying that to which it witnesses. Only because it
is called to witness does it enjoy; only through its enjoying does it witness.[136]

For the people of God to witness to the world it is integral that it be a people
like other peoples. No one can witness if they are invisible. Yet at the same time
the people of God cannot be a witness unless it is also invisible in the sense of
being mysterious and incapable of being grasped merely as a people or institution like any other.[137] It thus "exists in total dependence on its environment
and yet also in total freedom in relation to it."[138] It has no distinctive language
or social form.[139] It exists in supreme weakness and supreme strength.[140]

3.6 Yhwh's Disciple

A servant needs to know and to heed the master's will. Israel as Yhwh's servant is thus taught on an ongoing basis by the teaching that came to be collected in the Torah and also by the teaching of prophets. Yhwh indeed
covenants to keep speaking to the people to this end. Of course this puts it on
the spot; the question is whether the servant will take any notice of the master.
The capacity of prophecy to keep speaking to Israel and to find fulfillment is
enhanced by its being put into writing.

Taught by Yhwh

Yhwh's servant is someone who has a disciple's tongue, someone whose ear
Yhwh continually opens (Is 50:4-5).[141] He is someone to whom God's word
comes. As Yhwh's servant, Israel is someone continually (or at least recur-

---

[136]Cf. Barth's discussion of "the liberation of the Christian" (*Church Dogmatics*, IV/3.ii:647-
62).

[137]Cf. Barth, *Church Dogmatics*, IV/3.ii:725-26.

[138]Cf. ibid., IV/3.ii:734.

[139]Cf. ibid., IV/3.ii:735-42.

[140]Cf. ibid., IV/3.ii:742-62.

[141]Is 50:4-9 describes the prophet's own calling, but insofar as the prophet speaks as Yhwh's
servant, the description can also be applied to Israel as Yhwh's servant.

rently, century after century) addressed by Yhwh. As Yhwh's witness, Israel is someone who testifies to the word Yhwh speaks before and after acting.

Yhwh does that especially through the prophets. The Torah itself is contextual in the sense that its teaching emerges from contexts and presupposes contexts. It envisages life in the land, when the people want to have a king, when harvests have failed and people have to sell their labor, when the multiplicity of sanctuaries raises problems, when the rise of prophets raises problems, when Yhwh throws the people out of the land for ignoring the provisions of the covenant, when Yhwh restores them and renews them. It thus speaks directly to contexts up to seven centuries after Moses' day (as well as indirectly way beyond that). The contextual nature of this teaching reflects the fact that over those centuries Yhwh inspired a process whereby questions were rethought in new contexts. But the nature of that process is hypothetical, and the Torah sets forth the Mosaic era as quite different from anything that followed (Deut 34:10). "In fact, so unavailable is that Mosaic mode of revelation that even the site of the grave of the great prophet is unknown" (Deut 34:6), like the location of Sinai itself.[142] Putting the teaching into writing in such a way as to associate it with the beginnings of Israel's story, rather than with the contexts to which it directly relates, in due course encourages a different dynamic. Yhwh's teaching comes through an explicit process of interpreting Yhwh's teaching expressed in a given text. Israel becomes the interpretive community described in Ezra and Nehemiah.[143]

Prophecy contrasts with the Torah. The prophets overtly bring up to date Yhwh's expectations, and they challenge Israel about its response to Yhwh. They, too, mediate Yhwh's *tôrâ* and Yhwh's word: "Listen to Yhwh's word," Isaiah urges, and in parallelism, "attend to our God's teaching" (Is 1:10). The trouble is, people "have rejected the teaching of Yhwh Armies, spurned the word of Israel's holy one" (Is 5:24). "They are a rebellious people, deceitful children, children who have refused to listen to Yhwh's teaching" and who (implicitly) tell seers and prophets to stop telling them about Israel's Holy One (Is 30:9-11). "Bind up the declaration, seal the teaching among my disciples," Isaiah further urges (Is 8:16). A declaration *(tĕ'ûdâ)* is a solemn statement of God's will or requirements; perhaps it is significant that Isaiah here uses this word in parallelism with *tôrâ*, and not the much more common related words *'ēdōt* or *'ēdût* that have more distinctly legal connotations. But the parallelism also indicates that *tôrâ* does have the authority of something solemnly attested by Yhwh. "Word" and "teaching" are parallel again in the vision of a time

---

[142]Levenson, *Sinai and Zion*, p. 90.

[143]See *OTT* 1:732-40. There is no need to understand this pejoratively, with Wolfhart Pannenberg (*Systematic Theology*, 3:59-60).

when nations come to Jerusalem to be taught by Yhwh, when "teaching will issue from Zion, Yhwh's word from Jerusalem" (Is 2:3)

Covenanted

In Isaiah 59:21 Yhwh speaks to the prophet about a covenant with the reformed people,[144] a covenant concerning the prophet: "My spirit that is on you and my words that I have put in your mouth will not depart from your mouth and from the mouth of your offspring and from the mouth of their offspring (Yhwh has said) from now and forever." The implication is that having a prophet speak to them is a blessing. They may sometimes have doubted this, though it is supported by the context as it follows on an encouraging vision about Yhwh's taking action like a warrior to restore the people, and it introduces visions of restoration (Is 60—62), which include further reference to the way the spirit of Lord Yhwh has come on the prophet to bring them an encouraging message (Is 61:1). There will still be need to challenge the people, as is hinted by the barbed comment about people who turn from rebellion. But in a context where the people will continue to be under the control of a superpower and pressured by their neighbors, the task of prophecy will be fundamentally encouraging rather than warning. It will actually be like that of the "false prophets" before the exile. Yhwh promises to keep speaking to Israel.

Yhwh's promise holds together spirit and word. *Spirit* commonly stands for the unpredictable and dynamic aspect to prophecy, the aspect that evidences Yhwh's involvement and indicates that there is something more here than the merely human. Over against spirit, *word* then stands for the content of what the prophet says. The supernatural nature of the words is also emphasized: although it will be a prophet's mouth that speaks, the words that emerge will not be ones the prophet formulated but words God put there. It will be as if Yhwh is manipulating the prophet like a puppet, and the prophet will discover the content of the message the same way as everyone else does, by listening to it. This is not the First Testament's only model for understanding the relationship between a prophet's words and God's words, but it is one such model. Thus a prophet does not merely testify to supernatural experiences or behave in exotic ways, though one should expect that, and a purported prophet who behaves in normal ways would be an odd phenomenon. A prophet speaks.

In Isaiah the activity of Yhwh's spirit also links with having the insight of a king and with his commitment to *mišpāṭ ûṣĕdāqâ*, decisive acts of faithfulness

---

[144]The prose promise looks to be of separate origin from the preceding poetic oracle, but in the context I take the "them" to be "people in Jacob who have turned from rebellion" (Is 59:20).

(Is 11:1-5; 32:15-17; 42:1-4). That link again follows well from the verses that precede Isaiah 59:21, where Yhwh promises to come to implement *mišpāṭ ûṣĕdāqâ* (and with the prayer that precedes that in Is 59:9-15a, which acknowledges the absence of *mišpāṭ ûṣĕdāqâ* in the community). So the promise of Yhwh's spirit is a promise that the dynamic activity of God will put on the prophet's lips words that promise *mišpāṭ ûṣĕdāqâ* in the affairs of the world and in the community's life. The activity of prophets promises to Israel the involvement of God in their lives and promises the words they need to hear as the years pass. For the undertaking does not relate only to this one prophet, but envisages another generation of prophets to follow, and another after that.

What is the cash value of the "forever" (like that of the "forever" applying to priesthood and kingship)? It is often said that prophecy "died out" in the Second Temple period, though the evidence is circumstantial and may indicate only that prophecy took different forms. The person who speaks here is the "Third Isaiah," though that is only a model or a way of reifying whoever it was who did utter these words. Whoever it was, the nature of this person's functioning as a prophet, as a divine mouthpiece, is different from that which obtained for Isaiah ben Amoz. For all the talk about Yhwh putting words in the mouth, to a significant extent the words from this prophet, in Isaiah 56—66 (and not least in the chapters that immediately follow), constitute a re-preaching of the words of Second Isaiah, as Second Isaiah's ministry took up First Isaiah's. Yhwh's word in the mouths of prophets now looks more like the word in the mouth of a preacher on a scriptural text. An implication of this is that the very fact that this process continues as we are now studying Isaiah and hearing God speak out of it indicates that Yhwh's promise is still being fulfilled—and that is so not for the sake of prophet or preacher but for the sake of their community. It is with the latter that Yhwh makes a covenant.

Faced with Yhwh's Written Testimony

The regular way whereby Israel receives Yhwh's communication is in speech. Prophets stand in places such as the temple courts and address people who come there to worship. The spoken word facilitates some forms of communication. Yhwh finds potential in words. Jeremiah's first vision of calamity (first in the order in the book, at least) depends on the significance of some spoken words. Seeing the branch of an almond tree (*šāqēd*) prompts Yhwh's declaration, "I am watching [*šōqēd*] over my word, to put it into effect" (Jer 1:11-12). The sight of a basket of figs (*qayiṣ*) prompts the declaration that the time (*qēṣ*) has come for Israel (Amos 8:1-2).[145] Everyday words have a mysterious capac-

---

[145]See the introduction to section 4.3.

ity to become windows to epoch-making events, because both belong to one reality, the reality over which Yhwh is Lord.

By its nature, then, prophecy is an oral operation, but for a variety of reasons it does not stay that way. Isaiah closes off the account of his ministry with the command, "bind up the declaration, seal the teaching among my disciples" (Is 8:16). Such language might be a metaphorical way of referring to his disciples' committing his teaching to memory, but more likely part of the point of this instruction is similar to that of his earlier writing down the words "pillage hurries, looting speeds" and the later commission to inscribe things on a scroll as a testimony against them (Is 8:1; 30:8). When it comes true, this will prove that he spoke from Yhwh, and it will give the people reason to reconsider his teaching as a whole and maybe find a future as they repent. "Writing prophecies was a response to the non-reception of their oral delivery."[146]

Binding up the declaration and sealing the teaching suggests a close to Isaiah's ministry, or a new stage to it. Isaiah says he is now just going to wait for Yhwh to act (Is 8:17-18). The words have similar significance to the ones that came nearer the beginning of this account of his ministry (Is 6—8), where Yhwh declared the intention to punish Israel by keeping speaking but making Israel blind and deaf so that they do not respond. Here the punishment is superficially different, but its implications are the same. Yhwh's face is turning away from Israel. There are times in a relationship when all has been said and there is nothing else to say, and so it is for Yhwh in relation to Israel; and therefore Isaiah, too, has nothing else to say. All there is now for Isaiah to do is wait for Yhwh's word to come true, which will be the vindication of his ministry. One sign he continues to offer people is his silence. Another is his sealed scroll. But another is his children with their names that suggested threat, with a hint of promise. Yes, they are signs ('ôt) and portents (môpēt); signs are usually positive, portents usually threatening. And that in itself also reminds us to look for the rhetorical significance of this declaration about sealing the teaching and simply waiting for Yhwh to act, a rhetorical significance parallel to that of the declaration that Yhwh intends to make the people deaf and blind. The declaration that henceforth Yhwh and Isaiah will say nothing is another threat designed to jolt people into listening. It is not clear that Yhwh or Isaiah actually refrained from speaking after this moment.

If Yhwh and Isaiah do stay silent for a while, that will test the people in another way. Who are they to turn to for guidance? They were never inclined seriously to turn to Yhwh or to Isaiah. Indeed, in effect they have said they wish to hear nothing of Yhwh or Isaiah, or of Yhwh as Isaiah interpreted Yhwh, and

---

[146]Joseph Blenkinsopp, *Isaiah 1—39*, AB (New York: Doubleday, 2000), p. 416.

they are more interested in hiding from Yhwh than in discovering what Yhwh has to say (Is 5:19; 29:15-16; 30:9-11). They would not put it that way, and would have said that of course they want guidance from the prophet and his God. But that is the implication of their attitude. And if they now turn to Isaiah and get no response, they will have to turn elsewhere, to their traditional resources, mediums and spiritists. That is where they will have to go for "teaching and declaration" if teaching and declaration is available to them from Isaiah only in fixed and written form, or is not available to them at all because even that is sealed up (Is 8:19-20).

The Practicality of Writing

It may be for practical reasons that Jeremiah puts in writing a message to the exiles (Jer 29), though he could have sent them an oral message. Perhaps there is special point in sending a *sēper*, a written document (Hebrew has no separate word for letter). It puts that message into writing and, in the absence of the person, makes it more objective and inevitable. It may also be significant that Jeremiah is responding to a letter from a prophet in Babylon urging Jerusalem to take action against Jeremiah.

The book of Jeremiah refers to several compilations of his sayings. One is a collection of his prophecies "concerning [or against] Israel and Judah and all the nations" (Jer 36:2). The object of writing it is that "perhaps the household of Judah will hear of all the bad that I am intending to do to them, so that each of them may turn from their bad ways and I may pardon their wrongdoing and their failure" (Jer 36:3). Initially it may seem a puzzle why *writing* should achieve that. It shortly becomes explicit that this is the only way Jeremiah's words can reach the people where they are most conveniently assembled, in the temple courtyard, because Jeremiah is for some reason prevented from going there. If they are written, Baruch can read them there on Jeremiah's behalf (Jer 36:5-8).

But we may wonder whether this scene also speaks to a later situation. Within a few years Yhwh's "perhaps" will have been disappointed, the city will have fallen and Jeremiah will have been taken off to Egypt. In the exile another "perhaps" comes into being: "perhaps" the Judeans will *now* come to their senses. Perhaps they will now reconsider what prophets such as Jeremiah were saying before the exile. But the only access they could have to the words of Jeremiah would be access to these words in writing. As happens within the story in Jeremiah 36, then, the writing down of Jeremiah's words makes it possible for the household of Judah to turn from their wrong ways and find Yhwh's pardon. And of course it does that for succeeding generations, down to the present day; perhaps that was in the back of God's mind. "That Jeremiah himself is not present for the three readings of the scroll is a narrative way of indicating that his words have a life beyond his personal presence." They "take on a life of their own in the community."[147] No one now has a chance to heed the prophecies of Uriah (Jer 36:20-23), which (as far as we know) were never put into writing. The oral delivery of prophecies has strengths and limitations. It has the power of the oral word, but also its transience. Because of this transience, we often like things to be put in writing, and Jeremiah's putting his prophecies into writing gives Yhwh's word ongoing tangible existence.

Available for Consultation

At the end of a proclamation concerning the destruction of Edom and its surrender to wild animals, Isaiah 34 invites people to "Consult Yhwh's scroll and read it out; not one of these is missing, none is looking for her fellow. For my mouth has commanded; his breath has gathered them" (Is 34:16). The expression "Yhwh's scroll" comes only here. Other expressions such as "the scroll of Yhwh's teaching," referring to Moses' Torah (e.g., Neh 9:3), are more common (and compare that story in Jer 36 of Jeremiah writing Yhwh's words in a scroll and Baruch reading from them). Presumably the bidding refers back to material in Isaiah that is now in written form. Yhwh communicates with the community through their opening themselves to what they find in the written scroll as well as through their listening for the spoken word. *Consult* (*dāraš*, EVV "seek") is the term for seeking guidance and help from the Torah or from Yhwh in person, and the application to the written prophetic word is thus also distinctive. If the prophecy in Isaiah 34 were one that had been fulfilled, one could imagine such an exhortation as a footnote added to the chapter to invite people to note this fulfillment (cf. 2 Kings 23:16). But as far as we know the declaration was not fulfilled, and thus more likely this is a reaffirmation that despite its implausibility, it will come about.[148] The declaration projects itself into the day when people will be able to check out that the written word has been fulfilled. If it is a later addition to the prophecy, it is one that affirms this and urges readers not to be put off by the fact that they have not yet seen its fulfillment.

We are talking about a word that "my mouth" uttered (the momentary transition to having Yhwh speak in the first person underlines that). Talk in terms of Yhwh's "commanding" this event reflects the fact that Yhwh's speaking in the prophets is not mere prediction nor even mere declaration of intent but is

---

[147]Terence E. Fretheim, *Jeremiah* (Macon, Ga.: Smyth & Helwys, 2002), p. 508.

[148]The verbs are qatal, like many of the verbs in preceding verses that speak of the future; I take them as instantaneous qatal, declarations about events that are so certain they can be spoken of as already happening.

a word of command that makes things happen, as is underlined by the parallelism with talk of Yhwh's breath *(rûaḥ)* gathering them. It is these words of command that are preserved in Yhwh's scroll. Yhwh would look very silly not to make sure they get implemented.

Another collection of Jeremiah's written prophecies comprises promises about Jerusalem (see Jer 30:2); as we have the book, the whole of Jeremiah 30—33 comprises such promises. Putting promises into writing undergirds their implementation, provides evidence when they come true that Yhwh really was their author and had been active in events and that Jeremiah was a true prophet, and makes them available as the subject of reflection and prayer (see Dan 9).

We do not know how much of the Torah was in writing during Jeremiah's day, but Jeremiah speaks as if the people had available in some form a fairly fixed account of the paths that Yhwh had laid before their ancestors. It is this that prophets such as Jeremiah, the people's lookouts, build on. It is possible for people to discover and review what Yhwh has said and done in Israel's history, and therefore possible for them not to heed it, as Jeremiah accuses them of doing (Jer 6:16-17). The existence of a reasonably established account of Yhwh's deeds and Israel's vocation is a necessity to prophetic appeal to such.

Later prophets such as Zechariah and Joel may already be taking up the written versions of earlier prophets' words. Joel can be a "scriptural prophet" in the sense of one who takes up existing scriptural collections of material in such a way as to show that the declarations of the prophets have not turned out to be empty; they will see fulfillment.[149] Zechariah 9—14 has a similar relationship with earlier prophecy.[150]

The Fixedness of Writing

The story in Jeremiah 36 points to another significance of putting prophecies into writing. While an oral word is bound to be fulfilled, that is even truer of a written word.

Baruch's scroll eventually reaches the king and there ensues an unforgettable scene in his winter apartment where a fire burns in his brazier. "As Jehudi would read out three or four columns, he would cut it with a scholar's knife and throw it into the fire in the brazier until the whole scroll was in the fire" (Jer 36:23). Jehoiakim knows he has to move one way or the other in relation to the scroll. He either has to heed it or destroy it. He knows that the word of

---

[149]See John Barton, *Joel and Obadiah* (Louisville, Ky: Westminster John Knox, 2001), p. 19, also pp. 22-27, following Siegfried Bergler, *Joel als Schriftinterpret* (Frankfurt: Lang, 1988).

[150]So Nicholas Ho Fail Tai, *Prophetie als Schriftauslegung in Sacharja 9—14* (Stuttgart: Calwer, 1996).

a prophet is powerful in its effect, and that (as with ordinary human words) a written word is more powerful than an oral word. Jehoiakim gives unintentional testimony to this by his systematic destruction of Jeremiah's scroll. The prophet's words declare what Yhwh intends to do and thus begin to put Yhwh's will into effect, and Jehoiakim wishes to short-circuit that process. Whereas Amaziah had to try simply to stop Amos speaking words that the nation could not endure (Amos 7:10-17), Jehoiakim needs to do something about words that have now been put into writing.

Some of his staff urge Jehoiakim to stop (Jer 36:25). Perhaps they see the inbuilt illogic in this procedure. If these are really Yhwh's words, burning them will hardly stop them coming true. If they are not really Yhwh's words, they have no power anyway. For readers, they point by contrast to a more appropriate response to a written collection of prophetic words. Perhaps Jehoiakim is more aware of the PR side to the event. He needs to show it is he who is master, not this prophet. In the event, he does not even effectively destroy the scroll, because Yhwh "hides" Jeremiah and Baruch and bids Jeremiah dictate all the words again, "and there were added to these many similar words" (Jer 36:26-32). Jeremiah gives further testimony to the significance of putting the spoken word into writing by telling us how the second edition of this scroll included much more than the first; we may imagine the king and his entourage trembling some more if they knew this was going on. Jehoiakim's last state is worse than his first.

A third collection of Jeremiah's words is an account of "all the trouble that would come on Babylon, on one scroll" (Jer 51:60), sent to Babylon by the hand of a Judean official called Seraiah who was apparently Baruch's brother (Jer 51:59; cf. Jer 32:12). In the context that points to the preceding collected prophecies about Babylon (Jer 50—51), though this event is dated in 594 and many of the prophecies in Jeremiah 50—51 may actually come from later decades. But in principle Jeremiah is doing something that constitutes a mirror image to the event in Jeremiah 36. Jehoiakim takes action to attempt to ensure that Jeremiah's words about Jerusalem do not come true. Jeremiah takes action to attempt to ensure that his words about Babylon do come true. Jeremiah in fact takes a series of actions. He writes the words down. He has them read out in Babylon. He has Seraiah draw Yhwh's attention to them, in words that constitute a prayer for them to be implemented. He has him throw the scroll into the Euphrates, weighted to ensure it would sink, and has Seraiah declare that this is a sign of what Yhwh is doing to Babylon itself (Jer 51:61-64).

Yhwh declares the intention to bring upon Babylon "all the words that I spoke against it, everything written in this book" (Jer 25:13). Which book? Yhwh may be anticipating the book referred to in Jeremiah 36 and/or may be referring to the prophecies against the nations in Jeremiah 46—51. The interpretation of this passage in its context raises unsolved questions, but these do not affect the fundamental point, that Yhwh presupposes that Jeremiah's words are in writing and expresses a commitment to fulfilling them.

3.7 Yhwh's Home

It might seem obvious that Yhwh dwells in the heavens and/or in heaven. But that is not all that needs to be said. Like a monarch with more than one dwelling, Yhwh has chosen also to dwell on earth, on a particular mountain, in a particular city, in a particular sanctuary.

Yhwh's Mountain

Jerusalemites are people who "call themselves after the holy city" (Is 48:2), but the actual expression "holy city" otherwise comes only in Nehemiah 11:1, Isaiah 52:1, and Daniel 9:24 ("holy cities" comes in Is 64:10). "Holy mountain" (e.g., Is 11:9; 27:13; 56:7) is more common; perhaps the city is holy because the mountain is. But then the mountain is holy because it is the location of the holy place, of Yhwh's sanctuary.

At the beginning of Israel's story Yhwh is "God, the one of Sinai" (Ps 68:8 [MT 9]).[151] Sinai—at least, Horeb—was the holy mountain where Yhwh first appeared to Moses (Ex 3:1). It is the portal of heaven. Yhwh then journeyed with Israel to a land Yhwh intended to take possession of and lend to Israel. Within the Pentateuch, then, if Yhwh has a natural earthly "home," it is Mount Sinai, but the Pentateuch also envisages Yhwh choosing another place to dwell, though it is unnamed (see Deut 12).[152] So Yhwh is not by nature the God of Jerusalem or the God of Israel, either the land of Israel or the people of Israel. God's background lies elsewhere, independent of city, land and people. God's original earthly home was somewhere else, definitely earthly, but rather distant and inaccessible. While Elijah once found his way there, he was rebuked for it. No one else ever tried; Israel did not even preserve a tradition concerning its location.

But "the one of Sinai" did become "God, the God of Israel" (Ps 68:8 [MT 9]). While there was no natural link between Yhwh and this people, this land, this mountain and this city, Yhwh entered into a link that inextricably bound Yhwh to them. Indeed, the God of mountain, people, land and city is not merely Yhwh but—God *simpliciter*. And Mount Zion became a place that will stand forever, its surrounding mountains recalling the way Yhwh surrounds Israel

---

[151]On the basis of regular usage, it would be easier to translate *zeh sinay* "this [is] Sinai," but that makes poor sense in the context; for "the one of Sinai," cf. *HALOT* on *zeh.*

[152]Cf. Anselm C. Hagedorn, "Placing (a) God," in *Temple and Worship in Biblical Israel*, ed. John Day, LHBOTS 422 (London/New York: T & T Clark, 2005), pp. 188-211; see pp. 204-5.

(Ps 125:1-2). It is not surprising, then, that a majestic mountain like Mount Bashan casts a resentful eye at the mountain where God chose to dwell (Ps 68:15-16 [MT 16-17]). If the God of Sinai was to move to a mountain in the region of Canaan, it would surely be to Mount Hermon, the highest peak of the Bashan range. That looks like a proper mountain of God, fit to be a new portal between earth and heaven. How strange that the armies of heaven chose to take little Zion, that Yhwh should view that as a desirable residence! Theologically, then, Zion towers above the mountains around, and in due course it will be recognized to do so as peoples flock to it like some Everest because they know they can learn God's ways there.

Thus Psalm 132 brings together the fact that David is Yhwh's anointed servant with the fact that "Yhwh chose Zion, desired it as a dwelling [môšāb] for himself." Likewise Psalm 78:68-70 brings together Yhwh's choice of Judah and specifically Mount Zion and Yhwh's choice of David.

Yhwh's City

There is no mention of Jerusalem in Genesis 1—11, and its comments on the city are equivocal; this contrasts with the central place of Babylon in Babylon's creation story.[153] Further, whereas Genesis 12 explicitly sees people and nation, and thus land, as integral to Yhwh's revised plan to bring blessing to the world, city had no place there. Was it implicit to this plan? Was it not inevitable for Israel to have a capital city? Actually Israel managed without one for two hundred years, but then, the whole arrangement portrayed in Judges did not work and takes Israel to having a king like everyone else. Perhaps a king does imply a capital city. David certainly assumes so, and retrospectively the First Testament is prepared to see Yhwh's choice in the identification of Jerusalem as this city, as it sees Yhwh's choice in the identification of David as king. The focus on the city will also reflect the greater centrality of Jerusalem for Judeans, and thus for the Second Temple Judean community, when for a while Judah might be called a city-state, an entity only the size of a county and centered on its one city.

But originally, if Israel was to have a capital, Jerusalem was not the obvious candidate. It had no history in the relationship between Yhwh and Israel, like Shechem (Deut 27; Josh 24) or Shiloh (1 Sam 1—4). But because of the people's faithlessness Yhwh "left the dwelling [miškān] at Shiloh, the tent he set up among people" (Ps 78:60) and let the covenant chest be captured. It was from a northern clan that he chose the first king, but then rejected him, and Yhwh likewise "rejected the tent of Joseph" and instead chose "Mount Zion, to which

---

[153]See Robert P. Gordon, *Holy Land, Holy City* (Carlisle/Waynesboro, Ga.: Paternoster, 2004), pp. 5-16.

he dedicated himself" (Ps 78:67-68). Zion becomes heir to the position and traditions of other shrines and sanctuaries where Yhwh has appeared, spoken and received the people's worship—Sinai, Shechem, Shiloh, Gibeon, Dan. The wilderness sanctuary and the covenant chest come there. Communities that might value varying traditions are invited to see all as fulfilled in Jerusalem; they can and must make it their center.

So there is some apologetic in Psalm 78. Not only does Yhwh choose Zion in Israel rather than some mountain in another nation. Yhwh chooses Zion in Judah rather than some location in Ephraim. We do not know the psalm's date, but it would speak pointedly during the time of David and Solomon (to support the novelty of settling on Jerusalem as the nation's capital), or during the time of the two kingdoms, or after the fall of Samaria, or during the time of tension between Samaria and Jerusalem after the exile. But there are also several forms of illogic about it. There is good reason for Yhwh to reject Shechem and Shiloh, but not much logic about choosing Jerusalem, nor (beyond having made an unequivocal commitment) for maintaining that choice. There is reason for rejecting Saul, though not very good reason, and not very good reason for choosing David or for maintaining that choice—again, except having made a commitment.

Psalm 46 begins by speaking of Israel's extraordinary confidence in God when its world threatens to collapse as tumultuous floods engulf it. Whence comes that confidence? Alongside those tumultuous floods that suggest overwhelming, disaster-bringing forces, it sets a river with streams, which rejoices God's city. The expression "God's city" comes only here (Ps 46:4) and in Psalm 87:3, though expressions such as "city of our God" and "city of Yhwh" come, for example, in Psalm 48:1, 8 [MT 2, 9]. There the city is explicitly Zion, and presumably this psalm was used there, though the description makes one think of Dan rather than Jerusalem. In Dan a river with its streams indeed does rejoice the city; it burbles all around it. Perhaps the psalm was written with Dan in mind and came to apply metaphorically to Zion, which has no river or streams except for the channel emerging from the Gihon Spring, channeled via Hezekiah's Tunnel to the Pool of Siloam. The river becomes a metaphor for the provision that comes from God's own presence. The absence of a river in Jerusalem and the precarious nature of its water supply might make the metaphor more pointed. At the Beginning, a river flowed into the world from God's garden, dividing into four branches to that end; one of them is called Gihon, indeed (Gen 2:10-14). Here such streams provide for God's city. God's story has made its way from the garden where it began to the city where it will end. Specifically, the river provides for God's holy dwelling (miškān, plural). The term will refer to the temple in particular rather than the city as a whole where this dwelling is located (cf. Ps 84:1 [MT 2]; 132:5).

The Scene of Yhwh's Acting, Speaking and Listening

Psalm 48 goes on to make some outrageous statements about this city's location on "the most beautiful height." There is nothing especially beautiful about Mount Zion. Even before it was built up, it must surely have been rather less lovely than the average spur of the Judean hills or than the Mount of Olives. It is also lower than that ridge and pathetically lower than Mount Hebron or Mount Zaphon, the great mountain on the Mediterranean coast to the far north. It earns such epithets not because of what it is in itself but because of the one who has come to live there. It is "our God's city," "the great king's town," "his holy mountain." Because this God has deigned to dwell there and thus made it "his holy mountain," it has gained a status out of all proportion to its natural significance. It is for this reason that there is more joy there than anywhere else on earth, or at least more reason for joy. "The name of Zion . . . has a high emotional value."[154]

Zaphon claimed to be the great holy mountain. There was at least one other mountain named Zaphon apart from that one to the north; perhaps this had become something of a generic term or standard epithet for a holy mountain. Indeed, perhaps each "Zaphon" was assumed to be a this-worldly embodiment of a divine dwelling place in the heavens. Actually Zion is what Zaphon claimed to be, the place where the great king dwells. Perhaps it is significant that Yhwh appropriated *such* a mountain and not one like Hermon or Zaphon. It is in keeping with Yhwh's choice of little Israel rather than Babylon or Egypt, Britain or America. There is thus no doubt that its impressiveness comes from the one who decides to dwell there rather than from its inherent grandeur.

What is the evidence? It lies in the way Yhwh has been manifest there. Although it is not visually impressive or high up, Mount Zion is actually rather secure, and its fortifications would make it more so. Jerusalem is a city that is "built up . . . bonded together," and Yah's clans therefore rejoice to stand there and confess Yhwh's name in the place where Yhwh makes it possible for David's descendants to exercise their authority (Ps 122:1-5). But that confession presupposes that the city's real security does not lie in itself. Psalm 48:3-8 [MT 4-9], too, goes on to make clear that the people's haven is ultimately not their city but their God. It remembers how, back at the beginning, kings assembled when the Israelites passed over together (over the Red Sea and/or over the Jordan or over the land), how they saw and were stunned and devastated. But that story itself reaches its destiny (the psalm assumes) with the conquest of Jerusalem and Yhwh's taking up residence there. So this recollection can

---

[154]Rendtorff, *Canonical Hebrew Bible*, p. 585.

move on seamlessly to the story of Jerusalem. Yhwh did not stop using the east wind at the Red Sea but has continued to do so. That is not merely a matter of what people have heard in that story they passed on, but a matter of what they have seen for themselves, in this city. They have seen kings moving from assembling to panicking.

And the evidence for that lies in what one can see in Jerusalem. The towers, the rampart, the citadels: there they are (Ps 48:12-14 [MT 13-15]). They are symbols of the strength that lies in Yhwh, and they witness by their inviolate existence to the way Yhwh has acted in the city's history with decisive faithfulness. Thus the psalm goes on to declare not merely "This is Zion" but "This is God."[155] They are evidence that this God is—God.

So it is because Yhwh dwells in the city that it stands firm. That is not because God's presence gives some mystical protection but because of the practical consideration that its God is "Yhwh Armies," one who "helps" it as morning comes (Ps 46:4-5 [MT 5-6]).[156] To express the point more concretely, it involves Yhwh shouting a warrior shout, at which raging nations such as the Assyrians collapse. That happens "as morning comes," the phrase that described Yhwh's action at the Red Sea (Ex 14:27). The deliverance of Zion is a repeat of that deliverance.

And Israel knows that when pressures such as these arise, Zion is also the place where it can come and plead with Yhwh about them, sure of a hearing because Yhwh is at home there (see Solomon's prayer in 1 Kings 8:27-53, and the many psalms that presuppose this as the place to pray). It is then "from Zion, perfect in beauty" that God calls, shines out, comes and speaks, with fire consuming around him (Ps 50:1-3). This description, too, does not refer to any inherent beauty about Zion, but to the way Zion has become beautiful because God resides there. One might have thought that God would be summoning the world in order to pronounce decisions about its destiny and Israel's deliverance or blessing; it is "our God" who comes (Ps 50:3; cf. Ps 80:1-3 [MT 2-4]). Actually the world is here summoned to hear Yhwh call Israel itself to account. Zion is the place whence emerges God's critique of Israel. The psalm thus points toward Lamentations 2:15, where there will be a grievous and grieved irony about this description of Zion as perfect in beauty and joy of all the earth and about the parallel description in the terms of Psalm 48:2 [MT 3], emerging from Israel's failing to respond to such a summons.

The city of God is not a place in heaven or even a place on earth insulated from its pressures, but a place within history and its conflicts where God is at

---

[155]Cf. J. W. Rogerson and J. W. McKay, *Psalms*, 3 vols. (Cambridge/New York: Cambridge University Press, 1977), 1:227.

[156]On "help," see section 3.5 "Covenant."

work putting down opposition. The challenge to the people of God is to believe that this is so and to live in history with confidence, yet without thinking that we are responsible for fixing the world's destiny or for bringing in the kingdom of God.

Recognized

Zion is "my holy mountain," where Yhwh installed the king of Israel (Ps 2:6). It is from "his holy mountain" that Yhwh hears and answers prayer (Ps 3:4 [MT 5]). It is "from the sanctuary . . . from Zion" that Yhwh sends help and sustains, resulting in action "from his holy heavens" (Ps 20:2, 6 [MT 3, 7]). Yhwh dwells on Mount Zion and hears prayer there, and thus takes action in coming from the skies in the way Psalm 18 describes. In Psalm 87, Zion is first a place Yhwh founded and establishes. It indeed shares in the strength of the mountains on which it sits, but not merely on the basis of its natural geographical position but from the fact that it is "his foundation," that "the Most High himself establishes it." Specifically, its strength and security come from the fact that Yhwh loves Zion more than all the other dwellings of Jacob. In the Psalms, "dwellings" usually refers to Yhwh's dwellings, to sanctuaries,[157] so the psalm makes a statement about Zion as (to use Deuteronomy's expression) *the* place Yhwh chooses, over against those other sanctuaries. Yhwh *loves* this place, loves being here, is attached to it and committed to it. Such are the honorable things that are said about it. God honors it. It is God's city. Yes, it is secure.

Thus Psalm 128 prays for the person who reveres Yhwh: "May Yhwh bless you from Zion, and may you see the good things of Jerusalem all the days of your life, and see your grandchildren, well-being on Israel." Zion/Jerusalem is both the source of blessing and the recipient of blessing. The horizon broadens through the prayer.[158] Such a person experiences blessings that come from Zion, but also sees Jerusalem itself experiencing good and shares in that. The person who reveres God shares in these throughout life and lives long enough to rejoice in the birth of grandchildren such as guarantee that the family and community continues. That in itself would be a symbol of seeing God's blessing on the people as a whole.

Psalm 87 pictures peoples such as Egypt (for which Rahab stands: see Is 30:7), Babylon, Philistia, Tyre and Sudan as having been in effect born in Zion

---

[157]Actually it is usually intensive pl., suggesting "the special quality of this particular dwelling" (Othmar Keel, *The Symbolism of the Biblical World* [New York: Seabury, 1978], p. 151). See "A Place of Security" (p. 247).

[158]Cf. Leslie C. Allen, *Psalms 101—150*, rev. ed., WBC (Nashville: Thomas Nelson, 2002), p. 245, though he takes the last phrase as a prayer.

(LXX has them declaring that Zion is their mother). They have come to belong to Zion, or Zion belongs to them. One can imagine Israelite exiles in those lands rejoicing thus ("next year in Jerusalem"), but it seems unlikely that the psalm could simply refer to Israelites living abroad as "Babylon" or "Philistia" (let alone "Rahab"). Further, one can also imagine the psalm rejoicing in the prospect of those peoples rejoicing to recognize Zion.[159] That would fit with the Psalms' recurrent conviction that all the nations are due to come to acknowledge Yhwh (e.g., Ps 96—97). Metaphorically or theologically speaking, both Israelites living abroad and foreign peoples destined to acknowledge Yhwh were born in Zion. Yhwh declares so, performatively.[160] Each people has its name written in Zion's register of citizens. The psalm speaks both in corporate terms (the contexts suggest that "this one" both times points to those nations, but "each person" suggests individuals). They belong to Zion, Zion belongs to them. They have the right of return. Indeed, the psalm pictures them there, perhaps imagining a festival such as Sukkot (or Pentecost, as Acts 2 describes it) with Israelites resident abroad and foreigners coming to Jerusalem. It imagines them singing and dancing with astonishment at the loveliness of this dwelling (cf. Ps 84:1 [MT 2]). Yes, they were born there. This is the source of all their life, their refreshment and their blessing, whether they live here or there. Zion is set "in the midst of the nations," "at the center of the world" (Ezek 5:5; 38:12).[161]

Yhwh's Abandoned Daughter

Yhwh often refers to Jerusalem by the term of affection *Daughter Zion*. There is a special link between Yhwh and Jerusalem like that between a father and a daughter. But the term often appears in the context of reference to the city's suffering. How strange that the daughter should be abandoned, the city be desolate and captive (Is 1:8; 52:2). How strange that she is gasping for breath, fighting for life (Jer 4:31). How strange that Yhwh has trampled on her as if she were grapes in a wine press (Lam 1:15). Jerusalem was "great with people . . . great among the nations, a princess among provinces" (Lam 1:1), a place of majesty (*hādār*, Lam 1:6). It was "the glory of Israel" (Lam 2:1). But Lamentations makes those observations in the context of the city's destiny not having worked out in the way they would imply. As the nation as a

---

[159]It is then possible to take *lĕyōdĕʿāy* in the natural way, as meaning "*to* those who acknowledge me": i.e., to Israelites (e.g., Ps 9:10 [MT 11]; 36:10 [MT 11]).

[160]Marvin E. Tate, *Psalms 51—100*, WBC (Dallas: Word, 1990), p. 390.

[161]The LXX translates *omphalos*, but it is doubtful whether we should read into the Hebrew the idea of Jerusalem as the navel of the earth (cf. Hagedorn, "Placing (a) God," pp. 190-91; Gordon, *Holy Land, Holy City*, pp. 30-31).

whole experiences attack and defeat despite being Yhwh's holy nation, so its capital city experiences siege and invasion despite being Yhwh's holy city. No one in all the world thought that Jerusalem could ever be taken (Lam 4:12). It is a hyperbole and a projection of what Israel itself believed, on the basis of those stories of the city's miraculous escapes in the past. But now, "Yhwh, the nations have invaded your domain, defiled your holy palace, turned Jerusalem into ruins" (Ps 79:1). Jerusalem is like a lonely widow, a serf, let down, disillusioned, weeping, betrayed, homeless, distressed, over-whelmed, desolate, bereft, defeated, dishonored, helpless, mocked, de-spised, fallen, comfortless, desecrated, hungry, despised, uncared for, trapped, stunned, crushed (Lam 1).

Surely Yhwh's compassion must mean Yhwh will arise and restore Zion? "It is time to be gracious to it," argues Psalm 102:13-21 [MT 14-22]. What is the basis for saying that the time has arrived? The following lines imply that the basis for this lies in the association of Yhwh's name and honor with Zion. Let-ting Zion be destroyed brought discredit on Yhwh's name. What kind of God would let the city that bore the God's name be destroyed? That would give the impression of lacking the power to protect it. So the time must come for Yhwh to restore the city and correct that impression. Then the nations and their kings will look on Yhwh with awe and reverence instead of scorn. So the demands of Yhwh's own honor reinforce its people's appeal for Yhwh to start behaving with grace and compassion toward their city. Indeed, it is significant that the suppliant asks for compassion and grace not for the people but for the city it-self, and includes in the motivations for this prayer that its people themselves delight in its stones and look graciously on its dirt (!). If they can look like that upon this ruin, surely Yhwh can do so. The last two lines take the point further. The nations and their kings will not merely revere Yhwh from a distance and then get on with their lives in Babylon or Tarshish; it will be *in* Zion that they do so (Ps 102:21-22). The vision of the nations coming to Jerusalem (Is 2:2-4) will find fulfillment. Of course it must do so. Zion is the only proper place to worship Yhwh. Yhwh's home on earth is there. It is inevitable that people who proclaim Yhwh's name and praise and thus serve Yhwh will come to Yhwh's home to do so.

Psalm 137 gives powerful testimony to Zion's significance for Israel, not least when its people are in exile. It presupposes the reasons for the people's attachment to the city, an attachment that has much in common with the feel-ings of any group of exiles for their homeland. The nearest it gets to an expla-nation is the reference to "Yhwh's song," but that makes it clear that the exiles' sentiments imply more than the warm feelings I have when my plane de-scends into the smog and slums of Los Angeles. This is that city Yhwh chose, made a home in, made a commitment to. The expression "forever" had hung over Jerusalem. But Yhwh abandoned this city to peoples such as the Babylonians and the Edomites. "Jerusalem's day" was the day of Yhwh's anger with Jerusalem. It was the day when foreign peoples sought to destroy the community and its future by destroying the next generation as well as the present one (see, e.g., 2 Kings 25:7). Here the people do not complain at Yhwh, as they do elsewhere. Their focus lies on the human agents of Yhwh's wrath at the city, who they imagine (perhaps that is all it is) inviting them to sing one of those songs about Jerusalem being "perfect in beauty" (e.g., Ps 48:2 [MT 3]). The temptation might be to put Jerusalem out of mind. Jeremiah had, after all, urged them to settle down, to put down roots, to pray for the city in which they now dwelt, which half implies putting that other city out of mind. "Never!" says the psalm. It is still "the greatest joy in all the earth" (Ps 48:2 [MT 3]). They know Jerusalem is not finished.

No, "Yhwh is building up Jerusalem, gathering Israel's outcasts, one who heals the people who are broken in spirit and binds up their wounds." Yhwh "has made the bars of your gates strong, blessed your children within you, One who gives well-being to your territory, fills you with finest wheat" (Ps 147:2-3, 12-14). Yes, Yhwh does have compassion on Zion and restores its fortunes in such a way that it is like awaking from a dream and finding that its bliss is a reality, and the nations are astonished at what Yhwh has done. But the need recurs, and so does the prayer (Ps 126).

Yhwh's Sanctuary

There is a deep human instinct to identify places that we can associate with God, and when we have grounds for reckoning God has appeared somewhere, our instinct is to build a shrine there. Even in the absence of a conviction that God has appeared somewhere, the medieval period built great cathedrals, and so does the contemporary world (in Los Angeles there are the evangelical Crystal Cathedral and the new Roman Catholic Cathedral of Our Lady of the Angels). Worship is a human instinct (cf. Gen 4), and one that needs to be harnessed to a proper relationship with Yhwh.

So Israel is to worship at the place Yhwh chooses (e.g., Deut 12:5, 11, 14, 18, 21, 26), not just in places it identifies (likely following the instincts of people who are already in the land, with their tainted worship). And its sanctuaries are to be built as Yhwh says. This is clearest with the wilderness sanctuary (Ex 25—31; 35—40), which represents an ordered world in which everything is in its place, an embodiment of the orderly cosmos. The account of the clans gathered around the wilderness sanctuary portrays Israel as a properly ordered whole, with Yhwh at its center. When we come to the account of the building of the temple, the First Testament emphasizes how this was David's idea, not Yhwh's, and how it was planned in detail by David, not Yhwh. The description of the wilderness sanctuary thus anticipatorily critiques the temple.[162]

The sanctuary on Zion is Yhwh's shelter (Ps 76:2 [MT 3]; Lam 2:6). It is Yhwh's tent (Ps 15:1; 27:5-6; 61:4). It is Yhwh's fold (Jer 31:23; 50:7). But those images might suggest something temporary. More reassuringly, it is the place where Yhwh settles. That was David's implicit aim in wanting to build Yhwh a solid house of stone (at least, that was what made Yhwh feel uneasy about it). Psalm 132 recalls David's commitment to finding "a place for Yhwh, a dwelling for the Strong One of Jacob." He located the covenant chest there and provided such a dwelling, which becomes Yhwh's place to settle (měnûḥâ). The EVV have "resting-place," but the word implies not that Yhwh is fatigued but that this will become a proper place for Yhwh to stay permanently. To judge from 1—2 Samuel, the background is the chest's wanderings from Shiloh to Philistia to Beth-Shemesh to Kiriath-Jearim. It had a "place" there, but David wants to provide it with a better one, and a settled one. The chest symbolizes the presence of Yhwh or the relationship between Yhwh and Israel, and it comes to be located in Zion. "For Yhwh chose Zion, wanted it as a dwelling for himself." The transition from the earlier part of the psalm is extraordinary. There it was David who chose Zion (Ps 132:5). Here Yhwh does so (Ps 132:13). If one hesitated to infer that Yhwh's choice and desire followed on David's, then the account of this process in 2 Samuel 7 would be reassuring. There, too, building a house for Yhwh is David's initiative, and Yhwh is ambivalent about the idea but eventually agrees.[163]

In Psalm 132, Yhwh does not stay ambivalent. "This is my place to settle forever; here I will dwell, because I wanted it." When Yhwh makes a commitment, it is not half-hearted. Yhwh indeed comes to dwell there, and that "forever" (though events will conspire to make Yhwh reconsider this). That means it becomes a place Yhwh blesses with the food it needs and one that knows Yhwh's deliverance, presumably on the recurrent occasions when it is attacked by Israel's enemies. Yhwh promises then to "clothe its priests with deliverance," which I take to imply that the relationship with Yhwh that the priests encourage and guard, not least by their sacrifices and their prayers, is the means whereby the city finds its safety, which will certainly mean "its committed people will resound loudly." It will also thus be a place where Yhwh will continue to keep the commitment to David that to Yhwh is a greater pri-

---

[162]See OTT 1:392-401. Karl Barth notes the connection with Stephen's critique of the temple in favor of the wilderness dwelling and with the absence of a temple in Revelation's heavenly Jerusalem (see The Word of God and the Word of Man [London: Hodder, 1928], p. 72; cf. Christopher Rowland, "The Temple in the New Testament," in Temple and Worship in Biblical Israel, ed. John Day, LHBOTS 422 [London/New York: T & T Clark, 2005], pp. 469-83; see p. 480).

[163]See OTT 1:562-72.

ority than this commitment to a place (see 2 Sam 7): "I will make a horn flourish there for David; I have prepared a lamp for my anointed." Now it is this temple that becomes heaven's portal. Here Isaiah finds he has access to the heavenly temple with its assembly (Is 6).[164] The temple is holy, like heaven itself, because it is an outpost of heaven.

Psalm 65:4-5 [MT 5-6]) suggests the same two sorts of benefits issuing from the sanctuary. First, there are the "good things" (lit., "good") with which people are filled there. *Good* is especially a term for the good things of this life such as food to eat. They emerge from God's house in the sense that they are the gifts of the God who lives there. Israel comes there to speak to God about them, to thank God for the good things of last year and to ask for good things next year—and it experiences God answering. More literally, it enjoys them there as it celebrates the harvest at festival time, as people coming to the royal palace for a banquet.

Then there are Yhwh's "awesome deeds." That is especially a term for God's more occasional, miraculous, interventionist acts whereby in faithfulness Yhwh delivers people from the attacks of their enemies. For such deliverances, too, Israel comes to plead in the sanctuary, and for these it also returns to give thanks when they have become reality. The God who grants them comes from Zion to act to deliver. But it is specifically because Zion is the place where Yhwh's dwelling is located.

A Place of Security

Thus the sanctuary is a place of prayer. As a place where Yhwh actually lives, it is a place where people pray and toward which they pray for blessing and deliverance.

"I have seen you in the sanctuary, beholding your power and splendor" (Ps 63:2 [MT 3]). How had the suppliant done so? In the context of the First Testament, the line hardly refers to gazing at an image of Yhwh. Perhaps it refers to seeing other symbols of Yhwh's presence such as the covenant chest. Perhaps it refers to a metaphorical seeing of Yhwh, as is the case when Christians talk about seeing God. Perhaps it refers to the rituals, ceremonies and processions of the temple, accompanied by the telling of the story of God's deeds for Israel, expressive of Yhwh's power and splendor. All that brought home their reality.

Yhwh's house is a home, a place of security. Psalm 84 begins by commenting on how "lovely" or "beloved" it is. The psalm does not go on to speak of the beauty of its stones or its woodwork or of the sun gleaming off its ramparts, but of pigeons nesting there, suggesting it is loved as a place of security.

---

[164]See Levenson, *Sinai and Zion*, pp. 124-25.

That fits (paradoxically) with the title "Yhwh Armies," which the psalm uses several times, and with its closing declaration about the blessings of the person who trusts in Yhwh.

While one might naturally picture the dwelling of "Yhwh Armies . . . my king" as a palace, the psalm does not refer to it as a *hêkāl* but as a dwelling or house. Like a regular house it has a court or yard of the kind where animals would be kept, grain stored, household tasks undertaken and food cooked, the kind of courtyard of which the temple indeed has a huge-scale example, where its sacrificial altar stands.[165] For a family, its courtyard is a true place of safety and security. When you walk into the courtyard, you know you are home. No wonder a person longs and faints to get there. Of course there is still a further level of belonging implied in the freedom to enter the actual rooms of the house that surround the courtyard. Priests and other Levites do so and are in a position to keep joining in its worship. But for a layperson, even standing from time to time in the courtyard of this house (e.g., on an occasion such as Sukkot) is a wonder. People come to appear before Yhwh in Zion maybe once a year, maybe three times if they are in a position to do as the Torah actually requires. Such an occasion, when one stands at the threshold of this house, is the best day of the year. It is better than all the days one spends living among the faithless (perhaps there is a further hint of its security as their dwellings are described as only tents, over against a house). Or (on an alternative understanding of the reference to standing at the threshold), even fulfilling the relatively junior responsibility of guarding the threshold of these courts (for instance, making sure that only the pure enter) would be better than living at the heart of the community of the faithless. That is how some Israelites would have to spend their lives, living in areas dominated by Edomites or Babylonians or Moabites, like Elimelech and Naomi when they had to move to Moab. They would not have the option of living in Jerusalem; occasions when they went there were therefore most precious.

Psalm 133 speaks of Zion as a place of blessing. It does not start off talking about Zion but about how fine it is when families live together as one, but its last lines suggest that Zion is its theme all through. The occasion when the family lives together is when everyone comes together for a pilgrimage to Zion. There is then a reciprocal relationship between family harmony and Zion blessing. It is joining together for this pilgrimage that opens the way to the blessing that Yhwh commands from Zion. The "brotherhood" may be the members of the extended family or may be the broader fellowship of the fam-

---

[165]The word for "altar" is actually plural; I take this as intensive ("your great altar"), as is the case with the plural word for "dwelling" in the first line, though in the temple complex as a whole there was more than one altar.

ily of Israel gathered for a festival. But part of the blessing that Yhwh commands from Zion is the family and/or community harmony that comes from being united in a relationship with Yhwh.

Psalm 134 then makes that blessing reciprocal as it appeals to the people to bless Yhwh and appeals for Yhwh to bless them. When *bērak* has God as object, I usually translate "worship," on the assumption that it refers to going down on one's knees *(berek)*. Here the psalm uses the verb both with God as object and with human beings as object. Human beings bless God; God blesses human beings. Human prostration leads to divine giving. And the place from which the divine blessing issues is the place where the human prostration is offered.

Served by the Priesthood

"You are to be for me a kingdom of priests" (Ex 19:6). "Warn the people not to break through to Yhwh to look and a multitude of them fall, and the priests, too, who come near to Yhwh, are to sanctify themselves" (Ex 19:21-22). Excuse me? There is a tension between the idea that the people's king is Yhwh and the idea of having a human king, and a less publicized tension between the idea that the whole people has a priestly relationship with God and the idea of a priesthood within the people, and a wholly male priesthood, at that. Admittedly the separation of priesthood from the family and from the monarchy has a positive aspect. At least the head of the family and the head of the state is not also a person who can get in the way of the relationship between the family and God (as was possible in the time of the ancestors) and between the nation and God, in keeping with common practice in traditional societies.

The origin of the priesthood, like that of sacrifice, the holy city and the temple, involves an interweaving of human and divine. On one hand, Exodus 19 presupposes that there are priests in Israel, even though God has not commissioned the appointment of any. On the other, God recognizes their existence and does go on to appoint the Levites for divine service and to give regulations for the priests' work. As with the offering of sacrifice, the institution of the monarchy, the establishment of Jerusalem and the building of the temple, human initiative comes first and divine validation second. Something similar will be true with the invention of the position of bishop or senior pastor within the Christian church, as well as, for instance, the development of Christian sanctuaries, special Christian worship places, though we have less evidence that God has ever validated these. The circumstances of Levi's appointment (Ex 32:25-29) suggests (with some irony) that it had a particular vocation to see that the people would be faithful to Yhwh rather than make images or follow other deities. They showed themselves committed to Yhwh's covenant and therefore are made guardians of it. One of the ironies here is that subsequently the priests and other Levites bear considerable responsibility for ways of worship in the temple that use images or involve other traditional practices that the Torah and Prophets condemn, and for failing to teach the people in Yhwh's ways (as bishops and pastors have taken the lead in causing the church to stray).

How far is a priesthood of the whole people in tension with the priesthood of certain people within the people? It depends what the priests do. Different parts of the First Testament allocate different roles within the clan of Levi in different ways,[166] and their role changed and changed in emphasis over the centuries, as the role of ministers has changed over the centuries of Christian history.

On the basis of that demonstration of faithfulness to Yhwh that made them willing to kill many of their fellow Israelites at Sinai, Levi was entrusted with the Urim and Thummim (Deut 33:8-9), a means of obtaining guidance from God over some course of action (Num 27:21; cf. Judg 1:1-2; 1 Sam 14:37-42). In Deuteronomy 33:10, their first responsibility is that "they are to teach your decrees to Jacob, your teaching to Israel." The Torah is both the deposit and the resource of this teaching, which can be summed up as enabling people to keep distinctions between holy and ordinary, and between clean and taboo, and thus to keep the community's religious, social and moral life in order (cf. Lev 10:10-11; Deut 31:9-13; Neh 8; Ps 15; 24; Mal 2:4-7). Associated with that is the responsibility to make decisions about whether particular things actually are clean or taboo and thus whether particular people can come into the sanctuary (e.g., Lev 13:8, 15, 17; also 1 Sam 1:14-18), assessing the value of offerings (Lev 27) as well as making decisions over matters of dispute between people, including matters such as homicide (e.g., Deut 17:8-13). They thus protect people from approaching the presence of Yhwh in a dangerous way and also enable them to approach that presence in a safe way by mediating their offerings, their prayers, their praises and their confessions. We will owe to the priests the presence of the Psalms in the First Testament; in their origin these represent Israel's address to God, but as a collection of praises and prayers they have become models for praise and prayer that God accepts, and thus become address from God to the congregation.

The priests' second responsibility in Deuteronomy 33:10 is thus "to put incense before your nose and whole offerings on your altar." Yhwh chose Levi "to stand to minister in Yhwh's name, he and his descendants, for all time"

---

[166]E.g., Leviticus and Numbers distinguish between the role of the descendants of Aaron and that of the rest of Levi, whereas in Ezekiel the priests comprise more specifically the descendants of Zadok within that line, while Deuteronomy does not refer to any such distinction.

(Deut 18:5). They thus officiate at sacrifices in that after the animal has been killed, they undertake the actions with the blood and take the animal (or the appropriate parts of it) to the altar to burn. As well as guarding the sanctuary to make sure inappropriate people do not enter it, they will be responsible more generally for its supervision and for maintaining it in good order. They will, for instance, keep the lamps burning and keep the presence bread in its place (Lev 24:1-8). In light of anthropological models, the world of scholarship is inclined to see the key role of priests as "maintaining the order of life in the community" by exercising responsibility for ritual purity and proper order.[167] In Numbers 6:22-27, their responsibility is to bless the people (cf. Gen 14:19-20; Deut 10:8). During the monarchy, priests take over from prophets the role of anointing kings in Yhwh's name (e.g., 1 Kings 1:39), a role that epitomizes an ambiguity in their position. They serve Yhwh, but they also come to be officers of the king (e.g., 1 Kings 4:2).

The First Testament's description of the priests' role shows that they need not stand between the people and God in a negative sense but can rather facilitate the people's relationship with God. From a practical point of view the community needs people to be able to teach and advise and people to look after the sanctuary and its worship, and everything depends on how they do that.

◆ ◆ ◆

Israel and the Church

In the New Testament there is one theological motif that Paul sees as a new revelation, "a mystery kept secret for long ages" (Rom 16:25), the proclamation of Christ to the Gentile world as a result of his rejection by the Jewish world (cf. Rom 11:25). The new revelation does not lie in God's willingness and intention to be recognized by the whole world; Paul quotes the First Testament on this theme (e.g., Rom 15:8-12).[168] But the extraordinary means whereby that would come about had not been seen before. It was the Jewish people's general refusal to recognize Jesus as Messiah that led to the focus on sharing the news about Jesus with the Gentile world.

In light of that, what is now the significance of the Jewish people? (Theologically, the question concerns the significance of "Israel," but I speak in terms of "the Jewish people" to make clear that I refer to this people as a whole, most of whose members do not live in the State of Israel.) Paul van Buren notes five

---

[167]Patrick D. Miller, *The Religion of Ancient Israel* (Louisville, Ky: Westminster John Knox, 2000), p. 162.

[168]See Section 8.1 and 8.6.

recurrent Christian views.[169] (1) It is simply replaced by the church. (2) Its remnant has been integrated into the church by conversion. (3) It is only the type of the church. (4) It is the exemplary negative foil of the church. (5) It has no special character since Christ, being simply part of the humanity standing in need of justification. All these are essentially negative views. He then refers to Bertold Klappert's view that the church is dependent on the Jewish people's election and on that election's coming to fulfillment in Jesus Christ, through whom we come to participate in its election and promises.[170] Van Buren's response to this is that it would seem to imply Gentile observance of the Torah and participation in the promise of the land. The former surely does not follow, for Paul points out that the move from the Abrahamic promise to the new act God undertook in the time of Moses involved God's changing the terms on which the relationship worked, and it makes entire sense to see that happening again in the move from Moses to Jesus.[171] As for the latter, some form of Gentile participation in the promise of the land seems entirely natural, not least given the fact that this is the land where the gospel events took place. There is such a thing as salvation geography. Christians have an investment in this land. If only it had been possible for Palestinian Christians and Israeli Jews to live in peace in this land, this would have been a fine symbol of the vision of one new humanity in Ephesians 2:11-21.

The Jewish people was elected to be God's people, and God's gifts and call are irrevocable (Rom 11:29). So its story as God's elect cannot have come to an end. The church cannot have replaced it. It makes no difference if the Jewish people decline to believe in their election or to believe in God or to obey God, because its election was not conditioned by its response to God, though it required that response, but simply by God's sovereignty. Its unfaithfulness could not annul God's faithfulness (Rom 3:3). The Second Vatican Council saw the church as the core of a future humanity united and reconciled in the kingdom of God.[172] But this is the Jewish people's destiny, and it can only become the church's insofar as the church is an expansion of the Jewish people and a beginning of that new humanity.

So the church's task is to learn from the First Testament understanding of what it means to be Israel, not on the assumption that it replaces the Jewish

---

[169]See van Buren, *Theology of the Jewish-Christian Reality,* 2:10.

[170]Bertold Klappert, *Israel und die Kirche* (Munich: Kaiser, 1980).

[171]Mark S. Kinzer, taking a position related to Klappert's as reported by van Buren and suggesting that Judaism and the church are two parts of the one people of God that are in a state of schism, argues that observance of the Torah is appropriate for Jews who believe in Jesus but not necessary for Gentiles (*Post-Missionary Messianic Judaism* [Grand Rapids, Mich.: Brazos, 2005]).

[172]So Pannenberg, *Systematic Theology,* 3:469.

people but on the assumption that it has come to share its vocation, and it lives looking forward to the day when the Jewish people comes to recognize Jesus.

The fact that the election of the Jewish people operates in this way offers massive good news to the church. There was nothing about the church that commended it to God and made God elect it. In our culture there is a strong undercurrent of assumption that something about us made us deserve God's election. The New Testament agrees with the First Testament that election does not work thus. We do not deserve election. It issues purely from God's freedom. The New Testament also agrees that the main object of election is the community, not the individual. I say "main" object because one can sometimes see God electing individuals; Paul is a notable example. (His example also illustrates how election is nothing to do with deserve; no one less deserved election.) And both the election of an individual such as Paul and the drawing of the Christian community into a share in the Jewish people's election also once again illustrate how the object of election is not to include some people in a relationship with God and exclude others, but to include some people as a means of extending that to others. Election is inclusive, not exclusive.

4

THE NIGHTMARE

Built into what it means to be Israel is a response to God as father, king and restorer. The trouble is that Israel does not give God that response. There are then consequences, of which the prophets have a nightmare vision, a nightmare from which Israel wakes to find it was more than a nightmare.

4.1 Faithlessness

Whereas the ideal Israel lives in trust and obedience, the actual Israel does no such thing. From the beginning Israel forgets, rebels, hustles, craves, tests, envies, forsakes, despises, disbelieves, grumbles, disobeys, abandons, angers, provokes, compromises, nauseates (Ps 106).[1] Jerusalem becomes disobedient, sinful, rebellious, careless, polluted (Lam 1). Israel has failed, gone astray, done wrong, rebelled, trespassed, turned its back on Yhwh's commands, ignored Yhwh's prophets and refused to turn from its waywardness (Dan 9). Moral and religious failure is a reality of both past and present (Ezra 9). There seems to be no way to change it.

The Nature of Sin

The First Testament does not have a concept of evil as a self-existent entity. Its first explicit references to evil (ra') are illuminating. The sequence of the First Testament narrative suggests that one can understand evil only when set over against good (ṭôb, Gen 2:9, 17; 3:5, 22). Good preexists evil; there is good in Genesis 1, but no evil. Evil has no existence or definition in itself. Second, evil expresses itself as doing wrong to other people, as hurt or violence. This is implicit in the conclusions God comes to about the world and its evil in light of the later comments on violence (Gen 6:5, 11-12) and the account of human conduct that precedes (esp. Gen 4; cf. Gen 19:19; 26:29; 31:29, 52; 50:15, 17, 20). Third, evil is what is evil "to Yhwh" or "in Yhwh's eyes" (Gen 13:13; 38:7; cf. Ps 51:4 [MT 6]), or what is evil in the eyes of human beings (Gen 28:8). That offers another pointer to the fact that evil does not exist in itself; indeed, in this sense neither does goodness. Goodness is what Yhwh is, and evil is what contrasts with that. Evil thus consists in the absence of what God is: compassion, grace, long-temperedness, commitment, truthfulness, for-

---

[1] On the beginning of this story, see *OTT* 1:452-74.

giveness and a willingness to punish wrongdoing (Ex 34:6-7).

The First Testament also sets over against each other faithfulness and faith-lessness (ṣĕdāqâ and reša', and related words; e.g., Gen 18:23-26; Deut 9:4-5; Ps 1; Prov 10:6-7; Ezek 3:18-21). In a nice parallel with the data concerning good and evil, faithfulness words again appear before faithlessness words (Gen 6:9; 7:1; 15:6; 18:19); indeed, faithlessness appears in Genesis only in the antitheses in Genesis 18:23-26. English versions usually translate ṣĕdāqâ and reša' by words such as "righteousness" and "wickedness," but those translations fall short of conveying the relational and communal significance of the expressions. They denote behavior that properly fulfills one's obligations to people with whom one is in a relationship—God and other people—and behavior that fails to do so.[2]

Thus, while it is an exaggeration to say that we can gain no understanding of sin except in light of a knowledge of Christ,[3] Genesis supports the idea that sin can be understood only in the context of understanding grace. God is faith-ful, humanity unfaithful; God is merciful, humanity defiant; God is kind, hu-manity ungrateful; God is self-giving, humanity withdrawing and self-assertive; God is out-reaching, humanity turned in on itself. "Sin is man's self-alienation from the grace of God from which and in which he has his being. . . . Thus the grace of God itself is the presupposition of man's sin. . . . [Sin's] in-conceivable reality can be grasped only when we see it as rebellion against grace." It is not the transgression of a universal law but "a wanton rebellion against the God who has given Himself to mankind."[4] Paul Ricoeur similarly comments that we cannot understand sin without understanding redemption, or defilement without understanding purity.[5] Sin is not a topic in its own right; there is "no place which belongs to it." It is merely a No that presupposes and opposes God's Yes.[6] So we do not understand the gospel in light of the law and of our failure to keep it. We understand our failure through understanding the gospel and the true nature of God's law.[7]

---

[2]See section 2.6 "True Faithfulness."

[3]Cf. Wolfhart Pannenberg, *Anthropology in Theological Perspective* (Philadelphia: Westminster Press, 1985), pp. 91-92.

[4]Karl Barth, *Church Dogmatics* (Edinburgh: T & T Clark, 1936-1969), III/1:34-35. In keeping with Pannenberg's comment, he adds at the end of the last sentence "in the person of His son." I assume that this self-giving began in Israel, indeed, in creation, though no doubt there is a sense in which this is also a self-giving "in the person of His son." Cf. ibid., IV/ 1:358-413.

[5]Paul Ricoeur, *The Symbolism of Evil* (reprint, Boston: Beacon, 1995), p. 71.

[6]Barth, *Church Dogmatics*, IV/1:143.

[7]Ibid., IV/3.i:369-71.

The Scandal of (Israel's) Sin

While the First Testament assumes that the whole world is sinful, it is much more concerned about the sin of the people of God than about the world's sin. "Listen, heavens; attend, earth," Isaiah begins (Is 1:2). There is a scandal to be proclaimed before the whole cosmos, and the scandal is Israel's behavior in relation to Yhwh. When Amos warns the world about punishment for sin, this is but the lead-in to warning Israel about its sinfulness (Amos 1—2). This, too, suggests that we understand sin in light of considering God's relationship with Israel. Jeremiah utilizes a similar piece of rhetoric to that in Amos 1—2. "The days are coming," Yhwh declares, "when I attend to everyone who is physically circumcised, to Egypt, to Judah, to Edom, to the Ammonites, to Moab, and to all the people with shaven temples who live in the wilderness, because all the nations are uncircumcised—and the whole household of Israel is uncircumcised in heart" (Jer 9:24-25). Circumcision is the covenant sign; it marks someone as belonging to the covenant people and heir to the covenant promises. Jeremiah subverts the implications of that fact. First, there are many other peoples who are circumcised, so the fact that Yhwh will attend to the nations carries with it the uncontroversial fact that Yhwh will thus be involved in attending to peoples who are circumcised. In declaring that, Jeremiah has no difficulty slipping in reference to Judah as one of the circumcised people. Of course the nations are circumcised only physically—the disciplining of the inner person that circumcision could suggest does not apply to them. But then neither does it apply to Judah or to the household of Israel as a whole.

The conduct that evidences this comprises a bewildering mixture of activities. When Ezekiel lists them, they include worshiping in the traditional "Canaanite" fashion, committing adultery or making love during a woman's menstrual period, withholding a debtor's pledge, robbing someone, failing to feed the hungry or clothe the naked, charging interest on loans, and failing to make fair decisions between people (Ezek 18:5-9; cf. Ezek 22:1-31; 33:15, 25-26). Wrongdoing does not divide into separate categories such as the ethical and the ritual. That is reflected in the fact that all such acts count as "abominations" (e.g., Deut 17:1, 4; 25:13-16; Ezek 8:6; 16:2; 18:13, 24; 22:2, 11).[8] In this sense, wrongdoing is a whole. "Both the contempt for the ordering of the sanctuary and the ruthless denial of the neighbour's right to live . . . break up any relationship with God."[9]

---

[8]Leviticus does seem to confine the word to certain sexual practices (see Lev 18), Proverbs to certain moral acts, especially deceptive acts that as such are not amenable to human judgment (e.g., Prov 6:16-19; 12:22; 20:10, 23).

[9]Walther Eichrodt, *Ezekiel* (London: SCM Press/Philadelphia: Westminster Press, 1970), p. 309.

The wide embrace of the commitment Yhwh looks for means that living properly in one area cannot compensate for failing in another. The modern temptation would be to focus on social concern and not to accompany that by sacrificial religious life. Jerusalem's temptation was the opposite. The people made costly and pleasing offerings and sacrifices, but in other senses did not heed Yhwh's words or teaching (both terms can refer to prophecy or to the Torah)[10] (Jer 6:19-20). Neither implicit attempt at crossover credit is effective.

Falling Short

Like other aspects of truth, the nature of sin cannot be encapsulated in one expression or picture, and the First Testament has a series of images to help us grasp the breadth and depth of the failure of the people of God.

In English, *sin* is a distinctively religious word, suggesting offenses against God and God's standards. In contrast, *ḥāṭāʾ* can be used in a more everyday way to refer to shooting at a target and falling short or missing it (e.g., Judg 20:16). This suggests that in a religious context it implies falling short of Yhwh's expectations. Israel is a people who fall short, miss the target; their aim and their walk go astray (Is 1:4; cf. Ps 51:2, 4 [MT 4, 6]. This does not imply that they do their best but do not quite make it. Failure is an active matter, "sin as refusal."[11] It involves failing even to aim at the target, deliberately setting aside Yhwh's standards and expectations. Failure is thus closely related to transgression, a flouting of the law God has laid down about how people must behave. The original sin was an act of disobedience, and disobedience continues to characterize the people of God: "They did not keep God's covenant; they refused to live by his teaching" (Ps 78:10). "The first result of man's confrontation with God's command is that he is proved relentlessly and irrefutably to be its transgressor."[12]

And behind the act of disobedience is a problem about the human heart, the inner person, which makes a change in the heart necessary (e.g., Ezek 36:26). Behind the act of disobedience is wrong desire (Gen 3:6; cf. Rom 7:7). Greed, gluttony and lust dominate the second half of the seven deadly sins, and Proverbs' first concrete warning implicitly concerns greed, the desire for more stuff that impels thieves (Prov 1:10-19). It also incorporates a number of further observations on the problems with desire (Prov 7:18; 9:17; 25:16; 27:20).

Given that falling short can imply failing because one does not try, Valerie Saiving Goldstein suggested that the distinctive feminine form of sin lies

---

[10]See section 3.6.
[11]James W. McClendon, *Systematic Theology: Doctrine* (Nashville: Abingdon, 1994), p. 130.
[12]Barth, *Church Dogmatics*, II/2:742.

here.[13] "Sin has not merely the heroic form of pride but also, in complete antithesis yet profound correspondence, the quite unheroic and trivial form of sloth," which one might also describe as "sluggishness, indolence, slowness or inertia."[14] "One is not or cannot or dare not be good enough to be authentically human."[15] It is a desire to be left alone by God and to hold on to our stupidity, like Nabal (cf. Ps 14:1). It is a desire to avoid obligations to other people. Barth sees Amos's challenge as lying here. It is a desire to ignore the call to live according to the Spirit even as we are flesh and live in the flesh; David's affair with Bathsheba provides an example. It is a desire to be responsible for our destiny, and thus to give in to despair because we cannot, like the Israelites in Numbers 13—14.[16] It generates a desire to go back to Egypt.

Sloth in fact features at the heart of the traditional seven deadly sins of personal life—pride, envy, anger, sloth, greed, gluttony and lust—though its place in this list is actually somewhat controversial. It featured in John Cassian's list of eight deadly sins, but he referred to it as acedia, spiritual sloth;[17] sloth itself eventually appeared in Thomas Aquinas's list in the *Summa theologica*. It is certainly present in Proverbs as the down-to-earth weakness that finds every excuse to stay sitting on the sofa watching the ball game (e.g., Prov 6:6-11; 21:25-26; 22:13; 24:30-33; 26:13-16). The trouble is it means you end up with nothing to eat, you get nowhere and your roof falls in (Prov 15:19; 19:15; 20:4; Eccles 10:18). Its positive equivalent is decisiveness or diligence, which means you have food to eat and you get somewhere (Prov 10:4; 12:24, 27; 13:4; 21:5). Qohelet, on the other hand, knows about its opposite, about people who never stop working.

Rebelling and Going the Wrong Way

Again, sin can be described as straying or erring (*šāgag/šāgâ*). As sheep stray and planners err (Ezek 34:6; Job 12:16), so do people in relation to God (e.g., Job 6:24; Ps 119:67), perhaps accidentally but sometimes deliberately, and they may have to accept responsibility for it (Prov 5:23; 19:27; 28:10; cf. Is 28:7). Some occurrences of the common word for "wrongdoing," *ʿāwōn* (e.g., Ps 51:2, 5 [MT 4, 7]), indicate that Israelites could be aware of a link with the much less common verb *ʿāwâ*, which can also suggest deviating or going astray. The

---

[13]Valerie Saiving Goldstein, "The Human Situation: A Feminine View," *JR* 40 (1960): 100-12; cf. Judith Plaskow, *Sex, Sin and Grace* (Lanham, Md./London: University Press of America, 1980); Susan Nelson Dunfee, "The Sin of Hiding," *Soundings* 65 (1982): 316-27.

[14]Barth, *Church Dogmatics*, IV/2:403.

[15]Mark E. Biddle, *Missing the Mark* (Nashville: Abingdon, 2005), p. 49. The words are in italics in the original.

[16]Barth, *Church Dogmatics*, IV/1:403-83.

[17]See John Cassian, *The Institutes* (Mahwah, N.J.: Newman, 2000), pp. 217-38.

wrongdoing of Israel means they have "skewed their way" (Jer 3:21), diverged from the way, and that deliberately.[18] Indeed, whereas *šĕgāgâ* can imply unintended deviation from the path of rightness (e.g., Josh 20:3, 9), *ʿāwōn* is more inclined to imply a deliberate choosing of the wrong way. "All of us, like sheep, stray [*āwâ*]"; the parallel colon makes explicit that this does not imply that like sheep we can hardly be blamed, because "each person to his own way we turned" (Is 53:6).

Isaiah's first image for such wrongdoing is that it resembles the rebelliousness of children against parents. "I reared children, brought them up, and they—they rebelled against me." They are offspring who "have left Yhwh, despised Israel's holy one, turned away backwards" (Is 1:2-4). Indeed, Israel has been a "rebel from birth" (*pāšaʿ*, Is 48:8). If Psalm 51:1, 3 [MT 3, 5] is the confession of an individual, then the nature of Israel is replicated in that of the individual. Israel has a "willful and rebellious heart" (*sārar, mārâ*, Jer 5:23).

That recalls the description of the son in Deuteronomy 21:18-21. Similarly, Yhwh's distinctive description of Ezekiel's audience is as a "rebellious household," characterized by a defiant refractoriness (*mĕrî*, Ezek 2; 3:4-11, 26-27; 12). Yhwh, then, is the father, the head of the household, whose members would be expected to submit to his authority. But the family does not do so. They are a rebellious family, both parents and children, more likely to refrain from listening and obeying than to do so (Ezek 2:5, 7). They defy Yhwh's decisions and rules for the household's life (Ezek 5:6). Their stance in relation to the head of the household stands out against Ezekiel's when he eats Yhwh's scroll and enjoys the taste, despite the scroll's harsh contents (Ezek 2:8—3:3). In contrast, they are people with eyes that do not look and ears that do not listen, a common parental lament about children (Ezek 12:2). They are "a rebellious people, false-hearted children, children who are unwilling to listen to Yhwh's teaching" (Is 30:9), like children who profess obedience to their parents but secretly do the opposite to what their parents say. Insofar as the relationship between people and God is a personal one, analogous to that of children to parents or husband to wife or of a person with a close friend, sin is a matter of unfaithfulness. It is sin that makes God the Wholly Other (except that it does not, because even the sinner can cry out to God).[19]

The verbs *mārad* and *pāšaʿ* (e.g., Ezek 2:3) are also used to denote revolt against a king or mutiny against an emperor (e.g., Ezek 17:15; 2 Kings 1:1).[20] The former is a less common word but one more often used with its literal

---

[18]Cf. *TLOT*, pp. 862-66.

[19]Ricoeur, *Symbolism of Evil*, pp. 58, 69.

[20]The NRSV "transgress" for this verb in the second half of Ezek 2:3 thus does not bring out the relational connotation of the word; JPSV renders it "defy."

meaning, while *pāša‘* (with its derivatives, esp. the noun *peša‘*) is a more common word but one more often used with its religious meaning. So the former would more directly remind hearers that their position is like that of the subjects of a king, while the latter would have more immediate religious connotations. Yhwh is the king, the head of the nation or the ruler of an empire, whose citizens or junior powers would be expected to submit to his authority. But they do not do so. They are nations of rebels, "hard-faced and tough-minded" (Ezek 2:3-4), not amenable to correction.[21] The notion of rebellion links with the image of a covenant relationship between Yhwh and Israel. People have ignored the covenant relationship into which they entered with Yhwh, refusing to live by the terms of the relationship Yhwh established with them at Sinai (Jer 11:1-10). They are thus indeed like the underling nations of a big power who have conspired to rebel. "They abandoned the covenant of Yhwh their God and bowed down to other gods and served them" (Jer 22:9).

While rebellion is a forceful image, the image of going astray is finally more radical because it means a person ends up separated from God and lost. The lostness that issues from falling short and going the wrong way means these are also expressions of stupidity (*’iwwelet*); the three words come in parallelism in Psalm 38:3-5 [MT 4-6]. Stupidity is Proverbs' term for the vices it attacks, such as lack of discipline and self-deceit. The psalm presupposes that intelligent people make just as foolish decisions and choices as less intelligent people, choices that are stupid in relationship to God and to other people. Admittedly, while the choices of more intelligent people may be simply just as foolish as those of the less intelligent, the disasters they thereby bring on themselves and on other people through their stupidity may be greater. "People's stupidity ruins their way, and their heart rages against Yhwh" (Prov 19:3).

Self-confidence and Incorrigibility

If hiding is the fundamental feminine sin, rebellion or pride is the fundamental masculine one. While Isaiah begins by talking about rebellion, it goes on to focus on what English translations usually refer to as pride (Is 2:9-22), the first of the seven deadly sins. There really is something impressive about Judah and Jerusalem and its leaders. They are high and lofty, majestic and exalted, like high mountains or high walls or cedars of Lebanon or oaks of Bashan or tall sea-going ships. They are in a position to utilize other people's strategic, military and religious resources and to face the future with self-confidence. But that obscures reality and compromises the witness to reality that the people of

---

[21]The plural "nations" may refer to Judah and Ephraim (cf. Ezek 37:22) or to the succeeding generations of Israel, ancestors and children (cf. Ezek 2:3-4), or to the twelve clans, or to the exiles and the people in Jerusalem.

God is designed to give. By their very nature they risk obscuring the majestic loftiness of Yhwh, and while that risk might not be realized as long as they continued magnifying Yhwh, in practice they almost inevitably become impressed by—themselves; and they enjoy drawing attention to themselves. Sin involves a "fixation on the self" (and the related search for confirmation by others).[22] Loftiness makes people treat themselves as God or behave as if God can be safely ignored (Is 9:9 [MT 8]), and it makes them treat others as if they do not count (Ps 10:2; 31:18 [MT 19]). With poetic justice, loftiness must lead to downfall (Is 2:9, 11, 17; Prov 29:23).

But Ezekiel 16 provides a powerful illustration of pride embodied in a woman. Yhwh had fallen for Jerusalem and showered her with love when no one else could see her beauty. Yhwh's love was thus the origin of her beauty and fame. There is therefore great enormity about her unfaithfulness, even if some naturalness about it. The gift of love can change the one to whom it is given; it can convey the gift of beauty. But the gift of beauty can also change a person. It can convey a new confidence in oneself, a confidence that forgets the fact that one's beauty derived from the love of someone else. Ezekiel's analysis parallels that in Deuteronomy, which emphasizes that Yhwh's commitment to Israel issued purely from Yhwh's love. "It was not because you were more numerous than any other peoples that Yhwh got attached to you and chose you, because you were smaller than any other peoples." Yhwh's deliverance of Israel from Egypt issued "from Yhwh's love for you and his keeping the oath he swore to your ancestors." Yhwh did not give Israel the land of Canaan because of its faithfulness or uprightness but despite its resistance to Yhwh and its refractoriness. Yet Deuteronomy knows that enjoying all the good things of the land that Yhwh gives will have the paradoxical effect of making Israel confident in itself and inclined not to think about the fact that it was only Yhwh who made all this possible (Deut 7:7-8; 8:11-18; 9:4-7). And as they put Yhwh out of mind, it will also have the even more paradoxical effect of encouraging Israel to turn to other gods (Deut 8:19).

And the people reach the point when they cannot give up this promiscuity. Their involvement with the "Masters" (the Baals) puts them into the same position as a person who is defiled through something such as contact with a corpse. But in the case of such defilement, time and the appropriate offering can put things right. In the case of this defilement, the people do not give time its chance, because they persist in their defiling activity. Nor of course do they take the action that can remove the defilement. They will not turn to Yhwh. Indeed, they seem incapable of doing so. "Their deeds do not let them turn to

---

[22]Wolfhart Pannenberg, *Systematic Theology*, 3 vols. (Grand Rapids, Mich.: Eerdmans/Edinburgh: T & T Clark, 1991-1998), 2:250.

their God, for a spirit of promiscuity is within them, and Yhwh they do not acknowledge" (Hos 5:3-4). Their being possessed by a promiscuous spirit does
not denote the imposition of some outward force. It is their own deeds that do
not let them turn to Yhwh. There is in them an ingrained pattern of behavior
that prohibits turning. They are too attached to the activity that makes turning
impossible. So they acknowledge other deities as well as Yhwh, and therefore
do not really acknowledge Yhwh at all.

With some contradiction, Israel likewise declares in response to Jeremiah
that even though he warns them that in the end they will lose out from their
faithlessness, "It's hopeless, because I am dedicated to strangers, and after
them I shall go" (Jer 2:25). Presumably here Jeremiah is putting words on their
lips, as prophets do (e.g., Is 28:15), to express the way they are irredeemably
convinced that they must look to alien gods rather than Yhwh, and are incurably committed to them. The same is true when he has them speak like an animal that has broken loose, "We are wandering free, we will not come to you
any more" (Jer 2:31). Yhwh therefore asks, with puzzlement and/or sadness,
"To whom shall I speak and give warning so that they will listen? There: their
ear is uncircumcised; they cannot listen." Yhwh does not mean to excuse them.
"Yhwh's word has become to them a reproach that they do not like" (Jer 6:10).
It is their preferences that are coming to the surface.

Universal Faithlessness

Human sin is falsehood, lying to Yhwh, lying to one another and lying to ourselves.

How big is the problem of sin? Yhwh challenges Jeremiah to search the
streets of Jerusalem to see if there is one person who makes decisions in a
way that aims at truthfulness, acting with *mišpāṭ* and *'ĕmûnâ*. He cannot find
one, even when they act on oath. Jeremiah hypothesizes that it may only be
poor people (the *dallîm*) who "are foolish, because they do not acknowledge
the way of Yhwh, the decision of their God" about the way people should
live. After all, their poverty puts them under special pressure. Is there an
irony there? What chance do poor people have to exercise *mišpāṭ*? Are they
not the *victims* of the practices Yhwh speaks of? But anyway, he goes on to
investigate the important people (*haggĕdōlîm*), but discovers that the same is
true of them. Yhwh's decisions about conduct were designed to place constraints on them to help them walk in Yhwh's way, analogous to the yoke
tied on an ox, but "all alike have broken the yoke, snapped the bonds" (Jer
5:1-5). Again there must be some irony or exaggeration: where do people
such as Baruch fit in? But evidently the community is corrupt through and
through. Everything is extortion, violence and assault, hurts and wounds;
wickedness stays fresh there like water in a well (Jer 6:6-7). "From the least

to the greatest, all of them are profiteering, and from prophet to priest, all of them are engaged in fraud" (Jer 6:13; cf. Jer 8:10). The whole community is involved in seeking to make money off people in ways that ignore proper standards of honesty. That is true of ordinary people and the well-to-do, and it is also true of the religious leadership.

Everyone wants to profit from a bull market, notwithstanding the cost to other people. The people directly involved will no doubt be mostly the adult men, but their action affects their whole families for good and for ill. Their achievements and sins have an impact on three or four generations. "The children are collecting wood, the fathers are lighting the fire, the women are kneading dough, to make cakes for the Queen of Heaven" (Jer 7:18). Jeremiah's contemporaries seem unchangeably wrong-headed. "Do Sudanese change their skin or leopards their spots? Then you too can do good, who are trained to do ill" (Jer 13:23). The conclusion of Jeremiah's work as the people's assayer is that the entire community are rebels. Smelting results in there being no good metal there (Jer 6:27-30).

While one of the aims of Jeremiah's speaking thus may be to justify Yhwh's act of punishment, another may be to get them to prove Yhwh wrong. But they cannot do so. And it has been so from the beginning. Notwithstanding a wistful look back to the time in the wilderness, Jeremiah declares that Israel has been taking no notice of Yhwh and doing what it liked ever since leaving Egypt (Jer 2:2; 7:24-26). When Ezekiel reminds the household of Israel of its story, he does so in sardonic fashion. The rebelliousness of Israel did not begin at Sinai. Even in Egypt Israel defiled itself by utilizing the forms of worship that the Egyptians used and by refusing to abandon them when Yhwh said to (Ezek 20:6-8). If Exodus traces the original sin of Israel back to Sinai (Ex 32), Ezekiel traces it back to Egypt. That shows how deeply ingrained it is.

Indeed, "Judah's failure is inscribed with an iron stylus, engraved with an adamant point on the tablet of their heart" (Jer 17:1). The image has two frightening implications. The guilt of Judah's shortcomings is indelibly recorded on its inner being. But the reference to writing in the inner being also suggests that its failure is written into its nature. It will never be able to escape continuing to act in the way that has incurred this guilt. Jeremiah 31:31-34 will respond to both these implications in talking both of forgiveness and of inscribing Yhwh's teaching on the people's inner being. Both aspects of the inscription are thus rewritten. But for the moment, the two aspects to the inscription condemn Jerusalem both to ongoing failure and to consequent punishment.

Of course Jeremiah's investigation concerns the people of God in a particular context. The same is true of the confession that "all our righteousnesses are as filthy rags" (Is 64:6 [MT 5] KJV), which is not a statement about universal human sinfulness, nor a declaration that even our best deeds are spoiled by sin,[23] true though that may also be. It is a statement the prophet puts on the lips of the people of God. It may be a contextual statement on the part of a particular generation, the people who live in the exile, or may more likely be a statement about the way the whole community has become stained, an acknowledgement about the life of the people of God as a whole as it has turned out over the centuries. The church can thus identify with it as its own life over the centuries has also turned away from the potential of its beginnings and been characterized by faithlessness, failure, dissension and violence.

The Prevalence of Sin

In fact, the First Testament is less concerned with a doctrine of universal sinfulness than Christian doctrine is. As a symbol of that, the proof texts for such a doctrine tend to dissolve on examination. In Romans 3:10-12 Paul quotes from Psalm 14:2-3 to make the point that the whole of humanity has "turned aside" and "altogether become foul; there is no one doing good, there is not even one." But the psalm itself is making a complementary point, that there are occasions when Yhwh sees that particular cultures reach terrible depths of turning away from God and refusal to acknowledge God or call on God, to the despair of people who know that God is involved. The statements express the background to the subsequent prayer for God to take action to deliver the faithful. The Church of England uses Psalm 143:2, "Do not go to law with your servant, because no living person can be in the right before you," as an introduction to a confession of sin, but the psalm does not go on to confess sin, and more likely it is a recognition of power realities, like Job's. The extravagant confession "I was born in waywardness; my mother conceived me in failure" (Ps 51:5 [MT 7]) contrasts with the claim to relative faithfulness that appears in other psalms. The psalm acknowledges that waywardness and failure go back to the beginning of the suppliant's life, whether one thinks of that as birth or as conception, as they go back to the beginning of humanity's life and the beginning of Israel's life. But it is not clear that the psalm implies that every sinner has to speak in these terms any more than in the terms of any other psalm (indeed, it is not even clear that it is an individual rather than the community that speaks in Ps 51). Its words are thus compatible with the idea of original sin, that we are all affected by sin from the very beginning of our lives because of our solidarity with the human race going back to Adam, but they do not assert that. That idea is also probably implied by Genesis 1—11 (see esp. Gen 8:21). But the doctrine of universal sinfulness may be merely that, merely a

---

[23]Against BDB, p. 722a.

doctrine. The First Testament's comments on universal sinfulness challenge communities to look at their actual lives and face up to their implications.

But the First Testament does reckon that sin affects all humanity. "There is not a faithful human being on earth who does what is good and does not fall short. . . . God made humanity upright, but they sought out many schemes/ theories" (Eccles 7:20, 29; cf. Ps 130:3; Prov 20:9). Eliphaz asks, "Can a mortal be in the right before God, or a human being be pure before his maker?"[24] He adds that God "does not trust in his servants, and can lay a charge on his messengers" (Job 4:17-18). There are a number of stories about heavenly beings who betray Yhwh's trust, beginning with Genesis 6:1-3 and perhaps including Job 1—2 (one such story also underlies Is 14:12-20). A fortiori, human beings can hardly be trustworthy. The fragility and vulnerability of human nature means we can perish as quickly as flowers in the summer sun or as clothes ruined by moths, and that reflects not merely the frailty of our bodies but the weakness of our spirits (Job 4:19-21). Surely people should notice the crumbling of their dwelling, the hovering of the moth, the slackening of the tent cord, but some people, at least, the kind of people who lack integrity, are heedless, they have no insight, and they pay for it with their lives.

Harm (*'āwen*) and trouble (*'āmāl*) do not emerge from nowhere, Eliphaz goes on; "humanity is born for trouble and the sparks fly upward" (Job 5:6-7). *Harm* and *trouble* can refer to the harm and trouble that come to us, and in isolation these lines would then be a poignant statement about the universality of human suffering, but they follow statements about human sinfulness, so that the text implies that the harm and trouble are the ones we cause. Wrongdoing in the world does not come from some other place than from us. There is still a poignancy about the statement (cf. Rom 7:7-25). We have to accept responsibility for our wrongdoing, yet it is also something we are the victims of. It is the way we are by nature. The opening of his story describes Job as *tām*, which EVV render "blameless," suggesting the absence of something negative rather than the presence of something positive; the word could thus suggest "sinless." But Job later makes clear that he recognizes that everyone sins; *tām* is a statement about his being a morally and relationally whole person, not a sinless one.[25] Eliphaz's point then is that even a man like Job who is a person of integrity and reverence for God (Job 4:6) is nevertheless inevitably a sinner like everyone else. It is therefore not so odd that suffering comes to him. He reaffirms the point in stronger terms later: how can anyone be pure or be in the right in God's eyes? When looked at from the perspective of God's absolute

---

[24]"Be more righteous/pure than God" is a more natural translation, but it does not fit the context.

[25]See further the next section, "The Faithful and the Faithless."

and transcendent deity, human beings look "abominable and corrupt" (Job 15:14-16).

The Faithful and the Faithless

The First Testament is more interested in the fact that there are two sorts of people, the faithful and the faithless (e.g., Ps 1). Everyone belongs to one or other category, and you have to decide which group to belong to. Paul makes a related assumption. He, too, sometimes distinguishes them in absolute terms in a way that has been especially influential in Christian theology, so that the first category exists only in theory as actually everyone belongs to the latter category: "All sin and fall short of the glory of God" (Rom 3:23). But elsewhere he presupposes that there are particularly righteous and good people and particularly wicked people (e.g., Rom 5:7; 2 Thess 3:2), with the majority falling in between or moving between the categories. Job belongs firmly in the "particularly righteous" category. He is a sinner, because everyone is, but he proved he was a person of integrity who revered God. He did not even sin with his lips (Job 2:10; cf. Job 6:30), a particularly easy part of us to sin with. He passed the test that the adversary proposed.

The First Testament is less interested in the universal sinfulness of everyone than in the gross wickedness of (for instance) people who plan the destruction of others, who dedicate themselves to evil rather than good, to falsehood rather than faithfulness, to words that will consume others by their deceit (Ps 52:2-4 [MT 4-6]). Sin thus characterizes relationships within communities. It involves deliberation, it involves falsehood rather than faithfulness, and it works especially by words (e.g., Ps 109:2-5). Statements of the prevalence of sin are warnings: "A truthful person who can find?" (Prov 20:6). In terms of the seven deadly sins, faithlessness involves anger and envy. Anger can only do harm (Ps 37:8); quick-temperedness is stupid, makes one do stupid things and generates strife (Prov 14:17, 29; 19:11), whereas being long-tempered suggests wisdom, encourages harmony and is good for us (Prov 14:29-30; 15:18). Its positive equivalent is self-control (Prov 16:32). "Fury is cruel, anger is overwhelming, but who can stand before passion?" (Prov 27:4). It "makes the body rot" (Prov 14:30). People's envy of one another is what generates toil, and that is empty. It has no substance (Eccles 4:4). It can lead to spiritual and moral disaster (Ps 73:3; Prov 23:17-18; 24:1-2, 19-20).

The Psalms and Job assume that people can be righteous. It is particularly remarkable that the First Testament emphasizes this in the case of Job, who apparently lives outside Israel (for Uz, see, e.g., Jer 25:20; Lam 4:21); if readers asked themselves about his nationality, they would surely conclude he was a foreigner, like Agur and King Lemuel (Prov 30:1; 31:1). Yet Job was "a man of integrity and uprightness, one who revered God and turned away from wrongdoing" (Job 1:1, 8). "A man of integrity" paraphrases *tām*, which etymologically suggests "whole," though in English that would have misleading psychological overtones. Etymologically, "upright" *(yāšār)* suggests walking a morally straight road rather than a devious one. "Revering God" points to the reality of a commitment to God and to the ways God approves. "Turning away from wrongdoing" is the negative corollary, as well as another way of referring to walking the straight road, keeping on the right road.[26]

Job's "integrity" is the topic of conversation between God and the adversary and between Job and his wife (Job 2:3, 9) in such a way as to imply that it especially relates to Job's relationship with God. Job knows that he is Job and God is God, and behaves accordingly. It means (among other things), Job points out, that we accept the bad things from God as well as the good things of which Job had substantial experience. This suggests that "integrity" and "revering God" go together, the latter making explicit the Godwardness of the first. Similarly, "uprightness" and "turning from wrongdoing" go together, the latter offering the negative corollary of the first.

So it is possible to be a person of faithfulness and integrity, and to submit to Yhwh's probing to check that out (Ps 7:8-9 [MT 9-10]). A psalmist can say, "I wanted to do what is acceptable to you, my God; your instruction was within my heart," not merely written in the scroll to which the psalm has just referred (Ps 40:8 [MT 9]). Thus the leader who speaks in Psalm 18 sees Yhwh's deliverance of him as grounded (at least in part) on his faithfulness, integrity and purity of hands (that is, he has not fraudulently brought about anyone's death). He has kept Yhwh's ways and obeyed Yhwh's commands. He has not turned to other deities or other objects of trust. The same can be true of Israel. In Psalm 44:17-22 [MT 18-23], the community protests the trouble that has come to it despite the fact that "we had not ignored you or been false to your covenant; our hearts had not turned aside or our feet deviated from your path," and adds the observation that "if we had ignored our God's name and spread our hands to a strange god, would God not search this out?" There were many occasions when Israel had to admit that it had turned to other gods, but this was not always so. There were times when it could say that it had kept Yhwh in its thinking, kept faithful to the covenant, not turned aside to other gods, even in its inner thinking. It is experiencing trouble because of God's action or because God has failed to act.

Divided

In a particular context it may not seem so obvious who are the faithful and who are the faithless. We hear of many forms of conflict within the people of

---

[26]See section 6.6 "The Two Ways."

God, such as conflict between rich and poor, between people committed to a stricter version of Yahwism and people who follow a broader form of faith (they may be using images or worshiping other gods as well as Yhwh). Isaiah 66:5-6 reflects a conflict between people who tremble at Yhwh's word and "your kinsfolk who repudiate you, who reject you for my name's sake." The former characterize the latter as "people who sanctify themselves and purify themselves for the gardens, . . . eating the flesh of pigs" and declare that they will come to a shameful end (Is 66:17).

Given that the prophecy represents the words of one side only in the words of the other side, its formulation is striking. In the classic style that has been characteristic of the history of the church, each side regards itself as the true people of God and is excommunicating the other. Both sides belong to Israel, both belong to the family: they are *'aḥîm* (kinsfolk). But "our" side looks forward to seeing Yhwh's retribution on "*his* enemies." Similarly the other side's repudiation *(śānē')* and rejection or exclusion (*nādâ* piel; the word later means "excommunicate") is done "for my name's sake." That may mean that from our side's perspective we are suffering for Yhwh's name's sake, but it may mean that the other side sees itself as acting for the sake of Yhwh's name. Likewise they may simply be scorning our side's expectation that Yhwh is going to be manifest in splendor, or they may themselves be looking forward to that manifestation in the conviction that our side will then laugh on the other side of its face. Either way, our side reckons it will be their side that ends up shamed. Both sides are sincerely convinced that they are on Yhwh's side, or rather that Yhwh is on theirs.

History is written and prophecy is validated by the winners, by "our side." (If the other side had won, it would have written the history and validated the prophecy and it would thus be our side, though it may be questionable whether anyone would still be reading it.) This "our side" is one that did believe in worshiping Yhwh alone and in doing that without the aid of images and other traditional forms of worship. And eventually it did win, in the sense that its view became the official view of Judaism and Christianity, though the other side's views continued, and continue to attract people. The First Testament as we have it is a deposit of that victory, though Yhwh did not deal retribution in the spectacular fashion that the prophet hears; perhaps the gradual conversion of the community to a reformist aniconic MonoYahwism made that unnecessary.

It is the nature of the people of God to comprise what Jesus will call wheat and tares together. In Isaiah 41 Jacob-Israel as a whole is Yhwh's servant. In Isaiah 54:17 the community becomes a body of servants. In Isaiah 65:13-15; 66:14 Yhwh's servants are a group within the community, the subgroup the prophet identifies with.

Refusing to Turn

In Hosea's day there was a calamity in Ephraim, perhaps the earthquake referred to in Amos (Amos 1:1; Zech 14:5; cf. Is 5:25). Isaiah 9:8-21 [MT 7-20] describes how the entire people responded with magnificent determination. They would turn a disaster into a challenge and take it as a stimulus to build a city and a land that was more splendid than the one that had been devastated. But they had failed to ask whether there was some other significance to the event. It is odd, given the widespread human instinct to ask "why did this happen to me," the common assumption that God makes things work out in a fair way, and the frequent inference that trouble means a person has done something wrong (cf. Job's friends). On many occasions that inference needs resisting, but on this occasion it needed accepting. "My Lord sent a word against Jacob, it fell on Israel." Isaiah might mean that the calamity constituted a message from Yhwh, which they read as a challenge to be overcome but thereby misread. Or perhaps the calamity followed on a message from Yhwh, and there is a kind of ellipse in Isaiah's words as he moves from the arrival of the word to the people's response to the event. Or most likely Isaiah sees the message and the event as two aspects of a whole. In sending a message against Ephraim, Yhwh was sending a disaster, because the word and the event are closely related. The word is a declaration of intent that brings about the event; it does more than merely announce it. The people knew that, in the sense that they knew the calamity had happened, yet they did not really know it or understand it or acknowledge it. And thus Yhwh sent further "messages" in the form of attacks from the east and the west. Yhwh exalted their enemies and goaded their foes[27] to devour them and they still did not turn. Yhwh tried another chastisement, removing their leadership and introducing social and moral chaos for which the needy paid a terrible price. The social chaos of the community in which no one cares about anyone else and the clans attack one another is both the reason why Yhwh must punish and the expression of Yhwh's punishment.

Thus it is foolhardy to rejoice at what will turn out to be a temporary deliverance. As people shout exultantly on such an occasion, Isaiah declares the intention to weep bitter tears in light of the coming destruction of "my dear people" (*bat-ʿammî*).[28] People were working hard at strengthening the weak places in the city, and they had regard to the armaments in the Forest House, "but they did not have regard to the one who did it. They did not look to the one who shaped it long before" (Is 22:8-11). Chastising them did not work.

---

[27]The first verb (*śāgab* piel) is one that elsewhere refers to something or someone that is so high they cannot be overcome. The second (*sûk* pilpel) apparently suggests poking a person with something sharp (cf. *HALOT*).

[28]See section 3.7 "Yhwh's Abandoned Daughter."

Yhwh had summoned them to weeping and mourning but instead they are feasting and rejoicing: "Let us eat and drink, because tomorrow we may die" (Is 22:12-13). Isaiah likes to put on people's lips the implications of their actions. In other contexts people might literally speak of eating and drinking because death is coming,[29] but this is not the present context. People are celebrating because they have experienced an extraordinary deliverance, but they do not realize that their celebration resembles that of people who talk in terms of dying tomorrow. And that carries a terrible irony because they are indeed in danger of dying tomorrow as a result of these very celebrations that they indulge in when they ought to going in for quite different forms of response to what has happened (Is 22:14).

None of this is the end. "For all this his anger did not turn, his hand was still extended, but the people did not turn to the one who hit them, nor did they have recourse to Yhwh Armies" (Is 9:12-13 [MT 11-12]). Neither party would "turn." The verb forms are exactly the same (lōʾ-šāb), suggesting a stand off between God and people. Yhwh will not stop attacking them. They will not have recourse to Yhwh. The parallelism suggests that the form of turning that Isaiah has in mind involves the people recognizing that they are not the solution to their own problem; Yhwh is the solution to it, the one they need to have recourse to. But "they have refused to turn" (Jer 5:3). "They have stiffened their neck so as not to listen to my words" (Jer 19:15). In order to listen to someone, you turn your head their way. Judah resolutely keeps its neck firm and thus keeps its head facing the way it wishes to go and refuses to turn so as to listen to any voice that seeks to make itself heard so as to get it to turn in another direction. Israel is characterized by inner firmness (šĕrîrût lēb, e.g., Jer 9:13; 13:10; EVV "stubbornness of heart"). They are impossible to change.

After the fall of Jerusalem there was the chance for a new start. The Babylonians appoint a good man from among the Judeans as governor. People who have fled to take refuge in neighboring countries return and join the leftovers that the Babylonians have allowed to remain. (We may guess that it is people of initiative and leadership potential who fled and now return to join the ordinary people who were left behind.) There is a good harvest. A particularly noteworthy event is the arrival of people from Ephraim to grieve and make offerings in the ruins of the temple. Notwithstanding Jeremiah's declarations about an exile that will last a whole generation and about God treating the people in Judah itself as rotten figs, it seems that Yhwh might be restoring the community, even restoring a community that brings north and south together in their grieving for Jerusalem and their recognition of it (Jer 39—41).

---

[29]See Hans Wildberger, *Isaiah 13—27* (Minneapolis: Fortress, 1997), pp. 373-75.

All that is imperiled by the assassination of the governor, the slaughter of the Judean group around him, the Babylonian garrison and the Ephraimite pilgrims for good measure (Jer 41). Even that does not mean the situation is hopeless. Jeremiah can pray for the community, as he could not before the fall of Jerusalem, and he promises it protection from Babylonian wrath (Jer 42). But a substantial group of Judeans flee to Egypt for fear of reprisals, and there they also insist on resuming the worship of other deities that had brought about the disaster (Jer 42—44). We might have thought that things could not get worse after the fall of the city. We would have been wrong.

Deaf and Blind

These dynamics apply among the exiles, too, whom Second Isaiah addresses as deaf and blind, yet urges to listen and look. In fact, it is hard to think of a deaf or blind person who is as deaf and blind as Yhwh's so-called servant (Is 42:18-20). The image of deafness regularly implies obtuseness, an unwillingness to listen. Blindness is a more ambiguous image; it can imply a self-imposed stupidity (there are none so blind as those who won't see) but also a deprivation that issues from other people's action, for imprisonment deprives people of light and thus of sight. Yhwh's servant was to deliver people from this form of blindness (Is 42:7—to beg one or two interpretive questions). But long ago Isaiah ben Amoz first talked about blindness as an image for stupidity, a stupidity imposed by God for people's faithlessness (Is 6:9-10). When God just now talked about leading the blind in a way they did not know (Is 42:16), one might read the image either way.

Jacob-Israel is blind in both senses. The people are plundered and despoiled, trapped and confined (Is 42:22), but this experience of blindness is accompanied by another form of blindness that the people now manifest. In one sense they have their eyes and ears open. They can see the trouble looming for Babylon, they hear the reports about Cyrus's triumphant campaigns. But they cannot see the really important thing; they will not listen to what Yhwh wants to do. Yhwh intends to work through these events to "magnify his teaching, ennoble it" (Is 42:21). In a sense that should be an easy job. After all, the foreign shores are waiting for the teaching Yhwh's servant will bring (Is 42:4). The context there suggests that the nature of this teaching is to convey insight on what is going on in the world, how Yhwh is at work there, how Yhwh is implementing a purpose, what everything means. That also fits in Isaiah 42:21. Yhwh wants to show the world what is happening and how it makes sense, how puzzling events such as the rise of Cyrus actually fit into a magnificent purpose.[30] And when all that is

---

[30]The conventional translation "law" for *tôrâ* (e.g., NIVI) is particularly misleading here; contrast JPSV and NRSV "teaching" (though the NRSV reverts to "law" for Is 42:24).

explained, people will be amazed at what Yhwh is doing.

But Jacob-Israel itself has been unwilling to listen to Yhwh's teaching. Over the centuries Yhwh had been teaching them, through people such as the prophets, that Yhwh was the only God, that Yhwh was pursuing a purpose in their life and that they owed this God their undivided allegiance, but they had never been very good at living by that (Is 42:24). In fact, they had been willfully blind for centuries; this is what had led to the blindness of captivity. And they will still not learn. Yhwh has inflicted on them not merely the darkness of captivity but the blazing fire of battle, but they still will not acknowledge what has been going on (what were the real reasons for the exile) or take notice of Yhwh, accepting Yhwh's account of it (Is 42:25). So they are the bearers of a multiple blindness: a self-imposed blindness reinforced by a God-imposed blindness that caused the exile, a God-imposed blindness involved in the experience of exile and a self-imposed blindness that even now refuses to look at things God's way. And as long as they refuse to face the facts about the blindness that led to the exile and the hopelessness of their present blindness, they cannot expect to find a future. This need not imply that Yhwh will not act unless they first turn, and certainly events do not work out that way. Indeed, as often the logic is the opposite. It is not that their opening their eyes is a condition of Yhwh's acting, but that Yhwh's acting demands as a response that they do open their eyes. Indeed, the declaration of it and the event itself might be the means of Yhwh's opening their eyes.

To put it another way, there in exile in Babylon, Yhwh remarks sardonically, Israel has not had the "burden" of offerings and sacrifices as it had in Jerusalem, yet it is nevertheless weary with Yhwh and does not come to "call on Yhwh" (Is 43:22-24). That expression could denote praise or prayer. Perhaps the exiles had given up both, or perhaps they had engaged in them without their heart being in them; but the prophet has earlier hinted that the problem lay in their not calling on Yhwh to act to deliver them from exile. They lamented Yhwh's abandoning them, but did not turn to Yhwh about it (Is 40:27).

Compared with offering sacrifices, calling on Yhwh is rather a cheap form of worship, the kind Christians go in for, but they have been too tired of Yhwh to offer it. So while Yhwh has not been wearying them or making them serve with those costly offerings, they have been wearying Yhwh and making Yhwh serve by making Yhwh bear the burden of their shortcomings and wrongdoings (Is 43:24). That has been characteristic of Israel during the exile, in this refusal to turn to Yhwh, as it has been characteristic of its life from the beginning. Yes, they are right that Yhwh had delivered Jerusalem up to its destroyers, but they refuse to face the fact that this was entirely deserved (Is 43:26-28). It is as well that a declaration of Yhwh's nature as the one who wipes out rebellions stands at the center of Yhwh's confrontation about this (Is 43:25).

Resistant to Yhwh's Way

Isaiah 40—55 takes a long time coming out with reference to Yhwh's intention to restore Israel by means of Cyrus; he is not explicitly mentioned until Isaiah 44:28. The polemical tone of the preceding chapters has shown an awareness that the community will not just fall down and say "Hallelujah" in response to this prophet's ideas about Yhwh's act of restoration. The reason for the reticence and the confrontational stance is also then soon explicit. In the community's eyes, the prophet's ideas seem crazy. Religiously it might be hard to believe that Yhwh is going to do something to restore the community after abandoning it for half a century. Politically it might seem hard to believe that Persia is going to be so friendly in its stance. Why should it be any different from Assyria or Babylon? Theologically it might seem hard to believe that Yhwh's anointed, Yhwh's shepherd, is the Persian Cyrus rather than the son of David whom Yhwh is committed to put on the throne of Israel again. With characteristic brashness the prophet simply assumes an identity between prophetic and divine words and declares that in resisting the prophetic word the community is arguing with God, as it did at the first exodus (e.g., Ex 17:1-7; Num 20:1-13). It is behaving like a human being arguing with another human being (one pot with another pot), not with God, or like a piece of clay querying what its potter thinks he is doing, or suggesting he is useless ("he has no hands"!), or like a person insulting a father or mother about their potential as parents (Is 45:9-10).

Excuse me, says Yhwh, but do you think you might leave me to decide how to work with my children, with the pots I shape? Through previous chapters the prophet has been seeking to reestablish Yhwh's faithfulness and sovereignty in the community's eyes, and the present challenge recapitulates that attempt and drives home its point. Yhwh is the one who determines events that are to happen and is therefore in a position to reveal what will happen. Yhwh is the one who created the world and created humanity and spread the heavens with all those stars and planets that the Babylonians thought determined events on earth. Yhwh is the one who determines what they do (Is 45:11-13). The community just has to believe that it coheres with all this (which in theory the community believes) to add that Yhwh has aroused Cyrus and is going to ensure that he completes the campaign he is engaged on, that this is an expression of Yhwh's *sedeq* (Yhwh's faithfully doing right by Israel). It will thus issue in his seeing that Jerusalem gets rebuilt and sending the exile community off there again. Needless to say, Cyrus did act for his own selfish reasons; the last colon ("not for payment, not for inducement") declares that unbeknown to him the real reasons for his actions were quite otherwise.

But it is so hard to get the community to see things the prophet's way. It is so strong-minded (*'abbîrê-lēb*, Is 46:12): EVV again have "stubborn-hearted," but the prophet's adjective does not have inherently negative connotations. It is therefore "far away from the act of faithfulness [*şĕdāqâ*]" that Yhwh intends, the act whereby Yhwh does the right thing by this people.[31] They are miles away from understanding it and/or they risk not being the beneficiaries of it. There is no doubt that it will happen and that it will happen imminently, and therefore they need to be shaken into seeing that. The vision of Babylon's own downfall that follows (Is 47) has the same aim. Although that prophecy is formally addressed to Babylon, the audience in the house is again the people who belong to "Israel's restorer, Yhwh Armies, Israel's holy one" (Is 47:4), and the function of the prophecy is once more an attempt to convince them that the day of deliverance and restoration is here. Perhaps one of their problems is that *they* cannot imagine that things could ever be different, like, for instance, colonies of the British Empire a century ago. A change in their imagination will not be enough to bring about their restoration to freedom, but in the absence of that change this restoration will hardly happen. It would be ironic if Yhwh made it possible for the Judeans to return to Jerusalem and no one wanted to go. Indeed, the response was rather mixed. Some went, very many stayed. The sin of the people of God includes resistance to God's way of doing things.

The Mystery of Sin

The fact that Israel's story turns out to be a story of resistance and rebellion makes it an even greater mystery than that of humanity as a whole (*ḥîdôt*, Ps 78:2) (given what God did for us in Christ and in pouring out the Holy Spirit, the fact that the church's story turns out similarly constitutes a yet greater mystery). Whereas Israel was designed to be a people where the kingship of God was a reality and thus to be a microcosm of what the world was called to be, it rejected Yhwh's kingship and become a microcosm of what the world also is.[32]

Israel was set at the center of the nations, with countries all around it. While that statement makes a geographical point, it also makes a theological one. Israel was designed to embody God's vision for a nation. Instead it has become an embodiment of what the nations themselves are, and thus it is more faithless than the other nations because of the greater gap in its life between what God has given it and how it has responded. It has failed to live up to its voca-

---

[31]The NIVI has "far from righteousness," but Is 40—55 does not elsewhere accuse the people of moral and social shortcomings in the manner of eighth-century prophecy, and when it talks about *şĕdāqâ* it is usually referring to Yhwh's doing right by the people.

[32]See John Goldingay, *Theological Diversity and the Authority of the Old Testament* (Grand Rapids, Mich.: Eerdmans, 1986/Carlisle, U.K.: Paternoster, 1995), pp. 74-75.

tion (Ezek 5:5-8). Jerusalem was designed to be "the secure city, filled with judgment," in which faithfulness lodged, but it has become unfaithful to Yhwh and murderous in its own social life: "your silver has become dross, your wine mixed with water" (Is 1:21-22). There is an ambiguity about the description of Jerusalem as a city that was "secure," an ambiguity reflected in the fact that translations often rather take *ne'ĕmān* to mean "trustworthy." Perhaps there was a time when Jerusalem could be described as trustworthy and faithful, though it is hard to see when that was; its first Israelite kings, David and Solomon, initiated the practice of unreliability and faithlessness there. Perhaps, then, security or trustworthiness, judgment and faithfulness are characteristics that Yhwh destined for the city because they are Yhwh's own characteristics, whether or not they had ever been realized there.[33] Alas, the destiny is certainly not realized now. The city falls far short. Jerusalem embodies the regular ambivalence of the city. It is a holy city, but also a bloody city. The city with that exalted destiny has become like Sodom and Gomorrah in its offensiveness to Yhwh.

To use another image, Israel was a vine that was designed to produce fruit and was well tended to that end, but instead of producing plump, juicy grapes it has produced pathetic, sour ones (Is 5:1-7). What is the nature of good fruit and useless fruit? Yhwh "expected judgment [*mišpāṭ*], but there—a bloodbath [*mišpāḥ*], expected faithfulness [*ṣĕdāqâ*], but there—an outcry [*ṣĕʿāqâ*]" (Is 5:7). The similarity between the two pairs of words is a symbol of the contrast between their meanings. "I myself planted you as a vine with red grapes, all with choice seed, so how did you change for me into the turnings of an alien vine?" (Jer 2:21). Yhwh had treated Israel with the beneficence appropriate to children and thought that in response they would relate to Yhwh as children to their father, but they have behaved more like someone being unfaithful to their spouse (Jer 3:19-20). Who has ever heard of anything as extraordinary, not to say disgusting, as the conduct of young Ms. Israel, who has put Yhwh out of mind to "offer sacrifice to emptiness" and thus trip herself up? (Jer 18:13-16). Why would the young bride leave her husband? Why would a people put their God out of mind in order to worship something that has no reality or power except the power to trip them up? Why should they thus choose the proven road to walk an unpaved road that goes nowhere?[34]

Hosea 10:1-2 takes the vine metaphor in another direction. Here Israel is "a luxuriant vine" whose fruit multiplies as the vine itself does. To be less metaphorical, its land flourishes. The crops grow. It experiences great prosperity.

---

[33] Applied to David and Solomon's line in Jerusalem, *ne'ĕmān* means secure rather than trustworthy (1 Kings 11:38).

[34] See further section 2.6 "Sadness," "Letdown."

Ephraim is in a position to multiply fine religious constructions to facilitate its worship. It is hard to say whether there is any note of critique in those comments, though the word for "luxuriant" *(bôqēq)* might mean "wasting," and thus might hint that this is a story that will go wrong, like the song in Isaiah 5. And whenever Hosea refers to things multiplying *(rōb, rābâ)*, critique and/or wrongdoing and/or trouble are usually present or not far behind (Hos 2:8 [MT 10]; 4:7; 8:11, 14; 9:7; 10:13; 12:1, 10 [MT 2, 11]).[35] Nor is there any indication whether the construction involves altars and columns for proper worship of Yhwh as the one who made the vine's flourishing possible, or whether the multiplying is a sign that people are also multiplying their gods. In the former case, for a while things are fine but then they go wrong as the people's heart becomes "deceptive"; in the latter case, their heart always was deceptive. But there is no indication of the link between the flourishing and the deception. That itself hints at the mystery about the sin of the people of God. How is it that we can experience so much of God's blessing and then set about deceiving God and ourselves?

The Mystery of Persistence in Sin

Looking over the story of Israel's resistance to Yhwh thus provokes a sense of puzzlement. Yhwh had demonstrated the capacity to provide for the people and in turning to empty gods they had "become empty": that is resourceless *(hebel,*[36] Jer 2:4, 6-7). There is something unparalleled in this turning from Yhwh to other gods. People do not usually do it, even though their gods are no-gods. But here is a people changing a real God for a no-god, changing someone glorious for something that will be of no benefit. They are like people deliberately abandoning a perpetual spring in order to rely on a tank that just collects rainwater—a leaky tank at that, which will likely leave them dying of dehydration before the dry season is over (Jer 2:13). Or they are like people who have been attacked and wounded but are turning to physicians who are quite unable to be of any help to them, not least because they resemble ER doctors who are no match for the heavies waiting outside to pounce on the victim again (Hos 5:13-14).

The indictment of the resistant community in Isaiah 40—55 comes to a climax in Isaiah 48. They are people who invoke the God of Israel, but "not in truth and not in faithfulness" (Is 48:1). There is a mismatch between the worship they offer and the reality of their attitude to Yhwh. Yhwh is the person who embodies truth and faithfulness; they are nothing like the one they pray to. Yhwh has more than once spoken of the pattern of announcing intentions

---

[35]Hans Walter Wolff, *Hosea* (Philadelphia: Fortress, 1974), p. 173.
[36]On *hebel*, see section 6.6 "Limits."

and then fulfilling them and has set that forward as a reason why other peoples and their gods should acknowledge Yhwh, but Yhwh now says that this was "because of knowing that you are stiff, and your neck an iron sinew, your forehead brass" (Is 48:4). It is impossible to get them to change their minds. It is as if they have an iron bolt in their neck that makes them incapable of turning their heads to listen to a voice from another direction. To change the metaphor, they can look Yhwh straight in the eyes, brazenly, but not take any notice of Yhwh. If Yhwh had not declared intentions ahead of time, they would simply have attributed the events to their idols (Is 48:5). And because they will not accept that Yhwh has been so speaking and acting, neither will they fulfill their vocation to testify to it (Is 48:6). By implication, the real audience for those earlier references to Yhwh's announcing intentions ahead of time was the Judean community more than the Babylonians or their gods. It has always been the Judeans that Yhwh is trying to convince. The pattern continues in present events. Now, too, Yhwh is declaring new intentions about the future (those relating to Cyrus's restoration of the community), so that the Judeans cannot dismiss these as old hat.

Beyond the mystery about Israel's faithlessness, there is thus a further mystery about its persistence in this faithlessness. When people have fallen over, they do not just lie there, do they? When they have turned the wrong way, they turn back, don't they? When they are deceived, they eventually see it, don't they? How come they have no regrets? They are like a horse rushing into battle, but they are rushing to disaster. The birds of the air have a mysterious ability to know when to go south and when to go back north, but "my people do not acknowledge Yhwh's decision" (Jer 8:4-7). Isaiah had already made the point in portraying Israel as the victim of a mugging (by Yhwh!) who keeps getting up asking for more. "Why get hit again? Why continue rebelling?" (Is 1:5-6). When Yhwh sets about healing the wounds, this just stimulates more wrongdoing (Hos 6:11—7:1).

Subsequently Yhwh confesses to a sense of deep puzzlement at the stupidity of the people left in Judah after the fall of Jerusalem who then flee to Egypt. "Come on, don't do this," Yhwh attempts to argue or cajole (*'al-nā' ta'ăśû,* Jer 44:4).[37] Can't they see the lesson in what happened to their kinsfolk when Nebuchadnezzar devastated Judah? Why are they now bringing ill on themselves and risking the elimination of the leftovers of the community that remain? Why are they trying to make Yhwh angry by worshiping other gods? Do they actually want to be cut off and made a laughing stock and a standard for cursing throughout the world? Have they forgotten the ill deeds of their immedi-

---

[37]Admittedly, talk of "begging" (NRSV, JPSV) overestimates the force of the *nā'*.

ate ancestors in Judah and Jerusalem, for which they have indeed shown no contrition? (Jer 44:7-10). Yhwh's questions are not designed to elicit answers but to express the mystery of human stupidity and the stupidity of the people who belong to God and the frustration and anguish of God in trying to work with people.

4.2 The Consequences

The faithlessness of Israel is already the fulfillment of a nightmare for Yhwh— and for many people within Israel. But it also presages a nightmare future for the people of God. Sin means God turning from being our friend to being our enemy. The Torah warns of that (e.g., Deut 28; Lev 26); the "classical prophets" perceive a new, "menacing irruption of divine reality";[38] in Lamentations, the fall of Jerusalem is "the moment of absolute doom."[39] "Should my soul not take its redress on a nation such as this?" (*nāqam* hitpael, Jer 5:9, 29).[40]

As the First Testament has a number of images to describe sin itself, so it has a number of images to describe its effects. Sin stains us, makes us disgusting, alienates us from God, leaves us unhealed. It also has a number of ways of describing God's reaction: rejection, rebuff, abandonment, withdrawal, wrath and an active seeking out of Israel to express that wrath. It has a number of ways of seeing the impact of that: blinding, exposure, shame, war, wasting, annihilation, expulsion, withering, dissolution, death.

Defilement

According to Paul Ricoeur, "Dread of the impure and rites of purification are in the background of all our feelings and all our behavior relating to fault."[41] I am not sure whether this is an exaggeration; it is easy enough to see how it applies to killing and in the realm of sex, though not to theft. But perhaps this is an oddity about Western thinking. The First Testament does view moral faults as defiling in a way that may be suppressed in Western thinking, where purity and impurity are more often metaphors for righteousness and wrongdoing rather than realities or values in their own right. But discharges, blood and semen leave a literal stain, and for First Testament thinking this is a sign that they also leave a symbolic stain. Sin defiles, and dealing with sin requires dealing with defilement. There are "alliances of meaning" between these two.[42] The opening of

---

[38]Walther Eichrodt, *Theology of the Old Testament*, 2 vols. (London: SCM Press, 1961, 1967), 1:344.

[39]Peter R. Ackroyd, *Exile and Restoration* (London: SCM Press, 1968), p. 53.

[40]See section 2.7 "Redress."

[41]Ricoeur, *Symbolism of Evil*, p. 25.

[42]Ibid., p. 47.

Psalm 51 provides an example, with its threefold plea for wiping away, washing and purifying. On the other hand, the First Testament does not make a link between defilement and demonic oppression, as Babylonian religion does.[43] Defilement does not relate to supernatural bondage. There is another contrast with Christian thinking, which, while having little place for purity thinking, has often emphasized the power of the demonic and supernatural bondage.[44]

In the confession in Isaiah 64, after acknowledging that they have failed to live by Yhwh's expectations, the community go on, "All of us have become like someone stained, all our acts of faithfulness have become like a menstrual cloth" (Is 64:6 [MT 5]).[45] Sin puts people in the same position as someone stained by something such as contact with semen or with menstrual blood. This does not make them repulsive, as if they were an "abomination," but it does mean they are in quarantine until they go through the appropriate sacramental rites and the appropriate time has passed. Meanwhile, they cannot take part in worship, and their ordinary human contact is limited. Isaiah once saw himself as stained as regards his lips (Is 6:5); his mouth needed to be sacramentally cleansed before he could join in the worship of the seraphim or speak to the community in Yhwh's name. In Isaiah 64 the whole community recognizes itself as like a person whose whole being is stained. It was once the case that it lived a life characterized by faithfulness to Yhwh; it is not explicit when this was, but the statement matches the way Jeremiah can speak of a long-ago time when Jerusalem was faithful to her husband (Jer 2:2). The point lies in the contrast. The people have ceased to be like that. Their forms of worship defile them (e.g., Ezek 20:7, 18, 30). They therefore need washing.

Blood in particular obviously stains, and it does that in more than a literal sense. One cannot remove the stain of bloodshed. "Even if you wash with detergent and get much soap for yourself, your wrongdoing is ingrained before me" (Jer 2:22). Jerusalem is a bloody city, and its bloodshed as well as its making of images means it has become culpable (*'āšam*), under obligation to make reparation for its wrongdoing (Ezek 22:1-4). As usual, Ezekiel is being sardonic. How can one make reparation for killing people, except by one's own death? Thus "you have brought near your days[46] and come to your years. Therefore I am making you the mockery of the nations, the scorn of all the countries. Countries near and far from you will scorn you, defiled of name, abounding in tumult" (Ezek 22:4-5).

---

[43]Cf. ibid., pp. 47-48.

[44]Cf. section 7.4 "Natural and Supernatural."

[45]In section 4.1 "Universal Faithlessness," I quoted this line in its more familiar KJV translation.

[46]The days of Ezek 12:23.

Zephaniah 3:1-2 puts the point even more pungently. Jerusalem is a city that has failed to put its trust in Yhwh (it trusts in other deities and/or in its own political initiative) and has therefore not drawn near to its God to plead for help. It has declined to pay heed to what the teaching of its true priests and its true prophets said about that, and about its life in which the powerful and wealthy do well at the expense of ordinary people. And that makes it *mōrʾâ*. That participle points in two directions.[47] The verb *mārâ* means "rebel," and the participle might be an odd formation from that verb, which the context supports: the people's rebelliousness lies in its unwillingness to listen to Yhwh or trust in Yhwh. But more immediately Zephaniah adds that the city is polluted, and the odd formation *mōrʾâ*, with the inserted aleph, also points to a link with Mishnaic Hebrew *rŏʾî* "feces." That is how defiled the city is. It is polluted by the violence and oppression that characterize its life, soiled as by excrement.

People's sin not only defiles them but defiles the place where Yhwh lives. It stands in the midst of the community, whose stain can hardly not affect it. Moreover, Israelites are in and out of the sanctuary every day and are therefore bringing their stain with them, even (paradoxically) when they come to make offerings as part of removing it. Hence each year it was necessary for the high priest "to make expiation *[kipper]* on behalf of the sanctuary from the stains of the Israelites, yes, from their rebellions, for all their shortcomings. He will do the same for the meeting tent which dwells with them in the midst of their stains." He will also "go out to the altar that is before Yhwh and make expiation on its behalf . . . and cleanse it and consecrate it from the stains of the Israelites" (Lev 16:16-19).[48] The awfulness of Yhwh's very dwelling being polluted by Yhwh's people can hardly be overstated.

Corruption

Israel is "a corrupt nation" (Is 10:6; cf. Is 9:17 [MT 16]). The notion of corruption (*ḥănuppâ*) is hard to define,[49] but it is related to the idea of stain (cf. the parallelism in Ps 106:38-39). It goes beyond that in suggesting a stain deliberately brought on oneself by ignoring God or refusing to treat God as God (cf. the parallelism in Job 8:13). The Septuagint's "godless" (cf. EVV) is thus not inappropriate. It may also hint at pretending to be something other than one is or pretending that things are other than they are (cf. Prov 11:9; and KJV "hypocrisy").

Bloodshed and other forms of faithlessness are also abominations (*tôʿēbâ*),

---

[47]See Jimmy J. M. Roberts, *Nahum, Habakkuk, and Zephaniah* (Louisville, Ky: Westminster John Knox, 1991), p. 206.

[48]Cf. John G. Gammie, *Holiness in Israel* (Minneapolis: Fortress, 1989), p. 41; with Roy Gane's comments in *Cult and Character* (Winona Lake, Ind.: Eisenbrauns, 2005), p. 142.

[49]See *TDOT, NIDOTTE.*

practices that disgust Yhwh (Ezek 22:2). They turn the people of God into an abomination, something disgusting. In having recourse to other gods to seek their blessing on crops and herds and people, Israel "defiled my land, made my possession an abomination" (Jer 2:7). For Jeremiah and Ezekiel, Israel's worship is characterized by abhorrent things *(šiqqûṣîm)* and abominations that have defiled Yhwh's sanctuary. The abhorrent things are apparently forms of worship and aids in worship such as divine images that are used in the temple and at other sanctuaries (Jer 4:1; 7:30; 16:18; Ezek 5:11; 7:20). They are aids that might seem harmless in themselves, the equivalent of icons and candles, but they are guilty by association. They characterize the traditional worship of the land and thus suggest the worship of other gods, with which they are associated (Jer 13:27; Ezek 20:30; cf. 2 Kings 23:13).

Ezekiel speaks in similar terms about sexual practices. Men have sex with their stepmothers and rape menstruating women, they defile their own daughters-in-law or rape their half-sisters, and they have committed abomination with their neighbor's wife (Ezek 22:10-11). In the account of this series of acts there is hardly any concern with what we would call ethics. There is no concern for the women's rights, feelings or freedom, or for the rights or feelings of a man whose wife has been unfaithful. There is some concern with family order and community relations, which most of these acts ignore. But the main concern is with defilement and abomination. These acts resemble religious acts of which Yhwh disapproves. Sex and religion are interwoven, and people's sexual behavior is a metaphor for their religious behavior. By ignoring Yhwh's instructions regarding sexual behavior, people are offending Yhwh. Jeremiah likewise characterizes acts such as stealing, murder, adultery, false swearing, alongside honoring other deities, as "abominations" (Jer 7:9-10).

Isaiah 65 describes people involved in rites in sacred gardens or groves that aim to ensure the life-giving fertility of the ground. They take part in rites that involve seeking to contact dead people (specifically, members of one's family) to continue the relationship with them, make gifts to them and seek their help. They take part in rites that abandon the distinctives of proper Israelite religion such as the avoidance of pork. There was nothing unhealthy about these things, but avoiding them set Israelite religion over against the religion of the peoples around. Talk of fire and smoke usually implies anger, but it fits the context if here the imagery rather suggests that their sacrifices and incense are an irritant to Yhwh, more like barbecue smoke blowing in the face than like the smell of a good meal (cf. Is 1:10-15).[50] Either way, the people "have provoked me to my face" and they will pay for it, or rather be paid for it.

---

[50]So Joseph Blenkinsopp, *Isaiah 56—66*, AB (New York: Doubleday, 2003), p. 273.

Israel "reviled me in offending against me" (Ezek 20:27). Their offensiveness (ma'al) lay in ignoring Yhwh's teaching about how to offer their worship
and in deciding for themselves in light of the way other people offered theirs.
And that was tantamount to reviling Yhwh (gādap). The word usually refers to
speech; the idea is, then, that their actions have amounted to declaring that
they do not care what Yhwh says about worship; they will do it the way they
decide. And another result is that "I was broken with their immoral heart that
turned away from me and with their immoral eyes that turned away to their
pillars" (Ezek 6:9). Often they may not have consciously taken that stance but
simply have assumed that the kind of worship that "obviously" made sense
and seemed to work for them would be welcomed by Yhwh. But this presumably would be less likely to be so when they worshiped other gods, and also
sacrificed children, so that they "alienated" the place (nākar piel; Jer 19:4-5).[51]
They have worshiped alien gods there and thus made it an alien place, one
where Yhwh is no longer at home.

Rejection

The point can be made much more personally in light of the quasi-marital relationship between Yhwh and Israel. In a patriarchal context that means Yhwh
as the husband provides for his wife and she looks to him for that provision.
What she has done instead is looked to the "Master" or the "Masters," like a
woman going after lovers because she thought they would provide for her better than her husband.

There is some inconsistency in Yhwh's response to the situation as Hosea 2
describes it, inconsistency that constitutes good news. On one hand, Yhwh
bids the people confront their mother, which really means the people confronting themselves or individuals taking issue with the stance that the community
has long been adopting. They are to make a stand on the basis of the fact that
their "mother" has gone back on her relationship with her "husband." Hosea
actually speaks more literally of "her man" and "my woman," which are the
regular First Testament terms for "her husband" and "my wife," though they
are not the more technical expressions for husband and wife, ba'al and bĕ'ûlâ.
The connotations of the latter are more patriarchal, and in this context also
more religious, because ba'al is the people's "lord and master." When Yhwh
says "she is not my woman," as opposed to "not my wife" (Hos 2:2 [MT 4]), this
is not so much a legal point about the people's marital status as a substantial
point about their mutual relationship. She has decked herself up in her fancy
clothes, put her husband out of mind and gone after lovers, and her behavior

---

[51]In light of Jer 19:3 I take "this place" to refer to the temple or to the city in general (cf. Jer
19:12-13) rather than to the Hinnom Valley, its reference in Jer 19:6.

means she is not "his woman" and that for her he is not "her man."

The logical result is for Yhwh simply to view the relationship as finished. Indeed, the statement "she is not my woman and I am not her man" has been understood as a legal declaration, a performative statement that effects a divorce. The marriage being over, as her ex-husband Yhwh could then simply stay on his own or go and find another woman. Yet Yhwh does not simply shrug shoulders and move on, but as the cuckolded husband rather declares the intention of wreaking punishment and terminating the marriage. He will turn her back into the naked woman she would be if he were not providing for her (Hos 2:3 [MT 5]). Stripping her is thus a kind of legal act, but also no doubt an act of shaming, and in the context of reference to her sexual activity one with sexual overtones.

The actual punishment will fit the crime. In reality Yhwh is the one who makes the rain fall and makes the crops grow and the animals flourish. So if the Israelites have turned their backs on this giver, they will find that they lose the gifts. The rain will not fall. The land will become desert. The sheep will grow no wool. When the time for grain harvest and grape harvest comes, there will be nothing to harvest. Orchards will be turned into mere forests of trees that produce nothing to eat because (or and) animals will eat up their fruit. The people will celebrate no festivals and sabbaths because there is nothing to celebrate and/or because Yhwh will not be party to such observances. They may enjoy their worship, but Yhwh does not reciprocate the feeling: these are *her* festivals, *her* sabbaths, not Yhwh's. Yhwh will have no compassion on the people of the land because they are "children of promiscuity." Perhaps people also sought help from the Master in connection with human fertility and it was of such parents that the present members of the community were born, or perhaps Yhwh simply means they are "promiscuous children," that is, "promiscuous people."

Rebuff

There is another aspect to the illogical nature of the husband's reactions. Before speaking about the punishments, Yhwh declares that Israel must give up these other relationships. The warnings are indeed warnings. Israel must give up her involvement with the Master, "otherwise . . ." So the declaration "she is not my woman and I am not her man" is not a final statement. It is possible for Yhwh's punishment to be averted. Yet when Yhwh imagines Israel turning, this seems not to presage reconciliation and the restoration of the relationship. Is it that Yhwh feels another natural human instinct, that a person cannot necessarily respond with an enthusiasm that presupposes the turning immediately solves all the problems and makes it possible to return to the relationship as it was before? This might be especially a question when the return is selfishly motivated ("I was better off with him"). And/or do the words that follow, about the people not acknowledging that Yhwh was the source of their resources, imply that Israel is seeing the stupidity of its ways without having a change of heart? (Hos 2:7-8). Is this remorse rather than repentance? Is it another aspect of the people's punishment that it should attempt to turn back to Yhwh but find no response?

Like Saul, for instance, then, it will see it did wrong, but not find a way out of the consequences of its mistakes. When a man divorces his wife and she marries someone else, if she later becomes free of her second marriage, he cannot decide to remarry her. This would be an abomination that polluted the land itself (Deut 24:1-4).[52] Adapting the regulation, Jeremiah points out that similarly it is surely unthinkable that Yhwh's "wife" should return to Yhwh after a series of affairs that have themselves defiled the country. Israel has wanted so to return, but it cannot be allowed (Jer 3:1-5). Hosea 5:6-7 has the people seeking help from Yhwh (biqqēš) but finding that Yhwh has pulled away from them (ḥālaṣ, the only occurrence of this vivid verb in this connection). Does this mean that they will truly return but find they are too late, that Yhwh will not be accessible to them? That would be hard to reconcile with other statements by Hosea and other prophets, yet it is compatible with some other solemn warnings, and it safeguards the fact that we can never take God's forgiveness for granted. In relationships between couples it is possible for faithlessness to persist so long that eventually the offended party is no longer interested in starting again. It is time to move on.

But perhaps Yhwh is speaking of a turning that is not radical enough. It still accompanies a turning to the Masters for help. In a sense it is no turning at all. It is what the people have long been doing as they turn to Yhwh but also turn to the Masters. On this understanding, they will find Yhwh has pulled away because of insisting on being the only one they turn to, the only one they regard as God. In seeking help from the Masters as well as from Yhwh, they have been breaking faith with Yhwh, betraying their covenant commitment. The children they have acquired after seeking the help of the Masters through involvement in the sexual rites are a standing fruit of that betrayal. So Yhwh will devour them. It sounds like an inevitability, but the declaration again gives the people opportunity so to act that Yhwh will not do it.

Later Hosea 5:15—6:5 speaks of a turning that shows it is not radical enough in another way, in the fact that it does not last. Hosea has Yhwh turning away from them until they acknowledge their guilt and come back: "Come, let us turn to Yhwh, because he is the one who tore, and he can heal

---

[52]The aim of the regulation may be to discourage men from too easy divorce and to safeguard the second marriage and the woman's position.

us; he hit, and he can bind us up." It is an expression of some profundity in its recognition of Yhwh's sovereignty. "He will revive us after two days, on the third day he will raise us up, so that we may be alive before him." It is a fine expression of faith and hope. "Let us acknowledge, let us pursue after acknowledging Yhwh; his appearing is as sure as dawn. He will come like the rain to us, like the spring rain that waters the earth." Acknowledgment of Yhwh is just what Hosea has been pressing for (e.g., Hos 2:8, 20 [MT 10, 22]; 5:4). Does Yhwh then welcome them with open arms? The trouble is that Yhwh has heard all that before. "What can I do with you, Ephraim, what can I do with you Judah, when your commitment is like morning cloud, like dew that goes quickly? That is why I cut them down by the prophets, slew them by the words of my mouth" (Hos 6:4-5).

"Rejoice in Yhwh," bid the Psalms, at least partly in the context of great worship occasions in the sanctuary, and they even add that foreign nations are to rejoice and exult (e.g., Ps 97:1, 12). Do no such thing, says Hosea, perhaps at just such a worship occasion: "Do not rejoice, Israel, do not exult like the peoples" (Hos 9:1). Instead of the nations being imagined as joining in the joyful worship of the temple, Israel is bidden to stop rejoicing. Indeed, perhaps Hosea's point is that "rejoicing and exulting" is the kind of thing that the Canaanites do in their unrestrained worship, screaming and shrieking, something associated with the sexual aspect to it. He is then bidding them stop worshiping in the manner of the Canaanites. "I will drive them out of my house, I will love them no more, Yhwh says" (Hos 9:15). If the relationship between Yhwh and Israel is like a marriage and Israel has gone off with other men, then her husband for his part gives up on the love relationship and determines to throw her out of the house, the sanctuary where Yhwh lives.

Abandonment

Or Yhwh will destroy the sanctuary. Poised at or on or above (*'al*) an altar, Yhwh bids an unnamed demolition contractor (an aide? or Amos himself?) to strike the tops of its pillars with a wrecking ball so that the ground at the base shakes as they tremble and then shatter on the heads of the worshipers below (Amos 9:1). It would not be surprising if the unnamed sanctuary were the royal sanctuary at Bethel from which Amos had been warned off by Amaziah (cf. Amos 3:14), though its being unnamed here suggests it might stand for sanctuaries in general whose demolition he had announced (Amos 7:7-17). That is what Yhwh thinks of the people's worship. Yhwh has urged the people to seek the good rather than the bad if they want to live and experience Yhwh's grace, but they will end up finding themselves dying as Yhwh's eyes are set on them for bad not for good (Amos 5:14-15; 9:4).

Jeremiah makes explicit that this is not merely a threat that applies to northern sanctuaries. If the people do not turn, "then I will make this house like Shiloh and make this city a belittling for all the nations in the earth" (Jer 26:6). The ruins of the Shiloh sanctuary were there for people to see, a few miles north of Jerusalem, but it might have seemed inconceivable that the sanctuary at Jerusalem should suffer the same fate. The First Testament speaks of no explicit divine commitment to Shiloh of the kind there was to Jerusalem, whereas Jerusalem was supposed to be the place Yhwh had chosen as a dwelling place forever (Ps 132:13-14).

Thus, even though Israel is Yhwh's special people, Yhwh will stop treating them as such. Amos 9:7 declares that Yhwh sees them as no different from the Sudanese, a far-off people who might seem of consummate indifference both to Yhwh and to Israel, though they shared the experience of being Egypt's underlings. True, I brought the Israelites up from Egypt, Yhwh grants: "and the Philistines from Caphtor and the Arameans from Kir." Yhwh is not even professing no difference in attitude to Israel and to some far-off people uninvolved with Israel. The Philistines are Israel's great neighbors and rivals for possession of the land of Canaan on the west. They are actually in possession of much of the land promised to Israel, as their territory runs up the coastal plain and round into the Vale of Esdraelon. The Arameans occupy the land to the northeast and are friends and rivals of Ephraim in the eighth century. It is with such peoples that Yhwh compares Israel's position. Being chosen by God guarantees Israel's position in the long term, but offers no guarantee to particular segments of it or to particular generations. The pattern antedates Israel's own existence; the promise to Abraham turned out not to apply to all his offspring, nor to all Isaac's. Nor has it in the past applied to all the offspring of Jacob-Israel. At Sinai, thousands were killed; at Kadesh, the whole generation was told it would not enter the land. Being part of Israel offers no unconditional guarantees to people.

"I shall return to my place until they suffer for their guilt[53] and have recourse to me. In their trouble they will make that their priority" (Hos 5:15). Hosea anticipates Ezekiel's vision of Yhwh's splendor withdrawing from Jerusalem. We would be pressing the metaphor in asking for an answer to the question where Yhwh's place is located, though perhaps Yhwh refers to a withdrawal to heaven. The emphasis lies on the terrible fact of withdrawal from Ephraim and Judah. Whereas Yhwh can be thought of as punishing actively by "attending" to the people (e.g., Jer 5:9, 29; Hos 2:13 [15]), here Yhwh punishes by leaving rather than by coming. The presence of Yhwh normally

---

[53]Not "acknowledge their guilt" (EVV); there are no parallels for this meaning of 'āšam (see BDB; and G. I. Davies, *Hosea* [London: Marshall Pickering/Grand Rapids, Mich.: Eerdmans, 1992], p. 158).

acts as a protection for the people and a guarantee of blessing. Yhwh would, for instance, protect them from Assyria and make their crops grow. Now Yhwh will depart and leave them to Assyria's worst devices and to famine.

Yhwh is thus withdrawing *šālôm*, *ḥesed* and *raḥămîm* from the people (Jer 16:5). It is hard to imagine a more devastating declaration. Judah will know no more well-being. It will know no more divine commitment. It will know no more divine compassion. Yhwh soon adds that in the exile that will result, "I will show you no grace" (*ḥănînâ*), a hapax of similar meaning to *ḥēn*; Jer 16:13).[54]

Withdrawal

The reason for the exile is that Israel "disdained me [*māʿal*] and I hid my face from them and gave them into the power of their enemies" (Ezek 39:23). Attitudes between these two parties have gone awry on both sides. Israel has behaved in a way that suggests it does not care what Yhwh thinks. Yhwh has responded by turning away. When a person's face is turned toward us it implies that they will see what we need and give themselves for us. When their face turns away, it means they do not see and do not give.

Yhwh's withdrawal is a withdrawal into silence (Amos 8:11-14). Israel will experience a famine, "not famine for bread and not thirst for water, but for hearing Yhwh's words." The warning is vivid and frightening, though symbolic rather than concrete, which adds to its sinister tone. What words from Yhwh are these that people will seek and not find? One context in which people are accustomed to hearing Yhwh's words (plural) is the declaration of Yhwh's will at festivals, for instance in the form of "words" such as those Yhwh utters in Exodus 20:1-17. Events to come will mean there are no more festivals where such words from Yhwh are proclaimed and people hear them. As a result, "people will roam from sea to sea, from north to east, they will go about seeking Yhwh's word, but will not find it." Individually, people were accustomed to seek a word from a priest at a sanctuary, guidance about matters of behavior and piety, but they will find none. They will long to know what to do about questions that arise in their lives and have no way of discovering the answer. "On that day the beautiful girls and the young men will faint with thirst, the people who swear by the guilt of Samaria, who say 'As your god lives, Dan,' 'As the way to Beersheba lives.' They will fall and never get up again."

The two halves of the passage may well be of separate origin, but having been brought together, they interpret each other. The thirst of the young

---

[54]In LXX and Vg. it is the gods that people serve in exile that will show them no grace, which will also be true.

women and men is a thirst for hearing that word from Yhwh (is this a word
about the young people's relationships with one another: "Shall I marry him/
her?"). But they will hear none. The places they thought were the places to
hear this word have become places that stand for guilt. For people listening to
these words in Amos 8 a few decades later, the reference to Samaria's guilt
(ʾašmâ) would also be too close for comfort to the name of a god worshiped by
some people who came to live in Ephraim after the fall of Samaria, ʾăšîmā (2
Kings 17:30; cf. NRSV). Even in Amos's own day reference to the "guilt of Samaria" and to the god at Dan would imply that people were worshiping the
Master rather than Yhwh, and the reference to Beersheba may have the same
implication.[55] In Ephraim (Samaria, Dan) or in Judah (Beersheba), both the
seeking of a word from Yhwh that was compromised by the attitudes and lives
of the seekers and the seeking of a word from some other deity would be capable of making Yhwh decide not to speak. And in any case the fall of Samaria
will mean the fall of the sanctuaries where one might do that, and thus the
eventual fall through hunger and thirst of the people who cannot satisfy their
hunger or thirst.

People were also accustomed to seek words from prophets, whose ministry
overlapped with that of priests, but neither will they find any of these. People
have in any case tried to stop prophets prophesying, and just now a Bethel
priest has tried to shut up Amos in particular (Amos 2:12; 7:12-13). It will not
be surprising if Yhwh takes them at their word and they discover that they
cannot find a prophet when they decide they want one. From Yhwh's perspective, the point about prophets is to be means of declaring a divine word when
Yhwh wants to utter one, not just when people want to hear one. If they refuse
to have prophecy on those terms, they forfeit having it at all.

Wrath

There are a number of senses in which we might talk about Yhwh's wrath.[56] In
the New Testament, God's wrath is often, paradoxically, a somewhat dispas-
sionate response to human wrongdoing that involves willing for this wrongdoing to have its inherent negative outcome. In the First Testament, the
dynamics of that process resemble those of Yhwh's curse, whereas wrath can
be an elemental force like a whirlwind or a hurricane (e.g., Is 26:20), or more
often, the strong feelings that emerge from Yhwh's passionate involvement
with the world and with Israel. There is a personal relationship between Yhwh
and Israel, which means that Yhwh is, for instance, the head of this household.

---

[55]See, e.g., J. Alberto Soggin, *The Prophet Amos* (London: SCM Press, 1987), pp. 140-41, who
translates *derek* "the Power."
[56]For what follows, see also section 2.7.

When the household flaunts the authority of its head, he does not take it lightly. Yhwh gets angry. "I will pour out my fury on them like water" (Hos 5:10). Yhwh's fury is like a winter storm that Yhwh pours out, overwhelming and sweeping away anything in its path.

Sometimes, however, *wrath* rather suggests the fieriness of what people experience when disaster comes. Ezekiel 30 comprises a long description of calamity to come on Egypt at the hand of Nebuchadnezzar, whose significance for Judah is the fact that this makes Egypt a foolish support to rely on. There is no declaration of the reason for this devastation of Egypt.[57] This is not to say that Yhwh had no moral purpose in the act, only that the chapter's concern is with the calamitous nature of what happens. It is in this sense that it involves Yhwh's wrath being poured out on Pelusium (Ezek 30:15). Wrath stands in parallelism with terms such as *desolation, destruction, decimation, fire, anguish, breaking up, darkness, captivity* and *falling from power*. It emphasizes the fiery nature of the experience that comes to people rather than the fiery nature of the feelings of the agent of this experience.

A vivid way of making this point is to picture the experience of Yhwh's wrath as the drinking of a cup of poisoned wine. A cup of fine wine is a blessing cup, and hosts share such fine wine with their guests (e.g., Ps 23:5). Yhwh thus pours out blessing (Mal 3:10). Correlatively, trouble can be pictured as a cup of something much less pleasant that one has to drink (e.g., Ps 22:6). Even fine wine can of course have negative effects if drunk in excessive quantities, and the reference to Yhwh's cup causing people to lie naked may refer to that effect of alcohol (e.g., Lam 4:21). But some references to a cup of wrath imply another framework. Here the word for "wrath" (*ḥēmâ*) denotes "heat" and it is also a word for poison (e.g., Deut 32:24, 33; Job 6:4; Ps 58:4 [MT 5]; 140:3 [MT 4]), and references to convulsion also suggest that Yhwh is not merely threatening to make the people drunk. This cup makes people reel because its wine is mixed with something more sinister than herbs and spices (cf. Ps 60:3 [MT 5]; 75:8 [MT 9]). The heat of the drink is not so much or not only the hot fury felt by Yhwh but the burning sensation experienced by the person who drinks this cup. This poisoned cup was not really meant for Judah, but it had come to deserve it, and when Yhwh told Jeremiah to make the nations drink from a poisoned cup, he began with Jerusalem and Judah (Jer 25:18).

Yes, Jerusalem "drank from Yhwh's hand his fury cup . . . drained the chalice, the shaking cup" (Is 51:17). As a result Jerusalem lies unconscious and insensible, incapable of standing up. It had been attacked and devastated by a foreign army, and in some ways resembles a person who has had too much to

---

[57]In the context, in Ezek 30:6 and 18 *gěʾôn* likely denotes pride in the objective sense of majesty, and in Ezek 30:14 and 19, "acts of judgments" (*šěpāṭîm*) are decisive acts of power.

drink and has collapsed paralytic in the street—and none of her children has come to find her and take her home.[58] But her problem is not that she has had too much to drink. It is that her drink had been spiked. Yhwh had passed a cup to her in the manner of the host at a banquet, and she had drained it, but it was a poisoned chalice, one that generated a hot fever, not merely intoxicating but toxic. It was this that made her collapse. And the reason why her children could not come out and take her home is that they were themselves lying overcome, their energy exhausted with the effort not to let the city fall. So they were in no position to mourn for her (Is 51:18-20). None of her neighbors would do so. And neither could Yhwh, her suffering and distress were so great. Or is it neither *would* Yhwh do so? After all, it was Yhwh who had administered the poisoned chalice, had finally stopped simply absorbing the fury that she had inspired over the centuries because that seemed to get nowhere, and had let it receive expression.

Darkness

So none of this happens without Yhwh's personal involvement. Indeed, the reversal comes about because Yhwh swears an oath, the kind in which one implicitly calls down judgment on oneself if one fails to do what one says: "Yhwh swears by the majesty of Jacob, 'If I ever put out of mind any of their deeds . . .'" (Amos 8:7). As usual, the self-threat is left incomplete. English versions render the verb šākaḥ, "forget," and a declaration that Yhwh will not forget could sound harmless, but it implies the impossibility of ever escaping. What is more, the oath shows that there is no doubt that Yhwh is personally involved in fulfilling the nightmare warning.

Thus Isaiah 9:17-21 [MT 16-20] comments, "for all this his anger did not turn; his hand was still extended. Faithlessness burns like a fire that devours thorn and thistle." Faithlessness carries destruction within it. One can see how that is so in the destruction of relationships in the community as "the people is like fuel for the fire; no one had mercy on their brother. They snatch on the right but are hungry; they consume on the left but are not full. Each devours his offspring's flesh, Manasseh Ephraim, Ephraim Manasseh, they together Judah." Thus this faithlessness "sets on fire the forest thicket, and it rises as a plume of smoke." Yet such declarations stand in the midst of depictions of Yhwh's anger and the extending of Yhwh's hand: "By the fury of Yhwh Armies the land is burned up." Yes, "for all this his anger did not turn; his hand was still extended." These phenomena emerge from Yhwh's feelings and actions. The fire they engender is the fire of Yhwh's fury. It is expressed in the fact that Yhwh's

---

[58]In the Ugaritic story of Aqhat this is the task of a mother's offspring: see Aqht A, 1:31-32; *ANET*, p. 150.

hand is turning against the people (Is 1:24-31). That is a terrifying prospect. The nature of the terror is underlined by the description of rebels and sinners being crushed or of people who indulge in traditional religious rites being burned up.

This day of darkness and wrath is "Yhwh's day" against Israel. "Yhwh Armies has a day against everything exalted and high" (Is 2:12). It is "a day of slaughter," like the day when sheep are slaughtered (Jer 12:3), "the day of their calamity" (Jer 18:17). It is a day for putting down and destroying (cf. Is 2:10-17; Zeph 1:7—2:3; Lam 1—2). If you are a little people, it is a day of deliverance, a day to look forward to; if you are a powerful people, it is a day to fear. For Israel Yhwh's day can be good news or bad news; Zechariah 12—14 forms a powerful interweaving of these. Like any other nation, and like the church, Israel is inclined to assume that other peoples are the ones that are destined to be put down.[59] Prophets confront Israel with the opposite prospect.

If there was a formulated idea of "Yhwh's day" before his time, Amos 5:18-20 in particular turns it from good news to bad news by declaring that it will be a day of calamity for Israel and not for its enemies. "Hey, you who long for Yhwh's day: what, really, will Yhwh's day be for you?" Israel assumes it is on the side of the angels and thus that "Yhwh's day," the moment when Yhwh sorts everything out, will mean its vindication and triumph. It will mean light, which is a figure for deliverance and blessing. On the contrary, says Amos, "it will be darkness rather than light"; that is, terrible calamity. The nation has often been like someone pursued by a lion or a bear, but it has often escaped, and it might therefore reckon that God would also deliver it from its present crises. But that assumption will be quite illusory. It will be "as if someone runs from a lion and a bear meets him, or he comes home and leans his hand on the wall and a snake bites him." It may think that the worst has happened, but it will find there is a yet more terrible event to come: "Will Yhwh's day not be darkness rather than light, gloomy with no brightness to it?"

Isaiah thus imagines people who are under God's punishment wandering about wretched and hungry, angry and cursing because of their lot. Individually, "they may turn their face upward or look to the earth, but there—into distress and darkness, gloom, anguish, and dark they are being thrust" (Is 8:21-22). The natural opposite to looking upward is looking down into the underworld, and this may be the implication of Isaiah's words. They look up to the heavens or down into the underworld in a kind of parody of Yhwh's own searching look that ensures they cannot escape punishment (Amos 9:2; Ps 139:8), but all they see is darkness in either direction. There is no more light in

---

[59]See further section 8.5.

God's face than in the depths of Sheol. Their destiny is wholly anguish and darkness. It is as well this is not God's last word (see Is 8:22—9:1 [MT 9:1-2]).[60]

Attention

We have noted that talk of "not forgetting" quite understates the significance of Yhwh's action. Again, Yhwh asks, "should I not attend to such things?" (Jer 5:9, 29). The verb is *pāqad*; translations such as "punish" obscure the understatement.[61] Amos makes its threatening nature explicit. Yhwh does not abandon the Israelites, which would be terrible, but makes a commitment to pursue them relentlessly to destruction wherever they try to hide (Amos 9:2-4), which is more terrible. "I will search Jerusalem with lamps and attend to the men who are resting on their lees" like vintage wine left undisturbed so that it can reach its best (Zeph 1:12), search thoroughly and relentlessly through the city to make sure no one escapes my attention.

With horrifying logic Yhwh declares, "Only you have I acknowledged of all the families in the earth; therefore I will attend to you in respect of all your wayward acts" (Amos 3:2). Coming to know someone (*yādaʿ*) involves entering into a relationship and making an act of commitment. It is what Yhwh does in relation to Abraham, Moses and Jeremiah in connection with a role they are to play (Gen 18:19; Ex 33:12, 17; Jer 1:5). Here alone the image is applied to Israel. Perhaps the link with Abraham is significant. Abraham and his family were to be a bridgehead for Yhwh's blessing among "all the families of the earth" (Gen 12:3; 28:14; the only other occurrences of this phrase).[62] The connection in which Yhwh refers to acknowledging him is his charging his children to keep Yhwh's way by exercising authority in a faithful way.

Entering into such a relationship means being unable to ignore this person henceforth. When people adopt a child, they are committed to looking after that child but also cannot avoid taking notice when the child behaves wrongly and cannot avoid doing something about it. Responsibility rests on them. So Yhwh has to take notice and take action when Israel goes off the tracks. Amos has already established that the same is true when other peoples go off the tracks, though he does so to prepare the way for saying that Israel also gets away with nothing. A child might hope that its parents' commitment to it means it will get away with things. It is not so. Yhwh reverses that logic.

In particular, Yhwh says, "On the day I attend to the rebellions of Israel, I

---

[60]Is 8:22 [MT 9:1] is obscure; the English chapter division presupposes that bad news continues through this verse; the printed Hebrew chapter division presupposes that the good news begins in this verse. The MT makes Is 8:19—9:6 [MT 5] one paragraph.

[61]Vg. and thus KJV have "visit," a nice equivalent understatement.

[62]Hans Walter Wolff, *Joel and Amos* (Philadelphia: Fortress, 1977), p. 177.

will attend to the altars of Bethel," with the result that the horns will be hacked off from its altar (Amos 3:14). Demolishing the altar would be a devastating action in relation to the provisions of sacrificial worship, but the stress on its horns recalls the role of the altar as a place of refuge (e.g., 1 Kings 1:50-51; 2:28). Chopping these off suggests the removal of any escape. Bethel is a multi-altared sanctuary or a great-altared sanctuary (if the plural is intensive). The religious pride of the nation will be destroyed. In addition, the nation is a land full of great palaces, down in the valley for the winter and on the breezy heights for the summer, decorated with so much ivory they almost seem to be made of it. Attending to Israel's rebellions will also mean demolishing all these (Amos 3:15). Why is this the way Yhwh attends to Israel's rebellions? It signifies the destruction of the country's two forms of architectural splendor, the religious and the secular. Amos's point here is not to condemn either the religious deviancy or the royal opulence but to say that both are doomed. The punishment fits the crime (Hos 10:1-2). Yhwh will snap their altars the way they break the neck of each of the many animals that they sacrifice on those many altars,[63] perhaps nominally for Yhwh's honor, but in reality for the Master's. He will destroy their pillars. The luxuriant vine will become a wasting vine.

So "be ready to meet your God, Israel" (Amos 4:12). It is another understatement. Meeting with God is inherently a solemn business and needs preparing for. This was so at Sinai (Ex 19:17), the only other occasion when the First Testament speaks of meeting God. Indeed, "meeting with" human beings is frequently a solemn business; the verb very often refers to hostile meetings such as battles. Yes, there will be a hostile meeting between Israel and Yhwh. Israel had better prepare. There is going to be wailing, mourning and lament in the streets and on the farms, "for I will pass through the midst of you, Yhwh has said" (Amos 5:16-17) instead of passing by you (Amos 7:8); and if Yhwh stops passing by, that means the end (Amos 8:2).[64]

Zephaniah likewise invites people to a festival. A solemn liturgy is about to begin and the entire temple gathering needs to be quiet. Perhaps there was an actual liturgy that celebrated or even dramatized the coming day when Yhwh's reign would arrive in the world. Perhaps this happened at a great occasion such as Tabernacles. There is to be a festive sacrificial meal for which all are properly prepared and in which all will share. Except that they will not, because Yhwh has determined that they will be the ones killed as if they were sacrificial animals (Zeph 1:7-8).

---

[63]The verb ʿārap ("snap") comes from the word for "neck" and usually denotes breaking an animal's neck. Perhaps the expression again points to breaking the horns of the altars (cf. Amos 3:14) (so Wolff, Hosea, p. 174).

[64]Jörg Jeremias, The Book of Amos (Louisville, Ky.: Westminster John Knox, 1998), p. 97.

Blinding

Isaiah is bidden to go and say to the people of Jerusalem, "Listen and listen, but do not understand; look and look, but do not acknowledge" (Is 6:9). Part of the point was to jolt them into turning to Yhwh.[65] But Yhwh will also have looked in the face the fact that speaking to a people always leaves them in a different position; if they do not respond, their situation is worse than before. And Yhwh not only accepts that but positively affirms it. Yhwh wants to win Judah back, but if they refuse to turn, he wants to punish them. In doing so, Yhwh will utilize that fact about the way speaking to people inevitably changes their position. It is thus Yhwh's will that Judah is to become more and more incapable of responding to any exhortation to change its stance. So Yhwh goes on to instruct the prophet, "oil this people's mind, weigh down its ears, seal its eyes, lest it sees with its eyes and listens with its ears and its mind understands and it turns and finds healing for itself" (Is 6:9-10). Some of the imagery for this process is a little obscure, but the implications are clear enough. It will be as if people's minds are clogged up with oil or fat, or as if their ears are too heavy for them to incline them in the right direction, or as if someone has smeared over their eyes so they cannot open them. Isaiah's ministry will have this effect, and that by Yhwh's intent. It is the form their punishment will take.

He expresses the point again in different but equally horrifying terms in Isaiah 29:9-12. "Confuse yourselves, be confused; blind yourselves, be blind." The Judeans are confused and blind not merely because there is oil clogging up their minds and a kind of paste over their eyes but because Yhwh has overwhelmed and immersed them with a kind of sleeping sickness that makes them fall about as if they were drunk: "They are drunk, but not from wine, they stagger, but not from drink, because Yhwh has poured over you a spirit of deep sleep."

There is an irony in the talk of pouring out a spirit of deep sleep. Elsewhere, words for "pouring out" (here *nāsak*) suggest the pouring out of oil to heal or enrich (*yāṣaq*, Is 44:3; cf. *šāpak*, Ezek 39:29; Joel 2:28-29 [MT 3:1-2]; Zech 12:10) or the emptying out of a spirit that will bring renewal, like the irrigating of land (*ʿārâ*, Is 32:15). And "deep sleep" (*tardēmâ*) usually suggests a state of unconsciousness in which Yhwh gives someone a revelation or does something marvelous (Gen 2:21; 15:12; Job 4:13; 33:15). In contrast, this is a maleficent pouring and a maleficent sleep (cf. Prov 19:15). There is a further irony. "He has shut your eyes (the prophets), covered your heads (the seers)." The people who were supposed to be among the people's sources of insight are among those whose eyes are smeared or who have bags over their heads, so that the

---

[65]See section 3.6 "Shaken to Their Senses."

"insight" they offer is one of the causes of the blindness that afflicts the people as a whole. The entire way Isaiah talks is totally unintelligible to them, as if written in a foreign language, and they are reduced to asking other people to explain it when these people themselves do not read the language. This again suggests that those prophets and seers who are supposed to be servants of Yhwh have no capacity to comprehend what Yhwh is saying or doing.

So Yhwh does the pouring, yet they also do it. They confuse themselves and blind themselves by their refusal to look in the direction Yhwh points. In this sense "the judgment is not that God barrels ahead with fire and brimstone. He simply brings judgment to fulfillment when he allows human beings to bear the consequences of their own actions."[66] Admittedly "allows" may be an understatement; Isaiah portrays Yhwh's action as more active than that. The prophets and seers shut their own eyes and put a bag over their own heads, but Yhwh does that too.

Exposure

Zephaniah imagines howls of dismay from the different quarters of Jerusalem (Zeph 1:10-13). Oddly, the reason is that the tradespeople have been cut off. The image of the city is of a place dominated by money making, and they are people "who say to themselves, 'Yhwh does not do good nor does he do bad.'" They are convinced they will always be able to carry on as they do. But they will find themselves desolated and plundered. Whereas they are building fine homes with the profits from their business and planting fine vineyards whose fruit they look forward to enjoying, they will neither live in the fine homes nor drink the fine wine (cf. Amos 5:11). The resources they have accumulated, the planning they have done, the building and planting they have undertaken: all will turn out to be futile. The object of punishment is to demonstrate the real truth to its victims and to the world.

Isaiah 5:8-24 speaks in similar terms of people who think that they will find happiness by building bigger and bigger homes and accumulating more and more land. He first hints at an irony: The result of their accumulation of land at other people's expense will be that they own a huge estate, but find themselves on their own there. Their selfishness has earned its reward. But that is not the sharp end of his warning. Merely feeling lonely will not be the only judgment that comes on people who own much land and many homes. They will find that their vast estates fail to produce enough to feed their owners. The hyperbole in the description of these people turning the whole land into one estate is matched by the hyperbole regarding the produce of this estate. There

---

[66]Hans Wildberger, *Isaiah 28—39* (Minneapolis: Fortress, 2002), p. 85.

is a hint that the land itself is involved in bringing about this judgment. It knows there is something wrong here and refuses to cooperate with its occupiers. Or it senses the cry of the blood shed on it and responds to it (cf. Gen 4:10-12). There is also a hint of a certain appropriateness in this punishment. An eye is being taken for an eye. The people who own much land and several homes had deprived other people of the means of growing their food, and it is therefore appropriate that they themselves should find they cannot grow enough to eat. Because of the self-indulgence of their feasting with its drink, the people of Judah will die of hunger and thirst; because of their indulging their appetite, Sheol will indulge its appetite on them. While they will no longer able to indulge their appetite, sheep and foreigners will feed off what is left of their city.

Isaiah goes on to express vividly how people bring punishment on themselves: They are hauling punishment like people dragging a cart with ropes. Fancy putting that amount of work into such a task! And all the way along, they have been giving no thought to the plans that Yhwh is making and implementing, and thus have implicitly declared that Yhwh needs actually to do something if they are to be convinced about the existence of any such plans. They call good bad and bad good, darkness light and light darkness, bitter sweet and sweet bitter: they either deny the reality of the trouble that has already come or deny the reality of the trouble that is coming.[67]

At present Judah trusts in falsehood, political and religious, and thinks that will preserve it from death. Yhwh's act of destruction will expose the untruth in the people's stance (Is 28:17-22). They think that security from the Assyrians lies in alliances with other nations and/or in seeking the help of other deities (which was perhaps involved in the concluding of such alliances) and/or in Zion's own inviolability. Perhaps they were consciously thus making a covenant with the god Death, a kind of bargain with the devil to avoid falling into his clutches. Or perhaps they need to see that this is the implication of their act: they thought they were taking actions that would preserve life, but the actual result of their initiatives will be the opposite. Either way, they think they are taking the kind of responsible action that will divert the Assyrian storm. In fact they are acting like King Canute, who bade the tide not to overwhelm him because he was king. Relentlessly the Assyrian flood will overwhelm them like an epidemic or a herd of elephants or a force of slave traders or a hurricane from the Gulf of Mexico.

---

[67]Both the context and the two succeeding pairs of antitheses point away from the idea that people are reversing the meaning of moral good and moral evil (though no doubt they also did that).

Shame

So at last they will get the message, but doing so will be an experience of terror. Their resources will be exposed as totally inadequate, like a bed that is too short or a bedcover that is too narrow. Isaiah doubtless has in mind the inadequacy of their policies and their objects of trust, but the context also suggests the inadequacy of their theological perspective. Yhwh is about to act with dynamic power, and they are used to the idea of Yhwh doing that; indeed, they trust in it. Yhwh's act will recall David's great victories over the Philistines at Baal-perazim (2 Sam 5:17-25), and it is such victories that they need to have repeated, in keeping with Isaiah's own stance regarding Yhwh's commitment to David's household (e.g., Is 7:13). The trouble is that Yhwh is going to be acting with that kind of energy *against* David's household and the people of Jerusalem and Judah, instead of for them. Yhwh is thus going to act in a strange way, a way that is alien to people's expectations, and even to Yhwh's own character. The message *(šĕmûʿâ)* Isaiah has heard concerns destruction upon the entire land. The people therefore need to stop mocking Isaiah, or they will find themselves in a worse bondage than the one they are in (Is 28:21-22).

Judah has refused to live by a policy of apparently irresponsible relaxed trust that everything would turn out all right. Isaiah knows that trust in Yhwh is the key to a stable building. The leadership was confident that it had the equipment and the morale as well as the policies to take it through the crisis that threatened, but things will not work out that way (Is 30:15-17). They will find that they make speed indeed, but make speed backwards, pursued by even faster opponents, and that morale will collapse. Perhaps "Isaiah does not have a very high opinion of the 'morale' of Judah's elite troops,"[68] but more likely he is not merely offering an independent informed assessment of their equipment and spirits but declaring that however good these are, they will not be good enough. Israel's battles commonly turn out quite differently from anything one would have expected because Yhwh makes them do that. This can work in Israel's favor—or against it. On this occasion, unaccountably its army will be decimated.

The people think that their worship is a means to life, but they will find it actually leads to death. Isaiah 1:29-31 warns that the terebinths at which they love to worship will become like a tree that has withered during a drought (the kind of event that such rites were meant to safeguard against!), and is therefore vulnerable to fire. The thing that looks strong—apparently a reference to an idol, also made of an impressive piece of wood—will become like wood-shavings or chaff, or literally the bits of flax that are shaken out by the process of

---

[68]Wildberger, *Isaiah 28—39*, p. 162.

spinning, also highly combustible. And the maker of the idol will be like the spark that sets all this alight so that it burns up. So the maker and the worshiper will have the emptiness of their religious choices exposed, and they will thus be shamed (cf. Is 65:13; 66:5).

Prophets and psalms speak much of people coming to be ashamed of their false commitments, their trust in entities that let them down. Foreign peoples will be ashamed of their trust in their own strength or in that of their allies that has been shown to be foolish (Is 20:5; 37:27). They will be ashamed of their trust in their gods and their images that cannot do anything to protect them (Is 1:29; 42:17; 44:9, 11; 45:16; Jer 48:13). In shame they will acknowledge Yhwh (Is 45:24). But Judah, too, will be ashamed of its trust in its political allies (Jer 2:36-37). It will be ashamed because of the implications of its defeat (Jer 9:19 [MT 18]; 12:13). That will leave a people helpless and vulnerable, unable to look after itself, reduced to casting itself on the charity of others, like a woman who has lost her sons (Jer 15:9). Because people will not honor Yhwh they will find their own honor turned to shame and find themselves in darkness (Jer 13:16). When Judah is invaded and overwhelmed, it will be like a woman's being exposed and thus shamed. There is an appropriateness about the image because Judah has behaved like someone being sexually promiscuous (Jer 13:22, 26-27). Israel will therefore be put in its place in the sight of the nations and become a horrific warning to them of what Yhwh is capable of doing (Ezek 5:15).

War

Yhwh's day means the collapse of the nation. It will be as sudden as the unforeseen crumpling of a poorly constructed high wall and as complete as the shattering of a pot that does not even leave a shard big enough to scoop coals or ladle water (Is 30:13-14). Or it will have the nature of the most efficient harvest that one can imagine. Every grape will go (Jer 6:9).

War is one of Yhwh's chief means of bringing this about. Modern readers are often troubled by the way the First Testament speaks of Yhwh making war on foreign peoples and commissioning Israel to do so. It may take the edge off this sense of offense (or it may increase it) to recognize that the First Testament gives great prominence to the fact that Yhwh also uses other peoples to make war on Israel, and in addition makes war on Israel in person. Yhwh even turns Israel's weapons round so that they are attacking themselves, the ultimate in friendly fire (Jer 21:4-7). As far as the Babylonians are concerned, they are assembling themselves for a siege, but unbeknown to them Yhwh is acting as general of these forces that attack Jerusalem, instead of fulfilling the more natural role of general of the forces that defend the city.

Zedekiah has asked about the possibility of a marvel against the Babylonians, of the kind Yhwh did against the Egyptians in bringing Israel out of

Egypt (*niplā'ōt*, e.g., Ex 3:20). There will be no marvels. With a reversal whose rhetoric matches the terrible reality, instead of Yhwh's hand being strong and Yhwh's arm being extended on Israel's behalf against Egypt (e.g., Deut 4:34; 5:15), Yhwh's hand is extended and Yhwh's arm is strong against Israel itself. Instead of acting in love, mercy and compassion for Israel and in anger, rage and fury against Egypt, Yhwh is acting in anger, rage and fury against Israel. The weapons with which they are defending themselves will become the weapons with which Yhwh attacks them. "I have set my face against this city for ill, not for good (Yhwh's message). It will be given into the hand of the king of Babylon and he will burn it with fire" (Jer 21:10). Like the face of a human king, Yhwh's face is the source of good and ill. If Yhwh smiles, there is good. If Yhwh frowns, there is trouble. What Yhwh sees is not pleasing, and Yhwh is frowning.

The result will be that the bodies for burial will be so numerous that the city will run out of room even in Tophet and the Hinnom valley, so that corpses will be left out in the open for the birds and the wild animals. There will not even be enough people to frighten them away. Indeed, the graves of people who have been buried will be desecrated (sometimes a practice in war) so that their bones lie in the open. Ironically, this will take place before the sun, the moon and the planets that they worshiped. There will certainly be no more marrying and therefore no future rebuilding of the people (Jer 7:32—8:2). "Is this the city that they call 'perfect in beauty, joy of all the earth'?" (Lam 2:15), as Psalm 48:2 [MT 3] and Psalm 50:2 say?

The collapse of the nation includes the removal of all forms of leadership: officers in the military, prophets, elders, experts, advisers, skilled craft-workers (Is 3:1-9). It is what actually happened in due course with the exile, when the Babylonians deposed kings, in 597 and 587, and sought to transport the entire leadership of the city. Isaiah's warning constitutes "a threat of anarchy."[69] It will mean that government (if it can be called that) will fall into the hands of young bullies rather than senior people who have earned some standing in the community. Or the removal of all the leading men will mean rule being exercised by women (Is 3:12). This might now seem a step in a good direction, of course, but Isaiah is taking patriarchal assumptions for granted, and in that framework this development would be another sign of regular order collapsing. God has brought calamity on the community, and the collapse of structures of authority compounds the calamity for ordinary people. It means the basics of life disappearing; in a city, at least, supplies of food and water depend on there being some social order. It means people living for themselves and

---

[69]Hans Wildberger, *Isaiah 1—12* (Minneapolis: Fortress, 1991), p. 123.

"oppressing" each other (*nāgaś*, Is 3:5). Isaiah's word is the one used for the Israelites' "bosses" in Egypt (e.g., Ex 3:7) and for Israelites themselves behaving toughly toward needy people in order to maintain or improve their own economic position (Deut 15:1-3 [EVV "exact"]).

Wasting

War means the death of people but also the wasting of a land. "I loathe Jacob's majesty, I repudiate its fortresses; I will deliver up the city and its contents" (Amos 6:8). Yhwh loves Jacob's impressive mountain country (Ps 47:4 [MT 5]),[70] but is prepared to do the opposite, to loathe it and repudiate it (*tā'ab* niphal, *śānē'*) and behave accordingly. Perhaps it is the monstrous nature of this declaration that warrants its extraordinarily substantial and definitive introduction. "The Lord Yhwh has sworn by his very self (message of Yhwh, God of Armies)." It is the Lord Yhwh who speaks, not merely Yhwh. Yhwh speaks "by his *nepeš*," not even merely "by himself" *(bô);* the expression is unparalleled (but compare "by his holiness," Amos 4:2). And in case we are not prepared to believe it, Amos adds that this is indeed a "message of Yhwh, God of Armies." All this undergirds and guarantees the loathing and repudiation with which Yhwh looks at the natural and beloved impressiveness of the hills and the humanly made impressiveness of the fortresses. It underlines and guarantees Yhwh's determination to give over the city of Samaria and its people to the control of anyone who wants them (the final verb *sāgar* [hiphil] suggests shutting up, specifically imprisoning).

It is as if the vineyard owner arranged for the ravaging of his vineyard (Is 5:5-6). His natural concern is to make sure the vineyard is protected so that animals cannot come and forage off its fruit, but the vineyard has of course not produced any fruit so the owner can afford to neglect its protection. Actually he is more intentional than that. It is not just that he cannot be bothered with it. He purposely breaks down its wall so that animals can come and trample it. As often happens, the reality goes beyond the parable. It is as if the vintner was in a position to stop the rain falling so that the vines die and the vineyard gets taken over by briars and thistles. (Ezekiel 15 later reworks the image. Israel is a vine. But what do you do with the wood of a vine? It is useless except for making a fire. That is a warning fact for the vine people.)

Isaiah thus commissions women to mourn for the city (Is 32:9-14). In summoning the carefree and confident women and girls, on this occasion Isaiah may not be confronting them about their attitude. There is nothing wrong in itself with being carefree and confident, unless they are involved in the false

---

[70]On the expression here, see section 3.4 "Landed."

confidence that the prophets speak of elsewhere.[71] The point lies rather in the contrast between their upbeat attitude and the reality that is soon to assail them. Instead of being an embodiment of poise and coolness they will find themselves thrown off balance because the harvest is going to fail. They will have to take off their finery and put on different garb, become a different kind of woman, become mourners. The lovely fields will have become thorn and thistle and the fruitful vine will have become fruitless. There is no ingathering.

So far we might have thought of a purely natural calamity, but the subsequent lines point in a different direction. Natural catastrophes can be humanly wrought, and this seems to be the case in this instance. Catastrophe overwhelms city as well as country. Indeed, the city seems to have been destroyed and abandoned. It is no longer habitable. It becomes merely hiding places for wild animals: a great joy to them, Isaiah sardonically adds, but a grief to its one-time human inhabitants who made it a bustling, lively place where people loved to live. Its enemies have destroyed the city and have also ravaged the countryside, as armies do.

The kind of calamity that will thus eventually need to come on Judah will be too harsh to count as chastisement. It will be "not for winnowing or sifting" but like the searing wind off the desert that withers everything (Jer 4:11-12).

Annihilation

"As the shepherd rescues from the mouth of the lion two legs or a piece of an ear, so will the Israelites be rescued, the people who live in Samaria" (Amos 3:12).[72] That is, all that is left is some evidence that a sheep has been killed and that you have not secretly sold it (Ex 22:10-13 [MT 9-12]). There is no hope in that image. To use another, all that will be left of Jacob in its splendor will be the equivalent of the gleanings after the grain harvest or the handful of olives that are too inaccessible to reach (Is 17:4-6). More literally, a city that marches out a thousand strong will lose all but a hundred of its men; a city that marches out a hundred will lose all but ten (Amos 5:3). In effect, the city's menfolk will be annihilated. If relatives taking out corpses from a house (because it has been demolished? or during a plague?) find that against all odds one of the household has survived, he will urge them not to utter Yhwh's name because that will surely provoke Yhwh to finish off the job (Amos 6:9-10). "Not one of them will escape, not one of them will survive" (Amos 9:1). There is no hope here.

That declaration comes in a vision of Yhwh commissioning the demolition of a sanctuary (Amos 9:1-4), the last of five visions of destruction (cf. Amos 7:1-

---

[71]The NRSV's "complacent" thus probably gives a misleading impression.

[72]Unfortunately we do not know how to understand the picturesque succeeding phrase with its reference to a couch and a bed.

9; 8:1-3) that manifest increasing solemnity. In the first two Amos successfully intervenes to bid Yhwh forgive or at least forebear. In the next two there is no intervention. Finally Amos sees Yhwh in the act of commissioning actual destruction, with the implications of this being "the end" all worked out. It is not just the end of the nation as a whole but the end of any possibility of new growth from its stump, to use Isaiah's metaphor. The demolition of a sanctuary might directly bring about the demise of its worshipers, as happened when Samson brought the sanctuary down on the Philistines. But the vision may as much reflect the fact that when Yhwh acts to demolish the sanctuary, that signifies the termination of the relationship between people and God.[73] And the fact that this last vision has no twin, but comes alone, in itself suggests abruptness and finality. This really is the end. Amos indulges in rhetorical overkill to make the point. The sanctuary collapses, and all the people die as a result. Then Yhwh kills the rest of them (!) with the sword so that none escape. Then Yhwh pursues the ones who do escape (!). Amos could hardly underline more forcefully the fact that the disaster will overwhelm everyone. There is no hope here.

Jeremiah, too, warns that the leftovers are not rendered safe by being the leftovers. They can be gleaned again (Jer 6:9). Yhwh intends to give them to the sword (Jer 15:9). It is they who are to be treated as spoiled fruit, to be trashed (Jer 24:8). And even when leftovers of these leftovers escape (e.g., Jer 40:11; 42:2), they can be further pursued by the disasters that overtook the rest of the community (Jer 42:15-22). The Babylonian exiles have returned involuntarily (though as a result of their own actions) to the Babylon that their ancestors Abraham and Sarah left voluntarily at the beginning of their story as a people, the beginning of the story in Genesis 12—2 Kings 25. The Egyptian exiles have deliberately returned to the Egypt from which Yhwh once took their ancestors, fulfilling the desire of that exodus generation itself when they were finding the journey to the promised land too hard, "back in a bondage they misread as freedom."[74] They too are acting in such a way as to ensure that they will have no leftovers (Jer 44:7, 12-14). There is no hope here.

Expulsion

"Now: I am throwing out the country's inhabitants" (Jer 10:18). Because of their self-indulgence and failure to pay attention to what Yhwh is doing, "my

---

[73]Cf. Jeremias, *Amos*, pp. 156-57. Contrast the suggestion that the demolition of the sanctuary need not imply the destruction of the whole people (so Francis I. Andersen and David Noel Freedman, *Amos*, AB [New York: Doubleday, 1989], pp. 841-42).

[74]Walter Brueggemann, *To Build, To Plant: A Commentary on Jeremiah 26—52* (Grand Rapids, Mich.: Eerdmans/Edinburgh: Handsel, 1991), p. 198.

people are going into exile for lack of acknowledgment" (Is 5:13). Yhwh is ruthless and resolute in facing the implications of the collapse of the nation. Yhwh's wrath will consume children and young people, husbands and wives, senior citizens and the very old. The whole community will be taken captive and their property (which includes their wives) will pass to other people. Yhwh is going to trip up the entire community: parents and children, friends and neighbors (Jer 6:11-12, 21). And there in captivity, the people who have escaped death in the city to be driven into exile will wish they had rather been among the people who died (Jer 8:3).

One significance of exile is that the people who are prosperous in the community, who have become so through taking other people's land one way or another, will find that the punishment will fit the crime (Mic 2:1-5). The poor people have lost their land; the new landowners will now join them in their landlessness. They will never be in a position to join in the community process whereby land is allocated. Indeed, Micah may mean that there will be no community to meet, to decide on the allocation of the land. The land will just sit there. (Actually, exile will do something to reverse the earlier wrong, because it is the well-to-do who will be taken off into exile and the landless peasants who will be left behind and will be in a position to farm the land, whatever the theoretical question about its ownership.)

With some irony Micah imagines the landowners protesting at the idea that land allocations are being changed (MT) or measured out in a new way (LXX) as a result of foreign invasion (Mic 2:4); this is just what the landowners themselves had done. They yelp at their land being taken away, not having been worried by the yelps of the people they took it from. They complain at the land being allocated instead to a foreigner who they think of as someone unfaithful (*šôbēb*, lit. "a turner away"). They have not accepted that this is what they are, perhaps in two senses. First, the term may have political connotations (cf. Jer 49:4);[75] they may see the invader as going back on commitments to Judah. If so, the irony lies in the unfaithfulness of Judah's own relationships with Assyria, and later with Babylon. Second, the term would also have religious connotations, as it has in its one other occurrence, when it is applied to Judah (Jer 31:22). The irony is clearly the greater: fancy these people who have resolutely turned away from Yhwh describing anyone else as turning away!

Exile will bring yet another irony. The making of images in the manner of other peoples will find its poetic justice when the Israelites, decimated and scattered among the nations, there serve gods made by human hands (Deut 4:25-28). Israel has consistently "gone after other gods and served them." They

---

[75]See Gerald L. Keown et al., *Jeremiah 26—52*, WBC (Dallas: Word, 1995), pp. 324-25.

will now be able to do so more conveniently. "I will hurl you out of this country into a country that you and your ancestors have not known," and there "you will serve other gods day and night" (Jer 16:11-13).

Pollution

Israel's faithlessness in itself brought pollution on it, but its invasion and exile will bring a further stage of pollution. Indeed, as the nations advance on Jerusalem, Micah portrays them saying, "It is to be polluted, our eyes are to look on Zion" (Mic 4:11). Their own intention was more down-to-earth, but pollution was the implication of their intention. Their attack will mean foreign feet trampling the city and desecrating the sanctuary. Its sacred status will be defiled. Their eyes will look at things that no human eyes should see, and they will do so with gratification.

Conversely, expulsion from Jerusalem will signify pollution for the people who go into exile (e.g., Hos 9:2-5). Having relationships with other deities in and on the land is a terrible way to treat this land that belongs to Yhwh, and there will be several sorts of consequence. One is that it will not work. The land knows who it belongs to, and it will not want to have anything to do with these people who treat its owner in this way. Then, they will not be allowed to live in this land any more. Perhaps this is the way the first threat will be implemented, though Hosea does not speak of the land vomiting them out or of Yhwh throwing them out. The focus lies not on the agency of their exile but on the conviction that there would be something theologically improper about their staying there.

So Hosea says they will go into exile to Egypt and to Assyria. Do some people go to one place, others to the other? What about the fact that the Ephraimites did not actually go into exile in Egypt? Such questions would be prosaic and would miss the point. Hosea talks elsewhere of a return to Egypt (cf. Hos 8:13; 11:5) as a way of indicating that their relationship with the land of Israel has come to an end. They are to go back to the place from which Yhwh took them to bring them to the land, because they have gone back on the implicit purpose of that move, to live as Yhwh's people in "Yhwh's land" (that suggestive phrase comes only here). Further, Egypt and Assyria are often paired as the political resources to which Ephraim looks; they are the political entities to whom Ephraim turns for help, the entities with which Ephraim is unfaithful to Yhwh (Hos 7:11; 12:1 [MT 2]). So the people are to go to the places that they treat as resources, in fulfillment of their implicit desires. Hosea does make explicit the point of their being taken to Assyria, which will be their more literal destiny. Assyria is a land that conveys defilement.

Life in a foreign land is not inherently defiling (for instance, because the land belongs to foreign gods), nor is contact with foreigners defiling in the way, for instance, that contact with a corpse is defiling. The idea that life in a foreign land conveys defilement arises only in connection with exile to a foreign land (cf. Amos 7:17; Ezek 4:13). Defilement is a metaphor to characterize the grimness of exile. Exile will have an effect like that of contact with death, in that it will make people unable to approach Yhwh, not merely because they are in a foreign land but because of the reason they are there. Like someone in a temporary state of defilement in the course of regular life or through the death of a relative, they will eat, but their eating will not be part of their relationship with Yhwh and of their worship of Yhwh, as it otherwise would be. They will not be able to bring their food into Yhwh's house for a festive meal before Yhwh. Like people who are defiled, their worship could not please Yhwh. It will be—just eating. As far as they are concerned, the festivals will not exist. The introduction to this passage bids people not to rejoice or exult (Hos 9:1); it may be an address with which Hosea confronted Ephraim at a festival. Henceforth, when people are in exile, the dates of Passover, Pentecost and Sukkot will come and go and will mean nothing for them.

Withering

Intermingled with the idea that Yhwh uses war as a means of bringing about the collapse of the nation is the idea that Yhwh uses nature. As well as acting via the Babylonian army, Yhwh acts directly in bringing epidemic on the people of Judah and the animals on which they depend. In the midst of the siege of Jerusalem countless people will die in a great epidemic (Jer 21:6). But natural disaster can be independent of war. It can be another way whereby faithlessness sees its reward. Amos explains the way ecological disaster has affected Israel by drawing attention to the people's social, personal and religious failure (e.g., Amos 4:1-11). One way or another, attitudes to God and to other people affect what happens to the land and what grows in it, to its wildlife, and even to the fish in the sea. Whether we are talking about a "natural" process or an interventionist one, human actions have very far-reaching implications. Yhwh's punishment of Israel not only devours humanity and the humanly made environment. It also devastates nature. It is human beings (men, women and children) who are involved in wrongdoing, but animals, trees, crops, mountains and wilderness also experience Yhwh's furious, burning anger (e.g., Jer 7:20; 9:10 [MT 9]). When human wrongdoing makes Yhwh unwilling to bring a drought to an end, that affects the deer and the wild donkeys as well as the nobles and their servants in the city and the farmers in the countryside (Jer 14:1-6).

Hosea 4:1-3 takes up the juridical model for understanding Yhwh's relationship with Israel. Yhwh has a charge to issue against the people. They are under obligation to Yhwh and to one another. They owe Yhwh acknowledgment. The context suggests that truth and commitment are obligations owed to Yhwh, though they might also be obligations owed to other members of the community. The latter certainly come in Hosea's subsequent words. There, several of the failures in relation to the community focus on threats to life of one kind or another: There is murder and bloodshed; cursing is another means of bringing illness or death on someone. Lying, stealing and adultery are forms of behavior that in other ways ignore obligations to fellow members of the community. Perhaps an implication is that real acknowledgment of Yhwh will express itself in an acceptance of Yhwh's principles for relating to other people. Truth and commitment toward Yhwh will issue in truth and commitment in relation to other people. When it fails to do so, natural disaster will follow.

Here Yhwh does not quite make specific how this works out. Perhaps there are "natural" links between attitudes to Yhwh, attitudes to one another and the fate of the land. Or perhaps Yhwh makes nature wither as an act of punishment for the people's offenses. Jeremiah speaks of the people's wrongdoing "diverting" the rains and "holding back" good things such as harvests (nāṭâ hiphil, mānaʿ; Jer 5:25). Elsewhere he pictures a terrible drought afflicting Judah (Jer 14:1-9). Neither people nor prophet suggests that Yhwh caused the drought, but both imply that Yhwh could bring it to an end. As the people see it, the oddity in the situation is not that the drought happens but that Yhwh does not bring it to an end. Yhwh is behaving like "a warrior who cannot deliver."

The first half of Joel (Joel 1:2—2:17) is dominated by a terrible natural disaster, a locust plague that devours everything that grows in the land. People in the West can only imagine the horrendous implications of that, though scenes of starvation in Africa may give us something of the idea. Different kinds of locusts have eaten everything. There are no grapes, and therefore there is no wine. There are no figs (a key source of sweetness), and the future of the fig harvest is imperiled because the locusts have even stripped the bark off the trees. The grain and barley, important staple foods, are ravaged. There are no olives and thus there is no olive oil, another staple of life. Pomegranate, apricot[76] and date palm have also withered. Thus "is food not cut off before our eyes?" (Joel 1:16). Animals, too, have nothing to eat. Further, if there is no oil, no wine and no grain, there can be no offerings. And if there is no harvest there can be no harvest festival, so the atmosphere of celebration in the temple has been replaced by an atmosphere of gloom.

And the land the locusts have invaded is "my land." They have devastated "my vines" and "my fig trees" (Joel 1:6-7). Who speaks? It is hard to see these

---

[76]Not apple (EVV), which did not yet grow in the Middle East (cf. John Goldingay, *After Eating the Apricot* [Carlisle: Paternoster, 1996], p. 45).

as Joel's words. Elsewhere, whenever a prophet says "my land," the speaker is Yhwh (e.g., Joel 3:2 [MT 4:2]; Ezek 36:5), and the trees were hardly Joel's.[77] At this point the person protesting the locust invasion and urging people to lament it is Yhwh. The locust invasion, like the invasion of a foreign army such as the Assyrians, outrages Yhwh, even though Joel goes on to imply that Yhwh is behind the event, as Yhwh was behind the Assyrian invasion.

Dissolution

The disaster that comes on Israel thus involves the very dissolution of creation. Amos 8:8-10 speaks of what will follow from the practices that characterize business in Israel. Once again, the warning combines the idea that nature itself will react to Israel's life with the idea that Yhwh will directly cause it to do so. The earth itself will tremble with horror at what takes place on it, as if responding to the cry of the blood of the innocent poor that arises from it. It will rise and fall in a short time in the way that the Nile does over a long period, as dramatically if not as speedily as the land does in an earthquake, and cause mourning all over the land or the world. At the same time, Yhwh will personally act to bring about more cosmos wide mourning that undoes the regular working of the creation as the sun itself withdraws into gloom and heralds or compels festival to become wake. Yhwh will act in such a way as to replace all occasions for rejoicing and expressions of rejoicing by occasions for grief and lament, with the outward observances that characterize such occasions, but with the deepest possible sense of grief. It will resemble the mourning for an only child, a couple's only continuing family, the person who was destined to carry them into the future. They now bury their child instead of the child burying them.

Zephaniah similarly begins with a nightmare vision involving a repeat of the flood devastation (Zeph 1:2-4).[78] Yhwh intends to "gather up, make an end of[79] everything from the face of the earth." The "earth" is ʾădāmâ, the soil, so that the words involve the paronomasia that also appears in Genesis 2: humanity is cut off from the humus. But more broadly the announcement and some of the language recall the announcement of the flood and the promise that it will not recur. Yhwh seems to have had a change of mind. "What is pictured is nothing less than a cancellation of the covenant with humankind and

---

[77]Admittedly, Joel does later speak in his own person (e.g., Joel 1:13, and perhaps in Joel 1:13-20 as a whole).

[78]See also Is 24:1-6 and section 8.5 "Polluted by Wrongdoing and Wasted."

[79]ʾāsōp ʾāsēp is written as if it were an instance of the idiom whereby an infinitive absolute prefaces a finite form of the same verb for emphasis. Actually the infinitive comes from ʾāsap (gather), while the finite verb apparently comes from sûp (come to an end). But it is an odd form (see BDB), presumably chosen or even devised to underline the paronomasia.

animals in Genesis 9."[80] It is a reversal of the process of creation; human beings, animals, birds and fish are mentioned in the reverse order to that in Genesis 1 (and see esp. Gen 1:28).[81] But the words that follow suggest that this
applies not to the world in general but to Judah in particular. One might therefore compare Jeremiah 4:23-26:

> I looked at the earth—there, a formless waste;
>> to the heavens—their light was gone.
> I looked at the mountains—there, they were quaking;
>> all the hills were trembling.
> I looked, and there—there were no human beings;
>> all the birds in the heavens had fled.
> I looked, and there—the garden land was desert
>> and all its cities had been pulled down,
>> before Yhwh, before his angry burning.

The dissolution of Judah is itself an undoing of creation.[82] "All of us have
withered like leaves, and our wrongdoings like the wind carry us off" (Is 64:6
[MT 5]). The vine has withered, there is no fruit, the leaves have dropped, and
the wind is carrying them away. It is the people's wrongdoing that causes the
withering, so it is the wrongdoing that carries the people away.

Or it is Yhwh's roar that causes the withering. "Yhwh—he roars from Zion"
(Amos 1:2). Yhwh once roared or thundered from Sinai (Deut 33:2; Judg 5:4-5)
but then came to live in Jerusalem, and that became Yhwh's base for opera-
tions in the world. Unpredictably, perhaps, but vividly, in these opening lines
in Amos the result of the lion's roar is the withering of nature.[83] Perhaps withering is nature's equivalent to humanity's recoiling or freezing at such a fearful
sound. But what does it stand for? Initially Amos spells out the implications of
this declaration by picturing calamity to come on Damascus, Gaza, Tyre,
Edom, Ammon and Moab. Are Judah and Ephraim therefore safe? Not at all.
Amos goes on to speak of calamity for Judah (Amos 2:4-5). Historically, the
significance of this oracle may be to make sure that Judah also sees itself as
confronted by Amos's warnings. Rhetorically, it prepares the way for Amos's
indictment of Ephraim, which more closely parallels the preceding warnings
to the other peoples: "For three rebellions of Israel and for four [in other

---

[80]Robert Murray, *The Cosmic Covenant* (London: Sheed & Ward, 1992), p. 49.

[81]Cf. William Dyrness, "Stewardship of the Earth in the Old Testament," in *Tending the Garden*, ed. Wesley Granberg-Michaelson (Grand Rapids, Mich.: Eerdmans, 1987), pp. 50-65;
see p. 61.

[82]Cf. Michael Deroche, "The Reversal of Creation in Hosea," *VT* 31 (1981): 401-9 (he is referring to Hos 4:1-3).

[83]Cf. Soggin, *Amos*, pp. 29-30.

words, for rebellion after rebellion] I will not revoke it" (Amos 2:6). There will be no escape when Yhwh acts (Amos 2:13-16).

Death

The calamity will be a deathly one. Amos bids the Israelites listen to a dirge that he raises over them: "She has fallen, she will not get up again, maiden Israel; she is left on her ground, there is no one to get her up" (Amos 5:2). In a dream you are walking along the street and you come across a funeral procession. You wonder who has died and you listen to the mourners' lament and the eulogy, and you realize it is you there in the coffin. The people is personified as a girl, but falling and not being able to get up again is the language of violent death and specifically death in battle, such as that of Saul and Jonathan (2 Sam 1:19, 25, 27). The next line (Amos 5:3) fits with this image, with its talk of the literal decimation of an army. Indeed, "a stench of death permeates all the original oracles of Amos" in Amos 5:1-17.[84]

Hosea 13 likewise begins and ends with death. It begins with more talk of how Israel has already "died" (Hos 13:1). This may be a reference to the deaths at Beth-peor (Num 25), perhaps to deaths in Ephraim during more recent invasions. It warns of Yhwh's savaging the people like a wild animal (Hos 13:7-8). It describes Ephraim as like a baby not knowing how to emerge from the womb (Hos 13:13). Then it pictures the most horrific deaths that often go along with war. Yhwh could redeem the people from the power of Sheol, restore them from the power of death, but there is no indication that Yhwh intends to do so. Translations vary in how they take the lines that follow, but it certainly becomes clear that Yhwh intends to let death lose rather than restrain it (Hos 13:14-16 [MT 13:14—14:1]).

All the talk about death incidentally makes clear that the reason death has overwhelmed Ephraim, and worse death threatens it, is that Yhwh is sovereign in relation to death. In Canaanite theology the god Death had the power to do battle with the Master, and at least to threaten to win a victory over him; every year the withering of nature in the dry season symbolized that possibility. In the First Testament, death and Sheol have no such power. They cannot frustrate Yhwh's purpose. Only by Yhwh's summons or with Yhwh's compliance can they take hold of a people or of individuals. As usual, that is both good news and solemn news. Death cannot come without Yhwh's willing or allowing, but Yhwh can and does summon death to serve the divine purpose. Yhwh's capacity to deliver from death does not establish that Yhwh will do so. And whereas two chapters ago Hosea had spoken of *niḥûmîm* (remorse/relent-

---

[84]Wolff, *Joel and Amos*, p. 251.

ing) kindling in Yhwh's breast (Hos 11:8), here he has *nōḥam* hiding from Yhwh's eyes.

So death will come to Ephraim, like the death that comes each summer, especially when the hot desert wind withers everything that grows. Ephraim may flourish among his brothers, so much more powerful than any other clan in Jacob's family, or may flourish among the undergrowth.[85] But terrible death will come, such as to make people wish they could summon Sheol to fall on them. The stress on what happens to babies and pregnant women suggests that "Baal, the Canaanite god of fertility, brings Israel ultimately to her death (cf. [Hos]13:1)."[86]

Because they have resorted to the Master, to shame, as the key to life, Yhwh their splendor will abandon them, and that will mean death (Hos 9:10-17). They have behaved as if the great life-giver is not Yhwh but the Master. He is the key to human fertility as he is the key to the fertility of crops and soil. He is the creator God (Yhwh, perhaps, is merely the God who delivered Israel from Egypt, but when the issue is one of ongoing life, that act might not seem so significant). This is what they think, but they are wrong, and they will discover so. They have abandoned Yhwh, so Yhwh will ratify the breakdown in this relationship, and that will have devastating consequences for ordinary life. Yhwh is the Lord of life and thus of death. By leaving them, Yhwh will show that this is so. Even if they do give birth (or perhaps Yhwh refers to children already born) and bring up their children to maturity, that will only provide another opportunity to demonstrate the point, because people need the great life-giver for their lives to continue as well as to begin. And Yhwh intends to turn away from them and thus withhold the gift of life that they attribute to the Master. Their recourse to the Master will not be effective, of course, because he lacks the power they attribute to him. So people who turn to him will find no birth, no womb, no conception. War ("the slaughterer") will actually be Yhwh's means of demonstrating who is the Lord of life and death. The future is so awful that Hosea can only pray for Yhwh to have the severe mercy of granting them a miscarrying womb and breasts that can produce no milk (cf. Lk 23:29). It is too grim a life to bring children into. People are willfully looking in the wrong direction, and the one who granted life has gone. As the compassionate one, Yhwh consistently acts as the great life-giver to the whole world, even though most of it looks elsewhere. But when Yhwh's own people behave thus, they may not get away with what the rest of the world gets away with.

---

[85] *aḥîm* could be the regular word "brothers" or a form of the word for "rushes" (see BDB, p. 28a).

[86] Wolff, *Hosea*, p. 229.

4.3 Can the Nightmare Be Forestalled?

"The time has come for my people Israel. I will not pass over them again" (Amos 8:2). Traditionally translations have "the end has come," but this gives a misleading impression. The word *qēṣ* suggests neither the end of time nor the end of the people. It usually means the end of a period of time, and here it might suggest the end of the period of Yhwh's restraint. Etymologically it suggests a cutoff, and it might indeed imply that Israel is being cut off, though that does not imply annihilation (JPSV renders "the hour of doom). Contextually, Amos uses the word because of the verbal link with *qayiṣ*, "summer fruit."[87] Amos sees a basket of summer fruit, an encouraging sight, but Yhwh bids him think rather in terms of that other word that looks and sounds quite similar but whose implications are the opposite. Israel's time has come (cf. Lam 4:18; Ezek 7:2-3, 6-7). So is there no way of escape? It would seem self-evident that when Yhwh declares the intention to act, Yhwh also implements that intention. In practice, matters are more complicated. There are theological reasons. The nightmare involves the destruction of Yhwh's people. Can Yhwh really bring that about? Is there any way out for Yhwh? Is there any way out for Israel?

Last-Minute Deliverance?

In Isaiah 29:1-8, Yhwh declares the intention to lay siege to Jerusalem and capture it the way David once did. Yhwh is now the city's enemy and attacker. The city will be as good as dead (it will have a "near-death experience"),[88] and will speak almost like someone in Sheol. Indeed, it will speak exactly like someone in Sheol, its voice like the voice of a ghost. Yet what follows somersaults and makes us reconsider. Whereas Assyria seemed to be Yhwh's agent in reducing the city, suddenly Assyria has become only a bad dream. Actually the nations will spectacularly fail to conquer Jerusalem. The extraordinary tension between the impression one receives from the opening and the closing is reflected in the rhetoric. If we read the passage from the beginning, it is only with the last lines that we realize that Jerusalem is to be preserved. But when we then reread the prophecy, we realize that the intervening lines can be read in two ways. If Jerusalem is speaking from Sheol, then this is a voice Yhwh can hardly resist hearing. The Psalms often speak from the depths of Sheol. It is out of the depths, when death seems to have overwhelmed the living, that Israel speaks, and expects Yhwh to respond. The horde of willful terrorizers that will be put down is a horde of attackers, not just a horde of oppressors within Judah. Yhwh's attending to Judah with thunder, whirl-

---

[87]From the root *qîṣ* rather than *qāṣaṣ*.

[88]Joseph Blenkinsopp, *Isaiah 1—39* (New York: Doubleday, 2000), p. 401.

wind and fire can presage deliverance not just punishment.

The movement in the prophecy between threat, ambiguity and promise reflects theological realities. On one hand, the faithlessness of Jerusalem requires that Yhwh act against the city. On the other hand, Yhwh's commitment to Jerusalem requires that Yhwh stay faithful to the city. One way of holding together these two necessities is for Yhwh to take Jerusalem to within an ace of falling (thus honoring the first necessity) but then to rescue it (thus honoring the second). And rhetorically, this nightmare vision holds both necessities before the city itself. When the Assyrian flood overwhelms Judah, it will rise till it is neck high, threatening to drown the people, yet not quite doing so (Is 8:8).

A subsequent statement makes the point in a different way. Isaiah speaks again of the decimation of the nation, then goes on: "And therefore Yhwh will wait to be gracious to you, and therefore will arise to have compassion on you, because Yhwh is a God with authority; the good fortune of all who wait for him!" (Is 30:18). It is a somewhat incoherent statement, appropriately so, because it is again expressing that complex point. The human waiting to which the closing exclamation refers (ḥākâ qal) is a positive waiting, expressing an attitude of expectancy and hope. Its basis would lie in the middle two clauses with their complementary declarations about compassion and authority, the two sides to Yhwh's character that are crucial to action on Israel's behalf (compare the might and commitment of Psalm 62:11-12 [MT 12-13]). The last three clauses in the verse thus suggest a promise that Yhwh is certain to arise to act on Israel's behalf with compassion and authority, a comment on the good fortune of a people that can look forward expectantly to that, and an implicit exhortation to look forward in that way. "For him" is lô, and the numerical value of these two Hebrew consonants is thirty-six, which the Talmud takes up in the comment that "The world must contain not fewer than thirty-six righteous men in each generation who are guaranteed [the sight of] the Shekinah's countenance."[89] It is they who unwittingly keep the world in being.

Yhwh Waits

But what is the significance of the first clause with its reference to divine waiting? Only here is Yhwh the subject of such a verb (ḥākâ piel).

Yhwh's waiting is bad news. It suggests delay. Isaiah does not, for instance, say that Yhwh has been waiting and has now stopped doing so.[90] The fact that grace, compassion and authoritative action are coming in the future is good

---

[89] B. Sanhedrin 97b.

[90] It makes no difference if we translate the yiqtol verbs in the first two cola as present, with NIVI. (It looks arbitrary to translate one as present, one as future, with NRSV and JPSV, though this also makes no difference to the point.)

news in the later clauses, but more equivocal in light of that opening verb. In the context of the Second Temple period, the declaration could seem good news, if it were read to imply that waiting is now over, but in the rhetorical context of Isaiah 30 in Isaiah's day, the statement opens in a way that suggests a threat. The verse as a whole thus incoherently both warns and promises. Yhwh waits, but will act eventually. Yhwh will eventually act, but at the moment is waiting. In their ambiguity the lines thus occupy a telling place at the center of Isaiah 30, since what precedes encourages the warning side to this central verse, while what follows encourages the promise side. The central verse does not resolve this ambiguity but expresses it particularly sharply.

Isaiah 31 again makes the point. It begins with the familiar indictment regarding Judah's proclivity for trust in foreign military resources, closing with the declaration that as a result of seeking "help" elsewhere, the "helper" and the "helped" will both tumble to their end. It then goes on to describe a lion growling over its prey. Yhwh Armies is now a lion and Jerusalem is its victim. The community may call out against the beast whomever they wish (for instance, the Egyptians): who are they to think they could seize its prey? It might be that it would not take a particularly astute political analyst to see that Egypt would "prove to be an unreliable ally,"[91] but the basis of Isaiah's argument is theological. So Yhwh Armies descends from the heavens "to make war on Mount Zion." Or is it *"against* Mount Zion," since that was the meaning of the preposition ʿ*al* just previously when Isaiah described how "Yhwh will arise *against* the household of evildoers" and *against* their helpers (Is 31:2)? Another simile compares Yhwh to birds flying over the city; that offers no obvious encouragement, since birds take over when lions are finished with the prey. Yet another simile speaks of a fire in Zion, an oven in Jerusalem, and these look like a fire and an oven that will consume its people.

Once again, however, it transpires that the reference to the birds is the point at which the prophecy is in the midst of a somersault (Is 31:5). It turns out that the flying birds (which are cute *ṣippŏrîm,* not vicious ʿ*ayiṭ,* birds of prey) are an image for protection and that Yhwh Armies is acting to rescue and deliver, as at the exodus and the Red Sea; Isaiah uses the verb *pass over,* the only occurrence of the verb outside Exodus 12. There could hardly be a more spectacular somersault, and once again it retrospectively introduces an ambiguity into the preceding lines. It seems that after all, the lion is protecting its prey, Yhwh is fighting on Mount Zion to deliver its people, and the birds are the kind beneath whose wings their young can shelter. Assyria is going to panic and fall, not triumph.

---

[91]Blenkinsopp, *Isaiah 1—39,* p. 412.

Grace and Response

If Yhwh can hardly abandon Israel, what does that say about the role of Israel's response to God in this relationship? Does it have no final significance? After the talk of "passing over," Isaiah 31:6 urges, "Return to the one from whom you have deeply turned aside, Israelites, for on that day they will spurn, each of them, their silver idols and gold idols." On some occasions the impetus to turning back to Yhwh comes from the threat of trouble, but here, as on some other occasions, it comes from the promise of grace. Judah's turning back to Yhwh is not a precondition of Jerusalem's deliverance. Yhwh has made a commitment to the city that removes the option of abandoning it. But Judah's turning back to Yhwh is an indispensable requirement consequent on Jerusalem's deliverance. The logic is that which the New Testament follows when it sees our commitment to Christ as a required consequence of Christ's dying and rising for us. The paradox in this way of thinking is heightened by the way the passage goes on to speak of the converse of this turning to Yhwh, the people's abandonment of their idols. That might link with the religious rites involved in concluding foreign alliances, which are "sin" and not just a diplomatic convention, and/or it might speak to more systematically idolatrous practices in a period later than Isaiah's, which are then the quintessence of the people's sin. Isaiah does not say that they *must* give up the idols, but simply declares that they *will* do so. Yhwh intends so and is committed to achieving this development. The statement is not even a promise but a declaration of intent. Indeed, the logic of those prose lines is that the people are destined to spurn these idols and turn back to Yhwh, so they may as well start doing so.

Although Judeans are using the wrong methods to end Assyrian pressure on Jerusalem, Yhwh can hardly simply let Assyria have its way with the city. What Yhwh has to do is see that Assyria falls—a more ambitious project than any Judah had in mind—and do so in a way that demonstrates this is a divine achievement, not a humanly engineered one. The Egyptians are human (Is 31:3); the Assyrians will fall to a sword that is not human (Is 31:8). Ordinary soldiers and crack troops will end up dead or fleeing or laboring for the people they expected to defeat. Their "rock" (in the context, their king; cf. Is 32:2) and their generals will be paralyzed by a supernatural panic. The fiery oven is meant for the Assyrians, not for their intended victims.

Isaiah will later tell a story that relates the fulfillment of this declaration of intent, though typically in an event that matches the prophecy's significance without directly matching its words or imagery (see Is 37:36-38). That story is prefaced by Yhwh's declaring, "I will protect this city and deliver it, for my sake and for the sake of David my servant" (Is 37:35). Two considerations prevent Yhwh from finally abandoning Jerusalem. One is the consideration

Moses appealed to on Sinai, Yhwh's own reputation: Yhwh cannot afford to go back on a commitment to the city. The other (perhaps the same one formulated in another way) is the commitment Yhwh made to David. Yhwh has to keep such commitments. That is the trouble with being God. You have to keep your promises.

Thus "Zion will be redeemed with authority, those in it who turn back with faithfulness" (Is 1:27). To mention people "turning back" after referring to delivering them again brings out the fact that the people's experience of deliverance cannot be separated from the question of their response. As an act of smelting, the judgment involves removing impurity, removing people who reckon that improving their own financial position comes ahead of caring for the orphan and widow (Is 1:23). But the passage has already made explicit that if people turn from such a life, they can escape punishment (Is 1:16-20). So "people who turn back" to Yhwh go through the act of smelting and come out the other side. To put it another way, Isaiah suggests an awareness that one has to allow both for the deserve and destiny of the city as a corporate entity, and for the response of the people who actually make up the community. The city as an entity will experience Yhwh's judgment and deliverance. The people within the city will determine by their response how that event affects them. If there are faithful people there, they will experience the calamity, but they will come out the other side. If there are "rebels and sinners" there who persist in their style of life and in traditional religious practices, they will be consumed by the calamity. If there are rebels and sinners who turn back from such a lifestyle and such practices, they, too, will come out the other side.

Thus Ezekiel sees the community as comprising both faithless people and faithful people (Ezek 3:18-21). His task is to warn it of the approach of calamity, but Yhwh has no expectation that the faithless will respond. There is something fixed about their character. It is inconceivable that they will change. The only question is whether Ezekiel fulfills his commission as lookout. On the other hand, there are the people who were once faithful but who deviate from that commitment. There may also be something fixed about their character, but the possibility of their turning back can be imagined. Further, Ezekiel's task is also to warn the faithful about the consequences of failing to keep their faithfulness, and Yhwh can certainly imagine that they might respond and maintain that faithfulness.

Bad Things Need Not Happen to Bad People

There are reasons within the character of God that make it questionable whether Yhwh can really implement the nightmare in all its finality. But we would be unwise to assume that Yhwh will forgive because that is his business.[92] That might be the unforgivable sin. "Should I relent?" (*nāḥam* niphal):

confronted by insistent rebelliousness and philandering, and not least the killing of children, Yhwh can hardly relent of the intention to take action (Is 57:3-6). Yhwh will not do so (cf., e.g., Jer 4:28) or is tired of doing so (Jer 15:6). Unless . . . For the prophets also often affirm that Yhwh will relent (e.g., Jer 18:8, 10) or has done so (e.g., Jer 26:19).[93]

When Yhwh speaks of coming calamity, this can have various aims. It demonstrates that the event really does emerge from Yhwh. It aims to prepare people for life the other side of this event. It helps people who live the other side of the calamity to come to terms with it, understand it and look to the future. But paradoxically, it is also open to being falsified. Indeed, it aims to be self-falsifying. The prophecy is a warning, and a warning is designed to be self-falsifying. The response for which the revelation of Yhwh's nightmare looks is that people should change their ways. They must turn and walk in a different direction, "walk by my teaching" (Jer 26:3-4). Thus when Yhwh declares an intention, it is always subject to change in light of what Yhwh sees and hears. It may be enough to hear the appeal of a prophet or to see the suffering of the people. The question "should I relent?" can thus be a genuine one. It is a question asked within the heavenly court from time to time.

Jeremiah's experience at the potter's workshop helps him to picture that there is no need for nightmare to become reality. When the potter's work goes wrong as the clay resists his attempt to shape it, he does not throw it away but reworks it. And a nation is like such a piece of clay. "I may speak concerning a nation or kingdom about uprooting, demolishing, and destroying, but if that nation concerning which I have spoken turns from the ill it does, I will relent concerning the ill that I intended to do to it" (Jer 18:7-8). It can be reshaped into a worthwhile pot. But the clay does need to be malleable to the potter's shaping, otherwise Yhwh may go in for some other shaping. Therefore Yhwh commissions Jeremiah to bid the Judeans, "I am shaping ill against you and formulating intentions against you. Do turn, each one of you, from the ill of his way and make good your ways and your deeds." But they may say, "Dammit![94] Because we will follow our own intentions and each of us will act in the firmness of his ill heart" (Jer 18:11-12).

Yhwh is bringing ill on the people because of their own ill-doing. The word *ra*ʿ recurs to describe the people's deeds and God's deeds (and the people's

---

[92]For this saying, see section 2.6 "Cleansing."

[93]See section 2.4 "Yhwh's Relenting," "Yhwh's Reliability."

[94]For *wĕʿāmĕrû*, translations have "they say" or "they will say"; I interpret the verb in light of those in vv. 7-8 above, but the theological point is not affected by the way one interprets the verb. For the translation of *nôʾāš*, cf. *HALOT*; etymologically it should mean "It's hopeless" (cf. Vg.), but the context here and at Jer 2:25 suggests defiance (cf. LXX).

heart), as the words "intend/intention" apply to both (cf. Jer 26:3). But if they give up their ill-doing, Yhwh will give up the intention of doing ill to them. Shortly afterward, when commissioning Jeremiah to confront Judah with the nature of his message over twenty years, Yhwh similarly explains, "Perhaps the household of Judah will hear of all the ill that I am intending to do to them, so that each of them may turn from their ill ways and I may pardon their wrongdoing and their failure" (Jer 36:3). The use of the same word for their actions and for Yhwh's implicitly explains the point. Their ill-doing necessitates Yhwh's ill-doing; their turning makes it natural for Yhwh to relent (*nāḥam* niphal, Jer 26:3) and to pardon (*sālaḥ*, Jer 36:3). While Yhwh's ultimate purpose for Israel is predetermined, Yhwh's will for the immediate future is never fixed. It is always dependent on the human response. People need never despair. Yhwh is not like a judge declaring a sentence that will be implemented no matter what the guilty person's response.

During the years running up to 587, Jeremiah repeatedly declares that the city's fall and destruction are inevitable (e.g., Jer 37:6-10), and he adds that individuals who want to avoid being swallowed up by it must leave and surrender to the Babylonians (Jer 38:1-3). Yet when consulted by Zedekiah, he says, "If you do go out to the king of Babylon's officers, you will live and this city will not be consumed in fire. You and your household will live. But if you do not, . . . this city will be given into the power of the Babylonians and they will consume it in fire, and you yourself will not escape from their power" (Jer 38:17-18). People can choose to stay in the city and die sooner or later by the sword, by hunger or by epidemic, or they can leave the city and surrender to the Babylonians. That seems the way to death, but it is the nearest they have to a way of life. It would constitute a recognition that they were in the wrong, that both Yhwh and Jeremiah were in the right, and that the king to whom they were surrendering was Yhwh's servant. The people in the city still have a choice, though it may not seem much of a choice. A man who had fallen off a cliff and was hanging on to a tree shouted for help and heard a voice from heaven calling, "Jump, and I will catch you." After a moment's thought he shouted, "Is there anyone else there?"

Not only can Zedekiah personally escape, like other people who could leave the city, but the whole city's future is still open. The fact that Jeremiah has spoken so unequivocally does not mean that it is fixed irrespective of the human response. The point at which Jeremiah makes this explicit is the occasion when Zedekiah has turned to Jeremiah with an apparent openness: "I am about to ask you something. Do not conceal anything from me" (Jer 38:14). It is when there might be a response that Yhwh makes explicit the point that was always implicit, that a response can make a difference to Yhwh's intent.

Testing

Yhwh does not usually point out that the human response makes all the difference to whether a declaration of intent comes to be implemented, but the story of Jonah suggests that Yhwh, Jonah and the Ninevites all knew that the absence of explicit challenge to turn and find pardon did not mean there was no possibility of doing so. The prophet Joel—after giving a frightening portrayal of the advance on Jerusalem of an unprecedented, terrifying, unidentifiable, irresistible army headed by Yhwh in person—surprisingly (or not) does go on to urge people to turn to Yhwh (Joel 2:12-17): "Who knows, he may turn and be rueful and leave behind him a blessing" (Joel 2:14). There is still the possibility of a turning that may push Yhwh into a change of plan. Jeremiah 18:1-10 affirms that as a principle. But it is rather less common for prophets to urge people to turn or repent than we might think. Omitting such an exhortation has the capacity to leave people to make a response to Yhwh that is determined less by fear than by a true recognition of wrongdoing. It is thus an initial risky act of grace on Yhwh's part to invite them to repentance with the possibility that they might find forgiveness. Making the point explicit has the effect of encouraging people to respond in hope. Omitting to make the point explicit has the effect of making it more possible that repentance is genuine; it is less likely to be made simply to try to get off.

Jeremiah 26 presupposes that something like the possible escape promised in Jeremiah 38 had happened in Isaiah's day. As usual, the rulers of Jerusalem encouraged injustice, prophets and priests prophesied and taught for money, and yet they were all convinced that Yhwh was with them and that no calamity would come to them. On the contrary, Micah declared, because of this "Zion will be plowed like a field, Jerusalem will become ruins, the mountain of the house a wooded height" (Mic 3:12). This did not happen.

When Jeremiah utters similar warnings a century later, priests and prophets campaign for his execution as a false prophet: How could a real prophet say such things? But some of the Jerusalem elders point out that Hezekiah did not execute Micah for that prophecy. On the contrary, "did he not revere Yhwh and seek to make peace with Yhwh, and did Yhwh not relent about the ill that he had announced for them?" (Jer 26:19). Micah's unconditional-looking prophecy was designed to be self-frustrating. What happened is not that Yhwh then put the warning of punishment on hold so that it is fulfilled in Jeremiah's day (what is fulfilled in Jeremiah's day is Jeremiah's prophecies). Yhwh simply cancelled it. This does not mean Micah's message was not from God and had nothing for the community to learn from; indeed, the story in Jeremiah shows the community learning from it. The preservation of the prophecy and its incorporation into Scripture reflects the conviction that as the word of God it remained instructive for the community. By indicating God's reaction to that situation in Judah it reveals God's attitudes in a way that has the capacity to keep giving the community food for thought.[95]

While Yhwh's declarations of intent thus often look fixed and irrevocable, the prophets are Yhwh's means of testing Israel and discovering what it is really made of, in order to confirm whether the declaration should be implemented or to overturn it. "I made you an assayer among my people" (Jer 6:27). Yhwh does not take for granted what the people are like. It was Jeremiah's task to discover that. The implication is that Yhwh will decide what to do with the people in light of what Jeremiah's ministry reveals. So, when commissioning Jeremiah to confront the household of Judah with the entirety of his teaching over twenty years, Yhwh speculates, "Perhaps the household of Judah will hear of all the bad that I am intending to do to them, so that each of them may turn from their bad ways and I may pardon their wrongdoing and their failure" (Jer 36:3). Reading the scroll is another test, which Yhwh approaches with an open mind.[96]

A city has lookouts to keep watch for it and warn it of approaching danger. Paradoxically, Yhwh who is bringing danger on Jerusalem also appoints lookouts (*sōpeh*) for it so that people can escape the danger. But in Jeremiah's day they give no heed (Jer 6:17). "Lookout" is Yhwh's distinctive designation for Ezekiel himself as a prophet (Ezek 3:16-21; 33:1-9). As messengers, prophets are identified with the kings they represent, but as lookouts, they are identified with their communities. A prophet as lookout is one who can see calamity from Yhwh approaching. A lookout who failed to warn of such danger so that people could take appropriate action would bear responsibility for the fate of the city. He would be guilty of criminal manslaughter by neglect and would be liable to the same fate. If Ezekiel passes on Yhwh's warnings about the danger the people are in, they are responsible for their own fate; if he fails to do so, they will lose their lives and so will he. But Ezekiel's words can be effective in bringing deliverance to people. The point of Ezekiel's describing his own significance in this way is to being home that fact to his audience. He makes clear that Yhwh deals differently with the faithless, the faithful who slip up and the faithful who maintain their faithfulness, but this is not to imply that Ezekiel divided them into such groups or ministered to people separately. A lookout shouts his warning to the city as a whole, not to individuals.[97] It is up to the

---

[95]Cf. Terence E. Fretheim, *Jeremiah* (Macon, Ga.: Smyth & Helwys, 2002), p. 377.

[96]See further section 2.3 "Knowledge."

[97]Moshe Greenberg, *Ezekiel 1—20*, AB (Garden City, N.Y.: Doubleday, 1983), p. 95, against Gerhard von Rad, *Old Testament Theology*, 2 vols. (Edinburgh: Oliver & Boyd/New York: Harper, 1962, 1965), 2:231-32.

exiles as a whole to decide which group they belong to. A prophet's ministry tests them.

Shaken to Their Senses

Isaiah, too, is sent with a message that looks ultimately irreversible but may not be so (Is 6:9-13). His task is to be Yhwh's means of punishing Judah for its faithlessness, but this happens in two stages. Stage two will be the devastation of the land, and its agency will be the Assyrian king. It is stage one for which Isaiah is directly responsible. He has a role not unlike Moses' in relation to Pharaoh. He is commissioned to make Judah more and more incapable of responding to any exhortation to change its stance in relation to Yhwh, to pressure that might come from prophets such as Micah and Isaiah, and no doubt from some wise priests and intellectuals. He is to make it more and more difficult for the people to respond to such pressure. How that works we can infer from earlier parts of Isaiah and from later parts: he is to announce that Yhwh plans to bring calamity on the people. But this meets with a wholly skeptical response (e.g., Is 5:19-21). The people's moral and religious state after hearing his announcement is thus actually worse than before his announcing it.[98] In Isaiah 6:9-10 Yhwh speaks of that as itself part of the people's punishment.

But why is Isaiah to tell them that this is what he is doing, and why does Yhwh tell him that this is his task? And why does this come to be included in the book? For the readers, this may help to explain the mystery of Israel's perverseness and to warn them not to walk down their ancestors' road. For Isaiah, it may prepare him for people's unresponsiveness and enable him to stand firm. But for the people themselves, the declaration about Yhwh's intent itself may, paradoxically, shake them out of their willfulness and drive them to turn. Yhwh has tried challenging people to understand what is going on and found this has got nowhere. Perhaps telling people that they are not allowed to understand may have the opposite effect. This declaration about Yhwh's punishment thus has the same significance as any other. It is designed to be self-falsifying. Nothing will please Yhwh more than to be able not to implement it. But it is shrewder to speak as if calamity is inevitable, to see if this brings people to their senses.

But there is a real possibility that people will respond by insisting on carrying on in their usual way. They need, for instance, to revise their estimate of humanity: "Get yourselves away from human beings, those who have breath in their nostrils, because for what are they esteemed?" (Is 2:22). Instead of being impressed by human achievement they need to start behaving

---

[98]See section 4.2 "Blinding."

on the basis of the fact that only Yhwh stands on high.

When Yhwh speaks, then, this brings a challenge. When a prophet speaks as Yhwh's servant, the hearers have to make up their mind which of two groups they belong to (Is 50:10-11). There are no bystanders here. Either they are people who revere Yhwh and listen responsively to the prophet's voice, or they are people who want to build a fire under this prophet.

One could call the first group the faithful remnant, the group within Israel as a whole that provides Yhwh with the response that is withheld by the people as a whole. The destiny of the person who listens and responds to the prophet-servant's voice will resemble that of the prophet-servant. This destiny is to walk in darkness and see no brightness and be able to do nothing about that, but to keep trusting Yhwh, keep relying on Yhwh (Is 50:10). That is what a prophet does (as the preceding testimony in Isaiah 50:4-9 has declared), and that is what the listener must do. It is apparently the only alternative to being a kindler of fire. "Whoever is not for me is against me," the prophet-servant implies, speaking as one who brings about a division, one who makes people take sides. People who choose the other way also find themselves walking, but they walk in light not in darkness. It is the light of the fire that they kindle, but it is a fire that will consume them rather than consume the people they mean it for.

Seek

So "every prediction of disaster is in itself an exhortation to repentance."[99] In order to move Yhwh to relent, what people need to do is have recourse to Yhwh instead of seeking help from other sources, human or divine. If they will not do it before disaster, they must do it in the midst of it or afterward. When Yhwh has withdrawn and Ephraim and Judah have suffered for their guilt, "they will have recourse to me. In their trouble they will make that their priority" (Hos 5:15). Trouble will drive the people to seek help (*bāqaš* piel) from Yhwh rather than the Masters. The second verb is more striking: *šāḥar*, from the word for "dawn," perhaps originally referred to looking for the dawn or getting up early to do something. It is a sign you are serious about it.

After declaring that Israel is as good as dead, with 90 percent of its menfolk about to die, Yhwh nevertheless goes on, "Seek from me and you will live" (Amos 5:4). Here "seek from me" is *dāraš*, a synonym of *biqqēš*. Both verbs often mean "seek" in the sense of looking for or pursuing or aiming at something, with a suggestion of "activity, action, and energy."[100] They can also mean "seek from"; the thing sought is then information or guidance or action.

---

[99]Abraham J. Heschel, *The Prophets* (reprint, New York: HarperCollins, 2001), p. 14.
[100]S. Wagner, *TDOT*, 3:296.

These verbs that English versions render "seek" thus have different resonances from those that commonly attach to that idea in Christian usage. They
suggest having recourse to Yhwh as the source of provision as opposed to
seeking help from other deities. Seeking Yhwh with all one's heart and soul
then implies not so much deep emotion as true commitment to Yhwh as opposed to having a divided attitude that hedges one's bets by also seeking the
help of other deities or by political alliances. The exile will mean the exposure
of those other deities that have no capacity to see people's suffering, listen to
their prayer or receive their worship.

In a context like this, one would reckon the verb referred to seeking help
and guidance from Yhwh at the sanctuary. We already know that people took
part with enthusiasm in worship at sanctuaries such as Bethel and Gilgal, but
that Yhwh repudiates this worship (Amos 4:4-5). Thus, whereas Amos then
ironically encouraged people in this worship, here he directly discourages it:
"do not seek from Bethel" or Gilgal or Beersheba (Amos 5:4-5). His addition of
Beersheba[101] suggests that what is wrong with those northern sanctuaries is
not merely that they are not in Judah. Even coming to Jerusalem would not
solve any problems, as Isaiah and Micah's polemic against Judah imply. Nor
surely does Amos imply that people need to seek from Yhwh without visiting
sanctuaries at all, as if people were to forget the history of Yhwh's involvement
with them in these places. The explicit reason for not bothering with Gilgal
and Bethel is that they are destined for destruction. It is almost written into
their names: Gilgal resembles the word for going into exile (*gālâ*), while *bêt-ēl*
(house of God) can be reworked as *bêt-ʾāwen* (house of trouble; cf., e.g., Hos
4:15). Yhwh's sentence of death hangs over Bethel and Gilgal. But this does not
explain how one seeks from Yhwh without seeking from the sanctuaries.

Meanwhile, indeed, Amos heightens the questions his words raise. Having
implied that Bethel and Gilgal are definitely death bound, he suggests that if
people do seek from Yhwh, Bethel can be saved; so indeed can the household
of Joseph, the entire people itself (Amos 5:6). Yes, notwithstanding the previous
line, the future is still open. The question of what is involved in seeking from
Yhwh therefore gains urgency. It is implicit in the immediately following words
about the faithless way people in power exercise authority, though the link between these last two lines remains inexplicit. Perhaps one implication is that the
faithful exercise of authority was a gift from God planted in Israel, not something Israel had to bring into being, and that therefore Israel can pervert this gift

---

[101]For Ephraimites to go to worship in a Judean sanctuary might seem a step forward, and
   Amos may imply they sometimes did visit the sanctuary at Beersheba, this being another
   sanctuary that like Bethel, but unlike Jerusalem, had associations with Judah and
   Ephraim's common ancestors.

but not cause it to cease to exist. It can be cleaned off and restored.[102] This collocation would support the thesis that the way one "seeks from Yhwh" is by having recourse to the words of a prophet—in this context, to Amos himself.[103] Perhaps the implication is that at a sanctuary festival people do not get confronted about the faithless way authority is exercised, just as this does not tend to happen in church at Christmas or Easter. People need to listen to what the prophet says instead of what their pastors say on those occasions.

Pursue

Amos 5:14-15 comes back to talk about seeking, and offers some clarification of the way Amos talked about seeking from Yhwh:[104] "Seek good and not evil, so that you may live." Here *seek* must mean "pursue" or "aim at" (cf. Is 1:17). Seeking (a word from) Yhwh would have to lead into seeking good, which is spelled out as loving it in the sense of dedicating themselves to it (*'āhēb*), while not seeking evil is spelled out as hating it or repudiating it (*śānē'*). That is in turn spelled out in practical terms as "establishing authority at the gate," bringing to an end a situation whereby the exercise of authority is perverted by serving the interests of the wealthy and powerful at the expense of the needy and weak, exactly the opposite of what authority is designed to serve. If that happens, then it might be the way to life instead of death, to having Yhwh with the people rather than abandoning them and being against them, to Yhwh's being gracious to the nation whose chastisements have already turned it into a shadow of its former self.

The fact that the passage leaves open the possibility of Yhwh's canceling the destined final calamity is one factor that has generated the suggestion that these lines do not come from Amos himself, who elsewhere can speak as if calamity is inevitable, but that logic is questionable.[105] It only illustrates the regular prophetic tension between declaring that calamity is inevitable and also urging people to turn to Yhwh with the implication that there is the possibility of escape. Whatever may have been the case with the ministry of an individual prophet, the prophetic books thereby assure readers that it is never over until it is over. In any situation, if people seek Yhwh by seeking good and not evil, "perhaps" applies.

---

[102]Cf. Jeremias, *Amos*, p. 118.

[103]See Claus Westermann, "Die Begriffe für Fragen und Suchen im Alten Testament," *Kerygma und Dogma* 6 (1960): 2-30 (see p. 22); cf. Wolff, *Joel and Amos*, p. 238.

[104]I take it that this is so whether or not Amos 5:1-17 is a chiasm in which vv. 4-5 and 14-15 correspond (see, e.g., Jeremias, *Amos*, pp. 81-97), and whether or not Amos 5:14-15 comes from a disciple rather than Amos himself (so, e.g., Wolff, *Joel and Amos*, pp. 234-35), though in that case the clarification is not Amos's own.

[105]Cf. Shalom Paul, *Amos* (Minneapolis: Fortress, 1991), pp. 161-62.

Isaiah 1:16-17 talks about seeking in similar terms, first urging Judah to "Wash, get clean" (Is 1:16). The people cannot wash the blood from their hands in the sense of getting rid of their guilt (Jer 2:22), but they are responsible for washing it off in the sense of changing their lives. That is the way they get the wrong of their deeds out of Yhwh's sight. They must stop doing wrong and learn to do right. Jeremiah himself makes the point: "Wash your heart of wickedness, Jerusalem, so that you may find deliverance. How long will your evil intentions lodge within you?" (Jer 4:14). The attitudes in their hearts cause death to other people, their actions give expression to those attitudes, and they are responsible for both. They have blood on their hands and in their hearts, and they have to get it off both places. Thus "by commitment and truthfulness wrongdoing can be covered" (Prov 16:6), though prevention is better than cure, the proverb adds: "but by reverence for Yhwh there is avoiding of evil."[106]

Hosea similarly urges that it is "time to have recourse to Yhwh, until he comes and rains faithfulness for you" (Hos 10:12). The implication is that people have already experienced disaster, and in that context Hosea holds before them the possibility that Yhwh might show faithfulness to them, the *sedeq* that becomes a standard way to speak of Yhwh's restoring people from exile in Isaiah 40—55. Hosea speaks of that in terms of "raining" faithfulness, in keeping with the imagery of the passage. For on the one hand, the past has been one of really bad farming practice. The people have plowed faithlessness (*reša‘*), sown vicious patterns of behavior into their social life, and by a natural process have seen an outworking in the form of a crop of oppression (*‘awlâ*, Hos 10:13). So they have eaten "deceptive fruit," a harvest in the form of distrust and dishonesty within the community and/or in relation to Yhwh and/or in relationships with other peoples. Hosea has just spoken about sin that goes back to the days of Gibeah, or even sin that exceeded that of the days of Gibeah (Hos 10:9). That sin was presumably the atrocity told in the story in Judges 19—20. It is a terrible indictment of the people in this later century. That, by implication, is what has issued in calamity. It is therefore time to make a new start. It is time to have recourse to Yhwh, to look for Yhwh for help, to seek for Yhwh to come to them—the implication is that Yhwh has withdrawn—and to bring to maturity a different kind of crop in the form of restoration and blessing.

Turn

Alongside the word *relent* to describe the change that needs to come about in Yhwh is *turn* (*šûb*) to describe the change that needs to come about in Israel.

---

[106]The context suggests human commitment and truthfulness rather than Yhwh's, and the language suggests avoiding evil rather than avoiding calamity.

"If that nation concerning which I have spoken turns from the ill it does, I will relent concerning the ill that I intended to do to it" (Jer 18:7-8). If *relent* is an essentially affective word, *turn* is an essentially active word.[107] It is a key word in Jonah; if Jeremiah's declaration applies to Nineveh, perhaps a fortiori it also applies to Israel.

To judge from Hosea 14:1-8, one could describe Israel's relationship with Yhwh as all about turning. First, there was the turning away, the turning that Yhwh needs to heal. Hosea invites Israel to own the twofold nature of that turning. It involved turning to other political powers such as the Assyrians so that they might "deliver"—the thing that Yhwh alone can do—with the associated assumption that their military resources are the key to their deliverance. It also involved turning to other deities, to images that they themselves made, which contrast with the God who responds to their prayers when they are in helpless need, and who looks after them.

Second, Yhwh's anger has now turned from them. That will issue in Yhwh's healing Israel's turning. It is a significant mixed metaphor. Perhaps it implies an ellipse and indicates that Yhwh will heal the wounds that have come about through Israel's turning away and then falling; the passage presupposes one of the occasions when Ephraim had been put in its place by the Assyrians. But as it stands, it implies an awareness of the paradoxical nature of Israel's turning. Turning away is not an illness or a wound but a deliberate act, yet it also has the characteristics of an addiction that people can apparently be incapable of reversing. The people are responsible for the fact that they have refused to turn back to Yhwh (Hos 11:5), but they are incapable of doing so (Hos 5:4) and need treatment or healing to enable them to turn. It is further suggestive that "love" parallels "healing," hinting that love is the means to healing (Hos 14:4). It is as Israel sees itself loved so persistently and illogically that it will be won to a turning back to Yhwh. As Israel is invited to put it, Yhwh is one who has compassion for an orphan like Ephraim.

Third, Yhwh's turning will also issue in their returning to new life. The promise that they will return may refer to returning from exile, but if so, it soon gives way to talk of a return to flourishing life in the land. Yhwh will cause Israel to flourish anew like wildflowers or mighty trees in Lebanon or fragrant olives or spreading vines, and they will sit in the shade of these trees.

But fourth, the need for Yhwh to heal their turning does not remove the need for them to turn, as is the case when someone receives *treatment* for an addiction; hence the way the passage begins. That love of Yhwh's is one fact designed to draw them to turn. But initially Yhwh refers to a more immediate

---

[107] Again, the standard English translation *repent* is thus not very illuminating.

set of facts, the way they have "fallen" through their wrongdoing. The nation is in a state of collapse. Its turning to other nations and other deities is self-condemned.

In turning to Yhwh they are urged to take with them—words (Hos 14:2). Prophets are commonly skeptical about the value of words, which are less costly than actions and less reliable as indicators of real attitudes. Yet turning needs to be put into words. The words "I am sorry" may be too easy to utter but may also be very hard to utter, and they are indispensable to the healing of a relationship. The words that are urged on Israel involve a plea for forgiveness that acknowledges wrongdoing. They appeal to Yhwh to accept them in grace and promise to bring the offerings a penitent would bring. Possibly the "words" stand in antithesis to sacrifices, and the expression "bulls/fruit of our lips" indicates that people are challenged to bring to Yhwh words as the fruit of their lips. They will be the equivalent of the bulls that they offer in sacrifice but will replace these offerings, which Yhwh now rejects (cf. Hos 5:6). Yet the realistic skepticism of God and prophet extends from offerings to words, which are much cheaper than sacrifices and no more reliable as indications of people's real attitudes. In any case, in this chapter Hosea does not suggest an antithesis between words and sacrifices but between different kinds of words. What counts here is not that the people bring words rather than something else but that they bring the right kind of words about relationships with foreign powers and other deities.

Act

Jeremiah puts the point succinctly: "Turn, children who turned away; I will heal your turning," but he then adds that this needs to be a turning without wavering (Jer 3:22; 4:1). He can imagine what needs to happen by way of Israel's turning (Jer 3:22-25), but it is only imagination; though the fact that he shares his unfulfilled longing with the people shows that he still lives in hope and that the possibility of turning remains open. He begins from the fact that what he can hear is "the plaintive weeping of the Israelites," arising out of their turning away. The people have experienced reversals and they are lamenting them. But they are doing so in the wrong places to the wrong deity. Yet a people that turned one way can turn back. What is required is an acknowledgment of the facts. It is their turning from Yhwh that has caused their trouble, rather than suggesting a solution to it. Only in Yhwh, the God who is alive and thus active, lies the possibility of healing or deliverance. The traditional religious forms are just empty noise. Further, people need to acknowledge that declaring that "the Master is alive" is the shameful thing it is ("the shameful thing" being a circumlocution for the Master), precisely because it involves turning from the real God to a nonentity who is treated as reality. That involves acknowledging their own shamefulness. They need to acknowledge the disgust that the expressions of their worship cause to Yhwh, even if they see them as offered in Yhwh's honor. They need to make this a real turning to Yhwh and not just another short-lived affair. It also needs to involve a turning to one another in truth and faithful decision making in society, instead of against one another.

Two images make clear the radicalism of the action the people need to undertake (Jer 4:1-4). It is like a farmer seeking to realize the potential in some land that has never been sown. At present, all that the land grows is the natural thorn bushes of the desert. The farmer has to till it and get the thorn bushes out if he is to see a crop. That involves painful, back-breaking work, but there is no substitute for it. Or it is like circumcising your mind or heart. Regular circumcision on an adult is a painful business (see Gen 34); imagine self-administered open-heart surgery. But again the state of the people means there is no substitute for such radical work on their own lives if their turning is too be real, like a philandering husband doing the painful work of facing up to the facts about himself if he is to change his ways. Yet if they will undertake that, the possibility opens up that they will not merely find their own life put back together but will also see their original vocation fulfilled. Nations will look at them and turn to Yhwh for the blessing they see Yhwh bringing them.

Eliphaz lays before Job similar action that can lead to God's restoring him (Job 22:21-30). Of course Job is not guilty of any of Eliphaz's accusations, but to the appropriate person, Eliphaz's prescription is quite appropriate. He has summed up the nature of sin as involving a failure to be generous to the needy. Turning to God thus involves giving up such oppression. It involves ceasing to treat one's wealth as the thing of real value. Throwing one's gold in the river or into the dirt (that is, throwing it back where it came from) might seem wasteful—one could surely use it to benefit those needy people—and Eliphaz may be using a figure of speech; perhaps he means we should value gold as not better than dirt or rocks. But he has seen something important, and the point needs making forcefully. Only if one has changed one's attitude and one's life like this can one really be reckoned to have submitted to God by listening to God's teaching in such a way as to let it settle deep in one's thinking and shape that thinking. It is God who is the one whom we really value, and this revolution in our thinking means we can come to him with our prayers and find him answering them, so that we find ourselves coming back to fulfill our promises by bringing an offering in gratitude for what God has done.

If that is to happen, seeking Yhwh's help involves taking the kind of action in connection with community life that will change its past dynamics. There needs to be sowing for faithfulness (ṣēdāqâ, Hos 10:12). It is not the same word as the one that describes what they seek from Yhwh[108] but a word that is sufficiently like it to hint that faithfulness has to be all-pervasive if it is to be a reality at all. Indeed, perhaps what Hosea means is that people need to sow in such a way that they can expect to see Yhwh's faithfulness. Either way, while Yhwh can act in faithfulness despite human unfaithfulness (and Isaiah 40—55 will speak of Yhwh's doing that), as Yhwh's people we cannot trust for that. Only as we sort out faithfulness in the community can we press Yhwh for faithfulness to us. To put it another way, Hosea goes on, there needs to be reaping in proportion to commitment (ḥesed). Again, we can look to Yhwh for commitment only if there is mutual commitment among us. The two halves of the line divide these realities artificially to make the parallelism work; Hosea's point is that people are to sow for faithfulness and commitment and thus reap in proportion to that, to see these as developing, fruitful realities in their common life. They are thus to start afresh, like a farmer plowing and sowing and seeing a crop in land that has never been farmed before.

With All Your Heart

Such turning could merely affect public life, while in private people still prayed to other gods or sought help from their ancestors. The turning needs to reach down into the nation's heart, to the springs of people's actions and attitudes, so that it affects the whole of the nation's being and not just its public life: see Joel 2:12-13. Paradoxically, one of the signs that this is so will be outward. Repentance would be expected to involve fasting, weeping and lamenting. Such signs of grief and mourning are not infallible indicators of sorrow, but the absence of them would be an infallible sign of the absence of sorrow. Yhwh does not want people to tear their clothes—another sign of such grief— and not to tear their hearts, but neither is Yhwh interested in a repentance that does not manifest itself in whatever symbolic marks of deep feeling are appropriate in a given culture.

Repentance is corporate and outward. Yhwh is not merely interested in individuals turning away from wrongdoing and doing so inwardly, but wants to see the people as a whole doing this and doing it publicly. Yhwh wants the people to tear their heart: "your" is plural, but "heart" is singular. The people is not merely a collection of individuals who need to make individual responses to Yhwh. The people is itself an entity and needs to make its corporate response. The outward expression of that is the gathering of the people as a whole for the priests to lead them. The blowing of a horn (Joel 2:15-16) now has different and more positive significance from the one it had before (Joel

---

[108]See under "Pursue" on p. 323.

2:1). Nobody will be exempt from the calamity that Yhwh has threatened, even babies (cf. Is 13:16), and no events will be exempt from being turned from joy to mourning, even weddings (cf. Jer 7:34; 16:9).[109] So no one is excused from a response. The babies are there, the wedding couples are there; nothing is more important than this turning to Yhwh, not even getting married or feeding the baby.

The turning is theologically based. The first basis Joel refers to is the nature of Yhwh as gracious and compassionate, long-tempered and big in commitment, and rueful about bringing disaster (Joel 2:13). These are the characteristics of which Yhwh spoke at Sinai and which Yhwh then manifested in abandoning the declared intention of casting off Israel (Ex 32:14; 34:6). Given that it is Yhwh who issues the exhortation to turn, in effect Yhwh is pointing people to that self-revelation. Yhwh is implying, "Look at what I have revealed myself to be: turning to me will meet with a welcome." After all, Moses prevailed on Yhwh to abandon that intention when there was no basis in such a turning. Moses simply appealed to Yhwh's self-interest. And Joel implicitly invites people to do so. Perhaps when they turn, Yhwh will also turn, and rather than destroying everything will leave behind a blessing, the means of praise and the reason for praise *(bĕrākâ)*,[110] some grain and some grapes from which wine can be made for a libation (Joel 2:14). The same logic underlies the appeal Joel commends to the priests. They are to urge Yhwh to "spare your people" because Yhwh's association with this people means Yhwh cannot destroy it at no personal cost (Joel 2:17). While other peoples will directly sneer at "your people" when Yhwh brings calamity on them, they will be indirectly sneering at Yhwh. The argument is very similar to the one Moses uses (Ex 32:11-13).

It parallels a declaration in Jeremiah. Surprisingly, despite the statement that Israel can no more return to Yhwh than a wife who has left her husband and been divorced can return to him (Jer 3:1-5), Yhwh nevertheless urges Ephraim to own its guilt and come back. "I will not scowl at you, because I am committed (Yhwh's message). I do not keep things forever" (Jer 3:12). Yhwh's words do not use regular theological language, and they may rather suggest the language of human relationships. When an unfaithful man seeks to return to his wife, he may well find her response is a glare rather than a smile. It is hard for the victim of unfaithfulness not to hold on to things forever. Against those two possibilities Yhwh puts the fact of Yhwh's being committed (*ḥāsîd*); only once elsewhere is this word used to refer to Yhwh (Ps 145:17). The noun *ḥesed* itself suggests a commitment that goes beyond anything that the other party has a right to expect; for instance, it could suggest keeping a commit-

---

[109]Cf. Wolff, *Joel and Amos,* p. 51.

[110]Cf. section 4.4 "Rescue," "Potential"; also the use of the noun in Neh 9:5.

ment to one's marriage when one's partner has behaved in such a way as to forfeit any right to expect that.

Perhaps

Joel does not assume that people can take anything for granted just because they turn to Yhwh, even though he does not point to the other side of Yhwh's character as one who does not clear the guilty (Ex 34:7). "Who knows?" (Joel 2:14). In a personal relationship, someone who has betrayed another has to come back in contrition without knowing how they will be received. That is one of the pointers to the contrition's being real. It seems that the people did turn, since Joel goes on to speak of Yhwh's "responding" to them and sparing them (Joel 2:18-19). Yhwh's declarations about the future are not set in stone. It is possible to heed chastisements (such as a locust plague) and avoid a more terrible fate.

Zephaniah has a different "perhaps," "perhaps you will hide on the day of Yhwh's anger" (Zeph 2:2-3). It may be that the arrival of the day of Yhwh's anger is unavoidable, but if it is, perhaps people may be able to hide from its effects. Yhwh will shine a flashlight into every corner of the city to flush out faithless people (Zeph 1:12), and they will not be able to hide. But for others there is a possibility of finding refuge on this day. The people who may be able to do so are those who follow Amos's urging to "seek help from Yhwh," people who have recourse to Yhwh and not to other deities, nor to their political resources. It is this that constitutes Yhwh's command, the first and most crucial of Yhwh's ten commands. And they will be people who "seek faithfulness." That might suggest the other aspect to the seeking that Amos urges (see Amos 5:4-7, 14-15), a commitment to faithfulness to Yhwh and faithfulness in community life. But in the context it more likely suggests seeking *Yhwh's* faithfulness, opening themselves to Yhwh's proving faithful to Judah and thus not seeking help elsewhere, nor simply despairing (cf. Is 51:1). In other words, "seeking faithfulness" restates "seeking help from Yhwh."

Zephaniah adds the strange requirement that the "weak people in the land" should "seek weakness," and this makes the same point again (Zeph 2:3). Translations have the "humble" seeking "humility," which is not exactly wrong, but it masks the implications of the words ʿănāwîm and ʿănāwâ. These first refer not to an internal feeling or attitude but to an objective position. The ʿănāwîm are people who are weak and powerless, ordinary people who have no say in what happens in the community, or the community as a whole over against imperial overlords. The humility that such ʿănāwâ may generate is a realistic acceptance of one's position that then gives one some purchase with God, who is supposed to be on the side of the powerless. Here Zephaniah urges people who *are* weak to recognize and own their weakness and not pretend things are otherwise. He urges them to let that make them turn to Yhwh.

Weakness is actually the position of the entire people. "The weak people in the land" means everyone, and thus the oracle does reaffirm the possibility that the whole people might find somewhere to hide on the day of Yhwh's anger. That would fit with the fact that the rest of the chapter speaks of Yhwh's action against a number of other nations. It begins with a "because" (Zeph 2:4), as if it is the prospect of that action against other nations that needs to drive this "weak people" to seek help from Yhwh. The first people mentioned are the Philistines, Judah's near neighbors whose affliction might well bring fallout for Judah itself. Further, the background might be Judean expansion into Philistia in the late seventh century, so that the exhortation to seek Yhwh's help confronts Judean political aspirations.[111] But if we read the exhortation in light of what precedes, it more likely assumes that the weak are people within Judah. The whole people does not recognize its weakness; specifically the people who are supposed to be the powerful do not. But the people who do so recognize the weakness of the nation's position and who let that make them turn to Yhwh are the ones who may *perhaps* find a hiding place on the day of Yhwh's anger.

Prayer

Amos's series of visions relates to this question of "perhaps." He sees Yhwh making locusts to consume what grows in the land, and after they have finished their task he says, "My Lord Yhwh, do pardon. How can Jacob stand, for it is small?" And "Yhwh relented concerning this. 'It will not happen,' Yhwh said." In a second vision he sees Yhwh summoning fire that consumes the great deep and is consuming the land. Amos says, "My Lord Yhwh, do stop. How can Jacob get up, when it is small?" Yhwh responds in the same way. In a third vision he sees Yhwh at a wall, holding a tool: English translations have "plumb line," but we do not know for sure the word's meaning, and the context might suggest something more aggressive. Yhwh declares the intention not to "pass over" Israel again but to devastate its sanctuaries and the household of Jeroboam. In a fourth vision (or perhaps this is something that happens in "real life") Amos sees a basket of figs (*qayiṣ*). Yhwh declares that "the time [*qēṣ*] has come upon my people Israel,"[112] and again adds, "I will not pass over them again." There will be terrible death and grieving (Amos 7:1-9; 8:1-3).

The implication of these visions is thoroughly ambiguous. It leaves Israel with a "perhaps," but with nothing to take for granted. They may or may not

---

[111]Cf. Jimmy J. M. Roberts, *Nahum, Habakkuk, and Zephaniah* (Louisville, Ky.: Westminster John Knox, 1991), p. 199, though he draws a different inference.

[112]See the introduction to section 4.3.

imply an ever-heightening portrayal of disaster. There is a locust plague as the dry season approaches, which threatens human beings and animals with nothing to eat for months. Then there is a fire capable of consuming the great deep (fire consumes water!). But consuming the great deep implies destroying the sources of water in the world itself. And whereas the locust plague seems to happen only in the vision and thus can be stopped from happening, the fire might be in the midst of implementation; "stop" (*ḥādal*) could imply "don't do it" or "stop doing it." Then there is a literal act of demolition, yet we are not sure what Yhwh is holding. Is it merely a plumb line to test whether the building needs demolishing or a weapon to demolish it? Finally there is the declaration that the people's time has come, and perhaps that does mean its end has come, as English versions assume (cf. *qēṣ* applied to the individual in Ps 39:4 [MT 5]; Job 6:11). Amos has spoken before of the people's death and of the mourning that will follow (Amos 5:1-2, 16-17), and here may do so again.

There is foreboding in the interactions between Amos and Yhwh that parallels that in the visions themselves. After the first vision Amos urges Yhwh to pardon the people (he evidently presupposes that the locust plague is a punishment for rebellion), but the account does not tell us whether Yhwh does so. Yhwh simply agrees to abandon the plague, there being no indication that this is more than a postponement of calamity. On the other hand, that does mean Yhwh "relents." Here at least for a while Amos's appeal tips Yhwh over (with relief?—*niham* is a feelings word) from the act of destruction that would be quite justified and proper; the logic parallels Hosea 11:8-9.[113] After the second vision, Amos does not ask for pardon, just for Yhwh to desist, to stop the thing that has started. Yhwh does again relent. In the third and fourth visions (Amos 7:7-9; 8:1-3) Yhwh opens the conversation, declaring the intention never again to "pass the people by." Yhwh has not been involved in pardoning, only in doing nothing by way of punishment at the moment; the prospect of punishment therefore continues to hang over the people. Yhwh will now pass through, bringing death (Amos 5:17), not pass by. Further, in these third and fourth visions Amos does not ask for anything. Is this because Yhwh has preemptively excluded it? Are there times when prayer is possible and times when it becomes impossible, times when Yhwh will relent and times when Yhwh will not? If so, how does an intercessor know which is which? And is an intercessor bound to take any notice? What is the point of telling a prophet or a people that calamity is coming? Does it totally exclude the possibility that people might still beseech Yhwh to relent? Or is the declaration that things cannot be reversed the strongest way of urging people to press that they be reversed?

---

[113]Cf. Jeremias, *Amos*, p. 128.

The motivation for Amos's prayer in Amos 7:2, 5 is different from that of Moses in a situation that is otherwise somewhat parallel (Ex 32:11-13). Amos does not appeal to Yhwh's prior acts in relation to Israel and to the implausibility of action that will short-circuit Yhwh's own plan, or to the danger of imperiling Yhwh's own reputation, or to the necessity to keep promises made to Israel's ancestors. Like Moses, however, neither does Amos make any appeal to expressions of repentance on Israel's part. Neither Moses nor Amos is in a position to make such appeal. Israel's repentance is not a precondition for its being spared, though maybe it is a precondition for its being pardoned; in other words, it would be morally impossible for Yhwh to pardon Israel while it continues in its wrongdoing, but sparing Israel for a while gives time for repentance and pardon. Amos appeals simply to the fact that Jacob is small, and thus appeals to Yhwh's pity, which is perhaps not so far from the basis for appeal that Yhwh implicitly offers Moses in Exodus 34:6-7. In the previous chapter (Amos 6) Israel has been priding itself on its achievements and strength and its capacity to stand firm and maintain its position in the world. In reality, or before God, it is rather tiny and incapable of doing so, and Amos now makes that a basis for appeal to Yhwh.

In Joel 1, Yhwh's outrage at the locust plague that has devastated Yhwh's own land suggests a basis for hope. Yhwh is of course in some sense sovereign in the world. A natural or human army does not bring about such devastation of God's trees in God's land without Yhwh's at least letting it do so. Surely Yhwh cannot stand aside and let this army simply carry on with its work, any more than Yhwh can take that stance in relation to the Assyrians? There is a relationship between God and the world. A natural disaster is not merely a natural disaster. God is in control of the world, and events in nature happen because of Yhwh's desire, or at least with Yhwh's connivance. They are not "just one of those things." That in itself would make it appropriate to lament *before Yhwh* (and not simply to lament). Joel thus challenges people to "sanctify a fast" and "call an assembly" to "cry out" to Yhwh like their ancestors in Egypt. He does not assume that the situation is irreversible, and he himself calls on Yhwh (Joel 1:14, 19).

4.4 Is the Nightmare the End?

Suppose that the nightmare does become reality. Is it then the end? We have noted that the end (*qēṣ*) does not mean the end.[114] Actually the end is never the end, whether the end is the fall of Samaria or the exile or the Antiochene crisis. "We have come to an end [*kālâ*] by your anger," the community prays, and it

---

[114] And see the introduction to 4.3.

pictures its wrongdoing standing before God forever, but then it prays, "Turn, Yhwh; how long? Relent[115] about your servants" (Ps 90:7-8, 13), and that means its prayer deconstructs. A people who had come to an end would not be able to pray. The calamity that comes on Israel is something like an end because it is an act of retribution for the people's faithlessness. But it is not an end because it is also an act designed to correct and refine a people that Yhwh still intends to work with.

Leftovers

One sense in which the end is not the end is that leftovers always survive. "An end is determined. . . . My Lord Yhwh Armies is making the end that is determined" (Is 10:22-23; cf. Is 28:22). "End" is again *kālâ*, which etymologically does suggest completion, and implies total destruction. Oddly, however, Isaiah denies that implication: "Even if your people, Israel, were like the sand at the sea, leftovers are to return for it; an end is determined, flooding with *ṣĕdāqâ*" (Is 10:22). While the implication of "leftovers" is that the disaster will be a terrible event from which few will survive, the fact that it will leave leftovers means that the disaster will not constitute annihilation. That raises a question about the conventional understanding of the last line. English versions assume that this *ṣĕdāqâ* is Yhwh's judgment, but *ṣĕdāqâ* suggests doing the right thing by people, and the use of that word raises the question whether annihilation could be an act of *ṣĕdāqâ*.

As well as taking up Amos's talk of the time that has come to an end, Ezekiel takes up the Isaianic expression "make an end." When he prophesies against some of the Jerusalem leaders and one of them drops dead, Ezekiel asks, "Lord Yhwh, are you making an end of the leftovers of Israel?" and Yhwh's answer indicates that this is not so (Ezek 11:13-21). Jeremiah, too, takes up this verb. After sharing a vision of the cosmos dissolved (which stands for Judah destroyed), he adds a further word from Yhwh: "The whole land will be a desolation, but I will not make an end" (Jer 4:27; cf. Jer 5:10, 18). Yhwh will make an end of the nations among whom Israel is scattered, "yet I will not make an end of you" even though you are severely disciplined (Jer 30:11). Admittedly it could look close to it. Isaiah had already observed, "Had Yhwh Armies not left us a few survivors [*śārîd*], we would have become like Sodom, we would have resembled Gomorrah" (Is 1:9).

When he goes out to meet Ahaz, apparently preparing for invasion, Isaiah takes with him his son "Leftovers-are-to-return" (Is 7:3). The name is the phrase that comes in Isaiah 10:22, but the meaning of the name is much more

---

[115]Not "have compassion": see Marvin E. Tate, *Psalms 51—100*, WBC (Dallas: Word, 1990), p. 436.

ambiguous in itself. "Leftovers" is *šĕ'ār*, more technically translated "a remnant," but the ambiguity of the name is a sign of the fact that the word is not a technical term in the First Testament in the way it has become.[116] What message does the son bring? That only leftovers of the threatening allies, Syria and Ephraim, will return home after Yhwh has defeated them (cf. Is 7:8b)? That only leftovers of Assyria, the superpower they want to resist, will return home after invading the Levant (cf. Is 37:36)? That only leftovers of Judah will survive if Judah does not live by reliance on Yhwh rather than trying to fix its own future (cf. Is 7:17)? That at least leftovers of Judah will survive? That at least such leftovers must now turn back to Yhwh? That at least such leftovers will turn back in the future? All these are aspects of Isaiah's message, and part of the answer may be that it is Judah that decides which one(s) apply.

Isaiah 37:30-32 is realistic about the terrible devastation that will come to Judah at the hands and feet and mouths of the Assyrians. What their massive army does not eat, it no doubt tramples underfoot, accidentally and/or out of spite. When the siege of Jerusalem is lifted, the aftermath is not like that when that siege of Samaria was lifted (2 Kings 7). All that the starving city dwellers will find this year will be the late growth of the year's crops. Nor will there will be time for a plowing and sowing program this year, and therefore a proper harvest next year. But next year normalcy will begin to return, so there will be a proper harvest the third year. Indeed, the people will plant vineyards and eat their fruit; this either implies a miracle (fruit from the vines in their first year) or a period of continuing peace during which new vines can grow to maturity. The promise is realistic about the people themselves. They are only a group of survivors *(pĕlîṭâ)*, only leftovers *(šĕ'ērît)*. But they too will not just survive but thrive, put roots down and flourish. All this is guaranteed by Yhwh's passion *(qin'â)*. The same passion that had brought about the community's angry devastation is harnessed to its restoration.

The Aims of Punishment

Belonging to the leftovers, the group of survivors, is no indication that people belong to the faithful remnant. Yhwh declares the intention to allow a few people to escape the destruction of Jerusalem "so that they may tell of all their abominations among the nations where they go, and they will acknowledge that I am Yhwh" (Ezek 12:15-16). Evidently there is nothing faithful about these people who escape, these leftovers. While Ezekiel looks for such acknowledgment from the nations, here the context suggests reference to the survivors' acknowledgment. But it is not clear that it does them any good.

---

[116]Cf. Rolf Rendtorff, *The Canonical Hebrew Bible* (Leiden: Deo, 2005), p. 705.

Ezekiel's point is that in their abject and shamed state at last they submit to Yhwh, and perhaps that they reassure the nations that there was good reason for their having been treated as they were by Yhwh. He similarly promises that the exiles of 597 whom he addresses will see sons and daughters be brought out of the city when it finally falls, which is good news, yet is not unequivocally so (see Ezek 14:22-23). This group of survivors will not be people who are especially faithful; rather the opposite, as the exiles will recognize when they see "their ways and their deeds" (for Ezekiel, "way" [derek] is a neutral word, but "deed" [ʿălîlâ] is always pejorative). The exiles will see the lives of the people who survive and will see that Yhwh's destruction of the city was entirely justified. The survival of the few finds its justification in what Yhwh does through them, not in what they deserved.

This was no faithful remnant, nor even a remnant designed to keep Israel going because of Yhwh's grace rather than human deserve. Again, as he sees executioners setting out to slaughter Jerusalem's population, Ezekiel asks whether Yhwh is really going to eliminate the leftovers of people who have survived disasters such as the fall of Ephraim and the fall of Jerusalem that brought Ezekiel and others to Babylon (Ezek 9:8). Yes, Yhwh is going to do so. That is all they deserve. They have not responded to finding themselves leftovers. We could say that having been allowed to survive as a remnant, they have failed to become a responsive remnant, a faithful remnant.

On the other hand, there are people who do not deserve execution, people who sigh and groan about the abominations committed in the city, people whom we could call a faithful remnant (though Ezekiel does not use that language). Yhwh commissions a priest/scribe to go and mark them on their foreheads (Ezek 9:4). This faithful remnant is to become the remnant that survives.

If the end were the end, it would fail in most of its aims. Abraham Heschel comments that traditionally, "punishment has three aims: retributive, deterrent, and reformatory," though in Israel's story, at least, it is not very successful in the latter two;[117] the same is true if one adds restoration as an aim of punishment.[118] So among these four aims, the most effective is the one often reckoned to raise most ethical questions, though it does not do so in the First Testament or the Second. They do not doubt its appropriateness.

This might be related to the fact that the First Testament also adds a fifth aim, giving great prominence to the need to put wicked people down in order to rescue the oppressed. The aim of punishment is deliverance; these two often appear in parallelism (e.g., Is 61:2). That is an important aim in punishing op-

---

[117]Heschel, *Prophets*, pp. 238, 239.

[118]See, e.g., Christopher D. Marshall, *Beyond Retribution* (Grand Rapids/Cambridge: Eerdmans, 2001), pp. 97-143.

pressors within Israel and the oppressors of Israel. Apart from that, in aim Yhwh's punishment of Israel is occasionally deterrent (designed to make Israel a *māšāl*, a warning example to the nations). It is rarely restorative or liberative; the nation as a whole is rarely in a position to oppress other nations, so that restorative and liberative punishment would apply more to elements within Israel in their relation to others and to nations that oppress Israel. It is consistently retributive (it is *nāqām*), designed to affirm what is right and put down what is wrong. And it is consistently reformatory (it is *tôkēḥâ,* "correction," or *mûsār,* "discipline"), designed to put before people a challenge (Ezek 13:5) and a choice (Mal 4:1-6 [MT 3:19-24]). The tension over whether Yhwh will bring an end upon Israel derives from the tension between these last two aims. If punishment is retributive, then Yhwh can bring an end, and perhaps must do so. If it is reformatory, Yhwh cannot.

Discipline

Hosea was told to go and "love a woman who is loved by a friend and is adulterous, like Yhwh's love for the Israelites whereas they are turning to other gods" (Hos 3:1). This leads Hosea to buy her, and then to impose restraints on her sexual activity.

Now in Hosea 1 he had been told to "get" a woman, but not told to love her (neither has Yhwh been said to "love," only to have compassion, which is rather different). Perhaps he did so, but there is no mention of "love" until the subsequent talk about her other "lovers" (did she have affairs because she was looking for the love she never found with Hosea?). It seems that a different attitude is implied here. This loving and disciplining happens (or at least is mentioned) because of something it symbolizes (Hos 3:4-5). "The Israelites will dwell many days with no king, no leader, no sacrifice, no column, and no ephod or teraphim." The things Israel will live without are things it would want to have and will miss, like a man or a woman required to live without any sexual expression. Like sexual activity (depending on the way it is indulged in), king, leader, sacrifice, column, ephod and teraphim might be things of which Yhwh approves, or might not. The point is that they will find themselves having to do without these things that seem to them indispensable to life. All forms of government will collapse (the state will be brought to an end). All forms of corporate worship will cease (the sanctuaries will be destroyed). All forms of seeking guidance and help from God will disappear (ephod and teraphim perhaps stand for means of approaching God that families would use at home).[119] But in due course, Hosea goes on, that will make

---

[119]See Wolff, *Hosea,* p. 62.

them turn to Yhwh for help and turn to David as their king: so kingship and forms of seeking help from God are not ruled out in principle.[120] And at a later stage, they will be amazed and overawed at the fact that Yhwh is again willing to provide for them.

All this has as its background the fact that Yhwh continued to "love" them, to be dedicated and committed to them, even when they were involved in a quasi-adulterous relationship with someone else. The passage provides another approach to the question Yhwh has to keep wrestling with. Yhwh loves Israel. Israel is unfaithful. Yhwh cannot give up on love for Israel and carry on being Yhwh. Neither can Yhwh simply ignore Israel's faithfulness and carry on being Yhwh. The combination of love and discipline offers another way of squaring the circle.

Ephraim is thus due for a "day of *tôkēḥâ*" (Hos 5:9). The word indeed denotes punishment, but the kind of punishment that is corrective rather than simply punitive.[121] It is more the action of parents in relation to children or teachers in relation to students than, for instance, the action of a court. "I am disciplining them all," says Yhwh (*yāsar*, Hos 5:2). The NRSV again has "punish," but this word, too, denotes action designed to make students or children shape up rather than action designed to put them down (cf. Hos 7:12, 15). What Yhwh does is make hedges and walls spring up so that Israel cannot find her way to her lovers, or make her mysteriously unable to catch them up no matter how hard she runs. The aim is that she may give up and decide she might as well go home (Hos 2:6-7 [MT 8-9]).

Correction

So "wrath is the countenance of Holiness for sinful man," though it is designed to draw its objects to turn back to God, so perhaps "the Wrath of Holiness might be only the Wrath of Love."[122] When Yhwh acts "against" people, this "judgment" is often designed to work "for" them, to win them back. It has the nature of correction, to make them change direction. Israel's story is one of recurrent chastisement designed to make it "turn" (e.g., Jer 5:3). Eliphaz assumes that the same dynamic applies in the life of individuals (Job 5:17-18). In Proverbs human reproof and correction may be mostly verbal; here divine reproof and correction are clearly physical, like divine restoration and blessing. God is not just talk. There is a sense in which this promises to give meaning to Job's suffering. It is not just chance or retribution but part of God's dealing with Job in the way that a wise and loving teacher deals with a pupil. (But

---

[120]This reference to David may reflect Judean development of Hosea's own prophecies.

[121]Cf. BDB; JPSV has "chastisement."

[122]Ricoeur, *Symbolism of Evil*, pp. 63, 68.

there are at least two difficulties with Eliphaz's applying this theory to Job. On one hand, on Eliphaz's own admission, Job is a person of integrity and reverence, so that God's correction of him seems grossly out of proportion. And on the other, it involves killing all Job's servants and children. This is a drastic form of correction for Job, and only raises the question of its meaning for those other victims.)

So the extending of Yhwh's hand is designed to smelt, not simply to destroy (Is 1:21-28). It is designed to remove slag and thus leave good metal; evidently there is good metal to be purified. Smelting is a terrifying prospect, but it will have a positive end. The punitive act whereby Yhwh gains personal relief (*nāḥam* niphal; Is 1:24) is also an act that cleans up the city. Yhwh intends Jerusalem to be *qiryâ neʾĕmānâ*, not merely in the sense of "Secure Town" (not a promise to be despised) but also in the sense of "Trustworthy Town"; the ambiguous expression is disambiguated as Yhwh adds the title "Faithful City." And to that end, Yhwh declares the intention to restore the kind of leadership Jerusalem had at the beginning, presumably the time of David. Jerusalem's leadership in those early years also had some ambiguity about it and it may be that Yhwh looks back with rose-tinted spectacles or with a commitment to be more interventionist this time. Revolution requires more than the removal of oppression and its causes and results; it requires the development of a new order.

The tension between nightmare and vision continues in Isaiah 1:27 in the talk of redemption through authority and faithfulness (*mišpāṭ* and *ṣĕdāqâ*). Like the name "Leftovers-are-to-return," it is an ambiguous idea. Is Zion to be redeemed by Yhwh's acting authoritatively against its enemies, or by Yhwh's preserving it when acting in that way in relation to the world or by its own turning to a life that embodies the faithful exercise of authority in the community? In the context of Isaiah as a whole, each is a plausible idea, but the narrower context suggests another possibility, that Zion's redemption comes about through Yhwh's acting with authority upon it. Isaiah is then making his previous point in different words. Yhwh is about to act authoritatively in relation to Zion in a way that reflects a commitment to doing the right thing. In the circumstances, that has to mean Yhwh acting against Zion, even though Yhwh's relationship with Zion also ultimately has to mean doing the right thing by Zion in a more positive way by expressing faithfulness to Zion. One way of achieving both ends is to make the act of judgment also the means of redemption. Yhwh delivers Zion by purging it. The First Testament does not usually press the financial implications of the term "redeem" (*pādâ*), so perhaps it simply carries the general connotations of "deliver" and/or "rescue," or perhaps it suggests an act of deliverance reminiscent of the exodus, Yhwh's great redemptive act, and/or perhaps its relational implications are signifi-

cant: it is often parents or relatives who go about redeeming someone. Any of
these would add to the point that the negative act is also a positive act.

Refining

Amos 9 works out in a different way the tension between the demands of retribution and the demands of reformation. It opens with a devastating vision
of destruction of a sanctuary and the slaughter of a people; none will be able
to escape. Thus "the Lord Yhwh's eye is on the kingdom that has come short,
and I will destroy it from the face of the earth." But then Yhwh says, "Howbeit,
I will not actually destroy the household of Jacob" (Amos 9:8).[123] Does Yhwh
imply that the *kingdom* must go but the *household* can continue, that the state
must come to an end but the people can continue? Or perhaps the sinful kingdom (Ephraim) must go but the household of *Jacob* (Israel as a whole) can continue. Or perhaps *any* sinful kingdom must go but the household of Jacob will
not finally go. Yhwh goes on to explain, "Because now: I am commanding and
shaking the household of Israel among all the nations as one shakes with a
sieve and no pebble/ear falls to the earth." The image of the sieve suggests another approach to the surviving of elements of the people. While it is not clear
whether the sieve holds onto the pure material to keep it safe or holds onto the
rubbish in order to dispose of it, one way or the other calamity purifies the
people. Amos's point then parallels the talk of smelting in Isaiah 1. The exile
will see to the disposing of the people who in Amos's time are standing before
Yhwh saying "You will not let trouble reach us or overtake us" (if we take the
hiphil verbs as transitive) or who are ignoring Yhwh and simply declaring that
"trouble will not reach us or overtake us" (if the hiphils are declarative) (Amos
9:10). The attitude the people take now to the word of the prophet determines
what happens to them afterward. People who speak the way these people do
are not saying in so many words "Go and prophesy somewhere else" (Amos
7:12), but that is the implication of their words.

That the talk of annihilation should not be Amos's final word fits with implications of the earlier words. Amos's visions come in linear sequence, and
the visions in which he prevails on Yhwh to relent yield to ones in which calamity is apparently inevitable. Yet the former continue to have implications.
The fact that Yhwh is one who twice yields to the observation that Jacob is so
small (Amos 7:1-6) remains a fact that continues to signify something about
who Yhwh is. It makes it unlikely that Yhwh can simply annihilate Jacob.
Yhwh is like a mother who eventually says "that's it" to her recalcitrant children and walks out. It is likely that she will return. It is commonly reckoned

---

[123]The verse uses the idiom whereby the finite verb is preceded by the infinitive, lit., "[in] destroying I will not destroy."

that the material in the last chapter in Amos, at least in part, comes from later contributors to the book. If this is so, then wittingly or unwittingly they draw out implications from Amos's own work. If this material is self-contradictory, then it is faithfully working out implications of tensions within Yhwh's own character. Less contradiction would mean less truth.

Malachi 3:2-4 speaks first of Levi's purification by smelting, but continues, "and I will draw near to you to exercise authority [*lammišpāṭ*]" (Mal 3:5). The background is the people's complaint, "where is the God who exercises authority [*ʾĕlōhê hammišpāṭ*]?" (Mal 2:17). Yhwh did not like the question—indeed, found it wearisome—but does eventually respond to it. "I will be keen in testifying against sorcerers, adulterers, perjurers, people who defraud employees, widows, orphans, and push aside foreigners, and do not revere me, Yhwh Armies has said" (Mal 3:6). There will be refining.

Restoration

When the action that is designed ultimately to be restorative has come today, this does not mean restoration itself can therefore come tomorrow. This is not merely because it has not yet had chance to work but because Yhwh also affirms the principle of retribution. The terrible devastation Yhwh will bring on people, land, city and sanctuary means "I will eliminate from them the sound of joy and the sound of gladness, the voice of groom and the voice of bride, the sound of millstones and the light of the lamp" (Jer 25:10). Those are the positive marks of ordinary community life: its regular joys, its celebrations and its daily round taking people from bread-making at the beginning of the day to lamp-lighting at the end. They will all be gone. And that will be so for seventy years, for the Babylonians will be allowed to rule the Levant for that long (Jer 25:11-12). In other words, they will rule it for a lifetime (cf. Ps 90:10), a standard period for desolation to last (cf. Is 23:15).[124] The implication is that anyone alive who thinks they are going to see restoration in their lifetime can forget it. The object is not merely purification but also retribution.

But Yhwh's action against Israel is indeed designed to be restorative and not merely penal. It encourages "the pain of taking responsibility."[125] Israel might thus escape the ultimate nightmare after experiencing a hint of it; it is possible for them then to turn in expectation that Yhwh will restore them. They must turn and acknowledge Yhwh as the one who can heal after hitting, who can lift up after putting down, who will be as consistent and reliable as

---

[124]Cf. William L. Holladay, *Jeremiah*, 2 vols. (Philadelphia: Fortress, 1986 and Minneapolis: Fortress, 1989), 1:668-69.

[125]Marshall, *Beyond Retribution*, pp. 132-35, though Marshall focuses more on responsibility for wrongs we have done to other human beings.

the coming of dawn and as renewing as the spring rains (Hos 6:1-3).[126] Hosea's
exhortation takes up major themes of his confrontations and warnings but
now presupposes that some of the warnings have come true. He has spoken of
Yhwh tearing them like a lion (Hos 5:14), and Yhwh has evidently done so.
They are people attacked and wounded, and he has spoken of their stupid and
pointless hope that the Assyrian king can heal them (Hos 5:13), but the one
who hurt them can also heal them. He has spoken of people's inability to turn
to Yhwh (Hos 5:4), but now he nevertheless exhorts them to do so; perhaps he
implies that the disciplining may have broken through that incapacity. He has
spoken of their failure to acknowledge Yhwh (e.g., Hos 4:1, 6; 5:4), but in these
words he urges them to change that: literally, to chase acknowledgment (Hos
6:3). If they do so turn and acknowledge, they could finding healing, treatment, renewed life (ḥāyâ hiphil). In a matter of days they could be put back on
their feet. (The imagery does not suggest they are dead and need resurrecting;
they are injured and need healing.) They could revive "through him" (literally,
"before him"). It would be by standing before Yhwh that they find healing,
through the healing light that shines out from Yhwh's face. It would be like the
day dawning again, like the rain coming to soften the earth for plowing, like
the spring rain falling to make the crops mature. These were the very concerns
of the worship of the Masters that people were attached to; Hosea wants them
to see that Yhwh is the key to them. Yhwh had been the unacknowledged giver
of them, then the withholder of them, and will be the giver of them again (cf.
Hos 2:8-9, 21-22 [MT 10-11, 23-24]).

The trouble is that the exhortation does not find a response; the discipline
does not work. The people will not come to Yhwh like that, or if they will, their
commitment soon dissolves (Hos 6:4). They therefore risk chastisement becoming punishment, because in the absence of repentance their wrongdoing
will not be covered.

Limitation

Jeremiah's letter to the exiles of 597 (Jer 29) again declares that the exile will
last seventy years, not the two years Hananiah was promising. The exiles may
as well settle down. They can build houses knowing they will have chance to
live in them, plant orchards knowing they will have chance to eat their fruit,
marry and start families, identify with their new country and pray for its *shalom*. Jeremiah is not making a profound theological point about their identifi-

---

[126]In the absence of indications to the contrary, I take these as Hosea's words to his people,
rather than, e.g., the people's words to themselves or words Yhwh puts on their lips (LXX;
MT has no chapter or section division at this point and may imply the same). But the theological implications hardly change.

cation with the cities where they sojourn. He is simply spelling out the implications of the fact that they are going to be there for decades, not months. It may even be that we should not make too much of the fact that the letter is sent to the exiles. Jeremiah is at least as concerned with its implications for the people in Jerusalem whom Hananiah is telling that the exiles will soon be back; it is the converse of the way Ezekiel speaks as if addressing people in Jerusalem when he is directly addressing people in Babylon.

The figure generates two different forms of reflection over future years. On one hand, there were several senses in which Judah's devastation could be reckoned to last about that literal period, depending on whether one saw it as starting, for example, in 605 or 597 or 587 and finishing with Babylon's fall in 539 or the completion of the temple's rebuilding in 516. On the other, Judeans centuries later could be tempted to think that the country continued to be in a state of decay and shame, so that Daniel 9 raises the question of what has happened to the delimiting of devastation to seventy years. The good news is that even if the seventy has come to mean seventy times seven, at least devastation is not to last forever.[127]

Jeremiah's letter both warns the 597 exiles (and the people who read over his shoulder in Jerusalem) that the exile must last a lifetime and also promises them that this does mean a term is fixed to it. It will not last forever. "I will attend to you and put into effect for you my good word. For I do acknowledge the plans I am formulating for you (Yhwh's message), plans for *shalom* and not for ill, to give you a future with hope" (Jer 29:10-11). Yhwh has been attending to Judah all right *(pāqad)*, and this attending has been of a kind to make one shudder (e.g., Jer 6:15). But whereas Yhwh has *threatened* to attend to Judah, now Yhwh *promises* to attend to it (cf. Jer 27:22; 29:10; Zeph 2:7). Yhwh has already been putting plans into effect *(qûm* hiphil), but they concerned ill (e.g., Jer 23:12, 20); now they concern good. Judah has had a "future" *('aḥărît),* but it was a negative one (e.g., Jer 5:31; 23:20). Now it is a future with hope; "there is hope for your future" (Jer 31:17). Yhwh "acknowledges" these new plans, owns them and affirms them.

Likewise, for the first stage of his ministry Ezekiel's task was to warn the community about calamity to come, then it was to be silent because people would take no notice, but when a messenger arrives in Babylon with the news that Jerusalem has fallen, Ezekiel will suddenly be turned from silence to speaking. The moment will have arrived when Ezekiel is to talk about a positive future (Ezek 24:25-27). At the same time, there is more than one sense in which the positive vision came first, and Yhwh often declares something that

---

[127]John Hill sees this as implicit in the book itself: see "'Your Exile Will Be Long,'" in *Reading the Book of Jeremiah,* ed. Martin Kessler (Winona Lake, Ind.: Eisenbrauns, 2004), pp. 151-61.

expresses this vision before the nightmare comes true. Indeed, each of the prophetic books as we have them associates a message of hope with the declaring of the nightmare—beginning with the vision that closes Amos. There are limits set to punishment.

Rescue

Further, punishment is designed to bring about the deliverance of the oppressed. We have noted that the First Testament does not make judgment a pervasive model for understanding God's activity in bringing punishment, as it is in Christian thinking;[128] it is as much as parent or as a cuckolded spouse, for instance, that Yhwh brings trouble on Israel. Yet further, even when Yhwh does act as judge, this has different aims from the ones that attach to the role in Christian thinking. In Isaiah 3:13-15 Yhwh acts as judge because judgment is being neglected in the community, but also acts as accuser or advocate, taking a stand in the court. The picture may conflate two kinds of court. There is the community court where the elders decide on a dispute after listening to people advocating different sides; thus "Yhwh is rising to argue a case, standing to decide for peoples." A certain irony will emerge, because it turns out that the decision makers, the community elders, are actually the people subject to arraignment in this court. Here, arguing a case is an advocate's role. But Isaiah goes on to speak as if the prosecutor is also the judge: "Yhwh will come in authority to the elders of his people and its leaders." Now the scene resembles a court in a capital city (or in heaven), where the king (or the King) presides. Here the heavenly court gathers to make decisions about what is going on in the world. It is not explicit whether the court is going to decide for peoples in the sense of taking action against them or for them, but either way the passage contains a nasty shock. The rhetoric works like that in Amos 1—2, where Yhwh arraigns Ephraim's various neighbors only to turn on Ephraim itself at the climax of the indictment.

In Isaiah 3 people think they are hearing about a scene like that in Psalm 82, but find themselves in one like that in Psalm 50. "You are people who have ravaged the vineyard; the spoil of the weak is in your houses. How can you crush my people, grind the faces of the weak?" Israel is not the beneficiary of Yhwh's decision making but is subject to indictment like other peoples. Specifically, its leadership is subject to this indictment. Again the situation parallels that in Psalm 82, where the entities that were supposed to make decisions on behalf of the weak and the orphan are supporting their oppressors instead. Israel's elders are as bad as the heavenly beings that were supposed to see to the protection of

---

[128]Cf. section 2.7 "Redress."

the needy in the countries that they represented but failed to do so. And therefore they will be removed. The function of judgment is to rescue the weak.

Israel is a vine that has not produced the fruit. It has failed in precisely this way, by generating a life characterized by oppression. Yhwh therefore determines to destroy it (Is 5:1-7). Will Yhwh really destroy the whole vine? At the crucial moment someone says, "Don't destroy all of it," on the basis of the conviction that "there is a blessing in it" (Is 65:8-10). Perhaps this allusive statement means that there is a source of blessing there in the vine (cf. Ps 37:26),[129] and thus a potential reason to bless or praise God in the way one does when drinking wine.[130] Faced with a vine that looks wholly rotten, the temptation is to destroy the whole thing and start again, but the soft-hearted vinedresser or the vinedresser's laborer or friend says, "Don't be so radical." Is the laborer or friend the lookout or intercessor or prophet whom the divine vinedresser has commissioned to intercede for the vine?

Whatever the significance of the comment about blessing in connection with the vine, the interpretation of the image suggests something less down to earth. Back at the beginning of the story of Israel's ancestors, Yhwh undertook to make Abraham a blessing, and there were two ways in which this would be spelled out: Abraham's offspring would become a substantial people, and they would enter into possession of the land of Canaan. These two promises recur here (Is 65:9-10). Yhwh will cause offspring to come forth from Jacob / Judah and they will occupy the land from Sharon to the Vale of Achor, from the Mediterranean to the Jordan. Yes, there is a blessing in the cluster. Perhaps that statement has no literal meaning in connection with viticulture but is exclusively an allegorical statement whose significance we appreciate only when we have listened to the parable's interpretation and seen that the blessing as usual lies in these two experiences.

Potential

For all Yhwh's recurrent talk of total destruction, there were always people exempted from it: Noah's family, Lot's family, Ephraimites who moved south, Judeans who escaped the devastation in Jerusalem. The reason did in part lie in the people themselves. Noah was the one faithful person in his generation, though we are told that only after we are told that he found grace in Yhwh's eyes. That sequence at least allows the inference that his integrity issued from God's grace being shown to him rather than that God's grace was shown to him because he was a person of integrity (and in any case that statement de-

---

[129]So BDB.

[130]Is 65:8 plays with two possible implications of *bĕrākâ*, its usual meaning "blessing" and a meaning that might emerge from its verbal link with *berek*, "knee," and *bārak*, "praise."

constructs, because if God's grace were a response to his integrity, it would not be grace). Lot escaped from Sodom not because he was more faithful than the Sodomites but despite the fact that he was so stupid and because he was Abraham's nephew.[131] Ephraimites who moved to Judah may have done so because they responded to Yhwh's word, but on the whole Judeans who were preserved in Babylon were not people who had been any more faithful than Judeans who perished in Jerusalem. So is the declaration that there is new wine in the cluster a response to something visible that the vinedresser is ignoring, or is it a statement of faith about what might be possible?

When Isaiah 65:8-10 interprets the earlier allegory, the new wine or the blessing are explicated in several different ways. They are "my servants." Does that mean they are people who actually serve Yhwh or people who are destined to do so or people Yhwh cannot abandon because they have this status? They are "my chosen ones." Is that because this is the way Yhwh exercised the right of choice in relation to Jacob/Judah centuries ago or because they are choice people? The last phrase that describes them encapsulates the question: they are "my people who have sought help from me" (dāraš). Is God's commitment based on the fact that they are "my people," the people with whom Yhwh long ago entered into a relationship, or is it based on the fact that they (will) have "sought help from me"? As usual, one cannot answer these questions, and that preserves significant theological truths that may be best expressed as negatives. Yhwh does not destroy Israel as a whole, though exempting some people does not issue simply from their deserve but from Yhwh's longstanding commitment to this people. But it does not happen separately from Yhwh's intention to have a vine that produces fruit, and it does not happen without this people's response in seeking Yhwh.

The terms that describe the exempted group are ones that belong to Israel as a whole. The leftovers are not only "my servants" and "my chosen ones," expressions that can apply to a group within Israel, but "my people." The implication is not necessarily that there is a group within the community that can see itself as Yhwh's people, Yhwh's chosen ones and Yhwh's servants, over against the people as a whole who cannot. It is that a group aware of having been exempted from a disaster that has overcome the people as a whole can see itself as the seed of a new people. It survives not on the basis of its superior commitment but in response to someone else's prayer for mercy. And its survival implies a call to people to commit themselves to seeking help from Yhwh in the future rather than having recourse to other deities. But insofar as people who hear this message live in a context where people do not have recourse to Yhwh, it calls

---

[131]2 Pet 2:7 tweaks the story in another direction, to make another point; my comment is based on the Genesis version.

them to do so now. Then the vinedresser's friend may have a basis for bidding the vinedresser to reckon with the possibility that there might still be a blessing in the vine and/or in order that Yhwh's exempting of them may be fulfilled.

The prophet goes on to warn people who have recourse to deities other than Yhwh: they will hunger, thirst, be shamed and howl, and *their* names will become a standard for cursing. The people who are not liable to these calamities are "my servants." Previously in Isaiah 40—66 "my servant" and then "my servants" have been terms for the community as a whole. Here once again that term, along with "my chosen ones," is a term for the people within the Judean community who really belong to Yhwh, as evaluated by whether they actually serve Yhwh as opposed to serving other deities as well as Yhwh. While Yhwh treasures the idea that the people as a whole is the servant or are the servants, realism also requires the recognition that for all the effort to implement this vision, it does not work.

So calamity is not a fate that hangs over the community as a whole but one that hangs over people who choose not to give exclusive service to Yhwh. Jesus takes up both the expectation that calamity will come on the city as a whole (e.g., Lk 19:41-44) and the expectation that God will bring about a judgment that discriminates between the faithful and the faithless (e.g., Mt 25:31-46). But he implies that the former will be a this-worldly reality, the latter a feature of the End, and this realistically takes account of how things are in current human experience, where calamity tends to engulf the innocent as well as the guilty. But here, the calamity will leave a pared-down community in the land, all of whom bless themselves and swear their oaths only by the true God. On the other hand, as usual one point of the prophecy will be to falsify itself as people who do have recourse to other spiritual resources are frightened into turning back from that and giving exclusive allegiance to "the true God, "the God of ʾāmēn." That means not the real God as opposed to gods that do not really exist, but the trustworthy God, the God who can be relied on, as opposed to deities that exist but cannot be trusted to deliver what we call on them for.

◆ ◆ ◆

The Church and the Nightmare

Karl Barth speaks of Israel as the form of the elect people of God that delivers its witness by resisting its election, whereas the church is the form of that elect people of God that is called on the basis of its election.[132] The church (Jewish

---

[132]*Church Dogmatics*, II/2:195-305. Parenthetical references in this section give page numbers in *Church Dogmatics*, II/2.

and Gentile) is "the perfect form of the elected community of God," because it witnesses to God's mercy (p. 211). Barth argues this in large part on the basis on an exposition of Romans 9—11. On the basis of the First Testament, the formulation does not work. This is not only because Christ has not yet come but also because there Israel's resistance to its election is not the last word. It is not the case that "according to the witness of the Old Testament, the wrath of God apparently opposes His love as an independent and apparently even the definitive direction of the divine will for the people of Israel," that "every promise stands from the outset in the shadow of the much more impressive menace" (p. 420). That is not true of the self-revelation in Exodus 34, nor of the plot of the First Testament story, nor (least of all) in the Prophets.

But the formulation is suggestive with regard to the positive theological significance of Israel's turning from Yhwh. Here "Israel precedes the Church in confessing human unwillingness, incapacity and unworthiness in face of the divine love and in praising the sole sufficiency of the divine mercy" (pp. 200-201). In Romans 9—11 Paul will see a positive theological significance in the rejection of Jesus by the Israel of his day; indeed, it is something God willed, something out of which God purposed to generate much fruit. Israel's resistance to Yhwh in First Testament times has similar significance. "Israel is the community of God in so far as the Word of God's grace reaches it," but its witness to this word is not dependent on its accepting it (pp. 233, 234). Jewish obduracy contains more gospel than all the unbelieving wisdom of the Gentile world put together (p. 236). "The meaning of its election is that in the very act of becoming guilty towards God it must genuinely magnify His faithfulness" (p. 259). Its service is "to reflect the judgment from which God has rescued man and which He wills to endure Himself in the person of Jesus of Nazareth" (p. 206). Thus Israel plays a part in God's purpose to be in relationship with the world whether it is responsive and enjoys God's blessing or unresponsive and becomes a "vessel of wrath." Either way it fulfills a role in the pursuance of God's purpose to have mercy on all. If God's hardening of Israel's heart lies behind its unresponsiveness, even that forms part of God's purpose to have mercy on all.[133] "God does not wait till Israel is obedient before employing it in His service." It serves God whether obedient or disobedient (p. 207).

We noted at the end of chapter three that it can hardly be the case that the church has taken the Jewish people's place as God's chosen people. Rather, the church is a vast expansion of that chosen people that has Israel as its core. The dynamics of Israel's relationship with God then reappear in the church, as Paul presupposes in 1 Corinthians 10 and Romans 11. The church can see the

---

[133]See Barth's exposition of Rom 9—11 in ibid., II/2:195-305.

nightmare embodied in its life and experience. It too is characterized by faithlessness. It too knows the kind of consequences described in section 4.2, embodied in the demise of the church around the eastern Mediterranean and north Africa in the first millennium, and then in the demise of the church in Europe in the second millennium, and now in the demise that is in process of the church in the United States in the third millennium. For the last, the possibility of forestalling the nightmare is still open, as it was for Ephraim in Amos's day or for Judah in Jeremiah's. For the former two (and for the church in the U.S.A. if it does not turn), then God's persistence keeps leftovers in existence and promises that there might yet be a blessing in it.

5

THE VISION

Although narrative is constitutive of Israel's faith, it was not and perhaps could never be all there was to it. The presupposition of the narrative is that Yhwh has started on a project with Israel, a project that is yet unfinished, and Israel needed a vision of what God would do in the future as well as an awareness of what God had done in the past. The narrative itself could incorporate indications of its authors' hopes, and Genesis is explicit in the way it sees Israelite faith as lived in the conviction that Yhwh had a purpose in mind for the world and for the people and was committed to taking them there. But when Israelite authors really wished to focus on the future, it would not be in narratives that they expressed these hopes, but in prophecy or apocalypse. By their nature, narratives do not tell us directly or explicitly the hopes of their authors and hearers; these will remain matters of inference and of irresolvable argument about whether or not, for example, Chronicles' account of David implies a hope for the reestablishment of the Davidic monarchy. It is the nature of prophecy to make promise (or warning) explicit.

Israel would have needed a vision even if there had never been a nightmare. Certainly the First Testament's nightmare could hardly be the sum total of its perspective on the future. Alongside it is thus set its positive vision. Once Israel has the nightmare in its perspective, the vision has to take account of it, whether or not the nightmare has yet come true. Many articulations of the vision thus presuppose a hopeless situation. Indeed, "one can scarcely imagine the revolution in thinking that must have been necessary for exilic Israel to envision a hope for the future. . . . The terror of losing all the foundations and structures for social identity and religious vision is scarcely comprehensible."[1] The nature of a vision or dream is to offer symbols to the imagination, and thus to inspire hope in a situation in which newness is unthinkable.[2] It is not to create new symbols (an oxymoron?) but to enable the community to own again the symbols that it knows but is afraid to trust.

Eschatology has often seemed an appendix to Christian faith, without integral relationship to its central doctrines and with little integral relationship

---

[1]Gordon H. Matties, *Ezekiel 18 and the Rhetoric of Moral Discourse*, SBLDS 126 (Atlanta, Ga.: Scholars Press, 1990), pp. 110, 219.

[2]Cf. Walter Brueggemann, *The Prophetic Imagination* (Philadelphia: Fortress, 1978/London: SCM Press, 1992), p. 66.

to Christian life. It makes little difference to life. But looking for the consummation of the divine purpose embodied in cross and resurrection is at the heart of Christian faith. First Testament faith likewise does not flee the world but does strain after the future.[3] In light of the way Yhwh's promises have been fulfilled in the past, it looks to their being fulfilled again in the future. (But I generally avoid words beginning *eschato-* because they are used in enormously varying ways and give a false impression of precision in theological thinking.)[4]

5.1 Hope and Its Bases

Hope lies in Yhwh. It lies in Yhwh's longstanding and present purpose and intention, in Yhwh's honor, grace and compassion, in Yhwh's holiness and rights over Israel, in Yhwh's return to the people and Yhwh's insistence on reigning in its life and in its world.

Hope in Yhwh

The English word *hope* is both an objective word and a subjective word. It refers both to the promise of a positive future and to people's attitude as they look to such a possibility. In the First Testament, the noun "hope" *(tiqwâ)* is usually objective. "Hope is almost always *'hope for . . .'*"[5] Yhwh declares that "there is hope for your future" (Jer 31:17). Yhwh is committed to giving the people "a future and a hope," a future with hope, a hopeful future, a positive future (Jer 29:11). Indeed, Yhwh *is* Israel's hope (Jer 14:8). When the exiles declare that "our hope has perished" they do so in the midst of declaring that "our bones are dried up" (i.e., our life and strength are quite gone) and "we are completely cut down" (like trees felled by a storm) (Ezek 37:11). They are thus not talking about *feeling* hopeless but about *being* hopeless. They have no future.

On the other hand, the verb "hope" *(qāwâ,* usually piel) refers to the attitude of anticipation that people may show as they look to the future. There is again some difference from the way English uses the word. The Hebrew verb denotes expectancy, an attitude that believes something good is to happen and looks for it, rather than a longing for something good while lacking any grounds for a conviction that this good will come. We could hypothesize a link between the meaning of the noun and the meaning of the verb: because people

---

[3]Cf. Jürgen Moltmann, *Theology of Hope* (London: SCM Press, 1967), pp. 15-16, 19.

[4]Cf., e.g., Yair Hoffman, "Eschatology in the Book of Jeremiah," in *Eschatology in the Bible and in Jewish and Christian Tradition,* ed. Henning Graf Reventlow, JSOTSup 243 (Sheffield: Sheffield Academic Press, 1997), pp. 75-97; see pp. 75-79.

[5]Rolf P. Knierim, *The Task of Old Testament Theology* (Grand Rapids/Cambridge: Eerdmans, 1995), p. 248.

have hope (that is, because there is to be a positive future), they can hope (look forward to the future expectantly).

The way English uses the word corresponds more to the use of *hope* in classical Greek, as Barth describes it. There it denotes an optimistic attitude based on the content of a human expectation for the future. From that notion "there is no bridge to the hope of Old and New Testaments." That hope is not based on human prognoses but on "that which in virtue of His self-declaration the God of Israel was and is and will be and mean and do in the history of this people," with its implications for the people and the individual. Thus the First Testament's only warnings about hope concern the danger of putting it on the wrong basis.[6] Jeremiah, for instance, never uses the verb positively (Jer 8:15; 13:16; 14:19, 22). People have hopes that are false, expectations for which they assume they have grounds, but they are wrong. Yhwh shares that experience (Is 5:2, 4, 7). But when the hope *is* objective, the future guaranteed by Yhwh's word, then people's attitude can be expectancy and not merely longing. Hope will then not be shamed (Is 49:23). When Lamentations declares that "Yhwh is good to people who hope for him" (Lam 3:25), it is not implying that hopefulness is what makes a positive future possible but that the certainty of a positive future is what makes hopefulness possible. It is because of this that hopefulness issues in renewed strength now (Is 40:31). So, says Hosea, "you must turn to Yhwh your God, keep *ḥesed* and *mišpāṭ*, and hope in your God continually" (Hos 12:6 [MT 7]). Hosea may mean they need to hope persistently for Yhwh's eventual act of restoration or that the dialectic between hope and fulfillment is an ongoing characteristic of the life of Yhwh's people, alongside *ḥesed* and *mišpāṭ*.

Yhwh's Longstanding Purpose

Wondering about the possibility of there being a future for Judah, Jeremiah declares, "Oh, Lord, Yhwh! Yes—you yourself made the heavens and the earth by your great might and your extended arm! Nothing is too marvelous for you!" (Jer 32:17). "Creation itself is a sign and measure of Yahweh's capacity to do beyond what the world thinks is possible."[7] Indeed, arguably the starting point for the First Testament's hope and vision is the creation story. It assumes that Yhwh is still committed to realizing the vision of which that story speaks.

A forward orientation is thus integral to Israel's faith from the beginning of the First Testament story. Yhwh lays before Israel's ancestors promises about a move to becoming a great people who inhabit their own land and evidence

---

[6]So Karl Barth, *Church Dogmatics* (Edinburgh: T & T Clark, 1936-1969), IV/3.ii:908.

[7]Walter Brueggemann, "Jeremiah: *Creatio in Extremis*," in *God Who Creates*, ed. William P. Brown and S. Dean McBride (Grand Rapids, Mich.: Eerdmans, 2000), pp. 152-70; p. 165.

how great it is to be the recipients of Yhwh's blessing. Then, from the exodus onward Israel's confessions of hope can be based in God's acts in the past. "They all, without exception, fell back on the long history of the mighty acts of Yahweh, on the experience of Yahweh's presence in Israel's midst, and on his words of promise. . . . Hope depends on future fulfillment, but its rationale is grounded in past experience."[8]

Such forward orientation gains extra significance in light of the nightmare that Yhwh later holds before Israel. The vision becomes the other side of that nightmare. According to the prophets, Yhwh's promises for the future are then expressed in at least three sorts of contexts. Before calamity actually happens, they set warnings about calamity in the wider context of Yhwh's purpose for Israel and for the world, to discourage anyone from thinking that the fall of Ephraim or the fall of Judah will be Yhwh's last word. Second, when these events have happened, these same promises bring encouragement to people on whom calamity has fallen. These people may not themselves see the restoration, but the promises make it possible for them to see their experience in that broader setting. The third context is the time when the community has experienced some fulfillment of those promises, but nothing as splendid as the promises presaged. Yhwh then reaffirms them and reassures people that it is not over until it is over. The expression "in that day" often marks such promises, owning a contrast between the disappointment of current experience and the purpose of Yhwh that still stands. Further, the reaction to such disappointment is often to paint those promises in more glorious Technicolor, so that the transformation Yhwh will bring about becomes more creative and more extraordinary.

Sometimes these hopes simply concern a freedom to live ordinary life in the land, enjoying good harvests and peace with other peoples. Sometimes they suggest a new kind of life lived on a whole new basis, with Israel enjoying a new position in the world and with the natural order transformed. Sometimes they come to imply that the coming event belongs to a far-off day rather than one that people have reason to think might be imminent. It is doubtful if the First Testament ever thinks in terms of a coming event that will bring an end after which an "after" can hardly be imagined. Nor does it suggest that life will recommence on another plane or in another world, in heaven rather than on earth. This world is the wonderful home God has given us.

Yhwh's Grace and Compassion

From the beginning, then, waiting was integral to Israel's faith, but the pros-

---

[8]Knierim, *Task of OT Theology*, pp. 252-53.

pect of the nightmare coming true introduces a moment of more equivocal waiting. There is waiting involved on both sides. Yhwh is waiting, in a more negative sense than was the case in Isaiah 5, though with a contrasting certainty that the waiting will see a happy ending. Yhwh is now waiting to be gracious to Israel (Is 30:18-19).[9] But (Isaiah affirms), "he will arise to have compassion on you," so that the people who wait for him have grounds for encouragement. "He will definitely show you grace at the sound of your cry." Even in the midst of decimating and scattering them, Yhwh will not let them go (*rāpâ* hiphil) or destroy them, "because Yhwh your God is a compassionate God" (Deut 4:31). One might have thought that the decimation and the scattering were the end of the relationship, but that cannot be so because Yhwh is still the compassionate God who cannot resist people when they turn back or even when they do not. Yhwh will not let them go, will not let them alone, leave them on their own. Yhwh will not finally destroy them. Yhwh will not put the covenant out of mind. Yhwh cannot go back on a promise.

There are two senses in which Israel's relationship with Yhwh depends on grace. Grace was the original basis of the relationship. There was nothing special to commend aged Abraham and infertile Sarah to Yhwh, nor anything to commend Israel, such as its numbers or its capacity for faithfulness; Yhwh's attachment to Israel emerged from reasons within Yhwh rather than within Israel (e.g., Deut 7:7-8; 9:4-6). But now, the faithlessness and the nightmare mean that Israel's destiny is dependent on Yhwh's grace in a new sense. The demonstration of grace after the nightmare will not happen straightaway. Perhaps it may be delayed to show it is not cheap; forgiveness costs Yhwh something. Yhwh has to safeguard against the idea that faithlessness does not really matter or that Israel is not really called to responsibility for itself. But grace will definitely and necessarily come. Isaiah uses the infinitive absolute construction to emphasize the point: literally, "[in] showing grace he will show grace to you." Perhaps that means "he will show great grace to you."

This grace will express itself in compassion. That does not merely mean that Yhwh shows sympathy for the people. Yhwh is not merely someone who comes alongside people and comforts them *in* their affliction, but someone who removes the causes of affliction. "Comfort" can itself refer both to action that restores and strengthens and to words that do so. Logically, the second depends on the first, even if in Isaiah the classic references to this comfort come in the opposite order. Isaiah 40—55 begins with Yhwh commissioning aides to comfort the people and to encourage Jerusalem (Is 40:1-2). But the implicit basis of that message of comfort is the fact that "Yhwh is comforting his people,

---

[9]On Is 30:18 see section 4.3 "Last-Minute Deliverance" and "Yhwh Waits."

restoring Jerusalem" (Is 52:9); the verbs there are qatal, suggesting a future act that has as good as happened and is therefore grounds for strongly comforting words in the present.

The compassionate one is someone who has authority in the world and is therefore in a position to act in the world. "Yhwh is a God of *mišpāṭ*," and therefore in the future "you will not weep at all" (Is 30:18-19). Isaiah uses the same grammatical idiom to emphasize the point: literally, "[in] weeping you will not weep." Admittedly he goes on to qualify this promise slightly by implying that they might have cause to weep; at least, they will have reason to cry out in hurt *(za ʿāqâ)* as they did in Egypt. Perhaps therefore the implication is that they will not weep and receive no response and thus find themselves continuing to weep. Restoration does not mean life becomes problem free but that problems get solved. Grace lies not in being protected from the need to cry out but in finding that Yhwh listens to the people's cry and answers "as soon as he hears it" (the preposition is *k* rather than *b*).

When the community prays for God's mercy (e.g., Neh 9), implicitly it pleads for Yhwh's consistency of compassion and grace to overcome the people's consistency of faithlessness, so that the pattern of grace, sin, loss and restoration may never falter at the third stage.

Yhwh's Light

Yhwh gives Israel concrete hopes, such as promises concerning the return of exiles to the land, the rebuilding of Jerusalem, the restoration of the monarchy and the rebuilding of the temple. But these are accompanied by more all-embracing promises expressed in images that reach into the people's spirits. The image of light shining is one of these. After giving the most solemn account of the gloom and darkness for which people are destined (Is 8:21-22), Isaiah reverses the picture (Is 9:2-5 [MT 1-4]). "The people walking in darkness have seen a great light."

Darkness and light are images not for ignorance and revelation nor for wrongdoing and right doing, but for calamity and blessing. Darkness suggests gloom, distress and anguish. Light suggests brightness, well-being and happiness. Here Isaiah spells out the significance of light in terms of increase that replaces decimation and joy that replaces misery. It is the kind of joy people have when they know that a good harvest means they will have food to eat for the next year or when they know they will get something back for the time, effort and risk they have put into a battle. That image is an ironic one because Isaiah goes on to talk about war, but without explicitly speaking of anyone fighting a regular battle. The people's distress and darkness come from oppression by enemies of the kind they experienced in the time of the "judges," so that the replacement of darkness by light requires their liberation from these oppressors, a liberation like that in Gideon's day (see Judg 6—8). The promise thus puts the emphasis on the extraordinary wonder of the deliverance. While Gideon and his army played a part in the victory, they did so by means of a silly stratagem involving trumpets, jars and torches, and they were helped by the Midianites' being terrified by a dream about a loaf of bread and then by their capacity for turning on each other in their panic. Whether Israel plays a role in this new deliverance or not, it will not be the decisive role. It will again be God who does the shattering and sees to the burning of the weapons of war.

In the modern world the destruction of the accoutrements of battle sounds a wonderful note, and we may thus read more into it than is there. Isaiah may have in mind only the destruction of the oppressors' boots and battledress, the sign that the threat they represent is thoroughly disposed of. Yet the placing of the oracle in a segment of the book that moves away from historical references toward a more ultimate horizon gives it more radical implications. The oppressor comes to stand for all oppressors, and if all oppressors have their battledress destroyed, there will be no need for Israel to have any. The implications of this vision are then not so different from those of Isaiah 2:2-4. That is supported by subsequent references to Yhwh as a prince of *shalom* and to the birth or enthronement of a new king, which will herald the coming of endless *shalom* on David's throne (Is 9:6-7 [MT 5-6]).[10] That *shalom* is hardly confined to peace; it suggests the broadest well-being. But neither can it exclude peace.

Yhwh's Horror

Jeremiah kept insisting that the prophets who promised *shalom* did so falsely, and eventually he was proved right; the time when "there is no *shalom*" arrived (Jer 30:5). The good news starts with the fact that the person who is acknowledging this with horror is Yhwh, who (with the rest of the heavenly cabinet) is aghast at the panicked cry and terrified look of the people who have been overwhelmed by disaster.

Which disaster is this? One may certainly see it embodied in the fall of Jerusalem in 587, though the context in Jeremiah invites us to look at the imagery more broadly. At this stage in the book the fall of Jerusalem has not yet happened, and the oracle recalls Jeremiah's own earlier anticipatory horror at coming disaster (Jer 4:23-26) as well as previous expressions of horror at earlier disasters. Further, the setting relates the oracle to both Israel and Judah (Jer 30:4). All this invites us to see Yhwh's horror as a visionary reaction to any one of the many calamities that have characterized the whole people's story. The

---

[10]See section 5.7, where I also discuss the context and background of the passage.

disaster envisaged counts as the very Day of Yhwh, a day Yhwh brought about, yet although Yhwh is the one who has generated these calamities as responses to the people's faithlessness and seems to have no regrets about that, this does not stop Yhwh being distraught at them. And thus it also does not make Yhwh content to leave the people to drown in their suffering. It makes Yhwh declare that "that day," an unprecedented "time of distress" for Jacob, will be succeeded by a another "that day," a day of deliverance (Jer 30:7-8). Service to Babylon will be replaced by service to Yhwh and to David. The people's current experience is like a reversion to servitude in Egypt, and Yhwh's deliverance will be like a new exodus. And a key stimulus to that act is the fact that Yhwh is personally affected by the people's distress, as had been the case when their cry rose to Yhwh in Egypt. Their distress does not mean they can do anything about the situation; it may even disable them more. Yhwh's horror means Yhwh does so act.

Yhwh goes on to speak to Jerusalem itself in similar terms, again indicating the divine horror at its suffering (Jer 30:12-15). Yhwh's words recall the speech of the Psalms and may take up the motifs of the people's prayers. In anticipation (within the structure of Jeremiah) they lament the suffering that the fall of Jerusalem has brought upon them, the lack of any way of treating their wounds, the way their allies have abandoned them, and the terrible fact that Yhwh, too, has abandoned them rather than acting as their shepherd and seeking them out. Indeed, Yhwh seems to have brought about their suffering. Yes, says Yhwh, that is all true, including the suggestion that I abandoned you and brought about your suffering. But there was good reason for that. You have no grounds for crying out in the manner of Israel in Egypt (*zāʿaq;* cf. Ex 2:23) as if you do not deserve what has happened. You deserve everything.

The situation looks hopeless. But a hugely illogical "therefore" follows, a "therefore" that follows the logic of election (Jer 30:16-17):[11] "Therefore all your devourers will be devoured, all your foes, every one of them, will go into captivity," and your plunderers will become plunder, "for I will bring about recovery for you and heal you of your wounds." The agents of Yhwh's punishment will become the recipients of that punishment. They called you an outcast, Yhwh adds, someone whom nobody (no shepherd) seeks out; this final "for" provides some retrospective explanation for the illogical "therefore."[12] And the one who hurt will become the one who heals. At one level

---

[11]For other such illogical "therefores" see, e.g., Jer 15:19; 16:14. See Theodore M. Ludwig, "The Shape of Hope," *Concordia Theological Monthly* 39 (1968): 526-41; see pp. 534-35.

[12]Cf. Walter Brueggemann, "The 'Uncared For' Now Cared For," in *Old Testament Theology: Essays on Structure, Theme, and Text* (Minneapolis: Fortress, 1992), pp. 296-307; see p. 301.

Yhwh denies the logic of their prayers: there is nothing inappropriate about what has happened to them. At a deeper level Yhwh accepts the logic. Yhwh cannot resist the plea for healing.

Yhwh's Intention

Jerusalem is about to fall and Jeremiah is in prison. It is a bleak moment for the city and the prophet. As the city falls, the prophet might expect to lose his life to his own people as a last act of helpless and pointless anger against the prophet who had said this would happen and thereby made it happen. At this moment, Yhwh's word comes to him (Jer 33:2-3). Yhwh speaks as the one who is "making it" and "shaping it," as the one who shapes and establishes Judah's destiny. In the immediate future this means bringing about the calamity that is coming on Judah, but Jeremiah goes on to speak of the people's restoration, which suggests that its entire destiny is in mind here. Yhwh goes on to invite Jeremiah, "Call to me and I will answer you and I will tell you great things, things that are fenced off, which you do not know."

Yhwh has a plan for the future, and invites Jeremiah to look to Yhwh for insight on what the plan might be. The call that Yhwh invites is not a call for help but a call for revelation; the answer will come in the form of Yhwh's telling the prophet about things. These can be "great things"; Jeremiah may ask big questions about Israel's future. The questions can concern matters that are "fenced off." By its nature the whole of the future is barricaded and off limits. Only Yhwh has access to it, because it issues from Yhwh's will, so neither Jeremiah nor anyone else knows what it will be.

The invitation to ask about all this suggests something paradoxical in the relationship between God and prophet. Revelation may come because Yhwh takes the initiative, as happened at the beginning of Jeremiah's ministry, when he did not welcome Yhwh's initiative (Jer 1). It may come because the prophet takes the initiative in asking a question, as Jeremiah has done, though not necessarily getting a very satisfactory answer (e.g., Jer 12). Or it may come because Yhwh invites the prophet to ask a question and the prophet does so, as Yhwh invited Solomon to ask for whatever gift he wanted (1 Kings 3:5) or Isaiah invited Ahaz to ask for a sign (Is 7:11). The relation between God and prophet involves different forms of interaction, including God's saying "I make myself available to you; you decide the agenda."

In a sense it is nevertheless an odd invitation, for Yhwh long ago revealed to Jeremiah how the future will unfold, in its negative and its positive aspects. So why the invitation? There might be several related reasons. One is that being told about this long ago is one thing; having Yhwh speak about it now is another. A second is that knowing the principle about nightmare and vision is one thing, but knowing how it applies in a particular context is another. A third is that the basic idea is one thing, but having a more concrete picture of that is another.

The picture of the future that follows (Jer 33:4-9) perhaps implicitly issued from Jeremiah's responding to Yhwh's invitation. It begins by underlining the horrific nature of the scene in the city as the houses of the royalty and of the ordinary people have been pulled down to strengthen the defenses, and they (?) have become the tombs of people who have already died in the siege. Destruction, death and defilement are the realities of the scene even before the city's actual fall. Worse, these are not merely the signs of war or natural disaster. It is not merely Babylonian missiles that are hitting the fabric and the people of Jerusalem. Yhwh is hitting them. Yhwh is the shaper of the disaster that issues from Yhwh's furious anger and from the turning away of Yhwh's face, which means, for instance, that Yhwh is not listening to the people when they beg for mercy. But recovery and healing will also issue from Yhwh, to whom the city will (once more) be a name to rejoice over. Further, the structure of the oracle is significant. That account of the horror of the city's fall features only in its preamble; Yhwh's actual message concerns "relief and healing" for the city.[13] So the rhetoric also suggests that while both disaster and restoration come from Yhwh, the latter is more important to Yhwh. Yhwh "makes" the future, the bad but even more the good. That means Yhwh "shapes" it (yāṣar): the word describes the work of a potter, but then denotes the shaping of a plan in the mind of human beings or God. It also means Yhwh "establishes" it (kûn hiphil), that is, implements the plan (Jer 33:2).

Yhwh's Holiness

Toward the end of the most trenchant denunciation of the people in Isaiah 40—55 Yhwh declares, "for the sake of my name I will delay my anger, for the sake of my praise I muzzle it for you, so that I do not cut you off" (Is 48:9). One might have thought that the preceding denunciation would lead in to a declaration that Yhwh is now casting the people off, but it fails to do so. The people's recalcitrance makes Yhwh angry, but Yhwh is prepared to keep muzzling that fury and not give in to the instinct to cut the people off, "for the sake of my name . . . for the sake of my praise"; "for my own sake, for my own sake," Yhwh repeats, so that "my splendor" should not be profaned (Is 48:11). Yhwh is caught. Getting involved with Israel makes it impossible to abandon Israel. It would make Yhwh look really stupid or really incompetent, and neither of these would be a good idea. Paradoxically, there lies a deep security for Israel in the fact that its position is protected by the needs of Yhwh's reputation

---

[13]Cf. JPSV; contrast NRSV and NIVI.

rather than some less fundamental consideration. It may not be flattering, but it is a bottom line.

Paradoxically, Israel's future is secure because Israel exists for Yhwh's sake and not just for its own sake. Israel cannot get away from Yhwh. Sometimes it insists on being just like the other nations, not only in having the same form of government but "in ministering to wood and stone." That really arouses Yhwh's fury and insistence on reigning over Israel, on being the only one Israel serves. And so Yhwh will bring Israel out from its exile among these other nations (a convenient location for worshiping other gods, though Israel did find Canaan quite a convenient place to do so), and will do that in fury as Yhwh took the people off into exile in fury (this is a God consumed by rage) in order "in the wilderness of the peoples" to determine its future and "make you pass under the staff and bring you into the bond of the covenant. . . . And you will acknowledge that I am Yhwh" (Ezek 20:32-38).

In Saul's day Israel wanted to be like other peoples in its form of government, and Yhwh still has mixed feeling about that, as Ezekiel's use of the language of kingship reflects; here it is *Yhwh* who will reign over the people. But in subsequent centuries Israel has wanted to be like other peoples in its religion, and the exile gives it the chance to do that. It has escaped from Yhwh and from the land of Israel, and among the nations it can live the same way as they do. But Yhwh will not accept this. Yhwh will still not adapt to it, at least in regard to the use of images. Yet Yhwh's response is not therefore simply to let Israel go and to start with a different people but to insist on maintaining the relationship. The reason is the fact that this would bring discredit on Yhwh (Ezek 20:9, 14, 22). Yhwh's fury is Israel's good news, as it had been in Egypt, even though now it is Israel that is the object of that fury. In a "vehement assertion of the irrevocability of God's election,"[14] Yhwh refuses to be defied, and is set on imposing a new exodus on the people. It will lead to a new gathering in the wilderness and a new census to make sure everyone is there (it will be like a shepherd counting sheep as they pass under the shepherd's staff). There Yhwh will impose a new covenant obligation on the people (there is not much implication that they will be asked whether they want to commit themselves to this covenant, as they were at Sinai). There will be a new purging of the wilderness generation, so that rebels again experience the exodus, but not the entry into the land. Thus in the future in the land itself "my holy name you will no more profane with your gifts and your pillars. For on my holy mountain . . . the whole household of Israel, all of it, will serve me in the land. . . . As a pleasing fragrance I will accept you when I bring you out from the peoples

---

[14]Moshe Greenberg, *Ezekiel 1—20*, AB (Garden City, N.Y.: Doubleday, 1983), p. 386.

and gather you from the countries where you are scattered and show my holiness among you in the sight of the nations" (Ezek 20:39-41).

The issue is Yhwh's holiness, Yhwh's deity. Both Testaments use the expression "holy people" rather infrequently. The effect is to put the focus on the Holy One.[15] That deity is currently compromised by the way Israel worships. Israel follows the ways of other peoples and thereby confuses the distinction between Yhwh and other deities. It is also compromised by Yhwh's chastisement of the people, which implies failing to complete the self-set and self-announced task of self-revelation through Israel. If Yhwh were simply to abandon Israel and acknowledge a final inability to succeed with that task that Yhwh had begun, this would further compromise it. So Yhwh intends one way or another to achieve the original aim, to take a purged Israel back in the land and get them worshiping properly there. Thus Yhwh's holiness will be manifested in Yhwh's bringing Israel back to its land, and on Yhwh's holy mountain Yhwh's holy name will not be profaned by Israel's offering the kind of gifts in the kind of way that compromises Yhwh's holiness. The offerings they bring will be holy, worthy of the one to whom they are offered. And therefore they will be like a fragrance that delights Yhwh. That implies a contrast with the present, when they let off a disgusting odor.

Paul's argument in Romans 9—11 is in keeping with these. It is impossible to imagine these prophets, any more than Paul yielding to Christian "supersessionism," the view that the church is a new Israel that has replaced the old. Yhwh would not accept such a denigrating of the divine holiness. "In doing what He does for His own sake, He does it, in fact, *propter nos homines et propter nostram salutem* [for us human beings and for our salvation]."[16]

Yhwh's Return

God is the one "who is, and who was, and who is to come" (Rev 1:4)—not merely "who will be." "God's future is not that he will be as he was and is, but that he is on the move and coming towards the world. God's being is in his coming, not in his becoming," which will mean "the establishment of his eternal kingdom, and his indwelling in the creation renewed for that indwelling." Thus "*the God of hope* is himself *the coming God* (Isa. 35.4; 40.5)." And the coming of God's kingdom or reign is the coming of God in person as king.[17]

Specifically, the God of hope is the God who comes back. The most terrible element in the nightmare is Yhwh's abandonment of Israel. The crucial center of any vision for the future must be Yhwh's return. This theme emerges espe-

---

[15]Barth, *Church Dogmatics*, IV/2:511-13.
[16]From the Nicene Creed; Barth, *Church Dogmatics*, IV/1:212.
[17]Jürgen Moltmann, *The Coming of God* (London: SCM Press, 1996), pp. 23-24.

cially clearly in Ezekiel, the prophet who speaks most vividly about Yhwh's leaving the city (see esp. Ezek 11:22-23).[18]

Isaiah 35 overwhelms by its imagery: desert blooming, lame jumping like deer, waters bursting forth in the wilderness, sorrows and sighs fleeing. What arouses such reactions? It is the coming of Yhwh. When Yhwh's majestic splendor (*kābôd* and *hādār*) passes by and the desert sees it (unlike Moses), it will respond by blossoming, so that it comes to look more like the forests of Lebanon, the orchards of Carmel and the flowers of Sharon. After rain, the desert can blossom and flourish with some speed, and this blooming is like that blooming writ large. It is as if Yhwh's splendor calls forth from the desert a responsive splendor. It will put on such fine clothes, it will be as if is full of joy, like human beings dressed in their finery for an occasion such as a wedding.

Yhwh's splendor suggests Yhwh in person, in all the wonder that attaches to that person (Is 35:2). Paradoxically, the expression "Yhwh's splendor" both emphasizes the majestic and overwhelming nature of Yhwh and also safeguards against the danger of it. To have Yhwh appear in person would surely devastate anyone who was there, like looking at the sun, so that the presence of "only" Yhwh's splendor is like that of "only" Yhwh's face or hand or arm or name or goodness; it is something less than the entirety of Yhwh's presence, something that will not electrocute humanity. Yet speaking of the presence of Yhwh's *splendor* all but removes the safeguards, given that by its nature splendor dazzles and overwhelms. It was such a presence that Israel once knew in the temple, a reason for priests discretely to withdraw.

But how will the desert see Yhwh's splendor? What is Yhwh's splendor doing there? What follows begins to indicate that, and the passage will come back to the image of the transforming of the wilderness, but in the meantime it sharpens the question by leaping in another direction in order to come at the phenomena from another angle. "There is your God," the prophet shouts. Human beings join nature in witnessing the coming of God in splendor. The human beings are people whose hands have fallen limp, people who have difficulty putting one foot in front of another any more, people whose hearts pound. The chapter will eventually make clear that they are not a subgroup within a larger entity whose members generally are in good health with good morale. They stand for a community as a whole, the Judean community in Babylon destined to return to Palestine, but currently downcast and hopeless. The imperatives are plural, so presumably this is an exhortation to the people themselves to strengthen their own weak hands, firm up their own shaky

---

[18]John Kutsko (*Between Heaven and Earth: Divine Presence and Absence in the Book of Ezekiel* [Winona Lake, Ind.: Eisenbrauns, 2000], p. 23) calls the presence and absence of God "a central paradox for the prophet."

knees and encourage themselves (Is 35:3-4). Fortunately it is not merely an invitation to pull themselves up by their bootstraps, a bare exhortation to pull themselves together. They can be encouraged in that direction by the same factor that leads the wilderness spontaneously to burst with cedar and fig and crocus. "There is your God!"

Yhwh abandoned Judah in 587. One could picture that in terms of the people being thrown out of Yhwh's land or of Yhwh leaving the land, but either way the children and the parent are no longer living in the same house. Indeed, the children have had to settle for a rather inferior position in another house where they have no familial rights and no assured future, and where they are under house arrest. They are entitled to weak hands, feeble knees and pounding hearts. But their God is coming. The house arrest will not continue. Yhwh is coming to assert authority over their jailers and put them in their place so as to do the right thing by the weak and discouraged in delivering them.

The exiles are weak, needy and thirsty people. Their weakness, need and thirst are not merely physical. Indeed, in Babylon they were probably not physical at all. Like Jewish people and other ethnic minorities in many countries in the modern world, they had not merely survived but done quite well, outwardly. But in their spirits the situation was different. It was there that they hungered and thirsted as they feared that their God was dead or had abandoned them forever. The prophet declares that Yhwh is not turning a deaf ear to their prayers but is about to bring about a transformation of nature that shows that Yhwh is still active, is still creator. We do not know what the prophet thought this transformation would literally look like. As usual, prophecy is cast in images. Literal irrigation and reforestation is neither necessary nor sufficient to count as fulfillment. But something transformative would happen, and people would have to declare, "Yhwh has been here bringing that about" (Is 41:17-20).

Isaiah 35 closes with a highway to take the people back to Zion (Is 35:8-10), but its first promise is Yhwh's own coming back to Zion's exiled people. That promise recurs when the voice of an unseen construction authority commissions celestial engineers (apparently) to carve a highway for Yhwh through the wilderness of mountains and ravines that surround Jerusalem (Is 40:3-5). Indeed, when they see Yhwh's splendor, the mountains and ravines make their own response by falling and rising, like the wilderness and desert blossoming. The return of Yhwh's splendor to Jerusalem will indeed be something to dazzle the world. Does this imply an appearance that literally dazzles or events that astonish and indicate that Yhwh has been acting? Perhaps the latter is more likely, but the prophet does not say, and the audience would be wise to keep their eyes and minds open to all possibilities. The splendor will be visible to all, though this may not guarantee that, for instance, the willfully blind see it. With both eyes the city's lookouts will see Yhwh returning and will shout the good news to the city (Is 52:8). But "all flesh" will see it (Is 40:5). In different contexts, that phrase can imply all Israel or all the world or all living creatures. In the context of Isaiah 35, we might reckon it refers to all living creatures. In Isaiah 40:6-8, it will refer to the people, who cannot imagine they are ever going to *see* anything; it is quite a promise that they will all see. The broader context of Isaiah 40—55 expects Yhwh's act to lead to acknowledgment by the whole world.

Yhwh's Rights of Ownership

When the Judeans have restored the altar of the ruined temple, but have not yet begun to restore the building itself, Yhwh nevertheless urges them to start rejoicing, because Yhwh is coming to dwell in their midst (Zech 2:10-13 [MT 14-17]).

In the Psalms, one responds in faith and worship when one *hears* God's answer to one's prayer, but before one *sees* this answer. The prophet expects the same response to his word to the community facing the challenge to rebuild the temple. His promise relates directly to that expectation. Yhwh is coming to dwell in its midst. Is Yhwh not there already? In some sense that is so: the altar has been rebuilt and the community has gathered in the presence of Yhwh for worship. But there are gradations or variant forms of the presence of God, and the settled presence that will reverse the departure in 587 is still one to look forward to. In light of Yhwh's statement of intent, the temple builders are told, "Your hands must/can be strong" (Zech 8:9).

It is in connection with Yhwh's coming once more to dwell in the temple that Zechariah declares the land of Judah to be Yhwh's allocation (ḥēleq) and says that Yhwh will again choose Jerusalem (Zech 2:12 [MT 16]). The notions of "choice" and of "allocation" do not naturally go together. The land is "allocated" to the clans by lot (e.g., Num 26:52-56); they do not choose which part they would like. Perhaps Zechariah simply juxtaposes these ideas for what each positively affirms. Judah is the tract of land that definitively, distinctively and permanently belongs to Yhwh. The parallel clause gives the point more precision. Judah matters because it was within Judah that Yhwh exercises the right of choice and chose Jerusalem. There Yhwh will dwell in the people's midst. In between these two expressions is the doubly odd phrase "on the holy ground" (ʿal ʾadmat haqqōdeš): not "in the holy land" (which would be something like bĕʾereṣ haqqōdeš, but the Bible never uses this expression). Zechariah's phrase recalls Yhwh's words to Moses about standing on holy ground[19]

---

[19] ʾadmat qēdeš.

at Horeb. The fact that Zechariah's context speaks of Yhwh's dwelling in the people's midst and choosing Jerusalem suggests the familiar idea that Jerusalem succeeds or pairs with Sinai as the holy place where Yhwh dwells. It is the holy mountain (Zech 8:3).

Yet alongside that is the declaration that many nations will also come to attach themselves to Yhwh and be a people for Yhwh (Zech 2:11 [MT 15]; cf. Zech 8:22). "The nations" are the entities with whom Yhwh is extremely angry, whose horns Yhwh is cutting off, whom Yhwh is turning into plunder for the serfs they have plundered (Zech 1:15, 21; 2:8 [MT 1:15; 2:4, 12]). Here there is no reference to the benefit this will bring to Judah in projects such as rebuilding the city or its walls (contrast Is 60). "Attaching themselves" (*lāwâ* niphal) is elsewhere used of people joining in covenant (Is 56:6-7; Jer 50:4-5).[20] Thus the other nations will become "a people for me," the expression elsewhere used to describe Israel's own relationship with God (e.g., Zech 8:8; Jer 32:38). Those other passages go on to complete the statement of a mutual relationship by adding that "I will be God for them." In contrast, here the complementary commitment is that "I will dwell in your midst" (Zech 2:11 [MT 15]). The worldwide relationship of Yhwh and the peoples is accompanied by a particular dwelling in Zion.

There is thus no implication that Yhwh's involvement with the world is ceasing to be geographically specific. There also need be no implication that the people of Yhwh is ceasing to be ethnically based or ethnically aware. It is not a church constituted purely by individual decisions. All Israel still counts as Yhwh's people. Indeed, Judah is still Yhwh's *ḥēleq*; it is just (!) that all Moab, Elam and Sudan also so count. (One might see the situation today as analogous: as a Gentile Christian, I see myself as part of Yhwh's people, yet this does not cancel out the distinctive central position of the Jewish people, "God's ancient people.")

The collocation of oracles is bound by rejoicing and silence; perhaps it is Zion that rejoices and the world that stands silent. Here, "all flesh" links with Zechariah's recurrent reference to "all the earth" (Zech 2:13 [MT 17]): for instance, Yhwh's eyes run through all the earth; Yhwh is lord of all the earth (Zech 4:10, 14; 6:5). It is simultaneously joyful and awesome that Yhwh is coming to Jerusalem again. It is joyful that Yhwh is coming to dwell there, but it is awesome that the one who is coming is the one who by nature dwells in a holy habitation on another plane (cf. Deut 26:15). And the talk of Yhwh "arousing himself" makes clear again that Yhwh's return to Jerusalem is but part of a broader act of self-assertion, an aspect of imposing the divine purpose on a po-

---

[20]Cf. David L. Petersen, *Haggai and Zechariah 1—8* (Philadelphia: Westminster Press, 1984/ London: SCM Press, 1985), pp. 181-82.

litical scene that at present looks much too settled. Yet it is also joyful and awe-some for Judah and for the nations that the nations are to be welcomed as Yhwh's own people.

Yhwh's Reign

Whereas the First Testament sometimes looks forward to a Davidic king reign-ing in Jerusalem again, a more consistent feature of its hope is the fact that *Yhwh* will reign. "The real heart of eschatology" lies in "the promise and ex-pectation of what is known as the 'kingdom of God' and the 'lordship of God.'"[21]

"How welcome on the mountains are the feet of someone bringing news" (Is 52:7-10). Translations traditionally attribute "lovely" feet to these messen-gers, which is quite a concept. Even feet mollycoddled and bathed are not the loveliest part of the body, and the feet of a messenger who has run some miles from a battle are liable to be dirty and unpleasant. Although it is thus more likely that the messenger's feet are "welcome,"[22] it is a suggestive idea that *feet* become lovely because of the message they bring.

Initially, the prophet speaks of the messenger simply "bringing news," which might not make the messenger's feet welcome. The news might be bad. The positive nature of the news is then made explicit: the messenger is "an-nouncing that all is well, bringing good news, telling of deliverance, saying to Zion, 'Your God is reigning!'" In Greek the *angelos* thus becomes a *euangelos*, and such terms in the Septuagint provide the New Testament with its idea of the evangel or the gospel or the good news.

The news concerns *shalom*, deliverance and Yhwh's reign. In what sense is all this "news"? News concerns things that have happened. It is easy to see how an experience of deliverance is news; deliverance is a punctiliar event (there is a contrast with the way Christians can speak of salvation as an ongoing expe-rience rather than an event). Babylon is falling and that will mean the exiles are delivered from their enforced sojourn there and Jerusalem can be rebuilt.

In what sense is Yhwh's reign "news"? There is a sense in which Yhwh al-ways reigns, and thus that Yhwh's reigning is not news. Nothing happens in the world without Yhwh letting it happen. The world cannot spin out of Yhwh's control. Yet there are limits to the idea of Yhwh reigning, for instance, in the forest fires that have been raging a few miles from where I sit, or the fighting between Israelis and Palestinians, or a workers' union strike in protest against a proposed reduction in health benefits. In Israel's way of thinking,

[21]Moltmann, *Theology of Hope*, p. 216.
[22]JPSV. There is some overlap in form and meaning between *ʾāwâ*, "desire," and *nāʾâ*, "be love-ly"; indeed, they may be only one root.

Yhwh's reigning means that Yhwh's will is done and Yhwh's purpose fulfilled. That does not fit with forest fires and fighting and an increased gap between rich and poor. Yhwh does not reign here.

There is another sense in which Yhwh's reign is a more concrete reality, though not a positive one. When messengers reached Babylon in 587 with the news that the Babylonians had taken Jerusalem, they brought news about Yhwh reigning, acting as king, but it was not good news.

It was at the Red Sea that the idea of Yhwh being king or reigning entered First Testament theology, when the Israelites declared that Yhwh would now reign forever (Ex 15:18). In one or other of those two senses, Yhwh has been doing so, by keeping some control of events rather than letting them get out of hand, and by acting to bring calamity. But these messengers' announcement that Yhwh reigns presupposes that in another sense Yhwh has not been reigning in Judah's destiny over previous decades while the city lies in ruins, as Yhwh does not reign in Los Angeles. That news about Yhwh asserting kingly authority is thus big news, and specifically good news rather than bad news.[23]

Yhwh's Arm Bared

It is significant that Isaiah 52:7 uses a verb, and a qatal verb at that. The messengers do not use a yiqtol verb or a participle—which would be natural ways to say "Yhwh reigns"—nor do they say, "Yhwh is king." The qatal form of their verb is the one used when a human king accedes to the throne and people say, "x has become king" (e.g., 2 Sam 15:10; 1 Kings 1:11; 2 Kings 3:1). To translate "Yhwh has become king" could admittedly be misleading because it would imply that Yhwh had not been king for a while. Yet that may be close to the First Testament way of thinking, because reigning or being king is a dynamic concept that means the king's will and policies are effective. A king is not really a king when reigning is only a formal concept. "The worshiping community does not burst into song because they have suddenly recalled the uniform, uninterrupted truth that God is in control."[24] The good news is that Yhwh is now asserting kingly power again in the way that happened at the Red Sea, once again defeating the powers that work against the ultimate divine purpose that centers on Israel. "Listen: your lookouts, they are raising their voice, they will resound together, because with both eyes they will look at Yhwh's return to Zion" (Is 52:8). This victorious king is now returning to Jerusalem. In vision, Ezekiel had watched Yhwh leave just before 587, but Yhwh is now coming back. So "break out, resound together, ruins of Jerusa-

---

[23]See further section 2.2 "Kingship over All the Earth," "Kingship over Israel."

[24]Jon D. Levenson, *Creation and the Persistence of Evil* (reissued, Princeton, N.J./Chichester, U.K.: Princeton University Press, 1994), p. xxiii.

lem, because Yhwh is comforting his people, restoring Jerusalem" (Is 52:9). Obviously the king will want his city looking nice, so the ruins of Jerusalem can start rejoicing; Second Isaiah uses two favorite powerful verbs to inspire this rejoicing.

So "Yhwh is baring his holy arm before the eyes of all the nations, and all earth's farthest reaches will see our God's deliverance" (Is 52:10). In origin it had been humanity's task to implement God's rule in the world, and "we have to regard the future of God's kingdom as the consummation of the creation of the world. . . . As the future of the world and its consummation, then, God will be finally shown to be its Creator."[25] But here, no one consciously contributes anything to this reigning of Yhwh: not Cyrus (because he is just trying to carve out an empire); not Babylon (because it is being forcibly dethroned, not resigning from the throne in Yhwh's favor); not the Judeans in Babylon or Jerusalem (who have no power to do anything); not the prophet (who only announces something). The people of God no more bring about or further or extend or build up this kingdom or reign of God than they will bring about or further or extend or build up the kingdom or reign of God that Jesus will announce. "The actualization of the Kingdom of God is *not* a matter for human initiative, but entirely a matter of God's initiative."[26]

Christians do often speak of their activity as working for God's kingdom or as designed to further God's kingdom or extend God's kingdom. The New Testament never uses such expressions. The only thing Jesus' followers do for God's kingdom is announce it and suffer for it. The New Testament follows First Testament usage. "In contrast to secular kingdoms, God's kingdom comes without human cooperation (Dan. 2:34)."[27] God establishes it (Dan 2:44). Again, human suffering and proclamation are involved, on the part of Daniel and Nebuchadnezzar and Darius, but it is God who decides to reign.[28] A human response is required, but it is not human action that brings in God's rule (how would it then be God's rule, if we had to vote it in?). At the Beginning, humanity was commissioned to subdue and rule the created world on God's behalf, and that seems a daunting task; bringing about the reign of God in the human world would be an even more implausible one. History shows

---

[25]Wolfhart Pannenberg, *Systematic Theology*, 3 vols. (Grand Rapids, Mich.: Eerdmans/Edinburgh: T & T Clark, 1991-1998), 3:540-41.

[26]Johannes Weiss, *Jesus' Proclamation of the Kingdom of God* (Philadelphia: Fortress, 1971), p. 132. It is odd that the liberal view that Weiss opposed, that our Christian task is to work for the kingdom of God, has become so prevalent among evangelicals.

[27]Pannenberg, *Systematic Theology*, 3:35.

[28]On the tension in Daniel between human and divine action in this connection, see Danna Nolan Fewell, *Circle of Sovereignty* (Sheffield: Almond, 1988; 2nd ed., Nashville: Abingdon, 1991).

how neither the nations nor the people of God are inclined to bring about or further or extend or build up this kingdom. The history of the church reinforces the point. It is desperate that we should be thrown back onto God's power to bring in that reign, but not as desperate as being thrown back on the commitment of the people of God.

Christians came to emphasize the conviction that God is Lord already and thus not to look for a coming reign of God. Their hope came to be set rather on our resurrection as individuals. We abandoned the idea of the world's transformation.[29] The First Testament invites us to look for it.

5.2 Transforming the People

The nightmare involved Israel's faithlessness and the disastrous effect that had on its relationship with Yhwh and its life as a people. The vision therefore needs to involve the reestablishing of the relationship, and Yhwh promises to restore the marriage, to be present to the people, to heal their wounds. But the vision also needs to involve a change in Israel, and Yhwh thus also promises to act to win Israel back, to bring about its moral renewal, to reaffirm and deepen the nature of the covenant relationship (not least through pardoning the wrongs of the past). Then, out of a heart of flesh that replaces its heart of stone, it will produce good fruit rather than rotten fruit.

Rebuilding a Marriage

Isaiah 54 begins by addressing Jerusalem as not merely childless but desolate. It would not be surprising if childlessness led to desolation: what use is a wife who cannot bear the children that a man needs if his own sense of manhood is to find fulfillment, if he is to be able to hold his head high in the community, if they are both to have security for their old age? In a patriarchal culture, a woman does not have the option of reckoning that escape from the protection and ownership of a man offers a promise of liberation.

The chapter goes on to urge Jerusalem not to be afraid that she will continue to be shamed (Is 54:4-8). It discreetly avoids identifying factors that might lie behind her finding herself in her shamed position (such as her philandering), and it may just be referring to the shame of her abandonment half a lifetime ago. That abandonment resembles widowhood, as if her husband had died when she was young and thus left her for all these decades without security or standing in society. That will have meant a kind of shame. Widowhood also of course means loss and grief, mourning and sadness. But it also resembles—just abandonment, the feeling that one has been cast off. It

---

[29]Pannenberg, *Systematic Theology*, 3:527-30.

is tempting to tell people that they simply *feel* abandoned by God. Yhwh does not do that, but in response to Jerusalem's accusations acknowledges, "Yes, I abandoned you," and here does not even countercharge that she quite deserved it, but does take the edge off the implications of the abandonment in more than one way.

Both kinds of shame (and any others that may actually have been in the prophet's mind) are destined to disappear because Jerusalem's husband is not actually dead. "Israel and Judah are not widowed of their God, of Yhwh Armies" (Jer 51:5). It sure looks that way, but it is not so. Indeed, in Isaiah 54 Jerusalem's husband is her maker; literal reality bursts the bounds of the allegory. He has not given up on the project he initiated. She is destined to be restored to what she was before, and the one who intends this is Israel's holy one, Yhwh Armies, the God of all the earth. Here only does the First Testament describe Yhwh thus, and it is striking that this comprehensive term comes in the context of a personal commitment to Jerusalem in particular. Whereas "her husband" and "his wife" are usually literally "her man" and "his woman," here the prophet uses the more patriarchal term for a man marrying someone (*bāʿal*), one that implies "the man who gains authority over you,"[30] but in this context that implies some good news. Yhwh is going to exercise sovereignty in her life in order to restore her. The use of the verb "restore" (*gāʾal*) in the context of the marriage metaphor carries extra resonance. Jerusalem stands within Yhwh's family orbit. Yhwh is the one who acts protectively and if necessary sacrificially on behalf of those in this orbit, specifically a vulnerable person such as a childless widow, and she belongs there. Yhwh is like Boaz, a man who knows his family obligations (this is not merely a romantic whim that may not last) and is prepared to marry a childless widow.

There need be little doubt about this "husband's" capacity to restore the city. Does he have the will? After all, he left. But he did that in a storm of anger. His walking out was not really a final and irreversible departure. She is sitting there bereft, but he is calling to her. "Yes. I walked out. But it was only to walk round the block, before I did something I would regret even more. Yes, I really lost my temper, I let out all that emotion I had been keeping in check for decades or centuries, but that did not mean everything was over between us." Indeed, the logic may work the other way round; expressing anger can be a step forward in a relationship, not a step backward, a necessity if a couple are ever to make a new start. Yes, it had lasted half a human lifetime, but in the context of Jerusalem's actual lifetime it was a much shorter time. In the context of Yhwh's lifetime, of course, a thousand years is like only a day (cf. Ps 90:4; also

---

[30]See section 4.2 "Rejection."

2 Pet 3:8), though this is less consolation to individual human beings who are not in a position to live by that time scale.

Reaffirming Commitment

Great compassion now replaces fury, and lasting commitment replaces abandonment. There is to be no more angry blasting. Yhwh is not like a violent husband who promises that the abuse will never recur but cannot keep that promise because the abuse issues from an inner well of violence. The violence rather issued from within someone whose inner being is dominated by compassion,[31] and it could be expressed and thus spent. There is no more anger there. His wife can take the risk of trusting that this is so. Literal reality pokes through the allegory again as Yhwh talks not only about commitment but about compassion—which is not really an emotion that relates to restoring a marital relationship—and about gathering Jerusalem, that is, gathering its people back. Indeed, while *commitment* is sometimes a word applied to marriage, the more likely background of the prophet's talk about compassion, commitment and their relationship to anger is Yhwh's self-revelation at Sinai (Ex 34:6-7). There Yhwh emphasizes compassion, commitment, grace and truthfulness, and a slowness about anger; this recognizes that anger may be a reality, for reasons Yhwh goes on to detail in speaking of punishing wrongdoing, but it does subordinate it to those positive qualities. Here Yhwh acknowledges that the anger was real but does not make a point of justifying it, and rather declares that it was long postponed and that it has been short lived (Is 54:7-8).

An appeal to Noah helps to make the point (Is 54:9-10). Yhwh has a record to appeal to. Actually the flood was not said to be an expression of anger but of grief (Gen 6:5-8), but from the perspective of the world's population this makes little difference; it ended up dead. Yet this calamity was followed by an oath that Yhwh has kept for more than two millennia (to stay with the First Testament's reckoning). So there is risk in trusting Yhwh's word, but it is not a leap in the dark. The prophet underlines the point as we have it in Genesis by speaking of Yhwh swearing an oath. It is a striking image, for an oath is a very human undertaking, one that appeals to God as witness (so to whom does God appeal?) and opens itself to God's punishment if we fail (so will God's punishment be self-inflicted?). To put it another way, Yhwh covenants to make things work out well; "covenant" is the expression that does come in Genesis. Indeed, Yhwh is prepared to go beyond that oath from after the flood (when there was also no talk of compassion or commitment, any more than of

---

[31]See section 2.8.

anger). Yhwh not only guarantees the cycle of day and night, winter and summer, but also points to the immovability of mountains and hills. When the Judean mountains take themselves off to the Mediterranean, then Jerusalem can start worrying about Yhwh's commitment and compassion, Yhwh's covenant to *shalom*.

Therefore Jerusalem need not be afraid. It need not be afraid of the future. It need not be afraid of other people's contempt or hostility. It need not be afraid that its ex-husband may start storming around seething with anger again and set on more violence. All that is over.

Yhwh will also cause people to become aware of the magnitude of the grace shown to them. They will discover that the horror of their faithlessness has not caused Yhwh finally to cast them off. Yhwh's arms are open, ready to resume the relationship. In Isaiah's day Ephraim exults in majestic garlands that are actually wilting, and these will soon be trampled under foot (Is 28:1-4) and their wearers be taken off into exile. But that will not be the end of the story. Isaiah has already declared that the new growth that Yhwh will bring about will become an object of beauty and splendor (Is 4:2). That will be an improvement on attaching that significance to tawdry garlands, but it might still locate ultimate beauty somewhere other than the appropriate place. On that day it will be Yhwh who is the beautiful garland or glorious diadem that the people delight in, and the failure of leadership that resulted in the defeat will be put right (Is 28:5-6). The person who has to make the decisions in the community will have the gifts to do so: the promise would apply to a king, but could also be understood collectively as applying to whoever is involved in the leadership of the people. And the vulnerability that Yhwh used or created in causing Ephraim and Judah to be defeated will now be reversed. Yhwh will strengthen the city's defenders rather than causing them to give up. Isaiah's vision for the future is thus quite practical. There will still be disputes in the city that will need resolving. There will still be enemies that threaten the city and that reach the very gate before being turned back. But Yhwh will provide the means of resolving the disputes and the strength to defend the city.

Accessible

"I will not hide my face from them any more, because I am pouring my spirit on the household of Israel" (Ezek 39:29). The relationship between Yhwh and Israel had broken down on both sides. Israel calls on other deities as well as Yhwh, and thus does not give its whole self to its dependence on Yhwh. In response Yhwh does not listen to its prayer and does not wish to be available to Israel. Yet Yhwh declares that things could still be different: "You will call on me and come and pray to me and I will listen to you. You will have recourse to me and find me when you have recourse to me with your whole self. I will make myself available to you (Yhwh's message)" (Jer 29:12-14). The break-down in the relationship is not terminal. They will be able to look to Yhwh alone, their attention no longer being divided between Yhwh and other dei-ties. Yhwh in turn will be happy to be available to them (māṣāʾ niphal). No, Yhwh will not hide from them any more.

Yhwh goes on to promise to return the exiles to their land in response to these prayers. That shows that while the people may have to wait for that re-turn (wait seventy years, in fact), it does not mean they have to wait for the re-storing of their relationship with Yhwh. A regular relationship with Yhwh involves a material, sacramental side, the sacrifices; the relationship is not lim-ited to inner feelings and words. And one day they will be able return to that full relationship, offering sacrifices again in the temple. But the fact that they cannot do that now does not mean no relationship is possible. They can call on Yhwh and bring their needs before Yhwh now. If they do that with their whole hearts—that is, they are indeed giving their whole attention to Yhwh, not di-viding themselves between Yhwh and other gods—Yhwh will not be able to resist being available to them. Expressions such as "seeking God" or "search-ing for God" can give a false impression of the process involved, as if the one sought is hard to find and everything depends on the acuity, persistence or good fortune of the seekers. But the issue in seeking God is exclusiveness in seeking God's guidance and help.[32]

But then after the exile "I will put my sanctuary in their midst forever. My dwelling will be over them" (Ezek 37:26-27). It would seem obvious that Yhwh's "sanctuary" (miqdāš) or "dwelling" (miškān) is the temple that has been defiled and is to be restored. But while the wilderness and the Jerusalem sanctuary were indeed in the people's midst, they are not described in these terms. Whereas the sanctuary will be "in the midst" of a special slice of the land (Ezek 48:8, 10, 21), it is Yhwh who will dwell "in the midst" of the people, forever (Ezek 43:7, 9). Further, while Yhwh elsewhere promises that Yhwh's dwelling will be among the people (Lev 26:11), there are no other references to its being "over" the people. This coming to be "over" them contrasts with the moving of Yhwh's splendor from "over" the cherubim and the temple thresh-old (Ezek 9:3; 10:4, 18) and then halting "over" the Mount of Olives, on its way from the temple (Ezek 11:23). Yhwh has already promised to be a scaled-down sanctuary for the people in the exile (Ezek 11:16).[33] In Ezekiel 37:26-27, while Ezekiel may be alluding to the permanent presence of Yhwh's temple among the people, he is likely also promising something more subtle, a return of the

---

[32]Cf. Terence E. Fretheim, Jeremiah (Macon, Ga.: Smyth & Helwys, 2002), p. 411. See section 4.3 "Seek."

[33]See section 5.4 "A People Who Belong."

presence that will be among the people and above them, protecting them. And perhaps the "forever" also retrospectively suggests that the promise about a scaled-down sanctuary did refer to a temporary presence in the exile that will be replaced by a permanent presence among the people. It will of course be one mediated by the material dwelling (cf. Ex 29:46), but it will be distinguishable from it.

Yhwh will not merely exult in doing good to them (so EVV) but will exult "over them" in doing so, like a groom over his bride (Is 62:5; cf. Zeph 3:17). And so Yhwh will not merely replant them in their country, but will do so "with all my heart and will all my *nepeš*." There is massive personal engagement on Yhwh's part with Israel. Perhaps it is this personal engagement, this sense of being rejoiced over, that will win Israel's reverence and their continuing to walk after Yhwh—to mix the metaphors, as we have already been told that Yhwh is going to continue to pursue them (e.g., Jer 29:18)—rather than turning to follow someone else.

The promise of Yhwh's presence is indeed spelled out in the vision of a new temple. Protestants might be tempted to reckon that the exile means people come to see that what counts is individual personal religion. The First Testament continues to affirm the significance of the bricks-and-mortar dwelling that speaks of God's real presence among the people, as much to people who could hardly ever go there as to people in Jerusalem.[34] Near the beginning of Isaiah is that vision of the mountain where Yhwh's house stands, elevated so that it is the tallest of the mountains around instead of being a little spur on a hill that stands somewhat lower than other nearby mountains (Is 2:2-4). Its physical nature thus comes to reflect its theological and religious significance and to facilitate its fulfilling its missional role.

Promising a Presence

The book of Ezekiel closes with a gargantuan vision of a new temple in Jerusalem, which reads like architectural plans for contractors to follow (though with a lot of detail for them to work out). Indeed, the people are "to observe the entire plan and all its statutes, and do them" (Ezek 43:11). Yet it is actually a vision of something that could not literally exist. The plans would require a geophysical transformation of the setting, as do later elements in the vision in order to make Jerusalem the source of a wondrous supply of fresh water. The nature of the vision with all its practical detail (like those of the wilderness dwelling) is to imply that we are talking about something real. It is real in the mind of Yhwh, and that makes it very real. Yet its impracticality means it is not

---

[34]Cf. Peter R. Ackroyd, *Exile and Restoration* (London: SCM Press, 1968), pp. 248-49.

simply a project for the community to implement. It is a concrete imaginative realization of what God intends, promising something Yhwh will implement. It "combines both dream and reality."[35] "No word is said of any human participation in the construction; what is said concerns the freely willed event of the coming of the glory of Yahweh to a dwelling in the midst of his people."[36]

Yet it also stands as a stimulus and a measure for the temple restoration project that the community will eventually undertake. Perhaps the observance of Yhwh's instructions more likely refers to the community's keeping Yhwh's instructions about the way the temple worship is to be conducted.[37] In the meantime, however, for a community in no position to do anything toward such a project, it stands as a stimulus to hope.

The vision's background is a temple that really exists in a state of disorder and pollutedness, which is then assaulted and further polluted and profaned by the trampling of Babylon's military. The promise of Ezekiel's vision is that this is not the end of the story. Yhwh has a vision of a new temple where holiness and cleanness reign, and one of the significances of the vast detail in its floor plan (Ezek 40—42) is that this is a temple where everything will be in order, physically and religiously. Its plan shares a recognizable continuity with the present temple, lying in ruins, yet is an exalted version of that, with a neat foursquare symmetry (and adherence to a mostly metric scale) that contrasts with Solomon's temple when it was in good shape. The floor plan draws attention to the substantial perimeter wall that makes sure that there is a clear boundary between the sacred and the profane (Ezek 42:20). The gates with their alcoves for the gatekeepers also link with the need to make sure that the people who come in do not breach the distinction between sacred and profane, clean and polluted, what is proper and what is an abomination. Prohibiting human use of the gate by which Yhwh returned to the temple may safeguard the same point, as does the ban on the use of "uncircumcised" foreigners (such as the Gibeonites; see Josh 9:27) fulfilling certain practical roles in connection with Israel's worship (see Ezek 44). The provision of storerooms, vestries and refectories meets practical needs but also provides a buffer zone between the outer parts of the temple complex and the more holy areas (cf. also Ezek 46).

The nave of the temple building itself, the holy place (as opposed to the holiest place), is called the palace (*hêkāl*, Ezek 41; cf. 1 Kings 6), another reminder

---

[35]Paul M. Joyce, "Temple and Worship in Ezekiel 40—48," in *Temple and Worship in Biblical Israel*, ed. John Day, LHBOTS 422 (London/New York: T & T Clark, 2005), pp. 145-63; see p. 147.

[36]Walther Zimmerli, *Gottes Offenbarung*, TBü 19 (Munich: Kaiser, 1963), p. 177, as translated by Ackroyd, *Exile and Restoration*, p. 112.

[37]Commentators, indeed, routinely reckon that MT's reference to a "plan" reflects a textual error: see, e.g., Leslie C. Allen, *Ezekiel*, 2 vols., WBC (Dallas: Word, 1994, 1990), 2:243.

that Yhwh is the real King in Jerusalem and the temple is the real King's palace. It is the only palace in the new Jerusalem, though Yhwh will go on to assume that there may be human kings there too (Ezek 43:7, 9). Even the *nāśîʾ* (the prince) may eat before Yhwh in the eastern gateway, but not go through it (Ezek 44:1-3). Even Ezekiel himself does not enter the inner room, the holiest place (Ezek 41:3).

This new temple makes for parallels and contrasts with the regulations from Sinai, the wilderness dwelling and Solomon's temple. Whereas the building of the first temple was a not-very-inspired afterthought in Israel's story (see 2 Sam 7), the temple now becomes the center of the land. Its altar is a much more splendid affair than that originally prescribed by Yhwh (Ex 20:25-26) as the principle of simplicity is allowed to give way to the principle of splendor and impressiveness, for the encouragement of the exiles and the beleaguered Second Temple community (Ezek 43:13-17). Whereas the accounts of the consecration of the wilderness altar and the First Temple's altar emphasized anointing and whole offering more than cleansing (e.g., Lev 8; 1 Kings 8), here all the emphasis lies on cleansing (Ezek 43:18-27). The altar needs not only to be taken from the realm of the everyday to that of the sacred but also to be taken from the realm of the polluted to that of the pure. That is an aspect of the renewing of the community's worship. This is a solemn feature of the occasion, but also an encouragement. Yes, Israel's worship needs purification, but Yhwh provides the way for this purification.

Healing

To put it another way, Yhwh is "bringing about recovery and healing" (Jer 33:6). "Recovery" (*ʾărukâ*) literally denotes making new flesh grow so that a wound heals (cf. Jer 30:17; also 8:22; Is 58:8). It will be too late to do that for the people who have actually died in the city, but not too late to do it for the community as a whole and for their city. This word is later applied to the actual rebuilding of the city's walls (Neh 4:7 [MT 1]). There is something about such physical restoration; it symbolizes and encourages the recovery of the community. It is like the healing of a wound. The moment when everything seems hopeless and when death seems the only future is the moment when at last Jeremiah speaks of recovery and healing.

And, he adds (Jer 33:6), Yhwh will reveal a "fragrance" to them (*ʿăteret*) to replace the bad smell of current experience (and of the corpses?), or perhaps an "abundance" to replace the loss that characterizes current experience, or a "prayer" or an "answer to prayer" to replace the hiding of Yhwh's face.[38] The

---

[38] *ʿăteret* is a hapax that might come from any of three roots *ʿātar* and thus generate any of these three meanings.

fragrance or abundance or answer to prayer will consist in "well-being that is trustworthy" (*šālôm we ʾĕmet*), renewed flourishing that will not disappoint and fail. The city's fortunes will be restored and its devastated fabric built up again. Yhwh will gather the people from the nations where they are scattered, "and I will sprinkle clean water on you. You will be clean from all your pollutions, and I will cleanse you from all your pillars" (Ezek 36:25). And "they will never again defile themselves with their pillars and their detestations and all their rebellions. I will deliver them from all their settlements/turnings[39] in which they sinned, and cleanse them" (Ezek 37:23).

So the day of restoration will be "the day when Yhwh binds up his people's hurt and heals the injury caused by its wounding" (Is 30:26).[40] Whereas we may think of healing especially in connection with disease, Israel thinks of it more in connection with wounds. Enemy attacks mean Judah is like a man who has been mugged and is all black and blue, and has no one to dress his wounds (Is 1:5-7). If only they would turn and find healing! Then Yhwh threatens that they never will (Is 6:10). Jeremiah, too, talks much about recovery and healing, but generally so to deny the possibility or to deny the reality of what other prophets called healing (e.g., Jer 6:14; 30:12-13). But through Hosea Yhwh declares, "I will heal their turning, I will love them freely, because my anger has turned from them" (Hos 14:4 [MT 5]). Yhwh therefore continues to utter the invitation "Turn, children who turned away; I will heal your turning" (Jer 3:22). Yhwh heals the people that is broken inside as well as injured on the outside (Ps 147:3).

Yhwh wounds, and Yhwh heals (Deut 32:39). Healing is one of the First Testament's more embracing images, as it is in the Gospels. It suggests the breadth of God's concern for people's bodies and spirits. Healing is a wide-ranging image for God putting things right that were wrong. God's healing is "individual and communal; present and future; spiritual and psychic/bodily; religious and social/economic/political. Healing would include both forgiveness of sins and deliverance from the effects of sins, both the sins of Israel and the sins of others. Indeed, the healing of all creation is in view."[41]

Thus the Gospels can speak of healing as "salvation." There are further contrasts between this way of speaking and Christian speech on the one hand and First Testament speech on the other. In speaking of salvation, Christian speech

---

[39]The MT and Vg. have "their settlements" (*môšĕbōtêhem*), presumably referring to the exile as a place of sin. Sym has "their turnings," implying *mĕšûbōtêhem*; cf. LXX "their lawlessnesses."

[40]Translating "his wounding" (cf. NRSV) makes for a subtle and profound theological point, but elsewhere a genitive associated with *makkâ* is objective, not subjective (e.g., Is 10:26; 27:7), and the context offers the audience no signal toward this more subtle reading.

[41]Fretheim, *Jeremiah*, p. 425.

moved the other way;[42] instead of speaking of salvation as involving the body as well as the spirit and the present as well as the future, Christian speech understands salvation to refer to a spiritual reality and specifically to the enjoyment of eternal life in heaven. On the other hand, First Testament speech did not apply the word *salvation* to the "spiritual" realm at all. This does not mean it is not interested in the spiritual realities of a relationship with God (though it has hardly any expectation of eternal life), only that it does not refer to these as "salvation." *Salvation* denotes God delivering people from crises, enemies, illness and other perils. It is for this reason that I translate key words such as *yĕšûʿâ* "deliverance" rather than "salvation" (though in circles where people offer "deliverance ministry" or exorcism that might raise a different set of problems).

Whereas we generally think of healing as an individual matter, Jeremiah sees that communities need healing. Perhaps the implication is that healing is so important to us as individuals that it provides a particularly powerful metaphor for the restoration of a broken community. If Yhwh heals the community, then as part of that individuals will experience their own healing.

Promising Moral Renewal

When God so acts, at last the people's ears and eyes will work. "The deaf will listen to the words of the scroll on that day; taken out of gloom and darkness, the eyes of the blind will see" (Is 29:18). There are promises that relate to physical sight and hearing, but the reference to the words of the scroll suggests that Isaiah here refers to mental and ethical sight and hearing, which fits with the significance of this recurrent motif in Isaiah. At the moment the people will not listen or look, and Yhwh has therefore made them constitutionally incapable of doing so, not least by speaking to them words that they would ignore. But that is not the end of the story. Yhwh will unblock the blocked ears so that people can listen to the scroll that they cannot make sense of at the moment (cf. Is 29:11-12). The testimony can be unsealed (cf. Is 8:16). The people's moral blindness has taken them into a many-faceted place of gloom and darkness, and one of the facets that Yhwh will reverse is the moral one.

In Isaiah 35, the appearing of Yhwh's splendor calls forth not only a transformation of nature but the transforming of blind, deaf, disabled and dumb into people who can see, hear, walk (indeed, jump) and speak (indeed, shout). Describing people as blind and deaf can suggest they are unable to see what God is doing or hear what God is saying. It can be a self-imposed blindness and deafness, but also a God-imposed one (e.g., Is 6:9-10; 29:18; 32:3; 42:18-20).

---

[42]See also section 5.1 "Yhwh's Reign."

Now these people have such sight and hearing restored. Talk of being disabled or dumb then suggests inability to walk Yhwh's way or to speak the truth about Yhwh, while walking/jumping and speaking/shouting suggests that people's moral spirits as well as their morale are transformed. Isaiah does not exhort people to change but declares that they will change. This will come about because they see Yhwh coming to deliver them, see the event that stimulates that responsive transformation of the wilderness into a place with streams, pools and springs. As Yhwh's coming in majesty calls forth blossoming in nature, so it calls forth blossoming in humanity.

Deuteronomy 30:6 offers a very different image for this. In Deuteronomy 10:16 Moses had urged the Israelites to circumcise their heart. This powerful image involves a metaphor and a metonymy. Previously, Israel has simply been required to ensure that its males undergo literal circumcision, "in their flesh." That sacramental rite ensures their place in the covenant people. They were no doubt expected to walk before Yhwh and to live wholly committed lives, as Abraham was (Gen 17:1), but Genesis does not make that point. The covenant did not issue from their obedience. All they had to do to qualify for membership of the covenant people was accept the covenant sign. But commitment to Yhwh does need to follow, especially after Sinai. David's reference to a permanent covenant likewise does not refer to any response expected of him (2 Sam 23:5), though elsewhere his story presupposes that Yhwh's commitment to him and his successors does require a responsive faithfulness and it makes explicit that failure in this respect could issue in punishment, even though not in the withdrawing of Yhwh's commitment (2 Sam 7:4-17).

In Deuteronomy 10, Moses makes the point by pressing the people to take on a metaphorical circumcision. In the narrow sense that might have implied the men subordinating their sexual activity to Yhwh, quite an expectation in itself. But Moses jumps beyond that to the submission of their whole lives to Yhwh. The Sinai covenant indeed required this. Moses makes explicit that such submission needs to affect the inner person, the springs of a person's life, because that is crucial to their outward walk. Leviticus 26:39-42 has already envisaged them taken into exile and has indirectly urged them *now* to humble their uncircumcised hearts. Their confession, submission to Yhwh, and making restitution for their wrongdoing will lead to Yhwh's being mindful of the covenant obligation to them that goes back to the commitment to their original ancestors.

In contrast both with Deuteronomy 10 and with Leviticus 26, Deuteronomy 30:6 *promises* that when the curse as well as the blessing has come upon the people, Yhwh will restore their fortunes and "will circumcise your heart and the heart of your offspring to dedicate yourselves to Yhwh your God with all your heart and all your spirit, so that you may live," so that they will then listen to Yhwh's voice and do what Moses says in Yhwh's name. Perhaps the implication is that the events reflected in Deuteronomy 27—30 indicate clearly that there is no longer any hope of their taking this action.[43] So Deuteronomy 30:6-10 makes Yhwh the one who will bring it about, and thus grant them the prosperity that will accompany their obedience and turning to Yhwh with their whole being. The promises of inner renewal issuing in obedience to Yhwh alternate with promises of the restoration of the nation's fortunes, and the relationship between these is left unstated. The ambiguity is reflected in the way the successive promises begin with Hebrew's characteristic copula *w*, which can mean "and" or "but" or not deserve translation at all (JPSV renders it "then," but that makes it much more specific than it is).

Winning Israel Back

How will that inner renewal come about? Hosea had warned Israel that Yhwh would bring on them national disaster (defeat in Jezreel corresponding to the murders in Jezreel), that Yhwh's attitude would change (there would be no more compassion), and that the relationship between Yhwh and the people would come to an end (you are not my people, and I will not be yours) (Hos 1:4-9). Yhwh will reverse all that again. Israel has been serially unfaithful to Yhwh in looking to the Masters for the provision of its needs, and Yhwh has declared the intention to endorse its effective terminating of their relationship. Hosea 2:14-23 [MT 16-25] follows devastating confrontation of Israel by an unexpected turnaround: "Therefore, now: I am charming her, taking her to the wilderness and speaking to her heart-to-heart."

Yhwh speaks in very different terms from before, being much more inclined to seek to reestablish the relationship. The paradoxical "therefore" indicates that precisely because of that unfaithfulness, somehow Yhwh has to win Israel back to the commitment she manifested at the beginning, before she came to the land.[44] The story in Exodus to Joshua makes clear that there were serious qualifications to *that* commitment, but the advantage about the wilderness was that the Masters were not very operative there. There was no doubt that Yhwh alone brought the people through the wilderness and provided for them. In the wilderness Yhwh will be able to get their whole attention and provide for them in a way that makes clear who is the provider; this is not the Masters' territory. There Trouble Valley, the place where they first offended Yhwh in the land and provoked an act of punishment (Josh 7), will become "the opening to hope" that it should always have been, as a place on the way

---

[43]Cf. J. G. McConville, *Deuteronomy* (Leicester, U.K./Downers Grove, Ill.: InterVarsity Press, 2002), p. 427.

[44]On such illogical "therefores," see section 5.1 "Yhwh's Horror."

up from the Jordan Valley to the heartland of Canaan. There Yhwh will thus be able to set the relationship going again. Israel will sing the way Miriam sang after the deliverance at the Red Sea (Hos 2:15).[45] She will no longer worship the Masters, nor behave as if Yhwh was (just) one of them. Their mutual relationship will be reestablished as one between a man and a woman committed to one another, the one to provide, the other to look to her husband for provision (the patriarchal understanding of marriage of course continues).

Yhwh makes a new covenant commitment to the Israelites, to protect them from trouble from the animal world and the political world. As is often the case, Yhwh makes this covenant *for* or *to* (*l*) the people, not *with* them (Hos 2:18). That highlights its one-sided nature. It is an act of decisive, one-sided grace, a commitment on Yhwh's part rather than a mutual agreement between Yhwh and Israel. As Israel's man, Yhwh undertakes to reestablish their marriage and to do so with faithfulness and authority, with commitment and compassion, and with steadfastness. Did Yhwh not manifest those qualities before? Indeed, they overlap with the qualities Yhwh claimed at Sinai (Ex 34:6). Here Yhwh is undertaking to provide such spectacular manifestations of those qualities that they will win the kind of recognition that the people have been holding back. At last, the people will acknowledge Yhwh.

That will make it possible for Yhwh to put Israel's relationship with nature and politics on its proper footing. Regarding nature, Yhwh will set on the right basis the relationship of the heavens and the earth; sun and rain will behave in the way the earth needs in order for the crops to grow. The earth will produce its classic and basic crops, grain, wine and oil; it will be Israel's personal experience of the covenant concerning nature that Yhwh made to humanity as a whole (Gen 9). But the specific force of it is a commitment to impose restraints on the beings within nature that are a threat to nature (wild animals, birds and reptiles; cf. also Gen 3:15). Whereas in the past Yhwh has used such agents in bringing trouble to Israel, and/or is about to do so, Yhwh will then rein them in. Likewise, regarding politics, Yhwh has used and/or is about to use "bow, sword and battle" to bring trouble to Israel, but will then banish these from the land.

Thus the signs Yhwh gave through Hosea and Gomer's children will be reversed. History had given Jezreel a bad name, but etymology had given it a good name, "God sows." God will indeed do that. Yhwh will have compassion on Not-compassioned. Yhwh will address Not-my-people as "my people," and this time the mutuality of covenant commitment will be complete, as

---

[45]"Sing" in Hos 2:15 [MT 17] is ʿānâ iv (BDB; cf. NIVI); ānâ i "respond" is more common, but "sing" makes better sense in this context and is the verb used of Miriam in Ex 15:21. Hosea may play on the homonymity and use ānâ to mean "respond" in later lines.

Israel says "You are my God" (Hos 2:23; contrast Hos 1:9).

"You will be a people for me, and I will be God for you" had been Yhwh's words at Sinai (Jer 11:4).[46] Hosea declared that this relationship was as good as over, but also affirmed that this would not be the end (Hos 1:9—2:1 [MT 2:1-3]). In the context of the exile it is reaffirmed in the second person (Jer 30:22; Ezek 36:28) and in the third person (e.g., Jer 24:7; 30:22; 31:33; 32:38; Ezek 14:11; 37:23, 27). Indeed, "I will be God for all the clans[47] of Israel and they will be a people for me" (Jer 31:1). In a similar way the closing promise in Amos has Yhwh restoring "my people Israel" and speaking as "Yhwh your God": that is the last word in the book (Amos 9:14-15).

Reaffirming the Covenant

That formulaic description of the relationship between Yhwh and Israel is often described as a covenant formula.[48] From time to time the relationship is explicitly described as a covenant.

Now: days are coming (Yhwh's message) when I shall seal with the household of Israel and the household of Judah a new covenant, unlike the covenant that I sealed with their ancestors at the time when I took them by the hand to bring them out from the country of Egypt, which covenant of mine they themselves broke though I myself had married them (Yhwh's message). Because this is the covenant that I will seal with the household of Israel after those days (Yhwh's message): I am putting my teaching inside them and I will write it on their minds, and I will be God for them and they will be a people for me. They will no longer teach, each their neighbor or each their brother, saying "acknowledge Yhwh," because all of them will acknowledge me, from the least of them to the greatest of them (Yhwh's message). Because I will pardon their wrongdoing; their shortcomings I will not keep in mind any more. (Jer 31:31-34)

Jeremiah's promise helped the early Christians understand the significance of what Christ was doing (e.g., Heb 10:12-18). As usual this involved an inspired reinterpretation of the scriptural text; it is thus important to seek to understand the promise in its own right.

This is not a promise for the far-off future but one designed to encourage people in the sixth century whose relationship with Yhwh has collapsed, to reassure them that this is not the end. Right now ("days are coming": they are on

---

[46]The drift of them; Lev 26:12 comes closest to this actual formulation.

[47]In the narrative books mišpāḥâ usually refers to an (extended) family or local community, a subunit of one of the twelve clans, but elsewhere it often denotes something more like the clan itself, a subunit of the nation (cf. Jer 1:15; 2:4; 3:14; 10:25; 25:9); Jer 33:24 speaks of Ephraim and Judah as "the two mišpāḥôt."

[48]See, e.g., Rolf Rendtorff, The Covenant Formula (Edinburgh: T & T Clark, 1998).

the way, they are nearly here, you will see them) Yhwh is doing something about this situation. Indeed, here as elsewhere in Jeremiah 30—31 it would be natural to assume that "days are coming" refers to the time the previous chapter refers to, the end of the seventy years of chastisement.

Further, this is not a promise for Gentiles but for the twin households of Israel and Judah that ideally comprise one family, and it relates to the relationship that Yhwh entered into with them at Sinai at the beginning of their story. That was the moment when Yhwh married this people, when Yhwh became their lord and master; Yhwh again uses the verb *bāʿal* that describes a patriarchal relationship between a husband and a wife, which obviously provides a better image for the relationship between Yhwh and people than an egalitarian relationship would do. One might have thought they would be glad to be in such a relationship, but they broke its terms.

How did they do that? Its most fundamental requirement was that Yhwh should indeed be God for them and they be a people for Yhwh, that they should be committed to Yhwh alone, like a wife to her husband. That was the first requirement in the Ten Words that are associated with the covenant, the terms Yhwh laid down at Sinai; associated with it was the requirement that they should not attempt to worship Yhwh by means of images. The Ten Words went on to spell out further the expectations Israel's husband had. It is easy to see how they have broken Yhwh's covenantal requirements. Jeremiah has kept declaring it. They worshiped the Masters as well as Yhwh. They worshiped by means of images. They took Yhwh's name on their lips in swearing their oaths to each other but actually lived by deception and fraud. They failed to keep the sabbath. And so on.

They thus broke the terms of the covenant. There is some (perhaps advantageous) ambiguity about the expression. Breaking the covenant (*pārar* piel) could imply simply contravening it, or it could imply actually nullifying it (e.g., Num 30:8 [MT 9]). If a man is unfaithful to his wife, he contravenes the terms of his marriage relationship, but he does not annul the relationship. That happens only if she divorces him. Breaking the covenant is more like the former than the latter. When Israel breaks the covenant, this causes Yhwh to discipline Israel and behave in a hostile fashion, like a wife withdrawing from her husband and behaving in hostile fashion when he has been unfaithful (e.g., Lev 26:15), but this does not mean Israel or Yhwh has annulled the covenant.[49] The covenant stays in being, so that Yhwh can say that for all Israel's unfaithfulness and Yhwh's responsive hostility, "I will think about my covenant with Jacob, yes, I will think about my covenant with Isaac, yes, my covenant with

---

[49]Cf. Rolf Rendtorff, *Canon and Theology* (Minneapolis: Fortress, 1993), pp. 197-98.

Abraham." For all Israel's covenant breaking and that hostility, "I will not reject them, or loathe them so as to destroy them, breaking my covenant with
them, because I am Yhwh their God" (Lev 26:42, 44). "I am Yhwh their God":
on Yhwh's side, at least, the relationship holds.

If the covenant is to survive in the long term, however, something more will
be needed beyond punishing Israel, which is unlikely to achieve anything positive. So Yhwh will seal a new covenant with the people. This is a not a matter
of merely renewing the existent covenant, like a couple renewing their marriage vows. Nor is it a matter of two people marrying again after divorcing,
when again the terms of the relationship would not change but they would
commit themselves to trying to do better this time. There is a covenant relationship still in existence between Yhwh and Israel, but it has not worked, and
therefore the relationship needs to be set on a different basis.

Pardoning and Thus Transforming

The existent covenant involved Yhwh making its terms quite clear to the people. They were written on stone tablets. But that meant they were external to
the people. This time Yhwh will see that they reach inside them. They will be
written onto their minds. Then the covenant arrangement will work: Yhwh
will be their God; they will be Yhwh's people. Specifically, the people will keep
their side of the covenant, as they did not before. They will acknowledge
Yhwh as their God instead of serving other gods. All the people will do so,
from the least to the greatest. In other words, it will not just be the ordinary
people who acknowledge Yhwh; the people who are inclined to take the lead
in serving other gods, people such as kings and prophets and priests, will also
do so. Or it will not be just the leaders, but also the ordinary people who are
inclined to go in for other forms of spirituality in the privacy of their homes.
They will not need to confront one another about that in the way they do at
present. They will not need "marginal" prophets such as Jeremiah trying to get
the community to acknowledge Yhwh. They will do it.

Jeremiah does not indicate how this will come about. By its nature humanity has certain instincts written into its DNA, such as the instinct to walk upright rather than on all fours, the instinct to eat, the instinct for self-
preservation. We could imagine God reworking human instincts so that acknowledging God became instinctive. (It would not therefore become inevitable; human beings can choose not to walk upright or eat or preserve
themselves.) But Jeremiah offers a pointer in another direction in his closing
promise, "because I will pardon their wrongdoing; their shortcomings I will
not keep in mind any more" (Jer 31:34). Yhwh intends once again to restore
people to their freedom and take them to their land. But the difference between the exodus from Egypt and the exodus from Babylon will be that the

second involves a monumental act of forgiveness. The first exodus itself needed to involve no such great act of forgiveness, though Sinai required one. That is one way in which the second exodus goes further than the first. Jeremiah will later express the point even more forcefully. Someone could look for Israel's wrongdoing, but not be able to find it, "for I will pardon those I allow to be leftovers" (Jer 50:20). The effect of Yhwh's pardon is that the wrongdoing and failure no longer exist and thus cannot be found by anyone who goes looking for it (cf. Mic 7:18-19).

The prophecies of the fall of Babylon, interwoven with promises of the restoration of Israel, make very little reference to Israel's sin. It is as if Yhwh has indeed put Israel's wrongdoing out of mind.[50] But the fact that Yhwh thus pardons and restores is then the basis for an exhortation to the people to turn to Yhwh: "I am wiping away your rebellions like thick cloud. . . . Now turn to me, because I am restoring you" (Is 44:22). The fact that Israel is Yhwh's servant means that Yhwh is committed to Israel, and that commitment includes being willing to pardon Israel its rebellions and shortcomings. Yhwh may take the people into exile, but could never leave them there. It is inevitable that the records of the court in heaven include the details of those rebellions and shortcomings, but it is also theologically inevitable that Yhwh declare that these records should be erased. Yhwh can do that as easily as the sun can disperse morning mist or marine layer: but the prophet uses terms for thick cloud and thunder cloud, which the sun cannot so easily disperse, so that the line highlights the magnitude of what Yhwh is doing. In terms of the other metaphor, there is quite a fat file in the sheriff's office that Yhwh has to burn. Bringing about the people's restoration from their exile involves such pardoning of the people. The first is dependent on the second. And it is not the case that they must first repent and then Yhwh will pardon and restore. Yhwh first declares the intention to pardon and restore, and on that basis exhorts Israel to turn.

It is not explicit that failure to turn will mean that Yhwh changes the intention to pardon and restore, though neither is it explicit that Yhwh will pardon and restore whether they turn or not. The ambiguity over that is significant, because if the answer to the question were clear either way, it would reduce the significance of the relationship between Yhwh and Israel. If pardon and restoration operated irrespective of Israel's turning, this would make the relationship a one-sided one; if a wife forgave her husband his infidelity but he did not return to faithfulness to her, the relationship would not be restored. But if pardon and restoration were conditional on Israel's turning, this would make the relationship a contractual one, not a personal one; when two people com-

---

[50]Fretheim, *Jeremiah*, p. 624.

mit themselves to each other, they do so unconditionally yet on the basis of the fact that both are making this commitment. So Yhwh is taking the initiative in inviting Israel back into a mutually committed relationship. The invitation is not legally conditional on Israel's response, but it is logically dependent on it.

Forgiving people is one of the most powerful and creative acts human beings ever undertake or that God ever undertakes. Perhaps it is the fact that Yhwh's restoration of them involves not holding their past unfaithfulness against them that will bring about the people's inner renewal, changing their attitude to Yhwh and winning them at last to acknowledge Yhwh. The point is underlined by the further promise that follows, concerning the impossibility of Israel's ever dying out (Jer 31:35-37). It is thus that in forgiveness "not only has an old page been closed but a new one opened."[51] Israel contributes nothing to its restoration because faith in Yhwh is "an empty hand, an empty vessel, a vacuum," yet also a positive recognition of the grace of God reaching out to us.[52] "Every Christian proclamation is an expression in one way or another of 'I absolve thee,' the word that refuses to accuse, and thus liberates and makes new life possible."[53]

Removing Faithlessness

Zechariah 5:5-11 pictures this in another way. It concerns "faithlessness" (riš'â). Following on the preceding vision about swindling people, one might understand faithlessness in a moral sense, but Faithlessness is eventually given a house in Babylon, which rather suggests that it refers to worship of images, probably worship of other gods. Yhwh will remove such worship from the land, another promise Yhwh fulfilled. Faithlessness is embodied as a woman, because the word is feminine, and/or because in the past Israelites often had set a consort alongside Yhwh, and/or because for Judean men during and after the exile the temptation to alien worship often came through the possibility of marrying non-Israelite women, and/or because the "other" is often conceptualized by men as female. This Faithlessness is carried off in a container to Babylon, its cover weighted down to make sure it does not get out. Its attendants can build a house for it there, where it belongs. The fact that Faithlessness can be so easily controlled suggests some irony. "If this idolatrous being truly lacked power, why bother with her at all?" But "the woman/goddess in this vision symbolizes wickedness not because of anything she can do but because of what worship of her can do to the people

---

[51]Barth, *Church Dogmatics*, IV/1:598.

[52]Ibid., IV/1:631, though Barth is speaking of faith in Christ.

[53]Jürgen Moltmann, *The Church in the Power of the Spirit* (London: SCM Press, 1977), pp. 225-26.

who follow her within a community of Yahwists."[54] (Since Zechariah else-where expresses the expectation that all peoples are due to come to acknowl-edge Yhwh, we should perhaps assume that exporting Faithlessness to Babylon will be satisfactory only as an interim measure; the main point here is the removal of such worship from the land.)

This aspect of the prophets' vision found more immediate fulfillment than many other aspects. Whereas the First Temple community never acknowl-edged Yhwh with any consistency, the Second Temple community seems to have done so; serving the Masters becomes a thing of the past. Likewise, it gave up worshiping Yhwh by means of images and came to observe the sab-bath. It lived by the covenant. Yhwh was its God, and it was Yhwh's people. Yhwh's teaching came to be written in its inner being. It became no longer nec-essary to tell people they must acknowledge Yhwh and not serve other gods. They did so. Yhwh implemented the promised new covenant and removed faithlessness from the land.

Of course the fulfillment of these promises did not mean people were living sinless lives, nor that they were incapable of monumental wrongdoings. In-deed, they proved incapable of recognizing God's climactic act toward the es-tablishing of God's reign in the world, when Jesus came. That thus involved another monumental act of forgiveness on God's part. So the pattern of faith-lessness and forgiveness repeated itself, and the first Christians could use Jer-emiah 31:31-34 to illuminate the way God acted in Christ. Once again, and on a more spectacular scale, God was involved in writing the truth in people's in-ner beings: not just those of Jewish people, but of Gentiles, once again by for-giving their sins. There is thus more recognition of Yhwh in the world than there was in Second Temple times, through the spread of the message about Yhwh through more of the Gentile world than the synagogue had reached by Jesus' day. Admittedly this is more a matter of quantity than quality. It is not clear that the good news of forgiveness in Christ has made the Christian church more committed to the acknowledgment of Yhwh than the Second Temple community was. Thus the vision of Yhwh's teaching written in peo-ple's inner being remains a vision—and whereas Hebrews quotes Jeremiah 31:31-34 as having been fulfilled, Paul quotes it as still to be fulfilled (Rom 11:27).

Protecting Them from Themselves

Israel had a gift for devising expressions of its faith, like the church. Yhwh's act of renewal will deliver it from that. People will stop looking to the altars,

---

[54]Carol L. Meyers and Eric M. Meyers, *Haggai, Zechariah 1—8*, AB (Garden City, N.Y.: Dou-bleday, 1987), p. 314.

steles and incense stands that their hands have made and start looking to their own maker (Is 17:7-8). Isaiah contrasts the God who makes people with the people who make their religious artifacts. The subject and object of the verb *make* are here reversed. Isaiah does not declare that proper Israelite religion is so supernaturally devised that one can deny human involvement in the creation of its artifacts (or its words and concepts), but it hints that there is no supernatural reality behind the humanly made artifacts that people use in worship. That being so, there is something sad about people's "regarding" these or "looking to" them, and at last they will see this and regard Yhwh, look to Yhwh. Perhaps there is some encouragement or satisfaction in worshiping by means of something you devised, particularly something solid and visible that suggests God's presence. There is some vulnerability or loss of control involved in submitting to one who is your maker. But there is also some realism about it.

People will thus be better at dealing with crises than they have been in the past. Restoration will not mean that life becomes problem free, but problems will be open to being dealt with. The people will not stop having the experience of Yhwh giving them "the bread of adversity and the water of affliction" (Is 30:18-22). Those phrases might imply that adversity and affliction are their bread and water, the basics of their life, or that they have the kind of bread and water that people have in situations of adversity and affliction (for instance, not much of it). And they might imply that such experiences come because that is just how human life is or that they come as chastisement for human sin. Isaiah then indicates either that restoration does not mean that life stops containing puzzling experiences or that it does not mean the people become sinless. But the puzzling experiences do get resolved, and the sin does get dealt with. Either way, these experiences do not mean Yhwh "withdrawing" from the people: literally the verb (*kānap* niphal) seems to imply going into a corner or going to an extremity.

In that context, Yhwh is described as "your Teacher." The word is plural, and LXX assumes it denotes human teachers, but this fits ill in the context, and more likely the plural corresponds to that of the words *God* or *the Lord*. It hints that Yhwh is the great teacher, the source of all teaching. There is a superficial tension between the idea of being able to watch this Teacher (who is presumably therefore in front of the people) and the idea of hearing the Teacher's voice *behind,* but the two images combine to suggest Yhwh's perceptible involvement with the people. They parallel the idea that Yhwh is both the one who goes ahead of the people and their rear guard (Is 52:12; cf. Is 58:8). There the implication is that Yhwh will protect them from attack; here it is that Yhwh will protect them from themselves. They will be able to look forward and see the way Yhwh is directing them; they will also hear the words behind that complement an appearance with a voice, either telling them when to turn right or left or warning them when they have unilaterally done so.

Furthermore, "You will defile/declare taboo your silver-plated idols and your gold-clad images; you will scatter them like something foul, about which you say 'Filth!'" (Is 30:22). Evidently there is a specific connection in which they will need that protective instruction, or rather, these words suggest a specific way in which Yhwh's showing grace will work itself out. Isaiah does not so much tell them they will have to abandon worship by means of images as promise that the sight of the Teacher leading them in the right way and the awareness of a voice doing the same behind will mean they will at last see through their images. They will come to perceive them as something religiously defiling rather than religiously resourcing. Indeed, they will see them as an illness (the more literal meaning of *dāwâ*, translated "something foul") and as vomit or excrement (the more literal meaning of *ṣē'*, translated "filth"); the combination of words suggests cloths made repulsive by excretions from someone who is very ill.[55] They will just want to throw them away.

Reestablishing Faithfulness

Long ago, the "vine" had been designed to produce fruit that took the form of the faithful exercise of authority, *ṣedeq ûmišpāṭ* (Is 5:7) This was not a project that Israel had to aim at but something given as a gift to Israel by God as "internally established qualities," in the course of bringing the people into being. It was part of the definition of what it meant to be Israel. Israel did not create them, though it could pervert them (Amos 5:7).[56] "Righteousness flows down from heaven, and bids fair to flood the face of the earth" through the people (cf. Is 45:8), but they "shrink . . . from the divine flood, they refuse to let it spring forth into life."[57] Yet God does not give up. In restoring the relationship with Israel, Yhwh undertakes to do so "with the faithful exercise of authority" (Hos 2:19 [MT 21]). These are not demands that Yhwh places on Israel but gifts that Yhwh makes. "As the bride-price which the bridegroom will pay, He will confer these qualities on her, so that she will never offend again."[58]

Thus the weak and needy will rejoice in Yhwh "because the ruthless will be no more, . . . all the people who are vigilant at wrongdoing will be cut off" (Is 29:19-21). One of the classic expressions of sin in Israel, as in modern societies,

---

[55]There is no specific reason to link *dāwâ* with menstruation in this context, and I take *ṣē'* as equivalent to *ṣē'â* or *ṣō'â* (see Hans Wildberger, *Isaiah 28—39* [Minneapolis: Fortress, 2002], p. 168).

[56]Cf. Jörg Jeremias, *The Book of Amos* (Louisville, Ky: Westminster John Knox, 1998), p. 90.

[57]Martin Buber, *The Prophetic Faith* (reprint, New York: Harper, 1960), p. 102.

[58]JPSV footnote.

is the systematic, ruthless and cynical manipulation of the legal system so that it favors people with power and resources and works against ordinary people who lack these. The system that was designed to make life work in a fair way becomes a tool for increasing injustice rather than furthering justice. That inevitably demoralizes and disheartens ordinary people who have no way of negotiating the system and become its victims. As long as Yhwh allows this situation to continue, the psalms show us how this becomes something that deprives people of the kind of joy in Yhwh that issues from knowing Yhwh as one who protects the weak and needy. Their worship has to be dominated by lament rather than rejoicing. But on the other side of the coming calamity, Yhwh will see that this situation does not arise again. Yhwh will eliminate people who make the system work in that way. The weak and needy will not be deprived of their rights, and they will have reason for joying in Yhwh as the one who indeed does have a bias toward the poor.

Zechariah has another vision of a huge scroll flying over the land (rather than the earth), inscribed with a self-curse or oath (ʾālâ) calling down calamity on oneself if one steals or swears falsely in Yhwh's name (Zech 5:1-4). The two offenses on two sides of the scroll are perhaps a kind of hendiadys, two sides of a coin; the self-curse refers to theft by means of deception, which likely denotes fraud (deceit might refer to perjury more generally, but the language does not correspond to the terms used in the Ten Words in this connection). It is the kind of act that by definition cannot be seen (like the subject of the word ʾālâ in Num 5:11-31) and is thus not amenable to human judgment on the basis of evidence. But we do not know why Zechariah focuses on this particular wrongdoing (or these two wrongdoings). Perhaps they are a synecdoche and stand for right standards in community life in general. Charged with the act, one may swear that one is innocent and get away with the wrongdoing. This scroll therefore requires people to call down divine judgment on themselves if they engage in it. The judgment will consume not the people themselves (or their children) but their house, perhaps because this is the place at which or near which their gains (for instance, their animals) will reside. The self-curse may be that expressed in the Torah itself (ʾālâ recurs in, e.g., Deut 29:10-28, sometimes translated "curse," sometimes "oath"), where the Ten Words include proscription of theft and false testimony.

Jerusalem is destined to become City of Faithfulness, Town of Truth (Is 1:26). The people that is holy through the Holy One's association with it is destined to become a people that lives its holiness.

Generating Fruitfulness

This renewing act of Yhwh's will thus ensure that the story of Yhwh's vineyard comes to a happy end that contrasts with the unhappy end in an earlier vineyard song (Is 5:1-7). In Isaiah 27:2-6 the prophet again pictures the owner looking after the vineyard carefully and attentively, and making sure that no enemy can pay it hostile attention, but this time looking with pleasure and anticipation as its fruit ripens and looking forward to the coming day when people will be able to sing of "a pleasing vineyard" or "a vineyard for fine wine."[59] The time will come when the vineyard will amaze the world with its produce. "There is no fury in me," Yhwh adds, suggesting quite a contrast with Yhwh's earlier angry indignation. "Who would give me thorn or thistle? I would march in battle against it, set it on fire all at once." This determination that no thorn or thistle be planted here contrasts with the earlier surrender of the vineyard to these. If they should now appear, they would be the work of an enemy, against whom Yhwh will take harsh and decisive action.[60] Yet even that enemy has the alternative option of turning to Yhwh and finding *shalom* in this relationship: "he must hold on to me as stronghold, achieve friendship with me, achieve friendship with me." Nothing will stop the achievement of Yhwh's purpose: "The coming [days]: Jacob will root, Israel will blossom and flourish; they will fill the face of the world with produce."

To put it another way, "They will be called 'oaks expressing faithfulness,' planted by Yhwh to display splendor" (Is 61:3). "Oaks" (*'ayil*) are elsewhere associated with false religion (Is 1:29; 57:5) or with powerful self-assertiveness (Ezek 31:14); similar words for oaks have associations with the devastation of the people (*'ēlâ, 'allôn*, Is 6:13). Further, the word *'ayil* has a homonym that itself means "powerful people" or "leaders"; it is a term for the people with power who were taken off to Babylon (2 Kings 24:15 Q; Ezek 17:13). "Oaks of *ṣedeq*" could thus have many connotations. It could suggest that people who are weak and feeble will become people who are strong and that people whose strength has been self-assertive will become those whose strength expresses itself in faithfulness to Yhwh. It could suggest that people who have been inclined to follow other deities will be transformed and that people who have been exiled and devastated for their faithlessness will be restored to power but will exercise it in a faithful way.

All this is to assume that the oaks will express their own faithfulness in their lives. But *ṣedeq* more often refers to Yhwh's faithfulness (e.g., Is 62:1), and the splendor that the parallel colon in Isaiah 61:3 speaks of is presumably Yhwh's splendor. So perhaps the people will be oaks expressing faithfulness because their restoration, their new growth and their being in a position to hold their

---

[59]Most Masoretic MSS have *ḥemed*; the Leningrad MS has *ḥemer* (cf. 1QIs[a]).

[60]In itself the phraseology could indicate that Yhwh is attacking the vineyard itself as if punishing it for growing thorn and thistle, and NRSV heightens this impression, but this is hard to fit into the tenor of the passage as a whole.

head high will manifest Yhwh's faithfulness in doing the right thing by them. The image does still affirm the possibility of taking images associated with false religion and self-will, and redeeming them by associating Yhwh with them.

Prophets urge their people to turn. But they also become aware that their people are not going to turn. In a sense they cannot do so. Thus the prophets do not say to the exiles, "*Now* will you turn?" Hope lies not in the possibility that Israel will now turn back to Yhwh. It has to lie in Yhwh turning back to Israel. Yhwh is the subject of the key verbs when the prophets talk about the possibility of a hopeful future, and they rarely have conditions attached to them.[61] And Yhwh will still need to do a new work among the exiles themselves.

A Heart of Flesh

At present the people have a stone heart. The image suggests not a heart that is unfeeling but one that is quite inflexible. As a prophet, Ezekiel had only too much personal evidence of this condition of Israel's heart. Prophets had long been using every imaginable means to try to get through to Israel, to get people to change, but they had quite failed. The people's heart was as hard as Pharaoh's had been before the exodus. To replace that, Yhwh will give them a flesh heart (Ezek 11:19-20). His use of the term *flesh* provides a notable illustration of the different nuance of the word *flesh* in the First Testament. A flesh heart is good news not bad news, because flesh is soft and malleable. Press it and it gives. The people's flesh heart will be one that responds to being pushed by Yhwh or by Yhwh's servants.

The new heart will make them walk Yhwh's way. No doubt that includes putting right the moral and social wrongs in the community, though the context suggests that Ezekiel here has especially in mind the renewal of their relationship with Yhwh. That is suggested by the promise's starting point—the need to remove detestations and abominations from the land (Ezek 11:18)—and by the fact that Yhwh goes on to warn of the trouble that will come to people whose heart continues to be set on their "abominations and detestations" (Ezek 11:21). It also fits with Yhwh's promise that the result will be their being a people for Yhwh, and Yhwh's being God for them (Ezek 11:20). It looks as if Ezekiel conceives the situation differently from Jeremiah; he gives the impression that the covenant no longer obtains at the moment.[62] But then, they will do what Yhwh says about whom and how they worship, and thus the relationship will be a reality (cf. Ezek 14:11). So in a formal sense Ezekiel may conceptualize the situation and the promise differently, though the realities he pictures are the same.

---

[61]Cf. Fretheim's comments on Jer 30:1-3, *Jeremiah*, p. 415.
[62]See the comments in "Reaffirming the Covenant" (p. 382).

To put it another way, Yhwh will give them one heart or another heart, or both (Ezek 11:19). Here (and in Jer 32:39) MT promises "one heart" while LXX promises "another heart."[63] Later, when other aspects of the present promise recur, Ezekiel refers to the people having a new heart (Ezek 36:26-27). Other passages do refer to being given another heart (1 Sam 10:9) or having one heart (1 Chron 12:39; 2 Chron 30:12) or being faithful to Yhwh with a whole heart (šālēm, e.g., 1 Kings 11:4; 2 Kings 20:3) or with all their heart (e.g., Jer 3:10; 24:7).

Since the heart suggests the inner being, the thinking, the attitude and the will, having another heart or a new heart suggests a radical change in their thinking and attitude. Once again, they will no longer be inclined to follow the Master rather than Yhwh. In turn, having one heart can suggest a pair of related ideas. They will no longer be divided people—for instance, inconsistent in their loyalty toward Yhwh—and they will no longer be divided among themselves about whether or not to be faithful to Yhwh. They will thus be faithful to Yhwh with their whole heart or with all their heart.

In yet another formulation, Yhwh will put a new spirit in their midst or give them a new spirit or put Yhwh's spirit within them (Ezek 36:26-27). Talk of the spirit as opposed to the heart heightens the emphasis on the supernatural nature of what Yhwh will do because "spirit" points to what distinguishes God from humanity (Is 31:3). It suggests God's own dynamic. Ezekiel's particular nuance on this appears in the way he talks about spirit entering him and giving him new vigor and courage, standing him on his feet and turning him into someone who speaks for Yhwh (e.g., Ezek 2:2). Something like that will happen to the whole people to enable them to make that vigorous commitment to Yhwh that they have long been failing to make. Thus "I will make it that you walk by my statutes and keep my decisions and do them" (Ezek 36:27).

In Jeremiah 32:39 Yhwh's promise is of "one heart and one way" or of "another way and another heart" (LXX). The addition of the word way produces "a sort of hendiadys"[64] that brings out the link between the heart and the will. Changing their heart brings about a change in the "way" they live. It gives their life a new integrity and a new focus. They have been going the way of Egypt and the way of Assyria, going by a wicked way in the Hinnom Valley and in the ways of other deities, directing their way to lovers and teaching such ways to other people, changing their way, scattering their ways and perverting their way (Jer 2:17, 18, 23, 33, 36; 3:13, 21; cf. Jer 4:18; 5:4-5; 6:16, 27; 7:3, 5, 23; 10:2; 15:7; 18:11, 15). All that will be replaced by one way, and not one way that, for example, resolutely follows the Master or resolutely relies on

---

[63]Because "one" is ʾeḥād and "another" is ʾaḥēr, consonantally the difference in Hebrew is only the minute one between d and r.

[64]Gerald L. Keown et al., Jeremiah 26—52, WBC (Dallas: Word, 1995), p. 160.

Egypt, but "one heart and one way to revere me for all time, for their good and that of their children after them."

Throughout, it is the community that has a new heart and a new spirit. The prophets recognize that renewal is not merely a matter of changing individuals. Individuals are part of communities and are decisively shaped by their belonging to communities. God would not be satisfied with merely changing individuals as if individuals were self-contained entities that could, for instance, serve God separately from their being part of their community. God chose Israel as a people and wants to turn Israel as a people into an entity that glorifies God. If God changes individuals, that may do nothing for the corporate entity. If God changes the corporate entity, that will also bring about change in the individuals.

5.3 Israel's Response

The prospect of the nightmare becoming a reality presses on Israel the necessity to turn to Yhwh. That has the potential to avert it.[65] When the nightmare has actually become reality, once again that presses on Israel the necessity to turn to Yhwh. The dynamics of the second situation will overlap with the earlier one, but each will have a profile of its own.

The restoring of a relationship has to be two-sided. Israel's transformation requires action on Yhwh's part; it also requires action on Israel's part. Having promised a new heart, Yhwh later urges the community to "put away from you all your rebellions that you have committed and get yourselves a new heart, a new spirit" (Ezek 18:31). Literally Yhwh urges them to "make themselves a new heart" (ʿāśâ l), though that expression can be used in the manner of the English expression "make money" to refer to the acquisition of resources for which one may not be able to take the credit (e.g., Gen 31:1; Jer 17:11).[66] In the ordinary use of this expression, a tension is sometimes explicit or near the surface: Israel is not to say that it made/got all its wealth for itself (Deut 8:17), though it did, for instance, build the houses in question; Hezekiah made himself cities and flocks, because God gave him many possessions (2 Chron 32:29). So it is, too, with regard to the restoration of people to what God designed them to be. Yhwh will give them a new heart and spirit, but this does not happen by a unilateral act of the all-powerful divine surgeon. They have some responsibility. It is not merely a matter of opening themselves to what God wants to do, but of something more active than that. Like the Israelites *taking* Palestine, the exiles have to take positive action to "get themselves" a new heart. It is they who put away their rebellions and grasp a new life. Jesus' bid-

---

[65]See section 4.3.

[66]Cf. Allen, *Ezekiel*, 1:267.

ding will correspond to Ezekiel's when he tells the religious leaders of his day, "Make the tree good and its fruit good or make the tree bad and its fruit bad" (Mt 12:33).[67] It will perhaps correspond to it again when he urges the dead Lazarus, "Come out!" (Jn 11:43).

So Yhwh's taking the risk of turning back to Israel needs to be met by Israel's turning, its willingness to accept discipline and face shame and come to trust and revere Yhwh rather than anyone else. Israel needs to acknowledge who Yhwh is and who it is. It needs to see the dynamics of the process whereby things can be put right between it and Yhwh and they can move on.

Yhwh's Turning and Israel's Turning

To avert the nightmare, Israel would have needed to turn to Yhwh before disaster happened, to seek help from Yhwh rather than from other deities or other nations. They could thus have forestalled it; Yhwh would then have relented. But they did not do so, and therefore the turning must come after the disaster happens. Moses envisages that in exile, Israel can seek help from Yhwh if they do so with all their heart and soul, if they turn to Yhwh and listen to Yhwh and take what has happened to heart (*šûb* hiphil; e.g., Deut 4:25-30; 30:1-10). Solomon, too, envisages it: it will involve their taking it to heart (*šûb* hiphil) and turning and pleading with Yhwh and turning to Yhwh with all their heart and soul and calling on Yhwh (1 Kings 8:44-53). Jeremiah envisages it: in exile they need to call on Yhwh and come and plead with Yhwh and seek help from Yhwh with all their heart (Jer 29:12-14). "Turn to me and I will turn to you" (Mal 3:7). That will need to be expressed in the appropriate practical way, which for Malachi means starting to honor their obligation to tithe. In Jonah, there are two reasons for Yhwh's relenting about punishing Nineveh: the fact that the city turns from its wrongdoing and the fact that Yhwh is a merciful God.[68] In Israel's life, what is the relationship between these two considerations?

Hosea 14 simply juxtaposes the two factors. First it bids Israel to turn to Yhwh, to plead with Yhwh to carry its wrongdoing, to affirm that it will now trust in Yhwh rather than in alien gods or foreign powers. Then it has Yhwh promising, "I will heal their turning," their turning away to those other resources; "I will love them freely, because my anger has turned from them" (Hos 14:4). Yhwh will restore them and make it possible for them to flourish again. The fulfillment of Yhwh's vision requires Yhwh's act and Israel's act, Israel's turning and Yhwh's turning. But the passage leaves unstated the rela-

---

[67]Cf. Walther Zimmerli, *Ezekiel*, vol. 1 (Philadelphia: Fortress, 1979), p. 386.

[68]Cf. Ben Zvi, *The Signs of Jonah*, JSOTSup 367 (London/New York: Sheffield Academic Press, 2003), e.g., pp. 21-22.

tionship between these two turnings, suggesting the insight that there is no fixed relationship between them. Yhwh makes promises and urges Israel to respond to them but does not clarify the relationship between these two factors that will determine Israel's destiny.

The issue is neatly encapsulated in the complementary ministry of the two contemporary prophets in Jerusalem in the late sixth century, Haggai and Zechariah. For Haggai, the rebuilding of the temple is an obligation the people must accept (e.g., Hag 1:4-8). For Zechariah, it is a promise that Yhwh will fulfill (e.g., Zech 1:16). Yet conversely, Zechariah begins with an exhortation from Yhwh, "turn to me . . . and I will turn to you" (Zech 1:3). If Yhwh now says, "turn to me, and I will turn to you," then evidently the exiles' freedom to return to Judah does not in itself constitute Yhwh's turning to Judah. Indeed, even the rebuilding of the temple does not make it impossible for Yhwh to continue to urge, "turn to me and I will turn to you" (see Mal 3:7). Yhwh goes on to exhort the people not to be like their ancestors who declined to turn when the prophets urged them, or who turned only when the prophets' warnings overtook them (Zech 1:3-6).[69] The context makes clearer what "turning" means. The ancestors failed to turn "from your evil ways and from your evil deeds" by listening and giving heed to Yhwh (Zech 1:4). In Malachi, their turning is expressed in bringing the tithes that they are apparently withholding (Mal 3:7-8). Yhwh's turning is likewise expressed in acts, in making the people flourish and the ground fruitful and thus in doing good (Zech 8:3, 4-13, 15).[70]

One could almost translate Zechariah's opening exhortation, "turn to me and then I will turn to you," or even "turn to me so that I may turn to you" (Zech 1:3).[71] The form of words is very different from those in Isaiah 44:22, "turn to me, because I restore/have restored/will definitely restore/am restoring you." There the verb is qatal and any of those translations might be suggested, but however one understands the declaration, Yhwh's act is the basis for the appeal to return.[72] The logic is thus the opposite to that in Zechariah. There, Yhwh expects the people to make the first move. Yet Second Isaiah looks for a response from the people, and perhaps there will be no restoring unless they do respond. Conversely, in Zechariah the fact that Yhwh is speaking to them means Yhwh is making the first move—is turning to them—and

---

[69]But Meyers and Meyers (*Haggai, Zechariah 1—8*, pp. 89-97) see the present generation (the people Zechariah addresses), not the ancestors, as the subject of "they turned,"

[70]The promises in vv. 4-13 are book-ended by occurrences of the verb *šabtî*. The second is followed asyndetically by the verb *zāmamtî*, "I have planned," and one would usually take such a compound expression to mean "I have again planned" (cf. NRSV, NIVI), but in the context it seems likely that *šabtî* keeps something of its intrinsic meaning (cf. JPSV).

[71]The second verb is simple *w* plus yiqtol.

[72]See the comments in section 5.2 "Pardoning and Thus Transforming."

the subsequent visions are dominated by promises of divine action. Soon Yhwh will say, "I have turned to Jerusalem with compassion" (Zech 1:16).[73]

Taking a Risk

The prophets' ambiguity about the dynamics of the restoring of this relationship reappears in another form in Joel's invitation, "Turn to Yhwh your God, because he is gracious and compassionate, long-tempered, great in commitment, and rueful about calamity. Who knows, he may turn and be rueful, and leave behind him a blessing?" (Joel 2:13-14).[74] The opening imperative puts the obligation on the people. The reminder of Yhwh's self-revelation at Sinai then suggests that the basis for the restoring of the relationship lies in Yhwh's own nature. But the closing clauses note that the fact that one party in a relationship may turn does not guarantee that the other party will. The party that makes the move takes a risk; it can take nothing for granted. That applies to Israel; it also applies to Yhwh.

This ambiguity is hardly surprising because the dynamics of the making or restoring of *any* relationship are mysterious. How do relationships work? Reconciliation has to involve both parties, but one cannot lay down rules for how the reconciliation happens, even if it is clear that one of the parties is in the wrong. Either the offended party or the offending party has to make a risky move, but it may be either that does so.

Jeremiah 31:21-22 urges this question in a way that involves a triple paronomasia with the verb *turn*. Yhwh is making it possible for Israel to return to its own country (*šûb*), but it has to take to the road for itself. It has showed itself very skilled at turning in the sense of turning away from Yhwh and turning to other deities (*haššôbēb*, from the same verb). So why will it not use this skill in a more positive way. *Return!* Yhwh then further underlines this challenge by declaring that Yhwh is in the midst of a new act of creation that makes it possible for a woman (that is, Maiden Israel, the daughter inclined to turn away) to become one who "surrounds/changes/turns a man." The verb is ambiguous, but Jeremiah includes the saying (it may be a proverb) because the verb (*tĕsōbēb*) rhymes with "who turns" (*haššôbēb*). Perhaps the implication is that this mere woman is able to defeat the apparent "men" who currently control her destiny. That is a further basis for encouraging her to be a returner rather than a turner away.

"On that day there will be blowing on a great horn, and the wanderers in the country of Assyria and the people scattered in the country of Egypt will

---

[73]Again one should perhaps take this as an instantaneous or prophetic or performative qatal, implying "I am turning/I will definitely turn/I hereby turn."

[74]See section 4.3 "Act."

come, and will bow down to Yhwh on the holy mountain in Jerusalem" (Is 27:13). A blast on a horn is another ambiguous image: it could suggest the need to flee for safety (e.g., Jer 4:5; 6:1). But it is also associated with triumph and with worship, and a blast on a horn announces the beginning of the jubilee year (Lev 25:9). Here it will summon the Israelites to worship as if they are in Jerusalem within hearing of the temple, when in reality they are scattered over the thousand miles from Assyria to Egypt: not just within the bounds of the Israelite empire but residing in indisputably foreign territory. Further, the reference to Assyria suggests people scattered there from the eighth century to the sixth, and suggests people from Ephraim as well as from Judah. To describe them as "wandering" (ʾōbēd) recalls Jacob in the distant northwest (Deut 26:5), while "scattered" is a common description of the exiles (e.g., Jer 16:15), and in combination with others these two participles describe Israel's scattered sheep (Ezek 34:4, 16). It will be a great horn indeed that summons all these, though whether they will respond is a different question. The promise is a guarantee that the call will be issued. No one will be lost who longs to return. Yhwh takes the risk of issuing the summons. They have to respond to it.

Accepting Discipline

When Israel declares that it is turning back to Yhwh, on several occasions Yhwh intuits that the people's repentance is only word deep (e.g., Jer 14), but Jeremiah speaks of an occasion when Yhwh does not do so. Yhwh has heard Ephraim lamenting, "You disciplined me, and I let myself be disciplined, like an untrained bullock; let me return; I want to return" (Jer 31:18). On this occasion, Yhwh says, I have listened to them. There is nothing in the words that Ephraim has uttered that marks them as any more serious than those earlier words, but this time Yhwh has heeded them. Jeremiah does not say that this time they are serious, only that this time Yhwh is going to take the risk of treating them thus. Ephraim claims to have accepted the discipline that Yhwh has often talked about and imposed (e.g., Lev 26:18, 28; Jer 2:19; 6:8; Hos 7:12; 10:10).[75] It accepts that it was not actually as broken in as Yhwh once assumed (Hos 10:11) but says it has now accepted the training Yhwh attempted to give, which involved Yhwh getting up early each morning to give it (Jer 32:33). It has accepted the yoke against which it rebelled (Jer 5:5). Once again it wants to return (Hos 6:1) and break the habit of a lifetime (Jer 3:7, 10), and it wants Yhwh this time not to refuse it the chance to do so (Jer 3:1; contrast Jer 3:12, 14, 22). It affirms its commitment to Yhwh instead of putting Yhwh and Yhwh's name out of mind (Jer 23:27; Hos 2:13 [MT 15]). It had turned away from Yhwh

---

[75]See section 4.4 "Discipline."

and not relented (e.g., Jer 8:4, 6), but now it has relented. Once it had not acknowledged the truth (e.g., Jer 4:22; 5:4-5), but now it has acknowledged it. It
recognizes the shame in its life that goes back to its young days.

It is a wondrous vision of hope to imagine Ephraim making such a statement and meaning it. It is all very well for Yhwh to declare the intention to put
Babylon down or make it possible for Judeans to return to their own country;
that need not require human cooperation. Getting people to recognize the
truth about themselves is a different matter. On this occasion Yhwh behaves as
if Ephraim has done so. Perhaps this is because it is true repentance and Yhwh
intuits this, though the passage does not say so. If anything, it points in the
other direction. Yhwh decides to take Ephraim at its word because of a longing
for it to be true, and perhaps because if Yhwh takes people at their word, their
word may become true as they respond to such a show of grace. So Yhwh really listens, really brings to mind and really has compassion (Jer 31:18-20).[76]
And that is because Ephraim is the son Yhwh loves. A mother wants to give
her children the benefit of the doubt even when they may not deserve it. There
are feelings that emerge from inside that impel her in that direction.[77] Like the
prodigal's father in Jesus' story, she will certainly hasten to welcome them
back when they claim to have seen sense and return. Whether or not
Ephraim's turning is true, accepting discipline is what is needed.

In the last decades before the exile, Judah does not understand the necessity
that it experience wrath rather than *shalom*, but "in later days you will understand it clearly" (Jer 23:20). The cataclysmic falling of this wrath in the destruction of Jerusalem will make many people face the facts from which they were
previously hiding. Meanwhile, Jerusalem's failure is a failure of reflection,
thought and memory. "In all your abominations and promiscuous acts you did
not think about your young days," the days Yhwh took hold of her (Ezek 16:22,
43). Or alternatively she thought about the wrong aspects of her youth (Ezek
23:19). Fortunately Yhwh does not so fail. Yhwh thinks about the covenant (Ezek
16:60). But Israel will learn to think about itself. When Yhwh restores the people
"you will think about your evil ways and your deeds that were not good"; they
will face facts (Ezek 36:31). By taking them through the disaster of exile and then
restoring them, Yhwh will cause people to become aware of the enormity of
their faithlessness. It will act like a course of electric shock therapy that jolts their
minds into another way of looking at themselves and their actions. Yhwh will
soften their hearts, replace their inflexible spirits by malleable ones.

---

[76]Each time Jeremiah uses the infinitive absolute construction.

[77]The word translated "heart" (*mēʿîm*) can refer to the womb (see BDB), and the verb for
"have compassion" (*rāham*) is related to the regular word for womb (*rehem*). See Phyllis Trible, *God and the Rhetoric of Sexuality* (Philadelphia: Fortress, 1978), pp. 44-45.

Shame and Self-Loathing

Such reflection is the result, or even the aim, of Yhwh's acting and restoring the relationship with the people, and the reflection in turn generates shame and self-loathing. Acknowledgment thus leads to thinking, and thinking to shame (Ezek 16:62-63). These three verbs recur to describe the process whereby the people's inner person is changed, though they can come in other orders. They think, they loathe and they acknowledge Yhwh (Ezek 6:9-10). They think, they loathe, they acknowledge, they are ashamed (Ezek 36:31-32). One would expect a vision for the future to include the idea that the shame of the present would be ended; shame would be no more. And so it does (Is 45:17; 49:23; 54:4; Zeph 3:11). But before that, Ezekiel emphasizes the positive role for shame. It encourages change.

As far as Yhwh is concerned, at present Israel is a bad smell, but Yhwh is going to change that and make them a pleasing fragrance. And then, back in the land, "you will bring to mind your ways and all your deeds by which you have defiled yourselves, and you will be loathsome to yourselves for all your wrongs that you have done, but you will acknowledge that I am Yhwh when I deal with you for the sake of my name, not in accordance with your wrong ways and your corrupt deeds" (Ezek 20:42-44). They will come to recognize how things were and how they now are, and as a result they will come to be as loathsome in their own faces (as Ezekiel literally puts it) as they currently are loathsome to Yhwh's sense of smell. That will be an unpleasant experience, but a realistic one. It will mean they face up to the facts. And either side of that talk of coming to loathe themselves is reference to coming to acknowledge Yhwh, which is itself a serious business, but also an indication of bringing about the thing they themselves want. They want to relate to Yhwh. They need to be jolted into doing it the right way, the only way that will work. And for Yhwh's own sake that will come about. There is no doubt of the reason. It is not to make Israel feel good. Rather, the reason relates to the fact that what happens to Israel does not depend on Israel's commitment—or rather on Israel's "wrong ways and corrupt deeds." Everything is for the sake of Yhwh's name, Yhwh's holiness, the revelation of Yhwh's deity (see further Ezek 36:16-32).[78]

Jerusalem has to live with the shame and humiliation of its wrongdoing. Yet shame and forgiveness are somehow linked: "I myself will establish my covenant with you, and you will acknowledge that I am Yhwh, so that you may think and feel humiliation and not be able to open your mouth again because of your shame, when I absolve you for all that you did" (Ezek 16:62-63). Here

---

[78]Baruch J. Schwartz argues that the very restoration of the people is thus an extension of their punishment: see "Ezekiel's Dim View of Israel's Restoration," in *The Book of Ezekiel*, ed. Margaret S. Odell and John T. Strong (Atlanta, Ga.: Scholars Press, 2000), pp. 43-67.

the references to shame and humiliation are bracketed by references to Yhwh's covenant-making and absolution or atonement or cleansing.[79] The fact that Yhwh establishes the covenant with them, along with their lack of deserve, means they will have nothing to open their mouth in complaint about; they will not have shame that they will attempt to blame Yhwh for (as they do at present).[80]

Yhwh's promise to give Israel a new heart likewise leads into the declaration that they will reflect on their evil ways and their wrongdoings, "and you will be loathsome in your own eyes because of all your wrongdoings and because of your abominations. Not for your sake am I acting (the Lord Yhwh's message), be it acknowledged by you. Be humiliated and ashamed because of your ways, household of Israel." Yhwh then goes on to more reference to cleansing the people of their wrongdoing (Ezek 36:31-33). Again, Yhwh declares, "I will bring about the restoration of Jacob and have compassion on the whole household of Israel and be passionate for my holy name. And they will carry their shame and all their offenses that they committed against me, when they dwell on their soil in security with no one making them making them afraid, when I have brought them back from the peoples, gathered them from the countries of their enemies" (Ezek 39:25-26).[81] Even the wondrous picture of Yhwh returning in splendor to the temple and the commission to get on with the building of this temple is interrupted by the declaration that "they are to be ashamed of their wrongdoings"; it is when they have become so ashamed that Ezekiel is to make the plans known (Ezek 43:10-11).

Somehow it is almost impossible for Ezekiel to speak of restoration without speaking of shame. Yhwh's act of restoration is based on a concern for Yhwh's own name to be vindicated. Yet references to shame are embraced by references to restoration, compassion, commitment and forgiveness. Knowing about God's grace enables people to own their previous failings, and owning their failings opens them up to God's restoration.[82] Shame is "a gift from God."[83]

Coming to Trust

Whereas Israel's faithlessness included an inclination to rely on powers such as Assyria, they will now no longer "continue to lean on the one who hit them"

---

[79]On the verb *kipper*, see section 2.6 "Cleansing."

[80]Cf. Margaret S. Odell, "The Inversion of Shame and Forgiveness in Ezekiel 16:59-63," *JSOT* 56 (1992): 101-12.

[81]NIVI and NRSV "forget" involves altering MT's *nāśû* to *nāšû*.

[82]Again, see Christopher D. Marshall, *Beyond Retribution* (Grand Rapids/Cambridge: Eerdmans, 2001), pp. 132-35.

[83]Jacqueline E. Lapsley, "Shame and Self-Knowledge," in *The Book of Ezekiel*, ed. Margaret S. Odell and John T. Strong (Atlanta: Scholars Press, 2000), pp. 143-73; see p. 159.

but "will lean on Yhwh, Israel's holy one, in truth" (Is 10:20). There is a paradox about Judah's life. They have been treating as their source of security one who was going to hit them. Like the victim of an abusive husband or father, one could imagine the victim of these attacks continuing to rely on their attacker, because what else can they do? They can hope there will be no more attacks and that the attacker will now be the protector, as they always hoped. Isaiah's promise is that the dynamics of this abusive relationship will be terminated. The abuser has been put in jail, and this jolting experience will draw his victims to put their reliance in the place it always should have been. The idea that "leftovers will return" (šĕʾār yāšûb, Is 10:21) finds a new meaning. The people who have survived because they were lucky (not because they deserved it) will become the faithful remnant. Similarly, when Yhwh puts down Egypt and then restores it as an ordinary nation but not one with pretensions to superpower significance, Egypt "will no longer be an object of trust for Israel, bringing to mind the wrongdoing in their turning after them" for help (Ezek 29:16).

Zephaniah makes a similar promise to the city about its leftovers. "They will take refuge in Yhwh's name. . . . They are the ones who will pasture and lie down with no one disturbing them" (Zeph 3:11-13). The leftovers will be the "weak and poor." As usual, those are not moral or spiritual qualities, and as far as we know the ordinary people in Jerusalem were just as inclined to worship other deities or make images of Yhwh as were politicians, priests and prophets. Yet there are temptations that the powerless and resourceless escape. They are unlikely to become convinced of their own importance and dignity. In worldly terms they have no importance or dignity, so for them an event such as the fall of Jerusalem will not have the same shattering significance that it has for the people who matter. They will not be taken off into exile; indeed, they may be able to take over the homes and estates of the people who are taken off. But the downfall of the state will become their testing. Yhwh's promise to the personified city is that the weak and poor will find refuge in Yhwh, rather than in those other deities or in their newfound opportunities. Changes in social structures and these opportunities that the new situation brings could push them into the same wrongs that have especially characterized the people who used to be in power, the deceit and falsehood. But this will not happen. The people who are leftovers because they are fortunate enough to escape disaster will become the faithful leftovers. And they will find that this is the key to the security that everyone is tempted to seek by other means.

On that day Israel's impressive cities will become like the places that people abandoned before the Israelites. Events will make clear that it is as foolish for Israel to trust in its fortifications as it was for the people who lived in the land before Israel. There is a fortress that is worth trusting, but it is not a humanly made one, or even a humanly identified one. On a number of occasions the fine natural and human fortifications of Jerusalem failed to live up to people's hopes. The secret of deliverance lies elsewhere, in the God who is the people's fortress. Likewise the secret of a good harvest lies somewhere other than in the traditional rites offered in honor of the deities that allegedly specialized in making the crops grow. Indeed, these will prove as unreliable as those fortifications. It is a nightmare prospect, but a positive one in that it introduces Israel to living in light of reality, not self-imposed fantasy.

Owning Doubt But Revering Yhwh

Yhwh's action will mean the service of Babylon will be replaced by service of Yhwh and of David (Jer 30:9). But a century later, in the secrecy of their hearts or in the privacy of their homes, the contemporaries of Malachi say, "Serving God is futile" (Mal 3:14). Serving God (ʿābad) can cover both worship and obedience to God's word in everyday life. Either way, people mutter, there is no profit in keeping God's charge and walking in mourning (for the sins of the past? for the hard experiences of the present?). It is the arrogant who deserve to be reckoned the fortunate ones. They do well in life. They test God and get away with it. It is paradoxical that the people who speak thus are described as people who revere Yhwh. These are tough words they speak, Yhwh comments (Mal 3:13-15).

And Yhwh listened attentively, and one might have thought that their words would bring a declaration of judgment on their heads, but they do not do so. Instead Yhwh had a memo put on file for these people who "revered Yhwh and reflected on his name. They will be mine, Yhwh Armies has said, on the day I am making a personal possession. I will pity them as a man pities his son who serves him. And you will again see the difference between the faithful and the faithless person, between the one who serves God over against the one who has not served him" (Mal 3:16-18). Apparently Yhwh's special possession (sĕgullâ) is now not the people as a whole (as in Ex 19:5; Deut 7:6; 14:2; 26:18; Ps 135:4) but the faithful within this people (the New Testament will reapply it to the people as a whole: Eph 1:14; Tit 2:14; 1 Pet 2:9).

The people feel forgotten; Yhwh promises that they are not. For on that day the fate of the arrogant and the faithless will be like that of straw in a fire. "But for you who revere my name a faithful sun will shine with healing in its rays. And you will go out and jump like calves from the stall and tread down the faithless, because they will be ash under the soles of your feet on the day that I am forming, Yhwh Armies has said" (Mal 4:1-3 [MT 3:19-21]). The people who revere Yhwh will find that the sun does not burn them up but instead brings them warmth and thus healing, which is elsewhere an image for restoration from the ravages of war and loss (Jer 8:15; 33:6).[84] It might seem that the calves are trampling the wicked to death, but elsewhere it is Yhwh's business to put down the wicked; here the language is allusive. More likely the wicked have been burned up and the calves are treading on their burned remains.

The promise is accompanied by two warnings (Mal 4:4-6 [MT 3:22-24]). First, these people who revere Yhwh must apply themselves to the teaching Yhwh gave Moses at Horeb. Second, they need to remember that for them, too, Yhwh's day is "great and awesome," and could turn into bad news. It could mean that Yhwh strikes the land with devotion to destruction; ḥērem is the last word in the book and thus the last word in the Prophets, and the last word of the First Testament in English.[85] Yhwh is safeguarding against that by sending Elijah the prophet to the people, Elijah being available for such a commission because he was taken to heaven rather than dying (2 Kings 2:11-12). He will forestall the threat by turning the heart of ancestors to children and that of children to ancestors. The current generation has, after all, profaned its ancestors' covenant (Mal 2:10); indeed, the children of Levi are defiled and the children of Jacob have been turning away from Yhwh's statutes since the time of the ancestors (Mal 3:3, 6-7). It is easy to imagine the ancestors therefore wanting to disown their children. So the present generation need to turn back to their ancestors so that they may also turn back to them, as the present generation need to turn to Yhwh so that Yhwh may turn to them (Mal 3:7).[86]

Acknowledging Yhwh the Distraught Destroyer

Israel will thus also learn to think about who Yhwh truly is. "In the aftermath of the days you will perceive it clearly" (Jer 23:20; cf. Jer 30:24). Jeremiah is referring to the facts about Yhwh's wrath that other prophets deny. "I will give them a heart to acknowledge me, that I am Yhwh; they will be a people for me and I will be God for them, when they turn to me with their whole heart" (Jer 24:7). As is often the case, at both points we might understand lēb, "heart," to refer to the mind and will at least as much as the emotions. Conversely, yādāʿ, "acknowledge," covers the activity of acknowledging Yhwh and not just the mental awareness of knowing something about Yhwh or the experience of intimacy with Yhwh. At the moment people turn their backs on Yhwh, but when Yhwh acts, people "will acknowledge that I am Yhwh" (e.g., Ezek 6:14). It is a

---

[84]Andrew E. Hill, Malachi, AB (New York: Doubleday, 1998), p. 351. See section 5.2 "Healing."

[85]Not in the LXX, where the Twelve Prophets precede Isaiah, though LXX does change the order of the verses to avoid this effect. The Hebrew Bible repeats the penultimate verse to the same end.

[86]There is nothing in Malachi to suggest that children and parents need to turn to one another (so EVV), for which one might expect the singular nouns, whereas Malachi does thus use ʾābôt to refer to ancestors and bānîm to refer to their descendants in the prophet's day.

recurrent pledge in Ezekiel.[87] This common phrase also involves an ellipse. Ezekiel is not concerned merely with people's tautological acknowledgment that Yhwh is Yhwh. He is here concerned with people acknowledging that the one who has brought disaster on them is Yhwh. That carries with it a recognition that this was an act of punishment from that God. And it carries with it an acknowledgment of Yhwh, an acknowledgment that Yhwh is God and a submission to Yhwh. "Acknowledging that I am Yhwh" implies acknowledging that I alone am God, acknowledging that Yhwh is Lord of heaven and earth.[88]

So this recognition will come about in part through recognizing that Yhwh has been active in bringing calamity. "My anger will spend itself and I will release my fury on them and satisfy myself, and they will acknowledge that I, Yhwh, spoke in my passion when I expend my fury on them" (Ezek 5:13). When Yhwh has killed the worshipers at the local sanctuaries, they "will acknowledge that I am Yhwh." Others who are scattered rather than killed "will acknowledge that I am Yhwh. It was not for nothing that I spoke of doing this bad thing to them" (Ezek 6:7, 10; cf. Ezek 6:13, 14; 7:4, 9, 27; 11:10, 12; 12:15-16, 20). Exclusion of prophets and elders from Yhwh's people, their death when the city falls and the people's deliverance from their deceptiveness will have the same effect (Ezek 13:9, 14, 21, 23; 14:8). The setting of Yhwh's face against the people of Jerusalem for their faithlessness will cause the exiles to acknowledge that it is Yhwh (Ezek 15:7). Yhwh gave Israel statutes that would only lead to their defilement and death "so that I might devastate them, so that they might acknowledge that I am Yhwh" (Ezek 20:26).[89] Yhwh will bring the people who revolt and rebel out from the land where they are in exile but not take them back to the land, "and you will acknowledge that I am Yhwh" (Ezek 20:38). "You will be profaned in yourselves [MT]/I will be profaned through you [LXX, Syr., Vg.] before the eyes of the nations, and you will acknowledge that I am Yhwh" (Ezek 22:16). "They will put your vileness upon you and you will carry your idolatrous shortcoming, and you will acknowledge that I am the Lord Yhwh" (Ezek 23:49). Ezekiel's wife will die, but he will not mourn her, because the imminent death of Jerusalem makes the mere death of one's wife insignificant, and through that "you will acknowledge that I am the Lord Yhwh" (Ezek 24:24, cf. 27). When Yhwh makes the land desolate, "they will acknowledge that I am Yhwh" (Ezek 33:29).

In a strange way, there is reassurance in this tough process. When the exiles see the faithlessness of the kind of people who live in Jerusalem (some of

---

[87]See Walther Zimmerli, *I Am Yahweh* (Atlanta, Ga.: John Knox Press, 1982).

[88]See section 2.1 "The God Who Speaks and Acts," "Only God."

[89]In the context "devastate" might refer to being outwardly destroyed or to being inwardly appalled.

whom Yhwh allows to escape from the calamity for this purpose) they will be reassured that the city had to fall, and they "will acknowledge that not without cause did I do all that I will have done in it" (Ezek 14:23).

There is another motif in this talk about acknowledging Yhwh as destroyer. When Jerusalem falls, Yhwh will spare some of the community from death and they will escape to be scattered among the nations, and there they "will think about me among the nations where they are taken as captives, how I was broken by their promiscuous heart that turned away from me and their promiscuous eyes that turned after their pillars. And they will be loathsome in their own eyes for the wrongs that they did, for all their abominations" (Ezek 6:9). The recognition we have been considering could look like a mere submission to a frightening power. It is as well that it also comes about through the process of reflection (*zākar*) on the way Yhwh was broken-hearted at the people's unfaithfulness. The experience of disaster, escape and captivity will impel such reflection that recognizes what these events say about Yhwh. They are not merely the acts of a judge; indeed, arguably a judge would not be so harsh. They are the acts of someone who is heartbroken. And this realization also leads to the people's recognizing the loathsomeness of their behavior. They are like an adulterous husband whose eyes come to be opened to the pain as well as the anger in his wife's reaction to his wrongdoing and who is thus led to recognize how sickening his behavior has been.

Acknowledging Yhwh the Life-Giver

Acknowledgment of Yhwh thus relates to more than Yhwh's destructiveness. In Ezekiel, the future "is dependent not upon man's ability to respond but upon God's willingness to act. . . . The will of God is for life." That does not remove the need for human response, but even this response "is really no matter of human endeavour but entirely of divine grace."[90]

Yhwh's aim from the beginning was simply that people should acknowledge Yhwh as Yhwh. At the beginning, "I caused myself to be acknowledged by them in the country of Egypt" (Ezek 20:5). It was the reason for Yhwh's giving them the sabbath "as a sign between me and them" (Ezek 20:12, 20). The phraseology suggests a link with the covenant. This gift was part of the way "I caused myself to be acknowledged by them . . . in bringing them out of the country of Egypt" (Ezek 20:9). Of course that did not work. But the exiles "will acknowledge that I am Yhwh" when Yhwh brings them back into the land to worship Yhwh there (Ezek 20:42). "You will acknowledge that I am Yhwh when I deal with you for the sake of my name, not in accordance with your

---

[90]Ackroyd, *Exile and Restoration*, p. 109.

bad ways and your corrupt acts" (Ezek 20:44). When Yhwh gathers scattered Israel and resettles the people on their own soil, and they live in safety there, "they will acknowledge that I am Yhwh their God" (Ezek 28:26).

To Ezekiel, Yhwh says "I will make a horn flourish for the household of Israel, and to you I will give an opening of the mouth in their midst, and they will acknowledge that I am Yhwh" (Ezek 29:21). An animal's horn is crucial to its strength, and the horn is thus an image for strength. In 587 Yhwh had cut off Judah's horn (Lam 2:3), but Yhwh will make it grow again. Ezekiel will therefore have reason to speak with them on a new basis. Once he had kept silent because the people's resistance made Yhwh uninterested in speaking to them (Ezek 3:25-27). Now he will feel free to speak because the fulfillment of his declarations about the restoration of the community will enable him to hold his head high in the community. He does not seem to have in mind here the fact that they, in contrast to Ezekiel, will need to hang their heads low and keep their mouths shut (Ezek 16:63, the only other occurrence of *pithôn*, the word for "opening"). It is this restoring of their strength with its positive implications for Ezekiel that will lead to his speaking and to their acknowledgment of Yhwh.

Yhwh will make a *shalom* covenant with them, giving them a secure and prosperous new life on their land,[91] "and they will acknowledge that I am Yhwh when I break the bars of their yoke and rescue them from the hand of the people who enslave them. . . . They will acknowledge that I, Yhwh their God, am with them and that they, the household of Israel, are my people" (Ezek 34:27, 30). Israel's mountains will know great flourishing of crops, animals and human settlements, "and I will do better than your original state, and you will acknowledge that I am Yhwh" (Ezek 36:11). "The ruined cities will be filled with flocks of people, and they will acknowledge that I am Yhwh" (Ezek 36:38). The community brought back to life "will acknowledge that I am Yhwh" (Ezek 37:6). Yhwh will bring the community back to life and put them on their own soil, "and you will acknowledge that I Yhwh have spoken and will act" (Ezek 37:14). "I will put my splendor among the nations" in acting authoritatively against them, "and the household of Israel will acknowledge that I am Yhwh their God from that day" (Ezek 39:21-22). When Yhwh restores the people, "they will acknowledge that I am Yhwh their God when I exile them to the nations but gather them upon their soil and do not leave any of them behind there" (Ezek 39:28).

It is not just Israel that is involved in this pattern. When Yhwh puts down Egypt and then restores it as just an ordinary nation rather than one with su-

---

[91]See further section 5.5.

perpower pretensions, Israel will no longer be tempted to trust in it and "will acknowledge that I am the Lord Yhwh" (Ezek 29:16). Nor will it be Israel alone that thus acknowledges Yhwh. "All the trees in the countryside [i.e., the other peoples] will acknowledge that I, Yhwh, brought low the exalted tree and exalted the low tree, dried up the green tree and made the dry tree flourish. I, Yhwh, have spoken and will act" (Ezek 17:24). When Yhwh punishes other peoples, they "will acknowledge that I am Yhwh" (Ezek 25:5, 7, 11, 17; 26:6; 28:22, 23, 24; 29:6, 9; 30:8, 19, 25, 26; 32:15; 35:4, 9, 15; 38:23; 39:6). And when Yhwh restores and renews Israel, "the nations will acknowledge that I am Yhwh (message of the Lord Yhwh) when I show my holiness through you before their eyes" (Ezek 36:23). "The nations that are left around you will acknowledge that I, Yhwh, have built up the ruins, planted the desolation" (Ezek 36:36). The nations more generally "will acknowledge that I, Yhwh, am sanctifying Israel when my sanctuary is in their midst forever" (Ezek 37:28). "I will cause my holy name to be acknowledged in the midst of my people Israel and I will not cause my holy name to be profaned again, and the nations will acknowledge that I am Yhwh, the holy one in Israel" (Ezek 39:7).

Acknowledging Yhwh the Restorer

Second Isaiah's way of making the point is to speak of acknowledging Yhwh as the one who has "restored" them. The verb (gā'al) could be used for the freeing of indentured servants, reinstating them in their place in the community, through the action of a member of the extended family who paid the debt that had led to their losing their independence.[92] It is such action that Yhwh promises, though of course it will not involve paying money. Isaiah 52:3-6 draws comparisons and contrasts between past and present experiences with foreign peoples. First, there was the Israelites' time in Egypt, which ended up as an experience of oppression, but did not start that way. The Israelites went to Egypt voluntarily to "sojourn" there (gûr), to live there as resident aliens in the time of a famine. They were in a position like that of individual resident aliens in Israel who were living in this foreign land for some reason and thus had no land of their own, no (reasonably secure) guarantee of somewhere to live and somewhere to grow food, and were thus dependent on finding employment or charity. And that position in Egypt was fine for Israel for some time. On the other hand, there was nothing positive about Israel's forced exile at the hands of the Mesopotamian powers. The Assyrians oppressed the northern clans, and neither Israel nor Yhwh has gained anything from the Babylonian exile. There in Babylon its rulers exult over Yhwh instead of exulting in Yhwh, prais-

---

[92]See section 2.2 "Restorer."

ing Yhwh.[93] They continue to glory in the capture of Jerusalem and the defeat of Yhwh, ever brought home by the presence of that hostage Judean community in Babylon. Thus Yhwh's name is continually despised.

All that will change when Babylon in turn falls and the Judeans are free to go home, as Yhwh "restores" them. Through being treated as part of Yhwh's family to whom Yhwh has that moral obligation, the community in bondage there will find itself restored to its proper position, though without Yhwh paying a price for that. Centuries previously Yhwh had surrendered Egypt, Sudan and Ethiopia to Pharaoh as the price of freeing Israel (Is 43:3), but Babylon is even less deserving of such a deal than was Pharaoh, and it will receive nothing. Cyrus will take everything away, and the Judeans will be free.

That will lead to acknowledgment of Yhwh, but surprisingly it is not the Babylonians who will give it (contrast, e.g., Is 49:26). "My people" will do so. That perhaps reflects a contrasting reality that lies behind the talk of Babylonian rulers despising Yhwh. By implication they of course did so and their sitting in power was a standing insult to Yhwh. But it is unlikely that they actually thought much about their relationship with the obscure deity of this obscure ethnic minority in Babylon. The people who thought more about Yhwh and implicitly reviled Yhwh were the Judeans themselves. It is they who first need to acknowledge that Yhwh is the one, and they will do so when Yhwh does that work of delivering them.

"Now" a new day has dawned (Is 29:22-24). Shame in relation to its religious choices and its political choices was to be part of Israel's nightmare, but that will not be the end of the story. Those choices would issue in defeat and exile and thus in shame, but Jacob's children will "now" see a new act of Yhwh. This promise, too, reminds the people of their link with Abraham and Jacob, the recipients of the original promise whom Yhwh then "redeemed" (pādâ); even when applied to Abraham, that verb presumably suggests the exodus, the act whereby Yhwh redeemed Abraham's people. And this new act will lead them to "hallow" or sanctify Yhwh's name. This promise and the succeeding ones take up motifs from the story that follows the exodus.[94] Then, Moses and Aaron failed to hallow Yhwh (Num 20:12; 27:14). Then, the people needed repeated exhortations not to stand in awe of other peoples (ʿāraṣ, Deut 1:29; 7:21; 20:3; 31:6); Isaiah has already spoken of the need to be in awe of

---

[93]"Exult" renders the verb yĕhêlîlû, which looks like a form from yālal, "howl," but that fits ill in the context. Tg. suggests taking it as a form from hālal, which perhaps needs repointing as yĕhallēlû (cf. D. Winton Thomas, Liber Jesaiqe, Biblia Hebrica Stuttgartensia 7 (Stuttgart: Wörttembergische Bibelanstalt, 1968).

[94]Cf. Wildberger, Isaiah 28—39, pp. 116-17.

Yhwh rather than of other people (Is 8:13-14). Then, people went astray (*tāʿâ*) in heart (Ps 95:10; cf. Ps 107:4). Then, they complained (*rāgan*, Deut 1:27; Ps 106:25, the only other occurrences of the verb). This act of deliverance will have the effect on the people's spirit that the first act of deliverance did not. The people whose life has been characterized by going astray in spirit and complaining will now hallow and stand in awe, acknowledge insight and accept instruction.

It is "a test of the genuineness of the knowledge and confession of sin whether the man who is willing and ready to accuse himself of corruption and transgression, and therefore to bewail the fact that he is lost, can with the same or an even greater willingness and readiness accept and affirm the sentence of God on this other side" and thus "grasp the promise of God and look and go forward and not backward." For if we cannot accept God's word of grace, it is doubtful whether we have accepted God's assessment of us as wrongdoers. Our self-critique may be simply another expression of our pride, a way of evading God's assessment. If we accept God's Yes, it is a sign that it is truly God's No that we accepted.[95]

Recognizing Its Wrongdoing

The way Israel behaves in relation to Yhwh over the centuries has involved appalling offensiveness. Israel has rather consistently declined to treat Yhwh as God, whether in the realm of politics (where it was inclined to trust other political powers) or nature (where it was inclined to turn to the Masters) or worship (where it was inclined to offer worship in the way it saw fit, if it offered Yhwh worship at all). Yhwh of course does not have a problem about carrying that wrongdoing. But Yhwh does have a problem in getting Israel to see the wrong it has done. And once Israel sees it, it might have a problem forgiving itself for it, and might long to be able to offer Yhwh something to make amends for its wrongdoing. The vision of Yhwh's servant in Isaiah 53 speaks to both those problems.

The vision portrays "us," which I take to be Israel—and specifically Israel in exile—coming to see something that for a long time it could not see, quite understandably (Is 53:1-3). The servant the vision describes is someone quite unprepossessing, like a spindly plant growing in desert soil. There is nothing impressive about him, nothing to attract people. He is not an inspiring leader. He is not merely ordinary, but distinctively pathetic, like God in the movie *Dogma*. He is the kind of person you look away from. It has been suggested that the prophet is describing someone with a disfiguring skin disease; the

---

[95]Barth, *Church Dogmatics*, IV/1:593-94.

prophecy is too allusive to come to that concrete conclusion, but this suggestion gives the right idea regarding the servant's appearance and people's consequent reaction.

When we get ill, we are tempted to ask, "What did I do to deserve this?"
When other people get ill, we are tempted to ask, "What did they do to deserve
that?" When they fail to get healed, we are tempted to reckon, for instance, that
they have not prayed with enough faith or tried the right course of treatment.
The servant's contemporaries (like Job's friends) inferred from his ill-fortune
that he must indeed have done something to deserve it. Actually (they have
eventually come to realize) he was suffering in order to help them in some
way. This does not need to imply suffering instead of them. After all, the original audience of this prophecy was the Judeans in the sixth century, who were
suffering themselves. The servant did not suffer in their place. He suffered
with them. He carried their weaknesses, took up their great suffering. He
shared in their experience of displacement and loss. He is a figure like Jeremiah, who was attacked as a false prophet and treated as someone who
worked against Yhwh's purpose rather than for it, and who shared in the displacement and loss of exile when he did not deserve it. The servant has analogous experiences that people reckoned came because he was unfaithful to
Yhwh but that actually came because he was fulfilling his vocation from Yhwh
by sharing in people's displacement and loss. And they came because of the
way his own people treated him in return for the ministry he exercised because
of Yhwh's calling. Yhwh thus let their wrongdoing fall on him. Further, ironically it was of course the case that the people who were suffering because of
their unfaithfulness were the other exiles. He was suffering to identify with
them not only in their loss but also in the sin that had caused it. "He was hurt
because of our rebellions." They had wandered away from Yhwh like sheep
wandering away from their shepherd, turned to go their own way rather than
walking with Yhwh and in Yhwh's way (Is 53:4-6).

The people of God who speak thus had to come to a radically new assessment of the significance of the servant's affliction. That apparently happened
through the way the servant handled his experience (Is 53:7-9). There was
something uncanny about it, something that did not fit their assumptions
about him. Their assumption was that he was under God's deserved punishment for his wrongdoing, though he refused to acknowledge this truth about
what was going on. Do people in such a situation react to their punishment the
way he did? He accepted the affliction that came rather than struggling against
it (here he perhaps goes beyond Jeremiah). He would not open his mouth, the
vision twice notes, as if this were especially extraordinary. And it is. The correct First Testament reaction to suffering is to protest at it, as the examples of
Jeremiah, Job and countless psalms show. But this servant would not open his

mouth, and certainly was not guilty of doing wrong by means of his words.[96] What is going on here? Who is this person?

As is the case in relation to the world, the First Testament does not think there is a problem with God's forgiving the wrongdoing of the people of God when they turn from their wrongdoing, as if that compromised God's holiness. The holiness of God is dominated by mercy.[97] The First Testament does see a problem in how the people of God can be prevailed upon to turn back to Yhwh and be weaned from their rebelliousness and turned into a people that live in covenant. God's servant achieves that. He is someone who needs to expect to be attacked by the people of God and by the world, but through this extraordinary life with its acceptance of affliction and its triumphant vindication, the deep-seated obtuseness of God's people will at last be overcome.

Seeing a Revelation

The point about sharing in the people's deserved experience of suffering and letting them afflict him, then, is similar to the point about Jeremiah's going through such trouble. It was in order to put things right between Judah and God, to encourage a healing of that relationship, to get Judah to turn back to Yhwh. The servant suffers to make things well for the people of God (to bring them *shalom*), to bring them healing (Is 53:5). The NRSV and NIVI have this happening because the servant is undergoing "punishment." This could be misleading, and KJV's "chastisement" is better. The word *(mûsār)* is a term for the disciplining of a child by a parent or that of a pupil by a teacher, which are designed to bring the person to change or grow. It is not a term for the judicial action designed to effect retribution for an offense. Isaiah 53 does not use a judicial framework for understanding the relationship between God and people. The servant is not punished for wrongdoing committed by others, an idea that would be abhorrent to the First Testament. By its nature guilt is not transferable. In any case, we have noted that Israel itself was punished for its wrongdoing by being taken off into exile (see, e.g., Is 40:2). The servant was not "punished" except in the sense of sharing in the experience that constituted punishment for them. They have born their punishment. But it has not changed them. They are no more inclined to commitment to Yhwh than they were before. How might they be changed?

One way the servant's affliction might bring this about relates to the effect it has on them. Maybe they will be moved and comforted by his willingness to share their suffering and/or maybe they will be brought up short by the way

---

[96]The "because" in Is 53:9 is perhaps ironic—EVV render *kî* "although," but it is questionable whether it ever means that.

[97]See section 2.8.

he puts up with their affliction yet continues to seek to reach them in Yhwh's name. Maybe one or other of these will provide a moral breakthrough that enables them to see themselves and Yhwh afresh and to respond to that new seeing. It is as if he is the pupil who is chastised by the teacher when it is they who need to learn something; and through watching him accept that chastisement, they do learn it. The imaginary testimony that the vision relates declares that this has indeed happened. His silent acceptance of suffering with them and from them drove them to move beyond antipathy and distaste. There was something more going on here than their initial easy judgment assumed. They realized that instead of seeing him as faithless (evidently under God's punishment) and themselves as relatively faithful, they had to turn this assumption upside down. He was the faithful one. That meant they were the faithless. Some of their prophets had always been saying that, and this servant's acceptance of suffering with them and from them enabled them to see that those prophets were right.

And Yhwh was behind all that. After all, it is Yhwh who sends prophets and thus sends them into a ministry that involves suffering for the people they seek to reach. That is regularly the dynamic of prophecy. It is not the stated reason why prophets attempt to evade their vocation, but it would be a good reason. In a way, the community was not so wrong when it concluded that God struck this servant. Yes, "Yhwh let fall on him the wrongdoing of all of us" (Is 53:6). Yhwh required of him a ministry that was bound to mean people's opposition and attacks. "He determined the crushing of the one he weakened," and "Yhwh's determination will succeed by his hand" (Is 53:10). Thus when it is all over he will be able to see results from it (Is 53:11). He will look at the way Yhwh's determination has been fulfilled, and he will be filled with delight. English versions have "satisfaction," but that rather understates the significance of *śābaʿ*; JPSV has "enjoy it to the full."

In isolation, admittedly, that is a rather remote involvement of Yhwh in the process whereby the people find healing and restoration. But the community's opening comment (Is 53:1) was that there was a revelation of Yhwh's arm in these events. Yhwh did not merely initiate a course of action from the safe distance of the court in heaven. Yhwh was involved in person in what went on. Talk of Yhwh's arm suggests Yhwh acting in power and might. The prophet has just spoken of Yhwh's arm being bared (of Yhwh's sleeves being rolled up) in order to act against Babylon. Here we might expect that the revelation of Yhwh's arm lay in the victorious vindication of the servant (Is 52:13-15; 53:12), but the community's words point in a different direction. They imply that it would have been very difficult to recognize this act as being Yhwh's arm, given where it was undertaken. It is in the activity of the servant in accepting suffering that Yhwh's arm is revealed, not merely in the eventual triumph of the servant. Jeremiah again stands in the background. The way he spoke made clear that Yhwh shared in his ministry. His pain was also Yhwh's pain. His rejection was Yhwh's rejection. When a prophet reached out to the people in Yhwh's name, this was Yhwh reaching out to them, and when the people refused to respond to the prophet, they were refusing to respond to Yhwh. Yhwh would thus be grieving over the cost Jeremiah paid for his ministry, but also experiencing the pain of personal rejection and paying the price for reaching out to them. That process is repeated when Yhwh's arm makes itself known in the ministry of this servant.

Offering Reparation

There is another form of Yhwh's involvement, a paradoxical one in light of that activity of Yhwh's arm. The vision talks about the servant laying down a reparation offering (ʾāšām, Is 53:10).[98] A reparation offering presupposes that people have acted in a way that causes offense. They have not treated someone as who they are and they have thus taken away something of their proper honor. They therefore need to do something to make up for their offensive act. A reparation offering makes symbolic and substantial restitution for such wrongdoing and thus makes a key contribution to restoring a relationship to what it was before. It recognizes responsibility and guilt and seeks to make up for something that has been taken away.[99]

How does the servant do that? What the servant offers Yhwh is his own life and in particular his suffering.

It is not clear whether the vision implies that the servant actually dies as a result of his ministry. Being "cut off from the land of the living" is a metaphor that would naturally imply that, but need not do so. He was allocated a burial place, but the passage does not say that he occupied it. He exposed himself to death, but this might not mean he actually died. And while the talk of vindication, having children and living a long life could presuppose that he died and Yhwh has brought him back to life, this is not mentioned. Fortunately, the resolution of the question of whether he actually died does not affect the com-

---

[98]The second colon in v. 10 can be read in two ways. I take napšô as the subject of the verb tāśîm (which is not a regular word for "making" an offering), as JPSV seems to presuppose. The NRSV and NIVI take it as the object and construe the verb as second person ("If you lay down his person as a restitution offering"). The "you" is presumably Yhwh (so explicitly NIVI). Theologically this understanding would suit me very well, but the trouble is that Yhwh is referred to in the third person in the cola on either side, so this understanding seems unlikely and not one we can build on theologically.

[99]The traditional translation "guilt offering" does not make the point precise enough, though the interpretation of the ʾāšām is much controverted (see, e.g., DCH, TDOT, NIDOTTE, TLOT). The KJV usually translates "trespass offering," though here has "offering for sin."

ment about making a reparation offering, because such an offering need not require a death (see, e.g., 1 Sam 6). The servant's life could offer such reparation, whether or not it has come to an end in death. Either way, the statement presupposes possibilities inherent in the servant's experience of affliction.

His faithful commitment to Yhwh in his ministry constitutes a stark contrast to the community's faithless abandonment of Yhwh. We have noted that in this ministry he represents Yhwh to the people. He embodies Yhwh's commitment to them and Yhwh's challenge to them. But he is like a prophet in that he also identifies with his people. He embodies the community's commitment to Yhwh, the commitment it failed to offer. The vision raises the possibility that his remarkable commitment with its willingness to go to the death could make up for the people's failure of commitment.[100] The people's failure to honor Yhwh, to treat Yhwh as God, has put the world out of kilter. The servant's remarkable honoring of Yhwh might restore its balance.[101] So when a servant of God silently accepts the attacks that come from the people of God and resists the temptation to respond with deceit or violence, that can be an offering to God made on behalf of the attackers, which God may accept as making up for the attackers' faithlessness.

One evidence that Yhwh has indeed accepted this self-offering will be the servant's restoration. Against all the odds, he will see offspring and live a long life. His work will be fruitful in bringing into being the offspring Yhwh longs to see and longs to restore (e.g., Is 41:8; 43:5; 44:3; 48:19). The people will live and flourish rather than wither and die; they will see long days.

It is not clear whether Second Isaiah has someone in mind as the fulfillment of this vision, and that is one factor that leaves it as a vision open to fulfillment in a number of ways. On the basis of the New Testament, we can declare that Jesus fulfilled this vision, and also that the church is commissioned to do so (see, e.g., Phil 2:5-11; 1 Pet 2:21-25).

5.4 Renewing the People

The First Testament's vision for the future is not confined to the reestablishing of a relationship between Yhwh and Israel. That has an outworking in the reestablishing of the people in their land, of the land itself, of the city and of its leadership. The Second Helvetic Confession, chapter 11, and the Augsburg

---

[100]Quantitatively there was no comparison, of course, but reparation offerings need not work on the basis of offering equivalence, as the instructions in Lev 5 as well as 1 Sam 6 show. The reparation is symbolic as well as substantial, and either may have prominence.

[101]Christian thinking has taken Is 53:10 as an exposition of substitutionary atonement, but actually a reparation offering was not an atoning sacrifice (it was not a sacrifice at all), and it did not involve substitution, as, e.g., the story in 1 Sam 6 shows.

Confession, chapter 17, berated "Jewish dreams," and Hans Urs von Balthasar has berated this-worldly hopes as "Jewish."[102] But the scriptural hope is of "the redemption of the world," not "redemption from the world," in keeping with the fact that the redeemer is the creator of the world.[103] The fortunes of the people are to be restored. Uprooting is to be replaced by planting, rejection by belonging, death by life, scattering by gathering, dispersal by return, division by reunion, decimation by multiplying, humiliation by pride. And all that is guaranteed by Yhwh's word.

Fortunes Restored

It might seem that exile would mean the end of a people. It would seem to be so when the Ephraimites were transported to Assyria. It could seem to be so when Judeans are transported to Babylon. But Israel's story has already looked forward to such possibilities and declared that they will not, or at least need not, be the end. Even if the curse as well as the blessing overtakes the people, if the people then turn to Yhwh, "Yhwh your God will restore your fortunes and have compassion on you and gather you again from all the peoples where Yhwh your God has scattered you" (Deut 30:3-5).[104]

Set in Jeremiah at a dark moment, when the city is soon to fall, is a document dominated by promises concerning a better future. It begins, "Days are coming (Yhwh's message) when I restore the fortunes of my people Israel and Judah (Yhwh has said)" (Jer 30:3). Such assurances that these are indeed Yhwh's words characterize the chapters that follow. The assurances are as necessary at a gloomy moment as are equivalent declarations that back up warnings at moments that look less gloomy. Since Jeremiah has just spoken of an exile that will last seventy years, readers might reasonably assume that the recurrent expression "days are coming" refers to events at the end of that period.[105]

"Restore the fortunes," šûb šĕbût, is an umbrella expression in the First Testament for restoration after a catastrophe (e.g., Jer 31:23; 33:26; Ezek 39:25; Joel 3:1 [MT 4:1]; Ps 14:7). Literally it means "turn [with regard to] a turning." Because Israel's great cataclysm involved the people's exile from their land, restoration involves returning the people there (e.g., Deut 30:3; Jer 29:14; 30:3), and the phrase itself was traditionally translated "bring back the captivity."

---

[102]See Jürgen Moltmann, *History and the Triune God* (London: SCM Press, 1991), p. 92; he refers to von Balthasar, "Zu einer christlichen Theologie der Hoffnung," *Münchner Theologische Zeitschrift* 32 (1981): 81-102.

[103]Moltmann, *Coming of God*, p. 259.

[104]It has been a common critical view that this chapter dates from after the fall of Jerusalem. Its attribution to Moses implies that restoring the people was bound up in Yhwh's original commitment to Israel.

[105]Cf. Fretheim, *Jeremiah*, p. 415.

While it might carry those overtones in some contexts, in itself the phrase has that broader reference to turning round the people's fortunes.[106] Turning the turning also involves rebuilding the city of Jerusalem with its citadel and palaces and ordinary homes (Jer 30:18; 33:7; Amos 9:14; Zeph 3:20), repopulating the land (Jer 32:44; 33:11), and replacing wrath with healing and forgiveness (Ps 85:1-2 [MT 2-3]). It thus embraces the whole of life, the inner and the outer, without any assumption that either is more important than the other.

Sometimes restoration is envisaged as coming about through regular historical events behind which Yhwh's activity is seen—notably the defeat of Babylon by Persia. Sometimes no such links are suggested and one gets the impression of Yhwh acting in supranatural, interventionist fashion. The former reflects the fact that sometimes a prophet can look at events and see ways in which they can be the means of Israel's restoration. The latter reflects the fact that sometimes a prophet can see no signs of Yhwh's acting. "The whole earth sits quiet" (Zech 1:11): one might have thought that would be good news, but in this context it is not. The continuation of the rule of the world by a superpower, even a relatively beneficent one, means God is not acting, God is not ruling. But that does not mean Yhwh cannot act. God can intervene to put down a superpower and implement divine rule.

Building and Planting

Jeremiah was appointed to uproot and to demolish, to destroy and to overthrow, but also to build and to plant (Jer 1:10). When people have been exiled in 597, he can start talking more immediately about building and planting: "I will focus my eyes on them for good and bring them back to this land. I will build them, not overthrow them. I will plant them, not uproot them" (Jer 24:6; cf. Jer 31:28, 40). "I will exult over them in doing good to them. I will plant them in this country in faithfulness, with all my heart and with all my soul" (Jer 32:41). Building and planting are literal elements in the First Testament's vision, but they are also metaphors.

Long ago, it had been "survivors of the sword" who "found grace in the wilderness" (Jer 31:2). When Israel has again been flailed by Yhwh's sword, is it possible to believe that Yhwh has not finished with it? Yet the sword has been a feature of Israel's life from the beginning. One way or another it escaped unscathed from Yhwh's sword (Ex 5:3), from Egypt's sword (Ex 5:21; 15:9; 18:4) and from the swords of Edom and of King Sihon (Num 20:18-21;

---

[106]The traditional translation takes *šĕbût* as from *šābâ*, "take captive" (cf. BDB), but this does not fit some occurrences of the phrase (esp. Ezek 16:53; Job 42:10), and more likely *šĕbût* comes from *šûb* itself (cf. *HALOT*). The verb is usually in the qal and thus means "turn" in an intransitive sense.

21:21-24). But it did not escape unscathed from its own sword wielded on Yhwh's behalf, according to Moses (Ex 32:27-29), and from the sword of the Amalekites and Canaanites when people ignored Yhwh's warnings (Num 14:43-45).

Yhwh came to the Israelites in the wilderness to make sure they would reach the land of their destiny, and Yhwh appeared to them at Sinai and elsewhere. Yhwh had made a permanent covenant to Israel's ancestors, and the very fact of Israel's continuing to exist over subsequent centuries is an indication that Yhwh keeps keeping commitment. All that is a basis for hope when the people are understandably overwhelmed by disaster. Where there has been destruction there will be building; where there has been grief there will be music, dancing and merrymaking; where there has been uprooting there will be planting. The planting has happened before Jeremiah's inner eye, and he knows that it will issue in being able to eat the fruit. The day all this comes about is already a reality. He can already hear the summons to people to go up to Zion to worship Yhwh (Jer 31:3-6). The punch line in the prophecy lies here. Once more, the rebuilding of the community will not be mere human achievement. It issues from Yhwh's grace, dedication or love (ʾahăbâ), and commitment. And thus the joy that issues from it will not be mere merrymaking. Perhaps there is significance in the way the planters are described as "beginning to enjoy" their produce (ḥālal), because the verb denotes the participation that starts when one has acknowledged that the firstfruits belong to Yhwh.[107] But that is more explicit in the vision of a way the vineyard guards will be summoning people to worship (Jer 31:6), presumably to give thanks for this harvest. But the punch line has added force because these Samarian guards are summoning people "to Zion." Samaria has seen a true restoration, and thus the people of Israel as a whole has seen a true restoration of itself.

When they return, they will plant the land (Amos 9:14), but what is more, Yhwh will plant them on the land and they will not uproot again from the land Yhwh gives them (Amos 9:15; cf. Hos 2:23 [MT 25]; 14:5-7 [MT 6-8]).[108] They will not just sit on the land like something that can easily be removed. They will have roots down into the soil. They will become a fixture there.

The vision of the city in Isaiah 60 returns in its closing lines to the people of the city, assumed to be the capital of a country that is small enough for the city's people to possess all of it, like Jerusalem in the Persian period. The people are "the shoot I planted" (Is 60:21-22). Earlier the term *shoot* referred to new growth from Jesse's felled tree (Is 11:1), but here the image applies to the people itself, not to a messiah. It is the people that Yhwh planted in the land (cf.

[107]See Keown et al., *Jeremiah 26—52*, p. 109.
[108]Cf. Jeremias, *Amos*, p. 169.

Ex 15:17; Is 5:7; Ps 80:8, 15 [MT 9, 16]), in keeping with Yhwh's promise to David (2 Sam 7:10). Once more, that image can affirm the security of the people: plants have roots reaching deep into the ground and keeping the plant in place (e.g., Jer 24:6; 32:41). So this "plant" will "possess the land forever." Plants flourish and produce beautiful flowers and fruit, and this adds further significance to the image (cf. Is 4:2).[109] In this connection the vision emphasizes Yhwh's direct involvement in planting the people. They will become a thing of beauty. That will include, though perhaps not be confined to, their flourishing in a way that recalls the promise to Abraham. And perhaps a further element in their beauty will be their own ṣĕdāqâ, a quality that will characterize the people as a whole. One could perhaps read the term as a condition or qualifier: only insofar as the people are ṣaddîqîm will all this be true of them. But in the context of the vision, it is at least as much a promise, standing alongside the declaration that ṣĕdāqâ will rule in the city or that the city's administration will be characterized by this quality. The people who flourish in this land will also flourish in their faithful relationship with Yhwh and with one another. Either way, it makes explicit that possession of the land has a moral aspect to it. Yhwh's promise is not fulfilled where the land is occupied but where this arrangement is not characterized by ṣĕdāqâ.

This might all be hard to believe. People have heard it all before. Prophet and Yhwh are nevertheless (or consequently) still bold to add not only that it will come about, but that it will come about quickly. It is as sure as the fact that Yhwh is the real God. Fortunately Yhwh and prophet do also have an escape clause: "in due time," "in its time" (Is 60:22).

A People Who Belong

In Jerusalem itself, Jeremiah compared the Judean community under Zedekiah and the people who had already been exiled in 597 to two bowls of figs (Jer 24). It would not be surprising if the people in Jerusalem saw themselves as the sound figs, the exiles as the rotten ones; they had, after all, been taken off from the land like that. Jeremiah declares the opposite to be the case. He does not say that the exiles *are* better, but that Yhwh will so regard them so as to show partiality to them (nākar hiphil) and bring them back home: "I will gather you from all the nations and from all the places where I have driven you (Yhwh's message) and return you to the place from which I exiled you" (Jer 29:14). Neither does Jeremiah say that the people in Jerusalem are worse than the people in exile, though he does say that Yhwh intends to bring calamity to them. The difference is not between the quality of the two groups. It lies in the

---

[109]There the noun is ṣemaḥ.

fact that the exiles have experienced their calamity and are thus due for a message of hope, whereas the Jerusalemites have not and still think they may escape, so that they still need to hear a threatening message.[110] Yhwh intends to treat the people in Jerusalem in such a way that they *become* like loathsome figs that are so bad they cannot be eaten (Jer 29:17). The vision concerns the destiny of the two communities, not their present nature. And there is some arbitrariness about Yhwh's siding with the exiles, like the arbitrariness of Yhwh's original choice of Israel or of David, or God's choice of people who come to see the glory of God in the face of Christ. It just emerges from Yhwh's will, being based on Yhwh's having a big purpose to fulfill that extends far beyond the "deserve" of Israel and Canaan or Saul and David or the Jerusalemites and the exiles or particular Christian congregations.

Whereas it would likewise look as if the people who had been taken off into exile were finished and it would not be unreasonable if the people in Jerusalem think the future lies with them, Yhwh declares otherwise. In Ezekiel 11:15-20 Yhwh begins by referring to Ezekiel's fellow exiles as his relatives, members of his family (*'aḥîm)*; only here does Yhwh do so. The description is then underlined by terming them his kin, "people of his *gĕ'ullâ*," members of his extended family with whom he thus lives in a mutual commitment to stand by each other and protect each other.[111] Yet further, they are members of the whole household of Israel with him. The accumulation of these terms suggests Yhwh is referring to more than Ezekiel's personal bond with the exiles, which makes him care about their destiny. The exiles belong to the household of Israel. It is that family that has a commitment to mutual support and protection, and it is also a family to which Yhwh relates as *gō'ēl* (though it is Second Isaiah, not Ezekiel, who makes that point). They are relatives within the family of Israel, a great motivator for proper behavior.

According to Ezekiel, the Jerusalemites have been denying all that, denying that the exiles count as the household of Israel, as members of the family, as relatives. It is a plausible view, for they are the ones who have been taken off away from the city Yhwh chose, the location of the sanctuary where Yhwh was committed to dwell. Yhwh thus begins by affirming that they do belong

---

[110]In a later context, returned exiles would be able to use a prophecy such as this to buttress their own position over against that of people who had not been in exile; but that would be to turn upside down the dynamic of the passage. If the passage was created then to buttress the position of those returned exiles, it backfires on them. Further, the people who appear in the passage in Jer 29 are people who do go into exile, so presumably come to belong to the good figs.

[111]The use of *gĕ'ullâ* is unique to this passage and makes a pun on their being also fellow exiles. "Your kin" is *'anšê gĕ'ullātekā;* "your fellow-exiles" would be *'anšê gā'lûtekā*. LXX in fact translates as if the word were the latter, though Vg. corresponds to MT.

to the family and household. As is often the case in the First Testament story, the people who look as if they are in the privileged position change places with the people who look as if they do not count. Yhwh acknowledges having moved them far away from there, and the Jerusalemites bid them accept Yhwh's action, face their rejection and stay well away. Empirical evidence shows that the country is now given over to the people who have been allowed to stay there. It is their "possession" (môrāšâ). Before the exodus, Yhwh had said that the land promised to the ancestors would become the "possession" of the Israelites as a whole (Ex 6:8); the Jerusalemites are now excluding the exiles from that possession. But Yhwh affirms the intention to give them the land of Israel.[112]

Yes, Yhwh has taken them far away from the sanctuary, but Yhwh has become a scaled-down version of a sanctuary for them in their exile.[113] It is a bold metaphor.[114] Yhwh is capable of being present with the people far away from Jerusalem, as if Yhwh in person were the sanctuary. This is not as good as having access to the "proper" sanctuary, but it is not nothing (especially in a context where the "proper" sanctuary is about to be devastated and virtually put out of commission). Further, exile will not be the end. Scattering will give way to gathering. Indeed, the exiles will return to clean up the religion that the Jerusalemites accept. They are like sheep who have been scattered because of the neglect of their shepherds, but Yhwh will search out these sheep and bring them back to their proper pasture on the mountains of Israel and by its water courses (Ezek 34:1-15).

A People with a Future

Between 597 and 587, then, Jeremiah speaks as if the entire future lies with the exiles. One could imagine the exilic community using that to support a claim to be *the* future of the community, especially after the city's final defeat. But then Yhwh keeps reaching out to the Judean community. It is as if the cataclysmic falling of the ax means there can now be the mercy that Yhwh has withheld. The Babylonians appoint a Judean governor, who encourages the people

---

[112]Historically, it may be that Ex 6:2-8 was written later than Ezekiel, in which case the contrast works the other way round, Exodus agreeing with Ezekiel that the Jerusalemites' declaration is too exclusive.

[113]The EVV have "a sanctuary for a little while," but the temporal usage is rarer and the usage following a noun (lit. "a sanctuary, a littleness") is usually adjectival. If Yhwh's words went on to refer to the shortness of the exile, this would support the temporal interpretation, but they do not. Rather cf. LXX, Vg, and Tg.'s interpretation in light of the development of the synagogue.

[114]Perhaps Ezekiel is taking up Is 8:14. If critics are right to emend that text, the relationship between Is 8:14 MT and Ezekiel might turn out to be the reverse (as with Ex 6:8).

who remain (and the people who return from taking refuge in neighboring countries) to settle down "and things will be good for you" (Jer 40:9), as Yhwh had promised (e.g., Jer 32:42). There are leftovers in Judah (Jer 40:11, 15). After the next catastrophe, the assassination of Gedaliah, Judean leaders ask Jeremiah to pray "for all these leftovers" and seek Yhwh's guidance regarding what they should do next, and Yhwh responds, though of course they take no notice (Jer 42:2).[115] Yhwh thus keeps pursuing these leftovers (Jer 42:15, 19), though they keep resisting (Jer 43:5). They risk eliminating the leftovers (Jer 44:7, 12), but they have not done so. Only some survivors will return to Judah from Egypt (*pĕlēṭîm*, Jer 44:14, 28), but that means some survivors will. The fact that Yhwh threatens to dismiss the community in Judah as rotten fruit is not a basis for the exilic community to claim that only they belong to Israel.

Thus Rachel can be comforted and can give up weeping (Jer 31:15-17). There is more than one Ramah where one could imagine Rachel grieving over her descendants trudging into exile, either the Ephraimite exiles of 721 or the Judean exiles of 587. Traditionally it has been assumed that she did so at Ramah because that is where she was buried. She had died in childbirth and as she died had grieved, and no doubt Jacob had grieved the loss of the love of his life. But now she is imagined grieving on a much vaster scale. She refuses to find comfort because what comfort could there be? If we imagine Rachel at Ramah in Benjamin (for Judean exiles, a staging post on the way to Babylon in Jeremiah 40), there is particular poignancy in the scene. Benjamin was the son for whom Rachel gave her life, but the exile means that was pointless. Yhwh denies her whole framework. There can be comfort. The children's departure does not mean they are no more. Her labor will not be in vain.

But it could look as if Rachel's children are done. After 587, it would not be unreasonable for the entire household of Israel among whom Ezekiel lives to say, "Our bones are dried up. Our hope has died. We—we are cut off"[116] (Ezek 37:11). Their metaphor triggers a vision that Yhwh gives Ezekiel. Scattered over a battlefield are the whitened bones of a defeated army. They are cut off from life, cut off from their community, cut off from their land and cut off from Yhwh. They have no hope. But Yhwh declares that the army will come back to life. As if in a movie that has been reversed and speeded up, Ezekiel watches

---

[115]It might have been that the stress on "all the leftovers," who end up in Egypt, in Jer 42—44 was designed to give the impression that Judah itself was empty for the exilic community to take over without any rivalry over who counted as "*the* leftovers" who would form the nucleus of a new future, but if so, the actual presence of Judeans in Judah would make this argument fall apart.

[116]In the expression *nigzarnû lānû* the prepositional expression (lit. "for ourselves") serves to emphasize the implications of the verb for the subject. The EVV "clean cut off" thus does not quite represent the point.

as bones come together to form skeletons, skeletons gain flesh, breath enters these corpses, and they come back to life, "a vast multitude." There is a sense in which the fall of Jerusalem and the exile meant the death of the nation, but Yhwh can and will bring this nation back to life and take it back to its land.

As if looking for the fulfillment of that vision, in Isaiah 26:19 at the end of a long lament at the state of the community comes an exhortation: "Your [s.] dead must live; my corpse must arise. Wake up and resound, you [pl.] who live in the dirt, because your [s.] dew is radiant dew; you [s.] cause the land of ghosts to give birth." The exhortation addresses Yhwh and then bids people in the grave to come out, as if it were uttering the life-giving summons that Yhwh needs to utter. Or rather, that is the fruit it wishes to see from the dew of Yhwh falling on the ground where the dead are buried (in the Middle East with its long rainless summer, dew is a key factor in fruitfulness). Yhwh will thus cause the ground to give birth, as ghosts become living people again.[117] While it would fit the later development of belief in resurrection, accepted by the Pharisees and then by Christians, to take this as referring to life after death for individual dead people, the pronouns make that difficult. Moreover, in a First Testament context, once again the prophecy looks for Yhwh to bring the nation back to life.

The one passage that does envisage dead individuals brought back to life is Daniel 12:1-3.[118] It is often the case that eschatology relates to theodicy, and the promise of resurrection certainly does so. In Daniel 12, people who have died as martyrs will wake from their "sleep" to eternal life, while people who died in their beds despite their being persecutors or collaborators will awake from their sleep to eternal shame.

Another Exodus

Israel's exilic experience has involved being scattered like a flock made to flee by a wild animal. Now Jeremiah proclaims to the nations the shepherd's intention to gather the flock back together and make sure that no such scattering can recur (Jer 31:10-14). To be less metaphorical, Israel has been servants to a master much greater than themselves. Now Yhwh will act as the next of kin who pays the necessary price to restore these servants to their proper position. They will be Yhwh's own servants again, but that will not be an objectionable servitude. Yhwh is the kind of master that servants volunteer to serve permanently (cf. Ex 21:5-6). So the people will return to Zion where they serve Yhwh and

---

[117]On *rĕpāʾim*, "ghosts," see section 6.9 "Long Life."

[118]On the novelty of this belief in this context—it is not merely a logical development from earlier First Testament beliefs—see John J. Collins, *Encounters with Biblical Theology* (Minneapolis: Fortress, 2005), pp. 31-32.

find themselves wide-eyed at the goodness of what their master gives them. Once again this will involve practical provision (grain, wine, oil, sheep, oxen, rich food). It will involve joy and gladness. And all this will be set in the context of a celebration on Mount Zion that signifies a rejoicing in the master as well as in the goods, in the giver as well as in the gifts. It will be a rejoicing that involves no division between women and men or young and old, so it is apposite that rhetorically, at least, it also involves no racial divisions; it embraces the nations as well as Israel.

There is likely another reason for speaking to the nations of Israel's return. It is a mark of the fact that Yhwh is serious in intent. Commissioning the proclamation parallels Yhwh's swearing an oath. It gives Israel reason for rejoicing. Having made this announcement to the world, Yhwh will have to fulfill it. Otherwise Yhwh's own name will be discredited.

Is the proclamation hard to believe? Jeremiah 31:9 directs people to the evidence of the past. The exodus story tells how Yhwh adopted Israel as son (e.g., Ex 4:22; Deut 32:6; Hos 11:1). Yhwh even affirms Ephraim's position as senior son, an extraordinary continuing affirmation after the rejection of Ephraim for its faithlessness (Gen 48; 1 Chron 5:1-2; cf. Hos 11:1-3). The more recent past does not undo what Yhwh affirmed at the beginning. There is to be a real restoration. The exodus story provides a basis for believing that Yhwh will once again deliver the people from servitude and will take them to the land of promise, and it suggests ways Yhwh will do so. The people's escape from servitude to journey to the land of promise will recapitulate their original escape and journey.

After a terrible warning about hurling the people off the land into a foreign country comes a promise: "Therefore, now, days are coming (Yhwh's message) when it will no more be said 'As Yhwh lives, who brought up the Israelites from the country of Egypt,' but rather 'As Yhwh lives, who brought up the Israelites from the northern country and from all the countries where he had banished them.'" Yhwh intends to bring about a new exodus to take the people back to the land given to their forebears (Jer 16:14-15; cf. Jer 23:7-8).

If there are passages where *lākēn* does not mean "therefore," we might reckon this is one of them, yet the word's usual meaning suggests a nice link.[119] There is an illogical logical connection between the declaration that Yhwh is throwing the people out of the country and the promise of their return, a logic that issues from Yhwh's commitment to the people. This is the country Yhwh gave to their ancestors; indeed Yhwh had caused their ancestors to possess it as belonging definitively and permanently to them (*nāḥal* hiphil; Jer 3:18),

---

[119]On such illogical "therefores" in Jeremiah, see section 5.1 "Yhwh's Intention."

given it to them in perpetuity (Jer 7:7), and fulfilled a sworn oath in doing so (Jer 11:5). There is thus some contradiction involved in eliminating them from the country given to them and their ancestors (Jer 24:10). Yhwh is self-bound to restore them to it or to restore their descendants to it. Their return will not necessarily need to be more spectacular an event than the exodus (and it was not that), but it will be an event that is real in the people's present experience, not an event of many centuries ago. They themselves will enter into possession of the country as belonging definitively and inalienably to them (*yāraš*, Jer 30:3). More literally, Yhwh will bring them back to the soil of Israel.[120] The land in its earthiness will be theirs again. They will tread on it and work it.

A Greater Exodus

There is a different illogic about Isaiah 43:16-21, which describes Yhwh as the one who brought Israel through the Red Sea and defeated the army that sought to put Israel down; one line goes to the first of these facts, two lines to the second, which in the context of forced exile in Babylon has the emphasis. But the description is initially expressed by means of participles that suggest that Yhwh is by ongoing nature the God of that Red Sea deliverance and victory. And it continues in yiqtol verbs, which can naturally be understood to make the same point in a different way.[121] All this draws attention to that original act of deliverance and victory that encourages people to believe in the possibility of another such act in their own experience.

Then come Yhwh's actual words, which tell people *not* to think about all that, because Yhwh is in the midst of doing something new. Perhaps the implication is that people can forget the earlier event because the new one exceeds it, but there is no need to infer this. The original event, after all, involved a way through the wilderness, miraculous provision of water and a response of praise. What is more significant is the simple fact that Yhwh's deliverance and victory are not confined to a long-ago event but are to be repeated in the people's own experience. The long-ago event needs remembering because such remembering has the capacity to increase the conviction that God can so act, but needs forgetting because people must not think that Yhwh is only a God who acted way back then but cannot be expected so to act now.

The prophets' promises are an ever-renewed restatement of Yhwh's original promises. It is important to emphasize both that these are the old promises and that Yhwh is now doing something new. It is apposite that for the epigraph to his volume on the Prophets Gerhard von Rad takes Yhwh's declaration of intent

---

[120]Rather than *'ereṣ yiśrā'ēl*, Ezekiel regularly uses the phrase*'admat yiśrā'ēl*, which has more earthy connotations.

[121]Unless hearers understood them as yiqtols with past reference.

to do "a new thing," while at the same time Yhwh speaks as the God who once
made Israel a path through the waters and is to act in that way again (Is 43:18-
19).[122] That is true of the new exodus, the new covenant, the new settlement of
the land, the new monarchy, the new Jerusalem, the new temple, even the new
creation, the new heavens and the new earth. What God intends to do is described in terms of the renewing of the old. That is so for epistemological reasons. God can enable people to understand what the new will be like only by
describing it in terms of what they know. But it is also thus for theological or substantial reasons. God can act in the future only in ways that take forward what
God has done in the past. This new act will be an expression of God's faithfulness. The new "does not annihilate the old but gathers it up and creates it
anew."[123] But like the original creation or exodus or settlement, in another sense
God is not merely building on something that already exists. After the fall of
Jerusalem, nothing exists. Everything has collapsed. "The new thing is the surprising thing, the thing that could never have been expected."[124]

A Complete Exodus

In light of the fact that disaster will not be the end, Yhwh often urges Israel not
to be afraid: not to be afraid of other nations, not to be afraid of the future, not
to be afraid of Yhwh. The bulk of Jeremiah 46 declares that Egypt is on the way
to calamity, but the closing verses then urge Israel itself not to be afraid. Calamity for Egypt is reason for fear, whether it means the collapse of an ally Judah
was relying on before the fall of Jerusalem or the collapse of the country where
people found refuge before and after that event. The nightmare vision for
Egypt is a nightmare vision for Judah, too. But Jeremiah 46 reaffirms that things
will be all right. Egypt is not Judah's ultimate destiny. It can count as one of the
places of their captivity, one of the places where Yhwh dispersed them, and
therefore one of the places from which Yhwh will bring them back. There is
some generosity involved in this stance, because strictly Egypt was neither a
place of captivity (people chose to go there) nor a place Yhwh sent them (they
went there against Yhwh's word). But even refugees in Egypt can be brought
home. So there is nothing to be afraid of in Egypt. When Yhwh makes an end
of Egypt, Judah will not come to an end, even though it is being cut down.

It is indeed being cut down, but there will be survivors, and Yhwh will see
that every one comes back. Whereas Edom and other nations will drink
Yhwh's cup of poison so fully that it will be as though they had never been,

---

[122]Gerhard von Rad, *Old Testament Theology*, vol. 2 (Edinburgh: Oliver & Boyd/New York:
   Harper, 1965), p. 1.

[123]Moltmann, *Coming of God*, p. 29.

[124]Ibid., p. 28.

"On Mount Zion there will be survivors and they will be holy; the household of Jacob will dispossess the people who dispossessed them" (Obad 17). Obadiah has especially in mind the Edomites, who took over much Judean territory from the exile and onward, but he extends his attention to the land of the Philistines, of Ephraim, of Gilead and of Phoenicia. In other words, Israel will once again control the land that David controlled. "Deliverers will go up to Mount Zion to decide for Mount Esau, and the sovereignty will be Yhwh's" (Obad 21). That closing comment gives room for Yhwh to reign or exercise sovereignty *(mĕlûkâ)* in Yhwh's own way, which would presumably exclude any too Israel-centered an understanding of the implications of Obadiah.

"On that day Yhwh will thresh from the channel of the River to the Wadi of Egypt, and you will be gleaned one by one, Israelites" (Is 27:12). Threshing is often an unpleasant image and gleaning might seem a humiliating occupation, but here Yhwh is the thresher concerned to make sure of gleaning and beating out every stalk of grain so as to be able to bundle it and take it back home. And this is a harvester who can cover a monumental estate extending from the Euphrates to the Wadi Arish, the traditional bounds of the Israelite empire (e.g., Deut 1:7; 1 Kings 4:21 [MT 5:1]).[125] Israelites who live over much of this area that is thus in some sense theoretically "home territory" will in fact for centuries be under pressure from other ethnic groups. Yhwh promises that none need be lost.

In Jeremiah 31:7-9 Yhwh is commissioning the nations to urge Yhwh to deliver Israel (MT) or to proclaim that Yhwh has done so (LXX). The northern country implies Assyria or Babylon, but "the ends of the earth" recognizes that people have also been scattered elsewhere. Geographically, Yhwh intends to be thorough in the work of restoration. And Yhwh will not be satisfied to gather the people it is easy to bring back or the people who would be useful in building up the devastated country. Yhwh will also bring the blind and disabled (cf. Is 35:5-6). For more obvious reasons, perhaps, Yhwh will also bring the pregnant and the women actually giving birth, the people on whom the nation's future depends as Yhwh intends to turn it back into a numerous people.

The people is only the "leftovers" of Israel, but in keeping with the nations' bidding (!), Yhwh intends to see that they all get back (cf. Jer 23:3). And these leftovers will thus seem a great assembly. They will come with tears, though Jeremiah does not make clear what kind of tears. These might be the tears of people who are still grieving the loss involved in exile itself, like those of the mother who misses her offspring (Jer 31:15-16). But in the context they might also be tears of joy. These are people who will find themselves experiencing Yhwh's

---

[125]Cf. Hans Wildberger, *Isaiah 13—27* (Minneapolis: Fortress, 1997), p. 599.

grace (MT) or comfort (LXX) as they are guided on their journey in such a way as to ensure that they have water for their refreshment and that their path is straight and level, not like the average mountain track on which it is easy to slip.

A Return Along Yhwh's Highway

Yhwh is committed to returning to Jerusalem. The people will come back because they return on Yhwh's coattails. Once again the power of the vision of this return in Isaiah 35:8-10 comes from the different images it combines. It speaks of a holy way, of the absence of anything that pollutes, of the shouts and the joy on people's heads (the celebratory garlands), suggesting a festal procession. It invites the hearers to imagine the splendor of a Babylonian New Year festival procession or the lesser but more precious splendor of an Israelite festival. The people's return to their land becomes such a joyous celebration.

For this holy way is also a "highway." That could have been just another term for a processional way, but its regular use for a "proper" (if metaphorical) highway from Babylon to Israel or from Egypt to Assyria (e.g., Is 11:16; 19:23; 40:3) means it would more likely suggest a marvelous freeway to take people to their homeland across obstacles such as ravines and mountains. That fits with the promise that travel on this highway will also not be imperiled by the presence of dangerous animals that often threatened travelers. The people will be able to get to Zion without difficulty or danger.

The people who do so will be the restored and ransomed (forms from *gāʾal* and *pādâ*). While Yhwh's act in bringing the people out of bondage to a foreign power and restoring them to the service of Yhwh in their own land might itself be seen as redeeming and restoring, these terms go back to Yhwh's first entering into a commitment to Israel and bringing Israel out of Egypt, and here they have that resonance. The return to the land is a rerun of the original journey to the land. That was the act of one who had entered into a family relationship with Israel and was willing to make sacrifices on its behalf (for instance, giving up Egypt and Sudan for it); the centuries that have passed have not changed that relationship. Israel is still the restored and redeemed, and there is a certain inevitability about its return to the land Yhwh took it to so long ago.

That will thus reverse the present situation. Once, Pharaoh had made up his mind to pursue the Israelites *(nāśag)* after they escaped from Egypt (Ex 14:9; 15:9), and Jeremiah warned how they could have that experience again without a happy ending (Jer 42:16; cf. also Lam 1:3 and the alternatives in Deut 28:2, 15, 45). But now Israel's "pursuers" will be joy and gladness. It will be the present realities of suffering and sighing, on the part of people in exile or in servitude in their own land, that are turning tail and fleeing.

Yhwh's return to Jerusalem is heralded like that of a returning king, and the exiles return as the king's booty (Is 40:9-11); Yhwh is a shepherd who (in a daring metaphor) is coming back to Palestine like Jacob with all the flocks he has accumulated while away to the north and east. Perhaps the implication is that for all the talk about withering (Is 40:6-8), the people have flourished numerically in exile, as the Jewish people will continue to do over the centuries. Further, these are not just mature sheep but lambs and mothering ewes, which is not just a sign of flourishing but an indication that they will need careful shepherding on their journey, which they will receive.

All this is expressed as a piece of good news to be brought to Jerusalem. "Herald" is *mĕbaśśeret*, someone who brings news. This is not necessarily good news, but clearly it is good news in this context (cf. LXX *euangelizomenos*, JPSV "herald of joy"). Jerusalem is the city Yhwh abandoned half a century ago, expelling thousands of its people. Lamentations expresses the grief of the city, grief that has presumably continued to be expressed over the decades as people have prayed its prayers. One of their repeated plaints has been that the city has no one to comfort it in its loss and grief. Now its God has declared, "Comfort, comfort my people . . . encourage Jerusalem," tell her that she has come to the end of her time of hard servitude paying the price for her wrongdoing (Is 40:1-2). That is the negative good news. The positive good news is that her God is returning and is bringing her people back, too.

A United People

Older than a tension between Judeans in exile and people who had stayed in Judah is a tension between Judah and Ephraim, and the loss of Ephraim is older and more final than the loss of Judah to exile. In relation to that parting of the ways Yhwh declares, "I will fortify the household of Judah and deliver the household of Joseph" (Zech 10:6-7). The promise may imply acceptance of these two continuing to be separate nations, in the context of the separate existence of the Samarian province in the Persian period. Second Kings 17 speaks of the deportation of "Israel" to Assyria, as 2 Kings 25 will speak of the exile of "Judah," which would seem to imply the transportation of the whole people. But 2 Kings also provides the numbers of Judeans who were transported, numbers in the thousands rather than the hundreds of thousands. These were the important people such as the government and the priesthood, and other people from the capital, people whose departure meant that the nation stopped functioning as a nation; in this sense Judah was taken into exile. Presumably something similar had happened in 721. Assyria would not bother to transport hundreds of thousands of ordinary people; Sargon's annals talk in terms of 27,290 people.[126] Most of the people

---

[126]See *ANET*, pp. 284-85.

in Samaria in later times were thus presumably descendants of the northern clans. But 2 Kings 17:24-41 emphasizes the results of replacing the people who were transported by people from elsewhere in the Assyrian empire, and Ezra-Nehemiah sees them as polluted.

Humanly speaking, it would be impossible to imagine the northern peoples being restored as the people of Yhwh, separately or united to Judah. But "Yhwh has restored [*šûb*] the majesty of Jacob as well as the majesty of Israel" (Nahum 2:2).[127] "In those days the household of Judah will go to [?] the household of Israel and they will come together from the northern country to the country that I enabled your ancestors to possess" (Jer 3:18). Jeremiah's restoration book concerns "my people, Israel and Judah" (Jer 30:3; cf. Jer 30:4). It concerns "all the families of Israel" (Jer 31:1), "the household of Israel and the household of Judah," with the new covenant applying to both (Jer 31:27, 31). Yhwh "will restore the fortunes of Judah and the fortunes of Israel and build them up as they once were" (Jer 33:7). When Yhwh restores the Davidic monarchy, "Judah will be delivered and Israel dwell in security" (Jer 23:6).

Even more astonishingly, elsewhere Yhwh declares the intention to reunite the nation of Israel, divided into two for most of its life in the land. "The people of Judah and the people of Israel will assemble together and appoint for themselves one head, and they will grow from the earth, for great will be the day of Jezreel" (Hos 1:11 [MT 2:2]). Given the divided and often hostile relationship of the two nations over the centuries, it is quite a promise that they will thus voluntarily come together and appoint a new leader. The reference to Jezreel, the place where "God sows," gives the clue to the meaning of the promise that the people will "go up from the earth," for *ʿālâ* can refer to the growth of plants that "come up" from the ground (*ʿāleh* means "growth" in the sense of foliage). The vision sees the people as divided, leaderless and as good as dead as a result of the day of calamity they have experienced. They will become united, be led and flourish once more, because they will experience a day that is light not darkness, life not death. Ezekiel in turn holds before the people two sticks, one representing Ephraim, one Judah, holding them in such a way that they become one (presumably because his hand joins them). Indeed, "I will make them into one nation in the land, on the mountains of Israel, and one king will be king for all of them. They will never again be two nations. They will never again be divided into two kingdoms. . . . There will be one shepherd for them" (Ezek 37:22, 24).

People in exile and people back in the land can also be one. The actual task of rebuilding the temple after the exile has to be undertaken by people in Jerus-

---

[127]Here "Jacob" presumably refers to Ephraim, "Israel" to Judah.

alem, but the builders are to accept offerings from people who evidently had not taken the opportunity to return to Judah and still live in Babylon. People from far away places like Babylon "will come and build in Yhwh's palace" (Zech 6:15).

Chronicles, Ezra and Nehemiah sometimes draw attention to the fact that there were members of the northern clans in the largely Judean Second Temple community, and that is a sign that Yhwh has not finished with Ephraim. Yet Ezekiel's vision is a bigger one than that. The population of much of the former northern kingdom indeed came to identify themselves as Jewish people by Roman times. Yet the Jewish people itself has been divided into many groups, often hostile to one another, and the Christian church much more so. Thus such promises about the restoring of the northern kingdom have been called "perhaps the most conspicuous example in the Tanak of patently false prophecy."[128] They deserve comparing with Jesus' prayer for the church's oneness (Jn 17:20-23), perhaps the most conspicuous example of patently unanswered prayer in Scripture. Being one people is a reality of hope as well as a present theological reality deriving from Yhwh's oneness, but one on the way and open to dissolution.[129]

A Permanent Covenant

Yhwh's original covenants for Noah and Abraham were permanent covenants. The David covenant narrowed down this permanent covenant, but in the context of the exile Jeremiah broadens it again: "I will seal for them a permanent covenant that I will not turn from going after them in doing good to them, and I will put reverence for me in their heart so that they do not turn aside from me" (Jer 32:40; cf. Is 55:3; 61:8; Ezek 16:60; 37:26).[130]

Jeremiah's permanent covenant promises that Yhwh's grace will keep pursuing the people. Yhwh is absolutely committed to doing good to them. Then it makes a promise to put reverence for Yhwh in their heart as a people, so that they do not turn aside from Yhwh to serve other gods or rely on other nations. That reexpresses the idea in Jeremiah's own "new covenant" (Jer 31:31-34); reverence for Yhwh and acknowledgment of Yhwh are very similar ideas. One of the implicit reasons why this new covenant can be permanent lies here. It is impossible to imagine Yhwh in permanent relationship with a people that did not revere or acknowledge Yhwh. It would not work, as a marriage cannot really work if its partners are not mutually committed. Yet it is also impossible to imag-

---

[128]David C. Greenwood, "On the Jewish Hope for a Restored Northern Kingdom," *ZAW* 88 (1976): 376-85; see p. 384; cf. Allen, *Ezekiel*, 2:195.

[129]See section 3.1 "One People" and Moltmann, *The Church in the Power of the Spirit*, p. 339.

[130]The reference of the permanent covenant in Is 24:5 is less clear.

ine Yhwh giving up on the permanent covenant and thus going back on a word so solemnly given. So in sealing a permanent covenant, Yhwh is taking on a commitment to making this covenant work, and therefore to doing whatever it takes to bring Israel to a response of reverence and acknowledgment, along the lines indicated in Jeremiah's talk of a new covenant and Ezekiel's of a new heart.

What is the relationship of this permanent covenant to the earlier "permanent" covenant(s)? Ezekiel raises this question most explicitly, though not entirely uncontroversially: "The Lord Yhwh has said this: I will do with you as you have done, you who have despised the oath and broken the covenant, but I myself will be mindful of my covenant with you in your young days and will establish for you a permanent covenant" (Ezek 16:59-60). "Establishing" a covenant (qûm hiphil) can mean confirming, implementing or maintaining an existent covenant (Lev 26:9; Deut 8:18), and JPSV here renders "I will establish it [the original covenant] with you as an everlasting covenant." But it has to add the "it" and the "as," and the overt transitions in Ezekiel's words ("with you"—"for you") and the new expression "permanent covenant" rather suggests that the traditional translation is right; Ezekiel is envisioning a new covenant, perhaps not surprisingly, as Jeremiah explicitly does.

Like Jeremiah, he is aware that the Sinai covenant has not worked because people have not kept their side of it, and like Jeremiah, he recognizes that the situation requires a commitment to new action on Yhwh's part rather than some expectation of different action on Israel's part. Perhaps Ezekiel was unfamiliar with the idea that Yhwh had made a previous "permanent covenant" behind the Sinai covenant and he would have had no reason to see any tension in the idea that Yhwh replaces the earlier covenant with a permanent one; neither do references to an earlier permanent covenant appear in Isaiah and Jeremiah. Affirming that Yhwh had long ago made a permanent covenant and affirming that Yhwh was doing so now might then be two ways of making the same point: there was a permanent commitment on Yhwh's part to Judeans in the sixth century, so they had no grounds for fearing that their covenant was finished. Alternatively we could reckon that there is no unfaithfulness in Yhwh's replacing one permanent covenant by another if the new permanent covenant constitutes an enhanced version of the original one. Yhwh is not going back on the commitment to Abraham. Analogously, in extending the David covenant to the whole people and giving up the idea of a distinctive commitment to David's line (Is 55:3), Yhwh is not going back on the David covenant but enhancing it, because the David covenant always existed for the sake of the people as a whole and its fulfillment of its vocation.[131]

---

[131]See section 8.2 "Recognition for Yhwh's Sake."

After the fall of Babylon, Jeremiah pictures Israel and Judah together coming to meet Yhwh with weeping (again, tears of joy?). They will ask the way to Zion (apparently they do not know the way, being a generation born in exile) "and they will attach themselves to Yhwh by a permanent covenant that will not be put out of mind" (Jer 50:5). Who will not do the forgetting? Other allusions to a permanent covenant refer to a covenant by Yhwh, and the sentence could signify that Yhwh will never forget this covenant. But every other verb in this oracle refers to the people's turning to Yhwh: they come, they weep, they have recourse, they ask, they attach themselves. Thus more likely it is the people who will not forget this covenant. In isolation one might imagine them making sure of recalling Yhwh's permanent covenant to them, but in the context it is more likely that Yhwh hopefully envisages a covenant commitment on their part that they will not forget, that will not fail.

A People Multiplied

The promise to Abraham also undertook to make the people as numerous as the sand on the seashore (Gen 22:17). Hosea takes up that image and adds that in keeping with its etymology Jezreel ("God sows") will become a figure for fruitfulness not disaster (Hos 1:10 [MT 2:1]).[132] The trouble is that the exile meant that Yhwh "gave Jacob to devoting" (ḥērem), to the total destruction involved in the annihilation of a people in Yhwh's own name (Is 43:28). Against that background, in Isaiah 44:1-5 Yhwh declares the intention to make the people flourish again.

It is a plausible guess that in speaking about the application of ḥērem to Israel, Yhwh had been responding to its plaints about its situation. Yhwh had responded robustly: "Yes, you are right, I did that, and here are my good reasons."[133] Yet we recall Yhwh's expression of regret about acting thus, not a regret at doing it but a regret at having to do it. Judah and Yhwh both know that talk in terms of annihilation is an exaggeration, but they also know that Yhwh had long threatened that after the disaster Yhwh threatened to bring, there would be only leftovers of the people. That is all they feel, and Yhwh does not tell them they are exaggerating. But Yhwh does declare that things will not end there. They are like dry, thirsty ground that will grow nothing (one may again hear their plaints; see, e.g., Ps 90; 102). But rain or irrigation has a magical capacity to make a desert blossom. So Yhwh will pour water on this parched and arid land. Put a little more literally, "I will pour my breath on your children." Yhwh speaks of "my rûaḥ," but this is not a promise of mere

---

[132]Cf. section 5.2 "Winning Israel Back."

[133]Cf. Claus Westermann, *Isaiah 40—66* (London: SCM Press/Philadelphia: Westminster Press, 1969), p. 130.

"spiritual" growth. It will need to be accompanied by that, as Yhwh makes clear on other occasions, but here Yhwh reassures the people that their more fundamental need will also be met. If the people die out, the question about spiritual growth cannot arise. Talk of the pouring of Yhwh's blessing on them confirms this, because blessing is fundamentally a matter of flourishing growth (e.g., Gen 1:28; 9:1; 12:2). The next line reworks the original image to make the point a simile: they will bloom like flourishing trees whose roots can reach down to ample waters.

On the other hand, it would also not be enough if Israel flourished numerically but failed to own Yhwh. Yhwh promises this will not happen. Among these growing offspring, people will individually make their personal confession of Yhwh. Again, this is not spiritual in the sense of inward. Like the testimony-thanksgiving of the psalms, what counts in this connection is an outward, public confession of Yhwh. In Babylon people often took Gentile names (see Daniel and Esther). Names often declare identity, revealing the part of the world we come from. The Judean community will flourish, will flaunt its Jewishness with pride and flaunt its commitment to Yhwh with boldness (Is 44:5).

Their increase will mean they no longer miss Yhwh's covenant chest, which had presumably been carried off by the Babylonians or been destroyed when the Babylonians conquered Jerusalem. One of the significances of the chest is to suggest Yhwh's presence enthroned among the people, perhaps because it was the footstool of the invisible Yhwh. But when numbers flourish again in Jerusalem, "Jerusalem will be called 'Yhwh's throne'" (Jer 3:16-17). Ezekiel thus makes no mention of the covenant chest. "Such is Ezekiel's focus on God himself, that much else is simply eclipsed."[134]

A People with Its Head High

Micah 5:7-15 [MT 6-14]) juxtaposes two or three contrasting perspectives on Israel and the nations. In the first, Israel is turned from victim to victor. Hans Walter Wolff suggests that here and elsewhere in Micah "the word 'remnant' has lost any negative tone suggestive of a lamentable group of survivors."[135] What Micah is about to say will effect a transformation of the word's implications, but initially its significance surely is to presuppose a situation in which Israel is indeed mere leftovers, a shadow of its former self. But a transformation will come about in Israel's position in relation to the nations. It will be as

---

[134]Paul M. Joyce, "Temple and Worship in Ezekiel 40—48," in *Temple and Worship in Biblical Israel*, ed. John Day, LHBOTS 422 (London/New York: T & T Clark, 2005), pp. 145-63; see p. 152.

[135]Hans Walter Wolff, *Micah* (Minneapolis: Augsburg, 1990), p. 155.

wondrous as the way dew and rain come without being created by human beings, a transformation that takes Israel from being the victim of the lion (e.g.,
Hos 5:14—6:1) to being the lion itself. The passage presupposes that Israel has
been defeated by people such as Assyria and Babylon, and promises that these
enemies will be cut down. It does not quite declare that Israel will do the cutting down. It is explicit that Yhwh brings the dew, but who turns Jacob from
leftovers into lion? How far will Israel be like dew and like a lion? Who will
cut down its enemies? The passage sidesteps these questions in favor of making a different point, putting more emphasis on the reality of this transformation than its agency.

Israel's hand will be high, like that of the Israelites leaving Egypt (Ex 14:8;
Num 33:3; cf. Num 15:30; JPSV translates "defiantly"), and they will see their
enemies cut down, like the Egyptians. The implication is that Yhwh will do the
cutting down, though that is not explicit. On the other hand, Yhwh goes on to
speak about doing some cutting off (the same verb *kārat*, though now in the
hiphil). And Israel is the explicit victim of this verb; or rather, its victims are
Israel's military, defensive and intelligence assets and its spiritual resources.
The passage is talking about the future ("in that day") and thus raises questions about the relationship of the two parts of the passage, or the two passages. It seems that the future restored Israel will face the same temptations as
the Israel of Micah's day, the temptation to trust in military resources and alien
spiritual resources. That community is thus promised it will be able to raise its
hand defiantly in the face of its enemies, but warned about trusting in those
resources, perhaps as the means of doing its own cutting down of its enemies.
A surprising further change of tone in the last line perhaps links with this, as
at last it affirms that Yhwh is the one who puts down the nations; it is not Israel
who does.[136]

There is a parallel allusiveness in Daniel 7 when God grants the authority
to reign. The other reigns, symbolized as animals, are replaced by Yhwh's
reign; God then gives this reign to someone who looks like a human being and
who in some way stands for "a holy people on high," whose rule will last forever (Dan 7:13-14, 27). It is unlikely that such an expression simply denotes the
earthly Israel, but it is also unlikely that it denotes a body of supernatural beings quite separate from Israel. Insofar as it denotes Israel, it refers to it as a supernatural people; insofar as it denotes a supernatural people, it refers to it as
one somehow identified with Israel.[137] Daniel's dream envisions God's rule in
the world implemented by means of Israel, but not a mere earthly Israel, which
(like the church) would turn out to have the flaws of other earthly powers.

---

[136]See section 5.1 "Yhwh's Arm Bared."

[137]I have discussed Dan 7 in *Daniel*, WBC (Dallas: Word, 1989), pp. 137-93.

Isaiah 25 describes a banquet on "this mountain" to which all peoples are invited. But this concern for all nations does not mean Yhwh has stopped being concerned for Israel in particular. Alongside the world's grief at the body bags both from victory and from defeat is Israel's grief at the shame of its position in the world. But Yhwh "will take away from upon all the earth his people's shame." Thus people will be able to say, "There, this is our God; we waited for him so that he might deliver us." Bringing about this great celebration "on this mountain," on Mount Zion, and thus making "the city of our God . . . the joy of all the earth," will also mean that "the daughters [i.e., cities] of Judah are to rejoice because of your decisive acts" (Ps 48:1-2, 11 [MT 2-3, 12]). The people will be able to hold their head high as they had not for centuries. Israel is at least among those "poor" and "needy" who have been given shade from the heat and shelter from the storm of history (Is 25:4). They have waited for Yhwh and will now be in a position to rejoice in Yhwh's deliverance.

"As you have been a belittling among the nations, household of Judah and household of Israel, so I will deliver you and you will be a blessing" (Zech 8:13). People have been saying to their enemies, "May you be decimated like Judah and Israel." They will now be saying to their friends, "May you blessed like Judah and Israel," as Yhwh originally intended (Gen 12:3).

A Word That Stands Forever

Can this really be believed? When Yhwh commissions someone to proclaim comfort to Jerusalem, the response is to question whether such proclamation is possible (Is 40:6-8). It is too much to believe. When Yhwh gave Ezekiel his vision of the people as the remains of an army strewn over a battlefield and asked him whether these dried-up bones could live again, the prophet wisely declined to express an opinion. This prophet's equivalent vision pictures the people and their commitment to Yhwh a generation later as like grass and flowers withered by the hot, dry, wind from the desert. In 587 Yhwh's searing breath destroyed them. "We are just another people overwhelmed by the tide of history." How can one make a proclamation either to or about such a people?

The commissioning voice points out that there is nothing wrong with this assessment of the state of the people. In themselves they are withered and discouraged, and if the future depends on their commitment, it is bleak indeed. But the questioning voice has forgotten one small consideration. From the beginning, the destiny of the people of God did not depend on their commitment or their word but on Yhwh's. And the word of Yhwh will stand forever. Phrases such as "the word of God" do not refer to written Scriptures but to anything that God says. A declaration on God's part about returning to Jerusalem and restoring the city, for instance, like any other declaration of God's, will find fulfillment, even if this takes time and even if the act needs to be undertaken again and again, because with Yhwh there is no gap between word and deed. The people's commitment needs to meet Yhwh's, but the failure of their commitment and the withering of their life do not mean the end. Yhwh is a stubborn God who, once having decided on something and announced it, persists until it is achieved. Yhwh's stubbornness will not be overcome by Israel's withered-ness.

In substance, the objections of this responsive voice echo the people's own plaint as the prophet subsequently relates it, "My way has hidden from Yhwh, a decision for me passes away from my God" (Is 40:27). The prophet's response is to remind them about the power and understanding of Yhwh as sovereign over the world. It is therefore alright for them to become faint and weary as decades pass and Yhwh seems to do nothing because that does not have to be the end of the story (Is 40:30-31). People who wait a long time for the vision to find fulfillment can find the strength to keep going because they know that delay in the implementing of the vision does not imperil the certainty of its implementation. The character of Yhwh guarantees the vision. Waiting for Yhwh conveys the strength to keep going because it contains the reminder that the vision will find fulfillment.

Yhwh's intention will find fulfillment because Yhwh's word is performative. It makes things happen, like the rain and the snow (Is 55:6-11). They do not return to the storehouses in the heavens from which Yhwh sends them on their journey. Admittedly they do in due course, because all the waters in the world go on an everlasting circular journey,[138] but Yhwh's point is the one a later line makes explicit, that they do not return with their work undone. While sun and rain are both needed to bring crops to fruition, in the Middle East one can assume that the sun will shine, but one cannot take precipitation for granted. It is the wonder-working nature of rain that provokes thought. If the rains fail, the crops fail; if rain comes, crops grow (give or take the occasional locust plague). Humanity then has seed corn for next year and food for this year. And Yhwh's word is the same. When Yhwh does not make any decisions, this does not mean that nothing happens, as the pointless and aimless nature of most of world history shows. But when Yhwh decides to speak, declaring that something is to happen, Yhwh's word is the effective causal agent in deciding what happens in the world. It makes things happen.

There is another significance in the talk of rain and snow. The prophet has acknowledged the way the searing heat of the desert wind could wither everything that grows. That was what Yhwh's *rûaḥ* could do, as the agent whereby

---

[138]Indeed, NRSV renders *kî ʾim* "until" and thus makes the passage recognize this, but this is hard to justify, esp. in light of the recurrence of *kî ʾim* later in the passage where we cannot avoid translating it "but."

Yhwh's word about calamity could find fulfillment. It was what Yhwh's wind and word had done. Now the prophet reverses that imagery in the course of offering this final picture of the process of restoration.[139]

The moment that lies in the background is the moment when Yhwh spoke in the 540s, when Yhwh gave the rise of Cyrus its meaning. "Cyrus, without realizing it, is, in fact, fulfilling the purposes of the God who has called him. The basis of the prophet's interpretation is by no means a skilful weighing of the political chances" but an "affirmation of the Creator God as the controller of events."[140] When Yhwh determined by means of Cyrus to open up the possibility that Judean exiles could return to Jerusalem and rebuild their city, the rise of Cyrus became not just one more event in the history of the world. It is this declaration that establishes that the return will take place, as nature responds with applause and a flourishing of its own (Is 55:12-13). It will be looked back on forever as an extraordinary act of God. (And so it has been.) So the exiles had better believe it.

5.5 Renewing the Land

In prison for persistently telling people Jerusalem is going to fall, Jeremiah redeems a tract of family land from his cousin Hanamel (see Jer 32).[141] In a sense he is just doing what Israelite ideals require, yet this is no ordinary act of family solidarity. He and his cousin are living at a moment when the structures of life are collapsing around them, when on Jeremiah's own theory the community is about to be taken off into exile. The ideals in the Torah are presumably even less compelling than usual. No one could blame him for laughing at the idea that this is a moment when those theoretical community principles bind anyone. And perhaps other people (including Hanamel) were laughing at the ingenuousness of someone who thought they did. Indeed, perhaps Jeremiah would have so laughed were it not for the fact that Yhwh had told him Hanamel was about to show up with an offer that he hoped Jeremiah could not refuse. Jeremiah did raise an eyebrow at Yhwh at the end of a long resumption of the First Testament story so far, though only after he had paid out his money (Jer 32:24-25). It is because of Yhwh's involvement that he cannot refuse. Buying the land is a sign that there will be a future.

Admittedly, the bad news for the moment is that the future is postponed. Jeremiah's assistant, Baruch, is to put the land deeds in a clay jar "so that they

---

[139]See further section 5.5 "Where Breath/Wind/Spirit Is Poured Out."

[140]Ackroyd, *Exile and Restoration*, p. 133.

[141]Israelite land could not be regularly bought and sold, but under pressure of circumstances such as poverty, the "owners" of a particular stretch of land could let it pass to someone else within the extended family.

may last a long time" (Jer 32:14). Jeremiah knows that the exile will last so long that hardly anyone currently alive will see it. But the time will come when "houses, fields, and vineyards will again be bought in this country" (Jer 32:15). "This country" will include Benjamin as a whole, and Judah as a whole, of which Benjamin is an adjunct (Jer 32:44). Indeed, Yhwh "will turn Israel back to its pasture, and it will graze in Carmel and Bashan and eat its fill on Mount Ephraim and in Gilead"—in other words, in the whole area that Ephraim once occupied (Jer 50:19). It will not happen immediately, but it will happen. The promise to Abraham and the deliverance from Egypt are the determinative factors for Israel's destiny; they mean that exile from the land cannot be the end. "You will see a country that stretches far" (Is 33:17). The land is one Yhwh cares about passionately, and it will become a place for a full life, a place characterized by peace and flourishing.

A Place for Living

Yhwh's intention for the people's life in the land was that if they live by Yhwh's commands, the rains would come, their crops would flourish, and they would live securely and carefree in the land (Lev 26:4-13). If only! But the failure of this vision because of Israel's own shortcomings, anticipated by this chapter (Lev 26:14-45), does not mean it simply lapses. Yhwh created the earth/land itself (hāʾareṣ), not as a waste (tōhû) but as a place for inhabiting (Is 45:18). Yhwh refers directly to the creation of the earth: even if it was an empty, unformed waste when Yhwh began work (Gen 1:2), it was not destined to stay that way. Yet hāʾareṣ is also the term for "the land" of Israel, which was destined to become a microcosm of the whole earth, with Israel as a microcosm of the people of the world living under God's blessing. So the promise that Yhwh created hāʾareṣ not as a waste but as a place for inhabiting suggests a promise about the land.

In the sixth century it became something of a tōhû, but it will flourish again. Yes, the harvesting of grain, which begins in early summer, will last till the fruit harvest of late summer, and the fruit harvest will last till sowing time in the fall (Lev 26:5). In Amos 9:13-15 Yhwh's promise reaffirms and goes beyond that. These harvests will be so extensive it will be as if the wine that issues from these grapes is running like a river down the mountains and hills on which the vines grow. The devastations of the exile will be restored, devastation of cities and also devastation of vineyards and orchards wrecked by invasion. The displacement of exile will be restored, and that forever. Yhwh's original intention for a good life will find fulfillment. The splendid but not very useful forests of Lebanon will become orchards and the orchards that already exist will seem as feeble as forests by comparison (Is 29:17).

The further promises in Jeremiah 30:18-22 speak simply of "the city" and may relate to cities in general, but either way they have implications for the present and future of the country as a whole, not just that of Jerusalem (or Samaria), nor just that of Judah. Ephraim had long been reduced to a mere Assyrian and then Babylonian province. Nebuchadnezzar's invasion devastated the entire country. People's homes were burned down. Whole cities were destroyed by fire and left as mounds of ruins ("mound" is *tēl*, the modern word for the mound on which the ruins of a city stand). Their monumental buildings were demolished. The population was decimated. The country was put under an administration appointed by its destroyers. The voice of worship and merrymaking was silenced (cf. Jer 16:9). The community's relationship with Yhwh seemed to be over.

Yhwh promises the restoration of the whole. Jeremiah's vision pictures the entire country rebuilt, homes reconstructed and city after city being well built-up and well defended and thus well populated and secure. As he later puts it, Yhwh "will sow the household of Israel and the household of Judah with human seed and animal seed" (Jer 31:27), so that the human and animal population grows again. The ravages of battle, flight and exile are undone. The cities bustle with life again and hold their head high. They are not looking over their shoulders fearful that another invasion is around the corner. They are now governed by a ruler who is one of their own rather than a foreigner, and it is not even a Judean appointed from outside in the manner of the interim Babylonian governor Gedaliah. It is someone put in place by Yhwh who can thus confidently draw near to Yhwh like a priest, for instance in seeking Yhwh's guidance and aid in the tasks of king.

All that will presumably involve human activity; the builders will be regular construction workers not angelic ones. Yet it is not mere human achievement like the rebuilding of Europe after the Second World War or the rebuilding of the Twin Towers site, but an expression of Yhwh's mother-love for the places where the Israelites live. The people involved are not merely a nation but a congregation, and their experience of restoration thus issues in enthusiastic celebration that does not merely express justified human self-satisfaction. It expresses gratitude to this compassionate God, who did not leave things as they were when that would have been quite justified, and who had often threatened to do exactly that. Indeed, the promise does not close with talk about the country's new ruler. It was easy for the introduction of monarchy to put the king into the place that really belonged to the people as a whole; Yhwh's covenant became a covenant with king rather than directly with people. Yhwh's vision avoids that conclusion and closes with that covenant relationship with the people as a whole, Israel as Yhwh's people: Yhwh as Israel's God (Jer 30:22).

Peace

Thus there is another sense in which the people will not merely return to the land as it was in the decades—indeed, the centuries—up to the exile. That would not be enough. When Joshua completed the initial taking of the land of Canaan, "the land had peace from war" (*šāqaṭ*, Josh 11:23; cf. Josh 14:15). But over subsequent centuries that experience was at best intermittent, interrupted by conflict with other peoples and by civil war (e.g., Judg 3:11, 30; 2 Chron 14:1 [MT 13:23]). Yhwh promises that the return to the land will not be merely a return to the experience that led up to the exile. "Jacob is to return and be at peace, to be safe (*šāʾan*), with no one to disturb" (Jer 30:10). That no one would disturb the people or make them afraid is another promise about Israel's original destiny (Lev 26:6). It comes to gain a sardonic side (Deut 28:26; Jer 7:33), but then to be renewed in light of the deeply disturbing experience of Assyrian and Babylonian domination (e.g., Ezek 34:28; 39:26; Zeph 3:13) and also to be a vision for all the nations (Mic 4:4). Peace is both a matter of objective security and of a feeling of security. The objective peace, safety and banishment of anyone to disturb means Israel need not be afraid or dismayed (Jer 30:10).

So Yhwh will enable the people to live in their country "in security" (*lĕbeṭaḥ*, Jer 32:37; cf. Ezek 28:26; 39:26; Hos 2:18 [MT 20]; Zech 14:11). That, too, was part of God's original promise (Lev 25:18-19; 26:5; Deut 12:10; 33:28), and it had sometimes come true (1 Sam 12:11; 1 Kings 4:25 [MT 5:5]). But it was an aspect of a total relationship between the people and Yhwh, and the whole relationship comprehensively collapsed. Living in security thus becomes an aspect of the vision of restoration. "You will not see the aggressive people, the people whose speech is too unfathomable to listen to, stammering in a tongue that cannot be understood" (Is 33:19). When Yhwh gives the people a king who embodies faithfulness and leads them in a life of faithfulness, they will live in security (Jer 23:6; 33:16; cf. Ezek 34:25-28). And even when the fulfillment of that promise finds unexpected disruption (Ezek 38:8, 11, 14), this will not be the end.

For two centuries, the United States was the most secure nation on earth. September 11, 2001, was therefore a devastating experience for it. Suddenly its security was devastatingly breached. Danger and uncertainty were no longer features of Europe or Asia or Africa alone, continents that Americans might visit but from which they could return to the safety of the homeland. Suddenly they were features of the homeland itself. A comparison of the national poise and assurance that preceded September 11 with the anxiety and disquiet that issued from it helps us to sense the significance of this promise for a people. It will mean people will again say in Judah and its cities, "Yhwh bless you, faithful abode, holy mountain." Yhwh adds, "farmhands and those who go about with their flocks will live in it, Judah and all its cities alike, because I will satisfy the one who is weary and fill everyone who is faint" (Jer 31:23-25).

It is apparently the prophet who then adds, "Upon this I woke up and looked, and my sleep was sweet to me" (Jer 31:26). One is tempted to add, "I bet it was." The visionary dreamer had beheld a very ordinary scene, yet one that had the extraordinariness that characterizes peace for a country that has been devastated by invasion and war. When Israel's life was working properly, then Yhwh's presence in Jerusalem was the source of life and blessing for the whole country. Evidently this dynamic is now working properly and people are responding by praying for Yhwh's blessing on Zion itself. Even very ordinary people like farmhands and shepherd boys who look after the tough side to shepherding flocks are able to share in the blessings of life in the land again.[142] They are the people who most get faint and weary, so they are the people whose thirst Yhwh slakes and whose tiredness Yhwh refreshes.

Where Breath/Wind/Spirit Is Poured Out

Isaiah 32:9-14 gives an apparently terminal picture of the devastation of countryside and land, which will leave countryside as thorn and thistle, and city as the abode of wild asses. This seems like the end. When the oracle continues by declaring that this will be so "until *rûaḥ* from on high is poured on us," initially we could assume that this simply continues the bad news; the *rûaḥ* from on high is Yhwh's *rûaḥ*, and that *rûaḥ* is capable of implying a process of searing, burning and withering (cf. Is 30:28). But even that burning can imply purging rather than simply destruction (cf. Is 4:4), and here the book of Isaiah typically uses such ambiguity as a way of making a surprising transition from threatening news to good news in Isaiah 32:15-20.[143] On this occasion the good news concerns restoration succeeding devastation, not the reversing of the threat of devastation. Wind/breath/spirit stands for unpredictable dynamic power, and on this occasion the effect of the falling of this power is renewing, not destructive.

This renewal affects a striking combination of realms. Initially it affects the countryside itself, which has been devastated by an invading army. Here the coming of Yhwh's *rûaḥ* onto the land is not merely a symbol for its coming on the people (contrast Is 44:3). It transforms the land itself. Wilderness that is useful only for pasturing sheep will be turned into land on which fruit trees will grow. The transformation will not be merely spectacular, as when wilderness becomes forest (e.g., Is 41:19), but useful, like the turning of wilderness

---

[142]See William L. Holladay, *Jeremiah*, 2 vols. (Philadelphia: Fortress, 1986, 1989), 2:196.

[143]Vv. 15-20 may be an addition to make vv. 8-14 less final.

into a fertile Eden (cf. Is 51:3). But it will indeed be spectacular, so that people's present orchards will seem as dispensable as an area of forest (cf. Is 29:17).[144] There will be no competition or worry over water and irrigation because there will be lots of well-watered land for growing crops. Thus people will even be able to let their animals range free rather than fearing that they will eat up the year's supply of food and then starve later, or fearing they will be subject to attack or rustling.

We might be surprised to see this as an achievement of the *rûaḥ* from on high, but less surprised to see the next effect of the falling of that *rûaḥ* as the growth and maturing of authority exercised with faithfulness—a fruit of the Spirit, indeed. Yet we might also be surprised to see Isaiah presupposing a link between these two aspects of the work of the *rûaḥ* from on high, a point underlined by speaking of authority and faithfulness living in the pasturage and the orchards. They are at home there on a permanent basis, not just as occasional visitors. The order suggests the link is not the moral one, as if faithfulness must first be implemented, then the natural world can be restored. If anything, the order points in the opposite direction: God will restore the natural world, then the sociomoral world. Either way, both form part of the agenda of the *rûaḥ* from on high.

The fruit of faithfulness will be *shalom* and also quiet and confidence, Isaiah 32:17 adds, and does make something of a moral point. While the parallelism of *shalom* with quiet and confidence might suggest that *shalom* refers merely to peace, the linking of *shalom* with the flourishing of the natural world and the faithful exercise of authority recalls Psalm 72 and the reworking of its themes in Isaiah 11, and points to the broader meaning of *shalom*. The psalm's vision of the faithful exercise of authority, of the protection of the weak, of *shalom* and the associated flourishing of nature was hardly ever realized in Israel, as it is not realized in, for instance, the United States or Britain. Isaiah once again affirms that this will not be the end of the story.

The emphasis on quiet and confidence and a carefree life also takes up motifs from Isaiah 32:9-14. The women of Judah were confident and carefree but were to have a rude awakening. Yet this too is not the end of the story. *Shalom* is the community's destiny.

In Shalom Covenant

Indeed, Yhwh will seal with the people a *shalom* covenant (Ezek 34:25-31), a lasting *shalom* covenant (Ezek 37:26). Its terms involve a restatement of those

---

[144]See "A Place for Living" (p. 439). Cf. Wildberger, *Isaiah 28—39*, pp. 257-63, where he also suggests that the sinking of the forest and collapse of the city refer to the fall of the superpower, the first stage in Israel's restoration.

in Leviticus 26.[145] As is often the case, this covenant is not a mutual commitment between two parties but a one-sided commitment on Yhwh's part. Here, by *shalom* Yhwh does initially mean "peace." The flock will not be vulnerable to wild animals, the people will not be vulnerable to enemies (perhaps Ezekiel implies that the people will not be vulnerable to wild animals; literal and allegorical interweave). But *shalom* again goes beyond that. It means the rain will fall when it should; these original "showers of blessing" (EVV) are not merely "spiritual blessings" but physical ones. For that matter, they are not mere "showers" but proper "rain,"[146] rain that makes the ground fruitful so that the people no longer experience hunger. The people will no longer be under foreign rule or subject to foreign invasion and despoiling. No one will make them afraid and no one will deride them for living on a land that could not sustain them. Ezekiel goes on to envisage the rebuilding of ruins and the inhabiting of towns, the multiplying of human beings and domestic animals. And people will say, "this desolate land has become like the Garden of Eden" (Ezek 36:35). It would be understandable if the exiles could never imagine being in possession of their land again and could never imagine that building, agriculture or husbandry would ever be possible again. And even if these were possibilities, it would be understandable if the exiles looked back to the "land flowing with milk and honey" as a "land that devours its inhabitants" (Num 13:32). Yhwh promises that all these fears can be faced.

Ezekiel implies two ways of describing how Yhwh will bring about this transformation. At first he speaks of Yhwh personally banishing the wild animals from the land and making the rain fall—literally, "giving" it (Ezek 34:25-26). He then speaks of the trees "giving" their fruit and the land "giving" their increase. That is possible only because of Yhwh's giving, yet as a result of that act the trees and the land become agents of giving themselves. The thinking is thus analogous to the description in Genesis 1 of events at creation, when God personally acted but also bestowed natural capacities on the land by "blessing" it.

Ezekiel's final vision portrays this blessing coming in a wholly other way (Ezek 47:1-12). A river flows eastward into the wilderness from the new temple, so abundant that after a mile or so one could not cross it except by swimming. The river restores wholesomeness to the Dead Sea, which becomes so full of fish that "people will stand fishing by it from En Gedi to En Eglaim,"

---

[145]Historically the relationship between the passages may be the reverse; that is, Ezek 34 may antedate Lev 26. It would then still be true that Leviticus associates these promises with Yhwh's purpose from the beginning, and that Ezekiel is restating an older purpose.

[146]Elsewhere *gešem* is usually translated rain; indeed, it is the word for rain in the flood story (Gen 7:12; 8:2).

though thoughtfully the marshes will stay salty so as to supply people with salt. Trees grow in profusion either side of the river, their leaves and their fruit renewed throughout the year "because their water is issuing from the sanctuary" (Ezek 47:12; cf. Joel 3:18 [MT 4:18]). The allegory in the vision comes to the surface here. When Yhwh returns to the temple and the relationship between people and Yhwh is put on a proper footing there, that will issue in the people's whole life flourishing. The promise resembles that in Psalm 72, for example, but temple rather than king becomes the key to its realization (Rev 22 takes up Ezekiel's imagery to portray its new Jerusalem, though it is not so clear there that this is a hope for real human experience in this world). The land will be redistributed among the clans (Ephraim and Manasseh being treated as two), without any account being taken of how things were before the exile, or how big the individual clans were (Ezek 48). The bounds of the land approximately correspond to those of Solomon's day, so that the promise's fulfillment requires a political and/or military miracle as well as a geo-physical one. The promise contrasts as implausibly with realities of the exilic or Persian period as the promise to Abraham contrasts with the realities of his day.

Hosea 2 presupposes a breakdown in the marriage relationship between Hosea and Gomer, and between Yhwh and Israel, and between heaven and earth. It then envisions a threefold restoration of the relationships. This will include a renewed covenant commitment for the animate world, heaven and earth being in renewed conversation with each other (Hos 2:18-23 [MT 20-25]). The covenant that is renewed is a "cosmic covenant" rather than the Sinai covenant.[147]

Yhwh's Passion

The restoration and flourishing of the land issue from Yhwh's passion for it. Yhwh *loves* this land.

After a locust plague, in Joel 2:18-27 Yhwh speaks again to the people. It is a response, perhaps to the people's acceptance of a bidding to turn to Yhwh. It is stage one of a response to prayer, the response in words that people hear, which precedes and promises the response in deeds that people will in due course see. The response uses participles, yiqtols and qatals, all with future reference. The qatals speak of the acts as having happened because Yhwh is so committed to them that they are already as good as actual, and on the same basis the participles similarly speak of them as presently happening, while the yiqtols recognize that they are actually future.

---

[147]Robert Murray, *The Cosmic Covenant* (London: Sheed & Ward, 1992), pp. 27-32.

The first motivation for Yhwh's act of restoration is the passion Yhwh feels for the land of Israel. It is the only time Yhwh becomes passionate about the land. But it is a logical feeling for Yhwh to have in regard to "his land" (cf. "my land" in Joel 1:6), this land that Yhwh loves (Ps 47:4 [MT 5]).[148] The EVV think of the verb *qānâ* as indicating more specifically jealousy, which is a suggestive idea. It implies that Yhwh resents the way the locusts sent by Yhwh have taken over the land. Yhwh is going to take the land back. Either the passion or the jealousy are good news for Israel, in that as long as Israel are Yhwh's tenants on this land, Yhwh's jealous passion undergirds its ultimate security and makes it impossible for Yhwh ultimately to abandon it. All the tenants need do is keep their noses clean, and they too will be secure there. But alongside the comment on the land is also a comment about Yhwh's attitude to the people itself, on whom Yhwh "had mercy." That verb (*ḥāmal*) can suggest the act of sparing people and/or the attitude of compassion that makes someone do that. Here the narrower and the broader context suggest a focus on the atti-tude. The feelings of passion toward "his land" and of pity toward "his peo-ple" go together.

Both passion and pity will issue in the restoring of the land and its produce, at point after point reversing the earlier picture in Joel 1 and fulfilling the promises of the Torah (see Lev 26:3-4; Deut 11:13-15). Vines and trees will grow their grapes and figs again. Yhwh pictures the actual harvest—the fresh grain, the newly fermented grape juice, the newly pressed olive oil—that brings such pleasure to smell and taste, and brings anticipation of participating in its fur-ther results, the bread, the mature wine and the illumination. People will eat their fill of these basics of human life and sit back in satisfaction. That will mean Israel forgets about the ravages of the past; it will be as if they never hap-pened. It will mean that Israel's neighbors will stop looking in pity and con-tempt at a people who had evidently chosen the wrong god to rely on (Joel 2:17). It will mean that Israel itself becomes convinced of the opposite point, that Yhwh is in its midst and that there is no God but its God. The mutual re-lationship of "your God" and "my people" will be a reality. Whereas Israel has come before Yhwh lamenting the failure of its harvest, it will now come before Yhwh with wild joy. Again the prophet presupposes that apart from protection from the locust, the key to a harvest is rain, the autumn rain to soften the ground and make plowing and sowing possible, and the spring rain to make the crops ripen and take them through the dry summer. These rains will fall.

Joel's perspective once more extends beyond Yhwh's concern for Israel, promising that Yhwh's restoring of the land will also be good news for the an-

---

[148]I take it that in the psalm it is the heights of Jacob that are the object of Yhwh's love: see section 3.4 "Landed."

imals of the wild, for which Yhwh also cares. It will be good news for the soil itself, which can rejoice in the way Yhwh has acted in removing from it the feet of the northerner and/or in enabling it to grow grass for the animals and crops for the people again (Joel 2:19-20 [MT 21-22]).

Transformed

"The northerner" suggests the fearsome, threatening enemy from the north who often appears in the prophets, a frightening superpower that is Yhwh's agent in bringing desolation and destruction. It may be a figure for the locust swarm that has devastated the land, or it may refer to the more terrible enemy that this swarm anticipated, whose coming would bring Yhwh's day. Either way, it has "acted great," as the superpower does (Joel 2:20; cf. Is 10:12-15), and it will find Yhwh acting great (Joel 2:21) both in putting it in its place by banishing it from the land, and in restoring the land—acting wonderfully, too (Joel 2:26). Yhwh's interests and Israel's interests come together. When it is lucky the northerner will be banished far away, to the desolation of the wilderness, to the Mediterranean, to the Dead Sea, securely out of Israel's territory, beyond its borders. When it is unlucky it will be dead, the smell of its rotting corpses rising to high heaven. And all that is because it acted great and thus provoked Yhwh into acting great in order to demonstrate who is really the great one (Joel 2:18 [MT 20]).

The promises' concern with making up for the reversals of current experience supports the idea that a vision such as this has a concern with theodicy.[149] It speaks very directly to issues that concern the community, but it does not do so by promising it that its calamities are about to be reversed. There is no implication here that the events are about to happen, only the promise that they will happen one day (even though the expression "in that day" does not come). That fact is enough to bolster the community in its trust in God, even if this generation never sees the fulfillment of these promises.

A vision in Zechariah 10:8-12 goes further in bringing together a range of promises, of strength, deliverance, settlement, joy, increase, revival and gathering, and adds, "I will bring them to the land of Gilead and Lebanon, but they will not be enough for them" (Zech 10:10).

The passage speaks in extremes. The people *were* many, but they will be many again, even as Yhwh sows them (that is, makes them multiply) in their dispersion. That is hard to believe. They are scattered far away, but Yhwh will

---

[149]Cf. John Barton, *Joel and Obadiah* (Louisville, Ky: Westminster John Knox, 2001), pp. 30-31; and James L. Crenshaw's comments on the book as a whole, "Who Knows What Yahweh Will Do?" in *Fortunate the Eyes That See*, ed. A. B. Beek et al. (Grand Rapids, Mich.: Eerdmans, 1995), pp. 185-96.

reach to those distant places to gather them. That is hard to believe. They have put Yhwh out of mind and feel as good as dead, but they will be mindful of Yhwh again and come back to life, with their children. That is hard to believe. They will not merely return to Judah, surrounded by other Persian provinces controlling the promised land, nor will they merely return to the proper bounds of the promised land, but they will spread to occupy Gilead and Lebanon, lands that had provided Jeremiah with a figure for devastation (Jer 22:6),[150] and even that will not be enough. And that is hard to believe. It will all be like a repetition of the triumph at the Red Sea, as if Yhwh is passing through that sea again and subduing it. But that is the strength they will have, which will mean they walk freely with head high.

The flourishing that Yhwh will grant will be yet more splendid. Isaiah 30:23-26 takes the realities of current experience and portrays the future as like them with the down sides removed and the positives enhanced. In regular experience one can never be sure that the rain will come, or will come at the right time in the right quantities; on that day, the rain will come. In regular experience one can thus never be sure how good the grain harvest will be; on that day the grain will grow a hundredfold. In regular experience one can never be sure that the fields will grow enough grass for one's cattle to pasture well and thus grow fat and strong; on that day, the pasturage will be plentiful. In regular experience one can never be sure how good will be the provender available to one's working animals; on that day, they will eat as well as the human beings do. In regular experience water is at the bottom of the hills and settlements are at the top, so that people spend much of their time carrying water uphill; on that day, the "natural" order will be vastly improved. Surprisingly, Isaiah goes on to refer to a "day of great slaughter when towers fall," but perhaps that presupposes that mountains and hills will now have ceased to be places where one needs to build strongholds; the vulnerability that reflects will be no more. The darkness of night is a time of such vulnerability, especially to stratagem and deception, but now it will be no more dangerous than daytime, and daytime itself will be enhanced; no one will be able to act and expect to escape detection (cf. Ps 139:11-12). Conversely, Yhwh will heal the hurts that have come through the people's experience of attack.

These allusions to a reversal of Israel's experience in history do not make a contrast between regular experience (the annual round of nature) and a coming enhanced version of how nature works, but between experiences of loss that come about through the vagaries of experience in history of which the ex-

---

[150]Cf. Rex Mason, "The Use of Earlier Biblical Material in Zechariah 9—14," in *Bringing Out the Treasure*, ed. Mark J. Boda and Michael H. Floyd, JSOTSup 370 (London/New York: Continuum, 2003), pp. 1-208; p. 89.

ile is a symbol. But that makes us reconsider the notion of a contrast between "regular experience" and the way things will be in that day. Yhwh's promise from the beginning was that the rains would fall, the crops grow and life flourish. The failure of such promises also reflects the vagaries of experience in history that come because of Israel's faithlessness. It is thus when the relationship between Israel and Yhwh is restored that people will experience the blessings of nature that were promised from the beginning.

When the First Testament speaks of the land, it indeed refers to the actual land of Canaan, but when we look at the promises associated with this land, "our gaze is necessarily directed to the paradise lost and restored which is to be the dwelling-place of this people, to the miraculously renewed earth upon which this people will some day live amid the other happily and peaceably united peoples. . . . The one land is waiting for the other."[151]

5.6 Renewing the City

"Comfort, comfort my people, your God says; encourage Jerusalem" (Is 40:1-2). The city is vital to the people, so the people are comforted through the city's being encouraged. Conversely, the return of the exiles is a comfort for the city. Whereas the city had no place in Yhwh's earliest dealings with Israel's ancestors and with the people itself, some of the First Testament's most spectacular visions relate to the city. The story that starts in a garden ends in a city. While one stage in this development was the people becoming a monarchic state with a capital (and a temple there), paradoxically the vision also reflects the reduction of the people and its land to not much more than a city-state, which came about in the late monarchy and persisted through the Persian period. A vision for the people, for the land and for the city came to be less and less distinguishable. The flourishing of the people as a whole will mean the flourishing of Jerusalem in particular, the heart of the land, and vice versa.

So the city becomes the focus of the people. If the people's blessing is a model for the world's blessing, then, whatever the contextual reasons for this focus on the city, the results should be suggestive for a world dominated by the city.

Yhwh in the Midst

In the years before the exile, the city's officials are roaring lions "in its midst," while the presence of Yhwh "in its midst" is a warning to them and an encouragement to their victims (Zeph 3:3, 5). Yhwh promises or warns the city of an intention to "remove from your midst" the people there who exult in their dis-

---

[151]Barth, *Church Dogmatics*, I/2:96.

tinguished position on Yhwh's holy mountain—people whose majesty becomes more important than Yhwh's—but to leave "in your midst" leftovers comprising weak and poor people (Zeph 3:11-12). Then Zephaniah 3:14-19 gives a further and less equivocal promise about Yhwh "in your midst." Ms. Zion can rejoice with all her heart because Yhwh has reversed the decision against her and turned away her foes. Now "the king of Israel, Yhwh, is in your midst; you need not be afraid of trouble any more. . . . Yhwh your God is in your midst, a warrior who delivers."

Yhwh's being in the midst is reason for the city to rejoice. It is reason for Yhwh, too, to rejoice. The promise looks back to a situation when Yhwh had made decisions that meant trouble for the city, meant invasion and devastation. (in Zephaniah's day those decisions were in the midst of being made and were in danger of being implemented; these promises look beyond them.) Yhwh has now reversed those decisions and turned away the agents of their implementation. Yhwh is not the commander-in-chief of some foreign army directing it to attack the city but the commander-in-chief "in the midst" of the city who will see that it stays secure from attack. The encouragement to rejoice thus recalls the encouragement of a city's lookouts when they see that the besieging enemy has retreated. Yhwh is not merely the king of the world but the king of Israel in particular, not merely sovereign in the world as a whole but one whose sovereignty is committed to the destiny of Israel. This king is "in its midst." Therefore its people's hands need not droop (for example, as they set about rebuilding the city), as hands do when they give up the work they were engaged in because of their owners' discouragement or fear (e.g., 2 Sam 4:1; Neh 6:9). Paradoxically, people can rejoice now both because Yhwh is going to rejoice then and because Yhwh is going to quieten them down then, in making it possible for them to stop grieving over the desolation of the city and the termination of the festivals in the temple. The ministry of true prophets can be an encouraging one and not a confrontational one, no longer the "Hey" that characteristically opens a prophetic rebuke and warning—as it opens Zephaniah 3. The restoration of the city and the presence of Yhwh in the midst will bring to an end the taunting of the peoples around that gives voice to the shame in the city's own heart. It will also bring to an end the oppression in the city. The antithesis between "people who put you down" and "lame/strayed" (as well as the earlier "weak/poor") suggests this refers to the oppression of ordinary people by those officials as well as the oppression of the whole people by the superpower. It is putting people down ('ānâ) that turns them into the weak ('ānî), or it is the weak who are easy to put down. The presence of the shepherd king in the midst will reverse all that.

When Judeans have had the opportunity to return to Jerusalem and rebuild the temple but have not responded with huge enthusiasm and have given up the rebuilding project, Zechariah 1:16-17 reaffirms the fact of Yhwh's return (or turning) to Jerusalem.[152] Temple and city will be rebuilt, and they will be the sign that Yhwh is choosing Jerusalem again. In Second Isaiah, Yhwh's references to choosing Israel are probably reaffirmations that Yhwh did so choose in the past (Is 41:8-9; 44:1-2; 49:7), but Zechariah reworks the idea. Yhwh is choosing Jerusalem again. Does this mean Yhwh had de-chosen Jerusalem? Second Isaiah holds back from those words but uses expressions that imply it, as does the declaration in Isaiah 14:1: Yhwh "will again choose Israel." "Implicit in this way of speaking is a rather drastic view of discontinuity in the religious affairs of the community with the fall of Jerusalem and subsequent deportations."[153] After all, "election is related intrinsically to possession of the land" (cf. Deut 4:37-38), so that "if Israel is not dwelling permanently in the land, then its election has apparently been rendered meaningless"; conversely, "to be elected once again means to be brought in and settled in the land . . . once again."[154] Yhwh needs to reaffirm the election of Jerusalem, and Zechariah declares that Yhwh has done so.

Preserved and Purged

One of the motifs in the portrayal of the city's revival in Isaiah 49 and Isaiah 54 is its protection from the kind of foreign oppression it has experienced over the centuries. The nature of its revival will ensure that. When Yhwh fulfills the promise of restoration, "Judah will be delivered and Jerusalem will dwell in security. And this is the name by which it will be called, 'Yhwh is our faithfulness'" (Jer 33:16). It is not surprising that such a name could be seen as embodied in the destiny of the city, because it will provide an even more astonishing proof of that faithfulness than will the reestablishment of the monarchy, which Jeremiah speaks of in the verses on either side. It will turn out to be a more perceptible one, too, since the city was restored, and the Davidic monarchy was not.

The destruction of Jerusalem was like the cutting down of a vine and the demolishing of a vineyard. But "on that day: Yhwh's branch will become for beauty and splendor" (Is 4:2-6).[155] The vine will grow branches again and produce spectacular fruit: that is, the city's population will increase once more, on

---

[152]The verb is qatal. NIVI has "I will return"; JPSV "I return"; I follow NRSV in reckoning that Yhwh speaks of having already returned; hence the rebuilding will follow (those verbs are yiqtol). But the point I make here is not much affected.

[153]Joseph Blenkinsopp, *Isaiah 1—39*, AB (New York: Doubleday, 2000), p. 282.

[154]Wildberger, *Isaiah 13—27*, p. 35.

[155]The literal trees will no doubt have a hard time, too, as will the tree of Jesse when the Davidic king is deposed, but the branch is hardly the literal branch of a tree, nor in this context the branch from the Davidic tree as in, e.g., Is 11:1.

a splendid scale. Yhwh will even take the risk of making it exalted and majestic, the very qualities that necessitated its felling (e.g., Is 2:12; 3:18). The population that survives will not have to settle for merely subsisting as a shadow of their former selves. It will be a sign that they are more than merely chance survivors. Their surviving the blast of Yhwh's breath/wind/spirit purging the city need not mean they are more deserving than people who did not; we have noted that Yhwh designates them "rotten fruit" (Jer 24). But it would not suit Yhwh's purpose to destroy the city, and they are the lucky ones. Or perhaps the purging away of the leadership, not least by being taken off into exile, means that the city is thereby purged of the people especially responsible for its wrongdoing, for the way people have been deprived of their lives there and for the city's religious wrongdoing, its "filth" (Is 4:4).[156]

Either way, the body that remains is "written for life in Jerusalem" (Is 4:3). The term refers to a corporate entity. It is "what survives," "the leftovers," "the remainder"; each is a singular word (pĕlîṭâ, niš'ār, nōtār). The expressions do not presuppose that Yhwh predetermined which individuals should survive, but they do imply that Yhwh predetermined that a group within the city would survive. Yhwh's commitment to Jerusalem would make that necessary. Yhwh had chosen it as a place to live forever (Ps 132:13-14). So Jerusalem still has a citizenry and still has a citizen register on which its names can be written. And the purging of the city means that this roll can be declared holy. Jerusalem will not have ceased to be the holy city (Is 48:2; 52:1). Holy offspring will still inhabit it (Is 6:13). It is only the burned stump of a once fine vine or olive, but at least it is that, and even a burned stump may have the potential to grow again. The significance of this residue is enhanced by its being designated the repository of the holiness that belongs to the city and its people. That is so even before it is enhanced by the spectacular increase that began this oracle (Is 4:2). When the community there has been reduced to a small group, even then it can rejoice in its status as well as in Yhwh's vision for the future. It is a holy people.

Indeed, the holiness of the temple will extend in a new way through the entire city. Even the bells on its horses and every ordinary cooking pot in the city will be "holy to Yhwh" (Zech 14:20-21). Given that horses are key military resources, the implication is that all such resources are now under Yhwh's authority.[157] The distinction between the everyday and the sacred disappears. Holiness does not mean withdrawing from Jerusalem, as the Qumran covenanters concluded in their day. It means Yhwh making the whole city holy.

Isaiah 4:2-6 can therefore see the city as secure from the scorching blast of

---

[156]Unless "filth" is not another way of describing the disorder that issued in people losing their lives.

[157]Cf. Mason, "Use of Earlier Biblical Material," p. 195.

Yhwh's breath (*bāʿēr*, the word for "purging," often refers to burning). Yhwh promises to be its protection rather than its peril. It will be protected from the storm, the overwhelming flood of foreign armies attacking the city (cf., e.g., Is 28:2). The metaphors of fire and flood come together in the description of trouble that can overwhelm ordinary members of the community through the ruthless behavior of its powerful people (Is 25:4-5), and in Isaiah 4 that fits the reference to the purging of the city's bloodstains. The city will also need protection from itself. Yhwh will grant all that. It will be as if a vast canopy covers the entire city (a canopy of the kind you would have at a wedding, indeed—a *ḥuppâ*), but specifically over Mount Zion, the place of Yhwh's abode where the community gathers before Yhwh. It will recall the cloud and fire that accompanied the people on their journey from Egypt and then appeared at Sinai, suggesting Yhwh's presence protecting them from being overwhelmed, and guiding them toward their destiny. Now there will be no more journeying and no more need of guidance, but there will be the reality of presence and protection.

Second Isaiah can quite imagine that in the future there will be powers that threaten the city. These might be superpowers like the Babylonians or their successors, or local powers like the ones that will put pressure on Nehemiah. But the prophet can envision no more oppressive terror, no need to dread any further action from Yhwh; the very fact that the people are now Yhwh's students will imply that (Is 54:13-17). There will be no need for further discipline. If and when anyone does seek to cause trouble to the city, this will no longer be because they are unwittingly Yhwh's agents in disciplining it, and they will therefore fall to Jerusalem rather than Jerusalem falling to them. The fate of Antiochus IV will in due course provide the most spectacular example (even if the later victory of Titus will constitute a counterexample and reflect the fact that the students can drop out of class). Yes, Yhwh is the one who created (!) the destroyer to ravage them, someone who was like a smith with his tools working for Yhwh. But Yhwh's sovereign relationship with such smiths as their creator will now be Jerusalem's security. Such a destroyer and such tools will not succeed because there will no more be accusations that anyone can bring against the city that would warrant its chastisement.

Brought Back to Life

The exile did not mean the emptying of the city (any more than of the country as a whole); the First Testament's numbers for the people who went into exile are relatively small. But it will have been from Jerusalem that the bulk of the deportees departed, including the royal family, the rest of the administration, the elders and the priests. The exile thus cut the head off the population of the city, and the imposition of direct Babylonian rule with its administrative center elsewhere (perhaps because the city had been devastated by the siege) re-

moved much of its raison d'être. What use is the capital city in such circumstances? Other people who were not deported would no longer have a
livelihood in Jerusalem when it ceased to be the center of a state. When the
temple has been destroyed, who would come to Jerusalem for the festivals
(Lam 1:4)?

Isaiah 49:18-21 thus imagines the city rejoicing in the return of its people. A
city's population is like a woman's finery: the people will restore it materially,
but they will also bring life to replace deadness, rejoicing to replace lamenting,
bustle to replace lethargy.

This transformation is hard to imagine, and to encourage the hearers the
prophet pictures the city finding it hard to imagine. Portray the city so full that
people will be complaining because there is not enough room for everyone.
Imagine a woman with a house full of children, even though she knows her
children have all left home. Where has this new house-full come from? The
questions do not require an answer; they are expressions of wonder. Who on
earth will look after all these children? Mother Zion need not worry: "Kings
will be your foster fathers, their queens your nursing mothers" (Is 49:23).
Kings and queens would no doubt normally have little to do with bringing up
their children; they would have an army of nurses and tutors to do that for
them. Now they will do it themselves—for Ms. Zion's offspring.

Thus "old men and women will yet live in the squares of Jerusalem, each
with their cane in their hand because of their great age, and the squares of the
city will be full of boys and girls playing in its squares" (Zech 8:4-5). Zechariah
mentions senior citizens of both sexes and children of both sexes, and the mention of old and young may imply a merism: people of all ages will be there, behaving in the way characteristic of who they are. But perhaps one is to imagine
the addressees of the promise as the unmentioned grown-ups, the middle-
aged people, needing to go about their work, but rejoicing in the proper relaxation of children and grandparents. Old people and children are part of the
work force in a traditional society, but here life will make it possible for old
people to rest and young people to play. The squares are the very places where
judgment had meant death and destruction, not least for children and old people (e.g., Lam 2:10-12).[158] The devastation that has characterized the city has
become a thing of the past.

Is it really possible? "Can prey be taken from a warrior? Or can captives
escape from someone in the right?" (Is 49:24). These children of Ms. Zion's
are the prisoners of Babylon, and Babylon has two sorts of power over them.
Babylon is the mightiest strength the world has ever known; rumors about

---

[158] Albert Petitjean, *Les oracles du Proto-Zacharie* (Paris: Gabalda, 1969), pp. 372-73; cf. Petersen,
Haggai and Zechariah 1—8, p. 300.

the Persians are all very well, but Babylonian power is the reality that confronts the Judeans every day. And Babylon is not only a forceful warrior but a warrior in the right. It is Yhwh's agent, precisely in exercising authority over the Judeans, putting them in their place. Either form of power, the military/pragmatic or the moral/theological, would be enough to keep the Jerusalemites in Babylon. Who could take them from the power of this warrior? The answer is, Yhwh can do so. There is no doubt that Yhwh has more military strength. And if Yhwh decides that enough is enough ("Her time of hard service is over," Is 40:2), then Babylon ceases to be in the right and becomes like a prison governor trying to hold on to prisoners who have completed their sentence. The one in the right (*ṣaddîq*) becomes merely a terrifying and ruthless tyrant (*'āriṣ*) (Is 49:25). Yhwh has no problem intervening to sort out such a one.

If this "is impossible in the eyes of the leftovers of this people in those days, will it also be impossible in my eyes (message of Yhwh Armies)?" (Zech 8:6). The juxtaposition of terms is noteworthy. "Is impossible" is the denominative verb *pālā'* from the noun *pele'*, "a wonder." An act like this requires a miracle. "So?" says Yhwh. The magnitude of the miracle is increased as Zechariah sets alongside that word the description of the people as mere leftovers. But the other side of that noun is the description of God as Yhwh Armies, which in fact bookends the whole verse. It is Zechariah's conventional description of Yhwh, seventeen times in this chapter alone (easily the most occurrences in any chapter in the First Testament), but that underlines rather than reduces its force. It is precisely in connection with such implausible promises that God's being Yhwh Armies is so important.

So in all Judah's cities and throughout the land, "there will be a habitation for shepherds resting flocks" and "the flocks will again pass by the hands of the person counting" (Jer 33:12-13). It might seem odd to talk about a habitation for shepherds in the city, but Yhwh is neatly reworking another warning, an image for total devastation. Jeremiah has spoken of metaphorical shepherds turning the land into a desolation (Jer 12:10-11); devastated cities are turned into deserted places that become places for flocks to lie down (Is 17:2). One might therefore picture restoration as involving the expulsion of shepherds and flocks. Yet shepherds are an essential part of the Israelite community, and sheep are an essential part of their life. They share in the restoration of land and city.

Repopulated

The exile meant Jerusalem became something of a ghost town. Isaiah 54:1-3 promises that it will be turned into a bustling city again. This is good news for its present population (unless they fear being pushed out by the returners) and a challenge for the exiles (who are the people who are supposed to bring about this increase by returning). Over the centuries the city had to extend its buildings and its walls to the west beyond the natural strong confines of the Jerusalem of the Jebusites and David. The prophet promises that it will do so again. It will not have to choose between right and left (contrast Gen 13:9). All this relates directly not to the size of the physical city but the size of its population; the buildings will have to follow, as they have had to do in modern Jerusalem and in other modern cities. Further, the original Israelite occupation of Canaan will be repeated from this city base as its offspring move out to occupy cities they never built (cf. Deut 6:10) from which the population has fled (or perhaps the prophet pictures these fleeing people moving on to occupy other desolate cities).

It sounds impossible, and historically, the Jerusalem of the immediately following decades stayed a small and underpopulated affair. Even in Nehemiah's day, when the city was once more the government center, it was hard to get people to live there. The vision's implausibility is hinted by the exhortation not to hold back: is it really possible for this childless woman to plan for a large family? Yet this implausibility is precisely why the vision is important, and it operates by implicitly reminding its audience of the precedent for what it promises, like the earlier reminder about the people's original father and mother figures (Is 51:1-3). That foremother was an infertile woman who was now beyond the menopause, but that had not made any difference when God decided to act. The longer the relative childlessness of Second Temple Jerusalem went on, the more important it would be to hold on to that precedent and this promise. And by Jesus' day Jerusalem is indeed a big bustling city, the center of a renewed people covering an area that rivaled that of the traditional bounds of the land, from Dan to Beersheba and from the Mediterranean beyond the Jordan. The shame of childlessness in a patriarchal culture is gone; Jerusalem can hold its head high among the nations again.

In the 540s this would seem a wildly implausible promise, almost a hurtful one. A woman who cannot have children is likely to feel this a grievous deprivation, one that continues to pain her decade after decade. Decade after decade it raises questions about her womanhood. In a traditional society it also raises questions about her place in society; it brings shame on her. The society has no proper place for a childless woman. Further, it is a woman's children who are her security in her old age and her husband's security. He, too, may long to have children because of the delight that brings, and he may stand in shame in the community because his wife cannot bear them for him. It is unlikely that the dynamics of the situation would not affect the relationship of husband and wife. For the wife, then, childlessness is a basis for grief, shame and fear.

The prophet therefore takes up the most powerful of images and offers an extraordinary bidding in exhorting this childless woman to shout out as if the unimaginably wonderful thing has at last happened. Jerusalem, too, is characterized by grief at its loss, shame at its position in the world community and fear for its future. But all that is to be reversed.

The certainty of the people's arrival is declared by letting us overhear Yhwh's commissioning of the agents through whom the work will be done (Is 62:10-12). "Go through, go through the gates, prepare the people's way, build up, build up the highway, clear it of stones." As in Isaiah 40:1-11, the identity of these highway construction engineers is not explicit, though insofar as we should reify them I take them to be heavenly figures who act as aides in the implementing of Yhwh's purpose. Their anonymity points us in the direction of assuming that their identity is not the point. They stand for the certain and immediate implementation of Yhwh's intentions. It is as if Yhwh through the prophet is already commissioning the construction work. "Lift an ensign over the peoples: there, Yhwh is delivering to the end of the earth! Say to Daughter Zion, 'There, your deliverance is coming!'"

The commission overlaps with that in Isaiah 40, though is not identical with it. Here the engineers are directly concerned with a road for the people to travel as they return to the city, whereas in Isaiah 40 the road was Yhwh's and the people returned only in Yhwh's train. The first good news for the city is the return of its people. Associated with that is the holding of a standard over the peoples (plural) (Is 62:10). That might function as a summons for them to start facilitating the return of the Israelites themselves from the countries where they are scattered, even to the end of the earth. This is a sign that Yhwh's deliverance is on its way. Only then does the prophecy speak in terms of Yhwh's own coming, with the exiles as the reward and recompense of the battling work Yhwh has done (cf. Is 40:10). "There, his reward is with him, his recompense in front of him. They will be called 'the holy people, the restored of Yhwh.' You will be called 'Sought out, a city not abandoned'" (Is 62:11-12). On the one hand, the exiles therefore turn out to be not people given up to absorption in the rest of the world but still a "holy people." On the other, the city thus turns out to be not one abandoned by Yhwh but one Yhwh seeks out in order to do this work of restoring. A standard held over the peoples also suggests a summons to the peoples themselves to join in this journey to Jerusalem. It is a fulfillment of the vision that goes back to Isaiah 2:2-4.

Expanding

Zechariah 2:1-5 [MT 5-9] pictures someone measuring out Jerusalem, the sort of person who works for the city planning department whose work presupposes, for instance, that it knows the city's dimensions.[159] This will raise questions about the city's need to be protected by strong walls, though that is not the only point about the vision. It may also relate to Ezekiel's vision of a city whose dimensions can be clearly demarcated (Ezek 40—48).[160] A divine aide points out that a prosaic interpretation of such a vision, which the surveyor's work implies, is based on two fallacies. First, Yhwh still intends that gargantuan prospering of the city. Like the great cities of the Two-Thirds World in recent decades, it will grow so fast that there is no way official building policy and provision can keep up with it. Like freeway planning trying to catch up with traffic, by the time people have built new walls for the city, they would already have been outstripped by population growth. But anyway (and second), the city's protection will not be its literal walls. "I myself will be for it (Yhwh's message) the fiery wall round about, and I will be for splendor in its midst" (Zech 2:5 [MT 9]).[161] Jerusalem will be a city without walls, one that assumes it is secure (cf. Ezek 38:11). There is an abb'a' sequence about Yhwh's words. The city will flourish and be without walls, because Yhwh will be its wall and will be the splendor that draws and glorifies. Neither the growth nor the security of the city will come about through human exercise of responsibility. They are not open to being fixed. They will come about through divine miracle, the God inside and the God around. (Nehemiah would take a different view on both counts. He could not be constrained by the visions of prophets. One needs to be practical, too.)

The cluster of oracles that follows this vision in Zechariah 2:6-9 [MT 10-13]) underlines its message in a subtle way. It takes the form of an exhortation to Judeans in Babylon to flee from there. Presumably Zechariah is still actually speaking to Judeans in Jerusalem, but doing so in such a way as to have them overhear words to the exiles. His good news is that Yhwh is in the midst of spreading out[162] the Judean community, like a bird spreading its wings to fly or flee on the four winds of the heavens, back to Judah. The people in Jerusalem overhear Yhwh once again commissioning their fellow Judeans in Babylon to get out of that place that remains destined for calamity. The trouble is that this is a people who have responded really well to the encouragement in Jeremiah 29 to settle down in Babylon. The lack of prepositions in Zechariah

---

[159]The compound expression for a measuring cord (ḥebēl middâ) is different from the word used in a positive way in Zech 1:16 (qāw Q, qwh K), which denotes something a builder uses in connection with actual building.

[160]Cf. Petersen, *Haggai and Zechariah 1—8*, p. 169.

[161]Both times the divine ʾehyeh of Ex 3:14, "I will be there"?

[162]pāraś (piel) usually has a positive meaning, not the negative "scatter," and the positive fits the context.

2:7 [MT 11] says it pointedly: literally, "Escape, Zion, living [as] Ms. Babylon" (EVV add prepositions). The Judean community whose real nature is to be Zion is living as if it were Babylon.

How does Yhwh's statement relate to Yhwh's exhortation? If Yhwh has spread them out, is it inevitable that they flee? This is surely not so. The summons urges them to make their move in light of Yhwh's intent. If they flee, is it inevitable that they get home? This was not so in Jeremiah's day, when Yhwh was exiling the people, not bringing them home. Fleeing will succeed only if it meshes with Yhwh's act of deliverance. Both the divine and the human act are necessary for the event to come about.

The exiles are urged to "flee from the northern land." Babylon is the northern land because one travels north from Jerusalem to get there, and because the north is the direction from which invaders usually come (unless they are Egyptian), and because the north thus becomes a symbol for forces that threaten well-being and life itself. Zechariah urges the community in Babylon to flee, to escape. He takes up Jeremiah's urging (e.g., Jer 51:6), though he can do so with striking new implications because Ms. Babylon has now fallen and Judeans have been free to go home for nearly two decades. Yet little has changed. The Judean community in Babylon and in Jerusalem lives under a different empire's control, and a more beneficent one than Babylon itself, and paradoxically, that good news is perhaps one reason why many Judeans see no reason to make the trek to the land of Judea that they had never seen. For Jerusalem, however, one occupying power could feel much like another. The community still cannot control its own destiny and it has to pay hefty taxes to its occupiers (see the dissatisfaction expressed in a prayer such as Ezra 9; also Neh 5). And it lacks the people or the resources to bring about the rebuilding of the city.

It is thus still the case that "the nations are plundering you." Zechariah may be referring to the Babylonians' past plundering, but the participles point to something that is still going on; perhaps, then, he addresses Jerusalem. People who have chosen to stay in Babylon could hardly complain about their position; it is the Jerusalem community that could feel that it has merely passed from the control of one imperial power to that of another and continues to be like a group of serfs (the word recurs in Ezra 9:9; Neh 9:36). The position is to be reversed. The plundering of Egypt was succeeded by the plundering of Babylon, and that will be succeeded by the plundering of Persia. The prophet's promises will come true, and people will recognize that Yhwh sent him.

Well Taught and Well Governed

A city's strength and security depend on internal considerations as well as external ones, on human considerations as well as technological ones. Isaiah 54 sees it needing not merely outward adornment but the moral and spiritual renewal of its children—the ones who were sold for their wrongdoing (Is 50:1). Indeed, perhaps the beautifying of the city lies in the renewal of its children. They will become Yhwh's students (Is 54:13), like the prophet (Is 50:4), in the way Yhwh had wanted (Is 48:17).[163] Their renewing will involve not merely a once-for-all surgical procedure, such as is implied in Jeremiah 31 or Ezekiel 36, but an ongoing personal mentoring relationship. And thus the *shalom* that was a moral possibility (Is 48:18, 22) becomes a reality, by Yhwh's faithfulness and/ or by theirs (Is 54:13).

In Isaiah 60:17-18 the visionary once more draws breath and starts again with the city's wondrous physical transformation. Yhwh makes a list of raw materials for this work, though these are gold, silver, bronze and iron instead of bronze, iron, wood and stone, and then speaks of the administration of the building work and its overseers, the "bosses" (*nōgĕśîm*) who are most familiar as the overseers of the Israelites involved in building work in Egypt (e.g., Ex 3:7). The work on this building will have very different oversight. What then follows suggests a more general allusion to administrative oversight. The city will have *shalom* as its government and *ṣĕdāqâ* as its bosses. This will be a new experience, whether one contrasts it with the preexilic Israelite government of the city or the exilic and postexilic imperial authority of Babylon and Persia. One way or another, none of these had succeeded in bringing the city *shalom* or *ṣĕdāqâ*, the vision expressed in a passage such as Psalm 72 or Isaiah 40—55. Things had not been well. The bosses were not people characterized by faithfulness, by an insistence on doing the right thing for the city and its people. Now government will do the thing it is supposed to do. Controlling violence within the city would also be implicitly part of this vision, but succeeding cola suggest a reference to violence from outside and thus make another link with the relationship of the city to the superpowers and to neighbor provinces. The city's walls will be so strong they will *be* its deliverance, as they were not before, and its gates will be so solid that they that they become an object of praise—or more likely that they lead to praise of Yhwh.[164]

The latter ambiguity alerts us to a broader one that links with the tension between the attitude that Zechariah and Nehemiah take to walls. English versions have Yhwh making *shalom* your government and *ṣĕdāqâ* your bosses.

---

[163]There, the verb *lāmad*; in Is 54:13, the related noun *limmûd*. See section 5.6 "Preserved and Purged."

[164]*tĕhillâ* most often refers to praise of Yhwh; Joseph Blenkinsopp suggests a link with the city gate's being the point of entry for a religious procession, and he contrasts the familiar mundane names such as "Dung Gate" and "Fish Gate" (*Isaiah 56—66*, AB [New York: Doubleday, 2003], pp. 15, 217). But the verb *hillēl* is occasionally used for praise of a human being.

For consistency one would then render the subsequent line "you will call deliverance your walls and praise your gates." It would be a mistake to describe these as more radical promises. To say that earthly rulers will become agents of *shalom* and *ṣĕdāqâ* is an extraordinarily radical declaration. But it is a striking alternative radical promise. Whatever the form of any administration, *shalom* and *ṣĕdāqâ* will themselves dominate the city with the insistence shown by Israel's "taskmasters" in Egypt. Likewise Yhwh's deliverance will be the wall round the city. Even if the city has stone walls, it is Yhwh's deliverance that is its real protection. And praise will be its gates: that is, the praise of Yhwh as the city's protection and deliverance, sounding through the city, will be of key significance to keeping it shut to invasion.

Brand New

The same is true of the prophet's declaration that the splendid restoration of the city really involves an act of new creation (Is 65:17-23). Yhwh is "creating a new heavens and a new earth," in light of which "the former things will not be brought to mind." It is an astonishing new image. The story of God's creating the present heavens and earth (Gen 1) is likely not so much older than this prophecy; neither is the story of God's promise never again to destroy the order of the cosmos. On the other hand, Yhwh has asserted that the heavens are shredding like smoke and that the earth will wear out like a garment (Is 51:6), and Yhwh did this in the context of affirming the intention to do something new that will make it appropriate to put the past out of mind and rejoice in what Yhwh is creating now (e.g., Is 43:18-19). In isolation one could thus naturally take this declaration to refer to the creation of a new literal cosmos that surpasses the original one and causes such earlier realities to be put out of mind.

A number of considerations suggest that is unlikely. The most compelling is that in this passage the idea disappears as quickly as it arises. Yhwh invites people to rejoice in this creative work, but then goes on, "because I am creating Jerusalem as a joy and its people as an object of rejoicing." Is this a further, distinct act of creation, in which Yhwh is involved? How do these two acts relate to each other, and why is the theme of a new cosmos announced and then allowed to disappear? What is the significance of the "because"?

(Re-)creating Jerusalem apparently explains what (re-)creating the world means; (re-)creating the world is an image for (re-)creating the city. The creation of a new cosmos is another way of speaking of the creation of a new Jerusalem, a topic that has run through these chapters—as Paul's talk of a new creation is a metaphor for what happens when a person is "in Christ" (2 Cor 5:17). The new Jerusalem will be like a microcosm of a new cosmos. It will be as if Yhwh has determined to undo all that went wrong about the original creation and start again, not with a new paradise garden but with a new garden city, a place that is a joy to Yhwh and a joy to its people. History will be over and creation's purpose will be realized.[165]

Indeed, the new city will be an improvement on the original creation. It will not need sun or moon because "Yhwh will be yours as lasting light and your God as your splendor." To put it another way, "your sun will no longer go down and your moon will not pass away, because Yhwh will be yours as lasting light and your days of mourning will end" (Is 60:19-20). Even in the evening there will be light (Zech 14:7). "The alternation of night and day, which serves as a refrain throughout Genesis 1, is to be brought to an end, as YHWH will ceaselessly enlighten the world."[166] Positively, lasting light means beauty; negatively, it means mourning is over. The city has been clothed in mourning apparel for decades, dark, gloomy, disheveled and dingy. Yhwh's presence will mean an end to all that and its replacement by finery. The reference to the days of mourning coming to an end reflects the way the promise links with the city's present troubled situation; it goes on to add that the people will possess the land forever. It is again apparent that the promise does not relate to a different world and a different city from the one the community lives in, but it promises that the circumstances of its life will be quite transformed. The presence of Yhwh will shine so bright, it will be as if sun and moon have become unnecessary. To work the metaphor a different way, it will be as if the sun never sets and the moon ceases to be eclipsed by it each month. Yhwh's light will never cease to shine. (People who live in a modern big city where darkness never really falls because of the omnipresence of artificial light need to recall or imagine what it is like in the countryside or the desert when night falls, especially when there is no moon.)

The new world does not yet exist in people's experience, but it really is guaranteed. The book of Isaiah almost ends with a promise that "as the new heavens and the new earth that I am making are standing before me (Yhwh's message), so your descendants and your name will stand" (Is 66:22).[167] Because the new world is a reality before Yhwh, it is guaranteed to become a reality for the people.

Creation's Purpose Fulfilled

In traditional societies, countless children die as babies and few people live to old age. In the new heaven and new earth of the renewed Jerusalem, babies

---

[165]Cf. Knierim, *Task of OT Theology,* pp. 216-17.

[166]Levenson, *Creation and the Persistence of Evil,* p. 125.

[167]The verbs in v. 22a are participles, which I thus translate as present tense. The verbs in v. 22b are yiqtol. The EVV do not observe this difference.

will not die and old people will live to be a hundred (Is 65:19-20). The focus of the vision is that human beings can live out their lives to their proper end. There is thus another sense in which it does not take us back to the Garden of Eden. There is no life-tree here from which people can eat in order not to have death come upon them at the natural end of their lives. As usual, the First Testament accepts that death is part of human experience. What it does not accept, here or elsewhere, is that babies should die and that adults should die in middle age. The psalms protest at illness and early death and demand that Yhwh reverse the process whereby the former leads to the latter, and here the prophecy promises that Yhwh will do so.

Thus "there will not be heard in it any more the sound of weeping or the sound of a cry" (Is 65:19). People will no longer weep and cry in anguish, especially over the death of babies and spouses and adult children ("parents should not have to bury their children"). In modern cultures these are occasional realities; in traditional cultures they are common experiences. It would be an exceptional family that did not lose several "babies of days," babies who had not even been weaned. It would be an exceptional adult who lived to seventy or eighty (cf. Ps 90:10). It would be an exceptional old person who was not affected by the gradual degeneration of body and mind. All that will end. The novelty of the new Jerusalem will be not its buildings but the life span of its people. Parents will see all their children mature to adulthood and their own parents grow to a great age, as active as they were in their own youth. To die at a hundred will be like dying as a teenager, and to die before a hundred will be like dying under a curse. People will live the long lives of the early generations in Genesis. It will not seem pointless to bring children into the world because they are quite likely never to grow up. The parents' generation will be offspring blessed by God in their fruitfulness, and their children will be with them as life proceeds.

They will thus also see the maturing of their projects (Is 65:21-23). They will build houses and live in them, plant fruit trees and see their fruit. Elsewhere the imperiling of such projects comes from invasion and attack; alongside illness, another threat in the Psalms is the attack of enemies, inside the community or outside. Initially, at least, their imperiling comes from the fact of premature death. Why bother to build a house or to plant fruit trees if you are likely not to see their fruit? Actually people did not seem to ask that question, and the reason may link with one of the reasons for their not being as troubled by the fact of death as modern societies are: They saw a large part of their significance as lying in their membership of a bigger whole, a people that extended horizontally and vertically. In this connection building houses you would not live in and planting trees whose fruit you would not eat made entire sense. You were expressing your belonging to this whole and contributing to its life. But that did not stop there being a certain poignancy and sadness about the matter. It would be nice to live in the house and eat the fruit oneself. In this new cosmos, people will do so. People will live as long as a tree and their houses will wear out before they do (the prophecy picks up the verb "wear out," *bālâ*, applying to the earth itself in Is 51:6). So the effort involved in building and planting will be worthwhile for the builders and planters themselves.

In this context specific resonances attach to the subsequent declaration, "before they call I will answer, while they are still speaking I will listen" (Is 65:24). The prophet has promised that babies will not die and adults not fail to live out their years, but the restating of this promise implies that it is not simply that illnesses and perils cease to exist. The people's relationship with life and with God will be more dynamic than that implies. They will find themselves calling out to God (*qārāʾ*) although not having to utter a cry of anguish (*zĕʿāqâ*). There will be reason to call out. There will be threats to life. But they will find that in this dynamic relationship Yhwh answers before they even call. People were used to calling out to God about the needs of their children and their parents and themselves, and they had sometimes known God to respond and heal—but sometimes not. In the new world it will be otherwise.

There is another cause of early death, the fact of war, which perhaps directly affects ordinary people in a traditional society more than is the case in a modern society with a professional army. People were subject to attack from wild animals, too, so that even if human beings get along with each other, the scene does not realize the vision in Genesis 1 of the animal world subdued by humanity. The context again suggests resonances for the renewed talk of wolf and lamb lying down together (Is 65:25). One way or another, there will be neither calamity nor destruction anywhere on Yhwh's holy mountain. The reference to the serpent once more indicates that the vision does not expect that all troubles and temptations will have disappeared, but the scene will have been transformed. No wonder this new city is a reason for rejoicing, not only for the immediate audience—presumably the actual and potential population of this city—but also for God (Is 65:18-19).

Protected

"On that day this song will be sung in the land of Judah: 'We have a strong city; he makes deliverance into walls and rampart'" (Is 26:1). The strength of Judah's city contrasts with the apparent strength of Moab's. Moab assumes that lofty walls are the key to its security (Is 25:10-12). Judah does not assume—or will eventually realize it is not the case—that its walls and rampart are its deliverance; rather the converse. For all the strength of Nehemiah's walls, true strength lies in the fact that Yhwh acts to deliver this city. This is its walls and rampart. To put it another way, for all the security of the rock of Zion (cf. Jer 21:13?), Yhwh *is* the people's lasting rock—has been its rock from of old, and/or always will be its rock. This city is strong because the one who dwells there is strong. And thus a wise people will want to enter this city because Yhwh is there and not merely because it looks strong. Actually, the passing of the years with their defeats has made the city's own strength look rather less reliable than it once did. The ridicule of Nehemiah's opponents (Neh 4:1-3 [MT 3:33-35]) might not be all bluster. Thus the appropriate object of trust is the city's God, not the city's walls, and the people who come into the city need to be people of faithfulness and truthfulness in their relationship with that God (Is 26:4).

In the immediate context, the city Yhwh has made low makes us think of the Moabite city just referred to (Is 25:12). That is not actually described as a city, but it is a lofty fortification with walls that is due to be made low, brought down, taken to the ground, to the dirt. All those words recur here. A little earlier, a preceding hymn did speak of destroying an unnamed city (Is 25:2). Both earlier passages refer to events that have not yet happened, and this thanksgiving likewise is one that will be sung when a destruction has taken place; it does not relate to an event that has happened when the prophecy is uttered. The Moabite city might be a literal threat in the time of the prophecy, if this belongs to the Persian period when the surrounding peoples were all threats to Jerusalem, but perhaps it has become a symbol like Babel. Here, the city stands for the city as a human institution organized over against Yhwh, Yhwh's purpose and Yhwh's people, or perhaps this specific city embodies that capacity of the city in this particular context. Either way, Yhwh puts it down.[168] The weak and poor are able to tread it down, as feeble forces were able to win spectacular victories in the old days. Its threat has gone.

Micah 7:1-11 has pictured a city (Samaria or Jerusalem?) lamenting the social and moral collapse of its leadership and its people, but then had the city declaring, "I will look to Yhwh, I will wait for my God who delivers; my God will listen to me" (Mic 7:7). From what does the city look for deliverance?

It would naturally long for deliverance from the social collapse that it has lamented, though the First Testament does not usually speak of deliverance in this connection. Deliverance usually implies a calamity threatened or experienced. So perhaps there is an ambiguity about the city's lament. It spoke of itself as bare like an orchard after harvest (Mic 7:1), and initially that seemed to refer to its being empty of honest people. But harvest is an image for punishment, and these later lines presuppose such a calamity. The city needs deliver-

---

[168]The verbs are all yiqtol except for the isolated qatal *hēšaḥ* ("he makes low"). Among these yiqtols it seems unlikely to be an isolated verb with past reference and more likely to be a gnomic qatal (cf. NIVI).

ance from physical destruction as well as from moral collapse, the physical destruction that has issued from the moral collapse. And it looks for this from Yhwh. The fact that its calamity was quite deserved does not mean it cannot appeal to Yhwh. It knows that Yhwh's rejection is never final. It must carry Yhwh's indignation until that indignation burns itself out. It is impossible to know how long that may take, but the nature of indignation is that it does not last forever.

There will come a time when the fire dies down and the more positive side to Yhwh's character that is usually dominant again comes to the fore. By nature Yhwh is "the God of my deliverance," that is, "my delivering God" or "my God who delivers" or "God who delivers me" or "my God who delivers me." Yhwh will again listen and will again deliver. Falling over will not have the last word. At the moment "I sit in darkness" (Mic 7:8), but darkness will not persist forever; as usual, darkness and light are images for disaster and blessing. Having Yhwh contend against the people (Mic 6:1-2) will give way to the more natural situation of Yhwh's contending for it (Mic 7:9-10). It will again experience Yhwh's ṣĕdāqâ. It imagines an enemy city deriding it with the reasonable question, "Where is your God," implying that Yhwh has abandoned it forever. And it imagines that enemy city suddenly confounded because Yhwh has not done so at all. Everything will be reversed. The derisive foe will have the experience that Yhwh's city has had. "A day for building your walls" will come, because this is "a day when your boundary will extend," and the city will need walls that embrace a larger city than before (Mic 7:11).

Secure

Isaiah 33 ends in a similar way, with a picture of Zion as "a secure pasture, a tent that will not move, whose pegs will never be pulled up, none of whose ropes will break" (Is 33:20). This is not a new, transformed Jerusalem, but the regular Jerusalem in new circumstances. The city's history indeed raises the question whether Jerusalem is a city of security or not. Whether one thinks geographically or theologically, the answer has become uncertain. The geographical uncertainty is built into its story. Its site probably commended itself to the Jebusites and to David because of its natural strength, but David's ability to capture it also deconstructed the idea of its natural strength. During the Assyrian and Babylonian period it sometimes escaped by the skin of its teeth and sometimes fell, and it eventually did fall traumatically and perhaps finally. After the exile it regained its wall but that earned the mockery of its neighbors.

Its theological uncertainty is also built into its story. Yhwh made a commitment to it, but in Isaiah's own day proved willing to go within an ace of letting it fall, and subsequently allowed that to happen. But ambiguity will not have the last word.

The image for that is a paradoxical and bold one: Jerusalem will be like a tent that stands permanently in its place (Is 33:20). Mobility is of the essence of tent-hood and vulnerability is the price a tent-dweller pays for mobility, but this is a tent that will never have to move in order for its occupants to find new pasture. The reason for that comes in another bold metaphor. Jerusalem becomes a city surrounded by water, like Tyre, but these are waters that a hostile fleet cannot traverse, because they are a metaphor for Yhwh in person (Is 33:21). Yhwh *is* a sea surrounding Jerusalem, and Isaiah can josh sailors who think they might navigate these waters: "your tackle is not up to the task." So Jerusalem is theologically secure. Its attackers will become plunder for its occupants. Yhwh's majesty is much greater than the majesty of the vessels that might blockade the city. Yhwh is our leader *(šōpēṭ),* the one who makes the authoritative decisions that determine what happens. Yhwh is our commander *(měhōqēq),* the one who decrees events. Yhwh is our king, notwithstanding the existence of a human king in whom people delight (Is 33:17). Once more, Yhwh is not merely *the* king who rules over the world as a whole, but *our* king, our leader who acts to deliver *us.*

Thus the Jebusites' ill-judged mockery (2 Sam 5:6) will come true; the disabled will not only defeat the attackers but turn them into spoil (Is 33:23).[169] Isaiah 33 as a whole works by taking up words and motifs from preceding chapters, but also from throughout the first half of the book, which it rounds off.[170] The final line (Is 33:24) takes us back to the very beginning. There, Judah is a people characterized by wrongdoing, and as a result it has become a man who has been mugged and not treated; and Yhwh finds Jerusalem's festivals disgusting, a burden Yhwh is no longer prepared to carry (Is 1:4-6, 14). Now, this is a people whose wrongdoing Yhwh is prepared to carry, so it is no longer sick. The promise is thus again somewhat paradoxical and bold. Yhwh does not speak of the city being turned into a people that now lives in the way Yhwh approves. The problem that the first half of the book has exposed can be solved only by Yhwh's being even more gracious, even more prepared to live with the sinfulness of its people. The passage perhaps again implies that the only thing that can transform is a willingness to forgive. What is explicit is the sheer grace of the city's people's having its wrongdoing carried.

---

[169]The interpretation of 2 Sam 5:6 is uncertain, but there is certainly scornful reference to the disabled. The blind also appear there, as they do in the Tg. at Is 33:23 (cf. JPSV; Wildberger, *Isaiah 28—39,* p. 297).

[170]See John Goldingay, *Isaiah* (Peabody, Mass.: Hendrickson/Carlisle: Paternoster, 2001), pp. 184-91.

Lasting

After promising the sealing of a new covenant relationship on a more secure basis and the permanent existence of Israel as a people and nation, in Jeremiah 31:38-40 Yhwh makes as extravagant a promise about the city's permanence. "Days are coming (Yhwh's message) when the city will be rebuilt for Yhwh from the Hananel Tower to the Corner Gate." Yhwh goes on to give some detail about where the measuring line will stretch. At the moment the city is being destroyed and the environs have been dramatically desanctified by becoming a place for false worship and a place of burial. But the city will be rebuilt, and rebuilt "for Yhwh," and the environs will be made "holy to Yhwh" again. And the city will then stand "forever." Once more the vision picks up the words associated with Jeremiah's commissioning (Jer 1:10). Yhwh will send no more prophet to uproot and overthrow.

The promise that the city will stand forever includes implicit conditions. Jeremiah suggests as much when picturing it restored to the Davidic ideal in its splendor (Jer 17:19-27). The passage presupposes a time when the city has fallen and the kings have been deposed, but when there are people living in it, the situation that obtained in the sixth century and on through the Persian period. It promises that kings and leaders will return to the city in splendor, riding through its gates in their horse-drawn carriages, and that the city will never again have its population taken away. People from all over Judah will come to the city to bring all sorts of offerings to Yhwh's house. But that will only happen if in the meantime people keep the sabbath. That becomes a key mark of commitment to Yhwh, because it distinguishes Judah from other peoples around. In the absence of that, restoration will be replaced by fire. So "the survival of the community depends upon the observance of the sabbath." Fortunately, "generation in, generation out, the Jews have adhered to the law of the sabbath and thereby maintained their integrity as a people."[171]

In the close of Ezekiel the city also receives unexpected prominence. It is a new city, though not explicitly a new Jerusalem, for the name "Jerusalem" does not occur in Ezekiel 40—48. Arguably it is a city that is simply an adjunct to the temple (rather than the other way round), a "temple city." It receives an allocation of land that its inhabitants can cultivate, "with the city's name from that day on 'Yhwh is there'" (Ezek 48:35). This declaration about the city closes the entire book, "a magnificent theocentric note for this most God-centred of biblical books to end on."[172] One gets the impression that this is a situation to last.

In the event, Yhwh evidently had a change of mind. The city was uprooted

---

[171]Holladay, *Jeremiah*, 1:511.
[172]Joyce, "Temple and Worship in Ezekiel 40—48," p. 160.

and overthrown in, for instance, A.D. 70 and 135. There was nothing new about Yhwh's "forever" having less cash value than one might have expected. Israel was promised the land forever, but has spent more time outside it than inside it. Aaron was promised the priesthood forever (Ex 29:9; 1 Chron 23:13; cf. Num 25:13; Jer 33:18, 22), but exercised it for only a few hundred years. Indeed, in Eli's day Yhwh explicitly revokes one form of that commitment (1 Sam 2:30). It transpires that the promise was implicitly conditional, though "conditional/ unconditional" may not be an illuminating way to frame the question.[173] Perhaps the city's turning away from Jesus' declaration that this was the moment for God's reign to begin made that inevitable. Jesus became the prophet who uprooted and overthrew.

But this did not mean God cast off the city. Rather, the earlier pattern repeats itself. Yhwh again destroys, but Yhwh is again committed to rebuild. Yhwh's underlying "forever" still stands. An implication would be that its inhabitants can always forfeit Jerusalem again, but that Yhwh's underlying "forever" will again continue to stand.

Recognized and Recognizing

The city is destined to become for Yhwh "a name of joy, praise, and glory for all the nations of the world" (Jer 33:9). That had been the people's original destiny, as they had committed themselves to Yhwh (cf. Deut 26:19), but things had not turned out that way because they had failed to listen to Yhwh (Jer 13:11). Yet Yhwh has not given up on that intention. They will be those things for Yhwh and for the nations. There is good news here for Yhwh, for the people and for the nations. When Jeremiah speaks, the devastated Jerusalem is a frightening sight, and things will only get worse in the imminent future. The city is a measure of what no city wants to become. Insofar as it is associated with Yhwh's name, it brings discredit on that name. Yhwh's intention was and is wholly different. Jerusalem is to be a joy to Yhwh and a joy to the nations. It will indeed be a measure of what a city wants to be. Other cities will look on its splendor with open mouths and will offer praise to Yhwh for what they see. They "will hear of all the good that I am doing to them" and "will be in awe and will tremble because of all the good and because of all the well-being that I am creating for it" (Jer 33:9).

Jerusalem has indeed been afflicted and scorned. "Is this the city that was called perfect in beauty, joy to all the earth? . . . We have engulfed it" (Lam 2:15-16). That will now be reversed. The afflicters and scorners will come to bow down to the city (Is 60:14-16). Once again the literal inhabitants of the city

---

[173]Cf. Robert P. Gordon, *Holy Land, Holy City* (Carlisle/Waynesboro, Ga.: Paternoster, 2004), pp. 104-6.

would doubtless gain personal encouragement from these promises, but the vision does not speak of these former oppressors bowing down to those people. It is addressing the hypostatized city, which is distinguishable from and more significant than its inhabitants. Indeed, it addresses Zion not Jerusalem: the latter is the city's down-to-earth political name, the name that foreigners would actually use, whereas the former points to the city's transcendent and symbolic significance, to something greater than its own streets and stones.

Scorn will give way to submissive respect; bowing low is the posture a subject takes to a king. People will recognize the true significance of the city, which comes from its relationship with Yhwh. The city they have scorned is "Yhwh's city, Zion of Israel's holy one" (Is 60:14). Given the importance in Isaiah of "Israel's holy one" as a title for God, it is particularly significant that the city is here given its link with God so conceived. In bowing down, the former destroyers are recognizing Jerusalem as what it truly is, a city that belongs to Yhwh. It is a place where Yhwh dwells, and to which Yhwh is committed. It is Yhwh's earthly capital. That means, for instance, that it shares in Yhwh's majesty; that will once again replace its humiliation. It will enjoy the resources of nations and kings, in the way already described, but here in terms of a new and whimsical metaphor: Woman Zion sucks the breast of male monarchs.

The vision has already described the nations recognizing Yhwh. Their recognition of Jerusalem as Yhwh's city thus also implies recognizing it as the city of the one true God—they are not simply recognizing it as Yhwh's city in the same way as they might recognize Babylon as Marduk's city. Recognition as Yhwh's city in this sense thus adds to the city's splendor. But there is more. The fact that the nations thus acknowledge Yhwh does not get restated. Instead, the vision affirms that the result of this recognition will be that the city itself acknowledges Yhwh as deliverer and restorer. They are familiar words, but significant ones. The city had not acknowledged Yhwh from its beginnings; it had been a Jebusite city. It had not faithfully acknowledged Yhwh through much of the monarchy; its people had worshiped various other deities alongside Yhwh. It had not acknowledged Yhwh in this way during most of the sixth century, quite understandably; it knew Yhwh as destroyer not as deliver and restorer. But now Yhwh will have acted thus, and the city will be in a position to acknowledge it, and will do so. A large part of Yhwh's aim in delivering and restoring will be to draw the nations and their rulers to come to acknowledge Yhwh there, but its byproduct will be to draw the city's own acknowledgment.

Shining Beauty

As the exile wears on, Jerusalem is like a powerless member of a community, drifting to and fro on the wind, still uncomforted after all these years; the description perhaps again echoes her self-description in her prayers. But she is to be turned into a woman of substance, a woman bejeweled (Is 54:11-17a). I take the picture of the city covered in jewels as reflecting the way the prophet can imagine the Jerusalem stone of her walls, her gates and all her buildings gleaming in the sun as if covered in precious stones, from foundations to pinnacles; it might be a more encouraging prospect than a more otherworldly picture of the city literally covered in jewels. (But perhaps I am prosaic; while sometimes promises of renewal are down-to-earth and practical, sometimes they are larger than life, and both fulfill important functions.) The beauty that was once critiqued (e.g., Is 3:16—4:1) is now a source for pride.

Isaiah 60 develops this picture. It begins by inviting us to imagine that morning is about to come. At this moment everything is therefore pitch black. Then, with the speed of a Middle Eastern dawn, suddenly morning breaks. And Jerusalem is the place upon which light first dawns. The picture freezes at that point. In modern terms, it is as if the morning sun is indeed gleaming on the Dome of the Rock, but has not shone down into the streets and the ravines around the city. So people who want to stand in the light climb out of the ravines and up the streets to the height of the city where the sun shines and the stones and gold shine with reflected glory.

In reality, there is no need for the city to pry itself out of bed in order to shine. This happens automatically. When the sun rises, this makes the city begin to sparkle and shimmer. Pretending to bid it to shine is an indirect promise to the people who hear this prophecy that Yhwh intends to make it do so. More obviously, promising the city it will smile and tremble with astonishment, unable to believe its eyes, promises the people that they will do so.

Darkness and gloom have covered the people of God itself (e.g., Is 9:2 [MT 1]), and for people hearing this prophecy they still do. Isaiah had promised light, but it is not obvious that it has dawned. Or perhaps we might say that the people of God have experienced one or two false dawns (for example, the victories of Cyrus), but the process whereby morn breaks then seems to abort. Boldly, this vision sees the gloom and darkness as covering the world, not the city. Things are the opposite of what people might be inclined to think. It could look as if the superpower was in the light (enjoying power and prosperity), but compared with the light that is about to dawn, it is in the dark. When that light dawns, the nations will recognize what real light is. It is splendor of another league, because it is Yhwh's splendor that is dawning in this city (Is 60:1-3). The nations will recognize the tawdriness of their power, prosperity and splendor, and come to admire the real light that has dawned, the splendor of the new Jerusalem that the vision of Isaiah 60 describes. In a sense, this vision is another reworking of Isaiah 2:2-4. It also reworks the idea of the return of the city's scattered sons and daughters: now they return as a pleasing byproduct of the pilgrimage of their "hosts," who kindly bring them along to see the sight.

In the modern world, the resources of the nations have hastened to Europe and North America for the enjoyment of their populace. Here they hasten to Jerusalem, the camels standing for trucks that will turn Jerusalem into a parking lot. But they come for Yhwh's sake. The resources (gold, incense, animals) come to be the means of beautifying buildings and making offerings and thus to help Jerusalem proclaim Yhwh's praise. The flocks of sheep are on their way to Yhwh's altar. The city is a place of splendor, beauty and worship (Is 60:5-9).

Isaiah 62 goes on to make explicit that the city will receive more than a possibly grudging recognition. Whereas Yhwh's promise concerning the city's future is sometimes expressed in down-to-earth terms (the city will be rebuilt) and sometimes in hyperbolic terms (the city will be rebuilt of precious stones, not regular stonework), it is sometimes expressed in religious terms or in symbolic terms. The different formulations have different effects. They speak of literal reality as it can be literally understood, imagined and experienced. They speak of literal reality in a heightened way. They speak of the religious and ethical significance of the restoration. And they speak directly to the heart of the city, not least to its hurt heart. One role of metaphors is to add affect to ideas and down-to-earth reality. They speak to people's inner being.

Delighted In

Here in Isaiah 62 Yhwh begins from religious and theological ideas: the city's restoration will manifest Yhwh's faithfulness (ṣĕdāqâ, ṣedeq), it will bring Yhwh's deliverance, it will restore the city's splendor. More affect comes with the talk of a new name, which introduces the dominant motif of the verses. Jerusalem currently has a name. It is not merely "Zion" or "Jerusalem" but "abandoned" and "devastation." Again, those names have literal and theological implications. The city stands literally devastated. And that is so because Yhwh abandoned it: stopped protecting it, stopped ensuring its safety.

The new name will be "My delight is in it" (Is 62:4). A person's "delight" (ḥēpeṣ) is their purpose or will, but frequently with an affective dimension conveyed by words such as pleasure or delight. Isaiah 40—55 has often spoken of this purpose or will of Yhwh to be implemented in the people's destiny (e.g., Is 44:28; 55:11). That ultimate purpose or desire or delight is not devastation but splendor, and Yhwh promises that this desire will be realized in the city. Yhwh will be delighted with how things are there. To put it in explicitly personal terms, instead of being like an abandoned woman, the city will be like a married woman. We have noted how in a patriarchal society, a woman's status comes from her marital status. To be a divorced woman implies shame; that is even true about widowhood (illogically, we might reasonably think). No one quite knows how to relate to a mature single, divorced or widowed woman. Jerusalem will have its married status back. It will be able to hold its head high. It will itself become a crown or a diadem in Yhwh's hand, which half-implies that it will make it possible for Yhwh's head to be held high; after all, Yhwh's name was also shamed both through the city's unfaithfulness and through the consequent punishment that Yhwh imposed.

The prophecy tweaks the marriage metaphor in another way in having Jerusalem's inhabitants marrying their mother (Is 62:5). Much of its population, after all, has gone off to settle hundreds of miles away, and may feel no commitment to their mother, as is confirmed by their unwillingness to return to her when they have the chance. But more central to the passage and the metaphor is the fact that Yhwh as groom rejoices over the city like a man rejoicing over his bride.

Even a powerful nation that suspects it may be subject to attack from abroad may feel obliged to make it much harder for people from abroad to enter. The vision of the revived and secure Jerusalem in Isaiah 60:8-13 combines strength with openness. It includes the nations in the worship of Yhwh in a different way from Isaiah 19:25, for example, yet just as fully.[174] Peoples from far foreign shores who flock to the light (Is 60:3) wait for Yhwh (cf. Is 42:1-4) in the way one may wait for the dawn. They know that their present light is actually disguised darkness, their joy disguised sadness, their religion disguised agnosticism, their prosperity disguised emptiness; as yesterday's luxuries become today's necessities, the people who most resolutely fulfill their insatiable appetite for buying stuff are the people with lower quality of life, lower self-esteem and more depression and anxiety. So they flock to Israel in their sailing ships like clouds scudding across the sky or doves soaring to their cotes, with the biggest container ships at the head of the procession, and again incidentally bringing Jerusalem's children home (Is 60:8-9).

There is admittedly an iron hand within the vision's velvet glove; if the nations decline to come to the light, they will find that their darkness gets much deeper (Is 60:12). But their resources can come to have a new significance and a real value when they find their destiny in glorifying Yhwh's name and beautifying Yhwh's city (Is 60:13). The foreign peoples will themselves take on the task of rebuilding the city's walls, which evidently seemed an impossibly daunting task till a man with experience in Persian administration took it in hand. Their kings will thus minister to the city (Is 60:10). Arguably that is what they did when the Persian king approved and paid for the work on it. But we must not be literalistic, not least because the vision goes on to describe the

---

[174]Against Blenkinsopp, *Isaiah 56—66*, p. 212, who sees a painful contrast between Is 60:4-7 and the "religiously universalistic world view" of Is 19:25.

gates of the city as permanently open, day and night, so that resources can be brought in. In theory the point of walls is to act as a protection, to keep people out, so if the gates are open all the time, why the walls? Its walls are the splendor of a city—its crown—as are the walls of the Old City of Jerusalem. They do not ensure the strength and security but they do symbolize it. This city will be in no danger of attack and capture; its walls are a sign of that (Is 60:11).

The vision then returns to the beautifying of the sanctuary, with impressive timber from Lebanon's famous forests. Yhwh sits enthroned in the heavens but chooses to have a footstool on the earth, and this footstool is the sanctuary. That puts the sanctuary in its place: it is only Yhwh's footstool. But it also exalts it: it is Yhwh's personal footstool (Is 60:13)!

When Yhwh returns to it, "Jerusalem will be called 'True City,' the mountain of Yhwh Armies 'Holy Mountain,'" and "they will be a people for me and I will be God for them, in truth and in faithfulness" (Zech 8:3, 8; cf. Is 1:26). The first formulae suggest two aspects to the life of the restored city. In terms of its relationship with God and with other people in the community, the city will be characterized by faithfulness, reliability, truthfulness, steadfastness. The expression "true city," literally "city of truth," comes only here in the First Testament; it coheres with the fact that "truth" itself (ʾĕmet) comes five times in the chapter, more than any other chapter in the First Testament. In terms of its relationship with God and with the world outside, Mount Zion itself will be characterized by holiness; the expression "mountain of holiness" also comes only here. The feet of foreigners who do not worship Yhwh will no longer defile it (cf. Is 52:1).

Prayed For and Praised For

Again, one notes that all this takes a lot of believing. Will it really come about? The troubles of the time after the initial restoration of the city (see Neh 5) make clear that it stands as a promise only partially fulfilled. The vision implicitly summons lookouts to keep pressing Yhwh over the matter (Is 62:6-9). Here much of the imagery is indeed down to earth. It is only too real an experience that people subjected to invasion or conquest have their produce appropriated by their invaders or occupiers. By commissioning Babylon to invade and conquer, Yhwh had subjected Jerusalem to such treatment. Now Yhwh utters a solemn imprecation that guarantees this will not happen again. Instead, the proper order will obtain. The people who harvest and gather will be the people who eat and drink. But they will not merely overeat and overdrink in family celebrations at home. They will eat and drink in the courts of Yhwh's palace in the proper manner of a harvest festival such as Firstfruits or Pentecost or Sukkot, enthusing over Yhwh as the one who grants every harvest as well as the one who has in particular made possible a harvest that is not appropriated by foreigners. Jerusalem will thus become a reason for praise of Yhwh throughout all the earth as the world sees what Yhwh has done for it.[175] And this comes about in response to the never-silent lookouts bringing things to Yhwh's mind.

It will indeed mean that Jerusalem becomes a reason for praise and a place of praise. In the place that has become desolate and deserted "there will again be heard a joyful voice, a happy voice, the voice of a groom and the voice of a bride, the voice of people saying, 'Praise Yhwh Armies, because Yhwh is good, because his commitment is forever,' bringing a thank-offering to Yhwh's house; because I will restore the country's fortunes as they once were, Yhwh has said" (Jer 33:10-11). The words presuppose the city's fall and a situation in which people are lamenting the fact that Jerusalem is a ghost town, as are other cities. Jeremiah's warning (see Jer 7:34) has come true, but it is not the last word. Jeremiah spells out the implications of restoration in two main ways. First, he presupposes that the ghost town will again be a bustling city, and leaps on to a particular reality that comprises a touching symbol of a return to normal life. There is no more joyful community occasion than the festivity of a wedding, an event that symbolizes hope for the future, so there is no more encouraging symbol of the city's true restoration than the picture of wedding celebrations resuming. But seamlessly Jeremiah goes on to a second voice, the voice of worship. People will be "saying" something different from what they are "saying" at the moment (the same participial form recurs). At present their words are words of lament, but they will again be words of praise and thanksgiving. The words of praise resemble Psalm 136:1, the last line exactly corresponding to the refrain that recurs through that psalm, and it resembles the praise the people do offer when they begin restoring the temple (Ezra 3:11). The praise relates to who Yhwh consistently is, and it is thus praise appropriate to a hymn, but it is accompanied by a thank-offering that presupposes Yhwh's acting in gracious ways to this community or this family or this individual. The goodness of God to which hymnody testifies will again have become reality in people's experience, and they will testify to that. In passing, the promise notes that they will do so in Yhwh's house; so it will have been restored.

Whereas the nightmare meant joy went into exile (*gālâ*, Is 24:11, cf. vv. 7, 8), restoration thus means the renewal of joy—in Yhwh (Is 25:9).[176] And fasting will be replaced by feasting (Zech 8:18-19). Through their experience of devas-

---

[175]I thus take it that the praise is praise of Yhwh rather than praise of Jerusalem; cf. the comment on Is 60:18 in section 5.6 "Well Taught and Well Governed."

[176]Patrick D. Miller, *Israelite Religion and Biblical Theology*, JSOTSup 267 (Sheffield: Sheffield Academic Press, 2000), pp. 683-86.

tation, people have been observing fasts in the fourth month of each year, and the fifth month and the seventh month and the tenth month, apparently marking the different stages in the siege and fall of Jerusalem and its aftermath (see 2 Kings 25). But these will all become instead occasions for joy and rejoicing and festival. While formally Zechariah refers to the fasts, in substance what the reference does is remind people of the horrific events themselves. The fasts kept these alive in the minds of people who mostly had not experienced them. Declaring that the fasts will be turned into feasts implies that the events themselves will become truly past, parts of history and no longer realities that continue to confront people.

Just make sure that you commit yourselves to truth and peace, Zechariah adds (Zech 8:19). As there is no chapter in the First Testament that has more references to *ʾĕmet* (and to God as Yhwh Armies), so there is hardly any that has more references to *shalom*.[177]

5.7 Renewing the Monarchy

Whereas prophets sometimes speak of the future as one in which monarchy has been abandoned or severely circumscribed, sometimes they speak of a future king who will fulfill Yhwh's intentions regarding kingship. The king who belonged to Yhwh had been destined to be Yhwh's means of ruling the nations and of ruling Israel with decisive faithfulness, and neither aspect of this intention had come about. But perhaps that will not mean Yhwh simply gives up. That intention becomes the objective Yhwh will fulfill in the future. Yhwh declares this intention in the context of the failure of the monarchy while it still stands, and again in the context of the fall of the monarchy. There will be a king who comes as a new David, a new shoot from the old tree, one through whom Yhwh rules, who brings *shalom,* on whom Yhwh's spirit rests, who acknowledges Yhwh, who stands as a shelter from the storm, who shepherds faithfully, who before Yhwh can combine forcefulness and weakness.

The Messiah

In Christian and Jewish usage the default way of referring to this intention involves referring to Israel's "messianic hope," but neither of these terms corresponds to First Testament usage. The First Testament does not explicitly talk about a messianic *hope.* There are no examples of people saying "we hope Yhwh will send the Messiah one day" or of prayers for Yhwh to send the Messiah. It is a plausible view that in the Second Temple period, people praying the psalms that refer to the king implicitly turned these into expres-

---

[177]Ironically, 2 Kings 9 has more; so do chapters with many idiomatic references in greetings (e.g., 1 Sam 25).

sions of hope and prayer for the Messiah, but there are no psalms in the Psalter that explicitly express that hope (contrast Psalms of Solomon 17, which prays for the coming of the Messiah and describes what he will be like). The Messiah is the subject of divine promise, not of human hope. Further, he is never actually the subject of explicitly *messianic* hope or promise; that is, the word *māšîaḥ* is not used of the object of such hopes or promises. While the First Testament does refer to the Messiah (in the sense of a figure who will realize the kingly ideal), it never calls him the Messiah. When it uses the word *māšîaḥ*, "anointed," it uses it only to refer to a figure who already exists, a current king or priest as someone anointed for his task. It does not use the word to refer to a coming anointed person. While it does speak of a Davidic ruler whom God will raise up in the future, it has no regular term or title for this person, and that lack will be one reason why Jews and Christians came to adopt the term *anointed* to describe him. But a more profound reason will have been the fact that the four or five centuries during which an anointed king ruled in Jerusalem were succeeded by four or five centuries and more during which this was not so. So those passages in the Psalms about the anointed king whom Israel once had came to be referred to the anointed king whom Israel would have again some day.

Not only are the psalms not overtly messianic, neither are some passages in the Prophets that have been read that way. More than one First Testament passage speaks of a son whose birth will link with God's promise to David. Isaiah's promise about a young woman having a baby whom she will call "God-is-with-us" may have in mind a child to be born to Ahaz; this name will then testify to Yhwh's faithfulness to the promise to "David's household" (Is 7:13-14). But the opaqueness of the promise, while facilitating the New Testament's using it in a creative way to illumine the significance of Jesus, means we cannot build anything on it in its First Testament context.

Jürgen Moltmann declares that "the future hope of Israel and Judaism is already messianic."[178] The fact that the Hebrew word māšîaḥ never refers to a future redeemer is a linguistic symbol of the fact that this is so in only a marginal sense. One could plausibly reckon that eschatological hope comes to be central to First Testament faith (at least, if one knew what *eschatological* meant), but hope for a Messiah is not central to the First Testament. The basic nature of First Testament faith would be little affected if it were not there. Moltmann goes on to comment on the fact that Christian theology "split up the unity of Old Testament messianology into Christology on the one hand, and eschatology on the other."[179] But in the First Testament, messianology is a subset of es-

---

[178]Jürgen Moltmann, *The Way of Jesus Christ* (San Francisco: HarperSanFrancisco, 1990), p. xiii.
[179]Ibid., p. 4.

chatology, not vice versa. Indeed, "Israel's unique conception of God as the God of history is the root of eschatology."[180]

One Through Whom Yhwh Rules

Subsequent to Isaiah 7, the description of the birth of an undeniably royal child in Isaiah 9:6-7 [MT 5-6] raises different questions. It speaks of a son who "has been born to us," on whose shoulders authority has come to rest. For the most part this oracle thus presents itself not as a vision of the future but as a declaration about events that have already begun to happen and about their outworking. The book of Isaiah has already spoken about Yhwh's work of restoration and renewal in the future (e.g., Is 1:24—2:4; 4:2-6), but when doing so has used yiqtol verbs. When it has used qatal verbs, it has been referring to events that have happened. The presupposition would be that here, too, it speaks about events that have already taken place. The royal birth would be an actual birth, like ones referred to earlier (see Is 7:1—8:4), or the passage might refer to a king's enthronement, the moment of his adoption by Yhwh, his rebirth (cf. Ps 2). The person the passage speaks of might then be Hezekiah, whose birth or enthronement is a sign that Yhwh is beginning to restore Israel, specifically the northern clans ravaged by Assyrian invasion (cf. Is 9:1 [MT 8:23], though the interpretation of that verse is difficult).

If this is so regarding the oracle's original significance, the situation changes when we read it in its context in Isaiah. Here there is no reference to a historical context in, for instance, the time of Hezekiah, as there is elsewhere either implicitly or explicitly (see Is 28—31; 36—39). Further, if the oracle originally expressed hopes regarding what would happen in Hezekiah's reign, those hopes were not realized. Indeed, it would have been extraordinary if they had been realized, because the oracle describes the fruitfulness of this birth in larger than life terms in the way it speaks, for example, of the complete fulfillment of the Davidic ideal: "His rule is to increase, and for *shalom* there is to be no end, on David's throne and on his kingship to establish it and sustain it, in decisive faithfulness from now and forever" (Is 9:7 [MT 6]). It thus joins the many other First Testament prophecies that see some contemporary fulfillment but portray matters in much more glorious or devastating terms than the ones realized in these events. Indeed, this would seem quite an extreme instance. In Hezekiah's day, in contrast to the description in Isaiah 9, the people walking in darkness did not see much light (even if Hezekiah did invite people from Ephraim to a Passover in Jerusalem). Yhwh did not multiply the nation or break their yoke or their oppressor's rod. His reign was not the beginning of a

---

[180]Sigmund Mowinckel, *He That Cometh* (Oxford: Blackwell, reprint, 1959), p. 153; quoted with approval by Moltmann, *Way of Jesus Christ*, p. 8.

time of unbroken well-being and faithfulness. Yhwh's passion did not bring this about.

As is the case with many other such prophecies in the First Testament, nevertheless the community evidently decided not simply to forget this as a false prophecy, as happened with other prophecies,[181] but retained it as promising something that would eventually come about. Such a retention fits with the locating of this oracle in Isaiah. It appears without historical reference, and it is separated from its historical context in material that does relate to Hezekiah, if that is its original reference.[182] It comes at the end of the account of Isaiah's ministry in Isaiah 6:1—9:7 (MT 6), at the center of Isaiah 1—12.[183] That account tells of Isaiah's commission, of aspects of his ministry, then of his failure to get king and people to respond to Yhwh. He therefore gives up preaching and commits himself to waiting for darkness to fall, in fulfillment of Yhwh's word. This description of light dawning after darkness thus follows his warning about the way final distress and darkness will fall on the community.

If this past-tense statement originally spoke of actual events and their expected fruitfulness, in this new context it comes to refer more consistently to the future. Its past-tense verbs become "prophetic perfect" or "instantaneous perfect," ones which see a coming event as so real that it can be described as already actual or as happening before the speaker's eyes. After speaking of the fall of darkness on Yhwh's people, it looks forward to the dawning of light in a way that does not relate this to a particular context. It simply promises that darkness will not be the end. And it speaks of the coming arrival of a new Davidic king as if it were a past event. Obviously that would speak powerfully to people living after the exile, and this has been an alternative context for locating the passage's actual origin.

So perhaps a prophecy whose original context was Isaiah's own time, and which once had a concrete reference to an actual king, came to be rethought and set in a less historically specific context in Isaiah 6—9. The question whether its beginning refers to a king's physical birth or to his enthronement then becomes less significant. It is prosaic to press the point that a child's birth could only presage his bringing about a deliverance in twenty years' time. Indeed, it does not make explicit the link between the gift of a new king and the people's deliverance from their oppressors. These might be two parallel or sequential gifts of God, rather than the new king being the means of the deliver-

---

[181]For instance, those of the other prophets mentioned in Isaiah, Jeremiah and Ezekiel.

[182]Cf. the comments in Brevard S. Childs, *Isaiah* (London: SCM Press/Louisville, Ky: Westminster John Knox, 2001), p. 80.

[183]In Is 9:8 [MT 7]—10:4 there will follow a reversion to the confrontational material that occupied Is 5:8-30.

ance. In any case, the stress lies on the fact and the fruit of the king's "rule"; the word *(miśrâ)* comes only here, presumably being used (invented?) to accompany the familiar word "ruler" *(śar)*. At the moment the burdensome yoke of their oppressor lies on Israel's shoulder, but the descent of rule onto this man's shoulder enables and/or symbolizes that yoke's removal.

One Who Brings Shalom

The king's name both associates him closely with God and makes clear that he is not God. "He has been named 'A Wonderful Planner Is the Mighty God; the Everlasting Father Is a Ruler with *Shalom.*'" By implication, the king himself will be a ruler characterized by *shalom*, but his name is not actually a description of him. It parallels other names in Isaiah such "Leftovers Will Return" and "Pillage Hurries, Looting Speeds" (Is 7:3; 8:1). Such names comprise a statement (not just a string of epithets, as NRSV and NIVI imply in Isaiah 9:6 [MT 5]), a statement not about the person himself but about something to do with God, which the person in some way symbolizes. The king's name comprises a declaration that the mighty God is a wonderful planner and that this God, the everlasting Father, is a ruler characterized by *shalom.*[184] What God does through this king will demonstrate those facts. Isaiah recurrently emphasizes the fact that Yhwh is good at formulating a purpose or taking decisions or making plans and putting them into effect (e.g., Is 14:24-27). Here he adds that these plans are characterized by wonder (cf. Is 28:29), the kind he has spoken of in describing the removal of the burden from the people's neck (Is 9:4 [MT 3]) or that Gideon raised a question about in the crisis this passage looks back to (Judg 6:13)—exodus and Red Sea wonder (Ex 3:20; 15:11). Through this king the people will again know Yhwh as the mighty God who formulates a purpose to do something extraordinary, and then does it.

Further, king and people will know this God as the everlasting father who is a ruler bringing *shalom*. The mighty God is a father to the people as a whole (Ex 4:22), though in the context this may be an embarrassing point to make (Is 1:2-3). And in the context it may be more significant that the mighty God is father to the king in particular (Ps 2:7; 89:26 [MT 27]), in a father-son relationship that will last (Ps 89:29 [MT 30]). Either way, this Everlasting Father is one who rules in such a way as to ensure *shalom*. Both the narrower and the broader connotations of *shalom* are significant here. As a ruler who brings *shalom*, this mighty God takes king and people from oppression and conflict to release and peace. But in addition, this Father sees that his son's people enjoy blessing, fruitfulness, prosperity and well-being in their life together.

---

[184]See John Goldingay, "The Compound Name in Isaiah 9.5 [6]," *Catholic Biblical Quarterly* 61 (1999): 239-44.

The description of God as "a ruler with *shalom*" is picked up in the words that describe the reign of the king, whose "rule" will also be characterized by *shalom*. The promise involves a hendiadys. Its parallelism means that it does not make two separate statements, about his rule growing and about *shalom* having no end, but one statement, that his will be a rule characterized by *shalom* that will flourish and have no end. Further, Yhwh's words go on to make explicit a further aspect of this *shalom*, or to reformulate what ruling with *shalom* involves. It involves decisive faithfulness or faithful decision making (*mišpāṭ ûṣĕdāqâ*). The king's reign would not involve real *shalom* if it did not involve *mišpāṭ ûṣĕdāqâ*.

In the context of Isaiah's day or the exile or the Second Temple period, once more the vision expressed here would seem highly unlikely of fulfillment. Isaiah therefore adds that Yhwh's passion will see to its fulfillment. Passion (*qinʾâ*) involves the ardor of love and the ardor of anger. Yhwh Armies has the ardor of a father or mother for their children that will give all their energy to ensure that their children get the best and that anyone who attacks them gets vigorously repulsed. That ardor will see to the throwing off of oppressors and the gift of *shalom* with *mišpāṭ ûṣĕdāqâ*.

This vision is not cited in the New Testament, though the earlier verses about light breaking into darkness (Is 9:1-2 [MT 8:22—9:1]) are so quoted (Mt 4:15-16). Christians have often reckoned it a prophecy relating to Jesus. If one sees it that way, it sets Jesus an agenda. Neither in the world nor in the Jewish people nor in the Christian church does one see *shalom* or *mišpāṭ ûṣĕdāqâ* flourishing. It is as well that Isaiah affirms that Yhwh's passion is committed to their achievement.

One on Whom Yhwh's Spirit Settles

As the great tree, Assyria, is to be cut down, so the tree of David is to be cut down. Yet it is not impossible for a felled tree to grow again, though it may require a miracle. "A branch will grow from Jesse's stump, a shoot will develop from his roots" (Is 11:1-5). But the focus in the vision that follows lies in a series of bigger miracles than the mere coming back to life of the Davidic tree. First, it lies in what Yhwh's spirit will do to this king. "Yhwh's spirit will settle on him, the spirit of insight and discernment, the spirit of planning and might, the spirit of acknowledgment and reverence for Yhwh." Yhwh's spirit is Yhwh's dynamism, something with the liveliness of breath and the force of the wind. It is therefore odd to think of it "settling" on someone (*nûaḥ*). The last thing that breath, wind or dynamism do is settle. But this dynamism will do that.

It is also odd to think of dynamism conveying insight and discernment. People on whom Yhwh's spirit comes are people who act in spectacular ways, but insight and discernment are assets they are inclined to lack (see the book

of Judges). Indeed, if Isaiah had said that Yhwh's *insight* will settle on this king
so that it will have the fruits that the vision then describes (the capacity to
make plans, the instinct to make decisions for the poor, a commitment to acknowledge Yhwh), we might have been less surprised; it would have fitted
with Proverbs 1:1-7. By speaking of these as the result of Yhwh's *spirit* settling
on the king, Isaiah indeed adds a dynamism. This king will operate like the
whirlwind, in the manner of the leaders in Judges, but this will be a whirlwind
that does not die down, and the dynamism will work to different ends. This
king will fuse dynamism and insight; they will make a formidable combination. The Assyrian king had pretended to insight and discernment (Is 10:13),
but in reality lacked these. He thought it was his insight and discernment that
had played a key role in enabling him to do what he did, but in reality there
were other factors at work. Divine insight and discernment used him as an the
unwitting agent. This king, in contrast, will embody insight and discernment.

He will combine dynamism and the capacity to make plans that are powerful in their outworking. Like insight, planning with power is a divine capacity;
it is Yhwh who is the wonderful planner and the mighty God (Is 9:6 [MT 5];
10:21; 14:24-27). Indeed, arguably dynamism and the capacity to make plans
are the same thing. Yhwh operates with insight in making plans (cf. Is 31:2); so
will the king. In recent years, it has not only been Assyria that has pretended
to insight and the capacity to make plans and implement them. Judah has been
doing the same. It has been led by feeble fools. When Yhwh's dynamism rests
on this king, things will change.

One Who Acknowledges Yhwh and Decides for the Poor

Another key factor in this change is the fact that Yhwh's dynamism will generate acknowledgment of Yhwh and reverence for Yhwh (Is 11:2). Insight and
reverence for Yhwh are simply juxtaposed; Isaiah does not specify the relationship between them. In Proverbs, reverence for Yhwh is the foundation or first
principle of knowledge, but insight and discernment also generate reverence
for and acknowledgment of Yhwh (Prov 1:7; 2:1-5). There is thus a dialectical
relationship between these two. Reverence for Yhwh generates insight; insight
generates reverence for Yhwh. Isaiah allows for the same possibilities. In this
context, I take it that the *da'at* to which Isaiah refers is not mere knowledge but
acknowledgment—acknowledgment of Yhwh, which is explicitly referred to
later in the vision. Both Assyrian leadership and Israelite leadership had been
as short of acknowledgment of Yhwh and reverence for Yhwh as they had been
of insight and discernment or the capacity to make plans and implement them.
That, too, will change with this king. "His scent will be reverence for Yhwh,"
the prophecy adds (Is 11:3). The phrase may be a gloss, but it constitutes a striking paronomasia; "scent" (*hārîaḥ*) comes from a denominative verb derived

from the word for "spirit" that is of such importance in this passage. Either the king finds a sensuous delight in reverence for Yhwh or his reverence for Yhwh makes the king a sensuous delight for his people. Again one might expect there to be a dialectical relationship between these two possibilities.

In turn what follows both describes the outworking of that reverence and indicates why people would find delight in the king. It also suggests another contrast with the kings Israel had actually had. Acknowledgment of Yhwh and reverence for Yhwh express themselves in the way the king goes about making decisions for people. On one hand, "he will not make decisions by what his eyes see, judge by what his ears hear" (Is 11:3), that is, simply on the basis of the obvious evidence and the things people say. He will get behind that to the real truth (cf. Prov 25:2-3). On the other, he will make decisions that benefit the poor and weak (Is 11:4). If there is a link between these, it perhaps implies the recognition that people with power and resources are capable of presenting a case with plausibility even when it is actually based on falsehood. So looking behind the appearance and the words to the reality is one aspect of a bias toward the poor. But that bias is broader. In the Western world the theoretical principle of law and justice is that everyone is treated the same, though the practical principle is that the system should work for the benefit of the people who administer it, such as lawyers and people who can afford them. In the Middle East—not just in Israel—the theoretical principle of law and justice is that the king's task is to protect the weak, not merely to see that the rule of law is implemented (e.g., Ps 72). But in Israel, as elsewhere in the Middle Eastern world, that principle was implemented more in the breach than in the observance. In practice the system again worked for the benefit of people with the resources to make it do so. This king will realize the ideal that Israel and other nations recognized in theory.

And that means the king will be prepared to take tough action against the faithless: "he will strike the land with the rod of his mouth, with the breath of his lips kill the faithless" (Is 11:4). He will not tolerate a situation in which the jails are full of poor people but wealthy swindlers get away with their wrongdoing. The settling of Yhwh's spirit on him will have the effect it had on those leaders in Judges and on the young Saul (1 Sam 11). He will take their kind of decisive violent action to put down the faithless. His word will have the same power that God's word has: he will speak, and things will happen (cf. Ps 33:6). This is the way he will demonstrate that the unifying principles that hold him together are faithfulness and truthfulness. In a warriorlike way he will manifest such faithfulness and truthfulness in his relationship with God and with his people. "Faithfulness will be the belt round his hips, truthfulness the belt round his thighs" (Is 11:5).

The result of the king's decisive action will be peace and harmony "in all my holy mountain." That usually refers to Mount Zion (e.g., Ps 2:6; 48:2-3) though it might also denote the country as a whole (e.g., Ex 15:17; Jer 31:23). Perhaps the one stands for the other: Mount Zion as Yhwh's dwelling casts its beneficent shadow over the entire country. Isaiah's vision would certainly be for wrongdoing and destructiveness to disappear from the whole land, as "the country is full of acknowledgment of Yhwh." In the context, the vision of supernatural harmony in the animal world, with the wolf dwelling with the lamb, may well also stand for supernatural harmony in the human world, though this too might in turn have implications for the animal world itself.[185]

A Shelter from the Storm

One side of that vision identifies the key to this harmony as the aggressive action of the king in acting in faithfulness and truthfulness (Is 11:4-5). The other side identifies the key as the acknowledgment of Yhwh in the land as well as in the king's life. These are two sides of a coin. Proper acknowledgment of Yhwh involves taking the necessary aggressive action to protect and deliver the weak and put down the people who take advantage of them. Only when that has happened is Yhwh acknowledged. Ultimately that acknowledgment is certainly destined to characterize the world as a whole. Isaiah 2:2-4 has already indicated as much, and shortly Isaiah 11 will note that this king is to be the means of that coming about. But for the moment, in the context Isaiah is declaring that the *country* is to be "full of the acknowledgment of Yhwh like waters covering the sea" (!) (Is 11:9). Once again, Isaiah is promising a miracle. In a strange way, the declaration that the country is to be full of this acknowledgment is a bigger miracle than that the world should be so filled. The latter is such a big universal idea that it requires us to think in a quite different framework in which the usual rules do not apply. The idea that Israel should be filled with this acknowledgment is imaginable in the sense that we can dream of what it would look like, yet this underlines the distance to be traveled for it to become reality. The book started with a lament at the problem of Israel's incorrigible failure to acknowledge Yhwh (Is 1:3). Here Yhwh refuses to see this problem as insoluble.

Presumably this acknowledgment and the resultant peace and harmony will be what turns the king into an ensign for the nations as well as the means of effecting a miracle in Israel. Then "Jesse's root that is standing will be an ensign to peoples; nations will have recourse to him and his settling will be full of splendor" (Is 11:10). The king will thus be the means of implementing the vision of the nations streaming to Zion and of Yhwh's teaching streaming out

---

[185]See section 7.4 "A New World."

(Is 2:2-4). The nations come because they see what has been achieved through this king's work there. That is why they will have recourse to him, coming to ask him how such transformation can be effected in their own communities. The very last colon promising (lit.) that "his settling will be splendor" is allusive, but the context suggests two ideas. The repetition of words and images indicate that the opening and closing lines of the vision (Is 11:1-2, 10) provide a frame for it.[186] One aspect of this is the recurrence of the idea of settling. It is the settling of Yhwh's spirit that brings about a transformation such as draws the nations. And perhaps it is precisely that transformation, which the vision has described, that constitutes the king's splendor, which lies not in the usual grandeur of monarchy but in the transformation this king brings to the community's life.

The world has not yet seen a king who has brought about this transformation. Paul does set it before the Roman church as God's vision for it and prays for God to implement it in the church's life (Rom 15:12), but this did not happen. Once again the vision thus sets an agenda for Jesus as the Messiah.

For at present there are people who act in a way that makes it impossible for the hungry to eat and the thirsty to drink, not least through their manipulation of the legal system, and the government fails to stop that (see Is 32:6-8). Yhwh promises that this situation will change, and kings and ministers of state will start reigning and exercising leadership in a way that harnesses their authority to faithfulness within the community (Is 32:1-5). They will promote the faithfulness that wants the needy to have enough to eat rather than takes advantage of them (in postbiblical Hebrew, ṣĕdāqâ, "faithfulness," is the word for almsgiving or charity or an act of generosity). The selfishness of clever rogues in the community is as threatening to the life of needy people as being overwhelmed by a hurricane or getting lost in the desert, but the government will fulfill its job of making sure that the needy are sheltered from this storm or watered in this desert. In the context Isaiah emphasizes that Yhwh does not want the community—specifically these leaders—looking to people such as the Egyptians as their means of protection (e.g., Is 30:2), yet this warning is apparently not incompatible with expecting the leaders to be a means of protection for their people. To put it another way, Yhwh has shown a commitment to being a refuge from the storm and shade from the heat for the poor and needy (Is 25:4-5), and/but Yhwh expects king and leaders also to be that.

In between the promise that the government will be committed to faithfulness and protection and the promise that fools and scoundrels will no longer be honored is the declaration that eyes, ears, minds and tongues will now

---

[186]See J. Alec Motyer, *The Prophecy of Isaiah* (Leicester, U.K.: Inter-Varsity Press, 1993), pp. 121, 125.

function properly (Is 32:3-4). Their malfunctioning is a common Isaianic theme, but here Isaiah links their restoration to this vision about government. Perhaps one implication is that the leaders will encourage this restoration in the community, so that people in general will look at things in a new way, and that will contribute to fools and scoundrels no longer being honored. Another might be that the leaders themselves are the people especially affected by this malfunctioning, and their becoming protection and refreshment for their people will be a sign that their eyes, ears, minds and tongues are now working properly. Leaders are inclined to be people who look but do not see, who go through the motion of listening but do not actually pay attention. They may think and make decisions quickly but not necessarily with insight, or they may be faltering before the problems presented to them. All that will change. Now they will really see (see what God is pointing them too, see the needs of people). Now they will actually attend (listen to what God is saying, listen to what their people are saying). Now they will think and make decisions with insight as well as speed. Now they will be able to make an intelligent response in circumstances where at the moment they cannot.

My Servant David

To put it another way, kings have the task of shepherding the people, but they behave like shepherds who just do shepherding as a job rather than as people who are committed to the sheep. The coming king will be the latter kind of shepherd.

After a devastating indictment of Israel's shepherds and a promise that Yhwh will shepherd them in person, we are surprised to read the promise, "I will set up over them one shepherd and he will shepherd them, my servant David. He will shepherd them. He will be a shepherd to them. I, Yhwh, will be God for them, with my servant David prince among them" (Ezek 34:23-24). If the kings fulfill their vocation to act with decisive fairness by delivering people who are swindled and protecting the powerless, then "there will come through the gates of this house kings sitting for David on his throne, riding in horse-drawn carriages, he, his servants, and his people" (Jer 22:4). Jeremiah again shows that he has accepted some of the trimmings of monarchy that Samuel warned about (1 Sam 8:11-17).[187] But if the kings will accept this vocation, such expressions of splendor can be allowed, even rejoiced in.

When Ezekiel speaks of "my servant David," we cannot tell whether he implies that David himself will come back from the dead like Samuel in 1 Samuel 28 or Moses in Matthew 17, or that the new ruler will be a new David, a David-

---

[187]Cf. Jer 17:24-25; see section 5.6 "Lasting."

like figure. Either way, the promise implies that the ideal state that obtained during David's reign will return. While the image of David that emerges from his own story is an ambiguous one, the image of David that stayed with Israel focused on his strengths as a leader and his loyalty to Yhwh, and ignored his weaknesses as a man and the seeds of trouble that his reign sewed. Even in Samuel-Kings, David is the man who turns a fragile people into one nation and takes that united nation to its greatest triumphs. In the subsequent story in Kings, the great thing about David is that he was unwavering in the commitment to Yhwh required by the first two commands in the Decalogue, so that he sets the standard for evaluating later kings. In Chronicles, written later than Ezekiel, the great thing about David is his making the arrangements for the temple and its worship. In promising that the people will have David as their king or leader, Ezekiel is promising someone who will hold the nation together, give proper priority to its worship, and oversee its being offered to Yhwh alone in the way Yhwh ordains. Yhwh can take the risk of calling such a leader "king" (Ezek 37:22-24) as well as "prince" and "shepherd."

Apparently Yhwh's direct shepherding is an interim emergency measure. Direct shepherding did not work too well in the long run before, in the period between Joshua and David, and a David became necessary, though his successors left much to be desired. Someone who really acts as Yhwh's servant and who is a prince, not a king, would not be so much of a risk. Having made this promise, Yhwh resumes talk of personally looking after the sheep in the manner of a shepherd—making sure they are safe from animals and have good provision of food (Ezek 34:25-31). Apparently the idea of having David as shepherd-king need not too much compromise the notion of Yhwh's being shepherd-king. But the test of an alleged servant of Yhwh is whether the vision in Ezekiel 34:25-31 has found fulfillment.

Shepherding by Yhwh's Strength

Instead of being Yhwh's means of ruling the nations, Israel's leaders were often humiliated by other peoples, with all the grief, pressure and shame that issue from this. Micah 5:1-6 [MT 2-7]) promises that it will not always be so. It portrays a reversal of that grief and shame, though it presupposes a time when there is no longer a ruler in Israel at all, a time when God has given Israel up. In that context it declares that the promise to David is not finished. The insignificant village of Bethlehem had already once produced the greatest hero Israel ever knew, and it will do so again (there would be no need for this ruler to be *born* in Bethlehem; if he is a descendant of David, then Bethlehem will have produced him). His origins will thus lie centuries back in that ancient Bethlehem family, and his destiny eventually to become ruler will lie centuries back in Yhwh's promise to David that guaranteed that another Davidic ruler would sit on David's throne, when the mother who bears him has actually given birth.[188] The fragmented people will become one again; readers might think of the northern clans who had split off from Judah, and then of these clans transported by the Assyrians, and then of Judeans scattered by events during the last decades of the seventh century and the beginning of the sixth.

The people who will thus return are this ruler's "kin," his brothers and sisters. The expression recalls Deuteronomy's reminder that the king must not forget that his people are his brothers and sisters; he is one among siblings, not someone in a position to lord it over them or see himself as above the law (Deut 17:14-20). The fact that he is not described as anointed is probably not significant; the term could have been used without being controversial. His not being called "king" may be more so, since we have noted that there are strands in First Testament thinking that are inclined to safeguard the fact that Yhwh is Israel's only real king by not using this term of Israel's earthly ruler. Thus the present king is here spoken of as "leader" (*šōpēṭ*), the term for the leaders in the book of Judges, before Israel had kings. It is the more significant that Micah does not use the word *king* when speaking of a king to come. Declaring that God will grant people another Davidic ruler recognizes that Yhwh's promise stands; declining to call him "king" recognizes that history more than justifies the uneases about human kingship expressed in the story of how Israel came to have kings. Indeed, perhaps it is significant that there is no actual reference to David or to the capital city of Jerusalem with its palaces. The promise goes back to little Bethlehem in its insignificance, before Israel had the accoutrements of a state that went with the Davidic monarchy.

What this "ruler" will do is repeat the achievements of a great king like David in delivering the people from their enemies. He will shepherd the flock rather than feeding off it (cf. Ezek 34). He will do so on the basis of Yhwh's strength and majesty, avoiding the trap of setting himself up as a center of power and a symbol of majesty. Notwithstanding that, his fame will be acknowledged to the ends of the earth. And therefore his people will dwell in safety and will enjoy peace—the context suggests that here *shalom* has its narrower connotation. Specifically, he will save his people from the Assyrians if they ever invade Judah.

Jesus' birth in Bethlehem provides a neat link with this passage (cf. Mt 2:5-6), and the rest of the passage provides King Herod with good reason to be concerned at the birth of someone whom people might expect to fulfill its portrait. Ironically, the description of the acts of this ruler show little overlap with what Jesus came to do.

---

[188]It is not clear whether this is mother Israel or whether the phrase links with the kind of statements that appear in Isaiah about a young woman giving birth.

The New Shoot from an Old Tree

Israel has proved that the reign of a king is not necessarily good news for his people. If the king leads the country away from Yhwh toward reliance on other deities or other nations, he leads it into trouble. But if the king is faithful to Yhwh in these two respects and faithful to his people, he will mean deliverance and security for them—deliverance from crises and ongoing security. Yhwh will ensure that this comes about, promising in Jeremiah 23:5-6 to "set up for David a faithful shoot" who will reign with insight and decisive faithfulness in the land, and in whose days Judah and Israel will know deliverance and security. And he will be called "Yhwh is our faithfulness" (cf. Jer 33:15-16). "Faithful shoot" is the Hebrew equivalent to a recurrent Middle Eastern expression for a "rightful heir."[189] The "shoot" is not merely part of a plant (as the translation "branch" implies) but a whole new plant from the existent stock. It is ironic that a Middle Eastern political expression becomes a term for the Messiah. But Jeremiah's gloss on the phrase makes clear that he uses the word for "rightful" with the connotations that attach to *ṣaddîq*. The rightful heir will be someone who acts in the rightful way, acts with decisive faithfulness. Thus it can follow that in his days Judah will be delivered and Israel will dwell in security, and he will be called "Yhwh is our faithfulness." And the fruit of faithfulness is security (Is 32:17).

Presumably Jeremiah is not implying that the coming king will literally be called "Yhwh is our faithfulness," which does not correspond to the usual pattern of Yhwh names. "Yhwh is our faithfulness" is not a name in this sense, any more than the "name" in Isaiah 9:6 [MT 5]). Hence it can be applied to the city as well as the king (Jer 33:16)—both will embody it. But it is no coincidence that the last king of Judah was Zedekiah, which means "Yhwh is faithfulness" or "Yhwh is my faithfulness" or "Yhwh's faithfulness." In no sense was Zedekiah an expression of Yhwh's faithfulness, and he might have made you despair of monarchy as some Israelites did. One might have expected Jeremiah to do that, but he knows that Yhwh has made an irrevocable commitment to David's line and therefore instead he declares that Yhwh will fulfill that promise by generating someone who really will embody the fact that Yhwh is faithful.

After Ezekiel's thumping declaration about the utter withering of Judah's monarchic tree (Ezek 17:1-21), and in the context of his hesitation about speaking of Judah having kings in the future, we are surprised to hear Yhwh's consequent affirmation of intent about taking a shoot from that tree and planting it on the mountains of Israel. "It will produce branches and bear fruit and be-

---

[189]See, e.g., John A. Thompson, *The Book of Jeremiah*, NICOT (Grand Rapids, Mich.: Eerdmans, 1980), p. 489.

come a noble cedar; every bird will live under it, every winged creature live in the shade of its boughs" (Ezek 17:23). That will cause the other trees (i.e., people in general) to acknowledge Yhwh as the God who has "brought low the tall tree, exalted the lowly tree; I have dried up the green tree, made the dry tree flourish" (Ezek 17:24). In Daniel 4 Nebuchadnezzar is the mighty tree at the center of the earth, under which birds and animals shelter and feed. Babylonian sovereignty is the means whereby the world lives in a framework of order. But although in this respect Nebuchadnezzar is Yhwh's servant, that arrangement can hardly be Yhwh's final intention. It is Yhwh's anointed who is destined to be Yhwh's means of exercising sovereignty over the nations (cf. Ps 2). In Ezekiel 17, at a low point in the history of the monarchy, with one king exiled for his rebelliousness and another about to go the same way, Yhwh is not merely promising to reestablish the Davidic monarchy but to make it so flourish that it will fulfill the vision attaching to it.[190] The exaltation of the Babylonian king and the humiliation of Judean kings cannot be the end of the story. Yhwh will reverse that. And the world will come to acknowledge Yhwh as the one who did this.

One Who Accepts Weakness

Zechariah 9:9-10 nuances these points in encouraging Zion to rejoice because "your king will come to you, he will be one who is faithful and who finds deliverance, weak and riding on a donkey, yes, on a colt, the offspring of an ass." The election of a new government makes people who voted for them think that the destiny of the nation will now turn a corner (they are regularly disappointed). The accession of a king is likewise a moment for celebration, and it usually leads to disappointment. But Zechariah, like Jeremiah, promises a king who will be ṣaddîq. The NRSV has "triumphant," JPSV "victorious," but it seems more natural to reckon that it has its usual meaning "righteous," "just" or "faithful," as in Jeremiah 23:5.[191] The promise that the king will be ṣaddîq is conventional but still encouraging. The rest of the promise is unconventional. As it unfolds, it perhaps suggests that the rejoicing relates to the king's return to Jerusalem after a battle. It is odd to describe him as someone who finds deliverance (yāša' niphal)—NRSV has "victorious," JPSV "triumphant," but that hardly fits the usual meaning of yāša' nor in particular its usual occurrences in the niphal (e.g., Num 10:9; Ps 18:3 [MT 4]; Jer 8:20).[192] It forms a contrast with

---

[190]The point is, if anything, stronger if historically Ezek 17:22-24 comes from after 587 (see, e.g., Allen, *Ezekiel*, 1:255).

[191]Cf. Carol L. Meyers and Eric M. Meyers, *Zechariah 9—14*, AB (New York: Doubleday, 1993), p. 125.

[192]Again cf. ibid., p. 126.

or a complement for the picture of Yhwh as the warrior king bringing about deliverance (Zeph 3:17).[193]

The idea of the king finding deliverance, needing to be rescued by Yhwh, does fit with what follows. He does not come as a triumphant warrior king in a chariot (see, e.g., Deut 17:16; 2 Sam 15:1). He comes as someone weak (ʿānî). Again, NRSV and JPSV take this word to suggest an attitude of meekness, but it usually denotes a position of weakness, and that fits here. The king has been in the position of the king in Psalm 18:27 [MT 28], a weak person whom Yhwh has delivered, and he comes to his people as an ordinary man riding an ordinary man's animal, in a compact rather than a limo.[194] The picture contrasts with Jeremiah's promises about kings on horses (Jer 17:24-25; 22:4). Admittedly a donkey is a quite plausible animal for a king to ride (1 Kings 1:33, 38), but it is an everyday and unmilitary animal. This is a king who knows how a relationship with Yhwh and with life works. It embraces faithfulness but weakness, deliverance and ordinariness. This king knows that "the king does not find deliverance [yāšaʿ niphal again] through his great army" and that "the horse is a falsehood for deliverance" (Ps 33:16-17).

As the king personally looks unlike a man of war, Yhwh's response is to declare the intent to abolish weaponry from the nation, and indeed from the world: "I will cut off the chariot from Ephraim, the horse from Jerusalem; the bow of war will be cut off and he will speak of peace to the nations" (Zech 9:10). As usual this intent is combined with the assumption that Yhwh's king in Jerusalem is Yhwh's means of ruling the whole world: "he will rule from sea to sea, from the river to the ends of the earth" (cf. Ps 2; 72). The vision of peace is at the same time a vision of empire. The fact that the king abjures Solomon's horses does not mean he abjures Solomon's imperial rule; rather the opposite. The fact that he does not ride on a horse fits with the fact that Yhwh is cutting off this military animal. Indeed, the king's abjuring the horse might even be what tips Yhwh into cutting off horses and chariots.

5.8 Renewing the Priesthood

As is the case with the monarchy, in light of its failure one might have expected that Yhwh would simply abandon the idea of priesthood, and the failures do need to be taken into account. But Yhwh abandons neither. The destruction of the temple and the exile mean that many priests are taken of to Babylon, and

---

[193]Cf. Carroll Stuhlmueller, *Rebuilding with Hope* (Grand Rapids, Mich.: Eerdmans/Edinburgh: Handsel, 1988), pp. 124-25.

[194]The description also picks up that of Judah in Gen 49:10-11 in a passage that undergirds the position of Judah as the Davidic king's clan, but the motifs there, too, describe the life of an ordinary person.

there is little ministry left to be exercised by those who escape this. But Yhwh promises that Levi in general and the high priesthood in particular will be re-established, the former standing alongside a restored Davidic leader.

A Future for Levi Alongside the Future for David

The destruction of the temple and the exile of the priesthood would look like its end. But on its eve (in the order in the book of Jeremiah), Yhwh promises that as David will not lack for a descendant sitting on the throne over Israel, so "for the Levitical priests there will not fail someone before me performing whole offerings and presenting grain offerings and making sacrifices, for all time." If Yhwh's covenant to maintain the alternation of day and night could be broken, then so could Yhwh's covenant with David, "and that with the Levitical priests, my ministers." Beyond that, Yhwh promises their spectacular increase. As the stars and the sand cannot be counted, so Yhwh will increase the offspring of David "and the Levites who minister to me" (Jer 33:17-22).

The expression "there will not fail" (kārat niphal, lit. "there will not be cut off") comes from the earlier promise to David (e.g., 1 Kings 2:4; 8:25). There are two notable differences about this reaffirmation of that promise. One is that the earlier version had conditions attached to it. It would be "if your sons guard their way by walking before me in truth" that the promise would hold. The earlier, less specific promise to David in 2 Samuel 7 also required that the king should walk thus, but it did not make that a condition of the promise. Similarly here the condition is omitted, perhaps because it is now even clearer that conditional promises do not work. That relates to the second difference, the context in which Yhwh makes this promise. These are not the high and heady days of David and Solomon but the moment of the monarchy's collapse, when it is clear that those conditions have not been fulfilled. One might therefore infer that the promise has ceased to hold. Not so, says Yhwh. The second oracle makes it clear that Jeremiah is not simply presupposing that the promise is conditional. It does that by drawing an analogy with Yhwh's most spectacular unconditional promise, that relating to day and night (not a "covenant with day and night" but a "covenant of day and night"). Yhwh unilaterally declared that day and night would not cease, and did so in full awareness that no conditions could be imposed on it because world history had already demonstrated that such conditions would not be met (Gen 8:21-22). In a similar way, in a situation where it has become clear that kings will not keep conditions, Yhwh affirms that commitment without conditions.

Even more distinctive is the extension of the promise to the Levites in general. Indeed, one could read that as the main concern at least of Jeremiah 33:17-18, as it is stated at greater length and with more specificity. Certainly this parallel commitment to the Levites is the distinctive feature of Jeremiah 33:17-22 as a whole. Jeremiah refers to the three main types of regular sacrifice: whole offerings, grain offerings and fellowship offerings (Lev 1—3). They are Israel's regular expressions of self-giving and gratitude. Their collapse would mean the severe impoverishment of Israel's relationship with Yhwh as the people were unable to offer that sacramental worship. Yhwh promises that this will not happen. They will be there to minister to Yhwh. Indeed, Yhwh expresses that with extraordinary lavishness in comparing the flourishing of David and Levi to the size of the heavenly army, the stars, or the quantity of sand on the beach. That is an unnecessary extravagance in connection with the fulfillment of the David promise. It is more to the point with regard to the Levi promise; after the exile, a shortfall in Levitical numbers was a problem (e.g., Ezra 8:15). Yes, Yhwh is committed to Levi's future.

The High Priest Forgiven

Among Zechariah's visions is one of the current high priest, Joshua, the son of Jehozadak (Zech 6:11), who was in turn son of the last preexilic high priest, Seraiah, and was taken into exile when his father was executed in 587 (2 Kings 25:18-23; 1 Chron 6:14-15 [MT 5:39-40]). Joshua himself was presumably born in exile. In Zechariah's vision (Zech 3:1-5), Joshua stands in front of Yhwh's aide, "with the accuser standing at his right hand to accuse him." It becomes clear that the accuser claims that Joshua is stained; he is therefore incapable of exercising his ministry. There might be several reasons for seeing Joshua thus. He might be reckoned personally stained by having been in exile. If a priest was rendered incapable of functioning through being in contact with a dead body, how much more must the years in a land full of images have that effect? It might be reckoned that the whole priestly leadership, indeed the whole priesthood, was irredeemably stained by its involvement in the forms of worship described by Ezekiel, which Ezekiel and others saw as the cause of the exile. If Joshua's grandfather was so involved, it would not be surprising if the same was true of his father and thus of Joshua's own upbringing.

In the vision, the accusation comes from a prosecutor in the court in heaven,[195] but it perhaps also came from other sections of the community. These might be people not tainted by exile, or people not tainted by the use of images, or people who wanted the priesthood to function again and were not sure whether it could. Perhaps it also came from inside Joshua and the other priests themselves. The accusation is not false. Joshua is covered in guilt. Symbolically, his clothes are "filthy." It is a very strong statement. The adjective *ṣôʾ* comes only here, but the related nouns refer specifically to human excrement and vomit.

---

[195]On the accuser, see section 2.2 "The Adversary." There is no particular reason to relate the scene to a specific event such as Joshua's installation to the priesthood.

"But Yhwh said to the accuser, 'Yhwh dismisses you, accuser, Yhwh the one who chooses Jerusalem dismisses you: isn't this a stick rescued from the fire?'" (Zech 3:2). Apparently Yhwh is not chairing the court but has delegated that task to an aide, and it is not clear whether the accuser has even had chance to state his case, but Yhwh dramatically intervenes. That in itself heightens the significance of Yhwh's words, as does the form of speech as Yhwh self-refers, "Yhwh dismisses you." The verb (gā'ar) is usually translated "rebuke," but that rendering is too mild and narrow.[196] The recipient of a rebuke can ignore it; when Yhwh is the subject of this verb, it has a devastating effect on the object (e.g., Ps 106:9; Nahum 1:4). In a court context, one might think of it as suggesting a judge's peremptory dismissal of a case on the basis that Joshua has no case to answer. But Yhwh does not say that, and subsequent verses will make clear that in this sense the accuser is indeed not wrong. Rather Yhwh declares that in his enthusiasm for his task the accuser has missed the point. Joshua is like something that has fallen into the fire and then been pulled out, alive but with the marks of the fire on it. The image is one that Amos used to describe Yhwh's chastisement of Israel (Amos 4:11). Israel had failed to heed the chastisement and had every right to expect it would end up in total conflagration (Amos 5:6-7). So the image of burning is no more encouraging than the image of leftovers (Amos 3:12). But like Daniel's three friends, Joshua embodies the later promise that Israel could walk through fire but not be consumed by the flame (Is 43:2; Dan 3). The accuser is focusing on the marks; Yhwh is focusing on the escape.

There is a sense in which the exiles paid for their guilt or wrongdoing through their time in exile ('āwôn, Is 40:2). There is evidently some other sense in which Joshua, at least, has not done so and perhaps cannot do so. There is no suggestion here that the fire has had a refining, purifying effect. Joshua's guilt is still there. But Yhwh bids the members of the court to take off his filthy clothes and says, "I am removing your guilt from on you" ('ābar hiphil). The verb is the one Nathan uses to David, and David then uses to Yhwh (2 Sam 12:13; 24:10; cf. also Job 7:21). The qatal declarations are performative; they effect what they refer to. Yhwh is having the filthy clothes removed by issuing an order (presumably to members of the court), and that is a sign that by the same word Yhwh is removing the guilt.

The High Priest Reclothed

Yet this verb does have somewhat equivocal implications. On both occasions Yhwh removes David's failure or his wrongdoing/guilt/punishment, yet

---

[196]It is also usually translated as a jussive, but see the comment in section 2.2 "Yhwh's Embodiment."

does so in such a way as to leave him paying a terrible price for it. The possibility of carrying ʿāwôn is built into the high-priesthood (e.g., Ex 28:38), but the ʿāwôn that Joshua carries is very far-reaching. Might Joshua and the priesthood of which he is head, too, have their ʿāwôn put away, yet still be unable to continue to act as priests?

Perhaps the instruction to remove Joshua's filthy clothes anticipates that this will not be so; certainly the instruction to replace them with fresh robes does so. The change in the noun from (regular) "clothes" to special "robes"[197] is significant. So is the further intervention in the scene by the prophet himself, who comments, "they will put a clean miter on his head." English versions take this as an intervention in the proceedings of the court, in whose meetings a prophet can take part; he now urges the putting of a clean turban on Joshua's head. In MT, however, the prophet says what will happen rather than what needs to happen.[198] Perhaps the prophet is speaking to himself. Either way, the prophet's intervention emphasizes what follows. A turban signifies a position of special authority, though the words for "clothes" and "turban" are not technical terms for the high priest's garments.[199] Joshua is set in a position of honor and authority in the community.

Yhwh brings that about as "the one who chooses Jerusalem." Whether this is so is clearly a live issue in the context, and the fact that Yhwh does choose Jerusalem is a key underlying conviction for Zechariah (see Zech 1:17; 2:12 [MT 16]). It similarly underlies the present vision, though it is hardly the main point any more than it was earlier. The accuser would be easily able to make a case for Yhwh's rejecting Jerusalem, but if that were his argument, one would expect more indication of this in Yhwh's response to the accuser. This response—and Zechariah's own words—focus on Joshua and his position as priest, while the aide's subsequent words focus on the temple itself rather than the city. Perhaps the implication of referring to the city's chosenness is that the city where Yhwh lives needs a high priest and the priesthood he heads up. Rejection of the priesthood and thus of the temple worship would imperil the position of the city.

At last the aide himself speaks, and does so solemnly. He "challenges" Joshua: the verb is ʿûd (hiphil), one that, for instance, describes Yhwh's serious confrontation of the people through the prophets before the exile (e.g., Jer

---

[197]The word mahălāṣôt comes only here and Is 3:22 and may mean "festal robes" or "white robes" (see DCH).

[198]That is, the verb is yiqtol yāśîmû; the jussive would be yāśēmû (cf. Meyers and Meyers, Haggai, Zechariah 1—8, p. 191). LXX has imperative without the "and I said"; Vg. has "and he said," followed by imperative.

[199]The word for "turban," too, ṣānip, comes in Is 3:23 (and Is 62:3; Job 29:14); the regular word for the high priest's turban is the related miṣnepet.

11:7). "Yhwh Armies has said this, 'If you go in my paths and guard my charge, yes, if you rule my house and guard my courts,[200] then I will give you access among those who go among these who stand here" (Zech 3:6-7). Typical of the biblical pattern presupposed in Jeremiah's promise to Levi, Yhwh first makes an unequivocal demonstration of divine grace in making a commitment to restore Joshua for reasons that have nothing to do with Joshua's deserve, then adds that this had better be followed by an appropriate response. Whatever had been true of Joshua personally, his predecessors had a track record of failing to fulfill their ministry in a way that corresponded to Yhwh's will. They had often led the people in worship of other deities or in worship of Yhwh that involved images. Joshua's challenge is to fulfill his ministry in light of Yhwh's instructions. It is on that basis that he must exercise authority (dîn) in the temple. And if he does that, he will have access to the court of heaven before which he stands on trial, like a prophet.

How is that significant here? Priests were often involved in prophecy, in bringing Yhwh's word to the people, and the implication might be that he will have access to the deliberations of the heavenly cabinet like a prophet to make that possible. He might then not make the kind of mistake that Nathan made (2 Sam 7:3-4). But in the context, this promise would relate more to his task of overseeing the work of the temple. There will be tricky decisions to be taken, but he will have the resources to make them.

The Priesthood as a Sign

It has been suggested that Joshua has been given a quasi-monarchic authority, perhaps in connection with questions about the relative authority of Judean temple authorities and Persian power,[201] though his rule has been specifically related to the temple. But in any case, Yhwh's aide goes on to address Joshua and "your fellows who are sitting in front of you" (Zech 3:8-10). They are apparently some council that exercises authority in the community, perhaps priests who govern the temple, perhaps elders who exercise authority more broadly. They are "people who are a sign that I am bringing my servant 'shoot.'" Perhaps the idea is that their exercise of power in the temple or in the community is a sign that Israel will one day have a Davidic ruler overseeing all the affairs of the people. Further, the word for "sign" (môpēt) commonly has worrying implications; it suggests something threatening that Yhwh intends to do. For the Judean people the appearance of a shoot from the felled Davidic tree will be good news (there is no indication that Zechariah identifies Zerub-

---

[200]The EVV take these two clauses as the beginning of the apodosis ("then you will rule . . . and guard . . ."); but see, e.g., Petersen, *Haggai and Zechariah 1—8*, pp. 203-7.

[201]E.g., Meyers and Meyers, *Haggai, Zechariah 1—8*, p. 196.

babel, the current such descendant of David, as this shoot), precisely because it will be bad news for the imperial authorities and for other more local pretenders to power in Jerusalem. "Shoot" and "servant" may be closely related images for a coming Davidic ruler.[202] But it is suggestive that the phrase "my servant shoot" brings together what one might see as two key competing ideas for the fulfillment of Yhwh's purpose, the shoot, to which the first part of Isaiah looks forward, and the servant, which preoccupies the later part.

This gathering is a sign because in it Yhwh is indeed reestablishing the community, and specifically (if they are priests) the temple and its priesthood. Yhwh goes on to point to a stone "that I am putting in front of Joshua, and on one stone with seven eyes, here, am I setting an inscription (message of Yhwh Armies) and removing that land's guilt on one day" (Zech 3:9). In light of Zechariah 4 we could see this as a building stone, but in the present context it must be a precious stone of the kind associated with the high priest's garments. Like other elements in the picture, it is not identical with that physical equivalent (we noted that the words for robes and miter are not the regular words), and neither is its significance. The literal high priest's accoutrements included two stones, each inscribed with the names of six clans (see Ex 28:9-12). The implication of completeness is here suggested by the stone's seven eyes or facets, but we do not know the precise implication of that feature. Those other stones were not directly related to guilt, though associated with the high priest's turban was a frontlet relating to guilt, but this was the guilt that could attach to his own person or his exercise of his ministry (Ex 28:38). Joshua's own cleansing represents an extension of such cleansing.

Now the inscribing and the removal of guilt are brought into association. While Joshua and his fellow priests need their guilt removed, that is true of the whole land. If the priesthood is defiled by exile, it is also defiled by the way it performed before the exile; and if the priesthood is defiled by the way it performed before the exile, so is the land in which priests and people lived their faithless life. The single stone suggests the removal of that guilt in a single day. The vision perhaps again takes up motifs from the story of the setting up of the priesthood, which included the prescription for an annual rite whereby all the guilt of the year was to be taken away on one day (Lev 16). After this once-for-all removal of guilt "on that day," Yhwh declares, people will be able to live a normal, regular, blessed, community life, each family with its vine and fig tree, able to invite others there. There is another nice ambiguity about this "day." Is this the day when guilt is taken away or the day when the shoot arrives? The passage could be read either way, but Zechariah may imply that the removal

---

[202]See section 5.7 "My Servant David" and "The New Shoot from an Old Tree."

of the people's guilt means they can start living a normal life. More likely he affirms that this does not have to await the arrival of the shoot.

In Zechariah 4 the prophet sees a gold lamp with a bowl and seven lights and with two olive trees above it. The seven lights stand for Yhwh's eyes ranging over the earth; the two olive trees stand for two "sons of oil" attending on Yhwh. The two sons of oil are presumably a priest and a king, or at least a priestly and a royal figure (Zech 4:14). They will thus represent Joshua and Zerubbabel, the priestly and royal leaders who otherwise appear in Zechariah and in the story of the community in Zechariah's day, in Ezra 3—6; and/ or they represent the positions these two occupy or stand for.[203] The EVV paraphrase the expression "sons of oil" as "anointed ones," and the priest and king would indeed be anointed, but the word for oil is that for fresh, newly pressed oil (*yiṣhār*), not the word for anointing oil (*šemen*), and anyway Zechariah may intend a more subtle point. Anointing involves receiving oil rather than providing it, but olive trees provide oil rather than consuming it; NIVI mg. thus translates "two sons of oil" as "two who bring oil." Their vocation is to see that the lamps shine bright: that is, that Yhwh's eyes can range over the earth. When Yhwh sees and shines light, that suggests caring and providing for the people Yhwh sees and shines on, as is explicit when Zechariah's words are later quoted (2 Chron 16:9). The two figures are means whereby that happens. It is in this connection that they (lit.) "stand above" Yhwh, like the trees standing over the lamp, and like servants who stand before their seated master and are thus above him.[204] Perhaps they do that especially by their involvement with the building of the temple, the place from which Yhwh shines out into the world. It is this, Haggai also promised, that is the key to the future of the community.

Priest and Prince

Joshua is obviously involved in the building of the temple, as Zechariah 3 has made explicit. But Zerubbabel is also involved, as Zechariah 4 has also made clear in the material that separates the recounting of Zechariah's vision from its interpretation (Zech 4:6b-10a). Yhwh declares, "Not by might and not by power but by my spirit. . . . Who are you, great mountain? Before Zerubbabel—a level place" (Zech 4:6-7). The implication may be that as governor of Judah (e.g., Hag 1:1) Zerubbabel had military forces available to him, but more likely neither Zerubbabel nor the rest of the community has

---

[203]Wolter H. Rose (*Zemah and Zerubbabel*, JSOTSup 304 [Sheffield: Sheffield Academic Press, 2000], pp. 177-207) takes them as heavenly figures, but this seems an unwarranted complication.

[204]See BDB, p. 756a.

much might or power. It is all held by other people: the authorities back in Persia, the local Persian administration, the people of Samaria and other surrounding communities, perhaps other groups within the Judean community. Fortunately Zerubbabel has the backing of the divine *rûaḥ*, the kind of divine energy that is reflected in the wind (wind to blow the mound of rubble away?); or is it the divine insight residing in Yhwh's mind? Yhwh knows how to get things done and can get things done. And as the Davidic prince, Zerubbabel can expect Yhwh's spirit to be involved with his work in either sense (e.g., Is 11:1-5), and as the exodus people, the community can also expect that (cf. Hag 2:5).

The fact that Zerubbabel would neither be able to see how to undertake the building nor have the resources is therefore not a problem. Yhwh can turn a mountain into a plain, even turn a mountain of rubble on the temple site into a platform for rebuilding. "He will bring out the first stone;[205] there will be shouts of 'Beautiful, beautiful'[206] at it. . . . It is the hands of Zerubbabel that have founded this house, and it is his hands that will complete it" (Zech 4:7-8). A day will come when he completes the building, and people who are currently just horrified at the mess will be thrilled at the beauty. Whereas people might read accounts of the splendor of the First Temple's building and of the great things that Yhwh had done in the past (e.g., Deut 10:21)[207] and feel that their own time was a day of small things, they are going to see Zerubbabel undertaking the ceremonies involved in a great building project and they are going to rejoice.

It would not be surprising if there were tensions and rivalries between the priestly and royal leadership in the Second Temple community, and these have been seen under the surface of the text of Zechariah. The chapters themselves set the two leaderships alongside each other and see both as means of Yhwh's blessings flowing out from the sanctuary. Zerubbabel will see that the temple gets built, Joshua will see it gets properly supervised, but the priests' fulfilling their task is itself a sign that a son of David—Zerubbabel or someone else—will one day rule in Jerusalem.

Yhwh also told Zechariah to receive gifts from certain individuals who have returned from the exile community in Babylon. Out of silver and gold—presumably the nature of their gifts—he is to make a many-faceted crown and

---

[205]The EVV link *rô'šâ* with *rō'š* and take it to mean headstone, but it may rather link with *ri'šâ* and *ri'šôn* and refer to a stone from the First Temple; its ceremonial setting establishes the Second Temple's continuity with the First (cf. Richard S. Ellis, *Foundation Deposits in Ancient Mesopotamia* (New Haven/London: Yale University Press, 1968).

[206]Or more literally, "Grace, grace."

[207]Cf. Meyers and Meyers, *Haggai, Zechariah 1—8*, p. 252.

put it on Josiah's head (Zech 6:9-15).[208] Yet high priests do not wear crowns,[209] and Zechariah is instructed to accompany this crowning with a different promise: "There, a man named 'shoot.' From his place he will shoot out and build Yhwh's palace. He is the one who will build Yhwh's palace and who will bear majesty and sit and rule on his throne. A priest will be on his throne, and there will be counsel that brings well-being between them." It seems that the crown is really destined for the "shoot." The logic parallels that in Zechariah 3, where the affirmation of Joshua was a sign that Yhwh would bring "shoot."[210] Here the crowning of Joshua promises the crowning of "shoot." The link with building the temple suggests this cannot be a Messiah to come at some future time; one would assume it is Zerubbabel, though he is not named and not actually crowned. One can speculate about the reasons,[211] but the effect of distancing the designation "shoot" from a specific contemporary person is to make this promise available as a statement of Yhwh's intention that can be an encouragement to the ongoing community.

The fact that it is emphatically the "shoot" who is to build the temple might suggest that the high priest's position is being downgraded; Zechariah 4 made the high priest and the "shoot" two sons of oil, both equally involved in resourcing Yhwh's work among the people. But that may be reading too much into the promise; the prophecy also emphasizes the way their joint ministry will issue in planning for the community that issues in its *shalom* (Zech 6:13).[212]

A More Circumscribed Priesthood

Ezekiel offers another take on the issues raised by Zechariah 3:1-5. According to Ezekiel, the priests of Zadok's line did not share in the wandering away from Yhwh that characterized the people as a whole and the rest of Levi, so they are affirmed in their position (Ezek 44:15-31). Their great privilege is to "draw near to me to minister to me" and to "stand before me to bring near me fat and blood," the elements in offerings that distinctively belong to

---

[208]"Crown" is plural, but it seems to denote something put on one man's head and it is the subject of a singular verb in v. 14. I take this to be not numerical plural but plural of extension or a Phoenician-type singular, as Tg. and Syr. imply (cf. NIVI and NRSV mg.). If the word is numerical plural, there would be one crown for Joshua and one for the man who is designated "shoot" (cf. Meyers and Meyers, *Haggai, Zechariah 1—8*, pp. 349-50).

[209]The high priest had a gold medallion or frontlet (*ṣîṣ*) on his turban (Ex 28:36), but this could hardly be termed a crown.

[210]See Rose, *Zemah and Zerubbabel*, p. 46.

[211]Does it reflect the need to be discrete in relation to the authorities and/or not to encourage messianic fervor in the community? Has he been arrested? Is he dead? Or is he back in Babylon?

[212]The idea that the *ʿăṣat šālôm* refers to a harmonious relationship between priest and "shoot" seems a little bathetic.

Yhwh (Ezek 44:15). But in that connection they have to be careful to avoid the mistakes of the ministry of the First Temple. They have to maintain the distinction between the holy and the everyday in their own persons. They must thus, for instance, avoid contact with death and avoid marrying someone who would bring the everyday into the realm of the holy (that is, someone who had been married to a layman and then been divorced or widowed). To the same end, they must not carry the holy (for example, by not changing their clothes) into the area where it would affect people outside and thus make them unable to continue with their everyday lives. The distinction between God and the world must be safeguarded. And a key aspect of their task is to teach Yhwh's people about holy and profane, and clean and polluting. Beyond that, they are to fulfill the role of appeal judges, making decisions in accordance with the decisions Yhwh has made. And they are to see that Yhwh's teaching about festivals is kept and that the sabbath is kept holy. In recognition of their fulfilling these key roles, and in recognition of their not possessing land and therefore being unable to support themselves and their families, they are to be supported from the sacrifices and the offering of the first of all produce.

In Ezekiel's temple, Yhwh intends a new role for the main body of Levites (Ezek 44:6-14). It has been suggested that, notwithstanding the instructions in Leviticus and Numbers, these Levites were the ministers at sanctuaries outside Jerusalem (where worship might have been out of keeping with the Torah), who were deposed by Josiah (2 Kings 23:8-9). Ezekiel thus reaffirms their demotion, which might explain their later lack of enthusiasm for returning to Jerusalem (Ezra 8:15-20). One might have thought they would simply be cast out, but this is not what happens. They have to live with the consequences of their wrongdoing, but they are still to be "ministers [*mĕšārĕtîm*] in my sanctuary" though they are to have subordinate roles, in keeping watch at the gates to safeguard its purity and in fulfilling practical tasks (including killing sacrificial animals).[213] The origin of the distinction between priests and deacons in the church lies here. Chronicles upgrades the status of their role by describing them as taking the leadership in worship activities such as prophecy and singing. They thus take over tasks that in other frameworks could be undertaken by laymen or by foreigners. The Torah allocates no land to the clan of Levi and thus makes the Levites dependent on provision by the people. Ezekiel 45 allocates them land, as it allocates land to resident aliens, making them more secure and able to work for their own future rather than being dependent on "charity."

---

[213]Cf. Iain M. Duguid, *Ezekiel and the Leaders of Israel*, VTSup 46 (Leiden: Brill, 1994), pp. 58-87.

Levi Purified

The issues surface again in the prophecy of Malachi, who threatens dismissal
and shame for the priests of his day (Mal 1:6—2:9) but then speaks of a purifying of this priesthood. The people have been lamenting the fact that Yhwh is
not acting decisively in their world for the cause of right. Yhwh replies (Mal
3:1-4) by declaring the intention to send "my aide," later described as "my covenant aide"; both titles hark back to Exodus 23:20, 23; 32:34; 33:2. This aide
"will clear a road before me," which in turn harks back to Isaiah 40:3-5 with its
talk of Yhwh's returning to Jerusalem.[214] Then, "suddenly the Lord whom you
seek will come to his palace," the temple. The people are asking for Yhwh to
come and act, and Yhwh undertakes to do so, but they will find this a less
pleasant experience than the one they have in mind. "The covenant aide in
whom you delight: now, he is coming, Yhwh Armies has said, but who can endure the day of his coming?" The people recall those who thought Yhwh's Day
would be good news but who would discover things were otherwise (Amos
5:18-20). Back at Sinai, the leadership of the aide provided Israel with some
protective distance from Yhwh, who was personally incensed at the people's
behavior. On this occasion they will find the aide's presence as threatening as
Yhwh's own. Back at Sinai, the action of Levi had been one factor in the people's escaping a worse fate, but in this context the Levites are contributing to
the problem rather than alleviating it. Thus the people "cover Yhwh's altar
with tears, with weeping and groaning, because he no longer regards the offerings or accepts them from your hand with delight" (Mal 2:13). The situation
will get worse with the arrival of this aide. "Who can stand firm at his appearing? Because he is like a smelter's fire and like launderers' bleach. The smelter
and purifier of silver will sit and purify the Levites, refine them like gold or
silver, and they will become for Yhwh people who present offerings in faithfulness, and the offerings of Judah and Jerusalem will be pleasing to Yhwh, as
in days of old, as in past years" (Mal 3:2-4).

Experiencing his coming will now be as devastating as falling into a furnace
or a vat of bleach (lit., "potash"). But the aim of smelting or bleaching is to purify and refine, and the good news is that the aide will sit at his task purifying
and refining the Levites. Yhwh has not finished with them. They have forfeited
any right to reckon that their permanent covenant will in fact endure. But apparently Yhwh is still committed to it. Thus Yhwh's relationship with Levi
mirrors that with Jerusalem itself (cf. Is 1:24-31). The priesthood will go into
the smelter as the city once went into the smelter, but it will not be cast off, as

---

[214]It seems artificial to reckon that "aide" (both times *mal'āk*) refers to two different figures;
but see Hill, *Malachi*, pp. 286-89.

the city was not cast off; Yhwh's aim is to purify it, as it was to purify the city. Then the Levites will become people who present the community's offerings in faithfulness instead of letting them down and letting Yhwh down, as they have been doing, and Yhwh will be glad to receive these offerings. All will thus be as it once was back at the time when Yhwh first separated Levi to its ministry because of its commitment to faithfulness.

Nothing we know of in Second Temple history constituted anything quite like a literal fulfillment of Yhwh's undertaking, though it does seem that the priesthood offered faithful ministry through the bulk of the Second Temple period. Later Jews such as the Qumran community and the early Christians applied Malachi 3 to themselves, though neither saw anything that closely corresponded to what Malachi describes. Neither John the Baptist nor Jesus brought about a purging and renewing of the temple worship; it hardly needed one in the way that Malachi saw a need in his day. The prophecy stands as a declaration that Yhwh was not finished with the priesthood, but neither would Yhwh simply let it continue in its unfaithful state.

The Whole People as Priesthood

There is a more radical promise, though one in keeping with Yhwh's original vision. As is the case with kingship, the first time Yhwh mentions priesthood in connection with Israel, it is the whole people that is the priesthood (Ex 19:6). Having royalty or priesthood within Israel goes back on that vision. It is explicit that Yhwh goes with the idea of royalty within Israel because Israel insists on it; the fact that priesthood is another universal among humanity suggests that the same is true of priesthood. In Isaiah 61:5-9 Yhwh affirms the original vision. Whereas foreigners will look after Israel's flocks and vines, "you will be called Yhwh's priests, you will be described as our God's ministers."

Here, as at the beginning, priesthood is not a ministry to other people, though it may be exercised on other people's behalf. Being a priesthood is not a mission Israel has to the rest of humanity, any more than Levi has a mission to the rest of Israel. The First Testament has a vision for the rest of humanity coming to acknowledge Yhwh, but it does not link that with the idea of priesthood. Two aspects of the significance of priesthood are implicit here. One is that priesthood exists for Yhwh's sake. Yhwh's priests are our God's ministers (from the verb *šārat*). As is the case in English, in a political context "ministers" are people with an important and exalted position in relation to a person such as a king; *minister* is a more exalted term than *servant/slave* (*'ebed*). Again as in English, in a religious context *minister* is a more general word than priests; all priests are ministers but not all ministers are priests. But unlike English, Hebrew uses *minister* more often to refer to service of God than to service of other human beings.

Here are people whom the prophet has just described as weak, wounded and mourning (Is 61:1-3) and who are now described as covered in shame and disgrace and also as the victims of robbery and meanness. Yhwh seeks to build up their spirits by offering them the alternative picture of themselves as priests and ministers. In theory priesthood and ministry are for God's sake and for people's sake, but in such a situation God is evidently happy that the idea of being priests and ministers should be something to build up the priests and ministers themselves. We know from elsewhere in Isaiah 56—66 that God also intends that foreigners should be within the company of priests and ministers, for the same reason, that this signifies honor in being brought right near to God and into God's service. But in this context, Yhwh encourages Israel with the idea of its being a priesthood whose service is facilitated by the people who have put Israel down and looked down on it. Foreigners can look after flocks, crops and vines; Israel can focus on its ministry. The nations will provide the resources to make that possible. Thus "their offspring will find acknowledgment among the nations, their descendants in the midst of the peoples; all who see them will recognize that they are offspring Yhwh has blessed." Disgrace will give way to splendor and recognition as a people Yhwh has made a commitment to. Robbery and victimization will give way to wealth and joy as they are paid their proper "wages," that is, treated fairly (Is 61:5-7).

In the church, it came to be the case that the presence of the right ministry validated the church, and the ministry came to have authority over the rest of the church. This contrasts with the idea in Daniel 7 that the "holy people" receives authority (Dan 7:27).[215] That notion is better preserved in Judaism, where rabbis do not have such a position of authority over their congregations.

5.9 Is the Vision the End?

We have seen that the end presaged in the First Testament's nightmare is never the actual End. Mercifully, the events that take place are not as far-reaching as one might have expected; they do not involve total destruction. Nor are they as final as one might have expected; it transpires that there are further events to follow the end.

Something analogous is true of the First Testament's vision, though the differences between a nightmare and a vision make for differences in the dynamic of this process. If the nightmare had been fulfilled in all its horror, this would have excluded continuation. There is no continuation after termination. On the other hand, if the vision had been fulfilled in all its glory, this would not have excluded ongoing life; indeed, it would have required it. There can

---

[215]Moltmann, *The Coming of God*, p. 182. See section 5.4 "A People with Its Head High."

be continuation after fulfillment. This End is also a beginning. When Yhwh has brought to fulfillment the creation project, we can all sit under our vine and our fig tree and live happily ever after. (In Christian faith, thinking about the ultimate End has often been dominated by the theme of a final judgment; the ultimate End is a threat one needs to be wary of. In First Testament faith, thinking about the interim end is dominated by the notion of calamity, but thinking about the ultimate End is dominated by the theme of restoration, renewal and the fulfillment of that creation project.)

The actual nature of the end that came in First Testament times (and in Christ) opens up another set of questions about the end and afterward. It is a cliché of Christian talk about the End to speak in terms of the "already" and the "not yet." This model for understanding the fulfillment of God's purpose derives from the First Testament, where a consistent pattern has Yhwh making declarations about an imminent end that then both does and does not come. Yhwh's day arrives, but it also remains a future expectation. The end comes in the sense that Israel experiences some cataclysmic calamity or marvelous deliverance; it does not come in the sense that neither event is as ultimate or as final as the declaration ahead of time would have made one expect. The interim end is not the ultimate End. There is thus an "afterward" following on each interim end, as well as an "afterward" to follow on the ultimate End.

More surprisingly, there is a further sense in which the End may not be the end. Even when the prophets' promises have been fulfilled, there can be a new crisis that emerges not from considerations related to Israel's own life, but from Yhwh's wider purpose.

A Return Still to Come

So prophets promise the End, but what comes about is *an* end rather than *the* End. Ezekiel and Second Isaiah paint wonderful portrayals of the physical and moral recreation of the people, and Cyrus indeed encourages Judeans to go home and rebuild the temple in Jerusalem and thus give their relationship with Yhwh a new start. But nothing turns out as wonderful as such prophets had implied. Relatively few people return and Judah remains only the size of a county, surrounded by semihostile neighbors. In some sense Yhwh returned to Jerusalem in 537 and has been present among the people there. Yet Isaiah 40:1-11 spoke of a coming with vast flocks in a splendor that all flesh could see, and such a coming has not happened.

So a decade or two after the Judeans are free to return to Jerusalem, Zechariah hears a heavenly aide ask, "Yhwh Armies, how long will you not have compassion on Jerusalem and on the cities of Judah, with which you have been enraged now seventy years?" (Zech 1:12). Yhwh answers with comforting words to the aide, who then declares: "Yhwh Armies has said this: I feel a huge passion for Jerusalem, for Zion." Such strong feelings promise action. Now it is the rebuilding of the temple and the city that will be the sign and outworking of Yhwh's return there (Zech 1:16-17). Further, prophets therefore also speak of another new exodus. "On that day the Lord will increase his hand, a second time, to get the leftovers of his people that are left over, from Assyria, Egypt, Pathros, Sudan, Elam, Shinar, Hamath, and the coastland of the sea," raising an ensign over the nations to gather scattered Israel and Judah from the four corners of the earth (Is 11:10-14). Yhwh's extending or raising a hand[216] a second time suggests two sorts of link or contrast. There is a contrast between this raising of the hand and Isaiah's repeated references to Yhwh's hand being extended to punish (Is 5:25; 9:12, 17, 21 [MT 11, 16, 20]; 10:4). Similarly Yhwh's raising an ensign to the nations in connection with restoring Israel contrasts with the raising of an ensign to the nations in connection with that punishment (Is 5:26). There is also another contrast, with the raising of a hand and an ensign in connection with Israel's restoration on the eve of the fall of Babylon (Is 49:22). Metaphorically speaking, hand and ensign had been raised and the Persians had made it possible for Judeans to go home, but most had not done so. Yhwh needs to do the same thing again, and somehow more effectively, in such a way as to affect not only Judeans in Babylon but others all round the Middle Eastern and Mediterranean regions, and Ephraimites too.

To use other imagery, on the eve of the fall of Babylon a heavenly voice commissioned the building of a highway for Yhwh's return to Judah, with many Judeans returning with Yhwh (Is 40:1-11). But the fact that many had stayed and that Yhwh's people were also scattered more broadly meant the need of another highway. Isaiah 11:15-16 thus goes on to promise that "Yhwh will dry up the tongue of the Egyptian sea and raise his hand over the River with the power of his wind; he will break it into seven wadis, make a way for crossing in sandals. There will be a highway for the leftovers of his people that are left from Assyria as there was for Israel when it came up from the country of Egypt." This highway will overcome not only the mountain obstacles but also the river obstacles, in the manner of the first exodus when people had crossed the Red Sea dry-shod. And the Persian period indeed saw further returns to Palestine, even though the worldwide dispersion of the Jewish people also increased over the centuries rather than diminished, and any return of Ephraimites was very nominal.

Nor is that the only need. During the Persian period, Ezra and Nehemiah show how the country of Israel is characterized by recurrent conflict between the Persian provinces of Judah, Samaria, Ashdod, and Edom, with Moab and

---

[216]"Increase his hand" is an odd expression and the text may be faulty, but the general meaning is clear.

Ammon also involved. Isaiah 11 is more positive than the *realpolitik* of Ezra-Nehemiah in its vision of Judah and Samaria/Ephraim living in peace. It also sees them as able to regain Israelite control of areas currently controlled by those other peoples (Edom, for instance, controlled an area that included Hebron, traditionally part of Judean heartland), which by the end of First Testament times largely did come about.

A Last Act of Praise

The confession that follows in Isaiah 12 suggests the nature of the praise and prayer that fits this dynamic. The chapter gives people a song they will sing "in that day." In LXX the song looks back from the moment of complete fulfillment: "I will confess you, Yhwh, because you were angry with me, and you turned your anger and you had mercy on me." But in MT the song declares, "I will confess you, Yhwh, because you have been angry with me; may your anger turn so that you comfort me." Here there is an ambivalence that corresponds to an ambivalence in the different position it presupposes. It speaks from a perspective like that assumed by Zechariah, when the people have experienced a form of restoration but still live under Yhwh's wrath (cf. Dan 9:16) and still need Yhwh's comfort (cf. Is 61:2; 66:13). In that context, they make declarations about Yhwh's being their deliverance and about their trusting and not being afraid (of peoples such as Samaria, Ashdod and Edom whose pressure gives reason for fear). These declarations are encouraged by the experience they have had of Yhwh's deliverance, occasions when Yhwh has proved to be "my strength and my might" (or "my song," the more familiar meaning of *zimrāt*). On the basis of these they look forward to a sense of joy that will replace the awareness of being objects of divine anger. Then "you will draw water with joy from the fountains of deliverance." They will indeed experience something like another exodus, which was an occasion when deliverance and the provision of water were necessarily interwoven; no water, no completion of that deliverance (see, e.g., Ex 15:22-27; 17:1-7).

The second half of the song resumes the beginning but goes on to elaborate on the praise that will be possible on that day. People will call on Yhwh's name in worship and gratitude as Abraham did on arriving in the land (Gen 12:8). They will testify to other peoples of Yhwh's deeds so that these deeds are acknowledged throughout the world, among nearby peoples who are currently a threat and further off, more powerful nations that have been a threat in the past (cf. Is 11:11-16). They will proclaim that Yhwh's name "stands on high," in keeping with the declaration Yhwh made long before (*śāgab* niphal; Is 2:11, 17). They will sing of the way Yhwh's majesty (*gē'ût*) is thus definitively established and human majesty is put in its place, not least that human majesty that pretended it could achieve restoration when Yhwh's mind was still set on rebuke (ga'ăwâ, Is 9:9 [MT 8]). They will be full of enthusiastic noise in the manner of a royal procession or a football crowd at how great is Yhwh in Zion's midst (gādôl), putting in its place human greatness (gōdel, Is 9:9 [MT 8]; 10:12). Ambiguity will be resolved. The LXX's version of the song will be possible.

Israel's Responsibility

The last chapters of Isaiah presuppose a similar context to Zechariah, and Isaiah 59 again answers questions; here they look more overtly questions addressed to Yhwh in the community's prayers. Is Yhwh's hand too short to deliver us, in the way it acted at the exodus? That is, can Yhwh not reach us from the palace in the heavens anymore? Or does the problem lie somewhere behind that? Is it that Yhwh's ear is too heavy to listen? That is, is it too much trouble for Yhwh to bend this way so as to be able to hear us, and therefore take action? (There is an irony about this image, which in its other two occurrences in Isaiah 6:10 and Zechariah 7:11 describes Israel's own unwillingness to listen to Yhwh.) Why does there seem to be a separator that stops Yhwh paying attention to us? Why do we seem to be refused permission to come before Yhwh with our pleas? Why does the kind of decisive action that will express Yhwh's faithfulness to us never actually come about? Why does our life as a people continue to be lived under dark clouds rather than in the bright clear light that follows a storm? The tone of the questions is that of the prayers in the Psalms, but the language is that of Isaiah 40—55, so that the questions are asking why those promises of decisive action that would express Yhwh's faithfulness (i.e., mišpāṭ ûṣĕdāqâ) have not come true.

No, it is not a problem about Yhwh's hand or ears, but you are right that there are things separating you and Yhwh from one another (Is 59:2). The language is ironic, because separation is usually a positive idea in the First Testament. It denotes the secure separation written into creation (for example, that of light from darkness), the privileged separation of Israel from other nations and of Levi from the other clans, and the privileged separation of clean from stained that contributed to Israel's embodying its separation in its life. But now a negative kind of separating has come into being, a separation that divides the people of God from God rather than enabling the people of God to be the people of God. It was Israel's job to make separations, but now it has done so by its wrongdoing rather than by its commitment to Yhwh, and the effect is the opposite to the intention of Yhwh's making of separations and Yhwh's instructions regarding separation.

In Christian talk, the notion of sin separating people from God has become a way of summing up the problem to which Christ is the answer. Such reapplication of scriptural ideas is fine, except for the danger that it obscures the actual point that Scripture makes. The problem of sin causing a separation is a problem about the church, not about the non-Christian world. It refers to the way the church comes to be identified with the world and thus on the wrong side of the separation distinction, looking from a distance at what it is supposed to be, but separated from that. It finds that God's face is turned away to avoid listening to its prayers.

It is for this reason that Yhwh's promise of decisive faithful action does not come true and that the people of God live in gloomy darkness rather than bright sun. But this does not mean there are no prayers to be prayed. A prayer acknowledging how things really are occupies Isaiah 59:9-15a; I take it as one devised and prayed by the prophet on the people's behalf, one they are invited to pray. It acknowledges that the reason there is no *mišpāṭ ûṣĕdāqâ* in Yhwh's relating to the people is that here is no *mišpāṭ ûṣĕdāqâ* in the people's own life. The people have failed to hit or even aim at the targets Yhwh sets, rebelled against Yhwh's authority to determine the policies of the people of God, deliberately turned from the path Yhwh set in front of them. They have on their hands the blood of people whose death they have caused as a result of the fraud practiced in the community, the extortion and the treachery that robs people of their livelihood. If these are present, their seeking of God is a pretense. It masks an actual turning away from God, even though people believe they are turning to God and seeking God. And this is not merely a problem affecting a small number of people. In chilling words, the prophet declares that there is no place for truthfulness in the public square, in the realm of law, commerce and government, and that the fool who tries to behave honorably only gets taken advantage of.

In general, this critique is rather conventional and echoes that of earlier prophets; it has even been suggested that this is a piece of earlier prophecy reworked into the part of Isaiah relating to the time after the exile. But that helps to make the dreadful point: Nothing has changed. Only if it does change can they expect Yhwh's vision to find fulfillment.

Eventually all the nations are to flock to Zion to learn from Yhwh and seek Yhwh's government. That is the vision for future days, *'aḥărît hayyāmîm*, the future we cannot discern because it lies behind us.[217] But if we are to see it arrive, in the meantime our task is to "walk in the name of Yhwh our God" (Mic 4:5).

A Last Great Battle

In the introduction to section 5.9 we noted three senses in which the end is not the End. One is that it is the beginning, the start of the full life intended from creation. Another is that it is incomplete; there is more that needs to be done.

---

[217]Cf. Wolff, *Micah*, p. 119.

But there is a third sense in which the end is not the End. The First Testament can look beyond the proper fulfillment of its vision and see not only full life but the intervention of new calamity. One might have thought that Yhwh's restoration and renewal of Israel (Ezek 36—37) would be the absolute End, the last great event, so that from now on, Israel simply lives happily ever after. There would be no more history.

Unexpectedly, "after many days" (Ezek 38:8) there is to be a repetition of a pattern that people knew from the past (cf. Ezek 38:17). Yhwh's promises have been fulfilled, Israel has been gathered from its scattering and is living a quiet life in its own land. But then, once again fearsome hordes assemble and invade Israel from the north. They have names that recall legendary peoples in Genesis and distant peoples that readers knew of from the newspapers (or heard prophets talking about), but they are not groups that readers ever came across in real life.

Like previous fearsome hordes from the north, these will come both because they want to and because they are "appointed" (*pāqad*, Ezek 38:8). Like any invader, they come because of what they can get out of it; no invader makes war just to benefit the people it intends to "liberate." They come because they have made a wicked plan to take advantage of this settled people living a quiet life in their unfortified towns. They will transform them into spoil. But they come because Yhwh is "turning" them (Ezek 38:4), which implies they are going in another direction and were not intending to come this way. Yhwh intends to lead them off like oxen. In earlier centuries Yhwh would have been making use of the northern hordes' instincts in order to chastise Israel for its wrongdoing, but there is nothing to chastise them for now. Yhwh is bringing them simply in order to triumph over them and show who is God. "I will bring you to my land so that the nations may acknowledge me as I show myself holy through you before their eyes" (Ezek 38:16). The destruction will be so great, the weaponry will provide Israel with firewood for seven years (Ezek 39:9-10). The dead will be so many, it will take Israel seven months to bury them all to make sure the land is not affected by the pollution of their unburied corpses (Ezek 39:11-16). At the same time, all the land's birds and wild animals are invited to come and eat the flesh off all these bodies, as at a sacrificial meal (Ezek 39:17-20). "I will put my splendor among the nations, and all the nations will see my decision that I executed and the power that I had among them" (Ezek 39:21). Israel itself will henceforth acknowledge Yhwh as God, from that day forward, as history continues to unfold (Ezek 39:22). The End is not followed by nothing or by heaven or by something we cannot imagine, but by life lived in confession of Yhwh.

Over the centuries expositors have identified these hordes with peoples of their own day. In the second century B.C. the northern enemy was Antiochus

Epiphanes; two or three centuries later it was the Roman Empire (see the Targum and Revelation); for Luther it was the Turks,[218] and in the context of the cold war, Meshech was Moscow and its "head" ($r\bar{o}$'$\check{s}$, Ezek 38:2) Russia.[219] One can hardly fault a weak or marginalized or disappointed people for seeing the threatening major power of its day as the contemporary Gog and Magog. That is the process that continues through the First Testament Scriptures themselves into the New Testament and great theologians such as Augustine, who hold together the idea that the End has come with the idea that life carries on and new crises arise. Conversely, major powers need to see themselves as the contemporary Gog and Magog, in danger of falling for the temptation to attack peoples that are well resourced but less powerful with a view to becoming Yhwh's victims, the means of demonstrating Yhwh's holiness and power.

A Last Invasion

Zechariah 12 similarly pictures "all the nations of the earth" gathering, specifically to besiege Jerusalem and Judah, as if the sixth-century siege were being repeated. The cause is not stated; the oracle focuses on the action Yhwh takes to bring about the attackers' defeat. Historically, there was no subsequent context when a great imperial power needed to besiege Jerusalem, so one should not take the picture too literally. It is an event that will take place "on that day." The variety of images the prophet uses to describe what will happen also indicates that one should not take the picture too literally. In keeping with the proclamation of other prophets, Jerusalem becomes like a poison chalice for its attackers,[220] or like a rock that dislocates the back of people who try to lift it. Or the God of Jerusalem makes its attackers and their horses go mad or blind, and acts as a shield to the people of Jerusalem so that they stand invincible the way David always did. Or the clans of Judah are like a cooking pot in the fire or a flaming torch that sets fire to a cornfield. The tents (i.e., homes) of Judah get their deliverance first, lest they should seem overshadowed by Jerusalem itself. When all this drama dies down and the dust clears, there is Jerusalem itself still standing serene. The prophet looks beyond the present, the literal and the historical to the consummation of God's purpose when Yhwh will defeat the nations on an occasion when they again attack the city.

---

[218]E.g., Martin Luther, "Letter to Wenceslas Link," in *Luther's Works* (Philadelphia: Fortress, 1972), 49:219-21.

[219]See Hal Lindsey, *The Late Great Planet Earth* (Grand Rapids, Mich.: Zondervan, 1970).

[220]Zechariah uses a word for chalice that has a homonym meaning "threshold," and the subsequent reference to the rock points up the paronomasia: the peoples tumble as they seek to cross the threshold of Jerusalem; cf. Ben C. Ollenburger, "The Book of Zechariah," *The New Interpreter's Bible*, vol. 7 (Nashville: Abingdon, 1996), p. 826.

Thus, says Yhwh, "I will seek to destroy all the nations that are attacking Jerusalem. But I will pour out on the household of David and on the population of Jerusalem a spirit of grace and prayer for grace, and they will look to me" (Zech 12:9-10). The prophet goes on to describe at great length and in great detail the bitter wailing of the people, by clan group and by family and by sex, mourning as deep as a couple's mourning for their first and only child. But why and on whose behalf are they seeking for grace and wailing? The passage is uneven and puzzling in detail. Are they wailing about their own slain? But there has been no reference to their losses (contrast Zech 13:7—14:2), and the picture of Yhwh's action and protection surely excludes the idea that they have experienced such slaughter. Are they wailing about their sin? There is no indication of that unless we infer it from the separate oracle that follows (Zech 13:1). Are they wailing about a particular person who has been slain, such as the Messiah (cf. Jn 19:37, which reinterprets the text in light of what happened to Jesus)? But there has been no reference to such an individual's death. Are they wailing about the people they have slain among the nations? But there has been no reference to their actually slaying anyone. Are they wailing more generally about the slaughter among the nations, inspired by Yhwh to urge Yhwh to give up the project of destroying the nations, rather like Moses at Sinai urging Yhwh to have mercy on Israel itself? That gives the best link between the statement about Yhwh's attempt to destroy the nations and Yhwh's inspiring the people to lament, and it also fits with the "plot" of Zechariah 14.

That chapter, too, warns the city of a time when attackers will assail it, but its scenario is a tougher one.[221] Here it is Yhwh who gathers the nations, and they will capture the city, rape its women, plunder its houses and exile half its people. Traditio-historically, Zechariah 12 works with the idea of an attack of the nations on Jerusalem, to be repulsed by Yhwh (cf. Ps 46). Zechariah 14 works with the ideas of Yhwh's war against Jerusalem, which appears in the Prophets, and combines that with the idea of Yhwh's war against the nations, which appears in the story from the exodus to Joshua and in the Prophets.[222] Thus Yhwh attacks Jerusalem but then turns to defend it and attack its assailants. Elsewhere that can mean a narrow escape (as in Is 29:1-8; Ezek 38—39). Here it means the city's deliverance after it experiences terrible losses. Indeed Yhwh's attack on Jerusalem apparently involves devoting it to destruction (ḥērem, Zech 14:11), though (as in Ezek 38—39 rather than Is 29) there is no sug-

---

[221]I take Zech 14:1-11 and 12-19 as parallel descriptions of the same events, and I interweave references to the two sections.

[222]So Hanns-Martin Lutz, *Jahwe, Jerusalem und die Völker,* WMANT 27 (Neukirchen: Neukirchener, 1968); cf. Mason, "Use of Earlier Biblical Material," p. 173.

gestion that it is an act of judgment.[223] Rather, it is one of those inexplicable acts such as the Psalms refer to when they protest Yhwh's abandonment of the people. But then Yhwh will intervene, as the Psalms urge, standing like a Goliath on the Mount of Olives, splitting mountains and filling up valleys, suspending night and making water flow down from Jerusalem to east and west. Yhwh will hit the city's attackers with an epidemic (as happened to bring about the exodus) and with a panic that makes them fight each other, and the people of Judah and Jerusalem will be able to gather in all their wealth. "People will live there, there will be no more devoting to destruction, and Jerusalem will live in security" (Zech 14:11). Both the people of Judah and the nations are liberated from the prospect of Yhwh's again acting as warrior.

At that coming day "Yhwh will become king over all the earth" and "Yhwh will be one and his name one" (Zech 14:9). The context suggests that not only will Israel acknowledge "Yhwh our God Yhwh one" but that the nations will do so too. The land will be leveled yet Jerusalem itself kept elevated above this plain, in a position to draw the world (cf. Is 2:2-4). And "all who survive of all the nations who came against Jerusalem will come up year by year to bow down to the king, Yhwh Armies, and to keep the Feast of Sukkot," *the* feast, the high point of the year (Zech 14:16). It has been suggested that the fact that Yhwh is king was a special focus of the worship at this festival. It is also a plausible view that at this festival in the autumn people prayed for the rains that were needed soon to soften the ground for the beginning of the new agricultural year. Thus any nation that does not come before Yhwh at this festival will have no rain.

Postexilic Judah is a tiny community, but "smallness enables a people to dream greatness."[224]

The Millennium

The notion that the restoration could be followed by a further crisis and deliverance may be one background to the idea of a millennium. In some respects the First Testament way of thinking (the actual word *millennium* does not come in the First Testament) has a quite different significance (or rather, a number of different significances) from that of the Christian idea of the millennium (or rather, the various Christian ideas),[225] but in other respects it is suggestively similar.

We have noted that an important background to this way of thinking is the fact that the restoration from the exile was much less complete than one would

---

[223] Against, e.g., Mason, "Use of Earlier Biblical Material," pp. 172-200, whose treatment involves reading between the lines to see, e.g., the Mount of Olives as signifying a place of false religion. Contrast Meyers and Meyers, *Zechariah 9—14*, e.g., pp. 418-21.

[224] Stuhlmueller, *Rebuilding with Hope*, p. 157.

[225] See Moltmann, *Coming of God*, pp. 134-68.

have expected. Further, this act of God did not include the final putting down of the superpowers or their coming to acknowledge Yhwh. Not only is Assyria succeeded by Babylon, and Babylon by Persia, Persia is succeeded by Greece. Thus Daniel 7—12 promises a final overthrow of the sequence of earthly superpowers, to be succeeded by a superpower of heavenly origin. Here the martyrs will be brought back to life and able to share in glory on earth. The New Testament vision of a millennium that follows the destruction of the superpower, during which Christ and his martyrs reign on earth, recasts that promise. The millennium—a thousand years, perhaps because it constitutes the last day of the world's week (a day with God being a thousand years; cf. Ps 90:4)—precedes the new creation that has no end.

Christian thinking came to claim that the church *is* that fifth superpower, or at least that the church age *is* the millennium, or that the church age will end with the millennium. These are the "amillennial" and "postmillennial" understandings of Revelation; the "premillennial" view is that Christ will return at the end of the church age, and this will usher in the millennium. On any theory, the End thus comes after the millennium. Thus Eusebius of Caesarea declared that reign of Constantine was the moment when the saints of the Most High received the kingdom (Dan 7:18).[226] The fall of the Roman *Empire* meant that the Roman *Church* took up that position. There is a frightening irony here. In reality the church always shares in the ambiguity of the superpowers, needing to be succeeded by the real final superpower.[227]

In Christian thinking, the eternal life of the individual has often seemed more important than the final reign of God. It is doubtful whether this is so for Jesus; it is certainly not so in the First Testament. The New Testament implies that we enjoy eternal life in fellowship with other people, in the context of God's reigning over the whole creation. "So *the kingdom of God* is a more integral symbol of the eschatological hope than eternal life," though "*new creation of all things*" is even more so.[228]

It is thus appropriate that the First Testament has very little to say about the individual's resurrection to eternal life but much more to say about those more fundamental realities, the reign of God and the new heaven and earth. The detail, about the destiny of individuals, can be filled in later, in light of Jesus' resurrection. But the detail is less important than the big picture—of the reign of God, of God's purpose in creation being realized.

◆ ◆ ◆

---

[226]Eusebius "Oration in Praise of the Emperor Constantine" 3.2; cf. Moltmann, *The Coming of God*, p. 161.

[227]See section 5.4 "A People with Its Head High."

[228]Moltmann, *Coming of God*, pp. 131-32.

Promises Confirmed

Christians commonly think of Jesus as the fulfillment of First Testament promises, but the New Testament itself is much more restrained and subtle in the way it approaches this question. It does not suggest that all God's promises have been fulfilled, and subsequent history, unsurprisingly, shows that it was wise. The Messiah did not introduce the messianic age nor any restoration of Israel. Nations have not beaten their swords into plowshares.[229] The New Testament makes no such claims with regard to the vast bulk of promises in the First Testament.

On the other hand, it does declare that all God's promises find their "Yes" in Christ (2 Cor 1:20). That suggests a different perspective on Christ's significance. He does not so much fulfill God's promises as confirm them. His life, death and resurrection are the ratification of these promises. If we should be inclined to wonder whether the promises will ever come true (for centuries have elapsed since they were given), these events provide further evidence that God will fulfill them (further than the First Testament events themselves). In the gospel the promises of the First Testament find not merely their fulfillment but their own future, because in Christ God says "Yes" to them.[230] The prominence of God's promises in First Testament faith makes clear that an orientation to the future consummation of God's purpose is intrinsic to biblical faith.[231] What the New Testament adds is that Jesus is the guarantee that God will fulfill those promises, because "in him the promised kingdom of God already became present."[232] As that kingdom had been present from time to time in Israel's life, so it would be present from time to time in the church's life.

Christians are also inclined to reckon that the New Testament is the basis for reinterpreting the promises in the First Testament. It is doubtful whether the New Testament gives much basis for this view. In declaring that prophecies have been fulfilled in Christ, it often uses the First Testament in a way that has little or no link with its original meaning; the opening two chapters of the New Testament provide convenient examples. This is the way the Holy Spirit inspires its authors to gain an understanding of Jesus, but the fact that it uses the First Testament in this way does not imply that it is therefore changing the meaning of the First Testament. The First Testament still has the meaning that the Holy Spirit gave it when first inspiring it. It still sets an agenda for Jesus.

The First Testament speaks much about Yhwh's intentions for the land of

---

[229]Cf. Paul M. van Buren, *A Theology of the Jewish-Christian Reality*, 3 vols. (San Francisco: Harper & Row, 1980-1988), 2:29.

[230]Moltmann, *Theology of Hope*, p. 147.

[231]Cf. Pannenberg, *Systematic Theology*, 3:527-41.

[232]Ibid., 3:545.

Israel, the city of Jerusalem and the heavens and earth as a whole. In Christian thinking, the land of Israel, the city of Jerusalem and the heavens and earth can provide figures for what God does in the church, but this function of the promises adds to their inherent meaning; it does not replace it. God has not stopped being interested in the land, the city and the heavens and the earth. How could that be so? These promises are confirmed in Christ and they continue to invite us to look expectantly for God to fulfill them.

The pattern we have just been considering thus reappears in the New Testament. It declares that the last days have come, but once more it transpires that only the interim last days have come. Many more days are to follow before the ultimate last days. Although Good Friday was succeeded by Easter Day, this does not solve everything, and like the Jewish people, we still await the Messiah, crying out, "Come, Lord Jesus" (Rev 22:20). To put it another way, there is a sense in which we live between Good Friday and Easter Day, on "a Saturday [that] has become the longest of days."[233]

---

[233]Walter Brueggemann, *Theology of the Old Testament* (Minneapolis: Fortress, 1997), pp. 401-3; the quotation is from George Steiner, *Real Presences* (London: Faber, 1989), p. 231.

6

HUMANITY

Israel has a distinctive place in God's purposes. But it is a microcosm of humanity. It also shows us how humanity is, and/or how God sees humanity. The First Testament "is primarily not man's vision of God but God's vision of man." It is thus not so much "man's theology" as "God's anthropology." "Man cannot see God, but man can be seen by God."[1] It is a vision of relationship with God; of living in community, in family and as a self; of responsibility and wisdom; of blessing; and of suffering, mortality and limitedness.

6.1 In Relationship with God

Erhard Gerstenberger declares, "the 'I-Thou' relationship to the personal guardian deity is a fundamental human experience deriving from prehistoric times which moves the world."[2] In the First Testament, the Psalms particularly cohere with this comment as they assume such individual relationships alongside relationships with the people as a whole and with its rulers. God is interested in us as human beings and can know everything about us, our activity, our thoughts, our words and our whereabouts; there is nowhere beyond God's reach (Ps 139:1-12). It is ontologically impossible to be godless.[3] While the First Testament as a whole is for the most part the story of a people, it also portrays God's relating to families and individuals, and occasionally describes such relationships (for instance, with Naomi and Hannah). Genesis, too, may presuppose that the way God relates to people such as Adam and Eve, Cain and Abel, Abraham and Sarah, Isaac and Rebekah, and their families illustrates how God relates to other individuals, couples and families. The New Testament, at least, implies this understanding (e.g., Heb 11), and popular piety assumes it, though it is tricky to work out how to connect that with the once-for-all-time, unrepeatable aspects of God's dealings with these ancestors (e.g., Gen 22).

In the First Testament humanity is made in God's image and is addressed by God with a commission to rule the created world on God's behalf. God is committed to humanity, and humanity is under obligation to God, to serve God and serve God's world.

---

[1]Abraham J. Heschel, *Man Is Not Alone* (New York: Farrar, 1951), p. 129.

[2]Erhard Gerstenberger, *Theologies in the Old Testament* (Edinburgh: T & T Clark/Minneapolis: Fortress, 2002), p. 78.

[3]Cf. Karl Barth, *Church Dogmatics* (Edinburgh: T & T Clark, 1936-1969), III/2:141.

Humanity in God's Eyes

The Scriptures' first statement about human beings is that they were made in God's image (Gen 1:26-27; 9:6). That and that alone distinguishes humanity from the rest of creation. Since the second century A.D. the idea of the image of God has been used "in the general sense of a human destination to communion with God,"[4] but this probably has little to do with the meaning of the expression in Genesis.[5] It is an allusive statement and not one to which the First Testament returns, and it is thus unlikely to provide the key to understanding the First Testament's view of humanity. Yet it does at least imply that humanity needs to be understood in its relationship with God, and describing humanity as made in God's image has stimulated reflection on the fact that humanity is designed and destined for such a relationship.[6] That is indeed a fundamental statement about humanity as the First Testament sees it, even if exegetically it has little or nothing to do with the idea of the image of God. The broader context of the creation story makes clear that we are designed and destined for that relationship, and the rest of the First Testament presupposes it. In contrast, "modern anthropology no longer follows Christian tradition in defining the uniqueness of humanity explicitly in terms of God," but rather in terms of its relationship with the animal world.[7] That condemns anthropology to a serious shortfall in understanding. Indeed, the definition becomes harder to make on this basis. In a theological context, anthropology "asks what kind of a being it is which stands in this [i.e., creaturely] relationship with God."[8] Admittedly, in third millennium-speak the word *relationship* is an allusive one—a warm word, but one with little content, like the world *community*. It leaves unexamined what *sort* of relationship obtains between God and humanity.

The assertion that all humanity is made in God's image contrasts with the conviction expressed elsewhere in Middle Eastern writings that the king especially represents God.[9] On the contrary, the First Testament asserts, humanity is one in nature by its creation. Although the human community is characterized by divisions between king and subject, rich and poor, powerless and

---

[4]Wolfhart Pannenberg, *Anthropology in Theological Perspective* (Philadelphia: Westminster Press, 1985), p. 74.

[5]On which see *OTT* 1:102-4, and now J. Richard Middleton, *The Liberating Image* (Grand Rapids: Brazos, 2005).

[6]See Wolfhart Pannenberg, *Systematic Theology*, 3 vols. (Grand Rapids: Eerdmans/Edinburgh: T & T Clark, 1991-1998), 2:218-31.

[7]Pannenberg, *Anthropology in Theological Perspective*, p. 27.

[8]Barth, *Church Dogmatics*, III/2:19.

[9]See Middleton, *Liberating Image*.

powerful, haves and have-nots, all have in common their being the creation of one maker (cf. Prov 22:2; 29:13).[10] Many proverbs declare that being wealthy is a sign of Yhwh's involvement in your life because of your faithfulness, while poverty issues from being abandoned by Yhwh because of your faithlessness. It would be easy to infer that the wealthy therefore have no obligation to the poor, that Yhwh is the maker of the rich but not of the poor; perhaps that divide is part of the way Yhwh made the world.[11] These sayings confront that. We are all made in God's image. Our treatment of other people therefore suggests an attitude to the God who made them, for good or for ill (Prov 14:31; 17:5); the New Testament indeed appeals to our being made in God's image in this connection (Jas 3:9).

The way this designation exalts humanity is extraordinary when one considers who we are. "What are mortals that you should think about them, human beings that you should pay attention to them? (Ps 8:4 [MT 5]). Here, human beings are ʾĕnôš, humanity in its weakness, and children of ʾādām, humanity in its earthiness. To be human is to be unlike God. God stands for strength, resources, fertility, faithfulness, wholeness, eternity, wisdom. Humanity stands for limitation, poverty, barrenness, shortfall, shortcoming, mortality, ignorance.[12] So why should God give a thought to us, pay attention to us? Those words in Psalm 8 "should be followed not by a question mark but . . . with an explanation point"; the sentence "expresses boundless astonishment."[13] We have noted that the verb for "think about" (zākar) is often translated "remember" but refers to a mental activity that contrasts as well as overlaps with remembering. It denotes a purposeful activity and not one that happens by chance.[14] And it can denote reflection on the present and the future as well as the past. The second verb (pāqad) often means "to visit," either to bring good or to bring trouble; what these two activities have in common is the paying of attention and the taking of appropriate action. The psalm puts God, the heavens and humanity on a sliding scale. It has already described the heavens, the moon and the stars as merely the work of Yhwh's fingers; they are minute by that measuring scale. And by the scale of the cosmos, humanity it-

---

[10]H.-J. Hermisson, "Observations on the Creation Theology in Wisdom," in *Creation in the Old Testament*, ed. Bernhard W. Anderson (London: SPCK/Philadelphia: Fortress, 1984), pp. 118-34; see pp. 118, 120.

[11]Tomáš Frydrych, *Living Under the Sun*, VTSup 110 (Leiden/Boston: Brill, 2002), p. 128.

[12]Based on Mark S. Smith, "Like Deities, Like Temples (Like People)," in *Temple and Worship in Biblical Israel*, ed. John Day, LHBOTS 422 (London/New York: T & T Clark, 2005), pp. 3-27; see p. 21.

[13]Hans-Joachim Kraus, *Theology of the Psalms* (Minneapolis: Augsburg/London: SPCK, 1986), p. 148.

[14]Cf. section 2.6 "Motherly Compassion."

self is minute. How extraordinary that the God at the gigantic end of that scale should pay so much attention to the creature at its minute end. How astonishing that God should "acknowledge" or "take account" of human beings (*yāda'*, *ḥāšab* piel; Ps 144:3-4); the psalm underlines the point by noting how they are as insubstantial as breath and as short-lived as a shadow cast by a passing cloud.

Addressed by God

Yet more extraordinary is it that God should commission humanity to control the world on God's behalf (Ps 8:5-8 [MT 6-9]). Human beings are thus in a position that is little less than *'ĕlōhîm*. The LXX takes that to mean little less than "angels." But the declaration links with humanity's being put in a position of Godlike authority in the world, so more likely they are little less than God, crowned with a share in God's honor and glory. Like Genesis 1—2, the psalm reckons that human beings are virtually kings and queens through being put in this position of sovereignty. Indeed, it is more explicit on this, describing them as crowned with honor and glory and caused to rule.[15] This again puts in their place those who are kings and queens in the narrow sense.

Like Genesis 1—2, the psalm reckons that being human means being given a task in the world, of ruling the world on God's behalf. We are to see that the creation reaches its destiny as a place subjected to God's authority. Genesis is equivocal about how far creation was a finished event; the created world is characterized by an order, but it still needs some mastering. As people made in God's image, human beings are designed to fulfill the commission to rule the world on God's behalf and take it toward that consummation. Neither Genesis nor the psalm hints that "in the story of the human race, . . . the image of God was not achieved fully at the outset. It was still in process," so that its full actualization might be reckoned to come only with Jesus Christ.[16] Humanity really was made in God's image, even if it has not gone on to fulfill the vocation this carries with it. Nor do the devastating results of the original human disobedience mean humanity has lost its commission. The appropriate human response is indeed astonishment at how extraordinary this is, and a worshipful acknowledgment of how majestic in all the earth is the name of the sovereign Yhwh (Ps 8:1, 9 [MT 2, 10]).

Whatever the connotation of "image of God," the context of the description

---

[15]Cf. Bernhard W. Anderson, *From Creation to New Creation* (Minneapolis: Fortress, 1994), p. 121.

[16]So Pannenberg, *Systematic Theology*, 2:217, 218. Pannenberg's whole discussion well illustrates the sense in which "image of God" functions as a symbol and stimulus to thought rather than as a defined concept; cf. *OTT* 1:102.

introduces an understanding that runs through the First Testament. On one hand, the creator is the absolute lord, the God of heaven and earth, independent of the world and not susceptible to human manipulation. On the other, the creator is one who addresses and relates to humanity "as a 'Thou.'"[17] God is holy, utterly other than us, but welcomes us into relationship. Israel's theology and its rule of life were concerned to manage antinomies such as this. It is easier to believe either that God is too mighty to relate to us or is simply our buddy or daddy. Israel knew that either instinct oversimplifies God and God's relationship with us. Israel's rules about what was clean and what was taboo were concerned with "the careful management of the mystery of access, which in turn opens the mystery of life. At the center of this preoccupation is Yahweh, who is in Israel the undoubted source of life, but who cannot be lightly or directly or easily apprehended, except with the utmost care not to offend or violate."[18] It has been said that the difference between God and us is that God never thinks he is us. Humanity needs means of keeping in mind the difference between the Holy One and us. Distinguishing between the holy and the ordinary contributes further to that. Thus the sabbath is holy to Yhwh (Lev 23:2). The festivals are holy occasions (Lev 23). The meat from a sacrifice must be eaten on the day of the sacrifice; none may be kept for the next day (e.g., Lev 22:29-30).

God first relates to humanity as a "thou" in transmitting the power to procreate and fill the earth, though God also did that to the animals (Gen 1:22). Toward humanity in particular God goes on to speak to bestow authority, give gifts, explain something of the place of other living things in creation, prescribe limits and offer warnings (Gen 1:28-30; 2:16-17). God continues to relate to humanity as a "thou" when the first human beings ignore the constraints imposed upon them and decline to respect the image of God in each other (Gen 3—4). This way of relating to humanity is then nuanced by the covenant relationship God introduces (Gen 9:8-17). Just as human beings have life not because they choose to have it but because God chooses to give it, so they are in this covenant relationship with God whether they like it or not, because in origin the covenant is a one-sided commitment on God's part, imposed rather than negotiated.

Of course life and covenant are actually magnificent gifts, and insofar as the essence of being human includes being on the receiving end of God's goodness, the essence of being human includes gratitude. Indeed, "only as he thanks God does man fulfill his true being."[19] Being human involves respond-

---

[17]Walther Eichrodt, *Man in the Old Testament* (London: SCM Press, 1951), p. 30.
[18]Walter Brueggemann, *Theology of the Old Testament* (Minneapolis: Fortress, 1997), p. 289.
[19]Barth, *Church Dogmatics*, III/2:170.

ing to and reflecting the fact that God is the one who created, the one who for-gives and the one who delivers.[20]

Under Obligation

To be human is thus to be responsible to God for fulfilling the creator's com-mission. In deciding to relate to humanity on a covenantal basis, God imposed further expectations on humanity that nuance those stated in connection with the creation. There is a "transactional" dynamic to the relationship between Yhwh and humanity that confronts "all modern notions of humanness that move in the direction of autonomy."[21] "Man is not sufficient to himself, . . . life is not meaningful to him unless it is serving an end beyond itself, unless it is of value to someone else. . . . Man can be a nightmare but also a fulfilment of a vision of God."[22] This implies that the obligation God places on humanity itself issues from God's grace.[23]

The transactional dynamic also confronts the notion that human beings are defined by their rights. Rather they are defined by their responsibilities. Thus Walther Eichrodt begins his study of humanity in the First Testament by de-claring that the key distinctive feature of humanity is the awareness of respon-sibility.[24] Humanity's significance and vocation lie in obedience to God.[25] Human beings are chosen by God to be the means of executing God's purpose, and to that end have to listen to God—specifically, to God's summons.[26] Ethics is part of dogmatics, because "true man is characterized by action, by good ac-tion. . . . As dogmatics enquires concerning the action of God and its goodness, it must necessarily make thorough enquiry concerning active man and the goodness of his action."[27]

By implication, simply because God is God, God can determine what hu-manity should do. More specifically, it is the fact that God makes humanity that gives God the right to decide what humanity should do. As the maker of the world, God owns the world (e.g., Ps 95:5); you own what you make. All life, in the plant, animal and human world, comes from God and belongs to God. Even time itself belongs to God. As a symbol of all this, Israelites are to give their first sons to Yhwh, along with comparable offerings of animals and

---

[20]Cf. ibid., III/4:24-26.
[21]Brueggemann, *Theology of the OT*, p. 451.
[22]Heschel, *Man Is Not Alone*, p. 194.
[23]Cf. Barth, *Church Dogmatics*, II/2:552-65.
[24]*Man in the OT*, p. 9.
[25]Heschel, *Man Is Not Alone*, p. 205.
[26]Cf. Barth, *Church Dogmatics*, III/2:142.
[27]Ibid., III/4:3.

crops and fruit trees, and they are to hold off from using one day in seven and from farming the land one year in seven (Ex 20:8-11; 22:29-30 [MT 28-29]; 23:10-12, 19; 34:26; Lev 19:23-25). These belong ineluctably to God, and God could make any demands of them, even the sacrifice of human beings, as Yhwh (almost) did of Isaac.[28] Giving sons to Yhwh might indeed imply sacrificing them, but a subsequent instruction makes explicit that, as the firstborn of donkeys *may* be redeemed, human firstborn *must* be redeemed (Ex 34:20). The two laws thus make two principles clear: Human beings belong to God, but actually God does not require them to be surrendered in that way.

The stories of Israel's ancestors in Genesis 12—50 follow Genesis 1—11 in assuming that humanity as a whole lives under obligation, and the Prophets make the same assumption. Admittedly, beyond Genesis 1—11 the First Testament does not explicitly lay the law down to humanity as a whole. In Genesis there are many commands, but nearly all are addressed to specific people in particular contexts; there is little teaching on the content of human obligation as such. The instruction God gives within the Sinai covenant, including the Ten Words, is instruction for Israel, not for all humanity. God's command has a consistently concrete character.[29] Yet in some respects, Paul notes, Gentiles act in accordance with the Law, demonstrating that they have the law written into their thinking (Rom 2:14-15), and that fits the portrayal of and attitude to people in general in Genesis and elsewhere. God's commands in the Torah as a whole are not random and unprincipled. As Irenaeus saw it, the basics of the requirements in Exodus-Deuteronomy are an exposition of natural law;[30] this theme recurs in later theology.[31]

Work and Rest

Humanity is created to work. Having completed the work of creation, God stops working, not because of tiredness but because the initial job is done, and the ongoing task is given to the beings made in God's image who are to continue the process of subduing and ordering the earth that God has initiated. God's sabbath is humanity's working week.[32] It is now humanity's task to bring in the rule of God over the created world. Genesis 1—2 makes humanity responsible for that world as a whole and then concretely for the particular piece of land where God puts the first human beings.

---

[28]See Jon D. Levenson, *The Death and Resurrection of the Beloved Son* (New Haven/London: Yale University Press, 1993), pp. 3-17.

[29]Cf. Barth, *Church Dogmatics*, II/2:661-708.

[30]Irenaeus *Against Heresies* 4.13.1.

[31]See the discussion in Pannenberg, *Systematic Theology*, 3:58-96.

[32]Cf. Middleton, *Liberating Image*, pp. 212, 291.

Human beings live from the ground as they were formed from the ground and return to the ground. Human existence is defined not in relation to a capacity to make personal choices or in terms of personal awareness, but in connection with a relationship with ground. "Agrarian existence is fundamental, and not tangential, to human existence." It is the way we fit ourselves into the cosmic life cycle that owes its existence to Yhwh.[33] Human beings are not made simply to be in relationship with one another, but to be in relationship with the earth. We work out that relationship by growing things, making things and cooking things. When human beings give up relating, growing, making and cooking, they abandon aspects of their humanness. The answer is not to seek to introduce meaning into life by other activities such as hiking in the wilderness or visiting foreign countries or watching sports or studying theology. But neither is it simply to focus on one of the human activities, such as relating. Seeking to fulfill the higher levels of Maslow's hierarchy of needs without also fulfilling the lower ones does not work (any more than vice versa). Or rather, we must not see the "higher" needs as higher. The needs do not actually form a hierarchy. "In all toil there will be profit, but talk leads only to poverty" (Prov 14:23).

Israel is aware of other styles of life than the agrarian. While its ancestors lived from the soil, they did so with some precariousness as resident aliens. They knew that their relationship with the land was a nonideal one. In Egypt Israel lived and worked in subservience to an imperial power, and knew that this was no kind of life to live permanently. For a generation it lived a life on the move in the wilderness, but that issued from God's chastisement. Its deliverance from Egypt found its fulfillment in a life in the land, on the land. It is in living this normal human life that it models what it is like to be the people Yhwh blesses. Arrival in the land flowing with milk and honey means beginning normal life and giving thanks for being able to do so (Deut 26:1-11).[34] If most of Israel's rules for life were generated in an urban context, it is noteworthy that they nevertheless contain very few regulations for urban life. The First Testament's ideal is people living on their own land, working for themselves, growing their own crops. In Western culture we assume it is more important to own your own house and to have a good time than to grow your own crops. The First Testament makes the opposite assumption (Prov 24:27; 12:11; 28:19). The Zionist pioneers of the kibbutz movement lived in keeping with a fundamental aspect of the First Testament vision.

Looking on the gloomy side, Qohelet comments that all human effort and

---

[33]Rolf P. Knierim, *The Task of Old Testament Theology* (Grand Rapids/Cambridge: Eerdmans, 1995), pp. 196, 197.

[34]Ibid., pp. 210-11.

achievement in work issue from the desire to do better than the next person, which suggests they are pointless. On the other hand, doing nothing is stupid, since one ends up with nothing to eat. So the best thing is to settle for a handful with rest rather than aiming for two handfuls with the toil that costs (Eccles 4:4-6). The sabbath command thus points a person away "from everything that he himself can will and achieve and back to what God is for him and will do for him. . . . What it really forbids him is not work, but trust in his work."[35] It points us to God's grace, God's Yes, and to letting these have the first and the last word. It is thus a day of great joy. Given that, however, "there is nothing good for a person but eating and drinking and enabling oneself to find good in one's toil. Further, I myself have seen that this is from God's hand" (Eccles 2:24; cf. Eccles 3:12-14; 5:18; 8:15).

In this context (though not in all contexts) there is therefore a case for valuing people in accordance with their capacity to make the farm work. Thus if someone vows to give Yhwh the equivalent of the value of a human being, a male between the ages of twenty and sixty is worth fifty shekels, a female thirty. For someone from five to twenty years, the figures are twenty and ten shekels. For someone from one month to five years, they are five and three shekels. For someone over sixty, they are fifteen and ten (Lev 27:2-7).

In other contexts, all human beings are to be treated in the same way. One human being cannot take the life of another, and someone who does so pays with their own life; rich people are not to be able to buy themselves exemption by offering monetary compensation (Num 35:30-34). After all, the victim was made in God's image; the murderer has attacked God (Gen 9:5-6). Conversely, the Torah does not allow for capital punishment in connection with theft. Nor does it allow for vicarious punishment: for example, killing someone's child when their parent has caused the death of a child (see, e.g., Ex 21:31; Deut 24:16). In these respects, the Torah contrasts with some Middle Eastern law codes.[36] The only exception to the rule about capital punishment for killing someone relates to homicide by willful negligence (Ex 21:28-32). Then, the requirement of capital punishment does apply to an animal that "willfully" kills a human being. Another theological framework is operating here;[37] indeed, one can see several principles operating. Alongside the sense that death requires reparation, so that a death requires a death, is the sense that allowance should be made for the degree of responsibility or intent.

---

[35]Barth, *Church Dogmatics*, III/4:53, 54.

[36]Cf. Moshe Greenberg, *Studies in the Bible and Jewish Thought* (Philadelphia: Jewish Publication Society, 1995), pp. 30-38. But see Bernard S. Jackson's critique, *Essays on Jewish and Comparative Legal History* (Leiden: Brill, 1975), pp. 34-62.

[37]Though again see Jackson, *Essays in Jewish and Comparative Legal History*, pp. 108-21.

Service

Humanity's relationship with God is that of servant to master. It is an honorable position; made in God's image, human beings are not merely "powerless and insignificant servants of the gods," as Babylonians may have been encouraged to believe.[38] They have a significant position in the world and a significant task to undertake. As their master, God commissions, provides and protects; as servants, human beings do not do what they like but seek to fulfill God's expectations. Being created to be servants of a kind master also implies a deep security; human beings are not designed to serve any human master.

But "man is born free, and yet we see him everywhere in chains."[39] The "everywhere" includes the beginnings of Israel as a nation, in a "household of slaves" (e.g., Ex 20:2)—in this case, state slavery or serfdom. Yhwh was against slavery. Paradoxically, this does not exactly mean that Yhwh was for freedom. Yhwh's aim was to restore this people from their service of Pharaoh to their proper service of God. Leviticus 25:42 notes the inconsistency between the fact that Israelites are Yhwh's slaves (as people whom Yhwh brought out of Egypt) and the idea that they might sell themselves or be sold (the niphal verb might be understood either way) "as slaves are sold" (NRSV; lit., "[by] the selling of a slave"). "It is to me that the Israelites are slaves, as people whom I brought out from the land of Egypt" (Lev 25:55). "Every one of us has heard the Voice; every one of us has received the divine gift of freedom at Sinai. This is why no one has the right to sell himself into slavery."[40]

It follows that the First Testament places limits on the extent to which human beings can be ʿăbādîm to other human beings. It does not involve the lifelong ownership of one person by another, which makes owners free to do what they like to this person who is their chattel. These limits usually make it misleading to translate ʿebed "slave"; the word is normally closer to meaning "servant" or "[indentured] laborer." Thus while Exodus 21 begins by assuming that people do buy ʿăbādîm, it focuses on regulating the practice by offering the laborer some protection (compare the sabbath law, Ex 23:12) without so weighting the arrangement in favor of the laborer that no one would ever take one on. What it allows is only short-term indentured service, which comes about because someone gets into serious economic difficulty (for instance, through crop failure) and pays for help with their labor. Hammurabi's Code allowed for only three years' such service, which limited the amount of help a person in difficulty could receive; the First Testament allows for up to six

---

[38]Middleton, *Liberating Image*, p. 230.

[39]The opening words of chap. 1 of Jean Jacques Rousseau, *The Social Contract* (reprint, New York: Hafner, 1954), p. 5.

[40]Abraham J. Heschel, *God in Search of Man* (reprint, New York: Farrar, 1986), p. 215.

years. Israelites can have permanent foreign servants (Lev 25:44-46), though again it might be misleading to call them slaves; Abraham's servant (Gen 24) would be an example of someone in this position. Proverbs speaks of servants only in the singular and suggests that a "modest" household might have just one.[41]

As well as serving God (*'ābad*) by its actions in the world, humanity serves God by its actions in worship (Ex 23:25; Ps 100:2), for instance, in observances such as a pilgrimage festival (Ex 10:7, 8, 11, 24, 26; 12:31) and related observances such as Passover and Unleavened Bread (Ex 12:25-26; 13:5), and in sacrifices and offerings (Is 19:21, 23). It also honors God by its words. Once again this applies to the words in the world by which it testifies to Yhwh. It also applies to the words it utters in worship as it declares its praise of God, its trust in God, its protest and plea and trust when it is in need, and its thanksgiving when God has acted in response to such protests and pleas. While most of the First Testament's references to worship in action and in word relate to Israel, such worship antedates Israel. In the world's story it begins in Genesis 4:3-4. As God starts the world's story over, it begins again in Genesis 8:20-21. In the story of Israel's ancestors it begins in Genesis 12:7-8. And the First Testament also often refers to other nations "serving" their gods. Neither Israel nor other peoples needed to be told that they should worship; worship is built in to being human. Israel worships in fulfillment of a vocation that applies to all humanity.

Of course the worship of other nations falls short—as does the worship of Israel. People fail to keep hold of the awareness of God and of what God's service looks like, both in worship and in the rest of life. People start killing their children in the name of worship.

6.2 Community

The opening pages of the First Testament recognize a sequence of expressions of human community: the one-to-one relationship of a man and a woman (Adam and Eve), the nuclear family (Adam and Eve and their sons), the extended family (Noah and his wife, his sons and their wives—actually called a "household"), then peoples and nations (Gomer, Magog, Sudan, Egypt, Elam, Asshur and so on); it also speaks of Cain building a city, which points to the city as another expression of human community. Human experience is intrinsically communal as well as intrinsically individual. Different cultures have emphasized one or other of these expressions of community; the rest of the First Testament takes up all of them and does not suggest that we should give

---

[41]R. N. Whybray, *Wealth and Poverty in the Book of Proverbs*, JSOTSup 99 (Sheffield: JSOT Press, 1990), pp. 42-44.

value to one over the others. God's purpose is worked out and frustrated through individuals, couples, households, families, cities and nations. Key First Testament values such as commitment, compassion and love are nurtured, expressed, discouraged and ignored in them all.[42]

The Communal Nature of Humanity

The First Testament thus emphasizes the corporate nature of human existence and experience.[43] Without implying that the individual does not count or compromising the notion of individual responsibility, it never thinks of valuing the individual over the community. Our identity lies as much in being members of communities as it does in being individuals. It is not the case that individual persons are the only realities. Family, village, city, culture and nation, for instance, are as real entities as the individuals who belong to them. What I am is shaped as decisively by my membership in these communities as it is by my personal genes and attitudes. The acts for which I am responsible are not just my acts as an individual; they are also the acts of my community: for instance, when my nation makes war, or how my city treats the homeless, whether I agree with the policy or not.

The First Testament attitude thus contrasts with that of Western culture, which instinctively thinks of humanity in terms of individuals. Here, each of us is

> a bounded, unique, more or less integrated motivational and cognitive universe, a dynamic center of awareness, emotion, judgment, and action organized into a distinctive whole and set contrastively both against other such wholes and against its social and natural background.[44]

It is "a rather peculiar idea within the context of the world's cultures."[45] One might therefore contrast the Western view with the "Mediterranean" view. The latter emphasizes, for instance, sociality and group orientation rather than autonomy and individualism; duty and loyalty to group belonging and group decisions rather than rights and duties to experiment and change individually and socially; consensual decision making rather than majority

---

[42]Contrast, e.g., Gerstenberger's emphasis on the family, *Theologies in the OT*, pp. 85-86.

[43]I here invert the common critique of First Testament thinking noted by Walther Eichrodt, *Theology of the Old Testament*, 2 vols. (London: SCM Press, 1961, 1967), 2:231; rather cf. Walther Zimmerli, *The Old Testament and the World* (London: SPCK, 1976), p. 107. We should not allow recognition of the weaknesses in H. Wheeler Robinson's *Corporate Personality in Ancient Israel* (Philadelphia: Fortress, 1964) to obscure the importance of his insight.

[44]Clifford Geertz, *Local Knowledge* (New York: Basic, 1983), p. 59; cf. K. C. Hanson, "Sin, Purification, and Group Process," in *Problems in Biblical Theology*, ed. Henry T. C. Sun et al. (Grand Rapids/Cambridge: Eerdmans, 1997), pp. 167-91; see p. 169.

[45]Ibid., pp. 171-72.

voting; respect for hierarchy, seniority and family rather than efficiency, ability and success; family/group success, achievement and respect by others for the group rather than individual success, achievement, self-actualization and self-respect; maintaining honor and avoiding shame rather than avoiding guilt; preserving face rather than preserving self-respect; encouraging children to think in terms of "we" rather than "I."[46]

The fact that the First Testament shares an inclination to the latter profile rather than the former might simply have been an aspect of its culture that does not carry normative theological authority, like ways of speaking of human nature such as *nepeš*.[47] But in fact it seems to do justice to the nature of human existence as corporate as well as individual; our own culture half-acknowledges that it does point to an aspect of being human that we have neglected to our peril. And the latter profile fits with the nature of Christian faith, where being a Christian means being grafted into the corporate body of Christ, the fellowship of the Holy Spirit, as well as having an individual relationship with Christ. If Christ defines humanity, Karl Barth comments, humanness means not only being for God but being for other people. This is not merely an obligation but "something ontological."[48]

So to start trying to understand human nature without reference to a human being's relationship with other human beings, without an attitude that treats other people as neighbors, is to skew the study from the start.[49] Sin lies in a rejection of this attitude. "Israel is a community, a people, not a collection of individual selves. The conviction that personhood is shaped, nourished, and sustained in community is a central assumption that Judaism and feminism share. . . . The individual is not an isolated unit who attains humanity through independence from others or who must contract for social relations. Rather, to be a person is to find oneself from the beginning in community."[50] Conversely, there is no ideal of seeking or valuing solitariness in the First Testament. Indeed, when someone is hurt, their pain issues as much from their rejection by other people within their community as from their physical pain (see, e.g., Ps 22).

Honor

It coheres with humanity's communal nature that, like many societies, Israel

---

[46]See Hanson, "Sin, Purification, and Group Process," pp. 171-72, referring to Bruce J. Malina and Jerome H. Nehrey, *Calling Jesus Names* (Sonoma, Calif.: Polebridge, 1988), pp. 145-49.

[47]See section 6.4 "Describing the Person."

[48]Barth, *Church Dogmatics*, III/2:210.

[49]Ibid., III/2:226-27.

[50]Judith Plaskow, *Standing Again at Sinai* (San Francisco: Harper & Row, 1990), pp. 76-77.

assumes that a person should have a proper esteem and value not only in his or her own eyes, but also in the eyes of his or her community. Indeed, the former is dependent on the latter: it is hard to have value in one's own eyes if one is shamed rather than honored by other people. Honor comes from one's place in a community and family (e.g., seniority in age), one's moral and religious integrity as they can recognize it, one's deeds (e.g., acts of courage or generosity), and one's wealth (insofar as it is a sign of integrity and right deeds, of hard work and of divine blessing). Conversely, shame lies in failure to provide for one's family or to maintain its discipline, in economic failure and poverty, in faithlessness in relationships with Yhwh or with other people, and nationally, in disgrace or defeat in relation to other peoples. Admittedly, "a good name is preferable to great wealth; grace is better than silver and gold" (Prov 22:1). People do get rich by disreputable means and by trampling on other people, but a name for graciousness is more important. Avoiding shame is a source of moral energy.

Job had once been a person looked after by servants and honored by the young and the aged. That was because he took action to relieve the needs of the weak and needy, the orphan, the widow and the alien, the blind and the disabled—not least by breaking the jaw of the oppressor to wrest the prey from his teeth. His counsel was widely respected and his comfort in sorrow appreciated. He thus exercised considerable authority in the community. And he thought that this would continue forever (Job 29; cf. also Job 31).

But if one is overwhelmed by disease or defeat, this is made worse by the shame it brings. The suppliant in Psalm 13:2-4 [MT 3-5] or Psalm 25:2-3 does not want to be defeated or die, because of the shame this will mean. Someone who trusts in Yhwh for the success of the crops, rather than turning to Baal, risks not having anything to eat, but also risks shame. Shame ought rather to rest on people who are unfaithful to Yhwh or to other members of the community. Conversely, deliverance means not merely restoration to life but the shaming of one's attackers: "They will be shamed and will shake in dismay greatly, all my enemies" (Ps 6:10 [MT 11]). "When a faithless person comes, shame also comes" (Prov 18:3)—shame for the victims and/or in due course for the faithless person. "Someone who robs his father and evicts his mother is a son who acts shamefully and disgracefully" (Prov 19:26).[51] The first colon is internally parallel and will thus refer to robbing and evicting both parents, and the son will be a married man with a family of his own for whose sake he acts in this fashion.

In First Testament thinking, shame pertains to our relationship with other

---

[51]In the context I take the hiphils as declarative.

people, guilt to what we are in ourselves. In theory this might mean that if no one else knows the wrong I have done, I will feel no shame; yet it may more likely mean that I know I have lost my honor as a member of the community, even if they do not know. And/or I may be aware of guilt and may not be able to live with myself, even if I can live with other people. Even if no one knows, I do. Conversely, I may believe I am guilty of no wrongdoing, yet know that I have contravened community standards, and thus experience shame (homosexual or adulterous acts, for instance, may match this configuration). In that connection, psychologists may be inclined to see shame as a more elemental emotion than guilt; perhaps we feel that basic shame in relation to the judgment of an "internalised other, . . . the embodiment of a real social expectation."[52]

How the Community Makes Life Work

By its bestowal of honor and shame, the community buttresses the way life works. "The mention of faithful people becomes a blessing, but the name of faithless people—rots" (Prov 10:7; the line comes to a powerful ending with that verb). The NIV and NRSV imply that this comment relates to the "memory" of people ("mention" is *zēker*) and thus to their reputation after their death, but there is no need to limit it to that. More likely the proverb offers a promise and a warning to people that relates to them while they are alive (as it did undeservedly to Job; cf. Job 29—30). Faithfulness makes you the kind of person who becomes a standard for blessing that people invoke, while faithlessness makes you the kind of person that people despise. The community's ethos thus reinforces the impetus to faithfulness and the disincentive to wrongdoing. The point may be expressed in the terms of wisdom: "People are praised for their good sense, but one who is perverse in thinking comes to be despised" (Prov 12:8). "People who walk in integrity walk safely, but people who make their ways crooked get recognized" (Prov 10:9). It matters to us what others think of us. We vary in what group we care about, but every normal person has a group of people whose acceptance and approval they need. There is honor even among thieves, and when someone lets their fellow crooks down, they get taken out.

Behind the community's attitude is the fact that "the mouth of the faithful is a fountain of life" for the people (Prov 10:11). It encourages the flourishing of life rather than death. The preceding proverb suggests it does that by virtue of the fact that the speech of the faithful is both honest and wise—these being

---

[52]Bernard Williams, *Shame and Necessity* (Berkeley/London: University of California Press, 1993), p. 103. On the study of shame within psychological and anthropological frameworks and its application to the First Testament, see Johanna Stiebert, *The Construction of Shame in the Hebrew Bible*, JSOTSup 346 (London/New York: Sheffield Academic Press, 2002).

two sides of a coin. The wicked are concerned to deceive and do harm, and their speech is thus foolish. It is destructive of the community. The speech of the wise is life-giving.

Thus "when the faithful do well, the town exults, and when the faithless perish, there is acclamation" (Prov 11:10). That fact has the potential to encourage the faithful toward persistence and the faithless toward change. Behind that is the fact that "by the blessing of the upright, a town rises, but through the speech of the faithless it is torn down" (Prov 11:11). When read in light of that previous proverb, "the blessing of the upright" suggests their experience of blessing—when they do well, the town does well (for instance, because they are generous to the poor or support civic projects?). Read in light of the parallel colon, the phrase suggests their words of blessing. The way they go around blessing people, declaring and praying for God's blessing for them, builds up the community, whereas the crooked speech of the wicked generates breakdown in the community. The succeeding sayings take that further. The speech of the faithless lacks respect for other people; it perhaps involves speculating about the wrongdoing that has issued in their misfortunes.[53] In particular, it has no respect for their confidences; they sow distrust.[54] The upright are people who can keep their mouths shut in both connections (Prov 11:12-13). Why should people need to have secrets? Proverbs recognizes that people sometimes feel the need. Paradoxically, the community needs its members to respect such boundaries if it is to function properly.

Sense and Sensitivity

Proverbs' attitude to the poor has an equivalent dynamic as it both commends concern for the poor and warns against going surety for debts. Sometimes the two appear in different contexts: for instance, the commendation in Proverbs 19:17; 28:27; and the warning in Proverbs 6:1-5; 11:15. But the sages did not always keep them apart as if they had not noticed the tension between them. Proverbs 22:22-27 juxtaposes them and thus encourages the wise to avoid two extremes of behavior. On the one hand, there are people who take advantage of the poor, those who have no resources or power to stand up for themselves—and the passage warns other people not to do so, because Yhwh may take up their cause. But one should at least think twice before imperiling one's own position by an instinctive generosity. What good does it do to end up joining the poor yourself? Ask whether you have the means of honoring the surety before you agree to it. Some aphorisms warn about standing surety for "a

---

[53]See Roland E. Murphy, *Proverbs*, WBC (Nashville: Thomas Nelson, 1998), p. 82.

[54]Ellen F. Davis, *Proverbs, Ecclesiastes, and the Song of Songs* (Louisville: Westminster John Knox, 2000), p. 79.

stranger" (Prov 6:1; 11:15), which adds another nuance to the sayings. Perhaps they imply that one might take greater risks for another full member of the community as opposed to a foreigner who happens to live next door. And/or the warnings especially apply to loaning money as an investment, as opposed to loaning money as an act of charity.

And yet "there are people who scatter about and are increased more, and people who withhold what is right, yet end up in need" (Prov 11:24). In isolation the first colon might seems to refer to a willingness to spend in order to gain, but the parallel colon makes clear that the proverb refers to a form of scattering that has moral implications. "Those who bless others are enriched, those who refresh others are refreshed," Proverbs 11:25 goes on. It does not comment on how such generosity or an instinct to be a blessing to others, on the one hand, and carefulness and seeking to look after one's own needs, on the other, can have these paradoxical effects; it just knows that they do. Is it because of some law written into the world, or some act of God? The next saying implies a factor: "The man who withholds grain [in order to push up its value?]—the people curse him, but there is a blessing on the head of the one who sells it" (Prov 11:26). It is because of some effect the action has on the community, on the way it prays. The community needs there to be some compromise between the individual interests of the seller and the corporate interest in having grain on the market. The merchant may be tempted to make profit the key criterion for business policy, but the proverb's point is that because people are involved, self-interest includes looking to the interests of others.

Thus "a person who makes and keeps commitments [a person of *ḥesed*] benefits himself, and a cruel person makes trouble for himself" (Prov 11:17; cf. Prov 11:18-19). Paradoxically, people who think about others and behave in extraordinarily self-giving ways toward them, and/or stay faithful to them when they have ceased to deserve that, find that this rebounds on them. For instance, the people to whom they give themselves do respond, and/or other people are moved to relate to them in generous ways. On the other hand, people who think they are behaving in their own interests have the opposite experience.

The People, the Nation and the State

It is human beings as such that are made in God's image and made little lower than God, made to rule the world on God's behalf. There is no basis for believing that some peoples or nations or races are superior to others. While Israel is distinctively chosen by God, this is not on the basis of any superior qualities it has; nor does its election turn it into a superior people or make it immune to the same judgment that comes on other people. Israel needs to keep itself distinct from other peoples because that is involved in its vocation, rather than because of any inferiority of others. Nor does the equality of human beings imply any questioning or regret about the distinctive individuality of nations; if anything, in principle the First Testament rejoices in it.

On the other hand, the First Testament does not attach any distinctive positive significance to nationhood over against other forms of community. It is simply the family writ large, a symbol of the fulfillment of God's purpose to fill the world. Barth indeed comments that whereas there are commands of God that relate to marriage, parenthood and local community, there is no command of God in respect to the existence and relationship of peoples and our attitude to our own people—there is nothing sacred about peoplehood or nationhood.[55] Yet Genesis 1—12 does link God's words of blessing to nations as well as to individuals, couples and families, and Deuteronomy 32:8 associates God with the being of nations. Barth's comment looks like one that emerged from the contextual setting of his work. Yet Pannenberg's comment that the nation is about identity, community and power is also suggestive.[56] Nationhood can indeed become a substitute deity. Perhaps it is no more a locus of conflict and power play than marriage, family, local community and the interrelationships of heavenly powers,[57] but its dimensions means it can generate conflict on a monumental scale and thus become a symbol of the fact that human life is characterized by conflict. René Girard comments that "all masculine relationships are based on reciprocal acts of violence" (the first "sin" was an act of violence—see Gen 4:7), and further, that whereas we would like to believe that collective violence is an occasional aberration in the life of societies, it is more likely something written into their nature, something that once present is inherently self-perpetuating.[58]

In Israel's case, at least, the nation is a collection of clans. The First Testament interrelates these clans, so that the people as a whole is family based, the clans' elders being its government. In the context of the settlement the clans represent collections of family villages, local communities of people who were related to one another.[59] But the exodus community incorporates a mixed multitude, as the local communities incorporate resident aliens and Canaanites such as Rahab.

A nation becomes a state when it has a centralized government exercising

---

[55]Barth, *Church Dogmatics*, III/4:303; see further pp. 285-323.

[56]See Pannenberg, *Anthropology in Theological Perspective*, pp. 444-84.

[57]Cf. Kraus, *Theology of the Psalms*, pp. 125-36.

[58]René Girard, *Violence and the Sacred* (Baltimore/London: Johns Hopkins University Press, 1977), pp. 48, 81.

[59]Hence my preference for "clan" to "tribe" as a translation of šēbeṭ or maṭṭeh, since clans are related, tribes are not.

power over the nation and appropriating resources from it. In Israel, this happens with the monarchy, when Israel moves from being a people with power diffused geographically, economically and religiously to being a people with centralized power located in the king and his court, which controls politics, economics and religion. Then, in due course, and gradually, this independent state (rather, the two states that Israel becomes) loses its autonomy and comes under the colonial control of a sequence of imperial powers.[60] The First Testament is ambivalent about these developments. Theologically, in theory one might support direct divine government, without a state apparatus getting between God and humanity, but in practice this meant people "did what was right in their own eyes," not to say being at the mercy of other peoples with more centralized government. In theory, divine rule via a human king then had the capacity to conform the people's life to Yhwh's will, but in practice this meant the people doing what was right in the king's eyes and/or experiencing oppression from their own wealthy and powerful—though this may have been less true when the Hasmoneans revived the monarchy. Conversely, imperial rule was capable of being another form of oppression, but also of being Yhwh's means of fulfilling prophetic promises and of implementing Moses' Teaching.

"The Israelite people never managed to develop a political structure that matched the creativity and novelty of the culture and religion they exhibited," and even their vision for the future pictured only a revival of the egalitarian clan community or the monarchic state despite their failures. "The legacy of ancient Israel provides us with no distinctive politics and with no template for translating culture and religion into a viable polity."[61] Nor has another people improved on their efforts. Perhaps its significance is to model for us the wrestling with insoluble questions that is required of every people.

The City

Historically, the development of the city is tied up with the development of the state. Administratively, cities are necessary to the functioning of the state. They include monumental buildings such as palaces and temples. They are fortified so that they can be defended against external enemies. They presuppose or generate differentiation of roles (bakers, craftworkers, traders, etc.) but also a codependent relationship with the countryside around.[62]

If a city is "a collection of people and buildings, large for its time and place,

---

[60]See Norman K. Gottwald, *The Politics of Ancient Israel* (Louisville: Westminster John Knox, 2001), pp. 7-31.

[61]Ibid., pp. 244, 249.

[62]See Volkmar Fritz, *The City in Ancient Israel* (Sheffield: Sheffield Academic Press, 1995).

characterized by a division of labor, social diversity, distinctive activities, and a way of life,"[63] then for all their differences, there are commonalities between cities in the ancient Middle East and modern cities. In the Babylonian creation story, the city is created before humanity, and it is created for the gods' sake rather than for humanity. In contrast, in the First Testament the city slips into the story from a sidebar as a byproduct of the story of Cain, but subsequently "the topos of the city in the Hebrew Bible is huge" so that "one of the main foci of the Hebrew Bible is its focus on 'cities' or, if you prefer 'the city,'" from Genesis 4:17 to 2 Chronicles 36:23[64]—and then from Matthew 2:23 via Acts 4:27 to Revelation 21—22.

The city thus starts inauspiciously, as something Cain devises as a place of security in the land of Wandering, despite Yhwh's promise of protection there (Gen 4:15).[65] The second city-builder is Nimrod, in whose story the city becomes a place whence empire building and thus warfare issue (Gen 10:8-12). The third city-builders are the people of Babylon who want to make a name for themselves, and who succeed in a different way from the one they intended (Gen 11:1-9). The next city is Sodom, a place of violence, sexual sin and resistance to God's message (Gen 18—19). Isaiah 24—27 portrays the desolation and destruction of "the city" (Is 24:12; 25:2; 27:10), without identifying it; the image can thus be applied in different directions as Yhwh's warning about the destiny of the city. Its characteristics or experiences are all attributed to Jerusalem elsewhere in Isaiah—but also to other cities such as Babylon. "In the Bible *there is only one city*, but it has multitudinous representations, manifestations, and instantiations."[66]

In Israel's own experience, the city is ambiguous from the beginning. In Egypt, the Israelites are involved in building store cities for the Pharaoh. On the eve of their entering Canaan, Moses promises them that they will possess cities they did not build, but also commissions them to destroy cities. In occupying the land, they indeed destroy cities, and they leave the first of these unoccupied but in due course build up cities. These include other cities as well as Jerusalem in the context of a process of urbanization involving the development of a class system, the oppression of the weak by the powerful (though religiously, the city was perhaps no worse than the country), and the first

---

[63]Ben D. Nefzger, "The Sociology of Preindustrial Cities," in *"Every City Shall Be Forsaken,"* ed. Lester L. Grabbe and Robert D. Haak, JSOTSup 330, pp. 159-71 (Sheffield: Sheffield Academic Press, 2001); see p. 160.

[64]Robert P. Carroll, "City of Chaos, City of Stone, City of Flesh," in *"Every City Shall Be Forsaken,"* ed. Lester L. Grabbe and Robert D. Haak, JSOTSup 330, pp. 45-61 (Sheffield: Sheffield Academic Press, 2001); see pp. 45, 47.

[65]For what follows, see Jacques Ellul, *The Meaning of the City* (Grand Rapids: Eerdmans, 1970).

[66]Carroll, "City of Chaos," p. 56.

"proper" system of slavery (1 Kings 9:15-21). But the city is also a place of sustenance (Ps 107:4-9).[67]

Amos 1—2 declares Yhwh's intention to put down cities for their wrongdoing (Damascus, Tyre, etc.). When an imperial city comes onto the horizon, this—Nineveh, then Babylon—is the object of Yhwh's critique and curse. Nineveh is the bloody city (Nahum 3). But it can turn: the whole population and the king do so (not individuals).[68] As Jonah brings deliverance to Nineveh, the exiled Judeans are to pray for Babylon (Jer 29:7); they are also praying against it, according to Psalm 137.

There is nothing inherently questionable about the city. The Bible begins in a garden but ends up in a city, but it is a city where the Messiah dwells. "We have a strong city" (Is 26:1), one whose name is *Yhwh šammâ*, "Yhwh-is-there" (Ezek 48:35). Jerusalem is the model city. The city, even Jerusalem, is not heavenly or spiritual *as opposed to* earthly, though ideally it would be heavenly and spiritual *as well as* earthly. One implication will be that Jerusalem shows the city to be incomplete without God, without worship and without mutual service. But the city is indeed doomed if the Messiah does not dwell there. "If one sets out to track the city in Christian Scripture, one will in time come upon Babylon," a city threatening and under threat.[69] Thus, notwithstanding the First Testament's common city focus, Isaiah 32:15-20 can imagine a world where, after calamity has deservedly fallen on the city, restoration implies not the restoration of city life but simply a transformation of the countryside whereby even wilderness pasture becomes richly fertile. It is then this, not the city, that will be "the setting for a just an equitable social order, with an end to warfare and social conflict."[70]

6.3 The Family

A happy family life is a key good for the First Testament. The family is both a natural unit, one that we are born into and that we birth people into, and also a humanly created unit, one that we bring into being as we welcome someone from outside by marriage or adoption. The latter extend the mutual commitment within a family to a new relationship outside it. It thus involves a covenant.[71] A covenant is unnecessary within blood relationships; the blood

---

[67]William P. Brown and John T. Carroll, "The Garden and the Plaza," *Int* 54 (2000): 3-11; see p. 7.

[68]Cf. Ellul, *Meaning of the City*, p. 69.

[69]Christopher R. Seitz, *Word Without End* (Grand Rapids: Eerdmans, 1998), p. 288.

[70]Joseph Blenkinsopp, "Cityscape to Landscape," in *"Every City Shall Be Forsaken,"* ed. Lester L. Grabbe and Robert D. Haak, JSOTSup 330, pp. 35-44 (Sheffield: Sheffield Academic Press, 2001); see p. 44.

[71]See Gordon P. Hugenberger, *Marriage as a Covenant*, VTSup 52 (Leiden/New York: Brill, 1994).

relationship itself implies the commitment that a covenant brings. The family relationships into which we are born imply the lasting commitment of the family's members to one another. There is no argument for that. It is part of being human. No matter what happens, parents are committed to their little children; grown-up children are committed to their parents. Brothers and sisters are committed to one another, and even if there is such a thing as a friend who sticks closer than a brother or sister, it is the latter that one can rely on in times of trouble (Prov 17:17; 18:24). So are members of the extended family, as the gō'ēl practice illustrates. Both the household and the extended family are key providers of theological imagery. People's experience of God shapes their experience of family, and their experience of family shapes their experience of God.[72] God is husband and Israel is wife; God is restorer and Israel is an impoverished member of God's family; God is master and Israel is servant; God is motherly father and Israel is son or daughter; God is householder and Israel is resident alien in God's household.[73]

Birth

Our origin is in the dirt, the earth's matter; we are shaped from the dirt (e.g., Job 4:19; Ps 103:14). We are also formed in our mother's womb. The one finds concrete form in the other. It is an extraordinary process, Psalm 139:13-16 reflects, the shaping of a person with their inner and outer aspects, the more extraordinary because of its invisibility, as if it were happening in the depths of the earth. It is like an act of creation—usually the point in talking about creation is the sovereign freedom of the act rather than, for instance, its creativity. It is like someone weaving patterned cloth, making something complex and intricate. It is all invisible to a baby's mother, even though she can feel extraordinary things happening inside her, yet it is all visible to the one who is making it happen. It is all rather unpredictable—when will the baby be born? Yet God understands the entire process. In bringing human beings into existence in the womb, God acts like a potter molding clay, a cheesemaker pouring out the milk and letting it solidify or a weaver making clothes—an internal set (bones and muscles) and an external set (skin and flesh) (Job 10:8-11).

And then God makes birth itself possible: "You are the one who pulled me from the belly, who made me rely on my mother's breasts; on you I was thrown from the womb, from my mother's belly you were my God" (Ps 22:9-

---

[72]Cf. Leo G. Perdue et al., *Families in Ancient Israel* (Louisville: Westminster John Knox, 1997), p. 225; he notes that monarchy is the other chief shaper of theological reflection and discourse.

[73]See section 3.1.

10 [MT 10-11]). There are many mysteries about birth. One is that a mother does not consciously make it happen, and neither presumably does a baby—to judge from the baby's helplessness when born. There is a sense in which it is a purely natural process, but another sense in which it comes about because God makes it happen. That is not merely because back at the Beginning God made nature that way, so that it works by inbuilt processes, but because God is involved in each individual birth. God acts as midwife, pulling the baby out and putting it onto its mother's breast where it will manifest its instinctive trusting expectancy of finding milk there.

The psalm's language is more violent than it sounds in NRSV. Emerging from the womb is not a gentle event. God does not merely draw a person delicately from the womb, but pulls a person out, kicking and screaming (see the other occurrences of the verb, in Judg 20:33; Job 38:8; 40:23; Ezek 32:2; Mic 4:10). A baby does not slide effortlessly from inside its mother but has to fight its way out, to break out like waters (cf. Job 38:8)—perhaps the imagery takes up from the breaking of the waters that heralds a birth, heralds the baby's bursting out. God then gives a baby no choice but to rely on its mother's milk. Indeed, perhaps this is not a (unique) occurrence of *baṭaḥ* i (make to rely) but an occurrence of *baṭaḥ* ii, meaning "make me fall" (see DCH). Either way, life may be much less secure outside the womb than inside, so from the beginning of our lives we are thrown onto God.

Parenthood

In a traditional society such as Israel, the family (in the form of the individual household and the extended family occupying a group of houses) is the immediate context for reproduction and nurture (including education), for identity and mutual care, and for production and consumption. "Grandchildren are the crown of the aged, and parents are the pride of their children" (Prov 17:6). While in some sense children may be their father's property, this may not be an illuminating observation. While a father has the right to treat his children as a disposable asset in the sense of being able to turn them into someone else's indentured servants if the family is in economic straits, a father's responsibilities are much greater than his opportunities.[74] One of the marks of Job's dedication to his family and to God was his concern for his grown-up children (Job 1:5). The younger generation enjoyed celebrations together, and parties are dangerous events. At the conclusion to the party season, Job would send (perhaps send for them) so that he could sacrifice whole offerings for them, to "sanctify" them (*qādaš* piel). In this context these

---

[74]Cf. Christopher J. H. Wright, *God's People in God's Land* (Exeter: Paternoster/Grand Rapids: Eerdmans, 1990), p. 238.

are evidently means of purification as well as signs that they really were giving themselves to God, not belittling and thus blaspheming God in the course of their revelry.[75] This fatherly initiative could counterbalance one's children's failure. God would surely receive his enacted prayer for his children, as God will later invite and receive his prayer for his stupid friends (Job 42:7-9).

Parents know best. Proverbs assumes that mothers and fathers accept responsibility for teaching their children, and urge their children to listen to them (Prov 1:8). It takes a father and mother to raise a child; Proverbs would reckon that is not the same when parents delegate all responsibility to schools or child-minders or when one parent abandons their children to be looked after by the other because of a preoccupation with work or because the two parents cannot get on or because the culture overemphasizes the role of either father or mother in this connection. Proverbs later adds that children should continue to listen to them when their father and mother are old (Prov 23:22). The older generation can be dismissed; its failing physical powers can be assumed to imply failing mental powers.

If the parents and children of Proverbs are often figures for teachers and pupils involved in education outside of the structure of the family, this underlines rather than imperils the assumption that parents are children's first teachers. "Initiate a young person in accordance with his way; even when he is old he will not depart from it" (Prov 22:6). English versions interpret the "way" to be the "right way" (see esp. NRSV), but "in accordance with his way" ('al pî darkô) rather suggests the way he chooses, the way that is natural to him. Positively understood, this would suggest encouraging the development of the child's individuality,[76] but Proverbs would see that as a trap, and more likely the command is an ironic warning, like Proverbs 19:27.[77] If parents encourage children to live in accordance with their own inclinations, they will do so all their lives. After all, stupidity can be "bound up in the mind of a young person" (Prov 22:15). The NRSV and NIVI take that as a general statement, which as such would stand in tension with the general assumption in Proverbs that young people are characteristically naive and thus urgently in need of instruction but not that they are willfully foolish. But the line has no "but" (contrast NRSV and NIVI) and more likely the first colon is subordinate to the second (cf. JPSV): "When folly is bound up in the mind of a young person, the disciplinary cane will remove it from him." So "discipline your son while there is hope" (Prov 19:18). "The person who rejects his son is sparing with the cane,

---

[75]On the verb *bārak* and its use here, see section 6.9 "Mortality Rejoiced In."

[76]Cf. Davis, *Proverbs, Ecclesiastes, and the Song of Songs,* pp. 119-20.

[77]Cf. Richard J. Clifford, *Proverbs* (Louisville: Westminster John Knox, 1999), p. 197.

while the person who is dedicated to him is careful to discipline him" (Prov 13:24). Proverbs thus speaks of the application of corporal punishment to young people who do seem to be going and growing the wrong way (cf. Prov 26:3). The proverb does not declare that using the cane is a necessary or regular part of childrearing; it concerns how we cope with problems, and in speaking of "children" it more likely refers to teenagers, for example, than to infants. It directly addresses cultures like those of the modern West that would never use the cane. It does reckon that people learn through being disciplined, but this is a very subordinate emphasis. Its dominant emphasis lies on argument. The question is whether people will "accept" what they are taught (Prov 2:1).

"Children are a possession from Yhwh; the fruit of the womb is his reward. Like arrows in a warrior's hand—so are the children born in one's youth. The good fortune of the man who fills his quiver with them. They will not be ashamed when they speak with enemies in the gate" (Ps 127:3-5). The EVV assume these children are sons, which may be too specific; a man's daughters are also a blessing to him. But it is true that the capacity of children that the psalm goes on to note belongs more to sons. The sooner the sons are born, the sooner will they be big and strong and thus assets: for instance, if their father should be accused of some wrongdoing or otherwise threatened.

Conflict

Sayings about the importance of discipline in the family illustrate how the family is a locus of conflict, hurt and frustration.[78] "A stupid son is a vexation to his father and a bitterness to the woman who bore him" (Prov 17:25). Parents long for their children to live wisely, get huge joy when they do and deep pain when they do not (Prov 10:1). "One begets a fool to one's grief; the father of a stupid person does not rejoice" (Prov 17:21). There are practical reasons why this is so. A son who plays his part in harvesting the family's fields shows good sense; one who lazes away through the heat of summer brings shame to his family (Prov 10:5).

The conflict is not confined to relationships between parents and children. "A foolish son is his father's ruin; a wife's contentiousness is a continuous dripping" (Prov 19:13; cf. Prov 27:15-16). Why is the wife contentious? Proverbs implies that her husband is probably involved in sex outside his marriage, as happens in traditional and modern cultures. Other parts of the First Testament point to other aspects of husbandly and wifely stupidity that issue in conflict. Admittedly, when one compares the assumption that parents know best with the reality that the First Testament describes in its portrait of parents

---

[78]On this motif in the First Testament Narrative, see *OTT* 1:277-87, 588-96.

such as Abraham and Sarah, Isaac and Rebekah, Jacob, Saul, and David, this assumption in Proverbs points to the same irony as the ascription of wisdom to Solomon. Some parents deserve to be ignored. Parents fail as teachers as much as children fail as pupils—though perhaps it is mainly leaders who are parents that do that, while ordinary parents do better.

"There is a kind of person that belittles their father and does not bless their mother" (Prov 30:11). The line identifies the first in a quartet of sins—the other three are self-deception about our moral state, a sense of superiority and a cold-bloodedness in devouring the poor. The lines involve at least one ellipse: what is their point? "The eye that mocks a father, scorns obedience to a mother—ravens of the canyon will peck it out, vultures will eat it" (Prov 30:17). Such attitudes to one's parent leads to death; what the saying directly describes is the horrible aftermath of this death, to find no proper burial with one's father and mother (cf. Prov 20:20). That points to a second ellipse, if the lines are concerned not merely with an attitude but with the active neglect that would follow from that and would take the parents to their death. As they advance in age, parents are dependent on the good will of their children. They can no longer beat them. The children are of course themselves now adults and continue to be responsible to pay heed to their parents and to care about and for them (e.g., Ex 20:12; Lev 19:32; Ruth 4:13-17; Prov 23:22). The parents are dependent on the children for their survival. If the children are only interested in when the family property will be theirs, the parents are in a very vulnerable position, though fortunately (Proverbs comments hopefully) such an attitude rebounds on the children (e.g., Prov 17:2; 19:26; 20:21; 28:24). The enthusiasm for parenthood in Psalms 127 and 128 no doubt reflects that practical importance of parenthood, though it likely also reflects the broader human attachment to parenthood that makes this part of adult human identity, for women as well as men.

The place of punishment needs to be set in the context of this understanding. All being well, there will be no need for it, if a child responds to the exhortation to learn. Proverbs recognizes that a rebuke can be much more effective than a beating; everything depends on the nature of the recipient (Prov 17:10). In Proverbs 1—9 neither father nor mother nor Wisdom herself threaten to punish their listeners, though they do warn them that they can bring punishment on themselves.[79]

"A cane and a rebuke can give wisdom, but young people let loose can shame their mothers" (Prov 29:15). The proverb draws a contrast between two extremes, wisdom and shame, corporal punishment and total neglect

---

[79]Cf. Michael V. Fox, *Proverbs 1—9*, AB (New York: Doubleday, 2000), p. 133.

(the verb can apply to animals that are not under control but it might even suggest that the young people in question are thrown out). It concerns the dilemma, what do you do when your son behaves in an immoral way? The answer it suggests is, don't give in to the temptation to do nothing and leave him to it. You will pay for it. Conversely, "discipline your children and they will give you peace and bring delight to your heart," or "bring delight to your appetite," satisfy you in a more down-to-earth sense (Prov 29:17; the word is *nepeš*). "When you hit them with a cane, they will not die." On the contrary: "You should hit them with a cane, and rescue their lives from Sheol" (Prov 23:12-14). The emphasis on discipline presumably means that Israelite parents had a hard time imposing it, like Western parents. The third line seems to parallel and clarify the second, whose point then is not that a caning will not kill the young person but that a caning may rescue them from death.

Sameness and Difference

Whatever the actual meaning of being made "in God's image," it establishes a fundamental mutual likeness among human beings. Being made in God's image is a fundamental statement about humanity, and all human beings are made in that image. Thus, for instance, all are involved in being fertile and increasing so as to fill the earth and subdue it, and thus in ruling it (Gen 1:27-28).

At the same time, that declaration of mutual likeness is qualified in various ways in the First Testament. In the immediate context, it is qualified by the note that the people made in God's image are "male and female." The same was of course true of the animals, but Genesis has not drawn attention to that. The significance it points to is not that the sexual difference links with personal relationships (as twenty-first-century Western people like to think), but that it makes possible the fertility and filling and thus the subduing and ruling. The same applies to the creation story in Genesis 2, where the forming of Eve as a "help" to Adam makes it possible for the two of them to have children—which Adam could not do on his own. Men and women need each other because otherwise they would not be able to fulfill God's design that humanity should fill the earth and govern it, or serve the garden. Among societies in general, there are usually differences between the roles of men and women, but there are apparently no universals with regard to such gender roles except the ones that are physiologically determined—only women bear and suckle children. It is that difference that is implied in Genesis 1—2 in connection with the filling of the earth and the man's need of help if he is to look after the garden.

The relative status of men and women also varies, though there are invariably aspects of women's roles that are valued less then men's. Usually men's greater involvement in defense and production gives them a greater status.[80] We have noted how this is indicated in the relative monetary evaluation of males and females in Leviticus 27:1-7.[81] An implication of Genesis 1—2, in contrast, is that women's reproductive role entitles them to a greater status than they often have, a status equal with that of men, perhaps also in part for contextual sociological reasons.[82]

The mutual likeness is further qualified as the First Testament unfolds. Humanity comes to comprise different nations, some of which come to rule over others. Kings rule over subjects. Parents rule over children (adult as well as little children). Husbands rule over wives, which is explicitly a result of sin's entry into the world. There are differences in the treatment of men and women servants (Ex 21:2-11), though it is not clear that these are necessarily to the disfavor of the woman, who stays as a servant for her lifetime but has the status of a wife. The regulations presuppose the practice of a man paying a bride price to a woman's father if he is to marry her, presumably in compensation for the loss of her contribution to the family's work—which she will now make to her new family (e.g., Ex 22:16-17 [MT 15-16]).

According to the second-century B.C. Testament of Reuben 5.1, "Women are evil." This view can be read out of passages such as Genesis 2—3, Hosea 1—3, Ezekiel 16 and 23 and Proverbs 1—9,[83] but these passages need not be so read. There are no equivalent First Testament statements that explicitly make such a declaration,[84] and much of its treatment of women (for instance, its acceptance of women prophets) stands in tension with it.

---

[80]So Carol L. Meyers, "Procreation, Production, and Protection," Journal of the American Academy of Religion 51 (1983): 569-93 = pp. 489-514 in Community, Identity, and Ideology, ed. Charles E. Carter and Carol E. Meyers (Winona Lake, Ind.: Eisenbrauns, 1996); with her references.

[81]See section 6.1 "Work and Rest."

[82]So Carol L. Meyers, "The Roots of Restriction," Biblical Archaeologist 41 (1978): 91-103.

[83]See Gale A. Yee, Poor Banished Children of Eve: Woman as Evil in the Hebrew Bible (Minneapolis: Fortress, 2003).

[84]The nearest is Eccles 7:26-28, though it is an enigmatic passage. The speaker first declares that women are a trap and best escaped, then adds that he has not found one woman in a thousand. Not only are the statements enigmatic; the only other reference to women in the book (Eccles 9:9) encourages a man to enjoy life with the woman he loves, which implies he can find one. The context suggests that the first statement is an emphatic version of the warnings in Proverbs about the "other woman" (which are as much a comment on men's weakness as on women's capacity to entice). Then, whatever the second saying means, "it may in fact not be specifically directed against women: there is little difference in the judgement on the two sexes, and the slight variation in wording may simply be for stylistic reasons" (R. N. Whybray, Ecclesiastes [Grand Rapids: Eerdmans/London: Marshall, 1989], p. 127). Indeed, it may be a saying Qohelet is quoting (like many others in the book), which he goes on to comment on; v. 29 then confirms that in his view there is actually no difference between men and women. None can be trusted.

The First Testament has no concept of the single life. A married couple and their nuclear family would normally be closely involved with their extended family, living in the same village, and the idea of a single person living on his or her own would seem very odd. Everyone is a member of a family. If a single woman, for instance, did not enter a monogamous marriage, she might stay with her parents, or might become someone's second wife, or after her parents' death might become a member of her sibling's family. Everyone belongs, one way or another. Thus when Ruth shows up to glean, Boaz asks who she belongs to, and the answer is "Naomi" (Ruth 2:5-6). No one is on their own.

Marriage

In traditional societies such as First Testament Israel, marriage is embedded in the household and (extended) family. "Only in modern society has marriage become the basis of the family" rather than the family taking precedence over marriage. The married couple are part of a web of relationships whereby the community sees to its need for food, shelter, work and other needs, and their marriage relates to the property arrangements within the community. All this is reflected in the fact that the family is heavily involved in choosing the partners in marriage.[85] Perhaps one reason for the conflict in the Song of Songs is that the couple are insisting in their relationship taking precedence over their families' agendas. For most people, marriage "was not . . . a matter of individual decision and choice. . . . The choice of a partner for an unmarried woman was a matter of concern for the entire household to which she belonged, and for the one to which she was destined to be transferred." That limits individual freedom but it also sidesteps problems in the modern view of marriage and family. The family is not an absolute; only God is (Gen 12:1).[86] But the couple and the individual do not take precedence over the family.

"A house and wealth are inherited from parents, but a proficient wife comes from Yhwh" (Prov 19:14). One can claim no credit either for one's wealth or for one's good marriage. The former is subject to prediction but not action, the latter to action but not prediction. The acquisition of either thus encourages humility and gratitude, but the latter even more than the former. It is a gift from God. "Find a wife, find something good, and obtain favor from Yhwh" (Prov 18:22). The articulation of this point perhaps implies that both single and married men might wonder whether that is true. The proverbs that refer to adultery and that refer to nagging might suggest part of the background to this. Proverbs 31 and the Song of Songs will expand on different aspects of the point. On the other hand, "living on the corner of a roof is better

---

[85]Pannenberg, *Anthropology in Theological Perspective*, p. 431.
[86]Ibid., p. 438.

than a contentious wife and a shared/noisy house" (Prov 21:9; cf. Prov 25:24).[87] Living in a guest room on the roof is like being a lodger in one's own house (cf. 2 Kings 4:10); the picture of the man living on the corner of the roof underlines the way in which he has become a marginal resident in the house—but that is fine to avoid arguments. Indeed, "living in a wilderness," another marginal place where survival is possible but life not easy, "is better than a contentious and vexatious wife" (Prov 21:19). The story of Job's testing comes to one climax with his wife's urging him to "blaspheme God and die" (Job 2:9).

In Genesis 2:18-25 husbands and wives are partners, though we have seen that the partnership may relate mainly to the fact that you need a man and a woman to start a family. In Proverbs 31:10-31 the teacher, perhaps still Lemuel's mother as in Proverbs 31:1-9, offers a much broader vision of the wife's half of the partnership. If one asks what her husband is doing in this poem, he seems to be sitting in the city square with the other senior members of the community, which might have sardonic implications. These are mitigated or replaced by others if one considers Abigail, an embodiment of the poem, whose husband spent his time being a sheep herder, even if the sardonicness also appears in the fact that he is a brainless idiot (1 Sam 25). Meanwhile the "strong woman" in Proverbs 31 is making sure the family business is profitable, managing the staff in "her" household, seeing to the provision of clothing and food for it. She is directly involved in making things and doing things (she is not just a manager who gives other people orders), and she takes action for the relief of poverty in the community. She makes decisions about land and vineyards and trades in cloth and garments; her realm, the home, is the economic and manufacturing unit in a traditional society. She teaches her household *hokmâ* and *tôrâ*, and lives a life that embodies reverence for Yhwh. One significance of the poem is the very fact that it presupposes the home as the center of production, teaching and life, and not merely a place people come back to for relaxation and consumption.[88] This woman sees that her home produces more than it consumes, and its surplus can therefore be used for the benefit of the needy.

All this suggests that while Israel was patrilineal and patrilocal (descent was traced via males and newlyweds lived with the groom's family rather than the bride's), the First Testament's implications are less patriarchal than we might have thought.[89] Men and women were interdependent, with women as well as men being involved in the management of the family's work and life. The soci-

---

[87]The root of *heber* usually suggests uniting and thus companionship, but this usage is unique, and a possible Akkadian cognate *hubūru* denotes "clamor"—which arguably makes better sense (see, e.g., Clifford, *Proverbs*, p. 190).

[88]Davis, *Proverbs, Ecclesiastes, and the Song of Songs*, pp. 154-55.

[89]Cf. Carol Meyers, in Leo G. Perdue et al., *Families in Ancient Israel*, p. 34.

ety was relatively egalitarian. A wife was not simply her husband's property.[90] More likely we should see her as a kind of extension of her husband, part of his person; the two of them form one social and legal unit (cf. Gen 2:24).[91]

Sexuality

In the modern Western world, people often look to their relationship with their spouse as far and away the most significant place to find friendship, affirmation and support. It is this relationship that provides refuge from a cruel world, not least the world of work. There is nothing corresponding to this dynamic in the biblical world.

Analogously, many of the laws about sex and marriage are concerned with the economic implications of people's sexual relationships rather than with their ethical implications—as is the nature of laws.[92] So the First Testament assumes that it is not the case that what consenting adults do in private is their own business. A major concern of the attitudes to sexual relationships in a traditional society is the protection of the family. Adultery and sexual relationships within the family make families break apart. "The laws regulating sexual relationship focus, not so much on condemning pre-marital intercourse as such, but on requiring full responsibility from the male as a consequence of his act."[93] Thus the First Testament assumes there is a structure of order written into human relationships. People are to have sex with other people outside their family not inside it (not with "their own flesh"): for example, not with their parents or step-parents, their parents' siblings, their children, their grandchildren, their spouse's other children or their siblings or half-siblings, the spouses of their immediate family (Lev 18:6-17). The requirement that people have sex with others of the opposite sex and not with people of the same sex is part of the same order. The extraordinary measures (as they would seem to a modern Western person) that are prescribed to ensure that a man's name would not be eliminated from the people (Deut 25:5-10) offer a further illustration of the subordination of sex to the family. So does the extraordinary statute that makes adultery a capital offense (Lev 20:10; Deut 22:22-24). The Torah does not allow discretion to the woman's husband either to require redress or to forgive his wife.

This is not all that the First Testament has to say about relationships be-

---

[90]See Wright, *God's People in God's Land*, pp. 183-221.

[91]Cf. Anthony Phillips, *Ancient Israel's Criminal Law* (Oxford: Blackwell/New York: Schocken, 1970), p. 117; cf. Wright, *God's People in God's Land*, p. 221. On marriage in Gen 12—50, see *OTT* 1:268-77.

[92]Joseph Blenkinsopp, in Leo G. Perdue et al., *Families in Ancient Israel*, p. 59, and pp. 59-63.

[93]Brevard S. Childs, *Exodus* (London: SCM Press, 1974), p. 477.

tween men and women. Proverbs 30:18-19 notes that there are a number of things that are really amazing about the world, such as the "way" of an eagle or a snake or a ship, which are extraordinary in different ways; and there is certainly something extraordinary, wondrous, magical, about the way a man wins a girl or makes love to a girl. No one tells him to do so or how to do so, but he does!

The Song of Songs constitutes a celebration of a sexual relationship that has no focus on procreation and that also presupposes an egalitarian relationship between a man and a woman; here it is as much the way of a woman with a man that evokes wonder. In the Song "there is no male dominance, no female subordination, and no stereotyping of either sex." The woman is fully the man's equal, in work and in the relationship.[94] This is not to imply that Israel could imagine the modern Western kind of marriage in which sex and companionship is very important but procreation had no part. It is to imply that sex can be important in its own right. Brevard S. Childs declares that "the frequent assertion that the Song is a celebration of human love per se fails utterly to reckon with the canonical context" in that the rest of Scripture does not so celebrate sexual love.[95] One might agree that it fails slightly to reckon with the canonical context (the Song's implicit commendation as wisdom and the fact that the rest of Scripture would imply that this celebration would be implicitly a love that relates to marriage), but the fact that the First Testament nowhere else so celebrates human love is no argument that it cannot be doing so here.[96]

6.4 The Person

Key to understanding the individual human person is the relationship between the inner and the outer person, heart or soul and body or flesh. Both are intrinsic to the person; both are given life by God; both are involved in relationships with God.

Describing the Person

The way Western thinking traditionally understands the makeup of the human person differs from the understanding characteristic of the First Testament. Indeed, words such as *soul, spirit, flesh* and *self* have a variety of different meanings in English, and equivalent words have a variety of different meanings in Hebrew (the meanings of *nepeš* include soul, person, self and life). While Greek

---

[94]Phyllis Trible, *God and the Rhetoric of Sexuality* (Philadelphia: Fortress, 1978), p. 161.

[95]Brevard Childs, *Introduction to the Old Testament As Scripture* (Philadelphia: Fortress, 1979), p. 575.

[96]Cf. André LaCocque, in André LaCocque and Paul Ricoeur, *Thinking Biblically* (Chicago/ London: University of Chicago Press, 1998), pp. 238-39.

psychē often has similar meaning to Hebrew *nepeš*, Greek *sarx* (flesh) often has quite different implications from Hebrew *bāśār*. This is not in itself to imply that the two Testaments have different understandings of the human person, only that their languages work in different ways. Words are different from concepts, and while the study of words is an aid to theological study, it does not constitute theological study. Further, in itself the way the First Testament talks about aspects of human nature through the use of words such as *nepeš* is not of theological significance; one must not confuse culture with theological message.[97]

Further, Christian understandings of the constitution of the person have been deeply affected by Platonic thinking and then by a reaction against Platonic thinking, and also by the Enlightenment and by empiricist thinking. In this context an important starting point is the assumption that a human being is made up of body and soul, though there is more than one way in which we may make that distinction. Indeed, Joel B. Green distinguishes four views.[98] At one extreme is "reductive materialism," the conviction that the soul does not exist because the person is nothing more than the product of organic chemistry. That seems to remove the basis for understanding a person as capable of moral action, for instance, or of relating to God. At the other extreme is "radical dualism," the conviction that the soul is a separate entity from the body and is capable of operating quite satisfactorily in independence of it—even more satisfactorily, if the soul is taken to be the real person. That, too, seems impossible to reconcile with the Scriptures or with scientific study. Between these extremes are two other views. "Holistic dualism" distinguishes between soul and body but sees them as interactive and mutually dependent; both are integral to the person, though in special circumstances one can function without the other. "Monism" sees the person as a single entity that is involved as one entity in activities such as moral decision making or prayer; *soul* suggests capacities or activities of this whole person. I see either of these views as compatible with the way the Scriptures speak.

The only Hebrew word commonly translated "soul" is *nepeš*, but it more often denotes the whole person, and in this sense the monistic view is nearer to the way the Scriptures actually speak. In the Garden of Eden "Yhwh God shaped the man with dirt from the ground and breathed into his nostrils the breath of life, and the man became a living *nepeš*" (Gen 2:7). Apparently Adam

---

[97]See, e.g., Brevard S. Childs, *Biblical Theology of the Old and New Testaments* (Minneapolis: Fortress/London: SCM Press, 1992), p. 572, who thus criticizes works such as Eichrodt, *Theology of the OT;* Hans Walter Wolff, *Anthropology of the Old Testament* (London: SCM Press/Philadelphia: Fortress, 1974).

[98]See Joel B. Green and Stuart L. Palmer, eds., *In Search of the Soul* (Downers Grove, Ill.: InterVarsity Press, 2005), pp. 13-14.

was already a *nepeš* when he was not yet alive, when we would think of him as "merely" a body, made from the ground; it was when God breathed into him that he became a *nepeš* that was alive. Conversely, a person can still be thought of as a *nepeš* when God has withdrawn that breath. A number of regulations in the Torah refer to a dead person simply as a *nepeš* (e.g., Lev 19:28; for *nepeš*, EVV simply have "the dead"). You are still a person when you are a dead body.

Subsequently, Yhwh speaks as one who "gives breath to the people on [the earth] and spirit to those who walk on it" (Is 42:5), and Ezekiel 37:1-10 relates a vision of Yhwh doing that. Bringing dead people back to life involves causing sinews and flesh and skin to come on bones and then the spirit breathing into them. A man or a woman indeed comprises two elements, but these are not body and soul but person and breath. It is these that make a person or "self"; though in understanding *nepeš* to mean "self," we also need to be wary of some of that English word's connotations, as "self" tends to imply something experiential, subjective and particular, the individual person understood from a particular angle.[99]

Body and Soul

Seeing body and soul as relatively independent, conventional Christian thinking has commonly assumed that death chiefly affects the body; there is no problem about the soul continuing to live separate from the body. The Platonic view goes beyond that in seeing the real person as the soul and the body as a dispensable shell in which the real person lives till it can shed it like a butterfly shedding its cocoon. On either understanding, John Brown's body can lie a-mouldering in his grave but his soul can go marching on. As another song puts it, "I don't care where they bury my body, because my soul is going to live with God." But when Enoch and Elijah go off to be with God without dying, it is the whole living person that goes, not just the soul. Conversely, when the dead Samuel comes to see Saul, it is the whole dead (?) person who comes, not just the soul. When Jesus rises from the dead and goes to the Father, it is the whole person who does so; Jesus does not leave his body in the tomb.

Even for holistic dualism, the starting point is the assumption that human beings comprise soul and body. However these are understood, this is not an assumption that the Scriptures work with. A symbol of that is the fact that the First Testament does not treat *nepeš* and body as a natural pair of words; only a few times does it mention them together (see Prov 16:24; Is 10:18 [see NRSV]; in the New Testament, only Mt 10:28). It can equally talk about, for instance,

---

[99]Cf. Nancy S. Duvall, "From Soul to Self and Back Again," *Journal of Psychology and Theology* 26 (1998): 6-15; see p. 10.

heart and *nepeš* and flesh (Ps 84:2 [MT 3]) or eye and *nepeš* and flesh (Ps 31:9 [MT 10]), as the New Testament can talk of spirit and soul and body (1 Thess 5:23). "Soul and body" is not a biblical pairing. Indeed, the more common pairing is heart and flesh (Ps 73:26; Prov 15:30; Eccles 11:10; Ezek 44:7, 9). Thus, ironically, if there is a word that is equivalent to *soul* in English, it is the word for heart, *lēb/lēbāb,* which JPSV, for instance, does sometimes translate "soul." It is the heart that suggests the inner, invisible aspect to the person as opposed to the outer, visible aspect. The heart embraces the mind, the spirituality, the affections, the will and the conscience. Insofar as the Scriptures do think in terms of a duality of body and heart (a duality rather than a dualism), we might see this as an indication that in its way holistic dualism does represent a scriptural way of thinking.

It is then significant that the heart is a physical organ. *Soul* suggests a nonmaterial aspect to the human person, and it can imply that there is a kind of nonmaterial inner place "within" us where we know things, relate to God and to other people, feel things, make decisions, and formulate moral attitudes. It is rather the heart that is involved in such activities, and *heart* points to an awareness that such activities have a physical base (*nepeš* actually has the same implication; it can denote the throat as the place where we breathe and as a place that links with appetite). God and other heavenly beings know, relate, feel, decide and formulate moral attitudes without the use of a body, though they apparently have some analog to a body—at least, the Scriptures often refer to God as having eyes, nose, hands, feet and other body parts. But for human beings, knowing, relating, feeling, deciding and formulating moral attitudes intrinsically involve a body.

The Inner and the Outer

This links with the way Western thinking speaks of "experience," especially about "religious experience" or "spiritual experience." By those terms we often refer to something going on "inside" us, to inward experiences. But we also speak of experience in broader senses; if I said I had an odd experience while writing this book, readers might not take this to refer to something inward. Our emphasis on the first kind of experience implies the modern conviction that "the *real* 'me,' the essential person, lives somewhere inside my head,"[100] and that we relate to God in a way that involves the soul as opposed to the body. The First Testament assumes that what happens to us outside and what we do outside is at least as intrinsic to "the real 'me.'" The way we then relate to other people is also intrinsic to "the real me." The experiences we

---

[100]Nicholas Lash, *Theology on the Way to Emmaus* (London: SCM Press, 1986), p. 144; he calls it a "queer" view, a "pathological deformation, a personal and cultural disease" (p. 145).

have with other people, including the rituals we take part in, are also intrinsic to our persons.[101]

The First Testament rather suggests that soul and body are the invisible and visible aspects to the one person. The soul needs the body and the body the soul. This is closer to the Homeric and Aristotelian view of body and soul, and to that prevalent in many other traditional cultures. The body is the visible embodiment of the person. The human person is one whole. Body and soul exist in mutual dependence and have similar moral status. Duality may be all right; dualism implies a false prioritizing of one element in a duality over against another. The Christian Platonic view sees the body as having inferior inclinations from those of the soul: the body is fleshly in the sense that it is inclined to draw the person away from relating to God and to other people and from moral decision making. As the First Testament sees it, God creates both and uses both; our souls can lead us astray just as our bodies can lead us astray.

Admittedly, there is a converse point that could be made about the inner and the outer. While we speak of soul and body as the inner and outer person, there are limitations to this language. The soul is also the aspect of us that has the capacity to live outside the body and reach out to others. Paul can be absent from Corinth in body but present in spirit (1 Cor 5:3-4). In dreams or in daydreams I can be miles away from where I am physically. In this sense the body is the inner person, the soul is the outer person. Lactantius was not so wrong when he declared that "the body can do nothing without the soul. But the soul can do many and great things without the body."[102] To different degrees the soul does need the body to do these things, but it then acts as a kind of extension of the body beyond its physical confines. In some sense soul and body can therefore exist separately.

The New Testament pictures being dead as being in an odd and troublesome state because you are temporarily separated from your body (2 Cor 5:1-4). Such separation is possible but not preferable. Over against Lactantius, Wolfhart Pannenberg asks, "When the life of the soul is conditioned in every detail by bodily organs and processes, how can it be detached from the body and survive without it?"[103] The soul would have a hard time functioning without the body, as relating to God and to other people involves the voice, the hands and the feet. Even silent prayer (not a very scriptural activity) normally at least uses the body in the sense of the brain. Activities or experiences such as memory, grief, happiness, decision making and moral evaluation all in-

---

[101]Lash instances a birthday party (ibid., p. 147).

[102]Lactantius *The Divine Institutes* 7.11; cf. Joel B. Green, "Body and Soul," in *What About the Soul?* ed. Joel B. Green (Nashville: Abingdon, 2004), p. 8.

[103]Pannenberg, *Systematic Theology*, 2:182.

volve the brain. Body and soul live in perichoretic union, like Father, Son and Spirit, "a relationship of mutual interpenetration and differentiated unity," without structures of domination. They form a gestalt, in mutual covenant, a gestalt formed by the creative divine Spirit.[104]

Body, Flesh, Spirit

The body, then, is of the essence of the person. "Embodiment is the end of God's works in creation." In humanity's embodiment, God's work reaches its goal. It is also the goal of God's work of reconciliation and of the world's final redemption.[105] Then, "Israel's chief conception of the body is its wholeness."[106] It needs to be complete, all its parts need to be functional, and its leakages need to be attended to. As an animal cannot be offered if it has a defect (Lev 22:21-25), so a man cannot be a priest if he has a defect (*mûs*) such as blindness, lameness or an injured foot or hand; this would involve profaning the places that Yhwh has sanctified (Lev 21:16-23). Things need to be complete examples of the class to which they belong. Further, the human body is designed to be something beautiful. The Song of Songs is the great repository of enthusiasm for the physical beauty of both male and female, but Psalm 45:2 [MT 3]) has the best man (?) saying to the king on his wedding day, "You are the most handsome of human beings; grace is poured on your lips—therefore God has blessed you forever."

The First Testament often refers to the body as *bāśār*, conventionally "flesh," and it sees the flesh as weak, as suggesting the human and limited over against the divine and dynamic (e.g., Job 10:4; Ps 56:4 [MT 5]; Is 31:3; Jer 17:5-8). "The dominant anthropological note struck in the Psalter is that of human frailty and vulnerability" (e.g., Ps 38; 88), though alongside that, "an important biblical dimension of being human is that of hope in God."[107] But *bāśār* does not have the connotations of *sarx* in Paul; it does not suggest sinfulness. My flesh can long for God or cry out for the living God (Ps 63:1; 84:2). And my bones can rejoice (Ps 51:8 [MT 10]).

Over against *bāśār* is *rûaḥ*, which has the dynamism of wind and the life of breath. The spirit, the breath of Shaddai, is in a human being; indeed, it is the spirit of God, the breath of Shaddai, that makes a person by giving them life (Job 32:8; 33:4; cf. Is 42:5; Ezek 37:1-14). The presence of the breath/spirit of

[104]Jürgen Moltmann, *God in Creation* (London: SCM Press/San Francisco: HarperSanFrancisco, 1985), pp. 259-60, 263.

[105]Ibid., pp. 245-46.

[106]Jon L. Berquist, *Controlling Corporeality* (New Brunswick, N.J./London: Rutgers University Press, 2002), p. 49.

[107]Childs, *Biblical Theology*, p. 573.

Shaddai is also what gives people insight; the spirit within a human being fills that human being with words (Job 32:8, 18-20). The presence of Yhwh's spirit does not make someone spiritual in the sense of inwardly focused, nor ecstatic in the sense of taken out of themselves or taken over by someone else. It does give huge new energy to the whole person that they are. Yhwh's spirit works dynamically through people in enabling them to deliver Israel, because it was the dynamic of the original act of liberating creation.[108] Yhwh's spirit is the bringer of new life because it was the bringer of life in the first place; it is completing or restoring that work. And the continuance of a human life is contingent on God's continuing to let us keep the divine spirit or breath; when God withdraws it (Eccles 12:7), we return to the dirt or clay from which we were made (Job 33:6; 34:14-15; cf. Gen 6:3; Ps 104:29-30, which extends this to animals). The fact that God's spirit is breathed into human beings (and other beings) through creation "does not mean that God's spirit is a constituent part of the creature. Rather it means that creaturely life has an eccentric character, that it is referred to the divine power of the Spirit that works upon it. Living creatures have the breath of life in them, but it is not at their disposal. God is always the Lord of creaturely life."[109]

The emotions are also of the essence of the person, as the important place of emotions within God shows.[110] To be in relationships with people involves emotions such as love, gratitude, anger, envy and fear.[111] Occasionally the First Testament refers to the emotions by speaking of the heart, as English commonly does, though the emotions are more commonly connected with other organs such as the kidneys, liver, womb or the innards generally.

Heart

The "heart," then, more often refers to the inner center of the person. "The heart knows its own bitterness, and in its joy another person may not share" (Prov 14:10). Other people can share something of our sorrows and our joys, but only we actually experience either; how demanding empathy therefore is, and how seriously we have to give ourselves to it. The heart is invisible. "Even at play the heart may be sad, and at its end joy is grief" (Prov 14:13). An underlying sadness may coexist with an outward lightheartedness. And even if that is not so, present joy may give way to grief. The fact that we are on our way to death introduces a degree of sadness even into the joys we have in the meantime. Yet once the fact of death is brought to expression, the joy may become real joy.

---

[108]Cf. Pannenberg, *Systematic Theology,* 3:1-2.

[109]Ibid., 2:186.

[110]See sections 2.6-8.

[111]Cf. Wyschogrod, *Body of Faith,* p. 91.

More specifically the heart suggests the aspect of us that thinks things through, forms attitudes and makes decisions—what Western thinking would call the mind. Stupid people (that is, those who leave God and other people out of their thinking) are people who have no heart (Prov 10:13). They are "mindless" or "senseless." It is of the essence of our humanity that we use our minds in such connections, though it might be misleading to suggest that reason is the distinctive human capacity; emotions may be just as distinctively human. But given that the heart is also the inner person as a whole, Proverbs 10:13 also points to the idea that stupid people are people who are shallow—literally, they are lacking in heart. What you see is what you get; and that is all there is.

"Above everything that you guard, keep your heart, because the springs of life come from it" (Prov 4:23). The context once again suggests that the heart refers centrally to the mind, the place where we store up wisdom (Prov 4:21). "The person who trusts his own mind—he is a fool, but the person who lives by wisdom—he will be safe" (Prov 28:26). The end of the line makes clear in what connection the stupid person is relying on his own thinking—how can I get out of a dangerous situation? That is the situation in which it is vital to look outside yourself for wisdom (and thus, for example, to take Yhwh into account and take right and wrong into account). "The purpose in a person's mind is deep water" (Prov 20:5); the image suggests not so much inaccessibility as profundity (cf. Prov 18:4). We may have a hard time understanding our own desires and motivations. But (Prov 20:5 goes on) "a person of discernment can draw it out." This perceptive person "is a kind of midwife who brings ʿēṣā to the birth" as much for the benefit of the person who could otherwise not articulate it as for anyone else.[112] One should not underestimate the depths of the person, but neither should one give in to hopelessness about it. But further, "Who can say 'I have kept my mind pure, I am pure from my shortcomings?'" (Prov 20:9). While that statement might point to the fact that no one *is* free of sin, in the context of Proverbs it more likely witnesses to the difficulty of *knowing* one's own heart. It is hard to be sure of one's motivations. "All the ways of a person may be pure in his eyes, but Yhwh measures spirits" (Prov 16:2; cf. Prov 21:2). Yhwh understands us better than we understand ourselves.

Psalm 73 recognizes the tension between our minds or hearts and our lives. "The state of the heart determines whether a man lives in the truth. . . . Heart is the dominant key-word in this Psalm"; it comes six times.[113] It begins with

[112]William McKane, *Proverbs* (London: SCM Press, 1970), p. 536.

[113]Martin Buber, *Right and Wrong* (London: SCM Press, 1952), p. 37 = pp. 34-35 in *Good and Evil* (New York: Scribner's, 1953).

the declaration that God is good to people who are pure of mind or heart, people of unequivocal commitment to Yhwh. That is a painful declaration because the psalm that follows makes clear that the psalmist had not (quite) gone astray in behavior, but had become sour of heart or mind (the verb *ḥāmēṣ* is rare and the hitpael comes only here; its more common related nouns refer to leaven and vinegar). The psalmist has come to the conclusion that there is no point in being innocent of heart and mind. The hearts of the faithless have so abounded, with the result that there is no limit to the wrongdoing their minds are planning. But the psalm closes with a renewed affirmation that "if my body and mind/heart fail, God is the crag for my mind/heart and my allocation forever" (Ps 73:26). God is the crag where our heart and mind need to take refuge when we are overwhelmed by the pressures that the success and persecution of the faithless bring to body and heart or mind.

The inner and the outer person thus interact with each other. "A joyful mind makes the face look good, but through sadness of mind the spirit is defeated" (Prov 15:13). The inner person or mind or heart is the key both to one's physical appearance and to the energy of the person as a whole. Inner joy is reflected in the way the face looks out with a brightness that brings life. Inner sadness likewise has a debilitating effect on our whole person, our drive and dynamic. Inner joy means someone makes things happen in the world through the brightness the face exudes; inner sadness means the person loses the vigor to make things happen (cf. Prov 17:22). "The spirit of a person sustains him in sickness, but a crushed spirit—who can bear it?" (Prov 18:14). Conversely, "what brightens the eyes gladdens the mind; good news builds up the person": more literally, the frame or body (Prov 15:30). When we see something good happening or hear news of something good, that has an affect on the inner person, and it also builds up the person more generally. Physical pain of course also has an effect on the inner person.

Thus the deeds make known the person. "Even children make themselves known by their deeds, whether their action is pure and upright" (Prov 20:11). Even in their case actions speak louder than words. It is no use claiming to have a pure heart if one does not have a pure life. On the other hand, "there are people who behave rich but have nothing, people who behave poor but have great wealth" (Prov 13:7). Perhaps they are hiding the facts from themselves—they do not face the fact of their poverty or cannot bear to spend their money. Or perhaps they are hiding the facts from other people. Either way, one cannot certainly infer people's wealth from their behavior. Appearance and reality are sometimes at odds.

A Renewed Mind, Heart, Spirit

As human beings we often go wrong; and therefore the center of the person, our heart or mind, often needs renewal. So Psalm 51:10-12 [MT 12-14] prays, "create a pure heart for me, God, make anew a steadfast spirit within me. Do not throw me out from before you, do not take your holy spirit from me. Give back to me your joy that comes from your deliverance, uphold me with a wholehearted spirit." The words suggest a richly complex anthropology. First, heart and spirit are apparently equivalents; they appear in parallelism again when the psalm speaks of a crushed and broken heart and spirit (Ps 51:17 [MT 19]). They point to two ways of picturing the dynamics of the person. The heart suggests the person's inner nature, the aspect that cannot be seen and can therefore be unfaithful when the person is being outwardly faithful, or can be planning wrongdoing that its victim could not imagine. The spirit suggests the person's energy and drive (it has little to do with "spirituality").

The psalmist knows that wrongdoing stains the inner person as well as the outer person, though it would be unwise to reckon that the acts that brought stain had their origin in one location or the other. The whole person is affected by sin and the heart or mind thus needs to be made new in order for the person as a whole to be able to stand before Yhwh. To speak of its being created pure is to emphasize the sovereign power of the act that the suppliant knows is needed, as sovereign and powerful as the moment when God said "Let there be light," and there was light. It is this kind of sovereign word that can magically bring about an act of creation. The fact that the heart is crushed and broken underlines this need (Ps 51:17 [MT 19]). It is a thing that is broken that needs renewing. (The EVV have "contrite," which the rest of the psalm shows the heart and spirit were, but it is doubtful whether the words for "crushed" and "broken" should be reckoned to indicate this. They simply mean "crushed" and "broken," as when one of these words is applied to the "bones," Ps 51:8 [MT 10].)

For the spirit, the locus of dynamism, to be broken is the more devastating. But it likewise needs its energy and drive restored and properly directed toward a steadfast commitment to Yhwh rather than to other tempting gods. In this sense it needs to be made new—again, if the person is to be able to stand before Yhwh. Dynamism and steadfastness need to come together.

In making explicit the prayer not to be thrown out from Yhwh's presence (Ps 51:11 [MT 13]), the next line complicates that understanding of spirit. By its nature "heart" is at home referring to human beings or to God; both God and human beings have a heart with which to think and make decisions. In contrast "spirit" is a word more at home referring to God than to human beings. God *is* spirit, is dynamic energy (Is 31:3). The first line might raise the question whether the steadfast spirit it refers to is actually God's, or whether the suppliant will become a person of steadfast spirit only as the divine spirit works on the human spirit. The second line raises that question more explicitly in the plea, "do not take away your holy spirit from me."

Arguably, the expression "holy spirit" is a tautology; both "holy" and "spirit" are words that essentially refer to God in God's Godness. But they have different emphases. *Holy* points to the distinctive uncreated divine transcendence. *Spirit* points to the distinctive dynamic divine energy. The plea thus underlines the one in the preceding line. Being "steadfast" (*nākôn*) is not especially a divine characteristic, perhaps because it implies an agent, someone who made an object steadfast and firm, unable to be shifted (the word does apply to Yhwh's throne, e.g., Ps 93:2). But the verb (*kûn* hiphil) is one of which Yhwh is often the subject. Yhwh is one who makes things firm. Perhaps the implication then is that the human spirit needs the divine, holy spirit to continue to be operative on it for its energy to be trained steadfastly in the proper direction. (The psalm assumes an operating of Yhwh's holy spirit within the human person. While it is possible that the psalm might have been used by the king, this way of speaking would not have excluded its being used by ordinary Israelites. Insofar as Yhwh's spirit was present and active among the people as a whole [e.g., Is 63:10-14; Hag 2:5], individuals could assume they were part of that, not least by virtue of God's spirit being breathed into them at their creation [e.g., Is 42:5]. This of course does not preclude a new outpouring of the divine spirit on everyone [e.g., Joel 2:28 (MT 3:1)].)

The third line in Psalm 51:10-12 [MT 12-14] nuances the point yet further. Asking to be upheld reexpresses the plea about a steadfast spirit. Is the "wholehearted" or generous spirit God's or the human spirit? The adjective (*nādîb*) and related words elsewhere always refer to human beings, except for one reference to the wholeheartedness or generosity of Yhwh's love (Hos 14:4 [MT 5]). Here, then, it is likely the human spirit that needs to be characterized by wholeheartedness in its commitment to Yhwh, but the psalm may imply that this will come about through the operating of the wholehearted divine spirit on the human spirit.

Seeking God with the Inner and the Outer Person

"How much loved is your fine dwelling, Yhwh Armies! My whole being has longed, indeed exhausted itself longing, for Yhwh's courts." Psalm 84 underlines how the whole person is involved in a relationship with God. "My heart and my body resound to the God of life" (here in Ps 84:2 [MT 3], JPSV has "soul" for *lēb*). Both do so, because God is involved with both inner and outer person. The experiences and feelings of body and heart/mind, such as longing and exhaustion or might and strength, mirror each other because both are aspects of the one person. Thus here is an analogy between the way a human being comes to meet with God and the way in which, here at Yhwh's altar, "sparrow has found a home, too, dove a nest for herself where she has put her young"

(Ps 84:3 [MT 4]). The outward journey to Jerusalem mirrors the inner journey as people seek God in their spirits. "The blessings of people who live in your house—they still praise you." The psalm dreams of physically living in Yhwh's material palace, because a relationship with Yhwh involves the whole person. Birds find a home in Yhwh's palace, in the trees in the enclosure or in the crevices in the walls, and human beings can also feel at home there, because Yhwh is creator of birds and human beings. There is a two-way interplay between matter and spirit. "A day in your courts is good; I chose it over a thousand [others]. Standing at the threshold in the house of my God [is good]; [I chose it] over dwelling in a faithless person's fine tent" (Ps 84:10 [MT 11]).

The point is most explicit in the description of people turning Baka Valley into a spring, even if it is obscure what this means. "The blessings of the one whose might is in you—highways are in their mind. Those who pass through Baka Valley make it a spring; first rains wrap it in blessings, too" (Ps 84:5-6 [MT 6-7]). Perhaps people are inspired by the prospect of completing their pilgrimage to Zion, where they will see Yhwh and/or Yhwh will see them: "They walk from rampart to rampart; each appears to God in Zion/the God of gods appears in Zion."[114] They are thus enabled to find inner refreshment even when the journey is hard. Insofar as Yhwh is the inspiration of this process, perhaps it makes little difference whether we assume that the pilgrims transform the valley, with MT, or that Yhwh does so, with LXX.[115] We do not know where Baka Valley was (but see 2 Sam 5:22-24), nor what (if anything) the name meant. It is traditionally understood as the name of a tree, though there is no hard evidence for this. The LXX and Targum make a link between *bākā᾿* and wailing *(bākâ)*, suggesting that people's expectation of seeing Yhwh means they can turn Wailing Valley into a spring. That leads into that other aspect of the oneness of God, humanity and nature, for the transformation that pilgrims effect in September-October by their anticipation of the festival is mirrored when the rains actually come. This physical transformation would hardly ever actually happen while they were on their way for the festival, but might happen soon afterward. The psalm points to another happy word association here, for pools *(bĕrēkôt)* are blessings *(bĕrākôt)*.

As *᾿ēl-hay*, Yhwh is indeed "the God of life" and not merely "the living God" (Ps 84:2 [MT 3]). With Yhwh is the fountain of life (Ps 36:9 [MT 10]). Further, only Psalm 84:11 [MT 12] declares that "Yhwh God *is* sun." Other peoples described gods and kings in such terms, and here Israel does the same. Christians are inclined to find God located in Jesus as an earthly person from the

---

[114]MT has *yērā᾿eh ᾿el-᾿ĕlōhîm* (one will appear to God), but the further transition to singular is surprising; LXX implies *yērā᾿eh ᾿ēl ᾿ĕlōhîm* (the God of gods will appear).

[115]MT has *yĕśîtûhû* (they make it), but LXX implies *yĕśîtēhû* (he makes it).

past, or in Jesus as an invisible person in the present, or in a future heavenly Jerusalem. The psalm affirms that God is the God of life for us now, the one involved in earthly life now: "he gives favor and splendor. Yhwh does not hold back good from people who walk with integrity. Yhwh Armies, the blessings of the one who trusts in you!" (Psalm 84:11-12 [MT 12-13]).

The Stages of Human Life

Our lives as a whole are lived in time: there is a *before* us and there will be an *after* us. We are part of something bigger than us. One reason Israelites can be more accepting of their own death than Christians are is because they see themselves as part of something bigger than themselves, part of the people of God and part of the purpose of God that stretches from a Beginning long before them to an End long after them.

In addition, time shapes our individual lives. Individually, we have a beginning, a maturing, a declining and an end. We remember and we hope (we reflect and we expect). God is involved with all these stages of our life. Psalm 71 describes this most systematically. It speaks for a person standing as an adult between youth and old age. It looks back to a life upheld by God from youth, indeed from its very beginning, from birth. "You have been my hope, my Lord Yhwh, my confidence from my youth" (Ps 71:5). In speaking of Yhwh having been "my hope," the psalm refers not to the subjective human attitude of hope but to the objective fact of Yhwh's being someone in whom one could hope, someone who vindicated hope. Thus "on you I have depended from birth, from my mother's womb; you have been my support, you are my praise continually" (Ps 71:6). This life has been one of learning about God's marvelous deeds, experiencing them and proclaiming them. "God, you have taught me from my youth and until now I proclaim your wonders." The question is, will it continue to be like that, into old age with its vulnerability, when one lacks the strength to defend oneself? "Do not cast me off for my old age; when my strength fails, do not abandon me. . . . Even to gray-haired old age, God, do not abandon me" (Ps 71:9, 18). Will God continue to be faithful, so the suppliant can continue to proclaim God's acts to the next generation, "until I proclaim your strength to a generation to come, your might to everyone to come"?

Lifespans in Israel were generally short, as they have been in most societies except the modern West, and most people died by the time they were in their thirties.[116] But a family will ideally comprise three or four generations (hence, when things go wrong in a community, this has an effect "to the third and

---

[116]See, e.g., Meyers, "Roots of Restriction," p. 95; also Wolff, *Anthropology of the OT*, pp. 119-20. On attitudes to "the stages of the body," see Berquist, *Controlling Corporeality*, pp. 107-34.

fourth generation"): children and young people, adults, people in their fifties and sixties, and very old people. Jeremiah 6:11 suggests four stages of human life—infancy, youth, adulthood and old age—as it speaks of babies, young people, man and wife, and the elderly and people who are full of years—the last apparently distinguishing between the old and the very old (for whom, see Psalm 90:10; and compare the age structuring in Lev 27:2-7).[117]

Modern Western culture idolizes childhood and youth, and the First Testament can occasionally enthuse over these: Hebrew has no word for *adult*, which perhaps suggests that this is just "normal" human life. Proverbs may presuppose that older people have a wisdom that the young lack, though it is not very specific about asserting that the great asset of old age is wisdom. "The glory of youths is their strength, the splendor of the aged is their gray hair" (Prov 20:29). There is some tautology about the second colon. The First Testament does not treat gray hair as a symbol of wisdom, but simply of old age, so that the second colon implies that the splendor of the aged is simply their age. It is noteworthy how old people become proud of their age, but the line also thus hints at a contrast with young people, who have something else to glory in. Yet the line affirms that their gray hair *is* the splendor of the elderly and invites the young to recognize that (cf. Lev 19:32), even as the elderly recognize the glory of the strength that young people possess.

While the older men are the people who make decisions in the community, in particular helping to resolve community disputes, there is of course no guarantee that a person will grow wise through growing old. To support the truth of the advice he gave Job, Eliphaz pointed out that the gray-haired and the aged were with him and his two friends (Job 15:10), which obviously in fact does the opposite and discredits the aged. Wisdom, we might reckon, is good at seeing things in perspective in light of traditional teaching, but is less likely to be innovative. But Solomon is the notorious example of someone who started off wise and became stupidly innovative when he was older (1 Kings 11:4). Elihu rejects the wisdom of the aged in favor of the innovation of the young (Job 32:9; cf. also Eccles 4:13), but how ironic is that?

An anxiety about growing old is one's health. The ideal was of course to maintain one's strength and facilities, but it was chiefly great heroes who did so (Deut 34:7; Josh 14:11). The average Israelite found, as we do, that old age often meant declining faculties and the sense of being a burden to other people (e.g., 1 Sam 3:2; 2 Sam 19:35; 1 Kings 1:1; Eccles 12:1-5 may be a moving poetic description of this experience, but the interpretation of the passage is uncertain).[118] Thus Levites gave up their regular work when they were fifty, though

---

[117]See section 6.1 "Work and Rest."

they carried on with support tasks (Num 8:23-26), and one may guess that something similar happened in the case of people in general, at this age or later (again, cf. Lev 27:2-7). There would be no idea that one moved from full-time work to simply playing golf, but they did move from being full-time professors to being adjuncts. Older people would continue to take part in the work of the farm (see Judg 19:16), but one can imagine that they worked less than they had when they were younger and that more responsibility passed to their children. It would be nice to be in a position to give testimony to Yhwh's faithfulness through a whole life, even into old age with its frailties.

The Good Life

Life is a great thing, a great gift from the living God. R. Norman Whybray suggests twelve aspects to "the good life" as the First Testament sees it: security, a land to live in, power, food and sustenance, a long life, wealth, family, justice, laws, wisdom, pleasure, and trust in God.[119] Among these, food is the first thing God gives humanity (Gen 1:29), the first thing God gives to humanity again after the flood (Gen 9:3), a basic thing for which all look to God (Ps 104:27-28), and the first thing for which Jesus bids his disciples pray (Lk 11:3). There is nothing better than food (Eccles 2:24), nothing that so gives joy and builds up strength (Ps 104:14-15). It is the reason why land is important, and why the first human beings are farmers, as is the first man after the flood. It is as well, therefore, that God declares that the earth is to bring forth vegetation and fruit trees (Gen 1:11-12) and promises after the flood never again to curse the ground and affirms that the cycle of sewing and harvest will never cease (Gen 8:21-22). The rejoicing in this process (e.g., Ps 65) reflects its importance. "Go and eat your food cheerfully and drink your wine with a good heart, because God long ago wanted your action. At each time your clothes should be white, and the oil on your head should never be lacking. Enjoy life with the woman you love all the days of the transient life that you are given under the sun" (Eccles 9:7-9; cf. Eccles 2:24; 3:12-14; 5:18-19; 8:15). No sackcloth and ashes, please. "There is hardly a word so characteristic of the Old Testament as the word joy."[120]

Eliphaz suggests a profile of human good fortune, expressed in his testimony about the activity of God in our lives. We are protected from trouble, from death in famine or conflict, from the attacks of human beings and ani-

---

[118]James L. Crenshaw discusses the ambiguity in Qohelet's attitude to old age in "Youth and Old Age in Qoheleth," *Hebrew Annual Review* 10 (1986): 1-13.

[119]R. Norman Whybray, *The Good Life in the Old Testament* (London/New York: Continuum, 2002), p. 6.

[120]Ludwig Köhler, *Old Testament Theology* (London: Lutterworth, 1957/Philadelphia: Westminster Press, 1958), p. 151.

mals. We live in covenant friendship with the land and its animals. There is well-being in our homes and folds, our offspring are many, and we come to the grave in ripe old age. Further, we have confidence about all this as life unfolds rather than worrying about it, so that we live with laughter and without fear; and as we then see it is so, we "acknowledge" it—the verbs *yāda*ʿ and negatived *yārēʾ* recur (Job 5:20-26).

Job himself suggests his profile of the good life when he looks back on how things once were (Job 29:2-4). "If only it was as in the months gone by, as in the days when God watched over me, as when his lamp shone over my head, when I walked in the dark by his light, when I was in my prime and God's company was on my tent." The overarching reality in Job's family life was God's watching over, God's lamp shining, God's company *(sôd)*. Given that, darkness holds no fears. It can be faced, because God interposes light. "The Almighty was still with me." In the First Testament (and in the New) God's "being with" is not merely an inner awareness of God's presence but an experience of God's active presence issuing in blessing and protection. It was a time "when my lads surrounded me, when my steps were awash with cream and the rock poured out for me streams of oil" (Job 29:5-6). God's presence generated a settled and well-appointed family life in a well-to-do household. Family of course is not merely the nuclear family but the wider kinship group of which Job's grown-up children are part, even if they live in separate households in the vicinity and do things together without Job (see Job 1). While the people in one household may be a group not unlike our nuclear household, the broader web in which that household is set means that the nuclear family does not bear the intolerable burden that weighs down the modern nuclear family. So Job has a company of young people *(na*ʿ*ărîm* has referred in Job 1 both to his servants and to his children; if it includes the former, it is a friendlier word than ʿ*ăbādîm)*. Cream (more accurately, the traditional refreshing yogurtlike *leben*) and olive oil (in this context, suggesting oil used as face and body lotion) flow like water. Job had looked forward to this continuing as he lived on to a good old age in the bosom of his family, enjoying such resourcing and keeping his powers to the end (Job 29:18-20).

By all means put all your energy into doing what you have the chance to do, Qohelet urges (Eccles 9:10). On the other hand, he tells of testing enjoyment *(śimḥâ)*, the experience of good things *(ṭôb)*. He builds houses with substantial staffs. He plants vineyards and drinks their wine, constructs parks and orchards with irrigation schemes, breeds large herds and flocks. He collects treasures, sponsors musicians and other indulgences (perhaps a harem, but the translation is uncertain). But having done all that, he concludes that play and enjoyment are mad and get no one anywhere (Eccles 2:1-12). It is useless to expend effort to become the best architect in the world or the richest person in the world or the most insightful Old Testament theologian in the world, or to try to work out what the future holds, or to fret over the fact that sometimes the wicked do well and the faithful do badly. Accept things as they are in the present and enjoy the simple things of life. "This exaltation, in the Old Testament, of earthly possessions, many children, long life, friendship and love, as well as wisdom, beauty, honour, and political freedom . . . is a continual thorn in the flesh for a spiritual view of life" in the sense of a view that contrasts the spiritual and physical or makes it possible for the one to be independent of the other.[121]

6.5 Responsibility

For modern Western Christians, the reality of freewill is a key aspect of what it means to be human, and a key implication of Genesis 2—3. On this view "the problem of freedom is peculiarly 'the' problem of human existence, for freedom is the original element of personal being."[122] To be human is to be free rather than predetermined. I make my own decisions, and I am responsible for them. The First Testament's focus lies elsewhere, not least in Genesis 2—3, which emphasizes that we are not free to do what we like, rather than that we are thus free. (It does also assume that we are indeed free in that Western Christian sense, but that is not its concern, and it would probably not see that as freedom.)[123]

There is another contrast with the modern understanding of freedom. A myth of biblical interpretation used to say that early in First Testament times Israel believed so strongly in the communal nature of human experience that it did not really allow for the responsibility of the individual. Jeremiah and Ezekiel then mark a recognition of the truth that responsibility is individual not corporate.[124] In actual fact, the First Testament recognizes the reality of individual responsibility from the beginning; it is the presupposition of the earliest regulations in the Torah as of the latest. At the same time, alongside this it recognizes throughout the reality of a people's or a family's communal nature and communal responsibility, both horizontal (in relation to our contemporaries) and vertical (in relation to earlier generations).[125] In different contexts, the corporate or the individual needs more emphasis. This under-

---

[121]Eichrodt, *Man in the OT*, p. 33.

[122]Emil Brunner, *Man in Revolt* (London: Lutterworth, 1939), p. 256.

[123]See *OTT* 1:132-33.

[124]See, e.g., references in Joel Kaminsky, *Corporate Responsibility in the Hebrew Bible*, JSOTSup 196 (Sheffield: Sheffield Academic Press, 1995), pp. 117-19.

[125]See the discussion in Paul Joyce, *Divine Initiative and Human Response in Ezekiel*, JSOTSup 51 (Sheffield: JSOT Press, 1989), pp. 79-87.

standing confronts our predominant focus on individual responsibility.

Bound Up in Responsibility in a Community

So the first laws in Exodus treat both community and individuals as responsible for their actions. As a preliminary (Ex 19), Yhwh addresses the household of Jacob (a corporate entity) and the children of Israel (a family of individuals). The whole people (singular) respond (plural). Yhwh will appear so that the people may hear (singular) and believe (plural). Moses is to set bounds for them round the mountain, but individuals are responsible for their observance of these bounds and for the guilt that would attach to infringement. The Ten Words (Ex 20) initially seem to be addressing the people corporately ("I am Yhwh your God who brought you out of the land of Egypt. . . . You shall have no other gods . . .") but transition imperceptibly to the second-person singular, apparently addressing individuals ("You shall not murder . . ."). The following law about the altar (Ex 20:22-26 [MT 19-23]) moves between *you* singular and plural, as do the closing laws and exhortations (Ex 23:13-33; cf. Ex 34:11-26). In between, the laws in Exodus 21 address the individual Israelite and treat this individual as responsible for his or her actions. One point about the law about "an eye for an eye" (Ex 21:23-25) may be that punishments are to be related to wrongdoings and all people are to be treated the same, rather than a rich person being able to pay a fine to avoid being personally punished. The law about homicide assumes that intent makes a difference to guilt and responsibility; if you kill someone accidentally, you are not to be treated as a murderer (Ex 21:12-14; 22:2-3 [MT 1-2]). Likewise the law about an ox killing a human being distinguishes between an ox that is a known attacker, whose owner is therefore implicated, and an ox that has never acted thus before (Ex 21:28-29). Thus the instructions recognize several realities. The people *are* a collection of individuals who can be addressed in the plural. The people *is* also a body; this corporate body exists as a reality. And individuals are responsible for their own lives, independently of their membership of this body.[126]

As well as having responsibility for our own lives, then, we belong to communities and share experience and responsibility with them, as the story of Achan and his family infamously presupposes (Josh 7), and as the New Testament emphasis on the body of Christ affirms. When the United States or Britain makes war on another nation, its citizens share in their nation's responsibility for this war, in the cost of it and in any gain that comes from it, whether or not they personally endorse it. Likewise the citizens of the nation

---

[126]Contrast Eichrodt, *Man in the OT*, pp. 9-13, who puts exclusive emphasis on individual responsibility. In the modern world, too, corporate bodies such as companies as well as individuals can own property and can be held responsible for their deeds.

they attack share in the cost of the invasion whether or not they personally support their own government and the policies that may have led to the attack. "Many modern thinkers would criticize the system of punishment advocated in Joshua 7 as inherently unfair because it does not treat each person as an autonomous individual," but this narrative might offer "an implicit critique of the modern predisposition to view individuals as autonomous entities who only relate to their society when they freely choose to do so." Likewise they would prefer the individualistic implications of Ezekiel 18 (as they understand them) because "although moderns are not opposed to the idea of benefiting from the merits of one's ancestors, . . . the thought of suffering for other people's misdeeds is so distasteful that we reject any theology that advocates such a linkage," even though it is truer to experience.[127]

Whereas Ezekiel has a reputation for individualism, he stresses the fact that Israel as a whole is a rebellious household. When he envisages calamity coming (Ezek 4—5), at first it comes on the whole city. There is no talk of discrimination. That point is explicit in the vision of destruction as a forest fire and then as a sword: "I will cut off from you faithful and faithless. . . . My sword will come out of its sheathe to all flesh from south to north" (Ezek 21:3-4 [MT 8-9]). But the description of undiscriminating calamity is designed to drive the community as a whole to turn. Even when Ezekiel 18 talks in terms of the individual, it does so for illustrative purposes in the context of a concern to address "the household of Israel" (Ezek 18:25, 29, 30, 31). It is *you* plural who are under the threat of Yhwh's punishment and are urged to turn.

Can the Faithful Deliver the Faithless Community?

In general, the thinking of the First Testament is thus more realistically corporate than the thinking of modernity. It knows that the destiny of individuals is tied up with that of groups of which they are members. Often life is not fair to individuals because they are swallowed up by the destiny of the groups to which they belong, for good or ill. But perhaps life might similarly not be fair for communities, for good or ill, because of the individuals within them? Could the presence of faithful individuals deliver a faithless people? Perhaps Sodom might escape calamity because of the presence of a mere ten faithful people (see Gen 18:22-33)? Perhaps Jerusalem can escape calamity because of the faithfulness of a Josiah? Jeremiah raises that possibility as he pictures Yhwh commissioning a search through Jerusalem for "one person taking action on behalf of trustworthiness, so that I might pardon it" (Jer 5:1). Ezekiel likewise imagines there being one person prepared to build a wall and stand in the breach before

---

[127]Kaminsky, *Corporate Responsibility*, pp. 95, 187.

Yhwh on behalf of the land. If there were such a person, its destruction might be avoided. The idea is that the city is vulnerable to attack not merely by Babylon but by Yhwh. Its vulnerability to warrior Yhwh, the fatal gap in its defenses, lies in its faithlessness. But it might take only one faithful person to close that breach. Such a person could defeat Yhwh! After all, Yhwh would be only too glad to have a reason to call off the city's siege. But Yhwh has searched through the religious and political leadership and the regular citizenry or landowners of the community,[128] looking for such a person, but found none (Ezek 22:23-30). The Targum implies that this person would stand in the breach by praying, and that may be an appropriate understanding of the way the person's faithfulness would function. But Yhwh's survey of the situation has focused on these people's wrongdoing rather than their failure in prayer, so its implication is perhaps that a single person's faithfulness would constitute a claim that appealed to Yhwh in the way one does in praying (cf. Is 53:10).

In Jerusalem, even if not in Sodom, there are people for whose sake the city might have escaped, if one person were enough. There were at least Jeremiah and Baruch, and other people who, for instance, defended Jeremiah (see Jer 26). Ezekiel 9 likewise implies that there were people who could properly hope to escape from Jerusalem's destruction on the basis of their disassociation from its wrongdoing. Jeremiah and Ezekiel are speaking hyperbolically and rhetorically when they say there is not a single person. The devastating charge is designed to make people disprove it, to shake people out of their indifference.

Ezekiel declares that even the presence of archetypal upright men of ancient times such as Noah, Job and Daniel/Danel[129] would not deliver their people if the people were faithless as a whole (see Ezek 14:12-20). Ezekiel three times makes explicit that they would not even deliver their own sons and daughters. He makes his point about nations in general—the three heroes are pre-Israelite or non-Israelite—but then makes explicit that what is true of the world in general is also true of Jerusalem. That no doubt indicates that one function of the warning is to focus the minds of the actual children and grandchildren of faithful people in Jerusalem, especially of the great reforming king Josiah and his contemporaries (Zedekiah was Josiah's son), and/or to focus the exiles' minds on them. It warns the community against the idea that it can shelter behind the presence of a number of faithful people, as if they could save the entire community.

---

[128]The ʿam hāʾareṣ (lit. "people of the country"). In such contexts the term seems to mean something less inclusive than merely "Israelites"; it implies a group of people in a special position.

[129]Not the First Testament Daniel but a figure of ancient times known to us from a Ugaritic story.

Challenged to Respond as Individuals

At the same time, individuals cannot hide behind the community. Like Exodus, Proverbs assumes that individuals exercise responsibility for their lives. Trusting God and believing in God's power does not imply doing nothing. However constrained by personality, background or experience, I am able to exercise responsibility now, to make decisions about which way I will walk. My task is to take control of my ears, mind, mouth, lips, ears, eyelids and feet (Prov 4:20-27). I am responsible, that is, for what I listen to, how I think about it, what I say, where I look and where I go.[130]

Yhwh complains, "they do not speak honestly; there is not a person who has relented of his or her evil by saying 'what have I done?'" (Jer 8:6). Jeremiah is bidden to put his oracles into writing so that "perhaps the household of Judah will hear of all the bad that I am intending to do to them, so that each of them may turn from his bad ways and I may pardon his wrongdoing and failure" (Jer 36:3; cf. Jer 25:5; 26:3). Community life requires that each individual acts in a faithful way with his neighbor (Jer 7:5). "Listen [plural] to the words of this covenant. . . . Cursed is the person who does not listen to the words of this covenant. . . . But [your ancestors] did not listen or bend their ear but walked, each person, in the willfulness of their evil heart" (Jer 11:2, 3, 8; cf. Jer 16:12; 18:11-12). "Your eyes are open to all the ways of human beings to give to each person in accordance with his ways and in accordance with the fruit of his deeds" (Jer 32:19). "After I have uprooted them I will again have compassion on them and return them each person to his possession, each person to his land" (Jer 12:15).

The rebelliousness of the household as a whole does not make it impossible for individuals to dissociate themselves from the community's stance. Ezekiel presses them to do so by presenting them with the picture of a man in linen who marks people who lament the abominations of Jerusalem, who are to escape the city's punishment (Ezek 9). The possibility of individuals thus escaping functions to highlight the totality of the calamity coming on the people as a whole.[131] It may not presuppose that there actually are such people; it may leave the question open. If there are, the passage's promise corresponds to Ezekiel's declaration about the three upright heroes. Such people save themselves, but they do not save anyone else.

Yhwh's undertaking to restore Israel implicitly recognizes that this restoration requires people's response, and that this is not only a corporate response. "I will purge from you those who revolt and rebel against me. I will bring them

---

[130]Clifford, *Proverbs*, pp. 20-21.

[131]Joyce, *Divine Initiative*, pp. 61-66.

out from the countries where they are staying, but they will not come onto the soil of Israel. And you will acknowledge that I am Yhwh" (Ezek 20:38). At the moment the people as a whole is in a state of rebellion but Yhwh can envisage some people dissociating themselves from this rebellion. Then, the people as a whole will be restored, but Yhwh can envisage some people continuing in a rebellious stance. They will be brought out from the lands where the people as a whole are scattered (perhaps to avoid giving the impression that Yhwh could not rescue them and/or that it is possible to escape from Yhwh), but they will not be allowed to return to the land. Their fate will parallel that of the wilderness generation, which left Egypt but never saw Canaan.

Bound Up in Responsibility with Previous Generations

People are also one in vertical relationships with people who came before and will come after. "The faithful person who walks in integrity—the good fortune of his children after him" (Prov 20:7). Conversely, "the person involved in extortion makes trouble for his household, but the person who spurns gifts will live" (Prov 15:27). The father who uses crooked means to gain things for his family would naturally think he was making life good for them, but he and they will find that life works in the opposite way. "The person who repays good with evil—evil will not depart from his house" (Prov 17:13). Everyday experience makes clear that the blessings of one generation usually affect the next generation and the one after that, and so do the calamities. Many of the international conflicts of the twenty-first century (notably, those in the Middle East) issue from the acts or neglects of the nineteenth and twentieth centuries. We are the beneficiaries and the victims of decisions taken by previous generations, and we pass on blessings and trouble to coming generations, as the Decalogue affirms (Ex 20:5-6). The First Testament recognizes this and has Yhwh working on this basis, though it puts a positive slant on it as it has Yhwh reckoning to keep commitment to thousands (of generations?) but only making sin have an effect on the third and fourth (generations?) (Ex 34:6-7). Proverbs likewise comments on the good fortune of children whose parents teach them to base their lives on the same foundation as their own, so that Yhwh's love and mercy extends to the next generation as it has to this one: "In reverence for Yhwh is strong security, and their children will have a refuge" (Prov 14:26). Jesus takes up the negative side to this reality in seeing the Jewish leadership in its day as the true descendants of its ancestors and as paying the final penalty for wrong done through First Testament times (Mt 23:29-36; cf. 1 Thess 2:14-16).

In line with our natural instinct to be happy about being the beneficiaries of our ancestors' honorable deeds or achievements but not about being the casualties of their wrongdoing, there was a saying: "It is the parents that eat unripe grapes but the children's teeth that are blunt" (Ezek 18:2; cf. Jer 31:29). Many people viewed unripe grapes as a delicacy, despite the fact that their acidity left a rough taste in the mouth. The saying speaks as if one generation eats the grapes but the next generation experiences the rough taste. It thus speaks realistically about the way one generation's acts affect the next. They do that for good—for instance, the parents plant trees but the children enjoy their fruit. They also do it for ill—the parents neglect their trees but the children are the ones for whom the fruit fails.

In Jeremiah and Ezekiel's day, people quoted the saying to apply it to their particular historical experience. They accepted the thesis that the troubles that came on Judah after Josiah were the result of religious indulgences before Josiah, those of Manasseh's long reign (see 2 Kings 23:26-27; 24:3-4; Lam 5:7). (The example also shows how, as is the case with war, a people is bound up in responsibility with its leadership.) Indeed, Yhwh speaks of having declared, back in the wilderness, the intention to scatter Israel among the nations because of its wrongdoing in the wilderness (Ezek 20:23). The present generation is thus paying the price for its ancestors' deeds way back then. But that's not fair, is it? It contradicts principles implicit or explicit throughout the Torah (see esp., Deut 24:16). "A principle that is rejected in the case of judicial punishment is yet recognized as operative in the divine realm," as Deuteronomy itself recognizes (Deut 5:9).[132]

It is then easy for people to ricochet from irresponsibility when they are doing all right to despair when calamity falls on them. At the time of the fall of Jerusalem people are saying, "Our rebellions and our failures are upon us" (Ezek 33:10). They weigh heavily on them not merely subjectively but objectively. Their wrongdoings have brought devastating calamity upon the community. Thus "we waste away in them" (*māqaq*), again not merely psychologically but physically. Ezekiel puts on their lips the term he threatened would apply to them when they run out of food and water during the siege of Jerusalem (Ezek 4:16-17; 24:23; and cf. Lev 26:39).[133] His later image will be that the people are like an army annihilated in battle; all that remains is bones scattered over the battlefield (Ezek 37). So "how can we live on," how can we survive as a community or come back to life?

Challenged to Escape Their Past

Yhwh does not deny what the people say to Ezekiel; they are right, as is indicated elsewhere (e.g., 2 Kings 23:26-27), though of course if they had turned to Yhwh, they could have escaped this fate. They can ask God not to make the

---

[132]Greenberg, *Studies in the Bible and Jewish Thought*, p. 37.

[133]In Zech 14:12 EVV translate "rot"; cf. the related noun in Is 3:24; 5:24.

ancestors' failures a basis for later judgment (Ps 79:8). If they are in trouble because of wrongdoing that goes back to Manasseh, it is wrongdoing they have continued. As the people followed Manasseh in his faithlessness (cf. 2 Kings 22:17; 24:20), so king and people over subsequent generations followed the example of Manasseh and his generation. The people is one people. The generations are not hermetically sealed.

Yet in Jeremiah and Ezekiel's day, Yhwh responds, "there will be no more repeating this proverb for you in Israel. Now. All lives belong to me. The life of the parent and the life of the child, they belong to me in the same way. It is the person who sins that will die" (Ezek 18:3-4; cf. Jer 31:29-30). Ezekiel's spelling out of the implications shows that this is at least as much a challenge as a promise. If a person lives a faithful life religiously and socially, "he will certainly live." But if his son does the opposite, "he will certainly not live. . . . He will certainly die. His blood will be on him," that is, he himself will face the consequences of his actions. If his son in turn does not follow his father's example, in turn "he will not die for his father's wrongdoing; he will certainly live" (Ezek 18:5-17). The principle is, "it is the person who sins that will die. A child will not carry it for the parent's wrongdoing and a parent will not carry it for the child's wrongdoing. The faithfulness of the faithful will rest on that person and the faithlessness of the faithless will rest on that person" (Ezek 18:20). One generation is not punished for an earlier generation's sin; if it turns back to God from waywardness it can be forgiven and healed (2 Chron 7:14).

In our day, our stress on the individual means we have to be reminded of the reality of the communal, as is reflected in our slanted reading of First Testament thinking on this matter. In Jeremiah and Ezekiel's day, the need was the opposite. Instead of evading corporate responsibility, people were evading individual responsibility. They believed they could do nothing about their own destiny. It was predetermined by the acts of their parents' and grandparents' generation. Not so, says Ezekiel. Each generation stands before God with an open future, called as part of its humanity to accept responsibility before God for its destiny.[134] The fact that one generation lives God's way does not protect the next generation; it has to make that stance its own. The fact that one generation evades God's way does not lock the next generation into a destiny that the past imposes on it. Ezekiel's community cannot use the past as an excuse for continuing to behave in the religious or social ways that brought about the

---

[134]Cf. Gerhard von Rad's comments about Chronicles in his *Old Testament Theology,* 2 vols. (Edinburgh: Oliver & Boyd/New York: Harper, 1962, 1965), 1:349. For further discussion see, e.g., Herbert G. May, "Individual Responsibility and Retribution," *Hebrew Union College Annual* 32 (1961): 107-20; Barnabas Lindars, "Ezekiel and Individual Responsibility," *VT* 15 (1965): 452-67; Kaminsky, *Corporate Responsibility.*

exile. It cannot make bondage to the past the basis for claiming victim status in the present. Recognizing the past's influence on the present opens up the possibility of distancing oneself from it. That is true about our relationship with our corporate past (family, society, community) and about our individual past: when we come to acknowledge our mistakes and wrongdoing, we also gain some independence from them. But it looks as if Ezekiel's community did not want that.

It preferred to wallow in victim status. When a group of elders come to inquire of Yhwh, Ezekiel arraigns them because of the wrongdoing of their ancestors (Ezek 20). At first that looks like a confirmation of the popular view that Ezekiel is denying, but it becomes clear this is not so. Yhwh arraigns them because they are continuing in the same ways as their ancestors. That warning back in the wilderness does not mean that an inexorable fate hangs over them. It means they have to see the depth of the problem that confronts them and the seriousness of the danger they are in and therefore take action. Yhwh urged the children of the wilderness generation not to follow in the ways of their parents, and it was their own failure to do so that led to Yhwh's warning about scattering, not the declaration elsewhere that in any case the sins of their parents would inevitably be visited on them.

Yhwh imagines the people asking Jeremiah why Yhwh is threatening them with disaster (Jer 16:10). This is itself a striking idea. One might have thought that the work of prophets such as Jeremiah had made them well aware of the basis for their alleged guilt, even though they would have disputed what Jeremiah said. Perhaps the question indicates how resistant they were; Yhwh's word had gone in one ear and out the other. Or perhaps the passage works purely rhetorically and Yhwh formulates their implausible question in order to give an answer that makes an important point: "Because your ancestors left me (Yhwh's message) and followed other gods, served them and bowed down to them. They left me and did not keep my teaching. And you have done worse than your ancestors. Here you are, every one of you following the firmness of your evil heart so as not to listen to me" (Jer 16:11-12). They are not simply paying the penalty for their ancestors' wrongdoing nor simply paying the penalty for their own wrongdoing. They are doing both. They are doing the former, because of the disastrous long-term effect of their ancestors' acts on the subsequent generation, and because in the absence of some of that subsequent generation turning back to Yhwh and in the absence of some forgiveness, that earlier wrongdoing cannot simply sit there neither forgiven nor punished. They are also doing the latter, because they have affirmed their ancestors' stance for themselves and stood firm in it, so as even to outdo their ancestors in wrongdoing—if that can be imagined.

There is nothing very novel about such a challenge. From the beginning, prophets assume that people are capable of responding to Yhwh. The question is whether they will. Israel is to "turn" to Yhwh (Hos 14:1-2 [MT 2-3]; Joel 2:12-13) and is subject to critique for not doing so (Amos 4:6-11).

Guilt and Forgiveness

Psalm 51 acknowledges guilt that goes back to the earliest beginnings of one's life: "I was born with waywardness, my mother conceived me with failure" (Ps 51:5 [MT 7]). As Israel's sin goes back to its earliest beginnings as a people, even to a time before the "birth" brought about by the exodus, so does the sin of the individual. Our conception and birth happen in a sinful context and we live in an environment affected by sin from the very start. It is hard to say at what moment we become individually responsible for our sin, but whenever that is, our lives are affected by that reality, just as the rest of our lives are affected by the nature we inherit from our parents and by the context in which they bring us up. Sin is as natural to us as breathing. But none of this means we are not challenged to accept responsibility for our lives. (The psalmist's point is compatible with some understandings of the idea of "original sin" though that often carries other connotations. As Augustine notes, the psalm does not imply that sin is somehow intrinsically related to sex,[135] nor does it imply that our sinfulness is distinctively determined by our genes rather than by our environment.)

In EVV, "guilt" most commonly renders 'āšām and related words (e.g., Lev 4—5) and refers to the objective position of someone who has committed an offense. "The objective nature of sin" means that "intention is (relatively) insignificant."[136] What counts is whether I have actually dishonored or hurt someone, not whether I meant to do so. Guilt relates to the objective wrong of an act rather than a feeling of blameworthiness. Israel "refused to dissolve her concept of guilt into subjectivity,"[137] though the subjective sense of being in the wrong could be expressed in other ways (see, e.g., Ps 51:3-4 [MT 5-6]).[138]

The objective fact of guilt means that people who do wrong have to "carry their wrongdoing/failure" (Lev 5:1; 7:18; 17:16; 20:17, 19, 20; 22:9, 16; 24:15); "their blood is on them" (Lev 20:9, 11, 12, 13, 16, 27). Wrongdoing, guilt and punishment interrelate. People have to live with their wrongdoing and its consequences. This again does not denote living with the feelings that issue from

---

[135] Augustine *Expositions on the Book of Psalms*, Nicene and Post-Nicene Fathers, series 1, vol. 8 (reprint, Edinburgh: T & T Clark/Grand Rapids, Mich.: Eerdmans, 1989), p. 193.

[136] Mark E. Biddle, *Missing the Mark* (Nashville: Abingdon, 2005), p. 95.

[137] Von Rad, *OT Theology*, 1:268.

[138] Jacob Milgrom argues that in passages such as Lev 4—5 'āšam means "feel guilty": see *Cult and Conscience* (Leiden: Brill, 1976), pp. 7-12; but see, e.g., *NIDOTTE* 1:554.

that; it rather means that wrongdoers may find themselves executed (e.g., Lev 20:2) or cut off from the community (Lev 20:18) or childless (Lev 20:20-21) or losing their lives (Lev 22:9) or put under a curse (Num 5:11-31) or bringing a calamity such as an epidemic on the community (Num 8:19).

This list of consequences includes some that are humanly imposed and some that are divinely imposed and some that leave the means of implementation unstated. Even where execution is mandated (e.g., for insulting one's parents or committing adultery) it seems unlikely that this law really prescribes what Israel should actually do. Certainly Israel does not seem to have understood Leviticus thus; as far as we can tell it did not execute adulterers or people who insulted their parents.

There is a further principle that needs to be noted (see Ezek 18:21-32). As one's parents' commitment to Yhwh does not carry over its effect in our lives if we do not imitate their commitment, so our own commitment does not carry over its effect in our lives if we subsequently abandon it. If we turn from our faithlessness and live obedient lives, we will live. God will put out of mind our acts of rebellion. After all, "do I really want the death of the faithless (the Lord Yhwh's message) and not for him to turn from his ways and live?" If a criminal turns from wrongdoing, this does not mean being pardoned for the wrongs. But the way Yhwh operates is different. Turning means pardon. Whereas a judge may hate having people die yet still accept the obligation to impose the death penalty, Yhwh, who also hates having people die and loves having the excuse to let them live, is in a position to act in accordance with that hatred and love. But you must then maintain that commitment, otherwise you will find yourself back on death row. "And you say, 'The Lord's way is not right.' Do listen, household of Israel. Is it my way that is not right? Is it not your ways that are not right? . . . Therefore I will decide about you each person according to his ways, household of Israel (the Lord Yhwh's message). Turn, turn away from all your acts of rebellion and they will not be wrongdoing that makes you tumble. Put away from you all your rebellions that you have committed and get yourselves a new heart, a new spirit. Why should you die, household of Israel? Because I do not want anyone's death (the Lord Yhwh's message). So turn and live" (Ezek 18:21-32).

The Opportunity to Turn

But the people do have to turn. The trouble is that their declaration that Yhwh is not acting rightly, with the implication that Yhwh is punishing them for their ancestors' wrongdoing, indicates a refusal to acknowledge that they themselves have done wrong, and thus a refusal to change their ways.

Yet as far as God is concerned, it is never too late. "As if I want the death of the faithless rather than that the faithless turn from their way and live on."

Being the victims of Yhwh's punishment for wrongdoing does not mean they are at an end, as if there is no way out. "Turn, turn from your wrong ways. Why should you die, household of Israel?" Yhwh repeats (Ezek 33:11). As people's faithfulness does not save them if they rebel, Ezekiel reaffirms, so people's faithlessness does not put them down if they turn from it. They can trust in their faithfulness, trust that it will mean they live on and do not experience calamity, if they maintain it, but not if they abandon it. God will then put their former faithfulness out of mind and they will die because of their wrongdoing. But that is the other side of a coin. It means that "when I say to the faithless, 'You are definitely going to die,' and they turn from their failure and act with decisive faithfulness, . . . they will live on, not die. All the failure they are guilty of will not be kept in mind for them. They have acted with decisive faithfulness. They will live on" (Ezek 33:14-16). Yhwh does not have any problem about forgiving people their sin if they have turned from it. Ezekiel does not imply that their new faithfulness makes atonement for their wrongdoing, though neither does he make clear how this process does work. Perhaps we are to assume that God works the same way as human beings do on a good day. If a man does terrible wrong to his father but then comes back and wants to behave like a son again, the father's instinct is to welcome him back; the wrongdoing ceases to matter. Ezekiel assumes it is so with God.

On the other hand, if he does not return, he cannot assume that things will turn out fine, notwithstanding the love of his father. The Jerusalemites encouraged themselves by recalling that Abraham gained possession of the land when he was only one man. There are many of them, so surely their possession of the land is quite secure (Ezek 33:24). Ezekiel implies that there are several flaws in their argument. First, how many is "many"? He describes the speakers as "people inhabiting the ruins" of the land of Israel. The country had been devastated and large numbers transported. Are these "many" facing facts? Can they really leave the Judeans in exile out of account (cf. Ezek 11:14-15)? Can they dismiss their neighbors who have designs on Judah, peoples such as the Edomites (cf. Ezek 35—36)? Of course they can, if they know Yhwh is involved in enabling them to keep hold of the land in fulfillment of the ancient promise. But the Jerusalemites' declaration, "the land has been given to us as a possession," strangely, tellingly and fatally hides the agent of this giving. Yhwh's involvement with Abraham began from Yhwh's initiative and presupposed nothing about his previous commitment to Yhwh, but it needed to issue in Abraham's becoming a man of trust, integrity and faithfulness (e.g., Gen 15:6; 17:1; 18:19). But this is a people who ignore Yhwh's expectations about religious and social life (Ezek 33:25-26). Their abominations must mean they lose the land, not that they are secure possessors of it. Their exemption from the transportations up to 587 does not mean they are not vulnerable. Yhwh can still totally empty the land. The people there now must turn.

6.6 Wisdom

Like love, wisdom is a quality all humanity is designed to possess, though like other such capacities it is rarely seen in its fullness and it is understood through its absence as much as through its presence. It denotes the insight and discernment to see things as they are and to act in light of how things are. As such, it is foundational and central to a life that works; it is "the necessary (and almost sufficient) means" for creating such a life.[139] It is thus not closely correlated to intellectual capacity or achievement, or to knowledge, but is rather a virtue that correlates with the qualities and attitudes of the person. It is quite accessible, which makes it strange that people spurn it, and of the two ways that open up before them, choose the stupid way rather than the path of wisdom. Perhaps this links with the fact that it is also dependent on divine giving and thus on reverence for Yhwh and moral faithfulness. Further, while it is of huge benefit in everyday life, it cannot answer the big questions about life and human experience, so that the wise person's relationship with God also involves trust and submission and a willingness to live with mystery.

The Availability of Insight

The First Testament often manifests a confidence that humanity can articulate this wisdom and live by it. Life is intelligible. Much of Proverbs is concerned with observations about how life works. "Hope deferred makes the heart sick, while a longing that comes about is a tree of life" (Prov 13:12). "There are people who scatter about and are increased more, and people who withhold what is right, yet end up in need" (Prov 11:24). What is the point of such observations? Perhaps the descriptive contains an implicit prescriptive.[140] Perhaps acknowledging experiences opens up the possibility of seeing a new pattern behind what looks random.[141] "Modern man puzzles to a greater extent over the irregularities which he is unable to fit into the general pattern. The ancients, on the other hand, were amazed if, in the confusion of daily events, inherent laws could nevertheless be discerned."[142] But simply understanding and articulating how things are fulfills an important function. If we understand, then in some sense we are in control. When a therapist enables a client

---

[139]Fox, *Proverbs 1—9*, p. 3.

[140]So, e.g., McKane, *Proverbs*, pp. 434-35.

[141]So Gerhard von Rad, *Wisdom in Israel* (London: SCM Press/Nashville: Abingdon, 1972), p. 128.

[142]Ibid., p. 127.

to articulate what is going on in his or her life, a weight can drop from the client's shoulders.

Most of the detail of wisdom is not very complicated. It is easy enough to understand the exhortations to avoid criminal company or adultery, and easy enough to see why these are sensible principles. Proverbs assumes people can be taught right and wrong—otherwise the book would hardly have a reason for existing. People have moral responsibility and they can learn. Proverbs appeals to their capacity to do so. "The ear that hears and the eye that sees—Yhwh made both of them" (Prov 20:12). The ear is so important an organ because through the ear we receive teaching and reproof, but the eye comes a close second in this connection (e.g., Prov 3:21; 4:21). It is therefore important that both can be trusted, because God made them. They can mislead (it is possible to listen to the wrong teaching or be wise in one's own eyes), and Yhwh's making of them places a responsibility on us to use them properly. But the fact that Yhwh made them means they need not mislead.

So we discover further how things are by looking, and we can thereby achieve wisdom on our own. Yet to keep reinventing the wheel is a wasteful procedure. It is wiser to learn wisdom by also profiting from the wisdom of the past. Proverbs 2:1-5 implies that "without learning from a teacher [vv. 1-2], reflection will avail nothing, and likewise teaching without reflection and analysis [vv. 3-4] will avail nothing." The key to learning lies in having these two in interrelationship.[143] When they are, they can lead to God granting wisdom (v. 5). Then a person's ongoing commitment to a wise life can be instinctive and self-motivating, but at an earlier stage it depends on winning a young person's commitment to the quest for wisdom before he or she has personal experience of it and its value.

Proverbs has a basically optimistic stance about life. Its introduction (Prov 1:2-7) reckons we can discern how life works and then live in light of that understanding. In conveying knowledge, instruction, discernment and insight, its wisdom can provide someone with shrewdness or practicality or sensibleness (*'ormâ*), with the capacity to formulate plans and make decisions (*mĕzimmâ*). That capacity to gain life skills is of obvious relevance to the young person (Prov 1:4). One should envisage not so much (certainly not merely) people of grade-school or high-school age but people of college- or graduate-school age, the people whom parents want to live wise adult lives, the people the king wants to use in the administration of the state, and the people who may end up teaching the faith. Whatever their age or destiny, they are unformed and thus susceptible to being misled. Proverbs wants to shape them

---

[143]Sa'adia Gaon, as quoted in Fox, *Proverbs 1—9*, p. 132.

and see their feet planted firmly on the right way.

The concern with the young does not mean that mature people simply arrive at wisdom and stop growing. They too can continue increasing in the kind of wisdom that makes it possible to steer one's way through life (tahbulôt—the expression comes from the word for "ropes" and links with other nautical terms; Prov 1:5).

The Strange Fact of Stupidity

One of Proverbs' key desiderata is that people should want to learn. Surely no one wants to be stupid? Yet all the time, people are ignoring wisdom's insights. So insight turns out to be something simple, yet also mysterious. It is a matter of one's heart as well as one's action, the heart as the wellspring of the person. Insight has to reach into that inner invisible wellspring if it is to characterize the life, and how that comes about is a mysterious matter. At one level the assertion that "stupid people despise wisdom and instruction"[144] (Prov 1:7) is a tautology or a truism; it says nothing. At another level it expresses that mystery: how extraordinary and inexplicable it is that people should be so stupid as to reject *wisdom!* But "if you were to crush fools in a mortar with a pestle along with crushed grain, their folly would not leave them"; fools are closed to learning, and there is no point in trying to teach them (Prov 27:22; cf. Prov 9:7-8; 13:1; 23:9). "Wisdom is in the presence of the discerning person, but the eyes of the fool are at the end of the earth" (Prov 17:24). They will not focus and pay attention. Their stupidity can be so deeply engrained that nothing can be done about it. They make real decisions and are responsible for them, but they lack the ability to make wise—that is, right and good—decisions. That is true of moral stupidity. "Such is the way of a woman who commits adultery: she eats and wipes her mouth and says, 'I have not done wrong'" (Prov 30:20). Stupid people are those who act in ways that destroy the community by the way they treat the vulnerable (foreigners, widows, orphans) on the basis of the conviction that Yhwh does not take any notice. They are important people and they talk big, but they will find that Yhwh knows that the plans of human beings are *hebel*—they have no substance to them (Ps 94:3-11).[145]

Yet Wisdom still addresses fools and seeks to get them to respond (e.g., Prov 1:20-24; 9:4-6). Perhaps one implication is that one can never know whether a person who seems incorrigibly stupid actually is so. The first reflection is an a posteriori one, the second the a priori attitude that teachers generally have to take. Ms. Wisdom still calls out, "Fools, teach your heart" (Prov 8:5),[146] and a prophet shouts in desperation, "Listen to this, will you, stupid people, sense-

---

[144]Or perhaps we should translate *mûsār* "discipline" rather than "instruction."

[145]On *hebel*, see section 6.6 "Limits."

less, who have eyes but do not look, ears but do not listen. Will you not revere me (Yhwh's message)? Will you not writhe before me?" (Jer 5:21-22). It is so self-evident, yet it is not compelling. Wisdom herself stands like a prophet in the marketplace shouting at the top of her voice. The problem is not that she is facing stiff competition from other prophets. It is that the naive are not listening to anyone. They just like being naive. They are indistinguishable from the stupid people who are averse to knowledge and the scoffers or loudmouths who are convinced they know everything and need to listen to no one (these *lēṣîm* do not believe in *mĕlîṣâ*, mystery; see Prov 1:6). Thus Ms. Wisdom is involved in rebuke; but such people take no notice, decline to listen, prefer to trust in their own insight (Prov 1:20-33).

"Who can understand wanderings?" (Ps 19:12).[147] Human sinfulness is mysterious. Why do we turn and wander from the path God lays out? The psalm has expatiated on how joyful and life-giving God's word is. How odd that we rebel against it. But we do. Therefore Psalm 19:12-14 prays, "Free me from the hidden, yes, withhold your servant from the willful. May they not rule over me, then I shall be whole, and free of great rebellion." We need God to free us from the inclination willfully to turn from God's way, even (especially) if we attempt to do so in secret ways—secret plots or secret turning to other deities. We need God to help us not submit to the influence of willful people. We need God to help us with the outward talk of our lips (because talk is such an effective way to sin) and the inward talk of our hearts (which may contradict the conformity of our lives). "May the words of my mouth be acceptable and the talk of my heart come before you, Yhwh, my crag, my restorer."

Human Responsibility and Divine Renewal

There is a further mystery: the process whereby human beings change their minds. The very phrase points to the mystery—how can a person *change* their *mind?* This can seem practically and logically impossible, yet we aim for it and experience it. The tension is one to be probed and understood rather than resolved.

As Proverbs sees it, humanity is divided into the wise, the stupid and the young people who could go either way. Proverbs itself exists to push people the right way. It makes two assumptions that stand in tension with each other,

---

[146]"Fool" is *ʾĕwîl* in Prov 27:22, *kĕsîl* in Prov 8:5, but the words have similar meaning. Further, *hābînû lēb* is an unusual expression, but even if we construe it some other way, the point is not affected.

[147]The EVV have "their wanderings" or the like, but the text has no pronominal adjective. I take the noun to come from *šāgâ*, which more characteristically suggests a deliberate going astray (cf. LXX) rather than *šāgag*, which more easily suggests accidental error (cf. Jerome).

a tension we know in our own world. It assumes that people are responsible for their destiny. It argues with them and presses them to act in rational and responsible ways in the conviction that it may get somewhere. But it is also aware that humanity has that mysterious inclination to stupidity and that rational argument often does not work.

Deuteronomy both urges people to circumcise their hearts and promises that Yhwh will do so (Deut 10:16; 30:6).[148] Ezekiel both urges people to get themselves a new heart and promises that Yhwh will give them one (Ezek 18:31; 36:26). Each insists on Israel's responsibility for its moral and religious life and also pictures Yhwh as the one who accepts responsibility for enabling Israel to live in obedience. No, people cannot escape their past. But Yhwh can make that possible. Notable exegetes on Ezekiel assume that the exhortation to "get [or make] yourselves a new mind" has rhetorical significance, though they disagree on the nature of its rhetorical significance.[149] The verb is ʿāśâ, which usually means "make." The EVV translation "get"[150] reduces the tension with the idea that a new heart is God's gift (e.g., Ezek 36:26) as it suggests laying hold on this gift; God does the renewing, but people have to open themselves to it. Gordon H. Matties suggests that the necessity for both ways of speaking stems from "the dialogical and covenantal dimension of discourse in Ezekiel."[151] God must act; people must reach out to God.

The standard prophetic exhortation to turn to Yhwh and obey Yhwh (reexpressed as a challenge to get a new heart) and the visionary prophetic promise that Yhwh will give people a new heart might seem like two alternative ways of looking at the dynamics of God's relationship with people.[152] But Ezekiel does not seem to pretend to resolve the nature of their relationship, and both have to be allowed to stand. While exhortation is more prevalent in the earlier part of the book and promise in the latter part, the distinction is not a clean one. The exhortation to "get yourself a new heart" epitomizes the tension. It parallels and relates to the tension between individual and corporate respon-

---

[148]See section 5.2 "Promising Moral Renewal."

[149]See, e.g., in the nineteenth century Patrick Fairbairn, *An Exposition of Ezekiel,* 3rd ed. ([Edinburgh: T & T Clark, 1863] reprint, National Foundation for Christian Education, 1969), p. 200; and in the twentieth Joyce, *Divine Initiative,* pp. 125-26. Cf. Jacqueline E. Lapsley, *Can These Bones Live?* BZAW 301 (Berlin/New York: Walter de Gruyter, 2000), p. 19.

[150]For this translation of ʿāśâ see, e.g., 2 Sam 15:1; and cf. Leslie C. Allen, *Ezekiel 1—19,* WBC (Dallas: Word, 1994), p. 267.

[151]Gordon H. Matties, *Ezekiel 18 and the Rhetoric of Moral Discourse,* SBLDS 126 (Atlanta: Scholars Press, 1990), p. 207.

[152]Thus Lapsley (*Can These Bones Live?*) sees Ezekiel as moving from an anthropology that sees people as inherently capable of making moral decisions to one that sees people as inherently incapable of that and needing God to make it possible, or at least sees the book as encouraging such a movement of perspective.

sibility and that between intergenerational influence and freedom. But the exile did lead to a clearer articulation of three awarenesses in this connection. One is the depth of human resistance to doing right or of its incapacity for doing so. A second is the possibility and need that God might do something new to take further the original work of creation in order to put this matter right. The third is that the way God might do this is by the affective impact of a new act of grace and mercy that wins a change in people's inner beings.

This need for God to do something new is well-illustrated in Deuteronomy and Ezekiel, though one can also perceive it in Exodus, Isaiah 40—55, and Jeremiah, for example. In light of the fact that Israel's failure led to the exile, the exilic period sees the strongest affirmation that Yhwh must and will undertake a work of new creation in the people's heart if they are to live in commitment and obedience. Then the Second Temple period sees the strongest affirmation that people can and must respond to God and obey God (opinion differs only on whether this is an authentic expression of religious commitment or a decline into legalism). The New Testament writings present a renewed affirmation of the need for God to do something creative in people's hearts and a declaration that this is what God is doing in pouring the Holy Spirit on the community that believes in Jesus. But neither does this resolve that necessary tension, as is shown by the New Testament's stress on obedience to God, its recognition that this is not always forthcoming, and the subsequent history of the church. Neither the death and resurrection of Christ nor the pouring out of the Holy Spirit has turned the Christian community into an embodiment of goodness.

In general, it is only because Yhwh gave us ears and eyes that we can see and hear. But that is true in particular too. There is a mystery about when people can see and hear, when they have insight and understanding and respond to what confronts them, and when they cannot see or hear. It reflects the ongoing sovereignty of God the creator.

Wisdom and Reverence for Yhwh

An unexpected move in the introduction to Proverbs (Prov 1:1-7), with its focus on the practical nature of wisdom, brings it to a close with the declaration that reverence for Yhwh or submission to Yhwh is of key significance if we want to be people of insight. The expression *yir'at yhwh* is traditionally translated "the fear of Yhwh," but this is misleading. The noun *yir'â* covers both fear and reverence, and we have to infer from the context which applies. Further, in a wisdom context *yir'â* suggests not a feeling but an attitude expressed in action. It is closely associated with acknowledgment, submission and obedience. Reverence for Yhwh is an attitude; it leads to acknowledgment of Yhwh, which is an activity. Wisdom expresses itself in both. It is the beginning and heart of the learning process. Insight means living in accordance with how things are; Yhwh is, after all, the world's creator and sovereign, and this fact is a fundamental feature of how things are. Likewise the second main homily in Proverbs has Ms. Wisdom challenging people to pay attention because otherwise they will get into trouble. But in the middle it casually adds that this is so because people who turn their backs on knowledge are also people who do not choose reverence for Yhwh (Prov 1:29). Heeding Ms. Wisdom's advice is an expression of such reverence. "A person's folly subverts their way, but their heart rages against Yhwh" (Prov 19:3). The division of humanity into wise and stupid is also a division into faithful and faithless.

Much of Proverbs is comparable with the teaching of other peoples and seems to have learned from it, which suggests that it would not see their reverence for their gods as implying that their learning is doomed from the start. They have to make do with reverence for God, as opposed to Yhwh (e.g., Gen 20:11; Job 6:14), which would leave them short over against what Yhwh has revealed to Israel, but it does not leave them without a starting point in an awareness that they stand over against God and live their lives before God. Wisdom can be attained by non-Israelites such as Job, Agur and Lemuel's mother (Prov 30:1; 31:1).

There is also a converse. While you need to revere God if you are to find wisdom, Proverbs 2 goes on to make the opposite point, that if you seek wisdom with openness, attentiveness, energy and urgency, "then you will understand reverence for Yhwh and find acknowledgment of God—because Yhwh is the one who gives wisdom; by his word come acknowledgment and discernment" (Prov 2:5-6). How is it that seeking wisdom leads people to recognize Yhwh? Perhaps the idea is that seeking wisdom, especially when done with such vigor, teaches the seeker that the quest cannot be a success unless one turns to Yhwh. Job 28 notes that people put comparable energy into mining for precious metals and succeed in their quest. They know where to find them. "There is a mine for silver. . . . But wisdom: where is it to be found? Where is the place of understanding?" (Job 28:1, 12). The only person who knows the answer to that is God. So if you want to find the way to it, you need to recognize that "reverence for the Lord, that is wisdom, and departing from evil is understanding" (Job 28:28). Proverbs 2 similarly recognizes that people who apply all their energy to seeking insight will not thereby find it and will find themselves driven to bring Yhwh into the picture. And/or perhaps the implication is that people who seek and find wisdom will find that they have unintentionally found or have been driven to express reverence for Yhwh. And/or perhaps (if we read v. 5 in light of v. 6) it is that such people will realize when they find wisdom that they have found it only because the way opened up to it by the grace of the God who alone knows the way to it. Of course those descriptive statements about how things work are really more prescriptive ones. In Western culture, at least, people who seek wisdom commonly do not then come to understand reverence for Yhwh. Perhaps Proverbs would comment that they claim to be seeking wisdom but are actually failing to do so; if anything they are avoiding it. They count among the stupid. On the other hand, Proverbs does not imply that it is possible to bypass the energetic quest for wisdom. The fact that it is a gift of God does not mean that the simple can just sit there waiting for it to arrive. The chapter both validates the quest and recognizes that it will not succeed except by God's making it do so. Wisdom is not mysterious in that it involves reverence for Yhwh and commitment to faithfulness and integrity, but mystery lies in whether and why people will show such reverence and commitment.

So "the good fortune of everyone who reveres Yhwh, who walks in his ways, because you will eat the fruit of your hands; your good fortune!—and good things will be yours, your wife like a fruitful vine within your house, your children like olive shoots around your table. There—so is the man blessed who reveres Yhwh" (Ps 128:1-4).

Wisdom and Faithfulness

To the fact that "reverence for the Lord, that is wisdom," Job 28:28 adds, "and understanding lies in turning away from evil." Proverbs 1:3 likewise sees the fruitfulness of wisdom as lying in "faithfulness, judgment, and uprightness." The way those two cola in Job 28:28 complement each other suggests we should not treat "faithfulness, judgment, and uprightness" and "reverence for Yhwh" as two separate qualities or stances. Reverence for Yhwh or acknowledgment of Yhwh expresses itself in turning away from evil or in faithfulness, judgment and uprightness. Shrewdness and the capacity to make decisions (Prov 1:4) can be used to bad ends as well as good ones; the first is the characteristic the serpent possessed in spades (Gen 3:1; cf. Job 5:12; 15:5), while the second can denote scheming and intrigue (e.g., Prov 12:2; 24:8). It is thus significant that Proverbs 1:3 incorporates reference to "faithfulness, judgment, and uprightness" and that Proverbs 1:7 adds that reverence for Yhwh is the beginning or first principle of wisdom; the hearers are not to follow the example of the people of intrigue (who ignore the first) or the serpent (who ignored the second). Faithfulness, judgment and uprightness are, after all, the characteristics of Yhwh's own person, and they are, thus, the qualities or stances that Yhwh looks for in people. The same implication emerges from Proverbs 2. There the quest for wisdom leads to reverence for Yhwh as the one who "stores up resourcefulness for the upright and is a shield for people who walk in integrity" (Prov 2:7). The point is repeated by the chapter's two "then" sentences. "If you incline your ear to wisdom, . . . then you will understand reverence for Yhwh and find acknowledgment of God," and "then you will understand faithfulness and judgment, and uprightness—every good path, because wisdom will come into your mind" (Prov 2:2, 5, 9-10). Wisdom will lead you to submission to God and will lead you to integrity of life; these three are interwoven.

Someone who stands within the wisdom tradition, such as Eliphaz, is thus quite at home assuming that a person who ignores integrity and reverence for God will find that God "catches the wise in their cleverness as the plan of the twisters speeds on" (Job 5:13). Insight and decision making can be at the service of crookedness rather than being associated with commitment, but then they are self-defeating. "Evil people cannot discern how to make authoritative decisions [mišpāṭ] but people who have recourse to Yhwh discern everything" (Prov 28:5). The word mišpāṭ is both more concrete and broader than justice, though JPSV's "judgment" is nearer an appropriate one-word translation. Like people who leave God out of account and do not seek God's wisdom, evil people cannot be people of judgment because their moral commitment leaves out a key consideration that contributes to wise and proper decision making. On the other hand, if you are committed to goodness and if you are seeking to be open to God's guidance regarding what is right (and to doing it), you will have discernment with regard to everything. To put it in terms that appear elsewhere, you will have that knowledge of good and bad that humanity once forfeited through insisting on going straight for it and ignoring God. Perhaps the lack of discernment into mišpāṭ also extends to a failure to see how mišpāṭ will come to them because of their wrongdoing.[153] To put it another way, people need to make a commitment to walking the straight and faithful road; Yhwh brings it about that such people find wisdom (Prov 2:6-8).

An op-ed writer in the New York Times would expostulate, however, that people who reckon to take God into account often seem to make pretty immoral decisions. The mere fact that people reckon to be committed to goodness and to seek to be open to God's guidance regarding what is right does not in itself mean they make right decisions.

The Two Ways

"Behavior is a path" is the "ground metaphor" of Proverbs 1—9.[154] Our life is a journey, but in a different sense from the one that is current in Western thought. There, the focus lies on the journey itself, the process, rather than the objective or goal. In Proverbs the journey has a destination. For a Western person, on my life journey what matters is that I am working out the implications

---

[153]Cf. Clifford, Proverbs, p. 244.
[154]Fox, Proverbs 1—9, p. 128. He capitalizes the first phrase and italicizes the second.

of being "me," and unfaithfulness would lie in failing to walk my distinctive path. For Proverbs, to go astray means leaving the path of doing right; it involves leaving the wise way for the stupid way, following Ms. Stupidity rather than Ms. Wisdom. It is a choice between different loves: love for wisdom, for one's wife and for life; or love for stupidity, for possessions, for another woman and for death (e.g., Prov 1:22; 4:6; 5:19; 8:17, 21, 36; Eccles 5:10 [MT 9]; 9:9).

In the Western understanding, we think in terms of each individual's unique life journey. In Proverbs, the journey is one we take in the company of others. Of the two ways or paths that open up before humanity, neither is a narrow one with room for only one person to walk it. Both are walked by groups of people, and we decide which group we walk with.[155] The faithful and faithless are not two groups of people, determined to be thus before they were born. We keep deciding which group we belong to. It is always open to us to move from the one way to the other (hence Proverbs' repeated encouragements regarding the one and warnings regarding the other). Indeed, the various words for "way" or "path" often come in the plural. The straight way is not constricting; it does not require everyone to conform to the same way. Likewise there are many ways of finding the false "freedom" of the crooked way. There is a sense in which there are many ways that lead to light and life, and many ways that lead to darkness and death. Yet there is some unity about the two kinds of way. The image of two ways thus illustrates how Proverbs sees things in black and white. The contrast between wisdom and stupidity, faithfulness and faithlessness, makes it impossible to confuse them. There is no gray. Proverbs' view reminds us that there are social and political contexts in which that is especially so.

So one way is crooked (ʿiqqēš) and appropriate to people who are crooked in their ways (lûz) (crooks, as we say) and in their speech, people who speak things that twist and turn (tahpukôt). It is the way of wrongdoers, who are committed to doing harm to others (Prov 2:15-16). Although they think their way will bring gain, it actually leads to death (Prov 2:18). It goes through deep darkness, which means they cannot see what will make them fall over to destruction (Prov 4:19). They thus eat the fruit of their way, of the decisions they take (mōʿēṣôt, Prov 1:31). People have responsibility for their way—they make a decision to walk down it, and they keep making decisions on the way. And those decisions have their own outworking. Whereas Yhwh acknowledges the way of the faithful, the way of the faithless perishes. Psalm 1:6 does not say that Yhwh acts to make that happen; it is the innate result of their action as

---

[155]Cf. Richard J. Clifford, *The Book of Proverbs and Our Search for Wisdom* (Milwaukee: Marquette University Press, 1995), pp. 14-18.

their acts come to the destination they were bound for. It is the fruit the tree naturally bears (Prov 1:31).

The other way is straight and is appropriate to upright people, straight people, as we say, people who are on the level (e.g., Prov 2:12-15; 4:24-27).[156] It is "the way of understanding" (Prov 9:6), "the way of wisdom" or "the wise way," which one can walk easily and which never trips one with obstacles or potholes (Prov 4:10-11). The reason is that it is well-illumined. It is not like a path through a dark canyon where one has to be careful about tree roots or pitfalls, not to say wild animals or robbers. "The path of the faithful is like bright light, progressing in brightness until day is fully established" (Prov 4:18).[157] Admittedly this way to life involves challenge and discipline (Prov 6:23). It is more like training for a marathon than going for a casual walk.

Like the way of the crooked, the way of the righteous can be seen as reaching its destination "naturally." It means that whereas the faithless will be uprooted from the land, the upright will continue to live there (Prov 2:20-22). Holding on to wisdom means you go on your way safely and do not injure your feet or experience other kinds of harm (Prov 3:23-25). "Stupidity is a joy to mindless people, but people of insight make their journey straight" (Prov 15:21). There will be two senses in which that is true. They will pursue a life that is straight, that has integrity. And they will thereby ensure that the journey they have to take is a straight one, not complicated by dangerous and worrying twists and turns where they are not sure what trouble lies ahead. One has to be wary of being summoned off this straight way (Prov 9:15); the promise is that a straight person will find a straight way (cf. Prov 3:5-6; 11:3, 5; 15:21). Whereas the other way passes through darkness and naturally leads to death as people fall into a chasm they cannot see coming, this way passes through light and naturally leads to life; people do not trip because they can see. To use a different image, "the way of a lazy person is like a thorn hedge"—it is like a walk through thick briers, perhaps in the end impenetrable—because the lazy person let it get that way or treats it that way and rejoices in the excuse to give up and not bother trying to get anywhere. "But the path of the upright is [like] a highway," a road that is leveled and paved so that an army could march quickly along it and reach its destination (Prov 15:19).

But Proverbs adds another level of explanation. This will be so because "Yhwh will be your confidence and will guard your feet from being caught" (Prov 3:26). Yhwh thus "guards the way of people committed to him" (Prov

---

[156]See Fox, *Proverbs 1—9*, pp. 116-18, 128-31.

[157]In the first colon NIVI speaks of "the first gleam of dawn," while in the second colon JPSV speaks of "noon." I take the whole line to refer to the speedy Middle Eastern transition from the darkness of night to the brightness of a new day.

2:8), which rather implies that it needs some safeguarding. There may be two senses in which this is so. The way of the faithful is a narrow one. Those who walk it are always near the edge. The way of the wicked is always a temptation (Prov 4:14-15). Yhwh thus needs "to deliver you from the way of the wicked" (Prov 2:12) who try to divert you into their way. This fits Psalm 1:6, which speaks of Yhwh "acknowledging" the way of the faithful. The way of the faithless will find its own destination; Yhwh makes sure of the way of the faithful, makes a commitment to it.

The Times

There are proper times for things. There is a time when women gather at the well to draw water, a time when cattle are rounded up, a time when sheep conceive, a time when the rains come, a time when the sun sets, a time for dinner, a time for kings to go out to battle, a time for harvest, a time for the movements of stars and planets, a time for trees to fruit (Gen 24:11; 29:7; 31:10; Lev 26:4; Josh 10:27; Ruth 2:14; 2 Sam 11:1; Job 5:26; 38:32; Ps 1:3). For human beings, thus, there are times, as the wise mind acknowledges (Eccles 8:6).[158] There are times for birth and death, planting and uprooting, slaying and healing, demolishing and building, weeping and laughing, and so on, and God makes all these happen at appropriate moments (Eccles 3:1-11). This implies God is not arbitrary.[159] But as far as we are concerned, these events are rather unpredictable; we do not know when the "appropriate" time is about to arrive. Nor, in many cases, are the events within our control. "Time and chance come to all of them"—the quick and the strong, and also the wise. "Because, furthermore, human beings do not know their time," any more than fish caught in a net or birds in a snare. "Like them, human beings are caught at a time of calamity, when it falls on them suddenly" (Eccles 9:12-13). "A wise person went up to a city of warriors and brought down its secure stronghold" (Prov 21:22); but no one may remember what a city owes to a poor wise man who enabled a city to resist such an attacker (Eccles 9:13-16).

"Whatever happens, it was named long ago, and it was known what a person is, and he cannot contend with something stronger than him" (Eccles 6:10). Gerhard von Rad calls this verse "quite unambiguous" in its affirmation of determinism, but Roland E. Murphy more appositely comments that "the text is ambiguous, and uncertainty is reflected in many translations."[160] "Naming"

---

[158] "A wise mind acknowledges time *ûmišpāṭ*"; but it is difficult to discern the connotations of *mišpāṭ* in the context.

[159] Against James L. Crenshaw, *Ecclesiastes* (London: SCM Press, 1988), p. 92.

[160] Von Rad, *Wisdom in Israel*, p. 264; Roland E. Murphy, *Ecclesiastes*, WBC (Dallas: Word, 1992), p. 57.

and "knowing" might suggest "determining," but they significantly fall short of actually saying that; there can be a difference between foreknowing and foreordaining. And the naming and knowing of ʾādām may simply refer to humanity's being made from ʾădāmâ and being destined to return there. That is indeed determined, but that is hardly determinism, the view that "all human action is preordained and that freewill is therefore an illusion."[161] That is surely excluded by the fact that it is possible, by living faithlessly or stupidly, to die before your time (Eccles 7:17).

Nor, when we can control events, is it often possible for us to know their appropriate moment. So it is pointless to toil away at life because we can never know if our toil will get us anywhere. We cannot understand the logic of the way God runs the world. "I have considered all God's deeds, that no one can find out the deeds that are done under the sun. However much people toil in seeking, they do not find out. Even if the wise say they will know, they cannot find out" (Eccles 8:17). If we cannot understand the present, we certainly cannot understand the future. "Who knows what is good for a man in life, the few days of his empty life. . . . Who can tell a man what will happen under the sun after him?" (Eccles 6:12). God is the author of both good times and bad times, and we cannot find out which of these will come in the future (Eccles 7:14). Thus our decisions have to be made in ignorance of their possible implications or appropriateness. We live in "the fog of war."[162] Likewise it is no use asking why former days were better than the present (Eccles 7:10); one can see how true this was in Israel's story, when people look back to the days of Moses or Joshua or Deborah or David, as one can when the church looks back to the past. They just were.

So the sensible thing is to enjoy doing good things such as eating and drinking, which are the fruits of our toil and come to us as God's gifts, and to revere God in accordance with God's purpose (Eccles 3:12-14). There seems no reason to reckon that this verb here denotes "fear" of God rather than "reverence" for God, its usual meaning in wisdom writings and elsewhere in the First Testament, which also makes sense in this context.[163]

The Big Picture

"Further, he has put hāʿōlām in their minds; humanity cannot find out what

---

[161]Dominic Rudman, *Determinism in the Book of Ecclesiastes*, JSOTSup 316 (Sheffield: Sheffield Academic Press, 2001), p. 34; cf. Michael V. Fox, *Qohelet and His Contradictions*, JSOTSup 71 (Sheffield: Sheffield Academic Press, 1987), p. 192. Contrast Fox's changed view in *A Time to Tear Down and a Time to Build Up* (Grand Rapids/Cambridge: Eerdmans, 1999), pp. 197-98.

[162]Robert McNamara's expression to describe the unclarity in whose context one makes decisions in a war, which provided the title for the movie *Fog of War*.

[163]Cf. Whybray, *Ecclesiastes*, p. 75.

God does from beginning to end" (Eccles 3:11). The second clause likely spells out the first, though there is more than one way in which it might do so. "What God does from beginning to end" may spell out *hāʿôlām*—LXX has "eternity," something close to the word's common meaning, while NRSV paraphrases "a sense of past and future." Or it may be "humanity cannot find out" that spells out the word's meaning, if *ʿôlām* comes from a different root, *ʿālam*, and means "what is hidden." "All this I tested with wisdom. I said, 'I will gain wisdom.' But it was far beyond me. What happens is far off and deep, very deep. Who can discover it?" (Eccles 7:23-24).

Wisdom and mystery turn out to be related. Alongside the relative intelligibility of the details of life stands a huge inscrutability about the big questions that set the details into a framework. Why do things happen the way they do? What is the world as a whole about? What is life as a whole about, especially in light of the fact that it ends in death? The way things do not always work out as they should (to judge from the rules in Proverbs) sharpens those questions. Why does justice not work out in the world? Why is life so unpredictable? Qohelet probably implies that there are answers to those questions, but that if there are, we do not know them. In this sense, wisdom is denied us. We can discern the mystery, but not know it. Imagining himself as the archetypal wise man, Qohelet declares that he has been in a position to reflect on wisdom and knowledge over against madness and stupidity but has come to acknowledge that this, too, is grazing on/longing for/thinking about wind[164]—worse than that, since "as wisdom grows, vexation grows; one who increases knowledge increases suffering" (Eccles 1:16-18). Indeed, perhaps his point is that wisdom and knowledge *are* madness and stupidity, if we treat them as means of gaining ultimate understanding. For practical purposes wisdom is vastly superior to folly (e.g., Eccles 7:19), but it is ultimately useless, because in the end the wise die just as certainly as the stupid (Eccles 2:12-16).

Questions about knowledge and ignorance stand out in Yhwh's opening words to Job (Job 38:2-5), as forms of *yādaʿ* appear in each line. "Who is this who darkens the plan by words without knowledge?" Job has been speaking as a man without knowledge. "Do gird up your loins like a man so that I may ask you and you may enable me to know things." He does not know the nature of the plan or purpose (*ʿēṣâ*) Yhwh was implementing in creating the world (he has waxed cynical about this purpose as it works out in history in Job 12:13-25, seeing it as characteristically destructive in its operation). There is no

---

[164]Outside Qohelet, *raʿyôn* occurs in the First Testament only in the Aramaic of Daniel, where it means "thought." But in Hebrew, BDB's *rāʿâ* i would imply a comparison with grazing on something, while *rāʿâ* iii would point to valuing or longing for something,

fault in his lacking this knowledge, or not having been there when the world was created, or not being in a position to know about the world as it exists in his own day. He *is* at fault for pontificating on the nature of the world and of God's involvement in the world when he does not have the knowledge to do so, and thus for obscuring the nature of God's involvement in the world. "Where were you when I founded the earth?—tell me, if you know insight. Who determined its dimensions—because you will know—or who stretched the measuring line on it?" (Job 38:4-5).

Yhwh will later add that he is at fault because he apparently "would frustrate my judgment" (Job 40:8). "Judgment" *(mišpāṭ)* refers to the way God made decisions for the world in fulfillment of that plan. English versions have Job "impugning" these decisions, but it is doubtful if *pārar* can mean that. It refers to making a plan or a decision ineffectual. Job has wanted to change the way God goes about exercising authority in the world. He does, after all, know the answer to the questions about who did make and implement the plans for the world's creation and who still brings about events in the natural world. For reasons that are not yet explicit, his understandable lack of knowledge about the world and God's plan for it has led him astray in his attempts to understand his experience of things not working out in his life as they should have done (and/or the general human experience of this) and in his critique of God's actual way of doing so. Yhwh's speech then

> bypasses completely Job's particular concerns. . . . Yhwh in no way condescends to any kind of self-interpretation. . . . God refrains from saying anything in explanation of his "decrees." Rather, he poses counter-questions concerning creation, its order and its preservation. Thus God makes creation bear witness to himself. . . . This self-witnessing of creation is understood as a flood of urgent questions which refer man back to the mystery of creation and of divine guidance. . . . While Job is unable to answer any of these questions, the rebel thus, to a certain extent, puts the whole world back into the hands of God. . . . He now knows that his destiny, too, is well-protected by this mysterious God. . . . God has turned to Job, and Job has immediately understood him. . . . God has bet on Job . . . and has not lost his bet. It could have turned out that Job would have closed his mind to this speech, and then God would have been the loser.[165]

Limits

"Deep emptiness, says Qohelet, deep emptiness; as a whole, it's empty" (Eccles 1:2). Qohelet's favorite word, *hebel*, refers literally to a breath in its lack of substance, and it thus stands for what is metaphorically insubstantial or ab-

---

[165]Von Rad, *Wisdom in Israel*, pp. 225-26; the last sentences follow Barth, *Church Dogmatics*, IV/3.i:433.

surd, meaningless, deceptive, ephemeral, pointless—the resonances of the word are as significant as its precise meaning, about which we cannot pontificate. It becomes clear in the book that Qohelet does not think that every single or individual thing in the world or in life is like that. There are many things that are "good"; that is another of his favorite words. But "everything" as a whole (*hakkōl*, yet another of his favorite words) is deeply empty. Attempting to understand the world as a whole, the totality that we experience, is futile and empty. There is no big picture, no macronarrative, at least none available to us, only little pictures and short stories. The word *qōhelet*, commonly translated "teacher," "philosopher" or "preacher," links with *qāhāl* and thus suggests that the speaker is someone who identifies with the congregation (in a Christian context, one might render the term "churchman"—or "churchwoman," as the word is feminine). What we read in Ecclesiastes presents itself as the faith of the community. It is therefore an extraordinary form of faith, one that focuses on the limitations in what we can do or understand.

"What profit is there for people in all the toil they expend under the sun? . . . It is a bad business that God has given human beings to be busy with. . . . Everything is empty, a thinking about/grazing on/longing for wind" (Eccles 1:3, 13-14).[166] It has no substance and will never satisfy. The toil to which Qohelet refers may include the attempt to understand life as a whole, but a word such as *toil* suggests something broader than that: the attempt to change the world as well as to understand it.[167]

Looking at how things are "under the sun," anywhere at all in the world as we experience it (the expression is another that recurs in Qohelet), suggests that the world is getting nowhere. Or it is getting worse. "Don't say 'How has it happened that earlier times were better than these.'" Why is that? Not because it is not true. Simply because the question cannot be answered (Eccles 7:10).

The notion of progress has been fundamental to the modern world, but the idea is often a myth. While we make progress in the depth of our understanding of aspects of the world and in aspects of our capacity to control our environment, we gain no fuller an understanding of the meaning of the world or of life, nor do we grow in the capacity to be faithful to God and to one another. Technological advance made Europeans able to enslave and transport hundreds of thousands of Africans and enables people to kill each other on a vaster scale than was possible in the ancient world. Humanity stays the same, as the world stays the same, going through the same routine day after day,

---

[166]On these different possibilities, see section 6.6 "The Big Picture," though the noun here is *rě‘ūt*.

[167]"The philosophers have *interpreted* the world in various ways; the point however is to *change* it" (Karl Marx, *Theses on Feuerbach* no. 11).

year after year, with nothing genuinely new ever happening (Eccles 1:4-11). "What is crooked cannot be straightened, what is missing cannot be counted" (Eccles 1:15)—particularly if God made it crooked (Eccles 7:13).

Specifically, we can do little about injustice and oppression in the world, where there is faithlessness in the place where there ought to be the faithful exercise of authority (Eccles 3:16—4:3). We can be sure that the time will come when God will act with authority in relation to both faithful and faithless, but that offers little comfort in the short term, particularly to people who die before God's time comes. They thereby make us reflect that humanity is no better off than the animal world—we live and die, and that is it. Once again, Qohelet infers that all we can do is enjoy life as long as we have it and as long as we are in a position to enjoy it. But he also wonders whether the death that is to come for the oppressed is a merciful deliverance, and whether people who have not yet been born (and either experienced or witnessed the oppression in the world) are best off of all (cf. Eccles 6:3-6).

Trust

Qohelet is like the little boy in Hans Christian Andersen's story who declares, "The emperor has no clothes."[168] The order in creation does not offer insight on how to live our lives. Wisdom does not enable us to control our futures. And wisdom cannot help you cope with the fact of death.

Another reason why reverence for Yhwh is at the center of insight[169] is that it implies a recognition that whereas we always have only part of the picture, Yhwh does see the whole and can therefore keep us on a wise path when we would not be able to do so for ourselves because of that shortfall in our knowledge. There is also a link between reverence for Yhwh and trust (Prov 3:5-8): "Trust in Yhwh with your whole heart and do not rely on your own insight." That literal translation would be misleading if we understood the heart to suggest the emotions. As is often the case, "heart" implies the whole being, especially at its center and wellspring, but here the context suggests especially the mind. A previous line has already urged the listener to write commitment and faithfulness on the tablet of the "heart" in this sense (Prov 3:3; cf. JPSV), and this connotation continues. Proverbs goes on, "Acknowledge him in all your ways and he himself will straighten your paths. Do not be wise in your eyes; revere Yhwh and turn away from evil. It will be health for your flesh, refreshment for your body." Once again Proverbs reminds its readers that there are limits to

---

[168]Mark K. George, "Death as the Beginning of Life in the Book of Ecclesiastes," in *Strange Fire,* ed. Tod Linafelt (Sheffield: Sheffield Academic Press/New York: New York University Press, 2000), pp. 280-93; p. 285.

[169]See on "Wisdom and Reverence for Yhwh" on pp. 581-83.

the extent to which it is wise to trust our own insight, even if we are the sharp-minded people it values. Our own minds can take us so far, but they have limitations. Even when we give ourselves to wisdom in the way Proverbs urges, things often work out differently from the way we envisage and plan, and it is as well to build that fact into the center of the way we think. Trust thus goes alongside pragmatism, reverence and morality to make a powerful foursome that will stand in creative tension with each other. It is another aspect to the link between the thinking of Proverbs and Yhwh's speech in Job 38—41, where Yhwh challenges Job to trust even though he cannot understand.

The stress on trust in the Wisdom books makes clear "what a great difference there is between this search for knowledge and the search for knowledge which determines our present-day relationship to the world." This First Testament quest is not objective and cautious but is based on commitment, trusting in the world and life and experience and the order that it expresses, and behind that, trusting in Yhwh (e.g., Prov 16:20; 29:25).[170]

The importance of not treating our own thinking as an absolute connects with the importance of the link between morality and acknowledgment of God. It can seem sensible to go in for a little insider trading or the development of a loving sexual relationship with someone or the invasion of a foreign power that looks very dangerous. . . . But it can turn out to be stupid. It is wiser to take right and wrong seriously into account. It is trust, acknowledgment and faithfulness that will mean our paths turn out straight and make things go well for our bodies. Trust, acknowledgment and faithfulness are wise in a practical sense. They pay. Alas, "womanly wisdom builds her house, but stupidity can tear it down with her hands" (Prov 14:1). That can be true within an individual's life, or in a family.

Wisdom is thus a tree of life for people who take hold of it (Prov 3:18). The fact that human sin brought into the world the subordination of women to men and introduced great pain into parenthood does not mean God wants us to make no effort to ameliorate these, and the fact that it cut us off from the tree of life does not mean God wants us just to surrender ourselves to death. Wisdom is the way to life. At the beginning, humanity tried to grasp discernment separately from listening to what Yhwh said. Proverbs invites humanity to put these two back together. The wisdom it commends holds together discernment, trust and acknowledgment of Yhwh, the wisdom humanity turned its back on at the beginning.

Submission

A vital insight of Job is that we have to live without things making sense. Wis-

---

[170]Von Rad, *Wisdom in Israel*, pp. 190-91.

dom lies in reverence for the Lord (Job 28:28), in the sense that such submission to God can issue in the capacity to cope with one's life and the experiences it brings. We have noted that Job started his story as one who revered God and departed from evil (Job 1:1). Paradoxically, the fact that this constitutes wisdom and discernment is apparently also the lesson he needs to keep learning. "The true sorrow in all his sorrows . . . consists in the conjunction of his profound knowledge that in what has happened and what has come on him he has to do with God, and his no less profound ignorance how far he has to do with God. . . . We see this knowledge and ignorance of God in headlong collision and unbearable tension. This is the depth and essence of the suffering of the suffering Job."[171] There is no doubt that God is involved with him; God is the subject of so many of his verbs. They are summed up in the picture of God as his enemy, one who is resolutely and inexorably treating him as God's enemy. "Surely all ancient and modern skeptics, pessimists, scoffers and atheists are innocuous and well-meaning folk compared with this man Job. They do not know against whom they direct their disdain and doubt and scorn and rejection. Job does." He thus "finds words of repudiation compared with which all theirs are only pious platitudes."[172] And further, it means Job never turns away from the battle in which God has engaged him, never turns to try to imagine another God to whom he might have recourse. Although God treats him as an enemy, he still flees to this God.[173] But Yhwh's response to his words of repudiation is almost a shrug of the shoulders. It is to declare to Job that God is free.[174]

Psalm 73 offers a parallel testimony. For a while the psalmist has been overwhelmed by the fact that faithless people often do so well in life despite the fact that they despise God and persecute God's people. By the time of giving this testimony, however, envy and dismay have been replaced by renewed conviction that God does act against the faithless and a correlative renewed awareness of God's protecting presence. How did this movement come about? "I went to God's sanctuary [and] considered their end" (Ps 73:17). The explanation is tantalizingly brief, but it fits with an assumption that appears elsewhere in the Psalms, that the sanctuary stands for another reality from the one we experience in everyday life—a truer reality even though it contrasts with life as we experience it. In the world outside the sanctuary the King of Assyria is the great king, but the sanctuary witnesses to the fact that in reality Yhwh is

[171]Barth, *Church Dogmatics*, IV/3.i:401.

[172]Ibid., IV/3.i:404-5.

[173]So Roland de Pury, *Hiob* (reprint, Neukirchen: Neukirchener, 1962), pp. 23-24; cf. Barth, *Church Dogmatics*, IV/3.i:424.

[174]Barth, *Church Dogmatics*, IV/3.i:432.

the Great King even when it does not look like it (Ps 47:2 [MT 3]). Taking part in its worship and hearing its testimony, we are emboldened to reaffirm our faith in that true reality. In Psalm 73 the sanctuary reinforces the knowledge that God does put the faithless down and bring the faithful to honor,[175] so as to free the psalmist to go and live life in that knowledge despite all appearances to the contrary.

In Psalm 77 the logic is more explicit, though we should hesitate to read it back into Psalm 73. Wondering whether God has cast off forever, the psalmist makes a point of calling to mind Yhwh's wondrous deeds of old, the way Yhwh delivered Israel at the Red Sea and led the people like a flock by the hand of Moses and Aaron. The implication is that present experience of Yhwh's abandonment must not be allowed to override the implications of those deeds, which were determinative of who Yhwh is for Israel.

Living with Mystery

So seeking wisdom leads to the realization that the quest must fail. The declaration that "reverence for the Lord, that is wisdom" comes at the end of the poem on wisdom that separates the argument between Job and his friends from Job's final statement (Job 28:28). As well as recalling the book's first description of Job (Job 1:1), it anticipates the challenge of Yhwh's address in Job 38—41. There, in the context of Job's expectation that he ought to be able to get an understanding of life's mysteries (specifically, of his own life's mystery), Yhwh appears to remind him (in effect) that reverence for the Lord is wisdom—all the wisdom he is going to get. There was an explanation for Job's suffering, but Yhwh withholds it from Job, to the comfort of the story's listeners because they will probably receive no explanation of their suffering, so that Job's experience is like theirs. Job has to live on the basis of reverence for Yhwh and keep proving that wisdom lies here. We can live with mystery and enigma if we keep reminding ourselves of the link between wisdom and reverence for Yhwh. While Proverbs 9:10 speaks of reverence for Yhwh as wisdom's "beginning" (*tĕḥillâ*), Proverbs 1:7 describes it with more ambiguity as wisdom's "first principle" (*rēʾšît*), and this can suggest the essence or highpoint as well as the beginning. It is a beginning that the wise never leave behind. Indeed, perhaps they will come to say simply that reverence for Yhwh *is* wisdom. Humanity never gains intellectual mastery of those big intellectual questions, but reverence for Yhwh enables us to relax over that.

There is thus another paradoxical reason why the teaching of the wise is not just for beginners and why the wise continue to profit from paying attention

---

[175]I take it that it refers to a restoration to earthly honor; *kābôd* never refers to glory in heaven.

to wisdom. From its opening lines one might think that Proverbs has a rather oversimplified view of how life works, but immediately after commenting on the way the wise continue to profit from its teaching, it goes on to indicate that it recognizes things to be more complicated. Its wisdom is designed to enable people to understand its mysterious enigmas (Prov 1:6; *ḥîdōt* are not merely children's riddles). That declaration surely deconstructs. The very nature of mystery and enigma is that it cannot be understood; what one does is keep wrestling with it and rethinking it. We do not reach a point when we "understand" creation or the problem of evil or the nature of God or the nature of our relationship with God. What wisdom does is help us along in the process of reflection on these deep and mysterious realities. And thus mature people will profit from reflecting on Proverbs as much as young people do. Indeed, they will profit more from this aspect of Proverbs, for youth likes straight and uncomplicated answers and is intolerant of enigma and mystery. It is this aspect of wisdom that maturity puts people into a position to utilize.

There is then an ellipse in the last colon of Proverbs 1:2-7. Following on "reverence for Yhwh is wisdom's first principle," one might have expected "wisdom and instruction—the *faithless* despise them." Instead Proverbs says that it is stupid people who despise them. The ellipse implies that folly can be equated with a refusal to revere Yhwh, which Proverbs will certainly go on to declare. It is often reckoned that growth in insight depends on avoiding the constraint of convictions about God, and holding on to convictions about God can indeed inhibit growth in understanding. But Proverbs' recognition of mystery reminds its readers not to think they have the truth buttoned up. It is precisely the recognition of mystery and enigma that makes it possible for people who revere God to be open-minded, not closed-minded. On the other hand, people who refuse to revere God are fools in two respects. They refuse to face the fact that the really important questions remain mysteries (though this does not make them cease to be worth reflecting on). And they refuse to make God part of their study (and therefore they bracket key considerations in the understanding of anything).

Thus reverence for Yhwh leads to wisdom in the sense of helping you both to understand life and to accept the situation when you cannot understand. Qohelet is the great exposition of this fact, even if "acceptance" may be a misnomer.

6.7 How Life Works

Human beings commonly assume that life is not random and that cause-and-effect is supposed to operate in human experience, so that people who live sensible, good, godly lives do well and people who live stupid, evil, godless lives do badly. You need to be hardy to live without such an assumption. The

First Testament in principle agrees, and it is willing to appeal to its hearers' self-interest in its consequent exhortations regarding the way they run their lives. Our life is in our own hands. We are not the helpless victims of circumstances. "A lazy hand makes for poverty, while the hand of the diligent makes rich" (Prov 10:4). Trust in God means success and good health (Prov 3:5-8). By what dynamic or process does this cause-and-effect operate? The First Testament has several answers. It operates via a natural dynamic, a moral one and a personal one.

How Natural Forces Make Life Work

The First Testament assumes that good deeds have good outcomes and bad deeds have bad ones.[176] What is morally *ṭôb* issues in what is experientially *ṭôb*; what is morally *ra'* issues in what is experientially *ra'*. People "eat the fruit of their ways, eat their fill of their own decisions" (Prov 1:31). The trouble that comes to them is the natural outworking of what they do, as natural as the growing of grapes from a vine. "From their mouths people eat good things"— they are the natural result of the good things they say, from their honesty and openness with other people. On the other hand, "the desire of the treacherous is for violence" (Prov 13:2). Out of context that would simply mean that they desire to do violence to other people, but the parallelism of the line suggests the idea that the natural fruit of their words is to harm themselves. That is not their conscious desire, but it is the desire implied by the words and behavior that lead inexorably in this direction. It will be as if it is the intended result of the plans they formulated. The beguiling of crooks actually leads to death, not to a fuller life; people who lie in ambush for others turn out to have ambushed themselves (Prov 1:10-19). Acts that are designed to bring trouble to others actually bring trouble to the perpetrator. Their own plans are their downfall (Job 5:13; Ps 10:2). They fall into their own traps (Ps 7:15 [MT 16]; 9:15 [MT 16]; 35:8; 57:6 [MT 7]). The rocks they roll fall back on them (Prov 26:27). The wicked person's troublemaking "falls back on his head; onto his skull descends his violence" (Ps 7:16 [MT 17]).

"A person cannot stand firm through faithlessness, but the root of the faithful—it does not move" (Prov 12:3). The question is, how does something come to stand firm and not shift? A building does so because it is properly built, with walls standing on foundations that go down into the ground; a plant does so

---

[176]See Klaus Koch, "Is There a Doctrine of Retribution in the Old Testament?" in *Theodicy in the Old Testament,* ed. James L. Crenshaw (Philadelphia: Fortress/London: SPCK, 1983), pp. 57-87. Gene M. Tucker underlines this point in "Sin and 'Judgment' in the Prophets," in *Problems in Biblical Theology,* ed. Henry T. C. Sun et al. (Grand Rapids/Cambridge: Eerdmans, 1997), pp. 373-88.

because its roots similarly go down into the soil. The faithful person is like someone with foundations or roots of that kind. They "naturally" guarantee stability. Thus you can overturn the faithless and they are gone, but the house of the faithful stands firm (Prov 12:7). "Those who plow trouble, those who sow wrong, reap it" (Job 4:8). Like *ra*ʿ, both ʿ*āwen* and ʿ*āmāl* can apply both to the badness of a deed, such as the trouble it is designed to cause to someone else, and the badness of the trouble that comes to the person who does the deed. So there is a naturalness about the way the perpetrators of trouble become its victims. It is as natural as sowing and reaping, as if there is a power built into the acts themselves that make them rebound on their agents. "A relaxed mind means physical health, but passion makes the body rot" (Prov 14:30). There is a positive energy about such emotions when they can become the motive force for action, but otherwise their energy is apt to consume the person who feels them. "Vexation slays the fool, passion kills the naive person" (Job 5:2). It is a process built into nature.

Eliphaz seeks to reassure Job that life does work in a moral way, by means of a long and detailed account of the way the wicked meet their downfall (Job 15:20-35). They are tormented, short-lived, fearful, vulnerable, insecure, hungry. They lose their homes and their wealth, their experience proving the negative side to Psalm 1. Eliphaz is clear about the reasons for this: the wicked are ruthless in their relations with other people and defiant in their attitude to God. Only at the very end does he comment on the forces that bring it about, and even there does so only allusively. It is because "the company of the godless is barren; fire consumes the tents of bribery; they conceive wrong [ʿ*āmāl*] and trouble [ʿ*āwen*], and their womb prepares deceit" (Job 15:34-35). Eliphaz may refer to the wrong, trouble and deceit that the wicked generate for other people, but it looks more like an interpretation of the dynamic of barrenness and burning that draws attention to the link between their action and their experience. The godless and the people who use bribery generate wrong, trouble and deceit for other people and also for themselves. Their actions rebound on them. Bildad makes the same point briefly in his disquisition on the fate of the wicked, which focuses more resolutely on their actual death and its horrors (Job 18:5-21): "their own plan throws them down" (Job 18:7).

How Wisdom Makes Life Work

Sensible people take that natural dynamic into account in the way they live their lives. "The capacity to make decisions [*mĕzimmâ*] will watch over you, discernment will guard you" (Prov 2:11), in saving you from the ways of men and women who would lead you out of the path to life into the way of death. Paying attention to the teaching of the wise leads to long life and well-being (Prov 3:1-2); it even makes people look fine (Prov 1:8-9). Holding on to wisdom means you know there is nothing frightening to threaten you in the way it threatens the wicked (Prov 3:24-25), whereas ignoring wisdom will lead to calamity and anguish (Prov 1:20-33). It is backed up by an even more impressive consideration. Yhwh used wisdom in creating the world (Prov 3:19-20).[177] "Now are you impressed?" asks the teacher. Yhwh would not dream of undertaking something like that without using wisdom. Would you be wise to do so?

Given that wisdom is the key to a successful human life, if people refuse to have anything to do with wisdom, they will find themselves facing disaster and will have to live with that. People have to live with the consequences of their choices. If they decline to listen to Ms. Wisdom when she summons them to listen, they will find that she declines to listen when they summon her to listen. She will be laughing instead (Prov 1:24-28). (Perhaps that is a rhetorical warning, and in reality she will be weeping.)

What is it that gives you pleasure and enjoyment, makes you relax and laugh (śāhaq)? This is a key question, because what gives you pleasure and makes you laugh is likely to reach deep into you as a person; it points to the wellsprings of your life. For a fool it is wrongdoing; for a person of insight, it is wisdom (Prov 10:23). Thus gaining wisdom is something enjoyable, matching the way wisdom encouraged enjoyment in Yhwh at creation (Prov 8:22-31). In Psalm 119, Yhwh's teaching is the way to life. But so is one's parents' teaching. "So keep your father's command, my son, and do not abandon your mother's teaching . . . because the command is a lamp and the teaching a light, and disciplinary rebukes are the way to life" (Prov 6:20, 23). The immediate content of that teaching concerns the son's sexual activity, and the parents' teaching corresponds to that of Yhwh's teaching. The son is to avoid the forbidden relationship of adultery and any relationship with a woman who is an outsider (Prov 6:24-35; we do not know who Proverbs is referring to by that term).

Proverbs argues in a different way from the Torah. Actually, the Torah does not offer any argument to support this prohibition, as it does for some other commands and prohibitions. It simply affirms the common conviction that adultery is forbidden. It is so obviously forbidden that no argument is needed, any more than it is for the prohibition on murder. In contrast, Proverbs offers lengthy argument that begins from a realistic assessment of the temptation to have an affair. Men let themselves be captivated by a woman they fancy, and the attractiveness can win them. But the price to be paid is monumentally huge, far outweighing the enjoyment that comes from the affair. It involves playing with fire. It will mean shame in the eyes of the community and phys-

---

[177]On this passage, see OTT 1:88-89.

ical harm from the woman's furious husband when he has his revenge. Proverbs' argument is thus not that an affair is wrong but that it is really stupid. "The adulterer is lacking in sense; the man who does this—he destroys himself" (Prov 6:32).

Of course sexual restraint involves discipline. It does not come easily. It is thus a paradigm for Proverbs' understanding of wisdom in general. The very fact that the book spends nine chapters urging attention to wisdom points up the fact that there is a problem here. So does the chapters' skilled and imaginative use of rhetoric to seek to win over the audience's compliance. So does the overt stress on discipline and reproof. One can sometimes sense the teacher wanting to grab the listeners (or the nonlisteners) by their lapels and shout "PAY ATTENTION, WILL YOU?" (e.g., Prov 1:22-23).

How Faithfulness Makes Life Work

In light of the link between wisdom and faithfulness, it is not surprising that there is also a link between the way wisdom makes life work and the way faithfulness makes life work. "The faithful eat to their hearts' content while the stomach of the faithless is empty" (Prov 13:25). There are obviously many exceptions to that rule, but insofar as it is true, how does that come about? It is as if "faithfulness guards the person whose life has integrity, while faithlessness overturns the sinner" (Prov 13:6). Faithfulness and faithlessness are quasi-personal forces, the one standing guard, the other tripping up, the one acting as a friend, the other as an enemy. "Good and commitment will chase me" (Ps 23:6).

"Ill-gotten wealth is of no avail, but faithfulness saves from death" (Prov 10:2). As often happens, the proverb's second colon clarifies the meaning of the first. Its point is not that ill-gotten gain is of no use at all but that it is of no use in connection with delivering you from death (cf. Prov 11:4). It does not guarantee you live a long and happy life. One can think of many ways this might turn out to be true. Other thieves steal what one has stolen; other members of the community care for the faithful; when someone gets ill, God acts to heal the faithful but not the faithless. Thus "the faithless make deceptive wages, but those who sow faithfulness a true reward" (Prov 11:18). The wages of sin is death (Rom 3:23), we might even say, but the wages of faithfulness is life. Thus "people who trust in their wealth—they will stumble, but the faithful will flourish like foliage" (Prov 11:28). Wealth is good until it becomes an object of trust, or rather of false trust, as if it could deliver more than it can. It is good until it becomes a supreme value and can therefore override moral questions.

So "the person who diverts upright people into a bad way will fall into his own pit, but people of integrity will possess what is good" (Prov 28:10). "The upright will inhabit the land, people of integrity will remain in it, but the faithless will be cut off from the land, the treacherous will be torn from it" (Prov 2:21-22). It is not explicit who is the agent behind those passive verbs: it might be foreign invaders or it might be Yhwh. To put it positively, faithful commitment *(ḥesed wĕʾĕmet)* will mean favor with God and with other people (Prov 3:3-4). It has a definite effect, but that effect works via people and via God, which can be expressed in terms of an emphasis on the effectiveness of uprightness and integrity themselves. "Honor Yhwh with your resources, with the first of all your produce, and your barns will fill with abundance, your vats will burst with wine" (Prov 3:9-10).

In isolation, one could read this as encouraging a contractual relationship between people and God, but the promise belongs in the context of a relationship characterized by love and mutual commitment—a covenantal relationship, though Proverbs does not use the word *covenant.* One might even see it as suggesting "a sacramental view of the universe."[178] It is "world-affirming" and materialistic.[179] It expounds an implication of the fact that the world is God's world and works with moral order. It rejects the view that there is no link between God and the world, as if God were not the one who keeps the world in being and keeps it working, and the view that there is no moral order written into the way God makes the world work.

Psalm 37 is a particularly systematic exposition of the conviction that things work out for the faithful and not for the faithless. Its background is the way the faithful fret at the prospering of the faithless. They may fret simply because this raises the question whether there is any moral order in the world. Or they may do so because of the more direct implications of that prospering, the growth in power that could enable the faithless to dispossess the faithful and imperil their lives. It promises that the faithless will wither and disappear. The faithful are to keep the faith, keep trusting that Yhwh will protect them and keep living in faithfulness. They will find that they enter into possession of the land (that is, they will have their own share in the land, or they will be able to maintain possession of the land as a whole over against the Canaanites or later rivals for possession). They will therefore be able to maintain their life; they will have a place to live and food to eat. In the meantime, it is wise to settle for living with a little rather than copying the style of the faithless in the conviction that this will pay off. It will not. The faithful may fall, but they are not hurled headlong, because Yhwh upholds them (Ps 37:24). It is in that context that one should perhaps read the declaration that follows (even if it is hyperbole), that the psalmist has never seen a faithful person abandoned or his offspring seeking bread

---

[178]See Murphy, *Proverbs,* p. 24.
[179]McKane, *Proverbs,* pp. 292, 294.

(Ps 37:25). Yhwh does not abandon them but raises them up and restores them to their prosperity.

How Faithlessness Makes Life Work

A number of the passages we have noted make the converse point to the one about faithfulness. "The violence of the faithless sweeps them away" (Prov 21:7). "The faithless flee when there is no one pursuing, but the faithful are as confident as a lion" (Prov 28:1). "In the offense of an evil man lies a snare, but the faithful person resounds and rejoices" (Prov 29:6): the parallelism indicates that the person the evil man snares is himself.

Yhwh declares to Mount Seir, "I will ordain you for blood[shed], and blood[shed] will chase you; because you did not repudiate blood[shed],[180] blood[shed] will chase you" (Ezek 35:6). The threat begins with Yhwh's action, which works through the action of blood as an agent in its own right. But as the verse unfolds, Yhwh's own action fades into the background and Yhwh speaks only of the chasing capacity of blood itself. There is a power in shed blood, a power to pursue its rebounding on its perpetrators. It is Yhwh's agent, but it becomes a moral force in its own right, a quasi-personal force: "Misfortune chases sinners and good fortune rewards the faithful" (Prov 13:21). Calamity, like blessing (literally "bad" like "good"; $rā{}^c\hat{a}$ and $ṭôb$) is a moral force at loose in the world bringing about the appropriate recompense for the moral bad that people do. Thus because of this policelike chasing, "a false witness will not avoid conviction, and one who gives lying testimony will not escape/will perish" (Prov 19:5, 9). The last verb in the second of these almost-identical proverbs brings them to a forceful conclusion that is both disquieting and encouraging. The implication of both proverbs is that the lying witness will be on the receiving end of the penalties that were falsely sought. It is in this context that Deuteronomy urges the principle of "an eye for an eye," to discourage other people from ever giving in to this temptation (Deut 19:16-21). If the witness concerns something that will take the life of the person accused, then the life of the witness becomes forfeit. The nature of Proverbs is not to speak of judicial proceedings to this end; it simply declares the certainty that things will work out that way.

A factor in this is the way the community works. "The person who stops his ear at the cry of the poor—he, too, will call and not be answered" (Prov 21:13). In other contexts, the one who answers such a plea might be Yhwh, but this saying begins with the cry and response that one person utters to another. "A person's majesty brings him low, and the one who is lowly in spirit obtains honor" (Prov 29:23). "A king who makes decisions truthfully for the poor—his

---

[180]The Hebrew is allusive, and JPSV renders "for your bloodthirsty hatred," but the point is not affected.

throne stands firm forever" (Prov 29:14). "The eye that mocks a father, scorns obedience to a mother—ravens of the canyon will peck it out, vultures will eat it" (Prov 30:17). This may happen because "contempt for one's parents is depicted as so unnatural that nature itself carries out the punishment."[181] But it may happen because the action breaks down the family, and it is the family that is responsible for burial. People who despise their family will find they have no one to bury them.

It is easy for us simply to dismiss Proverbs' convictions, which are also those of Job's friends. But

> the opponents of official racial segregation in the United States and of apartheid in South Africa were sustained by the conviction that such injustice simply could not preserve itself in the face of the claims of simple human justice. The dissidents in the Soviet Union and Eastern Europe resisted in the knowledge that the massive structures of oppression would eventually show themselves to be hollow. The democracy movement in China is supported by the certainty that such repressive power will one day crumble.[182]

We noted that Psalm 37 makes a long series of affirmations about the way Yhwh not only makes sure things work out for the faithful but also makes sure the faithless wither and get cut off. It does that in the way reflected in that formulation. Yhwh is the subject of verbs concerning the destiny of the faithful: Yhwh gives them their requests, acts for them, brings out faithfulness and a decision for them, upholds them, acknowledges their days, is dedicated to acting for them, does not abandon them, does not let them be condemned, exalts them, helps them, rescues them, delivers them. Almost as many lines of the psalm concern the destiny of the faithless as concern that of the faithful, but Yhwh is never the subject of the verbs relating to the faithless. The exception that proves the rule is that Yhwh "laughs at" the faithless "because he has seen that his day will come" (Ps 37:13). Their destiny is something that Yhwh foresees, but foresees as something in which Yhwh is not involved.

How then does it come about? It resembles the withering of grass, which suggests it is a natural process. Or the faithless simply "perish" or "come to an end" or disappear. Or "their sword will enter their own heart," as if it recognizes moral propriety and turns itself against the one who wields it, and "their bows will break" rather than complete their dastardly deed. Even these inanimate objects prove part of a moral structuring of reality and behave with a personal seemliness that the faithless lack. The psalm's favorite way of de-

---

[181]Clifford, *Proverbs,* p. 266.

[182]Carol A. Newsom, "The Book of Job," in *The New Interpreter's Bible,* vol. 4 (Nashville: Abingdon, 1996), p. 487.

scribing the process is to speak of the faithless being "cut off" (*kārat* niphal; Ps 37:9, 22, 28, 34, 38), but it never specifies the agent of this cutting, and one wonders whether the verb has its common intransitive significance. It then simply means "come to an end," without pointing to there being an agent of this failing. Likewise "the arms of the faithless will be broken"—or "will break." Perhaps even "the rebels are destroyed" (*šāmad* niphal) signifies only that they perish (cf. KJV at Ps 83:10 [MT 11]).

How Yhwh Makes Life Work

While Psalm 37 or Proverbs can thus see a "natural" link between acting well or badly and having good or bad things happen, they can also speak of this in terms of Yhwh's involvement. And while Psalm 37 safeguards the centrality of love to Yhwh's person by directly associating Yhwh only with acts of blessing, other psalms and proverbs safeguard Yhwh's rigor by also directly associating Yhwh with the bringing of calamity. The declaration that ill-gotten gain does not avail but faithfulness saves people from death is followed by the affirmation that "Yhwh does not let the faithful person go hungry, but thwarts the desire of the faithless" (Prov 10:2-3). "Yhwh tears down the house of the grand and establishes the territory of the widow" (Prov 15:25). The grand (*gē'îm*) may not be high and mighty, but they are set over against the widow (who, equally, may not be humble) by the fact that they are in a position to look after themselves when the widow is not. But Yhwh can overturn the expectations that attach to both parties' positions.

Yhwh thus sees to "guarding the paths of judgment, watching the way of people committed to him" (Prov 2:8). "Yhwh's eyes are in every place, watching the bad and the good" (Prov 15:3). "Watching" (*ṣāpâ*) is the activity of people who want to cause trouble and people who want to offer protection (e.g., Ps 37:32; Jer 6:17). It thus looks to the future, to what the people we are watching will do, or what the watcher intends to do. The proverb confirms the hope of Laban, who is aware that it is risky to trust Jacob but also that Yhwh watches between people and knows whether they keep their mutual commitments (Gen 31:49), the implication being that if they fail to do so, Yhwh will see that consequences follow. If people are obedient to Yhwh's requirements, Yhwh will grant them the rain they need and thus a plentiful harvest, will grant them peace from enemies and protection from wild animals. If they are not obedient, Yhwh will send epidemic, invasion, defeat, trouble from wild animals, drought and thus famine. If that does not draw them to obedience, Yhwh will ruin their land, scatter them among the nations and demoralize them there (Lev 26; cf. Deut 28). When widow or orphan are abused and cry out to Yhwh, Yhwh listens and acts to punish their abusers (Ex 22:22-24 [MT 21-23]).

There is an appropriateness about the way Yhwh works, scoffing at people who themselves scoff. "Yhwh's curse is on the house of the faithless, but he blesses the abode of the faithful. At scoffers he himself scoffs, but to the weak he shows grace. The wise obtain honor, but the confident exalt belittling" (Prov 3:33-35). The talk of cursing and blessing suggests a link with the awareness that natural forces make life work, yet this is a not merely a curse or blessing with its own power but Yhwh's curse and Yhwh's blessing. Thus that appropriateness about the way Yhwh acts applies both positively and negatively. A worshiper can claim, "Yhwh has recompensed me according to my faithfulness, according to the purity of my hands before his eyes." Thus "with the committed you showed commitment, with the person of integrity you showed integrity, with the pure you showed purity—but with the crooked you twisted and turned" (Ps 18:24-26 [MT 25-27]). The psalm closely matches Yhwh's action toward the suppliant with the suppliant's action toward Yhwh. It does the same with Yhwh's action toward the "crooked," though it achieves a new effect by not repeating the same word as happened in the previous cola. One would not have been surprised if it had done so to avoid implying that Yhwh was crooked (*'iqqēš*), but it goes on to describe Yhwh's action by means of the verb *pātal*, which has similar implications (cf. Job 5:13). So Yhwh's action again matches that of the wrongdoer. "You play dirty; I can play dirty."

Thus "do not rob the poor because he is poor, do not crush the weak person at the gate, because Yhwh is the one who will take up their case and despoil the people who despoil them of their life" (Prov 22:22-23). The needy are vulnerable to people who are more adept at using the law at "the gate," the square at the entrance to the city where legal questions are resolved. Yhwh does not let the skillful legal swindlers get away with it, and acts in a way that corresponds to the wrongdoing. Yhwh, too, gets involved in the legal case, and despoils the despoilers (cf. Prov 23:10-11, if the restorer [*gō'ēl*] there is divine rather than human).

There is a power in shed blood. But the First Testament also has it working via Yhwh's own action. Abel's blood cries out to Yhwh from the ground (Gen 4:10), and Job bids earth not to cover his blood in such a way that his outcry is silenced. Although he thus speaks in anticipation of the apparent certainty that he will die, he goes on to refer to an advocate to argue his case with God, which should result in his not dying (Job 16:18-19). I take it that his trope involves his imagining his blood, though not yet shed, anticipatorily appealing not to God but to someone in the court of heaven who will thus be driven to speak with God on his behalf.[183]

---

[183]See section 2.2 "Yhwh's Embodiment."

How Yhwh Makes Bad Things Happen to Bad People

The double dynamic of this process is illustrated in the way Jeremiah speaks about ill-doing and the experience of ill. Babylonian and Egyptian lions have mangled Judah. How has this come about? "Is this not what your leaving Yhwh your God would do to you?" (Jer 2:17). Relying on other deities and/or on other political resources would have this "natural" consequence. Their political policies that leave Yhwh out of account will actually be their downfall. Thus "may your ill-doing [rā'ā] punish you, your turnings reprove you, so that you may acknowledge and see how ill [ra'] and bitter is your leaving Yhwh your God" (Jer 2:19).[184] The bad thing that Judah has done in leaving Yhwh will generate a bad experience on Judah's part. It will generate its own punishment.

Yet Yhwh is involved in bringing this about. "I am bringing ill on this people, the fruit of their plans" (Jer 6:19). The ill they experience is the fruit or natural outworking of the ill they have done, the decisions they have taken—not the outworking they had in mind, but the natural outworking, nevertheless. It is the natural outworking of the fact that they "have not given heed to my words, and my teaching—they have spurned it" (Jer 6:19). Thus it is a natural outworking that Yhwh is bringing. Events are not merely the natural consequences of their acts, nor even the result of the way God set the world going at the beginning. Yhwh is at work in these events now by means of natural processes, but is also personally responding to the people's personal rejection of Yhwh's personal communication. To put it another way, "I will pour over them their ill" (Jer 14:16). The ill they experience will come by Yhwh's deliberate act, but it will be as if Yhwh is drowning them in the ills they have done, which by their own nature issue in this trouble. The people do ill, so Yhwh does ill (cf. Jer 18:7-12; 26:3). Using the same word again points to the intrinsic relationship between the two acts. It almost hints at a necessity or an inevitability whereby one ill issues in another. But Jeremiah expresses the point in terms of personal decision making on Yhwh's part as on the people's. Events involve Yhwh's formulating an intention to do ill, just as they involve the people's formulating an intention to do ill. One ill does not automatically issue in another. They do ill; Yhwh does ill. They do good; Yhwh abandons the plan to do ill.[185]

Alas for Judah, Isaiah 3:9-11 laments, "because they have dealt ill for themselves." The declaration is backed up by a proverbial saying about how life

---

[184]On the translation and construction, see William L. Holladay, *Jeremiah*, 2 vols. (Hermeneia, 1986, 1989), 1:96.

[185]Of course this does not mean that all ill that happens issues from ill that people have done; the First Testament recognizes that bad things happen to good people.

works out, which these coming events will illustrate. "Say of the faithful person, it's good, because they will eat the fruit of their deeds." On the other hand, "Alas for the faithless person. It's ill, because what his hands have dealt will be done to him [MT]/will turn back to him [1QIs^a]." The saying points to several understandings of the link between people's acts and their subsequent experience. First, it is a matter of people doing good or ill for themselves. They are not merely the victims of fate or of Yhwh's fiat. The opening verb *(gāmal)* suggests rewarding someone for something or paying them their wages. They have brought what happens on themselves. But second, there is an inner link between what they do and what subsequently happens. In their relationship with God or with each other they do what is good or ill. That then issues in good or ill in their experience, in blessing or calamity. The double use of the words *good* and *ill* suggests an inner link. Third, the image of fruitfulness underlines that link and provides a metaphor for it. Blessing and trouble issue from doing the right or the wrong thing as naturally as figs grow from a fig tree. Fourth, the use of the words "faithful" and "faithless" *(ṣaddîq, rāšāʿ)* to characterize good and ill carries implications for how that comes about, because behaving faithfully develops faithful mutual relationships and thus "naturally" issues in the blessing that comes from such relationships, while living faithlessly has the opposite effect. Fifth, the 1QIs^a reading points to a more personalistic understanding of this process. It is as if our acts instill energy into our deeds and give them a boomerang force of their own that has a feedback effect on the actor. Sixth, MT suggests the presence of another personal energy, the concealed subject of the passive verb ("will be done"). Once again that hints that Yhwh's own activity is also involved in the innate or natural processes that are working themselves out.

How Yhwh Acts via This-Worldly Means

Yhwh is "God of redress" (Ps 94:1), one who can therefore be urged to rise up to pay back the important people who exult in their wrongdoing, act destructively in relation to the community and conspire to bring about the death of the innocent. That involves deliberate sovereign action. It issues from the fact that (contrary to the conviction of the faithless) Yhwh sees what is going on and hears people's cries. But the same redress can be described in terms of Yhwh's bringing people's wickedness back on them, which suggests something like diverting the force of that wrongdoing, like a tennis player utilizing the force in a powerful serve in returning it—indeed, God puts an end to them *"through* their evil doing" (Ps 94:23).[186] Their own wrongdoing is the means of their downfall, perhaps

---

[186]Cf. JPSV. The NRSV and NIVI have "for" their wrongdoing, but "through" is a more common meaning for *bĕ*, and it fits the parallelism.

because the way they treat others encourages attitudes that recoil on them.

In Job, the earthly story begins with Sabeans and Chaldeans killing some of Job's staff, and fire from heaven killing others, while a great wind brings death to Job's offspring (Job 1:13-20). But that happens because Yhwh and the Adversary raised a hand against them (Job 1:11, 12), and thus Job comments (though he had not heard their conversation), "It was Yhwh gave, and Yhwh has taken" (Job 1:21). The duality of agency is hinted by the way the fire and the wind are described. They are "God's fire" and "a great wind." The former expression might mean just "an extraordinary, powerful fire," but in the context it likely invites us to take it more literally, and that connotation can then carry over to the latter expression.

While Eliphaz can think of wrongdoing issuing in trouble for the perpetrator in the manner of sowing and reaping, he can then immediately picture the process as one involving God's direct action. These plowers "perish by the breath of God, come to an end by the blast from his nostrils" (Job 4:8-9). It comes about because God storms like a warrior into battle. Zophar describes how the wicked perish, their wealth disappears, and their offspring are reduced to begging. How does that come about? "They swallow riches but vomit them; God will throw them out of their belly" (Job 20:15). Vomiting is a particularly down-to-earth, natural phenomenon, and one that might have been pictured in a naturalistic way; there is something poisonous about riches improperly gained, and the stomach reacts against them (cf. Job 20:14, 16). But Zophar then goes for another level of explanation. The consuming of the wicked is indeed like consuming poison, but poison is a common figure for Yhwh's anger, and the burning of the poison is the burning of that anger: "he will let loose on him his angry fury, rain it on them as his food (Job 20:23). Yet there is still another level of explanation. "The heavens will expose their wrongdoing, the earth rise up against them." The very heavens and earth protest at what they see happening on the earth, and God (presumably) hears this protest. As a consequence "the flood will sweep away his household, torrents on the day of his anger. This is the portion of faithless people from God, their possession by his word, from God" (Job 20:27-29). God sends a flood that issues from God's anger, and the portion or possession (ḥēleq, naḥălâ) of the wicked, the land that securely belongs to them, is very different from the one they thought they were making sure of for themselves. The last line makes the point very emphatically, with two different words for God (ʾĕlōhîm, ʾēl) coming at the end of each colon, and with the expression "his word" pointing to the decision God made to bring this about.

How Yhwh Makes Our Experience Match Our Actions

Job agrees; that is his problem. Denying that he has done wrong, he comments,

"What is the allocation of God above, the allotment of the Almighty on high? Surely, calamity for the oppressor, trouble for people who do harm. Surely he would see my ways, count all my steps" (Job 31:2-4; cf. Job 31:6, 14, 23, 35-37). God is personally involved in bringing trouble on wrongdoers. God attends carefully to what they do, makes an evaluation of it and determines their fate. While Job quotes this thesis in order rather systematically to deny it, Elihu expounds it systematically with conviction. He does not directly declare that Job must have earned his suffering, must have done terrible wrong. He does declare that Job has done wrong in the way he has reacted to his suffering. He has claimed to have lived faithfully, accused God of having misused his authority in relation to him and asserted that there is no point in living in a way that pleases God. He has thus made common cause with the faithless, the wrongdoers, the rebels, who also mock the belief that God is involved in a moral way in the world (Job 34:5-9, 34-37).

Elihu argues that Job makes an incoherent allegation. Why would God bother to rule the world and then exercise sovereignty in a way that ignores right and wrong? It does not make sense (Job 34:10-15). Nor does it fit what one sees in the world. Experience provides the evidence that God does not leave rulers and other important people in their positions forever, as if favoring them because of their position. When they act faithlessly and impiously, he listens to the cry of the poor and puts their oppressors down (Job 34:16-30). Elihu thus uses a combination of deductive argument, from what must logically be so, and inductive argument, from what can be seen in the world, to rule out Job's own inductive argument from his own experience. He responds in a similar way to Job's assertion that there is no point living in a way that avoids sin. God, he says, is God, and is obviously not affected by Job's faithfulness or faithlessness. "Your faithlessness affects a person like you and your faithfulness affects a human being [like you]" (Job 35:8). Job's argument from his own experience is ruled out by the deductive argument from the nature of God.

Yhwh's own strategy involves pointing to facts about creation that Job knows about but has not taken into account. In creating the world, Yhwh set limits to dangerous and threatening powers such as the sea and the darkness, ensured that other dangerous and threatening forces such as hail, storm, lightning and thunder are under Yhwh's control for use in battle, and set in place the planets and stars to determine the orderly passing of the seasons (Job 38:8-38). Those facts provide the evidence that Job's private world cannot be the victim of uncontrolled chaos in the way that it seems, even if Job cannot see how that is so. Perhaps it is the case that Job's submission to Yhwh (Job 40:3-5) is merely the submission of one who has been overpowered, not one who has been convinced. This would fit with the fact that when Yhwh starts again, it is to focus on majestic human power and then on two mythic creatures who embody or symbolize frightening chaotic power (Job 40:9—41:34 [MT 26]). Job can put down neither of these, but Yhwh can do so. Job comes to accept that, and not merely submit to Yhwh (Job 42:1-6). He can live with the idea that the world is one in which chaos exists but is under Yhwh's constraint.

In the First Testament a theology of holiness and of mercy holds back a theology of tragedy, the idea that human beings can be victims of a fate jointly decreed by their own nature and by God.[187]

How Yhwh's Actions Relate to Our Plans

"Plans with counsel succeed; make war with advice" (Prov 20:18; cf. Prov 15:22; 21:5; 24:4-5). Yet "the horse is made ready for the day of battle, but the deliverance belongs to Yhwh" (Prov 21:31). Thus "it is a person's mind that plans his way, but it is Yhwh who directs his steps" (Prov 16:9; cf. Prov 20:24; 21:31). "There are many plans in a person's mind, but it is Yhwh's intent that will prevail" (Prov 19:21). All human planning can be frustrated by God's making things work out in a way other than what we planned. "If Yhwh does not build the house, the builders have toiled on it in vain; if Yhwh does not guard the city, the lookout has kept vigil in vain" (Ps 127:1). "There is no wisdom, no insight, no planning before Yhwh" (Prov 21:30); no such wisdom compares with Yhwh's, or no such wisdom counts for anything before Yhwh. And while the second colon makes clear that the saying's direct concern lies with wisdom applied to making plans, the first colon also implies a more far-reaching insight in light of which the humanly formulated wisdom of the First Testament itself deconstructs. Proverbs could give one the impression that it thinks it has everything figured out and could encourage us to think that we have everything figured out. But this usually unspoken qualification applies to all its teaching. Human beings must always keep themselves open to the activity of God, "an activity which completely escapes all calculation."[188] "Many people seek help from a ruler, but a person's decision comes from Yhwh" (Prov 29:26). It is impossible to know whether you will get the decision you need from the ruler, but anyway there is a higher authority that you can trust.

Further, "organizing the mind belongs to a human being, but the response of the tongue comes from Yhwh" (Prov 16:1). It is true that we can make plans but Yhwh's words can decide what actually happens, but this would be an allusive way to make the point, and nowhere else does the First Testament refer to Yhwh's "tongue" speaking.[189] Rather, the proverb refers to the way we

---

[187]Paul Ricoeur, *The Symbolism of Evil* (reprint, Boston: Beacon, 1995), p. 89.

[188]Von Rad, *Wisdom in Israel*, p. 101; cf. Murphy, *Proverbs*, p. 162.

[189]Is 30:27 proves the rule, because it refers to a tongue of fire.

sometimes say something different from what we intended, or say something we have not thought, so that our words seem a kind of gift. Therefore it is wise to "commit your acts to Yhwh so that your plans may stand firm" (Prov 16:3). "The lot is cast into the lap but its every decision comes from Yhwh" (Prov 16:33). Reference to casting lots comes most often in connection with the allocation of the land and of tasks in the temple, and it has the potential to reduce conflict over such questions (Prov 18:18). No one can be accused of manipulating the decisions. Yhwh's authority lies behind them.

"Yhwh made everything for its/his purpose, even the faithless for the day of calamity" (Prov 16:4). Perhaps that simply means that Yhwh sees that the faithless get their comeuppance. But it might rather suggest that Yhwh is capable of using the faithlessness of people to bring the calamity that Yhwh wishes, as Yhwh did in different ways with the Pharaoh whose mind Yhwh closed (so that the day of calamity made people acknowledge Yhwh) or with the Assyrian king whose faithlessness brought the calamity to Judah that Yhwh wanted to be brought.

God "catches the wise in their cleverness as the plan of the twisters speeds on"[190] (Job 5:13). When Paul quotes the first colon (1 Cor 3:19), the cleverness of the wise could be merely the location of their capture, but in its original context, their cleverness is also the means (cf. Job 36:8; Eccles 7:26; against *DCH*). In a single clause, then, Eliphaz encapsulates a two-level understanding of the event. Their cleverness captures them; God captures them. God could capture them in some other way that had no intrinsic relation to their own act (they might just drop dead), and God sometimes does that. Or they could trip themselves by their own plan, and it might be nothing directly to do with God; it might be just one of those things. But sometimes these two forms of causation come together. The second clause then underlines the point. Their plan speeds toward its implementation, but in doing so it is speeding toward disaster for them.

How Yhwh Protects and Delivers

The Psalms assume Yhwh is involved with the individual. Although many psalms may have been especially used by the king, few speak in terms that apply specifically to the king or another leader, and the stance that a person such as Hannah takes to God implies that these psalms' expectations would be ones also claimed by ordinary individuals. The individual calls out to Yhwh and Yhwh answers (e.g., Ps 3:4 [MT 5]). Yhwh does not ignore the cry of the weak (Ps 9:12 [MT 13]).

---

[190]For *nimhārâ*, EVV have translations such as "are brought to a quick end" (NRSV), but the verb means simply "hasten."

Thus the individual proves that "You, Yhwh, are a shield around me, my honor, one who lifts my head" (Ps 3:3 [MT 4]; cf. Ps 7:10 [MT 11]). I am assailed and dishonored, too shamed to lift my head, but you reverse all that, the psalmist says. Yhwh is involved in the life of individuals, providing protection and restoration to one's place of honor in the community, and thus restoration of one's self-esteem. Yhwh upholds the individual (Ps 3:5 [MT 6])—upholds them from the danger that threatens at night, and/or upholds them so that they can relax and sleep rather than worry. "You yourself bless the faithful, Yhwh, you surround them with acceptance like a shield" (Ps 5:12 [MT 13]); the psalmist uses a different word for "shield," denoting a much more impressive one, the kind that envelops a person (the shield in Ps 3:3 [MT 4] was the smaller, handheld kind, though Yhwh was still making it something that reached around the suppliant). To put it another way, Yhwh is a "haven" (miśgāb), a place inaccessibly and therefore safely high up (e.g., Ps 9:9 [MT 10]). "Yhwh is my cliff, my fastness, the one who enables me to escape. My God is my crag on which I take refuge, my shield, my peak that delivers,[191] my haven" (Ps 18:1-2 [MT 2-3]; cf. Ps 31:2-4 [MT 3-5]; 42:9 [MT 10]; 61:2-3 [MT 3-4]; 62:2 [MT 3]; 71:2-3; 91:2, 4, 9; 94:22; 144:1-2). Apart from "shield," all these expressions are variants on the same image. When a bird or an animal is in danger, it may well seek refuge in the safety of a high crag of the kind that it can reach and other creatures or human beings cannot. Human beings, too, may seek refuge in the literal mountains, which offer many an inaccessible hiding place.

For the Israelite, God is that refuge, far beyond the reach of enemies. "Will you hide me in the shade of your wings?" (Ps 17:8; cf. Ps 36:7 [MT 8]; 57:1 [MT 2]; 63:7 [MT 8]). This image might remind people of the cherubim in the temple or of the picture of the sun as having wings (cf. Mal 4:2 [MT 3:20]), but the wings that most immediately link with protection and shade are the wings of a mother bird sheltering her baby. In Psalm 30 Yhwh is one who establishes us (and therefore enables us to live in confidence), yet then hides the face (that is, withdraws blessing), puts down.[192] But Yhwh also heals, brings up from Sheol, and replaces mourning in sackcloth by dancing for joy (Ps 30:1-3, 7, 11 [MT 2-4, 8, 12]). Yhwh is involved in the our entire story.

"Yhwh is my light, my deliverance: whom should I fear?" (Ps 27:1). When the light shines out from Yhwh's face, this means people experience deliverance. Therefore holding on to wisdom mean you sleep unworriedly because

---

[191]qeren usually means "horn," but it denotes a hill in Is 5:1, and the context suggests this meaning here (cf. NIDOTTE); nowhere else is Yhwh described as a horn.

[192]BDB takes this as the sole occurrence of dālâ piel, which would literally mean "draw water." I rather take it as the piel of DCH's dālâ ii, "hang down," with a similar meaning to that of dālal, "be low" (and cf. dal, "poor").

Yhwh is your confidence (Prov 3:24-26). "Confidence" *(kesel)* is a striking word. This confidence can denote a kind of confidence that implies stupidity (Ps 49:13 [MT 14]; Eccles 7:25; cf. *kĕsîlût,* Prov 9:13). Such confident people *(kĕsîlîm)* are fools (e.g., Prov 1:22; and 3:35, soon to follow). Boldly, Proverbs turns confidence talk on its head. The people who boldly trust in their insight and capabilities are stupid. The people who simple-mindedly trust in Yhwh are wise.

Yhwh's military aid is not merely defensive. Delivering from enemies means putting them down. Psalm 35 urges, "contend, Yhwh, with the people who contend with me, fight with the people who fight with me, take hold of shield and buckler, arise as my help, draw spear and pike to meet my pursuers." Yhwh does not balk at the implications: Yhwh is prepared to break the teeth of the faithless (e.g., Ps 3:7 [MT 8]).

Thus one can hold back from taking personal requital for wrongdoing and hope in Yhwh, "and he will deliver you" (Prov 20:22). This does not happen "automatically" but because Yhwh takes action. Proverbs 24:10-12 challenges people about failing to get involved and claiming not really to know what was going on when others were being taken off to slaughter, as the modern West has in relation to events such as the Holocaust and the Rwandan genocide. But "if you say, 'Now, we did not know about this,' the one who weighs minds— he will certainly discern, the one who watches over your life—he will know, and he will repay the person in accordance with their deed." Yhwh knows the truth about all that. The allusiveness of the sayings leaves their implications rather open, in some ways worryingly so. Perhaps they declare that Yhwh will repay the people guilty for the slaughter, but perhaps they declare that Yhwh will repay the people who stood by. Either way, they declare that when we decline to get involved, Yhwh may intervene.

On the other hand, "when your enemy falls, do not rejoice, when he stumbles, your heart must not be glad, lest Yhwh see it and be displeased and turn his anger from him" (Prov 24:17-18). The positive ethos of the first line makes it hard to imagine that its basic concern is to make sure that the enemy is well punished; more likely the idea is that Yhwh's anger may turn from the enemy to this person who is rejoicing at the enemy's downfall.[193] It is thus the converse of another saying: "If your opponent is hungry, give him food to eat, if he is thirsty, give him water to drink, because you will be heaping coals on his head, and Yhwh will reward you" (Prov 25:21-22). The opening participle is not an ordinary word for enemy such as *ʾôyēb,* but *śōnēʾ,* from the verb conventionally translated "hate." So the saying refers to the way we respond

---

[193]Cf. Murphy, *Proverbs,* p. 182.

when people treat us as enemies but then themselves get into difficulties, and it promises Yhwh's reward. This does not happen automatically, but because Yhwh acts. (We do not know the meaning of the image in the third colon. It is not clear why such generous action should make Yhwh bring calamity on the attacker, but neither is the image an obvious way to refer to bringing someone to repentance.)

How Death Makes Things Work

Death is one of the forces that see that life works out in a moral way for people who are confident in their power and wealth (Ps 49:14-15 [MT 15-16]). "Like sheep they have headed for Sheol," not merely because they follow each other like sheep too stupid to do anything different, but because "death shepherds them" (or feeds on them there, on another understanding of $rā\hat{\ }a$). They leave one form of shepherding (Ps 23) for another. Thus "the upright have dominion over them at morning and their form is for wasting by Sheol instead of its having a lofty home," instead of their being able to continue in their magnificence. "Yet God will redeem my life from the power of Sheol, for he will take me." That was what the stupid wealthy thought they could do for themselves but cannot (Ps 49:7 [MT 8]). The psalm does not speak of God being directly involved in taking people to their death, though it would no doubt affirm that God was behind this process. Even the NRSV does not imply that God is directly involved; when it describes the sheep as "appointed for Sheol," even that renders a third-person *plural* verb.[194] God is not its implicit subject. The psalm makes God the subject of a verb only in connection with people's deliverance from death. Here presumably "redeem" *(pādâ)* has its more usual non-monetary implications (cf. Hos 13:14), since God does not actually pay anything to anyone. God will simply "take" the faithful from Sheol, preventing it from finally getting the faithful person into its clutches (cf. Ps 16:10; 18:5, 16 [MT 6, 17]; 30:3 [MT 4]). So the upright have dominion over them at morning when their deliverance and the fall of the faithless become a reality. In light of belief in resurrection, the lines could be understood to refer to that, but within the First Testament's own context they would rather suggest God's involvement in this life.

Psalm 52 similarly addresses a person who "exults in evil," with a series of images for God's personal involvement in bringing about his downfall (Ps 52:5-7 [MT 7-9]). "God himself will break you up forever, snatch you up and pull you from your tent, uproot you from the land of the living." The man is like a building; God will break him down. The man is like a plant; God will

---

[194]The verb is *šātat*, a byform of *šît*, which can be used intransitively (cf. Ps 3:6 [MT 7]), and this understanding avoids hypothesizing a change of subject (cf. JPSV).

uproot him. More literally, the man is like or is someone relaxing secure at home; God will burst in like the FBI pursuing a criminal and drag him out. "The faithful will see and revere, and will laugh at him: 'There is the man who does not make God his stronghold but has trusted in the abundance of his wealth; he finds strength in his destruction.'" He thought his wealth and his destructiveness were his strength, but they are actually his weakness, because God is the only stronghold.

There is thus a positive side to human mortality. In the context of a lament at people's deceitful attacks and a challenge nevertheless to trust in God, a suppliant comments, "Yes, human beings are a breath; mortals are deceit; going up on scales, they are less than a breath, altogether" (Ps 62:9 [MT 10]). Both aggressors and their victims are inclined to think that the former will be in power forever, but both need to remind themselves that is not so. Human beings can look weighty but actually lack substance. Death is the great leveler. "When the wicked die, their hope perishes, and the expectation of their resources [or: of their wickedness] has perished" (Prov 11:7). In Sheol the captives and the oppressed can rest because their oppressors no longer have any power over them: "small and great are there, and the servant is free from his master" (Job 3:17-19). When anyone dies, their hope perishes, but the wicked had hopes attached to their wrongdoing and/or their resources. They thought they could cheat death (cf. Ps 49). But they cannot.

6.8 How Life Does Not Work

So we assume that cause-and-effect operates in our lives and that life does work in a moral way. But the protests of Job (among others) insist on what we also know: that it is not always so; on a bad day we may reckon it is not so at all. The Psalms make this especially clear as they protest the experience of pressure, attack, sorrow, groaning, debilitation, disappointment, wasting, reproach, defamation and scheming (so Ps 31:9-13 [MT 10-14]). The suppliant is in dire "straits" *(sar)*, constrained and confined, closed in, needing God to make it possible to stand in a broad place instead—often the etymological implications of *sar* do not seem to carry over in usage, but here they do (Ps 31:7-8 [MT 8-9]). All this is made worse by the way it affects relationships with other people. The suppliant has become a reproach, that is, people are full of reproaches. They assume that the suffering is an indication of unfaithfulness in the suppliant's life. They might suspect secret recourse to other deities, as the psalm makes a point of denying that (Ps 31:6 [MT 7]). The suppliant has also become a frightening sight to people, and therefore something from which they recoil. They put the suppliant out of mind; they do not want to think about such suffering. It is like already being dead and forgotten. Or if they wish to think, their thoughts relate to generating further slurs, and not just slurs but further suffering, because if the person is under God's judgment for faithlessness, they should surely associate themselves with that action.

Psalm 102 provides another example of the way suffering can envelop the whole person. It affects the body; a fever burns up the body as if one is in an oven. Bodily suffering then has an effect on the inner person, so the heart is affected by this experience. That, too, is described in terms of burning, the burning of grass by the searing heat of summer. It is as if the suppliant is coming to the end of that burning process. It is nearly dark, is as if life is running out. The suppliant sits in ashes rather than before a laden table, and tears fall into the water the suppliant drinks. Oddly, we might think, the psalms make relatively little reference to actual healing. Their concern with sickness lies especially in its implications for relationships, and they lament the way that suffering distances us from other people. The suppliant lies there awake while everyone else sleeps, like a species of bird that stays awake at night while all the other birds sleep. But much worse than that is again the fact that other people often find illness impossible to cope with. It makes them wonder whether they will be the next to fall, and they seek to distance themselves from it. Or it makes them wonder whether suffering can come undeserved, and they seek to deny that by identifying the suppliant's suffering as indeed deserved.

How are we to think about all that? The First Testament notes the extent to which the rules about life are generalizations that do not always work, and it reflects on the significance of suffering that comes in contrast with what those rules would make one expect.

The Nature of Rules About Life

Wisdom describes how things are, how life works, in the conviction that life is not merely random. There is an order or logic about the world and about human life, an order or logic that we can discover and live in light of. Thus we can make decisions that enable us to fit into the way that life works rather than trying to work against it and inevitably fail. The trouble is that the rules of life are more like the rules of sociology or economics than those of physics or chemistry. Wisdom thinking is Israel's equivalent to the social sciences. Its rules involve looking for patterns in events that in reality are all unique. Yet if wisdom truly involves acknowledging how life actually works, it has to be realistic about the "exceptions" to its rules as well as about the rules. It therefore involves both the kind of generalizations that especially characterize Proverbs and the insistence on the exceptions that especially characterize Job and Qohelet. Neither the generalizations nor the exceptions would constitute wisdom without the other.

"There is a right [yāšār] way before a person, but its end is the way to death" (Prov 14:12; cf. Prov 16:25). It is possible to walk down the right road but find that it leads to disaster. You could look back and consider the process whereby you took this road and see no fault in it, yet it led to calamity. Qohelet expresses the point with greater boldness and without equivocation:

> I again looked under the sun: The race does not belong to the swift or the battle to the valiant, nor bread to the wise, nor wealth to the intelligent, nor favor to the learned, because time and chance happen to all of them. Because human beings, too, do not know their time. Like fish that are caught in a grim net, like birds that are caught in a snare—like them, human beings are caught at a time of calamity, when it falls on them suddenly. (Eccles 9:11-12)

Qohelet hardly believes that life works out with total randomness; his periodic more orthodox sayings suggest he is seeking to counterbalance the teaching of people who paint things as more predictable and intelligible than they actually are (at least, this is the contribution of his work in the context of other Scriptures). He does believe that hard-edged statements about life's consistency and predictability fail to take the exceptions into account, and as we ourselves look at life as it is under the sun we can hardly disagree. While the swift generally win the race and the better warriors win the battle, it is not always so, often because death catches them out when they had no reason to expect it.

Proverbs' talk about coping with not being well-off presupposes that people may do all the right things and be wise, yet end up poorly off (Prov 15:15-17; 19:1). Laziness issues in poverty, hard work in wealth (Prov 10:5); but Proverbs makes it clear that the clauses cannot be turned inside out. It has just noted that there is such a thing as wealth that issues from dishonesty, not hard work (Prov 10:2). Its urging of generosity to the poor implies a recognition that there is such a thing as poverty that does not issue from laziness. In the world's big cities there are many people who work hard but stay in poverty. It is tempting to turn generalizations in Proverbs into rules, and thus encourage people to infer that a great disaster such as an earthquake or hurricane or tsunami reflects the wickedness of its victims.[195] But Proverbs would be wiser. The First Testament's declarations about the way life works deconstruct; they surreptitiously grant the truth in what they overtly deny. This is not a weakness but a strength.

As far as we can see, there is some randomness about God's involvement in the world. (I am not bothered by this personally, but if you think it cannot be right, you can emphasize the "as far as we can see.") "To a person who seems good to him, he gives wisdom, knowledge, and enjoyment," that is, the wisdom and knowledge to find enjoyment. "To a person who falls short he gives

---

[195] Is 41—45 would suggest that this hypothesis is plausible when a prophet announces the calamity ahead of time, but not when it is an a posteriori interpretation.

the work of collecting and storing up—to give to someone who seems good to God. This, too, is emptiness" (Eccles 2:24-26). Is it emptiness because that is how it is for this person who falls short, or does this comment imply that "falling short" does not have the usual connotations of moral failure but simply means "does not please God" for reasons one cannot perceive, so that the event puts a question mark by all meaningfulness?

Therefore only stupid people think they are wise, that they understand how things work, that they have life under control, that they can make things happen (e.g., Prov 26:12), as the story of Ahitophel and his failed counsel famously illustrates (2 Sam 15—17).[196]

Moral Forces Not Working

So the moral rules do not always work. Famously, Job was a person of unequaled integrity and devotion to God, but also a man whose life fell apart. His friends inferred that this must mean he was actually a person secretly lacking in integrity. He could surely have confidence and hope on the basis of his reverence for God, the integrity of his ways. "Think now, what innocent man has perished, and where have the upright been cut off?" Eliphaz asks. "As I have seen, those who plow trouble, those who sow wrong, reap it" (Job 4:6-8). Where there is life there is hope. Job is a person of integrity, reverence for God, innocence. Yes, he is experiencing suffering, but he will not perish. It does not happen.

The trouble with rhetorical questions is that someone may answer them. They purport to presuppose an obvious answer but formally leave the answer open, and in response to Eliphaz's question readers were free to respond, "Well, actually, one could give quite a few examples." Faithful people do perish in their faithfulness, and faithless people live long lives in wrongdoing, so that other people are encouraged in wrongdoing. The faithless get what the faithful deserve and vice versa. Not even in death is that disparity removed; the faithless receive honorable burial. That does not mean there is no truth in the promises about things going well for people who revere God and going badly for the faithless, but they are not invariably reliable (Eccles 8:10-14). Job's personal problem is that he has the experience Eliphaz speaks of, but has not generated it in this way. God has worn him out, attacked him in anger, and handed him over to wicked people who then attack him and shatter him. "Those who prayed the prayers of lamentation were not exactly prudish when they reproached God with his severity. But here is a new tone which has never been sounded before. . . . Job stands face to face with a completely new expe-

---

[196]Cf. von Rad, *Wisdom in Israel*, 102-4.

rience of the reality of God, an experience of something incalculable and fearful."[197]

"My face is red with weeping, deep shadows cover my eyes, because[198] there is no violence on my hands and my plea is pure" (Job 16:16-17). There is no blood on his hands that would explain his suffering. The claim that his plea is pure may link with this, if "plea" has its regular legal connotations in keeping with Job's frequent picture of himself as a person pleading for vindication in court. But it may pick up the accusation that his attitude to God undermines prayer (Job 15:4). Or it may be an affirmation that he never prays to other deities, an implicit or explicit requirement in prayers of laments in Psalms. The descriptions of God's attacks on him correspond to those in Lamentations 3, reflecting Yhwh's bringing about the fall of Jerusalem. But Lamentations accepts the propriety of God's attack. Jerusalem knows that it has blood on its hands and that its worship was corrupt. Job knows no such thing.

To the claim that innocent people suffer, Eliphaz would likely respond, "Well, they could not really have been innocent." No one can claim to be totally innocent and upright, and therefore we must all accept God's implicit judgment on our lives—which is what calamity consists in. But the narrator has forestalled that argument by portraying Job as a man of unequalled piety and honor. His suffering is out of all proportion to his share in the general sinfulness of humanity.

Yhwh Not Working

"Rather than revise their theology," I once heard someone say, "the friends are prepared to rewrite Job's life." In a sense they do not need to revise their theology; they just need to give it more flexibility. "If they are wrong, as they are, it is in such a way that they are also right, just as Job is right in such a way that he is also wrong."[199] They preach timeless truths about God's wisdom and omnipotence and justice, but these once-living words have now become dead words, whereas "in Job's speeches we are plunged into the strain and stress of the ongoing history of Yahweh with him."[200]

But before they rewrite Job's life, they rewrite his children's lives, which might be more hurtful. We know that Job had been aware of the possibility that they might have sinned and blasphemed God secretly even if they did not do it openly, and that he had therefore prayed for their forgiveness for any such

---

[197]Ibid., 217.

[198]It is doubtful if *ʿal* can mean "although" or needs to mean it here: see Clines, *Job 1—20*, p. 387.

[199]Barth, *Church Dogmatics*, IV/3.i:454.

[200]Ibid., IV/3.i:457.

failure and led them in offering sacrifice against that possibility, to sanctify them again (Job 1:5).[201] Initially, the friends' response to Job's own suffering is that as long as it is not terminal, their theology is not imperiled; given human sinfulness, some suffering is not surprising or unreasonable. So, Bildad declares, Job needs to seek God seriously and keenly, like someone getting up early to do something they are committed to doing (šāḥar piel), and to pray for God to show grace to him (ḥānan hitpael). Then, if Job is as innocent and upright as he seems, God will arouse himself and restore or recompense (šālēm piel) his faithful home—that is, the home where he had lived faithfully (Job 8:5-7). But of course this framework will not work for his sons and daughters. They are dead. So (Bildad reasons) they cannot have shared Job's (relative) innocence and integrity. Their house cannot have shared the faithfulness of Mr. and Mrs. Job's house, otherwise they would not have died in its collapse. "If your children sinned against him, then he gave them into the power of their rebellion" (Job 8:4). Bildad's expression is a noteworthy declaration about the interweaving of moral forces and God's activity. Rebellion has a power of its own to bring about trouble to the rebels, but God actively gives them over to its power.[202] But Job knows, and we know (does Bildad?), that Job had faced the possibility that his offspring had sinned and reviled God, and had taken appropriate action for and with them. Bildad has indeed been rewriting their lives.

Actually, God has not been making these lives work out in a way that matches mišpāṭ and ṣedeq. After listening to each of the friends assert that the wicked receive their comeuppance, Job calls the bluff on this claim. Faithless people live on and get on in life and rejoice in the lives of their children; their family life thrives, and "God's cane does not come on them" (Job 21:7-9). Initially Job does not quite say that events in the world look totally arbitrary, that the faithless generally do well and the faithful badly, that there is no evidence of God's activity in the world. He is simply contesting his friends' implicit view that the generalizations of Proverbs always work. The obverse of the fact that faithful Job suffers is the fact that some faithless people do well all their lives. Just as the friends are ignoring the facts about Job that indicate that a faithful person can have their life collapse, so they are ignoring the evidence that faithless people can flourish and then die happy, for all the world as if they are enjoying the blessing promised to the faithful. And it is God who brings this about, or fails to do so.

---

[201]See section 6.3 "Parenthood."

[202]Paul's language in Rom 1:24-32 will recall this expression, though he there speaks of giving people over so that their sinfulness finds its outworking in more outrageous sinfulness, which is rather a different point.

As he goes on, Job comes nearer to implying that Proverbs' generalizations are not even true as generalizations: "How often does the lamp of the faithless go out, does disaster come upon them, does he allocate suffering in his anger?" (Job 21:17). So "why are times [for acting in judgment] not reserved by the Almighty?" (Job 24:1). Job goes on to describe the wickedness of the rich and the consequent suffering of the poor, like the homeless in a modern city scrabbling for food and huddled against the cold and the rain: "From the city men groan, people who are mortally injured cry for help, but God does not place blame" (Job 24:12). The people responsible for their plight simply get away with it. God does nothing to restrain or punish evil.

It is such comment and questioning that tip Eliphaz into rewriting Job's life (Job 22). It would be easy enough for him to see Job's theology as ideological; he needs to be able to maintain the position he does in order to avoid facing the fact of his wrongdoing, which is the real explanation of his suffering.

Wisdom Not Working

Bildad's response is to reassert God's awesome power (Job 25:2). God is one before whom Sheol trembles, one who showed such great power in creating the world and putting down the forces of disorder and resistance. Further, "these are [merely] the outskirts of his ways, and what a whisper is the word that we hear of him—who could understand his mighty thunder?" (Job 26:14).[203] We just cannot expect to understand God's ways, which are so much higher than ours. Yhwh will take up this theme in due course (Job 38—41).

Thus in Job and Bildad two sharply different perspectives confront each other, both affirmed by the First Testament and both speaking powerfully to situations when God is inactive in the face of calamity—or even causes it.[204] Bildad's is resolutely theological, in a narrow sense. He knows we must let God be God, in God's transcendent, creator holiness and absoluteness. The mighty, august God is ultimately one before whom we must bow when we run out of understanding. God is one characterized by fire, hidden in the cloud for our protection, speaking in the thunder and embodied in the whirlwind. Bildad acknowledges the reality of Job's experience and does not seek to explain it (for instance, by accusing Job of being a great sinner who has deserved it—Eliphaz's accusation), but reckons we cannot finally question God's ways;

---

[203]MT gives the impression that Job 26:5-14 are Job's words, but Job 27:1 seems to imply that someone else was speaking there. Job 26:5-14 may thus continue Bildad's address in Job 25:1-6, which Job perhaps interrupts in Job 26:1-4. Or perhaps Job speaks sarcastically in Job 26:5-14 (so J. Gerald Janzen, *Job* [Atlanta: John Knox Press, 1985], pp. 177-78). Either way, the passage is more the kind of thing Bildad says than Job does.

[204]I follow Newsom, "Book of Job," pp. 519-20, though I tweak the matter rather differently.

that is to make ourselves into God. We are nothing before the majesty of this God.

Job's theology is more experiential and ethical. He acknowledges the truth in Bildad's words, but he cannot let them overwhelm what he has experienced and what he has seen. There is something wrong with a theology that allows God to stand aloof from a situation where someone is hounded by trouble as if they were guilty of great wrongdoing when they are not. And (it seems) this experience has opened Job's mind to a broader problem that he had apparently evaded when he was doing well in life. The converse of his experience of suffering he does not deserve is the experience he sees elsewhere in the lives of people who wrong others by, for instance, ignoring or taking advantage of the weak and needy. They get away with it all their lives. It is necessary then to batter on God's chest till one gets a reply, even if the reply is a reminder of the other truth about God.

> One of the characteristics of acute suffering is its tendency to obliterate all other experience. It can become almost impossible to see, hear, or feel anything beyond one's own suffering, as though that suffering were all that existed in the world. In such a situation, images of God that stress the intimate, personal quality of God, likening God to one who suffers with the grieving, may not be what is needed. What one craves is reassurance that one's own suffering is *not* the whole of reality. The religious experience of the holiness of God, of God as wholly otherness, is capable of providing such reassurance. As Bildad's speech suggests, religious language that speaks of the transcendence of God often does so in terms of creation. God's power in overcoming chaos and establishing the reliable structures of the cosmos can be an important support for one whose own experience is a wilderness of pain and anxiety. Thus one should not assume that only the religious traditions that speak of God in personal and intimate terms are of importance to one who suffers. There is also solace to be found in the language of God's majesty and transcendence.[205]

Suffering as Corrective

So how can we make sense of suffering? Is there a logic to it? To judge from the Psalms, most suffering does not issue from the sufferer's personal sin, but some is explicable as resulting from our failure, waywardness and (moral) stupidity (see, e.g., Ps 38:1-5 [MT 2-6]). Our sin is then a crushing burden. This is not a comment on the psychological burden that sin feels or the way it affects a relationship with God. Rather it refers to the way it affects the body, because it leads to the expression of Yhwh's anger, to its total loss of soundness and well-being.

---

[205]Ibid., p. 520.

As he claims at some length, Elihu has a distinctive contribution to make to attempts to work out why suffering happens and how we respond to it. He speaks first of the way God reaches out to people in dreams and visions (as Job himself has; Job 7:14), but people do not always perceive that God is thus speaking to them (Job 33:14-18). "So they are then reproved by sufferings" in such a way that may take them to the verge of death (Job 33:19-22). The implication for Job is clear: his suffering is a form of discipline or reproof. Proverbs often speaks of discipline and reproof as key elements in parents' treatment of their offspring; it is hardly surprising if these also feature in God's treatment of us. So the dreams, the sufferings and the words of the aide are designed to enable Job to see the sin he has not faced and thereby to lead him on in his moral life and his relationship with God. He can therefore be restored to full life and to a good relationship with God. If the dreams did not reach the person, this process may do so as the person prays, recognizing and testifying to the fact that they have sinned but not been overcome by calamity because of it. And this is something that may happen to a person several times during his or her life (Job 33:25-30). Suffering is not punitive but disciplinary and redemptive, designed to win people back to God (see further Job 36:5-21).

Ironically, Elihu's thesis resembles that of the despised Eliphaz, Bildad and Zophar in combining insight, danger and irrelevance. It suggests insight because suffering can indeed make people examine the nature and bases of their lives, change their minds, their attitudes and their priorities, and draw them (back) to God, as other parts of the Scriptures note (e.g., Rom 5:3-5; 8:28). But it is notably hard to find Scriptures that declare that God *sends* suffering to this end as opposed to *harnessing* it to that end, though Hebrews 12:5-11 is an example. Taking this as *the* key to understanding suffering, and thus instinctively appealing to it when someone gets ill or loses a spouse or a child, threatens to generate a demonic understanding of God. Job's own story illustrates the point. We know from the prologue that this was not the explanation of Job's suffering.

Elihu later adds another insightful, dangerous and irrelevant argument. "Because of great oppression people may cry out, cry for help because of the power of the mighty, but not say 'Where is God who made me?'" (Job 35:9-10). "You do not have because you do not ask," James 4:2 will comment. People who do not ask for deliverance from their suffering or oppression may therefore fail to get it. And each of the three friends has urged Job to have recourse to God (Job 5:8; 8:5; 11:13), apparently reckoning that he does not do so. He has of course cried out, but crying out does not in itself constitute prayer. The Israelites in the wilderness kept crying out because they were under attack or had no food or water, but they were more inclined to cry out in protest at Moses than to cry out to Yhwh, and often got in trouble with Yhwh. Thus "they may cry out but he does not respond" (Job 35:12).

On the other hand, crying out in such a way that the cry does not seem to be addressed to Yhwh but is just a cry of pain does not rule out Yhwh's responding (see Ex 2:23-25; Is 40:27). It would thus be dangerous to suggest that a particular cry remained unheard because it was not formally expressed as a prayer. Indeed, while Job's own cries have talked about God more than to God, the missing cry Elihu speaks of is itself not addressed to God. Actually, it is surely exactly the kind of cry Job has kept uttering, as it asks about the absence of the God who made the suppliant, who in the past has given the suppliant strength or songs of praise for God's power and goodness,[206] and who has given the community insight through reflecting on the nature of God's world (Job 35:10-11). So Elihu's insightful point is irrelevant to Job.

Suffering as Testing

We have seen that in effect Proverbs affirms a version of the prosperity gospel: "Honor Yhwh with your resources, with the first of all your produce, and your barns will fill with abundance, your vats will burst with wine" (Prov 3:9-10). Yet it continues, "Do not object to Yhwh's discipline, my son, do not resent his rebuke, because Yhwh rebukes the one he loves, like a father the son in whom he delights," and it goes on to declare once more that wisdom is a more profitable acquisition than gold or silver (Prov 3:11-16). If the points were not implausible and controversial, would they need so much emphasis? Even Proverbs recognizes that there is more to be said than the prosperity gospel.

The book of Job comprises the most sustained discussion of the fact that the confident assertions in many sayings in Proverbs cannot be pressed. Job was a man of integrity and uprightness who revered God and shunned wrongdoing (Job 1:1). His life worked out accordingly; he had a large family and many possessions. Indeed, he was the biggest man in the East. So what is the relationship between his piety and his happiness? Is it because of the blessing it produces that he is a person of unparalleled integrity, uprightness and commitment to God? Let us imagine what would happen if these are taken away.

Despite not being privy to the scenes in Job 1—2, from the beginning Job knows that God is the one who has caused his suffering, shooting poisoned arrows into his system (Job 6:4). Indeed, that is the most painful aspect of his suffering. He experiences an incomprehensible inconsistency about the way God can treat people. Not only did God put much care and effort into bringing a person such as Job into being, but then "you granted me life and commitment, and your attention watched over my spirit." Initially the kind of care that went

---

[206]zĕmirôt can be understood either way.

into creating Job continued in his life. Alongside the gift of life was a divine commitment that brought a positive attentiveness and concern with Job. But it did not last. "You hid these things in your mind; I know that this was your purpose." Perhaps Job means that God then hid that commitment and attentiveness, but more likely he means that God had already been concealing the intention to show a different kind of attentiveness, a different kind of watching. "If I fell short, you would watch me, and not clear me of my wrongdoing. If I was faithless, woe to me, but if I were faithful, I could not lift my head, full of shame, sated with my weakness" (Job 10:12-15). If he is faithless, then he gets what he deserves. But if he is faithful, he gets the same treatment and cannot hold his head high as if his humiliation did not matter. God has wronged him, humiliated him, uprooted him, alienated him from society and family (Job 19:6-20). Job speaks like one of Kafka's antiheroes, hounded by God, finding no exit no matter which way he turns, powerless, resourceless, friendless and loveless.

Unfortunately, God's testing has the capacity to push someone over the edge. Job passes his first test and initially his second (Job 1:22; 2:10), but "afterward" (Job 3:1) things look different. It is doubtful whether his cursing the day of his birth and his vitriolic words about God in the debates that follow would count as neither sinning with his lips nor "ascribing *tiplâ* [something like 'impropriety'] to God" (Job 1:22), and God's rebuke of Job presupposes there was something wrong with his words. But it rather seems that his friends share responsibility for this with God and the Adversary. Can he no more bear their silence than God's, and then not bear their words?

Job's experience corresponds to that described in the Psalms: "Deep is calling to deep at the sound of your waterfalls; all your breakers and your waves have passed over me" (Ps 42:7 [MT 8]). Among other peoples, the overwhelming of the waters of the deep would suggest the attacks of other deities. The psalmist, however, knows there is only one God; the bad things that happen cannot be blamed on some other deity. They must have come from Yhwh. The same applies to Israel's corporate experience. Its defeat cannot have been brought about by any other god. Yhwh must be responsible for it. In Psalm 44:9-14 [MT 10-15], for instance, Israel thus makes Yhwh the subject of a sequence of horrifying verbs: you spurned us, disgraced us, turn us back, make us like sheep for food, scattered us, sell us, make us a reproach and byword. There is thus a possible apparent solution to the question of suffering that neither the psalms nor Job take up. One could attribute it to some other god and/ or turn to some other god for deliverance from the afflicting god. In Israel, when people got ill there was no one like a physician in our sense to go to. People knew that illness came from God and were thus more aware than we are that God is the healer. The question then was whether you turned to Yhwh or some other deity. At this point Job passes God's test. "My servant Job" has spoken what is right about me, Yhwh will eventually declare (Job 42:8).

Suffering as World-Shattering

Out-of-the-ordinary suffering makes moral sense if it punishes or disciplines or tests or corrects. But what if it does not? Job knows that there is no reason for his suffering to be punitive or disciplinary or corrective, and he does not know it is a test. It therefore puts him into a turmoil (*rōgez*, Job 3:26) because it makes his world collapse. He thought he knew how life worked. He lived a life of commitment, integrity and reverence for God, and he lived a life in which he knew God's blessing. He would not need to assume that there was a simple one-way causation there, as if the Adversary was right that he was only in it for what he got out of it. Rather he assumed that life was a whole; commitment and blessing, blessing and commitment formed part of that whole. God hedged him about. But now God hedges him about in another way, and for this there is no rationale that he can see. His world thus falls apart. "A human being does have servitude on earth; his days are like those of a day-laborer, like a servant who longs for the shadows, like a day-laborer who looks forward to his pay" (Job 7:1-2).

Genesis 1—2 correspond to equivalent Middle Eastern creation stories in seeing humanity as created to serve God, but the chapters differ in seeing this work in positive terms. Job speaks more like the Middle Eastern stories and moves in a gloomier rather than a more positive direction. Humanity was created for drudgery.[207] The ideal human life involves working one's own farm, or in the city having one's own business (for instance, baking). Being in employment is a poor second to that. As in our culture, people who simply have to labor for others, as people hired by the day, perhaps because they have got into debt and become indentured servants, have a much less satisfying work life. They do not enjoy their work life for itself but spend the day looking forward to the evening when they will be able to stop work, get their wages and start living their life. No doubt that is an exaggeration; there are indentured servants and day workers who enjoy their work. Likewise there are human beings who do not see their life on earth as like being drafted into service in the army ("servitude" is *ṣābāʾ*). But a person who experiences ongoing suffering may well look at it that way. "So I have been allocated months of emptiness; nights of toil have been assigned to me" (Job 7:3). In themselves, the days of laborers are empty, vain, useless (*šāwʾ*), and so are the lives of sufferers. Indeed, they are worse, because at least indentured servants and day-laborers

---

[207]Cf. Norman C. Habel, *The Book of Job* (London: SCM Press/Philadelphia: Westminster Press, 1985), p. 157.

get the chance to relax in the evening and sleep at night. For the sufferer, the nights are as toilsome as the days. They drag on as much as the days do for the servant or laborer (Job 7:4)—or are made terrifying by those nightmares God keeps sending (Job 7:13-14).

Psalm 8 marvels at the fact that God makes so much of humanity in giving us such a significant place in ruling the world. Job also marvels, but to different import. "What are human beings that you make much of them, that you give your mind to them and pay attention to them each morning, test them every moment?" (Job 7:17-18). A person who experiences God's attacks experiences a form of divine attentiveness that one would wish to escape. It is reasonable enough for God to keep close watch on the Sea or the Dragon, embodiments of frightful and dangerous power that threaten God's intention to have a world characterized by order and blessing (Job 7:12). But does a human being really deserve such attention? Are we so threatening to the world and to God's purpose? Testing is all very well (e.g., Ps 26:2; 139:23), but does it need to be continual and relentless? If Eliphaz is right, some experience of suffering issues inevitably from the fact that we are sinners. But "if I sin, what do I do to you, watcher of humanity? Why have you made me your target and have I become a burden to myself [MT]/to you [LXX]?" (Job 7:20). Why should God make such an issue of human sin? Even human beings find it possible to overlook one another's mistakes. Why can God not do so? Are they a threat to God somehow? Why can God not forgive Job and thus end the time when he needs to undergo God's attacks, so that he can be allowed to die—and no longer be vulnerable to God's attentiveness? "Why do you not carry my rebellion and remit my wrongdoing?—because then I could lie down in the dirt and you would search for me and I would not be there" (Job 7:21).

Elihu closes his argument (Job 36:22-26) by declaring, "Now: God is on high in his power; who is a teacher like him?" God is great in power and in the capacity to give instructions about how things need to be in the world. How impossible, then, to fault him for the way he acts. "Who has attended to his way for him, who has said 'You have acted oppressively'?" The first question uses the verb *pāqad*, which could point to people's prescribing what God *should* do (SO NIVI, NRSV). But it is familiar as a term to refer to God's attending to human wrongdoing (EVV "visit"), and the second colon supports the view that it refers to people passing judgment on what God *has* done. Rather then questioning what God does, Elihu reckons, someone like Job should be thinking about acknowledging God's great acts, the great acts people have lauded in the past. After all, "God is great and we cannot know; the number of his years is beyond searching." Elihu goes on to describe the greatness of God as creator, the one who forms the rain and thus the one who provides the world with food, and also who uses the violent aspects of creation to bring calamity on oppression

(Job 36:27—37:24). Everyone is aware of these acts, though we see them only from afar. We do not pretend to understand the God who brings them about. So Elihu concludes, "the Almighty—we cannot reach him, great in power and authority; abundant in faithfulness, he does not afflict" (Job 37:23).

No, you cannot understand what is going on, says Yhwh near the end of the book. And I am not going to tell you. You have to live without knowing.[208]

Suffering as Overwhelming by Death

Suffering implies a distancing from God. The First Testament does not picture God being with people in suffering, because it knows this is a contradictory idea. If God is with you, then good things happen. God is one who delivers. The idea of the presence of God in the midst of suffering is self-contradictory. Suffering means God has left us to our own devices. Indeed, the suppliant's experience rather suggests being plucked up and hurled off as by a tornado in an expression of furious divine anger. My whole body and person shake in dismay. God stands aloof. Either Yhwh is angry with me, or Yhwh behaves so (Ps 6).

"If only my anguish were properly weighed and my calamity put with it in the scales, because now it would be heavier than the sand of the seas—that is why my words were outspoken" (Job 6:2-3). Suffering can be such that there is no way to express the weight of the burden. Suffering can thus mean I am drawing near to Sheol; indeed, that death already overwhelms me.

> My whole person is full of troubles;
>> my life has come to the brink of Sheol.
> I am numbered with people who go down to the Pit;
>> I have become like a man who is helpless,
> Among the dead an outcast, like the slain,
>> lying in the grave,
> People of whom you are mindful no more,
>> and they are cut off from your hand.
> You have put me in the bottom of the Pit,
>> in utter darkness, in the lowest depth.
> Your fury presses on me;
>> with all your breakers you have afflicted me. (Ps 88:3-7 [MT 4-8])

No doubt sufferers who spoke thus knew they were not literally dead, but

---

[208]Job 42:5 does not seem to show that Job illustrates a "communion theodicy," the idea that suffering can bring someone closer to God (against Antti Laato and Johannes C. de Moor in their introduction to Laato and de Moor, eds., *Theodicy in the World of the Bible* (Leiden/Boston: Brill, 2003), p. xlviii. It is Yhwh's appearing (and putting Job in his place) that brings the denouement of the book of Job, not Job's suffering.

neither is their language mere metaphor. The power of death was indeed over-whelming them. "I have called on your name, Yhwh, from the deepest Pit" (Lam 3:55). Israelites do not make as sharp a distinction between life and death as we do, and they are generally much more troubled by the way death can force its way into the midst of what is supposed to be life than they are by the fact that life eventually ends in death.

The great thing about Sheol, Job creatively assumes, is that it is a place of relief for the weary, oppressed and afflicted—the group to which Job now be-longs. "I have no peace, I have no quietness, I have no rest, and turmoil has come upon me" (Job 3:26): but in the realm of death, there is relief. The pow-erful are no longer exercising their power, the wicked can no longer trouble the weary, prisoners of war are not undertaking forced labor, and indentured ser-vants are free of their masters (Job 3:14-19). "Surprisingly, perhaps, Job's por-trait of this place of peace in Earth is similar to the image many Christians have of heaven"; Job finds it attractive because it is "a place of escape from the trap of living with God."[209] But death looks different when it overwhelms you be-fore its time, and before you have had the chance to enjoy a full life. Who wants to go to bed and sleep when they still feel full of life? During life, Yhwh is sup-posed to be positively mindful of us, and we live within reach of God's hand; God attends to us (Ps 8:4 [MT 5]). Death means this ceases to be so. We are no longer crowned with glory and honor, exercising dominion in the world (Ps 8:5-8 [MT 6-9]). And that is all right at the end of a full life; after all, we are asleep, enjoying our rest. But it is not all right when this experience comes in the midst of so-called life.

Suffering as Hopeless

"Hope deferred makes the heart sick, while a longing that comes about is a tree of life" (Prov 13:12; cf. Prov 13:19). In his first address, Eliphaz twice speaks about hope. Job's own first words before his friends, beginning "Perish the day I was born" (Job 3:3), have systematically excluded hope, though he has not used the word. He will do so in a moment, picking up Eliphaz's use of it. "If only my request could come true and God grant my hope." But in fact, "my days have flown faster than a shuttle, they have come to an end without hope" (Job 6:8; 7:6).

First, with some irony, Eliphaz speaks of the integrity of Job's ways being his hope (Job 4:6). But then he speaks of God as our hope (Job 5:8-16). What is one to do in a situation like Job's? "I myself would have recourse to God, I

---

[209]Norman C. Habel, "Earth First," in *The Earth Story in Wisdom Traditions*, ed. Norman C. Ha-bel and Shirley Wurst (Sheffield: Sheffield Academic Press/Cleveland, Ohio: Pilgrim, 2001), pp. 65-77; see p. 69.

would lay my cause before God, one who does great things that cannot be fathomed, wonders beyond counting." Eliphaz starts from the wondrous creation power of God, continuing in God's continuing generous creativity of the natural world, causing rain to fall on the dry and arid surface of the ground and thus again doing something wondrous to them. He then moves on (seamlessly, as the First Testament does) to the application of that power to the realm of politics and to the affairs of people in general. In those realms God acts to turn socioeconomic positions upside down for the lowly, the people who have fallen on hard times, and for the mourners, who are also vulnerable if they are people who have lost their husband or father. God elevates both to safety, rescuing them from their vulnerability. God acts to turn upside down the plans of decision-makers, too, not least when they are calculated to increase the vulnerability of such people. But that might all seem rather general and remote. Does it apply to the ordinary individual? Eliphaz's opening words here imply it applies to individuals like himself and Job, and by the end of this section of his address he has personalized his statement. An individual needy person such as Job can claim that creative and historical generosity and power of God. Yes, "there is hope for the poor person."

This apparently means nothing to Job. "What strength do I have, so that I should be hopeful, what future do I have, so that I should prolong my life? Is my strength the strength of rocks, or is my flesh bronze? No, there is no help in me; resources have departed from me" (Job 6:11-13). Job's point is not that he would need inner resources of hopefulness in order to engender hope, but that in order to have hope, he would need to be able to see reason for hope in the form of sensing the strength to keep going and sensing some prospects for the future. But he can see none. He would need superhuman strength to be able to keep going, and his strength has gone. He cannot help himself anymore. God is supposed to be the locus of strength, help and resources (e.g., Job 9:4; 12:16; Ps 22:19 [MT 20]) and thus the basis for hope. But God has abandoned him. Nor are his friends offering him any help.

The close of the book suggests another angle on the question. I find that many students dislike the book's Hollywood ending because life isn't like that. And their instinct fits with the fact that the ending confirms those two declarations of Eliphaz. Yet Eliphaz surely must be right, even if he and his friends are stupid in the way they try to apply their insights to Job. Job's integrity and God's integrity were indeed Job's hope. Of course the students are right that life is not like that, but the effect of the ending is to make the book as a whole do honor to both truths: the truths of human experience and the truths about God. I refer students to Psalm 91, which declares that the person who lives in the shadow of the Almighty will prove that Yhwh is their safe refuge from trouble: "a thousand may fall at your left, ten thousand at your right: it will not come near you" (Ps 91:7). I then remind them of the story of Jim Elliot, one of five Christians who were killed by people they were trying to reach with the gospel of Christ in 1956. His wife Elisabeth Elliot titled his biography *Shadow of the Almighty*.[210] If there was ever a person of whom Psalm 91 was not true, it was surely Jim Elliot. Yet there is something authentic about his wife's appeal to that psalm in declaring that she would not let its disconfirmation in his life imply its disconfirmation. The other things she knew about God meant that somehow it must nevertheless be true. The close of the book of Job expresses the same awareness.[211]

6.9 Death

Thus there is no denial of death in the First Testament. It faces the fact that life will come to an end, and it has no expectation of a renewed life the other side of death. It often accepts that with equanimity, though the fact that death often assails people before their time means it is also capable of protesting about it. But/and it is enthusiastic about life and loves the idea of enjoying "length of days," having the opportunity to "fill out" one's days, living one's days to the full (Is 65:20).

Long Life

"Gray hair is a splendid crown; it is attained by a faithful life" (Prov 16:31). Thus "the light of the faithful shines bright, but the lamp of the faithless goes out" (Prov 13:9): while everyone's lamp goes out eventually, the faithful can expect the candle to have the chance to burn on and not to be extinguished before its time. To that end, "the teaching of the wise is a fountain of life for turning people from deathly snares," as is "reverence for Yhwh" (Prov 13:14; 14:27; cf. Prov 19:23). Thus "the way of life leads upward for the person of insight, to turn from Sheol below" (Prov 15:24). Insight does not make it possible to escape eventual death, but it does make it possible to live a life of its proper length and its proper quality rather than one that is dominated by Sheol while one is still alive and/or terminated by Sheol before its time. So "people who keep commands keep their lives; people who disregard their ways will die" (Prov 19:16; cf. Prov 10:8; 13:13). Whose commands are these? There are human commands that lead to death, commands that the wise will resist (e.g., Is 29:13), and there are commands that they will hasten to obey. In Proverbs, these are the commands of the king, of parents, of teachers; elsewhere they are

---

[210]Elisabeth Elliot, *Shadow of the Almighty* (New York: Harper, 1958).

[211]On the way the book's ending reframes the whole book, see Kenneth Numfor Ngwa, *The Hermeneutics of the "Happy" Ending in Job 42:7-17*, BZAW 354 (Berlin/New York: Walter de Gruyter, 2005).

the commands in the Torah and the commands of prophets, behind which stands God's command. Omitting to specify the origin of the commands puts the emphasis on the fact that "everybody gotta serve somebody," or at least that it is wise not to make our own assumptions and convictions the sole basis for our actions. We need something outside ourselves to guide us. Otherwise people are "disregarding their ways." They think they are acting in their best interests when they are doing the opposite.

Proverbs 28:16 speaks of "a ruler lacking discernment and big in oppression." We could understand this to indicate that one without discernment is oppressive, or that one who is oppressive is without discernment. Perhaps the second colon points in the latter direction: "one who spurns extortion will live a long life." On the other hand, "a person who wanders from the way of discernment will rest in the company of ghosts"[212] (Prov 21:16), sooner rather than later.

Thus there is something wrong when death seems to come too soon, even for someone who also speaks of it dragging: "My days fly faster than a shuttle and come to an end without a thread/hope.[213] Think: my life is wind; my eye will not again see good things" (Job 7:6-7). Or the days fly faster than a runner bringing messages for the king, or a skiff skimming along the Nile, or an eagle swooping on its prey (Job 9:25-26). Day after day passes speedily and inexorably (even though in another sense slowly and inexorably) without there being any change in the suffering these days bring.

On the other hand, a happy life comes to its satisfactory end when one has seen the birth of children and grandchildren (e.g., Ps 128:6; Prov 17:6; Ruth 4:16-17), when one can "come to the grave in ripe old age,[214] like a heap [of grain] coming up [to the threshing floor?] at its time" (Job 5:25-26). One dies the death of a righteous person (Num 23:10), dies in peace, with people to complete the appropriate mourning rites (Jer 34:4-5). Thus the new Jerusalem will not be characterized by an end to death but by the opportunity to live life to its proper end: "There will no more be heard in it the sound of weeping or the sound of a cry, there will be no more from there a baby of a few days or an old person who does not live out his days, because the young person will be someone who dies aged a hundred and the person who falls short of a hundred will be belittled" (Is 65:19-20). Life comes to an end after one has lived a full life.[215]

---

[212] rĕpāʾîm; not "shades" or "healers." See, e.g., Brian B. Schmidt, Israel's Beneficent Dead (reprint, Winona Lake, Ind.: Eisenbrauns, 1996), pp. 267-73; P. J. Williams, "Are the Biblical Rephaim and the Ugaritic RPUM Healers?" OTS 52 (2005): 266-75.

[213] Job utilizes both meanings of tiqwâ.

[214] If that is the meaning of the hapax kelah.

[215] See Rachel Z. Dulin, A Biblical View of Aging (Mahwah, N.J.: Paulist, 1988).

Mortality Accepted

"A covenant with death" (Is 28:15) "is the ultimate absurdity, since death alone brooks no compromise; yet every post-edenic human endeavour is an attempt to make a deal with death."[216] Therefore "the first task of every religion is to provide an answer, an oracle, in the face of death."[217] Genesis 1—3 might imply an awareness of this view, though perhaps also some critique of it. It does not begin with this question, though it does soon take it up. Our feebleness and mortality are not the First Testament's first affirmations about humanity,[218] but they are statements that soon feature. At the Beginning, humanity had access to a sacramental tree of life, which would apparently have made it possible for our inherently mortal selves to put on immortality (cf. 1 Cor 15:53), but we preferred a different tree and thus lost the possibility of access to that one.[219] It was not God's original intention that death should be the end; it was disobedience to God that caused it.

After that, the First Testament more or less forgets about this issue. By its nature this life is the context in which proper human existence is worked out. One characteristic that makes this possible is the fact that the First Testament is less "me-focused" than modernity. For the individual Israelite, it is God's purpose and then Israel's destiny that matter. One dies, but that does not mean the end of the family to which one belongs, or the community or the people or the purpose of God. And anyway, death is like going to bed and going to sleep—who objects to doing that? When the First Testament frets about death, its usual concern is the premature death that often comes to people. The threat of death troubles Job because death would deprive him of the opportunity to sort things out with God. But in general, the First Testament takes for granted and is accepting of the fact that human life comes to its natural end in death. It lacks the "reluctance to accept our mortality" that characterizes Western culture,[220] and the preoccupation with death in some other Middle Eastern cultures. Evidently fear of death is not a universal human phenomenon but a culturally contextual one. The First Testament does not see death as something that comes from outside ourselves, an alien force attacking us from without, like the god Death of other Middle Eastern religions or Paul's "last enemy" (1 Cor 15:26), or as something unnatural that is to be fought and defeated with

---

[216]Francis Landy, "Tracing the Voice of the Other," in *The New Literary Criticism and the Hebrew Bible*, ed. J. Cheryl Exum and David J. A. Clines, JSOTSup 143 (Sheffield: Sheffield Academic Press, 1993), pp. 140-62; see p. 143.

[217]So Joseph Blenkinsopp, *A Sketchbook of Biblical Theology* (New York: Herder/London: Burns and Oates, 1968), p. 88.

[218]So Edmond Jacob, *Theology of the Old Testament* (London: Hodder, 1958), p. 151.

[219]See *OTT* 1:143.

[220]Lloyd R. Bailey, *Biblical Perspectives on Death* (Philadelphia: Fortress, 1979), p. 1.

the resources of medical science, a little like a virus. Death is not a threat. It contains no menace or peril. Nothing alarming or frightening can assail us in the realm of death, because there are no metaphysical powers outside Yhwh's control. Nor do we fear meeting Yhwh after death, as if death means being confronting with our misdeeds and judged us. "Immortality? It's not anything I'd lose sleep over."[221]

The First Testament thus refers to the afterlife rather less frequently than other peoples;[222] Israel certainly experienced death differently from the Egyptians, "who invested more of their time, energy and wealth in preparation for it than any other people at any time in history."[223] In Israel, death "involved little material preparation and minimal ongoing provision"; Yhwh was "'God not of the dead but of the living' (Mark 12:27)."[224] This is not to say that many average Israelites were not preoccupied with death and the dead in the manner of other Middle Eastern peoples; biblical prohibitions and archeological evidence suggest this may have been so. But the First Testament itself takes death for granted as a natural and acceptable reality that comes from within.[225] The fact that humanity forfeited the possibility of eating from the tree of life and thus living forever is thus something about which Israel shrugs its shoulders but does not lose sleep. Resurrection life enabling life to continue in glorified form will thus be a wondrous uncovenanted bonus rather than the fulfillment of a yearning.[226]

The World Health Organization defined health as "a state of complete physical, mental and social well-being, not merely the absence of sickness and handicaps." But it is normal in the course of going through life to experience loss, grief, pain, anguish, distress, sorrow and disappointment. The fact that we do suffer these means it would be wiser to see health as "a subjectively ascertainable *attitude*" to one's fluctuating condition, "the strength to be human." That strength lies in "the acceptance, the affirmation, and the love of frail and mortal life."[227]

---

[221]The poet laureate Stanley Kunitz, quoted in *The New York Times*, May 19, 2005, p. B1.

[222]Cf. Philip S. Johnston, *Shades of Sheol* (Leicester, U.K./Downers Grove, Ill.: InterVarsity Press, 2002), pp. 72-73; Zimmerli, *The OT and the World*, pp. 114-15.

[223]Philip S. Johnston, "Death in Egypt and Israel," *OTS* 55 (2005): 94-116; see p. 94. Cf. Siegfried Morenz, *Egyptian Religion* (London: Methuen, 1973), p. 187.

[224]Johnston, "Death in Egypt and Israel," pp. 94, 116. I do not think there are stages in First Testament thinking on this subject, as if it were working its way toward NT truth (see, e.g., Hartmut Gese, *Essays on Biblical Theology* [Minneapolis: Augsburg, 1981], pp. 34-59).

[225]Bailey, *Biblical Perspectives on Death*, p. 4. Contrast, e.g., Eichrodt, *Theology of the OT*, 2:501-3; the protests about death to which he refers relate to death that comes before the proper time.

[226]See further "Human Life in Christ" at the close of this chapter.

[227]Moltmann, *God in Creation*, pp. 271, 273, 275; the second quotation summarizes the work of Ivan Illich in *Limits to Medicine* (London: Boyars, 1976); the third comes from Barth, *Church Dogmatics*, III/4:356-58.

Mortality Resisted

Psalm 39:4-7 [MT 5-8] prays, "Yhwh, make me acknowledge my end—the number of my days, what they are; I want to acknowledge how passing I am." The psalm is surely not asking Yhwh to "make me *know* my end," to reveal how short human life is; the subsequent words show that the suppliant is well aware of that. But acknowledging it is a different matter. At some level all human beings know they will die, but very many live in denial of the fact, and the suppliant does not wish to do so. "There, you have made my days handbreadths; my span is as nothing before you. Yes, every human being, standing firm, is altogether breath; yes, a man goes about in the shadow/as a shadow.[228] Yes, it is for a breath that people hustle; he heaps things up, but does not know who gathers them." The psalm puts into words the awareness about how passing I am. It is there in writing. It is thereby owned and acknowledged. Yhwh is the author of the shortness of life; Yhwh could have enabled humanity to live a thousand years and did not do so (cf. Ps 90:1-6). Perhaps that would have made no difference to the psalm's point. Genesis 5 implies as much with the recurrent mantra that follows its note on someone who lived nine-hundred-plus years, "and he died," "and he died," "and he died. . . ." This span would still have been nothing compared with Yhwh's eternity and might therefore still have seemed like a breath or a shadow. It would still be the case that we heap things up like the harvesters heaping grain in the field but do not know whether we will be the ones who gather them into the granary or whether we will have a heart attack first (cf. Lk 12:16-20).

So what can one do? For the psalm, that seems to be the wrong question. "So now, what do I look to, my Lord? My hope is in you." Between the two cola, the psalm moves from "what" to "who." The suppliant is going to end up in Sheol; there is no avoiding that. The appropriate response is to focus on the reality of a relationship with Yhwh now and on a life lived looking to Yhwh as one's hope. (Of course it will turn out that this points to a theological foundation for the fact that the suppliant will unexpectedly find that life does not end with death, because Yhwh is not the God of the dead but of the living: see Jesus' brilliant theological argument in Mk 12:27. But the psalm has not worked that out.) The suppliant is but "a sojourner with you, a transient like all my ancestors" (Ps 39:12 [MT 13]). But in Israel, the position of a sojourner is not one to be despised. What Yhwh has to say about sojourners suggests that they end up with much of the privilege of Israelites without so much of the re-

---

[228]BDB takes this as an idiosyncratic instance of the word *ṣelem* that means an image, but this involves a stretch of the word. More likely the noun is a homonym from *ṣālam* ii (cf. discussion in *HALOT*).

sponsibility, and presumably Yhwh will remember the kind of commitment the Torah enjoins on sojourners (e.g., Lev 25).

For Qohelet, however, death "casts its shadow over every meaningful interpretation of life." When it speaks of fate *(miqreh)*, "what happens to you" *(qārâ;* cf. Eccles 2:14-15), it regularly has in mind death itself.[229] "Death is the beginning of life in Qohelet."[230] "A name *[šēm]* is good, better than good oil *[šemen]*—and the day of one's death better than the day of one's birth" (Eccles 7:1). Perhaps the first saying simply prepares the way for the second. "You acknowledge that a good name is better than fragrant oil, do you not? Well, I say that the day of one's death is similarly better than the day of one's birth." Or perhaps the second builds more sardonically on the first. "You acknowledge that a good name is better than fragrant oil, do you not? Well, the day when you die means you have no more chance to ruin your good name, so it is better than the day of your birth when you receive the potential for earning one" (cf. Eccles 7:8).

Mortality Rejoiced In

Of course long life can be a curse. "I loathe my life," Job says (Job 10:1). "I reject/despise my life" *(mā'as,* Job 9:21). He is not in a position to reject it in the way that I can reject my dinner and not eat it, or at least it does not occur to him to reject it in that sense. The idea of suicide does not seem to be part of the Israelite worldview except in a circumstance that threatens intolerable shame (1 Sam 31:4-5). All Job can do is reject it but carry on living with it. Elijah, too, declares that he has had enough and wants Yhwh to take away his life, but Yhwh rather provides him with sustenance and then extends his dangerous vocation (1 Kings 19:1-18).

Job has already asked, "Why is light given to the sufferer, life to the person who is troubled in spirit, the people who wait for death but it does not come, who search for it more than for hidden treasure, who will rejoice with great joy, will be glad because they have reached the grave, to the man whose way is lost, whom God has hedged about?" (Job 3:20-23). He has still not agreed to blaspheme God and thus commit suicide. But he agrees with his wife's underlying convictions regarding long life. Life hurts more than death will. The hurt is not merely bodily, but mental and emotional. It is a hurt of spirit—in the context not a bitterness of spirit (EVV) in our sense (cf. 2 Sam 2:26; Is 5:20; Jer 2:19; 4:18), though of course that also characterizes Job. It is a sense of being lost, abandoned, wandering. The signposts have all disappeared and there is no way of knowing where one is going. Or—to change the image—

---

[229]Von Rad, *Wisdom in Israel*, p. 228.

[230]George, "Death as the Beginning of Life in the Book of Ecclesiastes," p. 282.

one is frozen in a place of pain and there is no way out of it. The Adversary had commented on the way Job has been hedged about by God in a positive sense (Job 1:10), but he now experiences a very different kind of hedging about. All he has to sustain him is his own groans. And the thought of this going on interminably is unbearable. Job has wished that light had not dawned on the day when his life began, that he had never been given the gift of life on that day. He also wishes that (like the daily dawning of light that repeats the first day of creation) the gift of life each day did not keep reprising that giving.

He makes the point with some poignancy and irony in response to Eliphaz. Eliphaz has talked about hope (Job 4:6; 5:16). The word sticks in Job's gullet. His only hope is quite other: "If only my request would come about and God would grant my hope, so that God would agree to crush me, let loose his hand to cut me off" (Job 6:8-9). Job's only hope lies in death, and he longs for it, but God does not respond to his longing. His lament is also a kind of parody of a prayer of lament.[231] It is not addressed to God; there would be no point in that, given that God seems to be his wild attacker (Job 6:4). And instead of expressing a longing for God's hand to be lifted from him or lifted to rescue him from crushing and death, he asks to be crushed and for that hand to cut him off. He cannot take the action that will drive God into slaying him, not because suicide is wrong, but because blasphemy is wrong. But neither can he persuade God to do so. Instead God seems to set a watch over him, as if he were some dangerous hostile force that needed to be hedged about to keep him under restraint (Job 7:12). Thus "for myself, I would choose strangling, death rather than my frame. I despise it; I shall not live forever; leave me alone, because my days are empty" (Job 7:15-16). By "leave me alone," perhaps Job simply means "stop attacking me" (cf. Job 7:19). But perhaps he indeed means "leave me alone." Instead of fearing being abandoned by God, he longs for it. But of course that reflects the fact that the presence of God simply means God attacking him.

Job prefers death to life, and God is the source of both. Job's own experience combines elements from both sides of that antinomy of life and death. It is characterized both by faithfulness and by chaos, which should be on opposite sides of the antinomy but have come together (and arguably his friends embody the opposite commixture). He embraces death, but he then experiences renewed life. Indeed, Yhwh's address suggests, "the embracing of death is also the embracing of life. . . . One lives, or obtains life, not by avoiding, but entering fully into, chaos/death."[232] Job's story also implies an analogous am-

---

[231]Cf. Newsom, "Book of Job," p. 387.

biguity about blessing, expressed in the very use of the verb *bārak* to suggest "curse." Blessing itself can engender curse—if Job had never been so blessed, he would never have been so cursed—and conversely, the human *běrākâ* of God turns out to be capable of expressing itself as protest and reviling.[233] As T. S. Eliot has one of the wise men (!) reflecting on their return from Bethlehem, "I had seen birth and death, / But had thought they were different."[234] They turn out to be interwoven.

Life and Death

It is an odd aspect of human experience that life and death are absolute opposites and yet can be hard to distinguish. Death and life stand as polar opposites in Proverbs, death associated with faithlessness, folly and chaos, life with faithfulness, wisdom and order. Proverbs' challenge is thus to choose the one rather than the other. Yet we have noted how it can seem that in the midst of life we can be in death, that death can overwhelm us. Suffering and abandonment by God is a kind of living death. In a modern Western context, it can be hard to determine when life begins: is it at conception or "quickening" or birth or what? And it can be hard to determine when life ends, as when a person is kept breathing by a machine. When a person is unconscious, they can seem to be dead when they are alive. It can be hard to tell when life becomes death. In Israel as in most societies, giving birth is a human experience that may well issue in death. Unless a seed "dies," it does not generate new life. Life and death overlap, but this overlap is disturbing and worrying. Israel will have been aware of these dilemmas, even if not in the same way challenged to take decisions about them. On the other hand, they were in immediate contact with death much more often than modern Western people are.

But by virtue of being brought into association with Yhwh, mortal Israelites are brought into association with the living God.[235] Contact with death therefore made it inappropriate to be in Yhwh's presence. People (and things) who had been in contact with death were quarantined until the effect had worn off and they had undergone a rite of cleansing, and the same applied to people with a deathlike disease such as the skin disease commonly referred to in EVV

---

[232]Suzanne Boorer, "A Matter of Life and Death," in *Prophets and Paradigms*, ed. Stephen Breck Reid, JSOTSup 229 (Sheffield: Sheffield Academic Press, 1996), pp. 187-204; pp. 201, 204, which this paragraph more broadly follows.

[233]Cf. Tod Linafelt, "The Undecidability of ברך in the Prologue to Job and Beyond," *Biblical Interpretation* 4 (1996): 154-72.

[234]T. S. Eliot, "Journey of the Magi," in *The Complete Poems and Plays of T. S. Eliot* (London: Faber, 1969), p. 104.

[235]See section 2.1 "The Living God."

as leprosy (e.g., Num 5:1-3; 19:11-22). Naturally, priests, and especially the high priest, had to be particularly careful about contact with death because of the effect this would have on their ministry (Lev 21).

A number of requirements in the Torah relating to cleanness and taboo become more intelligible if we understand them as having a related concern: to safeguard the distinction between life and death (I prefer the word *taboo* to negative expressions such as *uncleanness* and *impurity* because it conveys the positiveness but also the ambiguity of the things to which it refers, which are sacred and consecrated, but also uncanny, dangerous and forbidden.)[236] This seems a plausible rationale for the three-times repeated requirement that people should not cook a baby goat in its mother's milk, so that the means of life becomes the means of death (Ex 23:19; 34:26; Deut 14:21), or sacrifice an animal on the same occasion as sacrificing its young (Lev 22:28), or take a mother bird along with her young (Deut 22:6-7). Perhaps the reason menstruation involves a taboo is that it mysteriously combines life and death. It is a sign of life, in that only a woman who menstruates can give birth to life,[237] yet it involves the loss of blood, and blood is a sign of life lost (cf. Lev 17:11); when we lose blood, eventually we die. "Menstrual blood, more clearly than any other taboo substance or state, is situated at an ambiguous semantic crossroads" in the way it suggests both death and life, both in an everyday sense and through the importance of blood in sacrifice.[238] There is no basis in Scripture for the long (especially) Christian tradition that the taboo nature of this blood is something to do with moral impurity, and specifically some inherent moral impurity of women.[239] Rather, these conventions keep life and death apart, buttress the fact that life and death actually are opposites, and undergird people's place in the sphere of life rather than of death.[240]

Death

What is death? Death is the end of life. It has no positive nature; it is simply

---

[236]So Sigmund Freud, "Totem and Taboo," in *The Complete Psychological Works of Sigmund Freud*, vol. 13 (London: Hogarth, 1955), p. 18; cf. Kathleen O'Grady, "The Semantics of Taboo," in Kristin De Troyer et al., eds., *Wholly Woman, Holy Blood* (Harrisburg, Penn.: Trinity, 2003), pp. 1-28; see pp. 1-3.

[237]This seems a more plausible understanding than René Girard's idea that menstruation suggests a link between sex and violence, because it leads to quarreling and disorder (*Violence and the Sacred*, p. 35).

[238]O'Grady, "The Semantics of Taboo," p. 28.

[239]See De Troyer, "Blood," in *Wholly Woman*, pp. 45-64, and other papers in that volume.

[240]Cf., e.g., Calum Carmichael, *The Spirit of Biblical Law* (Athens/London: University of Georgia Press, 1996), pp. 126-41.

the absence of something. When people die, they do not cease to exist. We can see them on their deathbed after their life has gone, but they have ceased to have life. At death "the dust returns to the ground as it was, and the breath returns to God who gave it" (Eccles 12:7; cf. Job 34:14-15; Ps 146:4).

The body of a human being (*'ādām*) came from the ground (*'ădāmâ*), and anyone can see that it dissolves back into the ground after death. There is a relationship between my mother's womb and the earth itself: hence Qohelet's words about the person who does well in life but then has to die like everyone else, "As he came out of his mother's womb, naked he will return, going as he came." He can take nothing with him (Eccles 5:15 [MT 14]; cf. Job 1:21). Death does not mean returning to my mother's actual womb, but it means returning to the source of my being that is associated with my mother's womb, the origin of the raw material that grows into in a person in the womb. I came from the earth; I return to the earth.

The life of a human being came more directly from God, and it is also evident that when someone dies, the breath (*rûaḥ,* e.g., Ps 104:29) or the life (*nepeš,* e.g., Gen 35:18) disappears and returns to the God who is *rûaḥ.* And whereas the living may hope that the absence of God may give way again to God's presence, the dead are forever cut off from God's presence.[241] Death means an end to fellowship with God and to fellowship with other people. It means an end to the activity of God and the activity of other people.

Even more obviously, it means an end to my own activity. It means an end to awareness. "There is a confidence for the person who is joined to all the living, because things are better for a living dog than a dead lion, because the living know that they will die, but the dead know nothing. And there is no more reward for them, because their renown is forgotten. Both their acts of love and hate and their passions have long since perished. They have no more share forever in all that is done under the sun" (Eccles 9:4-6). The same transition recurs in Ecclesiastes 9:11-12, from the fact that nothing is quite certain or predictable to the fact that the one thing that is predictably unpredictable and certain is the fact that we die. Qohelet has no doubt that life is better than death, but he has rather an acerbic reason for believing so: it lies in the fact that the living know they will die. That apparently is their "confidence" or "security" (*biṭṭāḥôn*). The English versions' "hope" is misleading, if it suggests that "while there is life there is hope." Qohelet's point would rather be that the living have no hope, in the sense of hope that they may not die. A lion has great confidence, a proverb points out (Prov 28:1), but of course that is true only when it is alive; when it is dead, a living dog is better off, as is a living human being, who also now

---

[241]G. Tom Milazzo, *The Protest and the Silence* (Minneapolis: Fortress, 1992), pp. 138, 139, 141.

has confidence—that confidence about death.[242] During one's lifetime, one's acts of love and hostility, one's passions, may receive their reward (*śākār*), at least in the form of renown (*zēker*)—acts of love, acts of hostility and passions may all be positively regarded. But after one's death, all that is over. It is when you are alive that you can do things and make your mark; afterward, you can do nothing. "There is no activity or reasoning/planning or knowledge or wisdom in Sheol, where you are going" (Eccles 9:10).

Death is like a mountain landslide brought on by the overwhelming winter rains. It is God who is the destructive, suffocating, irresistible wall of rock and mud. That is the end (Job 14:18-22). In some sense, as Job portrays it, we have some awareness after death, like that portrayed in Isaiah 14:9-11—though maybe that is a figure. Certainly it is there to offer a contrast with the fact that we have no awareness of anything back in life, including matters that are dearest to us such as the destiny of our family. The dead know nothing (Eccles 9:5). They can grieve only for themselves. God thus puts an end to the human person, though Job more specifically notes that before this and by the prospect of its happening, what God actually puts an end to is the human person's hope.[243]

Emptiness

"Light is sweet and it is good for the eyes to see the sun. If people live many years they should enjoy them all, but think about the dark days, because they will be many. Everything that is coming is emptiness" (Eccles 11:7-8).

Unsurprisingly, Qohelet offers a contrary perspective on youth and old age to that which is explicit and implicit elsewhere in the First Testament (Eccles 11:9—12:8), one that links with his stress on mortality. His closing main section before returning to his declaration that everything is emptiness formally addresses young people and is no doubt intended for their reading, like much of the teaching in Proverbs, but it is also intended for people in general to overhear as it brings the whole book to a climax. Qohelet urges people to enjoy their youth and follow the inclinations of their minds and eyes in such a way as recognizes the fact that God will call them to account (*mišpāṭ*, Eccles 11:9). That might constitute a warning about the moral framework within which they are to enjoy their lives, though Qohelet has not previously talked about God's judgment. It may be a more characteristically quirky declaration that God will hold them responsible for making good use of their youth,[244] which

---

[242]Cf. Fox, *Qohelet and His Contradictions*, p. 258; *A Time to Tear Down and a Time to Build Up*, p. 292.

[243]Cf. Clines, *Job 1—20*, p. 335.

[244]Cf. W. Sibley Towner, "The Book of Ecclesiastes," in *The New Interpreter's Bible*, vol. 5 (Nashville: Abingdon, 1997), p. 353.

would fit with the earlier comment on its being God's gift and God's will that we live in such a way as to enjoy our lives (Eccles 2:24). It may even be a first reference to the fact that even for young people, death lies ahead. That would make the balance of the verse fit the balance of the next exhortation.[245] "Banish vexation/sorrow from your mind and put away trouble from your body, because youth and dark hair/dawn of life[246] are empty" (Eccles 11:10). Qohelet's interim conclusion turns out to cut the ground from his original enthusiasm for youth. The reason for avoiding vexation and trouble of mind and body is that the opportunity to do that is short—and that makes youth itself turn out to be empty.

"So reflect on your creator in your young days, before the grim days come and the years arrive of which you would say 'I have no pleasure in them'" (Eccles 12:1). Qohelet goes on to a vivid poetic portrait of old age. Much of the detail is uncertain of interpretation but it leaves no doubt of the sad decline that old age brings, until "the dust returns to the ground as it was, and the breath returns to God who gave it." It is this that leads into the reprised underlying judgment, "Deep emptiness. . . . Everything is emptiness" (Eccles 12:7-8).

Qohelet is particularly offended by death's unpredictability and its insusceptibility to our control. "There is no one who knows what is going to happen. . . . There is no one who has power over the wind/spirit/breath, to restrain the wind/spirit/breath, and there is no power over the day of death" (Eccles 8:7-8).

> The faithful and the wise and their acts of service are in God's hand. Whether it is to be treated with love or with hostility, no one knows anything that lies before them. Everything is as it is for everyone. One experience comes to the faithful person and to the faithless, to the good and to the clean and to the taboo, to the one who sacrifices and to the one who does not sacrifice. As is the good person, so is the person who falls short, the person who swears is like the person who shuns an oath. This is the grim thing about all that is done under the sun, that one experience comes to everyone. Further, the mind of human beings is full of grimness, and their mind is full of madness, while they live—and afterward, they belong to the dead. (Eccles 9:1-3)

Qohelet begins here from the vulnerability that characterizes the position of the faithful and wise as much as anyone else—for all their good deeds—then goes on to the uncertainty that also characterizes their position: no one knows whether around the corner lies disaster or blessing. That, too, is as true for the faithful and good as for anyone else, as true for people who are religiously ob-

---

[245]Cf. J. A. Loader, *Ecclesiastes* (Grand Rapids: Eerdmans, 1986), p. 130.

[246]*šahar* could have either of those meanings according to which root we connect it with, but the implication is the same.

servant in their worship and with regard to the canons about purity and are careful about oaths they might not be able to keep as they are for people who are careless about all these. Their goodness, their insight and their acts of service do not function as in insurance. One common experience *(miqrâ)* comes to them all. The common experience is the one that dominates Qohelet's horizon, the fact that we will all die.

The relative superiority of wisdom over stupidity with regard to the living of life pales into insignificance in light of the fact that death claims the wise as certainly as the stupid. Both are forgotten (Eccles 2:12-16). If one looks at one's life in the context of the life of one's family or community, then one's individual death does not seem so tragic; at the end of a fulfilling life one takes one's natural place with one's ancestors, in the bosom of Abraham (Lk 16:22). But if one looks at one's life individually, separate from that of other people, death makes it a mockery. To be more precise, it makes everything empty, which could make one repudiate life itself (Eccles 2:17).

Finality

Job is scandalized by the brevity of life as many people experience it. "A human being, born of a woman, short-lived, full of turmoil, comes up like a flower but withers, flees like a shadow and does not last. . . . His days are limited, the number of his months lies with you, you appointed the bounds that he cannot pass" (Job 14:1-5). He is not seeking to characterize all human life. "Short-lived [lit., short of days], full of turmoil" contrasts in particular with "full of days," the characterization of Isaac and David (Gen 35:29; 1 Chron 29:28), and eventually of Job himself (Job 42:17). But these features do sometimes or often characterize people's lives, in a way that his own experience has brought home to Job. If they are fortunate, human beings live quite a long life, seventy or eighty years, and the First Testament is satisfied with that. But there is an alternative human experience, when someone like Job lives a life devastated by illness or by the wicked, or in Job's case because he is unaccountably hounded by God, and then dies relatively young. It is such a person who comes up and withers like a flower in the hot Middle Eastern sun. There is no way we can go beyond what God has determined for the length of human life. (Modern medical capability both disproves and illustrates the point. We can live much longer than we once could. Yet we cannot finally defy death. There is still a limit set.)

That experience is then compounded by a second scandal, that death is then the end (Job 14:7-22). "There is hope for a tree, if it is cut down, that it will renew itself again and its shoots will not cease, . . . but a man dies and grows feeble, a human being expires, and where is he?" In nature, a tree that is cut down may well grow again, as the flowers that die will come up again next year. But when people are cut down (by illness? by God? by the wicked?), they die. They rather recall the irreversible drying up of a lake or a river (for instance, through an earthquake). They do not come back to life. Death is an endless sleep, not a sleep from which they awake next morning. One look at their remains in the tomb the next time it is opened proves the point. Human beings die and thus lose their strength, lie feeble and unable to do anything. Where are they? In the grave, in Sheol. "A cloud vanishes and goes; so a person who goes down to Sheol does not come up. He does not return home again; his place does not recognize him any more" (Job 7:9-10). And that is the end of all hope. "If I look forward to Sheol as my home, make up my bed in the darkness, address the Pit 'You are my father,' the worm 'Mother,' 'Sister,' where then is my hope, who can see hope for me? Will it go down to the gates of Sheol—together will we descend to the dirt?" (Job 17:13-16). Again, Job's plaint concerns not the fate of humanity in general who have no hope of leaving Sheol. If one dies in the bosom of one's family after a full life and goes to rest with one's ancestors, death seems all right and one can sidestep the fact that it involves making one's bed in darkness and becoming food for worms. But if one dies before one's time treated as a wrongdoer and one has never been able to find vindication, then there is no positive side to death, and its clearly negative side asserts itself in one's awareness. Death is the end of any prospect of ever finding vindication. That is the sense in which Job has no hope once he dies. It is this hope of vindication that dies when he dies. Or rather, it does not accompany him to Sheol. It simply evaporates.

Death is thus the great leveler between humanity and the animal world. "Who knows whether the breath of human beings rises up and the breath of an animal sinks down to the earth?" (Eccles 3:21). In Qohelet's day there were perhaps people who were speculating that human beings would enjoy a positive afterlife, as animals would not. Qohelet points out that there is no evidence for this.

◆ ◆ ◆

Human Life in Christ

According to Karl Barth, "In theological anthropology what man is, is decided by the primary text, i.e., by the humanity of the man Jesus."[247] In light of that, a human being is one who (1) lives in history before God, (2) lives in encounter

---

[247]Barth, *Church Dogmatics*, III/2:226.

with others, (3) is the subject of a material organism, (4) is allotted a delimited span by God.[248] This is a suggestive definition, and no doubt there is indeed a sense in which Jesus is the primary Christian text, yet Jesus does not bring a new anthropology. He embodies an anthropology already implied by the Scriptures.

The huge significant difference the New Testament makes to an understanding of humanity is its emphasis on the fact that after death we shall rise to a transformed life. Ironically, this is not a new piece of New Testament revelation but an affirmation of an aspect of Pharisaic theology, which itself builds on Daniel 12:1-3. What the New Testament decisively contributes is not the content of this aspect of the faith but a new basis for believing it. Admittedly Jesus bases it on the fact that a relationship with God surely cannot finally die—how could God stop being the God of Abraham, Isaac and Jacob? "He is not the God of the dead but of the living" (Mk 12:27). But the more common New Testament argument is that the resurrection of Jesus meets Qohelet's point. Before Jesus' resurrection there was no evidence that the breath of human beings rises up and that of an animal sinks down to the earth. It is a nice idea, but in the absence of evidence are we just fooling ourselves? So the Psalms, for instance, do not go in for some craven leap of faith into a belief in resurrection for which there is no evidence (it will not be craven after Jesus' resurrection!), but bravely continues to believe in God's involvement with us in this life.

Jesus' resurrection is not merely evidence. It is not the case that the First Testament was understandably mistaken in reckoning that life ends in death. It was right. It is Jesus' death and resurrection that makes our resurrection possible as well as believable, makes it possible for that relationship between God and Abraham to come back to life in this new form. A corollary is that humanity can also reckon on the alternative possibility of going to Gehenna rather than staying asleep in Sheol—or perhaps we should see Gehenna as a reframing of Sheol in light of the loss of resurrection life that it now stands for. That is also a New Testament revelation, or rather an element in Pharisaic belief that the New Testament affirms. We have noted that the end of Job makes an affirmation (like Dan 12:1-3) that somehow the unfairnesses of this life cannot be the end of the story. They are statements of faith that involve a leap across the dark into the light. The resurrection means that we no longer have to make such a leap of faith. Admittedly, and oddly, this does not seem simply to solve issues we have considered in this chapter. Christians still wrestle with them, intellectually and experientially.

---

[248]Ibid., III/4:43-44, summarizing *Church Dogmatics* III/2.

It was a risky business, "revealing the resurrection."[249] The prospect of life after death can be a constructive hope for communities and individuals under pressure, such as people living in the Antiochene crisis to which Daniel 12 speaks or undergoing grim personal suffering or coping with loved ones losing their lives. In other contexts it risks discouraging people from taking our earthly life as seriously as it deserves as God's gift. Either way, it risks our not experiencing life's pains or its joys, and thus squandering them, "selling them off cheap to heaven."[250] "It is only when one loves life and the earth so much that without them everything would be gone, that one can believe in the resurrection and a new world."[251] Christians' frequent failure to take this life seriously shows God's wisdom in delaying the revealing of the resurrection, and it points to the necessity to keep living by the First Testament's emphasis on this life as well as by the New Testament's evidence for the resurrection.[252]

---

[249] The phrase comes from the Orthodox liturgy.

[250] Jürgen Moltmann, *The Coming of God* (London: SCM Press, 1996), p. 50.

[251] Dietrich Bonhoeffer, letter to a friend, Advent II, 1943 (*Letters and Papers from Prison* [reprint, London: Collins 1962], p. 50).

[252] There are other texts apart from Dan 12:1-3 that the New Testament refers to in connection with proclaiming the fact of resurrection, and further texts that Christians have subsequently reckoned hint at the idea of a positive afterlife, but there are none that hint at that in themselves. (E.g., on Ps 49:14-15 [MT 15-16], see section 6.7 "How Death Makes Things Work"; on Ps 73:24, see section 6.6 "Submission; on Is 25:7-8 see section 8.6 "Life Victorious over Death"; on Hos 13:14 see section 4.2 "Death"; Paul's quotation of these two passages in 1 Cor 15:54-55 involves an inspired reinterpretation of them.) The considerations I note in these two paragraphs show why it is not surprising that God waited to "reveal the resurrection."

7

THE WORLD

The First Testament narrative focuses on God and Israel, its danger and its destiny, but it begins by putting in place a broader canvas: "In the beginning God created the heavens and the earth" (Gen 1:1).[1] Conversely, the Wisdom Books, the Psalms and the Latter Prophets may start from Israel or from the individual, but they are soon seeing them on this same broad canvas. These other parts of the First Testament vastly broaden the insights that emerge from Genesis on the world of God's creation. The First Testament is much concerned with the being of heaven and earth before God, and with God's relationship to them.

Yhwh is thus involved with nature and with the cosmos as a whole. Yet *nature* and *cosmos* are both narrower and broader in meaning than the expression "the heavens and the earth,"[2] or—to put the subject more fully—"the heavens and the earth, and all that is in them" (e.g., Ex 20:11), or—to put it more succinctly—"everything" (*hakkōl*, e.g., Jer 10:16). Our Greek-based word *cosmos* suggests the universe as an ordered whole, while the Latin-based word *nature* suggests the phenomena of the material world, particularly insofar as it constitutes a self-contained system containing its own principle of life.[3] The First Testament does look at reality from these angles: "the world of the Hebrew Bible is a spiderweb of a world. Interrelatedness is basic to this community of God's creatures. Each created entity is in symbiotic relationship with every other" and with God.[4] But these Scriptures look from other angles, too. The

---

[1] Actually, the translation of this opening verse of the Bible is controversial (cf. *OTT* 1:75), though this does not affect my point in the present context.

[2] See Rolf P. Knierim, *The Task of Old Testament Theology* (Grand Rapids/Cambridge: Eerdmans, 1995), pp. 186-91.

[3] Cf. Theodorus C. Vriezen, *An Outline of Old Testament Theology*, 1st ed. (reprint, Oxford: Blackwell, 1962), p. 220 (2nd ed., Oxford: Blackwell/Newton, Mass.: Branford, 1970, p. 422). On the word *cosmos*, see Gerhard von Rad, *Old Testament Theology*, 2 vols. (Edinburgh: Oliver & Boyd/New York: Harper, 1962, 1965), 1:152, 426-27; 2:338-39; and on *nature*, H. Wheeler Robinson, *Inspiration and Revelation in the Old Testament* (London/New York: Oxford University Press, 1946), p. 1; John W. Rogerson, "The Old Testament View of Nature," in *Instruction and Interpretation*, OTS 20 (Leiden: E. J. Brill, 1977), pp. 67-84; see pp. 69-73; Wilhelm Gräb, "Creation or Nature?" in *Creation in Jewish and Christian Tradition*, ed. Henning Graf Reventlow, JSOTSup 319 (London/New York: Sheffield Academic Press, 2002), pp. 277-90.

[4] Terence E. Fretheim, *God and the World in the Old Testament* (Nashville: Abingdon, 2005), p. 19.

usual theological term is *creation*, which has the advantage that it "has theological presuppositions already built in, it is a way of 'seeing *as*'"; it makes clear that the reality to which it refers is not self-existent.[5] The term does fudge the distinction between creation as an event and the creation that is the result of God's creative activity. But it is a useful fudge, given the fact that many passages (e.g., Job 38—41; Ps 104) also blur this distinction.

The suggestion that there is no place for "a doctrine of the universe, a cosmology" in dogmatics[6] sidelines too much material in the First Testament, which implies a doctrine of the universe, a cosmology, and one that is significant in various ways for humanity.

7.1 God's World

God made the world and the world belongs to God. "The heavens are yours, the earth also is yours" (Ps 89:11 [MT 12]). The storehouses in the heavens and their contents belong to Yhwh (Deut 28:12). The earth is full of Yhwh's "possessions" (Ps 104:24).[7] That is so because God made it (e.g., Ps 95:5). How silly to think that we could give something to God, who already owns everything (Ps 50:10-12)!

God's ownership of the world has a number of other implications. It means God is in a position to decide how it works and to make sure of its security and stability. It means it manifests God's greatness and grace. It means there is a unity about it; earthly experience can help us understand God's dealings with us. It means that we can share in the world (because God invites us to), though we cannot behave as if we own it. It means the world gives God its worship.

Regularity

In Genesis 1, the process of creation is orderly and rational, and it issues in a world that is orderly and rational. In Job, the mystery of nature comes more to the fore, and Job 38—39 especially emphasizes the "mysterious, bizarre, and unfathomable elements of creation."[8] Genesis 1 surveys a world that is a carefully ordered whole, Genesis 2 focuses on a garden, Job 38—39 casts its eye over an untamed wilderness. Yet Job 38—39 manages also to emphasize that Yhwh made the cosmos a place with its own order. Yhwh asks Job a series of questions about who makes the heavens and the earth work and who understands how they work. To each question the implied answer is that Job does not, though Yhwh does. "Job can only view the cosmos sliding inexorably into chaos," but

---

[5]A. R. Peacocke, *Creation and the World of Science* (Oxford/New York: Oxford University Press, 1979), p. 366.

[6]Karl Barth, *Church Dogmatics* (Edinburgh: T & T Clark, 1936-1969), III/2:19.

[7]*qinyāneka*: I prefer to translate *qānâ* "possess" rather than "create" (see *OTT* 1:47-48).

[8]Israel Knohl, *The Sanctuary of Silence* (Minneapolis: Fortress, 1985), pp. 166-67.

Yhwh challenges Job to recognize "the cosmic expanse as a complex work of aesthetic and moral import." The heavens and the earth are an ecological whole. And this "(re-)construal of creation" is the book's indispensable means of transforming the character of Job and of the community that reads the book.[9]

Yhwh's questions begin with a series about the process of creation, which establish the fact that by that process the inanimate world was measured out, securely founded and protected (Job 38:4-11). Naturally enough, they ask about the origin of light; this fits with the picture painted in Genesis 1. But it is a characteristic of Job 38—39 that each section, while linking with what precedes, takes the discussion in a new direction, and here the interrogation moves from speaking of the original creation to asking about the ongoing workings of heaven and earth. Yhwh asks about what happens each day, not about what happened at the Beginning. Has Job ever told the morning to dawn (Job 38:12)? The text thus makes a smooth transition from the process of creation to the day-by-day reality of heaven and earth, which dominates what Yhwh wants to say in Job 38:12—39:30. The ease of the transition corresponds to the fact that beneath the surface there is a continuity that belies the shift.

The questions presuppose some facts about the ongoing nature of heaven and earth as Yhwh manages it. As lord of heaven and earth, Yhwh (unlike Job) knows what is going on throughout heaven and earth and positively effects what happens, which is otherwise inexplicable. In Genesis 1, God commands light into being, and the chapter implies that this establishes an ongoing arrangement whereby light dawns on the world each day. The image of God as the watchmaker, who started the world off and could then leave it to keep going, fits Genesis 1. Job 38 rather invites us to see the dawning of light as an act that God undertakes afresh each day. The creation's regular events happen because Yhwh commands them or directly makes them happen by acting within nature. "God says every morning, 'Do it again' to the sun; and every evening, 'Do it again' to the moon. It may not be automatic necessity that God makes all daisies alike; it may be that God makes every daisy separately, but has never got tired of making them."[10] God "seeks out" each day: for instance, the day on which Job was born (Job 3:4). It does not come into being on its own initiative but because it has been summoned and called into being, as God called into being the first day.

Yet Yhwh also assumes that dawn has its "place." There is indeed a regular pattern here. Yhwh is a being of habit. Everything has its place in Yhwh's well-

---

[9]William P. Brown, *The Ethos of the Cosmos: The Genesis of Moral Imagination in the Bible* (Grand Rapids/Cambridge: Eerdmans, 1999), pp. 318, 320.

[10]Gilbert K. Chesterton, *Orthodoxy* (New York: Lane, 1909), pp. 108-9. Chesterton does also preface the first sentence with "It is possible that."

ordered cosmos. Everyone has his or her place. In the myth that is taken up in Isaiah 14:12, Dawn is a person who has a son, and in Job, too, Morning and Dawn are quasi-persons, the recipients of orders to get up and act the police officer at the beginning of each day.

Order

Hans Heinrich Schmid sees the physical order of creation and the moral order of creation as linked by the notion of ṣĕdaqâ, which he understands against the background of Egyptian cosmology and politics.[11] There, maʿat is the equivalent of ṣĕdaqâ, referring to the wisdom that both the divine king and the human king manifest in exercising government, which has its fruit in a wise ordering of the cosmos and of human life.[12] Schmid sees ṣĕdaqâ as similarly denoting "world-ordering." This understanding seems to involve too much inference for us to take it as a key to understanding ṣĕdaqâ in the First Testament, even if creation thinking may be the framework for thinking about ṣĕdaqâ. From the First Testament's own use of the word, one would never guess that ṣĕdaqâ denoted world-ordering. It means something more like faithfulness, doing right by the people in one's community.[13] But physical order and moral order do have a link, derived from their shared origin in Yhwh. It is because both issue from Yhwh that people who live by the faithfulness of the moral order experience the blessing of the physical order. It is because both issue from Yhwh that the government's support of the moral order also buttresses the physical order. The linkage between forms of order reflects a personal relationship rather than an impersonal principle.

If there is a word that "comes close to being *the* Hebrew word for world order" when used in connection with the creation and existence of the world, it is the word ḥôq,[14] the word for an enactment, a decree or an ordinance, which can suggest the order God has imposed on the world. The etymological link

---

[11]See Hans Heinrich Schmid, *Gerechtigkeit als Weltordnung* (Tübingen: Mohr, 1968); also "Creation, Righteousness, and Salvation," in *Creation in the Old Testament*, ed. Bernhard W. Anderson (London: SPCK/Philadelphia: Fortress, 1984), pp. 102-17.

[12]Cf., e.g., Walther Zimmerli, *Man and His Hope in the Old Testament* (London: SCM Press, 1971), p. 15.

[13]Thus Knierim makes the telling claim that many texts *implicitly* suggest that Yhwh's presence in the cosmic order is perceived in the presence of this order of Yhwh's ṣedeq/ṣĕdaqâ (*Task of OT Theology*, p. 200; my emphasis), but he quotes only two passages that express this point directly. One is Ps 85:10-13 [MT 11-14], where ṣedeq appears in the company of ḥesed, šālôm and ʾĕmet. The other is Ps 89:14 [MT 15], where it similarly appears in the company of mišpāṭ, ḥesed and ʾĕmet. While the First Testament no doubt sees the world as founded in and on ṣedeq, the latter is no technical term for order. For further critique, see Lennart Boström, *The God of the Sages*, ConBOT 29 (Stockholm: Almquist, 1990), pp. 92-96.

[14]Knierim, *Task of OT Theology*, p. 199.

that also exists in English between giving orders and imposing order is then suggestive. Yhwh has indeed imposed an order on the world. The establishing of a framework of constraint on the world provides a secure framework within which it can exercise its freedom. Thus Psalm 148:3-8 speaks of Yhwh having laid down a constraint for sun, moon, stars and rain, and it speaks of the stormy wind "fulfilling his word" (NRSV "fulfilling his command"). The planets and stars decide what happens on earth (for instance, determining the seasons) on the basis of "laws" (*ḥuqqôt*) or an "ordinance" (*mišṭār*) (Job 38:33).[15] The cosmos works on the basis of something like laws of nature, but they are laws set by Yhwh.

Israelites were quite capable of distinguishing between regular and normal events, and unusual and extraordinary ones. God brought about both sorts of events, but there were events brought about by God that fitted into a perceptible pattern and ones that did not.[16] Yhwh directs things, but there are rules by which these regular events take place. Job 28:26 similarly speaks of Yhwh making such a "decree" for the rain, a decree that ensures that rain falls on the earth, though perhaps it leaves to the rain exactly where and when it falls. Proverbs 8:27-29 uses the word in the context of a double use of the verb *ḥāqaq*. Yhwh marked out a circle on the face of the deep and thus put the horizon in its place (cf. Job 26:10). Yhwh marked out the foundations of the earth and thus made sure it was well-founded. In between, Yhwh laid down a marker for the sea—so that the waters might not transgress his word, Proverbs again adds. In Job 38:10, Yhwh similarly recalls, "I imposed my decree/limit on it," the limit constituted by the sandy shore that the sea is not to transgress.

If only humanity could be similarly bound, Jeremiah 5:22 implies! Yhwh is lord of the world, and the world is Yhwh's servant. Yhwh speaks to nature to commission it to do its job, for instance bidding snow and rain to fall or clouds to circulate so that rain falls (Job 37:6, 12). Creation has a vocation.[17] Yhwh summons it to court to hear the case against Israel; it is a better servant than the people of God is and it can be relied on to come to a right judgment (e.g., Ps 50:4-6). On the other hand, Jeremiah adds, how marvelous that the fixed order of the cosmos is "the standard and pledge of Yahweh's consistent preservation of Israel" (Jer 31:35-36; 33:19-26).[18]

---

[15]BDB has "rule" for this hapax legomenon (cf. NRSV), but related words refer to writing; cf. Norman C. Habel, *The Book of Job* (London: SCM Press/Philadelphia: Westminster Press, 1985), p. 523.

[16]See Rogerson, "The Old Testament View of Nature," pp. 67-84.

[17]Fretheim, *God and the World in the OT*, pp. 278-83.

[18]Robinson, *Inspiration and Revelation in the OT*, p. 9.

Security

In themselves the heavens and the earth have no permanency. "Those things could perish, but you yourself would stand, while all of them wear out like a garment; you could pass them on like clothes and they would pass on, but you are the one; your years do not end" (Ps 102:26-27 [MT 27-28]). Translations render "those things *will* perish," but there is no need for the yiqtol to have that implication, and no basis for thinking that the psalmist would believe that the world was going to perish. The point is rather that it has no inherent permanency like Yhwh's.

Psalm 104 is aware of the world's having two potential forms of insecurity: it might be overwhelmed by floodwaters or it might collapse like a building that lacks substantial foundations. Either possibility could be suggested by natural phenomena, on one hand the pounding of the waters on the Mediterranean shore or the flooding of Mesopotamia, on the other the landslides caused by storms or the shaking of the earth by thunder and lightning.[19] In many parts of the world, its security does not look as if it can be taken for granted. Flood or earthquake or volcano assails communities. More fundamentally, we might question the world's security by asking what keeps the cosmos revolving, or what would happen if a meteorite hit the earth. The First Testament declares that the world has an ongoing security from collapse or flood, issuing from a divine act in the past, and it invites humanity to trust in the security of the world, not merely on the basis of empirical evidence in the world itself but on the basis of conviction about Yhwh's reliability. Yhwh did make the world in such a way that it is well founded and secure (Ps 24:1-2). The waters that burst through the land as springs and that surround it could seem to imperil it, and do sometimes flood it and destroy life, but they will never finally do so. God knew that the inhabited world needed to be built securely over its swampy base, and drove down into it the pillars that would make sure the world had firm foundations.

Psalm 65:5-8 extends the argument. It speaks of "awesome deeds" whereby Israel's delivering God does right by the people and is thereby manifest as one to whom all nations might look. It is this God who is "establisher of mountains by his power, girder of might, stiller of seas' roar, of their waves' roar, of the peoples' noise." As is often the case, the participles refuse to be referred exclusively either to a past act of creation or to ongoing activity. Establishing, girding oneself and stilling characterize God's relationship with the world at the Beginning and on a continuing basis. The "noise" that peoples make now is a further manifestation of the dynamic force of disorder that God quelled at the

---

[19]See section 7.2 "The Realm Below and the Realm Above."

Beginning. It is therefore vulnerable to the same stilling. Conversely, the power God shows in Israel's story is a basis for sure trust in God's keeping the world secure. The extraordinary acts whereby God is manifest in power in the world take place now, not just in the past. They thus meet with the awed but echoing response of the whole world, including people who live as far away to east and west as it is possible to imagine.

The God who delivers Israel is one whose power extends to the ends of the earth in bringing it security, keeping it firmly established and stilling the forces that work against its order and God's purpose. From the Beginning God has been the one who made the world secure, established the mountains and stilled the raging of the sea, and that is obviously good news for the whole earth and not just for Israel. And God's acts on Israel's behalf do not make God a threat to other peoples; indeed they imply good news for them, as God continues to protect order in the world and to constrain the forces that make the peoples a threat to one another as one nation lords it over another. Thus all the ends of the earth, from farthest east to farthest west, stand in awe and acclaim Yhwh's signs. These acts of God on Israel's behalf did not directly benefit the rest of the world, but they do imply good news for it as they demonstrate that God does not allow superpowers such as Egypt and Assyria to rule forever. The ends of the earth thus recognize that Yhwh is their security and are drawn into trust in Yhwh.

Sameness or Volatility

A very different inference from the consistency of the world is expressed at the opening of Qohelet (Eccles 1:4-11). It is a sign of the pointless circularity that characterizes existence in its totality (God's own being excepted). The regularity of the cosmos can be a source of wonder and security, but it can also be a mirror in which one sees reflected the unrelenting sameness of human history. The idea of progress and growth is very important to human beings, but Qohelet sees it as a myth, and sees the circularity of the cosmos as a sign of that. The sun goes on the same tiring journey every day. The wind goes on the same circular round. Rivers keep seeking to fill the sea, but never succeed. All nature does is tire itself out getting nowhere. "There is nothing, properly speaking, *creative* about Qoheleth's cosmos. . . . The constant rhythms of day and night are not praised for their salutary roles in sustaining and ordering life (cf. Ps 104:19-23); they are rather disparaged for their incessant repetitions. According to the psalmist, the gushing streams provide for life, including the 'birds of the air' (vv. 10-12). For Qoheleth, they flow for nothing."[20] They are not a

---

[20]W. P. Brown, *Ecclesiastes* (Louisville: John Knox Press, 2000), p. 24.

cosmos, an interdependent ecology, nor a creation, part of an entity through which God is doing something. They are a series of disparate elements without effective relationship to one another or to some purpose outside themselves. In themselves that is indeed how they can look; any assurance that they are otherwise will depend on convictions from elsewhere.

Job 9 speaks in a way that contrasts with both Psalm 104 and Qohelet. The divine sovereignty Job sees in the world is a negative power, a terrifying violence. God may have provided the earth with strong foundations (Ps 104:5), but God can shift mountains or overturn them and cause earthquakes that make one question whether those very foundations are imperiled. God may have set the sun and moon and stars in the heavens to illuminate and to rule (Gen 1:14-18), but God can bid the sun not rise. God may marshal the star army, count them and summon each of these troops by name so that not one dares be idle on parade (Is 40:26), but God can also firmly constrain the stars so that they fail to fulfill these functions. God may be wise and mighty in power (as Is 40:26 again also says; that description comes otherwise only in Is 31:2), but Job does not find these attractive assets. On the surface, Job's point is that God's capacity to produce natural disorder does not encourage confidence in God's capacity to sustain moral order, but his underlying point is the converse one. Job has not actually experienced God taking such actions in nature. The mountains do not overturn and the sun does rise each morning. Psalm 46:3-4 [MT 2-3] speaks only hypothetically of the mountains falling into the sea and Psalm 75:3 [MT 4] specifically affirms that God keeps earth's pillars steady. Indeed, Job might be glad to see some convulsions in nature, for these can bespeak God's acting to vindicate and deliver (e.g., Ps 18; 97). Job agrees with Eliphaz (Job 5) that bringing about transformation in nature and supporting the moral structures of human life go together. It is the actual moral disorder he experiences that makes him imagine God realizing a capacity to bring about an equivalent terrifying natural disorder. God may overturn the cleverness of the wise, but who can overturn God's wisdom when it works against us?

For better or for worse, Job is playing into God's hands, for God will eventually use the evidence from nature to counter the evidence from Job's experience. Indeed, in the shorter term Job watches his argument deconstruct, for he goes on to speak of the way God's power was exercised in the original creation (Job 9:8-9). Lacking the gall to describe that in negative terms, he can use only the positive terms that God will use in Job 38. By the end of his description, his summary has God doing great marvels beyond fathoming or (re)counting (Job 9:10). His echoes of Eliphaz are ironic, though one might argue whether the irony is Job's at our expense or the author's at Job's expense.

Magnificence

Evidently much depends on your perspective. Psalm 104 is a particularly outstanding picture of "the unity, the coherence, the harmonious order of the cosmos."[21] "If the first speech of Yahweh in the book of Job gives us the fullest Old Testament review of Nature's mysterious details, the best picture of Nature as a going concern is to be gained from Psalm civ," in all its structuredness, harmony and mutual dependence on God.[22] It reflects how "wherever you cast your eyes, there is no spot in the universe wherein you cannot discern at least some sparks of his glory."[23] The psalm also illustrates the "exuberant and effusive" nature of Israel's celebration of the world that responds to "the reliability of life in a reliable, generous, gift-giving world."[24] Whereas Marcion reckoned that the world was not good,[25] the First Testament sees it as good, ordered and beautiful.[26]

"Yhwh is very great," Psalm 104 says, and goes on to illustrate the point with the facts about Yhwh wrapping light like a garment or traveling on wings of wind. It is not so much pointing to phenomena that should convince someone of Yhwh's greatness as acknowledging phenomena that inspire this testimony to Yhwh's greatness. In a traditional culture people do not argue from creation that there must be a creator. They know God is there, as surely and as improvably as they know they are themselves there or know other people are there. Knowing that God is there and is creator, through the nature of the heavens the psalmist sees some aspects of *who* this creator is. It must be the creator's splendor, like the majesty of a king, that is reflected in the creation (cf. Ps 19:1-6 [MT 2-7]). The light is the creator's garment, the heavens the creator's home, the clouds are the creator's transport, the wind its power, storm wind and lightning are the aides through which the creator's will is put into effect. So how great is the creator!

A majestic revelation of the kingly glory of Yhwh permeates the earth as well as the heavens in such a way as to make them share in what is actually Yhwh's majestic glory. More poetically put, "Yhwh our Lord, how majestic your name is in all the earth, you who bestowed your glory on the heavens!"

---

[21]Walther Eichrodt, *Theology of the Old Testament*, 2 vols. (London: SCM Press, 1961, 1967), 2:113.

[22]Robinson, *Inspiration and Revelation in the OT*, p. 8.

[23]John Calvin, *Institutes of the Christian Religion*, 2 vols. (Philadelphia: Westminster Press, 1960/London: SCM Press, 1961): I.v.1.

[24]Walter Brueggemann, *Theology of the Old Testament* (Minneapolis: Fortress, 1997), p. 157.

[25]Cf. Barth, *Church Dogmatics*, III/1:334-40. Walther Zimmerli begins his book *The Old Testament and the World* (London: SPCK, 1976), p. 1, by noting the effect of NT statements warning about the world (1 Jn 2:15, 17).

[26]Gordon D. Kaufman, *Systematic Theology* (New York: Scribner's, 1968), pp. 295-98.

(Ps 8:1 [MT 2]).[27] Translations often place Yhwh's glory "above" the heavens, but this obscures the point.[28] There is a majestic glory about earth and heaven that actually come from Yhwh. This is not to imply that people inevitably recognize this for what it is, as the very fact that the psalm speaks of Yhwh's "name" being there indicates. The psalm can hardly be referring to people recognizing the reality and the glory of God under some other name. It is in Israel and Judah that God's name is known (Ps 76:1 [MT 2]), and that is the means whereby the glory of heaven and earth can be recognized as what they are.[29] Rather, the knowledge that Yhwh is the God of majestic glory enables us to realize that the majestic glory of heaven and earth are actually reflections of Yhwh's or gifts from Yhwh.

But nature can indeed be a means of revelation. The story Jonah tells his fellow sailors constitutes a paradoxically effective testimony to the power of Yhwh, whom Jonah has characterized as "the God of heaven, who made the sea and the dry land" (Jon 1:9). How great Yhwh is, if Yhwh is able to bring about such a huge storm. In general, we should not be sentimental about the idea of God's appearing through nature. This happens not so much in familiar beneficent realities such as sun and moon, springs and rivers, trees and woods, but in terrifying forces such as fire, lightning, thunder and storm (e.g., Ps 18; 29; 68; 77; 97).[30] Being the creator of the heavens and the earth in all their impressiveness means Yhwh has the power to bring terrible calamity on Israel in its rebelliousness (Amos 4:12-13; 5:8-9; 9:5-6).[31]

The storm ceases when Jonah bids the sailors throw him into the sea, thus abandoning his attempt to evade God's commission. That causes the sailors to revere Yhwh even more, offering sacrifices and making vows as expressions of their recognition (Jon 1:11-16). Later in the story, nature is a means of communication with Jonah himself (Jon 4:1-11): After Yhwh's relenting about Nineveh's destruction, Jonah makes himself a shelter and sits gloomily under it. Yhwh assigns a plant to give him better shade, which Jonah very much likes. But then Yhwh assigns a worm to attack the plant, causing it to wither. Next day Yhwh assigns a *khamsin* wind to blow there, while the sun also beat down on Jonah, which causes him to become angry about the plant. That gives Yhwh opportunity to raise a question. If it is appropriate for Jonah to be so concerned about this short-lived plant, is it not appropriate for Yhwh

---

[27]I have assumed that the odd verb form *tenâ* is a form of *nātan* (though perhaps a corrupt one).

[28]For the idiom, see 1 Chron 29:25; also Num 27:20.

[29]Cf. Hans-Joachim Kraus, *Psalms 1—59* (Minneapolis: Augsburg, 1988), pp. 180-81.

[30]Cf. Eichrodt, *Theology of the OT*, 2:16-17.

[31]See section 2.1 "Creator."

to be concerned for the people in Nineveh—and their animals?

Full of Wonder and Full of Grace

Elihu speaks from another angle of human failure to learn from this so-called revelation. It is too overwhelming (Job 36:24—37:24). His starting point and finishing point is that we cannot expect to understand God or to understand the heavens and the earth. The greatness and the eternity of God in themselves make this impossible. The power and majesty shown in God's activity in the heavens and on earth underline it.

"Does anyone understand these processes of nature," he asks? "Yes, we do," the modern age is in a position to affirm. We understand considerable aspects of them. We are in a position to duplicate them. We can make it rain and we can split the atom and release something of the frightening dynamic of nature for good and for ill. We are in a position to change the way the earth and heaven interact. It seems likely that the way we have worked with nature on earth has altered the ozone layer and changed patterns of sunshine and rainfall. We may well have set going changes that will alter the levels of the oceans in different parts of the world and alter the very flow of the Gulf Stream in the oceans.

But Elihu's claim that we do not understand God or the world is contradicted by his exposition of God's nature and of the world's nature and by his invitation to Job to consider God's wonders. Evidently they are not wholly beyond comprehension. Indeed, this man who asks whether Job can expect to understand the deeds of the one who is complete in understanding has actually claimed to be complete in understanding himself (Job 36:4). In the same way physicists who understand much more of the cosmos's working may not then regard it as an enigma that is now solved, but rather bow before its mystery in a deeper sense, as theologians who write books on the Trinity may be drawn into a deeper bowing before its mystery. To understand the workings of the cosmos is to be drawn into worship, not to find reason to suspend worship. Nature does not cease to be full of wonder.

Elihu does recognize that it is also full of grace. Whereas Qohelet sees an image of futility in the cyclical process whereby water evaporates and then falls as rain, Elihu sees it as contributing to God's bringing of blessing to the world. It is God's means of giving food in abundance. Such realities are expressions of God's commitment. Like a psalmist, Elihu emphasizes that God's provision involves fullness, not mere adequacy. At the same time, he sees this as the way God *governs* the world. That raises other possibilities. Perhaps the workings of nature could be the means of prospering the upright and also of punishing the faithless. So it is. They can be a club rather than an expression of commitment.

Psalm 85 speaks by faith of such a demonstration of God's involvement: "commitment and truthfulness have met, faithfulness and well-being have kissed." The fruit of this will come as "truthfulness will grow from earth, faithfulness has looked down from heaven" and the land gives its produce. Yhwh's commitment and faithfulness are thus involved like divine aides in that flourishing of nature that comes through their gathering and beginning to work together, preparing the way for Yhwh to come in person to "give what is good . . . as he sets his steps on the way" (Ps 85:11-13 [MT 12-14]).[32] The flourishing of nature comes from the working together of the heavens that provide rain (and sun, though Israel takes that more for granted) with the earth that produces the actual growth. These are embodiments of divine faithfulness and right, of Yhwh's keeping promises to the people and doing the right thing by them. Yhwh indeed gives "what is good," which again suggests the goodness of the material things that God gives. And it is in this giving that Yhwh's splendor will be manifest in the land.[33] The psalm also affirms that Israel must be committed to Yhwh and must not turn to folly (MT) and/or must turn their minds to Yhwh (LXX), but the fruitfulness of earth does not exactly come about through the cooperation of divine and human activity. It is not divine and human characteristics that embrace and kiss each other but the interwoven facets of Yhwh's character.

Commitment in the Heavens and on the Earth

The opening of Psalm 36 describes the egregious character and behavior of wicked people and its close prays for protection from them. The center, Psalm 36:5-10 [MT 6-11]), addresses God with a description of God's commitment and truthfulness that suggests the confidence the psalmist feels or wants to feel when confronted by such people. The link between these is unstated for the moment as the section thus ricochets in another direction in characterizing those aspects of Yhwh's character and life in relation to heaven and earth: "Yhwh, your commitment is in the heavens, your truthfulness as far as the clouds." The EVV have "your commitment reaches *to* the heavens," but the psalm says more than that.[34] Yhwh's commitment is *in* the heavens. Yhwh's commitment is there because that is where Yhwh lives; the statement might be

---

[32]The *gam* in v. 12 [MT 13] suggests that it is indeed Yhwh who acts, not merely the aides or the forces of nature. This is reasserted in v. 13b [MT 14b]. NRSV and NIVI understand *wĕyāśēm lĕderek* to mean "and it will prepare a way," but this seems to ignore the *l.* "And it will set [its mind] to a way for his feet" is possible (cf., e.g., Is 41:20). But more likely the line closes with another reference to Yhwh's activity in bringing renewal.

[33]I assume that the suffix from *yiš'ô* (his deliverance) carries over to *kābôd* ([his] splendor).

[34]The line comprises two noun clauses, with no word for "reaches," and while the preposition in the second colon is *'ad*, that in the first is *bĕ*.

a way of saying "you as the committed one are in the heavens." Yhwh's commitment is there because the workings of the heavens are themselves an outworking of Yhwh's commitment (cf. Ps 89:2 [MT 3]). As much is suggested by the repeated refrain in Psalm 136, "his commitment is forever" (vv. 4-9 relate to the heavens and the earth). In a related formulation in Psalm 108:4 [MT 5], Yhwh's commitment is "great above the heavens."[35]

Psalm 36 goes on to compare Yhwh's faithful decisiveness or decisive faithfulness not with realities of the heavens but with realities of the earth, the highest mountains and the great deep. These realities are spoken of theologically, with the quasi-mythical language that appears elsewhere, though this has become metaphor. The "highest mountains" are "the mountains of *'ēl*." Behind the expression is the idea that there were mountains that the Canaanites saw as "mountains of El" as Zion was the mountain of Yhwh. A high mountain might be a place where God chose to be met. But here the word for God functions as a superlative, so that the expression suggests "awesomely impressive mountains." The "great deep" *(tĕhôm rabbâ)*, too, elsewhere signifies awesome primeval waters (Gen 7:11; Is 51:10; Amos 7:4), but here likely refers more prosaically to the waters beneath the earth or to the sea itself (cf. "deep" in Ps 135:6). The psalm goes on to make even more down-to-earth statements about Yhwh's committed truthfulness and decisive faithfulness: "you deliver human beings and animals." It is natural to see committed truthfulness and decisive faithfulness expressed in acts of deliverance, but surprising to see how the psalm works out the logic of perceiving Yhwh's involvement with the world. Genesis 1 invites us to think of God's *blessing* of the whole creation (cf. Ps 104), but we usually associate *deliverance* in a distinctive way with humanity. The psalm sees the oneness of God's involvement with heaven and earth as naturally extending to the animal world, even in acting in deliverance.

In a similar context of the attacks of enemies and the threat of destruction, Psalm 57 speaks of taking refuge in the shadow of God's wings and then declares, "he must send his commitment and his faithfulness," and urges, "be high over the heavens, God, your splendor over all the earth" (Ps 57:1-3 [MT 2-4]). While the words of the latter prayer might suggest a visionary or liturgical manifestation of God, which could encourage the psalmist in the short run, this would not ultimately meet the needs the psalm speaks of unless it was also a promise and a sign that this glory would be manifest in the world outside worship. Thus the psalm's heading suggests that we read it in the light of an experience such as David's when he was on the run

---

[35]Hardly "greater than the heavens" (NRSV, NIVI): see BDB, p. 759a.

from Saul.[36] The manifestation of God's glory needs to link with sending God's commitment and faithfulness from heaven, those qualities personified as aides whom we meet elsewhere (e.g., Ps 23:6). Thus God's glory will be manifested as the psalmist is delivered. It is such an act that demonstrates that "your commitment is great, up to heaven, your faithfulness up to the clouds" (Ps 36:5 [MT 6]). It is in acting thus that God sits enthroned high over the heavens. If it is in the temple that the psalmist finds refuge in the shadow of God's wings until destruction passes, this sacramental or symbolic experience of protection needs to become material reality. The psalmist cannot stay in the temple all day.

As in Heaven, So on Earth

It is possible to think of God's will being done in heaven and to ask for it to be done in the same way on earth. The psalmist looks at the matter in a different way. If God's splendor is not manifest on earth, it is not obvious that it is a reality in heaven. Psalm 57 looks for some divine self-assertion in heaven, which will have implications on earth. There is a parallel contrast with the use of the psalm in celebrating Easter. The psalm does not look forward for a demonstration of God's splendor in the exaltation of the Messiah. It does not associate the manifestation of God's splendor with a final Day of Yhwh. It expects to see God's splendor, commitment and faithfulness manifest in the here and now.

This is the context of the repetition of Psalm 57:7-11 [MT 8-12] in Psalm 108:1-5. There are detailed differences in this version: for example, here Yhwh's commitment is great *over* the heavens. But the bigger difference is that here the acknowledgment of Yhwh's faithful commitment opens the psalm rather than closing it, as Psalm 108 combines the section of Psalm 57 with Psalm 60:5-12 [MT 7-14]. The psalm expects to see this cosmic commitment embodied in an act of deliverance that fulfills a promise God has made, which follows in Psalm 108:7-9 [MT 8-10]. Conversely Psalm 108 gives a new basis to the appeal issued in these words in their context in Psalm 60. Its basis is not merely the neediness of the people (Ps 60:1-4 [MT 3-6]) but the faithful commitment of Yhwh, which the psalm asks to be demonstrated in heaven and on earth.

Psalm 36, too, begins from the threat of the wicked and declares, "in the shadow of your wings people can take refuge." But they find more than that. They "imbibe from the abundance of your house" and "drink from your delectable river" (Ps 36:7-8 [MT 8-9]). In general and in particular the language parallels Psalm 23, which also rejoices in Yhwh's protection as shepherd and

---

[36]If the psalm was used by an accused person finding asylum in the temple and awaiting God's judgment, in the company of accusers (see Kraus, *Psalms 1—59*, p. 530), again the manifestation of God will need to be one that has an effect in life outside the temple.

which declares, "You have smothered my head with oil; my glass fills me abundantly"—literally, "saturation." The word "saturation" (rĕwāyâ), with the implications of intoxication, comes from the verb for "imbibe" (rāwâ) in Psalm 36, and "smother" (dāšan) is related to the word for "abundance" (dešen, literally "fat") in Psalm 36. In both psalms this fine banquet takes place in Yhwh's house. Where is that? The psalmist is on earth, not in Yhwh's heavenly temple, but neither psalm suggests that "Yhwh's house" is the Jerusalem temple. It is important that one can take refuge in the shadow of Yhwh's wings anywhere in the world, which is possible because the whole world is Yhwh's. The implication is that we can also banquet with Yhwh anywhere in the world, though we should not simply "spiritualize" the image and refer it simply to aspirations regarding the inner religious life.[37] The psalm is concerned with the outward world and its pressures, and it presupposes that the whole world is Yhwh's house, for refuge and celebration.[38] The psalms presuppose a oneness of heaven and earth, humanity and animals, physical life and religious life, because Yhwh is the God of them all.

So the temple is a place where one can find protection and enjoy a superb festal meal, and this provides the imagery for the protection and enjoyment one finds elsewhere (or is it vice versa?). And/or Yhwh's commitment and protection are rich food and refreshing drink from a running brook that flows through the Eden-like garden of Yhwh's house.[39] The relaxed, indulgent enjoyment of the physical good things of life on earth is a gift from Yhwh that as such can become a figure for the relaxed, indulgent enjoyment of other aspects of a good life on earth that are gifts of Yhwh. This does not imply that the physical becomes *merely* a metaphor for the "spiritual" or that "spiritual" blessings or salvation make up for the fact that physically we have a hard time from the wicked. It is rather that God's involvement with the physical (earth and heaven, human beings and animals, protection and feasting) means that God will be involved in the physical world in putting the wicked down (Ps 36:11-12 [MT 12-13]).

---

[37]Cf. Gerhard von Rad, "'Righteousness' and 'Life' in the Cultic Language of the Psalms," in *The Problem of the Hexateuch and Other Essays* (New York: McGraw-Hill/Edinburgh: Oliver & Boyd, 1966), pp. 243-66 (see p. 260) = pp. 187-204 (see p. 199) in *From Genesis to Chronicles* (Minneapolis: Fortress, 2005).

[38]Cf. Peter Craigie, *Psalms 1—50*, 2nd ed., WBC (Nashville: Thomas Nelson, 2004), p. 292; and the treatment of this theme starting from Rev 21—22 in Gregory Beale, "The Final Vision of the Apocalypse and Its Implications for a Biblical Theology of the Temple," in *Heaven on Earth*, ed. T. Desmond Alexander and Simon Gathercole (Carlisle/Waynesboro, Ga.: Paternoster, 2004), pp. 191-209.

[39]I take the plural in *naḥal ʿădāneykā* as intensive: this is "the river of great luxury." BDB treats this ʿēden as a different root from that of the place "Eden," but the homonymy would make hearers associate the two.

The World's Worship

Because the world belongs to Yhwh, heaven and earth may or do or must join in the praise of Yhwh. Because Yhwh hears the needy and is going to deliver Zion, "Heaven and earth must praise him, seas and all that moves in them" (Ps 69:34 [MT 35]; cf., e.g., Ps 96:11-13; 98:7-9). In response to the declaration that Yhwh is in the midst of pardoning and restoring Israel, Isaiah 44:23 urges heavens to resound, depths of earth to shout (the merism also implies everything in between). Mountains and their forests (every single tree!) are to break out in resounding. Only a response of the whole of creation can come near to providing an appropriate response to the prospect of this event.

The idea of the cosmos praising Yhwh may seem pure metaphor to a modern reader, but it is less so within the First Testament. For modern readers, praise is essentially an activity of the spirit, the mind and the will, and it is essentially addressed to God. Inanimate, unthinking, unfeeling entities can no more praise than dead people can, and praise is just as natural when one is on one's own as in the company of other people. In contrast, the First Testament understands praise as essentially a matter of body and sound, not merely of mind and spirit (e.g., Ps 95:1-2, 6-7). One cannot praise God silently or in a way that does not involve body movement. The animate and inanimate creation thus has most of the capacities or potentials required for praising Yhwh. Perhaps the First Testament implies an awareness that there is a personal liveliness within nature.[40] But in any case, nature's physicality is its asset. As human beings can shout and groan or clap and bow, so animals can howl and birds can shrill, trees can swish their branches and wind can roar. Like humanity, the rest of creation can also naturally respond to God's awesome majesty and power. As humanity shrinks in terror, so earth trembles, mountains jump, heavens burst, seas and rivers run away, trees shatter, leaves fall (e.g., Ps 29:3-9; 68:8; 114:3-7). The moments when nature does so in these psalms are not everyday ones and the responses are not everyday. They are out of the ordinary. Yet they are just as "natural" as more everyday events, even if they are acts of God in the sense used by insurance policies.[41]

The First Testament also understands praise as intrinsically involving other people who see and hear, and therefore join in. Worship is a matter of glorifying God, and this involves an audience. Whether the worshiper has a conscious intention to praise God is neither here nor there. The significance of the praise lies in the effectiveness of the way it points to God's praiseworthiness.

---

[40]See more speculatively Walter Wink, *Unmasking the Powers* (Philadelphia: Fortress, 1986), pp. 153-71.

[41]Terence E. Fretheim, "Nature's Praise of God in the Psalms," *Ex auditu* 3 (1987): 16-30 (see p. 25).

The animate and inanimate creation can be seen and heard and thus can draw others into its praise. Its special gift, calling and capacity is to testify publicly to the power of the one who created it.

Nature is thus a means of expressing a relationship with Yhwh. The king of Nineveh commands that domestic animals join with humanity in fasting, covering themselves in sack and crying out to God as expressions of turning from wrong ways (Jon 3:5-9). As animals are quite capable of making sounds and gestures that suggest praise, so they are quite capable of making sounds and gestures that suggest grief. They can contribute to a general expression of mourning at wrongdoing that needs to characterize the city. Indeed, the closing verse of Jonah suggests more than this. As humanity's fate is bound up with nature's, so nature's fate is bound up with humanity's. If calamity comes to Nineveh, it will affect the people's animals and not just the people themselves. It is in their own interests that they should turn to Yhwh in grief and lament. Jonah 4:11 assures them that Yhwh indeed cares about them. They do relate to Yhwh, and Yhwh to them. The conversation between Yhwh and nature is two-way. Yhwh speaks to it, and it speaks to Yhwh. Earth has a voice.[42]

Wordless and Worded Praise

Psalm 148 makes the point most systematically, urging all the different components and forms in the heavens and on the earth to join in praise.[43] There is a chiastic structure about the psalm's challenge to praise. It opens with the bidding *hallĕlû yāh*. In specifying what that implies, it begins with praise sounding from the heavens, first on the part of its personal beings, then on the part of its impersonal entities.[44] It goes on to speak of praise sounding from the earth, first on the part of its impersonal beings and then on the part of personal beings. Then it closes as it opened, with *hallĕlû yāh*.

Inside that opening and closing bracket, each of the two main halves of the psalm begins with a bidding that relates to its distinctive realm. And each of these halves eventually closes off the systematic specifying of its audience with the jussive requirement, "they are to praise Yhwh's name." The very na-

---

[42]Cf. The Earth Bible Team, "The Voice of Earth: More Than Metaphor," in *Earth Story in the Psalms and in the Prophets*, ed. Norman C. Habel (Sheffield: Sheffield Academic Press/Cleveland, Ohio: Pilgrim), pp. 23-28; cf. Howard N. Wallace, "*Jubilate Deo omnis terra*," in *Earth Story in Psalms and Prophets*, pp. 51-64; see pp. 51-52, 62-63.

[43]See further Fretheim, *God and the World in the OT*, pp. 249-66, and the table surveying nature's praise (pp. 267-68).

[44]The "high heavens" are literally the "heaven of heavens" or the "heavenly heavens" (cf. Ps 68:33 [MT 34]). Such phrases might seem to suggest that there were various levels of heaven, but there are no explicit references to this in the First Testament, and more likely the expression is a poetic one to describe the whole heavens in their exaltedness.

ture of praise in the Psalter is to combine a challenge to worship with the reasons for worship, characteristically in a clause beginning "for," and so it is here. Each time this summary jussive brings a transition to the reasons for this praise.

The heavens' reason for praise is the fact that they came into being through Yhwh's command. Yhwh's sovereignty was expressed in their creation itself and in the terms of that creation. They were put in place as permanencies. The anthropocentric nature of the psalm's praise emerges here. The permanence of sun, moon and stars is good news for the people who are encouraging them to praise Yhwh. So is the fact that Yhwh definitively set a boundary or appointed a statute for the waters. They can never overwhelm the earth.

Earth's reasons for praise are more subtle. The whole animate and inanimate world is to praise Yhwh in particular for what Yhwh has done for Israel, for it is in Israel that the exaltation of Yhwh's name becomes a reality. Yhwh exalted Israel, but the result is that Yhwh is exalted in Israel as the people who are committed to Yhwh, the people who have known Yhwh near to them.[45] Thus the wordless praise of the whole cosmos can be complemented by the worded praise of this people. What the mere words of this little people cannot achieve, the wordless praise of heaven and earth can achieve. What the wordless praise of heaven and earth cannot do, the worded praise of Israel can do.

The fact that heaven and earth are summoned to praise Yhwh coheres with the fact that the psalms do not glorify nature itself. "Israel trusts in Yahweh and not in the world order. To the extent to which it is certain of the world order, it is certain because of its trust in Yahweh."[46]

The Oneness of God's Activity

There is another sense in which the cosmos gives praise to God. It glorifies God by its own being. God is a rock; God is a mother eagle. So "rocks and mother eagles are reflective in some sense of who God is. . . . In themselves they are capable of showing forth the strength or the care or the glory or the faithfulness or the majesty of God. . . . The use of natural metaphors for God opens up the entire created order as a resource for depth and variety in our God language."[47] Is it then a sacramental universe—is there something about the nature of the world as God created it that makes it a means of communi-

---

[45]When the root *qrb* is used of the relationship of Yhwh and Israel, it commonly denotes Yhwh's drawing near to act on Israel's behalf. This makes sense in the context. The phrase ʿam qĕrōbô thus signifies not "the people who are near to him" but "the people to whom he is near" (in "raising their horn," which presumably signifies making them strong).

[46]Knierim, *Task of OT Theology*, p. 199.

[47]Fretheim, "Nature's Praise," pp. 22-23.

cating God's grace?[48] The branch of an almond tree and the pot in which some meat is cooking can become signs of what Yhwh is doing in the world (Jer 1:11-16), and created things such as bread and wine are capable of being taken and turned into means of grace. This hardly implies that nature as such inherently possesses special qualities that make that possible,[49] but God and nature have a mutual revelatory relationship. Perceiving something about nature helps us see things about God more powerfully; knowing something about God helps us see nature more clearly.

The oneness of God's activity and the oneness of God's world facilitate understanding of God and of God's activity. It opens up the feasibility of comprehending things in the world that we experience, as we understand one thing in the light of another. It also makes the language of analogy possible and thus opens up the feasibility of understanding things that are not of this world, as we understand them in the light of things that we do experience in this world.

The oneness of God's activity in the human and the animal world provides means for understanding the way God relates to us. Psalm 23 provides a powerful example. Like many psalms, it works with a rich combination of images, and we cannot be sure where metaphor ends and literal description begins. Eventually it talks about being beset by enemies, and I assume that is a literal reality; if it is also a figure of speech, it is the figure that stands nearest to literal reality in the psalm. God and God's involvement with us are also literal realities, but they are at the other extreme from the reference to military pressure in the sense that we cannot talk about them literally. We need the language of analogy and metaphor. Two extended metaphors make it possible to describe how God becomes involved when we are under attack. Whereas the psalmist could have given testimony to the way God literally protects from defeat or death and grants triumph in that situation, instead the psalm speaks of these realities through images, from the animal world and from the world of human community.

It starts from the animal world with the assertion that Yhwh is a shepherd (Ps 23:1). In Israel as elsewhere this is a familiar image for kings and thus a natural one for God. In its other occurrences in the First Testament the object of shepherding is, more naturally, a flock, Israel, and "shepherd" is usually simply an epithet (e.g., Gen 49:24). It is very unusual for Yhwh to be looking after

---

[48]See, e.g., William Temple, *Nature, Man and God* (reprint, London: Macmillan, 1949), pp. 472-95; and section 6.7 "How Faithfulness Makes Life Work."

[49]Cf. Wolfhart Pannenberg, *Systematic Theology*, 3 vols. (Grand Rapids, Mich.: Eerdmans/Edinburgh: T & T Clark, 1991-1998), 2:137-38. In *Church Dogmatics*, III/1:233, Barth does describe Gen 2 as having a sacramental view of creation, over against the prophetic one in Gen 1.

a single sheep (cf. Jacob in Gen 48:15) and for the image to be developed in the way that happens in Psalm 23. This is not a mere appropriation of a routine metaphor but a creative exposition that explores the metaphor's potential in a unique way. The First Testament's other extended exposition of the shepherd image comes in Ezekiel 34, applied more to the human "shepherds" who looked after Israel, but that passage also brings out the distinctiveness of this one, because Ezekiel 34 is more an allegory than the exposition of a metaphor. Similarly, while many of the details of the psalm parallel exodus traditions, it is their setting in the exposition of the metaphor that gives these details their coherence here.

Yhwh fulfills two aspects of a shepherd's responsibility, providing for the sheep and protecting it. The former image extends the linkage implied by the metaphor. It now embraces the plant world and the animal world as well as the divine world and the human world. All are one. The shepherd makes sure that the sheep has good grass and drinkable water and thus that its life is sustained. In what way does Yhwh do that for the psalmist? The image of feeding recurs later in the psalm, and I take this as pointing to the significance of the metaphor, though admittedly it does so only by utilizing another. But that is an entirely natural way for metaphor to work. Literally, the psalmist is threatened by trouble (ra‘). Enemies threaten disaster. The psalm's testimony is not merely that Yhwh makes it possible to escape such threats. Yhwh ensures that the psalmist not only survives but triumphs, providing marvelously for the psalmist's needs. Here that further metaphor surfaces. In the midst of the crisis it is as if Yhwh is a servant preparing a fine meal for the psalmist.[50]

The one extraordinary experience of being feasted by Yhwh is then the basis for a confidence about living with Yhwh, and doing so on an ongoing basis: "I will live in Yhwh's house for long days" (Ps 23:6). The image again becomes more intelligible if we read it in its metaphorical context, for metaphorically the psalmist has been enjoying the hospitality of Yhwh's house, and the prayer's last line expresses the hope of continuing metaphorically to return there and thus continuing to enjoy that hospitality.[51] Literally, then, the psalmist is under attack from enemies, yet experiences not only deliverance but triumph. Religiously, the psalmist experiences that as brought about by Yhwh.

---

[50]The psalm gives no indication that it has a liturgical setting and that this is a literal meal connected with a sacrifice, at which the psalmist's enemies were present (so Kraus, *Psalms 1—59*, p. 306).

[51]Literally, "I will return in Yhwh's house." Perhaps we should read *wĕyāšabtî* (and I will live) instead of *wĕšabtî* (cf. LXX), or perhaps the construction is elliptical; *šûb* followed by *b* recurs in Jer 8:6.

Metaphorically, that is like being entertained and indulged in Yhwh's house, with the enemies looking through the window with chagrin, gnashing their teeth, and the psalmist is convinced that Yhwh's goodness and commitment will continue to "pursue" in this way. But another level of metaphor sees a shepherd's providing for sheep as offering an analogy for a leader's providing hospitality for a servant.

One wonders whether the shepherd's work is somewhat idealized. Metaphor can thus involve feedback, as happens in a different way when the psalm refers to the shepherd acting "for his name's sake." The shepherd causes the sheep to relax in grassy pasturage (not to be taken for granted in a country such as Israel) and takes it to waters that are very still, to natural or humanly dammed pools (rather than waters that flow swiftly, dangerously and frighteningly).[52] The shepherd provides for the renewing of its life in such a way that it does not lack for anything, and thus leads it by paths that take it the "right" way. Such traveling to find grass and water may involve a route through steep and dark ravines that can seem dangerous,[53] but the sheep knows that it is safe. It would be vulnerable to attack from predators (cf. 1 Sam 17:34-35), but the shepherd's club protects it and is thus one of its encouragements. The other "encouragement" is the stick with which the shepherd prods the sheep and keeps it on that right way.

Human Life Illumined from Nature

In our present context the psalm's significance is the unity it affirms about life on earth and the unity it affirms about life on earth in relation to life in heaven. All belong to God and thus illumine each other. The life of shepherd and sheep corresponds to that of God and human being, so that each can illuminate the other. Inanimate nature (grass, water) matches the needs of animate nature and thus contributes to that correspondence. There is a further correspondence between the dynamics of human life and the dynamics of God's relationship with humanity. Hospitality and entertainment, feasting and beautifying, eating and drinking provide natural images for God's involvement with us. God, the human world in its social relationships, the animal world and plant world are all one. There is an essential analogy between the way nature works and the way human life works. Different aspects of nature will illumine human experience.

The world thus illustrates the nature of wisdom in the world. "Do ask the animals and they will teach you," or ask the birds or the earth itself or the fish,

---

[52]*mê měnuḥôt*, "waters of stillness"; the second noun is intensive plural.

[53]For "death's darkness" as a form of superlative, see D. Winton Thomas, "*ṣalmāwet* in the Old Testament," *Journal of Semitic Studies* 7 (1962): 191-200; see pp. 198-99.

Job bids (Job 12:7-9).[54] "Go to the ant, you lazy man" (Prov 6:6). The marvelous way ants collect and store up their food in the summer and fall enables them to last through the whole year. Won't the human being who lies there in bed learn a lesson from them? Only humanity is made in God's image, yet the whole world comes into being by the hand of God and thus there is a unity about all creation alongside the distinctiveness of humanity in relation to the rest of it. So the world deserves not only human respect but human reflection. The world tells us about the nature of reality. It even tells us about ourselves (cf. Prov 30:24-33).

The world is, indeed, an expression of divine wisdom. Before creating the world, Yhwh made sure of having Ms. Wisdom, and she was then present all through the process of creation (Prov 8:27-29). To describe her role in this process she uses the allusive term 'āmôn, which I am inclined to translate "child" (NRSV, NIVI and JPSV use the words master worker and confidant).[55] Whatever the meaning of that expression, it seems a secure inference that she was not just standing there watching without influencing what Yhwh did, though even if she were, she ended up thrilled to bits with what eventuated (Prov 8:30-31). That in itself implies that the world was an embodiment of wisdom; otherwise she would not have liked it so much. So the world is a place to learn from. Because the world is God's creation, it cannot but be a revelation of God.

Psalm 92 illustrates the point further from the inanimate world. "When the faithless flourish, they are like grass": like the grass or the wildflowers that grow abundantly after rain but soon wither.[56] On the other hand, "the faithful flourishes like the palm" with its fruit, "grows tall like a cedar in Lebanon" with its impressive spreading branches (cf. Job 8:11-13; Ps 1:3-4; Jer 17:5-8). "They are transplanted into Yhwh's house, they flourish in the courts of our God." The idea that examples of these trees are transplanted into the temple area is an imaginary one; there were trees there, but not of this kind. The context with its reference to the flourishing and downfall of the faithless makes clear that this flourishing is not merely in the psalmist's religious life, though no doubt it will also happen there. The psalmist expects to live a long, healthy and productive life because Yhwh is involved in it. In making the point the psalm makes several significant connections: Yhwh is involved with earthly life. Yhwh is involved with the natural world, so that its experience provides

---

[54]It may be that Job is ironically quoting his friends, but even if so this probably does not undo the point; see the discussion in David J. A. Clines, *Job 1—20*, WBC (Dallas: Word, 1989), pp. 292-94.

[55]See *OTT* 1:121.

[56]On the construction in Ps 92:7 [MT 8], see Marvin E. Tate, *Psalms 51—100*, WBC (Dallas: Word, 1990), p. 461.

metaphors for the psalmist's. Both the natural world and the worshiper are at home in Yhwh's house and gain sustenance there for their physical lives. And Yhwh proves there to be the one who acts with uprightness and moral consistency in this involvement in the natural and the human world. Thus these people "proclaim that Yhwh is upright, my rock, in whom there is no deviance" (Ps 92:15).

Such convictions are the basis for a frightening prayer or prediction for Zion's attackers in Psalm 129:6-8.

Yhwh's speaking through nature and to nature goes along with Yhwh's speaking in the form of statutes and ordinances given to Israel. In Psalm 147:12-20, Yhwh is "giver of well-being," and does more than merely provide basic needs. Yhwh gives them *finest* wheat, and *fills* them with it, completely satisfies them. After this comment the psalm returns to the sovereignty of Yhwh over the climate that makes the wheat grow. Here the stress is on the tough side to winter in the Judean hills and on Yhwh's capacity to make sure that winter cold does not get out of hand. Eventually frozen waters flow freely. All this issues from the fact that Yhwh is involved. Once more, Yhwh does not leave nature to its own devices but sends out specific orders for snow, frost, hail, and cold, and for the warmth and wind that bring relief. As Yhwh's speaking brought the world into being stage-by-stage, so Yhwh's speaking and Yhwh's breathing lies behind all the weather phenomena that people experience. Acting by speaking ("he sends his word") does not mean Yhwh is semi-distanced from the process that the divine word brings about.

Like Psalm 19, the psalm then pairs the word spoken in the Torah with the word uttered to nature. The close juxtaposition of references to Yhwh's word suggests no polemical or defensive attempt to relate the unrelated. Rather it implies an assumed oneness between the commanding word spoken to the heavens and the earth and the commanding word spoken to Israel. Each provides a model for understanding the other. We can see how God relates to nature by considering how God speaks to us. We can understand how God relates to us by considering how God relates to nature. If Israel has a unique understanding of the word of command addressed to it, then presumably it has a unique opportunity to understand the nature of creation. This possibility is borne out by the thinness of understanding of heaven and earth attained without the help of Israel's understanding. We can understand God from nature, but we do so by keeping in dialogue with God's more explicit speaking of which Scripture is a deposit.

7.2 The Heavens and the Earth

"The heavens and the earth" comprise one realm we cannot reach and one to which we do have access; one realm that belongs to God and constitutes a home for God and one that belongs to humanity and constitutes a home for humanity. Heaven suggests "the side of creation that is open to God"; if there were no heaven, the earth would be a closed world, a world without transcendence, in which nothing new can ever happen.[57] The heavens proclaim God's glory, and they are the source of rain as both threat and gift. The earth is the home of the animal world as well as humanity, and the animal world exists in its own right, not just as an adjunct to humanity. The earth is also the scene and the means of God's generosity being showered on humanity, for our enjoyment—though that also places obligations on us. Then there is the realm below, where Yhwh does not make a point of acting, but over which Yhwh is also sovereign.

The Heavens

Both the heavens and the earth are awesome realities (cf. Ps 8:1 [MT 2]), but that is especially true of the heavens. The planets and the stars proclaim God's glory by standing there—or rather by moving around at God's word—as the work of God's own hands (Ps 19:1-4; cf. Ps 8:3 [MT 4]; 102:25 [MT 26]; 103:22). By day and by night the sun, the moon and the stars pour out to one another their inescapable witness to the fact that their maker is the glorious God. As is characteristic of the words of the psalms themselves, their words are both worship and testimony. They are worship, because they function to glorify God. But they do so by being testimony, addressed to others. They also function in another connection as worship and testimony, because as well as being heard by one another they are overheard elsewhere—all over the world over which they shine and travel, in fact. And because their movements are so important to life on earth, their testimony is inevitably overheard there.

In what sense is this so? In isolation Psalm 19 could suggest that by means of the wonder of God's heavens, the glory of God makes itself known through the entire world. It might then be significant that the word for God is ʾēl, a term that could be used of the high God in other religions. Yhwh does not appear in the first half of Psalm 19. The psalm would be starting from the fact that the whole world does acknowledge that the heavens reflect divine glory, though it eventually then adds testimony to the significance of Yhwh's having actually spoken in words.

If this is its conviction, what was true in First Testament times is simply not true now, at least in the Western world. The sound does not go out to all the earth and the words do not reach the end of the world, or at least do not do so effectively. In theory God's glory is known through the creation, but in practice

---

[57]Jürgen Moltmann, *God in Creation* (London: SCM Press/San Francisco: HarperSanFrancisco, 1985), p. 163.

this does not work. Nor actually is this simply a modern Western problem. Paul notes how God's great power and majesty can be perceived in the world God made, but that people declined to learn the truth from this revelation (Rom 1:18—2:16). Perhaps Psalm 8 has anticipated this point, for it speaks specifically of *Yhwh's* majestic glory being reflected in creation. That is so only for people who know of Yhwh by other means, through Yhwh's being known in Israel. Such people recognize that the glory of creation is the glory of Yhwh.

Psalm 19:5-6 goes on to cite a particular, spectacular example of the heavens telling God's glory, the daily journey of the sun. Each morning it emerges like a bridegroom from its divinely provided quarters and starts running on its way like a warrior. Sun is personified, but it is no god in the manner of other Middle Eastern peoples. This sun is controlled and cared for by God. Whether the bridegroom is getting up on his wedding morning or emerging from the wedding ceremony or getting up after his wedding night, all would be moments characterized by exhilaration, enthusiasm, wonder and energy. Nor is it explicit why the warrior is running, though soldiers did even more running in the ancient world than they do in a modern army (cf. Is 40:31; Joel 2:4-9). One significant reason they did so was to carry news (see, e.g., 2 Sam 18:19-32), and this might be what the sun is doing. The line that follows, on the other hand, may suggest another angle on the question as it points to the way the sun beats down inexorably from morn till night, not from one position but moving over all the world, so that no one (for instance, the wicked) can escape its heat. Suddenly things have become solemn. This is not a wedding but a war.

The heavens proclaim. But what do they proclaim? An odd aspect of Psalm 19:1-6 is that the creation gets more and more prominent as the lines unfold, and God gets less and less prominent. Does the creation end up (maybe against its will) glorifying itself more than God?

Yhwh points out to Job that the heavens are, of course, beyond human control (Job 38:31-33). Isaiah 40:25-26 similarly declares that the planets and stars are utterly subordinate to Yhwh, though it demythologizes them more completely than Job 38 does. There Yhwh speaks of them as if they were farm animals, which Yhwh can tie and untie, and lead and guide into position. But Yhwh does so in order to enable them to play a real role in ruling the world. We might link that conviction with the picture of the court of heaven, where potentially rival powers are firmly reduced to the status of aides. The constellations are Yhwh's means of determining what happens in the world, as they are released or led on their way like farm animals. They reveal times and seasons and indicate directions.

The Awesome God of the Storm

Back at the Beginning Yhwh divided the original waters into two, so as to make a space between them for the earth (Gen 1:6-13). In Psalm 29, Yhwh sits enthroned above the waters above, the ones held back by the sky dome. Around Yhwh are the other divine beings (literally, "sons of gods") that form the court of the one who really is God. They are summoned to acknowledge the one who sits enthroned above the waters and who thunders and storms from there.[58] The "sound" or "voice" of Yhwh (qôl) is the monumental clashing of thunder that can resound when some of the waters are let loose in a storm, accompanied by lightning ("fiery flames"). On earth, the reverberations of that sound have extraordinary effects. When a storm sweeps the mountains and the desert, thunder and lightning and wind split huge trees and make the earth seem to shake and frighten animals into labor and strip forests of their leaves. Such an event is not merely a happening within nature but an echo of the voice of God. The psalm does not explicitly link thunder and storm with a victory in battle, though this may be implicit.[59] Nor does it comment on what might cause Yhwh to storm in this way (contrast Ps 18). The focus lies on the fact that Yhwh does, and that the storm is a manifestation of Yhwh's glorious majesty and mighty power.

The bulk of the psalm might be scary. The last line offers encouragement (Ps 29:11). The might and majesty manifest in nature are not merely manifestations of frightening strength. They are associated with the blessing and well-being of Yhwh's people. The psalm prays or promises that Israel will be the beneficiaries when the true God of the storm acts. H.-J. Kraus quotes a Babylonian poem about Enlil (whose descriptions are elsewhere also applied to Marduk):

> His word makes the heavens quake, makes the earth shake. . . .
> The Lord's word is a rising flash flood that beclouds the countenance;
> His word, it sweeps away huge lotus trees [?].[60]

Yhwh is the God of storm, as other peoples believed Enlil, Marduk or Baal to be.[61] What other peoples attributed to such gods in relation to their peoples is actually true of Yhwh. Whether or not Yhwh shares power with the divine beings, Yhwh does share it with Israel. So they can contemplate the storm and simultaneously be humbled by the power of God expressed in the violence of nature and encouraged by the promise that this power is designed to work for them, not against them.

---

[58]See further section 2.2 "Yhwh's Underlings."

[59]Craigie emphasizes the circumstantial evidence: see *Psalms 1—50*, pp. 245-46.

[60]Cf. Kraus, *Psalms 1—59*, p. 347. See further T. H. Gaster, "Psalm 29," *Jewish Quarterly Review* 37 (1946-1947): 55-65.

[61]See further the discussion in Carola Kloos, *Yhwh's Combat with the Sea* (Amsterdam: van Oorschot, 1986), pp. 15-124.

The Faithful God of the Storm

There is thus reason for rejoicing here, and not just for Israel. In this connection, Psalm 97 expresses itself somewhat paradoxically, especially in light of Psalm 29. It challenges the whole world to shout for joy, but its proposed reason is surprising. It is the fact that Yhwh has become king. Is there good news for other peoples in the fact that Israel's God has asserted control of the world? Apparently so. Is there good news in the fact that the deep darkness of the thundercloud surrounds Yhwh? Apparently so. Is there good news in the fire of lightning and the travailing of earth in the thunderstorm, as if it were twisting itself in the process of giving birth? Apparently so. These phenomena in the heavens that have their effect on earth are not merely manifestations of extraordinary power. In Yhwh, power is adjoined to moral qualities and serves a moral purpose. Yhwh has determined to reign in the world, but the exercise of authority is associated with a commitment to faithfulness. The supports that hold up that throne of Yhwh's in heaven are faithfulness and authority. In other words, if you ask what Yhwh's reign is founded on or based on, where its security and strength lie, the answer is that they lie in the combination of faithfulness and authority (*ṣedeq ûmišpāṭ*), in faithful authority or decisive faithfulness. So in proclaiming Yhwh's power by their powerfulness, the phenomena of the heavens also proclaim Yhwh's commitment to faithfulness. It is in this combination that the revelation of Yhwh's splendor lies. But *ṣedeq* works within the context of a relationship and means Yhwh is committed to what is right for Israel. In turn, that means death for Yhwh's enemies. Surely the earth, the far shores, the peoples, are then implicitly threatened by this commitment? The thundercloud (*ʿānān*) most commonly appears in the First Testament as a sign of Yhwh's appearing to Israel, especially at Sinai (e.g., Ex 13—14; 19; 24; Num 9), and the stormcloud (*ʿărāpel*) also appears in this connection (e.g., Ex 20:21; Deut 4:11).

Apparently this logic does not hold. The same tension appears here as appears in Isaiah 40—55, where the prophet sets alongside each other a commitment to doing right by Israel and a declaration that nations will come to recognize Yhwh, without showing how the two interrelate. By implication, belonging to the nations of the world does not have to mean being counted as Yhwh's enemies, and Yhwh's commitment to doing right by Israel does not have to mean trouble for other peoples. The nations have to decide whether they will indeed rejoice in Yhwh or whether they will continue to glory in pseudo-gods. But the manifestation of Yhwh will expose the latter for what they are and thus shame their adherents. The "gods" (*ʾĕlōhîm*) are in reality mere "godlets" (*ʾĕlîlîm*), entities whose name makes it look as if they are gods when they are nothings.

When is this revelation of Yhwh in heaven and on earth? Prophets can speak of it as lying in the future, but some psalms see it as also lying in the past, in Yhwh's acts of deliverance in Israel's experience that indicate that Yhwh alone is God. The psalm's use of so many qatal verbs does not encourage the reader to take it as "eschatological" in the sense of belonging to some far-off future day. Nor does the parallel with other psalms encourage us to see it as something that the psalmist has simply seen enacted liturgically. As readers we might more plausibly reckon that the psalm is encouraging us to look for something happening before our own eyes, in our own experience.

The Gift of Rain

Elihu implies some understanding of the process whereby rain "works" (Job 36:27—37:13). Water evaporates from the earth and becomes located in rainclouds; then in due course this water is released from there and returns to earth, eventually to return to the heavens again. To Elihu this is a pointer to God's greatness. It is not merely a natural process taking place by its own momentum ("water evaporates") but something God is continually bringing about ("God draws up drops of water"—drop by drop, apparently). Elihu is not averse to describing meteorological processes impersonally, or rather to personifying meteorological forces ("the skies pour [the rain] down"). His is not a supranaturalist picture of God's involvement in the storm, and not a very metaphorical one. Here, God does not ride on the clouds as a carriage, though from his heavenly tent God does shoot flashes of lightning as arrows. What is striking is therefore the combination of the two forms of description. By implication, each stage can be described either way.

Water evaporating and then falling as rain could suggest a gentle natural process, especially in northern Europe. Elihu describes it as a frightening one, because he focuses on the rainstorms of a Mediterranean climate. It does not rain much there, but (as Albert Hammond lyricized about Southern California) they never warn you that from time to time it does pour. So it is in Elihu's homeland. Rain means overwhelming floods cascading from skies as somber as night, thunder reverberating across mountains and valleys, and lightning flashing through the grimly dark sky. It is a natural way to go about describing nature as God's means of expressing anger at wrongdoing. It puts humanity in its place, as the "elements" still do in every corner of the world. Thunderstorm, snow, cold, ice, tornado and heat still have the capacity to bring a community's life to a standstill, to "seal people's hands" so that they cannot do anything and to make even animals stay indoors. They even inhibit the task of doing theology or the formulating of things to say to God, whether by making the day too dark or the light too bright, and thereby they expose the pretensions of theologians.

In this aspect of the portrait, too, Elihu combines an account of phenomena that work themselves out within nature with an account that assumes that God is directly at work in them. It is when Yhwh blows cold on water that ice forms. The thunder is God's voice. The flashes of lightning are God's arrows. The wise person will see in thunder and lightning God thundering at wrong-doers and God flashing to consume them.

Of course Elihu's poem is largely irrelevant to Job. The readers of his story know that the lightning and tornado that destroyed his farm and workforce and family did not come on him because he was a wrongdoer. Elihu's meteo-rological theology cannot be applied to every storm. But other parts of the First Testament confirm that it can be applied to some. The appropriate response to storm, flood, thunder, hurricane and heat wave is therefore the one Jesus com-mends, that we should repent just in case (Lk 13:5).

Yhwh's own words to Job take up related themes. The questions concern not whether anyone (such as Job) knows where the rains come from, but who makes them happen. Who cut a channel for the torrents of water that fall on earth (Job 38:25-27)? Yhwh makes these extraordinary things happen. In the context, the "channel" for the torrent of water cascading from the heavens is not the empty wadi through which the rains will eventually roar, but the chan-nel that Yhwh has made from the reservoir in the heavens that brings these waters to earth. Parallel to it is the "way" down which thunderbolts travel. Rainstorms and thunder, as well as lightning and winds, thus also work in ac-cordance with a cosmic freeway map laid out by a visionary and turned into reality by an engineer long ago.

What is noteworthy about these rains is that they fall in their abundance on land where no human beings live. A significant motif in Yhwh's address sur-faces. Job has presupposed that the cosmos is organized is such a way as to re-volve around humanity in general and him in particular. Yhwh's address points to the evidence that this is not so. Middle Eastern peoples could never take rain for granted. Very often they did not have enough. Yet Yhwh distrib-utes rain very liberally. It is just that Yhwh does not make it fall where human beings need it. Apparently Yhwh has other priorities. Yhwh likes making grass grow. The poem does not even note that animals eat it. Long ago Job de-clared that Yhwh used wisdom to turn rain into a destructive agent—either by withholding it or by flooding with it (Job 12:13-16). Yhwh's questions point to evidence that this is too cynical an assessment of Yhwh's relationship with that aspect of nature, or rather it is an assessment too centered on human needs. The world is geared just to be itself, an ecological whole (Job 38:26-27). Job 38 "'decenters' creation; it is decidedly not anthropocentric. This is a world de-signed for the benefit of the whole community of life, indeed of inanimate na-ture (by our definitions) as well. Humans must find their niche within this dynamic, dangerous, but vibrant ecosystem."[62]

In turn, consideration of extraordinary rain leads to consideration of ordinary rain, or rain in general (Job 38:28-30). In their way, rain, dew, ice and frost are as mysterious as human life. Where do they come from? Previous questions have invited the answer that Yhwh knows about these things and brings them into being as Job does not, and that is no doubt implicit here. The world is just too extraordinary for Job. Yet these particular questions are more purely rhetorical. Yhwh probably does not mean "I am rain's father, dew's begetter, ice's mother, frost's bearer." Nor is the address attacking the convictions of religions that attach specific deities to these natural phenomena.[63] The simple description of the extraordinary way a vast expanse of water can freeze over suggests that these questions are more an expression of wonder and of recognition that—humanly speaking—such questions have no answers. The world is a wonder, but also an enigma.

There follow further questions concerning sovereignty in the heavens as this affects the earth (Job 38:34-38), questions presupposing that Yhwh is the one who gives orders to the elements, to rain and lightning, tells the clouds how to produce rain, works out how much rain is available and actually releases it like a person upturning a bottle.[64] This rain then softens the soil and breaks it up so it can be plowed (or turns the dusty soil back into moist earth that will not simply blow away). It would be so useful to human beings to be able to control the rain, but we cannot. "Human nature is more powerful than mother nature," declared the *Los Angeles Times* the week after a monumental hurricane. Oh no, it isn't.

The Animal World

When Yhwh's speech to Job is done with the heavens, it turns to the earth and its inhabitants. All are wild animals and wild birds. Again the question arises, do you know what is going on in the natural world? A new question also arises, can you provide for these creatures' needs? For instance, who provides the prey for the lion and the raven (Job 38:39-41)? Human beings feed domestic animals, but not such creatures of the wild. No human being could do so, but Yhwh does.

The poem chooses markedly carnivorous creatures. The prey to which it re-

---

[62]Dale Patrick, "Divine Creative Power and the Decentering of Creation," in *The Earth Story in Wisdom Traditions*, ed. Norman C. Habel and Shirley Wurst (Sheffield: Sheffield Academic Press/Cleveland, Ohio: Pilgrim, 2001), pp. 103-15; see p. 113.

[63]See Habel, *Book of Job*, pp. 542-43.

[64]With BDB I have taken the "hidden realms" as lying in the heavens, and understood the obscure word *śekwî* to mean something to do with the "sky." Connecting both in some way with the mind (NRSV) fits ill with the context.

fers comprises animals such as sheep, killed by the lion and taken advantage of by the raven when the lion is not looking. Here there is no yearning for a creation in which the lion lies down with the lamb. Nor is there any allusion to the threat and danger that lions are to humanity. Yhwh superintends the natural world as it is. Further, the focus lies on the need for lion and raven to provide for their young. It is the predator's motherly instincts and obligations that Yhwh enables her to fulfill. Can it really therefore be right that Yhwh cares not one whit for human beings? Does the a fortiori argument of Matthew 6:25-34 not hold?

What do you understand about the breeding habits of ibex and deer? Yhwh goes on to ask (Job 39:1-4). Job or his employees knew about breeding cattle and sheep. They knew how long is their gestation, how they could help them lamb or calve successfully, and how to help make sure they rear their young. They knew nothing about breeding these creatures of the mountains, and no one does anything to help them. But they manage just fine. The cycle of pregnancy, birth, growth and self-sufficiency proceeds without human supervision or human awareness, though by implication it is overseen by Yhwh. The political "times" when Yhwh uses armory such as hail are indeed complemented by the natural "times" according to which the life of ibex and deer unfold, which are also part of the natural ordering of the cosmos. To a human observer, such times may seem part of a depressing and meaninglessly repeated cycle, whether they are the political times or the natural ones (cf. Eccles 3:1-8). We do not understand them. Yhwh does, and is not depressed by them.

Yhwh evidently gets satisfaction out of observing these creatures, like a celestial wildlife expert. Perhaps Yhwh grieves at the loss of animals from the wild, of which the fate of the buffalo is a spectacular instance. Once more, by implication Yhwh as the one who gave these animals this home also sees that they find their food (cf. Ps 104:11). And Yhwh's words thus also confront Job's earlier expression of pity for the onager, and presumably implicitly confront his analysis of the position of the poor (Job 24:1-11). Job has pointed out that he has put considerable resources into seeing that the poor are looked after (Job 31:16-23). These verses point out that Yhwh in turn sees that there is food for the onagers, for whom Job has only scorn. They are perhaps not so poorly off as Job implies.

If Job's men venture into the desert, they could perhaps capture and train some wild donkeys, though not the buffalo (Job 39:9-12). This is no not-yet-tamed ox. You could never get it to do an ox's work. Of course, you could always kill it and eat it and use its hide. While human beings must not eat the flesh of animals "with its life, its blood"—which might preclude eating live animals or might imply draining the blood from the meat—we are allowed to kill animals to eat them; animals are not allowed to kill human beings to eat them, because human beings are made in God's image (Gen 9:2-6). But that permission to humanity comes not as part of creation but in the aftermath of the emergence of humanity's inherently violent nature.

Stupidity and Impressiveness in the Animate World

Yhwh is not sentimental about the animal world. While some animals teach human beings lessons in wisdom (e.g., Prov 30:24-28), others were made stupid. The "screecher," the ostrich (Job 39:13-18), can flap its wings with enthusiasm, but not fly. It is an unusual bird. Further, whereas the stork was fabled for the way it cares for its young, the ostrich was fabled for seeming to neglect its.[65] One might compare the myth that the ostrich lives with its head buried in the sand. While it searched for food, it allegedly left its eggs in the open where the warmth of the sun could hatch them, but it stupidly made no allowance for the fact that this would also mean their getting trodden on, and it thereby wasted the effort involved in laying them. It is all because God declined to give the ostrich the wisdom to behave any more thoughtfully and lovingly. The world has wisdom built into it, but only sometimes. Once again the poem has no compunction about involving God in responsibility for an aspect of the cruel side to creation; it rejoices in the wonder of creation, but does so without sentimentality.

There is a further distinctive feature of the passage about the ostrich. It asks no question. So what is its point? Is Job invited to see himself as resembling the ostrich, a being who has forgotten wisdom—indeed a being from whom God has withheld wisdom? The beginning of God's charge was that Job's words lacked knowledge (Job 38:2). A rhetorical question about what Job knows (e.g., Job 38:18; 39:1) is unnecessary here. An ostrich is in no position to rule the world. Case proven.

Yet for all the ostrich's earthboundness and stupidity, there is no denying its impressiveness when it runs. It has the potential to outpace a horse, and on that basis can laugh as loudly as the wild donkey and as the horse itself, or even as Leviathan (Job 39:18; cf. Job 39:7, 22; 41:29 [MT 21]). So if Job is an ostrich, is Yhwh also expressing appreciation for him, as Yhwh will later express appreciation for him over against the three friends who are even more stupid than he is? Or is the ostrich's laughter more an expression of its stupidity? For there is a rider on the horse, and the preceding context suggests this is not the war horse that will appear in the following verses but a horse ridden by a hunter, and that the ostrich's brio is about to find itself in a cage. Its laughter is the laughter of a fool (Eccles 7:6), the kind of play that Job might attempt

---

[65]In the first line I have taken ḥăsîdâ to refer (as usual) to the stork, but the reader may also understand it to open up the question whether the ostrich's wing is "committed/kindly" like the stork's (see BDB): see the following lines.

with Leviathan—to his cost (Job 41:5 [MT 40:29]). If Job is the ostrich, is Yhwh the horse, or is the wise author the horse, and Yhwh the rider?

Admittedly, the horse was chiefly a military animal, and the poem goes on to laud the horse's strength and fearlessness and warrior enthusiasm. Who made it that way? Isaiah 31:1-3 warns Judah not to trust in horses as a military resource. They are, after all, only physical resources, capable of being outpaced by Yhwh. Yet in themselves they are so impressive. In Job 39:19-25 Yhwh stands back from this aspect of nature and marvels, in the manner of the daily marveling at the process of creation that Genesis 1 describes. Once more we may be surprised at Yhwh's enthusiasm. We might have preferred Yhwh to be enthusiastic at the horse running free across desert plains, like the donkey, but it is war that brings out the character of the horse and thus raises the question who made it as it is. Yet even in war, the horse remains an animal with a mind, or rather a spirit, of its own, no more tamed than the other creatures Yhwh points to. It has no more respect for its own side ("it does not trust in the sound of the trumpet") than for the other side. It remains its own "person."

If the horse is the most impressive of animals, the hawk and the eagle or vulture are the most impressive of birds. If the ostrich is the most land-locked and the most stupid of birds, these two know how to soar and know how to care for their young (Job 39:26-30). It is Yhwh who teaches the birds to undertake their extraordinary migratory journeys up and down the Rift Valley and to soar high and build their nests on inaccessible cliffs. There they and their young are safe, but from there mice and desert creatures are vulnerable to the swoop that brings them to their bloody end. Where you find a corpse, blame the vulture. Yhwh teaches it to live like that.

One might then reckon that Yhwh's provision for these birds of prey forms an inclusio with Yhwh's provision for lion and raven, with whom the questions about earth's creatures started (Job 38:39-41). Or perhaps these corpses are the slain of war, so that horse and bird of prey work together. If the wars of horse and bird of prey are fought in the cause of right, this would make Job 38:12—39:30 close with another declaration that Yhwh makes nature work in a way that puts down wrong; but the point is not explicit.

Humanity's Place in the World

So the animal world was not created for humanity's benefit, as some of its members make clear. Onagers and wild donkeys wander about the desert (Job 39:5-8). How wasteful to let all those valuable animals loose in the wild when they could be making themselves useful. But they also have their place in the scheme of things. This profligacy can be attributed only to Yhwh, who seems to enjoy the fact that they make their home in the wild, in areas that seem most inhospitable. Finding their food there is tough, but they have their freedom, and that makes living there worth it. Better a hard life on the salt flats of the Dead Sea rift than the service of a driver in Jerusalem. Perhaps the author wonders whether they have a better life in their freedom than that of drivers, or authors of wisdom books or theologians. Here Yhwh reverses the value judgment implied when we set up an antithesis between city and open country, culture and nature. The city is a place of bondage from which Yhwh is absent, the wild a place of freedom where Yhwh provides.[66]

Yhwh follows up the entire series of questions in Job 38—39 with a challenge to Job to respond (Job 40:1-2). But Yhwh has silenced him. The eloquent Job now wishes to say nothing (Job 40:3-5).[67] I imagine him expecting that this will therefore be the end of the matter. He is therefore appalled when Yhwh starts up once more with another series of challenges and questions that look as if they might go on as long again as the first, though in the event they do not do so. Perhaps the implication is that Yhwh is not very satisfied with Job's quasi-submissive response. Teachers are familiar, after all, with the student who gives up arguing when overwhelmed by points we have made, without this meaning the student has really been convinced. Yhwh wanted to get Job to look at creation from another angle, an emic rather an etic one: The aim of portraying the life of various animals has been to provoke Job into looking at their lives from inside, instead of looking at life only from the perspective of what it is like to be Job. Job's response offers no indication that this aim has been achieved.

In an indirect way, the instructions concerning which animals can be eaten also make the point that the animal world exists in its own right and not just for humanity' sake. In the Western world, we assume that animals are there to be eaten. In a traditional society such as Israel, eating meat is rarer, and there are rules about the creatures that can and cannot be eaten. Creatures that can be eaten need to belong to recognizable categories (Lev 11; Deut 14), for instance, animals with cleft hooves that chew the cud, and fish that have fins and scales, and other creatures "equipped for the right kind of locomotion in its element" (i.e., earth, water or air) rather than being "neither fish, flesh or fowl."[68] Israel may not eat creatures that seem to be a cross between two categories. No doubt there were other considerations that entered into the avoidances,[69] but one of their implications is that there are many, many creatures that exist just for their own sake, or for God's sake—certainly not for Israel's sake.

The ban on having sex with animals has the same implication. It involves confusion (tebel) rather than observing the proper differences between species

---

[66]Cf. Brown, *Ethos of the Cosmos*, pp. 362-63.

[67]Cf. Ibid., p. 365.

[68]Mary Douglas, *Purity and Danger*, rev. ed. (London: Routledge, 1969), pp. 55-56.

[69]See section 3.3 "Distinctive and Separate."

(Lev 18:23), which is the implicit principle behind many other prohibitions on mixing things such as cattle for breeding, seed and material for clothes (Lev 19:19). These are not absolute principles; mixing is allowed in other connections. Bread for sacrifices can involve mixing flour and oil (the verb *bālal*, e.g., Lev 2:4-5); cattle fodder involves mixing elements (*bĕlîl*, e.g., Is 30:24). Further, one need not assume that Israelites were especially inclined to bestiality, any more than to sex with one's mother-in-law. The regulations are teaching put in the form of regulations for behavior, in this case teaching that establishes the independent existence of the animal world.

Part of the World's Ecology

Psalm 104:10-18 suggests more directly that even if humanity is central to God's provision in nature, God has other concerns. Earlier in the psalm, water is a peril; here it is a provision: God is "one who waters the mountains from his penthouse," to grow food for humanity and for our domestic animals. But the psalm, too, gives more space to the way this water provides for wild animals and wild birds. These are of no use to humanity, but God provides for them. It is the point implicit in Genesis 1 and central in Job 38—39; animals and birds are there in the world in their own right. Indeed, this section of Psalm 104 has a chiastic arrangement that makes the point with special force. The central lines concern domestic animals and human beings (the context and the parallelism suggests that the mountains here appear as the places where grain and vines grow) (Ps 104:14-15). One might have thought that these lines were going to be the climax of the section. But then not only do the subsequent lines revert to wild animals and birds, they especially focus on trees, birds, animals, high mountains and crags that are notably impressive, remote and irrelevant to humanity.

The psalm goes on to note how the moon and sun function to provide structuring for the life of earth, marking the time that belongs to human beings and their work and the time that belongs to wild animals and their doing what they have to do (Ps 104:19-23). The fact that God put moon and sun in their place at the Beginning to tell people and animals the proper time for different activities is the guarantee that this structuring continues to hold. While humanity comes second in the account here, again this hardly means it constitutes the climax, for most space is given to wild animals. "Are we humans really the goal of creation? The Christian doctrine of the incarnation obviously implies such a view, which we find also in the OT creation stories," because it was in a human being that the fellowship of creator with creature reached its fulfillment.[70] Perhaps so. But here humanity almost looks like an afterthought.

---

[70]Pannenberg, *Systematic Theology*, 2:74.

"Earth, with its diverse cast of characters, is a central actor in Psalm 104; humanity has only a bit part."[71] We should not think too much of ourselves.

The poem about wisdom in Job 28 has the same implication. It begins by wondering at the awe-inspiring nature of the inner recesses of the earth itself. There in its depths lie the riches and the resources of silver and gold and iron and copper and sapphire. The poem reflects on the mystery of the way such valuable treasures lie hidden deep in the earth and away from any paths that human beings or even animals regularly tread, so that miners are involved in adventurous, enterprising and hazardous expeditions in order to get hold of them.

If the talk in Genesis 1 of human mastery over the earth contributed to the ecological crisis,[72] this will have been encouraged by the Christian instinct to treat Genesis 1 as *the* biblical statement about creation. Accounts such as Job 38—39 also complement Genesis 1 by offering a less monarchic and human-centered understanding of God and creation and by seeing humanity much more as part of the ecology of the world.[73] While retaining ownership of the heavens, Yhwh has given the earth to humanity (Ps 115:16), yet even the earth is given us to use, not to own. The land itself continues to belong to Yhwh. Its human occupants are in no position to sell it, as they can sell things they have made such as houses in cities.[74] They may grow produce on it and even lease the rights to it to someone else, but once every seven years they forfeit the right to sowing (Ex 23:10-11), as a sign that it belongs to Yhwh. And Yhwh chooses that year to let the land's natural growth be available to the poor and to the animals of the wild. Then once every fifty years people are to allow control of the land to revert to its previous occupants (Lev 25). Time also belongs to Yhwh, and Yhwh similarly claims one day in seven as a sign of owning the whole, and chooses to use it for the benefit of children, servants, immigrants and animals (Ex 20:8-11; 23:12; Deut 5:12-15). We do not have the world or even time to do with what we like.

The Gifts of Creation

If Israel's relationship with the animal world differed from that of Western culture in one way, its relationship with what grows from the ground differs from

---

[71] Arthur Walker-Jones, "Psalm 104," in *The Earth Story in the Psalms and in the Prophets*, ed. Norman C. Habel (Sheffield: Sheffield Academic Press/Cleveland, Ohio: Pilgrim, 2001), p. 92.

[72] But see *OTT* 1:114-15.

[73] I recall my first Old Testament teacher, John Austin Baker, making this point before Lynn White gave his famous lecture about the negative effects of Gen 1 (see previous note).

[74] Cf. section 3.4 "Landed."

that of Western culture in another. In the West, no one has to wonder whether next year produce will be available. Israel could not take this for granted, and thus it is a topic for prayer, praise and wonder.

Psalm 65 speaks of how, when we are invited to come into Yhwh's courts, "we shall have our fill of the good of your house, your holy palace" (Ps 65:4). Blessing lies in enjoying good things, and that happens through coming to God's palace. There is again some ambiguity about what is meant by this palace. Here I take the psalm to refer to coming to spend time in the temple courts at a festival, where Israel recognizes Yhwh as the one who provides. The material provision of the palace courts would, of course, be splendid indeed. The closing lines of the psalm will make quite clear that these material things are valued in their own right; they are not symbols of religious blessings. "You have attended to the earth and made it abound; you greatly enrich it." You "establish their grain," the psalm comments (Ps 65:4). The verb, which is then repeated, suggests a link between God's activity in the world in the present and at the Beginning. Translations appropriately take these two verbs as instances of *kûn* (hiphil) meaning "prepare," but it is worth noting that they take up the earlier occurrence of the verb to refer to God's "establishing" the mountains (Ps 65:6 [MT 7]). Yhwh was involved in *hākēn* at the Beginning and continues to be so involved (cf. Ps 78:20; Job 38:41).[75] That in turn suggests we should take the grammar literally and infer that the people whose grain God establishes or prepares are the people whose awed response to God's deeds was reported earlier in the psalm. The earth that God has visited is not only the land of the people of Israel but the land of all of earth's peoples who (without knowing it) look to "our God" as their hope. By the end of the psalm we are thus having to ask whether its opening description of God as one "to whom all flesh can come" means just what it says.

The psalm speaks of God's enriching work in similar terms to the ones that apply to human experience (cf. Ps 23). It is as if nature is a person whom God has enriched and satisfied with drink and filled with other good things, other luxuries. Even the wilderness pastures are full to overflowing as the psalmist's glass fills to overflowing. The year is crowned like a person having perfume poured over his or her head. Nature rejoices, shouts and sings like human beings overwhelmed by the goodness of what God gives them to enjoy. By implication, these are the good things that come from God's house. They also make praise appropriate for God in Zion—so LXX says in the first line. Or they generate silence as praise for God in Zion, in keeping with the awe that the

---

[75]Brueggemann, *Theology of the OT*, p. 352. He notes that there is a beginning here for responding to Knierim's suggestion that we need a First Testament theology of food (*Task of OT Theology*, p. 226).

psalm's middle section describes—so MT implies there.

This God lives in a palace in the heavens but also has a residence on the earth for meeting with people and seeing that the world's needs are met, and from this twofold dwelling ensures that good comes to the whole world. "God's stream is full of water" (Ps 65:9). It is God's stream that waters the world. Whereas a visit from an earthly king is to be dreaded because it empties the fields when his chariot passes through, a visit from the heavenly king distributes largesse rather than receiving it.[76] This fits with the way God is the subject of a sequence of ten verbs either side of that reference to God's stream, leading into a declaration that "your cart tracks overflow with richness." God is the farmer making sure that the ground has the water it needs and the other forms of attention that make the harvest happen, with the result that when the farmer drives his cart back home it is so full of grain it overflows onto the cart tracks.

The Abundance and Goodness of God

Surprisingly, perhaps, the psalm then closes with two lines that make no mention of God. The portrait fast-forwards from fall and winter, the time of the fall rains that soften the ground for plowing and the winter rains that make things grow, to spring and summer, the time when grain and fruit ripen. So it rejoices in a picture of the wilderness pasturage flourishing to overflowing. These are not areas where farmers plow and sow—by definition, they do not regularly get enough rain to make that possible—but areas that grow grass to provide flocks and herds with their pasturage. In this picture, that grass is also supernaturally abundant and thus capable of supporting vast herds and flocks, making the hills seem to be clothed in them as the vales are clothed in grain (Ps 65:13). And this flourishing creation joins Israel and the nations in praise. After all, the trees have branches to wave and clap; crops have the capacity to wave like a congregation swaying; grain and grass has the capacity to murmur as the wind whistles through it. The hills and vales sing for joy, and they invite the human creation to join in.[77]

It is not true, we might shout out. The world's harvest is not enough to feed the world. You do not make your tracks overflow. Yes I do, God replies. There is enough food in the world to feed the world. The challenge is to you to get about distributing it.

That might add an extra resonance to the earlier statement in the psalm about forgiveness (Ps 65:3 [MT 4]). On the one hand, people who pray this psalm, acknowledging the acts of rebellion whereby we have kept the good

---

[76]See Tate, *Psalms 51—100*, pp. 143-44.
[77]Cf. section 7.1 "The World's Worship."

things of the world for ourselves, can believe that the record of these can be whitened out or washed off.[78] They can have their record of wrongdoing expunged and thus be assured that it no longer exists. On the other hand, we can of course only pray that prayer on the basis of putting our lives straight for the future. We cannot ask for forgiveness if we continue to take an inappropriate share of the good things that God gives. And that links with the importance of not "spiritualizing" the psalm, as if we now know that God is not so interested in food as the psalmist thought was the case. The psalm knew that God was interested both in the realm of the spirit (forgiveness) and the realm of the body (food). It will thus not let us focus too much on the former and thereby free us to neglect the latter, on the basis of seeing it as a less important realm.

So "taste and see that Yhwh is good!—the blessings of the person who takes refuge in him!" (Ps 34:8-10 [MT 9-11]). Taking refuge with Yhwh brings more than protection (cf. Ps 36:7-8 [MT 9-10]). It brings blessings (cf. Ps 1) that include every good thing (!) and no lack (cf. Ps 23:1, 6). It is this that stimulates the awareness that Yhwh is "good," the opening confession in Psalms 106, 107, 118 and Psalm 136. The declaration about God corresponds to the declaration by God at the creation (Gen 1). God looks at creation and says "it is good." Creation looks at God and says "God is good." "The creatures reflect the goodness of their createdness back to God and as a witness to God toward the entire world."[79]

So the world has not lost the goodness that God saw in it at creation. "Inasmuch as the world order revealed goodness, wisdom, glory, and righteousness, it also revealed God's presence in the world in an ultimate way, and did so more directly than human history ever could."[80] With depressing frequency we hear of earthquakes and floods in which hundreds or thousands of people die, but many more people die each year from human violence than from nature's violence. We have to see particular experiences of Yhwh's goodness not working out against the evidence provided by the creation as a whole that this goodness is a reality. God's goodness is revealed in the goodness of creation, even if humanity also needs God's goodness to express itself further in the self-revelation that tells us more of who God is and in acts of deliverance and renewal that also embody and undergird the revelation as a whole. When Yhwh appears to Job, Yhwh provides no information or arguments that Job's theologian friends (and Job himself) have not used in the preceding parts of the book. All that Yhwh does is reaffirm those declarations about the cosmos. Far from being put in question by Job's experience, they have to put Job's ex-

---

[78]On the verb *expiate*, see section 2.6 "Yhwh's Love."

[79]Fretheim, "Nature's Praise," p. 26.

[80]Knierim, *Task of OT Theology*, p. 201.

perience in perspective. The significance of Yhwh's appearing is to urge Job to maintain faith in that God-centered perspective.[81]

Praying for Material Blessing

The comparison of people who trust Yhwh with animals in Psalm 34:8-10 [MT 9-11]) further hinders us from taking too figuratively the idea of having our hunger satisfied. The same applies to the link between feeding the people and bringing them up from Egypt: "I am Yhwh your God, the one who brought you up from the country of Egypt: open wide your mouth and I will fill it" (Ps 81:10 [MT 11]). In other contexts "filling the mouth" might denote giving them things to say, but this context suggests things to eat. God relates to the people like a mother or father who sees a baby's open mouth and fills it. Bringing the people out of Egypt was a physical event, and so was feeding them on the way from Egypt to the promised land: "He fed them from the finest of the wheat; I will fill you from the rock with honey" (Ps 81:16 [MT 17]). The sequence of verbs here is jerky—in person, in suffix and in tense—which may suggest that the text is conflated. But the effect is to make the change of tense suggest the same link between the beginnings of the people's life and its continuance.[82] God has met the people's physical needs in the past, giving them the finest bread to eat. Yhwh will continue to do so in the future, if they walk in the right ways. Linking this line with what precedes also resolves the puzzle of why the psalm speaks of honey "from the rock." It is not clear why this should denote especially fine honey, which would make for good parallelism, but it makes for a good link with the recollection of the people's history. Once, God provided *water* from the rock, which would slake their thirst. Now, God will *fill* them (*śābaʿ*) with *honey* from the rock. The psalm expresses more vividly the promise of the priestly blessing: "Yhwh bless you and keep you; Yhwh shine his face to you and be gracious to you; Yhwh lift his face to you and give you well-being" (Num 6:24-25).

Such a promise would give a basis for prayer. Psalm 67 constitutes a prayer for Yhwh to do just that: "God be gracious to us and bless us, shine his face among us." This psalm again presupposes that God's blessing is physical and material, not merely "spiritual." It does assume that God is concerned for the nations to enjoy "spiritual" blessings, because it looks to their coming to recognize God as their lord and shepherd. But it keeps the word *blessing* for God's this-worldly gifts and thereby encourages us not to take them with insufficient

---

[81]Cf. ibid., pp. 202-3.

[82]One verb is *waw*-consecutive plus yiqtol, the other yiqtol. The EVV assume that both verbs have the same time reference (though they vary as to what that is), but the combination suggests a summary of the psalm as a whole.

seriousness. Its vision is that through God's people the nations come to recognize God as the one who gives earthly blessings.[83] If God's people lose the vision for being the means of that realization, the "spiritual blessings" will not follow.

As well as declining to see blessing as a spiritual matter, the psalm declines to see the fulfillment of God's purpose to bless as a reality that belongs to the End, and only to be brought about by God's act independently of ours. It knows that God has blessed us and believes that this is all that is needed for the extending of a recognition of God now. Its prayer is designed to urge God to bring that about. By implication, that may also depend on God's people being willing to share God's blessing. There is thus good reason to avoid suggesting that the fulfillment of God's purpose awaits a special act of God at the End—which would let us off the hook of being the means of God's blessing being recognized today. And that takes us back to the question of whether we share the world's resources with the rest of the world or focus on enjoying them for ourselves.

Creation and Government

The harvest has a prominent place in the prayer in Psalm 72, with a different dynamic, as it implies some other moral and political questions. This prayer for the king will be one that he overhears, and one may wonder if it is as much designed for the king and his subjects to hear as for God to hear. The psalm rejoices in uninhibited fashion in the good things of earth. It prays for the mountains and hills (in other words, the hilly country of Israel as a whole) to bring forth *shalom*, well-being or prosperity. It prays that they may do so with that same permanency that attaches to the planets. More specifically, it prays for abundance of grain in the land. Grain shakes on top of the mountains: only here is shaking a sign of blessing on the earth rather than a sign of trouble as the earth itself shakes. Grain is as dense as the trees in Lebanon, as the people in a city, as the wild grass in an open field.

But this enthusiasm and prayer is set in the context of a prayer for the king, and the conviction that the king's actions make a key difference to whether the prayer comes true. The psalm's great enthusiasm for prosperity and bounty thus implies a similar understanding of the role of government to the one that characterizes modern Western countries. The government's task is to ensure that the economy works. The psalm accepts that, but propounds a different view of the way the government goes about ensuring that the economy works, that the crops grow. It is not so much a matter of encouraging investment and

---

[83]See section 8.1 "Acknowledging Yhwh as Provider."

efficient management of human resources. It is a matter of ensuring that things work out fairly for the needy. This is the way in which the king will "come down like rain on mowing" (that is, grass that will be mowed for animal feed, not already mown grass, which does not need or benefit from rain), "like showers that water earth." By paying attention to the needs of the needy and poor, and therefore putting down the oppressor, the king will irrigate the earth and make the crops grow. The psalm apparently assumes that giving priority to this will ensure that the crops grow, that the economy takes care of itself (Ps 72:1-7). It assumes an underlying moral structure of reality. Matters on earth are interwoven, and attention to one issues in effectiveness in another.

There is then some irony about such a prayer for the king, especially one whose heading designates it a "Solomon-psalm." Solomon is one whose very name, *Shelomoh*, invites us to see him as the person especially responsible for *shalom*, and at one level Solomon accepted that responsibility. But he also encouraged the further development of a class structure in Israel and divisions between rich and poor that had been introduced by David, and added the mistake of encouraging the influence of other peoples' religions in Israel through his "diplomatic marriages."

In modern Western countries it is sometimes asserted that the relationship between economics and fairness within a society involves a "trickle down effect." Paying attention to the economy working at the national level, letting businesses make a good profit and letting business leaders receive good salaries will ultimately issue in increased prosperity for ordinary people. Anecdotal evidence suggests that actually the opposite is the case, or at least that the rich grow richer faster than ordinary people prosper or poor people catch up, so that the gap between rich and poor grows. In any case, the psalm sees the logic the other way round. The king is expected to put his energy into seeing that the society works in a way that is fairer for the less well-off. If he does that, the community will then find that its life as a whole is characterized by prosperity.

The psalm does not assume that there is some dynamic power or faithfulness within mother nature herself that makes the crops grow and generates prosperity or well-being. The government stands between God's power and faithfulness and the flourishing of nature, in a positive sense. The opening lines of Psalm 72 thus interweave prayer for the king to exercise authority with faithfulness for the sake of the needy by crushing the oppressor, with prayer for the mountains to yield well-being for the people. It prays that God may thus make the government the means of ensuring that society works in such a way as to enable nature to yield its produce. The king makes it possible for the faithful to blossom, and that makes it possible for nature to blossom. (The LXX prays rather that he may make "faithfulness blossom," which might be little different, though MT's expression presses the need for faithfulness to find concrete expression in what happens to actual people and safeguards against any implication that faithfulness somehow comes into effect "naturally.")[84]

The psalm does not indicate how this comes about. Perhaps it assumes that God acts in interventionist fashion to ensure that things work out this way. Perhaps it assumes that a cause-effect linkage is built into the way the earth works. Anecdotal empirical evidence suggests that there may be something in both these theories. Sometimes one explains what happens, sometimes the other does. (Many people who live "healthy lives" live long ones, but some die early of a heart attack. Many people who live "unhealthy lives" die young, but some live on, and sometimes they testify that it is because God has intervened in their lives.) Perhaps the psalm implies another aspect of the unity of all reality that is assumed in the capacity of nature to provide metaphors for human experience.

In the hymn "Jesus Shall Reign Where'er the Sun," Isaac Watts made a fine metrical version of Psalm 72 that subverts its distinctive convictions, abandoning its convictions about God's involvement in this worldly life. The psalm believes that God is concerned about and active in the everyday political and agricultural life of Israel and that there is both challenge and promise for the government there. Watts sees Jesus as fulfilling the psalm's vision, yet in the way he claims this, he so reinterprets the vision as to betray it, and he surrenders the world of nature to other powers—in our case, to humanity independently of God.

The Realm Below

The twofold division of the cosmos into the heavens and the earth conceals a threefold division, for earth itself divides into the world where living people abide and the underworld where dead people abide. The preference for a bipartite expression, "heaven and earth" coheres with its general reluctance to encourage too much interest in that realm, which was off limits, but the First Testament does talk about the world below as well as about the world above.

Heaven, earth and the world below all appear in Psalm 18, which presupposes that threefold structure of the cosmos. In the heavens above, Yhwh has a palace and a throne, from where to keep watch over what happens on earth below and to intervene from time to time. Below the earth is the realm of

---

[84]In Ps 72:5, further, MT has "may they revere you as long as the sun . . . ," while LXX has "may he live as long as the sun. . . ." The MT's prayer subordinates the king's exercise of power to the praise of Yhwh as well as to the needs of people. LXX's prayer fits the psalm's later talk of his ruling the world and receiving from it. Has MT de-ideologized the text or has LXX ideologized it (or messianized it, on the assumption that the king is the Messiah)?

death; into the earth is where we go when we die and are buried. Personally, Death is like a being with ropes and traps who seeks to capture us before our time (Ps 18:5 [MT 6]) or a greedy being never sated with swallowing people (cf. Ps 69:15 [MT 16]); Death is a personal being in Canaanite theology.

Geophysically, the realm of death is pictured in the light of the fact that there are vast reservoirs of water under the earth. While these are a prosaic literal reality (they are the sources of springs, streams and wells), they are also a metaphysical reality (they are part of the waters that once overwhelmed the earth, put under constraint by Yhwh). In that capacity they can threaten to overwhelm us before our time. Instead of Sheol's gates being unable to hold on to people who belong to God (Mt 16:18), Sheol reaches outside its gates and takes someone within its clutches while they are still alive. In a sense, indeed, the torrents of Belial do then already overwhelm us (Ps 18:4 [MT 5]). It is as if we are already in Sheol. And neither the powerful waves and torrents of the sea nor the ropes and snares of a hunter can be escaped. The name Belial may combine *bĕlî* and *yaʿal*, so as to suggest "worthlessness." But in this context people might link it with *bĕlî* and *ʿālâ*, which would suggest "without ascending"; Sheol is the place from which no one comes up (we do not know the etymology of the word *Sheol* itself).[85] Or they might link it with the verb *bālaʿ*, meaning "swallow," which would suggest the way death's torrents swallow people.[86]

The nature of the tomb is to be a place of darkness. Once you are put there, a rock is placed over its entrance and the tomb descends into darkness. That points to the nature of Sheol as a place of deep darkness. It is thus a place that makes people stumble about in confusion. Even its light is dark compared with real light (Job 10:21-22). It is also a place of silence. "Can dirt confess you, proclaim your truthfulness?" (Ps 30:9 [MT 10]). There is no celebrating or confessing of Yhwh there (Ps 6:5 [MT 6]). That might be simply because the inhabitants of Sheol are dead; there is no acting or thinking or remembering there (Eccles 9:10). Or it might be because Sheol lies beyond the realm where Yhwh chooses to be present or chooses to act (so that there is no act of God, no truthfulness, to celebrate). Psalm 88:10-12 [MT 11-13]) thus asks rhetorically whether Yhwh does wonders for the dead, whether the ghosts[87] rise to confess Yhwh, whether Yhwh's commitment and truthfulness and wonders and faithful

---

[85]The NIVI takes *šĕʾôl* as a term for "the grave," not a place like earth or heaven; but see Philip S. Johnston, *Shades of Sheol* (Leicester, U.K./Downers Grove, Ill.: InterVarsity Press, 2002), pp. 73-74.

[86]This would also connect with the way Belial becomes a name for Satan. See *DDD*; *TDOT*; D. Winton Thomas, "בליעל in the Old Testament," in *Biblical and Patristic Studies*, ed. J. Neville Birdsall and Robert W. Thomson (Freiburg: Herder, 1963), pp. 11-19.

[87]On *rĕpāʾîm*, see section 6.9 "Long Life."

deeds are proclaimed in that land of darkness and oblivion.

The Realm Below and the Realm Above

Human life on the earth itself is lived between two locations and forces. We live under the caring eye of Yhwh in heaven, but subject to the greedy desire of death and to the possibility of its overwhelming us. Fortunately the experience of attack from below always makes possible the appeal to the realm above. Psalm 18 reflects a particular experience of being threatened by the forces from below and delivered by the forces from above. It eventually becomes clear that this particular threat from below came via human enemies on earth, who imperiled the worshiper. Fortunately, the forces above can also involve themselves on the earth, with the result that the worshiper won an extraordinary victory, in the way the psalm goes on to describe. The psalmist cried out to Yhwh in the palace in the realm above, God heard, and things happened in the realm below. The psalmist then won a supernatural victory, but not a supranatural one. It was not like the deliverance at the Red Sea or even the capture of Jericho; it involved fighting. But it was an extraordinary victory, and it was Yhwh who brought it about against the odds, as happens on a number of occasions in the story from Genesis to Kings and in Chronicles.

The supernatural nature of the event is especially conveyed by the description of Yhwh's appearing (Ps 18:7-15 [MT 8-16]). Conflict on earth reflects conflict between the forces of heaven and the forces of Sheol, and this is "naturally" echoed and/or experienced and/or pictured in terms of the physical world. So when the forces of Sheol reach up to the earth, Yhwh comes down from heaven to earth. Yhwh's tearing apart of the sky so as to hasten down to earth is like the coming of a violent storm. Such a storm is accompanied by thunder and hurricane winds, an unnatural daytime darkness, flashing lightning and torrential rain that soon issues in flooding from below as well as from above. Yhwh is clothed in elements of the natural order, implying a "fundamental compatibility between Yhwh and the natural order."[88] Yhwh's arrival and entering into conflict with the forces of the world below cause the earth itself to shake when Yhwh's anger is expressed.[89]

The heading of the psalm invites us to read it in the context of the life of

---

[88]Fretheim, "Nature's Praise," p. 25.

[89]It is often reckoned that we should see in the Psalm the imagery of earthquake and volcano (cf. Kraus, *Psalms 1—59*, p. 260, following J. Jeremias, *Theophanie* [Neukirchen: Neukirchener, 1965]). But few worshipers (Canaanite or Israelite) would have experienced earthquake (the First Testament refers to only one literal earthquake, in Amos 1:1; Zech 14:5) and perhaps none a volcanic eruption; flood from the sea or tidal wave were also unknown in Palestine. If these have influenced the portrayal, it will be secondhand, via a tradition of

David, as does 2 Samuel 22. If we do so, we can see hints of occasions when Israel did experience an involvement of nature in the winning of victories (see 2 Sam 5:17-25). But they are only hints. The story of Deborah and Barak (Judg 4—5) hints at another such experience, though only in the verse account of the event. At the least, all this implies that there were very many battles that did not involve Yhwh intervening in a way that found a resonance in nature, as conversely most violent storms happened independently of battles. It is therefore striking that the psalm suggests such a powerful collocation of Yhwh's involvement in political/military events and in natural events. Perhaps the background is again Canaanite theology's picturing of Baal as storm god, which First Testament theology is applying to Yhwh's acts in political/military events. It then declares the conviction that Yhwh is indeed the real God of storm and lightning, thunder and flood.

7.3 God's Ongoing Activity in the World

The pattern of Yhwh's activity in the original creation continues in Yhwh's ongoing activity in the world. Wondrous acts of creation continue in ongoing provision. Occasional acts of deliverance are complemented by ongoing blessing. Nature and history, creation and politics, the creation of the world and the history of Israel, all are one.

God at Work

We have noted the ambiguity of the English word *creation*, which can refer both to God's original act of creating the world and to the resultant world itself. In the First Testament, Psalm 104 is the most systematic exposition of the continuity between God's original and ongoing activity in creation. A series of pictures of Yhwh run through the psalm.[90] Yhwh is a king robed in majesty, transported around the realm in a limousine, sending off aides hither and thither. Yhwh is a sheik stretching out a wide-spreading tent, and a builder constructing a luxury abode and a back house. Yhwh is a military general thundering at forces that dare resist, and making them shake with fear. Yhwh is a herdsman providing food and water for a variety of animals, and a farmer watering a variety of crops and seeing that they grow. Yhwh is the head of a family controlling the life of a household and providing it with all it needs.

---

imagery with its origins elsewhere rather than directly from experience. But this only pushes the question of its origins one stage back, and the imagery requires only the experience of violent storms and lighting and the earth movements that the consequent floods can bring. Cf. the comments in Luis I. J. Stadelmann, *The Hebrew Conception of the World*, Analecta Biblica 39 (Rome: PBI, 1970), pp. 144-46.

[90]See Hans-Joachim Kraus, *Psalms 60—150* (Minneapolis: Augsburg, 1989), p. 304.

This many-faceted portrayal is set in the context of a bracket of self-exhortation, commitment and prayer (Ps 104:1a, 31-35), which reminds the worshiper that Yhwh's original and ongoing work in creation are a major reason for praising Yhwh. In between this bracket, the psalm enthuses over the heavens and the earth, the sea and the land, the rain and the crops that the rain makes possible, the trees and the birds, the moon and sun, and the wonder and the solemnity of it all. Many of its features recall Genesis 1, though it centers on a conviction that superficially contrasts with Genesis. Its God is not one who rests once the original creation is finished. As by implication in Job 38—39, Yhwh is ceaselessly active, rebuking forces of disorder, seeing that creatures get plenty to drink, watering mountains, growing grass, producing bread, making darkness, feeding animals, withdrawing breath and giving it.

Psalm 104 strikingly interweaves all possible ways of making statements about God's involvement with heaven and earth, by means of qatal verbs (fientive and stative), yiqtol verbs, participles, noun clauses, infinitives, jussives and cohortatives, and doing all this in apparently unconscious fashion. Some of its qatal statements unequivocally refer to God's original act of creation, when Yhwh founded the earth and appointed a place and set a boundary for the waters and put the moon in its place, when Yhwh made everything with wisdom; it was then, apparently, that Yhwh planted the cedars in Lebanon and formed Leviathan to play in the sea. But the bulk of the psalm's yiqtol verbs, its participles and its noun clauses point to God's ongoing involvement with the cosmos and nature.

The greater part of the psalm comprises a series of sections with the same outline structure. In each, one or more qatal verbs introduce a sequence of verbs in other forms. I take the initial qatals to refer to God's original act of creation and the subsequent clauses to refer to God's ongoing activity in heaven and earth. God put on light, and continues to be manifest in the heavens (Ps 104:1-4). God established the earth, and continues to keep it safe (Ps 104:5-8). God exercised control over the waters, and continues to make them a blessing rather than a peril (Ps 104:9-18). God put the moon in its place, and continues to be lord over both day and night (Ps 104:19-23). God made everything in wisdom, and continues to provide for everything (Ps 104:24-30). Some verbs can be read either way, and that is part of their significance. Whatever negative effect human sin has had on the world, it does not alter Psalm 104:24.[91]

Both the combination of past and ongoing reference, and the uncertainty about determining the reference of some of the verbs, deconstruct the distinction between original creation and ongoing involvement or creating and sus-

---

[91]Cf. Barth, *Church Dogmatics*, IV/3.ii:698.

taining. This deconstruction is effected elsewhere through the use of participles to describe God's involvement with the world. These systematically refuse us the option of making the distinction. It is not so much a matter of original creation and continuous creation as a link between a sovereignty exercised once-for-all at the Beginning and a sovereignty exercised on an ongoing basis.[92] What happens in the world now is not a matter of mere chance. God is not merely the watchmaker who set the world going and then left it to run itself.

Wondrous Acts Continued in Daily Provision

In its testimony to Yhwh's present involvement with the world, Psalm 145 begins by celebrating Yhwh's great deeds and graciousness without specifying what the deeds are or how the graciousness manifests itself. When the psalm eventually becomes more concrete (Ps 145:14-20), we are surprised at the way it does so, as it speaks of Yhwh as "supporter of all who fall, raiser of all who bow down." One would imagine that the great and awesome acts of God with which Psalm 145 starts are Yhwh's once-for-all deeds in Israel's history, but if Yhwh is also supporter of the falling and restorer of the fallen, that suggests an involvement in people's lives that turns the once-for-all acts at the Beginning into an ongoing pattern in Israelite experience. That in turn suggests that Yhwh's ongoing acts constitute not merely an intervention in crises but an ongoing provision of everyone's basic day-by-day needs. Thus "the eyes of everyone wait for you, you are giver of their food to them at its moment, opening your hand, fulfilling every living thing's desire" (Ps 145:16). One way this may link with the great acts at the Beginning is that there is thus a stupendous generosity about them. God provides more than merely the wherewithal to survive. In giving food, God's hand is wide open, like a farmer allowing an animal to take as much fodder as it chooses. The result is that *all* living things (not just some of them) have their *desires* (not just their basic needs) *fulfilled* (more than barely met). "There is no creature . . . upon whom God's mercy has not been poured out," Calvin comments, so that the right way to seek the truth about God is not by trying to think about God but by looking at God's works.[93] And this generous provision of food is an example of Yhwh's doing the right thing and keeping a commitment, as was the case in those acts at the Beginning of Israel's story. In this Yhwh is being faithful and committed, *ṣaddîq* and *hāsîd*.

Much of Psalm 144 speaks of God involved in political events, bringing

---

[92]Cf. the discussion in Tim J. Gorringe, *God's Theatre* (London: SCM Press, 1991), pp. 15-18.
[93]Calvin *Institutes* I.v.6, 9, referring to Augustine's comments in *Expositions on the Book of Psalms*, 6 vols. (Oxford: Parker, 1849), 6:319.

about rescue and deliverance for David. But then it moves seamlessly to God's involvement in the ordinary life of family and farm: "Our sons like plants, full-grown, in their youth; our daughters like corners, carved, in a palace building; our barns full, producing things of every kind; our sheep thousandfold, ten thousandfold; in our fields our cattle laden; no breach, no departure, no cry in our streets" (Ps 144:12-15). Once more the psalm looks for an involvement that is extraordinary in its fruitfulness, as Yhwh's activity in deliverance has been extraordinary. And it closes by returning to the political, asking for no occasions when the city's walls are breached or its people have to leave it.[94] But in effect it thus asks, may there never be need of those special political acts of God. May we be granted the blessing of living in uninteresting times.

Providence

Psalm 107, too, celebrates Yhwh's involvement with earthly life in down-to-earth terms. Unlike Psalm 104, it talks about Yhwh's involvement with earth in a way that centers on humanity. It considers a series of human adversities and rejoices in the way Yhwh reaches out to people in their need, acting on the world. If people have wandered in the desert, Yhwh leads them and meets their needs—or rather does more than that, in quantity and quality, the first line suggests. If people have found themselves in the darkness and discomfort of imprisonment because they have rebelled against God and offended people in power, Yhwh breaks the prison doors and brings them out. If people are afflicted and low, unable to eat and near death, Yhwh heals and restores. If they are threatened at sea by a mighty storm, Yhwh stills the storm. In general, Yhwh can turn fruitful land into desert, but can also turn desert into fruitful land and decimated into manifold. And this increase is the result of Yhwh's blessing, the closing line asserts. Like Psalm 104, in the end Psalm 107 thus makes links with Genesis 1, and like Psalm 104 it also makes the point that God's acts at the Beginning continue in people's experience. God blessed at the Beginning and commissioned people to increase. God blesses now and makes them become many.

The experience of illness and the threat of death to which Psalm 107:17-22 refers is one that comes to people in general, though the other afflictions in the psalm are expressed otherwise. The first recalls the story of Israel on the way from Egypt to the promised land (Ps 107:4-9). The second recalls the experi-

---

[94]Unless this line continues the picture of the animals and denotes the presence of "no plague nor abortion nor bellowing in our broad meadows" (Leslie C. Allen, *Psalms 101—150*, rev. ed., WBC [Nashville: Thomas Nelson, 2002], p. 359). The last word is the problem in this interpretation, for there is no other text where it clearly refers to fields rather than the streets of a city. Kraus (*Psalms 60—150*, p. 540) seems to relate just the first two phrases to animals and to see the last as denoting a human cry in the streets, but this splits the line artificially.

ence of Israel in Babylon (Ps 107:10-16), as Isaiah 40—55 describes it. The fourth takes us back to creation itself, or rather to the theme of the threatening of the world by the forces of disorder that God put in their place before creating the world (Ps 107:23-42). As a whole the psalm implies that the kind of earthly deliverance associated with creation, deliverance from Egypt and deliverance from Babylon are not once-for-all past experiences but paradigmatic ones. Yhwh is involved in the earth now, feeding, freeing, healing and stilling. When people experience such provision, liberation, healing and deliverance, the psalm invites them to see this as God's work in keeping with those patterns, and therefore to acknowledge Yhwh's commitment and Yhwh's wonders and let their thinking be shaped by this acknowledgment. "What are thought to be chance occurrences are just so many proofs of heavenly providence, especially of fatherly kindness."[95] The background of the word *providence* lies in Yhwh's "providing for" Abraham in Genesis 22, a story which shows that providence may be not merely a general commitment to seeing that the world continues to work but a particular provision in situations of need.

An overlapping configuration appears interwoven in Psalm 147, where the first and last sections speak of Yhwh's building up Jerusalem and speaking to Jacob, while the middle section (Ps 147:7-11) focuses more on Yhwh's lordship in the natural realm. That is what enables the animal world as well as the human world to have its fill. A logical and chronological sequence appears, analogous to that in Genesis 1. First God produces clouds, through clouds God produces rain, through rain God produces grass, through grass God feeds animals. The psalm thus recognizes the logical sequential interwoven functioning of nature, yet it sees God as bringing about each stage. Once more God is no watchmaker winding up the universe and leaving it to function. When the next psalm refers to *kol-běhēmâ* (Ps 148:10), it pairs these with other animals and implies that the word refers specifically to cattle with their importance to human beings. But when Psalm 147 refers to animals, the parallel colon brings an unexpected allusion to God's responding to the call of the ravens, whose parents were popularly supposed not to feed their young (cf. Job 38:41), which suggests that these animals are the animals of the wild. Psalm 147 is not concerned with humanity alone and the world as it relates to humanity but with God's provision for all creation. A fortiori, human beings ought not to put their trust in resources that do not impress this God.

Human Responsibility for the World's Security

The oneness of humanity and the world has another outworking. The world

---

[95]Calvin *Institutes* I.v.8.

continues in being despite human inclination to wrongdoing (Gen 8:21). The implication is that human wrongdoing does imperil the world's security. It threatens the world's foundations. It is only because God has decided not to let it overwhelm them that collapse does not follow.

There is a metaphorical sense in which human wrongdoing threatens the world's foundations. The world is founded and kept secure by some moral and social structuring, and wrongdoing imperils that security. There are passages in the First Testament that have been read as themselves making this point. Yhwh says, "Whereas earth and its inhabitants are melting/tottering, I measured out its pillars" (Ps 75:3 [MT 4]): God has given it an order that guarantees it will not collapse. Because Yhwh began to reign, "the world is established. It does not shake. He decides for people with fairness" (Ps 96:10). The attack of the faithless on the upright is a situation "when the foundations are destroyed" (Ps 11:3). When powers of heaven fail to support moral and social order, "all earth's foundations shake" (Ps 82:5).

It would be a nice metaphor to suggest that the "foundations" of the world are both its physical structuring and its moral structuring. But some of the passages, at least, more likely reckon that moral and social disorder imperil the world because they threaten to make its destruction necessary, as Genesis 8:21 implies, unless Yhwh determines otherwise. Fortunately Yhwh does so determine; when the moral and social foundations are imperiled, Yhwh will not let this have its "natural" consequences. The implication of Genesis 8:21 is not that Yhwh's only choice is total destruction or helpless hand-wringing, and that Yhwh chose the latter and is thus committed simply to doing nothing in the face of moral and social disorder in the world. Yhwh will take sovereign action to decide with equity for the peoples and thereby ensure the world's continuing stability (Ps 96:10). When the ineffectiveness of the divine aides imperils earth's foundations by threatening world judgment, Yhwh intervenes in their working and thus keeps earth's pillars steady (Ps 75:3 [MT 4]; 82:5).[96]

A distinctive implication of Genesis 1 over against Genesis 2 is that God created the world a cosmos in which everything has its place. In practice, we do not always experience the world like that. The waters do not remain in their place; the earth does not produce its crops; the animals do not procreate; people do not observe the sabbath. There is need for its order to be maintained, but the doing of that is a human responsibility that we fulfill through the sac-

---

[96]In EVV, Ps 11:3 looks like another passage that uses this metaphor: the attack of the wicked on the upright is a situation "when the foundations are destroyed." But the word for "foundations" (šātôt) is a different one that comes only here. Presumably it comes from šit, which means "put/set." Jerome has leges (laws), which supports the idea that it refers to the destroying of the social structure, but also suggests that it does not actually use the metaphor of making "earth's foundations" shake.

ramental action Leviticus prescribes. Exodus and the Psalms imply that powers of disorder can still overwhelm the world and overwhelm the lives of individuals. The reasserting of order then has to be God's business, and the way human beings lay hold on its possibility is through prayer.

Deliverance and Blessing

God's original act of creation thus finds one form of continuance in God's making nature work. It finds another form of continuance in God's acts in history.

Much twentieth-century study of the First Testament emphasized Yhwh's activity in history, in the once-for-all historical events that brought Israel from Egypt to Canaan and on to being a monarchic state, and in the story of the empires of Assyria, Babylon, Persia and Greece as they impinged on Israel over subsequent centuries. By their nature, the great First Testament narratives focus on this story. While they begin with creation, this is the preamble to Israel's story. In Second Isaiah, conversely, Yhwh's comforting Israel is an occasion for heaven and earth to resound (Is 49:13). In prophecy as in narrative, creation is of interest in connection with what happens to Israel. By their different nature, the Psalms, the Wisdom Books and the teaching in Exodus-Deuteronomy focus more on Yhwh's ongoing activity in the world. Yet even when something closer to an interest in creation in its own right appears here, the predominant background of the question is still the significance of heaven and earth for humanity—as is the case with modern interest in creation. There is no disinterested contemplation of heaven and earth. Part of the point of the scientific enterprise is to enable us to gain a better understanding of who we are—or to support our convictions about who we are.

The First Testament narrative does refer to Yhwh's ongoing activity, and the other books do refer to once-for-all events in history, while the Prophets incorporate both these interests, so that the First Testament does not present these as an either-or. Once-for-all events can be of decisive importance for human experience, but all peoples spend most of their lives in "ordinary time," not living through great epoch-making events. Israel lived through the human cycle of birth, growth, work, marriage, parenthood, maturity, responsibility, wisdom, bereavement, senescence and death. They lived through the annual cycle of plowing, sowing, hoeing, reaping, watching, harvesting and rejoicing. If Yhwh was to be a God who related to the actual nature of human life, Yhwh must be a God who relates to that.[97] "Deliverance is Yhwh's; your blessing is on your people" (Ps 3:8 [MT 9]). While deliverance is the center of Israel's story,

---

[97]Cf. Knierim, *Task of OT Theology*, p. 176.

the Torah is framed by two books in which God's blessing is the dominant theme.[98] God delivers in order to fulfill the original purpose of blessing. "He who has been saved will one day thank God for his blessing."[99]

Yhwh is indeed both the savior and the giver of this life's good things, the lord of both history and nature. Hosea handles a situation in which people are inclined to assume that it was the Masters (the "Baals"), not Yhwh, who ensured that their grain ripened and their vines and olives produced wine and oil (e.g., Hos 2:8 [MT 10]). Yet Hosea's response is not to remind the people that Yhwh was the creator. It is to remind them that Yhwh was the one who had brought them out of Egypt (Hos 2:15 [MT 17]). Deuteronomy implicitly argues in the same way. People are to bring their firstfruits to Yhwh, and when doing so they are bidden to acknowledge not that Yhwh their God is the creator but that Yhwh their God has brought them into the land they were promised (Deut 26:1-11).[100] We hardly must or can decide whether or not the instruction envisages this happening once for all, on the part of the generation that first enters the land. Deuteronomy will envisage that, but it will also envisage every subsequent generation identifying with this experience. It is of this that their firstfruits provide evidence. The God of whom the First Testament speaks is one who relates to the whole of life and the whole of the world.[101]

By the end of the twentieth century, scholarship had learned that point well enough for us now to be subject to "a temptation to pan-creationism (like an earlier pan-covenantalism)."[102]

Nature and History

Modernity sometimes sets over against each other "nature" and "history." Nature is a realm of consistency and order. It may issue in surprises, but we can often predict what it will produce, and retrospectively, at least, even surprising natural events can be shown to reflect recurrent patterns of cause and effect. History reflects once-off decisions by human beings and chance collocations of circumstances. It is a realm in which we have less expectancy of finding laws at work. It is less amenable to prediction, even if with 20/20 hindsight we may

---

[98]Cf. Claus Westermann, *Blessing in the Bible and the Life of the Church* (Philadelphia: Fortress, 1978), pp. 29-30. See further *OTT* 1:288-93.

[99]Zimmerli, *The OT and the World,* p. 39.

[100]See Gerhard von Rad, "The Theological Problem of the Old Testament Doctrine of Creation," in *Problem of the Hexateuch,* pp. 131-43 (see p. 132) = pp. 177-86 (see p. 178) in *From Genesis to Chronicles.*

[101]On the factors that encouraged neglect of creation theology in the twentieth century, see Fretheim, *God and the World in the OT,* pp. ix-xi.

[102]Walter Brueggemann, "Jeremiah: *Creatio in Extremis,*" in *God Who Creates,* ed. William P. Brown and S. Dean McBride (Grand Rapids: Eerdmans, 2000), pp. 152-70; p. 153.

again be able to see why an event "had" to happen. On the other hand, disciplines such as sociology, psychology and economics presuppose that there are regularities and patterns to be discovered within human behavior and decision making, while Einsteinian science has drawn our attention to the contingent within nature. In the First Testament, too, "the aim of creation is history," in the sense of "the history of the covenant of grace." Moving from creation to what follows involves no transformation into something else; history itself begins with creation.[103]

The First Testament can see both "natural" and "historical" events as brought about by God, but it then distinguishes between the ordinary and the extraordinary, and between the ordinary and the especially significant. In considering the human, like the social sciences it looks for patterns and regularities in human experience; this interest is characteristic of Proverbs. The notion of law applies to the realm of human experience as much or as little as it does to the realm of nature. But both the ordinary and the extraordinary reflect God's involvement, and in this respect the First Testament invites us to rework both our understanding of nature and our understanding of history. Yhwh works both in cyclic time and in historical time.[104]

In the First Testament, "the world lies open to God."[105] Both the abstraction "nature" and the abstraction "history" are inclined to obscure that truth, as we view them as separate realms unfolding by other dynamics—the dynamic of nature that comes from its own inherent energy or the dynamic of history that comes from the energy of human beings. Proverbs provides a vivid illustration of the way the First Testament holds these two realms together as it portrays wisdom as the means by which rulers exercise their power (Prov 8:15-16) and also as the One who stood alongside Yhwh through the process of the world's creation (Prov 8:22-31). Nature and history are thus both realms in which God is active, but over against Greek and Roman narrative, Israelite narrative is distinctive for the systematic way it interweaves explanation of events in terms of human causality and of divine causality.

According to Ludwig Köhler, "History is under God's management. . . . All history has its source in God, and takes place for God."[106] If this were so, we

---

[103]Barth, *Church Dogmatics*, III/1:59-60.

[104]See Knierim, *Task of OT Theology*, pp. 192-98.

[105]Gerhard von Rad, "Some Aspects of the Old Testament World-View," in *Problem of the Hexateuch*, pp. 144-65 (see p. 154) = pp. 205-22 (see p. 212) in *From Genesis to Chronicles*.

[106]Köhler, *Old Testament Theology*, p. 93; quoted by Gerhard von Rad, "The Beginnings of Historical Writing in Ancient Israel," in *Problem of the Hexateuch*, pp. 166-204 (see pp. 170-71) = pp. 125-53 (see p. 128) in *From Genesis to Chronicles*. Von Rad adds, "the real actors in the drama are neither nations nor kings nor celebrated heroes." This seems to underestimate the importance of nations and kings and heroes.

would expect to read a different story. History does not look like a story that comes from God, at least not from a God with the qualities of Yhwh. In its understanding of the broad sweep and destiny of history, the First Testament indeed emphasizes the fulfillment of Yhwh's will, but its account of this same broad sweep of history implies that Yhwh's will is continuously frustrated, even if it is certain of ultimate fulfillment. Yhwh sets constraints for history; it is not allowed to get finally out of hand and frustrate the ultimate divine purpose to bring into being a good world. But most events happen independently of Yhwh's actual will. Conversely, in its account of the details of history, the First Testament emphasizes the fulfillment of human wills. Yet its account also indicates that Yhwh is capable of intervening in such a way as to bring about events that run quite against human or natural logic—as in the deliverance of the Israelites from the Egyptian army at the Red Sea or the affliction of Saul by an evil spirit or bad temper. Or Yhwh may act behind the scenes so that "events unwind . . . according to the laws of their own nature" while at the same time fulfilling Yhwh's will.[107]

In this connection, Yhwh possesses vast "natural" reserves of snow and hail, lightning and destructive winds to call on from time to time (Job 38:22-24; cf. Ps 33:7; 135:7; Jer 10:13). The cosmos has its "times" as well as its "ways" and its "places" for such things. In speaking of the "times" of snow and hail, lightning and wind, one might have had in mind the working of the "seasons," but here the "times" are political rather than natural—they relate to war and battle.[108] The cosmos has "times," regular times for pregnancy and birthing and occasional times for calamity and battle. It is geared to serve historical and existential needs. Both nature and history can be outworkings of Yhwh's sovereignty and thus both have their times, the times that Yhwh can determine from time to time.

Creation and Politics

Psalm 33:1-5 urges people to make noise and music for Yhwh, because "Yhwh's word is upright and all his work happens in truthfulness." What kind of word is *upright?* Yhwh's "word" includes Yhwh's "promise" (Hebrew has no separate word for "promise"), and promises could be the kind of words that one would characterize as upright or reliable. That fits with the declara-

---

[107]Von Rad, "Beginnings," in *Problem of the Hexateuch,* p. 201 = p. 151 in *From Genesis to Chronicles.*

[108]Hail in particular is a war motif (Josh 10:11; Is 30:30); hailstones can be pictured as Yhwh's weapons, in the same way as thunder and lightning. Snow is a wonder, but not a war motif; winter is not the season for war (2 Sam 11:1), and snow does not provide a military image. So the line about trouble and war likely refers only to the hail and not to the snow of the preceding colon.

tion that Yhwh's work happens in truthfulness; the deeds faithfully fulfill the
words. A word of command is also "upright" insofar as it commissions an upright deed, and that too will generate truthful deeds. Yhwh's command insists
on events in the world being upright, and Yhwh's promise makes a commitment that this will be so. To put it another way, Yhwh is one who is "dedicated
to the faithful exercise of authority"—or as translations traditionally put it,
Yhwh "loves justice and righteousness" (Ps 33:5). Here the exercise of authority is Yhwh's own rather than that which Yhwh also expects from human beings, though this will follow. Faithful exercise of authority is a principle of
Yhwh's working in the world. The psalm describes the outworking of those
statements about Yhwh's word and attitude in an outrageously extravagant
fashion. Yhwh works in a way that *always* manifests truthfulness, so that the
whole earth is *full* of evidence of Yhwh's commitment.

How so? Is it that world history is thus full—Yhwh is so active in world history? But *is* world history full of Yhwh's commitment? In what sense? Or is it
that the created world is so full—the created world works in a way that evidences Yhwh's faithfulness and commitment? That can also raise questions,
though perhaps not as many.

So Yhwh's plan and intention for the world is to see that events there are
characterized by uprightness and truthfulness. Yhwh is committed to a faithful execution of this intention. It necessarily follows that a people whom Yhwh
chooses to be a personal possession will have a particular experience of
Yhwh's commitment and truthfulness. But this experience can by no means be
confined to them: it is a feature of Yhwh's involvement in the world as a
whole.[109]

Psalm 33 will be centrally concerned with Yhwh's faithful exercise of sovereignty in history, but before going on to work out the implications of that, it
notes the basis of this declaration, which lies in the fact that Yhwh created the
heavens and the earth at the Beginning (Ps 33:6-9). The "word" that operates
in upright fashion now is the "word" by which Yhwh gained and expressed
control of the heavens and earth at the Beginning. To be more precise, the reference back to the Beginning is not merely a general reference to creation but
a reference to sovereignty. The heavens came into being because Yhwh spoke
a word of command, which specifically exercised sovereignty over the army
that lives in the heavens. The planets and the stars might seem to have power
of their own, but actually they are subordinate to Yhwh. The point about sovereignty continues in the declaration that Yhwh exercised control over the waters and the deeps, with their famous potential for devastation. The earth, too,

---

[109]On Ps 33, see further *OTT* 1:55-61.

came into being in response to Yhwh's word—specifically, a word of command, to which in response the earth "stood" (to attention/in attendance?). On the part of its inhabitants, the appropriate reaction is to be overwhelmed by a respectful awe.

So the manner of God's creation of the world is the undergirding of the statements about history that precede and follow.[110] Yhwh asserted sovereignty at the Beginning in such a way as to gain control of negative forces in the world, and asserts sovereignty in history in a way that coheres with that in its commitment to uprightness and the faithful exercise of authority. The way Yhwh is involved in history is thus a continuation of Yhwh's involvement in creation. It is a logical continuation and a morally inevitable one.

In describing the outworking of this sovereignty, Psalm 33:10-22 emphasizes its negative aspect: "Yhwh has thwarted the nations' plan, frustrated the peoples' intentions." But this emphasis offers good news for little peoples like Israel. When nations are planning something that works against Yhwh's purpose, Yhwh is quite capable of frustrating their plan. On the other hand, when the nations' potential victims are concerned to avoid becoming actual victims, this desire may also be vulnerable to Yhwh's sovereignty. They may be tempted to reckon that the key to survival is the quality of their own military potential. But this is not so. "No king delivers himself through the magnitude of his army. . . . The horse is a vain hope for deliverance" (Ps 33:17). The key is that sovereignty of Yhwh, the fact that "Yhwh's eye" is on them and is committed to them, along with the responsive orientation of their lives to Yhwh. The question is whether they are people who "revere him," people who "base their hope on his commitment." It is this that makes the difference when they need someone "to rescue their life from death and keep them alive when food is gone" (Ps 33:18-19). It thus applies not only to directly military questions, but also to the question of whether the people have enough to eat. The context suggests that the psalm refers to the food shortage that results from invasion and siege (e.g., 2 Kings 6:25; 25:3; Lam 2:19), though one might generalize it.

Nature and Israel's History

Yhwh's creation of heaven and earth thus undergirds the psalm's encouragement for peoples under attack (and its warning to them). Psalm 33 needs no eschatological hope for the implementing of Yhwh's purpose in the world. It believes that this purpose has already been implemented at creation, and all that is needed is for Yhwh from time to time to protect the world from the frustrating of that purpose by nations that desire to thwart it. The guarantee that

---

[110]Cf. Knierim, *Task of OT Theology*, pp. 208-9.

this thwarting will not happen is the fact and the manner of creation. The creation implemented Yhwh's purpose at the Beginning and ensures that this purpose will stand. (Perhaps the increasing assertiveness of the empires as history proceeds—Assyria, Babylon, Persia, Greece, Rome, Turkey, Britain, the United States—required a reconsideration of that assumption. It comes to be true that "Yahweh's own plan is more effective in bringing the plans of the nations to naught than in implementing the order of his creation in or through human history, or in reintegrating human history into the order of his creation."[111] As the visions in Daniel suggest, in response to the existence of these empires Yhwh will have to go in for a new assertion of sovereignty in order to implement divine rule.)

Yhwh's plan and intentions thus confront and defeat the nations' plans and intentions, and implement the moral commitments that provide the psalm's opening reasons for praising Yhwh.

It was as one sovereign over heaven and earth that Yhwh acted in Israel's experience. Yhwh is great, greater than all gods as one who acts with total effectiveness "in the heavens and on the earth, in the seas and all deeps" and as "the one who struck Egypt's firstborn" (Ps 135:5-8). If the one God is lord of political events and of natural events, one might expect the two to mirror each other. So when Israel left Egypt, "the sea looked and ran away, Jordan turns round, the mountains skipped about like rams" (Ps 114:1-4). The psalm is talking about the once-for-all events whereby Yhwh delivered Israel from Egypt and brought it into the land, but these events are portrayed in metaphor in a way that heightens nature's involvement. The Red Sea runs away. The Jordan not only stops but goes into reverse. The mountains not only shake but skip, and the psalm goes on to invite earth to join it in whirling[112] before "the one who turns rock into a pool of water, flintstone into a spring of water" (Ps 114:7-8). The psalm might have seen the Sea as the embodiment of the dynamic powers that God defeated before creation (cf. Is 51:9-10), but it forswears this move. It draws attention more broadly to the way the story of Israel's deliverance from Egypt, provision in the wilderness and entering into the land intrinsically interweaves these with God's involvement in nature. Without that involvement, there would be no beginning, middle or end to the story of deliverance. So it is appropriate that nature, along with nations, should respond to it.

These events involve signs, portents and wonders in nature. Those three

---

[111]Cf. ibid., p. 209.

[112]The verb *ḥûlḥîl* usually means "writhe" in travail, but in the context of vv. 4 and 6 might here mean "dance" as in Ps 87:7. The reference may be to the land of Canaan: cf. Ps 29, where Lebanon skips.

words overlap in meaning, though one can note some approximate differences between them.[113] Signs can be ordinary or extraordinary; the point about them is that even if they could have been "natural," ordinary events, they have significance attached to them. Yhwh can be manifest through a bush, at least through a burning bush—fire is a common means through which Yhwh is manifest. Yhwh is manifest in the wind, the *rûaḥ*. Yhwh is manifest in the thunderstorm. Commonly the attaching of special significance to a "natural" event happens before they take place rather than retrospectively. God or God's representative declares that some ordinary or unusual phenomenon will have special meaning. In Israel's history, the disasters that come upon Egypt as the Pharaoh resists pressure to let the Israelites leave his land are a series of signs. However ordinary or extraordinary they are, they gain their significance from the fact that Yhwh declared they would happen and declared what they would signify. Signs need not be bad news; the rainbow is the parade example of a beneficent sign, a declaration of God's commitment to the world. But the disasters that come on the Egyptians are also portents, and other events in nature can indeed be carriers of bad news (cf. Joel 2:30-31 [MT 3:3-4]). Wonders are undeniably extraordinary events that have been similarly announced ahead of time, events such as the Red Sea deliverance. But they are not confined to past history. "Yhwh will make the majesty of his sound heard and make the descent of his arm seen, in angry fury and devouring fiery flame, cloudburst and downpour and hailstone." Thus, "because of the sound of Yhwh, Assyria will shatter" (Is 30:30, 31).

Nature Reverberates

In delivering Israel, Yhwh thus proves to be the "wonder worker" who "made known your might among the peoples" as lord of nature (Ps 77:14 [MT 15]). But whereas Exodus and Psalm 114 have dynamic forces of water draw back when confronted by Yhwh, Psalm 77:16-20 [MT 17-21] speaks not of the parting of waters but of the pouring down of waters. A great storm brings whirling wind and thunder and lightning, and shakes the ground. Then at the end the description reverts to one that could be based on the kind of picture offered by Exodus, with Yhwh making it possible for the people to go through the sea, led by Moses and Aaron. As Israelites who sang this psalm pictured what actually happened, they thought in terms of the dividing of waters, but in this psalm they utilize the imagery of storm as a figure for what happened. It is a theological figure, for it presupposes that Yhwh is the God of nature, the God of storm. When we experience wind, storm, thunder, lightning, flood and

---

[113]See Robinson, *Inspiration and Revelation in the OT*, pp. 34-43.

ground shaking, we are experiencing the reverberations of Yhwh's passing by. So the psalm makes a polemical statement, perhaps two, and also in consequence makes one or two substantial ones. It is Yhwh, not Baal, whose presence and power reverberate in the storm. Yhwh is the one real power on earth and in heaven. The recurrent storm, and not only the occasional political event, reflect the presence and power of Yhwh. Yhwh is the lord of nature.

But Yhwh's acts in nature do not compel recognition. Despite the reference to Yhwh's might being "made known," the psalm goes on to recognize that "your way was in the sea . . . but your footprints were not acknowledged" (Ps 77:19 [MT 20]; both times the verb *yāda'*). People only hear wind and see waters parting, or hear thunder and see storm and lightning and feel ground shaking. The only footprints they see are those of their leaders. It is because these leaders have told them that Yhwh has promised to deliver them that they experience deliverance or storm as Yhwh's act and not a freak natural event. This may be especially significant in the setting of the psalm, for it is actually a lament. At present God is not acting in the way these lines describe, and their purpose is to remind the psalmist and God of how things once were and how by implication they are supposed to be. The psalm is also a reminder that the person praying has to look for the invisible indications that God is acting and has to be prepared to read nature as reflecting God's activity.

The pattern of Israel's subsequent experience also involves acts of Yhwh that are accompanied by signs that it is the God of heaven and earth who is acting. Psalm 68:7-10 [MT 8-11] also speaks of the earth shaking and the heavens pouring rain when God strode out before Israel, but then goes on to speak in the yiqtol of God spreading about rain in abundance and establishing the land with good things for the weak. These verbs would encourage worshipers to see the pattern of events at the Beginning repeated in their own experience. Once again the talk in terms of a storm that makes the earth shake offers a metaphorical description of an event that in the narrative involved no actual storm. Only once in the narrative books is there any hint of a storm coinciding with Yhwh's acting in events, in Judges 5:20-21, and that allusive reference comes in a poetic celebration of the event; the accompanying prose story in Judges 4 makes no reference to it. Here, too, earth shaking and storm have become motifs in accounts of Yhwh's appearing in order to intervene in events, perhaps because they were so in Canaanite stories about Baal.[114] As in Psalm 77, utilizing these motifs declares the conviction that Yhwh is the real God of nature. Yet it might be impossible to sustain this conviction unless people did experience the activity of God in actual fierce storms with their thunder and

---

[114]Cf. the comments in section 7.2 "The Realm Below."

lightning and the earth slips that flooding can bring.

In Mediterranean climates, the winter rains are both an indispensable bless-ing and a great threat, and Psalm 68 moves seamlessly between these two as-pects of them. In making that once-for-all journey from Sinai to Canaan, accompanied by the people, God shook the earth, but God also established the earth in Canaan.[115] In making that journey, God poured down rain that could flood land and people away, but God also abundantly watered this land, in the manner of a farmer watering the land that is his personal possession (Ps 68:7-10). God's needy people thus experience the "good things" that Yhwh pro-vides (as, e.g., Ps 34:10, 12 [MT 11, 13]; 104:28). Yhwh is one "who gives rain, early and late rain at its time, watches over for us the weeks appointed for har-vest" (Jer 5:24).

The First Testament thus speaks of Yhwh's thundering in three connections. The thunderstorms that people experience from time to time are reminders of Yhwh's awesome power in nature. Occasionally such thunderstorms have co-incided with moments of crisis and thus become means of Yhwh's delivering the people and bringing calamity on its foes. For both reasons they are thus signs of deliverance and calamity, as well as metaphors for God's acts in deliv-erance and punishment.

Restoration in History and in Nature

The community's restoration comes about on the same basis. Psalm 126 looks back to a time when "Yhwh showed his greatness in acting with us" (gādal hiphil; cf. 1 Sam 12:24) and the nations were astonished and "we were people rejoicing," laughing and shouting, as when Yhwh "did great things" at the ex-odus (cf. Ps 106:21). But it is actually looking back not to that initial deliverance of the people, but to a subsequent memorable moment when "Yhwh restored the fortunes of Zion" and "we were like people dreaming/people gaining health."[116] Having recalled that great occasion, the psalm asks God to do it again: "Restore our fortunes, Yhwh."[117] It perhaps suggests a time in the Sec-ond Temple period. The concrete outworking of God's turning will be some-thing that looks like the flowing of water in a wadi when the winter rains come, or the flourishing of plant life when there has been irrigation. Indeed, it will *be* something of that kind, to judge from the following lines, which de-scribe how "the people who sow in tears will reap with shouting." In a

---

[115]The verb kûn (hiphil and polel) in Ps 68:9-10 [MT 10-11] suggests the establishing as opposed to the shaking of the earth.

[116]There are two verbs hālam. The one meaning "dream" is more common and fits here, but LXX and Tg. imply it is the one meaning "be healthy."

[117]On this phrase, see section 5.4 "Fortunes Restored."

Canaanite context, weeping as one goes out to sow might suggest a sense that the god's own fate was mirrored in the fate of nature, but there is little ground within the First Testament for inferring such a reference. The plea for restoration rather suggests a context in which the harvest cannot be taken for granted. Weeping is an expression of fear over whether there will be a good harvest. Thus "when they go, they will go with weeping, carrying a bag of seed." But the psalm asks for a restoration that means a bountiful harvest, so that "when they come back, they will come with shouting, carrying their sheaves." Of course that can never be guaranteed. Investing precious seed, upon which the community's future life depends but which will seem to die, is always an act of faith and hope and anxiety and fear.

Psalm 147 similarly urges praise of Yhwh as "builder of Jerusalem," one who "gathers the outcasts of Israel." It then goes straight on to describing Yhwh as "healer of the broken-hearted, bandager of their wounds," one who restores the wounds of body and spirit. Yhwh is also one who "counts the number of the stars, gives them all their names"—at first, a more surprising transition, but one that reflects the link made in Isaiah 40:25-31. The restorer of people and city is able to be that on the basis of being the controller of the stars that shape the nations' destinies. This is the "God of stars and broken hearts."[118] Of course the psalm speaks larger than life, as the use of participles make possible. The gathering of the outcasts of Israel is certainly unfinished, and so are other features of the psalm. Yhwh has shown the capacity to do the things that the psalm speaks of, but most are incomplete. Israel still needs Yhwh to be "restorer of the weak, caster down of the faithless to the ground" (Ps 147:6). But Yhwh's power as creator is the guarantee that Yhwh can fulfill these descriptions.

At the climax of a sequence of declarations of intent to restore Israel, Yhwh issues a further command: "rain, heavens above; skies are to pour faithfulness, earth is to open and deliverance blossom, faithfulness is to spring up, all at once" (Is 45:8). Here the cosmos is not merely responding in praise to the restoration it sees Yhwh bringing about; it is the means whereby that deliverance comes about, its agent. Creation and salvation, nature and deliverance, are thus integral aspects of one whole. The world's creation was an expression of grace designed to introduce a story of faithfulness, but that purpose aborted. Israel's creation was brought about with the same intent but led to the same disappointment. Acts of destruction undertaken against Israel have had negative effects on the world of nature, and the restoration of Israel is to be accompanied by the blossoming of nature. Indeed, the world can be the means of

---

[118]Allen, *Psalms 101—150*, p. 380.

Israel's restoration. The cosmos is itself an expression and an embodiment of Yhwh's faithfulness and therefore can be Yhwh's agent in showing faithfulness to Israel (*ṣedeq*) and in generating faithfulness in Israel (*ṣĕdāqâ*). Yhwh's involvement in nature and in the story of Israel is so much one activity that the language of either can be applied to the other.

Yhwh's activity in nature may be something like the wielding of a club (and on Yhwh's own land), but it may be an act of commitment (Job 37:13). Nature is a means of bringing punishment upon Jonah, but it is also a means of his deliverance (Jon 1:17—2:10 [MT 2:1-11]). Yhwh "assigns" a large fish to swallow Jonah and transport him safely back to land, and then speaks to it to make sure it knows when to vomit him out. Apparently Yhwh does not specially create this fish. The form of expression suggests that it is part of nature that is as such there to serve Yhwh, and the saving and transporting of Jonah is simply the next task to which it is commissioned.

7.4 The Ambiguity of Life in the World

There is an irreducible ambiguity about life in the world. The world as God created it, rules it and manages it is full of surprises. It is not at all what we would have made it. When some scholars urge that it looks as if it was designed by someone, other scholars retort that there is just as much evidence to the opposite. It is full of incongruity and oddity as well as majesty and splendor.[119] Insofar as darkness is a negative, Yhwh is one who brings light, yet darkness itself can be a positive. Nature is a positive, a means of Yhwh's blessing people, but also a means of bringing trouble. Creation issues from Yhwh's creative action, but from the beginning there have been elements within the created world that have asserted themselves over against Yhwh. Strange creatures within the created world symbolize or embody dynamic power asserted against Yhwh. But Yhwh is committed to bring ambiguity to resolution and the world to its destiny.

Darkness Giving Way to Light

Yhwh is sovereign over darkness. But is Yhwh sovereign over it as something positive or wholly negative?

In Genesis 1, darkness is the backdrop against which the positive image of light emerges. It is light that is "good." Job's understanding corresponds with that of Genesis. The wonder of each day is that night, with its deathly, even preternatural gloom, gives way to the joyful brightness of light in a daily repetition of that moment when God first said, "Let there be light." Job just wishes

---

[119]See further Habel, *Book of Job,* pp. 534-35.

it had not done so on the day of his conception (Job 3:4-6).

"Since your days began, have you given orders to morning, told dawn its place?" Yhwh later asks Job (Job 38:12). The question does not merely concern the material working of the cosmos. Yhwh wakes the dawn "so that it might take hold of earth by its fringes and faithless people might be shaken out of it. Earth changes like clay under a signet and they stand out like a garment.[120] From faithless people their light holds back and their raised arm breaks" (Job 38:13-15). Daylight has the capacity to expose faithlessness and bring the punishment of the faithless. Yhwh's questions assume a link between the material, the moral and the experiential worlds because Yhwh is lord of all three. Yhwh dispels the literal darkness and thereby dispels the darkness in which the faithless hide, and thus terminates their time of enjoying light in the sense of happiness and successful exercise of power over people. Yhwh plans the workings of heaven and earth so as to achieve specific purposes, making the natural world work in a moral way. Darkness is the realm of wickedness and death; Yhwh lives in the realm of light, and thus light reflects Yhwh. The point is another marker of continuity from Job 38:1-11, where Yhwh emphasizes that creation involved setting limits to the aggressiveness of the sea. Here that divine control is exercised day by day as well as at the Beginning, over the raised arm of the faithless as well as over the onward reaching of the sea.

Job's friends would nod, thinking that this applies to Job in his supposed secret wrongdoing, but in due course it will become clear that the argument works the other way. If Job were a wrongdoer, God could have exposed him. Even with the friends' help, God has not done so, so Job is not a wrongdoer. Yhwh is more interested in getting Job to nod, because Job's own argument flowed from an awareness that the friends are wrong. Job has declared that God is not active in bringing moral light in the world and terminating the light of the faithless (e.g., Job 21). It is key to the address through chapters 38-41 that Yhwh is indeed so active and that Job must recognize this even if it does not work out in his own experience. He is challenged to let the workings of the physical cosmos be a clue to the workings of the metaphysical cosmos and thus to believe that the latter also works out in a moral way. There *is* night and Job has been living through it. Yhwh wills there to be a realm of darkness that can be a cover for faithlessness, but does not let night last forever.

In Job 38:16-21 Yhwh continues to question Job concerning light and darkness, now not about whether he is sovereign over them but about his knowl-

---

[120]Vv. 13-14 interweave at least two images. Earth's mountains and valleys are like the folds in a garment or bedcover, or the undulations made in wax by a signet or seal. These folds or undulations in the earth are brought into light by the rising sun, so nothing can escape being exposed and shaken out.

edge and experience of them, though the questions presuppose that the former depends on the latter. This knowledge and experience specifically relates to darkness and light in far-off realms. A fortiori, shortcoming there would imply the same in connection with heaven and earth as a whole. God asks about the deepest reaches of the sea, and beyond that Sheol itself, the place of deep darkness. The questions imply that Yhwh has been there, seen that and understood that. Job has pontificated about death and Sheol (e.g., Job 3:16-19), but he does not know what he is talking about. Yhwh does. If Yhwh does not do wonders in Sheol, it is not because of lack of access. There are "ways" round the cosmos, channels by which it works, and Yhwh knows these.

Darkness and Death as Part of Yhwh's Realm

Beyond this, Job 38:16-21 suggests a contrary symbolism. Light and darkness both have rooms beyond the eastern and the western horizon, from which they emerge, morning (cf. Ps 19:5) and evening. Here there is less implication of an antithesis between the realm of darkness and the realm of Yhwh. Not only is there an official "way" to where light dwells, but there is also a "place" for darkness in the structuring of this ordered cosmos. Yhwh is personally surrounded by deep darkness (Ps 18:11) and can give a positive significance to darkness in the alternating pattern of life on earth: Yhwh makes darkness as a time for the animals to come creeping out (Ps 104:20).

An Egyptian hymn to Aten has many parallels with Psalm 104; we are not clear whether there is a direct relationship between the two.[121] A major difference appears in the way they speak of darkness. Aten is the sun god; in Psalm 104 the sun is simply a part of Yhwh's creation. The psalm mentions the moon first, and thus opens up the possibility of a positive theology of night and darkness. In the Aten hymn, night is simply a time from which this god is absent. That is also a point at which Psalm 104 differs from Genesis 1. There are a number of parallels between the two, and again we do not know whether there is a direct relationship between them. In Genesis Yhwh is of course lord of the realm of darkness, but it does not expound a positive view of darkness in the manner of Psalm 104. There, both day and night have a positive place within Yhwh's creation.

The same is true of Leviathan and of death itself. It was in wisdom that Yhwh made the world and all that is in it, and the wise creation includes the

---

[121]If there is, von Rad implies that such material that is not "wholly original to Yahwistic belief" is somehow less central to a study of First Testament Theology: see "Theological Problem," in *Problem of the Hexateuch*, p. 140 = p. 184 in *From Genesis to Chronicles*. I assume that the psalm's acceptance into the First Testament means that in principle it has the same status as any other part.

strange creatures of the sea, and specifically Leviathan, now no threat to the order of the world (Ps 104:24-30). Indeed, the psalm eventually makes an astonishing declaration about the nature of Yhwh's involvement with everything. As the creator, Yhwh is not only the life-giver but the life-withdrawer. God gives, but also hides the face. God takes away breath as well as bestowing it and renewing the face of the ground. Apparently this, too, is an aspect of the wisdom with which Yhwh made the world and which Yhwh continues to express in it. The psalm again underlines the oneness of humanity with the animal world when it describes all animals as it might describe human beings: created through the sending out of God's breath (rûaḥ), dismayed when God's face hides and returning to the dirt when they die (Ps 104:27-30). The fact of death might well make the world long for a renewal and transformation that broke the cycle of life and death, along the lines suggested by Romans 8:18-23, but there is no suggestion that the cycle of life and death resulted from human disobedience to God, that heaven and earth are implicated in human sin, that they are "fallen."

Indeed, the psalm's hope is that Yhwh may rejoice in creation now, as Yhwh found joy during the original creation process (Prov 8:30). That hope is the more striking given the further description of Yhwh as "the one who looks on the earth and it shakes, who touches mountains and they smoke," and the allusion to human faithlessness with which the psalm almost closes (Ps 104:31-35a). There are indeed problems about the world, but they consist in the fact that its human inhabitants are resistant to God's will in a way that the rest of creation is not.

But problems in such human resistance and problems about the natural world can come to interweave, as they do for Jonah (Jon 1:1-10). A devastating storm assails the boat in which Jonah travels in a bid to evade God's commission and God's presence. Presumably the meteorologists at Jaffa could have explained the storm after the event, but the story also describes it as sent by God, and Jonah knows that it is because of him that the calamity has come upon the boat. As he puts it in his eventual testimony to Yhwh's deliverance, the waves and billows of the sea overwhelmed him. They are natural waves and billows, but they are *Yhwh's* waves and billows (Jon 2:3 [MT 4]). Further, they are the waves and billows of the deep (měṣûlâ), the deep represented by the Red Sea, the seas where Leviathan sports (Ex 15:5; Job 41:31 [MT 23]). It is the flood (nāhār) that overwhelms him. It is těhôm, the deep of Genesis 1:2, that surrounds him. These powers of nature are the embodiments of dynamic forces that could assert themselves against God, but on this occasion their tumult is definitely under God's control. Indeed, he gets rescued by a suspiciously Leviathan-like fish.

Nature as Threat

The world confronts Israel as it confronts us as something of majesty and beauty. This is so on the macro scale, whether we stand on the Golan Heights or on the Horns of Hattin looking across Lake Kinneret, or stand on Mount Carmel or on the Mountains of Gilboa or on Mount Tabor looking at the plains of Jezreel and Esdraelon. It is so on the micro scale, whether we examine a split pomegranate or a snowflake or a Sharon rose. Yet it also confronts us as a threat and a danger. Rains fail to come, or fall in such rushing quantity as to wash away soil and homes and to drown animals and people. Fires consume forests and locusts consume crops. Mosquitoes bring disease and death. An earthquake deep below the ocean generates a tsunami that overwhelms the coasts around and the people who live there. We would like to think that we control nature, but we do not, and neither—it might seem—does God. Nature has a mind of its own, like humanity.

The assumption that nature is a means of blessing and a means of punishment runs through the Torah and the Prophets. Israel enters a good land, one that flows with milk and honey (e.g., Ex 3:8; Num 14:7-8). The people had their origins in shepherding, but the good water supply in Palestine will mean they will also grow wheat and barley as well as vines, figs, pomegranates and olives, while its mineral resources will also enable them to work with iron and copper (Deut 8:8-9). Thus the time when things go well can be defined as the time when everyone is free to live under their vine and their fig tree (1 Kings 4:25). Yet Deuteronomy 28 realistically lists the troubles that will come upon people. As well as illness and epidemic and military defeat, these include various forms of pestilence and drought. Wild animals and reptiles are also a threat. "Nothing could be farther from reality than to imagine that there was a harmonious and balanced relationship between man and nature in Palestine."[122] The heavens and the earth have the potential to disrupt the order that Yhwh wills, to disrupt the order that Yhwh wills for humanity, and to be the vehicles of disaster rather than goodness (*raʿ* rather than *ṭôb*). Yhwh is implicitly committed to keeping such potential unactualized. But on occasion, Yhwh may choose rather to harness this potential so as actually to bring disaster when disaster is deserved.

When Yhwh thunders, this can be good news for Israel, but not always. It can be that "Yhwh roars from Zion, sends out his sound from Jerusalem, and shepherds' pastures mourn, Carmel's peak withers" (Amos 1:2). In Jeremiah 25:30, Yhwh roars from an abode in the heavens (cf., e.g., Ps 18; 29), but here Yhwh's abode is on earth, in Jerusalem (cf., e.g., Joel 3:16 [MT 4:16]). While we

---

[122]Odil Hannes Steck, *World and Environment* (Nashville: Abingdon, 1980), p. 62.

might take Yhwh's roar as the roar of a lion (cf. Amos 3:4, 8), "roaring" can also refer the crashing of thunder (e.g., Job 37:4; Joel 3:16 [MT 4:16]). Yhwh's "giving his sound" can also suggest both lion's roar and thunder's crash (e.g., Ps 18:13 [MT 14]; 68:33 [MT 34]). Amos's continuing words about the effect of this sound on the pastures and the hills points to the latter of these images; Amos is speaking of a manifestation in nature that devastates the world, though he describes it doing so in an unexpected way. The effect of the storm God's arrival is not the blossoming of nature that rain should bring, but the withering of nature.[123] This aspect of its effect is similar to that in Psalm 29, where forests are stripped of their foliage (cf. also the reversing of Is 41:17-20 in Is 42:13-17). And where are the pastures of which it speaks? To what people do these shepherds belong? Amos's hearers might expect that they belonged to people such as Aram and Edom. This is the significance when these verses recur in Joel 3:16 [MT 4:16]. The Yhwh who roars is the one who is a refuge for Israel and is protecting Jerusalem. But in Amos 1:2 this opening verse encapsulates the message of the chapters that follow, and by the same rhetoric. It is Carmel's peak that is affected by Yhwh's thunderous roar, not the peak of some mountain in Moab or Ammon. The word *Carmel* is the last word in the verse, with the same impact and effect as the turn to Israel in Amos 2:6—3:8, after the declarations about the other nations.

Then in Amos 4:6-11, for instance, failure of the rains and thus of the grain harvest is an act of punishment, though one designed to drive Israel to turn to Yhwh. The same was true of blight, mildew and a locust epidemic with their disastrous consequences for crops, and especially for fruit trees, and of epidemics that affected the human and animal population (e.g., Hag 1:5-6, 10-11). Yhwh "summons" nature as a means of punishment.

Nature and Yhwh's Day

Thus Yhwh has a "Day" of disaster that finds periodic realization in Israel's experience, in events such as the fall of Samaria or the fall of Jerusalem, but also a locust plague.[124] The background of Joel is an unprecedented calamity in which locusts of various kinds have systematically devoured the people's fruit trees and crops (see Joel 1).[125] They have thus devastated the people who care for them and depend on them. The countryside is ravaged; the grain is rav-

---

[123]Cf. J. Alberto Soggin, *The Prophet Amos* (London: SCM Press, 1987); see also Hans W. Wolff, *Joel and Amos* (Philadelphia: Fortress, 1977).

[124]On Yhwh's Day, see section 4.2 "Darkness."

[125]I assume that the prophecy refers to a literal natural disaster that has actually happened. But if the disaster has at that moment happened only in the prophet's vision, or if it is a figure for a military invasion, this does not affect the theological implications we infer here.

aged. The priests mourn; the ground mourns. The farmers are dismayed/ wither; the vines, the wine, all the trees of the countryside, grain, water-courses—all wither/are dismayed; joy withers/is dismayed.[126] Yhwh not merely allows the epidemic but causes it. And this is no regular natural disaster that Yhwh causes, but one of overwhelming finality, of the kind that Deuteronomy 28 warns (locusts feature in Deut 28:38). The fall of Jerusalem was a terrible disaster in itself, but also an embodiment of the End, of Yhwh's day (e.g., Lam 2:1, 21, 22). This plague is a sign of the End, as the fall of Jerusalem is in Lamentations. It is an event that will need telling about to future generations, in a grim parody of the way Israelite parents pass on to their children the story of Yhwh's deliverance from Egypt by means of "signs and portents, great and grievous" (Deut 6:20-23). Now there is a locust plague imposed on Israel itself that will need relating not just to children but to grandchildren and great-grandchildren (Joel 1:2-3).

Joel sees a link between this "natural" event and that Day of Yhwh. It is a sign of something else, something much bigger. "Alas for the day, because Yhwh's day is near. It will come like destruction from the Destroyer" (Joel 1:15).[127] In his subsequent warning about Yhwh's Day, Joel either portrays that calamity further or he takes it as an anticipation or warning of another calamity. Joel 2:1-3 goes on to elaborate the way the locust plague adumbrates Yhwh's day. Yhwh speaks on "my holy mountain," urging lookouts to warn people in the city about the terrifyingly disciplined and unstoppable army that is coming, Yhwh's army, coming on Yhwh's day. Once again the picture recalls Yhwh's action against a foreign nation, not least Yhwh's sending a plague of locusts that covered Egypt (Ex 10:1-15), and once again the horror of the prophecy is that this picture is turned back on Israel itself. The effect of this army is to turn a Garden of Eden into a desolate wilderness. It is the realization of "a day of dark and gloom, a day of cloud and darkness." The locust army (or some army that they figure) turns Eden into desolate wilderness. "Before them, earth quakes, heavens shake, sun and moon darken, stars withdraw their brightness." Yhwh gives voice, and who can withstand the huge army that does what Yhwh says? (Joel 2:10-11). Joel's language parallels that of Isaiah 13, and this heightens the effect. Isaiah 13 speaks in such terms about the chilling implications of Yhwh's day for Babylon through the advance of the Persians, coming as Yhwh's army. Indirectly that is good news for Israel itself. Here its implications are chilling for Israel as an unnamed and unidentifiable

---

[126]There are seven verb forms in Joel 1:10-20 that might be forms of *yēbēš* (wither); most might alternatively be forms of *bôš* (be dismayed/ashamed). The paronomasia suggests a link between the withering and dismay on the part of both the land and the people.

[127]"Destroyer" is *šadday*; see section 2.3 "Power and Authority."

force advances on it. The stability of the earth will dissolve, the promises to Noah will be suspended, the creation will be undone. And that is guaranteed by the identity of the army's commander-in-chief.

On the other hand, if people turn round, they may find that Yhwh "spares a blessing" (Joel 2:14). And/or on the other side of calamity Yhwh promises to make the land fruitful again and to restore what the locust plague had taken (Joel 2:18-27). As land and people were one in withering, dismay and mourning, so they will be one in joyful gladness (Joel 2:21, 23).

Yet once more Joel speaks of Yhwh's Day and again pictures it as cosmic catastrophe: "the sun will turn into darkness, the moon into blood" (Joel 2:30-31 [MT 3:3-4]); cf. Joel 3:15 [MT 4:15]). "Heaven and earth tremble" (Joel 3:16 [MT 4:16]). Again he speaks of a day beyond that when "the mountains will drop down juice and the hills flow with milk and all the watercourses flow with water" (Joel 3:18 [MT 4:18]). Like Amos in Amos 5:18-20, Joel has bidden Israel to face that fact that Yhwh's day will mean darkness, not the light they imagine, but he finally lets it mean light again.

Protection from Creation with Its Assertiveness

As well as being a threat, nature can be a pressure and a temptation. Psalm 121 begins with a lifting of the eyes to the mountains and the question "from where will my help come?" "Mountains" are a figure for strength, but the details here are more disputed. Lifting the eyes is not a gesture of fear but a gesture of expectancy or worship or confidence or pleading (e.g., Ps 123:2). The mountains are therefore hardly a threat but rather a potential resource or refuge (cf. Ps 11:1; Ezek 7:16).[128] Indeed, perhaps Jerome and the KJV were right to translate v. 1b "from where my help will/might come."[129] Is the psalmist tempted to look for strength in the wrong place? True security lies in the fact that Yhwh is "maker of heaven and earth." Yhwh is our real "guardian" and our real protection in danger. "The distinctive character of the Old Testament concept of creation comes out clearly here. It ministers not to a theoretical explanation of the universe but to the mastering of a concrete situation in life in a practical way. It represents not a piece of knowledge but a decision to submit oneself to God's creative will and power."[130]

The fact that Yhwh is maker of heaven and earth gives Yhwh the ability to ensure that we do not stumble. No dangers on earth need worry us (Ps 121:2-

---

[128]The reference is too general to suggest either Mount Zion (and in any case the plural is then odd) or mountains as places of illicit worship.

[129]For mē^ʾayin in an indirect question, see, e.g., Josh 2:4.

[130]Artur Weiser, *The Psalms* (London: SCM Press/Philadelphia: Westminster Press, 1962), p. 747.

3). It also gives Yhwh the ability to protect from dangers in heaven such as the killing heat of the sun (the moon is perhaps there just as a makeweight rather than for the sake of reference to lunacy or as reflecting awareness of the power of the moon god) (Ps 121:5-6). As a converse to the promise that God will give us everything "good" is the promise that we will be protected from all that is "bad" and thus will guard our lives. When people leave home to go to work in the fields and when they come back home (and in between), Yhwh guards (Ps 121:7-8).

Correlative to the participial descriptions of God as maker and guardian in Psalm 121, which run together God's activity in bringing the world into being and God's ongoing activity in the world, is a description of our experience in the world that associates it with the way the world came into being. At the Beginning, Yhwh asserted authority over natural forces that could have overwhelmed the world, but surprisingly, it might seem, those forces continue to assert themselves. Psalm 46 thus imagines nature itself in turmoil. Waters roar and seethe, mountains quake and topple. Its picture reflects the experience of a landslide, but that has already become part of the way the imagination envisages the imperiling or dissolution of the natural order. It does not assume that the victory God won before creation was a final victory. The threatening dynamic of the waters in tumult might indeed imperil the created world. Events such as an earthquake or a flood remind people that nature cannot be taken for granted.

But alongside that picture is one of water that delights and refreshes as "a river with its streams rejoices God's city" and of a mountain that "does not topple" (Ps 46:4-5). There is a city that is watered by a many-streamed river like the one in Eden and like the many-streamed Jordan that abundantly waters the city of Dan in the north. The waters below are under God's control and can therefore be a resource and not just a threat. This city on its hill does not topple like the ones in the worshipers' nightmare.

That reflection yields to the imagining of a situation in which nations have "roared" and are threatening Jerusalem like the sea pounding on a vulnerable shore. The destructive forces of nature become the destructive forces of politics. The story of Pharaoh's attack on Israel at the Red Sea (see Ex 15:1-21) and the story of Sennacherib's attack on Judah (2 Kings 18-19) illustrate the kind of moment when the psalm came true in everyday life. Such events are experienced as expressions of earthquake and tidal wave, of earth changing, mountains quaking and toppling, sea roaring and seething. They thus reprise the assertiveness of primeval forces before creation. Yhwh's deliverance of the community is then a reprise of Yhwh's original assertion of authority over these primeval forces. If nations roar, then Yhwh can also. If the earth can assert itself and quake, Yhwh can make it actually dissolve. God not only provides gently and protects firmly but delivers aggressively.

The bad news is that the original divine act of assertion was not final, but the good news is that it can be repeated. No doubt there is a subtle and complicated relationship between the acts. Stories about God asserting authority in primeval times encouraged trust in God at moments of natural disaster or political danger. Experiences of deliverance from natural disaster or political danger confirmed the truth of stories about a primeval victory. The community's worship mediated between these. It encouraged the ongoing declaration that Yhwh once won this victory and still wins this victory, so that the declaration could be made with force when political or natural situations required it to become political or natural reality. It also encouraged people to bring their experiences of Yhwh's natural or political deliverance into relationship with the acknowledgment of the God of heaven and earth so that the latter was not merely a liturgical confession that lacked contact with realities outside worship.

The Origin of Evil in the World

So where does evil in the world come from? In Genesis 3 it issues from an interaction between human beings and a being within God's creation that encourages human beings to disobey God, and they do so. In Genesis 4 evil might seem more straightforwardly human; no serpent appears to tempt Cain, but wrongdoing emerges from inside humanity. Yet there is again some mystery about it. It comes about because sin is crouching at the door like another animal, waiting to fulfill its desires. Human beings are responsible for what they do; no one forces them to do it, yet it does not simply emerge from inside them. This is the clearer in Genesis 6, where evil issues from the intervention of heavenly forces in the world, though Genesis does not explain how there came to be heavenly powers in apparent rebellion against God. We have seen that in Psalm 46 earth's waters roar and seethe, mountains quake at its rising. This self-assertiveness on nature's part did not come about only after human beings asserted themselves over against God, still less as a result of that. The assertiveness embodied in nature antedated creation. Before creating the world, or in the process of doing so, God needed to assert authority over existent dynamic forces and harness them to a positive purpose. Evidently God did not do so in a final way, and they still assert themselves. Indeed, Genesis 1—2 recognize that as created good, the animal and plant world still needed some mastering, and this mastering is humanity's vocation.

So humanity was not originally responsible for nature's assertiveness, but is made responsible for it. Indeed, if there is a cause-effect relationship between the assertiveness of nature and that of humanity, it is the former that brings about the latter (see Gen 3:1). Nature shares with humanity the ambiguity of its relationship with God, and the ambiguity of this relationship is reflected in the ambiguous interrelationship of these two. Both nature and humanity are capable of worshiping and serving; both are capable of resisting and rebelling. Humanity is called to fulfill its own destiny by enabling nature to fulfill its destiny in a way that turns its back on assertiveness and manifests fruitfulness (Gen 1—2). Instead, humanity yields to the assertiveness of the animal world and exploits the plant world, and humanity thus fails to realize its own destiny and hinders nature from fulfilling its own. Humanity was not the original cause of nature's unwillingness to glorify God, but it can now reduce its capacity to glorify Yhwh. "The heavens proclaim the glory of God with less clarity on a smoggy day in Los Angeles than on other days."[131] Conversely, assertive nature's pressure on human security takes humanity's attention away from the praise of God, even if God's subsequent subordination of nature then gives humanity opportunity to move from lament to confession.

Nature assumes that there should be a morality about the way it and its produce are used, and when this is not so, it weeps. The appropriate response to this awareness of nature's is that it should grow thorns and weeds instead of wheat and barley (Job 31:38-40). When humanity's rebelliousness against God brings consequences in the realm of nature (e.g., Is 24:1-7; Jer 12:4; Hos 4:1-3), this may then not simply be because Yhwh wills it, but because nature wills it. In one sense it further reduces nature's fulfillment of its vocation; instead it becomes drawn into its equivalent of God's strange work (cf. Is 28:21). Or to think of it another way, God harnesses nature's potential for disruptiveness and turns it into a means of implementing God's own strange work.

When we pray "Your will be done on earth as in heaven," we imply that heaven is a place where God's desires are fulfilled and that earth is a place where they are not, but both Testaments imply a more complex understanding. On one hand, there are forces in heaven that oppose Yhwh. On the other, on earth we are challenged to commit ourselves to doing Yhwh's will and not to confine ourselves to praying that this might be so. But the Lord's Prayer is realistic in recognizing that it is no good us thinking that we can overcome evil, that through us God's will can be implemented. We await divine action to achieve that. The Lord's Prayer is a prayer, not a disguised New Year's resolution.

Who Can Put Down Evil?

Perhaps dissatisfied with Job's initial response to being questioned (Job 40:1-2), God starts again. Does Job have an arm like God's? Could Job thunder like

---

[131]Fretheim, "Nature's Praise," p. 29.

God? (Job 40:9). Does Job have a big enough temper to let loose on the assertive (gē'eh) and put them down? (Job 40:11-12). The words pick up a claim regarding the original creation, when Yhwh set limits to the sea's assertiveness (gā'ôn, Job 38:11). Yhwh's act back then is the basis for claiming the power to continue to put down assertiveness. Can Job make any such claim? Or can Job trample down the faithless (Job 40:12)? Now the words pick up the claim regarding Yhwh's commissioning of the morning, which flushes out the faithless (Job 38:12-15). Can Job send the faithless off to Sheol? (Job 40:13). His questions have concerned whether God is governing the world in the right way. The right way (sĕdāqâ) is a matter of behaving properly in relation to people with whom one is in relationship, and in this sense Job cannot see that God is acting rightly by him. Yhwh's question is whether Job is himself in a position to do anything about this. Those who can, do; those who cannot do, whine.

To substantiate the point, Yhwh points to two further creatures, bĕhēmôt (Job 40:15-24) and liwyātān (Job 41:1-34 [MT 40:25—41:26]). The former is a straightforward Hebrew word, but it is plural in form and elsewhere refers to cattle (e.g., Gen 1:24-26; 2:20) or to animals in general (e.g., Gen 6:7, 20; 7:2, 8; also Job 12:7; 18:3; 35:11). Only here and in Psalm 73:22 is it an intensive plural referring to one animal, apparently "the beast."[132] In Psalm 73:22 the psalmist confesses to having been bĕhēmôt with God, to having behaved like "the beast" asserting itself against Yhwh. In isolation, the description in Job could suggest an animal such as the hippopotamus, a hugely powerful creature at home in water and impossible for one person to capture, but there is no other evidence that bĕhēmôt was simply a term for a particularly powerful earthly creature.

Translations are also unsure whether to take liwyātān as a proper name, Leviathan (NRSV, JPSV) or as a common noun, the crocodile (NRSV mg.; NEB). But there is no doubt that elsewhere liwyātān is an embodiment of powers asserted against God, pictured as a twisting crocodile or sea dragon. Talk in terms of the past defeat and killing of Leviathan (Ps 74:13-14) is another way of declaring that such dynamic powers were defeated before creation and were defeated at the Red Sea. But they evidently still assert themselves and they can still be aroused (Job 3:8). God has not eliminated them; they are an ongoing reality.[133] Leviathan remains to be defeated at the End (Is 27:1). But in the meantime, humanity can be unfazed by evil. It is not surprising, but neither is it ultimately threatening; its power is under restraint. God has reduced Leviathan to a creature playing in the sea for Yhwh's amusement (Ps 104:26), like Ms. Wisdom playing before Yhwh at creation (Prov 8:30-31)—or might Yhwh

---

[132]The word may alternatively be an unusual (Phoenician) singular form.

[133]See Jon D. Levenson, *Creation and the Persistence of Evil* (reissued Princeton, N.J./Chichester, U.K.: Princeton University Press, 1994).

have shaped Leviathan "to be laughed at" there? Either way, elsewhere playing is not the activity of Leviathan, nor is Leviathan a being to laugh at, and this seems to be a point of the passage. Like the *tannînim* in Genesis 1:21, Leviathan has become merely a creature that Yhwh made and not one to be taken too seriously. The frightening sea serpent becomes a plaything, as the sea with its threatening power becomes only as problematic an entity as a newborn baby (Job 38:8-11). In Job 40, too, Leviathan has been tamed. Perhaps the point of the taming is to gain some benefit from its powers as it is allowed to exercise them, within limits.[134]

If Leviathan is a sea monster that symbolizes power asserted against Yhwh, the same understanding makes sense of "the Beast," which the picture of Leviathan thus clarifies. The Beast is also a fearsome creature that symbolizes and embodies power asserted against Yhwh. Circumstantial evidence that this is the right approach to these two is provided by a fact that we shall shortly consider further, that the First Testament elsewhere speaks of other creatures that seem to be both creatures of the desert and demonic forces. Mysterious, frightening, animate creatures such as these supply a useful way of conceiving of mysterious, frightening, animate forces of evil (to call them personal may be too great a compliment).

The Beast

The Beast is "the first of God's ways" (Job 40:19). Translations usually paraphrase "the first of God's *works*," which is fair enough. Yet the statement is a provocative one, for Yhwh "possessed (?) Wisdom as his first way" (Prov 8:22).[135] The first thing God did before creating anything was to make sure of possessing Wisdom, but apparently the first thing God did after that, before creating the rest of heaven and earth, was to create the Beast. Further, perhaps Wisdom was the first of God's ways not merely in a chronological sense. Wisdom was the most important principle that Yhwh needed to assimilate before creating the world. Is the Beast then the most important of God's works, or the most impressive? The Beast, not Job, is king in God's creation![136]

But the maker of the Beast can also slay it, Yhwh goes on. It is "the first of God's ways; its maker must draw near his sword" (Job 40:19).[137] We have seen that a number of First Testament passages speak of God defeating the assertive

---

[134]So Mary K. Wakeman, *God's Battle with the Monster* (Leiden: Brill, 1973), p. 67.

[135]See *OTT* 1:46-48.

[136]Leo G. Perdue, *Wisdom in Revolt: Metaphorical Theology in the Book of Job*, JSOTSup 112 (Sheffield: Sheffield Academic Press, 1991), p. 226.

[137]The verb *yaggēš* is hiphil (so "draw near," not "draw near with") and jussive (so "must/may," not "does/will/can").

powers before or at creation and at various subsequent points, but that Psalm 104:26 speaks of God making Leviathan to play *(śāḥaq)*. Here in Job Yhwh uses the same verb in describing how "all the wild animals play" near the Beast, which is apparently their lordly protector, though this responsibility does not stop the Beast itself enjoying a doze in the shade by the riverbank (Job 40:20-21). But that opening line is the First Testament's boldest statement regarding a divine sovereignty that extends to making the power that asserts itself against God. It firmly declares that this is no embodiment of disorder that is even momentarily outside Yhwh's control, but a power that always has Yhwh's sword raised over it if it thinks of stepping out of line. The disorder that is present in the world is present because Yhwh made it that way (as, we know, the disorder in Job's life is there because Yhwh made it that way). But Yhwh keeps it firmly within bounds. And there are no further overwhelming forces, no flooding waters, that are greater than the Beast: it is quite relaxed about such pretensions, later lines make clear.

And "God can take it by the mouth with his rings, pierce its nose with his snares" (Job 40:24). God can get control of the Beast.[138] The NRSV takes the line as another of the rhetorical questions that are typical of Yhwh's addresses, but the sentence has no marks of a question. It makes sense as another statement of God's power in relation to the Beast, linking with the first line as a bracket round the intervening description of the Beast's activity. For all the Beast's power, God has no trouble taming it, like a wildlife hunter taming a small animal. The statement about the Beast again recalls the description of Leviathan turned into God's plaything.

But before all that, the very opening line about the Beast is the most enigmatic in its implications: "there is the Beast, which I made along with you" (Job 40:15). The regular *bĕhēmôt* (the domestic animals) and the first human beings were indeed created together, on day six of creation. But what are the implications of drawing attention to the fact? Does it again imply that the Beast need not be taken too seriously, because it was just part of creation like Job? Or that Job is an embodiment of self-assertiveness like the Beast, so Job had better note carefully the way Yhwh relates to the Beast? Or that it is therefore not surprising if the Beast attacks Job? If so, while Yhwh's address makes no allusion to the adversary of Job 1—2, the references to the Beast and to Leviathan express in a different symbolism the acknowledgment that Job's calamities reflect the involvement of hostile heavenly forces in his experience. Like that other symbolism, however, they assert that these forces are under God's control.

---

[138]I have followed the redivision of the lines in Habel, *Book of Job*, pp. 553-54, but I would interpret the last line in the same way on the basis of MT's division.

The Dragon

The account of Leviathan more resembles Job 38—39 in incorporating many of Yhwh's typical questions, though it apparently begins with a sarcastic statement.[139] As God can pierce the Beast's nose with snares (Job 40:24), so—the questioner hypothesizes—I suppose "you can pull out Leviathan with a hook and press down its tongue with a line" (Job 41:1 [MT 40:25]). The interrogation proceeds with a series of variants on the question whether Job can catch Leviathan and make it work for him or carve it up and sell it or turn it into a plaything—see Psalm 104:26 again (Job 41:2-9 [MT 40:25—41:1]). It is Leviathan itself that does the playing/laughing here (śāḥaq again; Job 41:29 [MT 21]). The impressiveness of its strength, like that of a giant crocodile, makes it inconceivable that Job should control it. The questions imply the point that was explicit in the passage about the Beast. What Job cannot do, Yhwh can. Insofar as Leviathan or the Beast are actual animals, Job cannot master them. How much less can he get control of the metaphysical entities they symbolize. This is a key claim within Yhwh's response to Job. Job has implicitly accused Yhwh of not having the powers of disorder under control. That is what his life experience indicates. Yhwh's reply is extremely confrontational, though no more so than Job's challenge, and when friends argue, they can take the risk of doing so in no-holds-barred fashion because they know that the friendship has room for that. Yhwh's reply is not bluster but a challenge to Job to recall the faith that he is committed to, which is supported by what he can see in the world. His faith asserts that Yhwh put the powers of disorder in their place before creation, and nature itself witnesses to that. The sea knows its place, the Beast knows its place, Leviathan knows its place. Job's life experience must not be allowed to belie it.

Yhwh then builds another a fortiori argument on that, though the sequence is jerky. "There is no one brave enough to stir it up: and who can stand before me? Who has confronted me so that I would pay/make peace? Under the whole heavens, things are mine" (Job 41:10-11 [MT 2-3]). Neither Job nor anyone else is going to risk arousing the monster. Nor can Job or anyone else stand before Yhwh (the one who controls this monster) with confrontational questions about the running of the world. Nor can Job or anyone else force Yhwh to deliver answers about why the world is how it is, or to deliver compensation for it or apology for it. Yhwh does not deign to be accountable to this court, and it lacks the power to force Yhwh into account. The court is *under* Yhwh, for goodness' sake, not in authority over Yhwh. Of course this has been exactly Job's complaint in earlier chapters.

---

[139]That is, there is no interrogative in Job 41:1 [MT 40:25] as there are in many following lines.

In due course the questions give way to admiring description of Leviathan reminiscent of the portrayal of the horse, though the description of this fire-breather also makes clear that Yhwh is not talking about a mere hippopotamus or crocodile. The description culminates in the judgment that "it can look at all that stands high; it is king over all the lofty" (Job 41:34 [MT 26]). Leviathan, too, might have been described as "the first of God's works" (cf. Job 40:19). It is not only the other animals' protector but also their sovereign. Yhwh's address thus closes with another implicit a fortiori argument. Leviathan is no sleeping gi-ant. It can stand over anyone who reckons to stand tall, any animal or human being (such as Job?). Perhaps the implication is that it can be Yhwh's agent in putting down all who assert their power and authority and status. Certainly it implies that this being that is a threat to all earthly power is no threat to Yhwh. For all its fearsomeness, like the Beast it is still something Yhwh made (Job 41:33 [MT 25]).

Yhwh's talk of the Beast and the Dragon illustrates the First Testament's striking way of speaking of destructive evil. It implies that phenomena in this world have a correlative reality in a supernatural world and vice versa. In sub-sequent sections we will see how this is also suggested by the way it speaks of the sea and the hydra, or sea serpent, of the snake and the jackal, and of adver-saries and people who do evil. In all these instances, there are literal, physical realities that are a threat to humanity. There are also metaphorical, metaphys-ical or subhuman realities that are such a threat. The link between the two may vary. The physical entity may be the means whereby the metaphysical or sub-human operates, or it may be a symbol for it.

Subhuman Evil

Thus the sea is a body of powerful natural forces that can be a threat in an area such as Mesopotamia as in a country such as Bangladesh. It may be that First Testament talk of the Sea as the embodiment of frightening and destructive power simply reuses talk that emerges from Mesopotamia as a land that is par-ticularly susceptible to flooding. But the sea's frightening dynamic power is apparent on the Mediterranean coast of Israel, while Israelites also knew the threat of tumultuous waters when they experienced flash floods inland. In Ugaritic writings, Sea and River are both quasi-personal powers. The cognate words in Hebrew do appear in the plural to denote the "seas" and "rivers" that are simply the subterranean waters that notionally lie beneath the earth (see Ps 24:2). Here the First Testament demythologizes Sea. But elsewhere it can think of Sea as a quasi-personal entity (e.g., Job 7:12; 26:12; Ps 74:13;[140] 89:9-10

---

[140]Especially if we understand the verb as *pārar* i rather than the (nonexistent?) *pārar* ii.

[MT 10-11]). The same is true of Death, a god for other Middle Eastern peoples, and in the First Testament sometimes an entity that traps, shepherds (in a hostile fashion) and consumes (Ps 18:4-5 [MT 5-6]; 49:14 [MT 15]; Is 5:14).[141]

The same passages that speak of the Sea as a quasi-personal entity also refer to other fearsome Leviathan-like creatures that embody or symbolize dynamic power asserted against God or independently of God. Genesis 1:21 reports that God created the great sea creatures, the *tannînim*, which in Psalm 148:7 are called to praise God. Ezekiel 32:2 derides the king of Egypt as one who fancies that he is a lion but is actually a *tannîn*, apparently a crocodile (cf. *tannîm* in Ezek 29:3). It is the same word that denotes a creature that is a figure for an overwhelming destructive power, analogous to the sea itself, over which God has to assert authority, in Job 7:12; Psalm 74:13 and also in Isaiah 27:1; 51:9. Again, at least part of the background is comparable talk that appears in Canaanite stories about Baal and Anat. The fact that *tannîn* can also denote the snake (Ex 7:9-12; Deut 32:33; Ps 91:13) supports the assumption that the sea monster was snakelike, a sea serpent or sea dragon.

To refer to this overwhelming destructive power, Job 26:13 and Isaiah 27:1 also use the more regular word for a snake, *nāḥāš*. But most references to snakes see them as figures for a harmfulness that is more nearby (Deut 8:15; Prov 23:32; Eccles 10:8; Amos 5:19), perhaps sent by God (Num 21:6-9; cf. Amos 9:3, where the word denotes a sea serpent). Specifically they are figures for human hostility and harmfulness (Gen 49:17; Ps 58:4 [MT 5]; 140:3 [MT 4]; Is 14:29), which can be expressed by means of snake-charming (Eccles 10:11).

All this adds depth to the reference to the snake in Genesis 3:1. In later tradition the serpent in Genesis 3:1 came to be associated with Satan (cf. Rev 12:9), though in Genesis it is simply one of "the wild animals that Yhwh God made." To say that the serpent *is* Satan misses the dynamic of the point that Genesis makes. Paradoxically, while this much-quoted passage does not overtly speak of supernatural rebellion against God, the less-quoted Genesis 6:1-3 does do so. Heavenly beings that once apparently worked with Yhwh in due course worked against Yhwh. Yet the deceptiveness of the serpent's work and its disastrous results might make one suspect the presence of supernatural power behind it (though in a sense such powers are lower rather then higher than us, so that we might designate them subhuman rather than supernatural). And Genesis 3 does overlap with ways the First Testament speaks of forces in rebellion against God. When one considers these other references to the snake, one can see that seeing Satan behind the snake only makes explicit resonances that could attach to the word in the First Testament. It does assume

---

[141]See Wakeman, *God's Battle with the Monster*, pp. 106-8.

that behind our human experience of trouble and evil there can be supernatural entities and forces. Realities that ought to be working in submission to God are working against God instead.

God won a victory over these forces at the Beginning, but this was not a final victory. To claim otherwise would be to ask people to ignore the facts of life. Flood and earthquake, shark and crocodile, snake and coyote, man and woman continue to imperil the ordered life of the cosmos as they assert their destructive power. There are people (or Job can imagine people) who are skilled at rousing Leviathan (Job 3:8). So when Leviathan has been roused, we have to call on Yhwh (or Yhwh issues this summons as a self-call) to reassert the power shown when Rahab was split, the sea serpent slain (Is 51:9-11). If God rebuked the powers of disorder at the Beginning (Job 26:11), God has needed to utter that rebuke on other occasions since (e.g., Ps 18:15 [MT 16]; 106:9) and keeps on needing to do that (e.g., Ps 104:7; Is 50:2; Nahum1:4). So statements about God's having crushed Leviathan stand in the midst of other statements recognizing that dark, hostile forces have overwhelmed the people in the present (Ps 74). If the first is true, how can the second be? If the second is so, how can the first be? Although there would seem to be some illogic here, it corresponds to reality.

Natural and Supernatural

Isaiah 51:9 sets in parallelism with *tannîn,* the sea serpent, that other entity with a name, Rahab.[142] Psalm 89:10 [MT 11] talks of it as being shattered, like Leviathan (cf. Job 9:13; 26:12, alongside the snake). The name Rahab is also used in a more down-to-earth connection, though a different one. In Isaiah 30:7 it is a pejorative name for Egypt, and so also apparently in Psalm 87:4. Although these passages speak of the Egypt of the monarchic period, they recall other passages that see Yhwh's victory over Egypt at the Red Sea as a victory over a monster such as Leviathan (Is 51:9). The fact that the Egypt of the exodus had been identified with the primeval monster would make the monster a natural metaphor for contemporary Egypt in Ezekiel's day (Ezek 29; 32).[143]

Other creatures of the desert are spoken of in analogous ways. The jackal is a creature that lives in once-inhabited desolate places. It thus regularly symbolizes destruction (Job 30:29; Ps 44:19 [MT 20]; Is 13:22; 34:13; 35:7; 43:20; Jer 9:11 [MT 10]; 10:22; 49:33; 51:37). And the word for jackal is *tan,* which recalls *tannîn.* In the company of the jackal in Isaiah 13:21; 34:14 is the goat *(śāʿîr).* Usually these are also simply wild or domesticated animals (e.g., Gen 37:31). But 2 Chronicles 11:15 has Jeroboam appointing priests for the *śěʿîrîm.* The NRSV

---

[142]This Rahab *(rāhab)* is a different person from Rahab in Josh 2 *(rāḥāb).*

[143]Wakeman, *God's Battle with the Monster,* p. 74.

renders "goat-demons"; so also in Isaiah 13:21; 34:14. In the latter passage they come in the company of entities that may simply be frightening animals, such as wildcats and hyenas (?) (*siyyîm, 'iyyîm*). But they also come there in the company of Lilith, a female demon who features in Canaanite and Babylonian texts. The similarity between her name and the Sumerian and Akkadian words for wind (*lil, lilitu*) fits with the fact that she was known as a storm demon. But the Hebrew and Aramaic word for night (*laylâ*) suggested to Jews that she was a night demon: compare the "terror of the night" in Psalm 91:5. Further, in other Middle Eastern texts *lilitu* is a female demon who ensnares men, and she later came to be identified with Adam's first wife.

The First Testament does thus recognize the paradoxical nature of our experience of the world. Much of human life is an experience of reliable order. When we plant apple trees, it is apples that these trees produce. We can calculate the times and the heights of the tide and be sure that it will do as we calculate. If we cut ourselves, we can be sure that blood will flow out. At the same time, sometimes crops fail, tides driven by extraordinary winds engulf oceanside communities, and strange diseases affect a person's blood. Sometimes human beings yield to outlandish deceptions, indulge in stupid acts of violence and fall prey to strange supernatural influences. We experience large-scale destructive forces within nature such as flood, earthquake, hurricane and volcano, and we experience attack from within the animal world. In both cases the precise form of the attack varies according to the part of the world where we live. In the First Testament the main perpetrators of evil are human beings, but evil can also come from elsewhere.

So we experience evil as brought about by other human beings, we bring it about ourselves, and we experience it as brought about by natural forces or by other creatures. But such accounts of evil do not seem to exhaust its nature. Sometimes evil has particular ferocity or deceptiveness or brings about particularly terrible disaster. Its effect exceeds that which human beings seem likely to have intended or achieved, or which can be attributed to impersonal natural forces. It is then that the First Testament speaks of supernatural or subhuman forces operating through human or political or natural means.

Such talk is common in traditional societies and in other ancient cultures, and the First Testament's way of speaking accepts that it is appropriate. Yet "Israel felt itself endangered or oppressed by demons far less than did the other cultures of the ancient Near East"[144] or the communities of which the New Testament speaks. The First Testament puts significant constraints

---

[144]Horst Dietrich Preuss, *Old Testament Theology*, 2 vols. (Louisville: Westminster John Knox/ Edinburgh: T & T Clark, 1995, 1996), 1:258. Cf. Jacob Milgrom, *Leviticus 1—16*, AB (New York: Doubleday, 1991), pp. 42-45.

around talk in these terms. One can easily make too much of supernatural and subhuman forces, and the First Testament avoids doing that. It can portray the great sea creatures as simply creatures that God made, made to play or to be laughed at. In this sense they are not creatures to be taken too seriously. Their power by no means rivals Yhwh's power. In the same way, it usually portrays the nations as simply nations. Egypt is called Rahab to emphasize its insignificance and to encourage Judah to laugh at its pretensions, not to encourage Judah to take it more seriously than it deserves. Yhwh exercised decisive authority over these forces at the Beginning and in connection with establishing Israel as a people. Neither in nature nor in politics can they threaten Yhwh or threaten Yhwh's people.

A World Brought to Fulfillment

There is no indication that Genesis 1—3 looks at creation "eschatologically," whatever that would mean, but Genesis does recognize that creation was the beginning of a project, not the end of one. Perhaps we should rather say that prophecy looks at the End protologically, as brought about by "the eschatological Creator God" who "is not the enemy but the perfecter of the first creation."[145] At present there are parts of the world (such as Jerusalem!) that receive so little water that they can sustain neither trees nor people: they will be transformed (Is 41:17-20; Zech 14:8). There is water so salty it is undrinkable: it will be transformed (Ezek 47:1-12). There is half of each day dominated by darkness: it will be transformed (Zech 14:6-7). There are animals that attack and eat other animals as well as imperiling humanity: they will be transformed (Is 11:6-8). "On that day Yhwh will attend with his sword, fierce and great and strong, to Leviathan the fleeing serpent, to Leviathan the twisting serpent; he will slay the dragon that is in the sea." The declaration that the slaying of Leviathan lies in the future is distinctive to Isaiah 27:1. Another distinctive feature emerges from the context. It immediately follows on a declaration that Yhwh will attend to the wrongdoing of earth's inhabitants, their killing of so many among Yhwh's people (Is 26:21). Further, it belongs in the broader context of Yhwh's attending to the army on high and the kings of earth (Is 24:21), and of Yhwh's wasting the earth and destroying the city (Is 24:1—25:5). It does not suggest that Leviathan or the dragon can be identified with specific powers, but "there can be little doubt that, in the context of 13—27 as a whole, a *political* connotation is present and intended."[146] Isaiah recognizes that fact of our own experience, perhaps now more vivid than it was in First Testament times through the multiplying of slaughter over the

---

[145]Eichrodt, *Theology of the OT*, 2:107.
[146]Joseph Blenkinsopp, *Isaiah 1—39*, AB (New York: Doubleday, 2000), p. 372.

past century, that God has not yet tamed the power of slaughter, but it promises that God intends to do so.

Thus the statement that God's relationship with the world involves "creation, conservation, and transformation"[147] does not say quite enough. Even before it went wrong and needed restoration, it was a project still on the way. "The world may have been created good, but not quite good enough."[148] Or the original creation was very good, but this does not imply it was complete—otherwise God would hardly have given humanity the task not merely of maintaining it but of subduing the world. So the renewed world is not merely a world restored to its Edenic state, but one taken to the destiny God intended when creating it.[149] God's creation commission was that humanity should subdue the earth (Gen 1:28), win it to the internal harmony that was apparently not built into it even though it could be described as "good," and God is still committed to the fulfilling of that creation project. There will come a day when "wolf will dwell with lamb, leopard lie down with kid, calf, lion, and fatling together; a little boy will lead them" (Is 11:6-9). In itself it is hard to tell whether this imagery directly refers to peace within the animal world or to humanity being secure from hostile wild animals or from hostile human attackers who are pictured as wild animals: "The imagery seems to have taken off on its own into a dream world in which wild animals have changed their nature and eating habits."[150] But it is significant that the dream takes place on Yhwh's holy mountain, which in the First Testament implies either Yhwh's abode in heaven or Yhwh's abode in Jerusalem; its harmony, without human beings or animals eating one another, is part of the dream vision in Genesis 1, of a world that reflects Yhwh's abode in heaven. The vision's broader context suggests a link with that creation project.

Isaiah 40—55 promises a restoration of Israel that is like a renewing of creation; Isaiah 56—66 promises something more like a renewing of creation that will constitute a basis for Israel's beginning to realize an ideal version of the known order of created human life; and Isaiah 24—27 promises a new creation in which the great limitation of the old, the reality of death, is overcome.[151] In

---

[147]Robinson, *Inspiration and Revelation in the OT*, p.17.

[148]Gene M. Tucker, "The Peaceable Kingdom and a Covenant with Wild Animals," in *God Who Creates*, ed. William P. Brown and S. Dean McBride (Grand Rapids: Eerdmans, 2000), pp. 215-25; p. 216.

[149]Cf. Jürgen Moltmann, *The Coming of God* (London: SCM Press, 1996), pp. 261-66.

[150]Robert Murray, *The Cosmic Covenant* (London: Sheed & Ward, 1992), p. 105. See further Ronald E. Clements, "The Wolf Shall Live with the Lamb," in *New Heaven and New Earth*, ed. P. J. Harland and C. T. R. Hayward, VTSup 77 (Leiden/Boston: Brill, 1999), pp. 83-99.

[151]In Is 25:6-8 the context suggests a concern with the abolition of "unnatural" death in war, not with "natural" death, but it may be that this is too restrictive an understanding.

each case the vision involves a life lived in the order of creation.[152] This perhaps helps us to bring together these perspectives from Isaiah with the perspective in Genesis 1, which probably emerged from a context similar to one
or another of them. While it does not explicitly look forward, perhaps it does
so implicitly.

◆ ◆ ◆

The World Brought to Its Destiny Through Christ

The New Testament is not very interested in the created world. This is not a
fault; it takes the First Testament for granted and does not need to repeat everything the First Testament says. (A problem arises only because Christians
treat the New Testament as if it were the Bible.) Paul does take up the ambiguity of life in the world and make a declaration about the world's destiny:

> I reckon that the sufferings of the present time are not worth comparing with the
> coming glory to be revealed to us, because the creation's keen expectation is wait-
> ing for the revealing of the children of God. Because the creation was subjected
> to emptiness, not willingly but by the one who subjected it in hope that the cre-
> ation itself will be freed from corrupting slavery to the glorious freedom of God's
> offspring. Because we know that the entire creation is groaning and laboring un-
> til now. Not only that, but also we ourselves, having the firstfruits of the Spirit—
> we ourselves also groan within ourselves, waiting for adoption, the redemption
> of our body. (Rom 8:18-23)

Back at the Beginning God subjected the creation to humanity, and this did not
work. The creation ended up subjected to emptiness. It is not so much that it
was created complete and humanity's failure spoiled it; rather it was created
as a project to be taken to completion and humanity failed to take it there. Ever
since its beginning, it has been groaning and laboring like a woman about to
give birth, but the birth never happens.

Jesus' death and resurrection are the decisive event that makes it possible
for creation to reach its goal, and the outpouring of the Spirit is the decisive
event that assures it and assures people who believe in Jesus that it will do so.
Elsewhere, Paul enthusiastically exclaims, "if someone is in Christ—a new creation! The old things have gone away. Look—new things have happened!" (2
Cor 5:17). In isolation, creation there becomes simply a metaphor for the
change that comes about in the individual for whom Christ died. But set in the
context of Romans 8, it becomes a declaration about stages in a course of ac-

---

[152]Knierim, *Task of OT Theology*, pp. 215-16.

tion. God has begun the process of bringing creation to its destiny, by implementing a new creation in the life of the church. We do not have to look beyond the life of the Corinthian church to which Paul writes to see that this is itself partial. There is plenty of ambiguity in the life of the church and in the life of individual Christians. New things have happened, but the old things have not gone very far away. Precisely that fact puts us into the same position as the creation. We do not simply accept the emptiness to which we are subjected, as if no alternative could be envisaged; we know there is an alternative, and we therefore rail against the emptiness (cf. Rom 7). Neither does our experience suggest that the new age has so arrived that the old has quite gone. And therefore we groan for the day when this will be so.

In doing so, we join in creation's groaning and creation joins in ours. It looks at us and knows that new creation will be a reality. What Christ has done guarantees that it will be taken to its destiny; humanity's failure to take it there will not have the last word. So, almost as keenly as we do, it looks forward to our "revealing" or our "adoption" or "the redemption of our body," because when that happens, it will be the signal and the trigger for it to come to its fulfillment.

The Revelation to John reaffirms that truth. The dragon and the beast will be no more (Rev 13). In the new heaven and earth there will be no more sea (Rev 21:1)—no presence of that symbol and embodiment of dynamic power that resists God. And there will be no more night (Rev 22:5); that symbol and facilitator of deception and wrongdoing will be gone.

8

THE NATIONS

The First Testament speaks often of "the nations," as they are and as they might be, and as facing the possibility of either Yhwh's blessing or Yhwh's destruction. The expression can denote the peoples of the world as a whole or the various political entities with which Israel itself lived in relationship or the empires that controlled Israel's destiny from time to time. The fact that the term has various referents in part explains the varied and complex way the First Testament speaks about "the nations."

Nations such as Britain and the United States have taken Yhwh's involvement with Israel as offering them an understanding of their own place in the world, in a way that is dangerously half-right. Israel had a unique place in God's purpose, one that no other nation can reckon to take up. There are no "new chosen peoples, new promised lands."[1] Yet Yhwh's taking one group of people and showing what Yhwh's blessing could mean for them indeed provided a model for understanding Yhwh's relationship with peoples (Gen 12:1-3). In this any nation can learn from Israel, though perhaps especially little nations that are insignificant in the world, as Israel was. But when great world powers claim this and see themselves as heirs to Israel's position in God's purpose, their posturing becomes demonic. There is much material in the First Testament that offers self-understanding to nations such as Britain and the United States, but it lies more in the way the First Testament talks about the nations in general than in the way it talks about Israel. Perhaps a small, oppressed people can find hints of its destiny in the story of what God did with Israel, but superpowers cannot do that.

It is odd that Christian faith declines to look for God's activity in blessing and judgment in the history of the nations over the past two millennia,[2] but perhaps this is because it would be too uncomfortable for the traditional Christian nations.

8.1 Belonging to Yhwh

"What about the Canaanites? and the Amorites, Moabites, Hittites?"[3] Not to

---

[1]See Conor Cruise O'Brien, *God's Land* (Cambridge, Mass./London: Harvard University Press, 1988), pp. 23-42.

[2]Cf. Wolfhart Pannenberg, *Systematic Theology,* vol. 3 (Grand Rapids: Eerdmans, 1998), pp. 496-517, though he focuses especially on church history.

[3]Regina M. Schwartz, *The Curse of Cain* (Chicago/London: Chicago University Press, 1997), p. ix.

say the Egyptians, Philistines, Assyrians, Babylonians, Persians and Greeks? The question arises out of the fact that Yhwh chose Israel as a special possession. What does this imply about God's attitude to the rest of the world? In the New Testament, Jesus chooses some people out of the world, yet that action is set in the context of God's loving the world as a whole, and it is apparently an expression of that love (Jn 3:16; 15:19). Likewise, choosing Israel does not mean that Yhwh rejected the rest of the peoples of the world.[4] They were created by Yhwh and they live in Yhwh's world. They are summoned to worship Yhwh, to recognize Yhwh as deliverer, sovereign and provider.

Summoned to Worship

Because the nations belong to Yhwh as their maker, they are destined to come and bow down to honor Yhwh (Ps 86:9). "All peoples" are thus urged now to worship Yhwh—paradoxically, as the one who "subdued peoples under us" (Ps 47:1-4 [MT 2-5]). The words "peoples" ('*ammîm*) and "nations" (*gôyyîm*) appear alongside each other (also the rarer *lĕ'ummîm*), applying to the same entities. While Israel can speak of the nations as if it were not one of them (thus *gôyyîm* comes to mean "Gentiles"), in fulfillment of God's promise to Abraham (Gen 12:2) Israel is also itself a *gôy*, like peoples such as Babylon or Moab. All are both peoples and nations. Like their English equivalents, '*am* draws attention to the familial-type links that hold a *gôy* together and contribute to its sense of identity, while *gôy* draws attention to the way a '*am* is a large-scale, structured entity that relates politically to other *gôyyîm*.

The nations belong to Yhwh and are drawn into acknowledging Yhwh, even though Yhwh has a special commitment to one nation, Israel. The nations are to join in praise of Yhwh, but the nations have been put down (or are to be put down, according to other texts). The double stance taken to the nations is taken up into the New Testament, where the world is both the object of God's love and the recipient of God's punishment. Translations of Psalm 47 make all these peoples "shout *with joy*," but that is an interpretation of the "shout," and it is not self-evident that Yhwh's subjecting peoples under Israel's feet is reason for all peoples to rejoice. Similarly, declaring that "God is king of all the earth" (Ps 47:7 [MT 8]) might imply only the kind of authority a master exercises over slaves, or the kind Nebuchadnezzar exercises over Judah. Yet the psalm goes on to describe how "the leaders of peoples gather, the people of Abraham's God" (Ps 47:8-9 [MT 9-10]). The MT seems to see the leaders of the peoples *as* the people of Abraham's God, while LXX has them gathering *with* the people of Abraham's God. Either way, the psalm is implying a more explic-

---

[4]See, e.g., Joel Kaminsky, "Did Election Imply the Mistreatment of Non-Israelites?" *Harvard Theological Review* 96 (2003): 397-425; and section 3.3 above.

itly positive statement about the relation of the nations' leaders to Yhwh, and thus about the nations' own relation to Yhwh. God's being king over the nations is good news for them as well as for Israel. The fact that Yhwh subdued certain nations (the inhabitants of Canaan or subsequently peoples such as the Philistines or Moabites or Assyrians or Babylonians) can be reason for other nations to rejoice if, for instance, the purpose Yhwh is prosecuting in this way is one that will mean blessing for nations in general.

The collocation of power in the heavens and power exercised for Israel appears in Psalm 68:32-35 [MT 33-36], with more explicit political connotations. "Kingdoms of the earth" are to "sing to God, make music to the Lord" as "the one who rides in the high heavens of old" and "sends out his sound, a mighty sound." It is worldly powers, not heavenly powers, that are here bidden to recognize Yhwh. They are indeed exhorted not merely to bow down to Yhwh, which might be the unwilling submission of defeated foes, but to join in music and song. That implies joining in the joy of Israel's worship. They worship "the Lord," which is not a very common epithet for God (given that "the LORD" in translations represents the name Yhwh). In a context such as the present one, the epithet hints at the attribution to Yhwh of an epithet that Canaanites gave Baal, *the* Lord and Master. It was Baal who sounded out power in the thunder. It was Baal whom Canaanites saw as the great sky rider (cf. Ps 68:4 [MT 5]).

The worldly powers are bidden to "give might to God," like the divine beings in Psalm 29.[5] Once again translations render "ascribe might," but this underplays the bidding; the psalm uses the ordinary word for "give" (nātan). By their nature worldly kingdoms possess power, so their giving power to Yhwh has a different significance from that which attaches to the recognition of Yhwh's power by people who have no earthly power. On the part of earthly powers, such recognition of the power that Yhwh exercises in the heavens implies a yielding of their own power. It has further implications on earth, because it transpires that the God whose own "might is in the skies" and who receives it from earthly kingdoms is also "giver of might and great strength to the people." God shares that might with Israel. But as the nations give it to God, they find their true selves in relationship to God.

Acknowledging Yhwh as Deliverer

Psalm 66 sharpens the point as it bids the whole earth to bow down before Yhwh on the basis of Yhwh's awesome deeds, which are again acts of deliverance done on Israel's behalf. They begin with Yhwh's victory at the Red Sea,

---

[5]See section 2.2 "Yhwh's Underlings."

the first demonstration of the power that makes it wise for the nations not to assert themselves against Yhwh. But this is not merely a feature of ancient history. On other occasions Yhwh has taken Israel to the very edge of disaster and, it might seem, over the edge, but in the end has then again proved to be "the one who puts us in life and has not given our foot to faltering," one who "brought us out into flourishing" (Ps 66:9, 12). Here "the earth" is distinguished from "your enemies," specific nations that oppress Israel and thus oppose Yhwh's purpose. "Enemies" could cover the original great power in Israel's story, and "the nations" (Ps 66:7) as a designation for the superpower of the day, and also "people" (*'ĕnôš*) more generally (Ps 66:12), as this could apply to individual foes such as Philistia or Edom. It is because such enemies wither before Yhwh that the world as a whole bows down to Yhwh. The psalm declares not what does happen but what should happen or can happen or will happen. The world's logical response to God's acts of deliverance for Israel is to bow down to Yhwh, not least because of the good news for the world that these acts imply. The point comes over vividly in the shortest psalm, Psalm 117, which urges all peoples to laud Yhwh "because his commitment is great toward us."

Psalm 96 similarly summons all the earth to sing about Yhwh's deliverance of Israel.[6] That event means the nations have some facts to face about their gods being trash. They are also going to have to surrender their splendor and strength instead of holding on to these, and to appear in Yhwh's courts to bring tribute to Yhwh like the representatives of some little nation appearing at the imperial court, trembling before its powerful sovereign. Yet the sovereign's proper exercise of power on Israel's behalf is also their encouragement. When Yhwh reigns, "the world indeed stands firm, it will not totter; he decides for the peoples with uprightness. He will govern the world in faithfulness and the peoples in trustworthiness" (Ps 96:10-13). The EVV have Yhwh "judging" the world, but this gives a misleading impression. The verb *šāpaṭ* is the word for "judging the poor"—that is, giving judgment with regard to them, exercising authority for their benefit. While the nations do not directly benefit from Yhwh's deliverance of Israel, it is good news for them because it establishes what kind of God Yhwh is and the basis on which Yhwh operates in the world. These character traits will work for the nations' benefit when they are in need—though they also hint at the negative consequences if nations fail themselves to be people of faithfulness and trustworthiness.

So the nations are drawn into the same acknowledgment of Yhwh as Israel itself offers. Even Yhwh's winning a victory over some other peoples is a par-

---

[6]"Announce" in Ps 96:3 is the verb *bāśar* (piel), which LXX translates *euangelizomai*.

adoxical form of good news for the nations of the world. It evidences that the moment will come when Yhwh takes up the reins of government over the world as a whole instead of continuing to leave it to insubordinate underlings, heavenly or earthly. Yhwh will become the world's decision-maker, one who exercises authority in a way characterized by faithfulness and uprightness. Yhwh combines majestic power with both a commitment to Israel and a concern for other peoples. What Yhwh does in Israel has inclusive, not exclusive, significance. It models how Yhwh wills to relate to peoples in general. They are thus both those who proclaim the good news of Yhwh's acts for Israel and those among whom this good news is proclaimed. Psalm 98 speaks in similar terms.

Acknowledging Yhwh as the One Who Looks Down from the Heavens

Psalm 113 begins by urging Yhwh's servants to praise Yhwh—an uncontroversial exhortation. The declaration that this praise will always be due, "from now to the end of the age," raises few further questions, though it does presuppose that the reasons for such praise will always apply. But Yhwh is also to be praised "from the sun's rising to its setting," which rather implies that the call to praise applies to people other than Israel. Why should that be so? It is so because "Yhwh is high over all the nations" as "his splendor is over the heavens." So what is the nature of the nations' praise? Does it comprise merely an acknowledgment of a superior power? But praise *(hallēl)* implies more enthusiasm than that, and the psalm goes on to declare that the unique deity that makes Yhwh a proper object of praise through the ages and through the world consists in the fact that Yhwh is not merely one who "sets his throne on high," who sits in power in heaven, but one who "bends down to look" and condescends to get involved on earth.

Often that involvement involves putting down the powerful, but here that is unstated. The psalm speaks only of the positive side to Yhwh's work. Yhwh bends down to discover what is happening on earth, like an adult bending to see what exactly is happening in the world of a child or a tiny animal. Yhwh then "lifts a pauper from the dirt, exalts a needy person from the trash heap," taking them from the place where they are living in humiliation at the dump whose "resources" provide them with food and shelter, and giving them the dignity of a place "among the nobles of his people" (Ps 113:7). Yhwh specifically exalts a particular kind of needy woman. A woman who cannot have children is always vulnerable to being marginalized or neglected or replaced, and she has no children who will look after her in old age. Yhwh "enables a barren woman to live at home," secure, "a joyful mother of children" (Ps 113:9). So who are these poor people and this barren mother? Does the description apply to all Israelites? The psalm's language deserves noting, for the English translations tend to describe Yhwh as exalting *the* poor and enabling *the* barren woman to live at home. The psalm speaks of one needy person and one barren woman. The woman's experience corresponds to that of Hannah and the language about exalting a needy person corresponds to her words (1 Sam 2:8). But there, one woman's experience stimulates a statement about Yhwh's characteristic activity. Implicitly, the fact that Yhwh sometimes does that is a promise that it can happen again. But implicitly the psalm recognizes that things do not always work out like that. Yet if Yhwh wishes to be acknowledged in the way this psalm speaks, this needs to become true for all people. And further, does the description apply only to Israelites? That will not be enough if Yhwh is to be acknowledged as lord of the whole earth as Yhwh is lord over the whole heaven. By no means is God's power "hidden in darkness."[7]

The object or principle behind Yhwh's faithful and upright exercise of authority is that Yhwh should be "a refuge for the broken, a refuge for times of pressure" (Ps 9:9 [MT 10]). The psalm may presuppose that Israel is the broken, but this moral principle will also apply when other nations are the broken, and may even be Israel's victims. The further object is that people who acknowledge Yhwh's name may trust Yhwh in times of pressure (Ps 9:10 [MT 11]). It is a possibility that Israel can certainly claim for itself, but it need not be limited to Israel when other nations are the ones under pressure.

Acknowledging Yhwh as Sovereign

So the nations are pictured appearing before Yhwh with a twofold confession (Jer 16:19-21). They will recognize that they have received from their ancestors a form of faith that was all they had to pass on, but the gods they called gods are not really gods but lies *(šeqer)*. Further, Yhwh says, "I am causing them to acknowledge, once and for all . . . my power and my might." Thus they will affirm that Yhwh has the power that the images and the gods they represent do not have. "They will acknowledge that my name is Yhwh," implying "I am the only real God."[8] The finality of their confession is underlined by a threefold repetition of the key verb *acknowledge* (along with the qualifier "once and for all," *bappaʿam hazzōʾt*, lit. "by this stroke/time"). And the causative form of the first two occurrences of the verb underlines the sovereignty of Yhwh over this process. Yhwh will bring it about. That means it is certain.

How does Yhwh do that? Hints from the context are suggestive and/or frightening. Jeremiah has spoken about Yhwh's bringing the Israelites back from all the foreign countries where they have been banished (Jer 16:14-15). It

---

[7]Calvin *Institutes* I.v.8.
[8]See section 2.1 "Only God."

will be an exoduslike event, one that replaces the exodus in people's own confession of faith. It would not be surprising if that had the same or more spectacular effects as the exodus in leading foreigners to acknowledge Yhwh (e.g., Ex 18:8-12). But Jeremiah has even more immediately spoken of Yhwh's sending fishermen and hunters to hunt the Israelites out because of their own addiction to images (Jer 16:16-18). The nations' double confession about images and about Yhwh follows on that act of exposure of Israel's images.[9] Perhaps both the act of grace and the act of exposure draw the nations.

Psalm 46:6-10 [MT 7-11] gives a clear description of the reality of the life of the nations, then a declaration about Yhwh's relationship to it. "Nations rage" and "kingdoms totter." Nations raging against each other and kingdoms consequently falling is the reality of history. But the psalm goes on to add a whole other factor: "he gives voice, earth dissolves." Whereas the raging and falling is an empirical fact, the statements about Yhwh's involvement come from somewhere else. One guesses that they come from the people's past experience of Yhwh's acts such as generated the stories of the exodus and conquest, from the telling of those stories and from their celebration in worship where they are taken as clues to ultimate reality. In light of experience, story and worship, the psalm leaps to a statement of conviction regarding how those specifics become a final generalization: "he brings desolations on the earth, one who halts wars to earth's ends; he will break the bow and snap the spear, burn shields in the fire." The generalization describes war ending not because people see its stupidity or become overtaken by a desire for peace, but because a more powerful war-maker asserts authority, like a teacher forcibly separating two battling schoolboys: "Stop; acknowledge that I am God—I will be exalted among the nations, I will be exalted in the earth." Imposing authority thus does mean that Yhwh comes to be recognized as God.

One day Yhwh will bring Gog against Israel in the manner of Assyria or Babylon (except that Israel no longer requires punishment by the hand of some agent of this kind), but there will be nothing to fear. Yhwh is acting this way again "so that the nations may acknowledge me when I show my holiness through you before their eyes, Gog." Thus "I will cause my holy name to be acknowledged among my people Israel, and I will not profane my holy name any more. And the nations will acknowledge that I am Yhwh, the holy one in Israel" (Ezek 38:16; 39:7).

Acknowledging Yhwh as Provider

Yhwh is the maker of the nations and all the nations belong to Yhwh; it is not

---

[9]Cf. William L. Holladay, *Jeremiah*, 2 vols. (Philadelphia: Fortress, 1986; and Minneapolis: Fortress, 1989), 1:480.

the case, for example, that Moab belongs to Chemosh, Babylon belongs to Marduk, and Israel belongs to Yhwh. It is therefore possible to urge Yhwh to exercise authority in relation to the other nations (*šāpaṭ*, Ps 82:8). Israel so prays, not for its own benefit (Israel is not mentioned in Ps 82) but because the "gods" who have responsibility for the nations under Yhwh are failing. They exercise authority in a way that encourages wrong by favoring the faithless instead of exercising authority on behalf of the poor, the orphan, the lowly, the weak and the needy. The psalm urges Yhwh to act like that for the nations.[10]

In the realm of nature, too, what Yhwh does for Israel contains promise for other peoples. In Psalm 67, with its abcb'a' shape, the opening and closing lines pray for God's blessing on Israel such as will cause the nations to acknowledge God's "way" and arouse its reverence for God. That could imply a purely selfish wish for God to bless Israel spectacularly, without the nations themselves being beneficiaries of Yhwh's deeds. The same significance might attach even to the repeated declaration that they will "confess" God (*yādâ* hiphil), for such confession might simply mean recognition. But the psalm's central tricolon makes explicit that the nations will actually "rejoice" and not just acknowledge the facts, and it gives the reason. It is "because you decide for peoples [or govern peoples] with fairness/straightness [*šāpaṭ, mîšôr*]" (Ps 67:4). It is thus that Yhwh will be sovereign in their destiny, as in Israel's. Likewise Yhwh will "guide" or "lead" them (*nāḥâ* hiphil), as Yhwh led Israel from Egypt and through the wilderness toward the land (e.g., Ps 77:20 [MT 21]; 78:14, 53), and as Yhwh leads an Israelite on a secure and safe path (e.g., Ps 5:8 [MT 9]; 23:3; 27:11; 31:3 [MT 4]; 61:2 [MT 3]). It is not surprising that the nations will resound with joy in their confession, confession, confession (the word is repeated three times, like "sing" in Ps 96:1-2).

The psalm's framework wish, then, is that God's demonstration of grace and blessing to Israel may be the means of the nations' coming to revere God. The grace and blessing issue from God's face shining among us (*'ittānû*, lit., "with us"). The preposition has complementary resonances to those of the expression "to you" in the priestly blessing (Num 6:25); both suggest that life issues from the shining of God's smile (e.g., Ps 118:27). A smile renews the inner life of the person who receives it, and it is the natural accompaniment or forerunner to acts of generosity. As in Psalm 65, these are acts of blessing, causing the earth to yield its produce, and when the promise of blessing has not worked out, acts of deliverance (even delivering Israel from the very nations the psalm refers to?). In both, the nations see God's "way," God's way of acting in relation to people. Both draw the nations' acknowledgment, praise and re-

---

[10]On Ps 82, see section 2.2 "The Judgment of the Gods."

joicing. Both are good news for them, too. Whereas the priestly blessing naturally focuses on Israel, these psalms look to the extending of God's blessing to
the world. God's acts again have inclusive, not exclusive, implications; reference to God's leading of Israel like a flock is an invitation to the nations rather
than a rejection of them, a pattern that can be repeated in their experience. The
psalm expresses in another form the convictions formulated in Yhwh's promise to Abraham (Gen 12:1-3), which also takes up the terms of God's original
blessing of humanity in the created world (Gen 1). It is not surprising that the
nations rejoice.

8.2 Acknowledging Yhwh's People

The nations' acknowledgment of Yhwh is tied up with an acknowledgment of
Israel. Israel lived most of its life as a small and insignificant player on the
world stage, at best open to being ignored by peoples around, at worst open
to being trodden into the ground by them. The First Testament declares that
this will not be the end. It is an understandable temptation for Israel to feel
overwhelmed by the power of the nations around. Yhwh promises there is no
need for that. The nations are destined to recognize the authority of Yhwh's
anointed. The servant who is despised will be acknowledged and the humiliated people will come to be honored, for their Lord's sake as well as for their
own. The masters will become servants, the tormentors and slave-traders will
become victims, the people at peace will be put on battle alert.

From Rebel to Servant

Psalm 2 starts from the assumption that "the nations," the great imperial powers, are supposed to accept Yhwh's authority, and it suggests they are unwise
to give in to the inclination to rebelliousness. Indeed, to do so would be really
stupid. The nations are inclined to boisterous assertiveness, bold planning
(that will actually lead nowhere), insistence on shaping their own destiny and
resistance to the people of God. This just makes God grin (cf. Ps 59:8 [MT 9]).
They would be wiser to opt for openness to what Yhwh says, reverent service
of Yhwh, awed joy before Yhwh and sincere submission. Otherwise, while
Yhwh laughs at their pretentiousness, they also lay themselves open to the
raging of Yhwh's fury and to being firmly brought back into line. Thus the object of this warning is to win them to see sense. "So now, kings, be sensible, allow yourselves to be put right, earth's leaders; serve Yhwh with reverence,
rejoice with trembling, submit sincerely" (Ps 2:10-12).[11] They will be wise to ac-

---

[11]The KJV, NIVI "kiss the Son" presupposes the most common meaning of *nāšaq*, but "son" is
Aramaic *bar*, not Hebrew *bēn* (as in v. 7). I take it as Hebrew *bar* used adverbially (cf. BDB,
141), and take the verb as *DCH's nāšaq* iii.

cept Yhwh's authority voluntarily and become people who serve Yhwh, "lest he be angry and you perish as regards the path, because his anger will soon blaze." They might then even find themselves the beneficiaries of the blessing declared in the psalm's last colon: "The good fortune of all that rely on him!" Not least by its "all," the psalm leaves this blessing open to their appropriation as well as Israel's. They can enjoy the good fortune they see in Israel and its king (cf. Ps 72:17, the related verb).

But further, that king is Yhwh's means of ruling the world: "Yhwh's anointed," "Yhwh's king," the one whom "I myself installed . . . on my holy mountain," the one to whom Yhwh said at his accession, "You are my son, I myself beget you today" (Ps 2:1-7). He is Yhwh's regent, with an authority not merely over Israel but over the world. It is through his exercising authority that Yhwh exercises authority, and the great nations are to recognize his authority and rule as an expression of their recognizing Yhwh's authority and rule. They do have a choice—a sort-of choice. They can submit to Yhwh by submitting to the king and do so voluntarily, or they can be forced to do so when "Yhwh frustrates the plan of nations, brings to nothing the ideas of peoples" (Ps 33:10). So if they resist the king's authority, they lay themselves open to the king's discipline, to his smashing them like a piece of pottery (Ps 2:8-9).

This is clearly a dangerous doctrine. Perhaps that is why God never inspired from the king the request suggested, "Ask of me" (Ps 2:8), and never implemented it. David's story does associate Psalm 18 with his experience: "you rescued me from strife with people, set me at the head of nations; people I did not acknowledge have served me" (Ps 18:43 [MT 44]; cf. 2 Sam 22:44). David's triumphs provide some illustration of the psalm's embodiment, and Psalm 2 is an even more enhanced imagining of it (cf. Ps 110), but the psalm is larger than life.

The psalm is clearly open to ideological appropriation. But it was only ever a theory; no Israelite king ever exercised such authority—even in David and Solomon's day—or therefore experienced the nations rebelling against him or acted thus to punish them. The psalm begins from a situation that never obtained, a rebellion against Israelite authority on the part of the nations that had evidently been under that authority. There was no time when the nations rebelled against Israel's authority, because there was no time when they were under Israel's authority and therefore could be tempted to do so, as if Israel were a superpower like Assyria or Babylon against which nations such as Judah did rebel. Perhaps the idea of the nations under Israel's authority forms an enhanced form of the portrait of David and Solomon's small-scale empire in Samuel-Kings and Chronicles. But Israel itself was a people whose political insignificance contrasted with the psalm's grandiose vision, but who knew that Yhwh was indeed the only God worth calling God, whose authority there-

fore extended to the nations, and they knew that Yhwh had mysteriously decided to work at being known by all the nations by means of little Israel. The
psalm reflects those facts.

A people that actually exercises power in the world, as the church sometimes has and as some "Christian" nations have, would need to be wary of the
way they use this psalm. There is no basis for another nation (e.g., Britain or
the U.S.A.) thinking it inherits such authority. We have noted that one aspect
of its theological significance might be that God applies it to a tiny nation that
has no human hope of ever exercising such power.[12] God does not apply it to
a superpower such as Assyria or Babylon, even though the Prophets can see
them as Yhwh's agents in particular contexts. It is thus a typical instance of the
way Yhwh reverses regular assumptions about power and works through the
underdog rather than the lion. That would be a further reason for questioning
whether Britain or the United States could ever see itself in this position. It
would more likely apply, for example, to Kenya or Guatemala or the Philip-
pines. Britain and the United States would be nations submitting, rebelling
and undergoing discipline, not nations enjoining submission or punishing rebellion.

The psalm does confront the pacifist strand in Christian (and non-Christian) thinking. The First Testament consistently assumes that God does not ab-
jure the use of force and violence and accepts the place of these in the affairs of
the nations and thus of Israel as a nation. Perhaps it is a judgment call when
we must love our enemies by lying in front of their tanks and when we must
love the oppressed by taking to the tanks in order to put down wrong.

Recognizing Israel's King

The book of Amos almost closes with a promise that "on that day I will erect
David's shelter that is falling[13] and repair their breaches, I will erect his ruins
and build it up as in days of old." The expression "David's shelter" comes only
here, and in isolation it might refer, for instance, to his tent sanctuary or his dynasty or his palace. But the subsequent lines suggest it denotes his realm or his
empire, which already stands in a reduced state in Amos's day and does so
more comprehensively in the exile and afterward. But Yhwh will rebuild it "so
that they may possess the leftovers of Edom and all the nations over which my
name was proclaimed" (Amos 9:11-12). Whereas David's sovereignty had extended to the nations around, in those later three periods these peoples are of-

---

[12]See the introduction to chap. 8.

[13]Not "fallen," surely, *pace* EVV, though the time reference of the participle *nōpelet* might de-
    rive from the yiqtol verb (the shelter will be in a state of falling in the future) or from the
    position of the speaker (the shelter is falling now).

ten thorns in the nation's side. Edom becomes a symbol of that, perhaps partly because it eats up Judean territory in the Persian period. All that will be reversed. Israel will once again control the area around it. Yhwh claims sovereignty over all these peoples, and it will be expressed in the Davidic king's sovereignty over them.

It would be a belated fulfillment of the prayer for the king in Psalm 72, which ends, "may all nations bless themselves by him. May they count him fortunate." Why should they do that? The wording again goes back to Yhwh's promise to Abraham (e.g., Gen 12:1-3) and takes up that promise's assumption about the interrelationship of Yhwh's work with Israel and with the nations. Yhwh will so bless Israel that the nations will covet the same blessing for themselves. The new note in the psalm is the focus of blessing on the king. In fulfillment of one of the elements in that promise to Abraham, Israel has become a nation like the nations. That in turn gives a more political turn to the relationship between Abraham's descendants and other peoples. So the psalm prays that the king may "have dominion from sea to sea, from river to earth's farthest bounds," with his enemies bowing before him in submission, kings of such far-off countries paying tribute, and their peoples praying daily for him to be blessed (Ps 72:8-15).

Again, the prayer is open to ideological appropriation. It offers the king a rationale for domination over other peoples if he ever has the chance to exercise it. But Psalm 72 is a canny psalm in the way it combines accepting the monarchy with making demands on it. It is formally a prayer, and how could the king object to a prayer? But in substance it lays the most searching demands before him, and here it immediately goes on to safeguard against ideological appropriation in the reasons it gives for the nations' homage and submission: "For he rescues the poor person who cries out, the needy, the person with no one to help." The reason for the nations' service of the Israelite king is the way the king serves his people, and specifically serves the vulnerable among them. One might risk the ideological instincts of a king who made that his priority. Is the implication that Yhwh will simply make things work out this way, compelling the nations to submit to the Davidic king because he has that priority? Or is it that the nations will themselves be drawn to such a king? Contrary to the more cynical understandings of *realpolitik,* might peoples and their leaders respond to the embodiment of such commitments? At least, does their seeking his blessing imply they might see the links between prosperity and care for the needy?

At the end of the psalm, the king becomes a standard of blessing that other nations aspire to, like Abraham. The psalm is a prayer whose implications extend beyond king to people and beyond people to world. Arguably its prayer for the nations' falling down before him thus deconstructs.

Eventually Triumphant

The First Testament encourages the expectation that a king should be a physically and intellectually impressive figure, tall, dark, handsome and insightful. Consider, for example, David (notwithstanding Yhwh's words about looking at the inner person), Absalom and the king of Tyre (1 Sam 16:18; 2 Sam 14:25; Ezek 28). It is a reasonable assumption, for God made body and mind, and one would expect God to bless the body and mind of one that God intends to use.

Yhwh's servant *will* be an impressive figure, but for some while will be dismissed because he is not such, so that initially he belies such expectations (see Is 52:13-15). Indeed, many peoples are appalled at the sight of him. But it is possible to face that fact—and its detailing in Isaiah 53—because of the reversal that will follow, which will mean that "at him kings will shut their mouths, because what had not been told them they will have seen, what they had not heard they will have considered."

Yhwh's servant "will act with insight; he will rise and exalt himself, he will be very high" (Is 52:13). He will have royal insight—the verb *śākal* is one that especially applies to the king. Indeed, it combines the ideas of insight and success, and hints at the fact that the former is of key importance to the latter. The servant is a David-like figure in this respect (e.g., 1 Sam 18:5, 13, 30; and the promise about David's shoot in Jer 23:5). And he will have super-royal majesty. Some of that, too, recalls David, as the fulfillment of old and not-so-old promises (Num 24:7; 1 Sam 2:10; 2 Sam 22:49). More strikingly, it also recalls descriptions elsewhere in Isaiah of qualities or achievements that lead to people being put down as their majesty threatens to rival Yhwh's majesty (e.g., Is 2:12; 3:16). Indeed, the very words that describe the position of Yhwh's servant are words that elsewhere describe Yhwh's own position as one who is exalted on high (see esp. Is 5:16; 6:1). Yhwh's servant shares in Yhwh's exaltation. That is not so surprising a declaration; a servant does share in the majesty of the master. The surprise in this picture lies in the appalling horror of the servant's journey to that exaltation.

"His appearance will be anointed beyond anyone and his look beyond other human beings." Describing the servant as of remarkable appearance continues to suggest he is a David-like figure (e.g., 1 Sam 16:18; 17:42), and describing him as anointed also fits with that aspect of the expectations of kingship, for the king was *the* anointed.[14] Alongside the declaration that the servant

---

[14]The LXX and Jerome derive the word *mišḥat* from *šāḥat* "spoil, ruin" (cf. BDB), but that would be the only occurrence of this noun. There is an established noun *mišḥâ* (of which this would be the construct) from *māšaḥ* "anoint," which usually refers to the anointing oil or to the anointed share (the share belonging to the anointed people, the priests). This makes better sense in the context.

will share in Yhwh's exaltation, however, is the affirmation that his anointed appearance and look are not merely the equal of David's or other kings' but their superior. Corresponding to that is the further assertion that kings will shut their mouths at him. He will realize the vision for the anointed king that appears in Psalm 2:1-2.

Further, "he will spatter many nations" (Is 52:15). Nations and kings appear together here as they do in Psalm 2, but here they are all the object of the servant's spattering,[15] which is more a priestly note than a royal one. It recalls the other context for thinking about anointing, for priests were also anointed, so in spattering nations this servant will be a more remarkable priest than any other as well as a more remarkable king than any other. It is not explicit what he spatters them with. It could be water or oil, but the account of covenant sealing at Sinai suggests it is more likely blood. Spattering with blood is not a means of cleansing or forgiveness but a sign of being sealed into a covenant relationship with Yhwh (Ex 24:8). Here Yhwh's servant is a means of the nations being sealed into such a relationship. Previously they have never heard of the possibility of their being in relationship with Yhwh. That was of course Yhwh's intention from the beginning of creation, but only rare people who happen to have been in the right place at the right time have come to know of it—people such as Jethro and Balaam, Rahab and Ruth, Uriah and Naaman. Now nations and kings will know. Thus their submissive astonishment at the work of Yhwh's servant has more explicitly positive connotations for them than the submission of which Psalm 2 spoke.

Although the First Testament does not envisage there being a problem about God forgiving the world, as if God's own holy nature forbad such an act,[16] there is a problem about getting people to come to acknowledge God and find forgiveness. It is the exaltation of this servant who has suffered that will bring the nations to that acknowledgment. On the other hand, although their submission does bring them blessing, Isaiah 52:13—53:12 (like Is 40—55 as a whole) does not put the emphasis on this blessing but on the way their acknowledgment contributes to the servant's exaltation. At the end of this servant poem the imagery ricochets back to the form it has at the beginning, and Yhwh declares that because of his faithful work "I will give him a share among the many; he will share out the powerful as spoil" (Is 53:12). He will be like a king who has fought victoriously as Yhwh's general. Yhwh will thus enable him to enjoy the fruits of triumph, plundering the army he defeats. Yes, na-

---

[15]The NRSV, JPSV "startle" presupposes that *yazzeh* comes not from the regular *nāzâ* but from a homonym otherwise unknown in Hebrew. This seems a hazardous and unnecessary hypothesis.

[16]See section 2.6 above.

tions and kings will shut their mouths at him (Is 52:15).

The passage describes the experience of Yhwh's servant and the significance that attaches to him, but it does not indicate to whom it refers. It is a kind of promise and a kind of job description. While the nearby context also does not unequivocally identify the servant, it has indicated that Israel was Yhwh's servant and also that the prophet was. Their experience contributes to the portrait and they are entitled (or warned) to find themselves in it. Christians traditionally see Jesus as *the* fulfillment of the servant vision, but the New Testament does not see the passage as a "prophecy" of which there is this one "fulfillment," nor does it use the passage to prove that Jesus is the Messiah. Jesus is one fulfillment of this vision, but in the New Testament he is not the only one. It sees Jesus as Yhwh's servant and also applies the passage to the vocation of the church (e.g., 1 Pet 2:21-22). So the function of the passage is to indicate to us the way servanthood can work, whoever the servant is. It can involve hurt and pain for the servant, but a hurt and pain that are productive for other people and are not the end of the story for the servant.

The portrait itself gives indication that it is not a kind of anticipatory picture of Jesus. There are elements that correspond closely to what Jesus would be and do, but other elements that do not. As a whole, the picture does not fit. Christians may rightly use the whole vision to illumine the significance of Jesus, but we can hardly claim that the literal significance of some details establishes that Jesus is its sole fulfillment while sidestepping the fact that he does not literally fulfill other aspects—which on that logic would undermine his claims. Isaiah 52:13—53:12 is a portrait based on what has been, not an anticipatory photograph of what is to come. It offers encouragement to anyone called to be Yhwh's servant—for instance, a prophet or the people as a whole. Yhwh is committed to the exaltation and fruitfulness of the servant portrayed here. It also offers encouragement to anyone unsure whether the world will ever come to acknowledge Yhwh. This servant will draw the nations into a covenant commitment to Yhwh.

From Contempt to Shame

Only rarely and on a local scale do other peoples and their kings acknowledge the authority of the king of Israel. Often, as Israel sees it, it is rather the object of disdain. In the context of the imminent fall of Babylon, in Isaiah 45:14-17 Yhwh thus speaks to Jerusalem and/or to the exile community that is on its way back to Jerusalem[17] about the nations' acknowledgment.

There is no doubt that at this moment the resources and riches of the na-

---

[17]The passage uses the feminine singular form for *you,* and thus refers to the city or the community that was mentioned in Is 45:13.

tions are changing hands. Cyrus thinks they are going to him, and the prophet has implied as much with regard to Egypt and its acolytes (Is 43:3). It is indeed Cyrus who will defeat them and become the king to whom they might be expected to bring their pleas, but he is only the tool in the hand of another, and Jerusalem is the city of Cyrus's sovereign, Yhwh, who has another idea.

Back at the beginning, Egypt had given financial support to Israel's departure from its country; in the meantime, all it has offered is empty political alliances and religious temptations. This time round, it may be Persia that defeats Egypt, but Egypt and its acolytes will come to Jerusalem and devote their resources to the city. "The toil of Egypt, the gains of Sudan, and the Ethiopians, people of stature—to you they will make their way, yours they will be; behind you they will follow as they make their way in chains" (Is 45:14). After all, if these peoples are going to accept anybody's authority and if their resources are going to go anywhere, it would be more logical for them to acknowledge the exile community and/or their city. The city, after all, needs rebuilding and beautifying, and these people can help in the task with their resources and their labor. It is to Jerusalem, not Cyrus, that they will bow down and offer submission, accepting the shaming of image-makers like themselves and fulfilling the expectations of Psalms 2, 72 and Psalm 110, though bowing to the city and its people rather than only to the king.

Bowing down to this community carries with it a bowing down to its God and vice versa, because communities and their deities are linked (the U.S.A. is a Christian country; Saudi Arabia is a Muslim country). "To you they will bow and with you they will plead: 'Yes, God is among you, there is no other, no God.'" The three peoples offer the acknowledgment that Yhwh alone is God for which the prophet continually presses, the acknowledgment upon which the Judeans themselves are tempted to renege. Further, they acknowledge that this God is "in you." It is in Jerusalem that Yhwh is acknowledged and served. Bowing down to Jerusalem makes concrete the peoples' purported bowing down to Yhwh; it is not merely an inward, private bowing down. Bowing down to Yhwh is what gives significance to bowing down to Jerusalem.

Yet further, these nations acknowledge that Yhwh is in the midst of turning from hiding to delivering, as the exiles themselves pleaded (Is 45:15-17).[18] "You are indeed a God who hides, God of Israel, deliverer." They will thus be enthusiastic about acknowledging Yhwh because they will see the point that the Babylonians will not see, the point that the community cannot imagine anyone seeing, the point that it has itself lost sight of. Perhaps, indeed, this imaginary submission of the southern peoples happens in the vision only to

---

[18]There is no pointer to a change of speaker, e.g., at the end of v. 14, and it makes sense to see vv. 15-17 as continuing the foreigners' words.

break through the community's own imagination, to help it to make the leap involved in affirming the point about God and Israel that the peoples make. *They* can see that God is in this community—can the community itself? *They* can see that this God is God alone—can the community itself? *They* can see that the God who has been hiding is now becoming once more the God who delivers—can the community itself?[19] *They* can see the Babylonian image-makers being discredited—can the community itself? *They* can see Israel finding deliverance through Yhwh—can the community itself? *They* can see that its shame is being removed and need never return—can the community itself?

Israel is to be Yhwh's witness before the nations, and one of the ways Yhwh seeks to turn them into that is by portraying these suppliants from other peoples witnessing to Israel, in an extreme form. They declare, "Israel finds deliverance through Yhwh, lasting deliverance; you will not be shamed or disgraced for lasting ages" (Is 45:17). Yhwh is not merely going to deliver Israel; it is going to find "lasting deliverance," literally "deliverance of the ages." It is not merely going to escape the shaming that comes on image-makers; it is not going to be shamed or disgraced "until the ages of eternity." Shame and disgrace are not mere theoretical possibilities. They have been existential realities for half a century. Deliverance reverses the shame that has issued from divine hiddenness, as well as reversing the hiddenness itself. And it does so with finality. Yhwh will never shame Israel again.

Actually Israel has known shame again, but the promise encourages Israel to believe that shame can never be Yhwh's last word.

From Master to Servant and Caretaker

The nations find their realistic, proper place in the world as beneficiaries of Yhwh, but able to reach their destiny only through recognizing that God is at work through Israel. That recognition involves a new way of looking at themselves and a new form of relationship to Israel.

After declaring at length the way Yhwh will put down Babylon, Isaiah 14:1-2 gives the reasoning behind this, which at a series of points involves Yhwh reversing the situation that obtains in the exile. Yhwh had withdrawn compassion from the people (e.g., Hos 1:6), but now "Yhwh will have compassion on Jacob." Yhwh had rejected the people (e.g., Jer 6:30), but will now "choose Israel again." Yhwh had removed the people from their land so that they had no settled home (*mānôaḥ*, Lam 1:3), but will now "settle them on their land" (*nûaḥ* hiphil). Other peoples had looked down on Israel (e.g., Lam 1:2-17), but now "aliens will join them, will attach themselves to the household of Jacob" (the

---

[19]On the idea of the hidden God, section 2.7 "Hiddenness/Withdrawal/Absence."

niphal verbs, *lāwâ* and *sāpaḥ*, are as vague in Hebrew as in English, and we cannot specify what form of joining they refer to). They had taken them off into exile, but now they will "take them and bring them to their place." They had behaved as their masters, but now "the household of Israel will possess them on Yhwh's land as male and female servants," like the servants of Abraham and Sarah—honored members of the household, though not quite members of the family. They had been their captors, but now they will leave their own land in order to take Israel home. They had been decision-makers; now Israel will make decisions for them.

That submission is made for Israel's sake, but also for Yhwh's (Is 49:7). At the moment Israel is a "servant of rulers." This is a sad description, for Israel was designed to be a servant of another master; the arrangement has gone seriously wrong here. Worse than that is being "loathed by the nations," people such as the Babylonians and no doubt others such as the Edomites of whom the prophets speak. The verb *loathe* is formed from the noun *abomination* (*tô'ēbâ*), and it would thus suggest that the nations look on Judah with disgust because of their ethical and/or religious behavior. Actually it is unlikely that the nations cared two hoots about the Judeans' abominations, but one may imagine that they looked down on the Judeans for their defeat and exile, and the prophet sees this as implying an indirect aversion for the abominations that had caused these events. But further, when the First Testament talks about the people's repugnance to other nations, it points to the way the community is externalizing its own awareness about itself, or the awareness the First Testament thinks it ought to have. It is "despised in spirit."[20] It has internalized any contempt that other peoples felt for it.

All that will be reversed. The kings whom Israel serves "will look, and they will stand up" to honor Israel and "will bow down" to acknowledge Israel. But they will not do that for Israel's own sake but "for the sake of Yhwh," for the sake of "Israel's holy one." It is to honor Israel's God that they stand and bow, whether or not they recognize that as they move from despising Israel to honoring Israel. Moreover, this happens because Yhwh, Israel's holy one, is a God who is "steadfast" and who "chose you." Israel is sure of neither of those facts, which adds to its sense of being despised in spirit. It knows Yhwh has abandoned it, and it wonders whether this is permanent. Against that awareness and that question are set those two facts about Yhwh: that Yhwh chose Israel in the first place and cannot but be faithful to that choice. They are effective counters to any sense of contempt that comes from some other quarter or any sense of contempt that Israel feels for itself.

---

[20] *libzōh-nepeš*, "despised of person."

Thus, Yhwh says, "I will raise my hand to nations, lift my signal to peoples, and they will bring your sons in their embrace and your daughters will be carried on their shoulder" (Is 49:22-23). Kings and queens who were used to having a huge palace household to look after their children will find themselves acting as nannies for Israelites returning from exile. They will bow down low before Israelites in the way that they were used to having their servants bowing low before them. Yes, honor will replace shame.

Recognition for Yhwh's Sake

It is because of its association with Yhwh that Israel will find peoples bowing down to it. But the days when Israel ruled a mini-empire are long gone, and it is hard to imagine them returning. Or is it? In Isaiah 55:1-5, Yhwh's promise is that those days will indeed return, though with a new twist. "I will seal for you a lasting covenant, my true commitments to David." The people as a whole will now have the kind of experience in relation to the nations that David once had. "I made him a witness to nations, a leader and commander of peoples." He was a witness to the nations by virtue of being a leader and commander to them. His achievements testified to Yhwh's activity as the one who gave him the victories that put paid to the threat of the nations around and carved out a small empire. One could also think of the David of the Psalms, at least, as a witness to them as, for instance, he testifies to Yhwh's expectations and to Yhwh's deliverance (e.g., Ps 2; 18). His victories were the fruit of Yhwh's reliable covenant commitment to him. Now that process is to be repeated, except that Yhwh's agent is to be the people as a whole. Witness to peoples is a vocation of Jacob-Israel in a more direct sense (e.g., Is 43:9-12), and in fulfilling this vocation it will find itself in a form of leadership in relation to a nation that it does not take seriously (cf. Is 45:9-13) and that does not take it seriously. "You will summon a nation you do not acknowledge, and a nation that has not acknowledged you will run to you" (Is 55:5).

Yhwh made a lasting covenant with David. That fact does not feature in the David narrative, though David does once use this expression to sum up Yhwh's commitment to him (2 Sam 23:5).[21] Psalm 89:1-4 [MT 2-5] also appeals back to a covenant Yhwh made for David, and (to put it in other words) to the true or steadfast commitments Yhwh made to David, but it does so in order to go on to upbraid Yhwh for not keeping this covenant commitment (Ps 89:38-51 [MT 39-52]). Isaiah 55 faces up to such plaints with audacity, repeating the declaration that Yhwh is making a lasting commitment but proclaiming its ex-

---

[21]2 Sam 7 does talk in terms of Yhwh's establishing a lasting throne for David's line (2 Sam 7:13, 16), and "lasting covenant" would be a fair summary of the kind of commitment Yhwh made in 2 Sam 7.

tension to the people as a whole. The Davidic covenant is being democratized[22]—which is quite appropriate, because Yhwh's covenant commitment originally applied to the whole people. If they had not insisted on having a king, the covenant would not have come to be focused on David. Now there are no kings, and Yhwh can revert to plan A. Yhwh has not only not abandoned that commitment to David but is bettering it by going back to the commitment that lay behind it. If Yhwh formally abandons the former but keeps the latter, in substance Yhwh thereby also keeps the latter.

The result will be that, like David, Israel will summon a nation that it does not acknowledge, and a nation that does not at the moment acknowledge it will run to do so. The expression may be a generic one, so that the prophet is alluding to nations in general, or it may refer to Babylon or Persia in particular, Israel's current overlord or the nation that is about to displace it. Either way, they are reacting to what Yhwh is about to do with the community, when Yhwh "glorifies" it before their eyes. Yhwh will exalt it to the position of splendor it had in David's day and more, and that will draw the superpower and/ or the nations in general to acknowledge it and to acknowledge its God: for all this is "for the sake of Yhwh your God, for Israel's holy one, because he will have glorified you" (Is 55:5). Once more the theological presupposition is that back at the beginning Yhwh had announced the intention so to bless Abraham so that all the families of the earth would pray to be blessed as Abraham had been blessed (Gen 12:1-3). That had reached a form of fulfillment in David; it will now reach a fuller form in the experience of the community as a whole. That will be the way they fulfill their vocation to be witnesses to Yhwh's activity (e.g., Is 43:8-13).

Hence the invitation at the beginning of Isaiah 55, "Hey, everyone who is thirsty, come for water, anyone who has no money, come, buy food, eat!" You want to find fulfillment as a people, to find restoration? You want water to drink, food to eat, a feast to partake in (cf. Ps 23:5), whether or not you can afford them? The prophet speaks metaphorically, though that does not mean the words refer only to "spiritual" realities. Yhwh has a destiny in mind for the whole life of this people. They are invited to come and "eat what is good." The "good" things, the "waters of deliverance" (Is 12:3), involve material provision and a place in Yhwh's purpose, and the former can provide a figure for the whole deal. Yhwh has in mind a whole new life for them. But they need to "listen, listen to me . . . bend your ear and come to me" (Is 55:2-3). At the moment they are planning their own future, and many of them will in due course see more future staying in Babylon than trudging to Jerusalem. That is like spend-

---

[22]Cf. Gerhard von Rad, *Old Testament Theology*, 2 vols. (Edinburgh: Oliver & Boyd, 1962, 1965), 2:240.

ing money on junk food. The people cannot bring about the restoration of Jerusalem, but perhaps they can prevent it. The repeated "listen, listen" (actually the imperative followed by the infinitive) takes up the expression in the ironic invitation Isaiah ben Amoz was commissioned to issue (Is 6:9). It contained a double irony—it was ironic on the surface, but beneath the surface asked to be taken quite literally. The exile happened because the exhortation met with no response, so that its surface irony was the one that found fulfillment. Second Isaiah wants to be taken literally, too.

From Tormenter to Victim

"Therefore do listen to this, you who are weak, drunk, but not with wine" (Is 51:21). When a prophet says, "Therefore," it is usually a scary moment, and the hearers might wonder whether Yhwh has more terrifying words to utter. The prophet then characterizes Yhwh as one who "contends" (rîb), and this would not make them feel any easier. Is Yhwh contending with them again? But the one who speaks is "your Lord" and "your God," and these epithets have already pointed in another direction. In a patriarchal context "your Lord" implies "your husband" (Is 51:22; Ps 45:11 [MT 12] is the only other time "your lord" comes), and "your God" recalls the covenantal relationship of "your God" and "my people," recently reaffirmed (Is 40:1). They are "his people," the colon goes on to affirm. Yhwh is not contending *with* them but *for* them. Yhwh does not intend that ever again they should drink a cup of poison: "I am taking from your hand the staggering cup, the chalice, the cup of my fury—you will not drink it again in the future." And through the Persian period that is now beginning they will not. Admittedly, in the future the city and its people will do so, in the Antiochene crisis in the second century, and when Rome takes Jerusalem in A.D. 70 and A.D. 135, and when six million die in the Holocaust. So perhaps this promise has a shorter validity than it appears to. But at least for this generation and for generations to come, the poison chalice is taken away.

"I am putting it into the hand of your tormentors, the people who said to you 'Get down so that we can walk over you, and you made your back like the ground, like a street for them walking by" (Is 51:23). Yhwh uses qatal verbs, which one would usually render "I took/have taken," "I put/have put." Perhaps these are statements about the future that are so certain that Yhwh speaks of them as already past. More likely they are performative statements—by these words Yhwh puts the act into effect. Either way Yhwh is definitely committed both to the taking away and to the imposing on someone else. Thus the supply of poison will not merely be trashed in some suitably impermeable deep-sea container but used to replenish the cup for another victim. Babylon needs to be put down.

It would be possible for Yhwh miraculously to soften the hearts of the Babylonians so that they have a strange change of policy and encourage the Judeans to go home to rebuild their city. Or Yhwh could impose a temporary paralysis on them so that they are unable to hold on to the Judeans and could give the city the protection of divine aides to stop further attack. But while sometimes acting in such ways, Yhwh more often works via the ordinary processes and rules of history. Here the prophet's implication is that it is appropriate that people who live by history die by history. It would be inappropriate simply to let the Babylonians off. There would be something artificial or phony or incomplete about it. There would be something immoral about just ignoring the atrocities they had committed simply because Yhwh had reversed those. The world would still be out of kilter. (Of course, if the nations repent, that is another matter.)

The nations deserve to have done to them what they did to others, though Yhwh does not say that will happen. The Judeans will not tread the Babylonians into the dirt as the Babylonians did the Judeans. But their city will be devastated as Jerusalem was. And this will be an answer to prayer. In their laments the community had spoken about the devastation of their city and the death of their children, about their lack of comforter and the actions of their tormentors (see Lamentations). Yhwh picks up their laments and promises a response (cf. Jer 51:34-35 for such a lament and Jer 51:36-37 for a response). The vision is a mirror image of the prospect envisaged for Ms. Babylon: see Isaiah 47. The two women will change places. One who is seated in elegance and power will find herself crouching in the dirt and one who is crouching in the dirt will find herself seated. One who drinks a blessing cup will find herself drinking a cup of poison and vice versa. The strong becomes weak, the weak strong. One who thinks she will never see bereavement will see her children killed in battle, and one who thought she had lost all her children will find herself sitting in the midst of a family again. The nations are put down not merely because they are the nations and are the enemies, on the wrong side in an ethnic conflict, but because they the faithless (Ps 9:5-6 [MT 6-7]). Amalek would never have been the victims of Yhwh's decision to eliminate them if they had not perfidiously attacked Israel.

From Slave-Trading to Watching Their Children Enslaved

In Joel 3:1-3 [MT 4:1-3], Yhwh looks to the time for restoring Judah from the ravages of destruction and exile, and from the losses and shortcomings in their destiny over succeeding centuries (to judge from the concrete references in later verses). Then, "I will gather all the nations and bring them down to the Vale of Yhwh-Decides,[23] and I will decide with them there about my people,

---

[23]*yĕhôšāpāṭ*, strictly "Yeho-Decides"; Yeho is a form of the name of Israel's God used only in compound names.

my possession, Israel, whom they scattered among the nations." There is no such literal location as "the Vale of Yhwh-Decides"; the point is that the gathering will need a wide-open space where a huge assembly can take place, and it is a gathering that will prove the truth in the declaration of faith made by the name of King Jehoshaphat, "Yhwh-Decides."

Yhwh goes on to imply another reason for declining to restore Israel in a way that sidesteps punishing the nations. They have not merely destroyed the fabric and infrastructure of a particular land. First, they have done what they liked with a people that belonged to Yhwh—"my people," "my possession." It is part of the protection of the people of God that nations who attack them are attacking people who belong to Yhwh. They risk a wrath like that of a lion whose cubs are attacked, or a mother whose children are abused. Further, what the nations have done has scattered Israel among the nations and imperiled the possibility of their functioning as Yhwh wanted, of their being an identifiable people at which the nations could look and to which they could be drawn. (Of course, Yhwh eventually developed another strategy, using the fact that Jewish people were scattered about the Mediterranean to draw the peoples among whom they lived to worship Yhwh, and thus providing a context in which it would be possible to spread the news about the Messiah who had come.)

There is worse. "They divided my land and cast lots for my people." As well as scattering Yhwh's people, they had divided up Yhwh's land (not Israel's land; cf. Joel 1:6) among themselves, that land that could arouse Yhwh's passion (Joel 2:18). But Yhwh was the only one who could allocate this land. Further, they had applied the lot not merely to the land but to the people, by this means deciding which Judean prisoners of war would belong to whom. They assumed themselves to possess these people as property. They could therefore treat them as currency. "They gave a boy for a whore, they sold a girl for wine and drank it" (Joel 3:3 [MT 4:1-3]). A boy for an hour with a prostitute, a girl for a pitcher of wine that the owner then downs without a thought. How could that simply be left as it was?

Phoenicia provided a particular example, apparently taking not only the possessions of people in Judah and Jerusalem, their silver and gold, but taking the people themselves to sell to the Greeks, who thus took them far away from their homeland. But Yhwh says, "I am arousing them from their place to which you sold them, and I will bring your deed back on your head. I will sell your sons and daughters into the power of Judah and they will sell them to the Sabeans [MT]/as captives [LXX] to a far-off nation" (Joel 3:7-8 [MT 4:7-8]). Yhwh will not simply sit there and tolerate such acts. Yhwh will bring the victims back home, which is the usual vision, but will also ensure that there are consequences that fit the wrongdoing. The people who sold children will see their

own children sold. It is unusual for the prophets to expect Yhwh to involve Israel in the punishment of the nations (cf. Obad 18; Mic 4:13; Zech 10:3-5; 12:6-
9; Ps 149:6-9).[24] As the Psalms show, in general Israel resolutely assumes that
punishment or redress is Yhwh's business. Perhaps we should see this statement as more a declaration about something that will happen in a way in
which the punishment will fit the crime. It is not directly a commission to
Judah to seek to take an eye for an eye but more a promise that justice will be
done and a warning to the nations about the destiny to which they are headed.
And in the event, it was other nations than Judah (not least the Greeks themselves) who brought trouble to Phoenicia in subsequent decades, and it was
specifically the Jewish communities in Greek cities that spread Israel's gospel
and were then the means of spreading the good news about Jesus.

From Peace to Battle

Yhwh goes on to issue a proclamation among the nations: "Sanctify a battle,
rouse the warriors, all the fighters must draw near and come up" (Joel 3:9-12
[MT 4:9-12]). There are times when turning swords into plowshares is an idea
full of hope, but times when hope lies in the opposite direction. When people
from one nation are selling people from another nation as slaves, this is not a
moment when Yhwh resolves to be long-tempered. It is a moment when Yhwh
promises the victims of such treatment that there will be justice and when we
may urge Yhwh to mobilize the forces of heaven against such acts. "Beat your
plowshares into swords, your pruning hooks into spears, the weak person
must say, 'I am a warrior'; come,[25] all you nations, gather together round
about." It is a moment when Yhwh summons earthly forces to action and to
turn their plowshares into swords, though Yhwh does so with some irony. It is
a challenge to a showdown. The people who turn swords into plowshares will
actually do so in vain. Yhwh challenges the forces of enslavement to mobilize
all their resources for a battle that they will believe to be one they fight on
God's behalf ("sanctify a battle"). Even the most feeble of fighters will need to
arouse themselves for action.

"There bring down your warriors, Yhwh." Yet when the moment comes, it
will not really be a battle but a tribunal. Once again Joel pictures the nations
gathering in the Vale of Yhwh-Decides, "for there I will sit to decide about all
the nations round about" (Joel 3:12 [MT 4:12]). There is no doubt concerning the
issue of this confrontation. Nations who think they are impressive and powerful will suddenly find themselves hauled before an authority of quite another
league. Yhwh will not need to stand and fight, only to sit and make a decision.

---

[24]Cf. Hans Walter Wolff, *Joel and Amos* (Philadelphia: Fortress, 1977), p. 79.

[25]The verb is preceded by another, ʿûšû, a hapax legomenon of unknown meaning.

Yhwh earlier spoke of this as an occasion when "I will make a decision with them" (*šāpaṭ* niphal; Joel 3:2 [MT 4:2]), as if they were going to be involved in determining what the decision would be, and there is a sense in which they have opportunity to do that; the right response to Yhwh could save their skins. But such language is ironic. Yhwh will impose a decision on them. It is as if two parties have come before a judge for the judge to decide what to do about them. This judge has a First Testament judge's proper commitment: not merely to be even-handed but to see that the unfairly treated are delivered. Yhwh will see to it that the right decision is made about the nations that scattered, divided and enslaved.

Psalm 79 includes a terrifying prayer for the nations' punishment that links with this promise: "Pour out your fury on the nations that have not acknowledged you, on the kingdoms that have not called on your name." It offers several reasons for its terrifying prayer. First, they have trespassed on Yhwh's space. "God, nations have come into your property, defiled your holy palace, turned Jerusalem into ruins." Foreigners were not banned from the temple, but their invading it as conquerors is a different matter, even if they come as Yhwh's servants bringing punishment on Judah. Second, as an extension of that, they have declined to acknowledge or call on Yhwh, as if they needed to recognize Yhwh's power or their reliance on it. Third, they have desolated the people's homeland, "devoured Jacob and desolated his home." We may guess that this was the most powerful motivation for their horrifying prayer, but we might be wrong. Fourth, they have shed the blood of Yhwh's people, and the brothers and sisters of the dead look for things to be evened out. "Why should the nations say, 'Where is their God?' May it be acknowledged among the nations before our eyes, the redress for your servants' blood that has been shed" (Ps 79:10). In these circumstances, Yhwh is one who disciplines the nations (Ps 94:10). The prophets provide some promises that respond to such a psalm, or that such a psalm could claim.

The nations are inclined to embody a human pretension that contrasts with the real truth about who has power in the world. That was the issue in the conflict between Yhwh and Egypt. The nations are people who put God out of mind and need to acknowledge that they are human, not God; and to make this point clear, they "must not prevail" (*'āzaz*, Ps 9:19-20 [MT 20-21]). Prevailing is Yhwh's business (cf. Ps 89:13 [MT 14]; contrast Judg 6:2). The nations pretend to authority and power; Yhwh must demonstrate authority and power to make the real facts clear. Nations may rage and roar like powerful oceans, but when Yhwh speaks a word of admonition they mysteriously melt and flee (Is 17:12-14). But Yhwh is relaxed about when to take appropriate action. Ahaz was understandably inclined to terror and panic as he was caught between the ambitions of Assyria and those of Syria and Ephraim, and Isaiah told him to relax (Is 7:4; cf. Is 30:15). He is to do as Yhwh does. "I will relax as I look at my place":[26] calmly Yhwh contemplates the way time will unfold from spring through summer to autumn until the right moment for action on the nations arrives (Is 18:4-6).

A Nightmare Vision for the Nations

Yhwh speaks to "my servant Jacob" as "the one who delivers you from afar, your offspring from their land of captivity. Jacob will again be at peace and be secure, with no one to disturb him." And Yhwh adds, "I shall make an end of the nations where I have scattered you, but I will not make an end of you, but I will punish you by way of judgment and certainly not leave you clear" (Jer 46:27-28). There are a number of reasons why the First Testament's vision includes a nightmare prospect for the nations.

First, putting down the nations that control and oppress Israel is logistically the necessary condition for Israel's own deliverance. The phrase "the one who delivers" stands alongside "I shall make an end." It is when the superpower is put down that its prisoners are freed.

Second, the putting down of the war-making nations is also a necessary condition for Israel's being able to live at peace once it has been restored to its land. The phrase "be at peace and be secure" stands alongside "no one to disturb." The disturbers need to be put out of action. That was how its story started. For most of its life, Israel was a tiny people in its world, dominated by other nations, but it lived its life in the awareness that Yhwh has defeated these nations in the past. Concretely, its story told how Yhwh defeated Egypt, the great power at the beginning of its story, then defeated different peoples that confronted it on the way to Canaan and the peoples of Canaan itself. "With your hand you dispossessed nations and planted them [Israel's ancestors]. You brought calamity on peoples and threw them out" (Ps 44:2 [MT 3]). Putting down war-making peoples is still a condition of peace.

Third, putting down the oppressors is part of the restoring of moral order in the universe. Yhwh could miraculously remove the Israelites from their places in exile and protect them from further attack with a wall of fire, but this would leave the oppressors unpunished and leave disorder in place. Thus "grave your shattering" stands alongside "therefore your devourers will be devoured" (Jer 30:12, 16), even though the devourers acted on Yhwh's behalf. Related to that is the possible necessity to show that Yhwh treats the nations the same way as Israel. Faced with the faithlessness of different peoples, Yhwh does not favor either Israel or the other peoples. All are treated the same way.

---

[26]I take it that *mākôn* refers to Yhwh's earthly dwelling, as, e.g., Ex 15:17; 1 Kings 8:13. The EVV "look from my place" (i.e., heaven) requires an odd use of *b*.

Fourth, putting down the oppressors corrects their misapprehension about Israel, and indirectly about Yhwh and Yhwh's involvement in the world. Of course they were not wrong that Zion was an outcast, was their prey, and that no one was acting like the shepherd of a lost sheep, seeking the people out so as to rescue them (Ezek 34:5-6). But the oppressors and the world in general need to be shown that these are not permanent realities. Zion cannot be dismissed. It will not be prey forever. The Good Shepherd is seeking it out. It is not a permanent outcast. It is integral to Yhwh's purpose in the world.

Fifth, Jeremiah's promise simply emerges from Yhwh's commitment to Israel. Israel is "Yhwh's servant," a member of Yhwh's household. There is a quasi-family relationship between Yhwh and Israel. Israel belongs to Yhwh's family, and therefore Yhwh is morally bound to act as its restorer (gō'ēl). Israel has a special place for Yhwh. "I am Yhwh—your God, and the holy one of Israel—your savior." At the beginning of Israel's story, Yhwh was prepared to surrender Egypt and its affiliates (to their rulers? to their non-gods?) in order to act as "your God," "Israel's holy one" and therefore deliver Israel and turn it more effectively into a people that belongs to Yhwh. It was "because of the fact that you were valuable in my eyes, you were important and I myself loved you." And Yhwh is prepared to do that again, surrendering Babylon to Persia in order to repeat that act of deliverance. "I will give people in your place, nations in place of your life" (Is 43:3-4).

"What can we say about the self-consciousness of a provincial cultic community tolerated by the Persian Empire which yet portrays history from Adam onwards as taking place all for her own sake?"[27]

8.3 The Superpower and Its Failure

The victim of God's punishment in the First Testament is most often the people of God, but when that is not so, the most common victim is the superpower of the day. Through most of Israel's history, a series of superpowers dominated the political, economic, cultural and religious life of the world as Israel knew it—Assyria, then Babylon, then Persia then Greece. The series continues in much of subsequent history all over the world as Rome, then Turkey, then Britain, then the United States has played this role. The themes that recur in the First Testament's comments on the superpowers are not very specific to the particular power in question at any one moment. Persia, for instance, is seen as a new embodiment of Assyria (Ezra 6:22), while prophecies relating to Assyria are reapplied to Greece (Dan 11), as the New Testament will see Rome as a latter-day Babylon (1 Pet 5:13). The comments thus offer raw material for a

---

[27]Von Rad, *OT Theology*, 1:347.

theological understanding of superpower as such and for reflection on, for instance, the rise and fall of the British Empire in the nineteenth and twentieth centuries or on the place of the United States in the twentieth and twenty-first. They are not so much concerned with the ethics of being the superpower, though they make some points about that. What they suggest is a theology of being the superpower. Perhaps if a superpower gets its theology of itself straight, it will have the necessary framework for its ethics.

The First Testament sees the superpower as Yhwh's servant, summoned by Yhwh, and having both a negative and a positive role in relation to Israel and the world. The problem is that it does not see itself as Yhwh's servant, and it has to be put in its place. It thus finds itself on the receiving end of Yhwh's retributive fury, expressed via the next superpower; which at least means deliverance for its victims. Its leader is the embodiment of its role, its mistake and its fate.

Yhwh's Servant

"I am making you a prophet for the nations," Yhwh said to Jeremiah; "I am appointing you this day over nations and over kingdoms, to uproot, pull down, destroy, and overthrow, to build and plant" (Jer 1:4, 10). As a prophet to the nations, Jeremiah is commissioned to send word to the kings of Edom, Moab, Ammon, Tyre and Sidon by the hand of their envoys who have come to Jerusalem to see Zedekiah, with whom they are apparently in alliance against Babylon. But the message concerns Babylon, the superpower that dominates their lives and Judah's life. Yhwh speaks as "the one who made the earth, the people and the animals that are on the face of the earth, by my great power and my extended arm." On that basis, Yhwh adds, "I give it to whomever I please," and at the moment "I myself am giving all these countries into the control of Nebuchadnezzar, the king of Babylon, my servant, and I am also giving him the wild animals to serve him" (Jer 27:3-6).

Yhwh's words offer a surprising contrast with the creation story and the exodus story. Genesis 1 and 2 in different ways dispute the common Middle Eastern view that kings have a godlike position in the world and assert that it is humanity that has this Godlike position. One expression of that is humanity's sovereignty over the animal world (Gen 1:26-28). It is thus remarkable that this sovereignty should be given to one person. Indeed, that strangeness draws attention to the broader strangeness of Yhwh's framework of thinking here. The creation stories give no place for the exercise of authority by some human beings over others. There are no presidents in the Garden of Eden. Humanity serves the garden; human beings are not in servitude to one another. But the way the world came to develop involved the realities of authority and servitude, and God here works within that framework. As the creator of the world, including humanity and the animals, God retains sovereignty over it, and in a context in which empire has developed, God asserts the right to use it and constrain it. The people need to settle down under Babylonian authority. The exile will last seventy years (Hananiah was talking about two years; Jer 28:2). It will not last forever, but it will last two or three generations.

Yhwh backs up this assertion with a reference to having made the world "by my great power and my extended arm." In the First Testament story these phrases do not appear in connection with creation but with the exodus (e.g., Ex 6:6; 32:11). Their appearance in the present connection again causes some shock. In the exodus story Yhwh used great power and an extended arm to act against the regional power and free the Israelites. Here the earlier work of that great power and extended arm in creation are the basis for subjecting the Israelites and other peoples to a superpower. All the nations are to serve him, his son and his grandson, until his country's time comes, too, and many nations and great kings make him a servant (Jer 27:7).[28]

But meanwhile, any nation that resists serving the superpower that Yhwh put in place is resisting Yhwh and will pay for it. That includes Judah. The God who wielded such power in creating the world and bringing Israel out of Egypt will wield that power to take Judah to Babylon. But if the people of God (or any other people) accept their servitude to the superpower, then they will be free to stay in their own land (Jer 27:8-22). Yhwh is not content with a mere generalization about submitting to Babylon. He goes on to tell Jeremiah to urge the kings, via their envoys, not to pay heed to their prophets, diviners, dreamers and so on when they tell them not to submit to Babylon. These advisers are prophesying falsehood. They risk Yhwh throwing them out of their own country into exile. Jeremiah is involved in these peoples' affairs purely because of their significance for Judah. He affirms that Yhwh is sovereign over their destiny. They have their prophets; even the fact that they are prophesying falsehood draws attention to the similarity between them and the Judean prophets. They can be exiled by Yhwh or allowed to stay in their own country.

And the agent through whom Yhwh will take such action in relation to Judah or these other peoples is "Nebuchadnezzar, the king of Babylon, my servant." The servants of Yhwh include Moses, David, Jeremiah himself and Israel as a whole, but also the Babylonian king. The superpowers, who think they serve no one but themselves, actually serve Yhwh.

---

[28]In the event, Nebuchadnezzar's grandson did not reign, though this more likely reflects the fact that Yhwh here speaks in images (as when speaking of a seventy-year exile) than that Yhwh had a change of mind (as Terence E. Fretheim suggests, *Jeremiah* [Macon, Ga.: Smyth and Helwys, 2002], p. 383).

The Agent Summoned by Yhwh

The superpower comes on the scene as a destroyer, but acts thus as Yhwh's agent, particularly in chastising the people of God because of its wrongdoing. Isaiah, too, speaks of the nations because of their role in relation to Judah. It is because of the need to chastise and then to restore Judah that Yhwh gets involved with the superpower. Under Yhwh's control, it has a moral role. Yhwh sends it "against a corrupt nation" (Is 10:6): the adjective suggests godless and perverted, polluting and polluted, in attitude to God or to other people.[29] Assyria, the original superpower, invades countries such as Israel and Judah for its own reasons, but in doing so, fulfills Yhwh's prevenient purpose. Yhwh is the actual commander-in-chief of the Assyrian army: "He will lift an ensign to nations from afar, whistle to it at the end of the world, and there it will be, coming speedily and swiftly" (Is 5:26).

The fact that the Assyrians are *the* world power is hinted by the talk of Yhwh's summoning "nations" (plural; cf. Is 8:9; 14:26; 30:28; Jer 1:15; 4:16; 25:9). The superpower is the embodiment of world forces attacking Judah. The Assyrians are about to campaign in the Levant in order to quell uprisings there, and they are acting in accordance with a policy formulated in light of the needs of the empire. They will have discussed the matter in the cabinet and consulted their god Ashur, and they come because they believe Ashur commissions them. But behind the words of the Assyrian god and king lie the initiative of Yhwh who is summoning them (cf. Jer 1:15) without their knowing it and manipulating them into doing Yhwh's will. Assyria is "my angry staff. A rod is in their hand, my fury" (Is 10:5). It is coming to Judah to rule it firmly, bearing the signs of authority given it by Yhwh.[30] Its rule over Judah will be the means of expressing Yhwh's furious anger with Judah. Yhwh is sending it to Judah, giving Assyria its orders (*ṣiwwâ);* he is its commander (Is 10:6). It is intent on being interventionist for its own reasons, because Judah has been resisting Assyrian policy, yet unbeknown to itself, it is doing something for Yhwh. Yhwh is about to finish off some work on Mount Zion (Is 10:12);[31] Assyria is just Yhwh's contractor. Jeremiah uses similar peremptory verbs of Babylon: Yhwh is sending for, taking, bringing (Jer 25:5-9). There is no doubt who is the Superpower here.

Or Assyria is just Yhwh's mercenary, crushing the wreath that decorates the

---

[29]See *TDOT, NIDOTTE* on *ḥānēp,* and section 4.2 "Corruption."

[30]While *šēbeṭ* (staff) could refer to a sign of authority or to a weapon such as a club, *maṭṭeh* (rod) cannot refer to a weapon, so presumably both cola refer to signs of authority. But Babylon is also unequivocally Yhwh's club *(mappēṣ),* the means by which Yhwh smashes nations, warriors and ordinary people (Jer 51:20-23).

[31]The verb *bāsaʿ,* here piel ("finish off"), usually suggests violence.

head of the Ephraimite leaders at their state banquet (Is 28:1-4): "Someone strong and powerful belonging to the Lord, like a hailstorm, a devastating tornado, like a storm of massive, flooding waters, he is putting it down to the ground with his hand." Yhwh is not prominent as the agent of this devastation, and is not explicitly the subject of any of the verbs. Yet the "strong" one through whom Yhwh is working is itself unnamed. The syntax and the substance of the lines stand in contrast. The syntax draws attention to the human agent through whom Yhwh acts, leaving Yhwh as the force behind the scenes. But the substance implies that the human agent is too unimportant to name, for the real agent in this event is the one who acts by means of the superpower. The tension between syntax and substance also puts the emphasis on the identity of Ephraim, the only dramatis persona actually named in Isaiah 28:1-4 (even the name "Yhwh" does not appear): "trampled underfoot will be the majestic garland of the drunks of Ephraim," the victim of the strong and powerful one, the victim of the Lord, and the victim of the devastating storm that both work together to bring. For the destroyer, as for a lion, it is a matter of fulfilling its predatory instinct. For the victim, it is a disaster. For Yhwh, it is an expression of an initiative (Jer 4:6-7).

Thus Jerusalem falls because Nebuchadnezzar takes it, but it falls because Yhwh gives it into his hand like a Christmas present (e.g., Jer 21:10). His success has nothing to do with his own military numbers or ability. "Even if you defeated the entire force of Chaldeans who were fighting with you and the people who were left among them were wounded men, each in his tent, they would rise up and burn this city with fire" (Jer 37:10).

Rebellion against the superpower can therefore be rebellion against Yhwh. Ezekiel 17 declaims an allegorical poem about Nebuchadnezzar transporting Jehoiachin to Babylon and replacing him by Zedekiah, who then made overtures to Egypt in the traditional Judean fashion (cf. Is 30—31); but Nebuchadnezzar will not stand for that. The allegorical history is told purely at the human level, in terms of decisions by Babylonian and Judean politicians. Ezekiel's interpretation of it largely does the same, though it starts in an odd way, by addressing Judah as a "rebellious household" (Ezek 17:11). Ezekiel has used that expression earlier (Ezek 2—3; 12), but there is a special point about it here. Politically, Judah is revolting against Nebuchadnezzar (Ezek 17:15). But religiously, Judah is rebelling against Yhwh. Similarly, Zedekiah's rebellion involves breaking the sworn covenant laid down by Nebuchadnezzar when he set him on the throne. Judah must be submissive rather than assert itself politically. Yhwh's comment is that he has despised "my oath" and broken "my covenant" (Ezek 17:19). Yhwh had affirmed the sworn covenant that Nebuchadnezzar made, because the process of chastising Judah was one Yhwh identified with. Ezekiel does not go as far as Isaiah and say that Yhwh was behind Nebuchadnezzar's action, though he might well be prepared to do so. His words would be compatible with the idea that Yhwh's action was retrospectively to rubber-stamp Nebuchadnezzar's action. Either way, the covenant is both Babylon's and Yhwh's, and Zedekiah will pay, not merely for breaking faith with Babylon, but for breaking faith with Yhwh.

For rebelling, Nebuchadnezzar will transport Zedekiah to Babylon, like his predecessor (Ezek 17:9). But Yhwh, too, declares, "I will spread my net over him . . . and take him to Babylon and come to a decision with him there about the offense [ma'al] he has committed" (Ezek 17:20). Zedekiah has committed an offense against Nebuchadnezzar, but the vast majority of the occurrences of this word denote offenses against God. It is Yhwh and not merely Nebuchadnezzar who will take him to Babylon to charge him with an offense. Indeed, Nebuchadnezzar's "taking" has been left behind in the chapter's rhetoric. Thus the end result will be that the rebellious house will acknowledge not merely that Babylon is the superpower but that Yhwh spoke these words through Ezekiel.

The Agent of a Positive Purpose for Yhwh's People

Yhwh's work through the superpower can have a positive significance. A superpower usually claims that its policies are designed to benefit the world it dominates, though things often look different to the alleged beneficiaries. Thus in a speech attributed to Titus, Josephus ironically suggests that the Jews were driven to revolt by Roman *philanthropia*.[32] Ironically, the superpower's self-perception can be right in a different direction from the one it imagines. Both its rise and fall can serve the destiny of Yhwh's own people. Yhwh thus declares, "Do not be afraid of Assyria, my people dwelling on Zion." Little Judah can be encouraged that the superpower currently oppressing it will not do so forever (Is 10:24-27).

The fall of Jerusalem did not mean the complete annihilation of the people. Yhwh had said there would be some leftovers, and "the king of Babylon allowed leftovers to Judah" (Jer 40:11). The superpower is the means of Yhwh's ensuring this. After that there is yet a further act of rebellion against Yhwh and against Babylon, Ishmael's slaughter of the Babylonian-appointed governor. Yet Yhwh promises the Judean community that if it now submits and stays where it is in Judah, "I will grant you compassion, and he will have compassion on you and restore you to your land" (Jer 42:12). If the people continue to resist Yhwh's authority that because of their faithlessness is expressed by

---

[32]Josephus *Jewish Wars* 6.333-36; cf. John J. Collins, "The Jewish World and the Coming of Rome," in *Symbiosis, Symbolism, and the Power of the Past*, ed. William G. Dever and Seymour Gitin (Winona Lake, Ind.: Eisenbrauns, 2003), pp. 353-62 (see p. 360).

means of the superpower's authority, they will again experience Yhwh's wrath expressed by means of the superpower's wrath. But as Yhwh can be tough by means of the superpower, so Yhwh can be compassionate by means of the superpower. Yhwh had once withheld compassion (Jer 13:14; 16:5) and used the superpower's refusal to have compassion to that end (Jer 6:23; 21:7). But Yhwh always intended to have compassion again (Jer 12:15; 30:18; 33:26), and superpowers are capable of being merciful toward subordinate peoples, for their own reasons, so Yhwh can also use that fact, and if necessary push them in that direction. The possibility of the Babylonians restoring the people to their land makes the point, for elsewhere Yhwh is the one who does such restoring (e.g., Jer 30:3; 32:37).[33] Yhwh can get the Babylonians to act positively as Yhwh can get them to act negatively.

In turn, the warning that Yhwh's day is coming for Babylon comes to a close with an explanation in terms of Jacob-Israel's destiny: "For Yhwh will have compassion on Jacob and again choose Israel, and will settle them on their soil" (Is 14:1).[34] The fall of Babylon serves Medo-Persian aspirations, brings punishment for Babylon's wrongdoing, demonstrates that Yhwh, not Babylon, is God, and opens up the possibility of Israel's restoration. Thus when Yhwh arouses Cyrus, "faithfulness calls [him] to its heel"—unwittingly he is the agent of Yhwh's doing right by Israel (*sedeq*, Is 41:2). It is "for your sake" that Yhwh is sending Cyrus off (Is 43:14-15). The fall of Babylon is to happen because of little Judah!

Is that a realistic expectation? Can Persia really be a resource for the Judeans? Can Yhwh really seize Judah from Babylon, like someone recapturing the prey from a lion? Just watch me, says Yhwh (Is 49:24-26).

Actually, Judah had been only too willing to treat the superpower as a potential resource, but it was right for the wrong reasons. It was right to resist pressure to rebel against Assyria, but seeking support from Assyria was a different matter, because it implied putting one's trust in the superpower rather than the Superpower (Is 7:1-9). The superpower would therefore be the Superpower's means of bringing calamity on Judah (Is 7:17-20). Jeremiah offers the same critique in the context of Assyria's dog days, by which time Judah ought to have learned its lesson the hard way. The superpower is a leaky tank compared with the Superpower (Jer 2:13, 18, 36).

Not Seeing Whose It Is

So under Yhwh's control a superpower can have a negative or a positive role;

---

[33]Cf. Fretheim, *Jeremiah*, p. 552.

[34]The EVV obscure the point by the chapter division (there is no chapter or paragraph division here in MT) and also by declining to give *ki* its usual meaning "for."

Yhwh can make it the means to fulfill warnings or promises. In both respects its acts bring a partial fulfillment of Yhwh's ultimate purpose in the world. It brings Yhwh's day. But all this is unwitting. The trouble is that the superpower does not realize whom it serves. It is not trying to serve Yhwh but doing its own thing. For more than one reason it would be appropriate for the superpower to call on Yhwh's name, and Yhwh declares that Cyrus is to do that (Is 41:25). That would imply asking for Yhwh's assistance in his tasks and acknowledging that Yhwh lies behind his achievements. And in a nominal sense Cyrus did call on Yhwh, but no more seriously than he called on Marduk.

Assyria likewise acted out of its own self-assertiveness and self-confidence. For that it will be punished in due course. In Yhwh's design the superpower is a kind of magistrate to punish wrongdoers, and when magistrates act to punish people, they have no personal interest in the matter (otherwise they would excuse themselves from the case). "But this is not what he envisions, this is not what he has in mind, because in his mind is destroying, cutting off nations not a few, because he says, 'Aren't my leaders kings, all of them?'" (Is 10:7-8). Serving Yhwh? In Assyria's mind it is not acting on the basis of an authority from Yhwh (or even Ashur?) but on the basis of sober calculation of its overwhelming military might, proven in other victories (Is 10:9). The Assyrian king allows his thinking to issue in big talk and allows his looking to envision high honor (Is 10:12). Beforehand he thought he had the potential to achieve all that he wanted, and afterward he complements himself on what he has achieved: "By the might of my hand I acted, by my insight, because I am smart." That was what enabled him to manipulate the boundaries of peoples and plunder their treasuries and cast down their inhabitants. It was as easy as robbing a bird's nest (Is 10:13-14). The trouble is that this ignores the one whose tool Assyria was: "Does the axe honor itself over the one who hews with it, or does the saw make itself greater than the one who wields it, like a staff wielding the one who raised it, like a rod raising the one who is not wood?" (Is 10:15). Retrospectively as prospectively the superpower treats its power and achievement as its own when it is merely God's agent.

Isaiah 36—37 makes the point more systematically, though narratively. Assyria has virtually conquered Palestine, the only remaining task being to reduce Jerusalem itself. During the siege Sennacherib's minister asks how Jerusalem thinks it will escape. It is no good relying on big talk or on Egyptian help. And it is no use relying on Yhwh, because Yhwh will be offended by Hezekiah's closing down many Yhwh sanctuaries (the "high places"), and because anyway Yhwh sent the Assyrian king. "It was Yhwh said to me, 'Go up to this land and destroy it'" (Is 36:10). They are two clever arguments for the narrator to attribute to the superpower's leader. But the minister then contradicts himself and makes a fatal mistake. "Do not let Hezekiah deceive you by saying, 'Yhwh will rescue us.' Did any of the gods of the nations rescue his country from the hand of the king of Assyria? Where were the gods of Hamath and Arpad? Where were the gods of Sepharvaim? Did they rescue Samaria from my hand? Which among all the gods of these countries rescued their countries from me, that Yhwh should rescue Jerusalem from my hand?" (Is 36:18-20). It is a mistake, because the minister has slighted and insulted the living God (Is 37:4, 6, 23-24). "You yourself have heard what the kings of Assyria have done to all the countries and devoted them. And will you escape?" (Is 37:11). Assyria sees itself as invincible and assumes that Yhwh can be discounted as if Yhwh were like the other gods represented by images (Is 37:18-19). It is thus blaspheming and reviling Yhwh (Is 37:23). It has set itself up as God.

The point is made in a subtle way by the words that follow. "Did you not hear long ago? I have done this. In days past I shaped it, now I have made it come about. It has happened, demolishing fortified cities into ruin heaps, their inhabitants helpless, dismayed and confounded" (Is 37:26-27). In the previous lines the king was speaking, and it would be natural to assume that he continues to speak here. But there is no further change of speaker when the lines continue, "I know your staying, your setting out, your coming in, and how you have raged against me" (Is 37:28). Here Yhwh speaks, which indicates that those preceding lines rather referred to Yhwh's shaping (i.e., planning) and acting. The rhetorical ambiguity reflects the pretentiousness of the king's attitude. We are hardly aware that these are Yhwh's words as the king is not aware that he speaks as if he were God.

Thinking It Is the One That Makes the Plans

The superpower's words thus give away its attitude to God. "As my hand has reached those idol kingdoms and their images, greater than Jerusalem and Samaria, shall I not do to Jerusalem and its images as I did to Samaria and its idols?" (Is 10:10-11). While the prophet may be suggesting that Jerusalem's predilection for images is the reason for Yhwh's punishment, or that Assyria sees Jerusalem as not good enough at image-making (!), as an element in the reason for the superpower's own punishment, the point more likely lies in the irreverence of the statement. Assyria speaks of Jerusalem as if it were an average (or rather, a below-average) religious center with its images, but thereby slights the true God who lives there. In its thinking, real human power counts for much more than theoretical divine power represented by an image (as one can see, after all). (Of course, ironically Assyria is half-right in that.)

The superpower can thus think it is in a position to formulate plans and implement them, when actually this is not so. Only a greater Superpower is in that position. "Shout out, peoples, and collapse, attend, all remote parts of the earth; prepare for battle, and collapse, prepare for battle, and collapse," Isaiah sarcastically urges (Is 8:9). "Peoples/remote parts of the earth" can again refer to the superpower, like plural "nations." The superpower can easily think it is the Superpower, but it is not. The frame around Isaiah 8:8-10 and the frame around Middle Eastern history is the fact that "God is with us," the conviction a girl will use as a name for her son when he is born (Is 7:14). This fact undergirds Judah's political destiny (e.g., Ps 46:7, 11 [MT 8, 12]) and thus affects people involved with Judah. It means God can protect Judah from Ephraim and Syria, and it is the X factor in the superpower's relationship with Judah. The superpower can raise the battle cry and put on its armor but then find itself falling apart. "Make a plan [ʿēṣâ]—it will be frustrated; speak a word—it will not happen" (Is 8:10). The superpower can make plans and announce them, but find them strangely foiled. Yhwh is the real planner. "As I envisioned, so it came about; as I planned, this will arise, to break Assyria in my land. . . . This is the plan that is planned concerning the whole earth, this is the hand extended over all the nations, because Yhwh Armies has planned—who will annul? His hand is extended—who will turn it back?" (Is 14:24-27).

Formulating plans is integral to the life of a superpower. A nation does not become a superpower without making plans, and it does not remain one without making plans. Those plans can be the means of implementing Yhwh's own intentions (Jer 49:30). But in due course Yhwh will formulate a plan to put the superpower down (Jer 50:45). That is Yhwh's plan for the world. Yhwh will declare it well ahead of time as a sign of determination to fulfill it and as subsequent evidence that events indeed issued from this plan (Jer 50:45; Is 46:10). And with some irony Yhwh's means of acting is the leader of the next superpower, who thinks he is merely fulfilling his own plan but is actually "the man of Yhwh's plan," which thus overrules the superpower's multiple plans (Is 46:11; 47:13).

So Yhwh declares that through Cyrus "I will implement my purpose" (ḥēpeṣ, Is 46:10; cf. Is 44:28). There might seem to be two purposes at work in the Middle East, Babylon's and Persia's, but Yhwh is overruling both in different ways. Babylon's strategy for holding on to power will fail. Cyrus will see himself as implementing his own purpose, and grammatically the declaration "he will fulfill his purpose on Babylon" (Is 48:14) could refer to that, but in the context of Second Isaiah's use of such words, Cyrus's purpose is sidelined. It is Yhwh's purpose that he is to fulfill.

Confident and Tough

When the moment of desolation for Assyria comes, people will comment, "This is the exultant city that dwelt in confidence, that said to itself, 'I and I alone am still here.' Hey, it has become a desolation, a lair for animals; everyone who passes by it hisses and waves his hand" (Zeph 2:15). The warning portrays two extremes of experience. On one hand, there is a supreme confidence in its position: how could one imagine that the superpower would ever fall? Surely it will be there forever? Then there is the extreme to which it is about to be taken when it becomes merely a refuge for animals and when human beings, people who perhaps admired it resentfully a little while ago, now look at it with horror or glee or a prayer for themselves that they may not come to the same fate.

The same experience will come to Assyria's conqueror. The Babylonians, too, are people who act out of a confidence in themselves: they are arrogant (*zēdîm*, Is 13:11), indeed the embodiment of arrogance, toward Israel's Holy One (Jer 50:29-32). This superpower, too, cannot imagine how its powerful and cultured position could ever be otherwise. The fact that Assyria fell does not mean that it must do so. Ms. Babylon, too, thinks, "I and I alone am still here" (Is 47:8, 10). "I will be here forever" (Is 47:7). Both statements deserve the horrified reaction people sometimes gave in response to Jesus' "I am." The noun clause is a statement only Yhwh can make (compare the divine *ănî* in passages such as Is 43:10-13). The verb "I will be" also belongs to Yhwh (see Ex 3:13-14): only Yhwh can say *ʾehyeh* or "forever," and Ms. Babylon is subconsciously speaking as if she were God. That is the nature of a superpower's self-understanding. Yhwh thus says to Ms. Babylon, "You did not call these things to mind; you did not think about its outcome" (Is 47:7).

There are other indictments of the superpower. One is that it characteristically acts tough and lacks compassion. To any ordinary nation, the superpower has an awesome might, a frightening power, one that belongs in another league from anything an ordinary nation pretends to (Is 5:27-29). It is hard to imagine having its strength, its persistence, its invulnerability—or its hardness.

On the eve of Jerusalem's fall, Yhwh warned the people left in the city that Nebuchadnezzar "would put them to the sword and not have pity on them or show mercy or have compassion" (Jer 21:7). And that would be in keeping with Yhwh's own attitude to Judah as expressed earlier: "The Lord . . . will not have compassion on its orphans or its widows" (Is 9:17 [MT 16]). To put it another way, to replace the light wooden yoke that is just enough to harness an ox's strength by giving it the minimum of constraint and keep it to the task the farmer intends, Yhwh is imposing a heavy metal yoke on Judah, treating it the way a farmer might treat a recalcitrant animal.

Yet although it had been the means of expressing Yhwh's anger, this gives Babylon no excuse for its conduct: "You did not show them compassion. On an elder you weighted your yoke heavily" (Is 47:6). The critique comes in the midst of a parabolic description of Babylon as a cultured, powerful woman, and it suggests that it is in her womanliness Ms. Babylon has failed. One expects a woman to be a person of compassion *(rahămîm)*—after all, she has a womb *(rehem;* the word came in Is 46:3). One expects a woman to care about the elderly members of her family. Whether the "elder" refers to people within Judah or to Judah itself, in what she did to Judah, Ms. Babylon has failed in her womanliness.[35] The prophet thus draws attention to another counterintuitive divine expectation of a superpower. As well as not having too high an opinion of itself, it has an obligation to compassion. It is expected to stay human, or to behave divine. It is expected to show stereotypical feminine qualities as well as stereotypical masculine ones. The one who shows no compassion will receive none (Jer 50:42).

Hans Barstad suggests we should have sympathy for Babylon, "a highly developed civilization, with an advanced political and economic structure" yet no resources of its own, so that "the whole existence of the empire depended entirely upon the import of materials like metals, stone, and timber, and all sorts of food and luxury items." The First Testament has no such sympathy.[36]

Put in Its Place

In light of its refusal to recognize who is God or to combine compassion with toughness, there is a moral and theological necessity for the superpower to be put down. The world cannot be left to the misapprehension that the superpower propagates. The real truth will need to be made clear to the superpower and to the world. The nations must be driven to "acknowledge that you are Yhwh, you alone" (Is 37:20).

So the God who manipulated the Assyrians into invading Palestine will manipulate them into leaving. "I am putting a spirit in him. He will hear a report and return to his country, but I will make him fall by the sword in his own country" (Is 37:7). A king who stays away too long risks finding he has lost his throne. Sennacherib will hear of such plots and will decide he had better get home, though he will still in due course fall in a coup. With some irony this happens when his own sons assassinate him as he is bowed down in the temple of his god Nisroch (Is 37:38). It transpires that this god cannot protect him but that he is vulnerable to the will of the God whom he thought could protect no one. The king who thought he controlled the environment will find he is

---

[35] Cf. Walter Brueggemann, *A Social Reading of the Old Testament* (Minneapolis: Fortress, 1994), pp. 111-33.

[36] Cf. Daniel L. Smith-Christopher, *A Biblical Theology of Exile* (Minneapolis: Fortress, 2002), p. 49, quoting from Hans M. Barstad, *The Myth of the Empty Land* (Oslo: Scandinavian University Press, 1996), pp. 63-64.

treated just like a domesticated animal: "I will put my hook in your nose and my bit on your jaws and make you return by the way you came" (Is 37:29).

Assyria has imposed its burdensome yoke on "my land' and "my mountains" (Is 14:25). Assyria was Yhwh's agent in chastising Judah, but thinking it could take possession of the land that especially belonged to Yhwh is a different matter. Breaking Assyria will mean removing the burdensome yoke from the people's shoulders, but in this context that seems to be the fortuitous consequence of Assyria's trespassing on Yhwh's rights. Likewise later, "Yahweh and Babylon have been in dispute over who should control Israel and the land of Israel,"[37] and Yhwh must resolve this dispute. Specifically, Yhwh is punishing the Babylonians for what they did to Yhwh's palace in Jerusalem. Yhwh thus has a task to do among the Babylonians, and is in the midst of attending to them (Jer 50:25-28; cf. Jer 51:11).

Think about the Assyrians, Yhwh bids the Egyptians (Ezek 31). Assyria was like a cedar of Lebanon, a huge, impressive tree that provided shade for all the birds and animals. It towered high above the other trees, but then "its heart became high in its majesty" (Ezek 31:10). English versions take this to suggest pride, but this may give a wrong impression. BDB suggests "reckless elation,"[38] a euphoria that issues in a confidence that things will always be like this and that puts out of mind who made them so (cf. Deut 8:14; Hos 13:6). That kind of elation is liable to make Yhwh take action to bring home the truth. So it was for Assyria, handed over to an even greater power, Babylon. The Assyrian tree fell, "so that no well-watered trees might grow high in their place or set their tops among the clouds" (Ezek 31:14). The idea is that other nations should learn the lesson from the fate of this first great Middle Eastern world empire. They would be wise to reflect on the fact that for human beings death is the equivalent to being cut down, and like felling, death is the great leveler. Death is the fate that awaits nations that aspire to Assyria's exalted position. Ezekiel is well aware of the irony in his statements, because the point of his oracle is to declare that although Egypt is nowhere near as impressive a tree as Assyria, it is going the same way.

The next superpower fails to learn the lesson—superpowers always do. The Babylonians are sinners and faithless, guilty of wrongdoing; the specific nature of their wrongdoing is their majesty as a confident and terrifying power that must be put down (Is 13:9, 11; cf. Jer 50:14). Babylon had challenged Yhwh to a fight (*gārâ* hitpael, Jer 50:24), and Yhwh will accept the challenge. Whereas Babylon was supposed to act as Yhwh's servant in its involvement with Israel,

---

[37]Walter Brueggemann, *To Build, To Plant: A Commentary on Jeremiah 26—52* (Grand Rapids: Eerdmans/Edinburgh: Handsel, 1991), p. 265.

[38]BDB, p. 926b.

it has been pursuing its own agenda in its preoccupation with carving out its own empire, and it is in the midst of losing the conflict with Yhwh that it has thus initiated.

The Exposure of Its Resources

When Babylon is taken, "Bel is shamed, Merodoch is dismayed; its images are shamed, its idols are dismayed" (Jer 50:2). The gods that were supposed to protect the superpower's capital and the images that represented them have failed. Their powerlessness has been exposed. The shame and dismay of the gods reflects that of their worshipers; the shame and dismay of the images reflect those of their makers.[39] "Days are coming (Yhwh's message) when I shall attend to its images" (Jer 51:52).

Thus as Cyrus advances, Second Isaiah pictures the Babylonians desperately seeking to bolster morale by making sure that their images do not fall over, then pictures the images being carried out of Babylon, off into exile, as had happened to the accoutrements from the Jerusalem temple. They are incapable of looking after the people they are supposed to carry. You can cry out to them, but they do not respond or deliver you from your trouble (Is 41:5-7; 46:1-2, 6-7). Their religious resources are not up to the challenge that Cyrus brings, and they need to be reinforced. But that shows the feebleness of the gods the images represent. They cannot handle events. The nations are summoned to a summit debate about the nature of divine involvement in international events. Their gods did not announce them ahead of time, because they were not their initiators. Yhwh was, and therefore could and did (Is 41:21-29; 43:9).

Isaiah 47 makes the point most scathingly. At the moment Ms. Babylon has a cultured woman's reputation for sensitivity and taste, and she occupies a queen mother's position of power. Both are to be reversed. Prestige and power give way to humiliation and ordinariness. She loses her secure location in the context of a family that will look after her, as the man who protects and provides for her disappears, and so do the children who were supposed to take up the task from their father. Ms. Babylon finds herself doing the menial jobs she formerly had servants to do, jobs that are not humiliating in themselves but are when you were once so much more. Initially there is no talk of destruction or death here, rather of reduction to the same ordinariness that characterizes the lives of others. Babylon is a place of power and culture, but it will cease to be anything of the sort. It will become just the little underling of another empire, another superpower. It is on its way from a brightness of destiny and a

---

[39]Cf. Fretheim, *Jeremiah*, p. 626.

position able to talk confidently, to silence and darkness. Silence is part of a human reaction to devastating disaster. There is nothing to say. On Judah's part, silence was one result of the fall of Jerusalem (e.g., Lam 2:10), and it had long been threatened that it would be overwhelmed with darkness (e.g., Is 8:22). These experiences will pass to its victors and captors. Babylon, which thinks it will always be there in power and impressiveness, will lose everything. The reason is that there is a powerful God who will not stay inactive when Babylon makes itself into God and who cares about the people the superpower has been dominating—Israel's restorer, Yhwh Armies, Israel's holy one (Is 47:4).

Babylon (Is 47:10-15 goes on) has vast resources of data and techniques which it reckons give it control of its destiny and thus give it huge confidence about its place in the world. But "your insight, your knowledge, this turned you." It will find itself overwhelmed by calamity. "Trouble will come upon you for which you will not know the countercharm; disaster will fall upon you that you will not be able to counter." It will attempt to stand firm in light of the insight and skill "in which you have labored from your youth." Yes, the prophet comments, "perhaps you may be able to succeed." But the comment is sarcastic. "You are collapsing in the midst of the abounding of your plans," and in this crisis "they must stand now and deliver you, the people who observe the heavens, those who gaze at the stars, who make known for each month some things that will come upon you." This is the life-and-death moment when the experts must come good. But the prophet knows they will not. "They are like stubble; fire is burning them." They cannot even rescue themselves from the blaze, let alone rescue their city and civilization. So much for the people in whom they have trusted and whom they have supported and resourced for the security of the state. "They are wandering each of them their own way; there is no one to deliver you" (Is 47:15) The superpower reckons it has resources of knowledge and techniques for anticipating and controlling events that enable it to fix anything. This undergirds its sense of invincibility. Supernatural forces support it, so that no higher power might question its policies. But it will find itself inexplicably vulnerable. Disaster will arrive under the radar and its resources will be exposed as powerless. There is no one to deliver a superpower.

Yhwh Uses One Superpower to Put Down Another

The way Yhwh puts a superpower down is by raising up another. Assyria is put down by Babylon. After Babylon, the Medo-Persian Empire is next, its first act as superpower being the putting down of its predecessor. The God who once lifted an ensign to summon one superpower can also lift an ensign to summon other forces to put that superpower down. Here Assyria's successor, Babylon, is the superpower and is destined to be put down by the Medes.

Once again Yhwh is acting in furious anger and giving an army its orders; they are Yhwh's consecrated ones, Yhwh's warriors, exultant agents and executors of Yhwh's majesty (Is 13:2-3). It is Yhwh who stirs the Medes against Babylon (*'ûr* hiphil, Is 13:17-22). The useful but frightening thing about the Medes is that they do not care about silver or gold, so you cannot buy them off. Further, they are totally ruthless and will not be put off their gruesome task; they do not care about civilian casualties, about babies or children or young people. They do not care about beauty and culture; they will have no problem about totally destroying Babylon, "the most majestic kingdom, exalted splendor of the Chaldeans," so that it "will resemble God's overthrow of Sodom and Gomorrah" and will never be inhabited again; "jackals will dwell in its castles, hyenas in its luxurious palaces." Once again one can picture this as the act of "a company of great nations from the northern country" (Jer 50:9). "Listen to the plan that Yhwh has formulated against Babylon, the intention that he has formulated against the country of the Chaldeans" (Jer 50:45). At one stage Yhwh had a plan that positively involved Babylon. Now there is a different one. "His plan against Babylon is to destroy it. . . . Yhwh has both planned and done what he said against the inhabitants of Babylon" (Jer 51:11-12). Yhwh summons the northern army that will destroy Babylon as Yhwh once summoned the Babylonian army from the north to destroy Israel (Jer 50:14-16, 21-29). As Jeremiah originally spoke of an army from the north without naming it, here initially he does name its vanquishers (contrast Jer 51:11, 28).

Isaiah 41:2-4 describes this as it happens, focusing on the question of who made this happen: "Who aroused from the east one whom faithfulness calls to its heel, gives up nations before him and makes him subjugate kings?" It is of course a rhetorical question, and Isaiah 13 has already answered it. Cyrus makes nations and kings like dust or driven chaff and feels no obligation to avoid trespassing (cf. Is 41:25), but all this happens because Yhwh surrenders nations and kings to him. "Who acted effectively?" One might have thought that Cyrus was the one doing so, and no doubt he, his army, his people and the Judeans in Babylon and elsewhere all thought this, but actually it is Yhwh who is so acting. The prophet immediately makes that clear, describing this actor as "calling the generations from the very first: I Yhwh am the first and I myself am with the last" (Is 41:4). A much wider initiative and purpose lies behind Cyrus's arising. One might even see Yhwh as the real warrior fighting a spectacular, rowdy battle or screaming at the head of the superpower's fighting forces (Is 42:13-17). One might have thought Cyrus was the one leading an army on its triumphant march of conquest, but there was someone else behind (or in front of) his achievements: "I will go before you and level the city walls, I will break up bronze doors and cut up iron bars, I will give you dark treasuries and hidden hordes" (Is 45:2-3).

Destruction from the Destroyer

So the superpower must be put in its place, but there is a necessity beyond that, a necessity for it to be put down and not just rebuked. "Hey, you ravager—and you are not ravaged, betrayer whom they have not betrayed. When you have finished ravaging you will be ravaged; when you have done betraying, they will betray you" (Is 33:1). Isaiah 33 is unspecific in its references to peoples and contexts, and commentators have linked it with every period from Isaiah to the Greek period and have thus seen the ravager/betrayer as everyone from Assyria through Babylon and Persia to Greece. The effect of the unspecific nature of the chapter is to make it apply to any superpower. It implies the principle that every great ravager does get ravaged, as that history from Assyria to Antiochus shows.

Thus the superpower is indeed vulnerable to the real Superpower: "The Lord Yhwh Armies will send wasting into its sturdiness" (Is 10:16). As the one who really controls the forces of earth and heaven sent Assyria itself (Is 10:6), so this sovereign will now send a means of dissolving the strength of its army. It may march resolutely and frighteningly to the very gates of Jerusalem, but then its stoutness will collapse (Is 10:27-32). To put it another way, Yhwh will burn up Assyria in a great conflagration that will consume the land so thoroughly that a child could count the trees that are left (Is 10:16-19). "The Lord Yhwh Armies" will personally wield an ax and have no trouble felling the tallest of trees and demolishing the thickest of forests (Is 10:33-34).[40] Or Yhwh will simply decimate the Assyrian army in its camp (Is 37:36).

Putting the superpower down expresses the dark side to Yhwh. It comes as šōd from šadday, as destruction from the Destroyer (Is 13:6).[41] The framework that made the superpower into Yhwh's agent now makes it Yhwh's victim. The result will be to reduce the confident, courageous and decisive superpower to paralyzing dismay and anguished fear. It will turn its land into a desolation, decimate its population, scatter its ethnic groups back to the lands whence they came, and bring the slaughter of children before their parents' eyes, the plundering of homes and the rape of wives (Is 13:9, 12, 14-16, 18).[42] The most honored of countries with all its majestic splendor, with its monumental buildings, will be turned into a desolation, not even settled by Bedouin or visited by shepherds, but home only to desert creatures, and it will be totally forgotten (Is 13:19-22; 14:22-23; cf. Is 41:11-12).

It would seem an impossible prospect to Judeans in Palestine or in Babylon

---

[40]Out of context Is 10:16-19 and 33-34 might be a threat to Judah, but in context they must apply to Assyria.

[41]On this title, see section 2.7 "Slayer."

[42]It is this prophecy for whose fulfillment Ps 137 asks.

itself. It is as difficult for its underlings to believe that a superpower could fall as it is for the superpower itself. With regard to Assyria the matter is therefore made the subject of a divine oath (Is 14:24). Jesus requires disciples not to take oaths but to make them unnecessary because all their words are trustworthy (Mt 5:33-37). Yhwh feels free not to be bound by this principle for the sake of people who need an oath to hold on to.

The point is made vividly by the reappearance of a declaration about Edom (Jer 49:19-21) as a declaration about Babylon (Jer 50:44-46). Babylon is the means of that action against Edom that will cause disquiet in the region, but now someone else is the means of equivalent action against Babylon that will cause disquiet through the earth as its cry makes itself heard among the nations. Earlier in the book Jeremiah has been working hard to get his audience to see Nebuchadnezzar as Yhwh's servant, but now he is working hard to make the opposite point, as "the purpose of Yahweh and the rule of Babylon are no longer compatible."[43]

Yhwh's Day Arrives for the Superpower

The finality of this destruction is underlined by describing it as the arrival of the very day of Yhwh. "Yhwh's day is near. . . . Yhwh's day has come" (Is 13:6, 9). Babylon's "hour is near to come. Its days will not drag on" (Is 13:22).

Yhwh's day had been threatened and brought about for Judah. It meant the very destruction of its world. Now the destroyer will have the same experience. Yhwh's day is regaining its right meaning as the moment Yhwh acts to punish Israel's oppressors and bless Israel itself. Once again Yhwh commissions a warrior army, consecrated to serve by implementing Yhwh's wrath, signaling from a place where a vast host can see the signal (Is 13:2-8). This time Babylon is not the army, as it had been a few decades before, but the army's victim (though that emerges from the poem's setting, not from references in the poem itself). As Assyria stood for a whole conglomerate of nations, so it is now as if the whole world is coming together to put this empire down. That army is about to enter the majestic gates of its capital. Its inhabitants dissolve in fear before it.

The event implies calamity for the whole inhabited world, the *tēbēl* (Is 13:9-16). Yhwh's day will be "harsh, with anger bursting out and burning" (lit., "harsh and outburst and burning of anger"). It will require sun, moon, stars and planets to cease to shine or be visible. Yhwh will destabilize the heavens, and the earth will shake out of its place. This might imply that the superpower's collapse has negative as well as positive significance for other peoples.

---

[43]Brueggemann, *To Build, To Plant*, p. 269; the first nine words are italicized.

The fallout from its punishment affects the whole world. Perhaps there is simply a practical inevitability about this. A calamity worthy of the superpower is bound to affect other people. It will involve a visitation on the world as a whole. This is as inevitable as the fact that, for instance, calamity affects "innocent children" (to the third and fourth generation) as well as their parents. And/or perhaps there is also moral aspect to this feature of the calamity—as is the case with the assumption that the generations that suffer share in their parents' wrongdoing. Trouble comes to the world associated with the superpower because it shares in its wrongdoing. Insofar as the nations are the superpower's victims they have reason to rejoice in its downfall, but insofar as they share in their own way in its human sinfulness they share in its devastation.

Zechariah also suggests the comprehensive nature of the event. He sees four horns that had scattered Judah, Israel and Jerusalem (Zech 1:18-21 [MT 2:1-4]). "Judah, Israel and Jerusalem" suggests the people of God as a whole over the centuries, and the fourfoldness of the horns likewise suggests all the superpowers that had oppressed this people over the centuries, like the four superpowers in Daniel 2 and 7. There a "critical turn against the rule of the world empires" comes. "In the long run neither the Babylonian nor the Persian Empire, much less the divided empire of the successors of Alexander, could fulfill the function of earthly representation of the divine government by establishing justice and peace." They had a wild beast character. The establishment of justice and peace would need to bear human features and would need God to come in person to bring it about (Dan 7:13-14).[44] The statue and the beasts have to be put down.

While Zechariah no doubt has an eye on the current friendly but still controlling power, Persia, as he has one eye on the Judah of its day, his vision, too, encompasses that more comprehensive horizon. It goes on to picture four blacksmiths that are to rout the horns (i.e., the armies of the nations they represent) and throw them down. Its promise is indeed the one taken further in Daniel. The whole story of the superpowers as superpowers is to come to end. Yet in Zechariah it is only the horns that are cut off. The superpower is pacified, not destroyed.[45] Its peoples may come to acknowledge Yhwh, as Zechariah envisions (e.g., Zech 2:11 [MT 15]).

In his final vision Zechariah sees four chariots (Zech 6:1-8), whose significance reinforces the message of the horns. The chariots also recall the horsemen of his first vision, but those were merely the means whereby Yhwh found out what was going on in the world. Chariots are military equipment, the an-

---

[44]Pannenberg, *Systematic Theology*, 3:51.

[45]Ben C. Ollenburger, "The Book of Zechariah," in *The New Interpreter's Bible*, vol. 7 (Nashville: Abingdon, 1996), p. 757.

cient equivalent of tanks, the means of Yhwh acting as "the lord of all the earth." They are four heavenly spirits/winds, complete and worldwide embodiments of Yhwh's dynamic energy, the means of imposing Yhwh's decree in the world as they wander about the world at will (the hitpael of *hālak* comes three times in Zech 6:7). But the fourfoldness of their activity is not systematically worked out—two of the chariots go north, one goes south, and none go east or west.[46] The focus of their activity lies in the directions where trouble was usually embodied. The south recognizes the importance of Egypt as the old enemy and a direction from which trouble sometimes subsequently came. But concentration lies especially on the north, the direction from which each superpower so far had come, the direction where traditional imagery located frightening alien peoples who embodied a threat to world order, the direction of the country where Judah had been exiled, and the direction where the chariots would find the current overlord, Persia. The last sentence of the vision underlines the fact that the north is the vision's focus: "Look, the ones going out to the northern land have settled my wind/spirit in the northern land." The notion of *settling* (*nûaḥ* hiphil) a *wind/spirit* is a paradoxical one and its precise meaning is unclear, but at least it implies that the chariots with their horses have implemented Yhwh's purpose and Yhwh's authority in the northern land. The vision again indicates that Yhwh has terminated the self-assertive sovereignty of the superpower.

Victim of Yhwh's Fury

Isaiah 30 begins by threatening Judah that its attempts to get protection from Assyria by allying with Egypt will fail, but it closes by declaring the downfall of this same Assyria (Is 30:27-28). "Yhwh's name is coming from afar." It is a powerful thing when Yhwh's name comes; it suggests the coming of Yhwh in person, in the multifaceted nature of Yhwh's revelation. Generally the presence of Yhwh's name is thus good news, but on this occasion it means bad news for "the nations"; the succeeding lines imply that this expression again refers to Assyria (see Is 30:31).[47] Indeed, it is really bad news. Yhwh comes with burning anger, bearing a heavy burden. The succeeding lines spell out its implications and show that it is really, really bad news. The anger occupies Yhwh's lips, Yhwh's tongue, Yhwh's breath (*rûaḥ*), as if Yhwh is a fire-breathing dragon. This breath is "like an overflowing stream"—we might take this as a stream of fire, but talk of its reaching up to the neck makes it sound more like flooding water, another common image for destruction alongside fire (cf.

---

[46]The EVV emend to make the chariots go in all four directions. But the focus on north and south corresponds to the focus on Assyria and Egypt elsewhere (e.g., Zech 10:10-11).

[47]See section 8.3 "The Agent Summoned by Yhwh."

Is 43:2; Ps 66:12). The fiery conceptualization of Yhwh also recalls the Middle Eastern portrayal of destructive power as a dragon, while the watery conceptualization recalls the alternative conceptualization of destructive power as overwhelming waters.

So Yhwh is taking on the persona of Dragon and Flood in order to deal with Assyria. And the burden Yhwh is carrying is a "yoke" or "bridle" destined for Assyria's neck. Usually the yoking of an animal is not a fundamentally unfriendly act—it does constrain the animal in order to get it to work, but work is not too unpleasant an activity, and the animal does get fed in return for working, as Isaiah has just now noted (Is 30:23-24). But this is a "false yoke,"[48] a bridle that is a means of leading astray. Once again Yhwh is going to lead the Assyrians without their realizing, but this time Yhwh is leading them over a cliff. The yoke is in fact false *(šāw')* in both senses of the word: empty or disappointing, and also devastating and desolating.

Nahum 1:2-11 describes Yhwh's devastation of the superpower with particularly terrifying vividness. He speaks as if he is describing something that has happened: I take the past tense to refer to something he has seen in his "vision" (Nahum 1:1), though this relates to the characteristic instantaneous qatal of the prophets. The event is certain and imminent (not least because Yhwh is committed to bringing it about), but he can describe it as if it had already happened—because in effect it has. Yet he does not merely give a straightforward description of the event; he does not simply say, "Nineveh has fallen." He rather portrays an imaginary cosmic outworking of Yhwh's wrath, which has made the most fertile parts of the land wither and made the most stable parts of the land shake. Yhwh's enemies therefore have no chance of standing firm when Yhwh appears. Indeed, the passage does not actually mention Nineveh (though Nahum 1:1 tells us that this is its subject). In Nahum "the real center of gravity is not in Nineveh; the real concern is with Yahweh's power, and to that extent Nineveh symbolizes all that might stand in opposition to that power."[49]

Babylon likewise has been the agent of Yhwh's wrath but is now its victim as Yhwh is punishing it (Jer 50:13, 15). It has brought Yhwh's cup of poison (i.e., brought death) to many nations, most of whom did not especially deserve it in the way Judah or Edom did, but the cup will pass to it: "Hey, you who make his neighbor drink, pouring out your poison until you make them drunk so that you may gaze on their nakedness; you are taking your fill of

---

[48]On the translation, see Joseph Blenkinsopp, *Isaiah 1—39* (New York: Doubleday, 2000), pp. 422-23, and cf. JPSV; and on yokes, see further section 8.3 "Confident and Tough."

[49]Richard J. Coggins, in Coggins and S. Paul Re'emi, *Israel Among the Nations* (Grand Rapids: Eerdmans/Edinburgh: Handsel, 1985), p. 13.

contempt instead of splendor. You, too, drink, and reel; to you will come round the cup in Yhwh's right hand and great contempt to your splendor" (Hab 2:15-16).

Redress

"This is Yhwh's redress [něqāmâ]; take redress from her, do to her as she has done" (Jer 50:15). "Israel is a sheep driven away, one that lions have chased; as the first king of Assyria devoured it and now as the last King Nebuchadnezzar of Babylon has gnawed its bones. Therefore Yhwh Armies, the God of Israel, has said this: 'Now. I am attending to the king of Babylon and his country as I attended to the king of Assyria'" (Jer 50:17-18; cf. Jer 50:41-46). Survivors of its destruction come to tell of "the redress of Yhwh our God, redress for his palace" (Jer 50:28). It is no longer possible to avoid Babylon's punishment, because "its case has reached the heavens, risen to the skies" (Jer 51:9). Although Babylon has been Yhwh's war club for smashing nations, Yhwh declares, "I will repay Babylon and all the inhabitants of Chaldea for all the wrong that they did to Zion before your eyes" (Jer 51:24).[50] After all, "aliens came into the holy precincts of Yhwh's house" (Jer 51:51). And "Yhwh is a God of recompense. He repays in full" (Jer 51:56). Once again Jeremiah implies that, while Yhwh could deliver Israel from Babylon without destroying the city or the power of Babylon, that would not restore moral order to the world political situation.[51] For Judah, defeat and exile meant having its conquerors and their allies pillaging its city. That will now be reversed as devourers become the devoured, plunderers become the plundered (Jer 30:10-17).

Nahum, too, begins with participial descriptions of Yhwh as "a passionate God, one who takes redress. Yhwh takes redress and is characterized by fury; Yhwh takes redress on his foes and rages against his enemies" (Nahum 1:2). The participles suggest that fury and taking redress is "a permanent attribute of Yhwh . . . a free-floating, unbounded characteristic."[52] For any reader in a position of power, fear is an appropriate response. The description again illustrates the positive power of strong feelings. Indifference means someone does nothing much; passion means a person acts with energy. Specifically, it means Yhwh acts to put things right. At the moment the superpower dominates the world and its resources, but Yhwh is a God of redress. Yhwh puts things right. As Mary will put it, "he is acting powerfully with his arm, he is scattering the people who are proud in their inner thoughts, he is bringing

---

[50]In Jer 51:20-23, 25-26 "you" is singular and refers to Babylon. In Jer 51:24 the plural refers to the Judeans.

[51]See section 8.2 "A Nightmare Vision for the Nations."

[52]Julia Myers O'Brien, *Nahum* (London/New York: Sheffield Academic Press, 2002), p. 53.

down rulers from their thrones and he is exalting ordinary people" (Lk 1:51-52).[53] Yhwh reverses things.

Yhwh's strongly felt anger is thus very good news for peoples controlled by a superpower. Although mercifully "long-tempered," Yhwh is also a God "great in might" and one who "certainly does not clear people"—does not let them get away with things forever. Nahum 1:3 takes up familiar phrases from Yhwh's self-revelation at Sinai and assures Israel that there is no need to draw gloomy inferences from them. Alongside the declaration that Yhwh is characterized by compassion and willingness to cover sin, that self-revelation made clear that Yhwh does not forever treat guilty people as if they were innocent. There is no tension between that idea and the idea that "Yhwh is good"—rather the opposite. It is precisely by acting decisively against the superpower that Yhwh manifests divine goodness. It is by so acting that Yhwh will prove to be "a haven on the day of trouble" for "people who take refuge with him." In that way Yhwh will "acknowledge" them—recognize them and treat them as Yhwh's own, "even in the sweeping flood" that overwhelms the superpower. It stupidly thinks it can "formulate intentions against Yhwh," make plans that work against Yhwh's purpose, for instance, in insisting on exercising control over Judah in the time of Hezekiah and Josiah—but it will find that it has taken on someone it cannot beat. "He is one who brings things to an end; opposition does not arise twice" (Nahum 1:9). You do not get two chances to defeat Yhwh.

So Yhwh is "against" Nineveh and intends to destroy its weaponry (MT) and/or its resources (LXX), the prey it has captured through its aggressiveness, both built up through oppressive relationship with the less powerful nations whose destiny it controlled. At the moment its aides, like lions, strike fear into the nations, but all that will end (Nahum 2:13 [MT 14]). Perhaps it was partly because Assyria did comprehensively collapse and Nineveh did comprehensively fall that Nahum was conclusively proven to be a true prophet—hence the presence of his book in the Scriptures.

Good News

In Nahum1:12-14 Yhwh reassures Jerusalem, "though I afflicted you, I will afflict you no more; now I will break his yoke from upon you and shatter your bonds." Ephraim has been devastated and its people transported, and Judah has also been subject to invasion and wasting. And Israel's affliction by the superpower issued from Yhwh's own decision. Here there is no reference to wrongdoing on Israel's part that led to this ravaging and wasting. The implicit

---

[53]I treat the Greek aorists as the equivalent of instantaneous qatal, and translate them as present.

argument rather parallels that in psalms that confront Yhwh over having abandoned Israel. Admittedly, neither is there any claim that Israel had not deserved what happened. The focus lies elsewhere. On one hand, Yhwh accepts responsibility for the superpower's being able to afflict Israel, whatever the reason for it; and on the other, whatever the reason for it, Yhwh is now bringing that to an end. And Yhwh means an end. Yhwh declares to the Assyrian king, "seed will be sown from your name no more; from the house of your god I will cut off carved image and cast image." The king is nothing. There will be no more sons of his line on the throne. The images of the Assyrian gods will be destroyed. Yhwh will personally see to the king's burial, Nahum adds, a sign that he really is dead.

The event is so real, the prophet can hear the herald bringing news of it to Jerusalem, pronouncing that the superpower's downfall will mean *shalom* for Israel to replace its devastation (Nahum 1:15—2:2 [MT 2:1-3]). He can commission Judah to celebrate its festivals—perhaps it had been impossible to celebrate them properly, or perhaps people had not felt much enthusiasm about them, or perhaps the deliverance will give a basis for a new level of enthusiasm for what the festivals stand for. As the Psalms again indicate, when abandoned by Yhwh and oppressed by the superpower, Israel would have beseeched Yhwh to grant it relief and would have promised to bring special offerings when relief came, and now it will have reason to fulfill those promises. This act of deliverance will not mean merely temporary relief from Assyrian pressure, of the kind Judah received in Hezekiah's day. It will mean the superpower is "totally cut off." It will be no more. Yhwh "is restoring the majesty of Jacob," turning Israel back to the splendid people it was designed to be.

In our own day, many of the citizens of the superpower doubt whether God is really the person Nahum says. Yhwh had better not be one who takes redress, because we will be on the receiving end of it. Others of its citizens may bow in dread before this portrayal, hoping against hope that Yhwh may not act thus in their day. But the underlings of the superpower may be encouraged. Their subordination will not be the final reality. The superpower is not merely their enemy but Yhwh's enemy. Even if the superpower has done nothing directly to offend Yhwh, its domination over smaller powers causes it to be adopted as Yhwh's personal enemy. Converse to that disapproval of Nahum's theology is the recognition that Nahum might be seen as resistance literature.[54] By portraying Nineveh fallen, it offers Judah an alternative world and grants its people hope as they picture Yhwh putting Assyria down. It does not invite them to the implausible task of putting Assyria down but opens up

---

[54]See O'Brien's discussion, *Nahum*, pp. 112-17, referring to W. Wessels, "Nahum," *Old Testament Essays* 11, no. 3 (1998), pp. 615-28.

the possibility of keeping on living. "Nahum becomes the voice of the Warsaw Ghetto."[55]

For the Judeans in Babylon subsequently, its fall will mean "Yhwh has brought forth faithfulness to us." They therefore are to "declare in Zion the deed of Yhwh our God" (Jer 51:10). The prospect of this event does also bring a challenge to the oppressed. "Flee from the midst of Babylon, get out of the country of the Chaldeans," like he-goats leading the flock, given the calamity that is about to overwhelm it. "Come out from its midst, my people; save your life, each one, from Yhwh's angry fury." They must not let fear immobilize them when they hear reports of political chaos within the country. That is the time to take decisive action. "Babylon is to fall, slain of Israel, as the slain of all the earth fell to Babylon; fugitives from the sword, go, do not stand there" (Jer 50:8-9; 51:45-46, 49-50). Jeremiah 25—29 urges the Judeans in exile since 597 to settle down under the Babylonians for a lifetime, and urges Judeans in Jerusalem to submit to Babylon. Jeremiah 50—51 declares that Yhwh will put Babylon down. Both perspectives are important.[56] At this moment, as in the last days of the preexilic period, it would be natural to be paralyzed by events, but this is a time for courage. Yhwh is acting to punish Babylon. The Judean community needs to believe that and act accordingly.

And for Other Peoples

Yhwh's fury about the superpower does not emerge solely from a commitment to Israel, and it is good news for peoples other than Israel (Nahum 3:1-5). Yhwh's fury with the superpower issues from its being a "city of bloodshed, totally deceitful," and one that has appropriated resources that belong to other peoples. It also issues from its immoralities, which the context implies is here a figure for trading. It is involved not merely in trading in goods, but in trading in people, beguiling and bewitching nations into selling peoples into slavery to it. The superpower's downfall means relief for all such peoples.

Although the nations were to serve Nebuchadnezzar, his son and his grandson, that situation was to obtain only until his country's time also came and many nations and great kings make him a servant (Jer 27:7). Here there is no comment on the moral significance of Babylon's eventual downfall or on this being good news for Judean exiles, for instance. It is simply an expression of Yhwh's sovereignty. As Yhwh had the power to give sovereignty to Nebuchadnezzar, so Yhwh has the power to take it away. While Nebuchadnezzar is someone whom other peoples serve, he is that because he is himself Yhwh's servant (Jer 27:6), and Yhwh has the authority to terminate this form of service

---

[55]O'Brien, *Nahum*, p. 115.
[56]Fretheim, *Jeremiah*, pp. 647-48.

on Nebuchadnezzar's part and give him a different role in which he will serve other peoples. No superpower retains its position forever. It is subordinate to Yhwh, and Yhwh decides when its "time" comes (Jer 27:7). So when Judah has lived in subservience to Babylon for the time decreed, "I will attend to the king of Babylon and to that nation (Yhwh's message) for their wrongdoing. . . . for many nations and great kings are making them into servants,[57] too, and I will requite them for their conduct and for the activity of their hands" (Jer 25:12, 14; cf. Jer 27:7). The subservience they have imposed on others will become their experience. "The Israelites are oppressed, the Judeans, with them; all their captors showed their strength over them, refused to let them go." But "their restorer is strong, Yhwh Armies is his name; he will firmly champion their cause, so that he may settle the earth but unsettle the inhabitants of Babylon" (Jer 50:33-34). Yhwh's intention to settle "the earth" indicates a positive concern for the world as a whole. Yhwh acts against Babylon for Israel's sake, but the whole world benefits.

Jeremiah thus commissions a proclamation among the nations that "Babylon is taken." Another northern power has attacked it, captured it and shamed the deities that were supposed to protect it. In imagination, the prophecy locates itself at the moment when this fall has happened but the devastation of the country that will follow is still to happen (Jer 50:2-3). And this is to be declared among the nations for whom Babylon is overlord. It is good news for them because they would prefer to be free rather than under Babylon's control. It is bad news for Babylon (which might like to conceal it—so Jeremiah forbids any concealment) because it brings Babylon shame and disgrace.

An implication is that other peoples, like Judeans, are unwise to identify too closely with the superpower, or at least are wise to be able to tell the time and to know when to abandon it. Jeremiah urges people in general, as well as Judeans, to "turn, each one, to their people; they should escape, each one, to their country" (Jer 50:16). Touchingly, it seems to be these foreign peoples in Babylon (?) that declare, "we tried to heal Babylon, but she could not be healed" (Jer 51:9). There is no one who can deliver a superpower. Therefore they, too, are urged to "flee from the midst of Babylon, save your life, each one, do not perish for its wrongdoing, because this is a time of redress for Yhwh; he is dealing retribution to it" (Jer 51:6).

The Superpower's Leader: Yhwh's Servant, Yhwh's Anointed, Yhwh's Shepherd

Leaders have special significance and special responsibility; a fortiori that will

---

[57]I take the verb as instantaneous qatal.

be true of the superpower's leader, who will also stand in special danger.

It is Nebuchadnezzar personally, for instance, who is Yhwh's servant (e.g., Jer 25:9; 27:6; 43:10). The only other individuals who are so designated with any frequency in the Torah and the Prophets are Moses and David (e.g., Ex 14:31; Num 12:7; Deut 34:5; Jer 33:19-26; Ezek 34:23-24).[58] Cyrus, likewise, is Yhwh's "shepherd" and Yhwh's "anointed." Yhwh is the one who created the world, decides what happens in it now and thus makes fools of people who pretend to know what is going to happen in it unless they get their information from this source. Yhwh is the one declaring now that Jerusalem is going to be restored, the one who deals with tumultuous forces that imperil the divine purpose—and is "the one who says of Cyrus, 'My shepherd' and speaks to 'his anointed" (Is 44:28—45:1). A prophet such as Ezekiel not long before Second Isaiah's day has looked forward to a time when Yhwh will set up a shepherd over Israel in succession to the long line of shepherds who have governed the people over the centuries, a new David (see Ezek 34; cf., e.g., Jer 23:1-5). *Anointed* is a similar though more technical term for the Israelite king as designated by Yhwh (e.g., Ps 2:2; 18:50 [MT 51]), and it too is destined to become a term for a Davidic king whom Yhwh will one day set over the people again. Second Isaiah applies these terms to the leader of the superpower. At this point in history he turns out to be the man after God's own heart. Yhwh takes Cyrus's hand like the president of the United States publicly taking the hand of the leader of some much less powerful country and thereby indicating the support of a much greater power and strengthening the standing of this leader. That leader will therefore be in a position to put down or disarm opposing or resisting forces. No one will resist this leader now.

Like their peoples (whose policies, indeed, they determined), these kings were not aiming to serve Yhwh, but unwittingly they were doing so. More specifically, Yhwh is quite capable of making the policies of the superpower's leader serve the destiny of the people of God, for chastisement or for restoration. Yhwh is "the one who says of Jerusalem 'It will be inhabited,' of the towns of Judah 'They will be built,' 'I will raise its wastes'" (Is 44:26), but the way Yhwh does that is through Cyrus's declaring that the city and the temple are to be rebuilt. "I have aroused him in faithfulness," that is, as part of my doing the right thing by Judah. "He is the one who will . . . send off my exile community," even though he gets nothing out of it (Is 45:13).

Yhwh has another aim in using the superpower's leader in this way. Addressing Cyrus, Yhwh declares that it happens "so that you will acknowledge that I am Yhwh; the God of Israel is the one who summons you by name" (Is

---

[58]Cf. John Hill, "'Your Exile Will Be Long,'" in *Reading the Book of Jeremiah*, ed. Martin Kessler (Winona Lake, Ind.: Eisenbrauns, 2004), pp. 151-61; see p. 154.

45:3). At the moment Cyrus does not acknowledge Yhwh and cannot be faulted for that—he lives in the wrong country. But events are designed to make it clear that "I am Yhwh and there is no other. Besides me there is no God" (Is 45:5). Indeed, one aim of Yhwh's girding Cyrus even though he does not acknowledge Yhwh is "that people will acknowledge from the sun's rise and from its setting [and therefore from everywhere in between] that there is none besides me. I am Yhwh and there is no other" (Is 45:6). Yhwh does not here specify how this will come about, though the implication of statements elsewhere is that the convincing evidence lies in the very fact that Yhwh is one who can declare ahead of time that this will happen and then make it happen.

The people of God may not approve of the way Yhwh uses its leader. There is something scandalous about calling him Yhwh's servant, shepherd or anointed. For the most part, Yhwh's response to people's (hypothetical?) objections is not to offer a rationale but simply to assert the authority to act in this way (Is 45:9-13). I'm the boss, says Yhwh, so shut up. But Yhwh does add another description of Cyrus that provides some rationale while also increasing the scandal. "Over my children and over the work of my hands you may give me charge" (Is 45:11). Cyrus counts as among Yhwh's children, like David (Ps 2:7). He counts as Yhwh's handiwork, someone Yhwh made for a purpose. Yhwh's sharp tongue invites people to reckon that Cyrus's father and maker is in a better position than they are to decide how to use him.

The Fallen Star

The superpower's leader has particular responsibility for the acts of the nation and thus pays a special price in connection with its downfall. In Isaiah 14:4-11 Judah is given a poem about him, to take up when it is all over (though the point about the poem is to be an encouragement now).[59] "Hey! The boss has stopped; the raging has stopped," they will be able to declare. "Yhwh has broken the rod of the faithless, the staff of the rulers, that beats peoples in wrath, a beating without relent, that dominates nations in anger, pursuing without holding back." The rod or staff that directs the beating of people sits in the leader's hand. The king of Babylon is the boss beating his charges (the term is the one for the Israelites' bosses in Egypt; e.g., Ex 5:6). In putting a leader down, Yhwh breaks the staff and terminates the beating. Now "the whole earth is at rest, is quiet; people break into a shout." We have noted that a superpower characteristically sees its rule as beneficent, but the objects of its rule characteristically see things rather differently.[60] Thus a cheer breaks the silence

---

[59]The EVV translate *māšāl* "taunt," but while the poem *is* a taunt, that is not the meaning of *māšāl*.

[60]See section 8.3 "The Agent of a Positive Purpose for Yhwh's People."

introduced by the putting down of the superpower's leader. Even the trees join in: "junipers, too, rejoice at you, cedars of Lebanon." Creation resounds with the world in its rejoicing, as it often does (e.g., Is 55:12), though the trees have their own down-to-earth reason for joy. They know that the leader will no more command their felling for his projects (Is 14:8). Further, their rejoicing at the fact that no one will be climbing their way also anticipates subsequent comment about the leader's climbing activity (Is 14:13, 14). The heights of Lebanon symbolize God's high abode, and the trees will be glad not to have this leader trespassing there again. The poem rejoices in the thought of the leader arriving down in Sheol instead and joining other rulers there, who greet him: "you have been made the same as us, your majesty has been brought down to Sheol." As a superpower has a hard time acknowledging vincibility, so a leader has a hard time owning mortality, but the moment for this will come. The leader ends up the same as everyone else, body rotting in the grave: "beneath you worm is spread and maggot is your blanket" (Is 14:9-11).

The taller they are, the harder they fall. A superpower's leader reaches higher than anyone else. The poem that follows (Is 14:12-21) draws a two-level analogy. Each day, Venus, the morning star, rises just before dawn and seems about to assert itself in sovereignty over the whole heavens, but the rising of the sun soon follows and eclipses Venus's brightness. Israel's neighbors saw this event in the heavens as suggesting a supernatural event. Venus stands for a god who seeks to gain sovereignty over the rest of the beings in heaven but is firmly put in his place by the highest god and cast down. Isaiah takes this story as an allegory for the attitude of the superpower's leader.[61] "You said to yourself, 'I will climb up to the heavens, above God's stars I will set up my throne." He had made himself into the highest power in the entire world, taking a godlike position over the world. It is as if he has scaled Zaphon, the high mountain where the gods have their earthly abode. He has destabilized the world, shaken off kingdoms, turned city and country into wilderness, demolished cities, controlled the destiny of peoples that he moved from their homeland. His downfall more than reverses that. "Hey! You have fallen from heaven, Shiner, child of Dawn, you are cut down to earth, enfeebler over nations" (Is 14:12). He goes from the extremities of the abode of the gods to the extremities of the abode of the dead.

The poem then makes the point in another way. The leader is destined to die in battle or to die in the way someone dies in battle, like Saul and Jonathan.

---

[61]Ironically, the passage (and the similar lament in Ezek 28:11-19) is commonly taken to refer to the fall of Satan. That follows the meaning of the Middle Eastern myth that the prophets utilize, but it does not follow what the prophets do with this myth in turning it into a parallel about a ruler's hubris and fall.

The trouble with that experience is that it may deprive a person of a proper burial as their corpse lies there on the battlefield. And the inner person can hardly rest if the outer person is not properly buried. This does not exactly stop one going to Sheol, but it does mean that the leader tumbles into the Pit bundled up with the bloody corpses (not to say separated body parts) of a miscellaneous crowd of war victims, rather than in the splendor of other leaders (Is 14:19). He has been an honored branch (cf. Is 11:1), but he is now a loathsome dead branch, which might make the reader think of a dead king or of similar words that mean a rotting corpse with its coagulated blood or an aborted fetus.

A Dishonorable End

There is a further moral aspect to the leader's fall. Even his own subjects have mixed feelings about him. He goes to the grave without honor because he has destroyed his own land and slain his own people (Is 14:20). Indeed, this is most specifically the reason for his downfall. Leaders destroy their own land and people by oppressing their own people, by requiring their subjects to be part of their war machine and by causing them to pay the price when eventually they are defeated. Evidently Yhwh cares about the land and people of Babylon.

Nahum 3:18-19 similarly pictures the implications for the Assyrian king of his empire's fall. "Your shepherds are slumbering, king of Assyria, your leaders settle down." While that might suggest that the Assyrian leadership is reprehensibly relaxed concerning questions of national security, more likely the prophet pictures the leadership as actually dead. Likewise "your people are scattered on the mountains and there is no one gathering them." The king is further invited to imagine himself mortally wounded. He is invited to face the fact that he was universally hated and that all this is deserved, because the whole world was victim to his aggrandizement.

Isaiah 14:20-21 points to yet a further aspect of the Babylonian king's downfall. Like ordinary people such as farmers or craftworkers or theologians, kings like to imagine their children continuing their work and keeping the family name going. Unlike ordinary people, many kings find that their own downfall costs their family their lives, lest one of them should aspire to succeed to the throne. Calamity for this leader will therefore include the elimination of the line and its name. There is a moral argument against that, which the First Testament elsewhere expounds. There is also a moral argument for it, or at least an advantage about the human instinct to exterminate the line when a king falls. At all costs this king's family should not have the opportunity to put on the throne someone with the family moral and political resemblance, who will again fill the earth with cities to control it.

The fate of the king of Tyre is described in similar terms. Tyre is not a political and military superpower like Babylon, but it is a monumental economic and trading force—Korea or Taiwan rather than the United States or the European Community. Its king is therefore exposed to the same temptations as the King of Babylon. The achievements of his city make him see himself as the most astute leader in the world. He has a godlike position in the world. But that makes it theologically inevitable that he should be put down (Ezek 28:1-10). It is also morally inevitable (Ezek 28:11-19). As few entities become world powers without being corrupted by power, so few entities become leaders in world trade without being corrupted. The king's "fall" has come about because he gave in to the temptation to trample on other peoples in order to make money.

Egypt, too, is a regional power rather than a global one, but its leader is open to analogous temptations. Like Tyre, its paradoxical vulnerability lay in a confidence that came from its physical position. The Egyptian king stupidly behaved as if he thought, "My Nile is mine. I myself made it" (Ezek 29:3). So Yhwh will treat him as if he were merely a fish that Yhwh can effortlessly catch. Once again it will have to be made clear who is God and who is not. And that needs to be made clear to Judah as well as to Pharaoh. It has long been tempted to look to Egypt to fulfill the role Yhwh was supposed to fulfill for it— to be its defense and support (e.g., Is 30—31). The Judeans believe his publicity, or he believes their flattery. They have grasped hold of him for support as if he were a strong cane, but he will turn out to be only a reed that breaks (Ezek 29:6-9). "Egypt will never again be the reliance of the household of Israel" (Ezek 29:16).

8.4 Ordinary Nations

While the relation between Yhwh and Israel on one side and the superpower on the other raises some issues, relations with smaller powers raise different ones. Regional powers such as Egypt and local powers such as Edom can again deceive themselves about their military and commercial strength and their insight, and dig their own grave through their willfulness and their violence. Admittedly it is impossible to claim that history always works out in a fair way for them, but it is the case that Yhwh cares about their suffering and promises that for them as for Judah, calamity need not be the end.

Self-imposed Folly

Egypt looks a relatively impressive power, but its actual weaknesses make it an unwise object of trust. Israel is tempted to consider Egypt as a trustworthy potential ally, but it is utterly vulnerable to Yhwh's manipulation. Isaiah 19:1-4 imagines Yhwh arriving in Egypt and causing great consternation among its gods and people. Somehow this will issue in civil strife at the level of family, local community, city and canton. The country will be utterly demoralized and will have no idea how to solve its problems. It will turn to its best spiritual resources but they will prove incapable of helping this once powerful country avoid coming under the control of an alien power. "Yes, fools are the leaders of Zoan; the most insightful of Pharaoh's planners—the plan is stupid," because it leaves out of account the fact that Yhwh is working out a plan here (Is 19:11-17). How could they present their counsel to Pharaoh on the basis of the insightful tradition to which they are heirs, when that tradition perforce ignores this key factor?

Egypt was a famous repository of insight. Israel respected and learned from it in the same way that Christians respect and learn from secular insight about philosophy or sociology or psychology. But when the world's insight leaves Yhwh out, it converts itself into stupidity. Applied to politics, that means the best planning in the world transforms itself into foolhardiness because it takes no account of the fact that Yhwh is a policymaker at quite another level from the leaders who help Pharaoh formulate foreign policy. Anyone who had real insight would acknowledge this fact about Yhwh and acknowledge the real factors that determine how political policies work out. People who fail to do that will end up in a state of panic about the policies Yhwh is implementing.

Thus far Isaiah sees Egypt's stupidity and wandering as self-imposed. But it also sees Yhwh as involved: "Yhwh has mixed in its midst a spirit of confusion" (Is 19:14). Behind the stupidity of the Egyptian leadership is an act of Yhwh that parallels Yhwh's original closing of Pharaoh's mind and the subsequent proposed closing of Judah's mind (Is 6:9-10). Isaiah does not give any reason for this act, though perhaps the reasoning is the same as the one attaching to the exodus. This is a way in which Yhwh is shown to be the one God. It will mean Egypt being overwhelmed by Assyria. Its advisers will be no more useful than drunks. Egypt will be totally helpless. The people of the Philistine coastland thus reflect that if that kind of thing can happen to a country such as Egypt, what hope have people who looked to Egypt for support? (Is 20:6).

For Edom likewise, its willfulness (*zādôn*, Jer 49:16; Obad 3)[62] is a source of Edom's self-deception and thus a factor in Yhwh's punishment. The word suggests something like a self-confident conviction that we can make decisions for ourselves or a refusal to recognize the decisions of the proper authorities in legal matters and an insistence on taking matters into our own hands (Deut 17:12-13), or on declaring something to be Yhwh's word when it nothing of the sort (Deut 18:20, 22). The willful are people who do not recog-

---

[62]Jer 49:16 also refers to "your horror" *(tipleṣet)*, but is this Edom's horrible nature (JPSV) or the terror it inspires (NRSV) or is it a reference to Edom's god? (so Holladay, *Jeremiah*, 2:376-77).

nize any authority of God over their lives (e.g., Ps 86:14; 119:21, 51, 85). Will-fulness is thus characteristic of Israel itself, and has been so from the beginning (Neh 9:16, 29). Edom is able to be thus self-confident because of the strength of its defensive position, but it is not too elevated for Yhwh to reach it (Obad 3-4). Edom's famous intellectual resources on which it relied in order to negotiate its way politically is failing it at its moment of greatest need. They do not provide it with the insight to negotiate a path through the threatened international crisis in such a way as to escape invasion and devastation, and that because it is Yhwh who is bringing about these events (Jer 49:7-13). Its in-tellectual resources are not up to counteracting that. "I myself have stripped Esau, uncovered his hiding places; he cannot conceal himself." So no one can escape, and as a result "his offspring is destroyed, with his kinsfolk and his neighbors—he is no more."

Yet the prophecy goes on, "Leave your orphans, I will keep them alive, and your widows can rely on me" (Jer 49:11). Whose words are these? It is charac-teristic of these oracles about the other nations that they contain some hint of mitigation of calamity, some suggestion of hope and mercy, and that would make one understand these as words of Yhwh that in a tiny way take the edge off the disaster. Or are they the words that there is no one to utter, as some of the ancient versions make explicit, so that they are a terrible expression of how awful the situation is? Certainly Yhwh's threats on either side offer no hope of mitigation. Jeremiah goes on to declare that "people who rightly would not drink the cup are certainly going to drink it, so are you in any way going to be clear?" (Jer 49:12). The words imply a recognition that the history of which Yhwh is sovereign does not work out in a fair way.[63] Some people experience calamity when they do not deserve it. If Yhwh does not intervene to limit di-saster in that connection, how much less can there be any escape for a people that thoroughly deserves it?

Apparent Impressiveness

In 609 in the last days of the Assyrian empire, Pharaoh Neco attempted to sup-port Assyria against the rising Babylonians. While he may not have had preten-sions to a Mesopotamian empire, defeating Babylon would preserve and increase his authority in his own region (including Judah). Four years later we hear a voice again commissioning troops, then asking why they are on the run instead of continuing to aim to create a world empire. It transpires that "that day is for the Lord Yhwh Armies a day of redress, for taking redress against his foes" (Jer 46:10). The voice summoning the troops, then asking somewhat sar-

---

[63]See further section 8.4 "Victims of History."

donically why they are on the run and commenting on their inability to find healing for their wounds, was Yhwh's, speaking as the supergeneral over this army that is more directly urged on its way by its earthly king. Behind the latter's machinations is a quite different design of Yhwh, for a day when "the sword will devour, will be full, will gorge on their blood," a day of terrible slaughter, not world-conquering victory. "For the Lord Yhwh Armies has a sacrifice in the northern country, by the River Euphrates": the blood will flow the way it does at a sacrifice. Yhwh is treating Egypt as an enemy to be slaughtered.

In the years after his defeat of Egypt in 605, several times Nebuchadnezzar took the conflict with Egypt onto its home territory. Jeremiah pictures Egypt's forces (MT) and/or its god (LXX) running for their lives on one of these occasions. Yhwh made them fall over each other (Jer 46:16). They blame "the king of Egypt," calling him "the big noise who let the moment pass" (Jer 46:17). His misfortune was to be confronted by another king, "the King, Yhwh Armies" (Jer 46:18). "King" is not a common title for Yhwh. Yhwh is king of Judah, so it would be wise to take more notice of Yhwh (Jer 8:19); Yhwh is king of the nations, so is much more powerful than their gods (Jer 10:7, 10). Only here is Yhwh's kingship set over against human kingship (Jer 51:57 will speak in similar terms in asserting Yhwh's power in relation to Babylon, though it does not set the divine king over against the human king). One is almost invited to feel sorry for the king who can only make a lot of noise but is unlucky to be set against such a more impressive king. But Yhwh comments, "I am attending to Amon of No, and to Pharaoh, to Egypt, its gods, and its kings, to Pharaoh and those who trust in him, and I will give them into the power of those who seek their life, into the power of King Nebuchadrezzar of Babylon and into the power of his servants" (Jer 46:25-26).

The passage resonates with all three possible antitheses that describing Yhwh as king may imply. Yhwh's attending to the Egyptian gods reflects the fact that Yhwh is God of the whole world and is much more powerful than other gods. Yhwh's attending to the Egyptian kings reflects the fact that Yhwh is king of the whole world and a much more powerful being than a mere human king. And Yhwh's attending to the people who trust in the king of Egypt reflects the fact that Yhwh is the real king of Judah. Of course ordinary Egyptians are people who have to trust in their king, and it might be that they are to pay the price for that. Again, that is unfair, but it is how life works. Yet the context makes little reference to ordinary Egyptians and focuses on kings and armies. In any case, talk of trust in Egyptian power resonates with a negative attitude to Judean trust in anything else but Yhwh (e.g., Jer 5:17; 17:5-8; for more specific reference to trusting in Egypt, see Is 31:1; 36:9). Nebuchadnezzar's invasion will demonstrate the emptiness of Egyptian power and Egyptian religion, and of Judean trust in Egypt. And by virtue of happening in fulfillment of Yhwh's word, it will demonstrate the power of Yhwh as God and King, power in the realm of religion and the realm of worldly politics, and demonstrate the possibility and advisability of trusting in Yhwh rather than those others. Yhwh's day will come for Egypt as Nebuchadnezzar invades the country, when the day of Yhwh is "the day of Egypt" (Ezek 30:9-10). But Judah saw Egypt as a resource, not a threat, so Yhwh's Day of calamity for Egypt was also bad news for Judah.

Among the reasons Jeremiah implies for Moab's destruction is that this nation of heroes and warriors needs to see who is the real King, as the falsehood of its trust in Chemosh is exposed (Jer 48:13-15). It has trusted in its achievements and its treasures (MT) and/or its stronghold (LXX) (Jer 48:7). It is time for this long-undisturbed people to experience exile (Jer 48:11-12); it has laughed at Israel (Jer 48:26-27). It has honored itself in relationship to Yhwh, exalted itself with arrogance and pretension (gāʾôn, gēʾeh, gōbah, gāʾôn, gaʾăwâ, rûm, ʿebrâ, bad, Jer 48:26, 29, 30). Its self-confidence will be replaced by shame (bôš), terror (ḥātat) and ridicule (Jer 48:1, 13, 20, 26, 39). Ezekiel 25:8-11 adds that it has inferred that Judah is no different from any other nation (exactly what Yhwh had determined should not happen; see Ezek 20:32). It too needs to come to acknowledge Yhwh.

Commercial Success

Jeremiah as a whole refers to Egypt more often than any book since Exodus, and its references could suggest why Yhwh might prefer to see Egypt lose in battle. Egypt is the old enemy, the old oppressor, the house of slavery out of which Yhwh had originally brought Israel (e.g., Jer 32:20-21; 34:13). In between that event and the killing of the great King Josiah, Egypt was a source of support against Assyria, and after that, against Babylon (Jer 2:18, 36). In the last years before the fall of the city, it was one of the places where Judeans took refuge (Jer 24:8; cf. Jer 26:21-23). Egyptian activity had delayed the conquest of Jerusalem by Babylon that Yhwh intended (Jer 37:5, 7). Egypt was then the refuge of some Judeans who escaped exile to Babylon as a place that seemed much preferable to Judah as a place to live, though Jeremiah declares that they will not find it so (Jer 42—45). Yhwh will bring Nebuchadnezzar to ravage Egypt and become its ruler and to destroy its temples and take off its divine images (Jer 43:8-13), and Yhwh will give Pharaoh Hophra over to his enemies, as happened to Zedekiah (Jer 44:30). Historically, it needs to be the earlier of these events that provide the rationale for Yhwh's putting Egypt down in Neco's time, but the broader context shows Egypt's ongoing key significance for Judah. Perhaps Yhwh was no more involved in Egypt's defeat than in events such as the defeats of France and the United States in Vietnam, but the event does remind a little people such as Judah neither to be excessively trusting in its big neighbors, nor excessively fearful of them.

In Israel's world in Ezekiel's day, alongside Egypt (to the south) stood Tyre (to the north) as a middle-range power. The focus on these in Ezekiel suggests that Yhwh reckons these two of greater importance than more local peoples, perhaps because they are regional powers that will raise more questions for Babylon as it seeks to assert its authority in Judah's world.

Tyre's interest in Jerusalem's fall was different from those of Judah's ancient enemies. With some cynicism, it simply saw this event as freeing it to increase its trading dominance of the Levant. But its fate will be the same, again with the result that it will "acknowledge that I am Yhwh" (Ezek 26:6). Tyre has not caused trouble to Judah, and rather stands as a symbol of prosperity, achievement and security. Jerusalem could naturally aspire to be like Tyre. Ezekiel subverts any such aspiration. Tyre will fall. Is anyone therefore secure? Isaiah had already pictured the horrified reactions of Tyre's neighbors and trading partners to its fall: "Is this your exultant one, whose antiquity is of old, whose feet would carry it afar to settle?" The event raises the question, "Who planned this against Tyre, bestower of crowns, whose merchants were leaders, its traders honored by the world?" The answer of course is that "Yhwh Armies planned it, to defile all splendid majesty, to put down all those honored by the world" (Is 23:7-9).

Tyre will thus be forgotten for a lifetime. But then it will be able to return to its trade like an old whore (Is 23:17): "At the end of seventy years Yhwh will attend to Tyre and it will return to its trade and have sex with all the kingdoms of the world on the face of the earth." Its fame and prestige as a trading nation meant it had to be put down, but there was nothing objectionable about being a skilled trading nation in itself, even though trading is a bit like prostitution— you are relating to people only for money. (The comment offers a thought-provoking perspective on the whole practice of exchanging goods for commercial gain. Why should one do that for money rather than as an expression of relationship? It is just like prostitution. It recalls the question, "How was it possible that Catholic doctrine defended private ownership of the means of production?")[64] So Tyre will be able to resume its vocation, but now "its profit and trade will be holy to Yhwh." Further, "it will not be stored or horded but its profit will be for the people who live in Yhwh's presence, for eating their fill and for choice clothing" (Is 23:18). People who do well in business customarily then store up their profits in the form of pension plans or large homes or the European beef mountain. Instead, to work out that dedication to Yhwh, Tyre's profits will be like offerings for the temple, which provide for the needs of the ministers there. There will be no skimping in the way they do that.

---

[64]José P. Miranda, *Marx and the Bible* (Maryknoll, N.Y.: Orbis, 1974/London: SCM Press, 1977), p. xvi; see further pp. 1-33.

Victims of History

While there are reasons that make such peoples deserve to be put down, the First Testament often describes their fall without providing such explanations. History is just like that. For instance, the forces of the king of Babylon invading Philistia will bring the day of Yhwh there. Jeremiah 47 describes the calamity coming on the Philistines at some length, yet gives no reason for it. Perhaps it reflects Philistine resistance to Nebuchadnezzar and represents a reaffirmation of Yhwh's power; perhaps it warns Judah not to follow such policies. But the oracle does not make such points. Perhaps this disaster comes upon Philistia because it has the misfortune to live next to Judah. Nebuchadnezzar is here in the Levant wielding Yhwh's sword against Judah for its faithlessness, and Philistia is caught in the crossfire. Initially the oracle focuses on the pathos of its situation. The Philistines are crying out like the Israelites in Egypt (*zāʿaq*, Ex 2:23). The panic is such that it makes parents stop looking to see what is happening to their children—how can that be imagined? People have nowhere to turn for help. The community is totally destroyed. All that is left is mourning. "Cut off from any help (v 4), Philistia can only await its doom, to be swept away by the flood of history."[65]

Except that the floodtide is not history on its own but the direct activity of Yhwh. The absence of reason for the destruction puts the emphasis on naked power. Faced with naked divine power, human hands are too weak even to rescue their children. No helper is of any use and no leftovers will survive. And that is so despite the fact that Yhwh shares in the awareness of the pathos of the events. This whole chapter is Yhwh's word, so the question, "How long until you are quiet?" is also Yhwh's question (Jer 47:6). Is Yhwh addressing the human hand that wields Yhwh's sword, bidding Babylon to recognize when enough is enough? If so, Yhwh does that in vain. Having commissioned this sword, Yhwh finds it has a mind of its own (cf. Zech 1:15). The terrifying picture puts together the certainty of the calamity that is to come, the sadness of it, the awareness that Yhwh caused it, and the fact that it may not abide by the constraints that Yhwh would like to impose.[66] Fortunately, as usual the nightmare is worse than the events that come about. One of the communities that Judah finds itself interacting with in the Persian period is Ashdod, the Persian version of Philistia.

On the way to an earlier defeat Neco had to take on Judah in the battle in which he killed Josiah, but Jeremiah does not hint that Neco's defeat is a punishment for that (Jer 2:16-17 seems to see that death as a lesson for Judah). Nor

---

[65]Holladay, *Jeremiah*, 2:339.
[66]Cf. Fretheim, *Jeremiah*, pp. 592-93.

does he more than hint that it was any pretensions to the creation of a wider empire that made Yhwh put him down. He may again imply the awareness that history is simply like that. If you take part in the war-based system whereby nations determine who is to rule in the world, you contract into an arrangement where there have to be winners and losers, and this time Egypt is the loser. Similar implications emerge from the way Jeremiah offers no explanation for the calamity to come on Syria, Kedar and Hazor (Arabian peoples), or Elam (in Persia)—or for the fact that Elam's fortunes will be restored (Jer 49:23-39). None of these peoples are involved in Judah's destiny, as enemies or allies, but all are likely victims of Nebuchadnezzar, as is explicit regarding Kedar and Hazor. The emphasis thus lies not on people's wrongful attitudes or their failure in relation to Yhwh or their hostility to Israel, but on the solemn facts about the way history works and the way nations become its victims through living in the wrong place at the wrong time. Here, too, they are not merely Nebuchadnezzar's victims but Yhwh's. Nebuchadnezzar defeats Kedar and Hazor, but does so on Yhwh's commission (Jer 49:28, 31). In a sense Yhwh does it (Jer 49:32), even if acting indirectly. Clearly Yhwh's sovereignty extends to peoples such as Kedar that are nothing to do with Israel (cf. Is 21:16-17). Paradoxically, while commissioning Nebuchadnezzar, Yhwh also warns Kedar and Hazor about what is coming and bids them flee, because *Nebuchadnezzar* has formulated a plan against them (Jer 49:30); the language of "planning" was earlier used of Yhwh (Jer 49:20). Similarly Jeremiah speaks both of Nebuchadnezzar setting up his throne in one of these countries (Jer 43:10) and of Yhwh doing so (Jer 49:38).[67] The former is a means of the latter.

The Cycle of Violence

Ezekiel 25:15-17 does accuse Philistia, like others, of taking redress from Judah, and that with malice of heart, which presumably implies that the basis for its action lies in such malice rather than in actual wrongdoing on Judah's part. Yhwh will therefore also punish Philistia; it, too, will thus come to "acknowledge that I am Yhwh." Either its attacks on Judah implicitly deny this or Yhwh's powerful action will any case now demonstrate it. And Yhwh's dispossessing the Philistines will mean that their coastlands can become territory where the leftovers of Judah can pasture their flocks as Yhwh "attends to them" and "restores their fortunes" (Zeph 2:4-7).

Jeremiah 49 and Obadiah describe how Yhwh will likewise bring calamity on Edom without giving much explanation for why Edom deserves it, but Obadiah 10 does accuse Edom of doing violence (*ḥāmās*) to its "brother" Jacob.

---

[67]Cf. ibid., p. 616.

The First Testament disapproves of such violence done by one nation to another (see Amos 1—2). It perhaps assumes that there is a further level of guilt involved in attacking Israel instead of recognizing it as Yhwh's means of implementing Yhwh's purpose in the world. There would be another level of this guilt involved in collaborating with the attack of foreigners on Jerusalem—contrast the subsequent vision of Israel as a people reestablished on Mount Zion as the holy mountain from which Yhwh rules in the world (Obad 16-21). But Obadiah also implies that Edom does worse because of that family link with Israel. It was bad enough that it stood aside when the Babylonians took Jerusalem and pillaged it, when Edom was "like one of them" (Obad 11). We do not know exactly how (if at all) Edomites were actually involved in the fall of Jerusalem; Obadiah's words may conflate those events with the way Edom expanded into Judean territory over subsequent centuries. Whatever the historical sequence of events, they involve looking with satisfaction at a brother's misfortune and taking advantage of it.

In Ezekiel 25:12-14, Edom has been involved in behavior that suggested seeking redress from Israel—we do not know what old scores it was seeking to settle. But now Israel itself will be the means of Yhwh's taking redress on Edom. The implication may be that redress is Yhwh's business (see, e.g., Deut 32:35; Ps 94:1) and that Edom was not aiming to act as Yhwh's agent but doing its own work. But the tables will be turned, and Yhwh will so use Israel. Edom will thus come to "acknowledge Yhwh's redress."

Ezekiel later goes on at greater length about the fate of Edom at Yhwh's own hands on the basis of its harboring an ancient enmity, its giving expression to it at Judah's moment of calamity, its ambition to take advantage of this moment by appropriating the land of Ephraim and Judah, "although Yhwh was there" (Ezek 35:10). Perhaps Yhwh presupposes that the restoration of Judah cannot be achieved without the putting down of Edom, a logical position when Edom is in the midst of expanding more and more into Judah's territory. But perhaps Yhwh presupposes that even if this were not pragmatically the case, the putting down of the oppressor is a necessary metaphysical balance to the elevation of the oppressed (cf. Obad; Ps 137). Perhaps Edom's protection is that destruction is to be brought by Yhwh in person and not by Israel. And again the aim is that "I will cause myself to be acknowledged through them [MT]/through you [LXX] as I decide about you" (Ezek 35:11).

So the day will come when "Egypt will be a desolation, Edom will be a desolate wilderness, because of the violence done to the Judeans whose innocent blood they shed in their land, but Judah will sit forever, Jerusalem to all generations" (Joel 3:19-20 [MT 4:19-20]). For long centuries Yhwh has been failing to do anything about the shedding of innocent blood or the blood of the innocent (*nāqî*) and has been thereby "clearing [people who have shed] their blood" (Joel 3:21 [MT 4:21]) and thus behaving as if clearing the guilty—*clear* is the related verb (*nāqâ* piel).[68] Yhwh's long-tempered self is always putting off punishment for the nations as for Israel, hoping to see the repentance that will make punishment unnecessary. Yet Yhwh's well-known self-description as one who is incurably long-tempered includes being also one who "certainly does not clear" (Ex 34:6-7), which Nahum applies to the world as well as to Israel (Nahum 1:3). Joel's expression affirms that Yhwh will indeed stop clearing [the people who have shed] blood. As happened to Israel, the time will come when Yhwh says, "That's it." Once more, the New Testament expresses itself even more directly as it pictures the martyrs asking when their blood will be avenged and promises that this will soon happen (Rev 6:10). God utilizes or takes part in the cycle of violence.

"Scatter the peoples who delight in wars," Psalm 68:30 [MT 31]) prays. Nations regularly provide rationalizations for engaging in war: it is in fulfillment of a mission, or in defense of freedom. The psalm calls the bluff of such claims.[69]

Suffering

Isaiah describes at length the suffering that comes on Moab when it is wasted. It cries and laments, weeps and wails and dissolves in tears. The prophet does not speak of this in order to crow over it. "My heart cries out for Moab," joining in Moab's own "cry" (Is 15:4-5): the verb is again *zāʿaq*, the verb for Israel's cry in Egypt. Shortly Yhwh explains, "because the waters of Dimon are full of blood, because I shall put more on Dimon, I shall drench the survivors of Moab, the leftovers of the land" (Is 15:9). Dimon refers to the well-known city of Dibon, but *dām* is blood, and Yhwh chillingly changes its name to "Blood City." Likewise "land" is *ʾădāmâ*, which in the context hints that it is also a place of blood. After this expression of grief at Moab's suffering (which in retrospect may be Yhwh's grief, since the "I" in the line just quoted is Yhwh), the prophecy declares that nevertheless this suffering will not be the end. As Yhwh sometimes warns Israel, there can be further calamity after calamity. "We have heard of Moab's majesty—very majestic—its magnificence and majesty and excess." But "the splendor of Moab will seem trifling, for all its great numbers. The remains will be small. The few will not be powerful" (Is 16:6,

---

[68]Cf. NRSV at Joel 3:21 [MT 4:21], following LXX and Syr., which I take to be paraphrasing rather than witnessing to a different text. NIVI, following Vg., refers the line to clearing Judah, but this fits ill in the context in light of the preceding reference to Judah as the ones whose innocent blood has been shed.

[69]I take the previous colon to refer to people who "love silver," which points to the actual rationale for many wars, but this does involve reading *rōṣê* for the hapax *raṣṣê*.

14). Subsequently, from Seir the prophet hears a voice asking a city's watchman about the night. Is the night of darkness and danger, of calamity and oppression over? Well, one such night may be over, but there is always another to follow (Is 21:11-12).

Between those declarations about Moab come more expressions of grief. Invasion and defeat mean an end to rejoicing over the harvest and over the prospect of new wine. The prophet has described the devastation of Moabite areas such as Jazer, Sibmah and Heshbon, but now adds, "Therefore as I weep for Jazer I weep for the vines of Sibmah, I drench you with my tears, Heshbon and Elealah. . . . Therefore my heart moans for Moab like a lyre, my soul for Kir-heres" (Is 16:9, 11). Moab has to face the reality of destruction, pain, mourning, desolation, death, decimation and flight, all linked to the need to overturn its majesty and sense of significance. A decent prophet has mixed feelings about that, no doubt satisfied that Moab gets its comeuppance but also joining with Moab in grief and weeping at destruction and suffering. In the same way he calls people to show mercy to the victims of war (Is 21:13-14).

And Yhwh acts thus. When calamity has overwhelmed Moab and "when the Moabites appear, when they exert themselves, at the place of worship, they will come to their sanctuary to pray but will not prevail" (Is 16:12). Events will expose their gods' powerlessness. But in light of its experience of invasion and devastation, Isaiah pictures Moab contemplating doing as Isaiah 2 says, sending "to the mountain of Ms. Zion" to ask for support and help: "Give advice, make a ruling, make your shade like night at midday, hide the banished, do not disclose the fugitive; banished Moabites must sojourn among you, be a shelter for them from the face of the destroyer." They will not be disappointed in what they find there: "A throne will be established with commitment and one will sit on it in trustworthiness, in David's tent one who governs, exercising government and prompt in faithfulness" (Is 16:1-5).

Jeremiah's oracle about Moab emphasizes the necessity of completing the work of destruction: "Cursed the one who does Yhwh's work negligently, cursed the one who withholds his sword from blood" (Jer 48:10). Yet like that oracle and oracles about Moab in Isaiah, Jeremiah grieves over the destiny of Moab (Jer 48:31-36): "I wail for Moab, cry out for all Moab, moan for the people of Kir-heres; with more weeping than for Jazer I weep for you, vine of Sibmah." Moab is "one who sacrifices at a sanctuary and burns incense to its god," but this gets it nowhere. Yhwh (apparently) wails, cries out (it is again the word for Israel's cry to God in Egypt), moans, weeps. Indeed, "my heart keens for Moab like a flute." Moab itself of course does these things as it goes through its horrifying devastation. Yhwh does the same, suffering with people such as Moab as well as Israel, and doing so irrespective of whether the suffering was deserved.[70] In light of that, it is not so surprising that Yhwh declares, "but I will restore the fortunes of Moab at the end of the days" (Jer 48:47). In the Persian period, like Judah Moab is a province of the Persian empire with some control of its own affairs.

Hope

With regard to Ammon, things are similar. Ammon has dispossessed Israelites living east of the Jordan as if there were no Israelites to inherit this land; Yhwh will therefore enable Israel to dispossess Ammon (Jer 49:1-6). It trusts in its resources and exults over the profaning of Yhwh's sanctuary, the destruction of the soil of Israel and the exile of the household of Judah. It too will acknowledge Yhwh (Ezek 25:1-7; cf. Zeph 2:8-11). Jeremiah also speaks explicitly of Yhwh's restoring Ammon's fortunes (Jer 49:6), and after the exile it, too, is a Persian province alongside Judah.

Israel was often inclined to rely on other nations for its political fortunes; this is a major reason Yhwh speaks so much about them. Ahaz, for instance, had turned to Assyria for support against the Ephraimite-Syrian alliance, while Isaiah had warned him that Assyria was a dagger in Yhwh's hand. The death of Ahaz would again raise questions about expectations of Assyria, especially as it apparently coincided with the death of an Assyrian king. Isaiah warns the Philistines not to make too much of the latter event, as if this terminates the power of Assyria and they can take the risk of declaring independence. "Do not rejoice, all Philistia, because the club that hit you has broken—because from the root of a snake there will come forth a viper, its fruit a flying fiery serpent" (Is 14:29). The death of one Assyrian king does not mean the end of domination by Assyrian kings. The Philistines will die of famine and war, but "the firstborn of the poor will pasture and the needy will lie down in safety." So when envoys come to Jerusalem from Philistia, perhaps to press Judah to join in resistance to Assyrian authority, how is Judah to respond? It is to say "that it was Yhwh founded Zion, and in it the weak among his people can find refuge" (Is 14:28-32). Paradoxically, security lies in being poor, needy and weak, because such people are driven to seek the reliable shelter that Yhwh established in Zion. Its security lies in Yhwh's having founded it, not in the (possible) implications of the more recent political events. On the stage Isaiah addresses Philistia, but the Judean audience in the house overhears Yhwh's reminder that real security lies somewhere else.

One might render the construct expression in the last line "his weak people" (cf. NIVI) and reckon that "poor, needy and weak" refers to the people as

---

[70]Cf. Fretheim, *Jeremiah*, p. 605.

a whole (Is 14:32). But the more obvious understanding takes the weak as a subgroup within the people, set over against the people in power. The people in power are inclined to reckon that they have to take responsibility for their destiny and for that of the people as a whole, in the same way as Philistia would. They may thereby dig their own graves. Being without power or influence can drive ordinary people to trust God more. But the openness of that expression does issue an invitation to the leadership. They can own that they belong to a weak people and cast themselves on Yhwh and on Yhwh's commitment to Zion, recognizing that in the short term we can never be sure of the implications of individual historical events (as the changing fortunes of global history since the rejoicing at the fall of the Berlin Wall illustrate). Yet further, if the weak can find refuge in Zion, is the implication that there is scope for Philistines to join this company?

Zechariah 9:1-8 declares Yhwh's assertion of authority over Damascus and Yhwh's defeat of Tyre, provoking a response of fear in Philistia as it correctly sees that this harbingers its own doom. That is all negative. But the passage then has Yhwh remove the blood from its mouth and the abhorrent things (*šiqqûṣîm*) from between its teeth—that is, Yhwh makes its life conform to Israel's rules about what one can eat, as if Philistia were part of Yhwh's people. Indeed, "it will be left over for our God [the verb *šāʾar* niphal]." A remnant of Philistia will not merely survive but "will be like a clan in Judah, and Ekron will be like the Jebusites," allowed to become part of the Judahite community. Those declarations make one reconsider the significance of earlier, tough-looking parts of this prophecy. The NRSV and NIVI have it beginning with Yhwh's word being *against* the land of Hamath, but JPSV has it beginning with Yhwh's settling *in* the land of Hamath (the preposition is *b*). Yhwh's eye is on people; this might be good news or bad news (or the ambiguous expression might signify their eye turning to Yhwh). In either case, the other peoples are like the clans of Israel—but are they like them in experiencing calamity or in experiencing God's love? In exposing the emptiness of Tyre and Sidon's wisdom and in stripping Tyre of its strength and its wealth, is Yhwh simply putting it down or delivering it from false objects of trust, as Yhwh delivers Philistia from false hopes and a false sense of importance and habits out of keeping with being part of Yhwh's people? The hovering in the passage between bad news and good news parallels that in prophecies about Judah itself in Isaiah 29. It simultaneously reassures Judah that Yhwh will act against its foes and invites it to see that this is not all that is in Yhwh's mind for them.[71]

---

[71]See Rex Mason, "The Use of Earlier Biblical Material in Zechariah 9—14," in *Bringing Out the Treasure*, ed. Mark J. Boda and Michael H. Floyd, JSOTSup 370 (London/New York: Continuum, 2003), pp. 1-208; see pp. 7-27.

8.5 The World of Nations Devastated

The prophets' regular first focus is on Israel and its wrongdoing and danger (even Amos only proves the rule, because there other peoples come first, but only for the sake of the rhetoric). They often go on to the coming devastation of other peoples. They can broaden the horizon yet further and portray the wrongdoing and devastation of the whole world of nations. Their rebellion and refusal to respond to God's covenant could mean the day of Yhwh's wrath falling on them.

Polluted by Wrongdoing and Wasted

The nightmare vision for Israel (Is 1—12) and for the nations (Is 13—23) becomes a nightmare vision for the whole world as the earth is emptied as by plague, wasted as by war, disfigured as by earthquake (Is 24:1-6). Religious status, social status or financial status grants no exemption from the scattering. The disaster is and is not a natural calamity. A complex network of factors explains it. It happens because Yhwh says so, because the world is under an execration, because it is undergoing punishment, because it is polluted as its human inhabitants have "transgressed teachings, violated statute, broken the ancient covenant/lasting covenant [běrît 'ôlām]."[72] The language is mostly rather different from that in Genesis 1—11, but the substance looks rather similar (and comparable to that of Rom 1—2). Genesis presupposes that the world as a whole knows the fundamentals of God's expectations of it. It does not talk in terms of statute and instruction (tôrâ) in connection with the relationship between God and humanity as a whole, but rather implies that humanity does not require a special revelation in order to know that God is there and to be drawn to worship. It knows that God has made a commitment to the world and that it is expected to fulfill a reciprocal commitment to God. It knows that we should care for the world and care about one another. It knows that things have gone wrong when humanity declines to live within the constraints God has set and when the world comes to be characterized by violence. In its look to the future, Isaiah 24 is the First Testament's equivalent to the look to the past in Genesis 1—11.

Thus, because of humanity's action the world is polluted or corrupt (hānēp).[73] Again that actual notion does not occur in Genesis, though in substance Isaiah may reflect similar thinking. Yhwh requires that Israel not pollute the land of Israel by condoning murder there, because such shedding of blood pollutes the land (Num 35:33-34). That recalls the idea that Abel's blood

---

[72]This does not imply annulling it, any more than "breaking a law" does so.

[73]Cf. section 4.2 "Corruption."

cries out from the ground when it has been shed by Cain (Gen 4:10). Isaiah implies the assumption that the world as a whole is God's and that it is not only the land of Israel that is affected by pollution, as it implies that it is not only Israel that is bound by covenant, instructions and statute. And if the whole earth is polluted by blood, it is not surprising if it becomes sterile, refuses to produce fruit and thus dries up, withers, and languishes.

Robert Murray suggests that Isaiah 24 reflects an ancient traditional way of thinking of creation as involving a mutual covenant relationship between God and humanity.[74] Genesis introduces no talk of a covenant until after the flood, when God makes a "lasting covenant" (*běrît ʿôlām* again) with humanity; nor is there any explicit reference to a creation covenant elsewhere in the First Testament. Perhaps Genesis presupposes that a covenant was hardly needed at creation, when there was a "natural" relationship between God and humanity.[75] It is after the flood that in light of human sinfulness (!) God promises never to suspend the rhythm of the seasons and the alternating of day and night (Gen 8:21-22). Jeremiah 33:20-21 speaks of the latter as a covenant, and in Genesis 9:1-17 God covenants never again to flood the earth.

Yet Isaiah 24:18-20 goes on to picture a flood overwhelming the earth, and also a fatal shaking of the earth, which the First Testament often declares an impossibility. It is as if the Noah covenant is suspended. Human transgression has led to curse devouring the earth once more (Is 24:5-6). Further, this is the moment when Yhwh will pay attention to the army on high as well as the kings on earth (Is 24:21-23). Like the covenant about a flood, the covenant concerning day and night is imperiled: sun and moon hide in shame. Allusion to heavenly beings also recalls the involvement of heavenly beings in the events that led up to the flood (see Gen 6:1-4). Like the narrative in Genesis 1—6, then, the nightmare vision in Isaiah 24 sees the world spoiled by the combined action of a variety of actors as creation is undone.[76]

Failing to Respond to God's Covenant

How can Yhwh bring such calamity on the world and thus fail to keep the commitment to Noah? That covenant did not make God's commitment conditional on humanity's responsiveness to God (God has already learned that this does not work). Yet Genesis 9 does lay down expectations of humanity, and it would not be surprising if the covenant presupposed that God's commitment would only work out properly if humanity did make its response to God. Is-

---

[74]Robert Murray, *The Cosmic Covenant* (London: Sheed & Ward, 1992), pp. 16-22.

[75]See section 3.2.

[76]On this theme in Is 24—27, see Patrick D. Miller, *Israelite Religion and Biblical Theology*, JSOT-Sup 267 (Sheffield: Sheffield Academic Press, 2000), pp. 670-77.

rael was very familiar with the idea of a mutual covenant that bound Israel as well as Yhwh, and Isaiah 24 may be taking up that model of the relationship between Yhwh and Israel and applying it in an innovative way to the world as a whole. It would assume that the unconditional covenant necessarily implied some expectations.[77] The point about the unconditional covenant was to put all the emphasis on the divine commitment, like a woman telling a man she will always love him. This presupposes that he will make the appropriate response; it does not rule out the possibility that he could behave in ways that make her stop loving him. A commitment to love is designed to inspire a response. Perhaps a warning such as the one in Isaiah 24 makes this assumption. It also implicitly heightens the stakes on Yhwh's involvement with Israel. Insofar as this prophecy is given to Israel and not to the world itself, it recalls the fact that Yhwh intends to reach the world through Israel (the theme announced in Gen 12:1-3). Is that process the only way this nightmare scenario can avoid finding fulfillment?

There is a converse implication for Israel. The nightmare scenario also promises Israel that Yhwh is involved with the world as a whole in a moral way. Subsequently, Isaiah 26:20-21 urges Yhwh's people to lock themselves in and hide "because now Yhwh is coming out from his place to attend to the wrongdoing of the inhabitants of the earth upon them; the earth will disclose its bloodshed; it will no longer conceal its slain."

Once again bloodshed is the paradigm of wrongdoing: "Bloodguilt points to the deepest level of ʿwn" (wrongdoing).[78] When people are killed, their blood soaks into the earth and their bodies are buried in the earth. The earth thus absorbs them and absorbs the fact that they were killed. The evidence seems to be gone. But actually this is not so. While Genesis speaks of this blood still crying out from the ground to God, Isaiah perhaps implies a slightly different metaphor in understanding Yhwh to be aware that there is wrongdoing to be dealt with, deciding that this is the moment to deal with it, and requiring the earth to produce the evidence that it otherwise inevitably conceals. Two factors, then, could conceivably bring it about that nothing happens after the killing of innocent people. One is that the earth conceals their blood; its cry goes unuttered or muffled. The other is that Yhwh stays at home in the heavens, not moving to take action. All that now changes as Yhwh "comes out from his place" and cross-questions the earth (Is 26:21).

In Isaiah 26 the prophet has been confronting Yhwh about the wrong done

---

[77]Cf. John Day, *God's Conflict with the Dragon and the Sea* (Cambridge/New York: Cambridge University Press, 1985), p. 146.

[78]Hans Wildberger, *Isaiah 13—27* (Minneapolis: Fortress, 1997), p. 572. Cf. Victor Maag, "Unsühnbare Schuld," *Kairos* 8 (1966): 90-106.

to his people, and the blood the passage has in mind is that of Israelites, "my people" (whether this means the prophet's or Yhwh's). So many of them have been wrongfully killed by their enemies. Now there will be action on their behalf (compare the prayer and the response in Rev 6:9-11). Living Israelites are to hide like the Israelites at the first Passover or like Moses on Sinai when Yhwh passes by, to make sure they are not caught by the aftershock or withered by coming too close (Is 26:20). But what will pass by is "wrath" (za'am), an elemental force like a hurricane. There are thus three agents or factors involved in bringing this calamity. There is the earth with its awareness of blood shed on it. There is Yhwh as one who cares about what human beings do. And there is the primal force of wrath.

Under a Curse

Genesis knows that human wrongdoing let loose various curses into the world (see especially Gen 3:14, 17; 4:11), and Isaiah 24:6 speaks similarly about an execration. To describe something as cursed ('ārûr) draws attention to the results of the curse for the people who experience it. To describe something as an execration ('ālâ) draws attention to the solemn commitment of the person who makes the curse, who is swearing an oath and calling down a self-curse in case of failure to fulfill the oath. As it often does, the First Testament offers alternative scenarios before people. Yhwh's preferred intention is that Israel's blessing should model what Yhwh could do for other nations (Gen 12:1-3), reversing the curse of Genesis 1—11. But the alternative possibility is that Israel's punishment should come to model what Yhwh will do to the whole world, repeating the curse of Genesis 1—11. This nightmare vision thus constitutes a mirror image of the prospect that Genesis 12 sets forth.

The implementing of the curse involves the summoning of warriors or—in Joel's image—of harvesters. The world is a vineyard that has only produced disgusting fruit, the kind Isaiah 5 spoke of. The clusters are ripe for cutting, the winepress is overflowing with grapes for treading; there is an impressive harvest, but it is a harvest of wickedness. As people look around, they can see no evidence of Yhwh's acting to vindicate truth and punish wickedness. But Yhwh will roar from Zion, as in Amos 1:2. Yhwh urges the harvesters to do their work (Joel 3:13-17 [MT 4:13-17]). The New Testament takes up Joel's imagery to describe the final dreadful harvest in terms rather bloodier than Joel's (Rev 14:14-20).

The "crowds" assemble there in "the Vale of the Determination" (Joel 3:14 [MT 4:14]). It is almost as if the Vale is itself a giant winepress, full to overflowing with armies that do not realize they are there only to be crushed. The earlier lines spoke of a decision Yhwh is about to make, but from another angle this is a matter of implementing a decision taken long ago. "Determination" is ḥārûṣ, usually taken as the only instance of a noun meaning decision. Similar words recur in the prophets to refer to a decision Yhwh has already taken, which is thus certain to be implemented. Isaiah uses this very word to refer to a destruction that has been "determined" (Is 10:22-23, where the word is certainly the passive participle of *ḥāraṣ*). This same word can also mean a threshing sledge (e.g., Is 28:27; 41:15), and this will indeed be the Vale of the Threshing Sledge as the heavenly armies thresh the "grain" that covers the vale.

Even if people cannot see the signs, its implementation is as certain as was the implementation of that earlier decision, which happened with the exile (cf. the parallel movement between Dan 9:26 and 27, using the same verb *ḥāraṣ*). "Sun and moon have gone dark, stars have withdrawn their brightness." The signs have appeared, the reverberations of Yhwh's roar. Joel can see them now, even if other people cannot. "Yhwh—he will roar from Zion, will give voice from Jerusalem,"[79] and once again that roar will herald Yhwh's taking action against the nations for their wrongdoing, this time without the irony that attaches to it in Amos 1:2 where it eventually introduces warnings for Judah and then for Ephraim itself. This time "Yhwh will be a refuge for his people, a stronghold for the Israelites," and they will see the evidence that "I am Yhwh your God, the one who dwells on Zion, my holy mountain." And henceforth "Jerusalem will be holy; foreigners will not pass through it any more" (Joel 3:15-17 [MT 4:15-17]). This does not exclude foreigners who have themselves come to acknowledge Yhwh; their feet do not defile. But foreigners will not pass through any more bringing their foreign gods with them or coming in order to shed innocent blood.

Destruction as Good News

Isaiah 14 has already declared that the same fate will overcome the king of Babylon, who aspired to ascend on high, even above these subordinate heavenly beings, but will be brought low, brought down to the Pit (Is 14:19; the word in Is 24:22). Even if the world has to wait till the End for the final shaming of the powers on high and the powers on earth, this need not mean they simply continue exercising their power unchecked until that day. From time to time God puts them down. Autocrats fall. And the fall of earthly powers is the visible equivalent to the fall of powers on high. The fall of any empire illustrates these realities. It is therefore possible for us to pray as Psalm 82 does for God to assert authority over these heavenly and earthly powers in the way God did in bringing about the fall of Assyria and the fall of Babylon.

It is no doubt also possible for us to pray for mercy if we belong to an

---

[79]In Amos 1:2 the context suggests these two yiqtols need translating as present, but the context here suggests future.

earthly power, though Isaiah 24—25 is more explicit about the fact that it will be possible for us to give praise, especially if we do not so belong. In response to the vision of destruction and dethronement, Isaiah 25:1-4 follows with a hymn of praise: "Yhwh, you are my God: I will exalt you, confess your name, for you have done a wonder, plans from of old, truthfulness, truth." The reason for the praise is extraordinary: "for you have turned a city into a heap, a fortified town into a ruin." The hymn offers another take on the significance of Yhwh's attending to laying waste to the earth, one that fits the idea that the earth was polluted by blood. City and fortified town stand for the center of power in the empire that holds power over weaker peoples. Yhwh's act will drive this strong and brutal power to honor and revere Yhwh. Isaiah does not quite say it will force it to do so, nor that its recognition will be merely a cowed capitulation; in isolation, we might think of the town of brutal nations *fearing* Yhwh, but following on the reference to *honoring* Yhwh, Isaiah more likely thinks of them *revering Yhwh.* The argument either side supports that.

Yhwh has done a wonder, an act like that at the Red Sea (Ex 15:11). It was an act that fulfilled longstanding policies of Yhwh and once again proved their power over against the policies of the empire. But they were not merely an expression of power but emphatically an expression of "truthfulness, truth" (*'ĕmûnâ 'ōmen*), of Yhwh's steadfastness (Is 25:1). How is that so? The argument that follows explicates how. The empire will have seen Yhwh's working in the opposite direction to its own policies. It did not care too much what happened to the poor and needy. But events have shown that they are Yhwh's priority. The policies of the empire made life either like the withering heat of summer or like the overwhelming storms of winter, but "you have been a stronghold for the poor person, a stronghold for the needy person in distress, shelter from storm, shade from heat, when the blast of cruel people was like a winter storm." And the empire has come to recognize that: "Therefore a strong people will honor you, a town of brutal nations will revere you" (Is 25:3, 4). It is to recognize the appropriateness of Yhwh's action, like Nebuchadnezzar recognizing the appropriateness of Yhwh's action against him after he has refused to break off his sins by practicing faithfulness and showing compassion to the oppressed (Dan 4:34-35 [MT 31-32]).

All that is reason for praise on the part of people who may identify with the poor and needy, or who may distance themselves from that oppressiveness and be drawn into a renewed acknowledgment of Yhwh as this God through seeing how God has acted on behalf of the poor and needy. Or perhaps this exalting of Yhwh *is* the honoring and revering of which the hymn shortly speaks. The worshiper belongs to those who represent the empire and survive to offer this honor and reverence. This offers hope to the readers of this volume, most of whom belong to an embodiment of the empire whose ruin Isaiah describes.

Yhwh's Day of Wrath upon the Nations

The day when Yhwh brings calamity on the nations is "Yhwh's day."[80] That precise expression comes sixteen times in the First Testament, but I assume that allusions to Yhwh's having a day or to the day of Yhwh's anger and other such expressions also refer to what is described most succinctly as "Yhwh's day." The variety in ways of speaking warns us against seeing "Yhwh's day" as a technical term with only one reference. Yhwh's day is any occasion when Yhwh acts decisively to implement the divine purpose by punishing wrongdoers and/or delivering the needy. Such moments recur through Israel's history; the First Testament does not speak in terms of there being just one "day of Yhwh." It refers to a moment within history that brings about a marked fulfillment of Yhwh's ultimate purpose. That happens at the fall of Babylon (Is 13:6, 9), the fall of Egypt (Jer 46:10; Ezek 30:1-3), the fall of Edom (Is 34:6; Obad 15) and the fall of Jerusalem (Lam; Ezek 7:10-12, 19; 13:5; 34:12). Whereas Amos turned the idea of Yhwh's day from good news to bad news by declaring that it is a day of calamity for Israel and not for its enemies (Amos 5:18-20),[81] other prophets reverse this transformation again. Yhwh's day is the occasion when the nations will be put down. "The day of our God's redress" is also "the year of Yhwh's pleasure" (Is 61:2); these are two sides of a coin. Yhwh's day is first against Israel, then against the nations (Joel).[82] It can then suggest a final day (Zech 14:1-3?). It is brought about by an army that is not identified with any that prophet or people can specify, one that embodies unknown and unnamable forces at Yhwh's disposal in the same way that Assyria, Babylon and Persia had once been (Joel 2:1-11). Joel's locust plague was without precedent in Israelite history; this invasion will be without precedent in world history (Joel 1:2; 2:2).[83]

The nations' leaders are their shepherds; correlatively, Yhwh "is leaving his lair like a lion, because their country is becoming a desolation through his oppressive fury, through his angry fury" (Jer 25:34-38). Isaiah 34—35 offers a picture of this day as a day of wrath. Whatever their prehistory, these chapters form part of the bridge between the first half of Isaiah, with its focus on the time of Isaiah himself, and the second half, with its more explicit reference to later events. Fittingly in that connection, it begins with talk of the nations and the heavenly powers, but it is then dominated by a declaration of punishment for Edom, for reasons that are not clear. While there were running bad rela-

---

[80]On theories regarding the origin of the idea of the "Day of Yhwh" see, e.g., Hans M. Barstad, *The Religious Polemics of Amos*, VTSup 34 (Leiden: Brill, 1984), pp. 89-108.

[81]See section 4.2 "Darkness."

[82]See section 7.4 "Nature and Yhwh's Day."

[83]Cf. Wolff, *Joel and Amos*, pp. 44-45.

tions between Israel and Edom through the centuries, there is not enough there to account for a distinctively vindictive stance toward the historical Edom. In due course Edom became a figure for Rome, and it seems that even here "Edom has become by then, in a certain sense, a cliché—Edom the evil neighbor."[84] Perhaps Isaiah could have spoken as easily about some other people, such as Moab; reference to Edom simply makes the threat more concrete. A striking feature of Isaiah 34 is the almost total lack of any rationale for Yhwh's act of punishment. The sum total of any such rationale is the phrase "for Zion's cause" (*rîb*, Is 34:8). That does indicate that Yhwh is acting because of the way Edom has behaved toward Zion, and it suggests the basis for prayers against Edom (cf. Ezek 35:5; Ps 137:7; Lam 4:21-22) or indicates Yhwh's response to such prayers. But the passage does not give us information about a context in which Edom earned Yhwh's wrath or earned Judah's opprobrium, nor does it speak of Judah's desire for such vengeance.

Furthermore, the declaration about Edom's punishment is directly addressed not to Edom itself, nor to Israel, but to the whole world of nations (Is 34:1-3). And the declaration that Isaiah bids the nations to hear is initially a declaration concerning calamity coming to them all. It seems that the punishment of Edom is but a concrete instance of Yhwh's punishing the world as a whole, designed for the world to learn from. And by implication, the point about it is that the nations should turn to Yhwh and be able to sigh in relief when Yhwh revokes their punishment, as happens to Nineveh in Jonah (and see Jer 18:1-10). They are urged to listen to Yhwh's declarations, imagine the scene the prophet puts before them, and flee from the coming wrath.

A Day of Fury and Devastation

Yhwh is a passionate person and does not view human wrongdoing with the coolness appropriate to a judge. Yhwh is not distanced from events like someone not personally involved but reacts with analogous ferocious anger to the burning fury David showed when Nathan told him a fictitious story about a man with great flocks and herds who appropriated a poor man's one lamb (2 Sam 12:1-6). Such vigorous rage energizes a person into action on behalf of the right and against the wrong. Cool serenity is not the personal quality required when one is confronted by outrageous wrongdoing. "The man who did this deserves to die," David said. For Yhwh, too, the people who provoke such anger are also people who must be killed. Only slaying can relieve the fury, and in this case slaying on the most monumental scale, so that the mountains seem to have dissolved in blood. The trouble is that killing takes only a moment, and

---

[84]Hans Wildberger, *Isaiah 28—39* (Minneapolis: Fortress, 2002), p. 325 (referring directly to Ps 137).

adrenaline takes time to subside, so that anger requires not merely the slaying but some way of making death worse than death. Thus the corpses are thrown away rather than buried, so that death is not the gateway to rest in Sheol but to ongoing restless homelessness. Instead of their bodies dissolving invisibly in the tomb, they decay in the Middle Eastern sun in a way everyone can see and smell (Is 34:2-3). Thus Yhwh will be satisfied. The killing will be an act whereby these peoples are devoted to Yhwh (*ḥāram* hiphil), as the Canaanites were supposed to have been.

Isaiah 13:1-8 speaks similarly of a day of Yhwh relating specifically to the fall of Babylon that will free Judeans to go home but sees this in the framework of a more worldwide cataclysmic event (Is 13:9-16). "Yhwh's day has come, harsh, with fury and burning anger, to make the earth a desolation and wipe out its sinners from it." It will bring cosmic cataclysm: "the stars in the heavens and their constellations will not shine their light; the sun is dark at its rising, the moon will not diffuse its light." Frightful massacre will follow among the faithless, the willful and the tyrants, such as will not spare their wives, their homes and their children. Israel was well aware that the world lives in defiance of God's purpose for it. Among other things, it is characterized by willful tyranny instead of a generous brotherhood. Because of an inclination to mercy and a longing that nations may change, for decades Yhwh puts up with the tyranny of one people over another and the general faithlessness of people to one another, but over those decades Yhwh's anger at the way peoples treat each other builds up inside and eventually insists on receiving expression. That is the nature of Yhwh's day. As Amos put it, it means light for people who need deliverance but darkness for their oppressors.

Yhwh's sword "will come down on Edom to act with authority on the people I have devoted." Because "Yhwh has a sword, filled with blood, gorged with fat, with the blood of lambs and goats, with the fat of rams' kidneys, because Yhwh has a sacrifice in Bozrah, a great slaughter in the land of Edom." In applying to Edom the imagery of slaughter, devoting and sacrifice, Isaiah makes explicit that although this is not an act of judgment in our sense (that cool, measured act of a court, distanced from the acts on which it has to adjudicate), it is indeed an act of punishment or redress. "For Yhwh has a day of redress, a year of recompense for Zion's cause" (Is 34:5-8).[85] The point about punishment is to put things right in the sense of restoring balance. Wrongdoing skews the world (and the heavens), puts it out of kilter and imperils its stability. Punishment restores its equilibrium and makes it possible that "all will be well, and every kind of thing will be well."[86]

---

[85]See section 2.7 "Redress."

[86]Julian of Norwich, *Showings,* chap. 13 (New York: Paulist, 1978), p. 149.

As usual, the earth pays a price for human wrongdoing, sharing in the fall-out from Yhwh's punishment of humanity. The land that humanity was given to serve and to eat from becomes irrevocably infertile, like Sodom and Gomorrah. "Its streams will be turned to pitch, its dirt to brimstone." Instead of humanity controlling the animal world, the animal world takes control of former human habitations. "Thorns will grow in its castles, nettle and thistle in its fortresses; it will be a home for jackals, an abode for ostriches. Wildcats will meet desert creatures, wild goats will call to each other, yes, there Lilith will relax, find herself a place to rest" (Is 34:9-15). We cannot really identify the creatures mentioned near the end here, and the subsequent mention of the Mesopotamian demon Lilith heightens the impression that these are demonic creatures.[87] The land to which humanity was supposed to bring order becomes the realm of disorder.

A Day of Death

"Yhwh's day is near against all the nations," says Obadiah 15-16. "As you people will have drunk on my holy mountain,[88] all the nations will drink continually, they will drink and swallow/splutter,[89] and be as if they had never been." For the nations, as for Israel, experiencing Yhwh's wrath is like drinking a cup of poisoned wine. "There is a cup in Yhwh's hand with wine foaming, full of mix-ins, and he pours from it; yes, dregs of it they will drain and drink—all the wicked in the land/earth" (Ps 75:8 [MT 9]). It is a good sign for someone to have a cup of wine in their hand that they want to share with their guests, but the information that the wine has lots of spices in it turns out to have sinister implications. These are additives that turn the wine into a cup of poison. Such is the cup in Yhwh's hand. "Babylon was a gold cup in Yhwh's hand making the whole earth drunk; nations drank of its wine; that is why nations go mad" (Jer 51:7). They are not merely intoxicated but poisoned. The nations are to drink their fill from that cup of poison and it will be the death of them.

Or it is like being attacked by a mighty warrior. "Yhwh will roar from on high, from his holy dwelling will give forth his voice. He will indeed roar against his fold; a shout like grape-treaders echoes to all the inhabitants of the earth, a yell is reaching to the end of the earth, because Yhwh has a case against the nations" (Jer 25:30-31). Yhwh goes on to picture disaster spreading from one nation to another, through the world, with the dead so numerous they lie

---

[87]Cf. section 7.4 "Natural and Supernatural."

[88]The *you*s in this line are plural. They might refer to Edom (the *you* singular of the previous line) or to Obadiah's Judean audience.

[89]It is not clear whether there are one or two roots *lûaʿ/lāʿaʿ*; see BDB.

unburied from one end of the world to the other. The leaders of the nations wail as they find there is no more escape for them than there is for ordinary people.

Jeremiah likewise pictures Yhwh holding this cup of wine, like the host at a banquet who will then invite his guests to share the cup. "Take this cup of wine (wrath)[90] from my hand and make all the nations to whom I am sending you drink it. They will drink, and they will convulse and go mad, because of the sword that I am sending among them" (Jer 25:15-16). So Jeremiah did so, giving the cup to Judah (!), and then to Egypt, the Philistines and other peoples of the Levant, the peoples of the desert, Elam and Media—and Babylon. "Now. I am beginning by doing ill to the city over which my name is pronounced, and you, can you really go free? You will not go free, because I am summoning the sword on all the inhabitants of the earth" (Jer 25:29). For different reasons all these peoples might think they would be exempt from disaster, but none will be—not even Yhwh's own people nor the superpower that is sure it will stand when all else fall. The order and the logic thus contrast with that in Amos 1— 2, where Yhwh moves from the nations to Judah and Ephraim.[91] If the nations must be punished for their wrongdoing, then Judah and Ephraim must be; if Judah must be punished for its wrongdoing, so must the nations, even the most powerful.

Ezekiel's prophecies about the other nations end by noting that they will all die—or rather, they will all be killed (Ezek 32:20-32). Legendary powers from long ago such as Assyria and Elam are there in Sheol, with remote and mythical powers such as Meshech and Tubal, and more immediate neighbors of Israel such as Edom and Phoenicia, and Israel's more immediate local power, Egypt, which at least has the consolation that the same fate comes to the other peoples. For all their power, they and their leaders end up in this same place of stillness with all their company, all their hordes, all their multitude. They are in remote parts of Sheol in recognition of their status as uncircumcised and as people who were killed in battle, which routinely implied stripping, mutilation, shame and being deprived of proper burial (cf. 1 Sam 31). The fate of the inner person corresponds to the fate of the outer person. They are there in Sheol despite the fact that they once spread terror in the land of the living and because they once did so. No matter how impressive or powerful or frightening a nation, it will end up in the same place as every other nation, dead. The portrait offers an implicit critique of nations,

---

[90]The construction is ungrammatical—hence this way of representing the sentence. "Wrath" interprets the word *wine*.

[91]Cf. Walter Brueggemann, *To Pluck Up, To Tear Down: A Commentary on the Book of Jeremiah 1—25* (Grand Rapids: Eerdmans/Edinburgh: Handsel, 1988), p. 218.

which by their nature come into being by violence, stay in being by violence and fall by violence.

A Day upon Repeated Wrongdoing

The beginning of Amos speaks of Yhwh roaring from Zion, with the result that the shepherds' pastures and forests of Mount Carmel wither (Amos 1:2). This could suggest that Jerusalem is the source of a calamity that does not affect Judah itself, though Amos 2:4-5 will clash with that inference. It could suggest that Jerusalem is the source of a calamity that specifically affects Ephraim, and Amos 2:6-16 (and the rest of the book) will confirm this. It could also suggest that Jerusalem is the source of a calamity that will affect pasturage and forest in general, there being no particular limitation to Israel, and that fits the way the book immediately develops (Amos 1:3—2:3). The peoples around Israel have been guilty of rebellion after rebellion ("for three rebellions and for four"), but they have now reached the point when they have done something that makes Yhwh (like a woman whose husband is repeatedly unfaithful) eventually say, "That's it," and determine to bring calamity on them. Before determining each calamity, Yhwh thus already declares, "I will not revoke it." There has been enough leniency and compassion.

The first rebellion involves Damascus and Gilead (Amos 1:3), and one might infer that Amos is condemning the nations for the way they have treated Israel. But the emphasis lies less on the objects of Damascus's action than on the enormity of the war crime that tips Yhwh over the edge: "they have threshed Gilead with iron threshing sledges." We do not know the precise meaning of that expression, but the image makes clear that it is an action of great enormity. Gaza's crime likewise involves uprooting a whole community and handing it over to another people (Amos 1:6), like European peoples transporting African communities to the Americas. The community might be an Israelite one, but Amos does not say so, and the emphasis lies more on the cynical enormity of the trafficking in humanity. The same is true of Tyre's handing over a whole community to Edom, though Tyre also incurred further guilt in that it had "not thought about the covenant of kinsfolk" (Amos 1:9). This seems more likely to refer to a covenant/treaty relationship between Tyre and Ephraim that Tyre had breached in the way it dealt with an Ephraimite community than that Tyre's action had meant a breach in the kinship relationship between Edom and Ephraim, which was a natural blood relationship and therefore not a covenantal one. But Edom itself is then condemned for its action toward its "brother," presumably Israel, but also for destroying its own compassion and letting its anger rage ceaselessly (Amos 1:11). The Ammonites' crime is also an attack on Gilead, but here Amos makes more explicit that what seals their fate is the nature of the attack: in the course of action to enlarge their own territory, they ripped open pregnant women (Amos 1:13). The practice is referred to a number of times (e.g., Hos 13:16) and has its equivalents in modern ethnic conflicts; while it has the purpose of killing the next generation as well as the present one, there is also a dehumanized hatred about it. Moab's crime is purely a wrong done to the king of Edom (Amos 2:1), but depriving someone of the chance to rest in peace is another dehumanized and dehumanizing act. "This offense against one who is dead forms the counterpart to the outrage against unborn life."[92]

A Day upon Rebellion

On the whole, then, there is more stress on the inherently repellent nature of the different peoples' acts than on their being perpetrated on Israel. "Rebellion" (*pešaʿ*) is then all the more striking a term to apply to these foreign peoples. The word can denote something more like crime or trespass or transgression. It suggests an offense in relation to other people's rights. And the acts that are critiqued in Amos 1:3—2:3 are what we would call war crimes. But Israel also used this noun and the related verb to refer to nations' failing to acknowledge the rights of a superior power, such as a sovereign with whom they stand in treaty/covenant relationship. Yet how can these nations rebel against someone with whom they have never entered into treaty/covenant relationship, and how does action between such people count as rebellion? At a later time Judah will be involved in rebellion after rebellion in its relationship with Babylon, and perhaps Yhwh sees these peoples the same way as Babylon would see Judah. Judah did not choose to be Babylon's underling, and these peoples did not choose to be Yhwh's, but that is what they are. And as Babylon had expectations of Judah, so Yhwh has expectations of these peoples, expectations they are assumed to be entirely familiar with. You do not need a special revelation to know it is wrong to engage in slave trading or ripping open pregnant women or forbidding someone a decent burial. It is the kind of thing that is built into being human. We are hardwired that way. Amos's condemnation of Edom makes the point vividly: Edom "destroyed its compassion" (Amos 1:11). It had the natural human compassion that members of a family have for one another, and in order to act as it did, it had to "kill" that compassion.[93]

For failing to behave in accordance with the way they are wired, the nations will suffer calamity. Devastation will consume the king of Aram and his household, destruction will consume the city of Damascus, death will come to

---

[92]Wolff, *Joel and Amos*, p. 162.

[93]"Kill" is J. Alberto Soggin's translation, *The Prophet Amos* (London: SCM Press, 1987), p. 40. The NRSV has "cast off," NIVI "stifle," JPSV "repress," but the verb is *šāḥat* piel.

the people in the Valley of Trouble and the ruler of the House of Delight,[94] and transportation back to the area Yhwh brought them from (!) (cf. Amos 9:7) will claim the people of Aram in general; similar blows will fall on Philistia. Fire will consume Tyre and the fortified cities in Edom. Fire will consume the capitals of Ammon and Moab, and their leaders will be exiled or killed. There is thus a difference between the nature of the trouble that comes, as there is a difference between the wrongs they have done. But the calamity does not correspond to the wrongdoing. Edom is to get away with trouble that affects only the buildings in its fortified cities, even though its crime sounds as wicked as any: "he pursued his brother with the sword and destroyed his compassion; his anger tore unendingly, his fury kept watch unceasingly" (Amos 1:11-12). On the other hand, a single act on the part of the king of Moab affecting the (dead) king of Edom is to result in the death of Moab's people as well as those of its ruler and the rest of its leadership and the destruction of a key city (Amos 2:1-3). Some Arameans will lose their lives, others will go into exile, without there being a basis in their levels of responsibility (Amos 1:3-5). Gaza exiles an entire community to Edom, but their fellow Philistines in Ashdod, Ashkelon and Ekron will also pay a terrible price (Amos 1:6-8). Wrongdoing thus meets its reward, but there is no tidy correspondence between act and punishment. Partly that reflects the fact that like other prophets Amos makes no distinction in responsibility or destiny between leaders, armies and ordinary people, and that is realistic about the way life is. Ordinary people benefit from the wise and good acts of their leaders and they suffer from their stupid and wicked acts, as children benefit from their parents' wise and good acts and suffer from their stupid and wicked ones.

A Day Well Announced

A locust plague provides Israel with a picture and an anticipation of Yhwh's day. Israel apparently responds in the proper way to Yhwh's wake-up call and Yhwh promises to restore the people, but this does not mean that Yhwh's day is cancelled. After restoring the land from the effects of the locust plague, Yhwh says, "I will pour out my spirit on all flesh" (Joel 2:28-32 [MT 3:1-5]). Pouring out spirit is a worrying image reworked. In literal usage the object of "pouring" is most commonly blood, and in metaphorical usage usually anger (e.g., Lam 2:4; 4:11), so that "pouring out one's spirit" would immediately suggest expressing anger. Is Yhwh acting in judgment on all flesh? But the result will be that "your sons and your daughters will prophesy, your old men will

---

[94]These may well be the names of two real places, in the Assyrian Empire by way of illustration, but they are chosen surely for the implications that can be read into their names. The causers of Trouble will receive their reward; Delight will become disaster.

dream dreams and your young men will see visions, even on servants and servant girls in those days I will pour out my spirit." Elsewhere the pouring out of Yhwh's spirit is a beneficent pouring (Ezek 39:29), and it becomes clear that this is so here.

Christian interpretation consciously or subconsciously takes the promise in light of the significance that the pouring out of the Spirit came to have for Christians, but the context does not suggest that its object is a "spiritual" transformation of the people in their relationship with Yhwh, as if prophecy, dream and vision stood for a closeness of relationship with Yhwh. Joel no doubt believes in such reality of relationship, but we would need clearer indication if this was the way to speak of it. In the context, "all flesh" refers to "all sorts of people in Israel"; it is not concerned with people outside Israel. But *flesh* often suggests humanity in its feebleness over against God, whereas *spirit* suggests the divine dynamism that contrasts with human frailty (Is 31:3). Joel does not say that there were no prophets in his day; we know specifically from Ezra-Nehemiah and from Haggai, Zechariah and Malachi that there were prophets in the late sixth century and in the mid-fifth, and we have no actual evidence that there were none in subsequent times. Joel affirms that it will be women as well as men, young as well as old, servants as well as householders, who will show that Yhwh's spirit has been poured over them like water or anointing oil. There is a kind of "democratization" of the gift of the spirit.[95] Why will this be? The context suggests that Israel's men and women, old and young, householders and servants, will all be receiving prophecies, dreams and visions that relate to the portents of cosmic disaster. "I will put portents in the heavens and on the earth, blood, fire, and columns of smoke; the sun will turn into darkness, the moon into blood, before Yhwh's day comes, great and terrible." Moses once expressed the wish that everyone in Israel could prophesy through Yhwh's spirit being on them (Num 11:29), and these different groups will be prophesying as Moses did when he announced portents in the heavens and on the earth, blood and fire and darkness.

The prophecies, dreams and visions will parallel the portents in the heavens and on the earth of which Joel speaks. He has declared that Yhwh's day is coming (Joel 2:1), and he now repeats that (Joel 2:31). He has spoken of its being near, and will soon repeat that (Joel 1:15; 3:14 [MT 4:14]). His own prophecies and visions and the disastrous locust plague announced the coming of that day on Israel; the coming of that day on the world as a whole will be announced by much more widespread prophecy, dream and vision, and more disastrous cosmic upheaval that suspends the working of nature more radically

---

[95]John Barton, *Joel and Obadiah* (Louisville: Westminster John Knox, 2001), p. 33.

than the locusts did. The restoration of Israel does not mean Yhwh's day is cancelled. And any delay in the fulfillment of declarations concerning it (including those in this book) does not imperil the idea that the day will come. It will happen, "as Yhwh said."[96]

But there is a way of escaping this disaster, because "everyone who calls on Yhwh's name will find safety, because on Mount Zion, in Jerusalem, there will be escapees, as Yhwh said, and among the survivors ones whom Yhwh calls" (Joel 2:32). Here there is no talk of Yhwh relenting about the coming of this day if people turn (though the fact that Yhwh does not speak of relenting does not exclude the possibility of Yhwh doing so). Instead there is talk of escape from it when it does happen. If people call on Yhwh for mercy, they can find safety (mālaṭ), like Lot fleeing the destruction of Sodom or David fleeing the attacks of Saul.

There will thus be a group that escapes (pĕlîṭâ). The term usually describes people within Israel who escape a disaster (e.g., Is 4:2), but here Joel sets these escapees over against the world. Earlier, there was to be no pĕlîṭâ from Yhwh's army (Joel 2:3); here, there will be such a group. There will be "survivors" (śārîd), a term characteristically used in the negative ("there were no survivors," e.g., Josh 11:8), so that the promise confronts a negative and turns it into a positive. "Calling on Yhwh" was not Joel's precise earlier formulation, but it is another way of speaking about crying out to Yhwh for help, in the way that people can "on Mount Zion, in Jerusalem." Perhaps anyone may do so, whether they belong to Israel or the nations, for it is open to the latter to be drawn to Zion, to Jerusalem (e.g., Is 2:2-4). Such calling recognizes that there is no one else to turn to, and Yhwh will respond to it. Or is this calling on Yhwh a response to Yhwh's own call? The second half of the passage is bracketed by reference to these two calls without clarification of the relationship between them. People's calling on Yhwh makes them people Yhwh calls; Yhwh's call invites them to be people who call on Yhwh.

A Day That Keeps Coming and That Never Comes

Psalm 48:12-13 [MT 13-14] invites people to go around Zion, count its towers and consider its rampart. The city is all there, intact, despite the attacks the psalm earlier refers to. Psalm 46:8-10 [MT 9-11] issues a similar invitation to "come and see Yhwh's deeds, how he has wrought great desolation[97] in the earth, terminating wars to the end of the earth." There were times when cities in Israel were overrun by the superpower, but there were occasions when they were marvelously delivered, and it is such occasions that the psalm invites

---

[96]Cf. ibid., p. 31.
[97]Intensive pl. (see GKC 124c).

people to consider. The nations had raged in vain. Their wars got them no-where. Yhwh has destroyed their weapons. "He breaks the bow and snaps the spear, burns shields[98] in fire." Peace will thus have arrived. Admittedly the psalm does not seem to be working with a longing for peace rather than war; its interest is in victory rather than defeat. War will come to an end because Yhwh has won and put the enemies down. Yhwh has destroyed the nations' offensive and defensive weapons; they cannot fight without these. *Now* they must "stop, and acknowledge that I am God; I will be high among the nations, I will be high in the earth" (Ps 46:10). *Now* they must acknowledge that the one who has defeated them is indeed God. It is sometimes said that violence can-not put an end to violence. This is not the psalm's view. And this brings good news; peoples to the end of the world can know that the superpower will not be able to invade them again. But that is a byproduct of Yhwh's victory, not the end in itself.

The two psalms speak as if the great desolation has happened and the ter-mination of war been effected. Evidently it has, but of course evidently it has not. The world is building up to one final day for Yhwh, but Yhwh's day keeps coming for different peoples as decades and centuries pass. It came for the United States in the Civil War and twice for many European nations and some Asian nations and others in the two great twentieth-century wars (it is typical that the so-called victors suffer almost as much as the vanquished). The horror of such events gives us a little idea of what the final Day will be like, as the prophets describe it. It will be an even more frightful expression of divine an-ger at the sin of human tyranny. It will bring desolation and massacre. It will involve something close to God's taking up again the bow laid down after the flood, a suspension of the order of creation whereby sun, moon and planets shine on the world, and whereby the heavens and the earth are firmly founded. Power structures are abolished and ordinary people, implicated in the general faithlessness, lose their lives. Security is replaced by flight and peo-ple who think they have found refuge discover they are wrong. Family life is not exempt from the devastation, as if it simply affected the men who go to war. As happened with those nineteenth- and twentieth-century wars, it af-fects children, homes and wives.

We have noted that Isaiah 34 overtly addresses the world of nations. Co-vertly it presumably addresses Judah, like the rest of the book. Like other ora-cles against other nations, the announcement of trouble for Edom is meant to encourage Judah. Whereas Yhwh had used the superpowers as agents in

---

[98] *ʿăgālôt* usually means carts (cf. Jerome), but never as war transport (for which one would expect *rekeb* or *merkābâ*). The LXX, Tg. more plausibly translate "shields"—in Aramaic, *ʿăgilāʾ*; perhaps one should repoint *ʿăgilôt* (cf. *HALOT*).

bringing trouble on Judah, the prophets make no such comment on the role of
Edom, which simply stood by laughing and made Judah's misfortune its own
profit. There is a case for Yhwh carrying that wrongdoing of Edom, as Yhwh
often carries Israel's wrongdoing. But there is also a case for Yhwh punishing
that wrong rather than give the impression, for example, that wrongdoing
does not matter. Edom becomes a working model of what happens to a people
that pursues its family with the sword and suppresses all compassion (Amos
1:11). Amos's comments about Edom indicate that Israel cannot afford simply
to rejoice in that; the working model is a warning for Israel too. The declaration
in Isaiah 34 indicates that Israel is invited to rejoice that wrong does get punished. Indeed, it introduces the positive promise that follows (Is 35). By implication, the kind of punishment that has fallen on Judah is to fall on a country
such as Edom, and that is part of that restoration of equilibrium envisaged by
Isaiah 34—35.

As Judah was never restored in the way Isaiah 35 described, so Edom was
never devastated as Isaiah 34 describes. The declaration stands as a promise of
the restoring of the moral order of the world by putting down evil as well as
exalting those to whom Yhwh has made a commitment. The New Testament
takes up and affirms the grimness of its picture (e.g., Rev 16—18). It is enough
to scare people into turning to Yhwh, so that it is never fulfilled.

8.6 Hope for the Nations

The nations are summoned to acknowledge Yhwh and rejoice in Yhwh.[99] Is
that opportunity subsequently lost by their wrongdoing? Is there any hope for
the nations? We have noted hints of hope for individual peoples such as Moab.
More generally, the First Testament reckons that Yhwh's deeds in restoring
Jerusalem and delivering Israel by putting Babylon down happen before the
eyes of all the nations, so that all earth's reaches can see this act of deliverance
(Is 52:9-10). It is of significance for the whole world. Like Israel, the nations are
faced with a choice that will determine their destiny, though the wrong choice
will not preclude restoration after disaster. They are destined to be drawn to
Zion to learn from Yhwh and have peace imposed on them, and to enjoy a
wondrous banquet that celebrates Yhwh's swallowing of death. And they are
destined to come to share in all the fullness of Israel's relationship with Yhwh.

Faced with a Choice

Yhwh can speak as if the nations' fate is sealed, but actually, like Israel's, the
nations' destiny depends on choices they make. "I may speak concerning a na-

---

[99]See section 8.1.

tion or kingdom about uprooting, demolishing, and destroying, but that nation concerning which I spoke may turn from the ill it does, and I may relent concerning the ill that I intended to do to it. And suddenly, I may speak concerning a nation or kingdom about building and planting, but it may do what is ill in my eyes and not listen to my voice, and I may relent concerning the good that I said I would do to it" (Jer 18:7-10). Jeremiah's particular concern is with the way Yhwh relates to Judah, and it is therefore striking that he states this principle in general terms. The way Yhwh relates to Judah is but an example of the way Yhwh relates to peoples in general. That fits with Jonah's portrayal of the relationship of Yhwh and Nineveh as a particular instance of Yhwh's way of relating to nations, where the dynamics of Nineveh's destiny match those Yhwh announces here.

The declarations about the fall of Babylon in a passage such as Isaiah 47 are formally addressed to Babylon, though we do not know whether the Babylonians ever heard them. The audience in the house is the Judean community there, and subsequent readers such as ourselves. But formally they address Babylon, and they thus parallel other declarations of Yhwh's intention to bring calamity, which are designed in part to drive the hearers to turn from their present stance and cause Yhwh to abort the plan for calamity. If the Babylonians discovered what Yhwh was saying and did turn, like Rahab, then Yhwh would surely have no alternative but to abort the plan as it applies to them, even if this was not Yhwh's plan in sending this encouraging message about Babylon for the Judeans to hear. Likewise if subsequent superpowers read Isaiah 47 and turn to Yhwh, presumably Yhwh will be glad to be trapped into canceling plans to bring calamity to them. If it seems implausible that Yhwh should be so flexible, then the story of Jonah reinforces the point. Jonah gives the Assyrians no hint that they can escape the disaster he announces, but they repent, and Yhwh has a change of mind. Jonah is not in the least surprised; that was why he had caught a plane going the other way. Who wants to be the means of God letting a superpower off the hook?

From creation Yhwh was the God of the nations in a positive sense, and from the time of Abraham Yhwh has envisaged a day when his seed would be a blessing to the nations as Yhwh so blesses Israel that nations seek the same blessing. Even by giving in to the temptations of a superpower, Assyria has evidently not removed itself from this prospect. The umbrella term for Israel's restoration, "turning the turning" (šûb šĕbût), is also the umbrella term for Yhwh's restoration of Moab, Ammon and Elam (Jer 48:47; 49:6; 49:39), and for Sodom and Samaria (Ezek 16:53). After Nebuchadnezzar's invasion, Egypt "will settle down as in former days" (Jer 46:26).

Given that promise, how can Yhwh immediately repeat words about bringing an end to all nations other than Israel? Perhaps the point lies in the comparison, and we should understand Yhwh to mean "I could make an end of all the nations among which I have banished you, but I would not make an end of you" (Jer 46:28; cf. Jer 30:11). The words are a sign of Yhwh's positive commitment to Israel, not a sign of Yhwh's actual negative intentions to other nations. There is thus some complexity about Yhwh's attitude to Israel's (and Yhwh's) neighbors, a complexity that goes back to Yhwh's commission of Jeremiah: "See, I am appointing you today over the nations and over the kingdoms to uproot, pull down, destroy, and overthrow, to build and plant" (Jer 1:10).

Promised Restoration

Yhwh later nuances the two sides to the role in relation to the nations that was part of Jeremiah's original commission (Jer 12:14-17). The promise not to make an end of Israel also applies to other peoples. "About all my bad neighbors who are touching the possession that I bestowed on my people Israel: Now— I am uprooting them from their soil and uprooting the household of Judah from their midst. But after I have uprooted them, I will again have compassion on them and restore each one of them to their possession, their country. If they really learn the ways of my people by swearing in my name, 'As Yhwh lives,' as they taught my people to swear by the Master [Baal], then they will be built up in the midst of my people. But if they do not listen, I will uproot that nation, uproot and destroy."

I take the neighbors (šěkēnîm) to be not far-off peoples such as Babylon but people such as Edom, Moab and Ammon, who would seem just as much of a threat after the exile as they were in Jeremiah's day. These words thus spoke to the subsequent community very directly. First, Yhwh refers to "their possession [nahālâ], their country," which recalls the declaration that Yhwh allocated the lands of the nations as their possession (nāḥal, yěruššâ, Deut 2:5, 9; 19; 32:8). Yhwh is the lord of their destiny, who provided for them and protected them from dispossession by Israel, though implicitly also set bounds for them. But second, they are thus "my bad neighbors" because they do not respect those bounds. They are people who are encroaching on Israel's land, the land Yhwh allocated to "my people" Israel. Third, Yhwh therefore intends to uproot them from their land as Yhwh is uprooting Israel from its land in taking it off into exile—though Yhwh also intends again to uproot (in a positive sense) Israelites from their land. If one is not to think so much or simply of people who will go to Babylon, these will be people who are driven to take refuge in nearby countries as a result of Babylonian invasion. But fourth, Yhwh then intends to have compassion on these peoples, too, and also to restore them to "their possession, their country." And fifth, Yhwh is not content to give them their land but leave them to the deities originally allocated to them. They can come to follow Israel's ways, instead of causing Israel to follow theirs. They can acknowledge Yhwh. They can be built up, and that "in the midst of my people." Earlier Yhwh has presupposed that these different peoples, Israel and its neighbors, should all live in their own "possessions," but this further promise compromises that and envisages neighbors who have committed themselves to Yhwh living in Israel. Ruth did that, and it offers a different vision from the separatist one in Ezra-Nehemiah. On the other hand, sixth, they do have to decide to follow Yhwh; Ezra and Nehemiah perhaps presuppose that the neighbors whom Judeans married declined to do that. If they do not do so or go back on their commitment to Yhwh, Yhwh will uproot them again, as would happen to Israel itself.

The description of Yhwh's servant implies this point (Is 42:1-4). "He will issue a decision to the nations. He will not cry out, he will not raise his voice, he will not make it heard in public. A broken cane he will not snap, a flickering wick he will not snuff; for the sake of faithfulness he will issue a decision." The key word is "decision" (*mišpaṭ*), a word that suggests the exercise of Yhwh's authority. Jacob-Israel is complaining that Yhwh has stopped exercising this authority on its behalf (Is 40:27). Yhwh is thus stung into doing so again. That is what is happening with the rise of Cyrus. So are the nations simply being informed of something that is of no direct use to them? The answer to such a question might be unclear to the last line of this section, which indicates that the servant's issuing or setting Yhwh's decision links with the foreign shores' waiting for Yhwh's teaching. "He will not flicker and he will not break until he sets a decision in the earth as foreign shores wait for his teaching." The declaration about Yhwh's servant picks up from the promise in Isaiah 2, which refers to the *nations* coming to Jerusalem, the place from which Yhwh's *teaching* will *issue*, and to Yhwh's *deciding* for them. In the broader context, then, Yhwh's decision making suggests reference to the nations' affairs. In the narrower context it suggests reference to Israel's destiny, but even that is something that responds to the foreign shores' waiting, even if that waiting is only half-conscious as the need for it becomes visible in the evident inadequacy of their gods.

Drawn to Zion

While Jacob-Israel is a broken cane and flickering wick whose strength and life are almost gone, so are the nations, and it is not much of a stretch to infer that they may benefit from the ministry of a servant such as this one. The subsequent prophecy (Is 42:5-7) presupposes this. Yhwh speaks as the creator of the whole earth and as the one who gives life to the people on it and then declares that the person addressed (in the context, Yhwh's servant) is summoned to be "a covenant for people." One would infer that this is again the people of the world, and that is confirmed by the parallel description of this person, "a light to nations." That will come about "by opening blind eyes, by bringing out captives from dungeon, people who live in darkness from prison." The captives whose eyes are blinded by the darkness are also the people of the world, created and given their life by Yhwh, turned into captives (by their empty gods?), but the object of Yhwh's enlightenment (cf. Is 49:6). Here the implications are the same as those of Isaiah 42:1-4, or perhaps its reverse. Jacob-Israel is of course also captive and blinded by the darkness. As the nations can benefit from a ministry intended for Jacob-Israel, so Jacob-Israel can benefit from a ministry intended for the nations (cf. Is 42:22). But the nations are the people in focus, and are thus invited into praise that responds to Yhwh's act (Is 42:10-12).

Isaiah 60 develops the idea that the calling of nations will be something Yhwh achieves through Zion. "The darkness will cover the earth, thundercloud cover the peoples, but over you Yhwh will shine; his glory will appear over you." The result will be that nations will come to your light, kings to your shining brightness" (Is 60:2). In keeping with Yhwh's original commitment to Abraham, Zion does not have responsibility for going out to win the world for Yhwh. Yhwh will so shine over Zion that the world in its darkness will naturally be drawn there. They will bring the exiles, Ms. Zion's children, with them. They will bring their resources, camels laden with gold and silver, not for the benefit of the city merely as city but because they will serve the worship of Yhwh in Yhwh's house there, where their flocks will make their way to Yhwh's altar. The telling of Yhwh's praise on Zion and the offering of sacrifices (word and sacrament) go together. Thus through the nations Yhwh will "add to the beauty of my beautiful house" (Is 60:7).

What good will this do for the nations? What kind of welcome will they find with Yhwh? "Yhwh is baring his holy arm before the eyes of all the nations; all earth's extremities are looking at our God's deliverance" (Is 52:10). The context in Isaiah 40—55 suggests they witness something that will benefit them. Indeed, they can be sure of finding a welcome, because they are responding to Yhwh's invitation in Isaiah 45:20-25, "gather and come, draw near all at once, fugitives of the nations." Egypt and its allies will have provided other nations with a model response to Yhwh (Is 45:14-17), and Yhwh now invites them to follow that example. The peoples of Israel's world have been overrun by Assyria, then by Babylon, then by Persia, but peoples who have run for their lives from these overlords are invited now to face the facts about their gods. "They have not recognized, the people carrying their wooden images and making their plea to a god who will not deliver." They are once again challenged to provide examples of their gods' capacity to say what they were going to do and then do it. Actually, Yhwh is the only one who can do that, and has proved it. "Faithful God, who delivers, there is none besides me." Directly it is Israel to whom Yhwh has been faithful (and the audience in the house for this prophecy is Israel, as usual). But Yhwh's invitation goes out beyond Israel. "Turn to me and be delivered, all earth's extremities. . . . To me every knee will bend, every tongue swear. Only in Yhwh—it is said of me—are faithfulness and strength" (Is 45:22-24). Yhwh is set on the world acknowledging the truth: Yhwh is the only God. They are going to bow down to Yhwh. "To him will come to be shamed all who rage at him; in Yhwh all the offspring of Israel will be in the right and thus will glory." Unless those who come to be shamed are a different group, these people are going to be ashamed of their past raging at Yhwh. But as they come to acknowledge those facts, the same coming means finding that the God who delivers Israel can also be their deliverer. Perhaps they are even included in that closing expression "all the offspring of Israel" (Is 45:24-25).

Of course the nations are also people who, for example, boast in themselves, despise Yhwh's name and oppress Yhwh's people (Is 52:4-5). Like Jacob-Israel, they need cleansing as well as confounding. The ministry of Yhwh's servant will effect that. "He will spatter many nations; kings will shut their mouths" because of the unprecedented nature of what they see in him (Is 52:15).[100] Once more the prophet combines an affirmation that the nations will benefit from Yhwh's act of deliverance that is initially of direct benefit to Jacob-Israel with a declaration that the nations need to be confuted and reduced to silence.

Coming to Learn from Yhwh

We have noted that the promise in Isaiah 42:1-4 takes up that in Isaiah 2:2-4 and Micah 4:1-4. At the moment Jerusalem is an insignificant little city in an insignificant little nation, with city and temple sitting on a protected but unimpressive mountain spur, overlooked by other peaks around. The nations come up to Jerusalem from time to time, but mainly to cause trouble. As far as they are concerned, Yhwh's house is simply the place where the Judeans worship their god, as other peoples have a temple for their god. The nations themselves are generally at strife with one another. The reality of history is wars and rumors of wars. "We cannot fail to see or realise that humanity appears strangely lost in its history."[101] History goes nowhere. In fact it is not history, or at least not story; it has no plot. Further, the background to this vision is a warning that things will get worse—and they did. Zion is to become a field that is plowed, Jerusalem a total ruin, the temple mount nothing more than a great wooded high place (Mic 3:12). The vision offers no other expectations for

---

[100]See section 8.2 "Eventually Triumphant."

[101]Karl Barth, *Church Dogmatics* (Edinburgh: T & T Clark, 1936-1969), IV/3.ii:694.

the present, but it has a conviction about a better future. In the aftermath of the present time things will be different. In the present Yhwh is involved in moving the nations around the chessboard, using them to bring calamity on Judah and on each other as they deserve it. But eventually Yhwh will do something different.

"It will come about, in the aftermath of the days: the mountain of Yhwh's house will come to be standing firm as the peak of the mountains, it will stand high above the hills." Zion will be exalted in the eyes of the nations and they will be drawn to it. Instead of being a place that Yhwh has abandoned and that they scorn, it will be one that is indeed the mountain where Yhwh's house stands, where Yhwh lives. "Peoples will stream to it, many nations will go and say, 'Come, let's go up to Yhwh's mountain, to the house of Jacob's God.'" They will come to the temple not, for instance, to bring their offerings, but "so that he can teach us about his ways and we can walk in his paths" (see, e.g., Is 42:24) rather than continuing to follow our own evil inclinations (Jer 3:17). Because teaching *(tôrâ)*, or Yhwh's word, will issue from Jerusalem to the nations, and Yhwh will decide disputes between them. The nations will give up war-making. No one will be under threat from anyone else. Whereas people are used to recycling their farm implements into weapons when an invasion threatens, like Western factories turning themselves into places to make tanks and bombers in the Second World War, now the recycling will happen in the opposite direction. And whereas people are used to fleeing from their fields and farms to the fortification of the city when an invading army approaches (knowing that they will return to find their crops plundered and their fruit trees willfully destroyed), now people will be free to sit and relax under their vines and fig trees (Mic 4:4). No wonder "foreign shores will wait for me; they will hope for my arm" (Is 51:4-5).

Presumably Yhwh is involved in the fulfillment of this vision and the elements I have identified in it are interwoven, yet the vision itself leaves much of that open. Only toward the end does Yhwh act, in making the decisions that enable the nations not to have to fight each other. Initially the passage offers a vision of a miracle and does not explain how its miracle will be wrought. Nor does it describe what it will actually look like; in the prophet's vision, no doubt the geophysical transformation here described actually happened, but the nature of a vision is not to make clear what the literal reality will be. Further, the vision does declare that people will come to Jerusalem because Yhwh's teaching will go out from there, but the "because" is allusive, and beyond that, oddly the vision does not clarify the interrelationship of any of these events.

The result is to focus the mind on the facts rather than the means or the logic. Anyone who believes that Yhwh is the only God and that Yhwh is present on Mount Zion could be depressed by its understandable insignificance in the nations' eyes. Anyone who believed that the nations are destined to acknowledge Yhwh could be depressed by the distance between that and reality. Anyone depressed by the conflicts between the nations could be depressed by the persistence of war in human history.

Clearly something new needs to come about on Yhwh's mountain before this vision can be fulfilled, as Isaiah implies with his subsequent exhortation to his people to come and walk by Yhwh's light (Is 2:5). There is some walking in Yhwh's paths that needs to begin there.

Seeing to this will be the task of the branch that will grow from Jesse's stock. "Yhwh's spirit will rest on him," and after his work "people will not do what is wrong or corrupt in all my sacred mountain, because the land will be full of the acknowledgment of Yhwh like the water covering the sea." Then "Jesse's stock that will be standing as a signal for peoples—nations will have recourse to him and his resting will mean glory" (Is 11:2, 9-10).[102] Instead of nations rebelling against his authority, in light of what they have seen they will willingly yield to it and seek his decision making, which will be the means of implementing Yhwh's decision making.

Life Victorious over Death

There are other good things for the nations on this mountain. There is a banquet to enjoy (Is 25:6-8). We should perhaps infer that this banquet celebrates the victory over the powers of heaven and earth described not long before, and thus celebrates Yhwh's assertion of kingly authority in heaven and on earth (Is 24:21-23). It celebrates the putting down of strong people and brutal nations (Is 25:3). The former passage ends up with the elders seeing Yhwh's splendor, as it had appeared after they ate and drank on Mount Sinai (Ex 24:9-11, 16-17). On this occasion "on this mountain," Yhwh will go more than one stage beyond that. There "Yhwh Armies will make for all the peoples on this mountain a banquet of rich meats, a banquet of vintage wines, marinated meats, refined wines." If submitting to Yhwh means peace among the nations, this will not be a solemn-faced affair. The peace dividend will not just be the economic one Isaiah 2 describes.

It is not merely an occasion for the peoples to enjoy a banquet. Such festivity can involve a form of denial, and victory celebrations especially do so. One people's victory celebration is another's occasion of loss, grief and mourning. Here that fact is taken up. "He will swallow up on this mountain the expanse of the covering that lies upon all the peoples, the spread that is draped upon

---

[102]I take the "resting" to refer to Yhwh's spirit's resting on him (v. 2); cf. Blenkinsopp, *Isaiah 1—39*, pp. 266-67.

all the nations; he is swallowing up death forever" (Is 25:7-8). War is one of the means by which death has the opportunity to reach out from Sheol into the world of the living and swallow people up before their time. In Ugaritic myth, Death is itself the great swallower, capable of swallowing a god. Here Yhwh puts that process into reverse: "he will have finally swallowed Death."[103] In the regular course of events, each year death could seem to have the victory over life, as nature "died" during the summer drought. As well as the searing desert wind withering all life, sometimes the autumn rain that was supposed to re-store life would fail to arrive. Events such as epidemics and wars would give Death further opportunity to swallow people before their time. From time to time Yhwh would put an end to such deathly events, but they would recur. There was no final swallowing of death.

Now there will be. Peace means Yhwh becomes the one who takes over death's role and swallows up death itself instead of letting death loose among the nations (cf. Is 24).[104] If Yhwh has won the final victory over the powers that make war and they are securely locked in prison (Is 24:22), there will be no more men going to battle and no more body bags, no more grieving over their death. "He will destroy on this mountain the covering that covers over all the peoples." Thus "the Lord Yhwh will wipe away tears from upon all faces." Yhwh's swal-lowing of death will mean an end to the death-dealing reality of war. Yhwh's putting down the power of nations is also a means of delivering the nations. Thus "Sovereign Yhwh will wipe the tears from upon all faces." This finally takes away the weeping that overwhelms the faces of the nations[105] and replaces grief with that richest banquet anyone has ever attended. Once again, the fact that Yhwh is the one who does this and does it on this mountain removes Israel from being an insignificant and despised people. Yhwh "will take away the re-proach of his people from upon all the earth." But this is not a meal that involves merely all Israel (nor simply the elders, as at Sinai) but "all the peoples."

All this will come about because "the hand of Yhwh will settle on this mountain" (Is 25:10). The words are reminiscent of the striking formulation about Yhwh's spirit "settling" on a king (Is 11:2).[106] The formulation is again

---

[103]On the way these myths provide resonances here, see Jon D. Levenson, *Creation and the Per-sistence of Evil* (reissued Princeton, N.J./Chichester, U.K.: Princeton University Press, 1994), p. 30.

[104]1 Cor 15:54; Rev 7:17; 21:4 reuse Is 25:8 to express a more general promise of a final swal-lowing of death and wiping away of tears, but in context it offers this more specific won-drous vision.

[105]The EVV use words such as *shroud* in Is 25:7, but the words for "covering" and "spread" are ordinary words without that specific meaning. I take them as metaphors that are explained in the next verse, where the word *upon* recurs.

[106]See section 5.7 "One on Whom Yhwh's Spirit Settles."

surprising. Yhwh's hand suggests Yhwh's mighty power. By its nature it does not "settle." It waves about. Does it suggest a particularly powerful, ongoing demonstration of dynamic power, as the subsequent reference to putting down Moab would suggest (Is 25:10b-12)? Or does it suggest that by "settling" on this mountain the dynamic power of Yhwh makes this mountain a place where conflict and oppression cannot arise again? It then again suggests an end to the apparently relentless sequence of war and peace, oppression and deliverance, in the history of Israel and the history of the nations. The sequence of waiting and deliverance has taken place for the last time.

Terms of Endearment

So the nations come to share in Israel's privileges. The prophets speak of the people of Yhwh and of the city of Jerusalem as Yhwh's daughter (e.g., Jer 4:11, 31).[107] It is a term of endearment, even when there is no "my," and pathos attaches to it when it appears in the context of calamity. It is grievous that "little girl Zion" is undergoing such affliction (e.g., Is 1:8). The prophets speak the same way about other nations, though Yhwh does not quite say of them that they are "my daughter." But the tone of endearment and pathos holds when the prophets apply the word *daughter* to other peoples under Yhwh's punishment: Tyre and Sidon (Is 23:10, 12), Babylon (Is 47:1; Jer 50:42), Egypt (Jer 46:11, 19, 24), Moab (Jer 48:18), Ammon (Jer 49:4), and even Edom (Lam 4:21-22).

The terms of endearment are more far-reaching in the five prophecies of how things will be for Egypt "on that day" in Isaiah 19:18-25. The move through them is dramatic. At first there is talk only of Yhwh and Judah as objects of fear, a nice reversal for Judah, but not much consolation for Egypt. Then there is talk of "five cities in the land of Egypt speaking the language of Canaan and swearing allegiance to Yhwh Armies; one will be called 'Destruction City' [MT] or 'Sun City' [1QIsa, Tg. Sym. Vg.]." Are these simply Judean cities? After that there is talk of "a Yhwh altar in the midst of the land of Egypt and a Yhwh column near its border," a public witness to Yhwh in the land. So "when people cry out to Yhwh because of oppressors, he will send them a deliverer and defender, and he will rescue them." Does this imply that the Egyptians are the oppressors against whom Israelites are again crying out? "Yhwh will make himself known to the Egyptians and the Egyptians will acknowledge Yhwh on that day." Is this merely the unwilling recognition that Pharaoh sometimes gave in Moses' day?

As this third prophecy continues to unfold, it becomes impossible to continue understanding it this way. "They will serve with sacrifice and offering,

---

[107]See section 3.7 "Yhwh's Abandoned Daughter."

and make vows to Yhwh and fulfill them." The exodus story had talked much of the service of Yhwh, but never of the Egyptians offering this service; it was the reason why the Israelites needed to leave Egypt, because that was a place where people could only serve Pharaoh. Now all that will change. The Egyptians themselves will serve Yhwh! They will make vows to Yhwh and fulfill them—that is, they will come to Yhwh with their prayers and promises; reference to the fulfilling of their vows presupposes that Yhwh will have answered these prayers. All that makes one reconsider the allusion to the five cities. Surely these are not merely cities full of people from Judah, but cities where the population as a whole has decided to make a commitment to the service of Yhwh. That enables us to give the more natural meaning to the expression "swear allegiance to" (šābaʿ niphal, followed by l). It refers to people who take this on as a new allegiance, replacing the one they had before.

The prophecy goes on to warn that "Yhwh will strike Egypt," but "striking in such a way as to heal." Yhwh's striking is not merely punitive but restorative. It is like Yhwh's striking of Israel, a chastisement or a wake-up call as much as a punishment. It is designed to make the Egyptians turn to Yhwh and pray, as was the case with Yhwh's chastisement of Israel. And "they will turn to Yhwh and he will let himself be entreated by them and heal them." Yhwh will then accept the Egyptians' prayers (ʿātar niphal) and restore them (Is 19:22). This then provokes a rereading of the first prophecy. There is an ambiguity about the Hebrew words for trembling and fear, which can denote an appropriate and constructive awed reverence as well as a debilitating alarm. Yes, Egypt needs to acknowledge the futility of its planning before the mightier planning of Yhwh Armies, but such recognition can become a creative awe and not be merely a crushing angst. Even the hand shaken in threat is designed to lead Egypt on, not simply to devastate it.

The fourth prophecy offers a further vision. Middle Eastern politics saw frequent conflicts between Egypt and the Mesopotamian powers. This conflict might seem built into Middle Eastern geopolitics. Isaiah declares this is not so. "On that day there will be a highway from Egypt to Assyria. Assyrians will come to Egypt and Egyptians to Assyria. The Egyptians will serve with the Assyrians" (Is 19:23). The Berlin Wall will come down. It will be possible to travel between these two great powers. But this will be so because both will be involved in that service to which the middle prophecy referred. There is no suggestion that this is merely a highway along which Judean exiles may return from Mesopotamia and Egypt to Palestine. It is a highway to facilitate worship.

Sharing Israel's Status

What is the place of Israel in all this? Physically, Israel stands between these two powers, often tempted to choose between them as allies or caught in the conflicts between them. Yhwh will turn the downside to this piece of geography into a positive. "On that day Israel will be third with Egypt and Assyria, a blessing in the midst of the earth that[108] Yhwh Armies will have blessed, saying 'Blessed be my people Egypt, and the work of my hands Assyria, and my possession Israel'" (Is 19:24). Assyria, Israel and Egypt are three allies or friends or partners, but Israel's location between the two powers sets it in the center of the world, in a position to be a blessing to both sides. There can be argument about how much to read into Yhwh's ancient promise that Abraham would be a blessing (Gen 12:2). It is clear here that Yhwh has in mind not merely that Israel will be a standard of blessing to which the world will aspire but a standard of blessing that Yhwh will apply to these other nations. They will be treated in the same way as Israel is treated, and that because they have analogous status to Israel. Israel is "my people," "the work of my hands," "my possession." Here, those terms are applied equally to Egypt and Assyria. The prophecy's radicalism is highlighted by LXX's version, which has "blessed be my people in Egypt and in Assyria and my inheritance Israel." It thus blesses the dispersion community in these two countries.[109] In MT the prophecy declares the blessing on the whole community and sees them as sharing in Israel's status as Yhwh's people, going far beyond the promise to Abraham in applying to Egypt and Assyria the terms that strictly apply only to Israel: "my people," "my handiwork" (for the latter, see Is 64:8 [MT 7]). The description of Israel as "my possession" just stands aside those.

Zechariah 8:20-23 pictures this more individually: "Peoples and inhabitants of many cities will yet come—the inhabitants of one will go to another saying, 'Let's go and entreat Yhwh and seek help from Yhwh Armies. Yes, I'm going.'" In picturing the nations coming to Jerusalem, Zechariah reaffirms and rewords the promise in Isaiah 2:2-4, but reexpresses it more concretely and combines it with other ideas. Before we get to nations, the talk is of peoples and cities. This suggests the various ethnic groups that surrounded Judah and the cities that formed the center of each of the Persian provinces in which they lived, such as the Samarians and the city of Samaria, the Philistines and the city of Ashdod, who stand politically and ethnically in parallelism with the Judeans and the city of Jerusalem. Zechariah goes on, "many peoples and numerous nations will come to seek help from Yhwh Armies in Jerusalem and to entreat Yhwh." That widens the horizon beyond the Levant to more far-off nations and imperial powers. The people come in the manner of Israelites, entreating Yhwh[110]

---

[108]I take the suffix on *běrăkô* to refer back to *hā'āreṣ*, notwithstanding the gender mismatch.

[109]Cf. Wildberger, *Isaiah 13—27*, p. 281.

[110]Lit. "entreat Yhwh's face" (?). I take *ḥālâ* ii as a different verb from *ḥālâ* i (cf. *DCH*). It occurs only in the piel with someone's "face" as object.

(that is, seeking help from Yhwh). "Ten people from the nations of every language will take hold, take hold of the coat of an individual Judean, saying 'We want to go with you, because we have heard that God is with you.'" It is the promise to Abraham fulfilled as individuals are drawn to his God.

During the Second Temple period there was no flocking of the nations to Zion, but there developed substantial interest in Jacob-Israel's faith on the part of individuals; it is part of the background to the spread of the good news about Jesus around the Mediterranean. Such Gentile adherents to Jacob-Israel's faith constituted a halfway stage in the spreading of that good news. For individuals thus to respond to Yhwh is not as good as communities doing so (the First Testament's attitude is the opposite of the usual Western one), but it is not nothing.

It does raise questions. Foreigners could be imagined speculating, "Yhwh will definitely keep me separate from his people" (Is 56:3). Such a speculation would fit some strands of the Scriptures and presumably expresses the conviction of some people in the community. But Yhwh's attitude is the opposite (Is 56:6-8). It is to welcome "the foreigners who attach themselves to Yhwh to minister to him and to dedicate themselves to Yhwh's name, to be his servants." Indeed, Yhwh declares, "I will bring them to my sacred mountain and enable them to rejoice in my prayer house." Foreigners can come to Yhwh's sacred mountain all right, and not merely to receive teaching. Yhwh's house is here a place for them to rejoice (in the way the Psalms envisage) and to pray. "Their whole offerings and sacrifices will be welcome on my altar, because my house will call itself a prayer house—for all peoples." Sacrificial offerings are often an accompaniment to rejoicing and prayer, and vice versa, and the mention of the offerings in the midst of the description of the temple as a prayer house suggests this is their significance here.

Ministers and Witnesses

The foreigners' attachment to Yhwh in Isaiah 56 has a more specific significance than the one described in Isaiah 14:1-2. They come to minister (*šārat*), the word used of priests and Levites. They come to give themselves to the proclamation of Yhwh's name, in the leading of worship. They come to be Yhwh's servants (not Jacob-Israel's servants, as in Is 14:1-2). Mention of Yhwh's name and Yhwh's service after reference to ministry suggests that all these indicate not merely foreigners' functioning as lay Israelites but their undertaking ordained ministry. The qualification for this is adherence to Israel's commitment to Yhwh: it applies to "everyone who keeps the sabbath rather than profaning it and holds fast to my covenant"; in this context observing the sabbath, the distinctive marker of Israel, is the way covenant commitment expresses itself. If they accept that form of separation from their own people, they need not be kept separate from Yhwh's people. They will count as members of Yhwh's people, in accordance with passages such as Isaiah 45:25 and Psalm 47:9 [MT 10] as we have understood them. Thus Yhwh, who gathers the scattered of Israel, fulfills the intention to "gather to it more besides the ones gathered," more than just the gathered of Israel.

Subsequently, Isaiah almost closes with some sending of witnesses to the nations (Is 66:18-24). The time has come "to gather all the nations and tongues, and they will come and see my splendor." Yhwh intends then to "put a sign among them and send from them survivors to the nations, Tarshish, Put, and Lud, drawers of the bow, Tubal and Javan, the distant coasts that have not heard report of me or seen my splendor." Apparently the people who are initially gathered are only representatives of the nations and they are then sent to tell all their fellows; or more likely "all nations and tongues" has in mind the known world, the provinces of the empire (cf. Dan 3:4). Tarshish, Put and so on then stand for distant countries lying beyond the empire's bounds, the real "all nations and tongues." The emissaries are survivors or fugitives (*pēlîṭîm*) because the prophecy presupposes a fulfillment of Yhwh's threat that disaster will come to the empire, and we already know that these survivors are due to come to acknowledge Yhwh (Is 45:20). So such survivors of the Middle Eastern political cataclysms of their day are sent to tell more far-away nations what they now know about Yhwh. And "they will declare my splendor among the nations. They will bring all your kindred from all the nations as an offering to Yhwh, on horses, in chariots, in coaches, on mules and on dromedaries to my sacred mountain, Jerusalem (Yhwh has said), as the Israelites bring an offering in a pure vessel to Yhwh's house. I will also take some of them as Levitical priests (Yhwh has said)" (Is 66:19-21).

This vision thus becomes a notch or two more spectacular. The survivors not only worship and not only see a signal that summons them to bring the survivors of Israel back home, but they see a sign that sends them back to these further far-off lands that have not yet heard anything of Yhwh nor seen Yhwh's splendor, where they will give their testimony to what they have seen. Yet further, the result will be foreigners from *all* the nations bringing back to Jerusalem Israelites who have settled all over the world. And when these foreigners bring the Israelites home, they bring them as an offering to Yhwh and themselves join in making the offering. They themselves function as Levitical priests.

And thus (Yhwh adds), "new moon after new moon, sabbath after sabbath, all flesh will come to bow down before me." What a fine ending for the book of Isaiah! But it is not the end. Yhwh has one more word. "And they will go out and look at the corpses of the people who have rebelled against me, for their worm will not die nor their fire go out, but they will be a horror to all flesh" (Is 66:23-24). That is the book's actual ending. Although this picture contributes to the postbiblical idea of Gehenna as a place where the damned suffer for eternity, its own point is more likely that ongoing generations will always need to be wary of the possibility that they might be cast into this ever-available fire. Nevertheless it was too much for the average scholarly reader, who in response to the reaction of the preview audience repeated the line about all flesh coming to bow down to Yhwh for the purposes of reading in worship, so that the reading closes in a positive way. The tough-minded version of the book deprives readers of the Hollywood ending and makes them face the fact that there is no inevitability about the positive ending. It is their choice that determines how it ends in relation to them.

♦ ♦ ♦

All Nations Will Come and Worship

As is the case with the theme of creation, the New Testament has much less focus on the nations than the First Testament does. And once again, this is not a fault, and it is only a problem because the church treats the New Testament as if it were the Bible and thus feels free to focus on itself and not be too concerned with the nations. After surveying material in both the First Testament and the New Testament on the idea of the people of God as the light of the world, on God's concern for the nations, Karl Barth concludes that "the former is richer, more explicit, more patent and more emphatic than the latter in relation to the problem of the universalism of the covenant, the glory of God, and the salvation of man as this is envisaged from the very first." He notes that the New Testament perhaps simply takes it for granted while the former needs to emphasize what is not self-evident, but whatever the reason, the far more vivid universalism of the First Testament needs close attention. Perhaps it was lack of this that encouraged the "fatal stagnation of missionary thinking in older Protestantism."[111]

Further, one should be wary of describing this expectation as "eschatological," since this is inclined to imply an unrealistic idealism. It is only eschatological in the sense that "its statements refer to facts and factors of present, this-worldly reality which are now concealed, and will be revealed as such only in the absolute future of the redeeming and consummating action of God." The universal statements are not eschatological and therefore perhaps idealistic but realistic and therefore eschatological. The scriptural writers

---

[111]Barth, *Church Dogmatics*, IV/3.i:60.

know God is concerned for the whole world, and therefore they have hope for it.[112] The nations are destined to walk by the light that shines in the new Jerusalem (Rev 21:24). "All nations will come and worship" (Rev 15:4). And that is a reality for this world. The temple is designed to be a prayer house for all nations (Mk 11:17).

Yet history is the story of how nation rises against nation (Mk 13:8). Jesus' understanding of the aimlessness of the history of the nations corresponds to that in Daniel (see esp. Dan 11). But the dragon's deception of the nations will not last forever (Rev 20:3, 8). The leaves of the tree of life are for the healing of the nations (Rev 22:2). Yhwh's reigning as king is a reality that belongs to the End, but it is not something that only happens once for all at the End. The return from the exile, the defeat of Antiochus and the coming of Jesus are assertions of God's kingly power, as are the Reformation, the restoration of a substantial Jewish community in Palestine and the development of a substantial body of Jews who believe in Jesus. Another would be the establishment of a political arrangement on Mount Zion and in Jerusalem that enabled Arabs and Jews to share the land that both see as theirs. We may expect to see such expressions of God's reigning as king, and also to look forward to the final establishing of that reign. Creation, the exodus, and the death and resurrection of Christ are the guarantees of it. The powers of evil fell from heaven on those days, and so did the powers on earth.

To that end—the fact that all nations will come to worship and that Yhwh intends to reign over the nations and that the Christ event is a further guarantee of that—the nations need to be apprised of the good news about Jesus so that they can start becoming his disciples (Mk 13:10; Mt 28:19).

---

[112]Ibid., IV/3.ii:489.

CONCLUSION

In this volume I have sought to stand back from the multiplicity of the First Testament's individual statements and ask "What portrait emerges from the whole?" What emerges is an account of a God who is transcendent but involved, sovereign but flexible, faithful but tough. It is an account of a people chosen by God to enjoy a special relationship that will also make it possible for God to reach out to the rest of the world. It is an account of a nightmare future that lies ahead of this people because of its relentless refusal to walk God's way. It is also an account of the glorious renewal of this people in all aspects of its life because God is never finished with it. It is an account of a humanity whose nature is to be in relationship with God and responsible to God, in community a well as individually, as it lives a life that can often be understood but sometimes remains unintelligible as it makes its inexorable way toward death. It is an account of a created world characterized by security and wonder, in which God continues to be at work, not least in restraining its dark side as God continues to be committed to taking it to its destiny. And it is an account of the world of nations, themselves threatened with calamity for their resistance to Yhwh but destined to come to acknowledge Yhwh.

In volumes one and two of this Old Testament Theology I have been directly concerned with what God has done and who God is. In discussing that, I have implied aspects of an understanding of the implications that has for our lives—for matters such as the way we worship, pray, do politics, do family, live our sex lives, exercise leadership, live in community. That will be the focus of volume three, "Israel's Life."

BIBLIOGRAPHY

Achtemeier, Elizabeth R. *Nahum—Malachi.* Louisville, Ky.: Westminster John Knox, 1986.

Ackroyd, Peter R. *Exile and Restoration.* OTL. London: SCM Press, 1968.

Albertz, Rainer. *A History of Israelite Religion in the Old Testament Period.* 2 vols. London: SCM Press/Louisville, Ky.: Westminster John Knox, 1994.

Albrektson, Bertil. *History and the Gods.* ConBOT 1. Lund: Gleerup, 1967.

Alexander, T. Desmond, and Simon Gathercole, eds. *Heaven on Earth.* Carlisle, U.K./Waynesboro, Ga.: Paternoster, 2004.

Allen, Leslie C. *Ezekiel.* 2 vols. WBC. Dallas: Word, 1994, 1990.

———. *Psalms 101—150.* Rev. ed. WBC. Nashville: Thomas Nelson, 2002.

Andersen, Francis I., and David Noel Freedman. *Amos.* AB. New York: Doubleday, 1989.

Anderson, Bernhard W. *Creation and New Creation.* Minneapolis: Fortress, 1994.

Anderson, Bernhard W., ed. *Creation in the Old Testament.* London: SPCK/Philadelphia: Fortress, 1984.

Augustine of Hippo. *Confessions.* In *The Nicene and Post-Nicene Fathers,* series 1, 1:21-207. Edited by Philip Schaff. Reprint, Grand Rapids, Mich.: Eerdmans, 1979.

———. *Expositions on the Book of Psalms.* 6 vols. Oxford: Parker, 1849.

Bailey, Lloyd R. *Biblical Perspectives on Death.* Philadelphia: Fortress, 1979.

Balentine, Samuel. *The Hidden God.* Oxford/New York: Oxford University Press, 1982.

Balthasar, Hans Urs von. *Theology: The Old Covenant.* Vol. 6 of *The Glory of the Lord: A Theological Aesthetics.* Edinburgh: T & T Clark, 1991.

Barr, James. "Some Semantic Notes on the Covenant." In *Beiträge zur Alttestamentlichen Theologie,* pp. 23-38. W. Zimmerli Festschrift. Edited by Herbert Donner et al. Göttingen: Vandenhoeck, 1977.

Barstad, Hans M. *The Religious Polemics of Amos.* VTSup 34. Leiden: Brill, 1984.

Barth, Christoph. *God with Us.* Edited by G. W. Bromiley. Grand Rapids, Mich.: Eerdmans, 1991.

Barth, Karl. *Church Dogmatics.* 13 vols. Edinburgh: T & T Clark, 1936-1969.

Barton, John. *Joel and Obadiah.* Louisville, Ky.: Westminster John Knox, 2001.

Bauckham, Richard. "Biblical Theology and the Problems of Monotheism." In *Out of Egypt,* pp. 184-232. Edited by Craig Bartholomew et al. Grand Rapids, Mich.: Zondervan/Milton Keynes: Paternoster, 2004.

Becking, Bob. *Between Fear and Freedom*. OTS 41. Leiden/Boston: Brill, 2004.

Ben Zvi, Ehud. *Signs of Jonah*. JSOTSup 367. London/New York: Sheffield Academic Press, 2003.

Berkovits, Eliezer. *Faith After the Holocaust*. New York: Ktav, 1973.

Berquist, Jon L. *Controlling Corporeality*. New Brunswick, N.J./London: Rutgers University Press, 2002.

Biddle, Mark E. *Missing the Mark*. Nashville: Abingdon, 2005.

Blenkinsopp, Joseph. *Isaiah 1—39*. AB. New York: Doubleday, 2000.

———. *Isaiah 56—66*. AB. New York: Doubleday, 2003.

———. *A Sketchbook of Biblical Theology*. London: Burns and Oates/New York: Herder, 1968.

Blumenthal, David R. *Facing the Abusing God*. Louisville, Ky.: Westminster John Knox, 1993.

Boda, Mark J., and Michael H. Floyd, eds. *Bringing Out the Treasure: Inner Biblical Allusion in Zechariah 9—14*. JSOTSup 370. London/New York: Sheffield Academic Press, 2003.

Boethius. *The Consolation of Philosophy*. New York: Modern, 1943.

Bonhoeffer, Dietrich. *Letters and Papers from Prison*. Reprint, London: Collins, 1962.

Boorer, Suzanne. "A Matter of Life and Death." In *Prophets and Paradigms*, pp. 187-204. G. M. Tucker Festschrift. Edited by Stephen Breck Reid. JSOTSup 229. Sheffield, U.K.: Sheffield Academic Press, 1996.

Boström, Lennart. *The God of the Sages*. ConBOT 29. Stockholm: Almquist, 1990.

Bovati, Pietro. *Re-Establishing Justice*. JSOTSup 105. Sheffield, U.K.: Sheffield Academic Press, 1994.

Brett, Mark G., ed. *Ethnicity and the Bible*. Biblical Interpretation Series 19. Leiden/New York: Brill, 1996.

Brown, William P. *Ecclesiastes*. Louisville, Ky.: John Knox Press, 2000.

———. *The Ethos of the Cosmos: The Genesis of Moral Imagination in the Bible*. Grand Rapids, Mich./Cambridge: Eerdmans, 1999.

Brown, William P., and John T. Carroll. "The Garden and the Plaza." *Int* 54 (2000): 3-11.

Brown, William P., and S. Dean McBride, eds. *God Who Creates*. W. S. Towner Festschrift. Grand Rapids, Mich.: Eerdmans, 2000.

Brueggemann, Walter. *Old Testament Theology: Essays on Structure, Theme, and Text*. Minneapolis: Fortress, 1992.

———. *The Prophetic Imagination*. Philadelphia: Fortress, 1978/London: SCM Press, 1992.

———. *A Social Reading of the Old Testament*. Minneapolis: Fortress, 1994.

———. *Theology of the Old Testament*. Minneapolis: Fortress, 1997.

———. *To Pluck Up, To Tear Down: A Commentary on the Book of Jeremiah 1—25*.

Grand Rapids, Mich.: Eerdmans/Edinburgh: Handsel, 1988.

———. *To Build, To Plant: A Commentary on Jeremiah 26—52.* Grand Rapids, Mich.: Eerdmans/Edinburgh: Handsel, 1991.

Brunner, Emil. *Man in Revolt.* London: Lutterworth, 1939.

Buber, Martin. *Good and Evil.* New York: Scribner's, 1953.

———. *On the Bible.* Reprint, New York: Schocken, 1968.

———. *The Prophetic Faith.* Reprint, New York: Harper, 1960.

———. *Right and Wrong.* London: SCM Press, 1952.

Calvin, John. *Institutes of the Christian Religion.* 2 vols. Philadelphia: Westminster Press, 1960/London: SCM Press, 1961.

Campbell, Alastair V. *The Gospel of Anger.* London: SPCK, 1986.

Carmichael, Calum. *The Spirit of Biblical Law.* Athens/London: University of Georgia Press, 1996.

Carr, David M. "Passion for God." *HBT* 23 (2001): 1-24.

Cassian, John. *The Institutes.* Mahwah, N.J.: Newman, 2000.

Chesterton, Gilbert K. *Orthodoxy.* New York: Lane, 1909.

Childs. Brevard S. *Biblical Theology of the Old and New Testaments.* Minneapolis: Fortress/London: SCM Press, 1992.

———. *Exodus.* London: SCM Press, 1974 = *The Book of Exodus.* Philadelphia: Westminster Press, 1974.

———. *Introduction to the Old Testament as Scripture.* Philadelphia: Fortress, 1979.

———. *Isaiah.* London: SCM Press/Louisville, Ky.: Westminster John Knox, 2001.

Clements. Ronald E. *God and Temple.* Oxford: Blackwell, 1965.

———. *Old Testament Theology.* London: Marshall, Morgan & Scott, 1978.

Clifford. Richard J. *The Book of Proverbs and Our Search for Wisdom.* Milwaukee, Wis.: Marquette University Press, 1995.

———. *Proverbs.* Louisville, Ky.: Westminster John Knox, 1999.

Clines, David J. A. *Ezra, Nehemiah, Esther.* London: Marshall, Morgan & Scott/Grand Rapids, Mich.: Eerdmans, 1984.

———. *Job 1—20.* WBC. Dallas: Word, 1989.

Coggins, Richard J., and S. Paul Re'emi. *Israel Among the Nations.* Grand Rapids, Mich.: Eerdmans/Edinburgh: Handsel, 1985.

Collins, John J. *Encounters with Biblical Theology.* Minneapolis: Fortress, 2005.

Cooper, Gillian, and John Goldingay. "Hosea and Gomer Visit the Marriage Counsellor." In *First Person: Essays in Biblical Autobiography,* pp. 119-36. Edited by Philip R. Davies. London/New York: Sheffield Academic Press, 2002.

Craigie, Peter C. "The Poetry of Ugarit and Israel." *Tyndale Bulletin* 22 (1971): 3-31.

————. *Psalms 1—50.* WBC. 2nd ed. Nashville: Thomas Nelson, 2004.

Crenshaw, James L. *Ecclesiastes.* London: SCM Press, 1988.

————. *Prophetic Conflict.* BZAW 124. Berlin/New York: Walter de Gruyter, 1971.

————. "Who Knows What Yahweh Will Do?" In *Fortunate the Eyes that See,* pp. 185-96. D. N. Freedman Festschrift. Edited by A. B. Beek et al. Grand Rapids, Mich.: Eerdmans, 1995.

————. "Youth and Old Age in Qoheleth." *Hebrew Annual Review* 10 (1986): 1-13.

Crenshaw, James L., ed. *Studies in Ancient Israelite Wisdom.* New York: Ktav, 1976.

————. *Theodicy in the Old Testament.* Philadelphia: Fortress/London: SPCK, 1983.

Cross, Frank M. *From Epic to Canon.* Baltimore: Johns Hopkins University Press, 1998.

Dahood, M. *Psalms.* AB. 3 vols. Garden City, N.Y.: Doubleday, 1966, 1968, 1970.

Davies, G. I. *Hosea.* London: Marshall Pickering/Grand Rapids, Mich.: Eerdmans, 1992.

Davis, Ellen F. *Proverbs, Ecclesiastes, and the Song of Songs.* Louisville, Ky.: Westminster John Knox, 2000.

Day, John. *God's Conflict with the Dragon and the Sea.* Cambridge/New York: Cambridge University Press, 1985.

Day, John, ed. *Temple and Worship in Biblical Israel.* LHBOTS 422. London/New York: T & T Clark, 2005.

Day, Peggy L. *An Adversary in Heaven.* Atlanta, Ga.: Scholars Press, 1988.

De Troyer, Kristin, et al., eds. *Wholly Woman, Holy Blood.* Harrisburg, Penn.: Trinity Press, 2003.

Dentan, Robert C. Review of *The Land,* by Walter Brueggemann. *JBL* 97 (1978): 577-78.

Deroche, Michael. "The Reversal of Creation in Hosea." *VT* 31 (1981): 401-9.

Dever, William G., and Seymour Gitin, eds. *Symbiosis, Symbolism, and the Power of the Past.* Winona Lake, Ind.: Eisenbrauns, 2003.

Douglas, Mary. *Purity and Danger.* Revised ed. London: Routledge, 1969.

Dozeman, Thomas. "The Holiness of God in Contemporary Jewish and Christian Biblical Theology." In *God's Word for Our World,* 2:24-36. Simon J. De Vries Festschrift. Edited by J. Harold Ellens et al. JSOTSup 389. London/New York: T & T Clark, 2004.

Duguid, Iain M. *Ezekiel and the Leaders of Israel.* VTSup 46. Leiden/New York: Brill, 1994.

Duhm, Bernhard. *Das Buch Jesaia.* Revised ed. Göttingen: Vandenhoeck, 1902.

Dulin, Rachel Z. *A Crown of Glory: A Biblical View of Aging.* Mahwah, N.J.: Paulist, 1988.

Dulles, Avery. *Models of the Church.* 2nd ed. Dublin: Gill and Macmillan, 1988.

Dunfee, Susan Nelson. "The Sin of Hiding." *Soundings* 65 (1982): 316-27.

Duvall, Nancy S. "From Soul to Self and Back Again." *Journal of Psychology and Theology* 26 (1998): 6-15.

Dyrness, William. "Stewardship of the Earth in the Old Testament." In *Tending the Garden*, pp. 50-65. Edited by Wesley Granberg-Michaelson. Grand Rapids, Mich.: Eerdmans, 1987.

Eaton, J. H. *Obadiah, Nahum, Habakkuk, Zephaniah.* London: SCM Press, 1961.

Eichrodt, Walther. *Ezekiel.* London: SCM Press/Philadelphia: Westminster Press, 1970.

―――. *Man in the Old Testament.* London: SCM Press, 1951.

―――. *Theology of the Old Testament.* 2 vols. London: SCM Press, 1961, 1967.

Eliot, T. S. *The Complete Poems and Plays.* London: Faber, 1969.

Elliot, Elisabeth. *Shadow of the Almighty.* New York: Harper, 1958.

Ellis, Richard S. *Foundation Deposits in Ancient Mesopotamia.* New Haven, Conn./London: Yale University Press, 1968.

Ellul, Jacques. *The Meaning of the City.* Grand Rapids, Mich.: Eerdmans, 1970.

Emerton, J. A. "The Syntactical Problem of Psalm xlv. 7." *Journal of Semitic Studies* 13 (1968): 58-63.

Eusebius of Caesarea. "The Oration in Praise of the Emperor Constantine." In *The Nicene and Post-Nicene Fathers*, series 2, 1:581-610. Edited by Philip Schaff. Grand Rapids, Mich.: Eerdmans, 1979.

Fairbairn, Patrick. *Ezekiel.* 3rd ed. Edinburgh: T & T Clark, 1863. Reprint, National Foundation for Christian Education, 1969.

Fohrer, Georg. *Theologische Grundstrukturen des Alten Testaments.* Berlin/New York: Walter de Gruyter, 1972.

Forster, E. M. *Howard's End.* Reprint, New York: Penguin, 2000.

Fox, Michael V. *Proverbs 1—9.* AB. New York: Doubleday, 2000.

―――. *Qohelet and His Contradictions.* JSOTSup 71. Sheffield: Sheffield Academic Press, 1987.

―――. *A Time to Tear Down and a Time to Build Up.* Grand Rapids, Mich./Cambridge: Eerdmans, 1999.

Freedman, David Noel. "Divine Commitment and Human Obligation." *Int* 18 (1964): 419-31.

Fretheim, Terence E. *God and the World in the Old Testament.* Nashville: Abingdon, 2005.

―――. *Jeremiah.* Macon, Ga.: Smyth and Helwys, 2002.

―――. "Nature's Praise of God in the Psalms." *Ex auditu* 3 (1987): 16-30.

―――. "The Repentance of God." *HBT* 10, no. 1 (1988): 47-70.

————. *The Suffering of God.* Philadelphia: Fortress, 1984.

Fritz, Volkmar. *The City in Ancient Israel.* Sheffield, U.K.: Sheffield Academic Press, 1995.

Frydrych, Tomáš. *Living Under the Sun.* VTSup 110. Leiden/Boston: Brill, 2002.

Frymer-Kensky, Tikva. *In the Wake of the Goddesses.* Reprint, New York: Fawcett Columbine, 1993.

Frymer-Kensky, Tikva, et al., eds. *Christianity in Jewish Terms.* Boulder, Colo./Oxford: Westview, 2000.

Gammie, John G. *Holiness in Israel.* Minneapolis: Fortress, 1989.

Gane, Roy. *Cult and Character.* Winona Lake, Ind.: Eisenbrauns, 2005.

Garrison, Jim. *The Darkness of God.* London: SCM Press, 1982.

Gaster, T. H. "Psalm 29." *Jewish Quarterly Review* 37 (1946-47): 55-65.

Geertz, Clifford. *Local Knowledge.* New York: Basic Books, 1983.

George, Mark K. "Death as the Beginning of Life in the Book of Ecclesiastes." In *Strange Fire,* pp. 280-93. Edited by Tod Linafelt. Sheffield, U.K.: Sheffield Academic Press/New York: New York University Press, 2000.

Gerstenberger, Erhard S. *Theologies of the Old Testament.* Edinburgh: T & T Clark/Minneapolis: Fortress, 2002.

————. *Yahweh the Patriarch.* Minneapolis: Fortress, 1996.

Gese, Hartmut. *Essays on Biblical Theology.* Minneapolis: Augsburg, 1981.

Ginzberg, Louis. *The Legends of the Jews.* 7 vols. Reprint, Baltimore/London: Johns Hopkins University Press, 1998.

Girard, René. *Violence and the Sacred.* Baltimore/London: Johns Hopkins University Press, 1977.

Gnuse, Robert K. *No Other Gods.* JSOTSup 241. Sheffield, U.K.: Sheffield Academic Press, 1997.

Goldingay, John. *After Eating the Apricot.* Carlisle, U.K.: Paternoster, 1996.

————. "The Compound Name in Isaiah 9.5 [6]." *Catholic Biblical Quarterly* 61 (1999): 239-44.

————. *Isaiah.* Peabody, Mass.: Hendrickson/Carlisle, U.K.: Paternoster, 2001.

————. "Isaiah i l; ii 1." *VT* 48 (1998): 326-32.

————. *The Message of Isaiah 40—55.* London/New York: T & T Clark, 2005.

————. *Models for Interpretation of Scripture.* Grand Rapids, Mich.: Eerdmans/Carlisle, U.K.: Paternoster, 1995.

————. *Models for Scripture.* Grand Rapids, Mich.: Eerdmans/Carlisle, U.K.: Paternoster, 1994.

————. *Old Testament Theology.* Vol. 1: *Israel's Gospel.* Downers Grove, Ill.: InterVarsity Press, 2003.

————. *Psalms.* 3 vols. Grand Rapids, Mich.: Baker, 2006-.

————. *Theological Diversity and the Authority of the Old Testament.* Grand Rapids, Mich.: Eerdmans, 1986/Carlisle, U.K.: Paternoster, 1995.

Goldingay, John, with David Payne. *Isaiah 40—55*. International Critical Commentary. London/New York: T & T Clark, 2006.

Goldstein, Valerie Saiving. "The Human Situation: A Feminine View." *JR* 40 (1960): 100-112.

Gordis, Robert. *The Book of Job*. New York: Jewish Theological Seminary Press, 1978.

Gordon, Robert P. *Holy Land, Holy City*. Carlisle, U.K./Waynesboro, Ga.: Paternoster, 2004.

Gorman, Frank H. *The Ideology of Ritual: Space, Time, and Status in the Priestly Theology*. JSOTSup 91. Sheffield, U.K.: JSOT Press, 1990.

Gorringe, Tim J. *God's Theatre*. London: SCM Press, 1991.

Gottwald, Norman K. "Literary Criticism of the Hebrew Bible." In *Mappings of the Biblical Terrain*. Edited by Vincent L. Tollers and John Maier, pp. 27-44. Lewisburg, Penn.: Bucknell University Press/London: Associated University Presses, 1990.

———. *The Politics of Ancient Israel*. Louisville, Ky.: Westminster John Knox, 2001.

———. *The Tribes of Yahweh*. Maryknoll, N.Y.: Orbis, 1979/London: SCM Press, 1980; reprint, Sheffield, U.K.: Sheffield Academic Press, 1999.

Grabbe, Lester L., and Robert D. Haak, eds. *"Every City Shall Be Forsaken."* JSOTSup 330. Sheffield, U.K.: Sheffield Academic Press, 2001.

Green, Joel B., ed. *What About the Soul?* Nashville: Abingdon, 2004.

Green, Joel B., and Stuart L. Palmer, eds. *In Search of the Soul*. Downers Grove, Ill.: InterVarsity Press, 2005.

Greenberg, Moshe. *Ezekiel 1—20*. AB. Garden City, N.Y.: Doubleday, 1983.

———. *Ezekiel 21—37*. AB. New York: Doubleday, 1997.

———. *Studies in the Bible and Jewish Thought*. Philadelphia: Jewish Publication Society, 1995.

Greenwood, David C. "On the Jewish Hope for a Restored Northern Kingdom." *ZAW* 88 (1976): 376-85.

Gutiérrez, Gustavo. *The God of Life*. Maryknoll, N.Y.: Orbis, 1991.

Habel, Norman C. *The Book of Job*. London: SCM Press/Philadelphia: Westminster Press, 1985.

———. *The Land Is Mine*. Minneapolis: Fortress, 1995.

Habel, Norman C., ed. *The Earth Story in the Psalms and the Prophets*. Sheffield, U.K.: Sheffield Academic Press/Cleveland, Ohio: Pilgrim, 2001.

Habel, Norman C., and Shirley Wurst, eds. *The Earth Story in Wisdom Traditions*. Sheffield, U.K.: Sheffield Academic Press/Cleveland, Ohio: Pilgrim, 2001.

Hanson, Paul D. *The Dawn of Apocalyptic*. Philadelphia: Fortress, 1985.

———. *The People Called*. San Francisco: Harper & Row, 1986.

Harland, P. J., and C. T. R. Hayward, eds. *New Heaven and New Earth*. Anthony

Gelston Festschrift. VTSup 77. Leiden/Boston: Brill, 1999.

Hauerwas, Stanley, and L. Gregory Jones, eds. *Why Narrative?* Grand Rapids, Mich.: Eerdmans, 1989.

Hays, Richard S. *The Moral Vision of the New Testament.* San Francisco: HarperSanFrancisco, 1996.

Henderson, Joseph M. "Who Weeps in Jeremiah viii 23 [ix 1]?" *VT* 52 (2002): 191-206.

Heschel, Abraham J. *God in Search of Man.* Reprint, New York: Farrar, 1986.

———. *Man Is Not Alone.* New York: Farrar, 1951.

———. *The Prophets.* Reprint, New York: HarperCollins, 2001.

Hill, Andrew E. *Malachi.* AB. New York: Doubleday, 1998.

Holladay, William L. *Jeremiah.* 2 vols. Philadelphia: Fortress, 1986; and Minneapolis: Fortress, 1989.

Houston, Walter. *Purity and Monotheism.* JSOTSup 140. Sheffield, U.K.: Sheffield Academic Press, 1993.

Hugenberger, Gordon P. *Marriage as a Covenant.* VTSup 52. Leiden/New York: Brill, 1994.

Humphreys, W. Lee. *The Tragic Vision and the Hebrew Tradition.* Philadelphia: Fortress, 1985.

Irenaeus. *Against Heresies.* In *The Ante-Nicene Fathers: Translations of the Writings of the Fathers Down to A.D. 325,* 1:309-567. Edited by Alexander Roberts and James Donaldson. Grand Rapids, Mich.: Eerdmans, 1981.

Jackson, Timothy P. "Restoring the Moral Lexicon: Ethics from Abomination to Liberation." *Soundings* 76 (1993): 487-523.

Jacob, Edmond. *Theology of the Old Testament.* London: Hodder, 1958.

Jacobsen, Thorkild. *The Treasures of Darkness.* New Haven, Conn./London: Yale University Press, 1976.

Janzen, J. Gerald. *Job.* Atlanta: John Knox Press, 1985.

Japhet, Sara. *The Ideology of the Book of Chronicles and Its Place in Biblical Thought.* 2nd ed. Frankfurt/New York: Lang, 1997.

Jenson, Philip P. *Graded Holiness: A Key to the Priestly Conception of the World.* JSOTSup 106. Sheffield, U.K.: Sheffield Academic Press, 1992.

Jepsen, A. "Beiträge zur Auslegung und Geschichte des Dekalogs." *ZAW* 79 (1967): 277-304.

Jeremias, Jörg. *The Book of Amos.* Louisville, Ky.: Westminster John Knox, 1998.

———. *Theophanie.* Neukirchen: Neukirchener, 1965.

Johnston, Philip S. "Death in Egypt and Israel." *OTS* 55 (2005): 94-116.

———. *Shades of Sheol.* Leicester, U.K./Downers Grove, Ill.: InterVarsity Press, 2002.

Jones, L. Gregory. *Embodying Forgiveness.* Grand Rapids, Mich.: Eerdmans, 1995.

Joyce, Paul. *Divine Initiative and Human Response.* JSOTSup 51. Sheffield: JSOT, 1989.

Julian of Norwich. *Showings.* New York: Paulist, 1978.

Kaminsky, Joel S. *Corporate Responsibility in the Hebrew Bible.* JSOTSup 196. Sheffield, U.K.: Sheffield Academic Press, 1993.

———. "Did Election Imply the Mistreatment of Non-Israelites?" *Harvard Theological Review* 96 (2003): 397-425.

Kaufman, Gordon D. *Systematic Theology.* New York: Scribner's, 1968.

Kaufmann, Yehezkel. *The Religion of Israel.* Chicago: University of Chicago Press, 1960/London: Allen and Unwin, 1961.

Keel, Othmar, and Christoph Uehlinger. *Gods, Goddesses, and Images of God in Ancient Israel.* Minneapolis: Fortress/Edinburgh: T & T Clark, 1998.

Kelly, J. N. D. *Early Christian Creeds.* 2nd ed. London/New York: Longmans, 1960.

Kessler, John, ed. *Reading the Book of Jeremiah.* Winona Lake, Ind.: Eisenbrauns, 2004.

Kinzer, Mark S. *Post-Missionary Messianic Judaism.* Grand Rapids, Mich.: Brazos, 2005.

Kitamori, Kazoh. *Theology of the Pain of God.* Atlanta: John Knox Press, 1965/London: SCM Press, 1966.

Kloos, Carola. *Yhwh's Combat with the Sea.* Amsterdam: van Oorschot, 1986.

Knierim, Rolf P. *The Task of Old Testament Theology.* Grand Rapids, Mich./Cambridge: Eerdmans, 1995.

Knight, George A. F. *A Christian Theology of the Old Testament.* London: SCM Press, 1959.

Knohl, Israel. *The Sanctuary of Silence.* Minneapolis: Fortress, 1985.

Köhler, Ludwig. *Old Testament Theology.* London: Lutterworth, 1957/Philadelphia: Westminster Press, 1958.

Korpel, Marjo C. A. *A Rift in the Clouds.* Münster: Ugarit, 1990.

Kraus, Hans-Joachim. *Psalms 1—59.* Minneapolis: Augsburg, 1988.

———. *Psalms 60—150.* Minneapolis: Augsburg, 1989.

———. *Theology of the Psalms.* Minneapolis: Augsburg/London: SPCK, 1986.

Kutsko, John F. *Between Heaven and Earth: Divine Presence and Absence in the Book of Ezekiel.* Winona Lake, Ind.: Eisenbrauns, 2000.

Laato, Antti, and Johannes C. de Moor, eds. *Theodicy in the World of the Bible.* Leiden/Boston: Brill, 2003.

LaCoque, André, and Paul Ricoeur. *Thinking Biblically.* Chicago/London: University of Chicago Press, 1998.

Lactantius. *A Treatise on the Anger of God.* In *The Ante-Nicene Fathers: Translations of the Writings of the Fathers Down to A.D. 325,* 7:259-80. Edited by Alexander Roberts and James Donaldson. Grand Rapids, Mich.: Eerdmans, 1981.

Landes, George. "Creation and Liberation." *Union Seminary Quarterly Review* 33 (1977-1978): 79-89 = pp. 135-51 in *Creation in the Old Testament*, edited by Bernhard W. Anderson. London: SPCK/Philadelphia: Fortress, 1984.

Landy, Francis. "Tracing the Voice of the Other." In *The New Literary Criticism and the Hebrew Bible*, pp. 140-62. Edited by J. Cheryl Exum and David J. A. Clines. JSOTSup 143. Sheffield, U.K.: Sheffield Academic Press, 1993.

Lapsley, Jacqueline E. *Can These Bones Live?* BZAW 301. Berlin/New York: Walter de Gruyter, 2000.

Lash, Nicholas. *Theology on the Way to Emmaus*. London: SCM Press, 1986.

Lee, Eunny P. *The Vitality of Enjoyment in Qohelet's Theological Rhetoric*. BZAW 353. Berlin/New York: Walter de Gruyter, 2005.

Lerner, Gerda. *The Creation of Patriarchy*. New York/Oxford: Oxford University Press, 1986.

Levenson, Jon D. *Creation and the Persistence of Evil*. Reissued. Princeton, N.J./Chichester, U.K.: Princeton University Press, 1994.

———. *The Death and Resurrection of the Beloved Son*. New Haven, Conn./London: Yale University Press, 1993.

———. *Sinai and Zion*. Minneapolis: Winston, 1985.

Lewis, C. S. *The Four Loves*. New York: Harcourt, Brace, 1960.

Linafelt, Tod. "The Undecidability of ברך in the Prologue to Job and Beyond." *Biblical Interpretation* 4 (1996): 154-72.

Linafelt, Tod, and Timothy K. Beal, eds. *God in the Fray*. W. Brueggemann Festschrift. Minneapolis: Fortress, 1998.

Lindars, Barnabas. "Ezekiel and Individual Responsibility." *VT* 15 (1965): 452-67.

Lindsey, Hal. *The Late Great Planet Earth*. Grand Rapids, Mich.: Zondervan, 1970/London: Marshall, 1971.

Lindström, Fredrick. *God and the Origin of Evil*. ConBOT 21. Lund: Gleerup, 1983.

Loader, J. A. *Ecclesiastes*. Grand Rapids, Mich.: Eerdmans, 1986.

Lohfink, Norbert. "Beobachtungen zur Geschichte des Ausdrucks עם יהוה." In *Probleme biblischer Theologie*, pp. 275-305. Edited by Hans Walter Wolff. Munich: Kaiser, 1971.

Lohfink, Norbert, and Erich Zinger. *The God of Israel and the Nations*. Collegeville, Minn.: Liturgical Press, 2000.

Longman, Tremper, and Daniel G. Reid. *God Is a Warrior*. Grand Rapids, Mich.: Zondervan, 1995.

Ludwig, Theodore M. "The Shape of Hope." *Concordia Theological Monthly* 39 (1968): 526-41.

Luther, Martin. "Letter to Wenceslas Link." In *Luther's Works*, 49:219-21. Philadelphia: Fortress, 1972.

Lutz, Hanns-Martin. *Jahwe, Jerusalem und die Völker*. Neukirchen: Neukirchener, 1968.

Maag, Victor. "Unsühnbare Schuld," *Kairos* 8 (1966): 90-106.

MacDonald, Nathan. "Whose Monotheism? Which Rationality?" *OTS* 55 (2005).

Macintosh, A. A. "A Consideration of Psalm vii. 12f.," *Journal of Theological Studies* n.s. 33 (1982): 481-90

Marshall, Christopher D. *Beyond Retribution*. Grand Rapids, Mich./Cambridge: Eerdmans, 2001.

Martens, Elmer A. *Plot and Purpose in the Old Testament*. Leicester, U.K.: Inter-Varsity Press, 1981.

Martin-Achard, Robert. *From Death to Life*. Edinburgh: Oliver & Boyd, 1960.

———. *A Light to the Nations*. Edinburgh: Oliver & Boyd, 1962.

Marx, Karl. *Theses on Feuerbach*. In Frederick Engels, *Ludwig Feuerbach*, pp. 82-84. New York: International, 1941.

Mason, Rex. *The Books of Haggai, Zechariah and Malachi*. Cambridge/New York: Cambridge University Press, 1977.

———. *Old Testament Pictures of God*. Oxford: Regent's Park/Macon, Ga.: Smyth and Helwys, 1993.

———. "The Use of Earlier Biblical Material in Zechariah 9—14." In *Bringing Out the Treasure*, pp. 1-208. Edited by Mark J. Boda and Michael H. Floyd. JSOTSup 370. London/New York: Sheffield Academic Press, 2003.

Matties, Gordon H. *Ezekiel 18 and the Rhetoric of Moral Discourse*. SBLDS 126. Atlanta: Scholars Press, 1990.

May, Herbert G. "Individual Responsibility and Retribution." *Hebrew Union College Annual* 32 (1961): 107-20.

McCarthy, Carmel. *The Tiqqune Sopherim and Other Theological Corrections in the Masoretic Text of the Old Testament*. Göttingen: Vandenhoeck, 1981.

McCarthy, Dennis J. "Hosea xii 2." *VT* 14 (1964): 215-21.

McClendon, James W., Jr. *Systematic Theology*. Vol. 2: *Doctrine*. Nashville: Abingdon, 1994.

McConville, J. G. *Deuteronomy*. Leicester, U.K./Downers Grove, Ill.: InterVarsity Press, 2002.

McKane, William. *Proverbs*. OTL. London: SCM Press, 1970.

Meier, John P. *A Marginal Jew*. New York: Doubleday, 1991.

Mendenhall, G. E. "The Monarchy." *Int* 29 (1975): 155-70.

Mettinger, Tryggve N. D. *In Search of God*. Philadelphia: Fortress, 1988.

———. *King and Messiah*. ConBOT 8. Lund: Gleerup, 1976.

Meyers, Carol L. "Procreation, Production, and Protection." *Journal of the American Academy of Religion* 51 (1983): 569-93 = pp. 489-514 in *Community, Identity, and Ideology*. Edited by Charles E. Carter and Carol E. Meyers. Winona Lake, Ind.: Eisenbrauns, 1996.

————. "The Roots of Restriction." *Biblical Archaeologist* 41 (1978): 91-103.

Meyers, Carol L., and Eric M. Meyers. *Haggai, Zechariah 1—8*. AB. Garden City, N.Y.: Doubleday, 1987.

————. *Zechariah 9—14*. AB. New York: Doubleday, 1993.

Middleton, J. Richard. *The Liberating Image*. Grand Rapids, Mich.: Brazos, 2005.

Milazzo, G. Tom. *The Protest and the Silence*. Minneapolis: Fortress, 1992.

Miles, Jack. *God: A Biography*. New York/London: Simon & Schuster, 1995.

Milgrom, Jacob. *Leviticus 1—16*. AB. New York: Doubleday, 1991.

Miller, Patrick D. *Israelite Religion and Biblical Theology*. JSOTSup 267. Sheffield, U.K.: Sheffield Academic Press, 2000.

————. "Power, Justice, and Peace: An Exegesis of Psalm 72." *Faith and Mission* 4, no. 1 (1986): 65-70.

————. *The Religion of Ancient Israel*. Louisville, Ky.: Westminster John Knox/ London: SPCK, 2000.

Miranda, José P. *Marx and the Bible*. Maryknoll, N.Y.: Orbis, 1974/London: SCM Press, 1977.

Miskotte, Kornelis. *When the Gods Are Silent*. New York: Harper/London: Collins, 1967.

Moberly, R. W. L. "Toward an Interpretation of the Shema." In *Theological Exegesis*, pp. 124-44. Brevard S. Childs Festschrift. Edited by Christopher Seitz and Kathryn Greene-McCreight. Grand Rapids, Mich./Cambridge: Eerdmans, 1999.

Moltmann, Jürgen. *The Church in the Power of the Spirit*. London: SCM Press, 1977.

————. *The Coming of God*. London: SCM Press, 1996.

————. *God in Creation*. London: SCM Press/San Francisco: HarperSanFrancisco, 1985.

————. *History and the Triune God*. London: SCM Press, 1991.

————. *Theology of Hope*. London: SCM Press, 1967.

————. *The Way of Jesus Christ*. San Francisco: HarperSanFrancisco, 1990.

Moran, W. L. "The End of the Unholy War and the Anti-Exodus." *Bib* 44 (1963): 333-42.

Morenz, Siegfried. *Egyptian Religion*. London: Methuen, 1973.

Motyer, J. Alec. *The Day of the Lion*. London: Inter-Varsity Press, 1974.

————. *The Prophecy of Isaiah*. Leicester, U.K./Downers Grove, Ill.: Inter-Varsity Press, 1993.

Mowinckel, Sigmund. *He That Cometh*. Reprint, Oxford: Blackwell, 1959.

Murphy, Roland E. *Ecclesiastes*. WBC. Dallas: Word, 1992.

————. *Proverbs*. WBC. Nashville: Thomas Nelson, 1998.

Murray, Robert. *The Cosmic Covenant*. London: Sheed & Ward, 1992.

Nelson, Richard D. *Raising Up a Faithful Priest*. Louisville, Ky.: Westminster John Knox, 1993.

Newsom, Carol A. "The Book of Job." In *The New Interpreter's Bible*, 4:317-637. Nashville: Abingdon, 1996.

Ngwa, Kenneth Numfor. *The Hermeneutics of the "Happy" Ending in Job 42:7-17*. BZAW 354. Berlin/New York: Walter de Gruyter, 2005.

Nicholson, Ernest W. *God and His People*. Oxford/New York: Oxford University Press, 1986.

Niebuhr, Richard. "The Idea of Covenant and American Democracy." *Church History* 23 (1954): 126-35.

North, C. R. "The Religious Aspects of Hebrew Kingship." *ZAW* 50 (1932): 8-38.

Noth, Martin. *The Laws in the Pentateuch and Other Studies*. Edinburgh: Oliver & Boyd, 1966.

O'Brien, Conor Cruise. *God's Land*. Cambridge, Mass./London: Harvard University Press, 1988.

O'Brien, Julia Myers. *Nahum*. London/New York: Sheffield Academic Press, 2002.

Odell, Margaret S. "The Inversion of Shame and Forgiveness in Ezekiel 16.59-63." *JSOT* 56 (1992): 101-12.

Odell, Margaret S., and John T. Strong, eds. *The Book of Ezekiel*. Atlanta: Society of Biblical Literature, 2000.

Ollenburger, Ben C. "The Book of Zechariah." In *The New Interpreter's Bible*, 7:733-840. Nashville: Abingdon, 1996.

————. *Zion, the City of the Great King*. JSOTSup 41. Sheffield: JSOT Press, 1987.

Osswald, Eva. *Falsche Prophetie im Alten Testament*. Tübingen: Mohr, 1962.

Otto, Rudolf. *The Idea of the Holy*. 3rd ed. London/New York: Oxford University Press, 1925.

Overholt, Thomas W. *The Threat of Falsehood*. London: SCM Press, 1970.

Pannenberg, Wolfhart. *Anthropology in Theological Perspective*. Philadelphia: Westminster Press, 1985.

————. *Basic Questions in Theology*. 3 vols. London: SCM Press, 1970, 1971, 1973.

————. *Systematic Theology*. 3 vols. Grand Rapid, Mich.: Eerdmans/Edinburgh: T & T Clark, 1991, 1994, 1998.

Paul, Shalom. *Amos*. Minneapolis: Fortress, 1991.

Peacocke, A. R. *Creation and the World of Science*. Oxford/New York: Oxford University Press, 1979.

Pedersen, J. *Israel: Its Life and Culture I-IV*. 2 vols. Reprint, London: Oxford University Press, 1954, 1953.

Peels, Hendrick G. L. *The Vengeance of God*. OTS 31. Leiden/New York: Brill, 1995.

Penchansky, David. *What Rough Beast?* Louisville, Ky.: Westminster John Knox, 1999.

Perdue, Leo G. *Wisdom in Revolt: Metaphorical Theology in the Book of Job.* JSOT-Sup 112. Sheffield, U.K.: Sheffield Academic Press, 1991.

Perdue, Leo G., et al. *Families in Ancient Israel.* Louisville, Ky.: Westminster John Knox, 1997.

Petersen, David L. *Haggai and Zechariah 1—8.* Philadelphia: Westminster Press, 1984/London: SCM Press, 1985.

Petitjean, Albert. *Les oracles du Proto-Zacharie.* Paris: Gabalda, 1969.

Phillips, Anthony. *Ancient Israel's Criminal Law.* Oxford: Blackwell/New York: Schocken, 1970.

Pinnock, Clark, et al. *The Openness of God: A Biblical Challenge to the Traditional Understanding of God.* Downers Grove, Ill.: InterVarsity Press/Carlisle, U.K.: Paternoster, 1994.

Plaskow, Judith. *Sex, Sin and Grace.* Lanham, Md./London: University Press of America, 1980.

———. *Standing Again at Sinai.* San Francisco: Harper & Row, 1990.

Pope, Marvin H. *Job.* 3rd ed. AB. Garden City, N.Y.: Doubleday, 1973.

Preuss, Horst Dietrich. *Old Testament Theology.* 2 vols. Louisville, Ky.: Westminster John Knox/Edinburgh: T & T Clark, 1995 and 1996.

Pury, Roland de. *Hiob.* Reprint, Neukirchen: Neukirchener, 1962.

Rad, Gerhard von. *God at Work in Israel.* Nashville: Abingdon, 1980.

———. *Old Testament Theology.* 2 vols. Edinburgh: Oliver & Boyd/New York: Harper, 1962, 1965.

———. *The Problem of the Hexateuch and Other Essays.* Edinburgh: Oliver & Boyd/New York: McGraw-Hill, 1966. New ed., *From Genesis to Chronicles.* Minneapolis: Fortress, 2005.

———. *Wisdom in Israel.* London: SCM Press/Nashville: Abingdon, 1972.

Reicke, Bo. "The Knowledge of the Suffering Servant." In *Das ferne und nahe Wort,* pp. 186-92. L. Rost Festschrift. Edited by F. Maass. BZAW 105. Berlin: Walter de Gruyter, 1967.

Rendtorff, Rolf. *Canon and Theology.* Minneapolis: Fortress, 1993.

———. *The Canonical Hebrew Bible.* Leiden: Deo, 2005.

———. *The Covenant Formula.* Edinburgh: T & T Clark, 1998.

Reventlow, Henning Graf, ed. *Creation in Jewish and Christian Tradition.* JSOT-Sup 319. London/New York: Sheffield Academic Press, 2002.

———. *Eschatology in the Bible and in Jewish and Christian Tradition.* JSOTSup 243. Sheffield, U.K.: Sheffield Academic Press, 1997.

Ricoeur, Paul. *The Symbolism of Evil.* Reprint, Boston: Beacon, 1995.

Ringgren, Helmer. *The Faith of the Psalmists.* Philadelphia: Fortress/London: SCM Press, 1963.

Roberts, Jimmy J. M. *Nahum, Habakkuk, and Zephaniah.* Louisville, Ky.: Westminster John Knox, 1991.

Robinson, H. Wheeler. *Corporate Personality in Ancient Israel.* Reprint, Philadelphia: Fortress, 1964.

————. *Inspiration and Revelation in the Old Testament.* London/New York: Oxford University Press, 1946.

Rogerson, John W. "The Old Testament View of Nature." In *Instruction and Interpretation, Joint British-Dutch Old Testament Conference, Louvain, Belgium, 1976,* pp. 67-84. OTS 20. Leiden: Brill, 1977.

Rogerson, John W., and J. W. McKay. *Psalms.* 3 vols. Cambridge/New York: Cambridge University Press, 1977.

Rose, Wolter H. *Zemah and Zerubbabel.* JSOTSup 304. Sheffield, U.K.: Sheffield Academic Press, 2000.

Rousseau, Jean Jacques. *The Social Contract.* Reprint, New York: Hafner, 1954.

Rudman, Dominic. *Determinism in the Book of Ecclesiastes.* JSOTSup 316. Sheffield, U.K.: Sheffield Academic Press, 2001.

Sarna, Nahum. *Studies in Biblical Interpretation.* Philadelphia: Jewish Publication Society, 2000.

Satterthwaite, Philip E., et al., eds. *The Lord's Anointed.* Carlisle, U.K.: Paternoster/Grand Rapids, Mich.: Baker, 1995.

Schaefer, Konrad. *Psalms.* Collegeville, Minn.: Liturgical Press, 2001.

Schmid, Hans Heinrich. "Creation, Righteousness, and Salvation." In *Creation in the Old Testament,* pp. 102-17. Edited by Bernhard W. Anderson. London: SPCK/Philadelphia: Fortress, 1984.

————. *Gerechtigkeit als Weltordnung.* Tübingen: Mohr, 1968.

Schmidt, Brian B. *Israel's Beneficent Dead.* Reprint, Winona Lake, Ind.: Eisenbrauns, 1996.

Schmidt, Werner H. *The Faith of the Old Testament.* Oxford: Blackwell/Philadelphia: Westminster Press, 1983.

Schuller, Eileen M. "The Book of Malachi." In *The New Interpreter's Bible,* 7:841-77. Nashville: Abingdon, 1996.

Schwartz, Baruch J. "The Bearing of Sin in the Priestly Literature." In *Pomegranates and Golden Bells,* pp. 3-21. Jacob Milgrom Festschrift. Edited by David P. Wright et al. Winona Lake, Ind.: Eisenbrauns: 1995.

Schwartz, Regina M. *The Curse of Cain.* Chicago/London: Chicago University Press, 1997.

Seitz, Christopher R. *Word Without End: The Old Testament as Abiding Theological Witness.* Grand Rapids, Mich./Cambridge: Eerdmans, 1998.

Shanks, Hershal, ed. *Aspects of Monotheism.* Washington, D.C.: Biblical Archaeology Society, 1997.

Smend, Rudolf. "Das Nein des Amos." *Evangelische Theologie* 23 (1963): 404-23.

Smith, Mark S. *The Memoirs of God.* Minneapolis: Fortress, 2004.

————. *The Origins of Biblical Monotheism.* Oxford/New York: Oxford University Press, 2001.

Smith, Morton. "The Common Theology of the Ancient Near East." *JBL* 71 (1952): 135-47.

Smith-Christopher, Daniel L. *A Biblical Theology of Exile.* Minneapolis: Fortress, 2002.

Soggin, J. Alberto. *The Prophet Amos.* London: SCM Press, 1987.

Sohn, Seock-Tae. *The Divine Election of Israel.* Grand Rapids, Mich.: Eerdmans, 1991.

Soulen, R. Kendall. *The God of Israel and Christian Theology.* Minneapolis: Fortress, 1996.

Stadelmann, Luis I. J. *The Hebrew Conception of the World.* Rome: PBI, 1970.

Steck, Odil Hannes. *World and Environment.* Nashville: Abingdon, 1980.

Steffens, Lincoln. *The Shame of the Cities.* Reprint, New York: Hill and Wang, 1957.

Steiner, George. *Real Presences.* London: Faber, 1989.

Stiebert, Johanna. *The Construction of Shame in the Hebrew Bible.* JSOTSup 346. London/New York: Sheffield Academic Press, 2002.

Stone, Beth Wheeler. "Second Isaiah: Prophet to Patriarchy." *JSOT* 56 (1992): 85-99.

Strong, John T., and Steven S. Tuell, eds. *Constituting the Community.* S. Dean McBride Festschrift. Winona Lake, Ind.: Eisenbrauns, 2005.

Stuhlmueller, Carroll. *Rebuilding with Hope.* Grand Rapids, Mich.: Eerdmans/ Edinburgh: Handsel, 1988.

Sun, Henry T. C., et al., eds. *Problems in Biblical Theology.* Rolf Knierim Festschrift. Grand Rapids, Mich./Cambridge: Eerdmans, 1997.

Tai, Nicholas Ho Fail. *Prophetie als Schriftauslegung in Sacharja 9—14.* Stuttgart: Calwer, 1996.

Tate, Marvin E. *Psalms 51—100.* WBC. Dallas: Word, 1990.

Temple, William. *Nature, Man and God.* Reprint, London: Macmillan, 1949.

Terrien, Samuel. *The Elusive Presence.* San Francisco: Harper & Row, 1978.

Tertullian. *Against Marcion.* In *The Ante-Nicene Fathers: Translations of the Writings of the Fathers Down to A.D. 325,* vol. 3. Edited by Alexander Roberts and James Donaldson. Grand Rapids, Mich.: Eerdmans, 1980.

Thomas, D. Winton. "בליעל in the Old Testament." In *Biblical and Patristic Studies,* pp. 11-19. Robert P. Casey Memorial. Edited by J. Neville Birdsall and Robert W. Thomson. Freiburg: Herder, 1963.

————. "ṣalmāwet in the Old Testament." *Journal of Semitic Studies* 7 (1962): 191-200.

Thompson, John A. *The Book of Jeremiah.* NICOT. Grand Rapids, Mich.: Eerdmans, 1980.

Torrance, Thomas F. "The Divine Vocation and Destiny of Israel in World History." In *The Witness of the Jews to God*, pp. 85-104. Edited by David W. Torrance. Edinburgh: Handsel, 1982.

Towner, W. Sibley. "The Book of Ecclesiastes." In *The New Interpreter's Bible*, 5:265-360. Nashville: Abingdon, 1997.

Trible, Phyllis. *God and the Rhetoric of Sexuality*. Philadelphia: Fortress, 1978.

Van Buren, Paul M. *A Theology of the Jewish-Christian Reality*. 3 vols. San Francisco: Harper & Row, 1980, 1983, 1988.

Van Leeuwen, Raymond C. "The Book of Proverbs." *The New Interpreter's Bible*, 5:17-264. Nashville: Abingdon, 1997.

———. "Proverbs 30:21-23 and the Biblical World Upside Down." *JBL* 105 (1986): 599-610.

———. "Wealth and Proverbs: System and Contradiction in Proverbs." *Hebrew Studies* 33 (1992): 25-36.

Volf, Miroslav. *Exclusion and Embrace*. Nashville: Abingdon, 1996.

Vriezen, Theodorus C. *Die Erwählung Israels nach dem Alten Testament*. Zürich: Zwingli, 1953.

———. *An Outline of Old Testament Theology*. Reprint, Oxford: Blackwell, 1962; 2nd ed., Oxford: Blackwell/Newton, Mass.: Branford, 1970.

Wakeman, Mary K. *God's Battle with the Monster*. Leiden: Brill, 1973.

Weems, Renita J. *Battered Love*. Minneapolis: Fortress, 1995.

Webster, John. *Holy Scripture*. Cambridge/New York: Cambridge University Press, 2003.

Weiser, Artur. *The Psalms*. London: SCM Press/Philadelphia: Westminster Press, 1962.

Weiss, Johannes. *Jesus' Proclamation of the Kingdom of God*. Philadelphia: Fortress, 1971.

Welker, Michael. "Security of Expectations." *JR* 66 (1986): 237-60.

Wells, Jo Bailey. *God's Holy People*. JSOTSup 305. Sheffield, U.K.: Sheffield Academic Press, 2000.

Westermann, Claus. "Die Begriffe für Fragen und Suchen im Alten Testament." *Kerygma und Dogma* 6 (1960): 2-30.

———. *Blessing in the Bible and the Life of the Church*. Philadelphia: Fortress, 1978.

———. *Elements of Old Testament Theology*. Atlanta: John Knox Press, 1982.

———. *Isaiah 40-66*. Philadelphia: Westminster Press/London: SCM Press, 1966.

Whybray, R. Norman. *Ecclesiastes*. Grand Rapids, Mich.: Eerdmans/London: Marshall, 1989.

———. *The Good Life in the Old Testament*. London/New York: Continuum, 2002.

———. *Wealth and Poverty in the Book of Proverbs*. JSOTSup 99. Sheffield, U.K.: JSOT Press, 1990.

————. "Wisdom, Suffering and the Freedom of God." In *In Search of True Wisdom*, pp. 231-45. Ronald E. Clements Festschrift. Edited by Edward Ball. JSOTSup 300. Sheffield, U.K.: Sheffield Academic Press, 2000.

Wildberger, Hans. *Isaiah 1—12.* Minneapolis: Fortress, 1991.

————. *Isaiah 13—27.* Minneapolis: Fortress, 1997.

————. *Isaiah 28—39.* Minneapolis: Fortress, 2002.

Wiles, Johnny E. *Wise King—Royal Fool.* JSOTSup 399. London/New York: T & T Clark, 2004.

Williams, Bernard. *Shame and Necessity.* Berkeley/London: University of California Press, 1993.

Williams, P. J. "Are the Biblical Rephaim and the Ugaritic *RPUM* Healers?" *OTS* 52 (2005): 266-75.

Wilson, Gerald H. "The Use of Royal Psalms at the 'Seams' of the Hebrew Psalter." *JSOT* 35 (1986): 85-94.

Wilson, Ian. *Out of the Midst of the Fire.* SBLDS 151. Atlanta: Scholars Press, 1995.

Wink, Walter. *Engaging the Powers.* Minneapolis: Fortress, 1992.

————. *Naming the Powers.* Philadelphia: Fortress, 1984.

————. *Unmasking the Powers.* Philadelphia: Fortress, 1986.

Wolff, Hans Walter. *Anthropology of the Old Testament.* London: SCM Press/ Philadelphia: Fortress, 1974.

————. *Hosea.* Philadelphia: Fortress, 1974.

————. *Joel and Amos.* Philadelphia: Fortress, 1977.

————. *Micah.* Minneapolis: Augsburg, 1990.

Wright, Christopher J. H. *God's People in God's Land.* Exeter, U.K.: Paternoster/ Grand Rapids, Mich.: Eerdmans, 1990.

Wright, N. T. *The Climax of the Covenant.* Edinburgh: T & T Clark, 1991/Minneapolis: Fortress, 1992.

Wyschogrod, Michael. *The Body of Faith: God in the People of Israel.* San Francisco: Harper & Row, 1989.

Yee, Gale A. *Poor Banished Children of Eve: Woman as Evil in the Hebrew Bible.* Minneapolis: Fortress, 2003.

Yoder, John H. *The Priestly Kingdom.* Reprint, Notre Dame, Ind.: University of Notre Dame, 2001.

Zimmerli, Walther. *Ezekiel.* 2 vols. Hermeneia, 1979, 1983.

————. *Gottes Offenbarung.* TBü 19. Munich: Kaiser, 1963.

————. *I Am Yahweh.* Atlanta: John Knox Press, 1982.

————. *Man and His Hope in the Old Testament.* London: SCM Press, 1971.

————. *The Old Testament and the World.* London: SPCK, 1976.

————. *Old Testament Theology in Outline.* Atlanta: John Knox Press/Edinburgh: T & T Clark, 1978.

Author Index